THE EARLY CHRIS

FROM PAUL

The Early Christians in Ephesus from Paul to Ignatius

Paul Trebilco

WILLIAM B. EERDMANS PUBLISHING COMPANY

GRAND RAPIDS, MICHIGAN / CAMBRIDGE, U.K.

© 2004 Mohr Siebeck, Tübingen, Germany

First published 2004 in Germany by
Mohr Siebeck, Tübingen

This edition published 2007
in the United States of America by
Wm. B. Eerdmans Publishing Co.
2140 Oak Industrial Drive N.E., Grand Rapids, Michigan 49505 /
P.O. Box 163, Cambridge CB3 9PU U.K.

Printed in the United States of America

12 11 10   7 6 5 4

ISBN 978-0-8028-0769-4

www.eerdmans.com

For Fiona, Stephen,
David and Philip

Contents

Contents

Part Two
The Pastoral Epistles, Revelation and the Johannine Letters

Chapter 5: What do the Pastoral Epistles tell us about
the early Christians in Ephesus?   197

Part Three
The relationships between the readers of the Pastorals,
the Johannine Letters and Revelation

Chapter 8: **The wider culture and the readers of the Pastorals,**
the Johannine Letters and Revelation: Acculturation,
Assimilation and Accommodation 351

Part Four
Ignatius' Letter to Ephesus

Preface

My interest in Ephesus was originally prompted by Professor James Dunn's suggestion that this was an area that had been overlooked in New Testament Studies. This dovetailed well with my hope that I could build in some way on earlier work on Jewish communities in Asia Minor and also tied in to my interest in unity and diversity in the New Testament, an interest that was originally stimulated by reading Jimmy's book of that title as an undergraduate. I am enormously grateful to Jimmy for his encouragement as I have worked away on this project.

In working on this book I am also hugely in the debt of Professor John Barclay. John has spent many hours talking about this project with me, and I have greatly appreciated his wisdom and insight.

I have spent rather too long on this book, including two periods of research leave and much time in between. The foundations of the project were laid in 1994 when I spent seven months at Tyndale House, Cambridge, and then five months as a visiting scholar at the Faculty of Divinity, University of Durham. From July 2001 to June 2002, I was a visiting scholar at the Department of Theology and Religious Studies, University of Glasgow. I am exceedingly grateful to each of these institutions for their hospitality and their excellent libraries. I am particularly grateful to Dr Bruce Winter, Professor James Dunn and Professor John Barclay respectively for making these periods of leave so enjoyable and worthwhile.

I am very grateful to the University of Otago for these periods of research leave, and for various research grants that have assisted with this work. I am also enormously grateful to two of my PhD students: to Chris Caradus, who has produced the camera-ready copy for this book, and undertaken the laborious task of constructing the indices with much skill and unfailing patience, and to Martin Williams who has proofread the whole work with exemplary care and attention to detail. I have greatly appreciated their support.

Chapters or sections of this book have been presented at conferences or seminars at a variety of institutions, particularly in Britain and Australia. I am very grateful for the responses received, which have helped to refine my thoughts. I am also very grateful to those who have read portions of this work, or who have spent time discussing it with me. In addition to Jimmy Dunn and John Barclay, I would particularly like to thank Professors Graham Stanton, Richard Bauckham and Wayne Meeks, and Dr Steve Walton.

I have taught a postgraduate paper based around this research several times here at the University of Otago, and am very grateful to the students who have focussed my thinking by their astute questions and responses to my material.

My heartfelt thanks go to Professor Jörg Frey, editor of the WUNT series in which this book appears and to Dr Henning Ziebritzki of Mohr Siebeck, for being willing to accept this book for publication. Professor Frey's detailed comments on an earlier draft of the book were exceedingly insightful, and have helped me to clarify and sharpen my argument in many places. Of course, all the oversights and errors of judgement that remain are mine! I am also very grateful to Ilse König for her assistance in the publication process.

I am grateful to Eerdmans for permission to revise and incorporate into sections 1 and 2 of Chapter 1 material that was originally published in *The Book of Acts in its Greco-Roman Setting* and to Dr Bruce Winter, the editor of *Tyndale Bulletin* for permission to reprint here as Chapter 12, in slightly revised form, two articles which were published in volumes 53.2 (2002) and 54.1 (2003) of that journal.

My wife Gill has been a loving and constant companion and support while I have been writing this book. I am enormously grateful for all she has done over many years whilst I have been (metaphorically) in Ephesus! I dedicate this book to our four children, Fiona, Stephen, David and Philip, with love and profound gratitude for all they have added to our lives.

Paul Trebilco
December, 2003
University of Otago, Dunedin, New Zealand.

Introduction

1. The significance of the early Christians in Ephesus

It is my contention that the life of the early Christians in Ephesus sheds a good deal of light on early Christianity in general.[1] As we will see a number of leading personalities of early Christianity have a connection with Ephesus and the range of New Testament and early Christian texts which are linked with Ephesus is probably greater than that for any other city in which there was an early Christian community.

Ephesus was also the capital of the province of Asia and the leading city of Asia Minor, where the church grew very rapidly. There is no doubting the importance of the church in Asia Minor in the first two centuries. Paul spent a considerable period of time in Asia Minor and Luke devoted a significant amount of Acts to Paul's travels in this region. That the early Church grew very quickly in Asia Minor is shown by the number of centres in which, according to our evidence, the early church became established by the end of the second century.[2] Thus, Aune notes that "In the aftermath of the fall of Jerusalem following the first Jewish revolt of A.D. 66-73, Anatolia had become perhaps the most important geographical center of Christianity in the ancient world."[3]

As the leading city of the province of Asia, and a key city in the wider area of Asia Minor, Ephesus clearly has a significant place in early Christianity. A number of scholars have recognized that Ephesus was a very important centre of early Christianity. For example, von Harnack saw Ephesus as the "third capital of Christianity" and added that "for a while it looked as if Ephesus was actually destined to be the final headquarters of the faith."[4] Beasley-Murray notes that: "the church in Ephesus was the most important in Asia Minor, and

---

[1] For bibliography on Ephesus see Oster 1987.

[2] See Oster 1992b, p938-54.

[3] Aune 1997, p131. Frend (1984, p38) notes that the province of Asia was "the main centre of Christianity for a century and a half after the Pauline mission". On p127 he writes: "The province of Asia emerged as the area where Christianity was strongest, with Ephesus as its radial point."

[4] von Harnack 1908, p76. It would be the third capital after Jerusalem and Antioch.

possibly the most influential church in the world at the end of the first century AD."[5]

Despite those who have recognised the importance of Ephesus for early Christianity (see section 2. below), the study of the early Christians in Ephesus has been somewhat overlooked by New Testament scholarship.[6] The focus has often been on particular issues connected with Ephesus, such as whether Paul was imprisoned in the city,[7] the relationship of particular documents to Ephesus,[8] studies of the broader questions of unity and diversity in early Christianity.[9] These issues have been important in their own right, but the broader picture of the life of the early Christians in Ephesus has not been given the prominence it deserves. Further, since we have a wealth of archaeological data available from the city, Ephesus offers the opportunity to develop a portrayal of the life of the early Christians in the context of all we know about the life of a major Greco-Roman city.

2. Recent Research on the early Christians in Ephesus

Recently, there have been some significant studies of Christians in Ephesus. Whilst the work of these scholars will be noted or discussed at the appropriate points, some more general, brief comments are appropriate here.[10]

Günther (1995) is the most comprehensive of recent treatments of Christians in Ephesus. After dealing with introductory issues, he discusses Ephesian Christianity in particular periods: from 41-54 CE (including the Pauline mission), to the end of Domitian's reign (96 CE, including Acts 20 and 2-3 Jn), from 98-117 CE (including Rev 2:1-7, Cerinthus and Ignatius), and from 118 to 197 CE (Justin's *Dialogue with Trypho*, and other evidence from Eusebius). Whilst there is much of value in his work, in my view many of his conclusions do not stand up to scrutiny. For example, he does not think a Pauline community became established in Ephesus at all, but rather that

---

[5] Beasley-Murray 1974, p73; he goes on " ... It is comprehensible that teachers of many kinds and of every shade of doctrine were drawn to Ephesus, to seek the patronage of the church and to influence its ways."

[6] This contrasts with the number of studies devoted to other cities and regions, most notably Antioch, Rome, Corinth and Egypt. For a discussion of previous work on Christians in Ephesus see Günther 1995, p4-12.

[7] See Chapter 2, section 3.

[8] This relates particularly to John's Gospel.

[9] For example Christianity in Ephesus was important in Bauer's analysis (1971, p67-94) and in Robinson's response (1988).

[10] There have been a number of other significant articles or books devoted to our topic; see for example Lemcio 1986; Mussies 1990; Schnackenburg 1991; Horsley 1992a; Fieger 1998. On recent work on Ephesus see also Schnabel 1999, p349-82.

Apollos was *the* key founding figure,[11] he views the Acts material as unreliable, and argues that 1 Jn cannot be used as evidence for Ephesian Christians (whilst 2-3 Jn can be).[12] On these points (and a number of others), I think the evidence argues in a different direction.[13] This means that overall, quite different conclusions about the nature of the life of the early Christians in Ephesus need to be drawn.

In his 1995 book, Thiessen looks only at Paul's mission in Ephesus and the Pastoral Epistles. He discusses issues of method, works through the Acts material in detail, and then discusses the Pastoral Epistles, paying attention to issues such as their connection with Ephesus and the historical situation of post-Pauline Christianity including matters such as leadership, social stratification and the position of the opponents. He concludes with a discussion of the struggle within post-Pauline Christianity at Ephesus over Pauline tradition. Much of what he says is valuable, but from our perspective, the fact that he does not draw on other early Christian literature (the Johannine letters, Revelation, Ignatius' letter) in his discussion of the life of the Christians in Ephesus, means that much else remains to be said about the topic of "Christen in Ephesus".[14]

Strelan (1996) discusses the significance of Artemis and other cults in Ephesus, and then against this background, explores Paul's mission in Ephesus, drawing on Acts and Paul's letter. He argues that in Ephesus Paul made little progress in converting Gentiles; rather Paul had success largely among Jews with the result that his Christian community in Ephesus was composed primarily of Jews, to the extent that we should speak of "Pauline Jewish Christianity" in Ephesus.[15] However, as we will argue, Acts suggests that the Pauline Christian community in Ephesus consisted of significant numbers of both Jews and Gentiles. Further, Rom 9-11 (especially 9:31; 10:1-4; 11:1f), written shortly after Paul's time in Ephesus, suggests that Paul thought his mission to Jews was largely unsuccessful. This does not mean that Paul did not convert a number of Jews, but it does undermine the view that suggests that Paul's community in Ephesus was predominantly Jewish, as

---

[11] Although note that he thinks the community founded by Apollos did not endure, and the Christian community in Ephesus was refounded by the Elder John of 2-3 Jn after 70 CE.

[12] For these points see Günther 1995, p52-3, 54-9; 53-67 and 108-111 respectively.

[13] See the critical reviews of Günther's book in Roloff 1997, p143-5; Schnabel 1999, p354-6. Roloff (1997, p144) asks two pertinent questions of Günther's treatment of Paul. Firstly, why did Paul stay so long in Ephesus, if his mission there was a total failure, as Günther thinks? And secondly, if Apollos did found the community in Ephesus, why, in light of Rom 15:20, did Paul attempt a mission there?

[14] For a review of Thiessen's book, including critical comments on his view of the Pastorals, see Roloff 1997, p142-3.

[15] Strelan 1996, p295.

Strelan believes.[16] Further, it is also a limitation of his work that he only discusses the material relating to Paul's mission and Acts.

Koester's works (1995 and 1999) about Ephesus are quite brief. Whilst I take a different view on some matters from him (for example, I will argue that the Acts account is historically valuable, and that the communities addressed in 1-3 Jn are to be located in and around Ephesus), his portrayal of the diversity of early Christianity in Ephesus is helpful, although I will eventually reconstruct the range of communities differently.

In my view then, the overall picture of the life of the early Christians in Ephesus can be clarified in more detail and in a different way than has been done hitherto. This is the task attempted here.

3. The aims of this book

In this book I will investigate the life of the Christians in Ephesus from the founding of the community in the city to the early second century. Clearly, the founding of the community is the obvious place to begin. The letter of Ignatius to the Ephesians, written around 105-110 CE, is the obvious point to conclude this study because, after this, there is very little information about Christians in Ephesus until the end of the second century.[17] The context for this investigation is the history and significance of Ephesus and of its religious life, including its Jewish community, in the first century from archaeological and literary sources. Accordingly, this is addressed in Chapter 1.

Clearly, a crucial issue is which documents relate to the Christians in Ephesus, and how reliable is the information they provide. We will outline below which books we think relate to Ephesus and will provide detailed argument for these views at the appropriate points.

The book has two main aims. The first is the descriptive task of attempting to outline what our sources tell us about the life and activity of the early Christians in Ephesus. Thus in Part One we will discuss Paul and his mission in the city as this is portrayed in his letters and Acts. In Part Two I will

---

[16] Further, Strelan's view (1996, p303-6) that by the phrase "the apostle to τὰ ἔθνη" Paul meant "apostle to those Jews living in those areas outside of Judea, or outside of Israel" (1996, p306) is very unlikely, particularly in the light of Gal 2:7-10. His treatment of Acts 19:10 (1996, p255-7) and 19:26 (1996, p137-9) is also very unconvincing. For further critique see Barclay 1998, p260-3.

[17] For a discussion of possible sources in the second century see Günther 1995, p161-204. On the earliest Christian inscriptions from Ephesus, which date to the 3rd century, see Antonopoulu 1999, p170-2. She notes there are 291 Christian inscriptions from the third century to 614 CE. On the earliest non-inscriptional material remains of Christianity in Ephesus see Foss 1979, p36. On Christianity in the third to fifth century see Foss 1979, p33-44.

discuss the Pastorals, the Johannine Letters and Revelation. I will present the case for linking these documents with Ephesus and for their dating. I will also discuss the views of various groups associated with Ephesus which emerge from these documents and which the respective authors regard as "beyond the pale". These are the Pastor's opponents in 1 and 2 Timothy, the "secessionists" who have left the community addressed in 1 Jn and the "Nicolaitans" spoken of in Revelation 2.

The second aim of the book is to present the argument that, apart from the very earliest period, there was never a single "Christian community in Ephesus". Rather, I will argue that there were different groups or communities of Christians in the city, and I will seek to describe in detail some facets of the life of these different groups. This emerges in Part Two, in which I discuss the various groups that are addressed by authors, or against whom the respective authors argue. But in Part Three I address this issue more directly and seek to demonstrate that the Pastoral Epistles and the Johannine Letters are not addressed to the same group of Christians (over some 20 years), but rather are addressed to different groups of readers. However, I will argue that John in Revelation is seeking to address both groups, and perhaps others as well, although he is aware that some of his readers may well not listen to his message. This will be argued in Part Three of the book by examining the situation of the readers of the Pastorals, the Johannine Letters and Revelation with regard to a range of issues, as these are expressed by the various authors. The issues examined are the relationship between Christians and the wider community in which they lived, material possessions, leadership and the locus of authority, the situation of women, and the terms used as "labels" for self-designation. These issues have been chosen because they can be seen as significant dimensions of the identity of a group and because they are issues on which there is sufficient evidence for comparative purposes.[18] By discussing these issues, I will also be building up a description of the life of these particular communities.

In a final chapter in Part Three, I will seek to argue that the readers of the Pastoral Epistles and the readers of the Johannine Epistles were not antagonistic towards one another and would have seen each other as part of the same wider movement, even if they also wished to maintain the integrity of their separate groups. I will also discuss further how John the Seer relates to the Pauline tradition in order to reinforce the argument that John is writing to all the Christians in Ephesus.

---

[18] It would be interesting to be able to discuss issues such as the ethnic make up of the readers of these documents, the readers' attitude towards Israel as the people of God and towards the Jewish law. But the evidence is insufficient across the three sets of documents to allow a comparison to be made on these issues.

In the two Chapters in Part Four I will return to the descriptive exercise and will discuss what Ignatius tells us about the life of the Christians he addresses in Ephesus. I will also argue that he is seeking to address and to unify all the Christians in Ephesus. A brief concluding chapter will seek to bring together the various matters we have discussed and, on the basis of what we have discussed about the life of the Christian communities in Ephesus, will make some observations relating to the ongoing debate about commonality and diversity in earliest Christianity.

4. Which New Testament documents are connected with Ephesus?

Whilst we do not have a long letter like Romans addressed to Ephesus, the range and number of documents which have some connection to Ephesus makes it a fruitful city for investigation. However, part of the difficulty of studying this topic is the problem of which NT documents have a verifiable connection with Ephesus. That the following documents are (or are not) connected with Ephesus will be argued at the appropriate points, where the dating will also be discussed. Here we simply note the documents which provide our primary evidence.

Clearly Paul preached in Ephesus and wrote about his experiences in the city, primarily in 1 Cor. Secondly, Luke writes about Paul's mission in Acts, and although this material needs to be examined for its historical reliability, I will argue that we gain much valuable information about the earliest Christians in Ephesus from this source. Thirdly, I will argue that 1 and 2 Timothy were written to Ephesus between 80-100 CE;[19] opponents are clearly in view in these letters. Fourthly, tradition associates the Johannine literature with Ephesus and I will argue that a strong case can be made for this geographical location. However, I will argue that we cannot use John's Gospel as evidence for a Johannine community in the city, since I have been convinced by recent arguments that the Gospels were written for all Christians and that we cannot deduce the history and life of a particular community from a Gospel. However, I will argue that 1-3 Jn can be used as evidence for the life of a "Johannine community" in Ephesus, and that we also learn of opponents of this community from these books.

Fifthly, the letter in Rev 2:1-7 is written to Ephesian Christians, and the rest of Revelation has Ephesian Christians in view, along with those in six other cities in western Asia Minor. We also learn from Rev 2:1-7 of the Nicolaitans. Finally, Ignatius wrote a letter to the Christians in Ephesus and again opponents are in view.

---

[19] Titus purports to be written to Crete (Tit 1:5).

A number of other documents of the NT have been associated with Ephesus by various scholars, but in my view the connection is too uncertain for them to be used in this study. Firstly, although it is likely that Paul was imprisoned in Ephesus, that he wrote any of the prison epistles (Phil, Col, Philemon) from Ephesus must be regarded as less than likely because the imprisonment itself is conjectural, some points argue against an Ephesian setting for these letters, and the data taken to argue for an Ephesian provenance can all be interpreted in other ways. Secondly, it is possible that Galatians was written from Ephesus, although it could have been written from Corinth, or at an earlier stage in Paul's ministry. But even if it was written in Ephesus, it would add little to our evidence for Paul's ministry in the city. Thirdly, a number of scholars have regarded Romans 16 as a separate letter which was originally addressed to Ephesus, but strong arguments have been given against this view. Fourthly, there is general agreement that in the letter now known as "To the Ephesians" the phrase "ἐν Ἐφέσῳ" in Eph 1:1 was not part of the original text. Accordingly, it cannot be used as evidence for the life of Christians in the city.[20] Fifthly, we will suggest that, although the first collection of Paul's letters may have occurred in Ephesus as part of the work of a "Pauline school", the evidence for this is not sufficiently strong for us to build on this possibility here.

Sixthly, Goodspeed argued that Luke/Acts was written in Ephesus primarily for Ephesian readers.[21] However, the evidence for this is very tenuous[22] and it remains unlikely. Sixthly, 1 Peter is addressed to Christians in Asia Minor (1 Peter 1:1), but given that its recipients were a circle of churches who lived in a wide geographical area, we cannot use it as evidence for the situation of Christians in Ephesus.[23] Finally, some scholars have suggested that Apollos wrote Hebrews, perhaps from Ephesus, which would mean that it might tell us something about the Christians in the city.[24] However this view is purely conjectural and has won little support,[25] and so Hebrews cannot be used here.

---

[20] The first five issues discussed here are covered in more detail in Chapter 2.

[21] Goodspeed, 1937, p27; see also Cook 1981, p15; Berger 1995, p755-65.

[22] Goodspeed notes the amount of space devoted to Ephesus and that Paul's only extended farewell to any of his churches is to the elders of Ephesus. However, neither factor need imply that Luke/Acts was written in Ephesus.

[23] Streeter (1926, p104, 131-4) and Weiss (1937, Vol 2, p685, 786) see Ephesus as the place of origin of 1 Peter. But this view has gained little support.

[24] See the list in Attridge 1989, p4 n28 and for example Montefiore 1964, p9-31. On Montefiore's view, Apollos wrote Hebrews after he had returned to Ephesus from the visit he made to Corinth recorded in Acts 19:1 and while Paul was away from Ephesus on the journey described in Acts 18:20-23.

[25] See Attridge 1989, p4; Barrett 1968, p8-11.

5. What makes a group a group?

In the course of this book, and especially in Parts Three and Four, we will often discuss a particular "group" or "community", terms which we use synonymously. Elliott offers a very helpful definition of a "group":

"The most generically inclusive term denoting a set of two or more individuals who are in reciprocal communication. Social groups are composed of persons whose relationship with one another are a consequence of an interrelated set of statuses and roles. Groups vary in size, duration, stability, mode of contact, objectives, manner of admission, formality, role prescriptions, degree of acquaintance among members, sanctions, etc., and can view themselves as 'in-groups' in contrast to 'out-groups' ('we' vs 'they') from which they distinguish themselves and for which they feel antipathy."[26]

Further, Elliott defines an "in –group" as "Any set of persons whose members perceive themselves as sharing the same distinctive interests and values and as constituting a collective 'we' over against nonmembers or 'out-groups' designated as 'they,' often with negative valuation."[27]

As these definitions imply, a crucial feature of a group is what its members share, or perceive themselves as having in common. This leads on to the question of what features or particular characteristics make a group distinctive? With regard to the sort of "groups" of early Christians that we are discussing here, we suggest that it is helpful to think of the shared features and characteristics, which can all be seen as facets of group identity, as including some of the following:[28]
• a sense of commitment to the group as an entity that must be joined and in which members continue to experience a sense of belonging and some form of shared social life;
• group boundaries of some sort (often defined by many of the characteristics on this list) and ways of maintaining them;
• in connection with boundaries, at least some sense of "us" and "them", and some understanding of attitudes to and interactions with "them";

---

[26] Elliott 1993, p130.

[27] Elliott 1993, p130. He defines an "out-group" (1993, p132) as "Any set of persons that is perceived by members of an in-group as holding different or competing interests and values from those of the in-group and that is designated by in-group members as 'they,' often with negative valuation." Botha (1996, p263) quotes the following definition of a group from Olmsted and Hare: "a plurality of individuals who are in contact with one another, who take one another into account and who are aware of some significant commonality. An essential feature of a group is that its members have something in common and that they believe what they have in common makes a difference."

[28] Some of these characteristics have been derived from Elliott 1993, p110-121 who gives a "Data inventory for synchronic social analysis of early Christian groups." See further Meeks 1983, p74-192; Botha 1996, p262-8; Elliott 1998, p273-313; Barton 1998, p174-6.

• common beliefs and perspectives, including ways of legitimating their existence as a distinct group;
• patterns of behaviour;
• shared rituals of various sorts, including rituals for entry into the group and forms of worship;
• shared attitudes and values;
• distinctive language and symbols, including language for self-designation;
• distinctive world-views and some form of shared narrative;
• loyalty to a particular tradition, and/or to particular people;
• some form of leadership and group structure or organisation;
• some understanding of the locus of authority;
• mechanisms for group discipline and for the management of internal conflict.

Of course, not all groups will exhibit all of these features, and not all group members will share all of the characteristics of the group as a whole.

When I use the term "group" or "community" of, for example, the readers of a particular document, I am suggesting first of all that the members of the "group" would identify themselves as belonging to that particular group. There is a strong sense of group consciousness then. Secondly, I am suggesting that we can analyse the group with regard to at least some of the features or characteristics listed above. Thirdly, I am suggesting that the members of a group would identify themselves as belonging to one particular group (Group "A") and not to another (Group "B"), and that the two groups, A and B, would be distinguishable because they would show differences with regard to at least some of the above features and characteristics.

This raises the question of when the differences with regard to features and characteristics are sufficient to say that the readers of two documents constitute two different "groups"? Of course this is clearest when documents themselves tell us that "we are one group and they are another" (though whether the perception is shared by the other "group" may be a different matter). This will be the case with "opponents" such as John the Seer's opponents, the Nicolaitans. Having seen that they are a "group", we can go on to discuss what makes them distinctive.

But sometimes a document does not address or say anything about the particular "other group" that we suspect is present in the locality. In one of the cases we are concerned with here, that of the readers of the Pastorals and of the Johannine Letters, each document has nothing to say about the readers of the other, and perhaps of course these documents could be to the same group but from different times (or to different groups in different places). But in this sort of case, we need to ask whether the two sets of documents are to the one group or not, and clearly this becomes a matter of judgement and of weighing the evidence. However, when two potentially different groups register quite differently with regard to a range of the above features and characteristics, we can suggest that we are actually observing two different groups.

In seeking to show that there are different "groups" of Christians in Ephesus, we will be analysing some of these shared features and characteristics of groups. Not all of these features will be accessible to us. In particular, from the documents we have we can ascertain some features of the theology of the *authors* concerned, but we are often unable to ascertain the theology of the group of *readers* addressed. Did the group share the author's theology, or did they reject that theology, or misunderstand it? Often we cannot tell. But, we *are* able to discern some of these characteristics with regard to the addressees of our particular documents from what the respective authors say. As noted above, we have analysed particular characteristics because in these cases there is sufficient information for us to be able to make comparisons.

We turn now to Chapter 1, in which I will discuss various facets of the history and significance of the city of Ephesus, and some significant dimensions of its religious life. This forms the context for our study of the earliest Christians in the city.

Chapter 1

The Context

In various ways the context of the city of Ephesus exerted an influence on the life of the early Christians in the city, on the development of their groups and on the ways in which they expressed their beliefs. In this chapter we will discuss some features of that context. Firstly we will discuss the history and significance of the city of Ephesus, and will then turn to three significant facets of the city which featured in particular ways in the life of the early Christians – the cult and temple of Artemis, the imperial cult and finally the Jewish community in the city. At various points in subsequent chapters I will also discuss particular facets of the city as they are relevant.

1. The City of Ephesus

The city of Ephesus is regularly mentioned in literary sources and some literary works were set in the city.[1] The first serious archaeological explorations were undertaken in Ephesus from 1863-74 by John Wood. In 1895 the Austrian Archaeological Institute of Vienna began systematic exploration of the site, work which continues today. Numerous buildings and over 4000 inscriptions have been discovered. Accordingly, we have a detailed knowledge of many facets of the life of the city.[2]

1.1 The History and Significance of Ephesus[3]

From around 1000 to 550 BCE the city of Ephesus was located at the northern base of Mt Pion,[4] near the place where the Cayster river met the Aegean Sea; from 550 BCE, it was situated near the Artemisium. Because of

---

[1] See for example Xenophon's *Ephesiaca*.

[2] For inscriptions from Ephesus Wankel 1979-84, 8 volumes, henceforth IvEph; these contain around 3600 inscriptions; see Horsley 1992a, p120-1. Newly discovered inscriptions are regularly published in JÖAI. The results of Austrian archaeological work have been published in the series *Forschungen in Ephesos*, in *JÖAI* and elsewhere. For discussion of recent archaeological work at Ephesus see Mitchell 1998-99, p149-51; see also Wiplinger and Wlach 1996.

[3] On the history of the province of Asia see Trebilco 1994, p292-302.

[4] See Strabo, *Geog.*640.

subsidence of the land in this latter area, Lysimachus founded a new city in 281 BCE on higher ground in the general area where the city was located in the imperial period.[5] Strabo reports that the people were reluctant to move and only agreed when Lysimachus blocked the sewers during a downpour of rain and so inundated the city.[6] Lysimachus fortified the new city with a wall which extended for more than five miles, and a new harbour was established.[7] The city was laid out on the Hippodamian system, with the only deviation being the so-called Kouretes Street, which followed an older path.

In the third century BCE Ephesus was in turn under the Seleucids, and the Ptolemies of Egypt.[8] After the defeat of Antiochus III, the city was made subject to the rule of Eumenes II in 188,[9] and seems to have flourished under Pergamene rule. Attalos II of Pergamum tried to deepen the harbour which was silting up, by making the entrance narrower through the construction of a mole. However, the mole increased the deposit of silt in the harbour and so made the problem worse.[10]

Ephesus came under the control of Rome after Attalos III of Pergamum bequeathed his kingdom to the Romans in 133 BCE, although Ephesus was granted its freedom by Rome. In the war between Rome and Mithridates, Appian tells us that the Ephesians gladly received Mithridates and in their eagerness to win his favour "even overthrew the Roman statues which had been erected in their cities - for which they paid the penalty not long afterwards."[11] Ephesus seems to have become Mithridates' headquarters and it was from here that he ordered that all Romans and Italians living in Asia

---

[5] See Knibbe 1995, p144-5. The exact location of the city at this time is debated. It has been thought that it was in the general area which was later occupied by the city in the Greco-Roman period; for this view see Keil 1964; Akurgal 1990, p142-71, 354-60; Erdemgil, 1992. However, it has now been suggested that Lysimachus' city may have been between the Hellenistic Harbour and the area later occupied by the Theatre; see Karwiese 1999, p393-8. This would mean that at some later time (perhaps from the last quarter of the second century BCE) the city developed significantly to include the area that it occupied during the imperial period.

[6] Strabo, *Geog.* 14.1.21; on Lysimachus' refoundation of the city see also Pausanias, *Descr. Graec.* 1.9.7; 7.3.4-5, who says Lysimachus brought additional settlers from Lebedos and Colophon.

[7] Lysimachus, whose general had captured the city in 302 BCE, called the new city Arsinoeia, in honour of his wife Arsinoe, but the old name prevailed; see Strabo, *Geog.* 14.1.21.

[8] See Magie 1950, p76, 933 n27, 936-7 n31; Kosmetatou 1999, p185-93. The city was briefly independent from 202 to 197 BCE.

[9] Ephesus lost its claim to freedom because it had received Antiochus III and had been his headquarters during the war; virtually all the other free cities were given their freedom by Rome. Ephesus seems to have recovered its freedom before the middle of the second century BCE, probably soon after 167 BCE; see Magie 1950, p109-111, 117, 954-6, n67, 1040 n16.

[10] See Strabo, *Geog.* 14.1.24.

[11] Appian, *Mith.* 21.

should be killed. The Ephesians complied and even "tore away the fugitives, who had taken refuge in the temple of Artemis, and were clasping the images of the goddess, and slew them",[12] thus disregarding the ancient right of asylum of the sanctuary.

An inscription informs us that in 85 BCE, after Ephesus had revolted against Mithridates, the city attempted to hold the loyalty of its lower classes by matching Mithridates' radical program. Debts owed to the city and to Artemis were cancelled, except for sums publicly lent on mortgages, on which Artemis remitted the interest. The city also made void all suits except those dealing with boundaries and inheritances and certain categories of non-citizens were to be given citizenship if they took up arms. Further, those to whom money was owed voluntarily released their debtors.[13] This gives us some insight into the disturbances in the city caused by the first Mithridatic war. However, Mithridates put down the revolt with great cruelty, but "gave freedom to the Greek cities", presumably including Ephesus, and made other provisions, in an effort to prevent defections.[14]

Ephesus was deprived of its freedom in 84 BCE by Sulla after he had defeated Mithridates and the city did not regain its freedom until c. 47 BCE. The fine imposed on the province by Sulla, in which Ephesus shared, the depredations of tax collectors, and the disruption to trade caused by pirates in the eastern Mediterranean must have greatly affected Ephesus' economy at this time.[15] During his rule Julius Caesar twice saved the money deposited at the temple of Artemis from being seized.[16] After the defeat of Brutus and Cassius, Antony was enthusiastically received in Ephesus in 41 BCE and he and Cleopatra spent the winter of 33/32 BCE in the city, which became a temporary centre of resistance to Octavian.[17] After Octavian's victory at Actium in 31 BCE, Ephesus seems to have remained at least nominally free.[18]

Ephesus was elevated to the status of the capital of the province of Asia in place of Pergamum by Augustus. We do not know Augustus' reasons for doing so; it may have been because of the strategic location of Ephesus as far as land and sea routes were concerned. In addition, while Pergamum was already a well-developed city, since it had been the capital of the Attalids,

---

[12] Appian, *Mith.* 23; Magie 1950, p216. This shows the hostility of the Ephesians to the Romans living among them, primarily because of the greed of tax collectors and merchants; see Rogers 1991, p4-6.

[13] See IvEph. 8.28f; on the inscription see Broughton 1938, p514-5, 559-60; see also Sherwin-White 1984, p242-3.

[14] Appian, *Mith.* 48; see also Magie 1950, p225.

[15] See Rogers 1991, p6-7; Pompey defeated the pirates in 67 BCE.

[16] See Caesar, *Civ.* 3.33 and 105.

[17] See Plutarch, *Ant.* 24.4.

[18] See Plutarch, *Ant.* 24.4, 56; Appian, *Bell. Civ.* 5.6; Friesen 1993a, p7.

Ephesus had a good deal of room for large scale building projects in the city centre.[19]

During Augustus' reign Ephesus experienced tremendous growth and participated fully in the general prosperity which resulted from the *Pax Romana*. As the whole province recovered and as communications with the interior of Asia Minor improved and new cities were founded there, the importance of cities at the head of the great roads to the interior increased. Ephesus, along with Pergamum, Smyrna and Cyzicus benefited greatly.[20]

We have a number of indications of the prominence of the city of Ephesus from the time of Augustus. In 29 BCE Augustus granted the right to dedicate sacred precincts to Dea Roma and Divus Iulius to Ephesus and Nicaea because, according to Cassius Dio, "these cities had at that time attained the chief place in Asia and in Bithynia respectively."[21] The city also received the much prized title "the first and greatest metropolis of Asia" which it uses in inscriptions of this period,[22] and as we have noted it was the capital of the Roman province of Asia.

Several authors also acknowledge the significance of Ephesus at this time. Around 20 CE Strabo wrote of Ephesus that "the city, because of its advantageous situation, ... grows daily, and is the largest emporium in Asia this side of the Taurus."[23] Pliny, in his *Natural History*, dedicated in 77 CE,

---

[19] See Friesen 1993a, p158; 1993b, p26-7; Knibbe and Alzinger 1980, p759; Elliger 1985, p61-2; Brenk 1998, p168; cf. Hemer 1986, p82-4. Pergamum was about 25 miles inland. The building work in Ephesus in the Hellenistic era had been quite slight. For other helpful measures taken by Augustus see Rogers 1991, p9-10, 94. A rescript of Antoninus Pius commanded all governors of Asia to land in Ephesus first; see Dig 1.16.4.5-6. Broughton 1938, p708 suggests this was an old custom which was set in law by Antoninus Pius. Friesen (1993a, p158) notes that although Augustus reorganised the province in 29 BCE and made Ephesus its administrative centre, the first provincial cult was established in Pergamum "as a way of claiming continuity with the past. Pergamum had been the center of Attalid rule and of Roman rule during the Republican period. A provincial cult founded anywhere else except Pergamum in 29 BCE would not have helped consolidate the authority of Augustus in Asia."

[20] See Broughton 1938, p796. An additional factor for Ephesus was the income derived from the cities and farming areas the city owned; see Jones 1971, p78.

[21] Cassius Dio 51.20.6. Augustus selected Pergamum and Nicomedia for the provincial temples of the Imperial cult.

[22] See for example IvEph. 647, 1541, 1543; see also Oster 1992a, p543.

[23] Strabo, *Geog.* 14.1.24 (641); see also 12.8.15. See Pleket 1994, p115-26, who discusses the economy of Ephesus mainly on the basis of inscriptions, and concludes (p122-3) that it was "a large, prosperous city, whose existence presupposes a dynamic and substantial interregional trade. Ephesus was an international 'entrepot', an international service city through which regular flows of goods passed." The wealth of some people in the city is reflected in the size and decoration of the homes on the south side of Kouretes Street which were built about the end of the first century BCE and frequently remodeled thereafter; many

after having spoken of Smyrna, wrote of Ephesus as "the other great luminary of Asia."[24]

Another indication of the wealth and growth of Ephesus in the first and second centuries CE was the number of donations made and public buildings constructed during this period.[25] In the Greco-Roman city monumental public buildings were all important and had become a dominant and crucial defining characteristic of the city and an indicator of status.[26] Building activity in Ephesus is particularly notable from the time of Augustus onwards. Through her buildings, the citizens of Ephesus expressed the greatness of the city. As Oster notes:

"The elevation of Ephesus in the dramatic urbanization policies of Augustus is revealed in its architecture. This revitalization included construction of aqueducts, repavement of streets, and Hellenization, including at times enlargement of agoras. As the political centerpiece of the province of Asia, Ephesus' burgeoning architectural program also encompassed triumphal monuments honoring C. Memmius, son-in-law of the Roman general Sulla, and M. Vipsanius Agrippa, adopted son and ally of Augustus. The new political realities of the early Empire were strikingly evident in the comprehensive romanization of the civic space in the State Agora (58 x 160m)."[27]

In the time of Paul the notable buildings of the city would have included the Temple of Artemis, the Magnesian Gate, the Upper or State Agora including an Augustan basilica and chalcidicum, the Bouleuterion, the temple of Dea Roma and Divus Iulius, the Prytaneion, the Memmius monument, the temple of Isis or Augustus, the monument of Pollio, an Octagonal structure, the Heroon of Androklos, the Gate of Mazaeus and Mithridates, the Tetragonos Agora, the Fountain House, the Palace of the Proconsul (?), the Theatre, the Harbour Gate, the Temple of Apollo, the Stadium and the

---

of the rooms were decorated with wall paintings and had high quality mosaics on the floors. For further details see Chapter 2 n208.

[24] Pliny, *N.H.* 5.120.

[25] See Broughton 1938, p719; 752-5; Alzinger 1974; Scherrer 1995a, p4-15; Note Rogers (1991, p141): "The visible leaders of the Ephesian aristocracy utterly transformed the architectural and visual character of the city through their building projects between the reign of Augustus and the time of Domitian."

[26] Mitchell 1993, 1, p80-1 notes the shift from political autonomy as an index of city status during the classical and Hellenistic periods to other criteria under the Roman Empire, in particular public building. In the most prosperous period of the Roman Empire, public building remained one of the few forms of independent political expression open to the cities. By the second century, which was the great age of construction, a city was expected to have a range of public buildings including fortifications, religious structures, political meeting places, places for cultural and educational activities, civic amenities, and decorative monuments.

[27] Oster 1992a, p543-4; see further Hueber 1997, p47-90.

Koressos Gate. Many of these buildings had been constructed or significantly renovated during or since the reign of Augustus.[28]

There was also clearly much goodwill in Ephesus towards the Julio-Claudian emperors, as shown by the creation of a new tribe named Sebaste, as well as subdivisions of the tribes with names such as Kaisarion, Tiberion and Klaudion.[29]

As we will note in more detail below, the third provincial imperial cult of the koinon of Asia was granted to the city of Ephesus by Domitian and the temple was dedicated in 89/90 CE. This changed the relationship between Ephesus and other cities of Asia, by increasing Ephesus' status. As Friesen notes: "Ephesus would henceforth be more prominent in provincial assemblies, it would have more claim to imperial favor, its wealthy citizens would have greater access to more distinguished offices, delegations from various cities would make annual trips to her festivals, and new sources of revenue would become available."[30] During the reign of Domitian a temple and cult of the Sebastoi was established and a very large bath-gymnasium complex (the "Harbour Gymnasium") was built in honour of Domitian, in conjunction with the establishment of Ephesian Olympic games which were also in Domitian's honour.[31]

Early in the second century CE it was said of Ephesus that it was a city which "grew in size beyond all other cities of Ionia and Lydia, and stretched herself out to the sea outgrowing the land on which she is built."[32] In the mid second century Aelius Aristides said that Ephesus was regarded by all as "the common chancellery (ταμιεῖον) of Asia ... and her recourse in need."[33]

Ephesus generally flourished during the second century,[34] although it was adversely affected by the plague in the latter half of the second century and by the policy of some of the emperors.[35]

---

[28] See the chart in Rogers 1991, p128-35 for details and references and the discussion, 86-107; see also White 1995, p51-4; Hueber 1997b, p251-69. For bibliography for these buildings see Oster 1987, Index. Of course many other notable buildings were constructed in the city after Paul's time. For a plan of the city see Karwiese 1995b.

[29] See Rogers 1991, p12. He also comments that this shows how "Roman terms and categories had penetrated the defining nomenclature of citizen status at Ephesus."

[30] Friesen 1993a, p38. For the dating see Friesen 1993a, p41-9. The first provincial imperial cult was built in Pergamum in 29 BCE, the second in Smyrna in around 26 CE.

[31] See Friesen 1993a, p34-7, 114-41; Kearsley 1999, p147-55.

[32] Philostratus, *Vita Apol.* 8.7.8; see also Seneca, *Ep.* 102.21.

[33] Aelius Aristides, *Orat.* 23.24; English translation Behr 1981, vol 2, p30. Aelius Aristides lived from 117 to 180 CE; see van der Horst 1981, p1.

[34] On how Ephesus responded to Trajan's rule see Schowalter 1999, p121-6. In this period notable new buildings included the Library of Celsus and the Nymphaeum of Trajan; see further White 1995, p53-6.

1.2 Population

The population of the city in the Roman period is generally estimated at between 200,000 - 250,000.[36] This would probably make Ephesus the third largest city in the Empire after Rome and Alexandria.[37]

1.3 The Strategic Location of Ephesus

Ephesus was located on a number of very important land and sea routes, with the result that it was a major centre of international trade. Sea traffic from the Aegean to the west, the Bosporus and Dardanelles to the north, from Palestine to the east, and from Egypt to the south all called in at Ephesus.[38] Ephesus was also a key centre for land transportation. As well as having good land routes to the north and the south,[39] two great highways led from Ephesus to the east. Firstly, the ancient Persian Royal Road, the *koine hodos*, the common highway, was a very important overland route which went from

---

[35] In the third century (ca. 262 CE) the city was invaded by Goths and the temple of Artemis was heavily damaged, never to be restored. On later Christian architecture in Ephesus see Hueber 1997, p94-107.

[36] Pleket 1994, p119 notes that Roozenbeek argues in an unpublished dissertation for a population of around 180,000 (not all of whom lived in the city itself), on the basis of the number of chiliastyes and on references in literary sources. Previous estimates (such as by Broughton (1938, p813) who considers 225,000 to be somewhat too low; Oster (1990b, p301): 250,000; Magie (1950, p585, 1446 n50): 200,000) were based on the belief that there were 40,000 male citizens in Ephesus in the second century CE (and hence a total population of around 225,000) but this rests on a misunderstanding of IvEph 951; see Warden and Bagnall 1988, p220-3. The inscription reads 1,040 rather than 40,000. This means these previous population figures are speculative; see further Aune 1997, p136-7. White (1995, p40-3) opts for 180,000. However, in support of the figure given in the text, we can note that we are more certain that Pergamum's population was between 180,000 and 200,000 in this period, and Ephesus was at least as large as Pergamum; see Mitchell 1993, 1, p243-4. On the difficulties of making population estimates see McGing 2002, p88-9. On changes in the population of Ephesus over time see White 1995, p41-65.

[37] See Duncan-Jones 1974, p260 n4; Stark 1991, p77-88.

[38] Oster (1990a, p1727) notes the importance of trade between Egyptian cities and Ephesus. Strabo, *Geog.* 14.1.24 mentions that the port of Ephesus was already silting up in the time of Attalus II. The harbour was also dredged in 61 CE; see Tacitus, *Ann.* 16.23; see also Oster 1992a, p543; Horsley 1992a, p134-5; IvEph 23, 274, 2061, 3066, 3071 which "testify to major efforts at keeping the harbour serviceable during and after the period of Paul's ministry there. ... These dredging operations were apparently successful since Aristides (*Orat.* 23.24) of the 2d century A.D. ... refer[s] to the accessibility of Ephesus' harbors." (Oster 1992a, p543). For a discussion of the harbours and the coastline of Ephesus see Zabehlicky 1995, p201-15; Fieger 1998, p47-50; Kraft, Kayan, Brückner, Rapp 2000, p175-233. The harbour is now silted up, and the city is more than 7 km inland.

[39] See Strabo, *Geog.* 14.2.29; Aelius Aristides, *Or.* 51.3f; see also Broughton 1938, p862-3.

Ephesus up the Maeander Valley to Tralles, Nysa, Antiocheia and onwards to the river Euphrates and beyond.[40] Secondly, from Ephesus one could travel to Sardis and then on the ancient Persian Royal Road which went to Susa; this became the primary means of linking Ephesus with the province of Galatia.[41] Thus the two great trade-routes from the Euphrates both ended at Ephesus. Local trade from the Maeander Valley and the interior of Asia Minor also came to Ephesus. Given this strategic location it is not surprising that Ephesus was chosen as the capital of the Roman province of Asia by Augustus and the base for the financial staff of the *aerarium* and the *fiscus*.[42]

Another indication of the strategic location and importance of Ephesus within the province of Asia is given by the fact that a college of *tabellarii* (messengers or couriers) was based in the city. Roman military control and the efficiency of their administration depended on rapid communications and so the Romans devised an elaborate series of communication networks. Ephesus, as the base for the college of *tabellarii*, was the centre of the Romans' communications network for Asia and courier routes would have radiated from Ephesus to all the administrative centres of the province.[43] In addition, the city was also the central bureau and treasury for the tax collectors in Asia, who had dispatch-bearers of their own who carried communication to and from Ephesus.[44]

Ephesus was also the centre of a *conventus*, or assize district. Since before Sulla's settlement of 85 BCE, Asia had been divided into twelve or thirteen assize districts, which were named after the most important cities where assizes were held. The Roman proconsul, or one of his legates, regularly held a judicial court in these principal cities of the province so that litigants and petitioners could bring cases to them for adjudication.[45] That Ephesus was the centre of a *conventus* would have contributed further to its prosperity.[46]

---

[40] For the route see Strabo, *Geog.* 14.2.29: "Since there is a kind of common road constantly used by all who travel from Ephesus towards the east ...." For the probable route see Levick 1967, map following p256; see also Magie 1950, p40.

[41] Levick 1967, p13. Aquilius rebuilt both highways when he organised the province of Asia in 129-6 BCE, precisely so that Ephesus, the chief port, could be connected to the distant parts of the province; see Magie 1950, p157; see also Ramsay 1890b, p27-62, 164-6.

[42] See Magie 1950, p157; Knibbe and Alzinger 1980, p759.

[43] See Mitchell 1993, 1, p129; IvEph 2200A, 4112.

[44] See Cicero *Att.* 5.13.1; *Fam.* 5.20.9; Magie 1950, p165. Oster (1992a, p543) comments: "The fact that Republican period milestones from Asia used Ephesus as the point of origin for measuring distances portrays the continuing significance of this site as a travel hub at the period contemporary with nascent Christianity."

[45] For a list of the conventus see Pliny *N.H.* 5.105-126; see also Cicero *ad. Fam.* 3.8.6; Magie 1950, p171-2; Mitchell 1993, 1, p64-5; 2, p33 and note 187. On the development and organisation of the system and its operation see Chapot 1904, p353-7; Habicht 1975, p64-91; Burton 1975, p92-106; Ameling 1988, p9-24. In Ionia the three assize centres were Smyrna,

2. Artemis of Ephesus

Ephesus was of course the home of many cults,[47] but the most significant and powerful deity in the city was Artemis of Ephesus. Artemis features in the narrative of Act 19 but the cult is also a significant part of the context for the life of the early Christians in the city.[48] Although Artemis was worshipped in many places, the cult of Artemis of Ephesus had its own distinctive characteristics and also changed over time.[49] It was the cult of the Ephesian Artemis which, more than anything else, made Ephesus a centre of religious life during our period. But the influence of the cult of Artemis extended beyond the religious sphere to the civic, economic, and cultural life of the city.

Ephesus and Miletus. We have evidence of the way governors conducted their business from Cicero and Pliny the Younger.

[46] Dio Chrysostom (*Or.* 35.15-17), speaking at Apameia Celaenae, gives a vivid idea of the regular influx of visitors associated with the assize and the economic advantages which accrued to an assize-city. On this passage see Jones 1978, p67-8. Being an assize city was also a mark of honour.

[47] Oster (1992a, p548) notes, "Ephesus' religious climate was similar to that of many other large cities in the Greek East." A plethora of Greco-Roman and some Anatolian deities were worshipped there, including Aphrodite, Apollos, Asclepius, Athena, Cabiri, Demeter, Dionysus, Egyptian Cults, Ge, God Most High, Hecate, Hephaestus, Hercules, Hestia, the Mother goddess, Pluton, Poseidon, Zeus and other minor deities; see Oster 1992, p548. There were also Temples such as a Temple of Hestia (part of the Prytaneion), a temple of Serapis, a Sanctuary of Zeus and the Mother Goddess (see Oster 1992a, p545). A number of heroes were also venerated, including Alexander the Great, Androclus (regarded as the Greek founder of Ephesus), Apollonius of Tyana (who performed an exorcism to rescue the city from a plague), Pixodarus Evangelus (who discovered the quarry for marble used in the construction of the temple of Artemis) and Publius Servilius Isauricus, proconsul of Asia 46-44 BCE; see IvEph 3066, 702; Friesen 1993a, p9-10). On other deities in Ephesus see Knibbe 1978, p489-503; Oster 1990a, p1661-98; Aurenhammer 1995, p251-80. On the Imperial cult in Ephesus see section 3. For recent discussions of Demeter see Suys 1998, p173-88; on Isis and Sarapis see Takács 1999, p269-74; on Egyptian cults in general see Walters 1995, p281-309; 1999, p315-24.

[48] On Pagan cults and pagan worship see in particular MacMullen, 1981; Lane Fox 1986; Mitchell 1993, 2, p11-31; Klauck 2000.

[49] Here I am much indebted to Oster 1990a, p1699-1726, who gives a very full bibliography. See also Oster 1976, p27-44; Fleischer 1973; Taylor, in Lake and Cadbury 1933, p251-6. The origin of the worship of the goddess in Ephesus is shrouded in obscurity. Although Artemis of Ephesus is similar to the Artemis of the Greeks, there were substantial differences and the two are not to be identified.

2.1 The Temple of Artemis

The Temple of Artemis, or the Artemisium, was outside the city wall and about two kilometres from the centre of Roman Ephesus. The temple which stood during the first century CE was the last and greatest of several temples built on the site, and was clearly the chief glory of the city.[50] It measured 130 by 70 metres,[51] and thus was about four times the size of the Parthenon in Athens. It contained 127 columns, 2m in diameter and 20m high. It was richly adorned with the works of the greatest painters and sculptors of the age. The temple featured in many of the lists of the seven wonders of the ancient world and was also the subject of a number of books, none of which are extant.[52] The epigramist, Antipater wrote as follows:

"I have set eyes on the wall of lofty Babylon on which is a road for chariots, and the statue of Zeus by the Alpheus, and the hanging gardens, and the colossus of the Sun, and the huge labour of the high pyramids, and the vast tomb of Mausolus; but when I saw the house of Artemis that mounted to the clouds, those other marvels lost their brilliancy, and I said, 'Lo, apart from Olympus, the Sun never looked on aught so grand.' "[53]

The reputation of the Temple and of the goddess in the city and province is also summed up by an inscription of around 44 CE which includes the phrase: "τὸ τε τῆς Ἀρτέμιδος αὐτῆς ἱερόν, ὃ τῆς ἐπαρχείας ὅλης ἐστὶν κόσμος - The temple of Artemis herself, which is the ornament of the whole province".[54] As a result of its grandeur and widespread fame, the temple was a great attraction to ancient travellers, as well as of course, to worshippers of Ephesian Artemis. The crowds who came to Ephesus to visit the temple must have contributed greatly to the prosperity of the city.[55]

---

[50] Aelius Aristides, *Or.* 23.25 writes: "When her temple has been erected greater than before ..." On the temples built on the site see in particular Bammer 1972; 1982, p61-87; 1984. Note also Wood 1877; Hogarth et al., 1908; Trell 1945; 1988, p78-99. According to Plutarch, *Alex.* 3.5, an earlier temple, built around 500 BCE had been destroyed by fire in 356 BCE, on the night of Alexander the Great's birth. The latest temple on the site was burned in ca. 262 CE by invading Goths and left desolate; total destruction was completed by Christians.

[51] See Oster 1992a, p545; Bammer 1972, Abb. 5.

[52] See Oster 1990a, p1713. The temple features in two-thirds of the twenty four lists of the seven wonders of the world compiled by Lanowski 1965, p1020-30.

[53] Antipater, in *The Greek Anthology*, 9.58; see also Pausanias, *Descr. Graec.* 7.5.4; 4.31.8.

[54] This is from the edict of Paullus Fabius Persicus; see IvEph 17-19, here 18b.1-3. A long inscription recording the reorganisation of the customs laws of the province of Asia was inscribed in 62 CE at the Temple of Artemis, showing how important Artemis and the Temple were for the whole province; See Engelmann and Knibbe 1989, p1-209.

[55] We can well understand the town clerk's point in Acts 19:35 when he says: "who is there that does not know that the city of the Ephesians is the temple keeper of the great Artemis."

We know little about the sacrifices and rituals held at the Temple during the Roman period. It has been thought that up until the first century BCE, the high priests of the cult were a class of eunuch priests who were given the title Megabyzoi,[56] but Smith has recently shown that it is highly unlikely that there was such a class of priests.[57] But we do know that by 104 CE the priestess of Artemis had become the chief official of the cult.[58] We know the title of a number of other functionaries who officiated at the temple, and a little of what some of them did. For example, the neopoioi played an important role in processions, and maintained the fabric of the temple and the hymnodoi sang songs in praise of Artemis at festivals.[59]

2.2 The Divine Attributes of Artemis of Ephesus

An indication of what was thought about the goddess comes from the meaning ascribed to her name Ἄρτεμις. Strabo wrote: "And Artemis has her name from the fact that she makes people ἀρτεμέας", that is, safe and sound, and Artemidorus adds ὑγιές - healthy.[60] There are other indications that Artemis was thought of as being benevolent to her followers. The term ἐπήκοος was used of Artemis, showing the conviction that she listened to prayer.[61] Artemis was also a giver of oracles in which she gave advice to her followers.[62] In another inscription Hestia Boulaia and Artemis of Ephesus were asked to save (σώζετε) the petitioner and his children.[63] Many people gave thanks to Artemis in inscriptions, probably for a variety of reasons.[64] In

---

[56] See Strabo, *Geog.* 14.1.23; Xenophon, *Anab.* 5.3.6; the term was of Persian origin.

[57] Smith (1996, p323-35) has shown that there is no epigraphical evidence for the title and the literary evidence is late and self-contradictory. It seems likely then that the actual title of the priest at Ephesus before the Roman period is unknown. Smith (1996, p332) notes that the title *archhiereus* is attested at Ephesus only during the Roman period.

[58] As shown by IvEph 27.265-8, the Salutaris inscription, which mentions the priestess, but not the Megabyzus; see Rogers 1991, p54; see also Picard 1922, p182; Baugh 1999, p453-60.

[59] Other titles include the Essenes (IvEph see Index); the neopoioi (IvEph 21, 1450, 1452), the hierokerux (sacred herald, IvEph 53); the kouretes (IvEph 1449); the epheboi (IvEph 6) and the kosmeterai (Mistress of Robes; IvEph 1449). See Oster 1990a, p1722 for a list of these titles. On the functions of some of these see Picard 1922, p163-97, 239-57; Rogers 1991, p45-8, 54-8. On the "Essenes" see Kampen 1986, p68-74.

[60] See Strabo, *Geog.* 14.1.6; Artemidorus, *Onir.* 2.35. This sort of etymology is not convincing, but it does indicate what people thought about Artemis. On Artemidorus see Olszewski 1999, p275-82; Schwabl 1999, p283-7.

[61] See IvEph 504; see also Weinreich 1912, nos 24-6.

[62] Picard 1922, p362-4; see also IvEph 533; 645.7.

[63] Keil 1939, p120 no 2.

[64] See for example IvEph 960.2,9; 961.1,7 (see New Docs 4, p127-9); 1588.3-4; 1578B.2. On Artemis' magical powers, which she used for the benefit of her devotees see Arnold 1989, p22-4; see also Knibbe, Engelmann and Iplikçioglu 1993, p130-2, no 25.

Achilles Tatius we read that "Yesterday, when I was weeping at the thought of my coming sacrifice, the goddess Artemis stood before me in a dream and said, 'Weep no more; thou shalt not die, for I will be thy helper'."[65] The romance written by Xenophon of Ephesus, probably in the second century CE, testifies to the devotion which Artemis could inspire, and to the belief that she aided her followers in their need.[66]

Artemis was also worshipped because of her lordship over supernatural powers.[67] She was acclaimed as Lady (Κυρία),[68] Saviour (Σώτειρα),[69] a heavenly goddess (οὐράνιος θεὸς ῎Αρτεμις ᾿Εφεσία),[70] and the Queen of the Cosmos (Βασιληῒς κόσμου).[71] She was also described as greatest (μεγίστη),[72] great (μεγάλη),[73] holiest (ἁγιωτάτη),[74] and most manifest (ἐπιφανεστάτη).[75] In statues of Artemis, she is often depicted wearing a zodiacal necklace, which is thought to have expressed her power over fate.[76]

It is often thought that Artemis of Ephesus was seen as a fertility goddess.[77] However, Oster has noted that this view of the cult stems in large

---

[65] Achilles Tatius 4.1.4; see also 7.14.6; 8.2.2-3.

[66] See Xenophon of Ephesus 1.2.2-4; 1.8.1; 1.10.5; 1.11.5; 2.11.8; 3.5.5; 5.15.2; text in Dalmeyda 1926; translation given in Hadas 1953. Xenophon may have written his *Ephesiaca* as early as 125 CE; see Schmeling 1980, p18-19. For devotion towards Artemis see also IvEph. 690.8-12.

[67] This list comes from Oster 1990a, p1724.

[68] IvEph. 27.363; 960.3, 9-10; 962.2; 1578B.2; 1588.3.

[69] IvEph. 26.4, 18.

[70] TAM 3, no 390, from Termessus.

[71] Oster 1990a, p1724.

[72] IvEph. 27.224-5, 324; Keil 1939, p119 no 1.3.

[73] In the romance written by Xenophon of Ephesus (*Eph.* 1.11.5), we have the expression "τὴν μεγάλην ᾿Εφεσίων ῎Αρτεμιν - Great Artemis of the Ephesians". In Achilles Tatius (8.9.13) we read "But the great goddess (ἡ μεγάλη θεός) Artemis has saved them both"; an inscription from the time of Hadrian (IvEph. 276) reads τῆς μεγάλης θεᾶς ᾿Αρτέμιδος; cf. Achilles Tatius 7.16. See also Act 19:27, 28, 34. For other inscriptions which use μεγάλη of Artemis see IvEph 27.224; 2026.10. For μέγας used of other gods in Ephesus see IvEph 1252, 3414-5, 3716, 3720; see also Lampe 1992, p64 n19. For the epithet "Great" of Artemis (not Ephesian Artemis) elsewhere see for example Ramsay 1890b, p410; 1904b, p138-9. We also have a number of parallels in inscriptions where other gods are called "Great". For example, "Μέγας ᾿Απόλλω Λειμηνός - Great is Apollo Lermenus"; see Ramsay 1889, p222, no 7; see also p226, no 21: "Μεγάλη ᾿Αναειτις - Great is Anaeitis". Both phrases begin their inscriptions, and thus are similar to acclamations. Note also Aelius Aristides, *Or.* 48,7. "And I cried out in my dream: 'Great is Asclepius' (μέγας ὁ ᾿Ασκληπιός)"; see also 48,21; 45,23; see also New Docs 1, p105-7; Peterson 1926.

[74] IvEph. 3061.6-7; 3072.2.

[75] IvEph. 27.344, 385; Picard 1922, p362-4; see also *New Docs* 4, 80-1.

[76] See Fleischer 1973, p70-2; Tafel 7-9, 18, 33-4; see also LiDonnici 1992, p407; in general Fleischer 1999, p605-9.

[77] Finegan 1981, p156 writes: "Although the Greek Artemis was primarily a huntress, the Ephesian Artemis was primarily a deity of fertility, and in this capacity, her symbol was the

part from the Christian polemic against Artemis, which interpreted the egg-shaped objects on the front of the cult image as breasts.[78] Yet, that these objects are breasts, and hence symbolic of fertility, is an interpretation found only in polemical sources,[79] and while modern scholarship has reached no consensus about what these objects actually are, it remains unlikely that they are breasts.[80] There is also evidence which suggests that this connection with fertility is unfounded. Prior to the Roman period and in the second century Ephesian Artemis is represented on coins as the Huntress with stags, and in the Salutaris inscription of 104 CE she is spoken of as accompanied by two stags.[81] Secondly, we should note the silence of all primary sources about this supposed link with fertility. The myths of Ephesian Artemis do not point in this direction, nor do any of the epithets given to the goddess,[82] and one inscription from Rome calls Artemis of Ephesus παρθένος.[83] Thus, while there was undoubtedly Anatolian and other influence on the goddess in the Roman period,[84] none of our evidence suggests that fertility was thought to be a prominent characteristic of Artemis at this time.

---

egg." See also Wernicke in *RE* 2, 1895, col 1372-3; Filson 1945, p75; Johnson 1979, p79; McRay 1991, p254.

[78] Oster 1990a, p1725-6; see also Baugh 1999, p452-3. For the Christian polemic see Minucius Felix *Octav.* 22.5; Jerome, *Comm. in Ep. Paul.* prooem, given in Fleischer 1973, p75. The depiction of Artemis before the Greco-Roman period shows a degree of variety. However, the depiction became more standardised later, with the upper part of her body covered in egg shaped objects, and from waist to ankles she is covered in bands on which are depicted animals and birds. The point at which this type became more or less fixed cannot be determined; the earliest dated representation of the type we have is found on cistophoric coins of Ephesus around 133 BCE; see Head 1892, no 144.

[79] See the preceding note for references.

[80] Fleischer 1973, p87; for a review of the suggestions of what the objects are see Karweise in *RE Supp* 12, 1970, 323-6; Trell 1988, p87-8; Fleischer 1973, p74-88; Mussies 1990, p182-5; Burkert 1999, p68-70. LiDonnici (1992, p391-411) argues the objects are breasts, but that they show that Artemis was a symbolic wife, protectress and nursing mother of Ephesus rather than a fertility goddess. Portefaix (1999, p611-17) supports the view which sees the pendants as the scrota of bulls.

[81] For the coins see Karweise in *RE Supp* 12, 1970, col 316, 337; for the Salutaris inscription (which will be dealt with in detail later) see IvEph. 27. 157-9; Rogers 1991, p159; see also p110. In Xenophon of Ephesus 1.2.4 it is said that horses and dogs were part of Artemis' festive procession, in which hunting weapons were also carried. On the probable change in the form of the cult statue in the mid-second century BCE see Brenk 1998, p157-71; see also Thomas 1995, p95-8.

[82] See Oster 1990a, p1726.

[83] IG 14, 964; see also Achilles Tatius 6.21.2.

[84] Oster (1990a, p1728) notes that some scholars opt for an Anatolian interpretation of the goddess in the Roman period, particularly by seeing Artemis as strongly connected to the Earth mother. However, by this time, Ephesus had been in constant contact with non-Anatolian forces for a long period and the processes of Hellenization and Romanization had affected the cult of Artemis.

2.3 The Characteristics of the Cult

Mitchell gives a helpful summary of religious activity in our period:

"Religious activity in the cities of the empire was, with rare exceptions, explicit and public, often involving the whole community in unified celebration of the gods. Its significance lay in rituals which all could observe and in which many citizens participated. These range from prayer, sacrifice, solemn ceremony, and religious processions to feasts, games and festivals."[85]

The cult of Artemis conformed to this pattern, as we will now attempt to show.

In Greek myth, the birthplace of Artemis, the daughter of Zeus and Leto and the twin sister of Apollo, was generally a grove known as Ortygia. Strabo tells us that according to the Ephesians there was an area known as Ortygia in the region of Ephesus and the Ephesians identified this grove with the nativity site of Artemis of Ephesus.[86] Clearly, by the time of the early Empire, the nativity myths of the Greek Artemis had been transferred to Artemis of Ephesus.

We know of two major festivals held in honour of Artemis of Ephesus. The Ἀρτεμίσια was held annually in the month of Artemision (March-April), both names being derived from Artemis. The Artemisia probably included athletic, theatrical and musical competitions.[87] One of the reasons for the popularity of the Artemisia may have been the custom described by Xenophon of Ephesus, who said in his romance that it had become traditional for young women to select their fiances, and young men their brides at this festival. As a result, according to Xenophon, at the time of the festival the city was full of local citizens as well as many visitors.[88]

A second festival was the celebration of the nativity of Artemis of Ephesus, held on the 6th of Thargelion (May-June). Oster notes:

"Because of Artemis' close tie with the city of Ephesus, and because legend reported that it was the site of her nativity, we can be sure that this was one of the largest and most magnificent religious celebrations in Ephesus' liturgical calendar."[89]

---

[85] Mitchell 1993, 1, p113.

[86] See Strabo, *Geog.* 14.1.20; see also Tacitus, *Ann.* 3.61.1.

[87] See Oster 1990a, p1708-9; Strabo, *Geog.* 14.1.20; Dionysius of Halicarnassus, *Antiq. Rom.* 4.25.4; IvEph. 1606.15; 1615.11; 4114.4. In general see Arnold 1972, p17-22. One of the functions of the Gerusia at Ephesus in the Imperial period was to provide funds to add a certain additional splendour to the celebration of festivals connected with Artemis; see Oliver 1941, p26, 37.

[88] See Xenophon of Ephesus 1.2.2-4.

[89] Oster 1990a, p1711; see also Knibbe 1995, p144.

The Salutaris inscriptions tells us that during this festival, as on other occasions, a procession which included people who carried images of Artemis along with other images, departed from the Artemisium, entered the city at the Magnesian Gate, continued to the theatre, left the city by the Koressos Gate and returned to the Artemisium.[90]

We also learn about some of the cultic acts performed during the nativity celebrations of Artemis from Strabo, who tells us something of what took place at Ortygia, the birth place of Artemis of Ephesus. Strabo writes: "A general festival is held there annually; and by a certain custom the youths vie for honour, particularly in the splendour of their banquets there. At that time, also, a special college of the Kouretes hold symposiums and perform certain mystic sacrifices."[91] We can suggest that on the day of the festival "the whole city of Ephesos would have been decked out to celebrate the birthday party of Artemis ... Visitors from around the whole Greek-speaking world [would have] come to see the annual re-enactment of Artemis' birth."[92]

2.4 The Temple of Artemis and Economics.

The Temple of Artemis was intricately connected with the economic structures of Ephesus and of the province of Asia. Large deposits of money were stored in the Temple. Dio Chrysostom provides a detailed account of this:

You know about the Ephesians, of course, and that large sums of money are in their hands, some of it belonging to private citizens and deposited in the temple of Artemis, not alone money of the Ephesians but also of aliens and of persons from all parts of the world, and in some cases of commonwealths and kings, money which all deposit there in order that it may be safe, since no one has ever yet dared to violate that place, although countless wars have occurred in the past and the city has often been captured.[93]

---

[90] See below for a discussion of the Salutaris inscription.

[91] Strabo, *Geog.* 14.1.20. The Kouretes were a special group of Artemis' priests. On the annual celebration of Artemis' mysteries and the role of the Kouretes see Knibbe 1981, p70-3; IvEph 26; *New Docs* 6, 196-202; Rogers 1991, p150-1, n15; 1999, p241-50; Portefaix 1999, p611-17; see also Horsley 1992b, p141-6. Note that from the time of the early empire there was probably a transfer of responsibility for the celebrations of the mysteries of Artemis from the temple of Artemis to the Prytaneion, through the direction of the prytanis; see Rogers 1991, p44; 1999, p245. However, Salutaris associated his benefactions with the Temple of Artemis, not the Prytaneion.

[92] Rogers 1991, p68.

[93] Dio Chrysostom, *Or.* 31.54; he clearly exaggerates the security of the Temple; see Oster 1990a, p1718, n443. On the Temple as a bank see also Plautus, *Bacchides* 306ff; Strabo, *Geog.* 14.1.22; Xenophon, *Anab.* 5.3.4f; Plutarch, *Demeter* 30.1; Caesar, *Bell. Civ.* 3.33,103; see also Thomas 1995, p98-100; Burkert 1999, p65-6. On the wealth of the temple see Pausanias, *Descr. Graec.* 7.2.6; 7.5.2. As noted above, in the second century Aelius Aristides (Orat 23.24) referred to Ephesus as "the common chancellery (ταμιεῖον) of Asia ...

Artemis also had her own financial estate, which was one of the largest in Asia.[94] The assets which belonged to the Temple came from gifts and bequests, and from revenue from property and livestock, such as the sacred herds, which were owned by the goddess.[95] Thus the Temple could, for example, lend money at interest and loan money on mortgages.[96] Hence Broughton describes the temple of Artemis as "the biggest bank in Asia".[97] Although we have evidence that the health of the financial affairs of the Artemisium fluctuated over time, mainly due to the wisdom, or otherwise, of those who managed the assets,[98] it is clear that Artemis of Ephesus exercised a great deal of influence on the economic activity of both Ephesus and Asia Minor in our period, and contributed greatly to the financial welfare of the region.[99]

---

and her recourse in need." This reputation probably stemmed in large measure from the resources of Temple of Artemis.

[94] See Broughton 1938, p645; Picard 1922, p69-87. She owned pastures, quarries, fisheries, and extensive estates.

[95] See for example Strabo, *Geog.* 14.1.26, 29; Xenophon, *Anab.* 5.3.9; Knibbe, Meriç and Merkelbach 1979, p139-47. Arrian, *Anab.* 1.17.10 records that Alexander the Great decreed that the tribute which Ephesus had formerly paid to the Persians should be paid instead to the sanctuary of Artemis of Ephesus. For the wealth of Artemis in the time of Lysimachus see Oliver 1941, p15, 17; Strabo, *Geog.* 14.1.21. Because of the great economic importance of the Temple, Lysimachus transferred the control of the sanctuary's wealth from the potentially irresponsible priests to the re-organized Gerusia.

[96] See IvEph. 8.33 mentions ἱεραὶ μισθώσεις - sacred leases for land belonging to the goddess; see also IvEph. 577; Oliver 1941, p25; Broughton 1938, p559-60; Oster 1990a, p1717-19. In either 304 BCE or around 285 Prepelaus, general to Lysimachus, guaranteed to the Artemisium its former privilege of keeping the standard weight. This was most important to an institution which made loans and received payments, since it helped to protect the institution against fraudulent currency. This shows the importance of the Artemisium as a bank; see Oliver 1941, p19-20, 53-4, no 1 = IvEph. 1449. See also Knibbe, Engelmann and Iplikçioglu 1989, p206-7, no 37 (time of Tiberius), which probably concerns money contributed by donors which was to be deposited in the Artemisium and was to be lent out together with other temple capital; see also SEG 39.1176.

[97] Broughton 1938, p890.

[98] The Artemisium was very wealthy in the time of Lysimachus but sometime after Lysimachus the city of Ephesus seems to have gradually assumed control over the finances of the sanctuary. Later, Augustus restored to Artemis an abundant income but the unscrupulous policy of those who administered the estate meant that by 44 CE the sanctuary lacked the necessary funds for the care and arrangements of the dedications. Steps were taken to remedy this situation by Paullus Fabius Persicus; see IvEph 17-19; Broughton 1938, p891; Oliver 1941, p14-21, 48; Knibbe, Meriç and Merkelbach 1979, p139.

[99] See Oster 1990a, p1719; Oliver 1941, p19. The income from Artemis' estates were used to maintain the temple and its cult, and for other purposes in the city; see Horsley 1992a, p147.

2.5 Artemis of Ephesus – A unique bond

Artemis was in a special sense, "Artemis of the Ephesians" (Acts 19:28, 34). There was believed to be a unique bond between Artemis and the city of Ephesus and its people. Artemis can be called ἡ ἀρχηγέτις[100] - the founder of the city, or προκαθηγεμών[101] - guide of our city. She can be described as [ἡ π]ροεστῶσα τῆς πόλεως[102] - the tutelary goddess of the city, and she can be called simply "the Ephesian goddess".[103] We have already noted that in the local nativity myth, Artemis was said to have been born near to the city. The frequency of her name in official documents and on coins indicates her relationship with the city, and the names of new citizens of Ephesus were inscribed on the wall of the temple of Artemis, showing the link between the city and the goddess.[104] Further, Artemis can represent Ephesus on coins celebrating treaties between Ephesus and other cities and thus personifies the city.[105] A result of this bond was that Artemis was thought of as protecting the city's fortifications and its general welfare. In an inscription written in the mid-second century CE the people of Ephesus ensured that the festivals and sacrifices of Artemis could be undertaken. They said that "in this way, with the improvement of the honouring of the goddess, our city will remain more illustrious and more blessed for all time." Kearsley comments: "The people of Ephesus appear to have believed that their own lives were deeply affected by

---

[100] IvEph. 27.20.

[101] IvEph. 26.8; cf. Pausanias, *Descr. Graec.* 10.38.6 and Mussies 1990, p185.

[102] IvEph. 24B.8.

[103] In the phrase τῇ Ἐφεσίᾳ θεῷ; see for example IvEph. 678.12; 3077.9; 3078.11; cf. 24B.22. For further titles see Picard 1922, p362-7.

[104] See for example IvEph. 1405.12; 1408.5,15; 1440.6-7; 1441.8-9; see further Rogers 1991, p47, 74 n39. For example, in IvEph 1449.7-8, the Council and the People agreed "to inscribe the grant of citizenship upon the sanctuary of Artemis, where also the other grants are inscribed", dated in 302 or 285 BCE. The practice began in the Hellenistic period, and probably continued in the imperial period. In a number of cities public documents were inscribed on the walls of a temple; see Magie 1950, p847 n31. Another example here is that buildings in the city were dedicated to Artemis, along with others. From an inscription dated 11-14 CE we learn that the Basilica on the north side of the "Staatsmarkt" was dedicated to Artemis Ephesia, Augustus and others; see Knibbe and Büyükkolanci 1989, p43-5. See also IvEph 424. Further, Artemis' statue stood in the Prytaneion (as well as that of Hestia), a key centre of the religious and political life of the city; see New Docs 6, p199; Fleischer 1973, p14-15.

[105] See Head 1892, no. 402-3, 405, 416-17, and Plate 38.1-4 (homonoia coins with Pergamum, Smyrna, Sardis and Alexandria). When Ephesus was de facto a free city between 87-84 BCE the city minted gold coins with a statue of Artemis on one side and the bust of Artemis on the reverse, again showing how Artemis could personify and represent the city; see Head 1880, p68-9.

the degree of reverence accorded Artemis."[106] All of this evidence shows the strength of the bond between Artemis and the city.

In 23 CE Tiberius granted permission for the communities of the province of Asia to build a second temple for the Imperial cult. The Senate finally decided that the honour should go to Smyrna; the claim of Ephesus was rejected because "the state-worship in Ephesus ... was considered to be already centred on the cult of Diana [Artemis]."[107] Thus the special bond between Artemis and Ephesus, and the overwhelming primacy of Artemis in Ephesus was recognized by the Roman Senate.

The Salutaris inscription is also significant in this regard. From the inscription, which was written in 104 CE, we learn that on procession day, 31 gold and silver type-statues and images, nine of which were of Artemis,[108] were carried from the pronaos of the temple of Artemis, outside the city wall, to the Magnesian Gate, which was the main entrance to the city from the south, where the procession was joined by the ephebes. The procession then went to the theatre, to the Koressos Gate and back to the Artemisium.[109] The procession occurred on the days the assembly met, on important festivals and on a number of other occasions. Rogers estimated that the procession would have occurred at least once every two weeks throughout the year,[110] and it is clear that Salutaris intended the procession to be a significant event in the city each time it occurred.[111] Further, since at least 260 individuals were involved in the procession through the streets, it "must have impeded, if not altogether halted traffic within the city at procession time."[112]

The inscription shows the vitality of the cult of Artemis in Ephesus in 104 CE. Further, Rogers has shown how Salutaris' foundation caused the people involved "to look (metaphorically) to the institutional structure of their city, to its Ionian foundation, and to the birth of the goddess Artemis, for their sense of social and historical identity in the complex and changing Roman world."[113] In particular, Salutaris' foundation, through focussing on the birth

---

[106] Kearsley in New Docs 6, 204; with translation of the inscription, which is IvEph 24, here B.32-4; the inscription makes it clear that the Roman Proconsul of Asia, Popillius Carus Pedo, had not been honouring the festivals of Artemis.

[107] See Tacitus, *Ann.* 4.55; see also Cassius Dio 59.28.1; Friesen 1993a, p15-21 who speaks of the "exclusive hold of Artemis on Ephesus" (p17 n47); see also Magie 1950, p501; in general Burkert 1999, p64.

[108] See the list of type-statues and images in Rogers 1991, p84-5.

[109] For the route see Rogers 1991, p85-107. The whole procession would have lasted at least 90 minutes; see Rogers 1991, p110

[110] See Rogers 1991, p83.

[111] The statues were to be carried "before everyone (πρὸ κοιν[οῦ])"; see IvEph 27 line 91.

[112] Rogers 1991, p86; at least 250 ephebes were involved in the procession.

[113] Rogers 1991, p41. The inscription also shows that Salutaris wished to encourage reverence for Artemis among children in the city; see Rogers 1991, p59.

of the goddess, taught the people to look "to the birth of the goddess Artemis at Ephesos, for a theological sense of how Ephesian social and historical identity was grounded in a 'sacred reality', which was impervious to all humanly wrought challenges."[114] We can see again then how central the goddess was to the identity of the city, and the intimate connection which existed between the city and her goddess.[115]

The city of Ephesus used the term νεωκόρος to describe her bond with Artemis. The word is found on a coin minted during Nero's reign, almost certainly with reference to Artemis,[116] in Acts 19:35, and on two coins of the Domitianic period the Ephesians called themselves "twice neokoros", that is of Artemis and of the Sebastoi.[117] On a number of inscriptions of a later date the city calls itself νεωκόρος τῆς ᾽Αρτέμιδος, as well as twice neokoros of the Sebastoi.[118] The term "νεωκόρος" was used by pagan and Jewish writers to refer to those who were responsible for the administration of a temple and its sacrifices.[119] It was also applied to peoples and to cities, and designated their relationship to a particular cult. When Ephesus applied this term to itself with regard to Artemis, it "was affirming its divine appointment as the keeper and protector of the religion and cult of the goddess, and as the recipient of the privileges and blessing which go with that office."[120]

---

[114] Rogers 1991, p69; see also p112-15; 145-7. The arrangements made by Salutaris were approved by the demos as a whole, so the foundation ultimately represented the attitude of the demos of Ephesus. It was also confirmed by Roman proconsuls.

[115] The Salutaris inscription is dated in 104 CE, but it is likely that the practice of carrying the images of Artemis in procession on the festival of the goddess existed prior to this; see Lightfoot 1889, Vol 2, p17.

[116] See Karwiese in *RE Supp*, 12, 1970, p330; Friesen 1993a, p53.

[117] See Friesen 1993a, p56. On the title neokoros, see Price 1984, p66-7; Friesen 1993a, p50-9. On the title with reference to the Imperial cult see section 3.1 below. The city was granted its second provincial cult under Hadrian, between 130 and 132 CE; on the Temple of Hadrian Olympios built at this time see Karwiese 1995a, p311-19. Hence the reference on these Domitianic coins must be to Artemis and the Sebastoi. This is confirmed by the fact that the coins also bear a statue of Artemis, or her temple. Another coin type also represented this Neocorate relationship; in these coins a woman, symbolising the city held a temple, symbolising the Temple of Artemis, in her hand; see Head 1892, no 314, 346, 384; Oster 1982, p215-16.

[118] See IvEph 2040.4-5; see also 300; 304; 304a; 740; 1910; 4336; Lampe 1992, p64 n20; *New Docs* 6, p203-6; cf. Taylor, in Lake and Cadbury 1933, p254-5. They must all be after 130 CE.

[119] For pagan usage see for example Pausanias, *Descr. Graec.* 10.12.5; Xenophon, *Anab.* 5.3.6. For Jewish usage see Josephus *BJ* 1.7.6; Philo, *Spec. Leg.* 1.32; *De Fuga* 17. See also *New Docs* 6, 205-6. On the development of the use of the term see Friesen 1993a, p50-9.

[120] Oster 1990a, p1702. Ephesus also used the word τροφός - nurturer, to describe this relationship when they spoke of themselves as "nurturer of its own Ephesian goddess"; see IvEph. 24B.22.

Oster summarises the strength of the bond between Ephesus and Artemis in this way:

"the quintessence of Artemis was forever related to the well being of Ephesus. Notwithstanding the individualistic and personal significance of the goddess, the principal force of her cult was upon the interrelated components of the city's urban life, e.g., the civic, economic, educational, patriotic, administrative, and commercial facets. ... There was no other Graeco-Roman metropolis in the Empire whose 'body, soul, and spirit' could so belong to a particular deity as did Ephesus' to her patron goddess Artemis."[121]

3. The Imperial Cult in Ephesus

The Imperial Cult was a very significant part of life in Ephesus in our period and also forms an important part of the context for the life of the early Christians in the city, including the context for the book of Revelation. In this section we will firstly discuss the provincial imperial cult of Asia in Ephesus and then turn to the municipal imperial cult in Ephesus and the various other ways in which the imperial cult was present in the city.

3.1 The Provincial Imperial Cult

In 31 BCE Octavian defeated Mark Antony at Actium. In order to show its allegiance to Octavian, in 29 BCE the koinon of Asia asked for permission to establish a provincial cult for him in Pergamum.[122] The cult came to be described as dedicated to Rome and Augustus (the name Octavian took in 27 BCE); this was the beginning of the provincial imperial cult in Asia Minor.[123] At the same time, Octavian also established a cult for Rome and Divus Julius in Ephesus.[124] This cult was for Romans living in the province, while the one in Pergamum was for the local inhabitants of Asia.[125]

In 23 CE the cities of Asia were granted permission by Tiberius for a second provincial imperial cult in Asia, with the cult being for Tiberius, Livia

---

[121] Oster 1990a, p1728.

[122] See Dio Cassius 51.20.6; Tacitus *Ann.* 4.37. On the imperial cult in general see also Thompson 1990, p158-64; Gill and Winter 1994, p93-103; Klauck 2000, p288-330, with extensive bibliography.

[123] For a discussion of whether the koinon of Asia or Octavian initiated the inclusion of Rome see Friesen 1993a, p8. On the nature of the cult and the temple that was built in Pergamum see Friesen 1993a, p8-15; 2001, p25-32. Cults of rulers were not an innovation at this time since there had been cults for kings, for individual Greeks and for Rome in the Greek cities in the Hellenistic period; see Price 1984, p23-52.

[124] See Dio Cassius 51.20.6-7.

[125] This was probably built between the Prytaneion and the Bouleterion along Kouretes Street; see Friesen 1993a, p11 n21; 2001, p26-7.

(his mother, and Augustus' widow) and the Senate.[126] In 26 CE, after intense competition between the cities of the province, it was decided by the Senate that the site for this second provincial cult would be Smyrna.[127] A provincial cult of Asia was established in Miletus for Gaius Caligula around 40 CE, but it was discontinued after his assassination.[128]

The right to establish the third provincial cult in Asia in Ephesus was granted by Domitian in the early to mid-eighties CE, and the temple was dedicated in 89/90 CE. It was built in the Upper Agora on a terrace that "constituted a major building project in an area that was already well-developed. It did not create a new district of the city, but rather redefined an existing one."[129] The cult was a "cult of the Sebastoi"; the emperors included in the cult were probably the Flavians, Vespasian, Titus and Domitian, with Domitia perhaps being included.[130] Since the two other provincial cults were for emperors of the Julio-Claudian line, the third provincial cult in Asia was needed because it enabled the province to show its reverence for the new ruling family of the Flavians. It is noteworthy that in the inscriptions which concern the dedication of the temple, the term *theos* was avoided for the reigning emperor. Domitian's name was removed from the inscriptions which commemorated the cult after his assassination in 96 CE and the cult, which shifted in focus to Vespasian, flourished for over a century.[131]

Games, which were a municipal, not a provincial initiative, were established in connection with the provincial cult of the Sebastoi in Ephesus.[132] They were begun as a festival for Domitian and identified him with Zeus Olympios,[133] but were discontinued after his *damnatio memoriae*. The games were later revived for Hadrian and were still being held into the third century. The harbour bath-gymnasium, the largest building complex in

---

[126] See Tacitus, *Ann.*.4.15, 37.

[127] See Tacitus, *Ann.* 4.55-56; see Friesen (1993a, p19-21; 2001, p36-8) for what is known of this cult. As noted above, Ephesus was rejected as the site for the temple because it already had the renowned cult of Artemis which dominated the cultic life of the city; similarly the request by Miletus that it be sited there was rejected because of its cult of Apollo.

[128] On this cult, see Friesen 1993a, p21-6.

[129] Friesen 1993a, p69.

[130] This, along with much other evidence, shows that the "imperial cult" involved the worship of a significant number of other members of the imperial household; see further Biguzzi 1998, p283-4; Friesen 2001, p130.

[131] See Friesen 1993a, p29-49; 2001, p43-52. Thirteen inscriptions concern the establishment of this cult; see IvEph 232, 232a, 233, 234, 235, 237, 238, 239, 240, 241, 242, 1498, 2048. They are all dedications from cities in Asia, set up in Ephesus. On the temple that was part of the cult, see Friesen 1993a, p59-75.

[132] See Friesen 1993a, p114-41.

[133] Note also the association of Domitian and Zeus Olympios (who is pictured holding the temple statue of the Ephesian Artemis) on a coin; see Friesen 1993a, p119-20.

Ephesus, was built to provide appropriate facilities for these Olympic games
in honour of Domitian. Thus this complex was related to the Cult of the
Sebastoi and was known as "the Baths of the Sebastoi" (τὰ βαλανεῖα τῶν
Σεβαστῶν).[134] The games were probably inaugurated in 89 CE.[135]

As we have noted above, the city of Ephesus used the term νεωκόρος, or
"temple warden", to describe her bond with Artemis, but also as an official
title for the city in relation to the cult of the Sebastoi. In two coins from
Domitian's reign the Ephesians call themselves "twice neokoros", that is of
Artemis and the Sebastoi.[136] The term had not been used as a title for a city in
relation to the imperial cult prior to the inauguration of the Sebastoi cult in
Ephesus and so this was an Ephesian innovation.[137] As Friesen notes, the
coins express the city's new religious situation: "The city now had two
dominant cults of equivalent significance: that of Ephesian Artemis, and that
of the Emperors."[138] Given the significance of Artemis for Ephesus, this
shows the importance given to the imperial cult. The title of "Neokoros" was
also significant with regard to inter-city rivalry in Asia. In using the title for
itself, "Ephesus proclaimed its unique status within the province as the
caretaker of the cult that was offered by all the cities of the province".[139]

The relationship between the imperial cult and other cults was also
expressed in a feature of the complex built for the cult of the Sebastoi in
Ephesus. The temple was built on top of a terrace; in front of the terrace on
the north side was a three-story façade, which featured a series of engaged
figures of deities along the length of the façade, including Attis and Isis.
Friesen has noted that a viewer, looking up at the façade, would have seen a
series of divine beings across the massive terrace, behind which was the
temenos of the Sebastoi. He suggests: "The message was clear: the gods and
goddesses of the peoples supported the emperors; and conversely, the cult of
the emperors united the cultic systems, and the peoples, of the empire. The
emperors were not a threat to the worship of the diverse deities of the empire;
rather, the emperors joined the ranks of the divine and played their own

---

[134] IvE 4.1104l 1125, 1155.

[135] See Friesen 1993a, p139.

[136] See Friesen 1993a, p56. The coins are given in Pick 1906, p236.

[137] See Friesen 1993a, p50-6. Ephesus seems to have adopted the neokoros imagery for
the Cult of the Sebastoi from the cult of Artemis. On the title see Friesen 1995a, p229-36.
Ephesus is called "neokoros" with regard to the cult of the Sebastoi in, for example, IvE 232,
232a, 233, , 237, 238, 241, 242.

[138] Friesen 1993a, p57.

[139] Friesen 1993a, p156. Friesen shows that other cities were not pleased with this
initiative by Ephesus; on inter-city rivalry and the imperial cult see Price 1984, p126-32. On
inter-city rivalry in general see Mitchell 1993, 1, p204-5; Broughton, 1938, p741-4. For the
rivalry between Ephesus, Smyrna and Pergamum see Dio Chrysostom, *Or.* 34.48; 38.23-4;
Aelius Aristides *Or.* 23.60; IvEph 1489.

particular role in that realm. ... [By the late first century CE] [t]he emperors and the (other) gods and goddesses each had their proper, complementary places in the life of the city, the province, and the empire."[140] Friesen suggests this imagery with regard to the significance of the cult expressed local Ephesian views.[141]

The provincial high priests of the imperial cult were leading people in the province of Asia. The high priesthood probably involved important cultic responsibilities and there was probably a provincial high priest for each provincial imperial cult in Asia.[142] We also know of a number of provincial high priestesses. Although a number of scholars have thought that women were given the title as an honour because their husbands were high priests, it is much more likely that the women concerned were functional high priestesses in the provincial cult.[143]

3.2 Municipal Imperial Cults

After the establishment of the provincial imperial cult in Asia Minor in 29 BCE, many municipal cults were established for Augustus (alone or with Roma), and new municipal imperial temples and sanctuaries continued to be built throughout Asia Minor in the first two centuries CE.[144] The imperial cult was also incorporated alongside other cults. For example, in Ephesus the Prytaneion served as the centre for the administration of many cults, and here

---

[140] Friesen 1993a, p75; on the façade see Friesen 1993a, p70-5. He notes (p75) that in 26 CE when Smryna was chosen for the second provincial imperial cult the argument was used that reverence for Artemis in Ephesus meant reverence for the emperors might be elbowed out. See also Brenk 1998, p168, who notes the façade seems to shout out "All the gods of Asia support the Emperor and the Flavian dynasty." However, he goes on "But it can also suggest the Emperor's incorporation, in a paternalistic way, not only of all the inhabitants of Asia into his cult, but also of their divinities." Friesen (1993a, p119) also notes that the architecture of the façade of the temple terrace shows the emperor is over the other cults. In this regard he notes, "the emperors, housed above the ranks of the deities, presided supreme over the world."

[141] Friesen 1993a, p75. We can contrast the inclusivity of the Imperial Cult with regard to other deities, with John's exclusivity in Revelation; but note also the Nicolaitans attitude of accommodation with regard to idolatry; see further in Chapter 7.

[142] On provincial high priests see Friesen 1993a, p77-81, 172-84. On their cultic responsibilities see Friesen 1993a, p89-92.

[143] See Friesen 1993a, p81-9 for a discussion and references to the literature, p185-8 for a list on known high priestesses. Women were included in provincial high priesthoods around the second quarter of the first century CE; see Friesen 1993a, p88-9; see also Oster 1992a, p544.

[144] See Price (1984, p58-9) where figures are given. Friesen (2001, p60) suggests that there were more temples to Augustus than to other emperors and also notes (Friesen 2001, p56-9) that the demarcation between municipal and provincial cults are sometimes unclear because of the involvement of cities in provincial cults.

the worship of members of the imperial families was associated with the worship of Demeter.[145]

In the cities of western Asia Minor, municipal imperial cults were not restricted to temples but were established in major public spaces. For example, imperial worship was found in the agora in Priene and in the courtyard of the bouleuterion in Miletus, and imperial cults were widespread in gymnasia and baths.[146] Clearly the cult was widely distributed and was intimately interwoven with organised communal life in Asia Minor.[147] The initiative for establishing these cults generally came from the cities themselves, although cities often informed the emperor of their wish to establish a cult.[148]

There were also numerous imperial festivals throughout Asia, which, like other festivals, involved the whole of a city and attracted many visitors. Such festivals, which generally lasted for a number of days, consisted of processions, sacrifices, feasts and games. Processions, which involved worshippers going well beyond sacrificial sites, meant that many public areas throughout a city were involved in activities connected with the cult. These festivals were "the key manifestation of the cult in action"[149] and show that the cult was important for the whole populace of a city and not just for the élite. The cult of the emperor also had a part in the activities of some private associations,[150] and imperial images have been found in private houses, in Ephesus and elsewhere.[151] Thus Friesen concludes: "imperial cults permeated

---

[145] See Friesen 2001, p63-5, who also gives another example.

[146] See Friesen 2001, p65-75.

[147] See the maps in Price 1984, pxxii-xxv, and also 1984, p78-100. Price (1984, p99) writes of "the extraordinary dense distribution of the imperial cult". See also Friesen 2001, p61. On sacrifices in the imperial cult see Price 1984, p207-33. For a critique of his distinction between sacrifices to and on behalf of the emperor, see Friesen 1993a, p146-52.

[148] See Price 1984, p66-7; Friesen 2001, p59. For the rarer initiative of the emperor (promoting, for example, the cult of relatives) or of provincial governors, see Price 1984, p68-71.

[149] Price 1984, p101. On the festivals see Price 1984, p101-132.

[150] See examples in Price 1984, p118. At Ephesus, the initiates of Dionysus set up a statue of Hadrian, "sharing the throne" with Dionysus; see IvEph 2.275 = SEG 26.1272. Friesen 2001 also discusses Hymnodes in Imperial Cults, which were groups dedicated to the worship of the emperors (p104-113), and imperial mysteries celebrated by groups (p113-116). Clearly imperial cult practices were undertaken by a number of groups.

[151] For example, busts of Tiberius and Livia were found in a vaulted niche in the hall of one of the recently excavated Terrace Houses in Ephesus; see Price 1984, p120; Robert 1982, p130. One of the houses also contained the graffito "Rome, the ruler of all, your power will never die" (IvEph 2.599). See also Friesen 2001, p116-120, who notes (p117) "Some householders would have included imperial figures in family shrines throughout the imperial period" and (p120) "many groups, families, and individuals were involved in the worship of members of the imperial family". On imperial cult images and worship see Cuss 1974, p104-112.

community life. ... Imperial cults were an aspect of urban life encountered often and in diverse forms."[152]

3.3 The Presence of the Imperial Cult in Ephesus

The imperial cult was a very significant feature of life in Ephesus. We have already noted the cult for Rome and Divus Julius established in Ephesus in 29 CE and the provincial "cult of the Sebastoi" dedicated in 89/90 CE. Further, a temple in the upper agora was probably the city's main temple of Augustus.[153] This municipal imperial cult "dominated the upper agora, the sector where social organization was administered. Governance, sacrifice, and administration took place in this area, all within the shadow of the Augusteion. Perhaps the emperor loomed so large here because Ephesus was the provincial capital and had a heightened sensitivity to the influence of the empire in everyday life."[154] In addition, during Augustus' rule, a royal stoa in the Upper Agora, which featured statues of Augustus and Livia in a room at one end, was dedicated to Artemis, Augustus and Tiberius.[155] A huge Temple of Hadrian Olympios, or an Olympieion, was built in honour of Hadrian when a second imperial cult was established in Ephesus between 130 and 132 CE.[156]

Traditional sanctuaries, at Ephesus as elsewhere, came to include the emperor.[157] Thus a temple of Augustus was constructed at the Artemisium in Ephesus,[158] and later a temple was built to Artemis and Hadrian on Kouretes Street.[159] We note also the number of imperial statues in Ephesus (as elsewhere).[160] With the exception of three statues erected by Roman officials in Ephesus, the rest, which number around fifty, were put up by residents of Ephesus.[161] Statues were generally erected to express gratitude to the

---

[152] Friesen 2001, p75. Friesen (2001, p128) also notes "the vitality of the festivals, the distribution of imperial cults throughout urban areas, and the importance of imperial temples all imply widespread participation." See also Klauck 2000, p313-23.

[153] See Friesen 2001, p95-103.

[154] Friesen 2001, p102.

[155] See Price 1984, p254-7; Friesen 1993a, p11 n21.

[156] See Karwiese 1995a, p311-19. Hadrianic Games were also established.

[157] See Price 1984, p146-56; Oster 1992a, p545; IvEph 429.

[158] IBM 522 = ILS 97; and CIL 3.7118.

[159] See IvEph 2.429; Alzinger 1970, p1650-2; Price 1984, p149-50. It is often called simply "the temple of Hadrian", but Price shows it was also to Artemis. See further Outschar 1999, p443-8.

[160] In general see Price 1984, p170-206. He notes (p198): "It is in fact clear that the visual representation of the emperor provided the crucial focus for the expression of attitudes to the imperial cult and to the emperor."

[161] Price 1984, p174; see IvEph 2.251-304; 5.1500-5. He notes (1984, p174): "The city itself was responsible for most of them, but some were put up by associations, such as the

emperor, and as an honour to him granted by his grateful subjects and they became the focus of much religious ritual.[162] In this regard we note an inscription connected to a statue of Hadrian in Ephesus which describes him as "their own founder and saviour" and goes on to say that the statue was erected "for his unsurpassed gifts to Artemis: he gave the goddess rights over inheritances and deposits and her own laws; he provided shipments of grain from Egypt, he made the harbours navigable and diverted the river Kaystros which silts up the harbours ..."[163] Recall too the imperial images which were part of the Salutaris dedication and were kept in the porch of the Artemisium and were part of the procession inaugurated by Salutaris.[164]

Architecturally and symbolically, then, the emperor was extraordinarily "present" in Ephesus. Price concludes with regard to Ephesus that the emperor's "name or image met the eye at every turn".[165] It is also noteworthy that in order to achieve this prominence of the imperial cult and image, there was considerable reordering of civic space in Ephesus. Thus, a significant part of the Upper Agora was redesigned during Augustus' rule resulting in an increased architectural impact of the emperor,[166] and when the provincial temple of the Sebastoi was added on one side of the Upper Agora in the 80s CE, this again constituted a major adjustment to central civic space.[167]

We should not think that reverence to the emperor in Ephesus was solely tied to cult and statues. Rogers has noted that from the middle of the first century CE, the Kouretes, who were responsible for the mysteries of Artemis and whose members were part of the governing order of the city, consistently call themselves not only "eusebeis", but also "philosebastoi", whereas before this time they simply called themselves "eusebeis".[168] Thus they not only made clear their piety to Artemis, but also paid their reverence to the Roman emperors. As Rogers notes, the inclusion of "philosebastoi" is indicative, not

---

youth of the city or the worshippers of Dionysus, while a number were erected by private individuals. The bases also sometimes record the procedures for the erection of the statues. For civic statues there were specific motions in the assembly (the bases record the name of the proposer), and thereafter the project was left in the hands of a specific local citizen (whose name is also recorded). A Roman official is only rarely recorded as having assisted the process."

[162] See the clear demonstration of gratitude towards the Emperor in the quotation from Menander Rhetor given in Price 1984, p175.

[163] IvEph 2.274; translation from Price 1984, p175.

[164] See IvEph 27, lines 270-3, 283, 419-25, 557.

[165] Price 1984, p136.

[166] See Price 1984, p140; this was to build the royal stoa, dedicated to Artemis, Augustus and Tiberius which contained statues of Augustus and Livia in a room at one end which is mentioned above; further a double cella temple next to the prytaneion is probably the temple for Rome and Divius Julius, built at this time; see Friesen 1993a, p11 n21.

[167] See Friesen 1993a, p;68-70.

[168] See Rogers 1999, p247-50 and for example IvEph 1008.

only of the creation of the imperial cult but also of the way the divinity of the emperor "had begun to have an effect on old cultic associations, traditional cults, and the ways in which members of those traditional cults chose to represent themselves to the public."[169] Thus we see another facet of the impact of the emperors.

We note then the omnipresence and significance of the emperor and the imperial cult in Ephesus. Friesen notes that the most distinctive feature of the imperial cults within Greco-Roman polytheism was "the ability of imperial cults to function at all levels of society. ... Imperial worship touched all or most aspects of life in the cities of Asia ... No other symbolic system had such a range of effective meaning."[170] Further, with regard to the function of the imperial cult within Greco-Roman society Price notes: "the cult was a major part of the web of power that formed the fabric of society. The imperial cult stabilised the religious order of the world. The system of ritual was carefully structured; the symbolism evoked a picture of the relationship between the emperor and the gods. The ritual was also structuring; it imposed a definition of the world. The imperial cult, along with politics and diplomacy, constructed the reality of the Roman empire."[171]

4. The Jewish Community in Ephesus

The Jewish community is another dimension of the life of the city of Ephesus that is important for our study. As we will see, we know of some Jews who became Christians and the evidence of Paul's letters and Acts suggests that the Christian group in Ephesus began among Jews. In general, in Asia Minor and elsewhere, as time went on links between Jewish communities and those who regarded themselves as members of Christian communities were close but could also be contentious. Further, issues connected with Jews and the Jewish community emerge in connection with the Pastoral Epistles, Revelation and Ignatius. In this section we will discuss what we know about the Jewish community in Ephesus.

4.1 The founding of the community

We do not know when the Jewish community was first established in Ephesus. Josephus claims in Contra Apionem 2:39 that Jews at Ephesus "bear the same name as the indigenous citizens, a right which they received from

---

[169] Rogers 1999, p248.
[170] Friesen 2001, p126.
[171] Price 1984, p248.

Alexander's successors", that is, Seleucus Nicator (312 to 281/0 BCE).[172] Further, in Ant 12:125-6 Josephus claims that the Jews of Ionia had been granted citizenship by Antiochus II Theos (262-246 BCE). While the claim to citizenship is dubious in both cases,[173] the implication that Jews were living in Ephesus at this period seems likely.[174]

In a letter to Zeuxis, the governor of Lydia, Antiochus III gave instructions for the relocation of 2,000 Jewish families from Babylonia to Lydia and Phrygia (Ant 12:148-53). The letter is probably authentic,[175] and is to be dated sometime between 212 and 205/4 BCE. Although none of these Jews were probably settled directly in Ephesus, it seems likely that some may have shifted to Ephesus in subsequent decades.[176]

4.2 Evidence from decrees preserved in Josephus and Philo

Josephus records a series of documents which concern Jews in Ephesus or more generally in Asia which range in date from 49BCE to 2/3CE, and some further evidence comes from Philo.[177] We will note that these decrees provide evidence for the maintenance of facets of Jewish identity by the community, conflict between the Jewish community and the city of Ephesus, the significance of the Jewish community, and that they were supported by the Roman authorities.

Although some aspects of these documents may be questionable, they contain sufficient material which is probably reliable for them to be used here.[178] In 49 BCE the consul L. Lentulus Crus exempted Jews who were Roman citizens in Ephesus from military service (Ant 14:228-30, 234, 240).

---

[172] See also Ant 12:119-21.

[173] See Trebilco 1991, p167-9; Tcherikover 1961, p328-30; Marcus in Josephus Vol 7, p737-42; Schürer, Vermes, Millar, Black, Goodman 1986, p127-30; Barclay 1996, p260-1. Mussies (1990, p186) argues that the Jews in Ionia were granted isonomia from Antiochus II Theos (cf Ant 16:160). This means, not that they had exactly the same rights as the Greek citizens of Ephesus but rather "that their own laws and customs and the local rights and laws would be equally respected."

[174] See Rogers 1986, p881; Kraabel 1968, p52.

[175] On its authenticity see Trebilco 1991, p5-6.

[176] See Falwell 1948, p218-19. Foss (1979, p45) thinks Antiochus III settled Jews in Ephesus, but this is to go beyond the evidence of Josephus. Rajak (2001, p304) thinks that at the time the Roman province of Asia was created in 129 BCE there were "established [Jewish] communities at Ephesus and elsewhere in Ionia". This seems a reasonable inference from the available data.

[177] See Ant 12:125-8; 14:223-7, 228-30, 234, 240, 262-4; 16:27-30, 59-60, 162-5 (which concerns Asia in general), 167-8, 172-3; CAp 2:38-9; Philo, Leg 315. Jews in Ephesus or Ionia are not mentioned in 1 Macc 15:16-25.

[178] The authenticity of these decrees has recently been defended by Pucci Ben Zeev 1998, see for example, p139-62, 262-72, 381f; see also Barclay 1996, p262-4; Gruen 2002, p85-6.

In 43 BCE Dolabella granted the Jews at Ephesus exemption from military service and allowed them to keep their customs and rites and to make offerings for sacrifices (Ant 14:223-7). Probably in 42 BCE[179] the council and people of Ephesus issued a decree in which they granted the proconsul's request that the Jews should be allowed to observe the Sabbath and live in accordance with their customs (Ant 14:262-4). In addition, Philo, in Leg. 315-16 cites a document written by G. Norbanus Flaccus, proconsul of Asia between 31 and 27 BCE, which permits Ephesian Jews to collect the Temple tax.[180]

According to Josephus, around 14 BCE M. Vipsanius Agrippa wrote to the city officials in Ephesus ordering that the Jews be allowed to collect and transport the temple tax to Jerusalem and that they should not be compelled to appear in court on the Sabbath (Ant 16:167-8).[181] It seems that a later conflict over Jewish rights between 9 and 2 BCE led the Jews of Ephesus and further afield to approach the proconsul Julius Antonius, who wrote to the city authorities in Ephesus to remind them that Augustus and Agrippa had permitted the Jews to collect the Temple tax and send it to Jerusalem.[182] In 2/3 CE Augustus published an edict outlining the rights of the Jews in Asia, including the right to follow their own customs, to send money to Jerusalem and to be exempt from appearing in court on the Sabbath.[183] Again, this witnesses to the fact that the Jews were experiencing difficulties with regard to these matters.

These documents suggest a number of conclusions. Firstly, we gain some insight into facets of Jewish identity.[184] That the Jews of Ephesus had a degree of communal life and organisation, which was crucial for the retention of identity, is clear from the fact that the community actively approached ruling bodies and gained the right of assembly, or permission to build a synagogue and administer their own finances (e.g. Ant14:262-4; 16:27-30,

---

[179] For the date see Pucci Ben Zeev 1998, p230.

[180] See also Ant 16.166, 171. On the tax see Levinskaya 1996, p145-6.

[181] For the date see Schürer, Vermes, Millar, Black, Goodman 1986, p119 n47; see also Gruen 2002, p98-9. This letter arose from the dispute between the Greek city authorities and the Jews of Ionia, which Josephus writes about in Ant 12:126 and 16:27-60; in the latter passage he says that the matters of being able to observe their own customs including the Sabbath, being exempt from military service and being able to send the Temple tax to Jerusalem were of concern to the Jews at this point; see Ant 16:27-30, 59-60.

[182] Ant 16:172-3; for the date see Magie 1950, p1581.

[183] Ant 16:162-5; date in Smallwood 1981, p143; Schürer, Vermes, Millar, Black, Goodman 1986, p119 n47 date this in 12 BCE. The edict was to be inscribed on the wall of the temple of the imperial cult at Ancyra, although Pergamum may be a better reading, see Rogers 1986, p881.

[184] On Jewish identity in the Diaspora see Barclay 1996, p399-444; Trebilco 1997, p287-300.

172-3). They also clearly met together regularly,[185] having obtained the right of assembly (Ant 14:227). The community in Ephesus retained strong links with Jerusalem and with the Temple, as is shown by the community taking active measures to ensure that they could send the temple tax to Jerusalem (e.g. Ant 16:167-8, 172-3).[186] The importance of Torah for the community is shown by the decrees in Josephus which show the Ephesian Jews arguing that they should be able to live in accordance with "ancestral tradition" or "with their own laws" and maintain their own customs (e.g. Ant 14:225-7).[187] Further, these decrees show that Ephesian Jews followed key Jewish practices and beliefs such as observing food laws (e.g. Ant 14:226) and the Sabbath (e.g. Josephus, Ant 16:167-8; they were also exempt from appearing in court on "their holy days"; see Ant 16:27-8) and they seem to have gained an exemption from military service so that they could keep the food laws and the Sabbath (Ant 14:223-30). The Jews took the initiative to ensure that they could follow these practices and beliefs, showing the significance they had for them. These factors – communal life and the right of assembly, the temple tax and the link with Jerusalem, observing the Torah including food laws and the Sabbath - show that the Jewish community in Ephesus maintained significant facets of Jewish identity.

Secondly, these documents often show that between 49BCE and 2/3CE there had been conflict between the city of Ephesus and the Jewish community. The Jews had experienced mistreatment and hostility over issues such as keeping the Sabbath and sending temple tax to Jerusalem, and over Jewish rights in general (see Ant. 14:230, 262-4; 16:27-8, 57-60, 167-8, 172-3; Philo, Legat 315).[188] The reasons for this hostility from the wider city of

---

[185] We will discuss below whether there was more than one synagogue in the city.

[186] Ephesus was probably also the centre for the collection of Temple tax from other Jewish communities in the wider area; see Duncan 1929, p40-2.

[187] In Acts 21:27-9, Jews from "Asia" accuse Paul of teaching "against our people, our law, and this place" (ie the Temple). These Asian Jews are primarily from Ephesus since they recognise Trophimus (see 20:4), who had also recently been in that city. It was probably Pentecost (see 20:16) so the Asian Jews would have come to Jerusalem as pilgrims. (That they are not present (legally they should have been) when Paul defended himself before Felix suggests that they had gone back to Asia; see 24:18-19; also 26:21; cf. Sherwin-White 1963, p52-3.) These Asian Jews, primarily from Ephesus, are seen to be zealous defenders of the law and the Temple. Hengel (1983, p105-6) concludes that the passage has a basis in history since the event and its setting correspond closely to what is known of the conditions of the time. As we will see in Chapters 3-4, Paul is also opposed by Jews in Ephesus; see Acts 19:8-9; 20:19. The fundamental reason for their opposition was probably that Paul was preaching a law-free Gospel to Gentiles.

[188] Ant 14.263 gives permission for Ephesian Jews to observe the Sabbath, probably in 42 BCE, and Ant 16:167-8 from 14 BCE says no one is to make the Ephesian Jews appear in court on the Sabbath. Rajak (2001, p324) notes "here is direct evidence that the city's decree of (?) 42 had been contravened, and apparently with impunity." For a different overall view

Ephesus may include the social distinctiveness of Jewish religious practices, that Jews were generally non-citizens, the lack of tolerance by the city, that Jewish rights were supported by Roman intervention in the affairs of the city, that the Jewish communities wished to send significant amounts of money (as Temple tax) out of the city and region to Jerusalem at times of local economic hardship and that local Greeks at times took advantage of wider political instability (for example, at the time of the Civil War) to act against the Jewish community.[189]

However, we hear of no further difficulties between Jewish communities and their cities in Asia Minor after 2 CE. Although this is predominantly an argument from silence,[190] it suggests that by the end of Augustus' reign better relations had been established between Jewish communities and their cities in various parts of Asia, and Ephesus seems to have been included in this wider phenomenon.[191] We can also note that we have no evidence that Jews in Asia Minor took any part in the revolts of 66-70 or 132-5 CE and the Diaspora revolt of 115-117 CE against the local authorities and Rome did not occur as far as we know, in Asia Minor. We can suggest that after 2 CE Jewish communities in Asia Minor, including Ephesus, generally lived peaceably and interacted positively with their wider communities, which was one factor that enabled them to flourish and to share in the prosperity of urban life in Asia in this period.[192]

Thirdly, the evidence provided by the decrees preserved by Josephus and Philo suggest that by the mid-first century BCE, there was a sizeable and significant Jewish community in Ephesus. Thus it seems to have been sufficiently noteworthy in the eyes of the city of Ephesus that Jews in the city were sending what must have been significant amounts of money to Jerusalem for action to be taken to stop this occurring (Ant 16:27-30, 163, 167-8, 172-3). Further, some Jews seem to have been sufficiently prominent in the city that it was irksome when they kept the Sabbath or refused to appear in court on that day. The result was that they were fined for observing

---

see Gruen 2002, p84-104, who concludes (p103): "the materials assembled by Josephus [regarding Jews in Asia] fall well short of demonstrating persistent persecution by Greeks or the salvation of Jews by Rome. The incidents were episodic and infrequent, engendered by special circumstances and readily solved."

[189] See Barclay 1996, p264-78; Stanley 1996, p101-24.

[190] But see MAMA 6, 264, which records that the Gentile Julia Severa donated a synagogue building to the Jews in Acmonia; further evidence for positive relations from Sibylline Oracles I/II, and Acts is discussed in Trebilco 1991, p183-4.

[191] See Safrai and Stern 1974, p443; Smallwood 1981, p143; Thompson 1990, p138-9, 144; Trebilco 1991, p183-4; Barclay 1996, p279-81.

[192] See Trebilco 1991, p173-85; Worth 1999a, p72-3. Acts tells us that there was some anti-Jewish feeling in Ephesus in the 50's CE caused at least in part by the fact that the Jews did not worship Artemis. We will discuss this incident in Chapter 4.

the Sabbath (Ant 14:262-4),[193] or were perhaps required to give a bond that they would appear in court on the appropriate day (Ant 16:164-5).[194] These seem to be the actions of the city against a significant community in their midst, rather than against a tiny and insignificant group which could be ignored or easily coerced.[195] Further, as Barclay notes, "these are Jews sufficiently articulate and well-connected (and with sufficient funds) to be able to take their protests to the highest authorities, with at least occasional success."[196] All of this suggests the community was prominent and significant within the life of the city.

In this connection, these documents also show that some Jews in Ephesus possessed Roman citizenship. According to Ant 14:228, in 49 BCE the consul L. Lentulus Crus released from military service "those Jews who are Roman citizens and observe Jewish rites and practise them in Ephesus". That the exemption applied to Jews with Roman citizenship is stated in related letters or statements to Ephesus in Ant 14:234,240. Ant 14:231-2 implies that the exemption covered all Jewish Roman citizens in Asia. [197] This number of documents strongly suggests that the restriction with regard to military service to Jews in Ephesus *with Roman citizenship* goes back to the Roman authorities. We do not know how many Jews in Ephesus were Roman citizens, but as Barclay notes, from the perspective of the Roman authorities, it must have been "sufficiently many to make it worthwhile to issue special directives about them".[198] Thus, it seems likely that the Jewish community in

---

[193] Ant 14:262-4 shows that Jews were fined for keeping the Sabbath; Ant 16:27-8 (which concerns the Jews of Ionia, and so clearly applies to Ephesus) suggests they had been forced to appear in court on the Sabbath. The two texts together suggest that they may have been fined if they did not appear in court on the Sabbath.

[194] Note that Ant 16:162-5 concerns the Jews in Asia in general.

[195] See Barclay 1996, p271-2. He notes with regard to Jewish communities in Asia (p276) "in general one can only explain Gentile hostility on the grounds that the Jewish community was of influence and importance – perhaps growing importance – within the life of the city."

[196] Barclay 1996, p271.

[197] See also Ant 14:231-2 (Delos); 14:236-7 (general). The later exemption by Dolabella seems to exempt all Jews and not just Roman citizens; see Ant 14:225-7.

[198] See Barclay 1996, p271. Smallwood (1981, p127-8) thought that the number of Jews affected must have been "infinitesimally small" and that the significance of Lentulus' action lay in the principle of toleration which it embodied (see also Saulnier 1981, p168-9,194). But it is not clear why Smallwood comes to this view. Others have taken the documents to imply that a significant number of Jews possessed Roman citizenship (see Schürer 1898, p85 ("in grösserer Zahl"); Safrai and Stern 1974, p152; Tcherikover 1961, p330; Schürer, Vermes, Millar, Black, Goodman 1986, p120). Binder (1999, p280) suggests that the number of edicts addressed to Ephesus about the exemption from military service "indicates that at least some of the Jews there were Roman citizens"; see also Gruen 2002, p87. We know of two Jews in Asia who had Roman citizenship in the first century CE; see MAMA 6, 264 (80s or 90s) and CIJ 770, which shows that the forebears of T. Flavius Alexander acquired citizenship in the

Ephesus was a significant community in the life of the city and that it had some prominent and influential members.[199]

Fourthly, Jewish rights in Ephesus (and elsewhere) were supported by the Roman authorities. This is clearest in Ant 14:262-4, a decree of the people of Ephesus, which states that the Jews in Ephesus had approached the proconsul that they might observe the Sabbath and follow their laws without interference, a request that the proconsul granted. The decree goes on: "it has therefore been decreed by the council and people that as the matter is of concern to the Romans, no one shall be prevented from keeping the Sabbath ..." Roman support was clearly vital.

4.3 A Jewish synagogue

No synagogue has yet been found in the city of Ephesus.[200] However, the existence of a synagogue in Ephesus seems to be implied in Ant 14:227, to be dated to 43 BCE, where the Jews are given permission "to come together for sacred and holy rites in accordance with their law".[201] Further, Acts provides evidence for a Jewish synagogue in the mid first century (Acts 18:19, 26; 19:8-9).[202] An inscription of the Imperial period mentions archisynagogoi and presbyters. It reads: "τῶν ἀρχισυναγωγῶν καὶ τῶν πρεσβ(υτέρων)

Flavian period; see Trebilco 1991, p172-3. Some Jews could have gained citizenship through emancipation by Roman masters.

[199] We can also note that Ant 16:31-57 suggests that some Jews in Ionia were wealthy. The Jews complain that they have been deprived of temple tax, have been forced to spend money on military expenses and liturgies (16:28) and that taxes have been imposed on them (16:45). In the speech Nicholas also notes that Jewish prosperity should not arouse envy (16:41). Barclay (1996, p268-9) notes from this evidence: "The Jewish community clearly had a reputation for prosperity. It contained extremely wealthy individuals, who would normally be held liable to contribute to 'liturgies', and it made sizeable collections of money for its annual tribute to Jerusalem ...it seems to have been extremely irksome to Greeks to witness this large and apparently wealthy community fail to pull its weight for the benefit of the city." Since Ephesus was the main city in Ionia, this evidence suggests that some Jews in the city were wealthy, although the evidence is indirect.

[200] Foss (1979, p45) notes that "the 'basilica' north of the Theatre Gymnasium may have been one [a synagogue], but the evidence is slight." He notes (p45 n47) that the evidence consists of a Jewish lamp of the second/third century that was the only lamp found in the building; see FiE IV/2, 187 no 159. On the synagogue in the Greco-Roman Diaspora see now Rajak 2002, p22-38; Fitzpatrick-McKinley 2002, p55-87, with reference to further literature.

[201] See Binder 1999, p280-1. Philo, Leg. 315, addressed to Ephesus, may perhaps also imply the existence of a synagogue.

[202] Acts also provides evidence for itinerant Jewish exorcists in Ephesus (19:13-16), and for the activity of some Jews during the riot in the theatre (Acts 19:33). These will be dealt with in Chapters 3 and 4.

πολλὰ τὰ {τα} ἔτη."[203] Another undated inscription reads]τὸ
θυσιαστήριον (altar or sanctuary), followed by a menorah.[204] It seems very
likely that this was from a synagogue.[205]

However, we may wonder if there were actually a number of synagogues
in the city.[206] When Acts speaks of "the synagogue" in connection with
Ephesus it does not necessarily mean that there was only one in the city. We
know that other large cities such as Rome had more than one synagogue, and
the wording in Acts could allude to the particular synagogue where Christians
normally met, until tensions developed with the Jews and Paul departed from
that particular synagogue with his supporters (Acts 19:8-9).[207]

4.4 Further evidence from inscriptions

Unfortunately we have very little inscriptional evidence for the Jewish
community in the city, and what we do have comes from after the first
century CE. However, we have noted that one inscription speaks of
archisynagogoi and presbyteroi and we can gain some helpful information
from the other inscriptions that have been discovered.

A second century epitaph for a Jew reads:
[τὸ μνημεῖόν ἐστιν] Ἰο[υλίου ?]
[   ] ἀρχιιατροῦ [καὶ]
[τῆς γυναικ]ὸς αὐτοῦ Ἰουλίας
[   ]ης καὶ τέκνων αὐτῶν·
     [ζῶ]σιν· ~
[ταύτης τῆ]ς σοροῦ κήδον—
[ται οἱ ἐν Ἐφέ]σῳ Ἰουδεοι. [208]

---

[203] See IvEph 1251; cf Horsley in New Docs 4, p113, 215 no 23; date in Horsley 1992a,
p122.

[204] See IvEph 4130.

[205] See Keil quoted in IvEph Vol 7, p433; Foss 1979, p45; New Docs 1979, p231. The
stone was found in the Cathedral of St Mary, and Foss suggests the synagogue was in this
area of the city. We do not know if it is significant that the stone had been used in building
the church.

[206] See Pesch 1986, 2, p167.

[207] See Horsley 1992a, p122; cf. Binder 1999, p282. Note that Acts speaks of more than
one synagogue in Jerusalem (note the implications of Acts 6:9), Damascus (Acts 9:2, 20),
and Salamis (Acts 13:5) but not elsewhere in Asia or beyond.

[208] See IvEph 1677, 6-7; see also Hicks 1890a, no 677; CIJ 745; date from Rogers 1986,
p881, n16. Noy (1993, p102) dates it as "second or third century"; New Docs 1979, p231
dates it as "late II?".

This is the tomb of Ioulios .... archiatros, and of his wife Ioulia,... and of their children, while living. The Jews in Ephesus are charged with care of this tomb.

Two points from this inscription are significant. Firstly, the man, whose name was probably Ἰουλίος holds the title ἀρχίατρος which designates an official municipal doctor. Such officially recognised public physicians were paid by the city and their principal task was to give medical attention to citizens. They were granted immunity from civic office by Vespasian, but Antoninus Pius limited the number of doctors to whom the cities might grant exemption to ten for a metropolis, seven for a conventus centre and five for ordinary towns, evidently because people had been evading office through taking up the medical profession. In an inscription such as the one under discussion from Ephesus probably to be dated after Antoninus Pius, it is probable that ἀρχίατρος designated one of these publicly recognised doctors, particularly since we have a series of inscriptions from Ephesus in which ἀρχίατρος almost certainly has this meaning. This strongly suggests that the Jew Ἰουλίος held this office.[209] Thus, at least in the second century, a Jew in Ephesus held a significant municipal office.[210] As an official of the city he may well have been a Roman citizen. Ameling describes him as standing "an der Spitze der sozialen Skala".[211] Secondly, we note that in this inscription the Jew Ἰουλίος entrusts the care of his tomb to the local Jewish community, which he calls [οἱ ἐν Ἐφέ]σῳ Ἰουδεοι. Clearly, the community is seen as one group.

A second inscription from the late second century is also interesting in this regard. It reads:

τὸ μνημεῖόν ἐστι Μ[άρκου] Α<ὐ>ρ[ηλίου] Μουσσίου ἰαιρέος· ζῆ· κήδονται οἱ Ἰουδαῖοι.

---

[209] On archiatroi see Wellmann, RE II, 1896, col 464-6; Keil 1905, p128-38 (the series of inscriptions from Ephesus); New Docs 1977, p10-25; Dig. XXVII.1.6,2-4; L.9.4,2; Mussies 1990, p188; Kalantzis 1995, p115; Künzl 1999, p205-9; Uzel 1999, p211-14. Another Jewish doctor is known at Venosa; see CIJ 600 (=Noy 1993, no 76; fifth century); cf. CIJ 5*; 1100. Noy (1993, p102) notes that a doctor working only for the Jewish community is unlikely to have received the title archiatros. We also note that under the early Empire, Ephesus had a well-known medical school, which was centered on the Museum; see Keil 1905, p128-38; Foss 1979, p21. Other archiatroi in Ephesus are listed in New Docs 1979, p231; they are IvEph 622 (c. 160), 1162, lines 4, 6, 7 (time of Antoninus Pius), 1164 (mid-II?), 3055, line 16 (late Imperial?), 4350 (late III or IV); see also Roozenbeek 1993, p103-6.

[210] For Jews in other cities in Asia Minor who held civic office or were significantly involved in the life of their cities, see Trebilco 1991, p47-8, 64-5, 173-83.

[211] Ameling 1996, p53.

This tomb is that of Marcus Aurelios Moussios, priest. He made this while living. The Jews are charged with its care.[212]

Here the Jewish community is seen as one group and is charged with caring for the tomb of a priest, Marcus Aurelios Moussios who was a Roman citizen.[213] The maintenance of tombs was an important matter in antiquity. That in these two cases this task of looking after a tomb was assigned to "the Jews" suggests that there was some mechanism by which this would happen. These two inscriptions therefore imply that the Jews of Ephesus had some formal organisational structure, and that the Jews of the city identified themselves as a coherent community.

There are also indications in the documents preserved by Josephus that on some occasions the Jews of Ephesus acted as a united body. For example, we learn from Ant 14:262-4, that probably in 42 BCE, "the Jews in the city (τῶν ἐν τῇ πόλει ᾿ Ιουδαίων)" of Ephesus petitioned the proconsul Marcus Junius Brutus that they might be able to observe their customs. Further, in Ant 16:172-3 Josephus records a letter, probably to be dated between 9 and 2 BCE, in which the proconsul Julius Antonius stated that "the Jews dwelling in Asia" had approached him when he was in Ephesus and asked that he might confirm their right to observe their own customs.[214] Although here the "Jews of Asia" seem to be acting in consort, that the letter is written to Jews in Ephesus suggests that they were a very significant group in view, a group within the wider group of Jews. Thus both these documents from the first century BCE and two inscriptions from the second century CE show that the Jews of Ephesus seem to be able to act as a united community.[215]

---

[212] IvEph 1676. The text was correctly read by Robert 1960, p381-4; for earlier reading see CIJ 746. Date from Horsley 1992a, p124.

[213] Smallwood (1981, p508) thinks that in these two inscriptions, the Jewish community was asked to look after the graves of non-Jews, "presumably because they were respected as reliable people". But as Horsley (1992a, p124) points out, these are epitaphs for Jews, where the Jewish community is asked to take responsibility for the upkeep of the graves of other Jews. We know of three other priests from Jewish inscriptions in Asia Minor; see CIJ 785 (Corycos); Reynolds-Tannenbaum 1987, p5, inscription *a* line 27 (Aphrodisias); Kroll 2001, p17-18, no 4 (Sardis). In this period priests may have had a minor part in synagogue worship, such as pronouncing certain benedictions, or they may have been preferred readers of the Torah. For those known from elsewhere see Robert 1960, p382-3; Brooten 1982, p95-8,249 n73. On the functions of priests see Leon 1960, p192; Brooten 1982, p90-9.

[214] See also Ant 16:167-8, and concerning the Jews in Asia, Ant 16:160-5.

[215] In Ant 16:168, dated to around 14 BCE and addressed to the magistrates, council and people of Ephesus, Agrippa states that anyone who steals sacred monies of the Jews and takes refuge in a place of asylum will not be handed over to the local magistrates, but will be "turned over to the Jews under the same law by which temple-robbers are dragged away from asylum". This suggests the Jews of Ephesus were recognised as acting together, and as being

Another inscription, published in 1989 and to be dated to the late second or third century CE,[216] concerns the burial of three Jews, one named Aurelius Sambathios Iudas, another whose name was probably Aurelius Sambathios, with his third name missing, and a third whose name has not been preserved. The inscription for the first person reads:

Τοῦτο τ[ὸ ἡμι]μόριόν ἐ[στιν] Αὐρ. Σαμ[βαθίου] Ἰούδα Ἐφ[εσίου] Ἰουδέου.[217]

This half of the tomb belongs to Aur(elios) Sam[bathios], son of Ioudas, an Ephesian (and) a Jew.[218]

We note that it is explicitly said that Aurelius Sambathios Iudas, is a Jew of Ephesus;[219] the same is also said of Aurelius Sambathios (whose third name is missing). The occurrence of the name "Sambathios" is significant. It is found among Egyptian Jews and it has been suggested that it applied to someone born on the Sabbath.[220] It suggests that at this later period, at least some Jews in Ephesus observed the Sabbath.[221] The name Sambathios has

---

able to exercise some judicial powers; see Binder 1999, p282. Again it suggests some form of united organisation.

[216] By Pleket, on the basis of the name Aurelius; see SEG 39, 1989, no 1222; see also Williams 1997, p260.

[217] The text is in Knibbe, Engelmann and Iplikçioglu 1989, p219 no 54.

[218] Translation from Williams 1997, p260.

[219] On the meaning of the term "Jew" see Williams 1997, p249-62. She suggests (p256) that here it functions "as a term of social and religious differentiation" and thus emphasises membership of the Jewish community.

[220] Horbury and Noy (1992, p128) note that names like Sabbataios, Sabbatis, Sabbatios and Sabbathion occur in a number of Egyptian inscriptions and papyri. They note: "The Hebrew Shabbethai (Ezra x 15, Neh. viii 7 שַׁבְּתַי), likely to apply to someone born on the sabbath, is found in the Elephantine papyri among 5ᵗʰ century B.C. Jews in Egypt. The LXX rendered it as Σαββαθαί or Σαββαθαῖος, but it could be spelled with *tau* instead of *theta*. The form Sabbatios occurs in the Letter of Aristeas (48, 49) and in 1 Esd. ix 14, ix, 48. ... Sabbataios is one of the forms which he [Tcherikover] showed were used mainly in Ptolemaic times, being superseded in the Roman period by Sambathion, which also spread to non-Jewish observers of the sabbath." For inscriptions with Σαμβάθιν see Horbury and Noy 1992, no 76; Σαμβαῖος see Horbury and Noy 1992, no 65. Tcherikover, Fuks and Stern (1964, p44) shows that the names beginning with Samb- became popular in the early Roman period. For other names with Sabbataios or similar see Horbury and Noy 1992, no 40, 58, 59, 60, 86, 93, 95, 96, 98, 106, 108; the name (or a variant) is found eight times (seven Jews and one God-fearer) in the Aphrodisias inscription; see Reynolds and Tannenbaum 1987, p147. On the name see further Tcherikover, Fuks and Stern 1964, p43-56.

[221] Horsley (New Docs 4, p231) notes Christian examples of the name, which places a question mark against the connection of the name with the Sabbath, as does the use of the name by non-Jews in Egypt (see Tcherikover, Fuks and Stern 1964, p43-56). However,

also been found in other inscriptions in Ephesus,[222] which may be Jewish, particularly in the light of this new inscription.[223]

A few other small finds associated with Jews have been found, including a Jewish glass flask, Jewish lamps and two magical amulets with Jewish characteristics.[224]

4.5 The city-wide organisation of Jews in Ephesus[225]

We have noted that the Jews in Ephesus seem to have adopted a city-wide organisational structure. Can we understand why they did this, particularly given that it is not the only possible structure they could have adopted?[226]

---

where the person named Sambathios is designated as a Jew, as in this inscription, the connection with the Sabbath is the most likely explanation for the name.

[222] Knibbe and Iplikçioglu 1984, p107 reads:] Μ. Αὐρ. Σαμβαθίου Λ. The editors suggest it is Jewish; it is undated but may be from the late second or third century. IvEph 2306k, which was found in the Church of St John and begins with a cross and so is Christian, contains the name Σαμβάθιος. IvEph 3307 reads Αὐρ. Σαμβάθιος Κρατέρου ὠνήσατο. It is from the late third century and the editors suggest it could be Christian or Jewish. For other Christian examples of the name see New Docs 4, p231.

[223] For other Jewish inscriptions from Ephesus, which are all later and do not provide any additional evidence, see IvEph 46, line 5 (the Apocryphal Letter between Abgar and Jesus, fifth or sixth century); 4135, l 25-6 (= CIJ 747, a Pastoral letter from Hypatios, the Bishop of Ephesus in the 530s, who mentions Jews); see also IvEph 3822 (= CIJ 755) from Hypaipa. Note that IvEph 2209 (=2281b) is said in the original publication to be "probably Jewish", but this view has been retracted in the Addenda et Corrigenda zu den Inschriften von Ephesos I-VII,1, p28.

[224] For the Jewish glass flask see Keil 1930, p39-41; also in Goodenough 1953, Vol 2, p108; Vol 3, no 961. It is decorated with a menorah, shofar, lulab and ethrog; and was discovered in the vicinity of the Cathedral of Saint Mary. Five Jewish lamps with menorahs have been discovered; they date from the second/third to the sixth century; see FiE 4.2, 1937 p114, no 180 (4th century, from the Grotto of the Seven Sleepers); p172 no 1872 (?6th century, Seven Sleepers); p187 no 157 (2nd/3rd century, basilica north of Theatre Gymnasium); p188, no 164 (4th century, no provenance); p188, no 167 (4th century, no provenance); see also Foss 1979, p45 n48; Goodenough 1953, Vol 2, p102-3, Vol 3 no 928, 929. For two undated magical amulets with Jewish characteristics which have been ascribed to the general vicinity of Ephesus see Keil 1940, p79-84; Kraabel 1968, p56-9. Kraabel (1968, p59) thinks they may "suggest the presence of Jewish elements in the magic of the Ephesus area" in the Imperial period. See further Kraabel 1968, p59-60; 69; Thompson 1990, p143; Frend 1984, p155 n34. A menorah was cut into the steps of the Library of Celsus, but we do not know when; see Worth 1999b, p53.

[225] See further Trebilco 1999, p325-34.

[226] For discussion of whether Jews elsewhere had a city-wide organisation, see Meeks 1983, p35-6; Schürer, Vermes, Millar, Black, Goodman 1986, p87-98. It seems clear, for example, that they had a city-wide organisation in Alexandria but not in Rome. Ant 14:235, 259-61 suggests the Jews in Sardis had a city wide organisation; see Branick 1989, p56. We do not know any details about the organisational structure of the Jewish community in Ephesus. It is unlikely that it formed a *politeuma* within the city; see Horsley 1992a, p122 and in general Lüderitz 1994, p183-225.

Firstly, the documents preserved by Josephus suggest that political expediency may have encouraged the Jews to adopt this structure (or reinforced this structure if it had already developed). Faced with challenges to their rights, the Jews of Ephesus needed to adopt a united front in arguing with the city authorities and the Roman administration. This is clear for example in Ant 12:125-8, where "the Ionians" agitated against the Jews of Ionia, which increased the need for Jewish unity so as to be able to defend the retention of their customs.[227] A second related reason was that of the Jewish Temple tax. As we have noted above, it is clear from the decrees preserved by Josephus that the cities of Asia attempted to prevent the Jews from sending the temple tax to Jerusalem. A prime reason for this seems to have been the difficult economic situation of the province of Asia for most of the first century BCE. The cities seem to have greatly resented a significant amount of gold being sent each year to Jerusalem, and the consequent harm this caused to the local economy. The cities therefore sought to prevent the export of the Temple tax by the Jews.[228] Faced with this sort of threat, the Jews of Ephesus needed to present a united front to argue their case. There may well have been other reasons that led to this city-wide sense of unity too - a sense of belonging together due to the common ties of their ethnicity, marriage within the community, observing the same customs and the life of the synagogue community or communities.

4.6 Later literary evidence

Justin's *Dialogue with Trypho,* written around 160 CE, was set in Ephesus according to Eusebius (H.E. 4.18.6), perhaps on the basis of a well-established tradition. Although we cannot regard Justin's work as a reliable record of an actual debate, that Justin probably situates both the *Dialogue* and Trypho in Ephesus suggests that Justin (and his readers) would have seen Ephesus as a suitable venue for a debate between a Christian and a learned Jew concerning matters like Jesus and the law.[229]

---

[227] See also Ant 16:27-60.

[228] Barclay 1996, p264-78.

[229] See Thompson 1990, p143. Kraabel (1968, p53) thinks Trypho found refuge in Ephesus after the Bar-Kochba revolt. Rajak (2001, p511) suggests that from the Dialogue itself "we might infer the setting to have been Greece, where Trypho is said to have been spending a lot of time (3)." Dial 1.1 simply locates in it "the walks of the Xystus", the Xystus usually being a place for gymnastics. Note that the gymnasium portion of the Harbour Baths in Ephesus, built in 89/90 CE, was called the "Xystos" (ξυστός); see Friesen 1993a, p127, 137; IvEph 1104, 1125, 1155. However, the covered colonnades of the Xystos was a popular context for philosophical discussion in other places, and was chosen for such discussions by, for example, Cicero; see Rajak 2001, p511. Eusebius describes Trypho as "the most distinguished Jew of the day".

Around 190CE, Polycrates, bishop of Ephesus, describes 14 Nisan as the day "when the people (ὁ λαός) remove the leaven".[230] Bauckham notes that this cannot simply be derived from Exod 12:15, but rather reflects contemporary Jewish practice and the language that is used for that practice.[231] We note also the use of the term "ὁ λαός" for the Jewish people; this term is found in Jewish inscriptions in Asia Minor,[232] and so probably reflects contemporary Jewish language. Accordingly, Bauckham notes that Polycrates "can speak of things Jewish in an accurately Jewish way."[233] This may in part be due to Polycrates living in close proximity to the large Jewish community of the city, and perhaps being part of a church with a strongly Jewish-Christian background. In this small way then we see the influence of the Jews of Ephesus on Christians towards the end of the second century.[234]

4.7 The size of the Jewish community in Ephesus

McGing has recently shown how very little hard data we have available to us with regard to the size of Jewish communities.[235] The only real indication that we have comes from the decrees preserved by Josephus, which suggest the Jewish community of Ephesus was reasonably sizeable;[236] perhaps it numbered in the hundreds by the first century CE? Comparative data from Sardis and Aphrodisias from a later period, at least suggest that some Jewish communities in Asia Minor could be of this size.[237] Some scholars have estimated that the Jewish Diaspora made up around 10% of the population of

---

[230] See Polycrates, quoted in Eusebius, HE 5.24.2-7.

[231] Compare m. Pesah. 1-2.

[232] See CIJ 776 from Hierapolis; the inscriptions from Smyrna and Nysa given in Schürer, Vermes, Millar, Black, Goodman 1986, p20 and 24 respectively; see also CIJ 662; 699-708, 720 (Nysa); TDNT 4, p39; Schürer, Vermes, Millar, Black, Goodman 1986, p89-90.

[233] Bauckham 1993a, p37.

[234] Note also that Irenaeus (Adv Haer 3.23) says that Theodotion, who translated the Torah and Prophets into Greek was an Ephesian. Kraabel (1968, p52) accepts this as credible, since Irenaeus grew up in Smyrna.

[235] McGing 2002, p88-106. He notes (p106): "I do not believe we have the first notion of how many Jews there were in the ancient world, even roughly speaking, nor do we have the means to discover it."

[236] See for example Ant 16:27 ("It was also at this time, when they [Agrippa and Herod] were in Ionia, that a great multitude of Jews, who lived in its cities ..."); see also 16:166. Philo (Leg. 245) writes of Asia and Syria that "the Jews are very numerous in every city". See also Horsley 1992a, p122. But clearly these texts do not give definite numerical data.

[237] The Sardis synagogue may have been able to seat one thousand people (it is only an estimate by the archaeologist), and the Aphrodisias inscription lists sixty-nine Jews and fifty-two "Godfearers"; see Trebilco 1991, p41, 152-3.

the Mediterranean,[238] while Ameling has recently suggested the Jews in Asia Minor made up under 5% of the total population.[239] Either figure would give a far larger number of Jews in Ephesus than this, but as McGing has shown, all our estimates are really guesses.[240]

4.8 Conclusions[241]

We do not know when Jews first settled in Ephesus, but clearly by the mid first century BCE, the community was well established. Documents from 49 BCE to 2 CE suggest that the community experienced hostility in this period, but it seems likely that interaction with the wider city in the first century CE was generally more positive. Further, the documents suggest that the community maintained facets of Jewish identity, that they received Roman support and that the Jews were a significant community in the life of the city.

Acts informs us about a synagogue in Ephesus in the mid-first century, although there may have been more than one Jewish synagogue at this time; two inscriptions relate to a synagogue (or perhaps to different synagogues) in later centuries.

Evidence from both Josephus and inscriptions show that the Jews could regard themselves as one group, "the Jews in Ephesus". Inscriptions also show that in the second century a Jew was an official city doctor and suggest that (at least) some Jews continued to observe the Sabbath. We do not know the size of the community, but it was probably sizeable, which means that the city-wide organisation of the Jews in Ephesus is noteworthy.

We can suggest that the Jewish community was a significant group in the "foreground" for the Christians in Ephesus and that some interaction between Jews and Christians would have been inevitable. We will build on this in subsequent chapters.

---

[238] See Meeks 1983, p34.

[239] See Ameling 1996, p30. He notes that others make an educated guess of between 5-10%.

[240] Accordingly, Strelan (1996, p181) estimates there were up to 25,000 Jews in the city. Robinson (1988, p114) thinks 75,000 is the upper limit. Binder (1999, p282) thinks "the other literary sources [apart from Acts] imply a sizable Jewish population in the city".

[241] We have further evidence for the integration of Jews into social, economic and political life in Asia Minor (discussed for example by Thompson 1990, p137-45). However, much of this additional evidence comes from after the first century CE. Further, given the diversity of Jewish communities in the Diaspora (see for example Jones 1998, p29-30) including Asia Minor, it would be methodologically unwise to take this evidence as applicable to Ephesus.

5. Overall Conclusions

Much more could be included in this Chapter. However, we have seen how significant Ephesus was as a city, and how important and vibrant were the cults of Artemis and of the Emperor, to take the two major examples of its multi-faceted cultic life. We have also seen that there is evidence for the significance of the Jewish community in the city. We will see that these elements of its context exerted influence at various points on the life of the early Christians in Ephesus.

Given the significance of the city of Ephesus and its strategic location, it is hardly surprising that it was chosen as a mission centre by Paul the Apostle. In Part One, we will firstly discuss what Paul tells us in his letters about his mission in the city, and then we will turn in Chapters 3 and 4 to discuss what the book of Acts tells us about that mission and about other features of the earliest period of the life of the early Christians in Ephesus.

Part 1

Beginnings in Ephesus

Chapter 2

Paul in Ephesus: the evidence of his letters

Paul is a major figure in the history of Christianity in Ephesus and our earliest written evidence concerning the Christian community in Ephesus comes from Paul's writings, so it is to these writings that we now turn. It is clear from Paul's letters that his ministry in Ephesus occurred after his first journey in Macedonia and Achaia. According to Acts 18:12, his departure from Corinth occurred when Gallio was proconsul in Achaia, probably from summer 51 to summer 52 CE.[1] Although there are differences among scholars as to how to solve the various chronological problems in Paul's career, these do not greatly affect the suggested dating of Paul's time in Ephesus.[2] The most likely date for his time in Ephesus described in Acts 19:1-20:1, which according to Acts was more than two years and three months, is from late 52 or early 53 to early to mid 55 CE, but a variation of two years either way does not greatly affect our current investigation.[3]

Here we will firstly discuss the evidence from 1 and 2 Corinthians and then will turn to the question of whether Paul was imprisoned in Ephesus and

---

[1] See Jewett 1979, p38-40, 164; Bruce 1990, p394-5.

[2] For a discussion of these problems see Donfried 1992, p1016-22; Alexander 1993, p115-23. A number of scholars (eg. Jewett) place the "second missionary journey" before the Jerusalem conference. However, the timing of Paul's arrival in Ephesus is relatively unaffected by this difference in reconstruction, since on this scheme his dated departure from Corinth is followed by a visit to Jerusalem, and then travel to Ephesus as it is for those who follow the order given by Acts. Knox and Lüdemann have argued for different chronological schemes again, but on Lüdemann's scheme (1984, p263) the timing of Paul's work in Ephesus is not necessarily greatly affected, since one of the options he gives for Paul's time in Ephesus is from Fall 51- Spring 53 (the other is Fall 48-Spring 50). Knox (1987, p68) however dates Paul's time in Ephesus from 46. Both Knox and Lüdemann argue that Paul appeared before Gallio on his last visit to Corinth (cf Acts 20:2f); but on this view see Bruce 1990, p395.

[3] There is some variation in dating Paul's arrival in Ephesus introduced by differing estimates of how long the travels listed in Acts 18:22-23 took, or on different reconstructions, how long after his time in Jerusalem Paul arrived in Ephesus. Jewett (1979, p164-5) dates Paul's time in Ephesus from late 52-early 55; Ogg (1968, p134-8) from the autumn of 54 to 57 CE; Haenchen (1971, p67,71) from summer 52 until autumn 54; Gunther (1972, p69) from late spring 53 or 54 to Pentecost 56; Murphy-O'Connor (1996, p29-30, 182) Aug 52-Oct 54; Barrett (1998, plvi-lxi) from Autumn 52 to Spring 55 CE.

wrote his captivity letters from the city. We will then discuss whether any of
Paul's other letters[4] provide evidence for his time in the city and will conclude
with a discussion of house churches, since these were a significant feature of
early Christian life in the city.

1. 1 Corinthians

It is clear from 1 Cor 16:8 ("But I will stay in Ephesus until Pentecost") that
1 Cor was written while Paul was in Ephesus, and it seems likely that 2 Cor
was written shortly after he had left the city.[5] Passages in both letters shed
some light on Paul's time there.

1.1 1 Cor 1:1

Paul begins 1 Cor with the statement: "Paul, called to be an apostle of Christ
Jesus by the will of God, and our brother Sosthenes (Σωσθένης ὁ ἀδελφός)"
(1 Cor 1:1). It is clear then that Sosthenes was with Paul in Ephesus at the
time of writing 1 Cor. Paul calls him ὁ ἀδελφός, a term which he regularly
uses in 1 Cor of believers.[6] That Sosthenes is singled out here for mention,
when there are clearly others whom Paul could mention (1 Cor 16:17, 19), and
that he is simply called "ὁ ἀδελφός" suggests he is very well known to the
Corinthians.[7] This makes it possible that he is the Sosthenes mentioned in
Acts 18:17 as a ruler of the synagogue in Corinth, in which case he had
become a believer.[8]

---

[4] In addition to the generally undisputed letters of Rom, 1 and 2 Cor, Gal, Phil, 1 Thess
and Phlm, we regard 2 Thess and Col (see section 4.4 below) as probably by Paul, and Eph
(see section 4.3 below) and the Pastorals (see Chap 5) as pseudonymous.

[5] See Martin 1986, p xxxiv. Paul wrote two other letters to the Corinthians, both of
which are probably lost. His first letter to the Corinthians was the "Previous Letter" (see 1
Cor 5:9), which dealt with some problems of sexual immorality, and probably also idolatry
(see Fee 1987, p6-7), and after 1 Cor he wrote the "Letter of Tears" (2 Cor 2:4; 7:8). They
were probably both written from Ephesus, although of course this is uncertain.

[6] See for example, 1 Cor 1:10, 11, 26; 2:1; 3:1; 16:12.

[7] Byrskog 1996, p240; Lindemann 2000, p26. Byrskog (1996, p240, 244) notes Paul
would refer to him "to establish or maintain good relations with the recipient of the letter …
if Sosthenes was known as a respected citizen of Corinth, he may also have provided some
important weight to the letter itself." It seems unlikely that Sosthenes is a co-author, since
most of the letter is in the first person singular; Witherington (1995, p79) suggests he may
have been Paul's personal secretary at this time.

[8] See Fee 1987, p30-1; Allo 1956a, p1-2; Lang 1986, p15; Collins 1999, p51.

But ὁ ἀδελφός is also a term Paul uses of his co-workers and associates in ministry, so Sosthenes may be one of Paul's co-workers in Ephesus.[9] Unfortunately we know no more about Sosthenes, since he is not mentioned elsewhere in the NT as a companion of Paul. But clearly a Sosthenes is with Paul in Ephesus, and was probably one of Paul's associates in mission in the city.

1.2 1 Cor 1:11

In 1 Cor 1:11 we read "For it has been reported to me by Chloe's people (ὑπὸ τῶν Χλόης) that there are quarrels among you, my brothers and sisters." Paul knows about the divisions in the Corinthian Christian community (1 Cor 1:12-13) from this source. Fee has argued that it is unlikely that Chloe's people were members of the Corinthian community. Firstly, the representatives of the Corinthians were Stephanus, Fortunatus and Achaicus (1 Cor 16:15-17). Secondly, if Chloe's people were from Corinth they would have probably been among those who followed Paul (since they reported to him), in which case Paul would have been most unwise to quote them as authorities on the situation in Corinth. Yet he here regards them as trustworthy witnesses, which suggests they were outsiders to the whole situation. Most likely then Chloe was a wealthy Asian, whose agents traveled between Ephesus and Corinth. Some of her people, who had become members of the Christian community in Ephesus, visited the church in Corinth and on their return to Ephesus reported to Paul on the situation in Corinth.[10]

Hence, it is likely (though no more than this) that Chloe's people were members of the Christian community in Ephesus. They were probably slaves or dependent workers in Chloe's household, since members of Chloe's family would have continued to use their father's name, even if he was dead.[11] We do not know if Chloe herself was a Christian, but Collins suggests that "Given the fact that Paul designates those who visited him by Chloe's name, it is

---

[9] See Ellis 1970-71, p445-52. Hays (1997, p15) thinks he is "sharing in Paul's missionary work" in Ephesus. If he is the Sosthenes of Acts 18:17, who was the ruler of the synagogue, a position of significance in the Jewish community, it is understandable that he would become a co-worker with Paul.

[10] See Fee 1987, p54, who here follows Ramsay 1900a, p104-5; see also Robertson and Plummer 1914, p10; Thiselton 2000, p121. Barrett 1968, p42; Conzelmann 1975, p32 are more cautious, and think Chloe's people may have been based in either Corinth or Ephesus. Theissen (1982, p92-3) rejects the view expressed in the text, mainly because Chloe's people are not mentioned in Rom 16 which he takes to be to Ephesus. However this is unlikely, so Theissen's objection is groundless. Fascher 1980, p89; Schüssler Fiorenza 1987, p394-5; Schrage 1991, p141 think Chloe's people lived in Corinth. Hitchcock's view (1925, p163-7) that Chloe's people were pagans is unlikely.

[11] See Theissen 1982, p57, 92-4; Schrage 1991, p141.

likely that Chloe was a Christian and, most probably, the patron of a church that gathered in her house."[12] Unfortunately we cannot be certain about this.

1.3 1 Cor 4:9-13

In the Corinthian correspondence Paul gives five separate catalogues of his suffering (1 Cor 4:9-13; 2 Cor 4:8-9; 6:4-10; 11:23-33; 12:10).[13] Do these tell us anything about Paul's time in Ephesus? It is possible that 1 Cor 4:9-13 reflects trials Paul had to endure in and around Ephesus, from which 1 Corinthians was written.[14] "To the present hour" (ἄχρι τῆς ἄρτι ὥρας; v11) and "to this very day" (ἕως ἄρτι; v13) may emphasize that some of what is mentioned here occurred in Ephesus. However, we must be cautious in using 1 Cor 4:9-13 here, since the expressions in v11 and v13 seem to be a deliberate contrast to the Corinthians' over-realized eschatology (v8), and thus are designed to underline the harsh realities of the Christian life in the present and to correct the Corinthians' view that the Christian had begun to reign.[15] The passage is therefore shaped with the Corinthians in mind. Yet Paul could not write this catalogue unless the items listed had a basis in his life. But did any of the items occur in Ephesus? 1 Cor 4:11 - we hunger and thirst, we are ill-clad and buffeted and homeless - expresses the deprivations and ill-treatment resulting from his general missionary way of life and does not necessarily describe his time in Ephesus.[16] Further, being "homeless" probably does not refer to Ephesus, where he may well have stayed with Prisca and Aquila (1 Cor 16:19, as he did in Corinth according to Acts 18:3). Rather, homelessness refers to the fact that as a missionary he was itinerant.[17]

---

[12] Collins 1999, p78; see also Witherington 1995, p99; cf Hurd 1965, p48. Schüssler Fiorenza 1987, p394-5 argues that "those of Chloe" means "the people or followers of Chloe" in Corinth.

[13] On these catalogues, particularly their literary function in Paul's letters, see Fitzgerald 1988. We will consider 2 Cor in the next section.

[14] For this suggestion see O'Brien 1991, p21; Duncan 1929, p67. I am here assuming that 1 Corinthians is a unity (on this see Fee 1987, p15-16) and so that the whole letter was written from Ephesus.

[15] See Fee 1987, p178. Commentators also note that these verses contain clear reflections of the teaching of Jesus.

[16] Paul may be referring to some particular occasions with some of the language used. Thus it is possible that κολαφίζεσθαι refers, along with other events, to the incident at Lystra recorded in Acts 14:19; see Fascher 1980, p151. However, Fitzgerald 1988, p143 n89 points out that in 1 Cor 4:9-13 Paul is not stressing the perils of being an apostle, but the ἀτιμία. Thus the blows in view here may be those offered as insults, rather than a reference to the incident of Acts 14:19.

[17] See Fee 1987, p179.

Paul also mentions "working with our own hands (ἐργαζόμενοι ταῖς ἰδίαις χερσίν)" (v12a).[18] Since this is never found in other hardship catalogues,[19] it clearly refers to Paul's own experience. At least from the time of his mission in Thessalonica, Paul had worked with his hands, originally probably out of necessity, but then also as a concrete expression of his mission.[20] This was a particular area of contention between Paul and the Corinthians.[21] It seems likely then that he continued to work with his hands in Ephesus (as Acts 20:34 also suggests).[22]

The three antitheses of v12b-13a may also be revealing: "When reviled, we bless; when persecuted, we endure; when slandered, we speak kindly." Again, this seems to be a description of Paul's missionary work in general, but given the evidence to be examined shortly that he faced opposition and endured suffering in Ephesus, it probably also includes his time in this city.[23] But the verse does not add anything to what we know from elsewhere in his letters, as we will see, apart from expressing Paul's response to such suffering.

1.4 1 Cor 4:17 and Timothy

In 1 Cor 4:17 Paul writes: "Therefore I sent to you Timothy, my beloved and faithful child in the Lord ..." Before Paul wrote 1 Cor he had probably dispatched Timothy to Corinth. This is suggested by 1 Cor 4:17, which is not an epistolary aorist but a real aorist in view of the fact that Paul does not mention Timothy as a co-sender of 1 Cor (1:1; cf 2 Cor 1:1), which suggests that Timothy had already left at the time of writing. Further, the indefiniteness with which Paul speaks of the timing of Timothy's arrival in Corinth in 1 Cor 16:10 makes it unlikely that he is the bearer of the letter.[24]

---

[18] The plural may well refer to Paul and Aquila, who were both tent-makers; see Acts 18:3.

[19] See Schrage 1991, p346.

[20] See 1 Thess 2:9; 4:11; 2 Thess 3:6-13; Hock 1980, p50-65.

[21] See 1 Cor 9:4-18; 2 Cor 11:9; 12:13-17.

[22] See Robertson and Plummer 1914, p87; Hock 1980, p26, 42. Acts 19:11-12 may also indicate that he worked as a tentmaker in Ephesus; see Trebilco 1994, p312-14 and n100.

[23] Note Barrett's comment (1968, p111): "These words ["up to this very moment" (v11)] may hint at a particularly acute period of suffering at the time of writing; xv. 32 might point to such a moment; cf. xvi.9. More probably however Paul simply means to point out that the apostolic story has no happy ending in this age." He is right that we cannot use the verse to argue for a particularly *acute* period of suffering in Ephesus prior to the time of writing (as Schrage 1991, p344 also emphasises), but clearly Ephesus is part of the overall picture of apostolic suffering.

[24] See Fee 1987, p188; Hurd 1965, p138; Collins 1999, p197. Timothy was probably travelling by a less direct route than the letter carrier(s) (cf. Acts 19:22, where Paul sends Timothy and Erastus to Macedonia). Stephanus, Fortunatus and Achaicus (1 Cor 16:17) probably carried 1 Cor to Corinth.

Since Timothy had been active in Macedonia and Corinth in the previous phase of Paul's work,[25] and since he had been in Ephesus before Paul sent him to Corinth as this verse shows, it is likely that he was with Paul for most of his time in Ephesus as one of Paul's co-workers. We should also note that according to 1 Cor 16:11 Paul expected Timothy to return to Ephesus before his own departure, which suggests he continued to work with Paul in the city after the visit to Corinth described in 1 Cor 16:11.[26]

1.5 1 Cor 15:32

In 1 Cor 15:32 Paul writes: "If with merely human hopes I fought with wild animals at Ephesus, what would I have gained by it? (εἰ κατὰ ἄνθρωπον ἐθηριομάχησα ἐν Ἐφέσῳ, τί μοι τὸ ὄφελος;) If the dead are not raised, 'Let us eat and drink, for tomorrow we die.'" In 1 Cor 15:29-34, Paul is seeking to impress on his readers the consequences of denying the resurrection of the dead. In verse 32 he focuses on the implications of such a denial for himself personally, thus giving a specific example of what he had said in v30-31. If the dead are not raised, then his struggle with wild animals at Ephesus had been in vain, and his actions "border on absurdity".[27]

There has been considerable debate as to whether Paul uses θηριομαχέω literally or metaphorically here.[28] It is generally agreed that the reference must be metaphorical. Firstly, and most significantly, Malherbe has shown that the term was used metaphorically by contemporary moralists to describe the wise man's struggle against his own passions and against his opponents. This strongly suggests that θηριομαχέω is to be taken metaphorically here.[29]

---

[25] That he worked with Paul in Thessalonica is clear from 1 Thess 1:1; 3:2-6; 2 Thess 2:1. He is evidently known to the Corinthians, since he needs no introduction in 1 Cor 4:17.

[26] That Paul himself visited Corinth after this point on his "painful visit" suggests Timothy returned to Ephesus with bad news, which necessitated a visit by Paul; see below. This also suggests Timothy returned to Ephesus. Paul wrote 2 Cor shortly after leaving Ephesus, by which time Timothy was with him again (2 Cor 1:1). Note also that it is not clear who the "brothers" are in 1 Cor 16:11, who will accompany Timothy back to Ephesus; see Lindemann 2000, p381-2. One possibility is that they are from Ephesus, having travelled with Timothy to Corinth, in which case they would be mentioned again in v12.

[27] Fee 1988, p762.

[28] Osborne 1966, p225-9 provides a good summary of the two positions. The literal reading is supported by, for example, Bowen 1923, p59-68; Michaelis 1928, p373; Héring 1962, p171-2; Carrez 1985, p776-7. Particularly prior to Malherbe's article, (Malherbe 1968) it was common to argue that the verb was meant literally.

[29] Malherbe 1968, p71-80. Paul need not have been directly dependent on the contemporary moralists for the language he uses here. θηριομαχέω was in fact used metaphorically by Ignatius in IgnRom 5.1, when he wrote that "I am fighting wild beasts from Syria to Rome, through land and sea, by night and day, bound to ten leopards - which is a company of soldiers - who when well treated become worse." Here the reference is clearly

Secondly, it is doubtful if Paul would have survived a real fight in the arena.[30] Thirdly, Paul does not mention a fight with real animals in 2 Cor 11:23-9, which he wrote after he had left Ephesus.[31] Fourthly, Paul's Roman citizenship[32] should have protected him against such a punishment. However, his Roman citizenship did not protect him from other unjust and illegal treatment. Thus in Acts he is beaten on occasions (Acts 16:22-3) and according to 2 Cor 11:25 he had been beaten with rods three times, a punishment from which Roman citizens should have been exempt. These incidents could indicate that Paul sometimes did not refer to his citizenship in order to prevent punishment, or that Paul suffered at the hands of Roman authorities who did not uphold the law.[33] However, if Paul had fought in the arena in exceptional circumstances, and survived, he would have lost his Roman citizenship,[34] yet Acts 22:25, 23:27 and 25:11, if reliable, show he still possessed Roman citizenship later in his ministry.[35]

---

to the soldiers who guarded him during his journey as a prisoner. Ignatius probably used the verb here because of his intense desire for martyrdom at the hands of wild animals in the future, which probably also led him to call the soldiers leopards; see Schoedel 1985, p178. Conzelmann p277 n130 suggests Ignatius' language is not evidence for a metaphorical usage of the verb, since Ignatius' death was close at hand. But clearly Ignatius' use of θηριομαχέω is metaphorical, even if he used the verb because of what lay ahead; see Fee 1987, p770 n52.

[30] The fact that Acts does not mention a literal fight with animals is also appealed to in support of a figurative interpretation. However, given that Luke mentions comparatively little of the suffering Paul endured (cf. 2 Cor 11:23-29) Luke's silence on this occasion counts for little.

[31] Nor does he mention such a fight in 1 Cor 4:9-13; 2 Cor 6:4-10; nor is it mentioned in 1 Clem 5.

[32] That Paul never mentions his citizenship, along with other factors, has led some scholars to doubt if he was a citizen. However, Hengel has put up a strong case that Paul was a Roman citizen; see Hengel 1991, p6-15.

[33] We know of other Roman citizens who suffered punishments from which they should have been exempt; see Hengel 1991, p7; Martin 1986, p377. We also know of some citizens who had to face the wild animals in the arena; see Eusebius HE 5.1.44, 50-2; Bowen 1923, p64. However, Harris (1970, p410 n1) comments: "in the case of Paul, who was guilty of neither rebellion nor murder, it must remain unlikely that popular pressure would ever have prevailed over constitutional custom".

[34] See Conzelmann 1975, p277 n129 who quotes Dig 28.1.8.4.

[35] Other points have been made in the debate:

1) Acts does not mention a literal fight with wild animals, but then there is much that Acts does not mention, as 2 Cor 11:23-7 shows; see also Bowen 1923, p62.

2) We have no evidence that Christians were thrown to wild animals in amphitheatres in the first century CE.

3) The Acts of Paul 7 from the second century CE relates a story of Paul fighting with a real lion at Ephesus (cf the story of Thecla and the lioness in Acts of Paul 3:27-39). On these stories see Metzger 1945, p11-21; MacDonald 1980, p270-5. However, they are clearly legendary.

The case that θηριομαχέω is here used metaphorically is therefore a strong one.[36] But such a metaphorical usage of the verb in no way lessens the gravity of the danger and hardship Paul endured.[37] If the occasion did not involve considerable danger, then it loses its relevance in the context of 1 Cor 15, for Paul must be referring to an extreme example of what he has endured.

This view of the metaphor also means we can decide whether εἰ ... ἐθηριομάχησα is to be taken as a condition of fact or contrary to fact;[38] he

---

4) In context, the reference in 2 Tim 4:17 to being rescued from the lion's mouth is also metaphorical and is probably derived from Ps 22:21 where the phrase refers to deliverance from great danger; see Hanson 1982, p161; Fee 1988, p297-8.

5) It seems likely that the stadium at Ephesus was not used for wild beast fights in the first two centuries CE, since the enclosed area at the east end which served as a substitute for an amphitheater cannot be dated earlier than the third century CE; see Harris 1970, p410.

[36] This is generally agreed now; see for example Allo 1956a, p416-7; Senft 1979, p203; Wolff 1982, p192; Klauck 1984, p116; Lang 1986, p230; Fee 1987, p770-1; Watson 1992, p172 Schrage 2001, p244; cf. Hunkin 1927-28, p281-2. MacDonald 1980, p265-76 argues that the autograph of 1 Cor did not contain the words "which I have in Christ Jesus" (15:31c). He argues that in the autograph Paul made it clear that the Corinthians were telling a legend about Paul's fight with a lion at Ephesus. The fight is thus neither literal, nor metaphorical, but mythical. However, his view presupposes that the Corinthians attached a well-known legend concerning a lion and a hero figure to Paul, which seems unlikely. Murphy-O'Connor 1986, p93 notes that reading ὑμέτερα as an objective adjective, as required by the normal reading of the verse, does not infringe the rules of grammar, so there is no basis in the text for MacDonald's proposed excision. Fee (1987, p770 n49) notes MacDonald's argument is "speculative at every key point" and neglects Paul's own argument in v30-31a. Osborne (1966, p229-30) on the basis of the commentary on Hab 2:17 found at Qumran (1 QpHab 11,16-12,5) in which animals are identified as "the Simple of Judah who keep the Law", suggests the opponents Paul faced were a well organised party of hostile Asian Jews, similar to those Paul faced elsewhere according to Acts (17:13; 21:27ff). His case depends on this identification reflecting "a common usage drawn from the well of postbiblical tradition common to both the Qumran community and the Christian community" (p230). However, an interpretation cannot be based on this far-fetched parallel alone and thus his suggestion is very unlikely.

[37] See Barrett 1968, p366.

[38] Those who thought ἐθηριομάχησα was to be taken literally often took εἰ ... ἐθηριομάχησα as a condition contrary to fact (it is possible for an apodosis without ἄν to occur with a condition contrary to fact in the protasis; see Barrett 1968, p366). Paul would then be referring to the *possibility* of his fighting with animals, not of him actually having done so, since he does not speak anywhere else of a fight with real animals. The verse would then mean "Suppose that I had fought against beasts at Ephesus (which did not happen, though I was ready to go through such a fight), and suppose that I had done so "kata anthropon", then ....?"; Héring 1962, p171-2; see also Harrisville 1987, p272. It would then be a threatened fate from which Paul escaped. But as noted in the text, this reading is unlikely. This reading of the verse was also taken to suggest that in Ephesus there was a violent outcry against Paul, stirred up by Jews, which included some calling that he should be condemned to the arena. Although Paul was spared this fate, Duncan thinks that "along

writes: "If .... I fought with wild animals" - had he done so or not? If Paul is using the verb metaphorically, then this suggests that the conditional clause is one of fact, referring to a real situation. Further, ἐθηριομάχησα stands parallel to "τί βαπτίζονται; - why do they have themselves baptised?" and "τί κινδυνεύομεν; - why are we putting ourselves in danger every hour?" In this context, the conditional clause in v32 probably concerns real dangers since it stands parallel to two other concrete situations.[39] Finally, Paul is here elaborating on v31, and thus on how he is in danger every day. It is difficult to see how something that never in fact occurred could serve as an adequate elaboration of this.[40] We conclude then that the condition is one of fact, and that Paul did fight with these metaphorical wild animals.

We are also able to come to a decision about the meaning of "κατὰ ἄνθρωπον" in 1 Cor 15:32. The phrase here means that if there is no hope of resurrection, Paul's struggle against "wild animals" is at the merely human level and he is nothing more than one mere man among others. Hence the best translation of 15:32a is "If with merely human hopes I fought with wild animals at Ephesus, what would I have gained by it?"[41] As Fee notes, Paul's point is "What sense does it make to live like this if we live only at the merely human level as others who have no hope for the future?"[42]

If θηριομαχέω is used metaphorically, to what does it refer? Given that Paul says the event occurred in Ephesus, he is referring to more than his own self-control, which is the way some of the contemporary moralists used the term. It is most likely that we should connect the phrase with Paul's mention of adversaries in 1 Cor 16:9, and suggest that these were the wild animals with whom Paul had fought,[43] although as we will see, we are not able to determine who these adversaries were.

---

with the outcry went arrest and imprisonment" (p131); see Duncan 1929, p66-7, 126-31; 1955-56, p163; cf. Carrez 1986, p52-3.

[39] Conzelmann 1975, p278; Wolff 1982, p192. Robertson and Plummer 1914, p362 (who accept a metaphorical meaning for ἐθηριομάχησα) note: "the climax, peril (κινδυνεύομεν), peril of death (ἀποθνήσκω), peril of a horrible death (ἐθηριομάχησα), is perhaps intentional."

[40] Fee 1987, p771 n50.

[41] This is the NRSV translation.

[42] Fee 1987, p771, who gives the many suggestions for the meaning of κατὰ ἄνθρωπον in n55. See also Malherbe 1968, p80; Héring 1962, p171; a similar usage is found in 1 Cor 3:3.

[43] See Malherbe 1968, p80; Fee 1987, p771; Hays 1997, p268. It is not unusual for those considered false teachers or opponents to be described as some sort of animal or as a beast; see Phil 3:2; Acts 20:29; Tit 1:12; IgnEph 7.1; IgnSm 4.1. Wolff 1982, p192 notes that ἐθηριομάχησα is an Aorist, and that this argues against Malherbe's identification of the wild animals with the adversaries of 1 Cor 16:9. This is not however an insuperable problem. It could be a complexive or constative aorist (see BDF, p171), or Paul could have one particular incident in view.

But were these adversaries other Christians[44] or pagans or Jews? The context is helpful here. In 1 Cor 15:30-1 Paul writes: "And why are we putting ourselves in danger every hour? I die every day! That is as certain, brothers and sisters, as my boasting of you." The context shows Paul is here speaking, not of a daily dying to self, but rather of physical danger; he means something like "Each day I face the reality of death".[45] His reference in v32 to fighting wild animals in Ephesus is thus one example of his being exposed to danger and coming face to face with actual death every day.[46] It seems very unlikely that other Christians would pose such a threat to Paul's actual life. The reference is much more likely to be to pagans or Jews, although to say anything more than this is only speculation.[47]

---

[44] In 1 Cor Paul was struggling with Christians in Corinth who were opposing him.

[45] See Fee 1987, p769; cf. Rom 8:36; 2 Cor 4:10; 11:23.

[46] See Fee 1987, p768-9; cf. Bowen 1923, p67-8.

[47] Lindemann (2000, p352) notes that Paul presupposes that his readers already know about the event in more detail, which is why we are unable to be certain about what he is referring to. A number of suggestions have been made in an attempt to be more precise about these "wild animals". 1) Barrett 1968, p366 notes: "It may be that the occasion was that of the riot in Acts xix.23-40; this must remain quite uncertain." See also Orr and Walther 1976, p90-1; Jewett 1979, p19. However, it is unlikely that the reference is to the riot in Acts. Firstly, according to Acts, Paul does not go near the theatre during the riot, so it is unlikely that he could describe the event as fighting wild animals, although the riot could have been more life threatening than Luke suggests. Secondly, the main point telling against the identification is that Luke places the riot at the end of Paul's time in Ephesus. Although Luke wants to avoid the impression (perhaps for his own reasons) that Paul was driven out of Ephesus, the narrative clearly implies that Paul left the city after the riot occurred. While it is possible that the riot occurred at any point during Paul's time in Ephesus, given the vague chronological introduction in Acts 19:23, it seems likely that it was towards the end of his time in Ephesus, as some scholars accept; see for example Schneider 1982, p274. Kreitzer 1987, p70 n26 notes "It seems to me that the incident [the riot] was so severe that it probably was towards the end of Paul's ministry at Ephesus and probably is [sic] responsible, at least in part, for his leaving the city." However, in 1 Cor, after the fighting with wild animals has occurred, Paul still envisages staying in Ephesus for some time (1 Cor 16:8), which makes it unlikely that Paul's "fighting with wild animals" was the riot; see also Lake and Cadbury 1933a, p245; Grosheide 1953, p375; Allo 1956a, p416; Harris 1970, p413. Thirdly, the way Paul speaks of "fighting with wild animals" suggests it was a well-known event. But if, as the view that 1 Cor 15:32=Act 19:23-40 requires, Paul wrote 1 Cor after the riot and before he left Ephesus, little time had elapsed (at least as Luke portrays events) for the Corinthians to have learned of Paul's "fighting wild animals" before he began writing 1 Cor; see Harris 1970, p413. It is more likely then that Luke did not know of or has omitted whatever it was that Paul was referring to in 1 Cor 15:32, although if some of the opponents with whom Paul fought were pagans, then the riot, which probably occurred after 1 Cor was written, could have been a later event in the on-going opposition. 2) Wolff 1982, p192 suggests that ἐθηριομάχησα could be an allusion to the pagan state as a beast, as in Rev 13. This is possible, but the background outlined by Malherbe seems more likely. 3) Duncan 1955-56, p163 argues that the wild animals were the Jews of Ephesus who attempted to secure Paul's

By using θηριομαχέω Paul seems to be alluding to the *extent* of the opposition he personally endured in Ephesus; his experiences in the city were like the life and death struggle with ferocious animals. Given that v32 is an illustration of v31 in which Paul speaks of dying every day, it seems that Paul was not simply involved in an ideological struggle with these opponents, but one that exposed him to severe physical dangers as well, probably as a result of fierce resistance to his preaching.[48] Even if we cannot be more precise about the opponents, or their actions, we can note that in these early days the Ephesian Christians must have been familiar with controversy and opposition from outsiders.

1.6 1 Cor 16:1-4: Ephesus and the Collection

In this passage Paul gives instructions concerning the collection for Jerusalem. Paul never mentions that the Ephesian Christians, nor other Christians in Asia, took part in the collection. Lüdemann interprets this silence in the following way: "It is most probable that Asia (Ephesus) did not organize a collection because the apostle could not (any longer?) gain a foothold there. Paul's intimations regarding his persecutions in this locality (1 Cor 15:32; 2 Cor 1:8) should also be noted."[49] This is a far-reaching claim, and if true would have wide ramifications for our understanding of Paul's mission, since it would imply he lost all support in all of Asia. Günther takes this even further, and suggests that Ephesus is not mentioned in connection with the collection because Paul's missionary endeavours in Ephesus failed, and so there was no "Pauline community" in Ephesus from which to make a collection.[50]

What do we make of these claims? Knox's reply to the claim by Lüdemann (which also applies to Günther) is worth quoting in full:

Yet can there be any question but that the Asian churches, particularly the church at Ephesus, were involved [in the collection]? To be sure, Luedemann thinks there is such a question. ... He cited 1 Cor. 15:32 and 2 Cor. 1:8 in this connection. I must differ from him at this point. There would be no disagreement between us, I feel sure, as to the fact that Paul worked (himself and through his aides) for a considerable period in Ephesus and in other parts of Asia (witness Colossae, Laodicea and Hierapolis; no doubt there were other cities) and that

---

condemnation on a serious charge, as a result of which he was in prison awaiting trial when he wrote Phil. However, this is simply speculation.

[48] See Fee 1987, p771; Barrett 1968, p23.

[49] Lüdemann 1984, p86. Lüdemann also thinks the effort to raise the collection in Galatia failed, because only Macedonia and Achaia are mentioned in Rom 15:26. See also Strelan (1996, p203-4) who thinks there was no collection from Ephesus. On the collection in general see Joubert 2000.

[50] See Günther 1995, p30, 47-53. In my view, he wrongly discounts much other evidence for the Pauline community in Ephesus discussed here, such as 1 Cor 16:8-9 and 16:19-20, and the evidence of Acts.

his relations with these churches were warm and close, even in the very period when the collection was being made (1 Cor. 16:19). And there is nothing to indicate that they had altered for the worse when he left Ephesus finally (so far as we know) for Troas, Macedonia and Corinth. It is not at all necessary to understand the crisis suffered there (2 Cor. 1:8-9) as involving an alienation from the Ephesian church or even that the occasion of the suffering had any connection with that church at all. Besides, from this trouble, whatever it was, Paul can say that he was delivered. He did fight wild animals in Ephesus, whatever that means, but again there is no hint that any alienation from the Ephesian church was entailed. Indeed, he speaks of this experience in the very letter in which cordial relations with that church are unmistakably reflected (1 Cor. 16:19). I have said in discussions of the date of Galatians that it is difficult to understand Paul's being able to speak so complacently in Romans 15 about his work from Jerusalem to Illyricum if he was at that very time in a state of alienation from the churches of Galatia; but that difficulty is enormously increased if Asia, too, were estranged. In considering the fact of Paul's silence about the collection in Asia, it may be well to reflect that we should know little about Paul's effort in Macedonia and Achaia if it were not for the Corinthian letters. But there is no letter to the Ephesians! And may not this fact itself point to his having his base or headquarters there?[51]

Thus, Knox concludes, rightly in my opinion, that Lüdemann (and hence Günther too) is wrong, and that Paul's relations with Ephesus were close and cordial. Further, given that Paul is writing 1 Cor from Ephesus and discusses the arrangements for the collection (1 Cor 16:1-4), it is most likely that the Ephesian Christian did contribute to the collection.[52] We certainly cannot argue that Paul's silence on the matter is significant.[53]

1.7 1 Cor 16:8-9

In 1 Cor 16:8-9 Paul writes: "But I will stay in Ephesus until Pentecost, for a wide door for effective work has opened to me, and there are many adversaries (θύρα γάρ μοι ἀνέῳγεν μεγάλη καὶ ἐνεργής καὶ ἀντικείμενοι πολλοί)."

Paul says he will stay in Ephesus until Pentecost.[54] At the very least this reflects Paul's Jewish heritage, and that for a Jew the year was divided by festivals. Fee notes that "it does not necessarily imply that he and the churches [of Ephesus and Corinth] kept this feast, but [rather] that it is a convenient time reference to a period in mid-spring. On the other hand, such a casual mention of it in this way (cf. Acts 20:16) may suggest that the church

---

[51] Knox 1987, p63-4; see also Dunn 1988, p875.

[52] See Duncan 1929, p248-9, whose further deductions about temple robbery are most unlikely.

[53] We will discuss the issue of the collection further in Chapter 4. Indeed, if we take Acts seriously as an historical source, we can note that the fact that Paul was accompanied by the Asians Tychicus and Trophimus (said in Acts 21:29 to be from Ephesus) to Jerusalem according to Acts 20:4, almost certainly with the collection, argues that Ephesus did contribute to the collection; see also Joubert 2000, p205.

[54] This suggests he is writing the letter in early spring.

very early saw Christian significance to this feast, probably as a result of the birth of the church on the Day of Pentecost."[55] But clearly we cannot say anything definite about the actual practice of the Ephesian Christians in this regard.

As Paul writes he faces opportunities and opposition in Ephesus, both of which provided good reason for Paul to stay in the city until Pentecost. Paul writes: "θύρα γάρ μοι ἀνέῳγεν μεγάλη καὶ ἐνεργής", literally "for a great and effective door has opened to me". The image of the door seems to be used to refer to opportunities for missionary work, as is also the case in 2 Cor 2:12.[56] The image of an open door which provided Paul with the opportunity for effective work reflects, at least in part, the fact that Ephesus was a large city in a strategic location which many people visited.[57] The city thus offered many opportunities for the preaching of the Gospel and perhaps Paul also found some of his hearers to be particularly receptive.[58] But we should not assume that the "open door" is only for evangelism; an integral part of Paul's mission was the nurturing of developing Christian communities so that they might become firmly established, and this is undoubtedly one dimension of the "effective" work in which he is involved.[59]

At what stage in Paul's time in Ephesus did he write 1 Cor? This will help us to evaluate what he says here. The evidence suggests it was towards the end of the period that Acts gives as over two years and three months, for the following reasons. Firstly, 1 Cor 16:5-9 suggests Paul feels that his time in Ephesus is drawing to a close, and he is planning to go on to Macedonia.[60]

---

[55] Fee 1987, p820. Wolff 1982, p222 does not think we can infer anything from this verse concerning whether the Christian communities of Ephesus or Corinth celebrated the festival.

[56] The image of a "door" is also found in Col 4:3; see also Acts 14:27; Rev 3:8. On the image see Robertson and Plummer 1914, p390.

[57] See Chapter 1.

[58] We cannot speculate further on what it was about Ephesus that offered such opportunities; cf Orr and Walther 1976, p358 who connect the statement with Ephesus being a centre for the worship of Artemis. But this is simply speculation. It is possible (though no more than that) that Epaenetus, who is said to be "the first convert in Asia" (Rom 16:5), was converted in Ephesus (though he is in Rome when Paul writes); he is mentioned after Prisca and Aquila in Rom 16:3-5 and so may be connected with them in some way. Günther 1995, p33 thinks that by saying the door was open, Paul is implying that before this it was closed. But this is to read too much into the expression, particularly in view of the fact that in 1 Cor 16:19-20 he passes on greetings from at least two house churches. Günther's view (1995, p47) that "Die Existenz paulinischer Gemeinden [in Ephesus] läßt sich nicht belegen" is very unlikely, given all we argue in Chapters 2-4.

[59] See Rom 15:15-16; 2 Cor 11:28; 13:9-10; Gal 4:19; Col 1:28-2:7; 1 Thess 2:11-12; 3:10-11; see also Bowers 1987, p192 n20 and more generally p188-97. Paul's strategy of revisiting communities also has this nurturing goal in mind; see for example 2 Cor 1:15-16; Phil 1:24-7

[60] See Fee 1987, p190 n44; Harrisville 1987, p14.

Note especially v8 - "I will stay in Ephesus until Pentecost", and his wish that the Corinthians will speed him on his journey "wherever I go" (v6) which suggests that he is not planning to return to Ephesus. Secondly, from 1 Cor 16:19 we learn that there are already a number of Christian communities in the province of Asia, so Paul seems to have been working in Ephesus (and the message has spread from there, or he and / or his co-workers have traveled from Ephesus to elsewhere) for a reasonable period of time.[61] Thirdly, 1 Cor 4:18 - "some are arrogant as though I were not coming to you" - suggests he has not been in Corinth for quite some time.[62] Fourthly, Lüdemann notes a number of points which show that when Paul wrote 1 Cor he had been absent from Corinth for a fairly long period after his founding visit. These are the exchange of letters prior to 1 Cor, the activity of Apollos between the founding visit and 1 Cor (1 Cor 3:6; 16:12), the new developments that had taken place in Corinth, and the fact that "many" had died since his departure (1 Cor 11:30). Without agreeing with Lüdemann's overall chronology, this evidence also suggests that Paul wrote 1 Cor towards the end of his time in Ephesus.[63]

Thus, Paul is probably looking back on an extensive time in Ephesus as he plans his next period of travel (1 Cor 16:5-9), and also looking forward to a future quite short period of promising work in the city. Clearly Paul sees himself as having been engaged in mission preaching which has brought results, and is continuing to bring results and as being involved in nurturing a community. This suggests that the Christian community has grown and become well established, for he considers that his work has been and is being ἐνεργής — effective.[64]

But his work is not unchallenged for their are "many adversaries (ἀντικείμενοι πολλοί)". Paul uses ἀντίκειμαι elsewhere with a similar meaning. In Phil 1:28 Paul exhorts the Philippians to not be frightened in anything "by your opponents (ὑπὸ τῶν ἀντικειμένων)" and in 2 Thess 2:4 we read of the man of lawlessness who "opposes (ὁ ἀντικείμενος) and exalts himself against every so-called god".[65] The verb then is used simply to

---

[61] See Conzelmann, 1975, p4 n31.

[62] See Fee 1987, p190: 1 Cor 4:18 most likely means that Paul's "failure to return after some years had caused some of them to treat him with disdain". Note also in Acts 19:22 Paul has already sent Timothy on ahead of him, since he plans to move on from Ephesus. In 1 Cor 16:10 Paul has sent Timothy to Corinth; see also 4:17, which is probably the same trip referred to in Acts 19:22. Again this suggests 1 Cor is written towards the end of Paul's time in Ephesus. That Paul wrote 1 Cor towards the end of his stay in Ephesus is argued for example by Dupont 1962, p301; Schrage 1991, p36.

[63] Lüdemann 1984, p101-2.

[64] See Wolff 1982, p222.

[65] ἀντίκειμαι is used in 1 Tim 5:14 of "the enemy"; in Lk 13:17 of those who opposed Jesus, and similarly of adversaries in Lk 21:15. It is used of the Antichrist in the Greek

describe the opposition between two parties; the context must be relied on to tell us more about the nature of the opponents (for example, as in 2 Thess 2:4). When there is no complement, as here and in Phil 1:28, it is difficult to know what type of opponents are in view.[66] Since we have no further information from 1 Cor about these opponents in Ephesus, we cannot comment about the exact nature of the adversaries, and we cannot be certain if they are Christians or non-Christians. However, given that the opponents in 1 Cor 15:32 seem to be non-Christians, and that these same opponents are probably in view here, we can suggest that again it is non-Christians, perhaps both Jews and Gentiles, whom Paul here describes as "adversaries".[67] Paul clearly considers them to be people who are diametrically opposed to his work.

It is noteworthy, however, that Paul speaks of "many adversaries (ἀντικείμενοι πολλοί)". He clearly thinks the opposition he is encountering was considerable.[68] We have already noted that these are probably the wild animals Paul refers to in 1 Cor 15:32. These references then point to the intensity and magnitude of the opposition to Paul in Ephesus.

1.8 1 Cor 16:12

In 1 Cor 16:12 we read: "Now concerning (Περὶ δέ) our brother Apollos, I strongly urged him to visit you with the other brothers,[69] but he was not at all

---

Apocalypse of Ezra 4:37, 43; of opponents in Letter of Aristeas 266.5 and in Lives of the Prophets 3:20. It can also be used of other forms of opposition; eg. in Gal 5:17 of the opposition between the Spirit and the flesh; in 1 Tim 1:10 of "whatever else is contrary to sound doctrine". It is used similarly in the LXX; see Ex 23:22; 2 Macc 10:26; Esth 9:2; 8:11; Is 41:11; 45:16; 66:6; Job 13:24; 1 Kgs 11:14. On the term see Spicq 1978, vol 1, p103-4.

[66] In Phil 1:28 where ἀντίκειμαι is used, it is strongly debated whether the opponents of the Philippians are pagans or Christians, and the issue must be decided from the letter as a whole; see Hawthorne 1983, p58; O'Brien 1991, p152-3.

[67] Lang 1986, p247, Robertson and Plummer 1914, p390; Heckel 1993, p262 n279 see them as both pagans and Jews. Barrett 1968, p389 suggests the opponents are "possibly non-Christians, possibly Jewish Christians"; see also Boxall 1998, p201. Duncan 1929, p29 thinks they were more likely to have been Jews than Gentiles, because of the strength of Jewish opposition elsewhere to Paul; see also Schnackenburg 1991, p44-5. Lindemann (2000, p380) thinks we cannot know if the opponents are pagans, Jews or Christians.

[68] Lindemann (2000, p380) notes that Paul also speaks of "many" opponents in 2 Cor 11:18 and Phil 3:18.

[69] The "other brothers" may be Stephanus, Fortunatus and Achaicus mentioned in 1 Cor 16:17, who probably brought the Corinthians' letter to Paul and are now returning to Corinth with Paul's letter; see Fee 1987, p824. Alternatively, the reference could be to Timothy (1 Cor 16:10), although the plural "brothers" in 16:12 would require him to have travelled with others; see Barrett 1968, p391; Wolff 1982, p223. Cf. Günther 1995, p35-7, who sees this as

willing to come now (καὶ πάντως οὐκ ἦν θέλημα ῎ινα νῦν ἔλθῃ). He will come when he has the opportunity."

We know from 1 Cor 3:6 ("I planted, Apollos watered") that Apollos had been in Corinth after Paul founded the community there.[70] 1 Cor 16:12 tells us that he had later left Corinth, since the verse concerns his return to the city. The question is, where and how did Paul urge Apollos to visit Corinth? It is most likely that Apollos was in Ephesus,[71] and Paul himself verbally urged Apollos to visit Corinth. This is certainly the most natural meaning of παρακαλέω in 16:12, which here suggests verbal communication.[72] This verse then provides evidence that Apollos had gone to Ephesus at some point prior to Paul writing 1 Cor.

However, it seems likely that at the time of writing, Apollos was no longer in Ephesus. This is suggested by the lack of greetings from Apollos in 1 Cor 1:1 and 16:20.[73] Perhaps he had moved on to another area since Paul had spoken with him? But the important point from our perspective is that he had been in Ephesus.[74]

1 Cor 16:12 tells us that Paul urged Apollos to visit Corinth. Given that a group who particularly looked to Apollos were part of the divisions in Corinth (1 Cor 1:12; 4:6) it is unlikely that Paul himself suggested that Apollos should return there. Rather it seems that in their prior letter to Paul the Corinthians had requested that Paul ask Apollos to return, as is also suggested by the fact that Paul begins 1 Cor 16:12 with "Περὶ δέ", which is the way he raises successive points that the Corinthians have written to him

---

evidence for an Apollos party in Ephesus, but there is no evidence for this and as we will note below, such a view is very unlikely.

[70] On Apollos in Corinth, and the factionalism there connected with Paul and Apollos see Richardson 1984, p104-110; Pogoloff 1992, p180-90; Carter 1997, p58-61; Ker 2000, p75-97.

[71] Lüdemann 1984, p102: "In the meantime [after his stay in Corinth], he had already made his way back to Ephesus and had been with Paul (1 Cor 16:12)." See also Lake and Cadbury 1933a, p234-5; Richardson 1984, p107; Williams 1990, p326; Fitzmyer 1998, p637. Thiselton (2000, p1332) suggests "it is likely that Apollos was with Paul at Ephesus between AD 52 and 54."

[72] See TDNT 5, p773-99; EDNT 3, p23-7. For examples of παρακαλέω used of verbal communication see 1 Cor 4:13; 14:31; 2 Cor 8:6; 9:5; 12:18. Paul can use the verb of exhortation in a letter, eg 1 Cor 1:10; 4:16; 16:15; 2 Cor 2:8. But nothing in 1 Cor 16:12 suggests Paul wrote a letter to Apollos, or sent a message to him via an intermediary.

[73] See Plummer and Robertson 1911, p393; Conzelmann 1975, p297; Wolff 1982, p223; Fee 1987, p824 n5. It may also be suggested by the past tense (οὐκ ἦν θέλημα – *he was* not willing; see Lindemann 2000, p382), but it is possible that this could apply to an action taken at the time of writing the letter.

[74] W.L. Knox 1925, p321 n8 thinks Apollos was with Paul at the time of writing; see also Allo 1956a, p462-3; Lang 1986, p247; Collins 1999, p79-80. Richardson 1984, p104 thinks "Apollos and Paul are within easy distance".

about.[75] Paul had indeed asked Apollos as requested. That he did so, says a lot about Paul, given the problems in Corinth. Fee notes Paul passed on the request "perhaps as a display on his part of the complete harmony between the two of them."[76] It reinforces that Paul does indeed see Apollos as brother and co-worker, not as a rival.

However, Apollos had decided not to go to Corinth, which also tells us something about Apollos.[77] As Witherington comments: "this suggests that Apollos did not want to add fuel to the fire of Corinthian party spirit and to their playing of favorites".[78]

The important point for us in this is that it suggests that Paul and Apollos were in agreement, or at the very least not at loggerheads. This is also suggested by Paul passing on the Corinthian request for a visit from Apollos, and by the way he speaks of Apollos here, including calling him "ἀδελφός". This confirms that the picture of the unity of their ministry which Paul presents in 1 Cor 3:5-9 is how Paul actually saw the situation, and not an idealized vision of how it should have been.[79] We can also note that Paul calls

---

[75] See Hurd 1965, p63-74, 206; Fee 1987, p274, 823-4; Barrett 1968, p391; cf. 1 Cor 7:1, 25; 8:1; 12:1; 16:1. Hurd 1965, p206 notes: "That they apparently had not similarly requested a visit from Paul is another indication of the strained relationship between Paul and the Corinthians."

[76] Fee 1987, p824. Note that Mitchell (1989, p229-56) has argued that Περὶ δὲ *need not* always be used in response to information received by the author in a letter, but given that Paul is unlikely to have urged Apollos to go to Corinth on his own initiative, this remains the most likely interpretation here.

[77] It is most likely that καὶ πάντως οὐκ ἦν θέλημα ἵνα νῦν ἔλθῃ refers to Apollos' will and not God's (cf. NRSV footnote). Without any qualifier the phrase needs to be understood in its context. Since Apollos is the subject of the final clause, it is likely that he is the one who has decided not to come now; see Wolff 1982, p223; Fee 1987, p824; Lindemann 2000, p381-2. But cf. Barrett 1968, p391-2; Bruce 1971, p160.

[78] Witherington 1995, p317; see also p86-7; see also Fee 1987, p824 ("Most likely he would have turned it down precisely because with Paul he resisted any implication that either of them was party to the internal strife being carried on in the church in their names"); Allo 1956a, p463. We do not know if Apollos did visit Corinth again; he is not mentioned in 2 Cor.

[79] Fee 1987, p824. Bruce 1971, p160 notes from 1 Cor 16:12: "It is evident from this reference that Paul's relations with Apollos were perfectly friendly." Watson 1992, p185: "One thing is clear: Paul has full confidence in him as a colleague." See also Knox 1925, p321 n8; Lang 1986, p247; Orr and Walther 1976, p360; Wolff 1982, p223. Hurd 1965, p206-7 points to the fact that Paul gave only a very brief reply concerning Apollos, and "did not go out of his way here to improve relations between Apollos and the Corinthian Church. He made no apologies for Apollos, and at the same time he made it perfectly clear that it was Apollos and not he who was at fault. Perhaps we are justified in saying that Paul's feelings towards Apollos were ambivalent." But this is to overlook 1 Cor 3:5-9, which together with 16:12, shows Paul was much more positive towards Apollos than this. Given that the Corinthians had asked for Apollos to visit, Paul probably did not need to "go out of his way here to improve relations between Apollos and the Corinthian Church", which explains the

Apollos συνεργός - fellow worker - in 1 Cor 3:9. Both passages then show how Paul actually viewed Apollos at the time of writing - as a brother and co-worker.

Given that Apollos had probably been in Ephesus until shortly before Paul wrote 1 Cor and that he was most likely involved in ministry in the city,[80] can we say anything about his work there? Might there have been an "Apollos party" growing in Ephesus? 1 Cor 16:12, along with 1 Cor 3:5-9, certainly do not support the view that Apollos worked against Paul in Ephesus[81] or that he encouraged in Ephesus the same sort of party rivalry between supporters of Paul and supporters of Apollos (1 Cor 1:12) that developed in Corinth. However, given that in Corinth this rivalry probably developed at the initiative of the Corinthians, is it possible that it arose in Ephesus without any encouragement from either Paul or Apollos? This is possible, but given that Paul and Apollos were both in Ephesus, and seem to be co-workers, it is unlikely that they would have stood aside while such factionalism developed.[82] But apart from the important conclusion from 1 Cor 3:9 and 16:12 that Apollos and Paul were working together (or at the very least, were not at loggerheads), we have no evidence concerning Apollos' work in Ephesus, or the effects of his presence there. We can, however, note that Apollos' impact in Corinth suggests that he was an early Christian leader of some significance;[83] this in turn leads us to suggest he had an impact in Ephesus.

1.9 1 Cor 16:19-20

It is generally agreed that this passage shows that 1 Cor was written from Ephesus. We can note the following points.

---

brevity of his reply on the matter. Richardson (1984, p104) notes Paul does not mention Apollos in 2 Cor 1:19 and takes this as evidence that the relationship between Paul and Apollos is "very strained". But it seems more likely that in 2 Cor 1:19 Paul is describing the founding of the Church in Corinth, in which Apollos was not involved (1 Cor 3:6).

[80] Although we have no idea how long he had been in Ephesus by this time; see also Falwell 1948, p137. If Apollos was still in Ephesus at the time of writing (which we have noted above is unlikely) then the reason he chose not to go to Corinth may have been because of the significance of the work he was doing in Ephesus; see Orr and Walther 1976, p361. But this can only be a suggestion.

[81] Note here that Apollos is not under Paul's wing; he is independent in the sense that he is not under Paul's command. But he is also not disregarding or going against Paul, but rather can be regarded as a co-worker.

[82] Compare Richardson 1984, p104-111, who thinks Apollos has a group of followers in Ephesus and that there was conflict between Paul and Apollos in the city. But Paul's attitude to Apollos in 1 Cor 3:5-9 and 16:12, written from Ephesus, makes this unlikely.

[83] Ker (2000, p77) notes "Apollos has sufficient stature as a leader in the Corinthian community for some to consider him superior to Peter or Paul (1.12)."

Firstly, "the churches of Asia send greetings (Ἀσπάζονται ὑμᾶς αἱ ἐκκλησίαι τῆς Ἀσίας)" (1 Cor 16:19a).[84] It seems likely that Asia here does not simply mean Ephesus, since if it did v20 ("All the brothers and sisters send greetings") would repeat these greetings.[85] We cannot tell how many churches there were in Asia by this time, or how widely spread they were through the province. However, we know that the churches in Colossae, Laodicea and Hierapolis were founded sometime in this period (Col 1:1; 2:1; 4:13, 15-16; Philm 1-2 (cf. Col 4:17); 10 (cf. Col 4:9); 23-4 (cf. Col 1:7; 4:10)),[86] and some of the seven churches of Rev 2-3 had clearly been established for some time by 95-96 CE, when Rev was written.[87] 1 Cor 16:19 clearly suggests that in the course of Paul's time in Ephesus successful evangelism had been conducted in the area around Ephesus and further afield.[88] Further, Paul here seems to imply (although we cannot put it more strongly than this) that the Christian community of Ephesus was the central Christian community of the province, since greetings are given from the churches of the whole province. This suggests that the Ephesian Christian community was a missionary centre, and maintained contact with Christians in other parts of the province.[89] This would not be surprising, given the location and significance of the city of Ephesus.[90]

Secondly, in 1 Cor 16:19b we read: "Aquila and Prisca, together with the church in their house (σὺν τῇ κατ' οἶκον αὐτῶν ἐκκλησίᾳ), greet you warmly in the Lord". Although we will discuss this couple in more detail in the next chapter, we can note several points here.

---

[84] This is the only occasion on which Paul sends greetings from all the churches of a province. He does so here probably in part in order to subtly lift the vision of the Corinthians to realise that they are part of a wider "family", as he does elsewhere in the letter (eg 1:2; 4:17; 11:16); see Fee 1987, p835 n7. That by "Asia" Paul means the province is argued by Robertson and Plummer 1914, p397; Knox 1987, p60. He also mentions Asia in 2 Cor 1:8; Rom 16:5; see also 2 Tim 1:15. On the possible range of meanings of "Asia" see Trebilco 1994, p300-2.

[85] 1 Cor 16:20 reads "All the brothers and sisters send greetings", which seems to refer to those brothers and sisters in the same location as Paul; see below.

[86] If Col was pseudonymous (but see later discussion), then these churches could date from a slightly later period. That Timothy is listed as a co-author of Col may suggest that he had gone there from Ephesus, and so was known to the Colossians; see Falwell 1948, p139.

[87] On the dating of Rev see Chap 7. Acts also gives evidence for a Christian community in Alexandria Troas (Acts 20:7-12); it may already have been in existence when Paul wrote 1 Cor (see Acts 16:8-11) or may have been founded on Paul's visit mentioned in 2 Cor 2:12 after he had left Ephesus (for this interpretation of 2 Cor 2:12 as implying the foundation of a community see Martin 1986, p41-2), in which case it would not be included here. See also 2 Tim 4:13; IgnPhd 11:2; IgnSm 12.1.

[88] See Senft 1979, p219.

[89] See Conzelmann 1975, p299.

[90] This confirms the picture given by Acts 19:10, 26, on which see Chapter 3.

According to Acts, they left Rome as a result of Claudius' expulsion of the Jews from the city (Acts 18:1-2)[91] and settled in Corinth; later they arrived in Ephesus with Paul (Acts 18:18-26).[92] They are in Ephesus as Paul writes 1 Corinthians and since they are known in Corinth, Paul here passes on greetings from them to old friends. Perhaps they had been with Paul during most, if not all, of his ministry in Ephesus. Aquila and Prisca probably played a very important part in the spread of the Gospel in Ephesus since, to judge by the frequency with which they are mentioned, they were two of Paul's most trusted and active co-workers.[93] This shows again that Paul's ministry in Ephesus was collaborative, as it was elsewhere.

We should also note the reference to a house church in Aquila and Prisca's home.[94] This points to the fact that, as elsewhere, the fundamental structure of the early Christian community in Ephesus was the house church. We will discuss the house church in more detail in section 5 below. We note here that preaching and teaching took place in the context of the house church and it is reasonable to suggests that Aquila and Prisca would have been involved in this, along with others. As the hosts of a house church, and from all we know about them from other references, it seems likely that Aquila and Prisca played a key role in the Christian community in Ephesus. It is clear then that the woman Prisca was one of the leaders of a house church, and one of Paul's leading co-workers in Ephesus; we will discuss this further in chapter 3.

Thirdly, these verses suggest that there was more than one house church in Ephesus at this time. Greetings are sent from Prisca and Aquila's house church and in addition from "all the brothers and sisters (οἱ ἀδελφοὶ πάντες)" (1 Cor 16:20). This could be a reference to greetings from Paul's co-workers who are often called ἀδελφοί,[95] but particularly with the inclusion of the word πάντες, it is more likely that the greetings were from all the other Christians in Ephesus and the surrounding area with whom Paul was in

---

[91] On the expulsion, and the difficulties caused by contradictory evidence, see Smallwood 1981, p210-16; Barclay 1996, p303-6.

[92] Later we find them back in Rome, where they hosted a house church (Rom 16:3-5). They are also mentioned in 2 Tim 4:19, in connection with Ephesus.

[93] According to Rom 16:4 Prisca and Aquila "risked their necks for my life". This event could have occurred in Ephesus (see Falwell 1948, p136-7; Günther 1995, p41-2), but we have no way of knowing this.

[94] Fee 1987, p835 suggests this was the house church to which Paul himself was attached in Ephesus.

[95] Fee 1987, p836 sees these "ἀδελφοί" as either "a redundant generalizing of those mentioned in v.19" or "more likely, it refers to Paul's various co-workers and traveling companions." Fee does not consider the point made in the text. Wolff 1982, p228; Klauck 1984, p127 also see the ἀδελφοί as Paul's co-workers. On co-workers as ἀδελφοί see Ellis 1970-71, p445-52. Speaking of οἱ ἀδελφοὶ πάντες seems to be somewhat different from speaking of one person as ὁ ἀδελφός, which we have argued in the case of Sosthenes and Apollos does designate them as a co-worker.

contact. This would include Paul's co-workers, but also other house churches in Ephesus.[96] If the average size of a house church was thirty people,[97] then the total number of Christians in Ephesus at this time connected with the Pauline mission may have been at least twice this number, although of course we have no firm evidence.

Finally, we can note that 1 Cor 16:19-20 suggests that Paul's relations with the Christians in Ephesus and elsewhere in Asia were close and cordial at this time.[98] There is certainly no indication of any discordant notes.

1.10 1 Corinthians as a whole

We can suggest that the theology of 1 Cor may reflect Paul's preaching in Ephesus at this time. We cannot build on this in any way, but we can note that it would have been surprising if Paul had written in one way to Corinth, and then preached with a quite different emphasis the next day in Ephesus.

We can also suggest that other features of 1 Cor may reveal something of the life of Ephesian Christians. For example, they probably celebrated the Lord's Supper according to the tradition Paul gives in 1 Cor 11:23-6, and 1 Cor 15:3-8 was probably a tradition Paul passed on to the Ephesians, as he had to the Corinthians.[99]

2. 2 Corinthians

2.1 Titus' two visits to Corinth, and Paul's "painful" visit

Titus' first visit to Corinth is probably mentioned in 2 Cor 8:6, where Paul writes: "so that we might urge Titus that, as he had already made a beginning, so he should also complete this generous undertaking among you." Thus, after 1 Cor had been received by the Corinthians, Titus probably visited Corinth in

---

[96] See Watson 1992, p188; Falwell 1948, p134-5. Barrett 1968, p396 comments: "These may be the part of the Ephesian church that did not met in the house of Aquila and Prisca. These need not be covered by the churches of Asia, since it would be quite natural to exclude Ephesus from this general category and reserve it for special treatment." (He also suggests the ἀδελφοί could be Corinthian Christians who had travelled to Ephesus.) See also Robertson and Plummer 1914, p398-9; Allo 1956, p467-8; Orr and Walther 1976, p365; Lang 1986, p249.

[97] This is the estimate of Robinson 1988, p120.

[98] See Knox 1987, p64.

[99] Schnackenburg (1991, p47-9) thinks there would have been similar social stratification in the Ephesian Pauline Christian community as there was in Corinth (eg. 1 Cor 1:26-8). But since we have no evidence at all from Paul on this matter with regard to Ephesus, it is wisest to refrain from importing Corinthian data to Ephesus.

order to implement the directions given in 1 Cor 16:2 about the Collection. This is what Paul means by "as he had already made a beginning".[100] Presumably Titus visited Corinth from Ephesus, since this is where Paul was at the time and Titus visited Corinth at Paul's request.

After writing 1 Corinthians, Paul made his "painful visit" from Ephesus (1 Cor 16:8) to Corinth (2 Cor 2:1-2, 12:14, 21; 13:1-2), which was part of what for Paul was an on-going crisis in the Corinthian church.[101] We cannot know what effect this visit, or the on-going Corinthian crisis had on the Christian community in Ephesus, but clearly this was a very difficult period for Paul himself.

After this painful visit, Paul wrote the "tearful" or "severe letter" (2 Cor 2:4, 9; 7:8, 12), almost certainly from Ephesus. It seems that Titus carried this letter to Corinth, and that Paul had arranged to met Titus in Troas on his return from Corinth. Paul then left Ephesus to go to Troas, but could not find Titus, and so went on to Macedonia in the hope of meeting him there (2 Cor 2:12-13). He finally met Titus, who reported that the situation in Corinth had improved (2 Cor 7:6-16).[102] All of this suggests that Titus carried Paul's "tearful letter" from Ephesus to Corinth,[103] and thus that Titus had been in Ephesus prior to this. This visit with the "tearful letter" seems to have been Titus' second visit to Corinth from Ephesus.

We do not know how long Titus had been in Ephesus prior to his first visit to Corinth. He is not mentioned in 1 Cor, which suggests that he was not with Paul at the time he wrote that letter,[104] although since Titus only seems to have become involved with the Corinthians after 1 Cor was written, it could

---

[100] See Harris 1970, p3 n1. The second half of 2 Cor 8:6 refers to the successful outcome of the painful letter. Hence his visit to Corinth with the "tearful letter" was probably his second visit to the city; see Harris 1970, p3-4. Harris notes (1970, p3 n1) that "the belief that Titus and ὁ ἀδελφός were the bearers of 1 Corinthians rests on a somewhat precarious identification of 2 Cor 12:18a with 2 Cor 8:6a and 1 Cor 16:11b, 12a." Hence the visit mentioned in 2 Cor 8:6 was Titus' first visit to the city that we know of.

[101] For the timing of the visit see the discussions in Hurd 1965, p56-7; Furnish 1984, p54-5; Martin 1986, p xxxiv; Thrall 1994, p49-77.

[102] See Martin 1986, pxxxiv; Harris 1970, p3-11. The most likely reconstruction of further events is as follows. Paul sent Titus and two others on ahead to Corinth with Paul's fourth letter (2 Cor 8:16-24), which was probably 2 Cor 1-9, a letter of reconciliation. Paul himself hoped to follow Titus (2 Cor 9:4-5). He probably then received word that renewed troubles had occurred in Corinth, so he wrote 2 Cor 10-13. He was again ready to visit them (2 Cor 12:14, 20-1; 13:1-2, 10) for what was his third visit and it seems he did so (and was presumably well received), since he wrote Romans from Corinth (Rom 16:23; cf. 1 Cor 1:14) and noted in Rom 15:26 that he had already added contributions to the Collection from churches in Achaia which would include Corinth.

[103] See Barrett 1973, p8; Martin 1986, p xxxiv; Fee 1987, p816.

[104] It is possible, but unlikely, that Titus carried 1 Cor, but 2 Cor 12:18, which could be interpreted in this way, probably refers to him carrying the "tearful letter"; see Martin 1984, p xxxiv.

be that Titus was with Paul in Ephesus when he wrote I Cor, but was unknown in Corinth and so was not included in the prescript or greetings.[105] He could have been working in Ephesus for quite some time. That Titus seems to have returned to Ephesus between his first and second visits to Corinth,[106] suggests he was working in Ephesus with Paul, and that he may have been involved in similar activity in the city before he went to Corinth on the first visit.

2.2 2 Cor 1:8-10

In 2 Cor 1:8-10 Paul writes: "We do not want you to be unaware, brothers and sisters, of the affliction we experienced in Asia (ὑπὲρ τῆς θλίψεως ἡμῶν τῆς γενομένης ἐν τῇ Ἀσίᾳ); for we were so utterly, unbearably crushed that we despaired of life itself. Indeed, we felt that we had received the sentence of death in ourselves (ἀλλὰ αὐτοὶ ἐν ἑαυτοῖς τὸ ἀπόκριμα τοῦ θανάτου ἐσχήκαμεν) so that we would rely not on ourselves but on God who raises the dead. He who rescued us from so deadly a peril will continue to rescue us; on him we have set our hope that he will rescue us again."[107]

Clearly Paul suffered extreme hardship on a particular occasion,[108] of such intensity that he thought a menacing death[109] was imminent and he was on the edge of despairing of life itself.[110] However, the severity of the affliction had led him to rely solely on "the God who raises the dead", and God had indeed delivered him from it.

In v8 Paul uses a disclosure formula to write of his affliction in Asia. It is unlikely that he is telling the Corinthians of the fact of this affliction for the first time, since the vagueness of the language suggests that they knew something of the event. Further, the general designation "in Asia" suggests the Corinthians knew exactly where it had occurred, and so Paul did not need to

---

[105] See Gillman in ABD 6, p581. Fee 1987, p836 comments that "it is possible that Titus would currently [ie at the time of writing 1 Cor] be working with him (see 2 Cor 2:13)."

[106] This seems likely since he was with Paul and available to be sent off to Corinth with the tearful letter.

[107] On the textual variants in the passage, see Martin 1986, p12-13.

[108] ῥύομαι ἐκ τοῦ θανάτου in 2 Cor 1:10a does not mean "preserve from death" in general, but "rescue from a(n actual) situation in which death was threatened"; see BDAG, p xxviii. Thus Paul has some specific event, or perhaps a sequence of events, in mind.

[109] τηλικοῦτος θάνατος; literally, so great a death; see Martin 1986, p15. Fitzgerald 1988, p157 points out that here (2 Cor 1:3-8), as in 2 Cor 11:23-33, Paul singles out one example of his suffering for greater and separate treatment. This points to how serious this experience of "such great a death" was for Paul.

[110] Héring (1967, p5) notes "the almost pleonastic use of language [in v8b] to depict the intensity of the suffering"; see also Harris 1970, p406-8. For a discussion of the formal contradiction between 1:8b and 4:8b see Bultmann 1985, p114; Furnish 1984, p124, 280-1.

be precise about the location. However, they probably did not realise the gravity of the event, nor the devastating effect the affliction in Asia had had on him, which is stressed in v8b; Paul writes to inform them of this.[111]

However, the affliction probably occurred after he had written 1 Corinthians, since if it had already happened he probably would have mentioned it in that letter, and the way he describes the two events in 1 Cor 15:32 and 2 Cor 1:8-11 is quite different. Thus, it is unlikely that this is the same incident referred to in 1 Cor 15:32.[112] Since it happened "in Asia" it occurred prior to Paul crossing from Troas to Macedonia (2 Cor 2:12-13; 7:5).[113]

We can note that Paul sees the possibility of further experiences of the same or of a similar type. As O'Brien notes, this is suggested by the fact that after having spoken of God's past deliverance (ἐρρύσατο – 2 Cor 1:10) Paul goes on in 2 Cor 1:10 to use the future tense twice (ῥύεσται - he will deliver). Further, Paul goes on in v11 to request prayer from the Corinthians, so that God will deliver him again in the future.[114] Thus Paul seems to be anticipating further afflictions of the same or of a similar type. We will bear this in mind in our discussion.

What was the nature of the θλῖψις Paul suffered in Asia?[115] Paul elaborates about the θλῖψις in 2 Cor 1:9 where the key phrase is "we felt that we had received the sentence of death (τὸ ἀπόκριμα τοῦ θανάτου)". The sense is that Paul, on reflection, accepted the sentence of death.[116] But what was "τὸ ἀπόκριμα τοῦ θανάτου"? A number of suggestions have been made.

---

[111] See O'Brien 1977, p248; see also Plummer 1915, p15-16. This is the new information imparted by the "disclosure formula" (on which see White 1972, p11-15; Furnish 1984, p112, 122), with which he begins v8, and which suggests he is imparting some new information. Furnish 1984, p122 however suggests that Paul perhaps assumed the bearer(s) of the letter would provide the Corinthians with further details about the event.

[112] See Barrett, 2 Cor, p63-4; Harris 1970, p411-13; Wolff 1982, p192; Klauck 1986, p20; cf. Warfield 1885-86, p30-5; see also Carrez 1986, p52-3.

[113] Furnish 1984, p122 suggests that Paul's intensity of feeling in referring to the event suggests it had happened fairly recently. See also Harris 1970, p421-3.

[114] See O'Brien 1977, p235, 249-50; see also Stanley 1961, p130; Harris 1970, p405-6. If the plural reading τηλικούτων θανάτων, in v10 was original, then this would strengthen the case here, but the singular reading is probably original; see Martin 1986, p12-13. Note that ἐσχήκαμεν in 2 Cor 1:9 is probably a narrative perfect, used like an aorist, and so is not further evidence for the on-going presence of the affliction; see Furnish 1984, p113.

[115] In 2 Cor 1:6 Paul writes that the Corinthians "endure the same sufferings that we suffer". This does not mean, however, that they suffer in exactly the same way as Paul. As O'Brien comments (1977, p247) "the addressees participate in the same Messianic woes, but not in the same θλῖψις." Thus, this does not help us to determine the nature of Paul's affliction.

[116] See Harris 1970, p408; Héring 1967, p5; Bultmann 1985, p28. This is the most likely meaning of αὐτοὶ ἐν ἑαυτοῖς ... ἐσχήκαμεν (2 Cor 1:9); the phrase then is not

Firstly, that the event is to be identified with that referred to in 1 Cor 15:32, which is taken to be a literal fight with wild animals in the arena.[117] However, as we noted above, it seems more likely that in 2 Cor 1:8-11 Paul is telling the Corinthians of an event which occurred subsequent to 1 Cor being written.

Secondly, that the reference is to the riot of Acts 19:23-41. This is possible, although in this case the riot must have been more life-threatening than Acts suggests,[118] or perhaps the riot as Luke recounts it was actually more life-threatening to Paul that commentators generally think.[119] Further, we have noted that Paul expected recurrences of the θλῖψις (2 Cor 1:10-11), which makes it unlikely that the reference is to the riot, unless Paul anticipated that the riot would lead to an outbreak of persecution. Finally, if the reference was to the riot we would have expected Paul to say that he experienced the θλῖψις ἐν Ἐφέσῳ and not ἐν τῇ Ἀσίᾳ. Given that Paul had already mentioned fighting wild animals in Ephesus (1 Cor 15:32) and adversaries in Ephesus (1 Cor 16:9) in earlier correspondence with the Corinthians, if yet another significant incident had occurred in the city it seems likely that he would have made that clear here. The view that the reference is to the riot of Acts 19:23-41 seems unlikely then.[120]

Thirdly, that the reference is to the onset of serious health problems, which continued to threaten Paul's life and which are often connected by scholars with Paul's "thorn in the flesh" of 2 Cor 12:7.[121] However, the connection with the thorn in the flesh is unlikely since the affliction mentioned in v8-11 is

---

evidence that it was a peril arising from within rather than without, and thus an illness, as Clavier 1953, p77 n2, (followed by Barrett 1973, p64) suggests.

[117] Warfield 1885-86, p30-5. If 1 Cor 15:32 is taken to refer to a literal fight with wild animals which did not actually occur, then it is unlikely that it can be equated with 2 Cor 1:8-11, which suggests a staggering event that did occur.

[118] See Steinmetz 1968, p323; Barrett 1973, p64; Bultmann 1985, p27, n7; Watson 1993, p7; cf. Murphy-O'Connor 1991a, p22. It is possible that the riot was more life-threatening than Acts suggests, since 2 Cor 11:23f shows that Luke does not give us (or does not have) a full record of what Paul suffered. Note that 1 Cor was probably written before the riot occurred, so that the affliction of 2 Cor 1:8 (which we have said occurred after 1 Cor was written) could be the riot. The riot has been connected with a time of unrest following the assassination of the proconsul of Asia, M. Junius Silanus in 54 CE (see Duncan 1929, p100-7; Carrez 1985, p773-6; 1986, p27-30), although this connection can be no more than a very tentative suggestion. For further discussion of this theory see Chapter 3.

[119] Kreitzer (1987, p67-8) notes of the riot: "My suspicion is that Paul was much closer to extreme bodily harm, perhaps even death, that we sometimes think in this episode."

[120] See Harris 1970, p415-17.

[121] See Clavier 1953, p77, n2; Allo 1956b, p11-12, 15-19; Harris 1970, p418-20; 1971, p57; Barrett 1973, p64-6; Steinmetz 1968, p323; Klauck 1986, p20-1. The connection with the thorn in the flesh is by no means obvious; see Martin 1986, p16. A considerable amount depends on the meaning of the "thorn in the flesh", on which see Thacker 1991, p67-9; Woods 1991, p44-53; Leary 1992, p520-2; Thomas 1996, p39-52.

clearly a paramount example of Paul "sharing abundantly in the sufferings of Christ" (2 Cor 1:5) and as Wolff asks: "Aber läßt sich das Wirken des Satansengels (12,7) in die 'Leiden des Christus' einbeziehen?"[122] Further, it seems that an affliction that Paul includes in the category of "the sufferings of Christ" (2 Cor 1:5) would be a matter that specifically related to believers, rather than a trouble that could afflict anyone.[123] This seems to rule out the possibility of a reference to illness here.[124]

Fourthly, that the reference is to an experience of persecution leading to imprisonment, during which Paul faced the possibility of death.[125] (See

---

[122] Wolff 1989, p25.

[123] See Thrall 1994, p115-116.

[124] Furnish (1984, p123, his emphasis) asks: "Is it not more likely that the onset of a disease would be identified with reference to its *symptoms*, to *how* it struck, rather than by a reference to *where* one was stricken?" But if the Corinthians knew something about the affliction, this would be understandable. Furnish also compares the illness of Epaphroditus (Phil 2:27), which is described quite differently from 2 Cor 1:8; see also Heckel 1993, p262 n279; Witherington 1995, p361-2. Note also ἐσχήκαμεν in 2 Cor 1:9 is probably a narrative perfect, used like an Aorist, in which case it does not support the suggestion that a recurring sickness is in view, see Furnish 1984, p113. Further, in 2 Cor 1:8-11, as in the surrounding section, Paul uses the first person plural. If this is a real plural, then it is unlikely that the affliction was an illness, since it would be unlikely (although not impossible) that a number people would suffer from the same illness simultaneously. However, it is likely that in using the plural here Paul does not mean to imply that others shared the experience, but rather is emphasizing that "his own life is a representative existence, exhibiting characteristics which constitute what is genuinely apostolic and Christian." (Watson 1993, p9). On the different interpretive possibilities for the first person plural in 2 Cor see Watson 1993, p8-9; Carrez 1979-80, p474-86; Byrskog 1996, p230-50. Other examples of the "authorial" or "literary plural" used in 2 Cor 1:8-11 are found in 2 Cor 5:11; 10:2. Thus, the use of the first person plural does not eliminate the possibility that Paul is here speaking of an illness. However, it is worth noting that elsewhere when Paul speaks of an illness he always uses the first person singular (2 Cor 12:7b; Gal 4:13f), which again argues against the affliction being an illness; see Heckel 1993, p262 n279. Further Byrskog 1996, p246 thinks that Timothy is the actual co-author of 2 Cor 1:1-14, which would rule out the reference to an illness here. Finally, in v8 Paul seems to speak of the inward character of the affliction; it was ἐν ἑαυτοῖς, which seems more appropriate to an illness. But as Thrall (1994, p116) notes "The point of the ἐν ἑαυτοῖς of v9 is not the inward nature of the θλῖψις itself but the fact that as far as Paul's own resources were concerned he had no chance of survival."

[125] See Duncan 1929, p131-9, 143, 193-9; 1956-57, p215-6 who sees a reference to an imprisonment here confirmed by 2 Tim 4:16, but regards the imprisonment as at Laodicea (on the basis of a manuscript note in Codex A and the Coptic Versions of 1 and 2 Tim) and as inflicted by a local Jewish court. But this is highly speculative (see Harris 1970, p414-15). See also Furnish 1984, p42, 55, 113-14, 123; Walters 1999, p319. Furnish sees Phil as written from this imprisonment, and uses Phil as evidence that the affliction was an imprisonment in Ephesus. However, he acknowledges (Furnish 1984, p123) that this interpretation remains hypothetical, "and its cogency depends directly on the strength of the prior hypothesis that the Philippian letter was indeed written from Ephesus." We will discuss this view below. Note also that although the words "ἐν ἑαυτοῖς" in 2 Cor 1:9 show that

section 3 below for a discussion of whether Paul was imprisoned in Ephesus.) One element of this has been the view that τὸ ἀπόκριμα τοῦ θανάτου was an official judicial decision.[126] However, Hemer argues that ἀπόκριμα here does not mean an official "sentence (of death)" but rather should be translated "verdict", with the term having no necessary judicial or forensic connotations. Paul had expected to survive until the parousia, but some drastic experience alluded to in 2 Corinthians 1:8f led him to petition God about the parousia, and the "verdict" was "death", that is, that Paul would not escape death before the parousia (2 Cor 5:1-10).[127] However, we should note that the connection with Paul's views on the nearness of the parousia is not explicit in 2 Cor 1:8-11. Yet Hemer's work is helpful in showing that a judicial interpretation of the phrase τὸ ἀπόκριμα τοῦ θανάτου is by no means certain. But, as we will see in section 3, it remains possible that Paul was imprisoned in Ephesus (although Hemer's work shows he probably did not receive a "death sentence"), and the affliction could be events connected with that.

Finally, given the general way in which Paul refers to the θλῖψις, a number of scholars have suggested that we cannot say what the nature of Paul's afflictions had been.[128] Our problem stems from the fact that Paul does not

---

Paul is focussing on his acceptance in himself of an ἀπόκριμα it is possible that this was caused by an imprisonment; cf. Danker 1989, p36: "'we have gotten in ourselves the death sentence.' The diction is carefully chosen. Paul is not referring to condemnation by secular authority. He notes that his experiences have taught him to face at the depths of his being the harsh reality of mortality." But the "experiences" could be connected with an imprisonment.

[126] See Deissmann 1901, p257. Stanley 1961, p129 translates ἀπόκριμα as "death-warrant".

[127] Hemer 1972, p103-7. That 2 Cor 1:10 shows that Paul expected to be delivered from the "answer" of "death" again in the future counts against Hemer's view; see Wood 1982, p151-2.

[128] See for example Héring 1967, p5 n12; Hemer 1972, p106 n16; Barrett 1973, p63-4; Heckel 1993, p262 n279. Bruce 1971, p179 notes: "If it was some external danger, the task of identifying it calls for speculation beyond the exegete's province." Danker 1989, p36 notes: "The record we have of his [Paul's] career is so fragmentary that all attempts to define them [the afflictions referred to here] are pure guesswork." Other suggestions about the nature of the θλῖψις have been made. Plummer 1915, p15-16 suggested the affliction may have been the Corinthian rebellion against Paul, and the comfort he refers to their submission and reconciliation to him. But this seems unlikely, and as Plummer himself notes (p16) "the language of vv. 8-10 does seem to be rather strong for the effect of painful news". It is also possible that the reference is to a shipping accident off the coast of Asia Minor, but as Klauck notes (1986, p20), in view of 2 Cor 11:23-6 Paul would probably not give prominence to such an event as something exceptional. Yates (1981, p243-5) thinks the θλῖψις was caused by Jewish opposition (cf. Acts 20:19); see also Wood 1982, p151-3. We can also note that it is possible that the incident referred to in 2 Cor 1:8-11 is the occasion on which Prisca and Aquila "risked their necks for my life" (Rom 16:4), since Prisca and Aquila seem to have been with Paul for most of his time in Asia, although by the time he writes Romans they are

inform the Corinthians of the details of the circumstances of the affliction, but rather speaks of its severity and significance.[129] This means that we do not know exactly what Paul was referring to, and a number of theories remain possible. However, it does seem likely that it was some form of external threat. The clause "so that we would rely not on ourselves (ἵνα μὴ πεποιθότες ὦμεν ἐφ᾽ ἑαυτοῖς) but on God who raises the dead" (2 Cor 1:9) suggests a set of circumstances where Paul might have extricated himself by personal effort, but chose not to do so.[130] Some scholars have argued that this language suggests we should think of some sort of danger or serious physical violence,[131] from which Paul could have tried to extricate himself, but rather chose to trust God who raises the dead.[132]

We conclude, therefore, that we can say no more than to suggest that the θλῖψις was some external danger, or some persecution, perhaps leading to imprisonment, or some other incident of which we know nothing. It is clear from the language of 2 Cor 1:8-11, however, that the experience of the θλῖψις in Asia, and God's deliverance from it, had had a profound impact on Paul.[133]

We have noted above that if the θλῖψις occurred in Ephesus, we would have expected Paul to have made this explicit, as he did in 1 Cor 15:32 and 16:9. It is often assumed that "in Asia" meant "in Ephesus", the capital of the province of Asia,[134] but this is by no means certain, particularly since elsewhere he explicitly mentions Ephesus by name (1 Cor 15:32; 16:8). That

---

back in Rome. Duncan 1929, p156-7 thinks the event referred to occurred in Ephesus, but this can only be speculation; cf Allo 1956a, p467. For some further suggestions see Allo 1956b, p15-19.

[129] See Furnish 1984, p122-4.

[130] See Martin 1986, p16. Barrett 1973, p65 notes that the periphrastic perfect subjunctive with the negative (μὴ πεποιθότες ὦμεν) here "suggests the discontinuance of an existing condition".

[131] O'Brien 1977, p249, n102: "the language does suggest some terrible danger from without" and p249: "that it was some severe persecution or deadly danger from without". See also Danker 1989, p35; Thrall (1994, p117) concludes "violent persecution, perhaps in the form of incarceration, remains the most probable explanation of the θλῖψις."

[132] One could understand a situation of sickness (not to be identified with the thorn in the flesh of 2 Cor 12:7) in which Paul could have "relied on himself" but chose rather to entrust his life to God, but we have already shown this interpretation is unlikely.

[133] See O'Brien 1977, p257. Dodd (1953, p80-1) argued that this event, which he thinks was a mortal illness, played a crucial role in Paul's spiritual life and brought about a "second conversion" which caused him to abandon the last vestiges of personal pride. This view however, depends on 2 Cor 10-13 preceding 1-9, which is debatable; see Thrall 1994, p117 n258.

[134] See Orr and Walther 1976, p19 ("Asia, probably in Ephesus"); Plummer 1915, p16; Bowen 1920, p116; Klauck 1986, p20.

Paul says it occurred "in Asia" suggests it was not in Ephesus; in any case, we cannot assume it was in the city.[135]

2.3 2 Cor 4:8-9; 6:4-10; 11:23-33; 12:10: Catalogues of Suffering

As noted above, four of the five catalogues of hardships which Paul included in the Corinthian correspondence are found in 2 Cor. Paul wrote 2 Corinthians shortly after leaving Ephesus, and so the question arises whether any of the hardships he gives in these lists occurred in Ephesus?[136] While the lists bear many affinities with other hardship catalogues, particularly those which concern the sage, they also reflect Paul's own personal experiences of suffering.[137] The litany of hardships and sufferings in 2 Cor 11:23-33 in particular seems too fresh in his mind and too specific to be simply a general catalogue. Further, particularly in the context of 2 Cor 11:21b-33, in which he is claiming that the true signs of apostleship were suffering and service for others, Paul needed to have a basis in fact for what he wrote here.[138] But did any of these events occur at Ephesus?

Some elements in the lists describe the general perils associated with missionary life.[139] However, some elements are very specific, but we simply do not know where they occurred, which underlines how fragmentary our knowledge of Paul's life is. On five occasions he received the forty lashes less one from the Jews, but in what centres did these take place?[140] Three times he

---

[135] Harris (1970, p403-4) comments that "in Asia" "in all probability refers to some part of the province other than the capital, Ephesus; otherwise ἐν Ἐφέσῳ (cf. 1 Cor. 15:32; 16:8) would doubtless have been used, all the more so since he was now writing from Macedonia, not Ephesus." See also Duncan 1956-57, p212; Furnish 1984, p122; Danker 1989, p35; Thrall 1994, p114. Duncan (1929, p193-9) argues that the θλιψις was an imprisonment which took place in Laodicea, but this is highly speculative. Luke seems to use Asia when he means Ephesus on some occasions. Thus Trophimus is called an Asian in Acts 20:4, but it is clear from Acts 21:29 that he was from Ephesus; see also Acts 20:16. But it is generally thought that Paul uses "Asia" to refer to the province; see for example Barrett 1973, p63. On the range of meanings of "Asia" see Trebilco 1994, p300-2.

[136] For the dating see Martin 1986, p xxxiv. Even if Paul wrote 2 Cor 1-9 before 2 Cor 10-13, it was only shortly beforehand.

[137] See Fitzgerald 1988, p207. Commentators note a number of references to specific events in these lists in 2 Cor.

[138] Martin 1987, p376 notes: "The only thing he could not afford to do in this debate was to overplay his sufferings without a basis in fact, and so lay himself open to the charge of protesting too much."

[139] For example, 2 Cor 6:5b (labours, sleepless nights, hunger); 2 Cor 11:23 (with far greater labours); 2 Cor 11:26-7.

[140] On this see Martin 1986, p376-7; Barrett 1973, p296-7. Acts portrays several occasions prior to the writing of 2 Cor when Paul could have received the thirty-nine lashes; see Acts 13:45, 50; 14:5; 18:12; Furnish 1984, p537. Falwell 1948, p124 thinks one of the lashings took place in Ephesus.

was beaten with rods; according to Acts he was beaten with rods at Philippi (Acts 16:22-3) but where did the other two beatings take place?[141] Where were each of his "far more imprisonments" (ἐν φυλακαῖς περισσοτέρως 2 Cor 11:23; cf. 2 Cor 6:5 - ἐν φυλακαῖς)?[142] The only imprisonment recorded in Acts up to the time Paul wrote 2 Cor is in Philippi, and this is only over-night (Acts 16:23-40).[143] Thus it is possible that in 2 Cor 11:23 Paul is using hyperbole.[144] However, a number of scholars have suggested that 2 Cor 6:5 and 11:23 provide indirect evidence of a recent imprisonment in Ephesus, which was where Paul had been most recently, and for a long period.[145] It seems likely that Paul was imprisoned in Ephesus, but we know nothing in detail about such an imprisonment.

Paul goes on to speak of "danger from my own people,[146] danger from Gentiles,[147] danger in the city, ... danger from false brothers and sisters"[148] (2 Cor 11:26). Was he troubled by Jews, Gentiles and "false brothers and sisters" in Ephesus? Again events that occurred in Ephesus could be included here, particularly given the length of time he spent in the city. Perhaps the events alluded to in 1 Cor 15:32 (wild beasts); 16:9 (opponents) and 2 Cor 1:8-11 (affliction) are in view in these "dangers", along with other incidents

---

[141] Roman citizens should not have been beaten, but sometimes were; see Cicero, In Verrem 5.62-66; Josephus, War 2.308. The stoning referred to in 2 Cor 11:25 is probably the incident at Lystra recorded in Acts 14:19, which was not a specifically Jewish punishment, but mob action in which Gentiles may have been involved (cf. Acts 14:5-6); the attempt at Iconium (Acts 14:5) probably came to nothing; see Barrett 1973, p297-8; cf. Danker 1989, p182.

[142] It is hard to know how many imprisonments are referred to by περισσοτέρως. See BDAG, p806: "far more, far greater (than Paul's opponents)". Hurd 1965, p24 notes from 2 Cor 11:23 "An unspecified but sizable number of imprisonments". It is impossible to be more specific, since clearly Paul is not being numerically precise here.

[143] It seems to be confirmed by 1 Thess 2:2.

[144] Furnish (1984, p354) who suggests that alternatively Paul may be indicating that other members of his group had been imprisoned. In Rom 16:7 Paul speaks of Andronicus and Junia as "fellow prisoners", but when and where was this?

[145] For example, Duncan 1929, p66-7; Allo 1956b, p295; Bruce 1971, p242; Furnish 1984, p113-15, 354; Lang 1986, p344; Wolff 1989, p139; see also Héring 1967, p84, but on the basis of 1 Cor 15:31-2, which he takes literally.

[146] A number of examples are given in Acts - 9:23, 29; 13:8, 45; 14:2, 19; 17:5; 18:6, 12; 20:3, 19; 21:11, 27.

[147] These are mentioned less often in Acts, but see Acts 14:15; 16:19-24, and of course the Ephesian riot (19:23).

[148] Compare Gal 2:4. These are people who claimed to be Christians who are hostile to Paul's Gospel, but whom Paul is unwilling to think of as Christians at all. The list concerns physical dangers; Héring 1967, p86 asks therefore if these people denounced Paul to the authorities. In this case physical danger and the bitterness of treachery would be combined; see Barrett 1973, p300. Paul probably has his rivals in Corinth (eg 2 Cor 11:13-15) particularly in mind in mentioning the "false brothers and sisters" here; see Furnish 1984, p537; Martin 1986, p379.

that occurred in Ephesus as well as elsewhere.[149] But we cannot do more than suggest this possibility, since the language used is general and Paul cites no specific incidents except for the one in Damascus (2 Cor 11:32-3).[150]

3. Was Paul Imprisoned in Ephesus?

The view that Paul was imprisoned in Ephesus and wrote one or more of the prison epistles (Eph, Phil, Col and Philm) from the city has had a number of supporters.[151] The NT does not explicitly say that Paul was imprisoned in Ephesus, but a number of passages are taken to support this.[152]

Firstly, Paul wrote 2 Cor 11:23 shortly after leaving Ephesus and speaks there of "far more imprisonments" (see also 2 Cor 6:5), and as we have noted above, up to this point in time Acts records only one imprisonment which occurred at Philippi. Given that when Paul wrote 2 Cor he had just spent over two years and three months in Ephesus, and had known some opposition in the city, it is likely that one of the imprisonments was in Ephesus.

Secondly, if ἐθηριομάχησα in 1 Cor 15:32 is taken literally, and the whole clause as a condition contrary to fact, then the verse can be taken to suggest that in Ephesus there was an outcry against Paul which included the call that he should be condemned to the arena.[153] Although Paul was spared this fate,

---

[149] See Hurd 1965, p24 n4.

[150] Bowen 1923, p63 notes "These κίνδυνοι belong, in part at least, to the city from which he writes, Ephesus." He takes the reference to be, in part, to a literal fight in the arena. Note that Paul experienced afflictions when he first arrived in Macedonia (2 Cor 7:5ff). In 2 Cor 11:23 Paul writes ἐν θανάτοις πολλάκις - literally, "in deaths many times". Thus Paul is referring to "situations in which I was in danger of death" (Barrett 1973, p296). This is then expanded in 2 Cor 11:24-27, where he refers to beatings and the hazards of travel and so on. But included in the ἐν θανάτοις πολλάκις could be the "fighting with wild animals" (even if understood metaphorically) or the θλῖψις in Asia.

[151] See Bowen 1920, p112-35; 277-87; Duncan 1929, p59-299; 1955-56, p163-6; 1956-57, p211-18; 1958-59, p43-5; Michaelis 1928, p368-75; Rowlingson 1950, p1-7; Stanley 1961, p66-7; Jewett 1979, p19; Furnish 1984, p42, 55, 113-14, 123; Carrez 1986, p27-30; Georgi 1986, p16, 18; Schnackenburg 1991, p46; Thiessen 1995, p111-38; Koester 1995, p122; Murphy-O'Connor 1996, p175-9; Walters 1999, p319. For a list of further supporters of the theory see Hurd 1965, p303 n6. The theory of an Ephesian imprisonment was first proposed by H. Lisco in 1900; see Duncan 1929, p59.

[152] See Duncan 1929, p66-71.

[153] If ἐθηριομάχησα is taken literally and the whole clause as a condition of fact, then this would presuppose that Paul was imprisoned in Ephesus, since anyone who fought wild animals would have been imprisoned first. However, this would require that Paul, a Roman citizen, not only fought with wild animals but also survived the ordeal, and so is a very unlikely reading of the verse.

Duncan thinks that along with the outcry went arrest and imprisonment.[154] However, we have noted above that it is much more likely that θηριομαχέω is used metaphorically here, and thus this verse provides no evidence for an imprisonment.

Thirdly, although 2 Cor 1:8-10 does not specifically mention an imprisonment, it points to some desperate danger, which could have involved an imprisonment. However, as we noted above, it is best to conclude that we simply do not know the nature of Paul's afflictions in Asia, and in any case it may or may not have been in Ephesus.

Fourthly, Rom 16:4 and 16:7 both point to some recent experiences. Since Aquila and Prisca were most recently with Paul in Asia, which suggests the event referred to in Rom 16:4 happened there, and since we have no reason to think that the imprisonment referred to in Rom 16:7 occurred in either Macedonia or Corinth, it is natural to think that both the events mentioned in Rom 16:4, 7 occurred in Ephesus.[155] However, the event alluded to in Rom 16:4 may not have involved an imprisonment, we simply have no information about the imprisonment mentioned in Rom 16:7, and we have no way of knowing where either event occurred.

Fifthly, Clement said that Paul was imprisoned seven times (1 Clem 5:6). However, this may be a deduction from 2 Cor 11:23,[156] or may reflect the fact that seven documents at Clement's disposal referred to Paul being in prison.[157] It is certainly not clear that Clement had any independent evidence at his disposal here, and he does not say that Paul was imprisoned in Ephesus.

Sixthly, in the *Acts of Paul* 7 there is a story of Paul's encounter with a lion in the arena in Ephesus. However, as Duncan notes, rather than offering any independent evidence, these passages are probably legendary developments of Paul's own phrase in 1 Cor 15:32.[158]

Finally, the Marcionite Prologue to Colossians asserts that Paul wrote that letter while in prison in Ephesus.[159] However, the value of this evidence is doubtful.

---

[154] Duncan 1929, p66-7, 126-131; see also Bowen 1920, p115; Michaelis 1928, p373-4. Dodd (1934, p85-6) argues convincingly against this point.

[155] See Duncan 1929, p68. This view is strengthened if Rom 16 was written to Ephesus (see for example Rowlingson 1950, p2-3), which, however, is unlikely.

[156] See Duncan 1929, p69.

[157] See Quinn 1978, p574-6.

[158] See Duncan 1929, p129-30; see also p69-70; Metzger 1945, p12-17.

[159] It reads "apostolus iam ligatus scribit eis ab Epheso - The apostle already in fetters writes to them [the Colossians] from Ephesus". But note that the Prologues ascribe Philemon and "Laodiceans" (our Ephesians) to Rome; see Duncan 1934-35, p294. On the Prologues see also Dahl 2000, p179-209. Many who favour an Ephesian origin for Col also argue that Philm and Eph were written in Ephesus, but it is questionable to accept the evidence of the Prologues on one count and reject it on another. Other arguments are also used to support the theory of an imprisonment. Firstly, it is noted that a building in Ephesus is traditionally

This is the extent of the direct evidence for an imprisonment in Ephesus. To this is often added other indirect evidence for an Ephesian imprisonment deduced from the prison epistles, on the hypothesis that they were written from Ephesus.[160] The cumulative case that an Ephesian imprisonment provides (according to this view) the most intelligible setting for some or all of the prison epistles, is then taken as strong corroboration of an Ephesian imprisonment.[161]

However, few scholars have been convinced by the arguments that an Ephesian imprisonment does indeed provide the most intelligible setting for some or all of the prison epistles and most favour other settings for these epistles.[162] Certainly the points in favour of an Ephesian setting for these letters cannot be used to strengthen the case for an Ephesian imprisonment, since it is possible for each point to be interpreted in accordance with an alternative geographical setting for the letters.[163] Further, as regards Phil, the reference to the *praetorium* (Phil 1:13) probably does not fit Ephesus. Ephesus was the capital of the senatorial province of Asia, and there is no

---

called Paul's prison, but this is a late tradition. Secondly, Acts 19:12 speaks of miracles worked by the application of clothing. This is understandable if Paul was in prison (see Stanley 1961, p66 n23) but this is not required by the text. Thirdly, an Ephesian imprisonment would also explain why Epaphras founded the communities of Colossae, Hierapolis and Laodicea, despite Paul seeming to be close at hand; see Stanley 1961, p66 n23. However, that the Gospel was spread by Paul's co-workers does not mean he was necessarily in prison at the time. Fourthly, that Paul avoided Ephesus and rather summoned the Ephesian elders to Miletus (Acts 20:17) may have been because of the previous difficulties he encountered in Ephesus, including imprisonment; see Michaelis 1928, p372.

[160] See for example, Duncan 1929, p72-161.

[161] See for example Duncan 1929, p72.

[162] For discussions of these issues see on Phil, Hawthorne 1983, p xxxvi-xliv; O'Brien 1991, p19-26; Fee 1995, p34-7. On Col see O'Brien 1982, p xlix- liv; Dunn 1996, p39-41. On Philemon see Bruce 1984, p193-6; Dunn 1996, p307-8; Murphy O'Connor 1996, p175-8. The reply to Duncan given by Dodd 1934, p72-92 remains valuable. Given that Ephesians is generally regarded as pseudonymous, it need not be considered here.

[163] Take the following points as examples. In the case of Philemon, Duncan (1929, p72-4) argued that the proximity of Ephesus makes it likely that Onesimus fled to Ephesus rather that Rome, which was over a thousand miles away. However, Dodd (1934, p80) countered that a run-a-way slave, "his pockets lined at his master's expense", could well want to get as far away from his master as possible. The request for lodging in Philem 22 is more easily explained if Paul is in Ephesus (Duncan 1929, p74-5), but Bruce (1984, p195-6) notes that many who experienced travel conditions similar to those of Paul's day "had no difficulty in believing that Paul did from Rome bespeak quarters at Colossae". Neither point is conclusive therefore. Similarly, the number of past and prospective communications between Paul and the Philippians mentioned in Phil argues for Ephesus as the place from which Phil was written rather than the more distant Rome (see Duncan 1929, p80-2). However, given that Paul was in prison in Rome for a considerable period of time, it is also compatible with a Roman origin for Phil. Again the point is not decisively in favour of an Ephesian provenance.

known instance of the proconsul's headquarters in a senatorial province being called a *praetorium* at this time. The appeal to inscriptional evidence for the presence of a member of the praetorian guard (*praetorianus*) in the vicinity of Ephesus has also been rejected as irrelevant here.[164] In effect then, with respect to the whole hypothesis of an Ephesian imprisonment, a great deal depends on the strength of the direct evidence that Paul was actually imprisoned in Ephesus.[165]

How strong is the case for an Ephesian imprisonment then? That Acts omits any mention of an Ephesian imprisonment is not a telling point against it, since Acts clearly does not mention many of the things Paul suffered.[166] The strongest piece of evidence is 2 Cor 11:23, but even this verse only makes an Ephesian imprisonment likely. 2 Cor 1:8-10 could have involved an imprisonment, but it is better to conclude that we do not know what the affliction was, and in any case it may or may not have been in Ephesus. All the other evidence is either weak or can be explained in another way, as we noted above. And even if Paul was imprisoned in Ephesus, we know nothing of the nature or length of the imprisonment. Was it just for a short period?[167] Did it allow Paul the sort of freedom necessary to write letters? Clearly the Ephesian imprisonment hypothesis must remain a hypothesis. Certainly, to suggest as Duncan does, that Paul was imprisoned twice in Ephesus and during the first (implied by 1 Cor 15:32) wrote Phil, and during the second (implied by the Demetrius riot of Acts 19) wrote Col, Eph and Philemon and was imprisoned a third time in Laodicea (connected with 2 Cor 1:8-11 from

---

[164] See Fee 1995, p35; W.L. Knox 1939, p179 and n4; Bruce 1989, p11-12. Bruce (1989, p12) notes concerning the *praetorianus*: "The *praetorianus* mentioned in three Latin inscriptions was a *former* member of the praetorian guard who later discharged police duties as a *stationarius* on a Roman road in the province of Asia." The inscriptions are CIL III. 6085, 7135, 7136.

[165] If it could be shown that it was *impossible* for Paul to have written one of the prison epistles from anywhere other than Ephesus, then this would become an argument in favour of an Ephesian imprisonment, but clearly this is not the case. Thus, a case that could have been cumulative had there been clear evidence for at least one of the prison epistles being written in Ephesus along with sufficient direct evidence for an Ephesian imprisonment, actually becomes circular, with the second hypothesis (that certain prison epistles were written from Ephesus) failing because of the weakness of the first (that Paul was imprisoned in Ephesus at all; see further Dodd 1934, p84). Clearly, if Paul was not imprisoned in Ephesus in the first place, he could not have written any letters there. The circularity of Duncan's case is particularly clear in Duncan 1929, p141: "Apart from the evidence of the Imprisonment Epistles not one of these outbreaks [of hostilities - viz 1 Cor 15:32; 2 Cor 1:8-11; the riot of Acts 19] has in the present chapter been shown *conclusively* to have been accompanied by imprisonment. Yet there must have been one or more imprisonments if the Epistles are to be assigned to this period."

[166] See Duncan 1929, p95-107.

[167] Allo 1956a, p416 argues this.

which he wrote the "fragments" preserved in 2 Tim 4) is to go far beyond the evidence into speculation.[168]

Thus we conclude that it is likely that Paul was imprisoned in Ephesus, but that we know nothing about any imprisonment(s). That he wrote any of the prison epistles from Ephesus must be regarded as less than likely because the imprisonment itself is conjectural, because some points argues against an Ephesian setting, and because the data taken to argue for an Ephesian provenance can all be interpreted in other ways.

But if we granted that Duncan, and a number of others, are correct, and Col, Phil and Philm were written from Ephesus, would this aid our present inquiry greatly?[169] It would certainly tell us more about what Paul endured in Ephesus. However, it would not add much to our knowledge of the Ephesian Christian community at this time. Philippians would tell us most if it were written from an Ephesian imprisonment. We would learn that some Ephesian Christians had been made confident in their faith because of Paul's imprisonment and further that the Christians were divided into factions because of Paul and his teaching, which had resulted in some people preaching Christ from envy and rivalry (Phil 1:12-18). We would also learn that some members of "Caesar's household" had joined the Christian community (Phil 4:22).[170] However, we noted above that the case for an Ephesian provenance is weakest in the case of Phil.[171] If Colossians was written from Ephesus the only thing we would learn about Ephesian Christians is details about some of Paul's co-workers in the city (Col 4:7-14),[172] and similarly we would only learn details about co-workers in Ephesus from Philemon (Philm 23-4). Thus, little is at stake for our current inquiry in this debate.

We conclude then that it is likely that Paul was imprisoned in Ephesus, but that the case that Paul wrote any of the prison epistles from Ephesus is not strong enough for them to be used as evidence for Paul's time in Ephesus or for the life of the Christian community in the city.

---

[168] This was his position in Duncan 1929, p298-9; he altered it slightly later. In Duncan 1956-57, p213-4 he left it an open question whether the second imprisonment was in Ephesus or elsewhere in the province. He also dissociated this second imprisonment from the Demetrius riot, which he put later; see Duncan 1958-59, p43; see also 1955-56, p163-6. Much is questionable in Duncan's work; for example his reliance on the "fragments theory" with regard to the Pastoral Epistles, his logic is frequently circular, and often possible hypotheses become the foundation stones for further hypotheses. See also Barrett 1973, p296.

[169] Manson 1962, p149-67 thinks that Philippians was written from Ephesus, but not while Paul was in prison in the city. However, it seems clear that Paul was in prison when he wrote Phil (1:7, 13, 14, 17) and as we have noted above, the reference to the *praetorium* (Phil 1:13) probably does not fit Ephesus. (Manson's view that Phil 1:13 refers to Corinth is unconvincing.) See also Murphy-O'Connor 1996, p222-4.

[170] On this see Duncan 1929, p110-11.

[171] See further Fee 1995, p35 n86.

[172] See for example, Schnackenburg 1991, p46.

4. Do any of Paul's other letters provide evidence
for his time in Ephesus?

4.1 Galatians

Was Galatians written from Ephesus? This is certainly a possibility,[173] although many scholars argue it was written from Corinth after Paul left Ephesus while others contend that it was written at an earlier stage in Paul's ministry.[174] But even if it was written in Ephesus, it would add nothing to our evidence for Paul's ministry in the city, since he gives no information relating to the Christians in the place from which he writes and no one else is mentioned in either the opening or closing of the letter.[175] The letter would, however, give us further evidence of the "anxiety for all the churches" (2 Cor 11:28) that Paul experienced while in Ephesus (eg Gal 4:19-20; 6:17).

4.2 Was Romans 16 to Ephesus?

A number of scholars have regarded Romans 16 as a separate letter which was originally addressed to Ephesus.[176] However, Gamble has argued that the textual history of the letter is best explained by the view that the original letter had sixteen chapters and thus that Romans 16 was the conclusion to the letter sent to Rome. Thus commentators such as Dunn and Fitzmyer regard the Ephesian destination of Romans 16 as unlikely.[177]

---

[173] For example, Manson 1962, p168-89; Murphy-O'Connor 1996, p180-2; Fitzmyer 1998, p636 and Koester 2000, p122 think Galatians was written from Ephesus.

[174] See Longenecker 1990, plxxii-lxxxviii.

[175] See Koester 1995, p120.

[176] Note that the oldest papyrus manuscript p[46] lacks Rom 16:1-23 and other manuscripts have Rom 16:25-7 after Rom 15:33 or 14:23, or after both 14:23 and in its present place. If Rom 16 was to Ephesus, it would be a letter of recommendation written by Paul for Phoebe which has lost its prescript in being attached to Romans. On this view it was originally sent to Ephesus and was added to Romans by someone other than Paul, probably at the time of the collection of his letters; see Fitzmyer 1993, p57, who gives a list of advocates of this view; see also Trobisch 1994, p72-3; Koester 2000, p143. The Ephesian destination of the letter is based on 1) the greetings sent to Prisca and Aquila (16:3-5) who were in Ephesus when Paul wrote 1 Cor (16:19; see also 2 Tim 4:19); 2) Epaenetus is described as the "first convert to Christ in Asia" (Rom 16:5); 3) Rom 16:17-20 seems more suited to an Ephesian rather than a Roman provenance. Manson (1962, p225-41) thought Paul sent Rom 1-15 to Rome and another copy of the letter which included chapter 16 to Ephesus.

[177] See Gamble 1977, p31-95; Jewett 1988, p147-8; Dunn, 1988b, p884-5; Fitzmyer 1993, p55-67; cf. Koester 1995, p122-4. Boismard (2000, p548-557) has suggested that Rom 16:3-20 belonged to the letter which we know as "To the Ephesians". However, this seems unlikely, and in any case Ephesians was probably not to Ephesus.

4.3 Ephesians

Does Ephesians helps us in this enquiry? Firstly, we note that it is most likely that the letter was not written by Paul. Evidence for this includes arguments concerning style, theology, and the probable use of Col as a literary source.[178] Rather Eph was probably written between 80-90 by a Pauline disciple and so on these grounds alone cannot be used as evidence for Paul's ministry in the city.[179]

However, regardless of views about authorship, there is general agreement that in the letter now known as "To the Ephesians" the phrase "ἐν Ἐφέσῳ" found in some manuscripts at Eph 1:1 was not part of the original text.[180] Other factors also make it unlikely that the letter was directed to Christians in Ephesus. We note that the letter completely lacks any personal greetings, that in 1:15 the writer says "I have *heard* of your faith in the Lord Jesus" and that 3:2 reads: "for surely you have already *heard* of the commission of God's grace that was given me for you".[181] If Paul wrote the letter to Ephesus, then these factors are very hard to account for, since we know he had an extensive ministry in the city. But an Ephesian address is also most unlikely if, as we have argued, the letter is pseudonymous, since most scholars suggest it would then have been written by a follower of Paul, who had some knowledge of Paul and his ministry. In this case that the letter speaks of a complete lack of personal knowledge of Christians in Ephesus by "Paul" would again be very hard to explain. The most likely possibility then is that the letter was originally written to somewhere other than Ephesus.[182] Since it was almost certainly not sent to Ephesus originally, we cannot regard the Christians in the city as the first recipients of the letter and so cannot read information about them from the letter.[183] However, it has been suggested that the letter

---

[178] See Schnackenburg 1991a, p24-9; Brown 1997, p627-30; Schnelle 1998, p300-3, 307-8; Best 1998, p6-40. On the use of Col by Eph see Schnelle 1998, p307-8; Schnackenburg 1991a, p30-33; cf. Best 1998, p20-5, 37-40.

[179] We note that in writing to Polycarp, bishop of Smyrna, around 105-110, Ignatius seems to allude to Eph 5:25, 29; see IgnPol 5:1; Best 1998, p15-16. This suggests a date for Eph no later than the 90s. Best 1998, p44-5 and Schnelle 1998, p303 argue for a date between 80-90 CE; Schnackenburg 1991a, p33 argues for a date around 90 CE; Collins 1988, p139 and Brown 1997, p630 for the 90s.

[180] See Metzger 1971, p601; Lincoln 1990, p1-2; Best 1997, p2-9. The words ἐν Ἐφέσῳ are missing from P^{46}, ℵ*, B*, 424c and 1739 and from manuscripts mentioned by Basil; the text used by Origen, Tertullian and Ephraem do not explicitly quote the words. Further, the position of ἐν Ἐφέσῳ in the vast majority of manuscripts makes the text difficult to understand grammatically.

[181] Note also that in 3:7-13 Paul's ministry is explained to the readers; see also 4:21.

[182] We will discuss the most likely location of the original addressees below.

[183] But what would Eph tell us, if it was written to (or as we discuss below, from) Ephesus? Eph 4:1-6:20 is a very general paraenetic section, and the letter does not lead us to postulate the existence of any "opponents". Further, although the purpose of Eph is debated,

provides evidence for the collection of Paul's letters and so indirectly gives evidence about Ephesian Christians. We will now discuss this possibility.

4.4 Did the first collection of Paul's letters occur in Ephesus?

2 Peter 3:15-16, Ignatius' Letter to the Ephesians and the Marcionite Prologues,[184] show that in the second century there was a collection of Paul's letters. However, it seems likely that the process of collecting some of Paul's letters must have begun much earlier.[185]

Did Ephesus have a place in this process? Firstly we will consider Goodspeed's unlikely suggestion. Then we will consider another suggestion that Ephesus had a place in this collection process.

Goodspeed suggested that Paul's letters were collected at Ephesus and distributed from the city, due to a resurgence of interest in Paul after Acts was written. Integral to his theory was that Ephesians was written as a general circular letter to introduce the Pauline letter corpus, with a lacuna being left in the text at 1:1 for the destination to be filled in by the courier.[186] On this theory Ephesians would not be to Ephesus, but to all the other churches to which the Pauline letter collection was sent, but Ephesus would be the place where Paul's letters were collected.

---

it seems most likely that its purpose is general; after a thorough critique (Best 1998, p63-75) of many other possibilities, Best (1998, p75) suggests it was written to former pagans (2:11; 3:1; 4:17) who, as Christians, have entered into a new group; Eph was written so they could understand the nature of the Christian group and the conduct required of group members. This very general purpose means we cannot determine much in detail about the readers from the letter, nor, if the letter was written from Ephesus, about the situation in Ephesus at the time of composition. Note that Muddiman (2001, p35-41, 45) proposes that Eph was written in order to achieve (p38) a "reconciliation between Pauline Gentile and Johannine Jewish Christians in Ephesus, 'thus making both one'." He points to similarities between Ephesians and (p39) "the literature of the Johannine circle in Ephesus". It may count against this interesting proposal that it is far from clear that the Pauline community in Ephesus at around 90 CE (Muddiman 2001, p35) can be thought of as "Gentile" and the Johannine community as "Jewish".

[184] See IgnEph 12:2, where he writes that "in every Epistle [Paul] makes mention of you in Christ Jesus." On the meaning of "in every Epistle" in Eph 12.2 see Best 1987, p3268-9. On the Marcionite Prologues see Dahl 2000, p179-209.

[185] Kümmel, 1975, p480; Best (1997, p17) notes: "When Clement writes from Rome to Corinth he is aware of both Paul's letter to his own church and the first letter to Corinth; a copy of the latter must therefore have arrived in Rome by this time." Paul himself began the process of his letters being shared with other communities; see Gal 1:2 (the churches of Galatia); 2 Cor 1:1b ("and all the saints in Achaia"), Col 4:16; see also 2 Cor 10:10-11.

[186] See Goodspeed 1933, p1-75; 1937, p48-9; see also Cook 1981, p15; Mitton 1955, p44-9. Goodspeed thought the collector of Paul's letters originally came from Colossae, since he knew Col so well.

However, Goodspeed's theory has not gained widespread support.[187] Firstly, if Ephesians was a circular letter, then we would expect to find the inclusion of ἐν without a place name in some texts, and other texts with different place names than Ephesus at 1:1, but none of the surviving manuscripts exhibit either feature. Secondly, this theory does not explain why copies without place names continue to exist. Thirdly, the suggestion that a lacuna was left in a circular letter is without parallel in antiquity.[188] Thus the form of the manuscript evidence for 1:1 argues strongly against Ephesians originally being a circular letter.[189] Fourthly, there is little to suggest that Paul was so completely forgotten as Goodspeed suggests and that the memory of Paul was only revived when Acts was written. Finally, we have no evidence that Ephesians was ever the first or the last letter of the first collection of Paul's epistles.[190] Accordingly, Goodspeed's theory is unlikely.

However, there is a second possibility, to which we now turn. Other scholars have suggested that Eph was written *from* Ephesus and that it shows that some Christians in the city had a role in collecting Paul's letters. We have noted in discussing Eph 1:1 that Eph was probably not originally sent to Ephesus. Rather it seems most likely that it was sent between 80-90 CE to a variety of readers (even if Goodspeed's detailed circular letter theory is not likely), probably chiefly in Asia Minor, who regarded Paul as a great apostle.[191]

Why then did the letter become associated with Ephesus? Scholars have suggested that this was because the letter was actually written *in the city*; scribes later recalled that the composition of the letter was linked to Ephesus, and so added "ἐν Ἐφέσῳ" at 1:1.[192] Additional reasons for this development

---

[187] See Taylor and Reumann 1985, p20; Lincoln 1990, plxxix-lxxx; Best 1997, p8, 18, 1998, p65-6.

[188] See Lincoln 1990, p3; cf 1 Peter 1:1; Gal 1:2.

[189] See Best 1987, p3250-1; 1997, p10-11.

[190] See Moule 1981, p262-3.

[191] See Brown 1997, p627; Schnelle 1998, p306; Best 1998, p2 (with some caution). There have been a range of more specific suggestions about original destination. Lincoln (1990, p1-4) argues for Hierapolis and Laodicea (based on Col 4:13; on this see Best 1997, p13-14). Kreitzer (1998, p381-93) suggests the letter was to Hierapolis and interprets Eph 4:9 against the background of the Plutonium of Hierapolis. Moritz (1996, p11-12), following Marcion (who identified Ephesians with the *Letter to the Laodiceans* mentioned in Col 4:16) argues for Laodicea. See also Taylor and Reumann, 1985, p19. For discussions of all the issues see Best 1987, p3246-79; 1997, p1-24; Lincoln 1990, plxxxi-lxxxii. The actual genre of Eph is strongly debated.

[192] Brown 1997, p630. He adds in p630, n28: "Or else it represented an early guess by a copyist as to a possible destination." On either view we would have to suggest that the scribe was either unaware of its unsuitability to go to Ephesus (since the letter says Paul does not know the readers personally) or else the scribe was content for this historical implausibility to stand. For a thorough review see Best 1987, p3253-7.

may have been that it was known that Paul had a long ministry in the city, but that there was no extant letter from Paul to Ephesus, and that the letter had a connection with western Asia Minor.[193]

If the letter was written from Ephesus by a Pauline disciple, it would then be evidence for a Pauline school of disciples, perhaps from the time of Paul onwards, which preserved and developed Pauline tradition in the city.[194] Further, since the author of Eph probably knows some of Paul's other letters,[195] it is suggested that this provides evidence for a collection of Paul's letters in the city.[196] Perhaps it was this Ephesian school which provided the context for the first collection of Paul's letters.

Colossians is also often brought into this discussion. It is argued that Col is also pseudonymous, written by a member of the Pauline school in Ephesus, perhaps around 70 CE, using material from Philemon, but perhaps other letters too.[197] The author is thought to be located in Ephesus because it is close to Colossae and to the Lycus Valley setting of the letter and because Ephesus was "the center of the Pauline mission in Asia Minor".[198] However, in my view it is more likely that Paul wrote Col (or perhaps it was actually penned by Timothy, although approved by Paul),[199] and so we cannot use Col as evidence for the "Pauline school" in Ephesus. But that Eph probably uses Col, does suggest the existence of a Pauline school in Ephesus (rather than say Corinth) since Ephesus is reasonably close to Colossae.

The Pastorals are also connected to this theory, as evidence of a Pauline school.[200] In Chapter 5 we will argue, as do many others, that the Pastorals

---

[193] Evidence for this connection is the mention of Tychicus in Eph 6:21f (mentioned in Col 4:7-8 (which is especially relevant if Col is authentic) and Acts 20:4, where Asia probably indicates Ephesus) and the familiarity with Col; see Schnackenburg 1991a, p29; Pokorny 1992, p37-8; Best 1998, p1-6.

[194] Lohse (1971, p181) locates the school in Ephesus and writes (p181, n12): "The rise of deutero-Pauline writings presupposes such a school tradition." See also Bornkamm 1971, p86; Pokorny 1992, p15-20, 37-8; Schnelle 1998, p350-3; Best 1998, p36-40 (who does not think the school is to be located in Ephesus).

[195] See Best 1998, p25-7 who thinks the author of Eph knew Rom, 1 Cor and probably Phlm and parts of 2 Cor. Schnackenburg 1991a, p36, thinks the author of Eph knows Rom, 1 and 2 Cor, Gal, Col and Phlm.

[196] See Brown 1997, p629-30. On the unlikely view of Trobisch 1994, p55-96 that Paul himself assembled the first collection of his letters (consisting of Rom, Gal and 1-2 Cor) for friends in Ephesus see Schnelle 1998, p350 n220.

[197] See Schnelle 1998, p287-8, 298. 352; Brown (1997, p616) favours a date in the 80s.

[198] See Lohse 1971, p181. However, Schnelle (1998, p288, emphasis original) writes: "In any case, Colossians originated in the area of *southwest Asia Minor.*"

[199] For discussions of the authorship of Col see Brown 1997, p610-15; Schnelle 1998, p282-8 (who argue it is pseudepigraphical); Schweizer 1982, p15-24; Dunn 1996, p35-9 (who argue for Timothy as the author, with Paul's approval).

[200] Since it seems unlikely that the Pastorals and Eph (and Col) were produced by the same school, this would be a different Pauline "school" from that which produced Eph; see

were written to Ephesus; some scholars think they were *also* written from Ephesus, which is certainly possible.[201] Roloff also argues that the author of the Pastorals knows 1-2 Cor, Rom, Phil, Col and probably Phlm, and so knows a collection of Paul's letters.[202] Thus it is suggested that the corpus of Pauline writings grew in stages (a collection to which Eph was added, to which collection the Pastorals were later added), and that it was all overseen by a Pauline school, or schools, located in Ephesus.[203]

What would this theory mean for our study? It would suggest that there was an influential school of Pauline disciples in Ephesus, disciples who valued his thought, and developed Pauline tradition. It would also suggest that one activity of this school was making a collection (however incipient) of Paul's letters in Ephesus, sometime between the 60s and the 90s. This would be a practical outworking of their valuing of Pauline tradition.

Both these points are historically possible. We will certainly argue later in this book for the continued existence of a Pauline group in Ephesus, for which our evidence is the Pastorals (which we date 80-100) and Ignatius' letter to the Ephesians.

However, we need to note that the evidence which connects a Pauline "school" (and its activity of letter-collecting) with Ephesus, is meagre. The strongest evidence for an actual connection of a school with Ephesus is firstly the probable use of Col (sent to nearby Colossae) by the author of Eph, and secondly that a later scribe associated Eph with Ephesus by adding "in Ephesus" in Eph 1:1.[204] But neither point actually *requires* Ephesus as the location of a Pauline school and the place where the corpus of letters was collected.[205] Col could have been used by an author writing in a range of locations, and Eph could have been written elsewhere – somewhere in western

---

Best 1987, p3264; Pokorny 1992, p15-16. This could raise the possibility of two different Pauline schools in Ephesus, but since we do not think there is clear evidence for even one such school in Ephesus, we will not pursue this.

[201] See for example Schnelle 1998, p333. We will discuss this further in Chapter 5.

[202] Roloff 1988, p39-40; see also Schnelle 1998, p351.

[203] See Schnelle 1998, p351-2. He also suggests "So too glosses such as 1 Cor. 14.33b-36, 2 Cor. 6.14-7.1; Rom. 7:25b; 16:25-27 point to a process of collection and to some extent of re-editing of the Pauline letters." Dunn (1988, p912-13) also argues that Rom 16:25-7 was a Post-Pauline addition, and it seems reasonable to connect the addition with the collection of Paul's letters.

[204] Note that Best (1987, p3260-1) thinks the middle of the second century is the earliest point at which we have actual evidence which suggests that Eph was known as "To the Ephesians". He also thinks that the association of Eph with Ephesus was quite late; see Best 1997, p22.

[205] Schnelle (1998, p352) suggests two other reasons for Ephesus as the place of the collection of letters: that letter collections of famous authors were known in Ephesus, and that Acts 19:19 indicates book production occurred in Ephesus; see also Trobisch 1989, p115. But these two points apply to many other cities too.

Asia Minor seems most likely (because of the link with Col and Tychicus), [206] but this need not involve Ephesus. Further, the place of composition of the Pastorals is uncertain, as we note in Chapter 5, and similarly the collection of Paul's letters could have occurred elsewhere.[207] We also note Brown's reserve about a Pauline school: "If one posits a considerable number of deuteroPauline letters, the existence of a Pauline school of disciples at Ephesus, who after Paul's death continued his heritage in the 80s, is not implausible."[208] But being "not implausible" is not sufficient for us to discuss a Pauline school at Ephesus at length in our argument here. And in the end, although the existence of a Pauline school seems reasonable, it remains a hypothesis. Thus because of the uncertainties about the link between Eph and Ephesus, and about the existence of a Pauline school in the city, we will not draw on either Eph or the hypothesis of a Pauline school, as evidence for our portrayal of the life of Christians in Ephesus.

5. The significance of house churches

Since the house church was fundamental to the life of the early Christians in Ephesus, as it also was elsewhere,[209] and since house churches are first mentioned in connection with Paul's mission in Ephesus, it is important to discuss features of the house church at this point. It is clear that the house church ("κατ᾽ οἶκον") was very important in Pauline communities and enabled

---

[206] Note Best's (1998, p37) uncertainty about geographical location when he writes of the Pauline school which he sees as responsible for both Col and Eph: "Its members probably lived somewhere in Asia Minor in the light of the geographical references in Col 4.13 to Laodicea and Hierapolis." See also MacDonald 2000, p18 who connects the composition of Eph with "the cities of Asia Minor".

[207] Note that Schnelle (1998, p352) thinks that collections of some Pauline letters were also made in Corinth and Rome; see also Manson 1962, p258. Best (1987, p3262) notes that Corinth may have been the place where Paul's letters were first made into a formal collection since 1 Cor heads many of the early lists of Paul's letters. He also notes (1987, p3272) that the variety of order found in the lists suggests a number of collections were made by different people in different places.

[208] Brown 1997, p616.

[209] On the house church see Filson 1939, p105-112; Banks 1980, p33-42; Malherbe 1983, p60-91; Branick 1989; White 1990, p103-110; Sandnes 1994, p93-99; Blue 1994, p119-222; Osiek and Balch 1997, p32-5; Fitzmyer 2000, p89-90; Barth and Blanke 2000, p260-4. Fitzmyer (2000, p90) notes that "There is no evidence, however, of a separate building reserved for liturgy in the Roman empire before the third century A.D." But prior to this, private homes were probably adapted for use by Christian communities. White (1990, p110) suggests that Christians continued to meet in "private or domestic settings" in the middle of the second century. On the development of the "Domus Ecclesias", which involves the physical adaptation of an existing edifice to make it more suitable for Christian assemblies, see White 1990, p111-123.

them to meet together for teaching and worship that was distinctively Christian (Rom 16:5; 1 Cor 16:19; Col 4:15; Phlm 2).[210] House churches were quite small household-based groups which met regularly, probably weekly (1 Cor 16:2), in someone's home.[211] The nucleus of the group would often have been a particular household, although new converts from outside the household and from non-Christian families, would join the group. As Branick notes "The private home ... afforded a place of privacy, intimacy and stability for the early Christians."[212]

It seems likely that several house churches came to exist in some cities.[213] Rom 16:5, 14-15 suggest there were at least three house churches in Rome.[214] Two verses are of particular interest with regard to Corinth. In Rom 16:23, written from Corinth, we read: "Gaius, who is host to me and to the whole church (ὅλης τῆς ἐκκλησίας), greets you" and in 1 Cor 14:23 we read: "If, therefore, the whole church (ἡ ἐκκλησία ὅλη) comes together and all speak in tongues, and outsiders or unbelievers enter ..."[215] These two verses suggest that on some less frequent occasions, "the whole church", that is probably all the Christians of the city, would meet together.[216] At other times, believers probably met in separate house churches. During the Pauline period, did Christians elsewhere sometimes meet in separate house churches and on other occasions as "the whole church", that is, in a meeting of all Christians in the city? However, we should note that both of these texts refer to the situation at Corinth. The formula "the whole church" is thus used of only one community. As a result, Sandnes notes:

"One should therefore be cautious in generalizing on this basis. The situation in Corinth may have been special. The situation might have been that some of the wealthy (Gaius?) in Corinth had the necessary space for a common gathering. This means that I question the use of the Corinthian model as a general pattern for other cities in the early Christian period. It goes beyond the evidence to assume that the Corinthian model holds for all cities where Christian house-churches developed. In Rome it may quite quickly have been difficult for all

---

[210] See also Acts 18:7-8; 20:8; Phil 4:22; 1 Cor 1:11. Of course, other groups – Jews, sometimes followers of mystery cults, associations of various sorts – also met in houses.

[211] This also reflects the fact that a community often began through the conversion of a household; see 1 Cor 1:16; Acts 16:15, 34; 18:8.

[212] Branick 1989, p14. That Christians met in houses correlated with the strong sense of "family" that was clearly part of Pauline Christianity; see Banks 1980, p52-61.

[213] See Malherbe 1983, p70. Lampe (1987, p367-8) notes the analogy from the Jews in Rome, where there were a number of different synagogue communities.

[214] See Branick 1989, p24-5. Col 4:15 suggests there was more than one house church in Colossae; see also 1 Thess 5:27.

[215] It is interesting that outsiders can be present; the earliest evidence for "closed" meetings including the Lord's Supper comes from Didache 9.5.

[216] See Klauck 1981, p33-9; Branick 1989, p23-4; Sandnes 1994, p96. As Branick (1989, p24) notes "Gaius is singled out for special mention due to his generosity in gathering the whole Corinthian church at his house."

the Christians to gather at any one place. I am therefore inclined to stress the independence of the house-churches at the expense of the Corinthian model."[217]

We have noted that, towards the end of the Pauline mission in Ephesus, there were at least two house churches (see 1 Cor 16:19-20).[218] We do not know whether "the whole church", that is, all the Christians in Ephesus at that point, could or did meet together.[219] At various points in this study we will note that Christians in Ephesus continued to meet in house churches throughout the period we are examining.[220] However, we will propose in subsequent chapters that, after the Pauline mission, the evidence of the Pastorals and the Johannine Letters suggests that all the Christians in Ephesus, that is, all the house churches which made up various groups, did not meet together. This issue will also re-emerge in our discussion of Ignatius' letter to the Ephesians. It is also important in this study to recall that all the Christians we will be discussing were part of house churches.

Leadership of the house churches was often, though probably not always, provided by the people in whose home the group met.[221] The Lord's Supper

---

[217] Sandnes 1994, p96-7. He also critiques Gielen (1986, p109-25), who rejects the distinction between the local city-wide church and the house churches and thinks "the church in the house" is a reference to the local city-wide church. But she ignores the likelihood that many house-churches existed in one city, as Rom 16:23 suggests was the case in Corinth, and so overlooks the relationship between different house churches in a city. It is more likely that the phrase "the church in the house" shows that the "local church" (ie the community of Christians in a city) was often divided into house churches; see Sandnes 1994, p97; see also Barth and Blanke 2000, p261-2. Sandnes (1994, p97-8) also notes that Justin, Apol 67.3 ("And on the day called Sunday, all who live in cities or in the country gather together to one place") has been taken to show that the Corinthian model applies to other cities. However, Sandnes shows that it is more likely that Justin means that it is normal procedure for Christians to come together on Sunday, rather than that he implies that all the Christians met in one place. Sandnes (1994, p97) notes: "What they [Christians] have in common is not the place, but the procedure of coming together … This means that Justin's statement must not be contrasted to gatherings in house-churches; rather it is a statement about the house-churches themselves." Further, in Martyrion of Justin 3, Justin denies that all the Christians in Rome could meet together in one place. Note however, that Paul regularly addresses all Christians in one place suggests that at least during his period of mission, there were strong links between house churches so that his letter could circulate from one to another.

[218] It is quite credible then that in speaking at Miletus Paul emphasised that the house church had been an important factor in his work in Ephesus; see Acts 20:20.

[219] We may wonder if they had the facilities to do so (see Branick 1989, p101) and if they saw the necessity of doing so?

[220] References to house churches in the later NT and in post NT literature are surprisingly rare; for the latter see the Martyrion of Justin 3; Pseudo-Clementine Recognitions 71.2. But as Barth and Blanke (2000, p262) note: "Since in the absence of specific church buildings no other rooms existed for the worship of the persecuted minority, there was no need to mention house churches."

[221] See Fitzmyer 2000, p82.

was celebrated in house churches; since at this stage the Lord's Supper was a full meal (see 1 Cor 11:20-22), and since there is no hint in the two places where Paul speaks of it (1 Cor 10:14-22; 11:17-34) that the management of the meal was in the hands of an official of any kind, the person in whose house it was held probably made the arrangements for the meal and had a presiding role over the Lord's Supper. As far as 1 Cor 16:19 is concerned, we can suggest that both Prisca and Aquila would have made these general arrangements, although the fact that Paul addresses his remarks about the Lord's Supper in 1 Cor 11:17f to the whole church suggests that responsibility for the proper conduct of the meal rested finally upon all members.[222]

The organisational form of the house church could lead to conflict. As we have noted, leaders of house churches would often be householders, as is also suggested by 1 Tim 3:4. But, as Lieu notes, this "was probably not always the pattern nor would every householder have held a structured role of authority. The tensions to which this could also lead are easy to envisage."[223] Note, for example, the tension between the householder in whose house the church met, who assumed a leadership role, and other leaders who had been appointed to a particular role. A further example is the conflict between local leaders of house churches, and itinerant teachers and prophets, which seems to be evident in Did. 11-13 and 15.1-2,[224] and the warning about the love of preeminence in 3 Jn 9.[225] While these texts probably reflect the concern that positions of authority attracted those who looked for preeminence, they may also reflect tension between these different forms of authority.[226]

Thus, Lieu notes that authority in the early church "was more than the question of different types of legally instituted leadership. A number of factors may lead to the exercise and recognition of power or influence".[227] Note the power exercised by prophets and teachers with charismatic gifts, the power of the householder which reflected social standing, the power of the appointed leader and the authority of those older in the faith or in years. Clearly there could be conflict between these different forms of power and authority, and they could well focus on house churches.

The size and structure of house churches had a considerable impact on church life. The maximum size of any house church depended on the number of people that could be accommodated in the largest house owned by one of its members. The average size of a house church is debated, and clearly relates

---

[222] See Banks 1980, p85.
[223] Lieu 1986, p133
[224] See Branick 1989, p93
[225] See also IgnSm 6.1; Hermas, Mand XI.12; Sim IX.22.1-3.
[226] See Lieu 1986, p134-5.
[227] Lieu 1986, p133.

to the size of houses in different places and the relative wealth or poverty of members of the church. However, the average number of people that could be accommodated in a wealthy person's house is probably 30-40,[228] but we should certainly not think that every house church had a person of this sort of wealth amongst its members. Clearly some house churches would be much smaller.

The size of the house church in turn laid demands on leadership, and on communication. If a group became bigger than could be accommodated in the largest house owned by one of its members, then it seems likely that it would divide into two house churches.[229] Since it seems likely that leadership at this point was generally plural, rather than being provided by just one person, this would immediately mean that there would need to be four leaders. Further, that a group consisted of two house churches in one area would then necessitate good communication between the two house churches, to ensure that they did not diverge with regard to belief, practice and so on.

That the basic unit of the Christian community was the house church means that variety, diversity and disagreement could develop amongst the Christians in one group which was made up of more than one house church. Thus, for example, differences could develop between house churches with regard to beliefs and practices, but also in such areas as socio-economic level, leadership style, attitudes to outsiders and mission in general, to name just some areas. Loyalty to a particular house church, or a leader or group of leaders, could also develop, loyalty that mirrored the strong ties of loyalty experienced in Greco-Roman households.[230]

In addition, if, for example, a new group of Christians arrived in a city, since they might form their own house church, they could remain independent of and autonomous from existing house churches. Alternatively if new missionaries arrived, they could set up a new house church, rather than necessarily integrate with an existing house church. This independence might

---

[228] Branick (1989, p38-42) argues that 30-40 people could be accommodated at a meeting in a wealthy person's house; Murphy O'Connor (1983, p156) suggests 50 was the maximum, 30-40 people more likely; Barth and Blanke (2000, p261) opt for 40; Blue (1994, p142-3; see also p175) argues for larger numbers: 75 in a large reception hall, with more being accommodated in adjoining rooms, but this is in a large mansion. On housing in this period see Osiek and Balch 1997, p5-32. In Ephesus two complete blocks of private houses (called Hanghäuser by the excavators) have been excavated on the north slope of Mt Koressos above Kouretes Street. In their earliest period they date back to the first century BCE and they remained in use until the seventh century CE, with considerable remodeling at various times. Some are the dwellings of shopkeepers, but most belonged to very rich people. They contain some impressive mosaics and frescoes. See further Strocka 1977; Jobst 1977; Bammer 1988, p104-119; Hueber 1997, p55-8; Osiek and Balch 1997, p11-12; Parrish 1999, p507-13. For a discussion of the chronology of the Hanghäus 2 see Wiplinger 1999, p521-6.

[229] We have defined how we understand a "group" in the Introduction.

[230] See Branick 1989, p26-7; Malherbe 1983, p69.

be for theological or other reasons (such as ethnicity), but might also be a result of the practicalities of the situation.

Another scenario to bear in mind here is the following: What if there were two or more distinct and different groups (each made up of house churches) in a city?[231] The basic unit of each group was the house church, and, simply out of necessity, it is unlikely that each "group" would ever all meet together (unless they were quite small); probably they kept in contact through individuals, or through leaders meeting together or in some other way. But how would two "groups", each made up of house churches with their leaders, maintain some form of contact, let alone form a coherent "single group"? All the members of the two groups would be unable to meet together, just as all the members of one group were probably unable to get together. Fostering unity and overcoming differences in this sort of situation would be challenging. Clearly, then the house church structure fostered the maintenance of difference, and the practicalities of house churches had an impact on the emergence and maintenance of diversity within the Christian communities of a large city. In general then, the house church structure of early Christianity facilitated diversity more easily than group-wide or city-wide unity.[232] We will need to bear these points in mind throughout this study.

6. Overall Conclusions

6.1 Information about Paul

Some of our discussions have led to negative conclusions – that we cannot use Romans 16, Gal, Eph, Col, Phil or Philemon in our discussions of Paul's time in Ephesus. Nor can we use the possibility that Paul's letters were first collected in Ephesus as evidence for Pauline influence there, since it remains uncertain that the collection of his letters occurred in the city. But we have gained some positive information about Paul, who was clearly a major figure in the history of Christianity in Ephesus, and about the Christian community.

Firstly, we note the paucity of information in Paul's letters about his time in Ephesus. When we compare the few verses that give us some information with our sources for Paul's relationship to, for example, the church at Corinth, we realise how much we are hindered by the lack of a letter written by Paul to

---

[231] Recall our discussion of "What makes a group a group" in the Introduction.

[232] Thus Lieu (1986, p132) notes that if a whole household converted to Christianity, "they would virtually constitute a community in themselves, [and] whole household relationships and loyalties inevitably continued to loom large. As such they would have allowed a degree of diversity within the church and could even become a focus for division."

Ephesian Christians. We are reminded of the occasional nature of our evidence for Paul's life. However, we do gain some information.

Secondly, we learn that Prisca, Aquila and Timothy probably worked with Paul for much of the time he was in Ephesus. We also know that Apollos had been with Paul in Ephesus prior to 1 Cor being written, that Sosthenes was with Paul at the time of writing 1 Cor (1 Cor 1:1), and that Titus carried the later "letter of tears" from Ephesus to Corinth (2 Cor 2:4; 7:6-11). We may suggest that each of these three "co-workers"[233] had spent a longer time working with Paul than simply the "snapshot" point in time for which we have evidence. For example, we can only ask if Titus had been with Paul for most of his time in Ephesus?[234]

All of this suggests that Paul had a significant and impressive team of co-workers and associates working with him in Ephesus. This seems reasonable, given that Ephesus was a big city, and that the Lycus valley churches, and perhaps some of the other six churches of Rev 2-3 were founded in this period from Ephesus, which functioned as a missionary centre. But it also means that the period of over two years and three months that Paul spent in Ephesus represented a concerted campaign by a number of early Christian workers. Paul was simply the leading figure in a group of close associates and co-workers who laboured together in Ephesus.[235]

We have also noted that Paul regards Apollos as a co-worker and brother, and shows no signs of anything but collegiality towards him. At the very least we can say that they were not at loggerheads. The evidence suggests that it is unlikely that there was an "Apollos party" in Ephesus.

Thirdly, from 1 Cor 16:9 we learn that as Paul reflected on his time in Ephesus he considered that the work of mission preaching and nurturing the Christian community in which he had been engaged, presented many opportunities, had brought results, and was continuing to bring results, for he considered that his work has been and was being ἐνεργής — effective.

---

[233] Titus is called a συνεργός in 2 Cor 8:23; Apollos in 1 Cor 3:9; Sosthenes is called ὁ ἀδελφός in 1 Cor 1:1; here the term almost certainly does designate him as one of Paul's co-workers; see Ellis 1970-71, p445-52. Epaphras founded the church in Colossae, probably during the period of time that Paul was in Ephesus. Paul describes him as "our beloved fellow servant" and a "faithful minister of Christ on our behalf" (Col 1:7; cf Col 4:12, 13); O'Brien (1982, p15) notes that he is thus "Paul's representative in Colossae". That he is a διάκονος suggests he is one of Paul's co-workers; see Ellis 1970-71, p438, 441-3. It is possible that he came to Ephesus and was converted, and was a co-worker with Paul in Ephesus before he returned to his home in Colossae. But this can only be a suggestion.

[234] Byrskog 1996, p248 suggests that "the mention of co-sender(s) known by the recipient served as a means to establish or maintain good relations between the correspondents. This explains best why Paul chose to include only certain persons, and not others who were with him at the time of writing." Thus, co-workers other than Sosthenes could have been with Paul at the time of writing.

[235] In general see Schnackenburg 1991, p49; Byrskog 1996, p249-50.

Further, 1 Cor 16:19 suggests that Paul's relations with the Christians in Ephesus were close and cordial, and we can also point out that there are no indications of any discordant notes.

Fourthly, 1 Cor 15:32 and 16:9 suggest that Paul encountered considerable and intense opposition in Ephesus, perhaps even to the extent of his life being threatened (if 2 Cor 1:8-10 applies to Ephesus). As Fee comments: Paul's "stay in Ephesus was anything but an Aegean holiday."[236] We cannot be certain of the exact source of the opposition, but the context of 1 Cor 15:32 suggests it was from pagans or Jews rather than from other Christians.

Fifthly, although the hardship catalogues provide us with no firm evidence, they suggest that Paul's time in Ephesus was marked by suffering. If the affliction referred to in 2 Cor 1:8-11, which was probably some sort of external danger, took place in Ephesus, then this would indicate that Paul experienced some dire event during which he despaired of life itself. However, it is not certain that this affliction occurred in Ephesus, and so it is not clear that Paul's time in Ephesus was marked by particularly acute suffering. Further, we do know that Paul also endured suffering elsewhere. One facet of Paul's suffering in Ephesus may have been an imprisonment, but we have no unequivocal evidence for this.

These hints are tantalizingly incomplete. 2 Cor 11:23-33 combined with the evidence from 1 Cor 15:32; 16:9 and 2 Cor 1:8-11 lead Fee to note: "One wonders at moments like these what a different picture of both the apostles and the early church we might have received if Paul had kept a journal of his stay in Ephesus!"[237]

Sixthly, Paul's letters also contain no information about the subsequent history of the Pauline community in Ephesus during Paul's life. In particular, did internal divisions develop in the community, as occurred in Corinth, or did outsiders come in and preach a different Gospel and seek to influence the community, as in Galatia? Unfortunately, we simply do not know.

6.2 Information about Christians in Ephesus

If information about Paul is sparse, then unfortunately the information we gain from Paul's letters about the Christians in Ephesus is even more limited. A passage like 2 Cor 1:8-11 which may or may not tell us something about Paul's time in Ephesus, certainly tells us nothing about the Ephesian Christian community. In particular, we lack detailed information about their theological perspective. However, we do learn some details about Ephesian Christians.

Firstly, we learn that Prisca and Aquila hosted a house church in their home in Ephesus and there was probably at least one other house church in the city.

---

[236] Fee 1987, p769.
[237] Fee 1987, p769.

Here, as elsewhere, the house church was the fundamental structure of the early Christian community. We have also discussed some features of the house church which will be significant throughout this study.

Secondly, we have noted that as Paul reflected on his time in Ephesus he considered that it had brought results, and was continuing to bring results. This suggests that the Christian community had grown and become well established.[238] 1 Cor 16:19-20 suggests that the Pauline Christian community was made up of more than one house church and thus may have numbered over 30 people.

Thirdly, we have also noted that 1 Cor 16:19-20 shows that there were other churches in Asia by the time Paul wrote 1 Cor; they probably included churches in the Lycus Valley and perhaps further afield as well. It seems that during Paul's time in Ephesus successful evangelism had been conducted in the area around Ephesus and further afield. Ephesus was probably the centre of missionary work in the area.

Fourthly, we can suggest that if the opposition to Paul had come from pagans or Jews, as seems likely, then the Ephesian Christians in these early days would have been aware that the Christian faith could provoke controversy and opposition from these quarters. Perhaps some Ephesian Christians had also experienced such opposition personally. Further, given that Paul seems to have suffered in some ways while he was in Ephesus, they would probably have been aware that a similar fate could await them. Beyond these probable points, we do not know what impact the fact that Paul endured opposition had on the Christian community in Ephesus, or how they reacted to Paul's suffering.[239]

6.3 The evidence of Acts

Since the events mentioned in 1 Cor 15:32 and 2 Cor 1:8-11 are not mentioned in Acts,[240] it seems clear that Acts does not give us the full story of Paul's time in Ephesus.[241] All we hear of opposition is the account of the riot,[242] and

---

[238] Note also that as Manson (1962, p212) comments, Paul's travel plans as outlined in 1 Cor 16:5-9 and 2 Cor 1:15-16 "assume that the work at Ephesus is, for the time being at any rate, completed; and no provision is made for any return to Ephesus." This suggests that Paul viewed the Ephesian community at this point in time as having attained a degree of maturity.

[239] We could also note that "Chloe's people" in Ephesus were probably slaves, but we do not know anything else about the socio-economic level of the Pauline Christians in Ephesus at this point.

[240] Unless the riot is the affliction mentioned in 2 Cor 1:8-11, in which case it was more life-threatening than Luke suggests.

[241] For example Barrett (1973, p139) notes of Paul's time in Ephesus: "persecution was fiercer, and Paul suffered more severely, than Acts (for whatever reason) permits us to see."

serious as this was, it seems clear from Paul's letters that he encountered more than this by way of opposition in Ephesus. Further, the hardship catalogues show how much suffering Paul endured, some of which may have occurred in Ephesus, and much of which is not mentioned in Acts.[243] Luke has downplayed (what was for him) the negative side of Paul's ministry. Yet we should also note that Luke was not setting out to write a biography of Paul. Clearly, then, we need to be aware of the limited nature of the Acts account of Paul's time in Ephesus. We turn now in Chapters 3 and 4 to discuss features of Luke's account.

---

[242] The Jewish exorcists of Acts 19:13-17 do not really constitute opposition.

[243] Note also that Acts does not mention the events alluded to in Rom 16:4, 7. For a list of information available from Paul's letters which is omitted by Acts, see Hurd 1965, p23-5.

Chapter 3

Acts and the early Christians in Ephesus: Beginnings and Success

1. The value of the evidence provided by Acts

In Acts 18:18-20:38 Luke gives material that pertains to Ephesus. The first issue that confronts us here is the value of this material. Can it be used as evidence for Paul's mission and the life of the early Christians in Ephesus?

1.1 The reliability of the Ephesian material in Acts

It is not my intention here to discuss the historicity of Acts as a whole, a subject which continues to be much debated.[1] Rather, since Luke could have very good sources for most of his work, but have deficient or inadequate sources for Ephesus, or the reverse could be the case, I will focus here on the historicity of Luke's material which relates to Ephesus.

There is much specific evidence which confirms that the material which concerns Ephesus should be taken seriously as a historical source. Oster has shown how well the material relating to Ephesus fits with what we know of ancient Ephesus and how much light can be shed on the text by a thorough knowledge of the city.[2] In particular, we can note that there is much accurate and vivid local colour in this narrative. What Luke says about magic in Ephesus, the silversmiths, the temple of Artemis, the significance and distribution of the cult of Ephesian Artemis, the fame of the city of Ephesus as the "temple keeper" of Artemis and the bond which existed between the

---

[1] For discussions about the historicity of Acts see Sherwin-White 1963, p172-93; Hengel 1979, p67-8; Hemer 1989a; Lüdemann 1988, p109-25; 1989; Marshall 1990a, p44-51; 1992, p89-98; Barrett 1999, p515-34; Ashton 2000, p171-8.

[2] Oster 1974; see also Oster 1976, p24-44; 1984, p233-37; 1990, p1661-1728. Subsequent work has reinforced Oster's conclusions. For example, on Ephesus as neokoros, or "temple warden" of Artemis (Acts 19:35), Friesen (1993a, p54) notes: "This element in the narrative – the appellation for the city – seems to reflect accurately the situation in the last half of the first century CE, for the speaker's argument rested on the assumption that the idea was common knowledge." Cf. White 1995, p37. Johnson (1992, p351) also comments: "Luke once more gets the local color precisely right"; see also Schneider 1982, p273; Conzelmann 1987, p164-5; Taylor 1996, p45-59.

city and the goddess, the use of the theatre for informal gatherings, the presence of the Asiarchs, the behaviour of unruly mobs in the Greco-Roman city, the role and meetings of the assembly, the attitude of the town clerk to a disturbance in the city and the way he defends the city's reputation, and much more is all abundantly confirmed as realistic by literary and archaeological evidence.[3] Thus much work has shown that Acts is generally reliable in the details it includes about Ephesian life, and the cult of Artemis and much light can be shed on the text by a thorough knowledge of the city.[4]

One point in particular is worth dwelling upon. In referring to Artemis of Ephesus in Acts 19, Demetrius speaks of τὸ τῆς μεγάλης Θεᾶς Ἀρτέμιδος (19:27) and the town clerk of τὴν Θεόν (19:37). A comparison with other authors of the period shows that ἡ Θεός found in 19:37 was probably the usual form of address for a goddess in Luke's time. Baugh notes that Luke's use of the form ἡ Θεά in 19:27 is contrary to normal classical and Koine usage when referring to goddesses.[5]

However, an examination of Ephesian sources which refer to Artemis of Ephesus shows that when her name is not specified ἡ Θεός is the predominant form; Luke's usage in 19:37 conforms both to current Koine usage and to this pattern of addressing Artemis of Ephesus. We would expect Luke to use the ἡ Θεός form in Demetrius speech in 19:27 too. But he does not; there, as we have noted, he has τὸ τῆς μεγάλης Θεᾶς Ἀρτέμιδος (19:27).[6]

The long inscription dating to 104 CE, which concerns the foundation established by C. Vibius Salutaris, is helpful in this regard. Here ἡ Θεός is found 13 times for Artemis;[7] ἡ Θεά is also used in phrases such as τῆς μεγίστης Θεᾶς Ἀρτέμιδος, but ἡ Θεά never occurs without her name

---

[3] See further in Trebilco 1994, p316-57. Gaius and Aristarchus are mentioned in the account as Paul's companions (19:29). This may be the same Gaius Paul baptised in Corinth (1 Cor 1:14), who was a host to Paul and the whole church in Corinth (Rom 16:23), although Gaius was a common name; see Johnson 1992, p348. Aristarchus (see also Acts 20:4; 27:2) is connected elsewhere with the Pauline mission; see Col 4:10; Phlm 24. Barrett (1998, p917) suggests that they may have provided information for Luke.

[4] Sherwin-White (1963, p87) notes that "The author of Acts is very well informed about the finer points of municipal institutions at Ephesus in the first and second centuries A.D." and concludes (1963, p92): "Acts does not show such detailed knowledge of any other city as of Ephesus." Millar (1967, p199) is also very positive about the historicity of Luke's account of the Ephesian riot. He notes: "No text illustrates better the city life of the Greek East, its passionate local loyalties, its potential violence precariously held in check by the city officials, and the overshadowing presence of the Roman governor."

[5] Baugh 1990, p291-2.

[6] The form Θεά (19:27) is not caused by attraction to μεγάλη; similar passages have Θεά consistently without attraction to feminine adjectives; see Baugh 1990, p292.

[7] See IvEph 27.12-13, 68, 215, 249, 271, 275, 313, 367, 396, 437, 462, 535, 553; for the text see also Rogers 1991 152-85.

Ἄρτεμις.[8] This illustrates what other sources also show was the stock usage at Ephesus in the first and second centuries CE: ἡ Θεός for simple references to Artemis, and "ἡ (adjective) Θεὰ Ἄρτεμις" as a formulaic title.[9] Thus the phraseology used by Luke in the speeches of Demetrius and the town clerk fits exactly the particular manner of speech used by Ephesians of the period. If the speeches had been created by Luke and on the whole reflected only his style,[10] then we would expect to find τῆς μεγάλης Θεοῦ Ἀρτέμιδος in 19:27, as can be found in other writers with reference to Artemis of Ephesus.[11] However, Θεά is predominantly found in parallel phrases *in Ephesus itself*, and this is what Luke has in 19:27. Baugh concludes that:

the 'vocabulary and phraseology' in Acts 19.27, 37 is probably not Luke's but authentic Ephesian speech. This is not to say that Luke's account is a verbatim record of the speeches, yet it does suggest that we have the substance of genuine statements in Acts 19. The difference in form between Θεός and Θεά may appear to be either an insignificant detail, or too trivial to sustain a conclusion about Luke's reliability. Yet I believe that it is an important substantiation of Luke's accuracy precisely because it is such a minor point which would have been overlooked by a less careful historian or by someone far removed from events at Ephesus.[12]

A strong case can be made then that Luke has some very reliable sources for his Ephesian material. However, we note that much of this relates to 19:21-40. Accordingly, Barrett argues that this passage "must be based upon information derived by Luke from Ephesus, either on a visit to the city or by inquiry, oral or possibly written, from Ephesian residents."[13] But if Luke has this sort of information for 19:21-40 from an Ephesian source that we have argued is reliable, it seems likely that he could have obtained all his information about Ephesus from the same source, or from sources of similar reliability in Ephesus.[14] Where we can check other material in Acts relating to

---

[8] See lines IvEph 27.224-25; see also lines 324, 407, 453-54; Baugh 1990, p293; Hemer 1989a, p122 n61.

[9] See Baugh, 293 and IvEph 276.8-9; 2915; Xenophon of Ephesus 3.5.5.

[10] As, for example, Dibelius (1956, p178-9) thought.

[11] See Strabo, Geog. 14.1; Dio Chrysostom, Or. 31.55 who both refer to Artemis of Ephesus as ἡ Θεός and Baugh 1990, p293. Strabo refers to all individual goddess in this way.

[12] Baugh 1990, p294.

[13] Barrett 1998, p917. Compare Günther (1995, p53-67) who generally does not think the Acts material is reliable. Similarly, Koester (2000, p122) thinks that Acts gives only scanty information about Paul's time in Ephesus: "nearly everything here is legendary."

[14] Again Barrett (1998, p903) suggests this: "The stories about Paul's successful healings (vv. 11, 12) and of the marked lack of success of the sons of Sceva [19:13-17] were no doubt told with delight–and probably with some exaggeration–by Ephesian Christians, and listened to by Luke with equal pleasure." Cf. Koester 1995, p128-31.

Ephesus (for example, Apollos' ability (18:24) and Ephesus' reputation with respect to magic (19:18-20)) it is corroborated as accurate by further evidence. Thus, we cannot claim that all of the Ephesian material in Acts is historically reliable, but the evidence does suggest that Luke has either very good knowledge of Ephesus, or reliable sources and that we should take Acts seriously as a historical source relating to Ephesus. In what follows we will not discuss all the features of or problems raised by the Acts material connected with Ephesus. Our interest is rather in the issue of historicity in relation to each passage, and in what this material tells us about the life of the early Christians in Ephesus, including figures such as Paul, Apollos, Priscilla and Aquila.

In the section of Acts relating to Ephesus, as elsewhere, Luke concentrates on Paul's arrival in a city ("beginnings"), his departure ("endings") and in between gives us what could be called "notable incidents". He gives us little insight into the on-going life of the church,[15] although some details can nevertheless be ascertained. Because this is the information at our disposal, our discussion will focus firstly on "beginnings", which includes not only Paul's arrival in Ephesus, but also the other information which can be ascertained from Acts about the first Christians in Ephesus. The most prominent theme which emerges from the "notable incidents" which Luke presents as occurring in Ephesus is that of Paul's success in the city, and we will also discuss this Lucan theme in this Chapter. In the next Chapter we will discuss the account of the riot, which is the focus for Luke's presentation of "endings", or Paul's departure from the city, and then will discuss Paul's speech at Miletus to the Ephesian elders.

2. Unknown founders of the Christian community in Ephesus?

When did the first Christians arrive in Ephesus? Luke records that the crowd at Pentecost included "Jews from every nation under heaven" (2:5) and gives a list of areas and regions they came from, which includes Asia (2:9).[16] Luke's

---

[15] See van Unnik 1960a, p35.

[16] The list contains a strange selection of countries, given in a strange order. There are a number of problems associated with the list, notably the mixture of ethnic names, countries and regions, and the principle of selection of the names, and peoples or places that are included and those that are left out. Luke has probably not invented the list, but seems to have modeled it on lists known to him. Barrett (1994, p124) notes: "Luke may have built upon an existing list and added other names that occurred to him on the basis of interests and connections of his own." This would explain the odd nature of the list. It seems most likely that, even if Luke took most of the list from a source, he has redacted the list so that it reflects the diversity of Jews present at the event. This means we can be reasonably certain that Jews from "Asia" were present on the occasion. For discussion of the list, different

basic point in giving this list is that the gift of the Spirit at Pentecost took place in the presence of Jews from all over the known world.[17]

One feature of these verses requires investigation. In 2:5 the people who witnessed the coming of the Spirit are said to be "devout Jews from every nation under heaven living in Jerusalem (εἰς Ἰερουσαλὴμ κατοικοῦντες)".[18] Similarly, in 2:14 Peter begins his speech "Men of Judea and all who live in Jerusalem (ἄνδρες Ἰουδαῖοι καὶ οἱ κατοικοῦντες Ἰερουσαλὴμ πάντες)". Since Luke uses κατοικέω of residence which is not limited to a brief stay,[19] these two verses lead us to think that the Jews present on the day who were not from Judea were originally from elsewhere but were now permanently resident in Jerusalem. However, in 2:9-11 Luke gives a list of where these Diaspora Jews came from which includes: "Parthians ... and residents of Mesopotamia (καὶ οἱ κατοικοῦντες τὴν Μεσοποταμίαν), Judea and Cappadocia, Pontus and Asia (καὶ τὴν Ἀσίαν), Phrygia and Pamphylia ... and visitors from Rome (καὶ οἱ ἐπιδημοῦντες Ῥωμαῖοι), both Jews and proselytes." Clearly, these Jews cannot be literally "οἱ κατοικοῦντες" in both Jerusalem and Pontus or Asia simultaneously.[20] The meaning seems to be that they were once resident in Mesopotamia or Asia, but now have made Jerusalem their home.[21] We have evidence that such a mixed population of Jews did live in Jerusalem at this time.[22]

---

possible solutions and references to earlier discussions see Barrett (1994, p121-2) who suggests Luke constructed the list using the precedent of passages in Jewish writers which outline the distribution of Jews throughout the world (such as Josephus CA 2:282; Philo, Flacc 45f; Leg ad Gaium 281f); Taylor (1999, p408-20) who thinks the best analogies to the list are official lists of places and peoples subject to the Persian Empire; Hengel (2000a, p161-80) who thinks the list is of Jewish origin and the nearest parallel is Philo, Leg ad Gaium 281-3.

[17] See Johnson 1992, p47. For a discussion of the historicity of the event and the likely traditions Luke used, see Barrett 1994, p107-110.

[18] On the textual variants see Barrett 1994, p117.

[19] See Lk 11:26; 13:4; Acts 1:19; 4:16; 7:2, 4, 48; 9:22, 32, 35; 11:29; 13:27; 17:24, 26; 19:10, 17; 22:12. Louw and Nida (1988, vol 1, p731) give the meaning as "to live or dwell in a place in an established or settled manner". See also Johnson 1992, p43.

[20] Lake and Cadbury 1933b, p113; Taylor 1999, p409 note the problem. Clearly, κατοικοῦντες cannot have the same meaning in v5 and v9.

[21] See Taylor 1999, p408.

[22] See Josephus, War 1:397, 437, 672; Acts 6:9, 22:3. Those from Rome who are described as οἱ ἐπιδημοῦντες Ῥωμαῖοι may have been genuine visitors in the city for a very brief period, although ἐπιδημέω can be used for those who live more or less permanently in a place which is not their own country; see Liddell and Scott 1940, p630; Louw and Nida 1988, vol 1, p732 who give the meaning as "to dwell more or less permanently in a place which is not one's own country." This is the meaning of ἐπιδημέω in Acts 17:21. So those from Rome could also be people who once lived in Rome, but are now resident in Jerusalem; see Johnson 1992, p44. Lake and Cadbury 1933b, p113 note that it is very doubtful whether there was clear difference in Luke's mind between κατοικέω and ἐπιδημέω, and that it was

The other possibility is that those from Mesopotamia and Asia were genuine visitors to the city, in which case they would be pilgrims in Jerusalem for the Pentecost festival.[23] We certainly know that large crowds came to Jerusalem for Pentecost, including pilgrims from the Diaspora.[24] However, Luke does not seem to have these pilgrims in view. Certainly if he did mean these people, he could have made that explicit. His use of κατοικέω strongly suggests he means permanent residents, not pilgrims. Further, Luke presents those converted on this occasion as foundation members of the new Church in Jerusalem (Acts 2:41-7). This strongly suggests that for Luke these people were not pilgrims, many of whom would need to return home quickly, but rather people who lived in Jerusalem on a fairly permanent basis.[25] Thus, although there would have been pilgrims from the Diaspora for the Pentecost festival, Luke seems to indicate that this was not the dominant group which was present when the events described in Acts 2 occurred.

Luke records that many Jews became Christians on this occasion. Of course, we do not know if representatives of all the different groups present became Christians, but Luke does record that 3,000 people who were present on the day of Pentecost believed (2:41) and others were added later (2:47), so it is likely that some Jews originally from Asia became Christians at this time. Since Ephesus was the leading city of Asia, and since, as we have seen in chapter 1 there was a significant Jewish community in Ephesus, it is possible that some of the Jews from Asia were from Ephesus and became Christians. We can suggest - although we can do no more than this - that some of these Christians returned to Ephesus at some stage, perhaps months or years after Pentecost.[26] Perhaps they formed the nucleus of the earliest group of believers in Ephesus.

We do not know what sort of theology such believers would have taken back to Ephesus. If they stayed in Jerusalem for a significant time, perhaps

---

his custom to vary his phrase without changing his meaning. However, Barrett (1994, p123, his emphasis) thinks they are "temporarily resident in Jerusalem: ἐπιδημεῖν is to be distinguished from κατοικεῖν".

[23] See Bruce 1988, p53.

[24] See Josephus Ant. 14:337; 17:254; War 1:253; 2:42-3.

[25] See Johnson 1992, p43; Williams 1990, p42; Schneider 1980, p251; Pesch 1986, 1, p100; cf. Causse 1940, p125-8.

[26] Michaels (1988, p9) notes on the origins of the churches in Asia Minor: "there had perhaps been pilgrims returning to 'Cappadocia, Pontus and Asia, Phrygia and Pamphylia' (Acts 2:9-10) after the sermon of Peter at Pentecost." (See also Bruce 1988, p57; Worth 1999a, p82; cf. Brown and Meier 1983, p104 n215.) The point is still valid, even if we see the people from Asia, not as pilgrims, but as Asian Jews who had settled in Jerusalem. Cranford 1980, p26 thinks the beginnings of the Christian community on Crete is to be traced back to Pentecost and Cretan converts there (Acts 2:11).

they would have been influenced by the Hellenists, but this is pure speculation.

3. Paul, Priscilla and Aquila arrive in Ephesus and Priscilla and Aquila's activity in the city (Acts 18:18-21, 26)

According to Acts 18:18-21, Paul traveled with Priscilla[27] and Aquila from Corinth to Ephesus, where Priscilla and Aquila remained. We will briefly discuss what Luke says about Paul's visit to Ephesus at this point and then will discuss Priscilla and Aquila's activity.

In Acts 18:19-21 Paul is said to go into the synagogue in Ephesus and argue with the Jews. He is asked to stay on, but declines, and promises to return if this is God's will.[28] The passage suggests that the Jews in Ephesus were receptive to Paul's message.[29] However, we have no confirmation of this first short visit to Ephesus from Paul's letters,[30] and doubts have been raised about the historicity of v19b-21a.[31] But little is at stake for us here, since this section offers us no detailed information.

---

[27] Luke always uses the diminutive form of her name, Priscilla.

[28] In 19:21 the Western and Byzantine texts read: "he took leave of them saying, 'I must by all means keep the coming festival in Jerusalem, but I will return ....'" Bruce 1988, p356 notes that if the festival was the Passover, then there was good reason for his haste (see Acts 18:20), since navigation could not begin until around March 10th and Passover was in early April in 52 CE. His hasty departure was thus to catch a ship. But it is unlikely that the Western and Byzantine texts are original here.

[29] Thus Luke shows that the prohibition on Paul preaching in Asia (see Acts 16:6) has now been lifted; see Williams 1990, p322. The receptiveness of the Jews in Ephesus is also suggested by Acts 19:8, where we are told that he spent three months preaching in the synagogue when he returned to Ephesus. We will discuss this in more detail in the section on "Success in Ephesus".

[30] See Trebilco 1993, p455. Note, however, that many scholars do think Paul travelled from Corinth to Jerusalem at this point as described in Acts 18:22, but that this was for the Apostolic Conference of Acts 15 and Gal 2; see Jewett 1979, p78-85. If Paul did travel from Corinth to Jerusalem at this time it could well have been via Ephesus.

[31] It has been argued that Luke has inserted v19b-21a at this point in order to present Paul as the first missionary preacher in Ephesus; see Haenchen 1971, p543; Schneider 1982, p254; Pesch 1986, 2, p155; Conzelmann 1987, p155. This is possible, since 18:19 is strange: "And they [Paul, Priscilla and Aquila] came to Ephesus, and he left them there; but he himself went into the synagogue, and argued with the Jews." Haenchen 1971, p547 asks "Did this synagogue then not also lie in Ephesus? Why did he not take the two with him? ... Finally, why does Paul go into the synagogue, only to depart at once with unreasonable haste, without taking advantage of the favourable mission opportunity which offered itself? All these difficulties disappear ... if we consider the words 'went into the synagogue ... if God is willing' in vv. 19-21 as an insertion." See also Conzelmann 1987, p155. One problem with this view is that, if Luke has added v19b-21a, then it seems likely that Luke

As we noted in the previous chapter, that Priscilla and Aquila were known in Corinth, but then traveled to Ephesus is confirmed by 1 Corinthians, written from Ephesus, since in 1 Cor 16:19 Paul passes on their greetings to the church in Corinth. We have already noted in Chapter 2 that 1 Cor 16:19 was written towards the end of Paul's more than two years and three months stay in Ephesus. Thus, Priscilla and Aquila arrived in Ephesus with Paul (who then departed (Acts 18:18-19)) and were still in the city when 1 Cor was written, which was probably over three years after their arrival,[32] and had a house church meeting in their home (1 Cor 16:19) – although of course they may have been absent from Ephesus for a period of this time. 1 Cor 4:12 ("we labour, working with our own hands") suggests that Paul continued to be a tent-maker in Ephesus, and since Aquila was a tentmaker, Paul probably worked in conjunction with Priscilla and Aquila as he did in Corinth (Acts 18:3).[33] Given all that we know about Priscilla and Aquila, Murphy-O'Connor plausibly suggests that they went to Ephesus from Corinth as part of Paul's missionary strategy, rather than for economic reasons.[34] All of this

---

would have indicated that Paul converted some people during the visit, and thus made him not just the first preacher in Ephesus, but the founder of the church. However, Luke does not record any conversions and further he makes it clear in 18:27 that there were Christians in Ephesus prior to any recorded conversions by Paul (see below). Given that Luke does not conceal this fact, he does not attempt to present Paul as the founder of the church in Ephesus. We can also suggest that it is not simply being the first preacher in a city which is important for Luke but rather founding the church; see Acts 13:43, 48; 16:11-15, 31-4; 17:4, 12, 34; 18:8. Thus the passage could well be historical, since if Luke had added it, it seems likely that he would have said Paul had converted people in Ephesus, not simply preached. (Note Barrett's comment (1998, p878-9) "Paul's visit must appear fruitless and pointless, and this is against its being a Lucan insertion.") We can also note that both Haenchen (1971, p543 n3) and Conzelmann (1987, p155) accept that v19a is historical, and Pesch (1986, 2, p154) thinks Luke used a source in v18-19b and v22-23; see also Schnabel 1999, p370. The source would then include the detail that Paul visited Ephesus at this time, en route from Corinth to Caesarea. If this is the case, then even if v19b-21a are an insertion (as Marshall 1980, p301 also thinks), then it is at the very least possible, and it is probably likely, that on his first visit to Ephesus Paul would indeed have taken the opportunity to visit the synagogue (see Marshall 1980, p301). Thus v19b-21a may be an insertion by Luke which actually clarifies what took place. However, as we noted in the text, it provides us with no detailed information about Paul or the Christians in Ephesus.

[32] This is allowing time for Paul's travel in Acts 18:22-23; Murphy-O'Connor (1996, p28-31, 171) estimates this time as a year.

[33] Two other factors in the Acts narrative have been connected with Paul's work as a tent-maker. Firstly, it is suggested that the handkerchiefs and aprons of Acts 19:12 were connected with his work as a tent-maker. Secondly, the Western text of Acts 19:9 has Paul arguing in the hall of Tyrannus from the fifth hour to the tenth. This would be when others were not working during the siesta, but also when Paul himself was not working.

[34] Murphy-O'Connor 1992, p50-1.

suggests a close collaboration in mission work between Paul and Priscilla and Aquila for most of the time Paul was in Ephesus.

According to Acts 18:26, Priscilla and Aquila were active in the synagogue in Ephesus and encountered Apollos there. Clearly they discerned something was amiss in his knowledge, and so "took him aside and explained the Way of God to him more accurately". We will discuss what was lacking in Apollos' knowledge shortly; here we note the teaching activity of Priscilla and Aquila. What can we conclude about them from these two Lucan notes and from the other New Testament references to them?

Firstly, the extent of their travel (Rome to Corinth (Acts 18:2) to Ephesus (1 Cor 16:19; Acts 18:18-21) and later to Rome (Rom 16:3-5)) and the fact that they can host house churches (1 Cor 16:19; Rom 16:5) has suggested to some that they are reasonably wealthy,[35] but we need to note that neither extensive travel nor hosting a house church are necessarily signs of significant wealth or social status.[36]

Secondly, Paul clearly regards them as amongst his closest and most valued co-workers and certainly they were in agreement with him theologically. In Rom 16:3, Prisca and Aquila are the first people to be greeted by Paul, with only the carrier of the letter, Phoebe, mentioned before them.[37] There Paul calls them συνεργοί, fellow workers in Christ Jesus. Paul uses the term of a number of his associates, such as Timothy (Rom 16:21), Titus (2 Cor 8:23), Epaphroditus (Phil 2:25) and Philemon (Phlm 1), with reference to those who labour alongside him in the service of God, probably in a whole range of activity including mission preaching, discipling new converts and pastoral responsibility for churches.[38] In Rom 16:3 then Paul states that Prisca and Aquila are part of this group who, as full colleagues, worked alongside Paul in ministry.

Paul also shows the great esteem in which he held Prisca and Aquila in the next phrase in Rom 16:3: "to whom not only I give thanks, but also all the churches of the Gentiles." The churches of the Gentiles were probably thankful for Prisca and Aquila's leadership and gifts because they were

---

[35] Thompson 1990, p118 writes: "From their mobility, occupation, and house churches we may conclude that these church leaders and devout Christians were fairly wealthy independent artisans."

[36] See Meggitt 1998, p129-35. For example, on p134 he notes: "All but the enslaved or the sick could journey at their own volition." See also Murphy-O'Connor 1992, p49. On Meggitt's work see Martin 2001, p51-64; Theissen 2001, p65-84 and the response in Meggitt 2001, p85-94.

[37] Käsemann 1980, p413, notes: "As the most prominent members of the community Prisca and Aquila are emphatically put first, and they receive almost extravagant praise."

[38] On the term see TDNT 7, p874-6; Dunn 1988, p892; see also 1 Cor 3:9; Col 4:10,11; Rom 16:9. Some of those described as συνεργοί probably worked with Paul, others independently of him.

considerably involved in missionary work among Gentiles along with Paul and on their own. They seem to have had a very considerable and widespread impact in the Gentile mission. It is noteworthy then that they were active in Ephesus for a considerable period of time alongside Paul.

Thirdly, on four of the six occasions when the couple are mentioned Priscilla is listed first (see Rom 16:3; Acts 18:18, 26, 2 Tim 4:19), which is unusual.[39] This may be an indication that she was of higher social status than Aquila,[40] or it may be that she was "the more prominent in Christian activity."[41] Further as Barrett notes: "Aquila is unique in the NT in that whenever he is named his wife is named too. ... It is most improbable that she [Priscilla] would have been mentioned so frequently by name if she had not been an outstanding person in her own right."[42] Certainly there is no indication that she had a different or less significant role in ministry than Aquila. Further, we note that in both Rom 16:5 and 1 Cor 16:19 Paul speaks of "the church in *their* (αὐτῶν) house". Since the male had special rights as head of the household, we would expect Paul to speak of "the church in Aquila's house";[43] that he does not again suggests that Paul saw Prisca as an important leader in the church.

Fourthly, and related to this point, since she is mentioned first when Luke speaks about Priscilla and Aquila teaching Apollos (Acts 18:26), it is clear that Priscilla is a teacher in her own right.[44] Luke notes that Apollos already knew the things concerning Jesus, so Priscilla and Aquila are to be thought of as teaching him matters beyond basic Christian teaching; since the one deficiency in Apollos' understanding mentioned in the text is that he knew only the baptism of John, Priscilla and Aquila would have taught him about Christian baptism, and perhaps other areas as well.[45] Clearly, Priscilla and Aquila were adept and knowledgeable in matters of the faith and in the Scriptures, and thus could instruct Apollos. Further, as MacDonald notes, "Even if we are to understand Priscilla and Aquila's taking of Apollos aside as bringing him into their home for some private teaching (cf. 1 Cor 16:19), we should not underestimate the significance of the act. The home was the basic

---

[39] The other two passages are Acts 18:2; 1 Cor 16:19.

[40] See Meeks 1983, p59; Thompson 1990, p226 n4; Martin 1994, p785; MacDonald 1999b, p241.

[41] Bauckham 1992, p244; see also Fee 1988, p300; Furnish 1979, p107; Murphy-O'Connor 1992, p42.

[42] Barrett 1998, p861.

[43] Furnish 1979, p106.

[44] See MacDonald 1999b, p241. That Priscilla is mentioned first in Acts 18:26 suggested to John Chrysostom (337-404 C.E.) that she took the lead in teaching Apollos. For John Chrysostom's view see Witherington 1988, p154.

[45] See Witherington 1988, p154; Meeks 1983, p133, who calls Priscilla and Aquila "theological instructors of considerable power."

cell of organization in the Pauline mission; it was the arena of celebration, teaching, and probably often also of conversion (cf. Acts 16:14-15, 40)."[46]

We also need to note here that in Acts Luke downplays the leadership roles of women. Details about the activity of women are offered very briefly and only in passing in Acts. Despite Luke showing that women make up a very significant group among converts to the new faith, "Luke attributes extremely minimal narrative discourses to women ... Women are virtually silent in Acts."[47] We note, for example, that very little information is given about the four daughters of Philip, who are mentioned in Acts 21:9. D'Angelo notes that although Acts gives the rationale for women as prophets in Acts 2:17-18, and the daughters of Philip are mentioned as prophesying (Acts 21:9), no prophecies are attributed to them. "This is the more conspicuous in that they are encircled by the prophecies of others. Immediately after they are mentioned, Agabus foretells Paul's arrest (21:10-12), while shortly before, anonymous disciples from Judea are said to warn in the spirit that Paul should not go up to Jerusalem (21:4)."[48] Thus MacDonald notes: "The author of Acts clearly does not want to emphasize women's prophetic activities."[49] The one form of women's activity of which Luke seems to approve is benefaction.[50]

Against this background, the portrayal of Priscilla as not only teaching Apollos, but also being mentioned first when this teaching activity is spoken of (Acts 18:26; cf 18:2), is especially noteworthy. As Martin notes with regard to Priscilla, "In a rare and unusual portrayal in Acts, we see a woman exercising decisive leadership and sustained intellectual engagement and instruction with a male who was himself an 'eloquent man, well-versed in the scriptures'."[51] MacDonald also draws a helpful wider conclusion: "The prominence of Priscilla in Acts should probably be taken as confirmation of the importance of her leadership during Paul's day; she was so well known as a teacher and missionary leader that her role could not be circumscribed."[52]

All of this would mean that the Ephesian Pauline community, and particularly the Ephesian women, had a role model of an active woman leader. We also note that the tradition emphasizes Priscilla's significance (as noted,

---

[46] MacDonald 1999b, p241.

[47] Martin 1994, p777. For women as a significant group among converts see for example, Acts 17:4, 12.

[48] D'Angelo 1990, p453.

[49] MacDonald 1999b, p239. In general on Luke proscribing and delimiting the role of women in Acts see Martin 1994, p763-99; MacDonald 1999b, p238-41.

[50] Note for example, Lydia's activity (Acts 16:15). MacDonald (1999b, p239) notes that in Acts "one detects a subtle attempt to play down leadership functions that may have sprung out of, or even gone beyond the boundaries of, the role of female patron."

[51] Martin 1994, p785.

[52] MacDonald 1999b, p241.

she is mentioned first in 4 of the 6 references) but, in that Priscilla and Aquila are always mentioned together, it also emphasizes their mutuality and partnership.[53]

Fifthly, we have noted that Priscilla and Aquila encounter Apollos in the synagogue. This clearly suggests that they are active in mission there and may well have had a considerable impact, although Luke says nothing about this.[54]

Thus we conclude that Priscilla and Aquila were highly esteemed coworkers of Paul who were probably in Ephesus for most of the duration of the Pauline mission in the city. We are justified in regarding them as among the leading missionaries of the Early Church.[55] We also note Priscilla's significance as a teacher and leader in her own right.

4. Apollos in Ephesus (Acts 18:24-8)

In Acts 18:24-8 Luke writes of the activity of Apollos, Priscilla and Aquila in Ephesus while Paul is elsewhere (18:22-19:1). Luke presents Apollos as a person of some ability. He was a Jew from Alexandria[56] and Luke describes him as "ἀνὴρ λόγιος", which here means either eloquent or learned and probably implies "rhetorical ability, perhaps also rhetorical training".[57] He was also described as being "powerful in the scriptures" ("δυνατὸς ... ἐν ταῖς γραφαῖς"; 18:24), which indicates his understanding of and ability to use the Scriptures in debate, an ability he later shows in refuting Jews in

---

[53] Martin (1994, p796, her emphasis) notes: "they appear to function as an energetic and effective wife-husband team, *together* exercising leadership and pastoral oversight in the church in their house, and actively engaged in a teaching ministry to and with both men and women. .. That Luke depicts the social interaction between Priscilla and Aquila based on links of mutuality rather than domination and subservience is unmistakable. The tradition provides a rare and inviting cameo of ... co-leadership ... and interdependency."

[54] We will discuss possible evidence of their impact below.

[55] Käsemann 1980, p413. Note that they are mentioned in 2 Tim 4:19.

[56] Much is made by some of his Alexandrian origins and that he may have had a theology similar to Philo, but as Barrett (1998, p887) notes: "Little can be made of the reference to Alexandria .... Philo was not a representative Alexandrian Jew, and it should not be assumed that Apollos must have been a philosopher and allegorist." See also Ker 2000, p77. If Apollos was instructed about Christianity in Alexandria (see v25), which is possible, then we can say nothing about the sort of Christianity he would have learned there, since we know nothing about Christianity in Alexandria in the first century. On the variant in 18:25, which places Apollos' instruction in the way of the Lord in Alexandria but is probably not original, see Barrett 1998, p887-8; cf. Nodet and Taylor 1998, p313-14.

[57] Meeks 1983, p61; see also BDAG, p598. In any case the two meanings are connected since to be educated in antiquity generally involved training in rhetoric. Pogoloff (1992, p180-7) thinks that as an educated Alexandrian (an "ἀνὴρ λόγιος") Apollos was well trained in rhetoric, and discusses the nature of Alexandrian rhetoric.

Corinth (18:28).[58] We are told that Apollos taught in the synagogue in Ephesus but that Priscilla and Aquila recognised that he needed further instruction so they took him aside and taught him further. We are next told that Apollos wished to go to Achaia, so the Ephesian Christians wrote a letter of recommendation for him. Apollos then travelled to Achaia and had a successful ministry there, "for he powerfully refuted the Jews in public, showing by the scriptures that the Messiah is Jesus" (Acts 18:28).

We have discussed Apollos' role in Corinth briefly in Chapter 2 and will expand on that a little here.[59] We learn from 1 Corinthians that Apollos worked in Corinth after Paul founded the community there, since Paul writes that "I planted, Apollos watered" (1 Cor 3:6). Apollos seems to have been independent of Paul, although Paul recognised him as a co-worker (1 Cor 16:12). It is clear from 1 Corinthians that Apollos made a significant impact in Corinth, which testifies to his ability. It is also likely that his work in Corinth led to an emphasis on wisdom and on effective speaking in that Christian community, although it seems likely that the factionalism that resulted was neither approved of nor encouraged by Apollos.[60] This means that we have some independent confirmation of what is said in Acts concerning Apollos' ability and that he travelled to Corinth.[61] That the Corinthians asked Paul, while he was in Ephesus (1 Cor 16:8), to urge Apollos to visit Corinth (1 Cor 16:12) shows that Apollos had been in Ephesus;[62] thus that Apollos had a connection with Ephesus is also confirmed by Paul's letters. Of course, these points do not confirm the historicity of the other elements of this section in Acts, but it does suggest there is some reliable tradition here.[63]

---

[58] Manson (1962, p255) suggests: "Luke means us to gather that Apollos had a masterly knowledge of the O.T."

[59] Note that at Acts 18:24 some manuscripts read Ἀπελλῆς rather than Ἀπολλῶς; however Barrett (1998, p886) concludes that the same person is mentioned in Acts and 1 Cor.

[60] On Apollos in Corinth see 1 Cor 1:12; 3:4-5; 4:6; see also Richardson 1984, p104-110; Pogoloff 1992, p180-90; Thiessen 1995, p44-5; Carter 1997, p58-61; Ker 2000, p75-97. On wisdom and effective speaking in Corinth, see for example 1 Cor 1:17, 23-24; 2:8; 3:18-23. The positive tone of Paul's remarks about Apollos in 1 Cor 3:5-9 and 16:12 suggest that Apollos was not the actual cause of the problems Paul encountered in Corinth; the problem was caused by the way some of the Corinthians reacted to Apollos. Perhaps the fact that Paul gives attention to wisdom and effective speaking in 1 Cor 1-4 is related to Apollos' probable ability in rhetoric, even if it was the Corinthians' own adoption of these themes that was the more proximate cause for them being on Paul's agenda.

[61] Johnson 1992, p335 notes the information on Apollos 'coincide[s] nicely (though not *too* precisely) with the picture provided of Apollos by Paul in First Corinthians.' See also Richardson 1984, p107.

[62] See the treatment of this verse in Chapter 2, section 1.8.

[63] Thus Barrett (1998, p859) writes of the story in 18:24-8 that "Luke probably found [it] in existence".

There has been much speculation about Apollos[64] and a number of points about the passage are debated.[65] The following observations are relevant here.

4.1 Apollos prior to his instruction by Priscilla and Aquila (Acts 18:24-5)

We will argue that Luke presents Apollos as a Christian prior to his meeting with Priscilla and Aquila; but Luke also indicates that there was an inadequacy in his knowledge, since according to Luke "he knew only the baptism of John" (Acts 18:25), that is the baptism administered by John. This suggests that he knew about Jesus' life (and see below) but that he knew nothing of baptism in the name of Jesus, as proclaimed, for example, by Peter on the day of Pentecost.[66] However, Apollos is not presented as a member of an illegitimate sect or something similar. The following points indicate that Luke considered Apollos was a Christian prior to his meeting with Priscilla and Aquila.

Firstly, Luke says that Apollos "had been instructed in the Way of the Lord"; this almost certainly refers to elements of the new faith. Luke uses the term "the Way" as a shorthand for the Christian "way of life" or "manner of life".[67] The term designates what is distinctive about the new faith, as compared with Judaism (see 9:2; 24:14, 22).[68] Thus in Acts 18:25 when Luke says Apollos "had been instructed in the Way of the Lord" we should think of distinctively Christian teaching.

Secondly, Luke says that Apollos "taught accurately the things concerning Jesus (τὰ περὶ τοῦ Ἰησοῦ)" (18:25). This resembles "τὰ περὶ τῆς βασιλείας - the things concerning the kingdom" in Acts 1:3 and probably includes both sayings and stories concerning Jesus.[69] What Paul said in Rome is described similarly (see 28:31); it clearly must be a description of Christian teaching and of content that is distinctive to the new faith.[70]

---

[64] For example, Manson (1962, p242-58) suggested that Apollos wrote Hebrews.

[65] Thus we do not know where he learnt the Scriptures; Conzelmann 1987, p157 suggests it was in Alexandria; see also Taylor 1996, p15.

[66] See Lake and Cadbury 1933a, p231; Conzelmann 1987, p158; Bruce 1988, p359.

[67] See for example Acts 9:2; 19:9, 23; 22:4; 24:14, 22.

[68] The "Way of the Lord" here is thus the Way of Jesus. Note also for Luke the expressions "the Way of the Lord" (18:25) and "the Way of God" (18:26) are almost certainly synonymous with "the Way" as is shown by the similarity between 18:26 ("explained the way of God to him more accurately (ἀκριβέστερον)") and 24:22 ("having a rather accurate knowledge (ἀκριβέστερον) of the Way"). See Lyonnet 1981, p153-4; Fieger 1998, p55. On the term "the Way" in 18:25, 26 see Lyonnet 1981, p149-64; Thiessen 1995, p55-6. Manson (1962, p255) thinks the "Way of the Lord" "means the way of life set forth in the teaching and by the example of Jesus".

[69] See Johnson 1992, p332; Manson 1962, p255.

[70] We can note that in the context "the things concerning Jesus" seem to include the baptism administered by John, but not baptism in the name of Jesus, since Apollos seems to be unaware of this; see Lake and Cadbury 1933a, p231.

Thirdly, sandwiched between these two clauses is the phrase "ζέων τῷ πνεύματι ἐλάλει". The fact that the clause is found between two phrases which concern Apollos as a Christian and as part of the new movement is decisive for its meaning. Hence this phrase almost certainly refers to another element of the new faith - that Apollos was "speaking fervently in the (Holy) Spirit",[71] rather than being a reference to Apollos' human spirit.[72] Further, Luke almost always uses πνεύμα (without ἅγιος) of the Holy Spirit rather than of the human spirit.[73]

Fourthly, we note that Apollos had only received John the Baptist's baptism, and not Christian baptism.[74] How can we explain this? That Apollos was already "fervent in the (Holy) Spirit", as we have argued, helps us to understand this note about baptism, for it explains one key difference between this passage and Acts 19:1-7: that the Ephesian 12 are baptised in the name of the Lord Jesus (19:5), whereas Apollos is not.[75] If Apollos did not possess the Holy Spirit before he met Priscilla and Aquila, but was only "ardent in spirit", then it is difficult to see why he was not baptised in the name of Jesus. He would have been comparable to the Ephesian 12 who (also had

---

[71] Alternatively, ἐλάλει could be taken with what follows, but the point made in the text would not be altered by this.

[72] That ζέων τῷ πνεύματι here means "fervently in the (Holy) Spirit" or something similar see Lake and Cadbury 1933a, p233; Käsemann 1964, p143; Bruce 1988, p359; Barrett 1988, p888; Fieger 1998, p61. Barrett (1998, p888) also notes "it is unlikely that one as interested as Luke in phenomena due to the Spirit would use ζέων τῷ πνεύματι to mean no more than an effervescent, lively human spirit." In addition, in 18:26 Luke says that Apollos preached boldly (παρρησιάζεσθαι) in the synagogue. In 4:13 Luke says that the boldness (παρρησία) of Peter and John was noted by members of the Council; in 4:8 Luke had said that Peter was "πλησθεὶς πνεύματος ἁγίου", and it seems clear that Peter's boldness (and implicitly John's also) was as a result of the Spirit. Acts 4:31 also makes the connection between being filled with the Spirit and speaking with boldness explicit. Hence, when in 18:26 Luke says that Apollos spoke with boldness in the synagogue, this seems to be because of the Spirit, since in Acts boldness is a result of the Spirit's activity. Thus Williams (1990, p327) comments: "That Apollos had received the Spirit may have been assumed by Luke in his reference to his preaching 'boldly' (v. 26; cf. 4:13; see 4:8)". This is therefore another indicator that "ζέων τῷ πνεύματι" should be interpreted as "speaking fervently in the (Holy) Spirit". Further, the phrase "τῷ πνεύματι ζέοντες" is found in Rom 12:11 and there it almost certainly means "be fervent in the Spirit". Although Paul's usage is not decisive for Luke, his usage in this way does add weight to our argument; see also Barrett 1998, p888.

[73] See for example Acts 2:4; 6:10; 8:29; 10:19; 11:12, 28; 20:22; 21:4; cf. the meaning of 19:21 is debated; see Barrett 1998, p919.

[74] Barrett (1998, p888) notes that ἐπιστάμενος means "being aware of, having experience of".

[75] Barrett (1998, p885 and 1984, p36-8) argues convincingly that Luke intended the two stories to be read together, interpreting each in the light of the other. They are united by two themes, the work of John the Baptist and the Holy Spirit.

experienced John's baptism but) did not know the Spirit, and so were baptised and then were filled with the Spirit. It is much more likely that, since Apollos had been filled with the Spirit (and also had been "instructed in the way of the Lord"), his earlier baptism by John was deemed sufficient and counted for Christian baptism and thus made baptism in the name of Jesus unnecessary, as seems to have been the case with the 120 who received the Spirit on the day of Pentecost.[76] The 120 were not baptised in the name of Jesus because they had already received John's baptism, which was then completed by baptism in the Spirit. That Apollos was not baptised in the name of Jesus seems to confirm that for Luke Apollos was already filled with the Spirit, and already a Christian. Thus we can adequately explain this feature of the passage. We conclude that Luke clearly presents Apollos as a believer before he met Priscilla and Aquila, although as we will see, there was a defect in his knowledge.[77]

However, it has been suggested that v25c-26 ("though he knew only the baptism of John ... more accurately") is an addition by Luke to his source.[78] Käsemann and following him Haenchen, have argued that Luke added v25c-26 in order to incorporate Apollos into the apostolic Church. It is noted that v25c-26 are disruptive in this context since they suggest that this eminent and eloquent student of the Scriptures who taught accurately concerning Jesus still needed some elementary instruction. If these verses are bracketed out, the contradiction disappears. For Käsemann and Haenchen, Apollos was in fact a Christian teacher independent of apostolic Christianity, whom Luke, through his addition to the passage, has depicted as still imperfect only so that he may be brought within the fold of the apostolic church in this passage.[79]

Käsemann's treatment of the passage can be subjected to a number of criticisms. Firstly, the whole concept underlying this view is that Luke was an advocate of "the one catholic church" and so endeavoured to present the

---

[76] Williams 1990, p327; Lampe 1951, p66. Bruce (1988, p364) also notes of the 120 at Pentecost: "Probably their endowment with the Spirit at Pentecost transformed the preparatory significance of the baptism which they had already received into the consummative significance of Christian baptism." Similarly for Apollos, John's baptism *plus* the receiving of the Spirit conveyed all that Christian baptism could have conveyed.

[77] Schweizer (1955, p245-54) is wrong, then, when he assumes that in v24-5 Apollos is still being characterized as a Jew. Schweizer argued that originally the story of his conversion would have been recounted in this passage, and Luke has modified it. Conzelmann notes (1987, p158): "But the Lukan style of characterization argues against Schweizer's view, as does the manner of expression, behind which we can detect no pre-Lukan stage." On Schweizer's view see also Barrett 1984, p34-6.

[78] Käsemann does not explicitly say that v26 is also an addition, but he clearly implies this in 1964, p147; see also Haenchen 1971, p555-7.

[79] Käsemann 1964, p143-8; Haenchen 1971, p556-7. Haenchen (p556) writes: "for Luke it was intrinsically impossible for a missionary to have worked independently .. alongside the apostolic Church."

church in the early period as united. Hence, for Käsemann, Apollos, who actually represented a separate strand of Christianity, was here incorporated under Paul's wing. But strong arguments can be mounted against the view that Luke advocates the idea of "the one catholic church".[80] Thus a crucial foundation of Käsemann's explanation of the passage must be questioned; that Luke edited the passage to incorporate the independent Apollos into "apostolic Christianity" in accordance with such a concept thus seems unlikely.

Secondly, in order to argue his case, Käsemann must ignore 1 Cor 16:12 in which Paul speaks warmly of Apollos, and 1 Cor 3:6-9 which shows that Paul did in fact see Apollos as "God's fellow-worker", and as one who was working alongside himself.[81] These two verses suggest that Apollos was not completely independent of Paul to the extent of needing to be incorporated into "the apostolic church", but rather was in fundamental agreement with Paul. Käsemann's view does not take these verses sufficiently seriously. In fact, the inference from Acts 18:26 that Apollos was loosely connected with the Pauline circle is supported by Paul's writings.

Thirdly, Käsemann's view suggests that Acts 18:24-8 presents Apollos as subordinate to Paul. However, Acts 18:24-8 does not require this conclusion. Luke does not present Apollos as joining Priscilla and Aquila as one of Paul's underlings, but rather as going on an independent mission to Corinth and this is borne out by 1 Cor 3:5-6. If Luke had wanted to subordinate Apollos to Paul he could have done so much more effectively by having Paul himself teach Apollos.[82]

Finally, it is unlikely that Luke introduced v25c ("though he knew only the baptism of John"). If we are correct that "ζέων τῷ πνεύματι" should be interpreted as "speaking fervently in the (Holy) Spirit", then if Luke added Acts 18:25c he would have *created* in Apollos a person who was filled with the Spirit without having received Christian baptism (but rather only John's baptism). This would have created a sharp contrast with Luke's normal presentation of people being baptised in the name of Jesus, and then receiving the Spirit (eg Acts 2:38). There are exceptions to this rule in Acts, but they are in extenuating circumstances,[83] of which there seems to be no trace here.

---

[80] See Barrett 1982, p35-6 and in particular 1998, pxciii-xcvii. Note for example, that nothing is said at all about apostolic succession in 20:17-35 (where it would have ideally belonged – it is rather the Spirit who appoints leaders (20:28)), and that 20:17-35 also predicts later trouble in the church, rather than that the church of Luke's time will be one and undivided.

[81] See Käsemann 1964, p145-7; Haenchen 1971, p556, who ignore these points.

[82] See Barrett 1984, p34.

[83] For example, 8:4-17 on which see Dunn 1970, p55-72. In 10:44-48 the gentile Cornelius is baptised *after* his reception of the Spirit as a sign of his being welcomed into the new community, but Apollos is a Jew. Those who first received the Spirit at Pentecost

This suggests Luke did not add v25c (but rather found it in his source), which in turn suggests he did not add v26 either, since the two are intimately connected. This also argues against Käsemann's explanation of the passage. Käsemann's whole analysis is suspect therefore and we do not need to see v25c-26 as Lucan additions. Rather, we can accept the story as credible, particularly given that in Paul's letters we have some independent confirmation of what is said in Acts concerning Apollos' ability and his connections with both Ephesus and Corinth.[84]

How is all of this relevant to our enquiry? Luke tells us that prior to Apollos' meeting with Priscilla and Aquila, Apollos spoke boldly in the synagogue. This could be taken to suggest that Apollos had a significant impact in the synagogue at this point, and that his preaching resulted in a group which followed him. What sort of beliefs would such followers have? Although, according to Luke, such converts would have been deficient as

---

(Acts 2:2-4) who probably also had only received John's baptism, are also in quite a different position from Apollos as those present, according to Luke, at the founding of the Church.

[84] We can also note that there seems no reason why Apollos could not be learned in the scriptures (Acts 18:24), and limited in his knowledge (18:25c) at the same time. Barrett suggests that both 18:24-8 and 19:1-7 concern diverse reactions to the disciples of John (1982, p29-39; 1998, p884-6, 898). He implies that Apollos and the twelve were historically in essentially the same position (knowing John's baptism only, but not being "Christians"). Luke's sources spoke of the different ways Apollos and the 12 were treated and this testified to the different ways of receiving John's disciples into the early church – some in the early Church argued that John's disciples simply needed further instruction prior to acceptance in the Church (as Apollos does); others argued that such disciples had to be baptised in the name of Jesus and receive the Spirit (as the 12 do). Luke explains the different treatment of Apollos and the 12 in his sources by "making Apollos more and the twelve less Christian." (Barrett 1982, p38). Thus in Acts Apollos is well instructed, fervent in the Holy Spirit and teaches about Jesus. The 12 by contrast have not even heard the Spirit exists. This redaction of his sources by Luke explains the different treatment in the narrative. But in fact the different treatment reflects the historical reality that John the Baptist's disciples were treated differently by different people in the early Church. This is an attractive explanation. However, it also raises the problem that Luke, through his redaction, would have created in Apollos a person who was filled with the Spirit without having received Christian baptism and who never receives Christian baptism. As noted in the text, this would have created a sharp contrast with Luke's normal presentation of people being baptised in the name of Jesus, and then receiving the Spirit (eg. Acts 2:38; as noted in the text, different treatment is always explained by extenuating circumstance, lacking here; or at the very least in Acts people receive both baptism and the Spirit at some point, even if the order varies). That Luke is happy to have such a contrast is possible, since as Barrett notes (1998, p885) we should not think that "Luke's mind worked within a rigid framework which assumed the absolute necessity of ecclesiastical regulations, including the requirement of baptism." But it seems simpler to suggest that Luke's sources actually spoke of Apollos as a Christian, including being ζέων τῷ πνεύματι, prior to meeting Priscilla and Aquila, while clearly this was not the case with the 12.

regards their knowledge (18:26a),[85] our discussion suggests that we are not to think of Apollos as converting people to some pre-Christian form of faith. Such converts may well have needed additional teaching, but nothing more that this. All his activity in Ephesus that we know of was as a Christian. This is an important conclusion.

Beyond this, we are left with unanswered questions. If Apollos did convert a number of people prior to his being taught "more accurately", what happened to these people? We do not know if Apollos was active in Ephesus for a period after he had been taught by Priscilla and Aquila and before he went to Corinth (Acts 18:27-8), but this seems likely; we have also noted in the previous chapter that 1 Cor 16:12 shows he had been back in Ephesus at some later point. Would he not himself have imparted the "more accurate" knowledge to any whom he had influenced or converted before being taught himself by Priscilla and Aquila? Or did Priscilla and Aquila teach these converts "more accurately" as well, or did Paul, when he worked in the synagogue later? In any case, it seems unlikely that there was a continuing group of Apollos' converts in Ephesus that stemmed from his activity prior to Priscilla and Aquila's tuition.

We also need to note that some scholars have seen the Ephesian 12 as Apollos' converts.[86] The link that is seen here is that both Apollos and the 12 know only the baptism of John.[87] However, there are important differences in the two stories as Luke tells them. Firstly, Apollos is, as we have argued, "fervent in the (Holy) Spirit" whereas the 12 "have not even heard that there is a Holy Spirit" (19:2). Secondly, Apollos is not baptised in the name of Jesus, while the 12 are. These differences make it unlikely that Luke wants us to see the 12 as Apollos' converts and as closely associated with him as regards their knowledge and understanding.

But has Luke's redaction altered the actual relationship between Apollos and the 12? We have seen that Apollos was almost certainly a Christian before he met Priscilla and Aquila. We will see that the 12 were probably

---

[85] Presumably, we are to think of Apollos "teaching accurately the things concerning Jesus", even though he knew only the baptism of John (18:25). This combination of statements has caused commentators much thought; see Haenchen 1971, p550, n10; Bruce 1988, p359-60.

[86] For example, Richardson (1984, p107) with reference to Acts 19:1-7: Paul "has re-baptized some of Apollos' converts in Ephesus." See also Taylor 1996, p27-8. Compare Fitzmyer 1998, p643.

[87] It has been suggested that Luke took the motif of the baptism of John from the story about the 12 and applied it in the story of Apollos, in order to make Apollos deficient in some way and thus to subordinate him to Paul and incorporate him into the apostolic church; see our discussion of Käsemann (1964, p136-48) above and see also Conzelmann 1987, p158. However, we have noted above that Käsemann's interpretation does not stand up to investigation.

disciples of John the Baptist before they met Paul. We have no reason to think that Apollos had any strong connection with John the Baptist,[88] and so no reason to suggest that Apollos and the 12 were connected historically. It seems more likely that both events occurred at Ephesus, and both concerned events near the beginning of the Christian mission in the city. Thus, because both stories mentioned John's baptism (albeit in slightly different contexts) and the Holy Spirit, Luke has given the two stories one after the other in his narrative.[89] But beyond this, there seems to be no historical connection between the two.

4.2 Apollos' instruction by Priscilla and Aquila (Acts 18:26)

As we have noted in discussing Priscilla and Aquila in Ephesus, Apollos preached in the synagogue in Ephesus where Priscilla and Aquila heard him and realised that he needed further instruction, which they proceeded to give him. What did Priscilla and Aquila teach Apollos? What does it mean that they "explained the Way of God to him more accurately" (18:26).[90] If he knew nothing of Christian baptism, as seems most likely, then it must have involved this at least. They may well have taught him in other areas, but given what Luke does and does not tell us, we have no firm basis for making other suggestions.

4.3 After Apollos' instruction by Priscilla and Aquila (Acts 18:27-8)

What was the nature of Apollos' activity in Ephesus after his conversion? Did he preach much in the synagogue after this point and before he went to Achaia? We know he later had a considerable impact in Corinth.[91] At this point did he have much of an impact in Ephesus?

According to Luke the believers in Ephesus wrote a letter of recommendation concerning Apollos to the Christians in Achaia (Acts 18:27),

---

[88] Beyond being baptised into John's baptism. Nothing suggests he was John's disciple, although admittedly our evidence about Apollos is limited.

[89] In Luke's narrative, it is helpful to read the two stories together (as we noted above), since then the contrasts between them aids interpretation. But this does not mean that Luke has redacted them to make the contrasts.

[90] Given that in v25 Luke says that Apollos had been instructed in "the way of the Lord", where "the Lord" is Jesus, and that he "taught accurately the things concerning Jesus", "the Way of God" in v26 must also be a reference to the Gospel, rather than to the (Jewish) way of God.

[91] See 1 Cor 3:5-6; 16:12.

which suggests that his work in Ephesus impressed the Ephesian Christians.[92] It seems then that before and probably after he had been taught by Priscilla and Aquila, Apollos made an impact in Ephesus. Further, we have already noted in Chapter 2 that 1 Cor 16:12 shows he was back in Ephesus at some later time, which suggests he was again involved in mission work in the city. Did an "Apollos party" develop in Ephesus, as it did in Corinth?[93]

In Chapter 2, section 1.8, we have suggested that 1 Cor 3:5-9; 16:12 do not support the view that Apollos worked against Paul in Ephesus or that he encouraged in Ephesus the same sort of party rivalry between supporters of Paul and supporters of Apollos (1 Cor 1:12) that developed in Corinth. Further, given that Paul and Apollos were both in Ephesus (although we do not know how long Apollos was in the city after he returned from Corinth (1 Cor 16:12)), and seem to be co-workers,[94] it is unlikely that they would have stood aside while such factionalism developed. So it is unlikely that there was an "Apollos party" in Ephesus which caused Paul similar problems to those he encountered in Corinth, and there is certainly no evidence for such an "Apollos party" in Ephesus (although this is hardly surprising given our limited evidence).

Further, in 1 Corinthians Paul never criticises Apollos' theological position and is in fact warm towards him (see 1 Cor 3:5-9; 16:12). The fact that he was taught by Paul's co-workers Priscilla and Aquila would support the contention that if Apollos did do any work in Ephesus it was of a "Pauline flavour". Hence, after Acts 18:26 we are to think of Apollos as in agreement with Paul on at least the foundations of the gospel, as Paul's positive remarks about Apollos show. We are certainly not to think of him as preaching a competing Gospel to Paul's. Although we can never disprove the suggestion that there was, for example, a house church founded by Apollos which had a continuing and distinctive life in Ephesus during and after Paul's mission, we have no positive evidence to back up such a suggestion, and even if such did exist, it may not have been particularly distinctive.

Three conclusions suggest themselves for this section then. Firstly, prior to his instruction by Priscilla and Aquila, Apollos preached in the synagogue in Ephesus as a Christian, but with inadequate understanding (18:25-6). Any converts he made at this time would have needed additional teaching, but we should not think of them as anything other than believers.

---

[92] Duncan (1929, p273) makes this suggestion. The further implications that Duncan draws about Apollos (p273-5) are based on his hypothesis that Phil was written from Ephesus.

[93] See above in the introduction to section 4 for a discussion of Apollos' impact in Corinth.

[94] This is Paul's view (1 Cor 3:5-9; 16:12), but would he have viewed Apollos so positively, and encouraged him to go back to Corinth (1 Cor 16:12) if Apollos had seen Paul as a bitter rival or enemy? Cf. Thiessen 1995, p45.

Secondly, it seems likely that Apollos had an impact in Ephesus prior to Paul's main work in the city (Acts 18:27); this may have introduced an element of diversity into the Christian community. However, we have no evidence for an identifiable "Apollos party" that continued to exist in Ephesus, nor for any on-going conflict between supporters of Paul and of Apollos in Ephesus.

Thirdly, Apollos, working alongside Paul although perhaps independently of him (cf. Acts 18:27; 1 Cor 16:12), but almost certainly not in opposition to him, may have been one of the factors in the growth of the Christian movement in Ephesus. He clearly had an impact in the city early on (Acts 18:27), and this may have been a continuing impact, since 1 Cor 16:12 suggests he had again been active in Ephesus. Paul's remarks about Apollos suggest it was an impact of which he himself approved.

5. Jewish Christians in Ephesus prior to Paul

We have noted that before Paul went on to Casearea, he entered the synagogue and argued with the Jews (18:19-21). However, Luke records no conversions and clearly does not envisage the Christian community being founded at this point. Yet in 18:27 we learn that οἱ ἀδελφοί in Ephesus wrote to the disciples in Achaia encouraging them to receive Apollos.[95] Who were these "brothers and sisters" in Ephesus? In Acts οἱ ἀδελφοί generally refers either to non-Christian Jews, or to other Christians; in this context the reference must be to Christians, since οἱ ἀδελφοί write to μαθηταί in Corinth.[96]

We do not know anything about the origins of this group. They seem to be within the synagogue, since they know Apollos, and this is where he has been active, so we can suggest that they were Jewish Christians, but may also have included Gentiles who were regarded by the synagogue as God-fearers.[97] It is

---

[95] Letters of recommendation are mentioned in Acts 9:2; 22:5; 2 Cor 3:1; see also Furnish 1984, p180. In 18:27 the Western text adds: "And some Corinthians who were on a visit to Ephesus and had heard him invited him to cross over with them to their native place. When he consented, the Ephesians wrote to the disciples to receive the man; and when he took up residence in Achaia he was of great help in the churches." On this see Bruce 1988, p358 n68; Barrett 1998, p890-1; it is unlikely to be original.

[96] ἀδελφός refers to a Christian in Acts 1:15, 16; 6:3; 9:17, 30; 11:1, 12, 29; 12:17; 14:2; 15:3, 7, 13, 22-23, 32-33, 36, 40; 16:2, 40; 17:6, 10, 14; 18:18; 21:7, 17, 20; 28:14-15. It refers to other Jews in Acts 2:29, 37; 3:17; 7:2; 13:15, 26, 38; 22:1, 5; 23:1, 5, 6; 28:17, 21. The context generally makes the sense clear; see also Bruce 1990, p108. Fieger (1998, p56) notes that this verse shows that ἀδελφοί and μαθηται are interchangeable terms for Luke.

[97] A mission to Gentiles in Ephesus is first mentioned in 19:9-10.

possible that the "brothers and sisters" in Ephesus were converted by Apollos, or Priscilla and Aquila,[98] or it may be that they had been Christians for some time. Or perhaps they were a group of mixed origins? Were some connected with those converted at Pentecost? Had some of them traveled to Ephesus after having been converted elsewhere or were some of them the result of a conservative Jewish mission or a mission connected with the Hellenists?[99] We simply do not know.[100] But their existence at least suggests that all of the Christians in Ephesus did not owe allegiance to Paul, and that there was a pre-Pauline group in the city.[101] We note also then that Luke does not actually present Paul as the founder of the Christian community in the city.[102]

We then seem to have a Jewish-Christian group, perhaps including some converted God-fearers, which existed within the synagogue in Ephesus prior to any known evangelist converting anyone there. They are the first known group of Ephesian Christians.[103]

That the believers in Ephesus wrote a recommendatory letter to Corinth in support of Apollos is interesting.[104] Käsemann notes that the community in

---

[98] Koester (1995, p128) and Günther (1995, p54-9) think they are a community founded by Apollos. But would followers write a letter of recommendation for their leader? This seems unlikely. Williams (1990, p323) thinks Priscilla and Aquila converted these Jews; see also Murphy-O'Connor 1996, p171 (who notes that a year elapsed between Acts 18:18-21 and Paul's return to Ephesus after his travels given in Acts 18:22-23); Barrett 1998, p886. Note that Luke records no conversions by Priscilla, Aquila or Apollos. However, although Luke does not explicitly say Paul founded the Christian community in Ephesus (and it seems clear that Paul did not found it from the existence of this group), he clearly wants to associate the Christians in Ephesus most strongly with Paul (eg Acts 19:1-7, 9-10, 17, 26). So the lack of mention of Apollos or Priscilla and Aquila in connection with these "brothers and sisters" of 18:27 may be part of Luke's redactional intent to associate Ephesian Christians most strongly with Paul.

[99] Similarly Luke does not tell us how the church began in Rome.

[100] Other unanswerable questions can be asked about this group. For example, was this group one factor in the opposition to Paul (1 Cor 16:9)? Further, when Paul withdrew from the synagogue along with "the disciples" (see 19:9), did all of this group leave with Paul? Or were they more inclined than Paul to remain in the synagogue?

[101] See Barrett 1998, p886. Luke does not make anything of this group (but nor does he deny their existence), which suggests he has not created them; he would have no apparent motive for this in any case.

[102] See Schnabel 1999, p369; cf. Haenchen 1971, p543. Irenaeus stated that Paul founded the church at Ephesus; see Haer. 3.3.4. But this is not required by Acts.

[103] Conzelmann 1987, p158: "This verse indicates the existence of a pre-Pauline Christian congregation." See also Haenchen 1971, p551 n5, who thinks the group existed prior to Priscilla and Aquila's arrival in Ephesus; see also Genouillac 1907, p208.

[104] Paul refers to letters of recommendation in 2 Cor 3:1 and in Acts 15:22-9 he is shown carrying such a letter; see also Rom 16:1; Col 4:10. Achaia presumably means Corinth here (see 19:1), although he may have visited other towns too.

Ephesus was "sufficiently influential (according to 18.27) to send letters of commendation to Corinth".[105] Certainly writing such a letter (and we have no reason to question the historicity of this note by Luke) suggests (although it does no more than this) that the Ephesian group was known to the Corinthian community, and that it was of reasonable size even at this stage – at least more than just a couple of people.[106]

6. Paul's first converts in Ephesus - the Ephesian Twelve (19:1-7)

6.1 Luke's purpose in telling the story

In Acts 19:1-7 we are told that Paul returns to Ephesus and there meets a group who are clearly Jews and who have been called the "Ephesian 12". After discussion it becomes clear that they have not heard of the Holy Spirit, but had been baptised by John the Baptist. Paul instructs them about the relationship between Jesus and John and then baptises them in the name of the Lord Jesus, lays hands on them, they receive the Spirit and speak in tongues and prophecy. We need to discuss several features of this passage and then will see what this passage contributes to our enquiry.

It has been argued that in this passage Luke presents Paul as "winning over the sects". Drawing on Käsemann's work[107], Conzelmann has argued that "Originally the annexation of the disciples of John the Baptist would have been related here; it is doubtful that the Spirit-less 'Christianity' as described here existed anywhere. For Luke, after the death of John the Baptist and after Jesus had superseded him in the history of salvation (Luke 16:16), there can no longer be a Baptist group. He has worked the matter out in his own way by making the disciples of the Baptist into a special Christian group."[108] Thus, in reality, for Conzelmann (as for Käsemann), the 12 were disciples of John the Baptist, but Luke does not want to present them as such because this would be to show that John the Baptist had a far greater influence than Luke wants to admit and (to quote Käsemann) to "endanger gravely the Church's view of his [John's] function".[109] Hence, Luke presents the 12 as "disciples" by adding the word μαθηταί to his source; that is, he presents them as Christians, but as incomplete Christians (or "semi-Christians"[110]) who were members of a sectarian group and who needed to be won over to

---

[105] Käsemann 1964, p138.

[106] On letters of recommendation see Jewett 1988, p147-52.

[107] See Käsemann 1964, p136-48.

[108] Conzelmann 1987, p159; see also Haenchen 1971, p557; Hughes 1972, p215.

[109] Käsemann 1964, p142.

[110] Käsemann 1964, p137.

full faith, which is what Paul does. Thus, according to Conzelmann, Luke here shows Paul winning over members of a Christian "sect", and thus adds another dimension to his portrait of Paul.[111]

However, this view hinges on the meaning of the term μαθητής in 19:1, which, it is argued, *must* here mean that Luke presents the 12 as Christian disciples (albeit incomplete sectarian Christians) prior to Paul's meeting with them.[112] On this view, what Luke has done by introducing the word μαθητής is to modify a story which originally concerned 12 disciples of John the Baptist so that it becomes an encounter with "sectarian" Christians.

This interpretation is indeed possible, but an alternative and simpler solution to the passage has been offered. Need μαθητής here mean "Christian disciple"? It has been suggested that Luke has told the story from the perspective of Paul. Paul met people who *appeared* to him to be μαθηταί - Christian disciples; hence Luke's use of the term is not to say definitively that the 12 *were* Christian disciples, but rather to show how they appeared to Paul at first.[113] However, Paul had some doubts and so examined their claims more closely. His natural assumption would be that if they were Christian disciples, then they had been baptised into Jesus and had received the Spirit. So Paul does not ask if they believed – he assumes this since he thinks they are "disciples". Rather he asks about their experience of the Spirit and learns that they have never heard about the Spirit.[114]

Paul's further question in 19:3 implies a connection between receiving the Spirit and baptism, a connection which is made explicit in Acts 2:38. If they

---

[111] Haenchen (1971, p557) notes: "In this guise, the readers could easily recognize the Baptist sects of their own day. It was not only a power of the past: the polemic of the Fourth Gospel against a messianic valuation of the Baptist proves that at that time the defensive battle against the Baptist sects was urgently required."

[112] See Haenchen 1971, p553: "μαθητής for Luke always signifies 'Christian'". See also Pereira 1983, p85-8; Thiessen 1995, p75-6; Taylor 1997, p72-5. If they are Christians, they seem to have no connection with the rest of the Christians in Ephesus, since they seem to be on their own and seem not to have met Priscilla and Aquila.

[113] See Marshall 1980, p305-6; see a similar view in Dunn 1970, p84-6; Roloff 1981, p281; Hartman 1997, p136; cf. Bruce 1988, p363; Porter 1999, p80-6. For a different explanation of 'disciple' see Murphy-O'Connor 1990, p367-8.

[114] That they do not know about the Spirit has been taken to mean that John the Baptist had never mentioned the Spirit, contrary to Mt 3:11 and Jn 1:33. But Marshall (1980, p306) notes "we should not in any case tie the teaching of John too closely to the garbled reports of it that may have been current in Asia Minor twenty years later." Further, their answer may simply mean that they did not know the Spirit had yet been given; see Webb 1991, p273-4. Johnson (1992, p337) notes it "can only mean that they did not know there was a Holy Spirit in connection with baptism." Taylor (1997, p72) suggests we follow a variant reading (λαμβάνουσίν τινες instead of ἔστιν: "we had not heard that anyone received a Holy Spirit"), but Barrett (1998, p894) rightly rejects this as a reading introduced to overcome the difficulty of the text as it stands.

are ignorant about the Spirit then this raises a question about the nature of their baptism, and Paul pursues this point. They answer that they have been baptised "into John's baptism", which seems to mean, "in the way commanded by John".[115] This suggests that they were followers of John the Baptist. Paul sees then that the 12 are in need of further instruction, and he provides this.[116] The 12 are then baptised in the name of Jesus and receive the Spirit.[117]

This view has the advantage of still seeing the 12 as historically disciples of John the Baptist, which seems the only likely interpretation of 19:2-3,[118] and also explains Paul's actions in v4-6, for he treats the 12 as in need of conversion.[119] This view also means that we should not think that *Luke* has

---

[115] Conzelmann (1987, p159) suggests that "The peculiar expression 'baptized into John's baptism' results from Luke's concern to avoid speaking about a baptism in John's *name*." For the concept of "being baptised into" someone or something see Rom 6:3; 1 Cor 1:13, 15; 10:2; 12:13; Gal 3:27. We do not know where they received John's baptism. Was it from John himself? Or was John's distinctive ministry continued by some of his disciples after his death? On 19:4 see in particular Michaels 1991, p248-50.

[116] Paul reminds them of the significance of John's baptism, and that John had pointed to the Coming One, who Paul now said was Jesus (19:4).

[117] As we noted in the section 4, the Ephesian 12 had no experience of the Spirit, and so were baptised in the name of Jesus, although they had been baptised into John's baptism. Apollos only knew John's baptism, but his existing experience of the Spirit meant he was not baptised in the name of Jesus. Possession of the Spirit is thus seen to be the crucial factor; see Bruce 1988, p364. This is the only case in the NT of people being baptised a second time. We should also note that the chronological relation of the gift of the Spirit to water baptism varies in Acts: before baptism - 10:47; at baptism - 2:38; 8:38f; after baptism - 8:15f. On the laying on of hands here see Marshall 1980, p307-8; it is a special act of fellowship that made it clear to the 12 that they were now fully part of the Christian community.

[118] In agreement with Käsemann 1964, p141-2. Taylor (1997, p73-6) thinks the 12 may have been disciples of Apollos, and had been baptised by him. "The immersion of John" (Acts 19:3) then would not mean that they were baptised by John, but rather refers to "the type of baptism done by John" (p73), in this case administered by Apollos. Thus Taylor does not think that disciples of John existed in Ephesus. However, given the differences between the 12 and Apollos (which we can argue are historically credible), it seems unlikely that there is any historical connection between them. As we have noted, Luke has brought them together because both stories relate to John's baptism and the Holy Spirit.

[119] Conzelmann (1987, p159), who follows Käsemann and Haenchen's understanding of the passage, thinks that v5-6 shows the story is not about "the correction of a type of Christianity", but speaks rather "of an annexation to the church". However, this observation tends to undermine Conzelmann's view of the passage since (on his view) it shows that Luke has inadequately altered his sources (or created a contradictory pericopae) and has left a story that gives the impression at its start that it concerns the winning over of sectarian Christians ("disciples"), but ends by speaking of conversions. Although it is conceivable that in Luke's view Paul would "rebaptise" "sectarian Christians", v3-6 seems to be a conversion narrative and suggest that the 12 were not Christians at all. Rather than seeing Luke as giving us such

altered the thrust of the passage in order to present the 12 as sectarian Christians whom Paul "wins over".

If Luke's purpose in including the passage was not to portray Paul as winning over the sects, can we suggest an alternative purpose that Luke had for including the story? Johnson has suggested that for Luke the passage is a foundation story, presenting the founding of the Christian community in Ephesus. Johnson notes: "The encounter with the Johannine disciples ... is essentially a standard 'foundation account' in which Luke shows the effective birth of Christianity in a new locale by means of conversion, baptism, the apostolic laying on of hands, the outpouring of the Holy Spirit and its manifestation in tongues and prophecy (cf Acts 2:1-4; 8:15-17; 10:44-48)."[120] It is likely that this is how Luke understands the passage, although we should also note that these are not the first Christians in Ephesus that Luke has mentioned, since he has already spoken of οἱ ἀδελφοί in 18:27. Yet this is the first occasion when Luke has given the sort of detail he supplies in 19:5-6, which suggests that for Luke this is the foundation of the Pauline group in Ephesus.

6.2 Historicity

What about the historicity of the passage? We have no independent corroboration for the passage nor for the 12 themselves, we are not given any specific details about the 12, such as names or origins and they have no further role in the story. This means we can only assess the plausibility of the story, but are unable to go beyond this.

On the view that Luke does not want us to see the 12 as sectarian Christians, but rather as disciples of John the Baptist whom Paul converts, it is possible to see the story as containing traditional elements. Firstly, we need to ask if the story as Luke reports it is historically credible? Is it likely that Paul met disciples of John the Baptist in Ephesus? What was the extent of John the Baptist's following? In particular, is it credible that he had followers in Ephesus around twenty years after he was active in Palestine?

Firstly, although we have no other evidence for a group of John's disciples like the Ephesian 12 in the first century,[121] since early Christian sources play

---

a contorted pericopae, as Conzelmann's view requires, it is better to see the story as more consistent, as the view presented above allows us to.

[120] Johnson 1992, p343. He notes on p344 that the Ephesian material does not actually imply that Paul himself established Christianity in the city. For Johnson the story of Paul's encounter with the disciples of John "has the effect of giving apostolic legitimacy to the Ephesian founding."

[121] See Taylor 1997, p105.

down the significance of John the Baptist, we should not take this silence as definitive.

Secondly, Josephus gives us an account about John the Baptist's death. He writes:

When others [ie "some of the Jews"] too joined the crowds about him, because they were aroused to the highest degree by his sermons, Herod became alarmed. Eloquence that had so great an effect on mankind might lead to some form of sedition, for it looked as if they would be guided by John in everything that they did. Herod decided to strike first and be rid of him before his work led to an uprising, than to wait for an upheaval, get involved in a difficult situation and see his mistake.[122]

It is clear from this account that John was a respected and significant figure who had a considerable following, and was sufficiently influential for Herod Antipas to execute him. The New Testament also speaks of crowds going to hear John (Mt 3:5; Mk 1:5; Lk 3:7, 10). John is clearly a teacher who has disciples (Mk 2:18; 6:28; Mt 9:14; 11:2; 14:12; Lk 5:33; 7:18; 11:1; Jn 1:22, 32, 35, 37; 3:25, 27) and he is addressed as a teacher (Lk 3:12) and rabbi (Jn 3:26) as well as a prophet (Mt 3:4; 11:9; 17:10-13; 21:26; Mk 1:6; 9:9-13; 11:32; Lk 7:26; 20:6).[123] Given the clear impact John made as a teacher and prophet during his lifetime, and that he had disciples, it is certainly possible that a group of John's disciples were in Ephesus some twenty years after his death.[124]

---

[122] Ant 18:118-119. Although we have material about John in other sources (apocryphal and Gnostic writings, Mandaean literature) Taylor (1997, p8) notes that recent studies have shown that the only historically valuable material is in the NT and Josephus.

[123] On John as teacher and prophet see Taylor 1997, p101-54; 223-34.

[124] Michaels (1991, p245-60) examines the references relevant to John the Baptist in the Acts material which relate to Paul and in Paul's letters. He argues that the subtle links between John and Paul in Acts are not a deliberate construction by Luke, but rather, with regard to 19:4 (as well as other passages in Acts) (p259) "Luke has preserved some authentic echoes of Paul's missionary preaching, including his [Paul's] citation and interpretation of John the Baptist". This reinforces the likelihood that in 19:1-7 Luke is drawing on tradition, in this case relating to Paul's interpretation of John the Baptist. Taylor (1997, p105-6) thinks it is unlikely that there were continuing groups of John's followers; but in my view we have no categorical evidence on the matter either way. A number of scholars have seen a polemic against followers of John the Baptist in John's Gospel, but this depends on being able to read the history of the community from the Gospel, which Bauckham has decisively challenged; see Chapter 6. But the concern to spell out with great care the subordination of John to Jesus in each of the Gospels (see Stanton 2002, p178-84; Taylor 1997, p11), does suggest that there was more interest in him in the early church than the evangelists explicitly state. Similarly, Johnson (1992, p338) notes that 19:3-4 is the fifth time in Acts that John's role as a precursor to Jesus has been clarified (see also Acts 1:5; 11:16; 13:25; 18:25). That Luke repeatedly takes up the issue, shows, as does Josephus, that John was an important figure in his own right. But this does not mean there were necessarily followers of John known to the evangelists.

Thus, the story is credible and it is quite possible that there were followers of John the Baptist in Ephesus around 52 CE.[125] But has Luke located in Ephesus a story which originally belonged elsewhere? Conzelmann has noted that the connection between Apollos and Ephesus in the preceding story about Apollos is firmly established historically by passages like 1 Cor 16:12, whereas we hear nothing else of these 12. He has therefore asked "if Luke was the first to locate the story about these disciples in Ephesus. This episode could have occurred anywhere (the closer to Palestine the better)".[126] Since we have no further evidence about these 12, we cannot show that the event described in 19:1-7 occurred in Ephesus, rather than being transposed there by Luke for his own reasons. However, the point raised by Conzelmann is a two-edged one. If Luke created the story, or localised a story that did not relate to a particular centre, one would think he would locate it in a place where John the Baptist's followers could be thought to have been, which is, as Conzelmann points out, "the closer to Palestine the better". Although, Luke could have located the story in Ephesus as part of his portrait of Paul's success in the city,[127] if it was strange for his readers to think of people who were connected with John the Baptist being found in Ephesus, then this would tend to undermine his point in the passage. It seems more likely that Luke has some basis for locating the story in Ephesus. Further, as Thiessen points out, there is no reason in the story itself to deny it being located in Ephesus, and he argues Luke is here using tradition which came from Ephesus.[128] We have also already noted that Luke has reliable historical sources for a good deal of his material relating to Ephesus, and he may well be using reliable Ephesian tradition at this point.

6.3 What does the story tell us about Christians in Ephesus?

If we grant the possibility that the story has some basis in tradition and that Luke has correctly located it in Ephesus (and as we have noted we can only argue for this in terms of probability) then three points in it are significant for our overall enquiry.

---

[125] Barrett (1984, p37) notes "There is good, though hardly overwhelming, reason to think that groups of John's disciples did persist after their master's death, and even after the death and resurrection of Jesus." Barrett 1998, p859, with regard to this story thinks that "Luke probably found [it] in existence". See also Hartman 1997, p138; Koester 1995, p127.

[126] Conzelmann 1987, p159. See also Käsemann 1964, p148.

[127] Conzelmann (1987, p159) suggests Luke could have "located the scene here [in Ephesus] in line with his tendency to portray Paul as the initiator." But as we have noted, Paul is not depicted as the founder of the Christian community in Ephesus, so this is unlikely.

[128] See Thiessen 1995, p83-4.

Firstly, for Luke the story contributes to the total picture of Paul's work in Ephesus. Here, Paul converts a group of people,[129] and although they are not the first Christians Luke has written of in Ephesus (cf 18:27), they are clearly a significant group for Luke. The group may then be one historical dimension behind Luke's portrayal of Paul's time in Ephesus as successful. We will discuss this theme in more detail shortly.

Secondly, Luke wants to say that these followers of John the Baptist became Pauline Christians.[130] But if they had been disciples of John the Baptist, as seems most likely, they would probably bring with them into the Christian community in Ephesus a different strand of thinking which was derived from their background. This could well include traditions emphasized by John which may then have been reinterpreted or incorporated, perhaps in distinctive ways, into their new beliefs.[131] We can also note that it was a sizeable group of "about twelve" men (ἄνδρες ὡσεὶ δώδεκα; 19:7), who perhaps had families, and may have formed one or more house churches, which may have had their own continuing and distinctive identity.[132] Again, this is a hint of some diversity among the Christians in Ephesus.

Thirdly, we see that people who followed John the Baptist, and perhaps knew something about Jesus (although we do not know how much the 12 actually knew about Jesus prior to meeting Paul) were present in Ephesus. Is this incident indicative of an on-going presence of followers of John the Baptist in Ephesus? To put the question another way, did Paul convert all of the followers of John the Baptist, or were there others who remained as

---

[129] Note the parallels here between the imposition of Paul's hands on the 12, with the resultant reception of the Spirit and speaking in tongues and prophesying, and the imposition of Peter and John's hands on the Samaritan converts in Acts 8:14-17. This emphasises Paul's success here.

[130] This is expressed in part by the fact that the coming of the Spirit accompanies the laying on of hands by Paul rather than the baptism itself. Johnson (1992, p338) notes: "The fact that it is the apostle Paul who is the medium for this bestowal has a legitimating function: these erstwhile Johannine disciples are brought within the apostolic community and authority."

[131] See Hughes 1972, p216-17 for a similar suggestion in relation to what is said about John in Luke's Gospel.

[132] It is unclear whether we are to see any symbolic significance in there being "about 12" in number. Williams (1990, p331) notes that Luke's indefinite expression ("altogether there were about twelve of them" (19:7)), suggests he did not attach any significance to the number twelve; see also Conzelmann 1987, p160. But note Johnson 1992, p338: Luke "clearly intends this one [number] to symbolically represent a realization of 'Israel' (compare Acts 1:15-2:13)." Williams 1957, p220 thinks that there were 12 (the "about" in 19:7 can be disregarded) and asks "Does this section point to the existence of a primitive 'college' of Twelve at Ephesus, reorganized perhaps by Paul, who governed the Church there?" But this seems to be entirely speculative. Thiessen 1995, p82-3 suggests that the number twelve emphasizes that they are a group which is independent of other Christians.

followers of John? Were such people an on-going influence on the church?[133] Unfortunately we have no evidence to answer these questions either way.

7. The success of Paul's work in Ephesus

We now turn to consider Acts 19:8-22 in detail, but here we will take a different approach. This material is best considered by noting that Luke wishes to highlight a particular theme with regard to Paul's ministry in Ephesus: that Paul's work in the city was successful, and that this points to the power of the Lord Jesus and of the Gospel.[134] We will discuss the way Luke builds up this picture of Paul's success in Ephesus, not only in 19:8-22 but also in 18:20, 19:1-7 and briefly in 19:23-40 (which we will consider in more detail in the next chapter).

Luke develops the theme of the success of Paul's work in Ephesus in the following ways:

1) In 18:20, on Paul's first visit to the synagogue, the Jews wanted him to stay for a longer period, but he declined. Clearly, he was well-received.

2) Paul converted 12 men in 19:1-7 who seemed to be "disciples" but who knew nothing of the Holy Spirit. He baptized them in the name of the Lord Jesus. When he laid hands on them, the Spirit came upon them and they spoke in tongues and prophesied, just as happened in Samaria when Peter and John laid their hands on believers (8:17).

3) According to 19:8-9, Paul preached for three months in the synagogue, and then encountered opposition from some Jews. Three months is a particularly long time for Paul to stay in the synagogue and shows that the Jews were receptive. This is confirmed by the note in v9 that when Paul finally left the synagogue, he took a number of believers, who are clearly Jewish Christians, and perhaps some God-fearers, with him.

4) According to 19:10 Paul then taught daily (cf. probably each Sabbath in the synagogue) in the hall of Tyrannus for 2 years (a very long time in Acts). As a

---

[133] As we have noted, many scholars have seen a polemic against followers of John the Baptist in John's Gospel, which they have located in Ephesus, and hence have connected that Johannine polemic with this passage and seen an on-going group of John's disciples in Ephesus. But see now Bauckham 1998.

[134] Thus Barrett (1998, p900) entitles 19.8-20 "Paul's successful ministry at Ephesus" and speaks of "the great success of the Christian mission described in 19.11-20" (p914).

result "all the residents of Asia heard the word of the Lord, both Jews and Greeks."[135] Paul was thus a successful teacher of both Jews and Greeks.

5) Paul's ministry in Ephesus is accompanied by miracles and exorcisms (19:11-12).

6) In 19:13-17 we learn that some Jewish exorcists tried to use the "name of Jesus, whom Paul preaches", to cast out evil spirits, since it was obviously so powerful. They were unsuccessful, which shows that the name of Jesus was not some magical device, but can only be used by those authorised to do so. The event shows that the power of Jewish exorcists was greatly eclipsed by the power of the name of Jesus, which Paul preached.[136] The incident also had a positive outcome: "When this became known to all residents of Ephesus, both Jews and Greeks, everyone was awestruck; and the name of the Lord Jesus was praised" (19:17).[137]

7) According to 19:18-20, new converts, of whom there were many, gave up their involvement in magic, presumably because the demonstration of the power of the name of Jesus in 19:13-17 had convinced them that any other power, including magic was worthless. Thus they confessed their practices and burnt their magic books. The new faith of the Christians was thus shown to be far greater and more powerful than one of the elements of pagan religiosity, namely magic.[138] The great value of the books emphasised again the success of Paul and the power of the Gospel. Luke is explicit about the impact of this incident: "So (οὕτως) the word of the Lord grew and prevailed mightily" (19:20).

8) In 19:23-40 we learn that Paul's work had been so successful that it had had an impact on the sale of souvenirs of Artemis, and so Demetrius, a silversmith, instigated a riot. In 19:26 Demetrius confirmed the impression already gained that Paul had been successful: "You also see and hear that not only in Ephesus but in almost the whole of Asia this Paul has persuaded and drawn away a considerable number of people by saying that gods made with hands are not gods." There was a danger that Artemis herself would be scorned. This testimony is even more impressive since it came from a hostile

---

[135] Luke also portrays the preaching of the Gospel in an area (rather than just a city) in Acts 5:16; 8:5-14; 11:26; see Schneider 1982, p268 and n17.

[136] Schüssler Fiorenza (1976, p13) notes: "According to Luke, then, the success of the Christian mission is based upon the powerful name of Jesus."

[137] In 19:10 and 17 it seems that Luke particularly wishes to emphasize that Paul has been successful among both Jews and Greeks, despite the fact that he has left the synagogue.

[138] See Schüssler Fiorenza 1976, p13.

witness. Another competitor with Christianity, the pagan cults, here represented by Artemis the chief deity of Ephesus, was shown to be threatened by the new faith. The threat not only has religious dimensions, but also economic and political ramifications as well.

9) Paul had also been able to make friends in high places (19:31).[139]

Much of Luke's theology is in evidence in this section, and much of it goes beyond what was historically verifiable, even for those who witnessed any particular event. Thus, for example, his view that Christianity is superior to Hellenistic magic and to pagan cults is a statement of Luke's faith.

But it is also clear that in this passage Luke wants to present Paul's time in Ephesus as a success.[140] Why? Primarily because this is the last area of work in which Paul can freely pursue his missionary efforts before he travels to Jerusalem and is arrested.[141] Luke emphasises this by mentioning travel to Jerusalem and then Rome in 19:21.[142] From this point on then the narrative concentrates on Paul's progress toward Roman imprisonment and the end of his story in Acts, and with this in view, Luke clearly wants to leave the reader with the image of Paul as a successful missionary in Ephesus.[143]

But has Luke created this picture of Paul's success in Ephesus? Or does this theological and apologetic picture also have some historical basis? We will now investigate this question.

---

[139] The Miletus speech also presents Paul as the paradigmatic missionary and church leader; see our discussion of the speech in Chapter 4.

[140] Luke gives summaries concerning the growth of the church in 2:47; 6:7; 9:31; 12:24; 16:5, and statements of Paul's success eg in 14:1; 17:12. However, in some places Luke does not present Paul as being particularly successful (eg in Athens, 17:34) which shows that it was not a constant theme on Luke's part.

[141] In the travels described in Acts 20:1-16 Paul turns to work of consolidation in already established churches, rather than missionary preaching.

[142] Luke will go on to show that Paul "must" indeed see Rome, but as a prisoner, not a free man.

[143] Haenchen notes this (1971, p558): "Luke in Chapter 19 once more shows his reader the Apostle at work, and indeed at the zenith of his labours. .. Thus understood the chapter is a unity, which makes the reader feel that if now the prison gates close behind Paul, his work is still done." Note also Johnson's (1992, p344) comment: "The Ephesian Church, established by an apostle, triumphant over the demonic powers of magic, independent of the synagogue yet drawing into itself both Jews and Gentiles, is the final evidence within Luke's text for the success and integrity of Paul's mission. That he so intends us to see it is shown further by the fact that it is to this Church that Paul directs his final testimony (20:17-35)." See also Schüssler Fiorenza 1976, p8; le Roux 1999, p307-13. Of course, for Luke Paul is successful not in his own right, but because of the power of the word of the Lord (19:10, 20) and the power of name of the Lord Jesus (19:5, 13-15, 17).

7.1 Luke and hyperbole

Luke clearly makes some statements in this section which are is hard to regard as literally true. For example, in 19:10 he says that "all the residents of Asia heard the word of the Lord, both Jews and Greeks." The population of the province of Asia in this period was in the millions;[144] it is hard to think that Luke meant us to understand that literally millions heard the Gospel in this period. We would be wrong to do so, because an examination of Acts shows that Luke uses the literary technique of hyperbole, an accepted form of speech,[145] a good deal.

Hyperbole can be defined as "an overstatement or a conscious exaggeration by the writer to gain effect." When using hyperbole "more is said than is literally meant",[146] so as to heighten the sense and emphasize a certain point. This is clearest in Luke's use of πᾶς, which is one of Luke's favourite words.[147] As was the case with other writers of the time, Luke regularly overstates the case to gain effect. This means we need to recognise that Luke is using an accepted literary technique at this point.

It is likely then that Luke is using hyperbole in presenting some of the elements of his portrait of Paul's success in Ephesus,[148] so as to emphasise

---

[144] See Broughton 1938, p812-16, who thinks the population of the province was around 4.6 million but notes (p814) "Any general estimate ... will have a very large margin of error, and perhaps is foolish to attempt."

[145] Hyperbole is widely used. It is found in the Hebrew Bible (see for example Gen 15:5; Ex 8:17; Dt 1:28; Jud 7:12; 20:16; 1 Sam 18:7; 1 Kg 1:40; Jer 4:23-6 see Bullinger 1898, p423-8; Eybers 1970, p38-49; Caird 1980, p110-17) and is a regular feature of Jesus' parables and teaching (see Huffman 1978, p207-20; for hyperbole in Jesus' parables see for example Mt 18:23-5; 20:1-16; Lk 15:11-32; 13:18-19; in Jesus's teaching, see for example Mk 10:25; Mt 7:3-5; 23:24) and occurs in the form of the *tobspruch* (Snyder 1977, p117-20; examples are found in Mk 9:42-7; 1 Peter 3:17). Philo (eg. De Spec. Leg 2.62) and Josephus (Cohen 1982, p385-405) use it regularly and it is discussed by classical authors in their treatments of rhetoric (See Aristotle, *Rhetoric* 3.11.15-16; Quintillian *Inst.* 8.6.67-76; 12.10.62; Cicero, *Phil* 2.63; Horace 2.3.502; for examples see Strabo, *Geog.* 3.2.9; Pliny the Younger, *Pan.* 52.3; Dio Cassius 67.8.1). It is clearly an accepted form of speech.

[146] Bullinger 1898, p423; see also Myers 1986, p96; Lausberg 1998, p263, 410-11.

[147] Note the following examples of the use of πᾶς in Acts which probably use hyperbole: Acts 1:19; 2:43; 4:16, 21; 8:9-10; 9:35; 13:24; 17:21; 18:2; 19:10, 17, 26; 26:11; see also 1:1; 2:5, 44; 8:40; 13:49; 15:21; 20:31; 21:21, 28; 24:5; 26:4. See also Cadbury 1920, p115; Lüdemann 1987, p121. Cadbury 1920, 115-17 shows that in his Gospel, Luke often adds ἅπας, πᾶς or ἕκαστος to his sources. Hence, hyperbole is also clear in the Gospel.

[148] It has been recognised by a number of scholars that Luke is using hyperbole in 19:10. Renié, quoted in Delebecque 1982, p225 n2 notes: "L'hyperbole en est à peine une tant Éphèse était fréquentée: marchands et pèlerins d'Artémis y affluaient. Les auditeurs, attirés par la renommée de l'apôtre, on dû étre fort nombreux et, de retour chez eux, ils se feront les propagandistes enthousiastes de son enseignement ..." See also Schneider 1982, p268; Murphy-O'Connor 1996, p173. Mitchell 1993, vol 2, p37 thinks that in 19:10 Luke

that Paul was indeed successful - but not as successful as a literal reading of some verses might suggest. When allowance is made for Luke's hyperbole, particularly in 19:10, 17 and 19:26 and perhaps elsewhere, is what Luke says about Paul's success credible? We will now discuss this.

7.2 A one-sided portrait

We noted at the end of the last chapter that it seems clear that Acts does not give us the full story of Paul's time in Ephesus. In particular, Paul seems to have suffered more severely, and the opposition to him was stronger than Luke indicates. This is not to indict Luke, since he was not setting out to write a biography of Paul, but it does mean that his account of Paul's time in Ephesus emphasised the positive side of Paul's time in the city.

This is not to say that Luke completely overlooks the negative side. The riot, while indicating success, also shows Paul encountered opposition. Further, in the speech to the elders at Miletus we hear of Paul "serving the Lord with all humility and tears, enduring the trials that came to me through the plots of the Jews" in Ephesus (20:19; cf. 20:31); Luke has not mentioned any of this in Acts 19. But it is clear from Paul's letters that his time in Ephesus involved opponents, suffering and perhaps imprisonment. The "negative side" was more pronounced than Luke suggests.

7.3 Yet according to his letters, Paul had some success in Ephesus

However, it is also clear from Paul's letters that he was successful in Ephesus. That Luke underplays the negative side of Paul's time does not necessarily mean that he has created the positive side. Again recall our conclusions from Chapter 2. 1 Cor 16:9 suggests that Paul considered that his work in Ephesus had brought results, and was continuing to bring results. This suggests that the Christian community had grown and become well-established,[149] and 1 Cor 16:19-20 suggests that the Pauline Christian community was made up of more than one house church and thus may have numbered over 30 people.

Further the greetings from "the churches of Asia" in 1 Cor 16:19 suggest that in the course of Paul's time in Ephesus successful evangelism had been conducted in the area around Ephesus and further afield in the province of Asia. Perhaps Paul himself went out on a preaching tour to some of the cities

---

probably means that people from the whole province, not the entire population, heard the Gospel as a result of Paul's activity.

[149] Fee 1987, p821 notes: "Paul's imagery [in 1 Cor 16:9] does coincide with the picture Luke portrays of the considerable success of Paul's mission in this city that finally brought about the conflict with the hawkers of souvenirs at the temple of Artemis (Acts 19:23-40)."

of the province.[150] It is certainly likely that some of his co-workers travelled in the province, since we know that congregations of a Pauline character were founded in Colossae, Laodicea and Hierapolis sometime in this period (Col 1:1; 4:13, 15-16).[151] We do not know when the other six churches of Revelation 2-3 were founded, but since some of the seven churches seem to have been in a state of decline by the time Revelation was written (probably 95-96 CE), they may well have been established in this period.[152] It is most likely then that productive evangelism was conducted from Ephesus into the surrounding area during this period. Thus, although Luke is using hyperbole in 19:10, we have some evidence that there was evangelisation in the province of Asia from Ephesus in this period. Note too that because of the strategic location of Ephesus, the fact that it was the provincial capital from the time of Augustus, an assize centre, and the home of Artemis of Ephesus and her famous temple, it was a centre to which people travelled. Paul's message would quickly be spread through the province, through the agency of people who had come to Ephesus for any of a number of reasons, had become Christians, and then returned to their homes, but also because people in the province would be used to hearing news from Ephesus.[153]

Thus, Luke's overall emphasis on the success of Paul's time in Ephesus does have some corroboration in Paul's letters, although we have noted that Luke downplays the negative side. Clearly then the picture Luke gives has some basis in history. But can we argue for the success of Paul's time in

---

[150] See Williams 1990, p332. In 19:22 we read that Paul sent Timothy and Erastus to Macedonia "while he himself stayed for some time longer in Asia." Does Asia here mean Ephesus, or does it indicate that Paul travelled around in Asia? In 19:26 Asia and Ephesus are clearly distinguished. 20:16 is inconclusive. In 20:4 Trophimus is described as an "Asian", but in 21:29 he is called an "Ephesian". The Jews from "Asia" who recognise Paul (21:27; 24:19) are probably from Ephesus. Thus on some occasions Asia means Ephesus, on others, Asia means a much larger area that Ephesus (19:26). It seems impossible to decide what Luke means in 19:22. Haenchen (1971, p569 and n5-6) argues that by Asia here Luke probably means only Ephesus, and notes that in 19:23 Luke presumes Paul is in Ephesus, although the point is not conclusive. See also Schneider 1982, p274. Zahn (1900, p687) thinks Paul makes excursions to other cities not far from Ephesus during this period.

[151] Paul had not been to Colossae (Col 2:1) but considers it to be part of his circle because the church was founded by Epaphras, one of Paul's co-workers (Col 1:7; 4:12-13), who was also known in Laodicea and Hierapolis. Conzelmann 1987, p163 notes: "Ephesus was the centre of an organized mission carried out by fellow workers of Paul, as Colossians indicates (even if not written by Paul). But Luke makes no mention of this, emphasizing rather the personal importance of Paul." See also Schneider 1982, p268; Bruce 1988, p366; Murphy-O'Connor 1996, p174. Col 2:1 ("and for all who have not seen me face to face") suggests that there were Christian groups in places other than Laodicea which Paul had not founded but for which he took responsibility. Some of these may have been in Asia.

[152] Bruce 1988, p366; Murphy-O'Connor 1996, p175; Barrett 1998, p906.

[153] In 1 Cor 16:9 Paul makes a similar point.

Ephesus in more detail, and in particular, for dimensions of this success which are not mentioned by Paul in his letters?

7.4 Features of Paul's success according to Luke

Luke's portrait of Paul success, found in the verses listed at the beginning of this section, can be categorised in the following way. It involves:

1) Success among Jews, although the success is followed by opposition (18:19-21; 19:8-10, 17);
2) Success among Gentiles, again followed by opposition (19:10, 17, 26-7);
3) Success in the province of Asia (19:10, 26);
4) Success in performing miracles and exorcisms (19:11-12);
5) Success in bringing about repentance from involvement in magic (19:18-20).[154]

We will now examine each of these dimensions of Luke's portrait of Paul's success in turn to see if the motif of success is likely to have an historical basis in each case.

7.4.1 Success among Jews, followed by opposition (18:19-21; 19:8-10, 17)

As we have noted above, when he first arrived in Ephesus, Paul is said to have gone into the synagogue and argued with the Jews. He is asked to stay on which suggests that the Jews in Ephesus were receptive to his message. After Paul's departure, Priscilla and Aquila were active in the synagogue, since it was there that they encountered Apollos. After returning to Ephesus, Paul preached in the synagogue for three months (19:8). The time period, which may well be from tradition, seems to be a lengthy one when compared with the time he preached in synagogues elsewhere and may indicate that Paul had some success.[155] We also recall here our findings from chapter 1 that the

---

[154] Acts 19:31 suggests that Paul was successful in gaining friends in high places. We will consider this aspect in the next section when we discuss the riot.

[155] Haenchen (1971, p560) regards the note of time as from tradition, and notes that the three months in the synagogue is "an amazingly long interval"; see also Duncan 1929, p26; Schnackenburg 1991, p44. Georgi (1986,p18) regards the note of a three month time period as a "reliable remark". In Pisidian Antioch Paul encountered opposition on the second Sabbath (13:42-4). In Thessalonica he preached in the synagogue for three weeks before trouble occurred (17:2-9). In Corinth no indication is given of how quickly they are opposed (18:6). The Jews at Beroea were more open (17:10-12). So the three months is certainly longer than in some places; see also Fearghail 2002, p48. Fieger (1998, p79) questions the reliability of the time period, since the number three is one of Luke's favourite numbers. But although Luke does not mean exactly three months, there is no reason to doubt it was a reasonable length of time.

Jewish community in Ephesus was well-established and was a significant community in the life of the city; we can understand why Paul spent a good deal of time in speaking with Jews. It is noteworthy that Luke says nothing about Gentile "Godfearers" in connection with the synagogue, in contrast to what he says about some other centres.[156] After opposition Paul withdrew,[157] taking "the disciples" with him, for the public nature of the opposition (19:9)[158] meant there was no longer the atmosphere of civil debate. We do not know, however, whether all "the disciples" who were part of an Ephesian synagogue left with Paul at this stage. Clearly, some Jewish Christians could have remained as part of the synagogue.

In his letters Paul never mentions preaching in synagogues; rather he calls himself an apostle to the Gentiles (Rom 1:5, 13-14; 11:13-14; 15:15-21; Gal 1:16; 2:7-9; cf. Rom 15:16). This has led some scholars to argue that he never in fact preached to Jews and God-fearers in synagogues.[159] However, it is clear from his letters that he also preached to Jews and was concerned for their salvation. This is clearest in 1 Cor 9:20 where Paul writes: "To the Jews I became as a Jew, in order to win Jews. To those under the law I became as one under the law (though I myself am not under the law) so that I might win those under the law." It is confirmed by Rom 1.16 where Paul speaks of the Gospel as addressed "to the Jew first and also to the Greeks".[160]

That Paul continued to preach to Jews is also clear from 2 Cor 11:24, written shortly after he left Ephesus, in which he tells us that on five occasions he received forty lashes less one at the hands of the Jews.[161] Such flogging was a punishment administered by the synagogue for a wide range of serious offences. That Paul endured this punishment five times shows that he

---

[156] Compare Thessalonica (17:4) Beroea (17:12); Corinth (18:4) and see Fearghail 2002, p47.

[157] Barrett (1998, p901-2) asks why the Jews did not object to Priscilla and Aquila's activity in the synagogue? But he notes that we do not know if they began to teach immediately after 18:19, nor how they presented their message nor the sort of provocation their teaching may have caused.

[158] It is unclear what πλῆθος in v9 refers to in the phrase "speaking evil of the way before the πλῆθους". It could refer to the Christians in the synagogue, the synagogue as a whole, or the general public in the city; see Barrett 1998, p904, who favours the third option; see also Fitzmyer 1971, p290.

[159] See the discussion in Trebilco 1991, p20.

[160] See also Rom 2:9-10; 3:9; 9:1-5; 10:1, 12; 1 Cor 1:24; 7:18 Gal 3:28. See also Bruce 1985, p2581; Strelan 1996, p199-203.

[161] The punishment is based on Dt 25:1-3. We have no record of where any of these floggings occurred, but Acts portrays several occasions prior to the writing of 2 Cor when Paul could have received the thirty nine lashes; see Acts 13:45, 50; 14:5; 18:12; Furnish 1984, p537. In 2 Cor 11:26 Paul also speaks of being in danger from his own people. Thus the consistent pattern in Acts of Paul being in conflict with the synagogue (see eg. 13:44-52; 17:1-5, 13-14, 18:5-7) is quite plausible.

did not lightly give up his Jewish connections and continued to attend synagogues and submit to their discipline.[162] This suggests that in most, if not all, of the cities Paul visited, he would go to the synagogue, even if he had been punished elsewhere.[163] This note of punishment also shows that Paul was often rejected by synagogue communities.

Thus it is historically credible that Paul preached to the significant Jewish community in Ephesus, but also that he was later rejected by some Jews (19:9). While Paul's letters show that he considered his mission to the Jews to have been mainly unsuccessful,[164] it is also clear that some of his congregations included Jews and that a number of Jews became Christians.[165] Thus we conclude that the report in Acts 19:8-9 that in Ephesus Paul preached in the synagogue for three months and had some success there is credible, although we cannot confirm the exact length of time.[166] Further we note that Luke begins the account in 19:8 by writing "Εἰσελθὼν δὲ εἰς τὴν συναγωγήν", using exactly the same words as in 18:19; this repetition suggests to Barrett that Luke may here be using the same source that he was using in the earlier section about Ephesus.[167] The probable use of a source adds weight to the likelihood that we have reliable tradition here. Thus by 55

---

[162] Stowers (1984, p64) writes: "This reaction could only have been caused by Paul's attempts to win Jews to belief in the crucified messiah. The infliction of this severe punishment five times reflects a certain persistence on Paul's part and probably the fact that Paul preached in synagogues on numerous occasions." See also Sanders 1986, p86-9. That Paul continued to consider himself a Jew, with the right to present his brand of Judaism is clear from Rom 9:1-5; 11:1; 1 Cor 9:19-23.

[163] See Stowers 1984, p64. We have other evidence that Paul was persecuted by Jews, probably because he continued to preach to them. See 1 Thess 2:15-16 (being driven out by Jews, probably from Thessalonica); Gal 4:29 (a typological reference to persecution of Christians "now" by others, designated as those "born according to the flesh" who are almost certainly Jews). Note other references to general persecution: Rom 8:35; 1 Cor 4:12; 2 Cor 4:9; 6:4-5; 12:10; Gal 5:11, some of which may have been from Jews. See further Trebilco 1991, p20-1.

[164] See Rom 9:30-3; 10:16-19, 21; 11:7, 11-15, 20, 25, 28; 2 Cor 3:14.

[165] There were probably some Jewish Christians in the congregations addressed in 1 Cor (see 1 Cor 1:23-4; 7:18; 12:13), Gal (see Gal 3:28) and Col (see Col 3:11).

[166] See Barrett 1998, p902: "Luke probably had before him a reference to a long stay in Ephesus; on this ground he probably felt it safe to extend the period of work in the synagogue (beyond for example the three weeks in Thessalonica, 17:2)." But since Luke has a reliable source for at least some of Paul's time in Ephesus, as the account of the riot shows, then it is likely that the mention of three months could go back to this source. Pesch (1986, 2, p167) thinks the Jewish community mentioned in 19:8 tolerated *Sondergruppen*, as is shown by their willingness to accommodate the disciples of John the Baptist (19:1-7; he assumes they had been active in the same synagogue as that mentioned in 19:8). This observation makes it more likely that they were prepared to tolerate Paul for three months, but it is weakened slightly by the fact that Luke does not connect the 12 to a synagogue.

[167] Barrett 1998, p903.

CE, the Pauline community in Ephesus almost certainly had some Jewish members.

We have also noted above that Paul's letters provide evidence that Paul was persecuted by Jews almost certainly because they did not accept his message.[168] Thus the picture in Acts 19:9 of some Jews disbelieving and "speaking evil of the Way before the congregation" is credible. He then withdrew from the synagogue and had to find a new base for his preaching activity.

7.4.2 Success among Gentiles (19:10, 17-18, 26-7)

Luke emphasises in 19:10, 17 and again in 26-7 (which will be dealt with in more detail in the next chapter) that Paul gained a hearing from Greeks (as well as Jews) and suggests in 19:17-18 that many became believers. It is clear from Paul's letters that he had a good deal of success in converting Gentiles. For example in 1 Thess 1:9 Paul writes that the Thessalonians "turned to God from idols to serve a living and true God." Further, it is clear that most of the Corinthians and Galatians were Gentiles.[169] But what about the situation in Ephesus? Do any of the indications and statements in Acts that Paul was successful among Gentiles in Ephesus stand up to investigation?

One element of Paul's success was that he "argued daily in the lecture hall of Tyrannus (σχολὴ Τυράννου)"[170] in Ephesus for two years,[171] and through this "all the residents of Asia, both Jews and Greeks, heard the word of the Lord" (19:10). Unfortunately, a "Hall of Tyrannus" has not been uncovered in

---

[168] See further Trebilco 1991, p20-7.

[169] See 1 Cor 1:23-4; 8:1-13; 10:7-30; Gal 4:8; 5:2-3; 6:12.

[170] According to the Western text Paul argued "from the fifth hour to the tenth" (19:9), that is, from around 11 am to 4 pm, perhaps during the midday siesta; on this see Martial, 4.8. Hemer (1989a, p56) notes that here the Western text incorporates a picturesque addition "which may be appropriate and indeed true, without therefore being necessarily original." If it is an historical reminiscence then this time of day was unfavourable, in the sense that many people would have been asleep (see Lake and Cadbury 1933a, p239) but it did mean that those who worked were able to come and listen to Paul.

[171] It is not certain that σχολή means a place here since its primary meaning is leisure or relaxation. It came to be applied to things associated with leisure, above all discussions, and thus came to mean "school", either the gathering itself, or the place in which they gathered; see Johnson 1992, p339. Horsley (*New Docs* 1, 130) suggests that the word here refers to a group of people meeting under the aegis of Tyrannos to whom addresses were given during their leisure hours. Malherbe (1983, p89-91) sees the σχολή as a guild hall rather than a lecture hall; guild halls were often named after a guild's patron. If it was a Hall, as seems most likely (see Barrett 1998, p904-5), we do not know whether Tyrannus was a lecturer or the owner of the building. On the hall see also Pereira 1983, p139-41. For nuns leasing a hall in Oxyrhynchos see *New Docs* 1, no. 82.

Ephesus, so we are unable to verify this detail.[172] However, the name Τύραννος is found in first century C.E. inscriptions from Ephesus,[173] which adds to the likelihood that the mention of Paul teaching in the Hall goes back to some reliable tradition.[174]

Some of the Greeks mentioned in 19:10,17, some of whom became believers, may well have been God-fearers, whose existence need not be doubted,[175] and among whom Paul often had some success.[176] Other Gentiles who heard Paul in the Hall of Tyrannus probably had no connection with the synagogue. This suggests that the Pauline community in Ephesus consisted of Jews and Gentiles, with some of the latter having had no connection with the synagogue.

A second dimension of Luke's presentation of Paul's time in Ephesus as successful, particularly among Gentiles, comes from his note that Paul spent over two years and three months in the city. This comprises three months'

---

[172] In Ephesus, we know of a building in the area of the Library of Celsus which was called an αὐδειτώριον, a word which is based on the Latin *auditorium*. The building was probably used by the proconsul as a court room; it is unlikely that the building was used as lecture hall, as has been suggested. On the inscription which is *I.Eph.* 3009, see Heberdey 1904, p52; Engelmann 1993a, p105-111. The undated inscription is probably to be dated in the 230's CE, although the auditorium could have been built well before this time. The site of the auditorium has not been located but it must have been between the south gate and the theatre street; see Engelmann 1993a, p105-106. Hemer (1973, p128) suggested the auditorium was a "lecture hall", but see Engelmann 1993a, p106. Rackham (1910, p351) suggested that the "school" was located in one of the gymnasia of Ephesus. Wexler (1981, p123-4, 133) thinks σχολή here may have meant "synagogue", but this seems highly unlikely.

[173] For Τύραννος in first century CE inscriptions from Ephesus see eg. *I.Eph.* 1001.5 (time of Tiberius); 20B.40 (54-59 CE, on which see Fieger 1998, p83-6.); 1012.4 (92-93 CE). In the 1st-2nd century CE it may have been used as a *cognomen* in successive generations of a small group of interrelated leading families in Ephesus; see Hemer 1989a, p120, 234; Lampe 1992, p70. The name Τύραννος is also found elsewhere; see for example TAM 5.1, 186.3 (Saittae); 252.3 (Kula); 741.3 (Iulia Gordus); TAM 5.2, 1384.1 (Magnesia ad Sipylum); Pape and Benseler 1911, p1565. In the Western Text the name is given as Τυραννίου (Tyrannius).

[174] Conzelmann 1987, p163 notes: "The detail about the lecture hall derives from local tradition." See also Williams 1990, p332. Presumably some sort of rent would have to be paid for the hall, although Luke does not mention such a detail. We argue later that Paul worked as a tent-maker while in Ephesus (see Acts 20:34), but probably the congregation contributed to the rent; see Haenchen 1971, p561.

[175] On the God-fearers see Trebilco 1991, p145-66 and more generally Trebilco 2001, p161-93; see also Mitchell 1993, vol 2, p32. Note that Luke consistently says that Paul addressed Jews and Greeks in the synagogue (Iconium 14:1; Thessalonica 17:4; Beroea 17:12; Corinth 18:4) or Jews and those who feared God or revered God (Pisidian Antioch 13:16; Athens 17:17). That this is historically credible is shown by the presence of God-fearers in synagogue inscriptions and in Josephus.

[176] See Acts 13:16, 43; 14:1; 17:4, 12; 18:4. See also Mitchell 1993, vol 2, p32, 43.

teaching in the synagogue (19:8), two years based on the hall of Tyrannus (19:10), and an unspecified period after sending Timothy and Erastus ahead into Macedonia (19:22).[177] This is the longest time Paul spent in any one city during his missionary travels.[178] This is credible, given the size and significance of Ephesus and the fact that it was a centre to which people from all over the province came.[179] Paul does not tell us in his letters how long he spent in Ephesus. However, we know that it was after his founding visit to Corinth that he went to Ephesus (1 Cor 16:1-8), and there was clearly a fairly long period between this founding visit to Corinth and the visit from Ephesus back to Corinth proposed in 1 Cor 16:5-8.[180] Paul seems to have spent this time (or a good deal of it) in Ephesus, which suggests his stay there was of a fairly long duration. Thus, the time of over two years and three months given by Acts is credible.[181]

The witness par excellence to Paul's success among Gentiles in Ephesus is Demetrius in 19:26-7: Paul's preaching has even affected the sale of souvenirs of Artemis, and provoked a reaction from the silversmiths. We will discuss the account of the riot in detail in the next chapter, but we can note here that a number of points argue strongly for the basic historicity of the narrative and suggest that the Christian community in Ephesus did grow significantly during Paul's ministry and that a number of Gentiles were converted.

7.4.3 Success in the province of Asia (19:10, 26)

We have already noted that we have evidence from Paul's letters and elsewhere (1 Cor 16:19; Col 1:1; 2:1; 4:13, 15-16; Philm 1-2 (cf. Col 4:17); 10 (cf. Col 4:9); 23-4 (cf. Col 1:7; 4:10); perhaps Rev 2-3) that the Gospel spread from Ephesus to the surrounding area during Paul's time in Ephesus. Thus, Luke's portrayal of Ephesus as a missionary centre for the province is

---

[177] The three years given in Acts 20:31 is probably an inclusive reckoning of time, counting in full the year of commencement; see Hemer 1989a, p256, 425; Haenchen 1971, p67.

[178] Compare the eighteen months spent in Corinth (Acts 18:11).

[179] Haenchen 1971, p560 regards the statement of time and place as having been taken over from tradition; see also Thiessen 1995, p91.

[180] See Chapter 2, section 1.7 and in particular Lüdemann (1984, p101-2) who points to the exchange of letters prior to 1 Cor, the activity of Apollos between the founding visit and 1 Cor (1 Cor 3:6; 16:12), the new developments that had taken place in Corinth, and the fact that "many" had died since his departure (1 Cor 11:30) as indications of the length of time between Paul's founding visit in Corinth and his writing 1 Cor and proposing to visit them again from Ephesus. Note that Luke does not know of, or does not wish to tell his readers of, Paul's painful visit to Corinth during this time; see 2 Cor 2:1; 13:2 and Chapter 2, section 2.1.

[181] Haenchen, 1971, p560 regards the statement of time and place as having been taken over from tradition.

credible, and is in keeping with the fact that Ephesus was the capital of the province and the hub of communications for the area.

7.4.4 Success in performing miracles and exorcisms (19:11-12, 13-17)

In 19:11-12 we hear of miracles Paul performed himself,[182] and then that handkerchiefs (σουδάρια) and aprons (σιμικίνθια) which had been in contact with Paul's body were taken to the sick, and they were healed of diseases, and evil spirits left them.[183] The belief that the bodies of particular people, or whatever touched them, had thaumaturgical powers was widespread in antiquity.[184] In the Gospels healing occurs when people touch the hem of Jesus' garment (Mk 5:27-34; 6:56) and in Acts people are healed by contact with Peter's shadow (Acts 5:15).[185]

We know from Paul's own writings that he performed miracles (Rom 15:19; 2 Cor 12:12),[186] and that miracles were performed by others in Paul's churches (Gal 3:5). Thus we need not reject the picture of him as a miracle

---

[182] This was probably though not necessarily by the laying on of hands.

[183] Σουδάριον is not found in the LXX or in any pre-Christian authors. It is based on the Latin word *sudarium*, which was a face cloth for wiping perspiration, or a handkerchief; see Glare 1976, p1859. It occurs in the NT (see Lk 19:20; Jn 11:44; 20:7) but these occurrences tell us little about its meaning. The word is found in Graeco-Roman magical literature, but never as a technical term for something used to perform cures. For its use see Preisendanz 1931, 7.826-27; 36.269-70; see also Betz 1992. Σιμικίνθιον is a hapax legomenon in the NT and is not found in the LXX or in any pre-Christian authors, and so its meaning is difficult to ascertain; see BDAG, p923-4. It is based on the Latin word *semicinctium*, which generally means a belt; see Leary 1990, p527-29. This meaning is quite likely for σιμικίνθιον, although commentators have often taken it to refer to some article of clothing which had been in actual contact with the apostle's skin. See Nestle 1901-02, p282; Lake and Cadbury 1933a, p239-40. Since we know that Paul worked as a tentmaker for at least some of the time he was in Ephesus (see Chapter 4 on Acts 20:34; cf. 1 Cor. 4:12), it may be that the handkerchiefs and aprons were connected with his work; see Hock 1980, p26, 42.

[184] See for example, Plutarch, *Pyrr.* 3.4-5. (Pyrrhus' right foot had healing power); Artapanus in Eusebius, *PE* 9.27 (the power of Moses' body to perform wonders); see also Oster 1974, p33-38; Schüssler Fiorenza 1976, p10-11. We should note that for Luke the power is not inherent in the apron or handkerchief, nor does he suggest that the power of God permanently resided in these objects, as if they were relics. For Luke, it was God who worked the wonders; see vv. 11, 20. See also Polhill 1992, p402.

[185] On this verse see van der Horst 1976-77, p204-12. Johnson 1992, p340 comments: "Luke himself, it should be noted, betrays no embarrassment about combining the 'word of God' with such 'popular religion'."

[186] See Holmberg 1978, p77, 155; Brockhaus, 1975, p192 n226. Fieger (1998, p99) also notes that 1 Cor 4:20 (ἐν δυνάμει) was written from Ephesus. Note also that for Paul his power is a power in weakness; see 2 Cor 12:9-10. Note however, that for Paul signs and wonders and mighty works (2 Cor 12:12) are at best but a limited part of the criterion of apostleship; at worst they can be highly deceptive; see Martin 1986, p436.

worker in Acts,[187] even if Luke gives a more prominent place to miracles than does Paul. Given that we know Paul performed miracles in other places, this passage suggests that miracles were an element in Paul's ministry in Ephesus.[188]

In Acts 19:13-17 we have the story of a group of itinerant Jewish exorcists who attempted to imitate Paul and use the name of "the Jesus whom Paul proclaims" to cast out evil spirits (19:13). Among the group were seven sons of a Jewish high priest Sceva, and we are told that the exorcism they attempted was unsuccessful (19:14-16). Luke seems to tell this story for a number of reasons. It shows that the name of Jesus is not a magical device but rather can only be used by those who have been given authority to call upon that name.[189] Further, the story shows the power of the Gospel Paul preaches. Not only are evil spirits cast out through Paul (19:12), whom the evil spirit acknowledges (19:15), while the seven sons of Sceva are unsuccessful in their attempted exorcism, but also the story shows that some Jews acknowledged the power of the name of Jesus whom Paul preaches, for they too want to use that name. In addition, for Luke the incident has a wider impact: "When this became known to all residents of Ephesus, both Jews and Greeks, everyone was awestruck; and the name of the Lord Jesus was praised" (19:17).[190] Thus the negative effect of the improper use of the name of Jesus was as significant as the positive effect of "the word of the Lord" (19:10).

Thus the story adds to the portrait of Paul's time in Ephesus as a success. Paul was so successful that Jewish exorcists tried to take over the name of

---

[187] See Acts 13:11; 14:3, 10; 15:12; 16:18. Haenchen, 1971, p563; Conzelmann 1987, p163 are unnecessarily sceptical at this point; see also Ashton 2000, p171-8.

[188] Barrett (1998, p903) thinks Luke is dependent on an Ephesian Christian source for this story.

[189] See Schneider 1982, p266; Garrett 1989, p92-3; Johnson 1992, p340-1; Fitzmyer 1998, p646. The story thus shows the triumph of Christianity over magic; see Garrett 1989, p89-99. The seven sons are in effect attempting to use Jesus' name as if it were a magical device. This theme is also in evidence in the stories of Simon Magus (Acts 8:9-24), the Jew Elymas (Acts 13:6-11) and the slave girl in Philippi (Acts 16:16-18).

[190] As Garrett (1989, p95) notes: "As the demon's defeat of the sons has shown, Jesus' name cannot be corrupted or misappropriated. Hence 'the name' deserves the grandest praise." This verse is clearly composed by Luke. The phrase "and this became known" (19:17) is Lucan; see 1:19; 4:16; 9:42; see also 2:14; 4:10; 28:28; Lake and Cadbury 1933a, p242; Haenchen 1971, p565. Acts 19:17 prepares for 26:26 – "this was not done in a corner". The role played by fear or wonder in the story is also Lucan; see Acts 2:43; 3:10; 4:16; 5:5, 11; 8:6; 9:35, 42; 13:12. In particular this verse recalls Acts 1:19 and 4:16. Johnson also notes that we have here the typical responses to a miracle story: "a) the spread of the news ... b) the response of awe and fear ... c) the glorification/praise of God'; see Johnson 1992, p341, who cites parallels. However, that Luke composed the verse does not mean that it has no basis in tradition.

Jesus which he invoked, but found they could not imitate Paul.[191] In fact the actions of these Jewish exorcists actually led to further praise of the Jesus preached by Paul and to further inroads being made against the power of magic, as we will see in the next story (19:18-20). But the story also shows that Paul's success is not due to himself but to the power of the name of the one he preaches.

Can we say anything about the historicity of the event? We know that in this period Jews had a reputation as exorcists.[192] Further, the Jews had a reputation for being practitioners of magic and were believed to know exceptionally powerful spells, which included the use of powerful names.[193] Given the presence of a significant Jewish community in Ephesus, as we showed in chapter 1, it would be understandable if itinerant Jewish exorcists visited the city. These features suggest that the story and its setting in Ephesus are plausible.

Ashton has also drawn attention to the conclusion in v20 which Luke draws from Paul's miracles and the incident with Sceva's sons: "So the word of the Lord grew mightily and prevailed". He notes that this conclusion "appears to conflict with his [Luke's] general determination to ascribe the success of the gospel, not to miracles, but to preaching, and especially to Paul's success in proving from the scriptures that Jesus was the Messiah.[194] Insofar as the content of this passage [19:11-20] 'goes against the grain' of the author's declared intention we should be the more reluctant to dismiss it."[195] This does not mean that the story is necessarily historical at all points, but it does make it unlikely that Luke created it and so inclines us towards seeing it as historical.

But we should note that we have no evidence to suggest that anyone named "Sceva" was ever a Jewish high priest, since he is not listed as a high priest by Josephus, who gives the names of all the high priests in the first century BCE and the first century CE until 70.[196] What do we make of the title then? The term ἀρχιερεύς is sometimes used of those who were never ruling high priests but rather were members of the Jewish priestly aristocracy. This may be the sense here, in which case the more impressive ἀρχιερεύς was used by

---

[191] See Haenchen 1971, p565.

[192] See Lk 11:19; Josephus, Ant 8:45-9; Justin, Dial 80.9-10; 85, 3; Schürer, Vermes, Millar, Black, Goodman 1986, p342-79; Garrett 1989, p91.

[193] See Simon 1986, p339-56; Johnson 1992, p222, 340; Fieger 1998, p111-14.

[194] See for example Acts 13:42-3; 14:1; 14:21; 16:14; 17:2-4.

[195] Ashton 2000, p176.

[196] On Sceva see Mastin 1976, p405-12; 1978, p97-9; on the textual variants of 19:14 see Strange 1987, p97-106; on this passage in codex Bezae see Delebecque 1982, p225-32. See also Johnson 1992, p340; Conzelmann 1987, p164. The name "Sceva" is Latin, which adds to the questions about the passage. On the list of high priests in Josephus see Mastin 1976, p405; Delebecque 1982, p226.

Sceva's sons in order to authenticate their activity.[197] Alternatively, the sons may have falsely described Sceva as ἀρχιερεύς in order to enhance their reputation,[198] since the title would suggest to others that the sons had contact with the supernatural and knew magical divine names.[199]

The story is thus plausible, and although there are doubts about Sceva, we have noted that the story is contrary to Luke's overall intention and so it is unlikely that Luke has created it.[200] The story thus probably adds one more historical element for Luke's portrait of Paul as successful in Ephesus and one more reason for the growth of the Christian community in the city.[201]

7.4.5 Success over the power of magic (19:18-20)

In Acts 19:18-20 we learn that some new believers, who had previously been involved in magic, now confessed and divulged their practices and burnt their books in public.[202] In the context, it is the demonstration of the power of the

---

[197] See Mastin 1976, p405-12. Thus Josephus describes Jesus son of Sapphas as τῶν ἀρχιερέων ἕνα (BJ 2, 566) and Matthias, son of Boethus is said to be τὸν ἀρχιερέα (BJ 4, 574) and ἐκ τῶν ἀρχιερέων (BJ 5, 527). We know these two were never ruling high priests. See also Schneider 1982, p270. Fitzmyer (1998, p646-50) thinks Sceva is a Jew who served as chief priest in the imperial cult in Ephesus.

[198] See Johnson 1992, p340; Delebecque 1982, p227. In this case, he and his sons may not have been Jews at all. Note that the Western text probably did not include Ἰουδαίου in 19:14, a reading which Strange (1987, p97-106) thinks is original. If this was the case, 19:14 describes a second group of exorcists (after the Jews of 19:13) and Sceva and his sons would be Gentiles. The problem that Sceva is not known to be a Jewish high-priest would then disappear.

[199] Our lack of any knowledge about Sceva has suggested to some that Luke has here taken over some sort of legend or an anecdote created by popular Christianity; see Conzelmann 1987, p163; see also Dibelius 1956, p19. This is possible, although no similar legends of priests casting out demons which Luke could have used as a model are cited to give this suggestion weight. But compare Testament of Levi 18:12: the sons of the true high priest will have authority to trample on the evil spirits; see Barrett 1998, p910.

[200] Barrett (1998, p909) thinks that Luke was using an oral or written tradition here and (Barrett 1998, p903) writes of the story in v13-17 that it was "no doubt told with delight–and probably with some exaggeration–by Ephesian Christians, and listened to by Luke with equal pleasure." If it were clear that Luke intended us to see the claim that Sceva was high priest as a scurrilous, then the case for historicity would be a little stronger. Mastin (1976, p408) describes the story as "wholly realistic".

[201] The Jewish exorcists are clearly itinerant, and so we do not know how long they were in Ephesus or if they had any impact on the Christians in the city.

[202] Some commentators (eg. Haenchen 1971, p567; Schneider 1982, 2, p270-71) have argued that the perfect participle (τῶν πεπιστευκότων) in v18 means that these people had been converted some time ago, and had continued to practice magic until the incident with Sceva's sons occurred. However, Garrett (1989, p95-6) has shown that Luke's meaning is that as a result of the defeat of the sons of Sceva, a great many people believed in the Word, some of whom had practiced magic and who immediately came forward to confess this. It is

name of Jesus in 19:13-17 that convinces them that any other power - magic, for example - is worthless.[203] The result is that these new believers renounce the practice of magic. What do we make of this incident? Again its theme is the success of Paul and of his Gospel, this time over the practice of magic. It is in fact the third encounter between the gospel and the practice of magic (see 8:4-25; 13:4-12) and as before "the gospel triumphs in explicit and dramatic fashion."[204] But is the account plausible?

Certainly Ephesus had a reputation as a centre of magical arts, and the city gave its name to the well known Ἐφέσια γράμματα.[205] The genuine Ephesian Letters were six magical terms which were thought to be words of power which could, for example, ward off demons and so could be used as written amulets or spoken charms.[206] Inscriptions from Ephesus also contain references to magicians and curses.[207] The books (βίβλοι, 19:19) of magic which were burned may have contained the famous Ephesian Letters and the sort of material preserved in the magical papyri, such as thaumaturgic formulae, incantations, hymns and prayers.[208] This side of the story is thus credible.

We also have a good deal of information about book burning in antiquity. Books were generally burned by rulers or others who found the books offensive, seditious, or dangerous, in order to repudiate the contents of the books concerned.[209] In Acts 19:19 we are told that the new converts burnt

---

these new believers who are referred to in the summary of 19:20, which refers to the numerical growth of the community.

[203] Garrett (1989, p97) notes that Luke's purpose is "to emphasize the sweeping victory of the Lord over the powers of darkness even in Ephesus, noted center of the magical arts."

[204] Johnson 1992, p341.

[205] They are well attested in the literature; see for example Clement of Alexandria, *Strom.* 1.15; 5.8; Plutarch, *Quaest. conv.* 7.5.

[206] See Arnold 1989, p15-16; McCown 1923, p128-40. The Ephesia Grammata are first mentioned in the fourth century BCE and in popular usage could be regarded as active and powerful protective spirits. The letters were also connected with Artemis of Ephesus and were said to have been engraved on the crown, girdle and feet of her statue; on the link between Artemis and magic see Portefaix 1999, p616-17. Jews also played a prominent part in the magic of the ancient world. On magic in general see Kee 1986, p95-125; *New Docs* 6, 193-96; Graf 1997; Klauck 2000, p209-31.

[207] See *I.Eph.* 3817A; 567-69; see also 1024.6f; 1044.20; Lampe 1992, p69.

[208] See Oster 1974, p61; see also Pseudo-Phocylides 149. The Greek Magical Papyri offer an abundance of comparative material regarding ancient books of magic; see Betz 1992. A few magical amulets with Jewish elements have been discovered at or near Ephesus; see Kraabel 1968, p56-9; above Chapter 1, section 4.4. It is possible then that some of those who had been practicing magic may come from a Jewish background; see Thompson 1990, p118-9.

[209] See Suetonius, *Augustus* 31; Livy 39.16; 40.29.3-14; Pliny, *NH* 13.84-88; Diogenes Laertius 9.52. For further references to book burning see Forbes 1936, p114-25; Pease 1946, p145-60.

their books in public (ἐνώπιον πάντων); Livy and Diogenes Laertius in their accounts of book burning both make a point of saying that it was carried out in public.[210] The public and communal nature of such an act seems to be an important part of the repudiation of the contents of the books concerned. However, in the Acts account the books were not forcibly seized by others as occurred in most of the other accounts from the Greco-Roman period, but rather were voluntarily burnt by their owners, and at great personal loss.[211] By burning their own books themselves and by doing so in public, the new believers in Ephesus were openly repudiating their own previous involvement in magic. All of this is plausible then.[212]

Further, 1 Thess 1:9-10 indicates that Paul clearly saw the necessity for his converts to turn from their former way of life, and other verses point to the decisive break between a pagan past and the believers present life for Paul.[213] We can thus note that the story fits all that we know of Ephesus and Paul. It seems reasonable to accept the story as credible then, although we note that we have no specific corroboration of the account.[214] But here again we can argue for the basic historicity of Luke's theme of Paul's success and the success of the Gospel in Ephesus, this time over magic.

The incident suggests two points about the on-going life of the church in Ephesus. Firstly, the value of the magic books was 50,000 silver drachmae. Since a drachma was a day's wage, this was a considerable amount of money.[215] Of course they were much poorer after they had burnt the books!

---

[210] See Livy 40.29.3-14; Diogenes Laertius 9.52; see also Cicero, *Natura Deorum* 1.63; Lucian, *Alex.*, 47.

[211] See Oster 1974, p62. For examples of authors burning their own books, for a variety of reasons, see Forbes 1936, p114-17; see also Lucian, Alex., 47, where he voluntarily burns his own copy of a book written by Epicurus, saying about the book: "Burn with fire, I command you, the creed of a purblind dotard!"

[212] Luke tells us that the new believers "confessed and divulged their practices (ἐξομολογούμενοι καὶ ἀναγγέλλοντες τὰς πράξεις αὐτῶν)" (19:18). Again this is in accord with what we know of ancient magic. As Bruce (1988, p369) notes: "According to magical theory, the potency of a spell is bound up with its secrecy; if it be divulged, it becomes ineffective. So these converted magicians renounced their imagined power by rendering their spells inoperative." See also Lake and Cadbury 1933a, p242.

[213] See for example Gal 4:8-11; Col 1:13-14.

[214] Haenchen does not think the story is historical. He writes (1971, p567): "Luke only wants to show how magic lost ground through the activity of Paul (= of Christianity), and according to his technique of narration he clothes this statement in the garb of an impressive scene." However, he does not take the points which argue for historicity sufficiently seriously and just because Luke makes a point in a story, does not necessarily mean he has created that story.

[215] Johnson 1992, p342: "Whatever the rate of exchange, fifty thousand of such coins [either denarion or drachma] obviously represents a fortune (cf. Mt 26:15). Luke would not have included the number had he not thought it particularly impressive." Note that no unit of currency is given in 19:19, but Barrett (1998, p913) notes that δραχμῶν must be supplied.

But, if the sum is reliable, the possession of this amount of disposable income to spend on magic books suggests that at least some[216] of the Ephesian Christians were well off.

Secondly, these people had come into the Ephesian Christian community with a worldview shaped by the contemporary magical arts. Such a pronounced background might have continued to influence their thinking as Christians.

We conclude then that a strong case can be put that there is an historical basis for Luke's account of Paul's success in Ephesus. We will incorporate dimensions of this in our overall conclusions below.

8. Overall Conclusions

We note first of all the tantilising lack of information about the on-going life of the Christian community in Ephesus. As we pointed out at the beginning of this chapter, Luke gives us an account of "beginning" and "notable incidents" which occurred in Ephesus, rather than a description of the on-going life of the Christian community in the city. However, we can note some points.

Secondly, we have evidence for the activity of some notable early Christians in Ephesus. Priscilla and Aquila worked in Ephesus with Paul, probably for most of the duration of the Pauline mission in the city. They were clearly leading missionaries in the early Church and we note Priscilla's significance as a teacher and leader in her own right. We have also noted the activity of Apollos in Ephesus. We can suggest that he had an impact before Paul's main work in the city (Acts 18:27), but also probably over quite a period of time, since he returned to Ephesus after time in Corinth. Although Apollos' work may have introduced an element of diversity into the Christian community, there is no evidence for an "Apollos party" at Ephesus. Apollos' work in Ephesus may have been one of the factors in the growth of the Christian movement in Ephesus; Paul's remarks about Apollos suggest it was an impact of which he himself approved.

Thirdly, it is credible that Paul's time in Ephesus, which Luke records as over two years and three months, was marked by some success, although we have noted that Paul also encountered opposition and endured suffering in Ephesus, features of Paul's time in Ephesus which Luke underplays. We can note a number of features of this success. We can suggest that Paul preached

---

Barrett also notes (1998, p914) "That Luke puts a price on them may reflect his strong dislike of the money-making side of magic and his clear rejection of it from the Christian side; cf. his treatment of Simon Magus (8:4-25)." See also Taylor 1996, p39-40.

[216] Luke describes the number of people as ἱκανοί. Barrett (1998, p912) comments that the word "is about as imprecise as 'a good many'."

to Jews in the synagogue in Ephesus, and that some Jews were converted. But it is also credible that Paul left the synagogue after some Jews spoke against him. We also have good grounds for accepting Luke's report that Paul then preached to Gentiles and had some success among them. Some of these Gentiles may well have been God-fearers. Thus the Christian community in Ephesus seems to have grown quickly, a point which is confirmed by Paul's statement about "effective work" in Ephesus (1 Cor 16:9). Further, by 55 CE the Pauline community in Ephesus had probably grown significantly and consisted of Jews and Gentiles, with some of the latter having had no connection with the synagogue.[217] We will discuss this further in the next chapter.

Fourthly, there are a number of suggestions of potential diversity. We do not know when the Christian community began in Ephesus, but perhaps some Ephesian or Asian Jews who were resident in Jerusalem were converted at Pentecost and returned to Ephesus at some stage, perhaps months or years after Pentecost. The first group of Christians in Ephesus for whom we have evidence were Jewish Christians of an unknown background. Their existence shows that all of the Christians in Ephesus even in the earliest period did not owe allegiance to Paul, and that there was a pre-Pauline group in the city.

The Ephesian twelve, who seem to have been disciples of John the Baptist prior to their conversion, may have had particular emphases to their Christian faith. They were a significant group and may have constituted a house church which perhaps had its own continuing and distinctive identity. According to Acts 19:9, after three months of activity in the synagogue, Paul left the synagogue along with "the disciples", but we do not know if all those who were Christians left the synagogue at this stage; some may clearly have remained. But this evidence suggests there was a significant group of Jewish Christians in Ephesus at the conclusion of the Pauline mission.

A number of Gentiles became Christians, some of whom may have been God-fearers, and others former devotees of Artemis.[218] Further, the believers who had a background in magic may have continued to be influenced in their thinking as Christians by the worldview of the contemporary magical arts.

However, one could overstate this diversity. Paul worked in Ephesus for over two years and three months, and probably the majority of the Christian community by the end of this period had been converted through his ministry, or through that of associates like Priscilla and Aquila. We can suggest then that by around 55 CE most of the Christians in Ephesus were "Pauline".

---

[217] In this we differ markedly from Günther (1995, p29-67) who does not think there was a Pauline community at the conclusion of Paul's time in the city. But we have noted at various points that his views are unlikely.

[218] Since their conversion affected the sale of souvenirs of Artemis; see the next Chapter.

Fifthly, miracles and exorcisms probably featured as one dimension of Paul's ministry in Ephesus and contributed to the impact of his mission. The story of the seven sons of Sceva attempting to use the name of Jesus in exorcism and inadvertently contributing to the success of Paul's time in Ephesus is plausible, although we can say no more than this about its historicity.

Sixthly, the account of the burning of magic books is credible and suggests that at least some of the Ephesian Christians were well off.

Finally, there may have been an on-going presence of followers of John the Baptist in Ephesus, but we have no evidence which confirms this.

Chapter 4

Acts and the early Christians in Ephesus:
Endings and Departure

We have noted in Chap 3 that Luke's account of Paul's time in Ephesus focuses on "beginnings", "endings" and "notable incidents". In this chapter we will firstly examine Luke's account of the riot in Ephesus, which is clearly a "notable incident" but also comes into the category of "endings", since shortly after the riot, Paul leaves the city. In Acts 20:17-35 Luke also gives a speech by Paul to the Ephesian elders at Miletus. This is a farewell speech, and so clearly also comes into the category of "endings". Our focus here will be on what this material tell us about Paul's time in Ephesus and the early Christians in the city.

1. The riot in Ephesus (Acts 19:23-40)

In Acts 19:23-40 Luke gives an account of a riot instigated by the silversmith Demetrius in protest against Paul's work.[1] In this section a number of Lucan themes are again in evidence. We note the following:

1) The success of the Pauline mission in Ephesus, for Paul's preaching has even affected the sale of souvenirs of Artemis, and provoked a reaction from the silversmiths. Demetrius acts as witness to this success in 19:26-7.[2]

---

[1] Luke introduces the riot with κατὰ τὸν καιρὸν ἐκεῖνον. Barrett (1998, p922) notes "this means no more than 'during Paul's Ephesian ministry', though Luke (20.1) takes it to have provided the cue for Paul's departure, which is likely enough." Some scholars (eg. Duncan 1929, p34) have attempted to link the riot of Acts 19 with the Artemision festival (on which see Trebilco 1994, p321-2). In 1 Cor 16:8 Paul says he wanted to stay in Ephesus until Pentecost, which falls in early June. This means Paul may have been in Ephesus in March-April when the Artemision festival was held (see Hicks 1890b, p414). However, Acts gives no indication that the riot occurred at the same time as a festival; see Strelan 1996, p62 n95.

[2] Conzelmann (1987, p165) notes: "For the Christian reader, the charge against Paul [in v26] is a testimony to the victorious advance of the mission." In v26 the context implies that "Asia" probably means the province, rather than the area of Ephesus and the surrounding Greek cities, since Demetrius is speaking of the wide effect of the Christian message; see also Lake and Cadbury 1933a, p246.

2) That Christianity is not a threat to the good order of the Empire, and so should be treated with toleration. Here, the town clerk's reasoned rebuttal of the charges brought against Paul is a continuation of Luke's picture that important representatives of political and social life are either positive or neutral towards the new faith. Luke wishes to show that the new faith was not politically dangerous and one feature of this is the favourable or neutral reaction of many Roman officials.[3] Thus in Acts opposition to Paul comes, not from the duly constituted gentile authorities, but only from crowds stirred up by the Jews or, as in this incident, motivated by less than worthy motives.[4] If the regular procedures of law were followed, then the new faith would be vindicated.

3) One dimension of the previous point is that the Asiarchs are said to be "friends" of Paul. This is part of the Lucan theme of the high social level of some of Christianity's new "friends". The point is that a group whose leader has such friends cannot be a danger to the Roman Empire.[5]

4) The superiority of Christianity over paganism and the weakness and confusion of the opposition to Paul. Because of the success of Christian preaching there is a danger that Artemis herself will be scorned (19:27). Yet the campaign against Paul was in confusion both in the city (19:29) and in the theatre (19:32), and most of the people in the theatre did not know why they were there (19:32). Then the crowd resorted to mindless repetition of slogans (19:34) and finally the town clerk had to tell them all to go home, before they made any further trouble (19:35f). The overall impression is that the victory of Christianity over paganism, represented by Artemis, is assured. Since this is clearly a theological matter for Luke which does not relate to the life of the Christians in Ephesus, I will not comment on it further.[6]

---

[3] See 16.35f; 18:14f; 22:25f; 23:29f; 26:31f; 28:18f; van Unnik, 1960a, p39; Bruce 1988, p8-9; Yates 1981, p241-2. Rather than being addressed to Roman officials, to try and convince them that Christianity was "safe", this aspect of Luke's message was probably addressed to Christians to draw their attention to the political innocence of Christianity and to encourage them to adopt an inoffensive lifestyle and an attitude of respect towards the ruling authorities; see Maddox 1982, p96-7; Stoops 1989, p88-90.

[4] See Lake and Cadbury 1933a, p236; Johnson 1992, p352; Bruce 1988, p379.

[5] See Schüssler Fiorenza 1976, p17. Johnson (1992, p349) points outs: "That such socially elevated folk became 'friends' (philoi) of Paul and showed concern for his welfare is consistent with Luke's recent efforts to show the success of the mission among the better classes (17:4, 12, 34)."

[6] Another theme that we will not investigate in detail is that a key factor in Gentile opposition to the new faith is economic self-interest. This is part of Luke's wider theme that responses to the Gospel are symbolized by attitudes toward material possessions. As Johnson (1992, p353) points out, in Luke-Acts the acceptance of God's call is accompanied by sharing possessions (Lk 8:1-3; Acts 4:32-7), while "opposition to the Gospel is expressed by

Given that Luke wishes to make these thematic and theological points in the riot narrative, what can we say about the historicity of the story? Firstly, we will point to some general indications of the historicity of the whole narrative and secondly will discuss arguments which have been raised against its historicity. Thirdly, we will discuss the theological points that Luke is making in this passage which are relevant to our investigation and see if we have any reasons to accept or to deny the historical elements which are involved or implied in these theological points. Finally, we will draw some conclusions for this section.

1.1 General indications of historicity

As we have noted at the beginning of Chapter 3, Oster, Sherwin-White and Baugh have shown that, in the account of the riot, Luke displays very accurate knowledge of Ephesus and commentators regularly point to the vivid local colouring of the narrative.[7] Thus, what Luke says (to pick just some examples), about the silversmiths, the significance of the temple of Artemis, the fame of the city of Ephesus as the "temple keeper" of Artemis, the presence of the Asiarchs, the behaviour of unruly mobs in the Greco-Roman city, the attitude of the town clerk to a disturbance in the city and the way he defends the city's reputation and much more is all abundantly confirmed by literary and archaeological evidence.[8] As we noted in the previous chapter, Barrett suggests that 19:21-40 is based on information gained by Luke either on a visit to Ephesus, or from Ephesian residents and this seems very likely.[9]

1.2 Objections to the historicity of the passage

A number of objections to the historicity of the passage have been raised; we will now consider each of these in turn.

1.2.1 Comparison with Paul's letters

Haenchen has noted that before Paul left Asia he experienced a severe affliction referred to in 2 Cor 1:8. However, in Haenchen's opinion, in Luke's day it was only known that great turmoil had preceded Paul's departure from

---

the love of money". Demetrius' concern about his loss of revenue is in keeping with the actions of others in Luke-Acts who by their material acquisitiveness show that they have rejected God's call; see also Lk 6:24; 16:10-31; Acts 1:17-20; 5:1-11; 8:18-24; 16:16-19; Johnson 1992, p353.

[7] See Johnson 1992, p351: "Luke once more gets the local color precisely right"; see also Conzelmann 1987, p164-5; Schneider 1982, p273; cf. Burkert 1999, p59-60.

[8] See further in Trebilco 1994, p316-57.

[9] Barrett 1998, p917; see also Fitzmyer 1998, p655.

Ephesus. Rather than speaking about it in a brief sentence, Luke vividly developed what he knew, drawing on his general knowledge of the Artemis cult, the Asiarchs, the constitution of the city, and the names Demetrius and Alexander, the first associated with the event by tradition,[10] the second coming from 1 Tim 1:20 and 2 Tim 4:14 where an Alexander is spoken of who was Paul's opponent.[11] Hence the whole account is basically created by Luke from the barest possible sources.

However, a number of points can be made against this view. Firstly, Haenchen underestimates the extent of verifiable detail in this section, even to the alternation between θεά and θεός which Baugh has noted.[12] Further, while Paul's letters do give an indication of opposition and suffering in Ephesus and "Asia" which Luke either does not know about or has chosen not to present, we cannot say that this riot did not occur just because it does not seem to correspond to either of the events alluded to by Paul in 1 Cor 16:9 or 2 Cor 1:8-11. If the riot is the event referred to in 2 Cor 1:8-11 (which is only one interpretative possibility) then it may have been more serious that Luke presents,[13] but we cannot say that the riot was Luke's creation just because Paul's letters do not confirm unambiguously that a riot occurred precisely as Luke states.[14] Further, that Luke is silent about some events which occurred during Paul's time in Ephesus (as we know from his letters) does not mean, of course, that he is unreliable when it comes to those events which he does record. However, the fact that we do know that Paul encountered opposition in Ephesus at some point (1 Cor 16:9) and potentially at others too, and also that he suffered a good deal at the hands of Gentiles in many places (2 Cor 11:23-26) means that this account cannot be dismissed as improbable, even if

---

[10] Haenchen (1971, p577) here admits to some "memory" of the event among Christians, concerning the name Demetrius. However, traditions generally concern not just a name, but also something that the person did. If the name Demetrius was remembered, then why not something more of what he actually did? Thus Haenchen goes some way here to undermining his own theory that the story was basically Luke's creation.

[11] See Haenchen 1971, p577.

[12] See Baugh 1990, p290-94.

[13] If the riot is the event Paul refers to as his "affliction in Asia" (2 Cor 1:8-11), and it is only one possible interpretation of 2 Cor 1:8-11 as we noted in chapter 2, then Luke has probably toned the account down, and made it sound less dangerous for Paul; see Johnson 1992, p352. If this is the case, perhaps Luke did not want to present Paul as suffering severely at the hands of Gentiles. But note Barrett's (1998, p918) comment: "To have a theatre full of people thirsting for one's blood might well have seemed life-threatening."

[14] Given that we can see that Luke's account in Ephesus is incomplete, Marshall (1980, p316) notes that "It is doubtful, therefore, whether we can press the argument from silence against Luke's account here." Thus we cannot say, for example, that the riot must be equivalent to 2 Cor 1:8-11, and therefore that Luke has greatly altered the story.

Paul's letters do not supply specific corroboration for it.[15] Thus, Haenchen's view is unlikely.

1.2.2 Paul is marginal to the story

Johnson has noted that "Paul's systematic removal from the center of the story"[16] is odd. However, this seems to argue for the historicity of the account. If Luke had created the story, it seems likely that he would have put Paul at the centre of the action, and perhaps had him address the crowd. That Paul is so marginal to it suggests it is not a creation.[17]

1.2.3 Demetrius' role in the riot

Haenchen has noted that after leading the crowd into the theatre, Demetrius and his friends disappear, so that in 19:32 the crowd is in confusion. He asks: "How can a man who is presented as so good an organizer veil himself in silence at the very moment when - before an enthusiastic public - he ought to come out with a concrete proposal?"[18] We can note that Demetrius does not actually disappear from the scene, since he is mentioned in 19:38, but it is certainly valid to ask where has Demetrius gone?

But to ask this question is to assume that Demetrius should have proceeded to take some official action against Paul. If that had been the case he could have approached the Assembly from the beginning and not caused a riot at all, or only secondarily.[19] Is it not more likely then that Demetrius' plan of action from the start was to cause trouble for Paul and thus to "scare him off"? Certainly his actions from the start seem to be aimed at stirring up an intimidating mob rather than taking legal action. Of course, it is possible that Demetrius did not have a concrete plan of action at all, or that he could not actually have had Paul expelled from Ephesus legally and rather wished to scare him away. Demetrius could then be quite happy with a mob that shouted for two hours. In any case, Haenchen's objection does not stand up to investigation.

---

[15] See further Taylor 1996, p58-9.

[16] Johnson 1992, p348.

[17] Schneider (1982, p276) notes that it remains unclear why the crowd did not seize Paul at once and take him to the theatre.

[18] Haenchen 1971, p576; see also Schüssler Fiorenza 1976, p18-19.

[19] Compare the situation in Philippi (Acts 16:19-21) where the slave girl's owners first go to the magistrates since their real intention is to take legal action, and only secondarily does a crowd join in. Similarly, legal action is taken first in Corinth; see Acts 18:12.

1.2.4 Alexander's sudden introduction in the narrative (19:33-4)

The Jew Alexander suddenly appears in Acts 19:33-4 and this leads to a degree of unevenness in the story.[20] However, most scholars argue that Alexander was put forward by the Jews in order to dissociate the Jewish community from Paul and the accused Christians. Since Paul was a Jew, and Jews were known to reject the worship of pagan gods, there was a risk that the general population would indulge in anti-Jewish agitation, since they would make no distinction between Jews and Christians. Hence Alexander is put forward to make it plain that the Jews had nothing to do with the present trouble; the Jews thus attempt to prevent any harm coming to the Jewish community as a result of the incident.[21]

However, when the crowd recognised that Alexander was a Jew they did not want to listen. There are probably two reasons for this. Firstly, the crowd would not distinguish between Jews and Christians and so Alexander would be connected with the activity of Christians which had provoked the riot in the first place. Secondly, the Jews were themselves known to share Paul's views about "gods made with hands" and so the crowd was concerned that as a Jew Alexander was not a worshipper of Artemis either.[22] But Alexander's attempted defence at this point suggests that the Jewish community themselves distinguished between their group and the Pauline Christians, which is quite plausible. Further, that the Jewish community would want to

---

[20] Haenchen 1971, p576-7. The unevenness in the story is probably a result of the account being very compressed, so that Luke gives us only the bare bones of the story, rather than an indication that Luke has created the account; see Kreitzer 1987, p67. We may ask what the Jews were doing in this gathering? Perhaps, since they were also opposed to Paul's work, they had been willing to join the crowd in this public protest. Stoops (1989, p87) argues that "The treatment of Alexander links the riot in Ephesus to the general experience of diaspora Jews and defines the social context against which the story should be read." He therefore uses the experience of the Jewish communities of the Diaspora, and in particular the arguments surrounding the rights of Jewish communities in the cities of the Roman Empire, to shed light on the content and the function of the report of the riot; see Stoops 1989, p73-91. But this is to put too much weight on this one factor as a guide for interpretation of the story.

[21] Haenchen, p574 n7, 575; Schneider 1982, p277; Rogers 1986, p882; Bruce 1988, p377. For a discussion of the meaning of συνεβίβασαν here see Barrett 1998, p932. Duncan (1929, p26-46) discusses the extent of Jewish opposition to Paul, but goes beyond the evidence in seeing them having a role in the riot.

[22] Luke does not say how the crowd recognised that Alexander was a Jew. Perhaps it was from the fact that a group known to be Jews had put him forward or that he was known to be a Jew, or by what he said in his defence. On the interpretation of the incident see eg. Roloff 1981, p293; Pesch 1986, 2, p181-2. Haenchen (1971, p577) asks "What exactly is the point of this Jewish intermezzo, which has neither reasonable cause nor sensible conclusion?" However, as we have noted, we can suggest a reasonable cause for the incident, and the fact that it is introduced suddenly does not require that it is unhistorical.

act in defence of its rights, is in keeping with other evidence which shows the Jewish community in Ephesus, and communities elsewhere, seeking to defend these rights.[23] The unevenness in the narrative does not mean it is unhistorical therefore but rather it is seen to fit well into the wider social and political context.

Thus we can explain why Alexander was put forward by the Jews and the reaction to him. But the other important point to note here is that Luke does not seem to have had a motive for including the "Jewish interlude", and makes nothing of it himself.[24] The involvement of the Jews is incidental to the whole event and does not add to the story of Paul in any way. In fact, that Luke seems to have had no obvious motive for including the "interlude" strongly suggests that he has not created either this part of the story or the whole account itself. For if he had created the whole story we would not expect to find an element in it which in no way furthers Luke's purposes in writing. Its presence here then strongly suggests that Luke is reliant on a tradition, which included this interlude, for his account of the riot, and thus argues strongly for the basic historicity of the whole riot narrative.[25] We have also noted that the extent of verifiable local detail in the account argues in the same direction. Certainly, the presence of the "Jewish interlude" greatly strengthens our case that the whole story does go back to a tradition.

1.2.5 The attitude of the town clerk (Acts 19:35-40)

Haenchen argues that the town clerk dismisses the complaint against Paul too easily by referring to the greatness of Artemis, and ignores the fact that the Christians have said that a god made with hands is not a god at all.[26] We can note three points. Firstly, the town clerk does not dismiss the complaints lightly, since he tells the crowd that they could be charged with στάσις (19:40), which was a very serious matter. A city that was charged with riotous behaviour could suffer severe consequences;[27] the fears of the town

---

[23] See Chapter 1; see also Trebilco 1991, p8-19; Taylor 1996, p51-2.

[24] Barrett (1998, p934) suggests v33-4 contain additional information which Luke added to a source and goes on "possibly Luke supplemented by local inquiry a narrative given him by a travel document (or similar source)". He suggests a consequence of this view may be that at the time of the riot Alexander was a Christian, or he became one subsequently. This is possible, but Luke gives no hint of this and makes nothing of it.

[25] Schneider (1982, p273) argues that Luke is dependent on a tradition for this account of the riot and notes: "Für diese Auffassung läßt sich "das Intermezzo" mit Alexander (VV 33f) anführen, das für Lukas keine Bedeutung haben dürfte."

[26] See Haenchen 1971, p577; see also Schüssler Fiorenza 1976, p17-19.

[27] A city involved in riots could lose the respect of Roman officials (Dio, *Or.* 38.33-37), guilds which caused trouble could be disbanded, city officials could be punished, and a city could even lose its freedom (see for example Plutarch, *Praec. ger. reip.* 813F, 825C). In 20

clerk were well founded and his actions entirely in accordance with contemporary advice to city officials.[28]

Secondly, the town clerk refers to the belief that Ephesus was the temple keeper of Artemis "and of the statue (καὶ τοῦ διοπετοῦς) that fell from heaven" (Acts 19:35). This answers the charge that Artemis was a "god made with hands". As far as the town clerk was concerned, the image was not made with hands but was "διοπετής", and the missionaries were mistaken.[29] Of course, the speech is a Lucan composition, but it seems likely that Luke would only give a pagan cult's answer to the Christian charge of idolatry because it was in his source. In any case, the answer is credible.

Thirdly, what of the town clerk's statement that the missionaries were "neither sacrilegious nor blasphemers of our goddess (οὔτε ἱεροσύλους οὔτε βλασφημοῦντας τὴν θεὸν ἡμῶν)" (Acts 19:37)?[30] Perhaps the meaning of βλασφημέω here is that Paul had not actually been aggressive or disrespectful to the goddess in anything he had said.[31] Alternatively, we can note that in the speech the town clerk does not give his support to the Christians, but rather supports the worship of Artemis, and argues against behaviour that would

---

BCE Cyzicus lost its freedom as a city after having permitted some Roman citizens to be put to death, apparently in connection with a riot (see Cassius Dio, 54.7.6; see also Magie 1950, p474. For another example see Tacitus, *Ann.* 12.58; see also Suetonius, *Aug.* 47.) Further, Tacitus tells us of a situation that got out of control in Pompei in 59 CE. During a gladiatorial show there was an "exchange of raillery" between local people and visitors from nearby Nuceria. This led to abuse, then to stone throwing and finally "to steel". Many of the Nucerians were killed or wounded. Tacitus (Tacitus, *Ann.* 14.17) notes that as a result "the Pompeians as a community were debarred from holding any similar assembly for ten years, and the associations (collegiaque) which they had formed illegally were dissolved."

[28] See advice on these situations given by Dio, *Or.* 34.24f, 33, 39; 46.14; Plutarch, *Praec. ger. reip.* 813E-F; Heliodorus, *The Ethiopians* 4.20.1-3; see also Mitchell 1993, vol 1, p65.

[29] See Bruce, *Acts*, 420; Mussies 1990, p190-91; cf. Oster 1974, p136.

[30] ἱερόσυλος meant literally to be a robber of temples, but it came to mean "sacrilege" as being the real crime involved in robbing a temple as distinct from other robbery. Duncan (1929, p38-45) argues that the charge of sacrilege against Paul was actually a Jewish charge that Paul was a "temple robber" of the Jerusalem temple, since his work resulted in a reduction in the payment of the temple tax. But this seems highly unlikely. Barrett (1998, p917) notes that "Paul could hardly have been satisfied with what is said in v . 37."

[31] Jewish writers regarded it as important to avoid gross offence against pagan deities. Two passages in Josephus illustrate this. Firstly in *Contra Apion* 2, 237 he writes: "Our legislator has expressly forbidden us to deride or blaspheme the gods recognized by others, out of respect for the word 'God'." Further, in his summary of the Law in *Ant.* 4.207, Josephus includes the following statement: "Let none blaspheme the gods which other cities revere, nor rob foreign temples, nor take treasure that has been dedicated in the name of any god." See also Philo, *Vita Mos.* 2.205; *De spec. leg.* 1.53; Stoops 1989, p87-88. The defence by Josephus and other Jews is understandable since we know that the charge of blaspheming Gentile gods was leveled against Jews at various times; see for example Josephus, *Contra Apion* 1.249, 309-11.

bring the city to the attention of the proconsul. He wants to dampen down the riot and is concerned that the Assembly is in danger of acting illegally and arousing the wrath of the Roman authorities, since nothing had been proved against Paul. It may well be then that he minimised the accusations against the missionaries.[32] Either explanation of this facet of the speech is historically credible.

1.2.6 "Proconsuls" (Acts 19:38)

In Acts 19:38 the plural ἀνθύπατοι is surprising. The number may be the effect of the previous plural (ἀγοραῖοι), or it may be a generalizing plural, meaning, "there are such people as proconsuls".[33] It has also been suggested that it might reflect the time of confused interregnum following the murder of Julius Silanus, proconsul of Asia, after Nero's accession in October 54,[34] although this can be no more than a very tentative suggestion.[35] But since ἀνθύπατοι could be a generalising plural, its occurrence here does not argue against the narrative containing historical information.

Thus we conclude that the objections to the historicity of the event are unconvincing.[36]

1.3 Are the specific thematic and theological points made by Luke in this passage based in history?

We will now discuss the thematic and theological points that Luke makes in this passage which have a bearing on our investigation and see if we have any reason to accept or deny the historical elements which are involved or implied

---

[32] See Marshall 1980, p316.

[33] See Lake and Cadbury 1933a, p251; Marshall, 1980, p321. The singular is used correctly by Luke in Acts 13:7,8, 12; 18:12. The generalizing plural is found, for example, in Plutarch, *Praec. ger. reip.* 813E: "You must also say to yourself: 'You who rule are a subject, ruling a State controlled by proconsuls (ἀνθυπάτοις), the agents of Caesar.'" The plural could also point to the fact that there was a constant change in who was holding the office, since it was normally held for one or two years; see Lampe 1992, p63 n18.

[34] See Tacitus, *Ann.* 13.1; Dio, 61.6.4-5; see also Hemer 1989a, p123, 169; Duncan 1929, p102-7; Carrez 1985, p773-6; 1986, p27-30.

[35] This view is criticised by Ramsay 1900b, p334-5. Ramsay notes that the two murderers of Julius Silanus would not have been able to assume the office of proconsul (as had been suggested), since constitutionally power would pass into the hands of the proconsul's three deputies until a successor arrived, and since the two murderers, Celer and Helius, were an eques and a freedman respectively they were not qualified to act as proconsuls. It remains possible then that the plural may refer, not to the murderers, but to the acting deputies; see Hemer 1989a, p123 n63; Bruce 1988, p379 n82.

[36] See also Barrett 1998, p917, who notes Haenchen's objections are "superficial and unconvincing".

in these theological points. In particular, has the fact that Luke is making a thematic or theological point through a particular section led him to create or modify the story, which would mean that what Luke says is historically unreliable at this point?

1.3.1 An Impact on the Artemis cult?

With respect to Demetrius' statement (19:26-7) about the success of the Pauline mission in Ephesus, we have noted in chapter 2 that Paul indicates in his letters that his time in the city had been effective and that other Christian communities in Asia were probably founded at this time.

What about the claim that Paul's preaching had affected the sale of souvenirs of Artemis and that "there is danger not only that this trade of ours may come into disrepute but also that the temple of the great goddess Artemis will be scorned" (Acts 19:27)? We have no evidence for this from Ephesus where the Artemis cult clearly continued to flourish throughout the first century,[37] although a decline in the sale of souvenirs is unlikely to have left any record in our evidence. However, the letter of Pliny the Younger to Trajan in 112 C.E. is interesting:

For this contagious superstition [i.e. Christianity] is not confined to the cities only, but has spread through the villages and rural districts; it seems possible, however, to check and cure it. 'Tis certain at least that the temples, which had been almost deserted, begin now [that is, since Pliny has been persecuting Christians and some have recanted] to be frequented; and the sacred festivals, after a long intermission, are again revived; while there is a general demand for sacrificial animals, which for some time past have met with but few purchasers. From hence it is easy to imagine what multitudes may be reclaimed from this error, if a door be left open to repentance.[38]

Pliny's letter shows that Christians were numerous in the province of Pontus and Bithynia and that the number of conversions was having an impact on pagan cults. It is also interesting that Christianity had an economic effect on those selling sacrificial animals. While the evidence is later and is not from Asia, it is noteworthy that the economic complaint of the silversmiths is comparable to the situation outlined by Pliny. It means that the claim made in Acts 19:26-7 of the impact of Paul's preaching on the worship of Artemis and the sale of souvenirs is realistic and cannot be dismissed as improbable.

Haenchen has argued that if Paul really threatened the cult of Artemis, then all the circles connected with the cult should have joined in opposition to him,

---

[37]The most obvious piece of evidence is the Salutaris inscription, *I.Eph.* 27, on which see Rogers 1991; see further Oster 1976, p29-44.

[38]Pliny the Younger, *Ep.* 10.96; on this see DeSilva 1992, p280; Cf. Price 1997, p244-5.

especially the priests and the city authorities.[39] However, this point actually argues for the historicity of the narrative. If Luke had created the event, it is likely that he would have shown the opposition to Paul came from a range of people, including the priests.[40] Further, we need not envisage that Paul had decimated, or even seriously threatened the sale of silver shrines, nor had a huge impact on the worship of Artemis.[41] Even a small impact on sales with the prospect of a growing problem may have been sufficient to bring Paul to the attention of Demetrius, particularly if Paul was active in the same area of the city as the silversmiths.[42] As we have previously noted, it is also likely that Luke here uses hyperbole in Demetrius' speech with respect to the inroads made into sales, as he seems to in 19:10, and 19:17.[43]

1.3.2 That Christianity is not a threat to the good order of the Empire

As we have noted, the town clerk's reasoned rebuttal of the charges brought against Paul is an important continuation of Luke's picture that the authorities are either positive or neutral towards the new faith.

It is difficult to argue for the historicity of this aspect of the speech. We can note that in his speech the town clerk acts in accordance with the sort of advice current in the period for city officials. In particular, as noted above, his consciousness that the city needs to avoid drawing the attention of the proconsul to itself is in keeping with advice given by a number of

---

[39] Haenchen 1971, p576.

[40] See Ramsay 1904b, p129-30 for this point. Marshall (1980, p315) notes: "In a pluralist, polytheistic society the priests of Artemis may well not have taken action against what may have appeared to them as a comparatively irrelevant sect."

[41] See Marshall 1980, p315.

[42] Note that ἀγυροκόπων - "place of the silversmiths", was found on two columns in Arkadiane Street (see IvEph 547), which is not far from the theatre and the Lower Agora; see New Docs 4, p8. The term ἀγυροκόπος is found in a number of inscriptions from Ephesus; see IvEph. 425.10 (see *ad* III.636); 547 (1); 547 (2); 586; 636.9-10, 2212.17; 2441; see also IvEph 585; see Hemer 1989a, p235-6; Lampe 1992, p66-9; New Docs 4, 7-10. We noted above that some scholars have attempted to link the riot of Acts 19 with the Artemision festival (which would then partly explain the reaction to Paul) but Acts gives no indication that the riot occurred at the same time as a festival.

[43] Kreitzer (1987, p59-70) notes that some unusual coins of Ephesus minted in 50-51 CE commemorating Agrippina's marriage to Claudius point to a close association between Agrippina and Artemis. He suggests the coins, and the Imperial honour they show was granted to Ephesus through the association of Artemis and Ephesus with the Empress, may have helped to foster an aggressive pride and popular fervour among the Ephesians with regard to Artemis and her temple, and thus help to explain the climate of hostility Paul encountered as shown by the riot. Although the coins may only be a minor factor in the hostile reaction to Paul, if there was this aggressive pride concerning the honour of Artemis at this time, then even a small impact on the sale of shrines may have led to the riot.

contemporaneous authors.[44] However, little is at stake for us here, since all the passage would show is that on one occasion a town clerk was positive towards the new faith, which need be no indication of an on-going attitude towards the Christian community in Ephesus.

1.3.3 The social level of Christianity's new "friends"

In Acts 19:31 some of the Asiarchs are said to be "friends" of Paul who sent him a message urging him not to go into the theatre. Who were the Asiarchs? Liddell and Scott define "Ἀσιάρχης" as "priest of the Imperial cult in the province of Asia".[45] However, in a recent study, Friesen has argued that "Asiarch" was not another name for a provincial highpriest (ἀρχιερεὺς Ἀσίας),[46] nor was it directly related to the provincial cult of the emperors. He notes that the first reference to Asiarchs on coins or inscriptions comes in 89/90 CE, and suggests that the office was either redefined or reinvigorated in the eighties of the first century CE and this caused the Asiarchate to begin to enter the archaeological record at this time. From this point on we have more idea of what the office involved.[47] Although Strabo show that the office was known in the Augustan period, the exact nature of the Asiarchate in the late republican period through until the eighties of the first century CE is unclear.[48]

Yet, while there is uncertainty about the precise functions of the Asiarch at the time Paul was in Ephesus, it is clear that the Asiarchs known to us in Ephesus were wealthy and influential people of high status who belonged to

---

[44] See above in section 1.2.5. It is also interesting to note the parallels between the advice given by the clerk to the crowd to do nothing rash, and the similar suggestion of Gamaliel to the Jewish Council in 5:35, 38-9; see Soards 1994, p104.

[45] Liddell and Scott, p256. This view permeates the secondary literature on the subject, and is found for example in Taylor in Lake and Cadbury 1933b, p258; Haenchen 1971, p574 n1; Lüdemann 1989, p217; Stoops 1989, p85.

[46] Friesen notes (1993a, p106): "The attempt to equate Asiarchs and provincial highpriests creates a scenario otherwise unknown in the Graeco-Roman world: two distinct and unrelated titles for the same prominent, provincial office." See also Friesen 1999b, p303-7; 1999c, p275-90.

[47] Friesen 1993a, p107-8. On p113 he notes: "In the second and third centuries CE, Asiarchs performed a variety of public services that were especially related to municipal life in Asia. Their duties were sometimes priestly and sometimes involved provincial temples, but imperial cults were not a necessary component of the Asiarchate." The public services included supporting gladiatorial contests and supplying funding for cities to mint coins; see Friesen 1993a, p98-9. On the change in the eighties, see Friesen 1993a, p155.

[48] See Friesen 1993a, p113. Kearsley (New Docs 4, p46-55; 1994, p363-76) agrees that the Asiarchate was separate from the provincial highpriesthood, but has also argued that the Asiarchate was a municipal magistracy in which people served for a fixed period of time. However, for a critique of this later position see Friesen 1993a, p110-12.

leading aristocratic families of the city.[49] By mentioning them here Luke is indicating that Paul had wealthy and powerful friends in Ephesus.

Since one of Luke's themes in Acts is to show that important representatives of political and social life support Paul, or at least do not oppose him, some scholars have thought that the note that some Asiarchs were friendly to Paul is unhistorical, since the note so clearly serves Luke's apologetic interests.[50] Since we have no independent attestation of the point, we cannot show that it is historical. But is it credible?[51]

Acts mentions Paul's contact with the proconsul, Sergius Paulus in Cyprus, and Sergius Paulus' subsequent conversion (Acts 13:4-12).[52] Mitchell suggests that this explains Paul's itinerary at this point. According to Acts, Paul went on from Cyprus to Pisidian Antioch, by-passing the thriving communities of Pamphylia, and Mitchell suggests this was because Pisidian Antioch was Sergius Paulus' *patria*, as we know from a number of inscriptions. Mitchell notes: "We can hardly avoid the conclusion that the proconsul himself had suggested to Paul that he make it his next port of call, no doubt providing him with letters of introduction to aid his passage and his stay."[53]

---

[49] See Strabo, *Geog.* 14.1.42; Friesen 1993a, p92; Kearsley in ABD I, p496; see also Worth 1999a, p117-20. We also note that they had no clear connection with the imperial cult in our period.

[50] See Lüdemann 1989, p217; Haenchen 1971, p576. Note also Haenchen (1971, p574 n1): "That these men elected for the promotion of the provincial cult were 'personally well disposed to the resolute enemy of the gods' (so Bauernfeind, 234) is highly unlikely." See also Schüssler Fiorenza 1976, p18. That the Asiarchs were not necessarily connected with the Imperial cult, as Friesen has argued, weakens this line of argument. Haenchen (1971, p574) has asked how it was that the Asiarchs appeared so quickly in order to aid Paul. Luke does not supply such details, but since the gathering of the crowd in the theatre probably took some time, there is no reason why some of the Asiarchs could not have heard what was happening and been able to warn Paul.

[51] It has often been thought that there were a number of Pauline Christians of at least some social standing (see for example Theissen 1982, p73-95), the most notable of whom was Erastus, who was ὁ οἰκονόμος τῆς πόλεως in Corinth (Rom 16:23). οἰκονόμος denotes a financial officer of the city, but it is not clear how high the position was within the administrative hierarchy, since the position could be filled by slaves and freedmen (although a number of scholars think that it is possible that he was a person of some wealth and notable social status; see Dunn 1988, p911; Fitzmyer 1993, p750; cf. Meggitt 1998, p135-41). However, Meggitt 1998, p75-154 has recently argued (p153) that "The various pieces of evidence presented by proponents of the 'New Consensus' to substantiate their belief in the presence of affluent groups or individuals in the Pauline churches are not convincing." Although he may have somewhat overstated his case, he has clearly posed a significant challenge to what had become something of a "New Consensus". In any case, none of the people who figure in the Pauline letters are of the standing of Asiarchs.

[52] Mitchell 1993, vol 2, p6-7.

[53] Mitchell 1993, vol 2, p7.

Unfortunately, we cannot confirm that Paul went from Cyprus to Pisidian Antioch from his letters. However, Luke himself does not make the connection between Sergius Paulus and Pisidian Antioch, which suggests that Luke has not created this route, but rather that it reflects Paul's actual travels. Further, that Paul did get to know Sergius Paulus is suggested by the fact that this connection explains his itinerary in Acts (Cyprus to Pisidian Antioch, without stopping in Pamphylia) which is otherwise a mystery unaccounted for by Acts. Thus we have good grounds for claiming that Paul did get to know Sergius Paulus, which would then again show Paul's ability (albeit according to Acts, though with a strong likelihood of being historical) to win friends in the upper echelons of society.

It is possible then that Paul had wealthy and powerful friends at Ephesus.[54] But we must ask, if Paul was good friends with the Asiarchs, why did he suffer in the city as much as his letters suggest? But answers can be given to this question - perhaps he met up with the Asiarchs after the events he alludes to in 1 Cor 15:32 and 16:9, or perhaps they were powerless to intervene if the Jewish community was the main source of the persecution Paul mentions in his letters. And certainly during the riot, according to Acts, they can advise Paul not to go into the theatre, but they cannot restrain the mob.

It is also important to note that even if the Asiarchs were friends of Paul, we do not know if they would have supported the Christian community in Ephesus after he left. We conclude then that it is quite possible that Paul had influential friends in Ephesus, although we do not know if they had any continuing relationship to the Christian community.

1.4 If the account of the riot contains some historically reliable information, then what do we learn from it about Christians in Ephesus?

We have seen then that the points raised against the historicity of the account do not require the conclusion that the narrative is historically unreliable. Further, we have seen that there is good reason to argue for a core of tradition behind the account. Not only is there much very vivid local colour here, but the details of the story are also credible. Admittedly, there are few details for

---

[54] A significant detail which points to a reliable source here is the use of the plural, Ἀσιαρχῶν; this agrees with Strabo, writing a generation before the dramatic date of this story, referring to the Asiarchs of Tralles as a group; see *Geog.* 14.1.42. Sherwin-White (1963, p90) notes: "If the author of Acts had not known the peculiarities of the organization of Asia, he might well have made an error. In some other eastern provinces the corresponding title went only with the office of President of the Council. There was only one Lyciarch, and only one Pontarch or Bithyniarch." Kreitzer (1987, p67-8) accepts that the Asiarchs acted benevolently towards Paul, but suggests that the note of them being Paul's friends was an after-the-fact reflection on the fact that they did help Paul on this occasion.

which we have specific confirmatory evidence, but corroboration like that supplied by the extent of verifiable detail in this section, even to the alternation between θεά and θεός in reference to Artemis, the letter of Pliny about the decline of pagan cults in Pontus and Bithynia, and the way in which the town clerk heeds advice given by contemporary writers about how an autonomous city should avoid drawing the attention of the Romans to itself are helpful here. Further, we have noted that if Luke had created the story Paul would probably have played a more significant role in it and that the presence of the "Jewish interlude" strongly suggests that Luke is reliant on a tradition for the whole account of the riot. These points argue strongly for the basic historicity of the narrative.

We can suggest with some confidence then that Luke is drawing on tradition here, and that the story tells us something about Paul's time in Ephesus and about Christians in the city.[55] We are not arguing that the riot happened exactly as Luke portrays it, but we do want to suggest that the thematic and theological themes Luke emphasises through the story are based on what happened rather than that his apologetic interest has created the story itself. What then does the passage tell us about Christians in Ephesus?

Firstly, as we have noted in the previous chapter, the riot combines with other elements in the Acts material relating to Ephesus to suggest that the Christian community in Ephesus had grown quickly (19:26-7), and a number of Gentiles had been converted, since the conversion of Jews would not affect the trade in souvenirs of Artemis (19:18). Hence the Gentile section of the community had probably grown significantly during Paul's ministry.

Secondly, we have already discussed the passages in Paul's letters that indicate that he experienced opposition in Ephesus. Luke's account also shows the opposition to the gospel from outsiders which Paul and others experienced. It also suggests that the Christian community may have experienced some on-going opposition from Gentiles, if their attitude to Paul was transferred to the community he left behind, although such opposition may have died down after Paul's departure from the city. Certainly the Christians would have understood the likelihood of suffering.

Thirdly, we have noted that in Acts 19:33-34 some Jews in Ephesus attempted to assert and preserve their distinctive identity compared with the Christians to prevent any serious hostility against themselves. This suggests

---

[55] Conzelmann's (1987, p164-5) comment is helpful: "Haenchen supposes that the author created the whole account based on only a minimum of information (including a vague recollection of one Demetrius). Nevertheless, while Luke does compose scenes, he does not invent stories such as this." Schneider 1982, 273 notes: "Gegen E. Haenchen ist mit H. Conzelmann zu vermuten, daß Lukas mit seinem Bericht im Episodenstil eine überlieferte Geschichte übernommen und ausgebaut hat." Others accept the account as historical; see for example Marshall 1980, p317; Kreitzer 1987, p66-8.

that, by the end of Paul's mission in Ephesus, the Jewish community saw itself as separate in some ways from the Christians and may also imply that the Jewish community was opposed to the Pauline Christians. It also seems likely that by this time the Christian community also saw itself as a distinct group, though probably a group with very strong links with the Jewish community.[56]

Fourthly, the account suggests that Paul won the friendship of some Asiarchs (19:31), but we do not know if they continued to support the Christian community after Paul had left the city. If such support had indeed continued, this would have been particularly advantageous for the Christians.

Fifthly, we noted in Chapter 2 that Paul's ministry in Ephesus was collaborative and we have further confirmation of that here. Gaius and Aristarchus, who are said to be Macedonians, are mentioned in 19:29 as Paul's "travelling companions" (συνέκδημοι). Aristarchus, who is probably also mentioned in Acts 20:4 and 27:2 and so is a Thessalonian, is connected elsewhere with the Pauline mission (Col 4:10; Phlm 24); Gaius is probably otherwise unknown.[57] The word συνέκδημοι suggests that they were "trusted and authorized assistants of Paul".[58] Acts 19:29 shows that someone in the crowd knew them and knew that they were connected with Paul. This suggests that they were associated in some way with Paul's mission and had been active in Ephesus. Perhaps they too are "co-workers" with Paul in some sense, even if only briefly since they are also "travelling companions".

2. Events subsequent to the riot

2.1 Paul's departure from Ephesus

According to Acts 20:1 Paul left Ephesus shortly after the riot. In 19:21-2 Luke depicts Paul as making plans to leave Ephesus for Macedonia and Achaia and then Jerusalem before the riot took place.[59] By speaking of these

---

[56] This is not to suggest that a definitive and enduring "parting of the ways" had occurred, since there was probably on-going in-depth contact and complex inter-relationships between the two groups, but it does suggest the formation of defined groups; see further Fearghail 2002, p52-4.

[57] Gaius is probably not the same as the person mentioned in 1 Cor 1:14 and Rom 16:23, since it was a common name. Nor can he be the Derbaean of 20:4, since he is from Macedonia.

[58] Barrett 1998, p929.

[59] Paul's plans at this time were concerned with the Collection for Jerusalem; see Rom 15:22-6, which confirms the travel plans outlined in Acts 19:21. Timothy had not been mentioned in Acts since his return from Macedonia to rejoin Paul in Corinth (Acts 18:5). We do not know if he accompanied Paul to Ephesus in 18:18-19, or joined Paul in Ephesus

intentions and preparations at this point, Luke implies that Paul was not suddenly driven from Ephesus by the riot, since he had already made his preparations to leave. But was it as simple as this? Did the riot mean that Paul had to leave Ephesus, when he had in fact not intended to depart at this point? We cannot be sure, since Paul does not unambiguously refer to the riot in his letters, although 1 Cor 16:8 suggests that at one stage Paul was planning his departure from Ephesus, but it remains possible that the riot forced a premature departure. Certainly Acts 20:1 suggests that immediately after the riot Paul did leave, and so it is possible that Paul was either required to leave, or thought his departure was prudent.

Luke's account leaves many unanswered questions concerning the Christians in Ephesus after Paul's departure. Did Demetrius actually bring charges before the proconsul before or after Paul left the city? What sort of future did the Christians in Ephesus face? Would they have to go "underground" from this point on? Unfortunately we can only raise these questions.

2.2 Trophimus and the Collection (Acts 20:4; 21:29)

In Acts 20:4 we have the list of those who accompanied Paul to Jerusalem, almost certainly with the collection, as agents of the different communities.[60] Tychicus and Trophimus are said to be Asians. Tychicus was later associated with Paul's letters to Asia Minor.[61] Trophimus is mentioned in Acts 21:29 in connection with the trouble in Jerusalem, and it is there said that he is from Ephesus.[62] In the list in Acts 20:4 he is therefore probably a representative of the Ephesian community, and Tychicus may have been too, although he could

---

later; see Pesch 1986, p157. We have noted in Chapter 2 that he was probably with Paul for most of his Ephesian ministry. It is uncertain if the trip referred to in 1 Cor 4:17; 16:10-11 was the same journey referred to here in Acts 19:22. In Acts 20:4 Timothy travelled with Paul from Greece en route to Jerusalem. It may be that he returned from Corinth (1 Cor 4:17; 16:10) to Ephesus before Paul's departure from Ephesus as Paul had hoped (1 Cor 16:11) and then continued to travel with Paul. It is unlikely that the Erastus mentioned in this verse is identical with Erastus the city treasurer of Corinth mentioned in Rom 16:23; see Bruce 1988, p372; Lake and Cadbury 1933a, p244.

[60] See Marshall 1980, p323-4; Conzelmann 1987, p167; Johnson 1992, p355. We do not know why Luke does not speak of the collection (cf. the clear hint in 24:17), although a number of suggestions have been made. Perhaps the failure of the Jerusalem church to rally to Paul's aid when he was arrested was an embarrassment; see Johnson 1992, p357.

[61] See Eph 6:21; Col 4:7; cf. 2 Tim 4:12; Tit 3:12. Barrett (1998, p948) sees him as one of Paul's colleagues.

[62] He is also mentioned in 2 Tim 4:20. The name Τρόφιμος is found around 25 times in the inscriptions from Ephesus; see *I.Eph.* 8.2, p196-7.

have represented another community in Asia.[63] This suggests that the Ephesian Christians did contribute to the collection, although we have no other evidence to confirm this.[64] But, as we noted in Chapter 2, section 1.6, the fact that Paul was organising the collection while he was in Ephesus (see 1 Cor 16:1-4) strongly suggests that the Ephesians would have taken part in it.

These details also mean that we know the name of one Ephesian Christian, Trophimus, who since he seems to have been chosen as a representative of the Ephesian community, was probably a key leader. He may have been one of Paul's converts. Since the Jews in Jerusalem object strongly when they think that he has gone into the temple (Acts 21:29-30) he is clearly a Gentile.[65] As we have noted, it is also possible that Tychicus was from Ephesus.

3. The Miletus speech (Acts 20:17-35)

After time in Macedonia and Greece (Acts 20:1-5) Paul sailed from Philippi to Troas (Acts 20:6-15), and then went on to Miletus (20:15-17). There, according to Luke, Paul gave a speech to Ephesian elders (20:18-35). We will now examine this speech. What does it tell us about Paul's time in Ephesus and the early Christians in the city?

3.1 The Location

In Acts 20:15 Luke says that Paul and his companions went to Miletus, but in v16 he adds that Paul had decided to sail past Ephesus, "so that he might not have to spend time in Asia" because he was eager to be in Jerusalem on the day of Pentecost. However, when Paul was in Miletus he sent a message to Ephesus and called the elders of the church to Miletus, where he addressed them (20:17).

From Ephesus to Miletus is about 32 miles as the crow flies,[66] and much further by road. Haenchen suggested that the messenger may have taken two days to travel from Miletus to Ephesus, but that the elders would have taken

---

[63] The name Τύχικος is found three times in the inscriptions from Ephesus; see IvEph 2223; 2948a; 3818a. Gaius was from Derbe, which suggests that that community contributed to the collection too.

[64] Knox (1987, p65) notes that the fact Tychicus, Trophimus and Gaius accompanied Paul to Jerusalem suggests that Asia and Ephesus in particular did contribute to the collection. As noted in Chapter 2, section 1.6, we do not know why Paul never mentioned that Ephesus was involved in the Collection.

[65] We do not know if it is significant that the person who is definitely from Ephesus, chosen as their representative, is a Gentile and not a Jew.

[66] See Haenchen 1971, p590.

longer.[67] If Paul was in a hurry, and so did not visit Ephesus, how do we explain this delay of at least five days? The issue is further complicated when we note that Luke has almost certainly not told us the real reason for Paul's journey to Jerusalem, which we know from Paul's letters to have been to deliver the Collection.[68]

A number of explanations have been offered for Luke's note of haste followed by the apparently contradictory delay in Miletus.

Firstly, it may be that the fastest boat that was available from Troas when Paul wanted to travel was not stopping at Ephesus, but rather at Miletus.[69] As Barrett notes with regard to Acts 20:16, Paul may have then "made a virtue out of necessity".[70] In this case his only opportunity to see the Ephesian elders would have been to call them to Miletus. But would the boat have stayed for the required time of over a week at Miletus, a less significant city than Ephesus?[71] Clearly, we do not know.

Secondly, since the real reason for the journey to Jerusalem was to deliver the Collection, this may well have provided a good reason for haste and for avoiding Ephesus. As Barrett notes "carrying a quantity of money must have been an anxious business, and Ephesus no very safe place."[72]

Thirdly, Paul may well have been aware that a visit to Ephesus could imperil his commitment to go to Jerusalem, since it could involve protracted delays caused either by those who opposed him (cf. 1 Cor 15:32; 16:9), or by the time needed to help the church there. Thus, when Luke says that Paul did not want to "spend time" (χρονοτριβέω) in Asia, he may well have been referring, not to a visit of a number of days, but to a longer period of apostolic work which a visit to Ephesus could well have entailed.[73] If this was the case, then Paul may have decided he could spare a period of a week for a stay in Miletus, as he could spare this length of time with the church in Troas (20:7-

---

[67] See Haenchen 1971, p590; Dupont (1962, p27) estimates the total time as three days, but does not say how he has calculated it. Hemer (1989a, p125) also thinks two or three days would be sufficient.

[68] It is possible that Paul did want to reach Jerusalem by Pentecost (although this has been doubted, eg. by Haenchen 1971, p588; Barrett 1998, p945) given 1 Cor 9:19-23, and that he refers to Pentecost (admittedly as a date) in 1 Cor 16:8.

[69] See Hemer 1989a, p125.

[70] Barrett 1977, p108. Bruce (1988, p387) suggests Paul decided he did not have time to see Ephesus again, but that his ship "was due to spend several days in harbor at Miletus; this gave him the opportunity to see some of his Ephesian friends."

[71] See Trebilco 1994, p360-2.

[72] Barrett 1977, p108; see also Haenchen 1971, p588. Barrett (1998, p960) suggests Paul did not wish to save time (he asks if he would have been so keen to attend a Jewish feast?) but that his route can be explained by the fact that he may have felt safer in Miletus than the huge city of Ephesus.

[73] See Lambrecht 1979, p331-2; Taylor 1996, p93-4.

12), but not the weeks or months a visit to Ephesus might have involved. This would make good sense of the whole narrative.

Fourthly, Paul avoids Ephesus not for lack of time, but because he had in fact been banned from Ephesus or because the potential danger to Paul in Ephesus was so great that he could not return there. Hence he had to call the Ephesian elders to see him in Miletus. Luke however, does not want to admit this and so substitutes Paul's haste as the reason for avoiding Ephesus.[74] This is possible, and although, as we noted in chapter 2, Paul may have been imprisoned in Ephesus, we have no evidence that Paul was permanently banned from any city, although this lack of evidence may be fortuitous. Further, Paul was clearly willing to risk great danger,[75] and so it is by no means certain that he would avoid Ephesus just because of potential suffering.[76]

Thus, all of these explanations are guesses, and there seems no way of favouring one over the others. But that we can offer a number of possible explanations for Luke's note of haste followed by an apparently contradictory delay in Miletus, means that this is no obstacle to the historicity of the event described.

But did Paul give an address to Ephesian elders in Miletus at all? There is no evidence for this in Paul's letters. However, Barrett notes:

"A farewell to the great city and Pauline centre Ephesus would be an appropriate piece to compose, but why, if Luke was writing fiction should he attach the story to Miletus? There seems no reason for this, and it would have been easy to imagine a fine scene in Ephesus, of which Luke had already told so much. It is perhaps more probable that Luke found a tradition that Paul had spoken to the local church at Miletus (as he did at Troas, 20.7-12), and thought it appropriate to bring there (the nearest point on the itinerary) a representative

---

[74] See Johnson 1992, p352; On p356 he notes: "We must wonder, therefore, whether it was actually the danger to Paul in Ephesus which might have been the real determining factor." Conzelmann (1987, p167) thinks Paul was expelled or banished from Ephesus. But it is speculative to write that (p171) "It is clear that Paul could no longer enter Ephesus." Carrez (1986, p27-30) thinks that Paul was imprisoned in Ephesus, but after the murder of Silanus he was released, perhaps by the payment of money. Because of this irregularity, he does not return to Ephesus, but rather calls the elders to Miletus. But this whole theory is speculative. Günther (1995, p54) takes the fact that Luke has Paul address the Ephesians at Miletus as evidence that Paul's missionary efforts had failed in Ephesus. But a great deal of evidence counts against this.

[75] See the hardship catalogues discussed in Chapter 2, especially 2 Cor 11:23-33. Barrett (1998, p945) notes that, according to this view, Luke is attempting to play down the degree of opposition to Paul's work in Ephesus, and then notes that "it is hard to see why he [Luke] should wish to minimize the perils endured by his hero."

[76] We can suggest that it would have been reasonably easy for Paul to slip in quietly to the city, meet with a few people, and depart again, given that Ephesus was a city of around 250,000 people. Horsley (1992a, p134-35) relates Paul's sailing past Ephesus to the silting up of the city's harbour, which was dredged in 62 CE.

group from the metropolitan church. A speech at Miletus could thus be historical, the sending for the Ephesian elders not. Such a suggestion is only a guess, incapable of proof."[77]

The problem with Barrett's suggestion that Paul addressed the local church in Miletus is that we have no independent confirmation for the existence of a church in Miletus at this time. It is possible that a church was begun in Miletus during Paul's time in Ephesus, since in 1 Cor 16:19 Paul passes on greetings from "the churches of Asia" which could include Miletus, and Luke notes that the Gospel spread to other parts of Asia in this period (see Acts 19:10, 26). However, Miletus is not one of the seven churches of Rev 2-3, and there is no evidence for a Christian community there in the NT.[78] Secondly, Barrett suggests a parallel with the address to the church at Troas (20:7-12), but in this case we do know of an occasion when Paul may have founded the church there (2 Cor 2:12). Thus, without evidence for a Christian community in the city, Barrett's suggestion that Paul actually spoke to the church at Miletus remains only a possibility, with no other evidence to support it.

But Barrett's point that if Luke had invented the narrative, there seems to be no reason for putting the speech in Miletus,[79] when the most effect would have been gained by having Paul give a great farewell address in Ephesus is a valid one. The setting in Miletus is most likely historical then; Paul probably did give a speech in Miletus, and this was known to Luke from tradition. Given our lack of evidence for a Christian community in Miletus, the most likely hearers of a speech were Ephesian Christians. That we can suggest a number of likely reasons why Paul might have addressed Ephesian Christians in Miletus rather than Ephesus, as we have noted above, means the setting given by Luke is at the very least credible. We cannot show that Paul did address Ephesian Christians at Miletus, since there is no indication of this in Paul's letters, but we have seen good reason for arguing that Paul spoke in Miletus, probably to Ephesians. Further, we have shown how accurate Luke's knowledge is of Ephesus, particularly in 19:23-40 but on other matters as well, which suggests he has a reliable source for Paul's ministry in the city; this means we can suggest that Luke gained information about an address Paul gave to Ephesian elders in Miletus from the same source.

---

[77] Barrett 1977, p109; see also Barrett 1998, p960; Schnabel 1999, p380-1.

[78] Miletus is only mentioned in the NT here and in 2 Tim 4:20: "Trophimus I left ill at Miletus", which need imply nothing about a Christian community there even in the time when the Pastoral Epistles were written.

[79] Barrett (1998, p960) notes with regard to 20:16, the question of the location in Miletus and the note of Paul's haste and then time spent in Miletus: "writers do not often voluntarily concoct the sort of problem that we see here". There is no mention of Miletus in the speech, nor any allusion to the city; see Dupont 1962, p26-7. Miletus was sufficiently famous for its wool for it to be mentioned in the LXX in Ezek 27:18.

However, does this speech give us any information about Paul's time in Ephesus, or the Christians in the city? We will now examine the contents and origin of the speech with a view to trying to assess this.

3.2 The contents and origin of the speech[80]

The genre of the speech is usually identified as that of a farewell address.[81] Watson notes the following features common to farewell addresses, which are found in this speech: "The testator assembles the elders of the community, his sons, and/or family (v. 17); rehearses his irreproachable conduct, protests his innocence, and calls others to imitate his life (vv. 18-27, 33-35); announces his impending death (vv. 22-25, 29, 38); appeals to the community tradition and explains the reward and punishment meted out for obedience or disobedience to it (v. 32); transmits the tradition to his descendants or disciples (v. 28); gives moral exhortation (vv. 28, 35); warns of persecution and false teachers to come after his death (vv. 29-30); and closes with prayers and tears (v. 37)."[82]

However, that the speech conforms to the genre of the farewell address says nothing about the historicity of the scene or the address itself, since a speaker could follow the form of the farewell address, consciously or not, in speaking to an audience.[83] As Barrett notes, "real farewell speeches are apt to take the same form as fictitious ones".[84] The inclusion of a farewell address at this point enables Luke to give an "insider's" interpretation of Paul before his arrest and trials, and thus to present to the reader a summary of Paul's character, and of how he worked in his churches.

It is also clear that, although Luke gives the speech as addressed to the Ephesian elders, it is undoubtedly more general than this. It is the only speech in Acts in which Paul addresses Christians and it comes at the end of Paul's missionary work as his last speech before he is arrested. Further, as we have

---

[80] A number of proposals concerning the structure of the speech have been made; see for example Dupont 1962, p21-6; Soards 1994, p105-8; Porter 1999, p116-17.

[81] See Munck 1950, p155-70, who also discusses the features of the genre; see also Dupont 1962, p11-21; Barrett 1977, p109; Lövestam 1987, p2-3; Kurz 1985, p251-68; Johnson 1992, p366. Examples of farewell speeches include Gen 47:29-49:33; Jos 23:1-24:30; 1 Sam 12:1-25; 1 Kgs 2:1-10; Jub 7:20-39; 21:1-25; Test 12 Pat passim; 2 Bar 44:1-46:7; Tob 14:3-11; 1 Macc 2:49-70. For Greco-Roman examples see Kurz 1985, p253-5. Since a farewell address is generally delivered by someone close to death, which is not the case here in Acts 20, it has been questioned whether the Miletus speech should be regarded as a farewell address; see Burchard 1975, p889; Lambrecht 1979, p332-3. However, there are some other examples of farewell addresses where the speaker is not close to death; see 1 Sam 12:1-25.

[82] Watson 1991, p185.

[83] See Munck 1950, p163.

[84] Barrett 1977, p109; see also Lövestam 1987, p3.

noted, its form fits the farewell address genre. Thus, for Luke, the Ephesian elders are almost certainly representatives of the whole church and in particular of its leaders. In the speech as Luke gives it, Paul addresses all the leaders of his congregations, and all the leaders of the church of Luke's time.[85] With this in view, it is understandable that in the speech Luke presents Paul as "the chief and exemplary evangelist and pastor, who by word and example instructs the new generation in their duties."[86]

There is almost universal agreement that the language and style of the speeches in Acts belongs to Luke rather than to the people to whom the speeches are attributed.[87] The Miletus speech contains a number of Lucan words which show that, in the form we have it, it has been written by Luke. Lambrecht gives a list of 46 examples of Lucan language, style and ideas in v17-38.[88] We will note a number of examples in the course of this section.

However, it is also clear that the speech contains a number of specifically Pauline words and phrases, and many echoes of Paul's actual teaching. Cadbury lists 14 words or phrases in the speech which he regards as "Pauline expressions".[89] While further examples will be noted below, we can point to the following particularly noteworthy examples here. Firstly, in v19 it is said that Paul served the Lord with all "humility (ταπεινοφροσύνη)". The word is used by Paul, but this is the only time it is found in Luke-Acts.[90] Secondly, in v31 it is said that for three years Paul "did not cease night or day to warn (νουθετῶν) everyone with tears." Apart from this passage, νουθετέω is exclusively a Pauline word in the NT.[91] Thirdly, φείδομαι is used by Luke

---

[85] See Lövestam 1987, p1; Dupont 1962, p20; Schnackenburg 1991, p51.

[86] Barrett 1977, p108; see also Haenchen 1971, p596. But that Luke gives the speech this general application has no bearing on whether Paul actually gave an address like this. Certainly, it could contain traditions originating in an actual address, and be used by Luke in a general way.

[87] See Baugh 1990, p290; Gasque (1975, p229) notes: "Now, no one (as far as I know) denies that the *language* of all the speeches is, generally speaking, Luke's."

[88] See Lambrecht 1979, p325; see also Dupont 1962, p29. For example, ὑπηρετεῖν in v34 is only found in Acts. Dupont (1962, p28) notes that the speech given in Acts 20 would have lasted two and a half minutes. Clearly it is a summary which again suggests it is Luke's words.

[89] Cadbury in Lake and Cadbury 1933b, p412-3. Others who note that the speech contains a number of Pauline words and has many parallels in Paul's letters include Dupont 1962, p29; Barrett 1977, p109-116; Marshall 1980, p330; Carrez 1996, p372-3; Porter 1999, p117. Johnson (1992, p367) notes: "It is unmistakably Paul [delivering the speech], and a Paul who presents himself to this community in terms remarkably like the ones we recognize in the letters we know Paul himself wrote to his communities. ... But it is important to recognize that Luke accurately represents not only a number of distinctively Pauline themes, but does so in language which is specifically and verifiably Paul's."

[90] See Phil 2:3; Col 2:18, 23; 3:12. On the term see Dupont 1962, p40-3. On the concept of humility, which is very characteristic of Paul, see Dupont 1962, p43-51.

[91] See Rom 15:14; 1 Cor 4:14; 1 Thess 5:12, 14; also Col 1:28; 3:16; 2 Thess 3:15.

only here but Paul uses it seven times.[92] Fourthly, in v32 we read: "I commend you to God and to the word of his grace, which is able to build you up and to give you the inheritance among all who are sanctified." Building up the church by the word of grace is Pauline,[93] as is the idea of an inheritance (κληρονομία) given by God to his people.[94] Yet it is generally agreed that the Pauline words and phrases here are not sufficient to claim that Luke actually knew or used any of Paul's letters.[95]

However, we cannot simply look at the level of language and identify some words as Lucan and others as Pauline. The situation is more complicated than this and we need to note two other phenomena. Firstly, there are a number of places where the language itself is Lucan or at least different from that attested by the Pauline letters but the concept or meaning of the language is close to that found in Paul.[96] For example, in 20:21 Paul's teaching is summarised as testifying to Jews and Gentiles "of repentance to God and of faith in our Lord Jesus Christ (τὴν εἰς θεὸν μετάνοιαν καὶ πίστιν εἰς τὸν κύριον ἡμῶν Ἰησοῦν)". Repentance is a word that Paul uses rarely (see Rom 2:4; 2 Cor 7:9, 10) and when he does so it is not qualified as εἰς θεόν. However, a verse like Rom 10:9 suggests repentance is in order, since people have not treated Christ as Lord, and other verses like 1 Thess 1:9 and Gal 2:15 reinforce this.[97] As Barrett notes "the formula looks like a summary of what Paul had said by one

---

[92] See Rom 8:32; 11:21 (twice); 1 Cor 7:28; 2 Cor 1:23; 12:6; 13:2.

[93] See Rom 15:20; 1 Cor 14:3-5, 12, 17, 26; 2 Cor 12:19; 1 Thess 5:11. οἰκοδομέω and οἰκοδομή are used in a metaphorical sense in Luke-Acts only in Acts 9:31 and here in 20:32. That edification is the work of God is also Pauline; see for example 1 Cor 3:7. See also Dupont 1962, p250-60.

[94] See Rom 4:13f; 8:17; 1 Cor 6:9f; 15:50; Gal 3:18, 29; 4:1, 7, 30; 5:21; Col 1:12; 3:24; but see also Lk 10:25; 18:18; cf. Acts 26:18; see in general Dupont 1962, p261-83.

[95] See Dupont 1962, p29-30; Barrett 1977, p109-110. For the view that Luke does not know Paul's letters see Barrett 1976-77, p2-5; Bruce 1988, p387-8; Johnson 1992, p4-5; Barrett 1998, pxxvii-xxviii, xliv-xllv. Barrett (1998, p964) gives a list of 30 verses in the Pauline corpus to which allusions can be found in the speech, and notes "This is an impressive list, but on examination it proves to contain nothing that is truly convincing as a literary allusion to the written Pauline corpus." There are a number of parallels between the speech and the Pastorals, which are given in Wilson 1979, p117-18; he notes (p117): "Almost every detail of Acts 20.17-33 can be found in the Pastorals." Barrett (1998, p965) concludes on the basis of this evidence: "there can be little doubt that Acts and the Pastorals were produced in similar circumstances and at times not very remote from one another." We cannot go into this subject in detail here, apart from suggesting that the most likely explanation for the parallels is that Acts and the Pastorals are drawing on very similar Pauline traditions. But as Barrett notes (1998, p965) in the Pastorals Paul is the preeminent apostle, whereas Acts is very reticent in the use of ἀπόστολος for Paul (using it only in 14:14), which argues against Luke being the author of the Pastorals. See further in Chapter 5.

[96] As far as this can be judged from such a small sample as Paul's letters.

[97] See Dupont 1962, p82-3. Johnson (1992, p361) notes the similarity between Acts 20:21 and 1 Thess 1:9-10 concerning repentance.

who was by no means completely ignorant of his teaching but took it in his own way, which was not quite Paul's (even though Luke may have thought it was)."[98] While Barrett is right that the summary "was not quite Paul's", it is very close to Paul, and does not seriously mis-represent him.

The second phenomenon is that in other places the language is Pauline, but the meaning is slightly different from that found in Paul. Take Acts 20:26 for example: "to testify to the gospel of the grace of God." As Barrett notes: "*Gospel* is a Pauline word; *grace* is a Pauline word; the Gospel of God recalls Rom 1.1; 15.16; 2 Cor 11.7; 1 Thess 2:2,8,9; but the combined phrase is not Pauline. [Here] ... Luke uses words that are superficially Pauline, but improbably represents words that Paul actually used. They are significant as the (by no means misleading, except to a somewhat pedantic reading) deposit of Paulinism that permeated to the next generation."[99]

Thus, in the speech we have a lot of Lucan language, a significant amount of language which is not Lucan but Pauline, some instances of Pauline thought (or something very close to it) in Lucan language, and other examples of Pauline language used in somewhat unPauline ways. For us, what really matters here is the presence of Pauline language and thought (with some of the latter in Luke's words) in the speech.[100] It is not simply Luke's thought that

---

[98] Barrett 1977, p112. Note other examples of a Pauline concept in Luke's words a) "ὑμεῖς ἐπίστασθε" in the opening of the speech (20:18; see also 20:34). This is a Lucan expression; see also Acts 10:28; 15:7. But Paul expresses the same concept regularly, but using the expression οἴδατε; see 1 Thess 1:5; 2:1, 5. 9, 10-12; 4:2; 2 Thess 3:7-8; Gal 4:13-14; Phil 4:15; see also 1 Cor 11:2, 23; 15:1; see Dupont 1962, p31-3. b) In v22 in largely Lucan language Paul expresses misgivings concerning his present enterprise. That these were real is clear from Rom 15:30-1. c) v24 expresses Paul's ready surrender of himself for the Gospel's sake. There are parallels to this in 2 Cor 4:7-12; 6:4-10; 12:9-10; Phil 2:17; 3:8; Col 1:24; 4:17.

[99] Barrett 1977, p112; see also Dupont 1962, p103-5 who notes (p105) that the expression "trahit la plume de Luc; mais la doctrine qu'elle suppose est authentiquement paulinienne." Comparable expressions to Acts 20:26 are found in Lk 4:22; Acts 13:43; 14:3; 20:32. Another example of Pauline language combined in a way that is different from that found in Paul, but characteristic of Luke is in v25: "preaching the kingdom." Paul uses κηρύσσω and βασιλεία, but never in this combination, which is however typical of Luke (see Lk 8:1; 9:2; Acts 28:31; cf. Lk 4:43; 16:16; Acts 8:12; 19:8), although he generally speaks of "the kingdom of God"; see Dupont 1962, p115-19.

[100] Note the summary by Dupont (1962, p29): "Tel qu'il se présente à nous, ce texte doit être attribué à Luc. Il veut sans doute transmettre l'essentiel de la pensée de l'Apôtre; mais l'élaboration et la présentation relèvent de l'auteur des Actes." Conzelmann (1987, p173) thinks that the only source Luke had here was the report about a meeting at Miletus as such and that Luke has thus "composed the details as well as the speech itself." But such a view does not account for all the Pauline language and thought in the speech. Haenchen (1971, p596, with reference to 20:31, 33-5) states that the speech presents "the enigma that Paul here to an extraordinary degree presents himself as an exemplary model". He regards this as sufficient reason to see the speech, not as "Paul's self-attestation", but rather as "Luke's

is presented in the speech. How do we explain this, given that Luke does not seem to know Paul's letters?

In the preceding section we concluded that we have good reason for arguing that Paul spoke in Miletus, probably to Ephesians. If we allow this possibility, it raises the question of whether there are traditions in the speech which go back to Paul. There are two basic possibilities here. Firstly, some of the Pauline language and thought in the speech could be due to "traditional contact with what Paul said",[101] and thus be derived from local Ephesian tradition. Secondly, some features in the speech could be due to Luke using general Pauline tradition, which Luke has clearly drawn on elsewhere in Acts.[102] Such tradition could have been derived from any of Paul's mission centres (since there was much consistency, for example, in Paul's manner of operating), or could have had no specific geographical anchorage. Can we decide between these two possibilities, or argue for each in particular cases?

Nothing in the speech demands that the tradition Luke was drawing on was specifically and undeniably Miletus tradition,[103] or that it was connected with Ephesian Christians in particular. There is no unequivocal allusion in the speech to the cities of Ephesus or Miletus, although even if there were some elements like this it could still be argued that Luke created such details as local colour.[104] Yet at the very least, the presence of so much Pauline language and thought shows Luke is using general Pauline tradition in the speech,[105]

---

witness about him" (p596). However, Haenchen overlooks the point that the call to imitate the speaker is a common feature of farewell addresses; see for example TZeb 1:2-7; 5:1-5; 7:1-4; TJos 10:1-6; TBen 3:1; 4:1. Further, Paul himself calls on others to follow his example; see 1 Cor 4:15-16; 10:31-11:1; Gal 4:12; Phil 3:17; 1 Thess 1:6; 2 Thess 3:7-9; see also Dupont 1962, p20-21. Haenchen notes this, but does not give such passages sufficient weight. They show that it is highly likely that Paul would call on leaders to imitate him. The presence of this motif in the speech certainly provides no grounds for arguing that ideas in the speech do not go back to Pauline tradition. Finally, Haenchen's view does not take account of the amount of Pauline language in the speech.

[101] See Barrett 1977, p110.

[102] See Barrett 1977, p110. Barrett notes (1977, p110) "this tradition may not have been a historical source of high quality, but it was by no means completely out of touch with the historical Paul." His tentative conclusion on p115 that "there is probably no direct Paulinism and no authentic Pauline material in the speech at all" is, I think, too severe and underestimates the cumulative case for genuine Pauline traditions in the speech.

[103] This is noted by Barrett 1977, p110.

[104] The account is found in a "we" section (see 20:15, 21:1) but 20:17-38 is given entirely in the third person. Barrett (1977, p110) suggests it is therefore independent of the itinerary.

[105] The general picture which Luke paints using this tradition is in harmony with the picture which we can deduce from Paul's letters. Barrett (1977, p116-7) summarises in this way: "The situation that Luke depicts, and the words he puts into Paul's mouth, are open to considerable historical objection; yet, when full allowance has been made for this, it must be recognized that the general picture of Paul that is presented is in harmony with that which

(although he may have supplemented this material himself) but does he also have tradition that is connected with the Ephesian Christian community?[106]

In my view there are a number of elements in the speech which arguably are connected with Paul's time in Ephesus or with Ephesian Christians, and for which Luke was probably reliant on local tradition. We have argued in the previous section that Luke has some genuine local tradition underlying his narrative in Acts 19, so it would not be surprising if he had additional Ephesian tradition which related to a farewell speech delivered to Ephesian Christians, which he utilised here.[107] These will be examined in section 3.3 below.

There are other cases in the speech for which we cannot show that Luke was reliant on local Ephesian tradition, although this may well have been the case we simply cannot show it. However, in these cases Luke has probably applied general Pauline tradition to the Ephesian community and we can argue that the tradition is appropriate for that community. We will examine these in section 3.4 below. However, we must first discuss one other interpretation of the speech.

That Luke is here expressing Pauline tradition has not been accepted by a number of scholars. Haenchen draws attention to the assurance that Paul bears no guilt with respect to the church, because he has declared the whole purposes of God to them (v20, 26-7). He thinks this is repeated with too much emphasis for it simply to belong to the style of the farewell speech. Rather it points to the fact that Paul bears no guilt for "the catastrophe which

---

can be deduced from the letters. These too attest that Paul was a conscientious and diligent pastor, so concerned for his flocks that he shed tears over their needs and errors; that he was prepared to hazard his life for the Gospel, and that the Gospel as he understood it rested upon the grace of God and was responded to in faith; that he worked with his own hands rather than accept support or payment from his converts (at least in some cases); that he directed his ministry to both Jews and Gentiles; that he did occasionally (but very seldom) introduce into his teaching a saying that could be attributed to Jesus."

[106] See Barrett 1977, p110. Barrett (1977, p110) also takes what he regards as the formlessness of the speech as a sign that Luke had access to some traditional material which he worked up into the discourse. However, Watson (1991, p191-208) has shown that the speech is not as formless as Barrett supposed.

[107] Thus Fitzmyer (1998, p675) notes: "The speech is again a Lucan composition, but the fact that he [Paul] so addressed the presbyters of Ephesus and the character of the speech he made are the sort of things that Luke might well have derived from his Pauline source." We should note that there are features of the speech in Acts 20 which are not mentioned in Acts 19. Note a) his tears (20:19, 31); b) the plots of the Jews (20:19); c) teaching from house to house (20:20); d) working with his hands (20:34). These will be dealt with below. This shows that in Acts 20 Luke is not simply summarising what he has already said in the earlier section. Rather, it seems most likely that he is here drawing on different local traditions from those used in Acts 19.

after his death began to loom up in the Church of ' Aσία".[108] For Haenchen
the catastrophe was that the congregations founded by Paul in Asia Minor
were largely lost to "the Gnostic heresy". For Haenchen, this is what v30 is
about: "the defection to the Gnostic heresy could not well be more clearly
described in this prophesy. The reader moreover had it before his very
eyes."[109] Hence in the speech we hear, not Paul addressing the elders of
Ephesus, but Luke addressing his church, absolving Paul from responsibility
for the churches in Asia Minor being lost to Gnosticism. Luke has created the
speech, and is here calling the leaders of his day back to Pauline apostolic
faith.[110]

However, the interpretative key for Haenchen here, as he explicitly notes,
is Walter Bauer's *Orthodoxy and Heresy in Earliest Christianity*. Haenchen
accepts Bauer's thesis that the Pauline churches of Asia Minor were lost to
Gnosticism at the end of the first century. For Bauer and Haenchen the book
of Revelation shows this.[111] However, subsequent work has shown that
Bauer was mistaken on this point. Thomas Robinson has shown that,
particularly in western Asia Minor where we have sufficient evidence to test
Bauer's thesis, heresy was not as widespread and strong as Bauer contended.
Robinson concludes: "Bauer's reconstruction of primitive Christianity in
western Asia Minor must, to a large measure, be set aside."[112]

---

[108] Haenchen 1971, p596.

[109] Haenchen 1971, p593. Others see this verse as a reference to Gnosticism; see for
example Beyschlag (1971, p426 n66) who thinks this is the earliest mention of early
Christian Gnosis; Schüssler Fiorenza (1985, p128 n20) who concludes from this verse that
"Gnosis is therefore present in Christian circles within Ephesus between 80-100 C.E."

[110] Haenchen 1971, p596. Wilson (1979, p118) drawing on Klein's work, suggests that
Luke has a different motive: "The problem was not that Christians were accusing Paul of
failure, but that the gnostics were claiming Paul as the authority for their teaching. The
speech asserts that, despite their claim that Paul is their authority, in reality they are excluded
from the genuine Pauline tradition and do not have the Pauline 'deposit'. The repeated claim
that Paul has withheld nothing from the elders (Acts 20:27, 30, 35) is not a claim of
innocence, but an assertion that Paul's appointed successors alone have his true teaching, and
they have all of it. There is only one Pauline tradition, so that any claim to possess a secret
Pauline tradition is opposed by Paul himself!" The speech would thus emphasize the
completeness of Paul's Gospel. But this view again depends on the Pauline churches of Asia
Minor being lost to Gnosticism and so there being a need for such a claim about the
completeness and authenticity of Paul's Gospel contained in the tradition of the Christian
community in centres such as Ephesus. But as we point out in the text, it is unlikely that
Asia Minor was lost to Gnosticism.

[111] See Bauer 1971, p82-8.

[112] Robinson 1988, p204. Note also Lincoln (1990, plxxxiii-lxxxiv): "Bauer's view that
Pauline Christianity never gained much influence in Asia Minor is increasingly questioned."
See also Fitzmyer (1998, p681): "Luke is not thinking specifically about Gnostics and the
gnostic heresy, because there is no real evidence that gnosticism had yet reared its head."

Thus, Haenchen's interpretative key for this passage is unusable, and his whole reading collapses.[113] We do not need to see the speech as a Lucan creation in which Luke addresses his church about Gnosticism. Our view that the speech contains both local Ephesian tradition and general Pauline tradition which Luke has probably supplemented, is more cogent. We will investigate particular passages in both of these categories which shed light on Paul's time in Ephesus or the Ephesian Christian community.[114]

3.3 Cases in which Luke is probably dependent on local Ephesian tradition

3.3.1 Paul's tears and trials in Ephesus (Acts 20:19)

In Acts 19 Luke does not explicitly state that Paul suffered in Ephesus (he is not actually harmed in the riot), but he does hint at difficulties in Acts 20:19 where we read that in Ephesus Paul was "serving the Lord with all humility and with tears, enduring the trials that came to me through the plots of the Jews (ταῖς ἐπιβουλαῖς τῶν Ἰουδαίων)."[115] ἐπιβουλή is used in Acts of Jewish plots against Paul (Acts 9:24; 20:3; 23:30), while Paul himself does not use the word. In Acts Paul regularly suffers at the hands of Jews (13:45; 14:2; 18:12; 21:31 etc).

However, it is likely that Luke is drawing on tradition at this point, and probably tradition connected with Ephesus. Firstly, Paul's catalogues of hardships discussed in Chapter 2 (1 Cor 4:9-13; 2 Cor 4:8-9; 6:4-10; 11:23-33; 12:10) and other passages (eg 2 Cor 7:5) show that he suffered many "trials", and that it is likely that he did endure a number of incidents which could well have been called "plots". Secondly, given that Paul himself speaks of being punished by Jews (2 Cor 11:24,26) and alludes to such difficulties in 1 Thess 2:15, it seems possible that "plots" by the Jews did in fact take place in a number of cities, including Ephesus. Thirdly, we have already seen that Paul encountered opponents in Ephesus (1 Cor 15:32; 16:9) some of whom could well have been Jews given the size and significance of the Jewish

---

[113] He also does not take sufficient note of the Pauline language and thought in the speech.

[114] There are a number of features of the speech which are general and which present Paul's way of operating as a missionary. These features fit the "last will and testament" pattern of the speech. Much of this could apply to Ephesus (eg. Paul's humility while in the city (20:19)), but it does not substantially add to our knowledge of Paul's time in Ephesus or about the early Christians in the city, and so will not be dealt with here.

[115] There are a number of parallels to these concepts in Paul's letters. Paul speaks of himself as serving the Lord (Rom 7:6; 12:11; 14:18; Phil 2:22; Col 3:24; 1 Thess 1:9; cf. Rom 1:1; Gal 1:1; Phil 1:1) as being humble-minded (2 Cor 7:6; 10:1; 11:7; 12:21; Phil 2:3; 4:12; Col 3:12) and as shedding tears (2 Cor 2:4; Phil 3:18). In these features then Luke could be drawing on general traditions about Paul.

population in the city. Fourthly, we can note that in Acts 21:27-9 it is Jews from Asia who were leaders in the action taken against Paul in Jerusalem (see also 24:18-19).[116] They recognised Trophimus the Ephesian, which suggests that some of the Asian Jews were from Ephesus. This in turn raises the possibility that some Jews in Ephesus opposed Paul.[117] While Luke could have created this detail, he does not seem to have a clear motive for making Asian Jews *in particular* the main agitators against Paul in Jerusalem.[118] This suggests the involvement of Asian Jews at this point is historical, and reinforces the possibility that Ephesian Jews in Ephesus caused trouble for Paul.

We can conclude that it is likely that here Luke is dependent on local Ephesian tradition and that Paul did indeed suffer at the hands of Jews in Ephesus (as well as at the hands of Gentiles; see the Demetrius riot), although we have no specific confirmation of this from his letters.[119] Thus it is likely that, after Paul had voluntarily left the synagogue along with the disciples because some Jews were speaking against his work (19:9), at least some Ephesian Jews continued to be opposed to Paul's on-going mission.

3.3.2 Teaching in public and from house to house (Acts 20:20)

In Acts 20:20 we read that in Ephesus Paul was "teaching you publicly (δημοσίᾳ) and from house to house (καὶ κατ' οἴκους)".[120] In Acts 19:9 we

---

[116] See Duncan 1929, p29, 53-5; see also Thompson 1990, p226 n7.

[117] Although it is possible that the Ephesian Jews who were in Jerusalem (as residents? on pilgrimage?) may have been more zealous against Paul than were Ephesian Jews in Ephesus.

[118] The Asian Jews' zeal for the Temple and the law (21:29) fits in with what we know of Asian Jews (see Trebilco 1991, p12-36), but then other Diaspora Jews would have shared this zeal.

[119] Lake and Cadbury (1933a, p260) note with respect to Acts 20:19: "It is natural to suppose that the Jews were responsible for some of the difficulties at Ephesus mentioned in Paul's letters." Note also that Luke does not mention these plots of the Jews in Acts 19. This suggests that Luke has not created this element of the Miletus speech, since then we would have expected him to have related some incident in Acts 19 that backed up this statement in the speech. Duncan (1929, p27-9) asks if the Jews attempted to build up a case against Paul at Ephesus as they did, according to Acts, in Corinth (Acts 18:12-17). On p26-46 he discusses the extent of Jewish opposition to Paul, but goes beyond the evidence in seeing them as having a part in the riot.

[120] δημόσιος is only found in Acts; see 5:18; 16:37; 18:28; 20:20. Luke also uses the phrase "κατ' οἴκους" in Acts 5:42, where we read: "And every day in the temple and at home (κατ' οἶκον) they [the Jerusalem apostles] did not cease to teach and proclaim Jesus as the Messiah." The meaning in both 5:42 and 20:20 is probably that teaching centred on both a public space (the temple or a public area) and the house. According to Luke then, the activity of Paul in Ephesus is comparable to that of the Jerusalem apostles earlier, except that one venue for Paul's teaching was a public space rather than the temple (see Dupont 1962, p81-2;

learn that Paul "argued daily in the hall of Tyrannus" and we have noted in the previous chapter that this is credible. This is probably the "public" venue that is alluded to here. But this text also suggests that Paul taught in different houses ("κατ᾽ οἴκους") and this may well refer to two related but distinguishable activities. Firstly, it refers to Paul's teaching activity in house church gatherings,[121] gatherings which would almost certainly have included celebrating the "Lord's Supper" (1 Cor 11:17-32). We have already noted the significance of the house church in Pauline communities in Chapter 2 and we know from 1 Cor 16:19-20 that more than one house church existed in Ephesus at this time. It is quite credible then that in speaking at Miletus Paul emphasised that the house church had been an important centre of teaching in his work in Ephesus. This would point again to the importance of the house church for Ephesian Christians.

But teaching "κατ᾽ οἴκους" is probably also a reference to Paul's practice of teaching in the context of people's houses. Stowers has underlined the significance of the private home as a major context for Paul's preaching and teaching activity.[122] Paul's letters show the significance of the private home in this regard (eg Rom 16:23; 1 Cor 1:16) and Acts confirms the picture (see Acts 16:15, 32; 18:7; 28:16f).

Stowers notes that, in the Greco-Roman world, "The private home was a center of intellectual activity and the customary place for many types of speakers and teachers to do their work. ... The private home provided a teacher or speaker with much more than just a place to speak and hospitality. The patron or host could provide the speaker with an audience and a kind of social legitimation."[123] He notes that sophists and philosophers regularly used private homes as venues for their teaching, and in doing the same Paul was following recognized practice.[124] Thus an invitation to teach in someone's house would provide Paul with a sponsor, an audience and credentials, and a venue away from the controversy of the synagogue or the competition of a public space.[125] So when Paul speaks here of "teaching you ... from house to

---

see also Acts 2:46; "κατ᾽ οἴκους" also recalls the conduct of Saul the persecutor in Acts 8:3). Thus, 20:20 expresses a Lucan theme. But we have strong grounds for seeing it as historical too, given the significance of the house as a venue for Paul's teaching, as noted in the text.

[121] Haenchen (1971, p591) thinks 20:20 refers to house-churches. Note that Paul has just taught in a house church in Troas, Acts 20:7-11, where "breaking of bread" and teaching were involved; in this case the house church met in an apartment house of three storeys.

[122] See Stowers 1984, p59-82, especially, p65-70. Paul also probably carried his teaching into everyday activities such as his leatherwork trade; see Hock 1980.

[123] Stowers 1984, p65-66. Stowers (1984, p81) notes that "Public speaking and often the use of public buildings required status, reputation, and recognized roles which Paul did not have."

[124] See Stowers 1984, p70.

[125] See Stowers 1984, p68.

house (καὶ κατ᾽ οἴκους)" we should think of teaching activity in private homes, as well as preaching in a house church gathering.

3.3.3 Working with his hands for his own support, and to support others (Acts 20:34)

In Acts 20:34 we read: "You know for yourselves that I worked with my own hands to support myself and my companions." We know that on occasions Paul refused to accept money from his converts (eg 1 Cor 9:4-18) so as not to put an obstacle in the way of the Gospel (1 Cor 9:12). This meant that he either relied on other churches to support him (2 Cor 11:8; Phil 4:15-18) or worked with his own hands (1 Thess 2:9; 4:11; 2 Thess 3:6-13; 1 Cor 4:12; 2 Cor 11:7; see also Acts 18:3 in Corinth). The view expressed here in Acts 20:34 is very similar to that given by Paul in a number of passages, especially 2 Thess 3:6-10.[126]

Given the evidence from Paul's letters that he worked with his hands, and Acts 18:3 and 20:34, it is thus highly likely that Paul worked as a tentmaker in Ephesus. That Luke could here be dependent on local tradition is suggested by the fact that we know that Aquila and Prisca were with Paul in Ephesus (1 Cor 16:19) and that he wrote 1 Cor 4:12 ("and we grow weary from the work of our own hands") from Ephesus, as we noted in Chapter 2.[127]

Acts 20:34 says that Paul's hands ministered not only to his own necessities, but also "to those who were with me". The purpose of this note is to show that Paul accepted his own advice given in v35: he had sufficient to give to those in need, and so to know from experience that it was more blessed to give than to receive. Dupont notes "Rien n'oblige à penser que le travail de Paul assurait la subsistance du groupe entier de ses collaborateurs, ceux-ci n'ayant qu'à se laisser entretenir par leur chef! Pour que la leçon porte, il suffit que l'Apôtre ait eu l'occasion d'en aider l'un ou l'autre dans une circonstance particulière."[128]

---

[126] Johnson 1992, p365; see also 1 Cor 4:12; 9:15-18; 1 Thess 2:9; 4:11.

[127] See Dupont 1962, p300-1. κοπιάω, used in Acts 20:35, is normally used by Paul of the work of ministry, but the usage in 1 Cor 4:12 is the same as here; see Barrett 1977, p116. Luke uses the term only in Lk 5:5, where it is applied to fishing. Paul also uses κόπος of manual labour; see 1 Thess 2:9; 2 Thess 3:8. If the handkerchiefs and aprons of Acts 19:11-12 were taken from Paul's workshop, then this adds force to the likelihood that he worked as a tentmaker in Ephesus. Thompson (1990, p119-20) argues that the fact that Paul worked as a tentmaker gives us some clues about the social level of some Christians in Ephesus.

[128] Dupont 1962, p305-6. It seems unlikely that Paul would have earned enough as a tentmaker to support others fully. Haenchen (1971, p594 n3) sees the comment that Paul supported others as an exaggeration, but does not consider the point Dupont makes. In his

3.4 Cases in which Luke is probably dependent on general Pauline tradition, but which he has appropriately applied to the Ephesian community

There are other instances for which we cannot show that Luke was reliant on local Ephesian tradition, although this may well have been the case and we simply cannot show it. However, in these cases, at the very least, Luke has applied general Pauline tradition to the Ephesian community, and we can argue that the tradition is appropriate for (or can plausibly be related to) that community. We turn to these examples now.

3.4.1 Elders in Ephesus (v17) who are also called overseers in v28

In Acts 20:17 Paul is said to address the πρεσβύτεροι of the church at Ephesus,[129] but we have no evidence in Paul's letters for πρεσβύτερος being used as a title for leaders.[130] However, Paul's writings show that in at least some of his congregations there were local leaders,[131] although it is also clear that no developed nomenclature for leaders was in general use. Thus in Acts 20:17 Luke is probably using a term which was current in his own day - πρεσβύτερος - to refer to leaders who were known by a different designation in the earlier period.[132] But, judging from Paul's other communities (eg 1 Cor 16:15-16; 1 Thess 5:12-13; Phil 1:1), it is almost certain that the church at Ephesus had some form of leadership.

It is also noteworthy that in 20:28 the πρεσβύτεροι are called ἐπίσκοποι. This strongly suggests that in Luke's time the two words were used of the same people and that "bishops" did not exist as a separate group.[133] The title πρεσβύτερος (20:17) indicates the dignity and standing of the leaders,[134] while ἐπίσκοπος (20:28) is not used here as an official title, but rather indicates the function of the presbyters.[135] Thus, all the "elders" fulfil the role

---

letters Paul does not explicitly say that he helped his co-workers in this way, but Acts 20:34 is in keeping with Eph 4:28.

[129] It has been suggested that the 12 of 19:1-7 may point to the existence of a "college" of twelve established by Paul as leaders of the church at Ephesus and that Luke may intend readers to identify the "elders" of Acts 20:17-35 with this group of "about 12"; see Michaels 1991, p250; see also Neil 1973, p203; Williams 1957, p220. However, that Luke intends there to be any special connection between the "12" and the "elders" seems very unlikely.

[130] See Conzelmann 1987, p173.

[131] Thus, for example, in 1 Thess 5:12-13 we read of "those who are over you in the Lord"; see also 1 Cor 16:15-16; Phil 1:1.

[132] See Marshall 1980, p241, on Acts 14:23. See also Schnackenburg 1991, p49; Marshall 1999, p173. Johnson (1992, p360) notes that the presbyterial structure of the local church from the beginning is assumed by Luke; see Acts 11:30; 14:23; 15:2,4,6,22,23; 16:4. See also Jas 5:14; 1 Pet 5:1; 2 Jn 1; 3 Jn 1.

[133] See Barrett 1977, p113-4; Haenchen 1971, p592-3; Johnson 1992, p362.

[134] Dupont 1962, p141-3.

[135] See Lövestam 1987, p6. This is the only time Luke uses the word ἐπίσκοπος.

of "overseeing" and probably both terms were used in Luke's time for leaders. But given that Paul speaks of ἐπίσκοποι in Phil 1:1 it is possible that in Acts 20:28 Luke (whether knowingly or not) gives the term Paul actually used on occasions in speaking of at least some leaders in his congregations.

We can also note that since no one individual is singled out in Acts 20:17-38, Luke envisaged a joint leadership structure in the Ephesian community, in which the leaders jointly had oversight.[136] Again, this is in keeping with the pattern of leadership in Paul's communities, and probably accurately reflects the situation in Ephesus in Paul's day.[137]

All of this suggests (with the same degree of probability that exists for all that we say in this section about the speech, given that none of it can be connected with certainty to Ephesus) that at the conclusion of Paul's time in Ephesus, his Ephesian community had a number of leaders and that the leadership structure was a joint one.

3.4.2 Testifying "to both Jews and Greeks" (v21)

Luke mentions on five occasions that Paul preached to "Jews and Greeks", although three of these come in the Ephesian material (Acts 14:1; 18:4; 19:10, 17; 20:21). In other places Luke emphasizes that Paul preached to both Jews and Gentiles (see 13:44-8; 14:27; 17:4,11-12, 17, 18:5-6). διαμαρτύρομαι (20:21) is generally Lucan, although Paul uses μαρτύρομαι of paraenesis.[138] It is clear from Paul's letters that he preached to both Jews and Greeks as we noted in the previous chapter, and we find in Paul comparable expressions to that used in Acts 20:21.[139] When in 1 Cor 16:9 Paul speaks of a "wide door for effective work" being opened to him in Ephesus he is referring to his evangelistic opportunities in the city, which probably involved both Jews and Gentiles, as they did elsewhere. Here, then, Luke seems to be appropriately applying general Pauline tradition to Ephesus.

---

[136] See Haenchen 1971, p593 n1.

[137] See again Phil 1:1; 1 Thess 5:12-13.

[138] διαμαρτύρομαι is found in Acts 2:40; 8:25; 10:42; 18:5; 20:21, 23, 24; 23:11; 28:23. Paul's only use of the term is in 1 Thess 4:6. μαρτύρομαι is found in Acts 20:26; 26:22; Gal 5:3; Eph 4:17; 1 Thess 2:12.

[139] See Rom 1:16; 2:9-10; 3:9; 10:12; 1 Cor 1:24; 10:32; 12:13; Gal 3:28; see also Johnson 1992, p361.

3.4.3 Fierce wolves from without and the rise of those distorting the truth from within (v29-30)

In v26 Paul claims to be "innocent of the blood of all of you (καθαρός εἰμι ἀπὸ τοῦ αἵματος πάντων)" (v26). This is a Lucan expression,[140] which implicitly envisages the defection of some of the Ephesian Christians. This will involve the defectors in judgement, but Paul will be innocent in this regard, since he has declared the whole counsel of God to the Ephesians (v27). This defection becomes explicit in v28-31 to which we now turn.

The pastoral metaphor is introduced in v28: "Keep watch over yourselves and over all the flock (τῷ ποιμνίῳ)". Paul does not use ποίμνιον and he uses the related ποίμνη and ποιμαίνω only in 1 Cor 9:7 and ποιμήν is used in Eph 4:11. Luke uses ποίμνιον only here and in Lk 12:32, but he does give the parable of the lost sheep (Lk 15:3-7). It seems fair to conclude that neither Luke nor Paul use the metaphor much.[141] However, the fact that Paul does not use ποίμνιον at all and that the pastoral metaphor is hardly a favourite with Luke means we cannot be at all certain about the origin of the language used here.[142]

In v29-30 Paul predicts that after his departure[143] trouble will arise for the congregation from two distinct quarters.[144] He writes: "I know that after I have gone, fierce wolves (λύκοι βαρεῖς) will come in among you, not sparing the flock. Some even from your own group will come distorting the truth in order to entice the disciples to follow them."

Some of the language in v29-31 is Lucan,[145] some is used by both Luke and Paul,[146] some is Pauline.[147] That φείδομαι and νουθετέω, both important

---

[140] It has parallels in Acts 5:28; 18:6. On the background of the term see Dupont 1962, p128-32 and for example Gen 42:22; Dt 21:7; 2 Sam 1:16; 4:11; 1 Kgs 2:31-3; Ezek 3:17-21; 33:2-9; TLevi 10:1-2. The declaration of innocence is one of the regular features of farewell addresses; see Prast 1979, p36-7, 116-119.

[141] Dupont 1962, p145-50.

[142] Barrett (1977, p114) is convinced that the pastoral language here is not Pauline. The metaphor is strongest in 1 Pet 2:25; 5:1-4 and Jn 10:7-18; 21:15f. It is very common in the OT; see Dupont 1962, p149 n1.

[143] There is evidence for ἄφιξις meaning "departure"; see Dupont 1962, p199-201; Bruce 1990, p434-5.

[144] Farewell speeches often include predictions by the speaker of a falling away or general misfortune that will occur after the speaker's death; see for example Jub 7:26-7; TLevi 4:1; 10:2-5; 14:1-3; TJud 18:1-6; TIssac 6:1-4; TNap 4:1-5; 2 Tim 3:1-5; 4:3-4; 2 Pet 2:1-3; 3:3-4. The presence of such an element here does not tell either way on the historicity of this element of Paul's speech.

[145] εἰσέρχομαι is used by Luke 49 times in his Gospel, and 32 times in Acts; it is only used four times by Paul (Rom 5:12; 11:25; 1 Cor 14:23, 24). λύκος is used only twice by Luke (Lk 10:3; and here) and not by Paul. ἀνίστημι is used by Luke 74 times, by Paul only six times. διαστρέφω is used by Luke five times (Lk 9:41; 23:2; Acts 13:8, 10; 20:30), but only once by Paul (Phil 2:15). ἀποσπάω is used by Luke (Lk 22:41; Acts 20:30; 21:1) but

concepts in this section, are not found elsewhere in Luke, does suggest that
Luke is not creating this section, but rather is using some Pauline tradition.
However, the number of Lucan words suggests that he has generally (but not
always) translated the Pauline tradition into his own language. The alternative
explanation - that Luke is trying to make the speech sound Pauline, but has no
Pauline tradition to use - does not seem to be credible.

Who are the λύκοι βαρεῖς?[148] In the OT bad leaders in particular are often
spoken of as wolves.[149] In Mt 7:15 we read "'Beware of false prophets, who
come to you in sheep's clothing but inwardly are ravenous wolves'" (cf. Mt
24:5; Lk 21:8; Jn 10:12; IgnPhd. 2.1-2). However, it is not clear from the
context of Acts 20:29 who these "fierce wolves" are who will come in from
the outside. They are spoken of in general terms which makes it impossible to
identify them more closely, but they are distinguished from those insiders
who will distort the truth (v30). All we can say is that they seem to be
Christian teachers from another community,[150] since "εἰς ὑμᾶς" suggests
they will do their damage as those coming from the outside into the group of
Christians. Further, it is the image of the church as a flock (v28-9) which leads
to the use of the image of wolves, with the word "wolves" being used in
contrast to true shepherds.[151] Beyond this we cannot say, since the text is

---

not by Paul. μαθητής is used by Luke 39 times in the Gospel and 30 times in Acts, but not
at all by Paul. The expression "night and day" is found in the accusative in Luke, here and in
Lk 2:37 and Acts 26:7, while in Paul it is found in the genitive (1 Thess 2:9; 3:10; 2 Thess
3:8); see Dupont 1962, p228 n4.

[146] παύω is used 9 times by Luke, three times by Paul. βαρύς is used by Luke twice
(Acts 20:29; 25:7) and Paul once (2 Cor 10:10). γρηγορέω is used three times by Luke
(only here in Acts) and four times by Paul. μνημονεύω is used by Luke in Lk 17:32 and
here in Acts 20:31, 35; Paul uses it six times. We note that some of these words are rare.

[147] φείδομαι is used by Luke only here and by Paul seven times (Rom 8:32; 11:21
(twice); 1 Cor 7:28; 2 Cor 1:23; 12:6; 13:2). νουθετέω is found eight times in the NT -
only here in Lk-Acts, but seven times in Paul (Rom 15:14; 1 Cor 4:14; Col 1:28; 3:16; 1
Thess 5:12, 14; 2 Thess 3:15). ἕκαστος is used by both Luke and Paul, but the expression
in Acts 20:31 "to admonish everyone with tears" is not paralleled closely elsewhere in Lk-
Acts, but is very similar to 1 Thess 2:11-12. This is an instance where both Lk and Paul use
the word, but only in Paul do we find close parallels to the actual concept being employed.

[148] Barrett (1998, p978) notes that βαρεῖς is somewhat surprising as a description of
wolves, and notes that it can also mean "powerful" and suggests Luke's point may be that
"the heretics are formidable rather than ferocious."

[149] See Ezek 22:27; Zeph 3:3; Pr 28:15 (LXX); Gen 49:27. On the wolf in Greek and
Latin literature see Dupont 1962, p210-11. Later, false teachers are often called wolves; see
Did 16.3; IgnPhd 2.1-2; 2 Clem 5.2-4; Justin, Apol. 1.16.13; Dial. 35.3; 4 Ezra 5:18; 1
Enoch 89:13-27; see also Lampe 1973, p256.

[150] Dupont 1962, p207. The influence they are said to have suggests they are teachers, as
does the comparison with the current elders who will "distort the truth in order to entice the
disciples to follow them" in v30.

[151] See Bruce 1990, p435; Barrett 1998, p978.

more interested in their impact on the congregation - that they will rampage and destroy, without concern for the church - rather than their exact theological position.[152]

In v30 the reference is to some Ephesian elders themselves perverting the Gospel and "drawing away" others after them.[153] This would involve the break-away elders in attempting to set up new and rival communities. Again, few details are given, and the emphasis is not on the nature of the teaching, but its seriousness.[154] What is involved is the corruption of the Gospel, and division in the church.[155]

As we have seen Paul only rarely uses the pastoral metaphor, which underlies the language of fierce wolves attacking the flock, and never speaks of "fierce wolves".[156] Nor does he speak of "perverse things (διεστραμμένα)". However, there are parallels in Paul's letters to what is said in Acts 20:29-30, so it is quite possible that Luke is drawing on Pauline tradition here, and translating it into his own language. Just prior to this point in Acts Paul had written 2 Corinthians, which shows that he had much difficulty from outsiders who have come into the congregation (especially 2 Cor 10-13). Note 2 Cor 11:4, 13: "For if someone comes and proclaims another Jesus than the one we proclaimed, or if you receive a different spirit from the one you received, or a different gospel from the one you accepted, you submit to it readily enough. ... For such boasters are false apostles, deceitful workers, disguising themselves as apostles of Christ." Galatians shows the impact of outsiders on Paul's communities; take for example 1:7: "but there are some who are confusing you and want to pervert the gospel of Christ" and 3:1 "O

---

[152] Scholars have speculated further about these "fierce wolves". Lampe (1973, p256-66) thinks the "wolves" refer to Judaizing "false prophets", but this is only one possibility; see also Lövestam 1987, p5. Barrett (1977, p115) suggests that "We must think of inadequately Christianized representatives of pagan religions, or possibly (laying less stress on εἰς ὑμᾶς) of those who attacked with the weapons of persecution." See below on those who would see a reference to Gnosticism here. However, these suggestions remain speculative.

[153] "Drawing away" others after them recalls Acts 5:36-7, which concerns two Jewish agitators. Lk 21:8 (cf. Mk 13:5-6) is also similar. Lampe (1973, p255) thinks it involves non-Christians persuading Christians to apostatize, but it seems more likely that it involves Christian leaders who teach different ideas setting up rival groups.

[154] See Dupont 1962, p219. He notes that some authors see them as Judaisers, others as Gnostics, but v30 is too vague and general to allow any such identification. The discourse does not seek to be precise, but to show the seriousness of the threat.

[155] Barrett (1977, p115) suggests that "both heresy (διεστραμμένα) and schism (ἀποσπᾶν) are involved, but the heresy is given as the cause of the schism - naturally the other side would put the matter differently."

[156] As noted above, neither Luke nor Paul use this pastoral metaphor much. Barrett (1977, p115) suggests that since the pastoral metaphor is not Pauline, neither is this phrase, but the evidence is so limited that it is difficult to comment on this.

foolish Galatians! Who has bewitched you?"[157] In Philippians (eg Phil 3:2-4) and Colossians (eg. Col 2:4,8) we again see the impact of outsiders, and in Rom 16:17-20 Paul gives a general warning against those, probably from outside, who would introduce dissension.[158] Particularly if Paul was aware of the existence of organised rival missions to his own, it is easy to imagine him warning the Ephesian leaders about them. Thus, although Acts 20:29 generally contains different language from that used by Paul, the intention to warn congregations about outsiders is clear in Paul's letters.[159] Certainly the rival teachers against whom Paul writes in his letters could well be described by Luke as "fierce wolves" who will "not spare the flock".

What about the warning about troublemakers from within the community? The language of v30 is Lucan,[160] but the concepts expressed are not foreign to Paul. He has recently written 1 Corinthians and in that letter had to deal with dissident elements within that congregation (esp 1 Cor 1-4; eg 4:18). Further, the Paul who can write that he is "under daily pressure because of my anxiety for all the churches" (2 Cor 11:28) is only too aware of the potential for trouble to arise within his churches.[161] 1 Cor 11:18-19 is also important here: "For, to begin with, when you come together as a church, I hear that there are divisions (σχίσματα among you; and to some extent I believe it. Indeed, there have to be factions among you (δεῖ γὰρ καὶ αἱρέσεις[162] ἐν ὑμῖν εἶναι), for only so will it become clear who among you are genuine." Here Paul gives one reason why he believes the reports he has received that there were indeed divisions among the Corinthians. Although Paul argues against divisions in Corinth (1 Cor 1:10-17; 3:1-23), he here seems to affirm that they are necessary. Fee explains this as a reflection of Paul's "now and not yet" eschatological perspective. Thus, "Paul expected 'divisions' to accompany the End, divisions that would separate true believers from those who were false. ... Paul ... probably sees their present divisions as part of the divine 'testing/sifting' process already at work in their midst. Such 'divisions' are not a good thing, but they are an inevitable part of the Eschaton, which has already been set in motion by Christ. Thus by this evil thing, their 'divisions,' God is working out his own purposes; those who are truly his, the 'tested/approved,' ... are already being manifest in their midst, and

---

[157] See also Gal 1:6, 8-9; 4:17; 5:7, 10, 12; 6:12; cf. also 2:4.

[158] See Fitzmyer 1993, p745-6. See also Eph 4:14; 5:6 and in general Dupont 1962, p215-19.

[159] Dupont (1962, p218) notes Paul's letters show "une préoccupation identique à celle du verset qui nous occupe dans le discours de Milet."

[160] See Dupont 1962, p215.

[161] Predictive prophecy is also found in Paul's writings - eg. 1 Thess 4:13-18.

[162] Paul uses the term only here and in Gal 5:20. Here it is roughly synonymous with σχίσματα of 1 Cor 11:18, and so must mean something similar, such as divisions or factions; see Fee 1987, p538; Barrett 1968, p261; Cranford 1980, p24.

presumably they will escape the final judgement that is coming upon the world (v. 32)."[163]

Given this theological view, it seems that Paul expected some in his communities to be tested and found wanting. This makes it quite likely that in a farewell speech Paul could have warned members of one of his congregations about those of their number who would pervert the Gospel, and lead others astray after them.

We conclude that we can put a strong case that the essence of v29-30 goes back to Pauline tradition.[164] Certainly, although v29-30 is generally (though not always) in Lucan language, Paul expresses the concepts involved in his letters. In fact, Luke could here be dependent on local Ephesian tradition; given what Paul says in his letters as we have noted, and the prevalence of "false teachers" in Paul's communities, it is very likely that Paul said something like v29-30 to Ephesian Christians at some point. But we cannot show that Luke is dependent on local tradition here, primarily because we have so little from Paul himself concerning his time in Ephesus. But at the very least, Luke could be dependent on general Pauline tradition, but it is very likely that Luke appropriately applied it to Ephesus, since, given what we know from Paul's letters, it is credible that Paul predicted the arrival in Ephesus of false teachers from elsewhere and the defection of some Ephesian Christians themselves.[165]

But the further question arises, would Luke have retained the tradition about false teachers if nothing like this had happened? Given that Luke presents the early church as generally united, and that this is the only occasion in Acts when he mentions false teachers,[166] he must have included the note here because false teachers were actually a problem after Paul's time. Johnson has noted that the prophecies in Luke-Acts are brought to fulfillment,[167] and Peterson shows how prevalent the motif of fulfillment is in Luke-Acts.[168] This suggests that we are to think of prophecies like this one in

---

[163] Fee 1987, p538-9. He also notes that this comment is probably inserted here in anticipation of 1 Cor 11:28-32.

[164] It is not certain whether v29-30 should be seen as a prophecy by Paul, or as an insightful "reading of the signs", but in either case we have parallels in Paul's letters. Predictive prophesy is found in Paul (eg. 1 Thess 4:13-18), and Paul has much to say about prophesy (eg. 1 Cor 14:1-12). Paul certainly read the signs and had forebodings of trouble with respect to his trip to Jerusalem with the Collection; see Rom 15:30-2.

[165] Barrett (1998, p979) thinks that in 20:30 "Luke is probably now thinking of the church at large." But the passage suggests that if it applied anywhere, it applied in Ephesus.

[166] But lack of harmony is mentioned, for example, in 6:1-2; 15:36-9; 21:20-21.

[167] Johnson (1992, p8) notes: "Paul's final words in Acts, 'this word of salvation has been sent to the Gentiles, and they will listen' (28:28), is meant to be understood as a prophecy that is - like all prophecies in Luke-Acts - brought to fulfillment."

[168] See Peterson 1993, p83-104.

20:29-30 as also being fulfilled, but after the events described at the end of Acts. We can suggest then that events turned out along the lines of v29-30 and that there was trouble in the Ephesian church from both insiders and outsiders after Paul's time and prior to Luke writing Acts.[169] One feature of this seems to have been the attempt by leaders to set up new and rival communities.

We have noted above that we cannot be certain that Paul did deliver a farewell address along these lines to Ephesian elders at Miletus, since this is not confirmed by Paul's letters. We have also noted that Luke is probably using Pauline tradition in the speech, but that nothing in the speech is directly related to Ephesus or Miletus (which is itself entirely understandable given the personal and hortatory nature of the speech). Given this lack of specificity with regards to Ephesus, it could be asked then whether we have grounds for claiming that false teachers arrived *in Ephesus* rather than elsewhere.

However, the fact that Luke presents the hearers of the speech as Ephesian elders strongly suggests that if the contents of v29-30 applies to any community after Paul's day, it at least applies to Ephesus. Luke includes the tradition about false teachers because this actually came true in Ephesus. It may, of course, apply more generally as we have seen, but at the very least Luke must see it as applying to Ephesus.[170] We are on strong grounds then when we claim that after Paul's time false teachers from without and within were a problem in Ephesus.

Yet we cannot say that these were Gnostic teachers, or that the community capitulated to Gnosticism. There is insufficient evidence from elsewhere to support this view, and nothing in the text requires it.[171] Luke may have been aware of the claim made by some to esoteric knowledge, a claim which Haenchen sees refuted in v20 and 27,[172] although these verses are quite comprehensible as dependent on Paul's conviction that he proclaimed the

---

[169] Barrett (1999, p530) suggests Acts was written in "AD 90 or thereabouts". Williams (1957, p234-5) writes: "it may be taken to imply that Luke knew that the Church in Ephesus after Paul's day had trouble with false teachers." In the speech Paul says that he will suffer in the future (see 20:23-5) and we certainly know that that happened. Again a case can be made that this goes back to tradition. Further, Rom 15:30-32 shows Paul's fears at this time that he will not be well received in Jerusalem. Bruce's comment (1988, p392) concerning v25 is relevant here: "Luke would not have reported [these words] and repeated them so emphatically if he had known that, in the event, they were falsified." See also Barrett 1977, p113.

[170] It may help to express this point negatively. If trouble had arisen in some of Paul's communities in Luke's time, but not in Ephesus, it seems unlikely that Luke would have included this section in the speech addressed to the Ephesian elders.

[171] See our discussion of Haenchen's view that the speech is a Lucan creation in which Luke addresses his church about Gnosticism.

[172] Haenchen 1971, p596.

whole Gospel which did not need to be supplemented.[173] But we cannot say that the Pauline Ephesian community capitulated to Gnosticism. However, as we have noted, the evidence does suggest that Paul predicted the Ephesian Christians would be troubled by false teachers from without and within, and Luke confirmed that this did indeed happen by addressing this tradition to the Ephesian elders.

3.4.4 Three years in Ephesus (v31)

This reference to Paul's stay in Ephesus as lasting for three years is consistent with the earlier notes of time (three months in 19:8; two years in 19:10; "a while" in 19:22). The three years here is probably an inclusive reckoning of time. We have no confirmation from Paul's letters of the period of time he spent in Ephesus, but it was clearly of considerable length.

3.5 Conclusions

We have shown that there are good reasons for arguing that Paul spoke in Miletus, probably to Ephesians. We have noted that, although nothing in the speech demands that the tradition Luke was drawing on was specifically Ephesian tradition, there are a number of elements which arguably are connected with Paul's time in Ephesus or with the Ephesian Pauline Christian community. In these cases we can put a strong case that Luke was either dependent on Ephesian tradition, or has applied general Pauline tradition to the Ephesian Christian community appropriately and with good reason.

An analysis of these verses has led us to a number of conclusions. Firstly, we see again that in Ephesus Paul preached to both Jews and Greeks. Secondly, the house church had been an important factor in Paul's work in Ephesus and was an important element in the life of Ephesian Christians. Thirdly, Paul worked as a tentmaker in Ephesus. Fourthly, it is likely that Paul suffered at the hands of Jews in Ephesus (as well as at the hands of Gentiles; see the Demetrius riot). Fifthly, at the conclusion of Paul's time in Ephesus, his Ephesian community had a number of leaders and the leadership structure was a joint one. Sixthly, given what Paul says in his letters, it is credible that he predicted the arrival in Ephesus after his departure of false teachers from elsewhere, and the defection of some Ephesian Christians themselves. Further, Luke seems to have confirmed that this did indeed happen after Paul's time and prior to Luke writing Acts, by addressing this

---

[173] See for example Gal 1:6-9; 3:1-5. Acts 20:20 also relates to Paul's view that he is under obligation to preach the Gospel; see eg. Rom 1:14-16; 1 Cor 9:16; 2 Cor 4; see also Dupont 1962, p62-7.

tradition to the Ephesian elders. However, the speech does not give a basis for the claim that the Pauline Ephesian community capitulated to Gnosticism.

4. Overall Conclusions

We have argued that both the account of the riot and the Miletus speech contain reliable information with regard to Paul's time in Ephesus and the early Christians in the city. We have also reached a number of significant conclusions which can be reiterated here.

Firstly, we have again seen that Paul's ministry in Ephesus was collaborative.[174] That a number of leading early Christians were part of the mission in Ephesus almost certainly contributed to its success. We should not think of "Paul's mission in Ephesus", but rather of the mission in the city of a team of key early Christian leaders. Secondly, we note the significance of the house church for the life of the early Christians in Ephesus. Thirdly, in Ephesus Paul preached to and encountered opposition from both Jews and Gentiles, and the Christian community may have experienced some on-going opposition from both quarters. Fourthly, Paul had some notable friends during his mission, but we do not know if they continued to support the Christian community after Paul had left the city. Fifthly, we have seen again that the Gentile section of the Christian community in Ephesus grew quickly. We noted in chapter 3 that the Jewish section of the Christian community was probably also significant.

Sixthly, by the end of Paul's time in Ephesus, his Ephesian community had a number of leaders and the leadership structure was a joint one. Seventhly, by the end of Paul's mission, the Jewish and Christian communities in Ephesus saw themselves as distinct groups, as least to some extent. Finally, Paul predicted that after his departure, "false teachers" would arrive in Ephesus from elsewhere as well as the defection of some Ephesian Christians themselves. It seems very likely that this did indeed happen after Paul's time and prior to Luke writing Acts.

---

[174] We learn from Acts 19:22 that Timothy was with Paul in Ephesus, a detail we gather from his letters. An Erastus is also named as Paul's assistant; he and Timothy clearly have pastoral responsibility in the churches they are to visit in Macedonia (Acts 19:22), and probably had some significant responsibilities in Ephesus too. We have noted above that it is unlikely that the Erastus of Acts 19:22 is the same person as is mentioned in Rom 16:23. The name is found again in 2 Tim 4:20.

Part 2

The Pastoral Epistles, Revelation and the Johannine Letters

Chapter 5

What do the Pastoral Epistles tell us about the early Christians in Ephesus?

1. Authorship

The majority of scholars argue that the Pastorals are not the work of Paul, although a significant number of scholars continue to advocate Pauline authorship.[1] The Pauline authorship of the Pastorals has been questioned for a number of reasons.

1.1 Historical Situation

The historical situation presupposed in the letters cannot be fitted into Paul's career as it is known from Acts and his undisputed letters.[2] If the Pastorals are by Paul, then he must have been released from imprisonment in Rome (Acts 28:16, 30-31), worked further as a missionary (2 Tim 4:13, 20; Tit 1:5, during which time he wrote 1 Tim and Titus probably from Macedonia, 1 Tim 1:3), before being rearrested and taken to Rome (2 Tim 1:8, 16-17), where he wrote 2 Tim. The Pastorals are our only source for all of this activity subsequent to Acts, although this is not a great difficulty in itself since Acts is clearly not an exhaustive account of Paul's life.[3] But we also note that there is

---

[1] See the list given in Marshall 1999, p58 n67. Recently note Johnson 1996, p2-32; 2001, p55-90; Mounce 2000, pxlvi-cxxix; in favour of Pauline authorship. For representative discussions in favour of pseudonymity see Bassler 1996a, p17-21; Davies 1996a, p105-118; Harding 2001, p10-27. For a review see also Marshall 1997, p7-17.

[2] These are Rom, 1 Cor, 2 Cor, Gal, Phil, 1 Thess, Phlm.

[3] 1 Clem 5.7, written around 96 CE says of Paul that "reaching the limit of the West, he bore witness before rulers"; however this is inconclusive. Other evidence (eg Eusebius HE 2.22) seems to be based on the NT itself. That Paul was released from the imprisonment in Rome mentioned in Acts 28 is conjectural therefore, although Luke's silence on the matter does not rule it out. Most scholars who believe Paul wrote the Pastorals locate them after the end of Acts; see the discussions in Prior 1989, p61-90; Towner 1994, p16-20; Mounce 2000, pliv-lxiv, lxxxiv-lxxxvi. Attempts have been made to fit the Pastorals into Paul's earlier career in Acts, but these do not explain the marked difference in style between the Pastorals and the undisputed Paulines which would then belong to the same period; see Marshall 1999, p71-2; see also Towner 1994, p17-19.

some tension between the picture of Timothy and Titus given in the Pastorals and that given by Paul's letters and Acts.[4]

1.2 Vocabulary and style[5]

The Pastorals contain words not found elsewhere in the NT at a rate two and a half times higher than that of the undisputed Pauline letters.[6] These words and phrases are often found regularly in the Pastorals, where they are theologically significant.[7] Further, words which do occur in the undisputed Paulines often have a somewhat different meaning in the Pastorals,[8] and there are differences in the usage of prepositions and connecting particles from the UP.[9] Although there continue to be debates about this matter, Marshall notes that "the shape of the vocabulary of the Pastorals is different from that of the genuine Pauline letters."[10] Similarly with regard to syntax, Marshall notes "it is difficult to avoid the conclusion that there are differences in syntactical

---

[4] See Barrett 1963, p9-10. For Timothy note Acts 16:1-3; 17:14f; 18:5; 19:22; 20:4; Rom 16:21; 2 Cor 1:19; Phil 2:19-20; 1 Cor 4:17; 16:10; 1 Thess 3:2, 6. The image we get is that Timothy was a trusted and efficient colleague. 2 Tim represents itself as written considerably later than any of the UP, but there Timothy is treated as young and inexperienced (2 Tim 1:11; 2:3, 7, 14, 22). On Titus compare 2 Cor 2:13; 7:6, 13f; 8:6, 16. 23; 12:18 and Gal 2:1, 3 with the fact that in Titus he is given elementary instruction. However, Mounce (2000, pxcvi) explains such material by suggesting that the Pastorals, while "private in form, are public in intention, speaking through Paul's delegates to the churches."

[5] The fundamental work here was done by Harrison 1921, but his work has been developed and critiqued by many others.

[6] See Harrison 1921, p18-44. There are 176 hapax legomena in the Pastorals. Note also that the Pastorals have a vocabulary of 848 ordinary words, over a third of which do not appear in the seven undisputed Pauline letters (see Hultgren 1984, p14); this is a much higher proportion than for any other Pauline letter.

[7] For example, the following are lacking from the undisputed Paulines: "the saying is sure"; a good or clear conscience; εὐσέβεια; σωφρονισμός σωφρόνως, σωφροσύνη.

[8] For example, "in Christ", "δικαιοσύνη" used of uprightness of living in the Pastorals (1 Tim 6:11; 2 Tim 2:22; cf Tit 3:5-7), see Taylor 1993, p64.

[9] For example, ἄρα, ἄρτι, διότι, εἴτε, ἐπεί, ἰδού, καθάπερ, νυνί; δέ, οὐχί, ὥστε and the preposition σύν are found in the undisputed Paulines (often frequently) and are not found in the Pastorals; see Barrett 1963, p6. Out of 214 particles in the ten Pauline letters, 112 are not found in the Pastorals. It was argued by Harrison that the Pastorals are closer to second century literature, both Christian and pagan, but this argument has been vigorously critiqued.

[10] Marshall 1999, p61; see also Fee1988a, p24. The evidence continues to be disputed; see for example Mounce 2000, pxcix-cxviii. However, his argument that much of the new vocabulary is explained by a different context and subject matter does not give sufficient weight to the point that in the undisputed letters Paul also writes lists of vices (eg 1 Cor 6:9-10), and writes of opponents and gives positive teaching, but does so using different vocabulary from the Pastorals.

structure and phraseology between the Pastorals and those letters whose Pauline authorship is not in serious doubt."[11]

1.3 Dealing with opponents

The method of dealing with the opponents is different from that adopted by Paul in his undisputed letters. There, Paul argues his case, often utilizing the opponents' language. In the Pastorals the author generally only denounces the opponents and their teaching,[12] rather than arguing with them in detail (the only exceptions are 1 Tim 1:8-11; 4:1-5; 6:6-8).[13]

1.4 Church structure

Although there was some form of leadership in the Pauline churches (based probably on the first converts, and the leadership of older people; see eg 1 Cor 16:15-18; Phil 1:1; 1 Thess 5:12-13), many scholars argue that the organizational development of the church in the Pastorals seems to have reached a stage beyond that of the undisputed Paulines. For example, one significant difference from the undisputed Paulines is that in the Pastorals the gift of the Spirit for ministry is connected with the laying on of hands and with some kind of official position in the church (1 Tim 1:18; 4:14; 2 Tim 1:6-7).

1.5 Theology

Three significant areas in which the theology of the Pastorals is different from that of the undisputed letters can be noted here. Firstly, with regard to Christology, Jesus is never called "Son of God", and the Pastor develops the concept of epiphany, which is used only once in the other Pauline letters,[14] to say that Jesus has appeared as the epiphany of the unseen God and will reappear in the future.[15] Further, both Jesus and God are regularly called Saviour,[16] a term which is used by Paul only of Jesus in Phil 3:20.[17] Secondly,

---

[11] Marshall 1999, p62.

[12] Paul does denounce opponents (eg Gal 1:8-9; Phil 3:2, 18-19; 1 Cor 16:22) but also argues at length with them; it is the latter which is missing in the Pastorals.

[13] See Johnson 1978-79, p1 n3. Brox (1989, p39) notes: "Man kann den Tatbestand so umschreiben, daß die Pastoralbriefe nicht eigentlich die Irrlehre, sondern die Irrlehrer bekämpfen."

[14] See 2 Thess 2:8.

[15] For epiphany language see 1 Tim 6:14; 2 Tim 1:10; 4:1, 8; Tit 2:11, 12-13; 3:4. See further Chapter 8.

[16] For Jesus as Saviour see 2 Tim 1:10; Tit 1:4; 2:12-13; 3:6; for God as Saviour see 1 Tim 1:1; 2:3; 4:10; Tit 1:3; 2:10; 3:4.

the term εὐσέβεια - piety or godliness, which expresses a proper attitude of respect to God and to others - is not found in the undisputed Paulines, but occurs regularly in the Pastorals where it is used to describe belief in God and the way the Christian life is to be lived.[18] Thirdly, in the Pastorals there is an emphasis on sound or healthy teaching (1 Tim 1:10; 4:6; 2 Tim 4:3; Tit 1:9; 2:1), which forms a "deposit" that must be held on to. The tradition needs to be protected and passed on (2 Tim 2:2) and emphasis is also put on the importance of knowledge of the truth, where "truth" refers to correct belief in Christ (1 Tim 2:4; 4:3; 2 Tim 2:25; 3:7; Tit 1:1).[19] While Paul certainly looked for correct teaching (eg. Rom 6:17), there does seem to be a considerable change in tone in these letters with regard to "sound teaching".[20]

1.6 Explanations of the data

A range of positions have been adopted to explain this data.[21] Firstly, it is argued that Paul wrote the letters, but the difference between the Pastorals and other Pauline letters is due to factors such as changed subject matter, that the Pastorals are written to individuals whom Paul knows well and not to churches, that he was writing to a more thoroughly Hellenised audience, that Paul incorporated in the Pastorals a considerable amount of traditional material which differed in vocabulary and style from his own material, or that he was utilizing special language because of the nature of the opponents in view in the letters.[22] However, many would argue that the differences

---

[17] It is also found in Eph 5:23.

[18] It is found in 1 Tim 2:2; 3:16; 4:7, 8; 6:3, 5, 6, 11; 2 Tim 3:5; Tit 1:1; see also Marshall 1999, p135-44.

[19] See Malherbe 1980, p19-35.

[20] In general Taylor (1993, p70) notes "The theological differences between the Pastorals and the undisputed letters are substantial, so substantial that for a host of commentators the distinctions in theology are determinative." The general lack of knowledge of the Pastorals by the Apostolic Fathers (apart from Polycarp) is not decisive with regard to authenticity. As Marshall (1999, p5) notes "There is nothing unusual about the low degree of proven usage of the Pastorals in the context of the general difficulty of establishing knowledge and use of the accepted Pauline letters." Further, no conclusions about the origin of the letters or their authenticity can be drawn from the fact that the Pastorals are lacking from P[46], and that they were probably not in Marcion's canon; see Marshall 1999, p6-8.

[21] See the slightly greater range of possibilities in Marshall 1999, p63-6.

[22] See for example Towner 1994, p30-5. Prior 1989, p37-59 has argued that 2 Tim is distinctive in style because, unlike most of the other Paulines which were co-authored (Timothy is mentioned in six letters) and written to groups, the Pastorals were written solely by Paul and to individuals. But as Marshall (1999, p65) notes "This theory collapses in view of the essential homogeneity of the authentic letters which can hardly have all been written by one helper but rather reflect the single mind of Paul himself."

between the Pastorals and the undisputed Paulines are of such a magnitude that they cannot be explained in this way.[23]

Secondly, some argue that the differences between the Pastorals and other Pauline letters is due to Paul's use of a secretary, to whom Paul gave the general outline of the letters, but the final product is due to the secretary.[24] However, this procedure is different, for no clear reason, from Paul's normal practice of dictation, which produced his relatively homogeneous undisputed letters, and no secretary is mentioned in the Pastorals. One variant of this option is that Luke wrote or compiled the Pastorals.[25] Supporters of this view note the similarities between the Pastorals and Luke-Acts with regard to vocabulary, and in areas such as the overall view of Paul, eschatology, social ethics, interest in good order and the law. However, these common features are too general to support this hypothesis and the substantial differences between Lk-Acts and the Pastorals with regard to style and some elements of theology argue against this view. [26]

Thirdly, it has been suggested that a pseudonymous author has incorporated "Pauline fragments" in the Pastorals, which explains the presence of personal notes in the letters.[27] However, this theory is unlikely, since these so-called "fragments" are couched in the same vocabulary and style as the rest of the letters.[28] If the author has used any such fragments, he

---

[23] As Marshall (1999, p79) notes, "the way in which the thought is expressed, both linguistically and theologically, poses great problems" for the view that Paul wrote the Pastorals. Murphy-O'Connor (1991b, p403-18) suggests that 2 Tim is more Pauline than 1 Tim and Tit, but none of the points he raises (regarding manner of address, christology, ministry, the gospel and absence of discussion of the opponents) are strong enough to suggest a difference in authorship. Accordingly, I consider the three letters as a group.

[24] This theory has been adopted by (for example) Kelly 1963, p21-7, 30-3; Mounce 2000, pcxxix.

[25] This view is favoured by Moule, Quinn and Wilson.

[26] See Taylor 1993, p71; Marshall 1999, p87-8. Differences with regard to theology are seen with regard to Christology, the Spirit, Paul as the apostle in Pastorals compared with the infrequency with which he has this title in Acts, Luke's lack of concern for the organisation of congregations and the lack of the sort of short words in Luke which would argue for common authorship.

[27] The list of fragments varies, but generally include 2 Tim 4:9-21; Titus 3:12-15. Also frequently considered are 2 Tim 1:15-18; 1 Tim 1:20; 5:23. Harrison (1921; 1955-56b, p250-61) is the best known supporter of this view; see also Barrett 1963, p4-12.

[28] See Cook 1984, p120-31. There is no exact parallel to this procedure in antiquity, and would these fragments have survived only as fragments? We can also ask what happened to the rest of the letter(s) of which they were fragments? It is also difficult to envisage a process whereby letters were dismembered and then recombined. Further, those who support this theory disagree about exactly which passages are fragments, which casts doubt on the whole exercise.

has rewritten them, in which case they are impossible to delineate, which makes this view implausible.[29]

Fourthly, the majority position today is that the letters are pseudonymous.[30] In my view, while questions can be raised about some of the factors which have led scholars to argue against Pauline authorship, the cumulative case that Paul did not write the Pastorals is strong.

So we conclude that the Pastorals were written by an author we will call the Pastor. He clearly saw himself as standing in the Pauline tradition and is seeking to apply that tradition (although with additions and developments from the genuine Paul) into a new and challenging situation with the aim of consolidating the Pauline identity of the recipients.[31]

2. Date

On the view that the letters are pseudonymous, determining the date of composition becomes a matter of weighing a range of factors.

Firstly, it is clear that the church structure presupposed in the Pastorals has developed beyond that in the undisputed Paulines. Thus, for example, leaders are required to have certain character attributes (eg 1 Tim 3:1-13), someone can aspire to church office (1 Tim 3:1), and testing is involved before someone is appointed to an office (1 Tim 3:10; 5:22). These are all signs of greater institutionalisation.[32] But how far has church structure developed?

We will note in Chapter 14 that between 105-110, Ignatius *advocates* the adoption of a three-fold structure of a single bishop, presbyters and deacons in Ephesus and elsewhere in Asia; the evidence shows that this three-fold structure is not fully accepted. Currently, for example, Onesimus is "bishop" in Ephesus but he is far from the undisputed leader of Christians in the city. Ignatius thus claims there should be one acknowledged bishop in each place but currently the reality is different. This means that the church structure Ignatius encountered in his travels in Asia Minor was only a little more developed than the structure presupposed in the Pastorals (where we will argue in Chapter 10 the same person can be called an "overseer" or a "presbyter", although the terms are not exactly synonymous). We should

---

[29] Most recently Miller 1997 has argued for this position and suggested that the Pastorals are composite documents built up over a period of time and lacking coherence; for a critique of his work see Marshall 1999, p16-18; Harding 2001, p18-19.

[30] See for example, Barrett 1963; Dibelius-Conzelmann 1972; Houlden 1976; Karris 1979; Hanson 1982; Hultgren 1984; Bauckham 1988, p469-94; Brox 1989; Quinn 1990; Taylor 1993, p60-72; Young 1994a; Bassler 1996a; Davies 1996b; Marshall 1999; but see below, where we will discuss Marshall's variant of this view.

[31] Harding 2001, p3; see also Schnelle 1998, p335; Marshall 1999, p80.

[32] See Käsemann 1964, p86-9; Dunn 1975, p347-50.

therefore see some distinction, but not a vast difference, between the church structures in the Pastorals and in Ignatius.

The situation in the Pastorals seems to be comparable to that envisaged in 1 Clement, written to Corinth from Rome around 96 CE, where again the offices of "overseer" and "presbyter" seem to be equivalent and where there is a plurality of overseers.[33] We need to recall here that church structure probably did not developed at the same rate and in the same way in every location, and so we cannot construct a chronological trajectory of developments. However, the similarities between the Pastorals and 1 Clement and the comparison between the Pastorals and Ignatius suggest a date of around 80-100 CE for the Pastorals.[34]

Secondly, Collins notes that the Pastorals "reflect an ecclesial situation in which the communities for which they were written were trying to find a niche in the Greco-Roman world".[35] Thus in the letters attention has turned in a new way (in comparison to the undisputed Paulines) to relations with the non-Christian environment, to how the Christian community is perceived and how it might live in ways in which the wider world considered acceptable. The Pastor is also concerned, again in a new way, to proclaim his faith and his ethical teaching in language that is comprehensible to the outside world.[36] These factors point to a considerable engagement with the wider world, which will be discussed in Chapter 8. These points are not decisive in themselves, but when viewed alongside the changes in church structure, confirm the conclusion reached from that evidence of the passage of a significant period of time after the composition of the undisputed Paulines.

---

[33] See 1 Clem 42.4; 44.1 with 44.4-5; 47.6; 54:2; Marshall 1999, p177; Hultgren 1984, p43. For the date of 1 Clement see Brown 1997, p666.

[34] We also note that Polycarp's letter to the Philippians (ca 120-130 CE) has probably been influenced by the Pastorals (see Poly, Phil 4.1; 9.1; cf 1 Tim 6:10, 7; 2 Tim 4:10), which means the Pastorals were written before 120 CE; see Brown 1997, p665; Schnelle 1998, 353. Harrison argued that the vocabulary of the Pastorals was closer to second century writers than to Paul. For example, of the 175 *hapax legomena* in the Pastorals, 93 are found in the Apostolic Fathers and Apologists. Of the 131 other words which are not found in Paul, 118 are found in the second century authors. However, the *hapax legomena* are virtually all used in the first century, many in the LXX, and as Marshall (1999, p60 n72) notes "there is as much correspondence between the Pastorals and the LXX as there is between the Pastorals and the second-century writers." See also Carson, Moo, Morris, 1992, p360-1. Thus, vocabulary does not argue for a later date.

[35] Collins 2002, p9; see also Schnelle 1998, p330.

[36] See Chapter 8 for evidence, such as the use of the epiphany schema and titles like "Saviour".

Thirdly, Quinn notes that if the Pastorals were written in the second century, it is striking that they do not actually quote Paul's own words.[37] This argues against a second century dating, given that 1 Clement, written in 96 CE, knows of 1 and 2 Cor and Romans and so gives independent evidence for a collection of (some of) Paul's letters at this time.[38] Certainly, the later one dates the Pastorals, the more surprising it is that they do not quote from (rather than simply allude to) Paul's letters and so this evidence argues against a date later than around 100 CE.

Fourthly, the opponents are not to be identified with second century Gnostics (as we will show below)[39] and so their presence does not require a second century dating. There are also similarities between the opponents and the teaching Paul opposed in Corinth,[40] but there are sufficient differences between the two groups of opponents (eg. with regard to the opponents in the Pastorals' attitude to the law (1 Tim 1:6-11)) to make it difficult to argue that the Pastorals *must* be close to the Corinthian correspondence in date and clearly such views could develop at any point during or after Paul's death. Schnelle thinks the opponents represent an "early form of a Christian gnosticism",[41] and they point to the period around 100 CE, although I doubt that we can be as precise as this. Generally we can suggest that the opponents are compatible with a dating between 80-100.[42]

Finally, given that the letters are pseudonymous, it seems clear that the Pastor has been able to draw on a living and vital source of traditions about

---

[37] See Quinn 1990, p18. He notes "At most one reads in several places two or three words running that appear to be slogans from a Pauline tradition; none of these slogans is a proper citation of one of his letters."

[38] See Schnelle 1998, p352-3. Of course, the Pastorals themselves probably give evidence for a collection of Paul's letters; see Bassler 1996a, p23; Schnelle 1998, p332, 340.

[39] Those who see the opponents as Gnostics, often date the letters well into the second century; for example, Koester (2000, p306) thinks of Gnostic opponents and dates the letters between 120-160 CE. Bauer (1971, p222-8) argued that the letters were written against Marcion's document entitled "Antitheses", but this is very unlikely. On Gnosticism see Klauck 2000, p429-503, with extensive bibliography.

[40] Although there are "new" features too, such as the speculative use of the Old Testament.

[41] Schnelle 1998, p333.

[42] A number of other points are raised in discussions of dating, but in my view are inconclusive. For example Hultgren (1984, p29) thinks Acts is known to the author because of 2 Tim 3:11 and that information about Timothy, Apollos, Prisca and Aquila and others in Acts also informs the Pastor. However, while this is possible, the Pastor's knowledge on these matters may be due to tradition rather than actual knowledge of the text of Acts. Secondly, we may also ask how the letters might have "surfaced" and become authoritative and whether this gives any indication of date? Perhaps the most likely suggestion is that, as private letters, they would emerge after the death of Timothy and Titus. This too would suggest a date in the 80-100 period, perhaps nearer 80 than 100, although clearly here we are speculating. See further discussion in Schnelle 1998, p336.

Paul's life, travels and teaching.[43] This sense of the vitality of the Pauline tradition suggest a date well before Ignatius.

We conclude then that the evidence argues for a date between 80 and 100 CE.[44] Given this dating, it seems very likely that Timothy and Titus were both dead when the books were written and thus that the letters were doubly pseudonymous. Timothy and Titus were probably chosen as the first addressees because they were remembered as key Pauline coworkers who "represented Paul's apostolic presence"[45] and who had implemented Paul's instructions in crucial situations facing his churches.[46] They seem well suited recipients for letters which seek to apply the Pauline tradition to a new day.

3. Place of Origin

We do not know where the letters were actually written. We will argue that the letters reflect the situation in Ephesus and Crete, and they could clearly have been written in or near Ephesus itself.[47] 2 Tim purports to come from Rome (2 Tim 1:17), and it was certainly possible for someone in Rome to know about the situation in Ephesus; but it too could have been written from Ephesus. Thus, the location of the author of all three letters could be Rome, or Ephesus, or somewhere else; in fact, we have no definitive data with which to make a decision.

As we have noted in Chapter 2, the Pastorals are often thought to have been written in Ephesus and so taken as evidence of a Pauline school in the city. It is suggested that one activity of this school would be to preserve Pauline tradition; since the Pastor knows 1-2 Cor, Rom, Phil, Col and

---

[43] See Roloff 1988, p45; Schnelle 1998, p333. The author of the Pastorals probably drew on Pauline letters (see Schnelle 1998, p351) but it also seems clear he drew on oral traditions.

[44] Brown 1997, p668 notes that the majority of those who think the Pastorals are pseudonymous "would accept the period between 80 and 100 as the most plausible context for their composition." Other dates are Collins 2002, p9: "composed toward the end of the first century sometime after 80 C.E." Quinn 1990, p19: 80-85 CE; Young 1994a, p23 "composed in the late first century"; Dornier 1974, p94: 80-90. The following opt for around 100 CE: Hultgren 1984, p29-30; Roloff 1988, p45-6; Brox 1989, p58; Merkel 1991, p10; Schnelle 1998, p333-4; Harding 2001, p44. Davies 1996a, p110 dates the Pastorals towards end of the first or at the beginning of the second century; Hanson 1982, p13: 100-105 CE; Kümmel 1975, p272 just after the turn of the second century; Bauer 1971, p84-5 dates them after the time of Marcion.

[45] Collins 2002, p10.

[46] See 1 Cor 4:16-17; 16:10-11; 1 Thess 3:2-3; Phil 2:19, 23 (Timothy) 2 Cor 2:13; 7:14f; 8:23 (Titus); Schnelle 1998, p334-5.

[47] See Barrett 1963, p19; Schnelle 1998, p333, 352. Brox 1989, p58 suggests Asia Minor more generally.

probably Phlm,[48] another activity of the school would be the collection of Paul's letters. However, the question here is whether the Pastorals are not only written to Ephesus, but *also* written from Ephesus and as we have noted, the place of composition is uncertain. Thus, that there was a Pauline school in Ephesus responsible for the Pastorals must remain a hypothesis. However, the Pastorals are evidence that the addressees of the letters in Ephesus saw themselves as in the Pauline tradition, which suggests a Pauline community continued to exist in the city.

4. Was Ephesus the intended destination of 1 and 2 Tim?

Where are the intended readers of these three letters? In 1 Timothy 1:3-4 Paul urges Timothy to remain in Ephesus because of the danger of opponents there. It is clearly envisaged that Timothy has responsibility for the community in Ephesus, where he is to attend to matters relating to the organisation of the community (1 Tim 3:1-13; 5:17-22). Both 2 Tim 1:18 and 4:12 again mention Ephesus, and Onesiphorus, who seems to be an Ephesian Christian (2 Tim 1:16-18) is greeted in 2 Tim 4:19. Thus although it is not said explicitly that all the addressees are in Ephesus, given these points and the strong connection with 1 Timothy, it is most likely that we are to think of 2 Timothy as also addressed to Ephesus. Thus, in both letters, the addressees in the second person plural (eg 1 Tim 6:21; 2 Tim 4:22: "Grace be with you (μεθ᾽ ὑμῶν)") and the more general exhortations (eg 1 Tim 4:6: "If you put these instructions before the brothers and sisters"; 2 Tim 2:14: "Remind them of this ...") are addressed to Christians in Ephesus and the opponents are thought of as present there.

In Titus we read that Titus has been left behind in Crete to organize churches there after a speedy missionary tour (1:5). It is clear that the Christian community in Crete was less structured than in Ephesus. Thus, it is most reasonable to associate 1 and 2 Tim with Ephesus and Titus with Crete.

A number of other factors support the location of the readers of 1 and 2 Tim in Ephesus and Tit in Crete. Firstly, Thiessen has shown that a number of the people mentioned in the Pastorals have a documented connection with Ephesus: we note Timothy, Titus, Prisca, Aquila,[49] Tychicus (2 Tim 4:12; Acts 20:4; 21:29), Erastus (2 Tim 4:20 and Acts 19:22) and Trophimus (2 Tim 4:20; Acts 20:4; 21:29).[50] This shows the author had an interest in people who were connected with Ephesus, which reinforces the likelihood that the readers were actually in Ephesus.

---

[48] Roloff 1988, p39-40; see also Schnelle 1998, p351.

[49] See Chapter 2 for these four people.

[50] Thiessen 1995, p251-3; cf. Hultgren 1984, p21-5.

Secondly, we will argue in the next section that the opponents are very similar in Ephesus and Crete and that their closest parallel is with the views that Paul faced at Corinth. Even if no particular person (a teacher?) traveled from Corinth to Ephesus and Crete,[51] it is quite understandable that a similar sort of teaching would occur in Ephesus as had appeared in Corinth,[52] and that it would soon be found in Crete also.[53]

Thirdly, that 1 Tim and Tit are to two different communities is borne out by the similarities in their contents. As Marshall notes: "The similarities between these two letters render one of them unnecessary if they are both written to the same location, and therefore separate destinations are plausible."[54]

However, a number of scholars who regard the Pastorals as pseudonymous, do not regard 1 and 2 Timothy as specifically written to Ephesian Christians, but rather as more general letters written to instruct Christians over a broad geographical area. On this view Ephesus and Crete are representative of more established churches and newer churches respectively, and so the teaching is more paradigmatic and general. In particular, this view sees the teaching combatted by the Pastor as *deliberately* representative of teaching which was facing the church in the Pastor's time, rather than as revealing an actual historical problem facing particular congregations in Ephesus or Crete. On this view the opponents' teaching was a construct, with the letters providing a definitive paradigm for combating such teaching wherever it occurred in the post-apostolic church.[55] The letters would not provide us with information about Ephesian Christians therefore.

The arguments used to support this view that the Pastorals are general letters are very weak. Firstly, it is noted that the Pastor sees the false teaching as both a present (1 Tim 1:3, 20; 2 Tim 2.20; Tit 1.10f) and a future phenomenon (1 Tim 4.1; 2 Tim 3.1). It is argued that this makes sense only if we do not limit the purpose of the letters to any one generation, locale or heretical movement and so that the teaching must be paradigmatic. But there is no difficulty with seeing the opponents' teaching as a present phenomenon, since that is regularly the case in Paul (see for example Gal 3:1f). What about

---

[51] We have no clear evidence for this and will note that the opponents in Ephesus have grown up within the community. But clearly there could have been some external influence.

[52] Note that the Pauline Christian community was founded in Corinth immediately before the community in Ephesus. There are differences between the opponents in Corinth and Ephesus however; for example, the speculative use of the OT is not found in Corinth. This suggests that the opponents grew up in Ephesus independent of Corinthian influence.

[53] See Marshall 1999, p85.

[54] Marshall 1999, p86; see also Hultgren 1984, p28-9; Meier 1973, p323-4 n2. Given these strong links with Ephesus, Quinn's suggestion (Quinn and Wacker 2000, p21-2) of a link with Rome is unlikely.

[55] See for example, Dibelius-Conzelmann 1972, p66; Trummer 1978, p163-4.

the future predictions as well? There is a strong tradition in the early church that the End would be accompanied by a time of intense difficulties (cf. 2 Thess 2:3-12) which included the "falling away" of some believers (see M t 24:10-12; Jude 17-18; 2 Peter 3:3-7).[56] The presence of this theme of a future falling away in the Pastorals may simply reflect this tradition. Further, it seems that the Pastor actually saw these future predictions as being fulfilled in his present,[57] and thus that the specific situation he addressed was a part of this predicted falling away. In themselves then, these passage do not require the conclusion that the situation is paradigmatic rather than real and we do not need to see the teaching as a general phenomenon.

Secondly, it is noted that the polemic is stereotyped, which is said to coincide with the general purpose of the letters.[58] However, the adoption of the standard polemical schema (see below) does not mean that the opponents are not real, and the Pastor's polemic also contains some very specific dimensions which cannot be paralleled in general polemic and seem to point to a specific situation. An albeit incomplete portrait of what can be seen as a real teaching can be drawn up from the letters.

Thirdly, the lack of an historical movement which fits what is said about the opponents is taken as evidence of the author's paradigmatic intentions. While the author does draw on what was familiar, the end result is not a description of historical opponents. However, this point presupposes that we know more than we actually know about historical movements in this period, and in any case there are close parallels between the opponents portrayed here and the situation Paul faced in Corinth,[59] which again suggests the Pastor writes of a real situation. Further, as Towner notes: "When it is noticed that the author does in fact counter forcefully the over-realized eschatology of the false teaching with his own forward-looking eschatology,... the case for an historical heresy and encounter is strengthened."[60]

Thus the evidence used to support this view of the letters is weak. Further, as we have already noted, the opponents' teaching clearly contains some very particular features, which argues against the view that the author was opposing a paradigmatic construct and we have also noted that a number of the people named have a connection with Ephesus, which suggests that the

---

[56] Fee 1988, p98.

[57] Note that in 2 Tim 3:1f the future tenses of v1-2 give way in v6 to a description of what has happened in the community as the tense indicates, thus showing that the author considers the predictions of v1-5 as having been fulfilled in the present, and that the people described in v1-5 are currently plaguing the community. Similarly, it is generally thought that the asceticism described in 1 Tim 4:3 was currently occurring in the community, and thus that the "later times" of v1 had arrived.

[58] See Trummer 1978, p160, Dibelius-Conzelmann 1972, p2-5, 66.

[59] See Towner 1989, p33-44.

[60] Towner, 1989, p44-5

author had access to traditions about Paul in Ephesus, and about the church in Ephesus in general.[61]

We conclude then that the view that sees 1 and 2 Timothy as general letters is very unlikely. Rather, 1 and 2 Timothy were sent by the Pastor to Christians in Ephesus with particular application to their situation, and can provide us with information about Christians in the city. On the other hand, Titus is best seen as sent to different recipients who seem to be in a broadly similar situation, although there are differences particularly with regard to the less developed ecclesiastical situation in Titus.[62]

We should also note that although the letters are written to individuals, they are clearly meant to be "overheard" by communities (1 Tim 6:21; 2 Tim 4:22; Tit 3:15) who are intended to apply what is said to themselves.

5. The "opponents"

In a number of passages the Pastor turns his attention to teachers who are in his view false, and who have created a crisis situation among the addressees (1 Tim 1:3-11, 18-20; 4:1-7; 6:3-5, 20-21; 2 Tim 2:14-18; 22-26; 3:1-9; 4:3-5; Tit 1:10-16; 3:8-11). One of the key reasons that the Pastor wrote the letters was to give instructions to his readers about how they should deal with these opponents.[63] Other factors discussed in the letters, such as the organisational structure of the church, are at least partly called forth by the need to combat the opponents and to increase the stability of the community.

What can we say about these opponents? Our first difficulty is that we do not have a sympathetic explanation of the opponents' position. Rather, we have to try and reconstruct their teaching and its motivation and the practices which the opponents advocated on the basis of the Pastor's highly polemical remarks about these teachers. This is the task of mirror-reading which regularly faces us in this study.

5.1 General polemic

Much of what the Pastor writes about the opponents is general; in fact it seems very likely that much of the language used in a number of passages against the opponents[64] is typical of the polemic that philosophers used

---

[61] See also Hanson 1982, p22.

[62] See further Marshall 1999, p1-2. On the similarities and differences between the opponents' teaching in Ephesus and Crete see section 5.6 below.

[63] See Towner 1994, p22.

[64] The Pastor writes about his opponents in 1 Tim 1:3-7, 18-20; 4:1-7; 6:3-10, 20-21; 2 Tim 2:14-4.5; Tit 1:10-16; 3:9-11.

against the Sophists. Karris has proposed that this polemic consisted of accusations of greed, of being deceivers, of not practicing what they preach, of the opponents' success among women, criticism of being involved in verbal disputes and quibbles, and the use of catalogues of vices.[65] The Pastor has adopted at least part of such a schema as a way of denouncing his opponents. The probable adoption of such a schema suggests that we generally cannot use these adopted features of the Pastor's polemic to gain information about the opponents.[66] Reconstructions of the opponents' teaching that do not recognise the use of this schema are thus unconvincing.[67]

Another difficulty we face in trying to understand the opponents' teaching, and one that we have noted under our discussion of authorship, is that the Pastor generally (but not always) refrains from direct confrontation with the teaching of the opponents.[68] He seems to have been more concerned to present what he saw as the deficiencies of the opponents and to combat the moral effects of their teaching than to analyze its contents.[69] This and the use of stock features of polemic make it difficult to try to piece together a coherent teaching that the Pastor opposes.

However, on some occasions the polemic does seem to reflect more than the standard polemical schema. For example, sometimes features of the standard schema are reshaped, seemingly to fit the actual situation.[70] Further, some features that are not characteristic of the polemic between philosophers and Sophists are present in the letters. Thus a core of information about the opponents remains and it is to this that we must turn for a description of the opponents. What then can we say about them?

---

[65] Karris 1973, p549-63; Johnson 1978-79, p1-26; Dibelius-Conzelmann 1972, p20-1, 65-7.

[66] Towner 1989, p262 n22 agrees. Thus for example, the vice catalogue in 2 Tim 3:2-5 (see also 1 Tim 1:9-10; 6:4-5) has the opponents in view, but since this is such a standard part of the schema against opponents we cannot conclude that the opponents in view in the Pastorals sinned in the areas described; see Karris 1973, p560. Towner (1989, p28) notes: "By and large the purpose of this catalogue was to identify the opponents as belonging to the apostates of 'the last days'." See also McEleney 1974, p211-12.

[67] See for example Cranford 1980, p27-40.

[68] See also Towner 1989, p24-5; Barrett 1963, p12. The Pastor does engage with the opponents in 1 Tim 1:8-11; 4:1-5; 6:6-8. This is in contrast to Paul's sustained and detailed theological argumentation against his opponents, often utilizing the opponents' language and themes.

[69] See Barrett 1963, p131; Marshall 1993, p17.

[70] For example, the vice catalogue of 1 Tim 1.9-10 shows signs of modification so that it corresponds with the Decalogue; see McEleney 1974, p206-10. Karris (1973, p557) thinks the phrase "Myths and genealogies" was part of the schema; however, the separate use of genealogies (Tit 3:9) and the phrase "Jewish myths" (Tit 1:14) suggest that the Pastor has an allegorical type of exegesis of the OT in view; see Towner 1989, p263 n23.

5.2 The opponents are Christians

In the Pastor's view, the opponents are false or deviating Christians, rather than pagans or Jews. This seems to be implied by the reference to Hymenaeus and Alexander in 1 Tim 1:19-20, where it is said that they have "suffered shipwreck in the faith (περὶ τὴν πίστιν ἐναυάγησαν)". Other passages accuse the opponents of swerving (ἀστοχέω) from the faith (1 Tim 1:5-6) or from the truth (2 Tim 2:18),[71] and in 2 Tim 3:8 the opponents are said to be of "counterfeit faith" (ἀδόκιμοι περὶ τὴν πίστιν).[72] The comment in 1 Tim 1:20 that some of the opponents had been delivered "to Satan, so that they may learn not to blaspheme" suggests that in the Pastor's opinion the situation of at least some of the opponents was not irredeemable, even if it required extreme measures.[73]

However, we should note that the opponents probably still saw themselves as Christians. They probably did not think they had "made shipwreck of their faith" (1 Tim 1:19), but rather that their teaching was correct, and that the Pastor was mistaken.

5.3 The opponents are within the congregations, and are leaders

The letters suggest that the opponents have arisen from within the congregations rather than being outsiders (cf. 2 Cor 11:4; Gal 2:4). Firstly, Timothy is told to order or command (1 Tim 1:3; 4:11; παραγγέλλω) and charge (2 Tim 2:14; διαμαρτύρομαι) certain people not to teach any different doctrine, implying that the opponents are members of the community and receive instruction and direction within the community, at least in principle.[74] Secondly, as we noted in the previous section, the Pastor says that he has delivered Hymenaeus and Alexander, who are clearly key opponents, "to Satan, so that they may learn not to blaspheme" (1 Tim 1:20); this indicates that they came under the jurisdiction and discipline of the community.[75] Thirdly, in 2 Tim 2:19-21 we have the image of a "mixed" church which suggests that the opponents' emerged from within the community.[76] These

---

[71] See also 1 Tim 4:1; 6:10, 21; 2 Tim 4:4. The opponents are compared to Jannes and Jambres in 2 Tim 3:8. According to tradition, these were Pharaoh's magicians who opposed Moses (see Towner 1989, p264 n37). The reference emphasizes the opponents' opposition to God; Towner 1989, p264 n37; Kelly 1963, p196.

[72] Note also 2 Tim 4:3, which suggests the opponents and their hearers did not want to cease calling themselves Christians, since they do still want to have doctrine and teachers, but rather they wanted to follow their own version of the faith; see Barrett 1963, p117.

[73] See also 2 Tim 2:25-6 which speaks of the opponents repenting and coming to know the truth.

[74] See also 1 Tim 4:6; 2 Tim 4:2; cf Tit 1:13; 3:10.

[75] See Towner 1989, p25; Barrett 1963, p22. Cf 1 Cor 5:5.

[76] Towner 1989, p25-6; 1994, p23.

points strongly suggest that these opponents are members of the community, rather than Christians from elsewhere who had visited the group. Whether the opponents' teaching had grown up in complete independence of outside influence is of course another matter.

We note also that the discipline of delivering opponents to Satan (1 Tim 1:20)[77] has as its goal "that they may learn not to blaspheme". Thus the action seems to be remedial and the goal is repentance. That repentance and restoration to the community is the goal is also suggested by 2 Tim 2:25-6, where the Pastor expresses the hope that "God may perhaps grant that they will repent and come to know the truth, and that they may escape from the snare of the devil". Thus, the Pastor hopes that the opponents will yet return to "sound doctrine" and to the community.

It is also likely that some of the opponents in Ephesus were leaders in the community.[78] Firstly the opponents want to be known as teachers (1 Tim 1:7) and seem to have been teaching the community,[79] which, according to the Pastor, was a task that fell predominantly to the presbyter-overseers (1 Tim 3:2; 5:17). Secondly, this would in part explain the detailed statements about qualities expected of leaders (1 Tim 3:1-13; 5:17-25; Tit 1:5-9). Thirdly, when the Pastor speaks of those who are upsetting "whole households" (Tit 1:11) the reference may be to house churches, and so to leaders of these groups.[80]

5.4 The success of the opponents and the crisis they have created

A number of passages suggest that the opponents had been quite successful in gaining a following. In 1 Tim 4:1-3 we read: "Now the Spirit expressly says that in later time some (τινες) will renounce the faith by paying attention to deceitful spirits and teaching of demons, through the hypocrisy of liars whose consciences are seared with a hot iron. They forbid marriage and demand abstinence from foods ..." It is generally agreed that this speaks of the Pastor's present situation.[81] The opponents are the "liars" who have caused "some (τινες)" to "depart from the faith".[82]

---

[77] This probably involves excluding the opponents from the community for a period; see Marshall 1999, p415.

[78] See Fee 1988a, pxxi; Mounce 2000, plxxx.

[79] 2 Tim 3:7 also clearly indicates that the opponents were teachers.

[80] See Towner 1994, p23. Recall also that teaching was often undertaken in the context of the house (see Stowers 1984, p59-82), and so the reference may also be to teaching activity in the house; again this would suggest the opponents were leaders.

[81] See Towner 1989, p25.

[82] That the Pastor means this to be a reference to the present and to the community he is addressing is also suggested by the fact that in 1 Tim 3:14-15 the Pastor said he was writing so that "if I am delayed, you may know how one ought to behave in the household of God, which is the church of the living God". He then goes on in 4:1f to write of some departing

Other passages indicate the impact of the opponents, although only in general terms. In 1 Tim 1:6-7 we read: "Some people (ὧν τινες) have deviated from these and turned to meaningless talk" and in 1 Tim 6:21 that by professing what is falsely called knowledge, "some (τινες) have missed the mark as regards the faith". In 2 Tim 2:17-18 we are told that Hymenaeus and Philetus, who are clearly opponents, are "upsetting the faith of some (τινων)".[83] Marshall suggests "The opposition is regarded as sizeable, is winning support and is dangerous. ... the writer is dealing with a powerful movement which has already made serious inroads into the life of the congregations."[84]

It also seems very likely that the opponents were particularly successful among women.[85] This is clear in 2 Tim 3:6 where we read that the opponents "make their way into households and captivate silly women (γυναικάρια)".[86] In 1 Tim 5:11-15 we read that younger widows "learn to be idle, gadding about from house to house (περιερχόμεναι τὰς οἰκίας); and they are not merely idle, but also gossips and busybodies, saying what they should not say (οὐ μόνον δὲ ἀργαὶ ἀλλὰ καὶ φλύαροι καὶ περίεργοι, λαλοῦσαι τὰ μὴ δέοντα) (1 Tim 5:13)." The Pastor then adds in 1 Tim 5:15 that some younger widows "have already turned away to follow Satan (ἐξετράπησαν ὀπίσω τοῦ σατανᾶ)". Since the Pastor makes a link between the opponents' teaching and women in 2 Tim 3:6 and since in 1 Tim 4:1 the Pastor connects the opponents' teaching with "paying attention to deceitful spirits and teachings of demons",[87] this reference to straying after Satan suggests the women have done so by accepting the opponents' teaching. This in turn suggests that the "gadding about from house to house ... saying what they should not" refers in part at least to some women spreading the opponents' teaching. Further, 1 Tim 2:12-15 also strongly suggests that some women were promulgating the opponents' teaching,[88] and were among the leaders of

---

from the faith. The implication is that they are departing from the household of God he is addressing. See Fee 1988a, p96.

[83] In 2 Tim 3:13 the opponents are described as "deceiving others and being deceived", which is a feature derived from the polemical schema. In 2 Tim 4:3-4 we read that "the time is coming when people will not put up with sound doctrine". Neither passage gives further data about the extent of the influence of the opponents. In Tit 1:11 we are told that opponents are upsetting "whole families", which we have argued refers to the situation in Crete.

[84] Marshall 1999, p42. The Pastor names opponents in 1 Tim 1:20; 2 Tim 2:17; 4:14; it seems likely that these individuals were known by the readers; see Barrett 1963, p47-8, 121; Roloff 1988, p105.

[85] See Marshall 1993, p17.

[86] On women in the Pastorals see Chapter 11.

[87] See also 1 Tim 1:20; 2 Tim 2:26 for the connection between the opponents and Satan or demons.

[88] Fee 1991, p57-8.

those opposed by the Pastor. This subject will be dealt with in more detail in Chapter 11.

However, exhortations against the opponents are directed to the whole congregation (1 Tim 1:6ff; 4:1, 6; 6:21; 2 Tim 3:2), which suggests both men and women were involved in the teaching. Nor do we have evidence which suggests that the opponents were primarily concerned to attract women to their teaching.[89] But if the opponents had particular success in households,[90] and if some features of their teaching were particularly attractive to women (as we will argue in Chapter 11) then it would be understandable that women were well represented among their followers.

None of the passages discussed in this or the preceding section enable us to quantify the extent of the following of the opponents, but clearly they were having a considerable impact on the addressees.

That some of the opponents are leaders (probably of house churches) within the community, who are teaching other members of the community, and that many community members seem to have followed the opponents suggests that the opponents have created a crisis situation for the Pastor. This can also be seen from the number of passages in which the Pastor writes about the opponents and their impact,[91] and the way, for example, he tells Titus that the opponents "must be silenced since they are upsetting whole families" (Tit. 1:11).[92] That the Pastor sees himself as facing a very severe crisis in turn explains the urgent tone the Pastor adopts as he writes.

5.5 What can we say about the opponents' theology?

We have already noted that the features of the polemic which the Pastor seems to have adopted from the standard schema cannot be used to reconstruct the opponents' theology. However, there are some further clear references to the opponents' teaching.

---

[89] As was claimed, for example, by Dibelius-Conzelmann 1972, p116. Towner 1989, p26 suggests the view that the opponents were making special efforts to win women converts comes from the superimposition of tendencies found among later Gnostics upon the Pastorals.

[90] 2 Tim 3:6 suggests that the opponents targeted Christian households, and had some success in this sphere. Towner (1989, p26) comments: "The author's widespread interest in promoting the stability of this social institution may well represent his paraenetic response to this potential or actual disruption." See also Tit 1:11, although the reference here may be to "the capitulation of whole house churches" (Marshall 1999, p197).

[91] See for example 1 Tim 2:8-15; 5:13-15.

[92] See also 1 Tim 1:3; 6:2b-5, 20; 2 Tim 3:5; Tit 1:13; 3:10-11, which are all strongly worded; see also Malherbe 1984, p235-43.

5.5.1 Jewish dimensions of the opponents' teaching

In Ephesus the teaching of the opponents seems to have had a Jewish dimension. In 1 Tim 1:3-4 Timothy is instructed to order certain persons "not to occupy themselves with myths and endless genealogies that promote speculations (προσέχειν μύθοις καὶ γενεαλογίαις ἀπεράντοις, αἵτινες ἐκζητήσεις παρέχουσιν)." What are these myths and genealogies? Some commentators think the reference is to the myths used by Gnostics, in which case the genealogies would refer to the lists of emanations used to account for the creation of the world and the origins of humanity. However, there is little to support the claim that "myths and genealogies" refer to the advanced Gnostic systems of aeon and archon speculation.[93] Further, the details found in later Gnostic systems are simply not present in the Pastorals and we will note that it is very unlikely that the opponents are Gnostics.

In addition, the connections made by the Pastor point in another direction. In Tit 1:14 the Pastor criticises the opponents for "paying attention to Jewish myths (προσέχοντες Ἰουδαικοῖς μύθοις)".[94] Although the term "myth" need not mean the same every time the Pastor uses it,[95] it seems likely that Jewish myths are also meant in 1 Tim 1:3-4, since the Pastor goes on in 1 Tim 1:6-11 to speak of "some people" who desire to be "teachers of the law (νομοδιδάσκαλοι)", and then goes on to discuss the role of ὁ νόμος. Hence the Pastor connects the "myths" with Judaism and the law, which suggests there was a Jewish dimension to the opponents' teaching and that both "myths and genealogies" are to be understood against a Jewish background. In 1 Tim 4:7 and 2 Tim 4:4 the author again speaks of "myths", without further specifying their content, but the reference may again be to "Jewish myths".[96]

---

[93] Towner 1989, p28; Spicq 1969a, p322-3; Mounce 2000, plxx. For the connection with Gnostic views see for example, Schmithals 1983, p117. It is not clear what role these "myths and genealogies" played in the opponents' system in the Pastorals. Towner (1989, p28) suggests "One aspect of their function, at least, was to support the ascetic practices, namely prohibition of marriage and abstinence from certain foods." In a footnote he notes the connection of 1 Tim 4:3 with v7. But the connection seems quite weak.

[94] Some of the opponents are also said to be "of the circumcision party" in Tit 1:10 and in Titus 3:9 the readers are told to "avoid stupid controversies, genealogies, dissensions and quarrels over the law", again suggesting a Jewish dimension. Further, Tit 1:15 may have Jewish purity rules in view.

[95] See Barrett 1963, p132.

[96] Barrett (1963, p12) notes that some have argued that these references to Jewish myths are included by the author in an attempt to make the letters seem Pauline, since Paul was known to have argued with Jews and Judaizers. However, nothing in Paul's letters suggest he attacked "Jewish myths".

What are we to understand by the reference to Jewish "myths and genealogies", which in context are clearly connected to the law?[97] Towner suggests that the reference to myths and genealogies concerns "some sort of speculative exegesis of the OT. ... The Jewish features within these contexts strongly suggest that the best parallels lie in the Jewish (rabbinic?) form of speculative exegesis of especially the genealogies and the creation accounts".[98] The genealogies would probably be broader than simple lists of descendants. The term can be used to refer to the parts of a history which are concerned with people, and so "genealogies" can be personal histories or biographies.[99] The opponents probably used such historical material to support their teaching, although we cannot say which stories they used.[100] For the Pastor such things promoted only speculation and vain discussion (1 Tim 1:4, 6), which diverted people from what in his eyes really mattered and so he rejected them totally (1 Tim 4:7).

Given the Jewish parallels for this sort of language, it is possible that the opponents were Jewish Christians,[101] but clearly Gentile Christians could also use the OT in this way. But the reference to the opponents being "of the circumcision"[102] in Tit 1:10 suggests that they were either Jewish Christians and/or Gentile Christians who had been circumcised.[103] However, there is no indication in the letters that the opponents advocated circumcision and no indication that "works of the law" were regarded by the opponents as significant for salvation.[104]

We also note that in both 1 Tim and Tit the references to the Jewish character of the opponents are found when the teaching is first introduced (1 Tim 1:4, 7-11; Tit 1:10; it is also found in the closing recapitulation in Tit

---

[97] Note also that in Tit 3:9 the "genealogies" may be connected with the "quarrels about the law"; see also Barrett 1963, p40-1.

[98] Towner 1989, p28; see also Spicq 1969a, p322-3; Gunther 1973, p78; Quinn 1990, p100-1, 245-8. Some early Gnostic sects found these accounts were particularly useful; see Towner, 1989, p265 n45. Mounce 2000, plxx suggests they are "haggadic midrash: allegorical reinterpretations of the OT, perhaps as fanciful interpretations of the OT genealogies ... especially of the patriarchs and their families."

[99] See Quinn 1990, p245.

[100] The Gnostic sect known as the Ophites used genealogies like this. See further Quinn 1990, p101-1, 111, 245-8.

[101] See Towner 1994, p24-5.

[102] Comparable usage is found in Acts 10:45; 11:2; Col 4:11; cf. Rom 4:12.

[103] See also Marshall 1999, p44. They are clearly within the church and so must be Christians rather than Jews.

[104] Marshall 1999, p46 notes the general rejection of human works in 2 Tim 1:9 and Tit 3:5 and suggests that if Jewish "works of the law" were being made a condition of salvation by the opponents, we would expect the Pastor to make the application specifically.

3:9); as Marshall notes "it is presumably intended to colour our reading of what follows."[105]

We have noted the reference to the law in 1 Tim 1:7-11. This passage speaks of the opponents "desiring to be teachers of the law" (v7). This would suggest that they expounded the meaning of the law and its application and 1 Tim 1:8-9 suggests how they applied the law. The opponents did not, in the Pastor's opinion, use the law "lawfully" or "legitimately" (νομίμως) because they said the law applied to everybody,[106] whereas for the Pastor "the law is laid down not for the innocent but for the lawless and disobedient", whom he lists. This suggests that the opponents thought the Jewish law was still valid for Christians to some extent, certainly in ways the Pastor thought were now wrong. Probably the Pastor objects to the way they used the law as a source for their speculations (1 Tim 1:3-4) and in order to argue for their asceticism with regard to food which may reflect food laws (1 Tim 4:1-3);[107] the opponents seem to have argued that both of these elements of their teaching were relevant to all Christians. By contrast, the Pastor regards it as illegitimate to use the law to regulate the life of Christians – it is not for the righteous (δίκαιος –1 Tim 1:9). Again this suggests that the opponents were Jewish Christians and/or Gentiles influenced by such Jewish Christians who maintained the validity of at least some significant parts of the law for Christians.

5.5.2 Knowledge

In 1 Tim 6:20 Timothy is told to "Avoid the profane chatter and contradictions of what is falsely called knowledge (τῆς ψευδωνύμου γνώσεως)". This strongly suggests that the opponents claimed to have particular knowledge. Further, in Tit 1:16 we read of the opponents: "They profess to know God (θεὸν ὁμολογοῦσιν εἰδέναι), but they deny him by their actions. They are detestable, disobedient, unfit for any good work." Marshall suggests that these two verses "may reflect a claim that the only, or the true, way to know God was through acceptance of the teaching and practices of the opponents."[108]

Further, a characteristic expression in the Pastorals is "ἐπίγνωσις ἀληθείας"- knowledge of the truth (see 1 Tim 2:4; 2 Tim 2:25; 3:7; Tit 1:1).

---

[105] Marshall 1999, p44; see also p195 n115.

[106] As well as arguing for the validity of the food laws, as we have noted they seem to have been developing esoteric myths and genealogies from the law (see 1 Tim 1:4). The Pastor asserts in 1 Tim 1:8-11 that the proper function and role of the OT is not as a source of such myths and genealogies, but rather to expose sin.

[107] See for example Mounce 2000, plxx.

[108] Marshall 1999, p44.

The term ἐπίγνωσις is only found in this phrase, which suggests that this expression is used in opposition to those who claim to have γνῶσις; it is thus an additional indication that the opponents spoke of their gnosis. The opponents profess to have knowledge (γνῶσις) of the truth, but, as 2 Tim 2:25 expresses it, their need is that God will grant that they will repent and come to a real knowledge (ἐπίγνωσις) of the truth.[109] We have already noted the references to Jewish myths and genealogies, and these may have been one feature of the gnosis.[110]

5.5.2.1 The resurrection is already past

In 2 Tim 2:18 the Pastor writes that Hymenaeus and Philetus "have swerved from the truth by claiming that the resurrection has already taken place (λέγοντες [τὴν] ἀνάστασιν ἤδη γεγονέναι)." This was probably a key element of the "gnosis" claimed by the opponents, as is shown by the number of links between 2 Tim 2:18 and 1 Tim 6:20-21.[111] Towner notes three similarities between the two passages.[112] Firstly, in both passages the context is an exhortation to Timothy to guard the gospel.[113] Secondly, in both cases the opponents' teaching is described as βέβηλοι κενοφωνίαι - profane chatter (1 Tim 6:20; 2 Tim 2:16).[114] Thirdly, in the Pastor's opinion, the result of the teaching in both cases is that some people have missed the mark (ἀστοχέω) concerning the faith (1 Tim 6:21) or the truth (2 Tim 2:18). It seems reasonable to connect the two passages and thus to conclude that, in the Pastor's opinion, one element of "what is falsely called knowledge" (1 Tim 6:20), is the belief that the resurrection has already taken place (2 Tim 2:18).[115]

---

[109] Barrett (1963, p109) sees an "anti-gnostic ring" in the use of ἐπίγνωσις. Simpson (1954, p66) argues that ἐπίγνωσις indicates full recognition or discernment and is not synonymous with γνῶσις; however it is hard to determine whether γνῶσις (which he only uses in 1 Tim 6:20) and ἐπίγνωσις are synonymous for the Pastor. That he always uses ἐπίγνωσις with "ἀληθείας", may suggest that otherwise the two terms are synonymous in his view.

[110] See Barrett 1963, p13.

[111] See Towner 1989, p30.

[112] See Towner 1989, p30-1.

[113] 1 Tim 6:20: "guard what has been entrusted to you"; 2 Tim 2:15 "rightly explaining the word of truth".

[114] These are the only occasions when the phrase occurs in the NT.

[115] This seems to be further confirmed by the fact that Hymenaeus, who features in 2 Tim 2:17 as one who holds that the resurrection is already past is mentioned in 1 Tim 1:20 as an opponent. This implies that the teaching about the resurrection which features in 2 Tim was also in view in 1 Tim and that 2 Tim 2:18 can be used to identify one element of the gnosis of 1 Tim 6:20. Tit 1:16, which says that the opponents "profess to know God" is probably also to be connected to the mention of gnosis in 1 Tim 6:20.

5.5.2.2 The nature of this gnosis concerning the resurrection

We see then that according to the Pastor, the opponents taught that "the resurrection has already taken place" (2 Tim 2:18). The opponents probably did not deny the resurrection, but rather claimed that the fullness of the resurrection had already been realized in the present in some spiritual sense and thus that they had already received the benefits of resurrection life and lived in the Age to come.[116] They probably excluded the concept of the future resurrection (cf. 1 Cor. 15.12) and may have claimed that salvation was fully obtainable now. Perhaps they believed that the spiritual resurrection associated by Paul with baptism was the only resurrection. Or perhaps they argued that with Jesus' resurrection the life of the age to come had fully arrived and so believers must now live the life of the world to come, which meant that marriage was no longer appropriate (1 Tim 4:1-5). This would explain the reference to them upsetting some believers in 2 Tim 2:18; this would be through a denial of a future resurrection.

Their teaching can thus be summed up as an "over-realized eschatology", over-realized in the sense that they seem to have denied that there was any "not-yet" dimension to their eschatology and thus to hold an eschatology that is more fully realized than, for example, Paul's.

5.5.2.3 The Pastor's eschatology

Some of the Pastor's teaching can be seen as an answer to this over-realized eschatology. This dimension of the Pastor's teaching in turn confirms that we are right to see the opponents as teaching an over-realized eschatology.

In 2 Tim 2:11 the Pastor quotes a tradition which states: "If we have died with him, we will also live with him (εἰ γὰρ συναπεθάνομεν, καὶ συζήσομεν)".[117] For the Pastor, the Christian life is grounded in participation in the death and resurrection of Christ, but the resurrection of believers is seen as a future event. The salvation which has been begun is to be completed, and so endurance is important in the present (2 Tim 2:12).[118] In the present, then, salvation is incomplete. Since this passage is one element of the teaching of which Timothy is to remind the congregation (2 Tim 2:14), and since the Pastor goes on to speak of the opponents' belief that "the resurrection is already past" (2 Tim 2:18), it seems likely that 2 Tim 2:11 has the opponents in view. The wider context of 2 Tim 2:18 thus suggests that we are correct to see the heart of the opponent's teaching as an over-realized eschatology.

---

[116] See Barrett 1963, p106; Lane 1964-65, p164-7; Cranford 1980, p3; Fee 1988, p256; Towner 1989, p31.

[117] Compare Rom 6:8.

[118] See Towner 1989, p31.

Further, in a number of other passages the Pastor emphasises that salvation has been inaugurated because of the Christ event.[119] Yet the Pastor also emphasizes a future dimension to salvation and asserts that it is unfinished (1 Tim 4:16; 2 Tim 4:18; Tit 1:2; 2:13; 3:7). Thus the Pastor writes of the hope of the return of Christ (1 Tim 6:14; 2 Tim 1:12, 18, 4:1, 8, 18; Tit 2:13) when salvation will be complete and the age to come will be present in fullness (1 Tim 4:8; 6:19; 2 Tim 4:8, 18). Hence, the present age is a time of deception (1 Tim 4:1; 2 Tim 3:1; cf 2 Tim 4:10), which looks forward to the return of Christ. Further, the Spirit has been given so that "we might become heirs according to the hope of eternal life" (Tit 3:7). Thus, eternal life is something the Christian may hope to inherit in the future (2 Tim 1:10; Tit 1:2; 3:7) but may also be grasped now (1 Tim 6:12, 19; cf 1 Tim 4:8). The Pastor thus retains the tension between the "now" and the "not yet" which is characteristic of Paul.[120] Again, this can be seen as a reply to the opponents' over-realized eschatology.

The use of epiphany language is also relevant here. The Pastor uses ἐπιφάνεια or ἐπιφαίνω to refer to the first coming of Christ (2 Tim 1:10) or the results of that coming (Tit 2:11; 3:4) as well as to the second coming of Christ (1 Tim 6:14; 2 Tim 4:1, 8; Tit 2:13). Salvation is depicted as intrinsically related to both of these epiphanies. Thus in Tit 2:11 we read: "For the grace of God has appeared, bringing salvation to all (Ἐπεφάνη γὰρ ἡ χάρις τοῦ θεοῦ σωτήριος πᾶσιν ἀνθρώποις)." Here the reference is to the past appearance of Christ, through which God's grace has been made clear. In 2 Tim 4:8 we read: "From now on there is reserved for me the crown of righteousness, which the Lord, the righteous judge, will give to me on that day, and not only to me but also to all who have longed for his appearing (ἐπιφάνειαν αὐτοῦ)."[121] Here epiphany language is used in connection with future salvation. Thus the use of epiphany language emphasises that salvation began with Christ's first "appearance" but will be brought to completion only with his second "appearance".[122] Again this emphasis that salvation has begun, but still has a future dimension, this time expressed by the two-fold use of epiphany language, can be seen to be in opposition to the opponents' over-realized eschatology.

We conclude then that one prominent dimension of the opponents' theology was that "the resurrection has already taken place" and that this can be seen as an over-realized eschatology that asserted that there was no future

---

[119] See for example, 1 Tim 1:15-16; 2:3-6; 2 Tim 1:9-10; 2:8-13; Tit 2:11-14; 3:4-7.

[120] See further Taylor 1993, p68-9; Towner 1994, p28-9; Barrett 1963, p23-4; Marshall 1990b, p87-8.

[121] The context, particularly 2 Tim 4:1 shows that ἐπιφάνεια here refers to the future appearance of Christ; see Dibelius and Conzelmann 1972, p121.

[122] Towner 1994, p28-9.

dimension of resurrection. Rather the believer was already living the resurrected life.

5.5.3 The origin of this over-realized eschatology

A number of scholars have suggested, in my view correctly, that the opponents' position resulted from a misunderstanding of Paul's teaching.[123] As is widely recognised, Paul emphasised the "now and not yet" dimensions of salvation. However, as we have noted, it seems that the opponents of the Pastor emphasised that the Eschaton had arrived in fuller form, that "the resurrection has already taken place" (2 Tim 2:18) and perhaps that salvation was fully obtainable now.

Given that the Pastor is writing to a community that can be understood as being in the Pauline tradition, and that the opponents seem to be within the community, rather than teachers who have come in from the outside, the opponents' theology can best be understood as a (perhaps deliberate) misunderstanding of Paul's teaching. We can suggest that over a period of time, a group among the addressees modified the Pauline tradition into the theology which the Pastor opposed in the letters.

In support of this view, Towner notes the similarity between the theology the Pastor opposes and the over-realized eschatology which is clear in 1 Corinthians.[124] The Corinthians seem to have misunderstood Paul's teaching that Christian experience in the present was a foretaste of future salvation, but that an element of futurity remains (Rom 6:3-8; Eph 2:5; Col 2:12). The focus of the Corinthians shifted from the future eschatological completion of salvation to their present experience of the Spirit, and they seem to have concluded that they had already "arrived" (1 Cor 4:8). In this light we can understand Paul's repeated attempts in 1 Corinthians to convince them that on this score they are mistaken and to reassert the forward-looking dimension of their faith. There are thus strong parallels between the Corinthians' position and the teaching the Pastor opposes. This reinforces the likelihood of the suggestion that the theology of the Pastor's opponents was similarly a development from Pauline tradition.

This suggestion also makes sense of the comments in the Pastorals that the opponents reject the truth (1 Tim 6:5; 2 Tim 3:8; 4:4; cf. Tit 1:14) and that Paul himself has been rejected (2 Tim 1:15; 4:10, 16). As Marshall notes, these two groups of passages suggest that in the Pastor's time "there was active and open opposition to Paul and his teaching, just as there was in

---

[123] See Towner 1989, p31 for further references.

[124] Towner 1989, p33-6; see also Marshall 1993, p17. We have noted above that this point does not mean that the Pastorals *must* be close to the Corinthian correspondence in date.

Paul's own lifetime."[125] It seems likely then that the opponents were reacting against Pauline positions. Of course, it is quite likely that the opponents claimed they were faithfully following Paul, but in the Pastor's view they were in fact rejecting Paul.

5.5.4 Women and the opponents' teaching

As we have noted, 1 Tim 2:8-15; 5:3-16 and 2 Tim 3:6-7 suggest that the opponents had a considerable impact among some women, particularly younger women, and some of these women have themselves been spreading the opponents' teaching (1 Tim 5:13; 2:11-12). The instructions given concerning women aim to counteract this so that some women are no longer key members of the opponents' group.[126]

Towner argues that over-realized eschatology in Corinth led to emancipatory activism by women (1 Cor 11:2-16; 14:33b-35). The promised eventual dissolution of social barriers in the new community (Gal 3:28; 1 Cor 12:13) was taken as a present reality by the Corinthian "enthusiasts". Thus the presence of over-realized eschatology affected various aspects of community life. Towner argues that we see the same phenomenon in the Pastorals and that the opponents' over-realised eschatology led to them advocating strongly emancipationist attitudes and behaviour for women.[127] This would explain why the opponents seem to have been particularly successful among women, and would also explain why the members of the widows' group (along with other women) have been propagating the teaching, since it seems very likely that the widows would be attracted to the emancipationist teaching of the opponents.[128] In order to counter the emancipationist views of women, the Pastor argues for culturally acceptable roles and conduct of women, against the opponents' teaching that had turned conventional roles upside down.[129]

---

[125] Marshall 1999, p43.
[126] See Fee 1991, p59; see further in Chapter 11.
[127] Towner 1989, p35-6, 38-41.
[128] See Bassler 1984, p23-41.
[129] Towner 1989, p38f.

5.5.5 Ascetic practices[130]

In 1 Tim 4:1-3 it is said that in the later times some who depart from the faith will "forbid marriage and demand abstinence from foods (κωλυόντων γαμεῖν, ἀπέχεσθαι βρωμάτων)" (1 Tim 4:3). Clearly the Pastor thinks that this prophecy has come true in his present time and so the passage provides evidence that the opponents promoted ascetic behaviour. A number of other passages may also be related to the opponents' asceticism.[131] Tit 1:15 suggests that the opponents forbade some things (such as food but perhaps other things too), as being unclean. In 1 Tim 5:23 Timothy is told to no longer drink only water, but to use a little wine for the sake of his stomach and in 1 Tim 6:17 the Pastor emphasises that God gives humanity all things to enjoy. Both verses can be understood against the background of the opponents' asceticism. That some women may have chosen to remain as widows and not remarry (1 Tim 5:14), and that others may have been unwilling to bear children (1 Tim 2:15) may also be connected with the opponents' asceticism.

Can we understand the opponents' views on marriage and foods? We will consider these matters in turn.

We can suggest that the opponents' rejection of marriage is connected with their over-realised eschatology. If the believer was living the resurrected life, then this could lead to a dualism that set the "spiritual" on a higher plane than the material. Those who espoused this teaching could either become libertine (as seems to have happened at Corinth) or they could become ascetic, and thus ignore the things of the material world, or regard them as belonging to the old age.[132] It may be that the influence of Jewish or Judaising elements here in Ephesus led to the different result compared with Corinth.[133] Perhaps the belief was that for those who had "arrived", for whom the resurrection had already occurred, marriage was unspiritual and fitting only for the old order.[134]

But we should also note that one of the reasons the opponents may have believed that the resurrection had already occurred (2 Tim. 2.18) was that

---

[130] For a very helpful discussion of asceticism in the Pastorals see Streete 1999, p299-316. She argues (p307) that the Pastor "proceeds to offer a counterasceticism to that of the so-called false asceticism of his opponents ... the author's advocacy of an 'appropriate' or 'proper' asceticism is centered upon '*sophrosyne* as a principal virtue'." (Quoting from Brown 1992)

[131] See Barrett 1963, p81; Taylor 1993, p74; cf. Rom 14:2, 21; Col 2:21f.

[132] A similar divergence in approach is clear among later Gnostics.

[133] Towner 1989, p37.

[134] Perhaps they were aware of the tradition found in Mt. 22.30 where Jesus says that in the resurrection there will be no marriage or giving in marriage; see Lane 1964-65, p166. 1 Cor. 7.1, 29ff could also be used in support of this view, if one believed that the resurrection had already occurred "spiritually". There are other parallels in Gnosticism, and probably at Qumran; see Towner 1989, p37-8.

they believed the material world was tainted, or perhaps evil,[135] and an impediment to salvation.[136] Thus, perhaps because of this foundational view, they went on to affirm that resurrection could only be spiritual, and that such spiritual resurrection has already occurred. Perhaps this foundational negative view of the physical world led directly to a rejection of marriage, which was clearly part of the material order.[137]

Why did the opponents demand abstinence from (some) foods? Here there are two possible answers. Firstly, as in the case of forbidding marriage, belief that the resurrection had already occurred could lead to the view that the material world belonged to the old age and so contact with it should be curtailed in particular ways.[138] The possibly connected view that physical matter was evil or tainted would lead to the same result.

Secondly, we have noted that there was a Jewish dimension to the opponents' teaching; the demand for abstinence from foods could be another Jewish feature of the teaching. Of course the OT commands abstinence from various foods and the question of which food could be eaten played a major part in Jewish Christian and Gentile Christian relations (see Acts 10:28; 11:3; 15:20, 29; 21:25; Gal 2:12). Other NT passages show that this was an issue in various places (Rom 14:2f; 1 Cor 8:7-13; 10:23-33; Col 2:21b). This may alone be the basis for the demand for abstinence from food, or it may be an additional reason alongside the view that the resurrection had already occurred and that matter was evil.[139]

---

[135] As we go on to note, this suggestion is likely because it could easily lead to the view that the resurrection was only spiritual, but it is made more likely by that fact that the Pastor underlines in 1 Tim 4:4 that creation is good.

[136] See Bassler 1996a, p80; Oden 1989, p59.

[137] See Bassler 1996a, p82. We note that at Corinth some denied a future bodily resurrection (1 Cor 15:12, 35) thought they were already reigning in the kingdom (1 Cor 4:8) and at least some looked down on sex (1 Cor 7:1-7) and marriage (1 Cor 7:25-38). It seems most likely that these views were all connected at Corinth, which suggests a similar phenomenon or cluster of beliefs is at work among the Pastor's addressees. Goulder (1996, p245-50) thinks the opponents insisted on marital abstinence because they wished to have spiritual visions. However, to argue this, he must read a good deal more of the letter as polemical than seems likely. We have noted that the opponents had a considerable impact among women (see 1 Tim 2:12-15; 5:11-15; 2 Tim 3:6-7; Tit 2:5) and that this may well have been connected to their emancipationist tendencies and their prohibition of marriage (which freed women from the bonds of patriarchal marriage), along with other factors; see Verner 1983, p177-80; Bassler 1996a, p81. In response, the Pastor advocates marriage (1 Tim 2:15; 3:2, 4-5, 12; 5:9, 14; Tit 1:6; 2:4-5).

[138] Lane 1964-65, p166, writes: "Had not the risen Jesus indicated by his own example that the food to be taken after the resurrection was fish or honeycomb? [Lk. 24.42f, reading a variant; cf Jn 21.9-14; Acts 10.41] Further appeal could be made to Paul's dictum that the Kingdom of God was not meat and drink [Rom. 14.17]."

[139] See Dibelius and Conzelmann 1972, p65-7; Hanson 1982, p88.

That a Jewish background is likely with regard to the demand for abstinence from foods is shown by Tit 1:15 where the Pastor says: "To the pure all things are pure, but to the corrupt and unbelieving nothing is pure. Their very minds and consciences are corrupted." Clearly this is again a reference to the opponents. The mention of the circumcision party in Tit 1:10, Jewish myths and "human commandments" (ἐντολαῖς ἀνθρώπων) in Tit 1:14, and the way in which these "commandments" are corrected by saying everything is "pure" (καθαρός), a word frequently used in the LXX and the NT in the context of purity rules,[140] suggests that the applicability of Jewish purity laws is denied by the Pastor in v15. The opponents' view that "nothing is pure" (Tit 1:15)[141] may then have been the basis from which they demanded abstinence from (some) foods. To the Pastor however, all things are pure. Given all of this, it seems likely that there is a Jewish dimension to the demand for abstinence from foods in 1 Tim 4:3, where the Pastor may be opposing the imposition of Jewish food laws.[142]

Thus rejection of marriage and abstinence from food may have both been linked to the view that the resurrection was already passed or to the probably associated view that the material world was evil. Or this may have been the reason for the negative view of marriage, with a Jewish background being an additional factor explaining the rejection of "foods".[143]

This sort of asceticism is paralleled in some later Gnostic groups which had a distaste for the material world. They believed that procreation was evil, with the result that marriage and family life were denigrated.[144] Some Gnostic groups also abstained from eating certain foods.[145] However, such attitudes

---

[140] See for example Lev. 11.32, 36-7; 13.6, 13, 17; Deut. 14.11, 20; Mt. 23.26; Lk. 11.41; Rom. 14.20. Mk 7.19 uses the verb καθαρίζω.

[141] This is undoubtedly an example of hyperbole, which is found quite often in the Pastorals. Fiore (1986, p18) notes: "Hyperbole adds attention and importance to the exhortation." He cites as examples of hyperbole 1 Tim 1:7, 14; 6:4-5; 2 Tim 1:15; 3:8, 12; 4:16; Tit 1:12, 15; 3:3.

[142] Gunther (1973, p101) also notes: "Since true nourishment is by words of the faith and of good teaching (1 Tim 4:6), the inference may be drawn that positive food laws were also being taught." Marshall (1999, p51) thinks the opponents "derived a radical set of ascetic restrictions regarding purity" by interpreting the law allegorically.

[143] Dibelius and Conzelmann (1972, p65) and Fee (1988, p8-9) think both factors account for the attitude towards food; see also Barrett 1963, p132.

[144] See Trummer 1978, p166-8; Taylor 1993, p87. Some Gnostic groups forbade marriage, for example Saturninus (see Irenaeus, Adv Haer 1.24.2), Marcion, and Apelles (Tertullian, de Praescriptione 33). Some therefore see the emphasis on celibacy as having a Gnostic background; see Cranford 1980, p30. We note the Pastor's emphasis on the value of marriage (1 Tim 2:15; 3:2, 4-5, 12; 5:9, 14; Tit 1:6; 2:4) and food (1 Tim 5:23; Tit 1:15) which can be seen as a counter to the position of the opponents on these matters.

[145] For example, Saturninus, who abstained from animal flesh; see Irenaeus, Adv Haer 1.24.2. The Pastor goes on to speak about the goodness of creation (1 Tim 4:3-5) which can

were almost certainly not unique to Gnostics and we will note below that it is very unlikely that the opponents were Gnostic. Further, we can explain these features of the opponents' teaching without recourse to Gnosticism.

5.5.6 Greed

In 1 Tim 6:5, the Pastor states that the opponents imagined that godliness (εὐσέβεια) was a means of monetary gain. Similarly, in Tit 1:11 it is said that the opponents are "upsetting whole families by teaching for sordid gain what it is not right to teach". The Pastor thus accuses them of trying to gain a following in order to gain an income.[146] We should note here that the accusation that opponents were only interested in business and money is part of the polemical schema against sophists and so may simply be taken over from that schema by the Pastor.[147]

However, three points argue that there is some substance to the charge in this case. Firstly, Towner notes that 1 Tim 6:3-21 is carefully constructed, with the accusation of greed (v3-10) providing motivation for the teaching directed to the wealthy of the community (v17-19).[148] The Pastor may have taken over the charge of greed from the polemical schema, but it is an important point for him and he has shaped the section around the charge. Towner thus sees the charge as a reliable indication that this was a feature of the opponents. Secondly, the Pastor includes in the list of qualifications required of a leader that they should not be a "lover of money" (ἀφιλάργυρος; 1 Tim 3:3) nor "greedy for money" (αἰσχροκερδής; 1 Tim 3:8; Tit 1:7). Since some of the opponents were leaders, this suggests that desire for monetary gain may have been a feature of the opponents. Thirdly, we will note in Chapter 9 that the level of argumentation against the love of money is noteworthy in the Pastoral Epistles. One reason for this is that the author considered that the love of wealth was a real problem among his addressees because, as he saw it, great problems stemmed from it (1 Tim 6:9-10). An additional reason for his attitude to the "love of money" may also be that he thought one of the reasons that the opponents had "shipwrecked their faith" was because of the love of money.

If the opponents did regard "godliness as a means of gain", then this would suggest that the asceticism which the author combats as one feature of the

---

be taken as a rebuttal of Gnostic beliefs about creation and the essential evil of matter (see Barrett 1963, p67) but this passage need not refer to gnostic views. On 1 Tim 4:1-5 see Trebilco 2000, p204-220.

[146] See Dibelius and Conzelmann 1972, p83.

[147] See Dibelius and Conzelmann 1972, p83.

[148] Towner 1989, p27 and p264 n38; cf. Kidd 1990, p93-100. Dibelius and Conzelmann (1972, p83) note the charge is part of standard polemic, but also suggest it was occasioned by some specific actions on the part of the opponents.

opponents' teaching (see 1 Tim 4:3) is not asceticism for its own sake, nor is it connected with a renunciation of all "worldly wealth". Rather, the asceticism may well be the rejection of only *certain* things, and thus as we suggested above, may be connected with Jewish law.

5.6 Is there a distinction between the opponents' teaching in 1 and 2 Timothy (which are said to be to Ephesus) and Titus (which is said to be to Crete)?

Up until this point we have generally looked at the evidence of 1 and 2 Timothy in order to build up a picture of the opponents in view there. We have drawn on Titus, but generally only to illuminate the meaning of words or to fill out the picture obtained from 1 and 2 Timothy. We now need to ask whether the Pastor envisages a significant distinction between the opponents' teaching in view in 1 and 2 Timothy on the one hand, and Titus on the other? Does this correspond to the purported geographical distinction between Ephesus (1 and 2 Tim) and Crete (Titus)?

When we examine the books individually with regard to the features of the opponents which are not derived from the polemical schema, we see that there are small differences between 1 and 2 Timothy on the one hand and Titus on the other.[149] In particular, the over-realized eschatology spoken of in 2 Tim 2:18 and the impact of the opponents on women, and the involvement of women as teachers of the opponents' doctrine (1 Tim 2:8-15; 5:13-14; 2 Tim 3:6-7)[150] are absent from Titus. However, there are significant common dimensions in the description of the opponents across all three books, such as that the teaching has Jewish dimensions (1 Tim 1:4-11; Tit 1:10, 14) and the greed of the opponents (2 Tim 3:1-5; Tit 1:18). Further, Tit 1:15 probably reflects asceticism, and so this is also a common feature (1 Tim 4:1-5), and Tit 1:16 probably reflects the claim to "knowledge" and so is parallel to 1 Tim 6:20.

Given these small differences and significant commonalities, that we are dealing with small books, and that the balanced eschatology of the Pastor (which we argued was a counter to the opponents' over-realized eschatology), is also found in Titus, we can suggest that the teaching of the opponents envisaged in Titus, while related to that in Ephesus (1 and 2 Tim), is to be thought of as slightly (but only slightly) different. Given the geographical

---

[149] Sumney 1999, p253-302 argues that there are separate and different groups of opponents in each of the three letters. But the Pastorals as a whole share so much in common, and there are sufficient links between them with regard to the opponents to make it very unlikely that the Pastor envisaged three separate groups. Our view that the opponents in Titus were related but slightly different from those in 1-2 Tim, recognises some of the points Sumney makes.

[150] Tit 2:3-5 concerns women, but concerns behaviour that does not discredit the word of God rather than their involvement in the opponents' teaching.

proximity of Ephesus and Crete, it is entirely understandable that very similar opponents would be found in the two localities, but that there were also small differences.[151]

This is in keeping with other distinctions between 1 and 2 Timothy on the one hand and Titus on the other. Note for example, the direction to appoint elders in Tit 1:5f, whereas in 1 and 2 Timothy, the system of leadership seems to be well established. Further, the reference to a Cretan prophet in Tit 1:12 again underlines the point that the situation referred to in Titus exists in Crete and is slightly different from Ephesus.

This supports our approach of using the evidence of 1 and 2 Tim to build up a picture of the community in Ephesus, while being cautious in using Titus to illuminate the situation in Ephesus, since in some facets Titus may be unique to the situation in Crete.[152] But it also favours the view that real situations in Ephesus and Crete are being addressed, rather than that the letters contain general polemic.

5.7 Identifying the opponents?

Can we identify the opponents and relate them to other known movements? We have noted that the opponents probably referred to (at least part of) their teaching as "gnosis" (1 Tim 6:20); some have taken this to mean that full-blown Gnosticism is in view here.[153] However, this is unlikely for a number of reasons. Firstly, the term "gnosis" or its equivalent, is found in contexts which cannot be called "Gnostic". For example, דעת is used at Qumran, particularly in the Wisdom texts,[154] and "knowledge" was often discussed in other wisdom texts of the Second Temple period; clearly none of these texts

---

[151] See Marshall 1999, p85.

[152] Some scholars see the "false" teaching in the Pastorals as a basic unit. Thus Spicq (1969a, p88): "Ces caractères intellectuels et moraux de l'hérésie sont communs aux trois épîtres". See also Barrett 1963, p133. Some disagree and see differences in the opposition to Paul. Thus Kelly (1963, p10-11) notes: "even if, as is highly likely (especially if the situations implied are in any sense historical), it [the false teaching] took somewhat different forms in Ephesus and Crete, its broad pattern seems to have been much the same at both centres."

[153] See for example Schmithals 1983, p115-117. Attempts to identify the opponents have ranged from Judaizers to Marcion and Gnosticism; see Gunther, 1973, p4-5 who gives 19 different identifications of the opponents. On Gnosticism see Perkins 1993.

[154] See 1 QpHab 11.1; 1QS 3.15; 10.9, 12; 11.6, 15; 1QH 2.18; 11.24; 4Q416 2iii13; 4Q418 9,9a-c,13; 4Q418 43-45i,6; 4Q418 55,5, 10; (4Q416-18 are part of 1Q/4Q Instruction); 4Q298 3-4ii8 (=4QcryptA); 1Q27 1i6; 4Q299 8,7; 4Q299 35,1 (=Book of Mysteries); 4Q413 1-2 (=Hymn of Knowledge); 4Q525 14ii19 (=4QBeatitudes). On these texts see the studies in Hempel, Lange and Lichtenberger 2002; see also Harrington 1996; 1997, p245-54. Davies 1943, p113-39 remains useful.

are "Gnostic".[155] We also note that the opponents Paul faced in Corinth probably spoke of gnosis (as well as wisdom), but they should not be seen as "Gnostics".[156] The use of the term "gnosis" by the opponents of the Pastor does not imply any necessary connection with "Gnosticism" therefore. Secondly, there is no evidence in the Pastorals that it was through receiving this gnosis that one participated in salvation or in the "resurrection" which, for the opponents, was already past.[157] Thirdly, there is no indication in the Pastorals that key features of later Gnostic systems were part of the opponents' teaching. Thus, there is no indication that for the opponents gnosis had come to mean a knowledge which released the soul from enslavement to the material world, or that aeon and archon speculation was involved.[158] Fourthly, there is no evidence that the opponents' negative view of creation, which is suggested by 1 Tim 4:1-5, was based on "a belief in devolution in the godhead. The writer does not have to prove to them that the world was created by God rather than by some demiurge, but simply that all of God's creation is good (1 Tim 4.4)."[159] Thus we conclude that the opponents should not be seen as "Gnostics".

However, this discussion is complicated by the debate about how Gnosticism developed and when along the process of development we can speak of "Gnosticism" proper. Gnosticism is clearly a group of beliefs, that have coalesced. But these individual elements can be present without sufficient evidence for the "Gnostic package"[160] as a whole. It may be then that the elements found in the Pastorals which later belonged to the "Gnostic package", are part of this "pre-Gnostic" period, before Gnosticism as a whole developed. The most we can say is that we have here "the presence of 'Pre-Gnosticism', i.e. of elements that later went to make up the Gnostic package but which are not yet themselves compounded together in the characteristically Gnostic fashion."[161] Thus, while many scholars have argued that the opponents are a form of Gnosticism, probably in a relatively undeveloped stage,[162] we probably should see them as belonging to a time

---

[155] See for example Wis 1:7; 2:13; 6:22; 7:17; 10:10; 14:22; Sirach 1:19; 21:13-14, 18.

[156] On Paul's opponents at Corinth see 1 Cor 8:1,7, 10, 11; 13:2, 8; see also Towner 1989, p29-30.

[157] See Towner, 1989, p32. On the Gnostic phrase "knowledge of the truth", see Quinn 1990, p282; for Gnostic interests with genealogies see On the Origin of the World 2.5.98-105; Irenaeus Adv Haer 1.30.9.

[158] Admittedly this is an argument from silence.

[159] Marshall 1999, p50.

[160] The expression is from Marshall 1999, p49.

[161] Marshall 1999, p49-50.

[162] Marshall 1999, p47 n59 gives a list; see for example Roloff 1988, p234. Barrett 1963, p13-16 suggests that the opponents are Jewish gnostic Christians. For a critique of these views see Marshall 1999, p47-50.

before this, before we can speak of "Gnosticism" in any way, even as "undeveloped". In addition, as Marshall notes, "the identification of the heresy in the Pastorals as a form of Gnosticism is not only an unnecessary hypothesis but also a distortion of the evidence."[163]

If the opponents do not represent "Gnosticism", then where are we to locate them in the movements of early Christian thought? The Jewish dimension of their teaching is particularly pronounced. They claim to be teachers of the law and we have suggested that their "myths and genealogies" are based on the OT. Asceticism could clearly be connected with Jewish thought, since it is known at Qumran for example.[164] But identifying the opponents as a form of Jewish Christianity does not readily explain the teaching about the resurrection or the freedom given to women.

We have also noted that the opponents' teaching about the resurrection can be seen as a misunderstanding of Paul's eschatology. One factor in this was also that Paul's teaching about the unity of men and women in Christ (Gal 3:28) could be taken to mean the obliteration of all distinctions.[165] Further, the opponents' asceticism (particularly their opposition to marriage) could be developed from their over-realized eschatology.[166]

Clearly, the author sees himself as within the Pauline tradition, and the way in which the Pastor insists that the Pauline "deposit" has been given to Timothy suggests the opponents also claimed their views were based on Paul's theology and authority.[167] This reinforces the likelihood that (at least) some of the opponents' views had roots in and were developed from Paul's

---

[163] Marshall 1999, p51; see also Mounce 2000, plxxv.

[164] Thiessen 1995, p319 notes it is explicitly related to commandments. Thiessen (1995, p317-38) argues that the character of the opposition in the Pastorals can all be understood in terms of a form of Jewish Christianity without recourse to Gnosticism. However since Gentiles can be part of groups that can be described as "Jewish Christianity" (ie. this is not an ethnic term), it is perhaps better to speak of dimensions of thought that can be derived directly from Jewish thought.

[165] Marshall 1999, p46 also notes that Paul was opposed by groups of Jewish Christians, and that elements of the opposition found in the Pastorals can be seen earlier in Paul – the stress on the law (Gal, Phil, Col), misunderstanding of the resurrection (1 Cor), restrictions on food (Rom, 1 Cor, Col) and sexual asceticism (1 Cor). "Consequently, all the factors in the situation can be accounted for in terms of a combination of Jewish and Christian elements. Moreover, there is nothing which requires us to postulate a significant difference in time from that of Paul himself." (p46)

[166] As we have noted, their forbidding of some foods could be a consequence of over-realised eschatology, or it could have Jewish dimensions, or both.

[167] See Marshall 1999, p47. He also notes that the Pastorals "refer to people who were opposed to Paul and disciplined by him." It is perhaps best to see these as indicating the Pastor's reaction to the opponents – given their current views, they are opposing Paul and would have been disciplined by him.

theology in directions in which Paul did not go, perhaps as a misunderstanding of Paul's theology or as a deliberate development from it in new directions.

We would be better then to see the opponents as a development from Pauline teaching, independent of "Gnosticism" which had not yet coalesced as a movement. Further, we can suggest explanations for the prominent Jewish dimensions of the opponents' teaching. Of course, this may be simply a development from within the Pauline tradition itself. But we can note that we concluded from our discussion of Acts that at the end of the Pauline mission the Pauline community in Ephesus had a significant Jewish element, including some Jews who had been followers of John the Baptist. Perhaps some of these Jewish Christians (or Gentiles influenced by them), who seem to have had a variety of backgrounds, were part of the group we have called "the opponents" and developed over time some of the Jewish dimensions of the opponents' teaching.[168] Alternatively, we note that there was a significant and sizeable Jewish community in Ephesus; clearly this community may have exerted an influence on the Pauline Christian community.[169] Perhaps both these factors were significant with regard to the development of the prominent Jewish dimensions of the opponents' teaching.

We can also note in this regard that the Jewish dimension of the opponents' teaching is the main "new" dimension in comparison with the opposition to Paul at Corinth, which we have argued is a similar phenomenon to that opposed in the Pastorals.[170] We can only wonder if it is significant that we know of a significant Jewish community in Ephesus, whereas it is not clear how significant or sizeable the Jewish community at Corinth was at this time.[171] Of course, there are many other variables involved, but we can

---

[168] We have also noted in Chapter 3 that Apollos may have converted some Christians in the synagogue in Ephesus and we have discussed the "Ephesian 12", who were also Jewish Christians; see also Thiessen 1995, p86 and n311.

[169] In Chapter 1 we discussed the probable influence of the Jewish community in Ephesus on Polycrates, bishop of Ephesus around 190 CE; see also Bauckham 1993a, p36-7. This would be a parallel example. But note there is no evidence in 1 and 2 Tim that circumcision was an issue. If the Jewish community was exerting an influence on the Christians in Ephesus, then it did not include circumcision. We also know of a Jewish community in Crete, so they could have influenced the development of the opponents' teaching there. See 1 Macc 15:22-3; Acts 2:9-11; Philo, Leg 282; Schürer, Vermes, Millar, Black, Goodman 1986, p71-2; see also Barrett 1963, p130-1. Marshall (1999, p46) notes "it is the combination of a non-Pauline version of Christianity [particularly with regard to resurrection and asceticism], including perhaps misunderstanding of Paul's teaching, with a Judaising outlook, that creates the unusual character of their teaching."

[170] Marshall (1999, p90) notes that the opponents' teaching has its closest links "with the teaching that circulated in Corinth and Colossae … The 'new' feature is the speculative use of the Old Testament".

[171] On Jews in Corinth see Schürer, Vermes, Millar, Black, Goodman 1986, p64-6; Acts 18:4-7, 12-17.

suggest that some of the exegesis of the OT which the Pastor calls "myths and genealogies" was developed either by the significant group of Jewish Christians who were part of the Pauline community in Ephesus, or because of the influence on the Pauline Christians of the Jewish community in the city.

Another additional explanation for the opponents' stress on asceticism and the emancipation of women has been suggested. *The Acts of Paul and Thecla*, a second century text, promotes celibacy and asceticism, gives a prominent place to women and stresses that the resurrection has already taken place because believers have come to know God. MacDonald has argued that the Pastorals are directed against the picture of Paul and his teaching that was later expressed in *The Acts of Paul and Thecla*.[172] The Pastorals need not be dated as late as *The Acts*, but *The Acts* show that views like those of the opponents did develop within the Pauline tradition. *The Acts* give evidence that some women within the Pauline tradition were able to experience a significant degree of emancipation from married life and domestic duties.

This view also sees the opponents' teaching as related to the Pauline tradition, albeit as an alternative development of the Pauline tradition to that found in the Pastorals, and strengthens the view that sees the opponents as a development from within the Pauline tradition.

Thus we can suggest that the Pastor's opponents in Ephesus developed their views from within the Pauline tradition and within the Pauline community of Ephesus, perhaps being influenced in this process of development by the Jewish community in the city. This explains the evidence: that they are clearly Christians, who continued to advocate for some Jewish elements for their faith that the Pastor thought were wrong, and have developed an over-realised eschatology and some ascetic practices.

5.8 Are there other features of the Pastorals that are directed against the opponents?

There have been a number of other suggestions about facets of the opponents' teaching combated by the Pastor. However, these generally rely not on points the Pastor says expressly characterise the opponents (such as Jewish myths) but rather on matters that the Pastor asserts; it is argued that he makes these assertions with the opponents in mind. Methodologically, this is more difficult to sustain. But we can note that the following features have been suggested.

Firstly, the Pastor emphasises that Paul was a preacher of the Gospel to Gentiles (1 Tim 2:7; cf. 3:16) and that God's saving will is directed to all people (1 Tim 2:4-6; 4:10; Tit 2:11). This may indicate that the opponents

---

[172] See MacDonald 1983; MacDonald 1988, p181-7; 1996, p170-8; Young 1994a, p13-23.

were Jewish-Christians who attached little significance to mission to Gentiles. As Marshall notes, "They may have insisted to such an extent on Jewish and ascetical practices that their form of Christianity had little appeal to Gentiles."[173] Certainly, a lack of enthusiasm for the Gentile mission could be in keeping with the strong Jewish dimensions of the opponents' teaching.

Secondly, it has been suggested that the opponents practised some form of "enthusiasm" and ecstatic prophecy, and claimed special inspiration by the Spirit.[174] In response to this the Pastor is alleged to play down the role of the Spirit. However, there is no clear evidence that the opponents claimed inspiration by the Spirit[175] and, as I hope to argue elsewhere, the Spirit plays a significant role in the Pastor's theology.[176]

5.9 What happened after the letters were written?

Can we say anything about what may have happened after the Pastorals were written? In particular, did the opponents continue and if so in what way?

As far as the Pastor is concerned, at the time of writing the opponents do not belong to God's people. This is clearly implied in 2 Tim 2:19, where the two quotations are from Num 16:5 and 16:26, although the second quotation is not exact. Barrett suggests that the whole story of Num 16 is in mind here.[177] In that story Korah, Dathan and Abiram set themselves up against Moses and then are separated from the faithful in Israel and swallowed up by the earth. By alluding to this story the Pastor is saying that Hymenaeus,

---

[173] Marshall 1999, p45; see also Mounce 2000, plxx. It is much less likely that this material is an attack upon the view that was later held by certain Gnostic groups, that a predetermined group of spiritual people would inevitably be saved and another group of "material" people would be damned; see Barrett 1963, p50; Taylor 1993, p68.

[174] See Ford 1970-71, p342-4.

[175] It is unjustified to see in 1 Tim 4:1 the Pastor's refutation of the opponents' claim to be inspired by the Spirit; the passage is better seen as a parallel to 2 Cor 4:4; 11:3, 13-15 where it is said that deceit is due to demonic or Satanic influence.

[176] See further Karris 1973, p557-8; Marshall 1999, p45. Other features of the opponents' theology have been suggested. Firstly, 2 Tim 1:9 and Tit 3:5 stress that human works in general do not contribute to salvation. However, if Jewish works of the law were being made a condition of salvation by the opponents, we would expect some discussion of this; see Marshall 1990b, p84; 1993, p17, 19; 1999, p46. Secondly, in 1 Tim 2:5 the Pastor stresses that there is one mediator between God and humanity, Jesus Christ. This may be polemical against a plurality of mediators, but this seems unlikely. Traditional material found in the Pastorals (1 Tim 1:15; 2:3-6; 3:16; 2 Tim 1:9-10; 2:8-13; Tit 2:11-14; 3:4-7) has sometimes been used in reconstructions of the opponents' theology. However, these passages do not seem to have been composed by the author for this occasion to combat the opponents' teaching, but rather contain traditional formulations the author utilises to develop his own theological position. Thus there is no evidence that in these passages the Pastor is combating things the opponents said.

[177] Barrett 1963, p106-7.

Philetus and their followers do not belong to God's people: God knows who are his, and these opponents are not included. Thus, all Christians should withdraw from such people (2 Tim 2:19). However, the opponents could well have seen themselves as the "true believers". It is certainly unlikely that they thought they had ceased to belong to God's people.

We note also that the Pastor generally does not counter the opponents' teaching by refuting their positions in extended theological discussion.[178] Rather, he advocates that the opponents and their speculations are to be avoided (1 Tim 4:7; 6:20; 2 Tim 2:14, 16, 23; Tit 3:9) and in Tit 1:11 he states that the opponents are to be silenced. Further through his polemical characterisation of the opponents as hypocritical liars whose consciences are seared (1 Tim 4:2) and whose teaching is meaningless talk (1 Tim 1:6) and so on, the Pastor seems to be attempting to create a stereotype in order to keep his hearers from associating with these opponents.[179] But despite this evaluation of the present plight of the opponents, the Pastor also hopes that they will repent, but only God can grant them repentance (2 Tim 2:25).[180] Overall then, the Pastor's main goal with regard to the opponents is to warn his readers in order that the opponents' teaching might not spread. Further, he does not seem to envisage that he can convince the opponents themselves to change their minds – although he does not rule out that this might happen.

But what happened? That the letters were preserved indicates that the Pastor gained a hearing. But what happened in the medium-term future after the letters were written? We can suggest three possibilities. Firstly, that the opponents saw the error of their ways from the Pastor's perspective and abandoned their teaching. Secondly, that the opponents remained within the communities addressed (as they seem to be at the time or writing, since they are present for Timothy to command them (1 Tim 1:3 etc)), as a sub-group who believed and acted somewhat differently from the rest of the community. Thirdly, that the opponents split away from the main group of addressees and formed a distinct group of their own.

Can we say anything about the likelihood of these options? We are of course weighing possibilities here, but we can at least do that. Option one seems unlikely, given that the Pastor does not seriously attempt to tackle the opponents' teaching head-on, and that the Pastor addresses the situation as a significant crisis caused by a significant group with developed beliefs. The Pastor would be deeply unhappy with the second option, and the strength of his polemic, and that he seems to have some readers whom he thinks agree with him (those who identify with Timothy, and those who will be the leaders spoken of in 1 Tim 3, for example) suggests option two is unlikely.

---

[178] We have noted the exceptions of 1 Tim 1:8-11; 4:1-5; 6:6-8.

[179] See Towner 1994, p26.

[180] Compare also Tit 1:13.

Thus, the third option seems the most likely one. This is supported by the facts that the opponents already had leaders and so had some group structure, had a developed teaching, and by the indications that house churches as distinct groups may have followed the opponents (see 1 Tim 5:13; Tit 1:11; perhaps 2 Tim 3:6), who thus were already well on the way to having a separate identity. Accordingly we can suggest that there may have been in Ephesus, from sometime between 80-100 CE for at least some period of time, a separate identifiable group which had its roots in the Pauline tradition, but which developed new dimensions of belief and behaviour.

6. Overall Conclusions

We conclude that the Pastorals were written by a person who saw himself as standing in the Pauline tradition and was applying that tradition to the problems of his own day. He was writing around 80-100 CE to Christians in Ephesus; that he wrote in Paul's name shows that Paul was an authoritative figure among his addressees and so demonstrates the on-going importance of Pauline tradition in the group.[181] Clearly then, a Pauline community continued to exist in the city.

In the letters, the Pastor dealt with a group of people that he saw as his opponents, who were a specific group among the addressees who also looked back to Paul as the key figure in their past. One of the Pastor's key reasons in writing 1 and 2 Timothy was to counter these opponents who had created something of a crisis for the Pastor.

The teaching of the opponents is best seen as having its roots in Paul's theology and as involving a development from Pauline tradition into some new directions. We can suggest that the prominent Jewish dimensions of the opponents' teaching may have developed because the Pauline community in Ephesus had a significant Jewish element, as is suggested by the account in Acts, or the opponents' teaching may have been influenced by the significant Jewish community in Ephesus. Or perhaps both these factors were significant.

We can also note that we can make a connection between Acts 20:30 and the opponents in the Pastorals. In Acts 20:30 Paul says to the Ephesian elders gathered in Miletus that "some even from your own group will come distorting the truth in order to entice the disciples to follow them." We do not know whether Luke was aware of the actual group of opponents spoken of in

---

[181] See Roloff 1997, p145.

the Pastorals, nor if he knew the Pastorals themselves,[182] but in any case it seems reasonable to make this connection.

We can also suggest, though we can do no more than this, that the "opponents" continued to exist after the Pastor wrote these letters, but perhaps as a distinct group which had split from the rest of the Pauline community.

The Pastorals will also be used in Chapter 8-13 where we will discuss different themes which emerge from the Pastorals, the Johannine Letters and Revelation.

---

[182] Dating of Acts becomes a crucial question here; it may well have been written before the Pastorals. Of course, some scholars have argued that Luke wrote the Pastorals, but this seems unlikely.

Chapter 6

What do the Johannine Letters tell us about the Early Christians in Ephesus?

We now turn to the Johannine Literature. We will argue that although John's Gospel was written in Ephesus, it cannot be used as evidence for the life of a community in the city, since it was not written specifically for that one community. However, the evidence suggests that the Johannine Letters were also written in Ephesus and, after discussing how we should read the rhetoric of these letters, we will discuss the secessionists who are in view there.

1. Why John's Gospel cannot be used here

Bauckham has challenged the view that each Gospel was written for a specific Christian community. Rather, he has argued that the Evangelists, rather than writing for their own communities, envisaged that their works would circulate around the churches and so envisaged a very wide-ranging and general Christian audience. This means that the present state of "the Johannine community" and its history cannot be read off the pages of the Gospel of John, as has been done, for example, in the very influential works of Martyn and Brown.[1]

Bauckham and the other contributors to the book, *The Gospels for All Christians,* marshal a whole range of evidence, which cannot all be discussed here. We note the following key points. Firstly, we note the evidence for close and regular communication between various early Christian communities, one feature of which is the extensive evidence for the exchange of letters, carried by messengers, from one church to another. Another element of this is the evidence for close contacts between churches in the late first century or early second century CE.[2] The evidence for rivalry and conflict in early

---

[1] See Martyn 1979; Brown 1979a. Many other examples could be cited.

[2] See Bauckham 1998b, p32, 38-43. In addition to Paul's letters, note 1 Peter, 1 Clement, Ignatius' letters, Polycarp's Letter, and we can suggest that many others have not survived. For close contacts between churches note Papias' comment about travelling Christians (discussed below) in Eusebius, HE 3.39.3-4, the evidence for communication between Churches shown by Ignatius' letters (see Chapter 15, section 3.5), and Hermas, Vis 2.4.3. Note also the high level of mobility in this period, on which see Malherbe 1983, p62-70. For

Christianity, and that different teachers actively promoted their ideas elsewhere, also shows the extent of the mobility of both people and ideas, and shows that we should not think of "exclusive enclaves of churches out of communication with others".[3] Given this level of communication between groups, it is unlikely that an author would write a Gospel solely for the community in which he lived.

Secondly, the evidence we have for the sort of people who would write a Gospel – figures who were influential in early Christianity – suggests that they were people who travelled widely and had experience of more than one early Christian community. The outlook of such people would thus be the movement as a whole, not just one particular community, and so it would be unlikely that they would write a Gospel solely for the community in which they lived, but would rather have in view the different contexts they knew well.[4]

Thirdly, the strong sense of being a worldwide movement or network which is evident in early Christian literature, also suggests an author would not write solely for a local community.[5]

Fourthly, the evidence for the publication and circulation of books in the NT period suggests books circulated through the existing social networks of authors and readers, and that books had wider audiences than just a local group or an immediate circle of some sort. What we know of the circulation of Christian literature supports this view.[6]

Fifthly, the Gospels are not letters, which had a particular intended audience, but rather are closest to the genre of the Greco-Roman bios, or (ancient) "biography", and all we know of this genre suggests people wrote

---

close contacts in the Pauline period see Branick 1989, p31; Thompson 1998, p49-70; Rom 12:13; 16:1-2; 1 Cor 16:10-12; cf Phil 2:25-30; Col 4:7-9; Eph 6:21-22.

[3] Bauckham 1998a, p3; see also p43-4. Note the evidence for conflict in Paul's letters, Rev, Ignatius.

[4] See Bauckham 1998b, p33-8, who gives examples like Barnabas, John Mark, Philip the evangelist, Aquila and Prisca, the itinerant apostles in Rev 2:2; note also the evidence for travel by leaders in 2 Jn 10-11, 3 Jn 3-8 and Did 11:1-6, Polycarp (see Phil 13:1). Note also Bauckham's later comment (1998c, p251): "I do not suggest that these people [the Evangelists] were modern individualists, but that their group-orientation was as much to the whole Christian movement as to any particular community. There is a great deal in the texts to suggest that such an orientation was common and expected, and also very little to suggest exclusive orientation to a particular network of like-minded churches distinguished from others".

[5] See Bauckham 1998b, p33; see for example 1 Cor 1:2; 9:5; 16:3; 1 Thess 2:14; 1 Pet 5:9; Rev 7:9-14; see also Meeks 1983, p107-110.

[6] See Alexander 1998, p71-111. She notes (p104) "The network model [of the circulation of books] itself implies not a monolithic structure but a multiplicity of intersecting lines of communication."

bioi for wide audiences.[7] Certainly, we have no parallel for a biography being written solely for a single community.[8] This does not mean that the Evangelists did not have particular types of readers in mind, "but they would be a category to be found throughout the churches, not a specific community."[9] Nor does it mean that the interpretation of the Gospels should be divorced from the context of early Christian life and thought. But the best context for interpretation is not that of one particular community, but all we know of early Christian communities in the late first century.[10]

Finally, it could be thought that the results of studies of Gospel "communities" are a vindication of the method. However, Bauckham notes that scholars have not generally argued that a particular feature of a Gospel can *only* be understood as addressed to a particular community rather than to a general audience. The results of studies of Gospel communities and of this way of reading the Gospels "are the results of applying to the text a particular reading strategy, not of showing that this reading strategy does better justice to the text than another reading strategy."[11] The results do not vindicate this method of approaching the Gospels therefore.

Bauckham suggests then:

"That someone should write one of the most sophisticated and carefully composed of early Christian literary works – a Gospel – simply for the members of the community in which he was then living, with its specific, local issues in view, thus becomes a quite implausible hypothesis. Knowing that his work was bound very quickly to reach many other churches, the audience he would address would be the Christians in any and every church to which his Gospel might circulate. His intended readership would be, not a specific community or even a defined group of communities, however large, but an open and indefinite category: any and every Christian community of his time in which Greek was understood. ... Since a Gospel does not address a specific community, we cannot expect to learn much from it about the evangelist's own community".[12]

---

[7] See Burridge 1992; 1998, p113-145; Bauckham 1998b, p26-30.

[8] See Burridge 1998, p131-4.

[9] Bauckham 1998a, p5; see also Burridge 1998, p143-5.

[10] This includes, for example, the expulsion of Jewish communities from synagogues, which must have been a fairly general phenomenon across a range of Christian communities. But this does not mean that all indications of the circumstances of the readers in a Gospel must apply to the whole of the intended audience; see further Bauckham 1998b, p23-5, 46; Barton 1998, p194. Nor are we suggesting that a Gospel author was not influenced by the community (or communities) of which he was a part when he wrote his works, but because these works were written for a general audience we cannot reconstruct the particular community from which the Gospel was written.

[11] Bauckham 1998b, p22. For a critical discussion of the methodology involved in discerning "Gospel communities" from the Gospels see Barton 1998, p173-94. For a critique of the studies of "Gospel communities" from a theological perspective, see Watson 1998, p195-217.

[12] Bauckham 1998a, p3-4.

Thus, in my view, we should not read John's Gospel as a narrative about the community to which John belonged and cannot reconstruct the history and contemporary life of "the Johannine community" from John's Gospel. While there have been some reactions to Bauckham's work, and some details of his argument may be disputable, in my view none of these reactions have overturned Bauckham's case.[13] Accordingly, we will not use John's Gospel as evidence for the life and history of a community in Ephesus.

But can we not say that the community from which John the Elder wrote his Gospel had, for example, been expelled from the synagogue, and had some women leaders, two of the key areas in which studies of the Johannine community have developed their work?

It may well be the case that the Christian community in which John the Elder lived in Ephesus (and which is reflected in the Johannine Letters) *had been* expelled from the (or a) synagogue in Ephesus (or perhaps had never been part of it, if they arrived in Ephesus after 70CE, but was now experiencing hostility from it). But my point is that we cannot use the Gospel of John as *evidence* for this, since it is not written for one community (but potentially for all communities), and is not reflective of the experience of just one community. Everything taken to be reflective of "Christian community" in the Gospel cannot be said to apply to just this one community, and we have no way of knowing, when interpreting an "open" text like a Gospel, exactly which features of the text may apply to any particular community, including the author's own. Thus, passages like Jn 9:22 and 16:2, in my view, cannot be taken as autobiographical of the history of the community in which John the Elder lived. Rather, they reflect what I take to be widespread experiences of Christian communities in the period that the Gospel was written – expulsion from synagogues. Hence from the Gospel we cannot say whether this was actually a trauma that the community from which the author wrote had experienced. To use such passages to speak of the history of just one community (in Ephesus) is to read the Gospel as if it were a Letter.

Similarly, it may have been that there were women leaders in the Johannine community, although if this was the case we may ask (as we will ask in Chapter 11), why they are so invisible in 1-3 Jn? But again, that women feature prominently in the narratives of the Fourth Gospel does not *necessarily* mean they featured prominently in the community to which John belonged. They *may* have featured prominently in a number of places and so,

---

[13] See Esler 1998, p235-48 (and see the response by Bauckham 1998c, p249-53); Marcus 2000, p25-8; van Eck 2000, p973-1008; Sim 2001, p3-27; Stanton 2002, p56. Marcus (2000, p27-8) notes that we do know of works that were written for local addressees. But while writing something down does not necessarily imply absence from one's readers, Bauckham's point is that, given many features of early Christianity, it is unlikely that the audience for whom an Evangelist wrote was just his own community with whom he was present. In support of Bauckham see also Dunn 2000, p325; Hägerland 2003, p309-22.

in writing as he does of women disciples of Jesus, John might be reflecting a general feature of early Christianity (although if this was the case, we would expect women to feature more positively in other texts from the period of composition of the Gospel, which they generally do not). Since the Gospel is not (in my view) written for his own community, this trend (if such it was) might or might not be in evidence in the actual community from which he wrote his Gospel. Or it might be (and this seems more likely) that John himself is seeking to make a theological point to his general Christian audience about the importance of women in discipleship and ministry and so is resisting a widespread trend towards patriarchy that is very obvious in the period in which he wrote.

Thus (and this becomes significant in Part Three), in my view, we cannot draw on the Gospel in discussion of matters such as Jewish-Christian relations in Ephesus, or the question of women in leadership in the Ephesian community to which 1-3 Jn is written.

However, we will now argue that John's Gospel was written in Ephesus; this and other evidence will lead us to argue that the Johannine Letters, which are clearly closely connected with the Gospel, were also written in Ephesus. Since the Letters were clearly written to a specific group or groups they can be used as evidence for the life of a community in the city.

2. That John was written from Ephesus

The Johannine Letters are clearly able to be used as evidence for the life of a Christian community (made up of several house churches).[14] But do these letters belong in Ephesus? Since most scholars see a very strong connection between the Gospel of John and the Johannine Letters, most would locate the letters in the same place as the author of the Gospel; it is also likely that the Letters were written to a community resident in the same general location as the author, or in the case of 2-3 Jn, nearby. This holds even if one does not think the same person wrote all four documents, since even if they are produced by different people, they clearly come from the same "circle" or group of authors. Accordingly, in this section we will consider the evidence for the authorship and provenance of the Gospel. In the following section we will discuss the authorship of the Johannine Letters and argue that they come from the same locale as the Gospel.

Where was the Gospel of "John" written? Since authorship and place of origin are clearly related we will need to deal with both issues, although our emphasis will eventually be on the latter issue.

---

[14] For example, it is clear that 1 Jn 2:18-25 reflects the recent experience of the community to which 1 Jn is written.

Recent studies of the Fourth Gospel have made it clear that a complex process of composition stands behind the Gospel, and one that probably involved the author moving from one centre to another. Because of the reliable knowledge of Galilee and Jerusalem which is evident in the Fourth Gospel, it seems likely that the author originally came from somewhere in Palestine.[15] However, as Bauckham notes, "The only Church, so far as we know, which ever claimed to be the place of origin of the Fourth Gospel was Ephesus. This means that if any of the external evidence is of any value, the most reliable is likely to be that of writers who can witness to the local tradition of Ephesus and its neighbourhood in the second century."[16] Accordingly, following Bauckham, we will begin this discussion by looking at the evidence from Polycrates and Papias.

2.1 Polycrates, bishop of Ephesus

In the last decade of the second century CE, during the paschal controversy, Polycrates, bishop of Ephesus, wrote a letter to Victor of Rome. In the letter Polycrates defended the quartodeciman observance in Asia as supported by the highest authorities in local tradition.

"As for us, then, we keep the day without tampering with it, neither adding nor subtracting. For indeed in Asia great luminaries have fallen asleep, such as shall rise again on the day of the Lord's appearing, when he comes with glory from heaven to seek out all his saints: to wit, Philip, one of the twelve apostles, who has fallen asleep in Hierapolis, [as have] also his two daughters who grew old in virginity, and his other daughter who lived in the Holy Spirit and rests at Ephesus; and moreover, [there is] John too, he who leant back on the Lord's breast, who was a priest, wearing the sacerdotal plate (πέταλον), both martyr and teacher (μάρτυς καὶ διδάσκαλος). He has fallen asleep at Ephesus. Moreover, Polycarp too at Smyrna, both bishop and martyr; and Thraseas, both bishop and martyr, of Eumeneia, who has fallen asleep at Smyrna. And why need I mention Sagaris, bishop and martyr, who has fallen asleep at Laodicea? Or the blessed Papirius, or Melito the eunuch who in all things lived in the Holy Spirit, who lies at Sardis, awaiting the visitation from heaven, when he shall rise from the dead? These all observed the fourteenth day for the Pascha according to the Gospel, in no way deviating therefrom, but following the rule of faith. And moreover I also, Polycrates, the least of you all, [do] according to the tradition of my kinsmen, some of whom also I have followed closely. Seven of my kinsmen were bishops and I am the eighth. And my kinsmen always kept the day when the people put away the leaven. Therefore I for my part, brethren, who number sixty-five years in the Lord and have conversed with the brethren from all parts of the world and traversed the entire range of holy Scripture, am not affrighted by threats. For those better than I have said, We must obey God rather than men."[17]

---

[15] On the accurate knowledge of Palestine as it was before 70 CE, see Brown 1966, 1, pxlii-xliii.

[16] Bauckham 1993a, p28. See also Bruce 1977-78, p360.

[17] Quoted in Eusebius, HE 5.24.2-7; cf. 3.31.3; translation from Lawlor and Oulton 1927, p169.

It is necessary to discuss what Polycrates says in detail here since, as we will see, Polycrates provides significant evidence with respect to Ephesus. Although this evidence has often been noted in recent discussions of the authorship and provenance of the Fourth Gospel, its full significance has generally not been appreciated.[18]

Bauckham has studied the passage from Polycrates in detail and shows that on the following points it is very relevant to our inquiry. Firstly, there are a number of indications that Polycrates was dependent on local tradition here.

a) With regard to Philip's daughters, Polycrates is clearly not dependent on Acts 21:8-9, since he speaks of three daughters, not four.[19] It is more likely that he is dependent on Ephesian tradition, which is also suggested by the fact that he says one of the daughters was buried in Ephesus.

b) Polycrates calls Philip, who in Acts 21:8-9 is "Philip the evangelist", one of the twelve apostles. He thus seems to have identified Philip the apostle and Philip the evangelist as the same person. Bauckham notes that early Christian exegetes frequently assumed that two people mentioned in scripture who had the same name were the same person.[20] He suggests that the identification of the two Philips probably followed an exegetical tradition of the Ephesian church. With regard to Philip then we see a combination of local historical tradition and local exegetical tradition. Certainly, the note about Philip should not be seen as undermining the credibility of the whole passage.[21]

c) Polycrates notes that John "has fallen asleep at Ephesus". This must be based on local tradition; we will note that Polycrates ascribes the Fourth Gospel to this John, so the passage suggests that the tomb of the author of the Fourth Gospel was known at Ephesus.

Secondly, in speaking of John as "he who leant back on the Lord's breast", Polycrates is clearly dependent on John 13:25 or 21:20. Bauckham thinks the allusion is most likely to Jn 21:20, since there the beloved disciple is introduced for the last time, and then is referred to again in Jn 21:24, where he is identified as the author of the Gospel.[22] The phrase quoted by Polycrates

---

[18] See for example Brown 1966, plxxxix; Barrett 1978, p101-2; Culpepper 1994, p128. They all think the statement about "John" refers to John the son of Zebedee.

[19] Bauckham 1993a, p30. By contrast Proclus, a Montanist, knew the tradition associating Philip and his daughters with Hierapolis (as did Papias, see Eusebius HE 3.39.9), but he referred to four daughters, all of whom were prophets, thus showing his dependence on Acts 21:8-9 (see Eusebius, HE 3.31.4).

[20] Bauckham 1993a, p30-1; he notes that Eusebius (HE 3.31.2-5) also identified the two Philips. Another example is the identification of Mary Magdalene and Mary of Bethany by most early Christian writers.

[21] This is the view of Barrett 1978, p101 n1 and Culpepper 1994, p128.

[22] Note that Bauckham (1993a, p24-7) does not think the Fourth Gospel shows that the beloved disciple, who is portrayed as the author of the Gospel (Jn 21:24), is to be identified

from John's Gospel indicates the special intimacy with Jesus which qualified the beloved disciple to be the author of the Gospel. Bauckham notes that by means of the phrase "he who leant back on the Lord's breast", "Polycrates not only identifies John as the author of the Fourth Gospel, but also suggests the special value of the Fourth Gospel as deriving from a disciple who was especially close to the Lord."[23]

Thirdly, Polycrates goes on to speak of John as μάρτυς. This is probably not a reference to John as a martyr, since when Polycrates speaks of Thraseas, Sagaris and Polycarp as martyrs his order is ἐπίσκοπος καὶ μάρτυς, with μάρτυς appropriately last. However, John is called ἱερεὺς ... καὶ μάρτυς καὶ διδάσκαλος. If μάρτυς designated John as a martyr, then it is strange that μάρτυς comes before διδάσκαλος. Particularly in view of our previous point, it is much more likely that μάρτυς "alludes to his authorship of the Gospel, which in John 21:24 (cf. 19:35) is treated as equivalent to the beloved disciple's witness."[24]

Fourthly, Polycrates may stress the point that John wrote the Gospel because of the importance of the Fourth Gospel in the quartodeciman controversy. In this letter Polycrates refers to 14 Nisan as "the day when the people put away the leaven". He is thus identifying the day as the day of preparation for the Passover (cf. Jn 19:14),[25] when leaven had to be removed from the house before sunset. Thus, "the significance of observing 14 Nisan can only be, for Polycrates, that, according to the Johannine chronology, it was the day Christ was crucified. Thus his reference to observing the fourteenth day 'according to the Gospel' must be to John's Gospel as authoritative on this point."[26] This reinforces our view that in this passage Polycrates is referring to John as the author of the Fourth Gospel and also points to the importance of John's Gospel for Polycrates.

Fifthly, Polycrates writes that John "was a priest, wearing the sacredotal plate (ὃς ἐγενήθη ἱερεὺς τὸ πέταλον πεφορεκώς)". The πέταλον was a

---

with John the son of Zebedee. Rather, the beloved disciple is to be seen as a Jerusalem disciple. For a discussion of the identity of the Beloved Disciple see Charlesworth 1995, who argues that the Beloved Disciple was Thomas.

[23] Bauckham 1993a, p31.

[24] Bauckham 1993a, p32; he goes on to note that μάρτυς καὶ διδάσκαλος designates John as the author of the Gospel and the author of the Johannine letters respectively. Bauckham also notes that μάρτυς has often been taken to refer to Rev 1:2,9 and thus to John the seer as a witness to the Gospel. This would identify the author of the Fourth Gospel with the author of Revelation. But the explanation given in the text is more likely, particularly since it is the Fourth Gospel which is in view both before ("he who leant back on the Lord's breast") and after ("These all observed the fourteenth day for the Pascha according to the Gospel"; see below) this section. Consequently, we do not need to suppose that in Ephesus at this time John the Seer had been identified with John the author of the Fourth Gospel.

[25] Since the day began at sunset, Jews ate the Passover meal at the beginning of 15 Nisan.

[26] Bauckham 1993a, p33.

distinctive item of head-dress worn only by the high priest. That John is said to have worn the πέταλον, means that he was thought by Polycrates to have officiated as high priest in the temple.[27] This has generally been interpreted either metaphorically,[28] or historically. Bauckham proposes that the most satisfactory explanation of the phrase is that Polycrates, or Ephesian Church tradition, identified the John who had died in Ephesus with the John of Acts 4:6, where a John is said to be a member of the high-priestly family. This identification was made, "not because he [Polycrates] had any historical information to this effect, but as a piece of scriptural exegesis".[29] The tradition that John, who is also identified by Polycrates as the beloved disciple, was a high priest is thus exegetical.

Such an exegetical procedure is in keeping with the well-attested practice of early Christian exegetes of identifying two people mentioned in scripture who had the same name.[30] In the case of John, this identification would have been facilitated by Jn 18:15 which, when taken to refer to the beloved disciple, says that he was known to the high priest. One could also understand the inference from Acts 4:6 that this John must have himself been high priest at some time. According to Bauckham, "The motive for identifying John the beloved disciple with this John will have been - in addition to the general exegetical tendency already mentioned - the natural desire of the Ephesian Church to find their own John, the author of the Gospel they prized, mentioned somewhere else in the writings of the emergent New Testament canon."[31]

This identification is important with respect to the question of authorship of the Fourth Gospel and Ephesus. It shows that when the Ephesian church looked for its own John, whom they believed to be the author of the Fourth Gospel in other NT writings, they did not identify him with John the apostle, the son of Zebedee, but rather with an otherwise unknown John of Acts 4:6. That they did not identify him with John the apostle is made clear by the fact that John the son of Zebedee also appears in the narrative in Acts 4:13 as one of the disciples who is interrogated by Annas, Caiaphas, John and Alexander.

---

[27] See Bauckham 1993a, p33-40.

[28] That is, as a metaphorical way of referring to John's position of authority in the Church.

[29] Bauckham 1993a, p42. Bauckham notes that Polycrates quotes Acts 5:9 elsewhere, which supports the suggestion that Polycrates is exegeting Acts 4:6 here.

[30] Bauckham 1993a, p42; apart from the two Philips and two Marys mentioned earlier, he notes the identification of Zechariah, the father of John the Baptist with the Zechariah of Mt 23:35 in the *Protevangelium of James* 23-4. Prominent figures of the post-apostolic period were also identified with people of the same name who appear in the NT. Thus Clement of Rome was identified with the Clement of Phil 4:3 (see Eusebius HE 3.4.9). A number of other examples can be given.

[31] Bauckham 1993a, p43.

"The Ephesian Church's own tradition about their own John evidently made them quite sure that he could not be John the son of Zebedee and obliged them, even at the end of the second century, to resist this identification which was already proving irresistible elsewhere and seems to have become universal in the next century."[32] We note also that in the Polycrates' letter, although Philip, who is mentioned first, is called an apostle, "John" is not called an apostle, which also strongly suggests John the apostle is not in view here.[33]

What this shows which is of interest for us is the strength of the local Ephesian tradition that "John", who was not the son of Zebedee, was buried at Ephesus and had written the Fourth Gospel.[34] Even if it was Polycrates himself who made the identification of the author of the Fourth Gospel with the John of Acts 4:6,[35] that he did so shows that there was a strong local tradition that the "John" who had written the Gospel which was so important to the church of Ephesus in the quartodeciman controversy was buried in Ephesus, and was seen as an authority figure for the Ephesian church. Further, we have noted above other features of local Ephesian tradition in this passage from Polycrates.

Bauckham thus concludes: "The John to whom Polycrates ascribed the Fourth Gospel was a very definite person. His tomb was at Ephesus. Polycrates could have explained how he was related to him. He was not the son of Zebedee, one of the twelve, but he was a personal disciple of Jesus. He must be John the Elder, a disciple of the Lord, to whom Papias referred in the famous passage of his prologue (ap. Eusebius, *Hist. Eccl.* 3.39.4)."[36]

2.2 Papias

In the light of this reading of Polycrates, Bauckham re-examines the evidence from Papias. Firstly, we need to note what Papias, the bishop of Hierapolis, wrote about John the Elder. The passage which Eusebius quotes was probably written by Papias between 125 and 135 CE:[37]

"And I shall not hesitate to append to the interpretations all that I ever learnt well from the presbyters and remember well, for of their truth I am confident. For unlike most I did not

---

[32] Bauckham 1993a, p43-4.

[33] See also Hengel 1989, p7.

[34] We will also note below that the likelihood that John the Elder was the author of the Fourth Gospel means that we can avoid some of the problems associated with the suggestion that John the Son of Zebedee came to Ephesus and was the author of the Fourth Gospel.

[35] As Bauckham (1993a, p43) thinks is quite likely.

[36] Bauckham 1993a, p44.

[37] See Hengel 1989, p16; Culpepper (1994, p109) suggests 130; Barrett (1978, p105-6) suggests around 140.

rejoice in them who say much, but in them who teach the truth, nor in them who recount the commandments of others, but in them who repeated those given to the faith by the Lord and derived from the truth itself; but if anyone ever came who had followed the presbyters, I inquired into the words of the presbyters, what Andrew or Peter or Philip or Thomas or James or John or Matthew, or any other of the Lord's disciples had said, and what Aristion and the presbyter John, the Lord's disciples were saying. For I did not suppose that information from books would help me so much as the word of a living and surviving voice."[38]

This passage strongly suggests that Papias knew the Fourth Gospel, since he gives the first six disciples in an order which reflects John's Gospel.[39] It is also clear that Papias here speaks of two Johns – John the son of Zebedee, and another John, here called "the elder". Both groups are called "disciples of the Lord". Papias seems to be using the term "the elders" to refer to the generation of teachers who knew the apostles but outlived them.[40] They were the people "who were teaching in the churches in Asia in the late first century CE and whose traditions, which they had received from those who had been personal disciples of the Lord, Papias recorded in his work. At the time when he was collecting oral traditions, the only personal disciples of Jesus still alive were Aristion and John the Elder."[41] John and Aristion were also called

---

[38] Eusebius, HE 3.39.3-4.

[39] See Hengel 1989, p17-21; Bauckham 1993a, p44-5; cf. Koester 1995, p138, who does not consider this point. It reflects the sequence in Jn 1:35-51 and 21:2 and diverges from the lists in the Synoptics and Acts. For James and John in fifth and sixth place, compare Jn 21:2. Matthew, a non-Johannine disciple who is important for Papias as author of a Gospel is added in seventh place. Culpepper (1994, p112) thinks that Papias either followed John's Gospel "or that both John and Papias independently attest an Asian tradition of the list of disciples which diverged from the synoptic tradition's elevation of Peter." But the similarities with John strongly suggest Papias is following a written source.

[40] Bauckham (1993a, p60) discusses the meaning of the term "the Elder" in Papias. John was called "the elder" to distinguish him from John who was one of the twelve and also a "disciple of Jesus". Papias collected the traditions of the elders who had known disciples of the Lord who were no longer alive as well as the traditions of Aristion and John the Elder who were still alive. The most probable meaning of the term "elder" in Papias' statement, then, is that the elders are not the same people as Peter and Andrew and the other disciples listed. The elders are the senior Christian teachers in various cities of Asia at the time when Papias was collecting traditions. Papias, living in Hierapolis, did not normally have the opportunity to hear them himself, but when any of their followers visited Hierapolis "he inquired about the words of the elders, [that is] what [according to the elders] Andrew and Peter had said ..." As Bauckham (1993a, p60) notes: "This interpretation is much more obviously consistent with the statement Papias had made just before, that he himself had learnt from the elders ..., than is the interpretation which equates the elders with Andrew and Peter and the rest of the disciples of the Lord." See also Barrett 1978, p106-9; Bruce 1977-78, p348; Chapman 1911, p13-16.

[41] Bauckham 1993a, p60. Note that Papias writes that he would ask what Andrew or Peter, or the other disciples of the Lord *had said*, and "what Aristion and the presbyter John, the Lord's disciples *were saying*". It is clear then that at the time when Papias was collecting

"elders" because they were part of this wider group of late first century teachers and tradition-bearers, but in contrast to the other elders, they had been personal disciples of Jesus. This means that John the Elder was still alive when Papias was collecting oral traditions, which could be sometime between the 80s and 100.[42]

Papias here does not say anything about the Fourth Gospel. However, Bauckham argues convincingly that Papias said that John the Elder, the disciple of the Lord, wrote the Fourth Gospel in the context of his well-known remarks on the origin of the Gospels of Mark and Matthew.[43] Bauckham notes that Papias' comments on Mk and Mt have two interests in common. Firstly, both are concerned with the way these two Gospels are based on the testimony of an eyewitness, a concern which also comes through in HE 3.39.3-4 (quoted above). This is likely to have been a major concern in Papias' discussion of the Gospels. Secondly, the comments about both Mark and Matthew are concerned with order; it seems likely that Papias said neither Mark nor Matthew arranged the λογία of the Lord "in order". As Bauckham notes: "The only reason Papias could have had for arguing this point is that he knew another Gospel, also recording eyewitness testimony, which in his view did arrange the λογία of the Lord in the correct order. This must be John.[44] .... John's is the extant Gospel which differs most markedly in this respect from Matthew and Mark."[45] Further, Papias' prologue (given above, from HE 3.39.3-4) seems to indicate that he preferred the Johannine order, since, as we have noted, his list of seven disciples is a Johannine list. Bauckham thus suggests that Papias said "something quite significant about the Fourth Gospel to justify his preference for its order."[46] It is reasonable to suggest that Eusebius did not report this, at least in part because he did not like Papias' conclusion that the Johannine order was correct and the others unreliable in this respect.[47]

Bauckham then notes that if Papias said something about the origin of the Fourth Gospel which Eusebius omitted, we might expect to see some trace of it in other writers who knew Papias' work. Strong arguments can be put

---

oral traditions all other disciples of the Lord whose teaching could have been accessible to him were already dead, while Aristion and John the Elder were still alive.

[42] For the dates see Bauckham (1993a, p60 n102) who thinks it was the 80s, and Barrett (1978, p107-8), who argues for c. 100.

[43] Given in Eusebius HE 3.39.15-16.

[44] See also Hengel 1989, p157 n118; Wright 1913, p300.

[45] Bauckham 1993a, p50.

[46] Bauckham 1993a, p52.

[47] Bauckham 1993a, p52-3; Eusebius' contrasting solution to the problem is given in HE 3.24.5-16. See also Hengel (1989, p21) for suggestions of other things Eusebius omitted.

forward that the Muratorian Canon, probably of the late second century,[48] is closely dependent on Papias in the last paragraph of what it says about Jn.[49] This can be seen in the Canon's comment about the order of John.[50] Further, the likelihood that the Canon is borrowing from Papias is suggested by its quotation from 1 Jn 1:1,4 in support of the view that John was an eyewitness and so wrote "in order", since Eusebius (HE 3.39.17) notes Papias quotes from 1 Jn. We also note that the Canon almost certainly refers to the author of the Fourth Gospel as John the Elder, not John the son of Zebedee, since John is spoken of as "one of the disciples" in contrast to Andrew who is "one of the apostles".[51] We may suggest that in this the Muratorian Canon also follows Papias, since "one of the disciples" is the phrase Papias uses (in Eusebius HE 3.39.4) for all who had been personal disciples of Jesus (whether members of the 12, or others such as Aristion and John the Elder). In using it in contrast to "one of the apostles" the Canon is suggesting that John was not "one of the apostles" and so was John the Elder.[52]

So the Muratorian Canon seems to be dependent on Papias, and to portray John the Elder as the author of the Fourth Gospel. This suggests that Papias attributed the Gospel to John the Elder, the disciple of the Lord. We have also suggested that Papias quoted from 1 Jn (as Eusebius also says) in support of John being an eyewitness of the events described in the Gospel and that the overall purpose of what Papias wrote was that he preferred the chronological order of Jesus' ministry in John's Gospel since John's Gospel was "in order".

Bauckham concludes: "In Asia, the tradition from Papias early in the second century to Polycrates at its end was that this John, the beloved disciple and the author of the Gospel, was John the Elder, a disciple of the Lord but not one of the twelve, who had died in Ephesus. We know of no dissent from this tradition in Asia before the third century. It is not certain when the identification of this John of Ephesus with John the son of Zebedee was first

---

[48] See Bauckham 1993a, p53 n86, with references to discussions which support this disputed date.

[49] See Bauckham 1993a, p53-6. Note that in its account of the origin of the Fourth Gospel, the Muratorian Canon is probably an elaborated version of what Papias wrote. Bauckham (1993, p45 n68) notes that no weight can be given to the statement in the so-called "Anti-Marcionite prologue" that John dictated the Gospel to Papias. See also Culpepper 1994, p129-30.

[50] With regard to John's Gospel the Canon says: "Thus he professes himself not only an eyewitness and hearer but also a writer of all the miracles of the Lord in order." Translation from Grant 1946, p118.

[51] That the Muratorian Canon mentions Andrew, the first disciple of the Lord mentioned by Papias, again suggests the Canon is following Papias.

[52] Bauckham also supports this interpretation of the Muratorian Canon by looking at Irenaeus, Adv. Haer 2.22.5 and Clement of Alexandria (ap. Eusebius HE 6.14.7); see Bauckham 1993a, p57-63.

accepted in Asia, but it does not appear to have happened for more than a century after the writing of the Gospel."[53]

This is important for us because it suggests that Papias, writing perhaps between 125 and 135, thought John the Elder was the author of the Fourth Gospel and thus backs up the later tradition found in Polycrates, a tradition that directly locates John the Elder, the author of the Fourth Gospel, in Ephesus. Thus although the association between the Fourth Gospel and Ephesus is from 190 CE, the tradition that John the Elder wrote the Gospel goes back, we may suggest, to Papias. Since we do not have the statement by Papias which Bauckham reconstructs about John the Elder, we cannot say that Papias himself located John the Elder in Ephesus. But that Polycrates was using local tradition, and that some elements of this tradition can be traced back to Papias (notably the authorship of John the Elder) certainly adds weight to Polycrates' statement about the location of the Gospel being in Ephesus and suggests that that tradition significantly predates Polycrates. Further, since Papias was from Hierapolis, it seems likely that he possessed "Asian tradition" and it seems reasonable to suggest that he knew about John the Elder and his authorship of the Gospel (as we have been able to reconstruct that tradition) because John was reasonably close by. This then too supports Polycrates location of John in Ephesus. We also note that it seems likely that Papias quoted 1 Jn, a point to which we will return.

Before we proceed further we need to address a question which has been posed about the information from Papias. If "John the Elder" of whom Papias writes (according to Eusebius HE 3.39.3-4) was in Ephesus, then why does Papias, who lived in Hierapolis, say that he *asked* people who came to him about what "Aristion and the Elder John ... were saying". Why did he not go directly to Ephesus and speak to John himself?[54]

Indeed it is often argued from this passage that Papias had not heard "John" in person. This is in fact the conclusion that Eusebius (in HE 3.39.1) draws from Irenaeus Adv Haer 5.33.4 when he contradicts Irenaeus.[55] However, in Eusebius HE 3.39.7 we read: "Papias says that he was himself an actual hearer of Aristion and of John the elder. Therefore (γοῦν) he mentions them very often in his writings." Part of the issue here is how to translate γοῦν. Barrett translates it as "at least", and thus suggests Eusebius qualifies the statement that Papias claimed to be a hearer of John the Elder, by saying "At least, he [Papias] mentions them very often in his writing". Barrett suggests: "This is no proof at all of personal acquaintance, as Eusebius was

---

[53] Bauckham 1993a, p65.

[54] Barrett (1978, p108-9) raises this objection.

[55] In HE 3.39.1 Eusebius clearly thinks the "John" referred to by Irenaeus is the apostle, for he goes on to write in HE 3.39.2: "Yet Papias ... makes plain that he had in no way been a hearer and eyewitness of the sacred Apostle."

too honest not to admit."[56] However, Hengel notes "We cannot infer from the particle *goun* that Eusebius is exaggerating in his first statement about John's audience and that Papias did not hear John at all. In later Greek the particle often has no restrictive significance but is merely used instead of *oun*."[57]

It seems most likely that in HE 3.39.7 Eusebius is referring to a distinct statement made by Papias, in which he said he had himself heard Aristion and John.[58] Eusebius goes on to refer to the fact that Papias in his work frequently quoted Aristion and John, which suggested that his claim to have heard them in person was no idle exaggeration.[59] This makes sense of the whole section in Eusebius and so we can suggest that HE 3.39.7 is good evidence that Papias had met John the Elder.[60] It seems likely then that Papias had two sources of information concerning Aristion and John: first hand information, since he knew them personally (HE 3.39.7) and they were still alive when he was collecting his traditions (HE 3.39.4), and secondary sources of information from followers of Aristion and John who passed through Hierapolis (HE 3.39.4).[61]

Accordingly, we can suggest that when Papias says that he asks travelling Christians what "Aristion and John the elder, disciples of the Lord, say", this does not mean that he himself has never heard these two "elders". Rather,

---

[56] Barrett 1978, p109.

[57] Hengel 1989, p22. Further a number of later authors (given in Hengel 1989, p159 n122) agree that Papias heard John.

[58] In HE 3.39.7, Eusebius cannot be referring to what Papias said in the section he has just quoted (HE 3.39.3-4), since there Papias does not claim to have heard Aristion and John. As Chapman (1911, p30) noted: "We must attribute great denseness to the acute historian [Eusebius], if we suppose that he considered the citation by Papias of many traditions of these two 'disciples of the Lord' [that he received from others] as equivalent to a statement that Papias had heard these words from their own lips, and not from the visitors to Hierapolis."

[59] Chapman (1911, p30) suggests the following paraphrase of Eusebius in HE 3.39.7: "But of Aristion and John the Presbyter he says he was a personal hearer, - in fact he seems to show that he really knew them well by the frequency with which he mentions them by name and sets down their traditions in his book."

[60] Irenaeus seems to refer to the same section in Papias' writings. In Adv. Haer. 5.33.4. he writes "And these things are borne witness to in writing by Papias, the hearer of John, and a companion of Polycarp." This is quoted by Eusebius who gives the Greek as "ὁ Ἰωάννου μὲν ἀκουστής" (HE 3.39.1). Eusebius in his Chronicle says "αὐτήκοον ἑαυτόν φησι γενέσθαι" (quoted by Chapman, 1911, p31). Eusebius is not citing Irenaeus in the Chronicle, where he does not say that Papias made any statements to this effect; see Chapman 1911, p32. Chapman (1911, p32) notes: "The likeness of αὐτήκοον to ἀκουστής suggests that both are echoing the same assertion of Papias, who will not have spoken of 'knowing' or 'seeing' or 'resorting to' or 'meeting', but of 'hearing' the last survivors of the Lord's disciples."

[61] Chapman 1911, p30-1. He notes a similar situation existed with the elders: Papias knew the elders personally (HE 3.39.3) and also asked their followers who came to Hierapolis about the elders' words (HE 3.39.4).

having heard them himself in the past, he is now keen to hear from contemporary travellers what they are currently saying.[62]

That Papias had met John the Elder adds credence to what Bauckham has reconstructed with regard to what Papias says about John's authorship of the Fourth Gospel. Further, it supports our view that John was in Ephesus, near enough to Hierapolis for Papias to have heard him in person on occasion when he was collecting his tradition. [63] It is certainly compatible with other evidence that he was at Ephesus.[64]

In conclusion then, we suggest that Papias thought John the Elder was the author of the Fourth Gospel; this supports the later tradition found in Polycrates, a tradition that directly locates John the Elder, who is seen as the author of the Fourth Gospel, in Ephesus. That Polycrates was using local tradition, and that some elements of this tradition can be traced back to Papias adds weight to Polycrates' statement about the location of the Gospel being in Ephesus and suggests that that tradition significantly predates Polycrates. But even if one disputes the claim that John the Elder wrote the Fourth Gospel, what we have shown is that the evidence of Polycrates about the Gospel's location in Ephesus needs to be taken very seriously. This is strong evidence, going back to tradition, that John's Gospel is to be located in Ephesus. But is there any other support for the Ephesian provenance of the Gospel and thus of the letters? We will turn now to Irenaeus and then to the Acts of John.

2.3 Irenaeus

Irenaeus (ca. 130-200) was born in Asia Minor but migrated to the West and became bishop of Lyon in 177 CE. Around 185 he wrote *Against Heresies*, in which he sought to refute Marcion, the Gnostics, the Montanists and probably Gaius. He was also a great champion of the Fourth Gospel, who claimed that the Gospel was written in Ephesus and reported that "John" lived in Ephesus

---

[62] Chapman (1911, p31) suggests that since Papias could not hear all the interesting sayings of Aristion and John with his own ears, he still wanted to learn about their sayings from visitors to Hierapolis as well.

[63] Bauckham 1993a, p44.

[64] Eusebius (HE 3.39.2) clearly interprets Irenaeus' statement that Papias was a "hearer of John" to refer to John the Apostle, and so points out that Papias did not say this. This does not mean that Eusebius is contradicting our interpretation of Papias, but rather Eusebius is showing that in his opinion, Aristion and John the Elder were not Apostles, which is what Eusebius goes on to say in any case. Further, (as we will argue below) it is likely that Irenaeus is actually referring to John the Elder, since this is clearly the person that Papias had in view in the passage referred to in HE 3.39.7, and Irenaeus seems to be referring to this same passage. As we will note, Bauckham (1993a, p67-9) has argued that Irenaeus regards John the Elder as the author of the Fourth Gospel, not John the Apostle. Alternatively, in HE 3.39.1 Eusebius may simply be commenting on what Papias says in the passage he has just quoted – where Papias does not say he heard John the Elder himself.

to an old age. We have argued that, prior to Irenaeus, Papias held that John the Elder was the author of the Fourth Gospel, and just after Irenaeus wrote *Against Heresies,* Polycrates held the same view on authorship and adds that John was in Ephesus. Irenaeus is thus the first writer to claim that John's Gospel was written in Ephesus. What do we make of Irenaeus' evidence?

It is difficult to know whether Irenaeus refers to John the son of Zebedee or John the Elder as author of the Fourth Gospel, although the latter seems most likely. It is clear that Irenaeus knew of the person "John" from Papias' writings,[65] and from Asian tradition he learned as a young man in Smyrna (Eusebius, HE 5.20.6; 5.24.16; Adv Haer 3.3.4). Irenaeus refers to "John", whom he thinks was the author of all the Johannine writings including Revelation,[66] as "the disciple of the Lord", or "disciple" sixteen times, and never as "John the apostle".[67] By contrast, for Irenaeus, Paul is "Paul the apostle" or just "the apostle". Bauckham suggest that "John the disciple of the Lord" was traditional terminology in Asia, and that Irenaeus is here reflecting his earlier years in Smryna. We have seen that the phrase "the disciple of the Lord" could apply to the twelve as well as to others; Papias uses it in its most inclusive sense. Given the emphasis on eyewitness in Irenaeus (as found for example in Eusebius HE, 5.20.6, the letter to Florinus given below), the phrase "the disciple of the Lord" is more significant than the term "apostle", since Paul was "*the* apostle", but not an eyewitness. But Irenaeus only uses the term "the disciple of the Lord" of an individual in connection with John.[68] All of this is compatible with Irenaeus thinking of "John" the author of the Fourth Gospel as John the Elder.

However, Irenaeus does call the author of the Fourth Gospel "the apostle".[69] But we can explain these passages as a reflection of Irenaeus' convictions about apostolicity in the battle against Gnostics. For Irenaeus "apostle" means one who is a reliable and has been authorised by Christ, in contrast to the secret tradition claimed by the Gnostics. As Bauckham notes: "It is understandable that Irenaeus should assimilate to this concept of apostolicity his own favourite evangelist and the most important source of eyewitness tradition from the ministry of Jesus in his native Asia. But since Irenaeus can treat the seventy as 'other apostles', in addition to the twelve (*Haer.* 2.21.1), there is no need to suppose he included the Fourth Evangelist

---

[65] See Adv Haer 5.33.4.

[66] Adv Haer 1.16.3; 3.16.5; 3.16.8; 4.20.11; 4.30.4; see also Hengel 1989, p3, 139 n10.

[67] Bauckham 1993a, p67. For the statistics see Burney 1922, p138-9.

[68] Bauckham 1993a, p68.

[69] Note Adv Haer 1.9.2-3; twice he puts John alongside "the other apostles" (in Adv Haer 2.22.5 (where he also calls John "the disciple of the Lord") and in his Letter to Victor, in Eusebius HE 5.24.16); and in Adv Haer 3.3.4 includes John with the apostles. See also Burney 1922, p139-40, who notes that John is never simply called "John the Apostle".

among the twelve."[70] Thus, we may suggest that Irenaeus calls "John" "the apostle", because of his wider context, but it does not mean he has abandoned his view that John is first and foremost "the disciple of the Lord" and thus Papias' John the Elder. To quote Bauckham again on Irenaeus: "He himself valued the Asian tradition too highly to identify John of Ephesus with John the son of Zebedee, but it is understandable that others, influenced by the same concept of apostolicity, should have welcomed the opportunity to do so."[71]

So it is likely that Irenaeus confirms the suggestion that John the Elder is the author of the Fourth Gospel. This would reinforce the tradition about authorship found in Polycrates and that we have sought to reconstruct from Papias, which, in the case of Polycrates also involved John the Elder being located in Ephesus.

However, even if Irenaeus does think John the son of Zebedee was the author of the Gospel (which seems much less likely than that he thought John the Elder was the author), he still makes the connection between the Gospel and Ephesus clear. We note the following passages.

Firstly, in Adv Haer 3.1.1 (=HE 5.8.4) Irenaeus says that John wrote his Gospel after Matthew, Mark and Luke. He writes: "Afterwards, John, the disciple of the Lord, who also had leaned upon His breast, did himself publish a Gospel during his residence at Ephesus in Asia." In this passage Irenaeus discusses the authorship of each of the Gospels in turn. It is significant that while he implies that Mk was written in Rome,[72] he does not say where Mt and Luke were written. Thus, his comment that John wrote in Ephesus is not something he has created in order to be able to locate each Gospel in a certain place. It is much more likely that it goes back to local Asian tradition. It is also clear from this passage that Irenaeus identifies the author of the Fourth Gospel with the Beloved Disciple; we have argued that in calling John "the disciple of the Lord" he is referring to John the Elder.[73] But it is most significant for our purposes that Irenaeus claims "John" wrote a Gospel while living in Ephesus.

Secondly, in Adv Haer 3.3.4 (=HE 4.14.3-8) Irenaeus writes:

"And Polycarp also was not only instructed by apostles, and conversed with many who had seen the Lord, but was also appointed bishop by apostles in Asia in the church in Smyrna. We

---

[70] Bauckham 1993a, p68.

[71] Bauckham 1993a, p68-9. This is one factor that explains the widespread attribution of the Gospel to John the Son of Zebedee after Irenaeus.

[72] Adv Haer 3.1.1. reads: "Matthew also issued a written Gospel among the Hebrews in their own dialect, while Peter and Paul were preaching at Rome, and laying the foundations of the Church. After their departure, Mark, the disciple and interpreter of Peter, did also hand down to us in writing what had been preached by Peter."

[73] Culpepper (1994, p124) thinks Irenaeus identifies John here with John the Apostle.

also saw him in our childhood, for he lived a long time and in extreme old age passed from life, a splendid and glorious martyr. He constantly taught those things which he had learnt from the apostles, which also are the tradition of the church, which alone are true. To these facts all the churches in Asia bear witness, and the present successors of Polycarp, and he is a far more trustworthy and reliable witness of the truth than Valentinus and Marcion and the others who hold wrong opinions. ... There are also those who heard from him that John, the disciple of the Lord, going to bathe at Ephesus, and perceiving Cerinthus within, rushed out of the bath-house without bathing, exclaiming, 'Let us fly, lest even the bath-house fall down, because Cerinthus, the enemy of the truth, is within.' ... Then again, the Church in Ephesus, founded by Paul, and having John remaining among them permanently until the times of Trajan, is a true witness of the tradition of the apostles."

Here again is the connection between John (again called "the disciple of the Lord") and Ephesus, although a written Gospel is not mentioned. Irenaeus also notes that he had known Polycarp; this suggests that the tradition about John and Ephesus may have come to Irenaeus from Polycarp, although he suggests that the story about Cerinthus has come from Polycarp to Irenaeus via particular people who heard this actual story ("those who heard from him"). That Irenaeus' source about John (and perhaps John's Ephesian connection) may have been Polycarp is also suggested by a letter Irenaeus wrote to a friend, Florinus, in which Irenaeus referred to being taught by Polycarp (d. c.155), and to Polycarp's knowledge of John. Irenaeus recalled:

"For while I was still a boy I knew you in lower Asia in Polycarp's house when you were a man of rank in the royal hall and endeavoring to stand well with him. I remember the events of those days more clearly than those which happened recently, for what we learn as children grows up with the soul and is united to it, so that I can speak even of the place in which the blessed Polycarp sat and disputed, how he came in and went out, the character of his life, the appearance of his body, the discourses which he made to the people, how he reported his intercourse with John and with the others who had seen the Lord, how he remembered their words, and what were the things concerning the Lord which he had heard from them, and about their miracles and about their teaching and how Polycarp had received from the eyewitnesses of the word of life, and reported all things in agreement with the Scriptures. I listened eagerly even then to these things through the mercy of God which was given me, and made notes of them, not on paper but in my heart."[74]

Here Irenaeus recalls the experience both he and Florinus had of sitting at the feet of Polycarp. The "John" of whom Irenaeus here says Polycarp spoke is undoubtedly the same John that he referred to in Adv Haer 3.3.4 as "the disciple of the Lord". As Culpepper notes "Since he appeals to Florinus' memory of their shared experience, it is most unlikely that Irenaeus would have fabricated any of this. Presumably, Florinus' memory was as clear as Irenaeus'."[75]

---

[74] Quoted in Eusebius, HE 5.20.5-7.
[75] Culpepper 1994, p126.

We see then that Irenaeus claims that Polycarp had direct contact with "John",[76] probably John the Elder, a tradition that Hengel argues is credible;[77] Irenaeus also claims that he himself had had contact with Polycarp. In the first and second of the three passages quoted above, Irenaeus locates John in Ephesus, and in the first passage says he has written a Gospel. We have noted that Irenaeus' source of information seems to have been Polycarp, although we will suggest he has other information too.

However, Irenaeus' accuracy on these matters has been questioned. Irenaeus claims elsewhere (Adv Haer 5.33.3) that Papias had reported that John had passed on a particular saying of Jesus. The saying is clearly spurious, but was accepted by Irenaeus on the authority of Papias, who had attributed it to John. In reporting this saying, Irenaeus writes: "All these things are borne witness to in writing by Papias, the hearer of John, and a companion of Polycarp, in his fourth book".[78] Eusebius quotes what Irenaeus writes, but then says "So says Irenaeus. Yet Papias himself, according to the preface of his treatise, makes plain that he had in no way been a hearer and eyewitness of the sacred apostles, but teaches that he had received the articles of the faith from those who had known them."[79] Eusebius then quotes the famous statement from Papias which mentions two Johns that we have discussed above.[80] As Culpepper notes "While Irenaeus does not claim to have had direct contact with Papias, as he had with Polycarp, his acceptance of a spurious tradition on the basis of Papias's contact with the apostle raises the question of whether his understanding of Polycarp's relationship with the apostle is similarly distorted."[81]

We should underline the point that Irenaeus does not say he had direct contact with Papias, and perhaps we can understand his willingness to accept a spurious saying of Jesus; many other writers of the period also accepted sayings of Jesus which we now know were spurious. By contrast, Irenaeus *does* claim to have had direct contact with Polycarp. Since Irenaeus writes in his Letter to Florinus about very detailed memories that Irenaeus and Florinus

---

[76] Note also Eusebius HE 5.24.16: "For neither could Anicetus persuade Polycarp not to observe what he had always observed with John the disciple of our Lord ..."

[77] Hengel (1989, p15) notes that Polycarp's martyrdom occurred between 156/7and 166/7 when he was very old, so he may have been baptized as a child between 70 and 80 and so could have known an aged John for some years.

[78] Adv Haer 5.33.4.

[79] Eusebius HE 3.39.2.

[80]Eusebius HE 3.39.3-4. We have noted above that Eusebius clearly interprets Irenaeus' statement that Papias was a "hearer of John" to refer to John the Apostle, and so points out that Papias did not say this. It is more likely, however that Papias meant he was a hearer of "John the presbyter" who was living in Papias' day.

[81] Culpepper 1994, p126; see also Barrett 1978, p105. Note, that when Culpepper speaks of "the apostle" I would claim the reference is to John the Elder.

shared of their time of instruction with Polycarp, we have already noted that Irenaeus is very unlikely to have created what he writes about his direct contact with Polycarp and that one thing Polycarp said concerned Polycarp's discussions with John. Therefore, we can reasonably suggest that Irenaeus' source for claiming that John was in Ephesus and that John wrote the Fourth Gospel, was Polycarp, and that Irenaeus recalled what Polycarp said correctly.

Further, since Irenaeus grew up in Smyrna, and so quite close to Ephesus, he may also be reliant on traditions from other sources which he himself encountered while he lived there. His sole source then may not have been Polycarp. We also note Bruce's comment that Irenaeus "nowhere undertakes to prove that John the apostle lived in Asia: he refers to his residence incidentally, as something which was common knowledge."[82] This again suggests Irenaeus was dependent on an established tradition here.[83]

We note however that Polycarp does not mention John in his *Letter to the Philippians*. Although he quotes 1 John, he says nothing about John and shows no knowledge of John's Gospel.[84] However, Polycarp's letter is brief, and his two references to Paul are in the context of allusions to Paul's letter to the Philippians; of course John did not write to Philippi.

We can draw some concluding remarks from this discussion. Firstly, we have suggested that Irenaeus provides further evidence for the authorship of the Fourth Gospel by John the Elder, which was the view of Polycrates and which we have suggested was also the view held by Papias. But what is more significant for our overall study is that Irenaeus, like Polycrates, clearly locates the Gospel in Ephesus. We have argued that it is reasonable to suggest that Polycarp was the basis for this tradition found in Irenaeus and so we should take seriously Irenaeus' statement that the Fourth Gospel was written

---

[82] Bruce 1977-78, p360. Note Bruce thinks that Irenaeus refers to John the Apostle.

[83] Note that a strong case can be made that Irenaeus knew Papias' work; see Bauckham 1993a, p58-62; Chapman 1911, p16. We have already noted Irenaeus, Adv Haer 5.33.4: "And these things are borne witness to in writing by Papias, the hearer of John, and a companion of Polycarp, in his fourth book". Further, in Irenaeus, Adv Haer 2.22.5 after a discussion about the length of Jesus' ministry, we read "... as the Gospel and all the elders testify; those who were conversant in Asia with John, the disciple of the Lord, [affirming] that John conveyed to them that information. And he remained among them up to the times of Trajan. Some of them, moreover, saw not only John, but the other apostles also, and heard the very same account from them, and bear testimony as to the [validity of] the statement." (See also Eusebius, HE 3.23.3.) Irenaeus may here be thinking of Papias (and others) when he speaks of "those who were conversant in Asia with John"; see Culpepper 1994, p124. Although we do not know what Papias said about John, we have argued above that it included that John the Elder was the author of the Fourth Gospel; Papias may well have said other things that backed up what Irenaeus had heard from Polycarp.

[84] See Barrett 1978, p105; Culpepper 1994, p126-7. As we will note, Polycarp's letter cites 1 Jn 4:2-3 and 2 Jn 7, but says nothing about the author. The later *Life of Polycarp* makes no allusion to John either, but this is an argument from silence.

in Ephesus. We have suggested that Irenaeus may well have had additional sources too.

Secondly, we have suggested that Polycarp of Smyrna knew John. This suggests that John lived nearby, which is compatible with Ephesus being John's home.

Thirdly, given that we have argued that Irenaeus writes of John the Elder, the other source that locates John the Elder in Ephesus is Polycrates. We do not know that Polycrates was directly dependent on Irenaeus; this seems very unlikely given that they were writing at very similar times, but quite some distance apart. So we can suggest that Polycrates and Irenaeus probably independently bear witness to the "Asian tradition" that the location of John (the Elder) and thus the Fourth Gospel, was Ephesus.

Finally, we have suggested that Irenaeus saw John the Elder as the author of the Fourth Gospel. However, if, in fact, Irenaeus thought John the son of Zebedee was the author of Fourth Gospel then it may be that on this matter he is quite independent of the Papias-Polycrates tradition, and so of what we could call the "Asian tradition". In this case, we would have two different but contemporary traditions of authorship, but it is notable that both traditions would locate the different Johns in Ephesus. However, if Irenaeus does think that John the son of Zebedee is the author of the Gospel (we think it is unlikely that this is how Irenaeus is to be understood), it may be that he has deduced this from Papias' lost comment on the matter, and so has misunderstood Papias.

2.4 The Acts of John

The association of a "John" with Ephesus is attested by the Acts of John, which locate John, who is clearly regarded as the Apostle and son of Zebedee, in Ephesus. Understandably, the work does not mention that John wrote a Gospel. We will show that, even though the Acts of John concern a different "John" from the person we think wrote the Gospel, they provide further evidence for the *location* of the Gospel in Ephesus.

The date of composition of the Acts of John is debated, but a number of scholars have recently argued for the mid second century as the most likely. Since the author draws on the Synoptic tradition, John's Gospel and Acts,[85] this provides a *terminus a quo*. Further, Lalleman suggests that there are similarities between the docetic Christology of the Acts of John and the Christology combatted by 1 Jn and Ignatius,[86] and opts for a date of 125-150

---

[85] See Lalleman 1998, p69-134.
[86] Lalleman 1998, p270.

CE.[87] Perhaps 150 CE remains most likely, although clearly it could be slightly earlier.

The provenance of the Acts of John is also debated. Many scholars have accepted an Egyptian provenance, and a few have argued for Syria.[88] However, Lalleman has recently argued against these possibilities and for an Asia Minor provenance. He notes that one of the key arguments against Asia Minor is that some have thought that the author does not know the city of Ephesus, particularly because the destruction of the temple of Artemis is recounted in Acts of John 38-42 when the temple was actually sacked, but not destroyed, in 262 CE. But it is clearly not impossible for an Ephesian author to have written this story in the second century, and Lalleman suggests someone from elsewhere in Asia would "have less scruples about doing so".[89] He suggests that other arguments in favour of a provenance in Asia include the prominence of women in Asia and in the Acts of John,[90] and recent discussions which show that the author had some knowledge of the city of Ephesus.[91] Lalleman goes on to suggest that the author is not from Ephesus

---

[87] See the review in Lalleman 1998, p268-70. Junod and Kaestli (1983, p694-700) conclude it was written between 150-200 CE; their view is accepted by Culpepper 1994, p188. Bauckham (1993a, p66) favours "around the middle of the century". Elliott (1993, p306) notes it is normally dated to the "late second-century" but some favour an earlier date. Pervo (1992, p48 n 7) favours a date of 150-200. Bremmer (1995b, p55) notes the prominence of older women and widows in the Acts of John and writes: "The special interest in these socially marginal categories seems to fit the second century better than the third, when Christianity was already growing explosively and making strong inroads into the higher layers of Greco-Roman society." Lalleman (1995, p117-18) on the basis of the motif of polymorphy in the Acts of John and the Apocryphon of John, suggests that the Apocryphon of John is dependent on the Acts of John, and that the Acts of John are early, specifically (p118), "The oldest form of the *ApoJ* was known to Irenaeus and thus predates his writings (+ or – 180); consequently, the *AJ* must be older still."

[88] See the discussion in Lalleman 1998, p256-61. He evaluates the arguments of Junod and Kaestli 1983, p692-4. The strongest argument for Egypt remains that the Acts of John use the rare word δικρόσσιον (71:1-2; 74:3; 80:3; 111:12) for a piece of clothing. However, Lalleman (1998, p258) shows that the Coptic translation of the Acts uses a periphrasis to render the word, which makes it unlikely that it is a specifically Egyptian piece of clothing; cf. Bremmer 1995b, p55-6. But it remains the fact that δικρόσσιον is only attested in Egypt.

[89] Lalleman 1998, p262.

[90] See Trebilco 1991, p104-126; van Bremen 1996; van Tilborg 1996, p154-64; Acts of John 30-6.

[91] See Engelmann 1994, p297-302; Lalleman 1998, p263-4. They argue that the Acts of John 38, 43 reveal accurate knowledge of Ephesian festivals, including the belief that Artemis was born in Ephesus and so her birthday was celebrated in the city, that we know Ephesians wore white at the festival of Artemis (IvEph 27, line 442; AJ 38), and that saying that John "goes up" to the temple (AJ 38) is understandable since this can mean "go upstream" (which is geographically correct) rather than "go uphill" (which is incorrect, since the temple is in a low lying area). Bremmer (1995b, p51 n40) regards Engelmann's work as "not convincing", but does not elaborate.

(since he thinks an Ephesian would not describe the destruction of the temple of Artemis in the mid-second century), and argues tentatively for Smyrna, since John receives a much more favourable welcome in Smyrna than he does in Ephesus.[92]

What do we conclude with regard to provenance then? It does seem likely that the author had a reasonable knowledge of Ephesus but given that the author could have travelled to the city from his own home, arguments from his knowledge of the city are not definitive. Thus, either Egypt or Asia Minor remain likely places of composition.

But in either case, the Acts of John are helpful evidence for us. For it is clear that the Acts of John disagree with the authors we have discussed thus far about which "John" featured in Ephesus, and thus about authorship of the Gospel of John. This different tradition in the Acts of John then adds weight to our view that the Fourth Gospel was indeed written in Ephesus. We have two possible explanations here. Firstly, it could be that we have two different and independent traditions (independent since they imply different authors for the Gospel), but traditions which *in both cases locate the author in Ephesus*.[93] This would mean that we have double attestation as far as location is concerned. For we have argued that Polycrates believed John the Elder wrote the Gospel in Ephesus, and that Papias also claimed John the Elder was the author, which strengthens this tradition. We have suggested that Irenaeus also saw John the Elder as the author of the Gospel, and that he definitely locates the Gospel in Ephesus, thus providing additional evidence for this Asia Minor tradition about John the Elder in Ephesus. The independence of this Papias-Polycrates-Irenaeus line of tradition and the Acts of John would give us double attestation with regard to the John-Ephesus link (with a different "John" in each case), and this would strongly reinforce our view that Ephesus is the home of the Fourth Gospel.

Alternatively, it could be that the tradition behind the Acts of John misunderstood the Papias-Polycrates-Irenaeus line of tradition and so spoke of John the Apostle. But this misunderstanding would probably pre-date 150 (the most likely date of the Acts), and so would strengthen the evidence for the existence of the Papias-Polycrates-Irenaeus line of tradition.

In either case, the Acts of John provide further evidence which locates "John" (and hence, we will argue, the Johannine Letters), in Ephesus.

We can also note here that Bauckham suggests the view that John the son of Zebedee was the author of the Fourth Gospel came first of all from Egypt. This comes from the Acts of John (if they are from Egypt), but also from the

---

[92] See Acts of John 18-19 (Ephesus) and 55.2, 56.2 (Smyrna); Lalleman (1998, p265-6) also draws on the newly discovered *Fragments on Polycarp*.

[93] Lalleman (1998, p270) notes the author of the Acts of John "presupposes a tradition concerning the activity of John in and around Ephesos."

Epistle of the Apostles (similarly from Egypt and to be dated around the middle of the second century), and from Valentinian teachers of the second half of the century.[94] So it seems likely that there was an Egyptian tradition which identified the author of Fourth Gospel with the son of Zebedee.[95] That the Fourth Gospel was the work of this John seems to have spread through the churches from the late second century because of the influence of the Acts of John, Clement of Alexandria and others in the Egyptian tradition.[96] This explains why the tradition which we have argued comes from Papias, Polycrates and Irenaeus that John the Elder was the author of the Fourth Gospel did not win the day. Particularly as the issue of apostolicity became more important in the battle with Gnostics and others, the tradition that "John" was John the son of Zebedee won out. But what is most significant for us is that all the evidence locates "John" in Ephesus.

2.5 The use of John's Gospel in Asia Minor

At the very least, the evidence for the use of John's Gospel in Asia Minor is compatible with an Ephesian provenance for the Gospel. Ignatius does not mention John with regard to Ephesus, but in Chapter 14 I will argue that Ignatius' silence about John does not undermine the view that Ephesus was the home of the Johannine tradition. Further, we have noted above that in the passage quoted by Eusebius in HE 3.39.3-4, Papias of Hierapolis gives the first six disciples in an order which reflects John's Gospel, which strongly suggests that Papias knew the Fourth Gospel. Although it is debated whether Justin Martyr knows John's Gospel,[97] and we do know that the Gospel was used outside Asia from the middle of the second century,[98] its use in Asia is noteworthy. Hengel comments:

"This special significance of the Johannine Corpus (including the Apocalypse) for theology in Asia Minor becomes especially visible in the paschal dispute and the Montanist movement: the typology of the passover lamb and the chronology of the passion in the Fourth Gospel support the Quartodeciman custom of the paschal feast as practised in Asia Minor; the new prophetic movement starting from Montanus and his prophetesses could hardly have come into being without the link between the Gospel and the Apocalypse; ... In the Montanist prophecy the Paraclete promised in the Farewell Discourses spoke to believers, and according to Maximilla the heavenly Jerusalem of Apocalypse 21 was to descend in Pepuza. However,

---

[94] See Bauckham 1993a, p65-6.

[95] Probably the Gospel came to Egypt with some oral information, perhaps concerning "John", and this led to the Fourth Gospel being related in Egypt to the only John who was one of the twelve.

[96] See Bauckham 1993a, p67.

[97] Hengel (1989, p12-14) argues strongly that Justin knows and uses the Fourth Gospel; cf. Culpepper 1994, p112-14.

[98] See Culpepper 1994, p123.

J.J. Gunther is surely misleading in stating that 'the creation of a Johannine Asian myth started with Montanism'. This new prophetic movement, beginning about 157 (?), already presupposed it."[99]

Thus, we see there is considerable evidence for the impact of John's Gospel in Asia Minor in the mid-second century. Although this, together with the use of the Gospel by Papias, does not require an Ephesian provenance for the Gospel, if there had been no discernible influence of the Gospel in Asia Minor in this period, then this would question an Ephesian provenance.

2.6 'Reading John in Ephesus' by van Tilborg

While in his recent book *Reading John in Ephesus* Van Tilborg has not sought to prove that John's Gospel was actually written in Ephesus, he does seek to demonstrate how many features of the Gospel can be illuminated against the context of what we know of life in first century Ephesus from inscriptions and other sources.[100] Thus, at the least, van Tilborg shows that John *could* have been written in Ephesus, although he does not show, as it cannot be shown, that John's Gospel can *only* be interpreted in the context of Ephesian life. But his work is one more piece of evidence which makes an Ephesian provenance for the Gospel likely.[101]

2.7 Internal Evidence

Much of the internal evidence often cited in favour of a particular location for John's Gospel is dependent on reading the history of the "Johannine community" from the Gospel,[102] a procedure which we have rejected. In my view, the only significant internal evidence for the provenance of the Gospel is the similarity between the Fourth Gospel and Revelation, which suggests that they are related in some way, even if the connection is not particularly

---

[99] Hengel 1989, p5. See also Hartog (2002, p188, quoting Farmer and Farkasfalvy): "'The Gospel of John was the Gospel of Asia Minor', as the Quartodeciman controversy reveals."

[100] See van Tilborg 1996. His focus is on how Ephesian readers would have read John's Gospel, and aims to give (p4) "an insight into the concrete embedding of the text in the history and life of the city of Ephesus." He discusses prosopography, Jesus and the authorities in Ephesus, John in relation to city life in Ephesus, group formation in John and Ephesus and "The Passion narrative and the God Emperor."

[101] Van Tilborg (1996, p3 n6) also notes that "the name *Joannes* is found in Ephesus more than any other biblical name and more than in other cities: the apostle, theologian, and evangelist John is mentioned in the Ephesian inscriptions at least 18 times ... furthermore, the name *Joannes* appears in some variations another 30 times". Although such data is not definitive, it remains interesting.

[102] See for example, Brown 1966, pciii-civ.

direct.[103] Since Rev was written to churches in Western Asia Minor, this point supports, but does not require, an Ephesian provenance for the Gospel.

2.8 Other proposed locations

Alexandria, Syrian Antioch, Palestine and the area of Trachonitis and Batanaea are the main alternative contenders to Ephesus.[104] The most serious contender here is Syrian Antioch. However, the similarities between Ignatius and the Fourth Gospel are insufficient for us to argue that the Fourth Gospel must have come from the same area as Ignatius.[105] Further, while the links between the Gospel and the Odes of Solomon are significant, it is likely that the Odes are at least two generations later than the Fourth Gospel and are dependent on it. The links cannot be used to argue that the Odes and the Fourth Gospel must both come from the same milieu, and it seems more likely that the links between the Gospel and both Ignatius and the Odes are better explained by Johannine thought making its way to Syria.[106]

Thus the alternatives to Ephesus, none of which have any ancient support, are all quite weak.

2.9 Conclusions

Thus, in my view, when it comes to the provenance of John's Gospel, Ephesus has by far the strongest claim.[107]

3. That the Johannine Letters were written from Ephesus

We have argued that John, probably "the Elder", wrote the Fourth Gospel and we have suggested that the Ephesian provenance of the Gospel is strongly supported. As we will note shortly, there are strong connections between the Fourth Gospel and the Johannine Letters, which suggests that, since the Fourth Gospel is to be located in Ephesus then the Johannine letters are also to be located there. Further, we will now discuss the authorship of 1-3 Jn and will argue that John the Elder whom we believe wrote the Gospel also wrote

---

[103] See the discussion in Chapter 13.

[104] See Brown 1966, pciii-civ; Barrett 1978, p128-31. On the final suggestion given above and made by Wengst, see Hengel 1989, p114-116; cf. Charlesworth 1995, p8. Ringe (1999, p13-14) favours Alexandria.

[105] See Hengel 1989, p152 n85.

[106] Hengel 1989 p143 n26.

[107] See also for example Brown 1979a, p66-7; Smalley 1984, pxxxii; du Rand 1994, p68-70. Strecker 1996, pxl thinks Ephesus was "the seat of the Johannine school".

1-3 Jn. Hence, since the four works are probably by the same author, they are to be located in the same place. In the next section we will note further evidence which supports our view that 1-3 Jn are to be located in Ephesus.

3.1 The authorship of 1-3 Jn

The similarities between 2 and 3 Jn, such as the opening phrase "whom I love in the truth", the very similar closing greetings (2 Jn 12 and 3 Jn 13-14), and that the body of each letter begins with "I was overjoyed" (2 Jn 4; 3 Jn 3), as well as the fact that the author of both letters simply identifies himself as "the elder" suggests that they are written by the same author.[108] We have argued that John's Gospel was written by John the Elder, and since the author of 2-3 Jn simply identifies himself as "the elder" and as there are close affinities between 2-3 Jn and the Gospel,[109] it seems most likely that they are by the one person.[110]

What about 1 Jn? We note that the author does not identify himself. However, there are strong similarities between 1 Jn and 2-3 Jn,[111] which suggest that the three letters are written by the same person. That the author of 1 Jn does not introduce himself to his readers as "the elder", or in some other way, is often used as an argument against the common authorship of 1 Jn and 2-3 Jn.[112] However, this can be readily explained by the fact that 1 Jn is addressed to the author's own group (as we will note in more detail below), a group in which the author needs no introduction and where he does not need

---

[108] The other option is that one is an imitation of the other; against this see Brown 1982, p16.

[109] For example in the use of ἀγάπη, ἀγαπᾶν, ἀλήθεια, φίλος, ἐντολή. See further in Chapter 13.

[110] Strecker (1996, pxxxvii-xliii) thinks that John the Elder mentioned by Papias is the Elder who wrote 2 and 3 Jn; see also Burney 1922, p137; Schnelle 1998, p441. It is possible that John the Elder of the Gospel of John and "the elder" of 2-3 Jn are separate people. But that the author of 2-3 Jn calls himself simply "the elder" suggests that the readers know who he is. If this was a different person from "John the Elder" (whom we think wrote the Gospel) but someone in the same circle (as is required by the similarities) then this title in 2-3 Jn would clearly be very confusing. The only way to explain the simple title "the Elder" in 2-3 Jn is then to suggest that "John the Elder" was dead by the time 2-3 Jn was written. This is possible but the explanation offered in the text seems more likely.

[111] See 2 Jn 5 and 1 Jn 2:7 ("no new commandment"); 2 Jn 5 and 1 Jn 3:23 ("love one another"); 2 Jn 6; 1 Jn 5:3 (the connection of love and commandments); 2 Jn 6 and 1 Jn 3:11 ("from the beginning"); 2 Jn 7 and 1 Jn 2:18, 22, 26 ; 4:1, 3, 6 (deceivers and Antichrist); 2 Jn 7 and 1 Jn 4:2 ("confess Jesus Christ come in the flesh" though note the difference in the Greek); 3 Jn 11 and 1 Jn 3:10 and 4:6 ("of God"); 3 Jn 11 and 1 Jn 3:6 ("seen God"); see further Brown 1982, p16-19; 755-6; Marshall 1978, p31; Rensberger 1997, p19 who argue for common authorship of all three letters; cf. Grayston 1984, p6-7 and Strecker 1996, pxl who argue for different authors for 1 Jn and 2-3 Jn.

[112] See for example Schnelle 1998, p454-5.

to bolster his authority by referring to any title, whereas 2 and 3 Jn are both genuine letters to groups which are part of the wider Johannine community and are geographically removed from the author, so that he needs to state his relationship to them, and the basis from which he can claim to address them with instructions, at the beginning of the letter.[113]

But what about the relationship between the Gospel of Jn and 1 Jn? The oft-noted differences between the two documents include matters of style (particularly with regard to the lack of clarity of expression in 1 Jn),[114] and theology (eg. relating to the atonement, eschatology and the Spirit).[115]

Although this evidence has led a number of scholars to argue for different authors for the Gospel and 1 Jn[116] (in which case the similarities are explained by seeing both authors as part of a Johannine school or circle), in my view common authorship of the Gospel and 1 Jn by John the Elder (and hence for us, that the Elder wrote all four works), is the most convincing explanation.[117] This explains the very strong connections between the Gospel and 1 Jn with regard to vocabulary, idioms and distinctive theological ideas.[118] On this view, the differences between the Gospel and 1 Jn need to be accounted for, although we should note that at times these differences have been exaggerated.[119] These differences can be explained in a number of ways.

Firstly, the passage of time and the development in the thought of the author as a response to the change in situation which has occurred between the two works being written, assist us in explaining the differences between them.[120] For example, with regard to 1 Jn we can suggest that the situation caused by the secessionists (see further below), has led the author to emphasise some traditional elements which had not been emphasised in the

---

[113] Brown 1982, p17-19 answers other possible objections to the common authorship of 1 and 2 Jn.

[114] On this Hengel (1989, p107) writes: "The reason why the letter [1 Jn] contains more stylistic difficulties and obscurities than the Gospel is connected with the fact that the author, an old man, dictated it quickly and in understandable agitation, whereas the Gospel grew slowly and was corrected in the final redaction. In Paul, II Corinthians, which is the most passionate letter, presents the most syntactical problems." See also Schnackenburg 1992, p30.

[115] See Smith 1974-75, p234-5; Brown 1982, p21-8; Schnackenburg 1992, p34-9; Edwards 1996, p50-3.

[116] See for example Dodd 1937, p129-56; Grayston 1984, p7-12; Rensberger 1997, p17-18.

[117] See for example Marshall 1978, p32-42; Hengel 1989, p124-35; 1993, p306-25.

[118] See the extensive chart in Brown 1982, p757-9, and p20-1; see also Brooke 1912, p i-ix. As examples, note 1 Jn 4:2 and Jn 1:14; 1 Jn 4:9 and Jn 3:16; 1 Jn 5:1; Jn 1:12-13.

[119] Marshall (1978, p32-42) and Schnackenburg (1992, p36-8) both show that these differences are not as great as often thought; with regard to differences in style, note also the way Brown (1982, p23-4) relativizes the impact of Dodd's statistics.

[120] We will argue below that the Gospel was written before 1 Jn.

Gospel,[121] or has led him to develop his thought in 1 Jn in somewhat different ways in comparison with the Gospel.[122]

Secondly, the differences between the Gospel and 1 Jn can also be explained by the difference in genre. Clearly, 1 Jn is written to the author's own group,[123] as a letter, or hortatory tract (the debate about the exact genre of 1 Jn does not effect our point),[124] whereas the Gospel is of a quite different genre, and addresses its readers as a narrative text about Jesus' life.[125] Since it is not attempting to connect belief in Jesus to a narrative about his life, 1 Jn can address issues in a different and more direct way through its letter-like genre. This difference in genre then also contributes to an explanation of the differences between 1 Jn and the Gospel.[126]

Thirdly, and connected to the previous points, are differences in subject matter. The Gospel seeks to *lead to* belief in Jesus (see Jn 20:31), and in so doing needs to address very significant Christological controversies, particularly with respect to "the Jews". But the Gospel does this through giving a narrative of the life of Jesus, and so its plot focuses primarily on his life. By contrast, as we will argue below, 1 Jn is written primarily to reinforce the assurance of the readers in the wake of the departure of the secessionists and its subject matter focuses on issues of assurance and current belief and practice in the Christian community. These difference in subject matter again assist us to understand the differences between the works.[127]

---

[121] Note the claim made in 1 Jn 1:1 and 3:11 to be presenting the Gospel as it was "from the beginning"; see Brown 1997, p389.

[122] For example, he seems to have re-emphasised future eschatology (eg 1 Jn 2:28; 3:2; 4:17), while still holding to the realised eschatology of the Gospel. We will argue below that this may well have been in response to the changed situation facing the author, in particular, the emergence of what he saw as "the antichrist" (2 Jn 7; 1 Jn 2:18, 22; 4:3) which led to the conclusion that "it is the last hour" (1 Jn 2:18). See also Schnackenburg 1992, p36.

[123] This is most obvious in 1 Jn 2:19: "They went out from *us*, but they did not belong to *us* ...."

[124] On the genre of 1 John see Brown 1982, p86-92; Hills 1991, p367-77; Strecker 1996, p3; Stamps 1997, p621-2. Even though it is not a letter, the twenty addresses to "you" (plural) show that it is clearly addressed to a specific audience. Further, that specific opponents are mentioned in 1 Jn 2:19-22 shows it is not a general tractate or encyclical addressed to all Christians, as some have argued.

[125] Parts of the Gospel show greater resemblance to 1 Jn than others; for example Jn 13-17 is closer to the hortatory nature of 1 Jn than some other parts of the Gospel. However, the fundamental differences between a narrative and a letter or tract remain.

[126] One example here is that κύριος occurs 41 times in the Gospel, but not at all in 1 Jn. However, κύριος is most often used as a vocative of address in the Gospel ("O Lord"), a usage which is not appropriate in 1 Jn; see further Brown 1982, p25.

[127] One example is the use of κρίνω and κρίσις, which occur 30 times in the Gospel, but not at all in 1 Jn. But note that the words are often used with respect to judgement on "the Jews" who do not believe in Jesus; this situation is not reflected in 1 Jn. Thus the difference in subject matter explains the difference in thought and word usage; see further Brown 1982,

Finally, we note the difference in audience. In 1 Jn the author seeks to provide assurance to his own specific community; the gravity of the situation facing the community, caused by the departure of the secessionists, is such that the author seems to have felt compelled to commit his advice and exhortations to the community to writing. By contrast, John's Gospel is, we have argued, written for general circulation to all Christians.[128] Hence the difference in audience can explain some of the differences between the two works.[129]

Thus, given that explanations can be offered for their differences, common authorship of the Gospel and 1 Jn, and hence that all four Johannine works were written by the Elder, is the most likely view.[130] Since we have located John the Elder in Ephesus, then clearly we also think 1-3 Jn were written in the city, with 1 Jn being to a community in Ephesus, and 2-3 Jn to communities close by.[131]

---

p25. That there is no debate with "the Jews" in 1 Jn may also explain the lack of direct quotation of the OT in the letter.

[128] Even if one rejects Bauckham's view, discussed earlier in this chapter, John's Gospel would be written for the Johannine community as a whole, which includes the groups addressed by 2 and 3 Jn, as well as 1 Jn, and not just the one group within the wider Johannine community addressed by 1 Jn. So on this view too, a difference in audience between 1 Jn and the Gospel remains.

[129] If in 1 Jn, the author is writing to a community he knew well then this may explain, for example, the fact that 1 Jn seems closer to what Smith (1991, p12-13) calls "primitive preaching (e.g., 1 Cor. 15:3) in its emphasis on the saving effect of Jesus' death, indeed of his blood (1 John 1:7; cf. 2:2)." Perhaps it was precisely his knowledge of his own community which led him to emphasize more traditional perspectives (perhaps this was what he thought they needed to hear at this point in time), whereas the Gospel, aimed at all Christians, seeks to break new ground at times, or to bring out different and new theological possibilities (such as seeing Jesus' death as exaltation).

[130] Other reasons for the differences between the Gospel and 1 Jn include the different length (the Gospel is almost eight times longer) and the possibility that parts of the Gospel reflect sources. We will have reason to draw attention to some differences between 1 Jn and 2-3 Jn in Part Three of this book, but these can be explained in large part by the differences in audience and genre, with 1 Jn being written to the author's own community, and having more tract-like qualities, and 2-3 Jn being written to groups beyond the author's own community, as genuine letters.

[131] See further below. Even if we were to postulate different authors for 1 Jn on the one hand and the Gospel and 2-3 Jn on the other, then the similarities of both language and theology between all these works requires the view that there was a very close association between the author of 1 Jn, and John the Elder (the author of the Gospel and 2-3 Jn) and thus that they belonged to the same circle or group and were definitely in the same geographical location (see Brown 1979a, p94-5; Caird 1966, p4) of Ephesus. But in our view the strongest explanation is that one author wrote all four documents.

3.2 External support for the Johannine Letters being located in Ephesus

In addition to these points about authorship, the location of the Johannine Letters in Ephesus is supported by the fact that the oldest clear allusion to 1 Jn is by Polycarp of Smyrna in his Epistle to the Philippians,[132] probably to be dated around 115-120 CE.[133] In Phil 7:1-2, after having spoken of false teachers who do not acknowledge the cross (6:3) Polycarp writes "For everyone who does not confess that Jesus Christ has come in the flesh is an anti-christ; and whosoever does not confess the testimony of the Cross is of the devil. ... (2) Wherefore, leaving the foolishness of the crowd, and their false teaching, let us turn back to the word which was delivered to us from the beginning."

Brown describes the first part of this quotation as "uniquely close to two Johannine passages",[134] 1 Jn 4:2-3 and 2 Jn 7.[135] The phrase "from the beginning" in 7:2 quoted above is probably an allusion to the phrase, "from the beginning" found in 1 Jn 2:7, 24; 3:11. Further, the phrase "of the devil" in Polycarp 7:1 is also found in 1 Jn 3:8. Finally, Hartog notes that the Johannine Letters are the only NT writings to use the term "antichrist" (1 Jn 2:18, 22; 4:3; 2 Jn 7) and Polycarp is also the only Apostolic Father to use the term. He notes: "Thus, the tests of 'density' and 'singularity' point toward Polycarp's knowledge of 1 John."[136]

It seems very likely then that 1 and perhaps 2 Jn were available to Polycarp. Thus before 115-120 these letters are known near Ephesus.

In addition, the first undeniable quotations of 1 Jn and 2 Jn are from Irenaeus, who wrote about 180 and who (as we have noted above) is said to have listened to Polycarp as a young man in Asia Minor (Eusebius, HE 5.20.6).[137] That both the first allusion and the first quotation come either from Asia Minor (Polycarp) or from a person with strong connections to Asia Minor (Irenaeus) supports Ephesus as the place where the Johannine Letters were written, and certainly does not support any other provenance.

---

[132] Strecker 1996, pxxix; also Briggs 1970, p416; Brown 1982, p8-9; see discussion of other possible parallels in Brown 1982, p6-9; Strecker 1996, pxxix.

[133] Hartog 2002, p169, 238 argues for a date of 115 CE. This is dependent on the unity of the Epistle, for which he argues convincingly on p148-69. However, even if one accepts the Two-Letter theory, many would argue for a date before 120 CE for chapters 1-12; see Hartog 2002, p157-8.

[134] Brown 1982, p8.

[135] 1 Jn 4:2-3: "Every spirit that *confesses that Jesus Christ has come in the flesh* ...Every spirit *that does not confess Jesus* is not from God. And this *is the spirit of the Antichrist*." 2 Jn 7: Many deceivers have gone out into the world, those who *do not confess that Jesus Christ has come in the flesh;* any such person is the deceiver and *the Antichrist*."

[136] Hartog 2002, p189.

[137] He quotes 2 Jn 11 in Adv Haer 1.16.3; 1 Jn 2:18-19, 21-22 in Adv Haer 3.16.5; 2 Jn 7-8 and 1 Jn 4:1-2; 5:1 in Adv Haer 3.16.8. For other later quotations see Brown 1982, p9-13.

Further, as we noted above, it is also significant that Eusebius (HE 3.39.17) reports that Papias from Hierapolis "utilized testimonies from the first letter of John and, likewise, from that of Peter".[138] We have argued above for the veracity of this tradition. We also know that Papias was a contemporary of Polycarp (Eusebius, HE 3.36.1-2) and so that Papias used 1 Jn also increases the likelihood that Polycarp did know 1 Jn.

We will argue below that the closest known parallel to the secessionists combatted by the author of 1 and 2 Jn are the docetists in Smyrna and Tralles against whom Ignatius writes in ca. 110 CE. Although Docetism was also known in Syria and Rome, this parallel near to Ephesus is significant.[139]

One final note is appropriate here. The authorship of all four Johannine documents is a matter of on-going and strenuous debate. Clearly, the view proposed here is contentious. I hope to have shown that to some extent, the issues of authorship and provenance are distinct. In the case of the Gospel, we have the two traditions – Papias-Polycrates-Irenaeus and the Acts of John – which disagree about authorship but agree about provenance, which means that Ephesus as the provenance of the Gospel of John is doubly attested. In addition, we have evidence for the impact of John's Gospel in Asia Minor which supports a provenance in this area. Further, we have evidence for the use of 1-2 Jn near Ephesus. Thus, the location of these works in Ephesus is more strongly attested than is the case with authorship, and we can proceed with confidence then to place 1-3 Jn in Ephesus.

3.3 Ephesus as the centre of a group of house churches

The Johannine Letters suggest there are a number of house churches throughout a local area.[140] As we have noted, the author of 1 Jn does not suggest that there is any geographical distance between himself and his readers so it is likely that he lives among those he addresses as "little children". Since 1 Jn is not a letter, but more of a tractate, this is understandable. Further, as we will discuss in Chapter 10, the author regularly speaks of "we", by which he means the community to which he writes, and of which he is a member.[141]

By contrast, 2 and 3 Jn were written to outlying house churches (or groups of house churches) some distance from the elder (who we think is in Ephesus)

---

[138] Brown 1982, p9 n12 notes that the designation "First Epistle" reflects Eusebius' fourth-century knowledge and need not be taken to imply that Papias knew 2 and/or 3 John.

[139] See Strecker 1996, p75. Note that Günther (1995, p102-111) argues that 2 and 3 Jn belong in Ephesus, but locates 1 Jn in Syria.

[140] See Strecker 1996, p3.

[141] Brown 1982, p32 suggests the author of 1 Jn "lived in the central locale of Johannine Christianity with many house-churches and numerous adherents – the place where the secessionist movement had begun." See also Schnackenburg 1977, p281.

and whom the elder hopes to visit (see 2 Jn 12; 3 Jn 13-14), although it seems likely that the distances are quite small. It also seems likely that Gaius and Diotrephes, mentioned in 3 Jn, belong to two separate house churches in the same location; since Diotrephes had refused to give hospitality to travelling missionaries, the elder is writing to request Gaius does so. Thus in 3 Jn 6 when the Presbyter writes to Gaius that "You will do well to send them [the brothers and sisters] on in a manner worthy of God", he is asking for support to enable these missionaries, for whom the elder clearly feels some responsibility, to continue their travels. This suggests several days journey separated the house churches of 3 Jn from those of 1 Jn.[142]

This suggests that there was a centre with a number of house churches to which 1 John was written – which is a further explanation of why the author put down his instructions in writing since he could not be simultaneously present in them all – and that within reasonable travelling distance there were other similar communities. They were perhaps in provincial towns.[143] Thus, 2 and 3 Jn testify to events in the wider movement of which the centre is (we believe) the Ephesian Johannine community.

There is also clearly a very strong affinity between the group (which is made up of house churches) to which 1 Jn is written and the groups to which 2 and 3 Jn are written. As we have seen, very similar language is used (which thus reflects the language of the whole movement) and just as "deceivers" have appeared in the centre of the movement (1 Jn 2:18-22) so it is feared that they will make their way to the outlying house church (2 Jn 7). Thus we can use 2 and 3 Jn to shed light on the whole movement, of which we suggest Ephesus is the centre, taking note that they speak both of events in Ephesus (and bear testimony to the life of the community to which the elder belongs) as well as of life in that wider movement.

3.4 That John travelled to Ephesus and established a community there

We have noted that the author of John's Gospel, whom we have argued was John the Elder, has reliable knowledge of Galilee and Jerusalem.[144] Thus, some scholars have argued that John lived in Palestine for quite some time

---

[142] Thus Barrett (1998, p922) thinks "3 Jn may well have originated in or in the neighbourhood of Ephesus". Oster (1992a, p543) notes "the city was also the hub of regional urban development. Ephesus had successfully annexed several adjacent suburban areas; NW to Metropolis, S toward Magnesia and Priene, and E 40 km into the Cayster valley." See also Magie 1950, p46-9; Broughton 1938, p607-27; Foss 1979, p3; White 1995, p41-3. What we know of the city of Ephesus is compatible with the picture gained from 2-3 Jn in this regard; but this is also true of many ancient cities.

[143] See Brown 1982, p101-2.

[144] On the accurate knowledge of Palestine as it was before 70 CE, Brown 1966, 1, pxlii-xliii.

and later travelled to Ephesus. One suggestion here is that he moved to Ephesus around the time of the Jewish War (66-70 CE), perhaps with a group of other Christians. Although we have no direct evidence for the arrival of such a group in Ephesus, it remains a reasonable suggestion.[145]

Given the evidence we have from the Johannine Letters for a community to which the author of these letters belonged, then it seems most likely that a community, which we can call "the Johannine community" (by which we mean the house churches addressed in 1-3 Jn, not a community read from the Gospel) existed in and around Ephesus. This could include people who travelled from Palestine with John, other Ephesians who were already Christians who joined the group, and new Ephesian converts. It seems likely that this community existed from at least 70 CE, and we will argue in Part Three that it was a distinct and separate community from the Pauline community in Ephesus.[146]

4. Date of John's Gospel and of the Johannine Letters

When were the Johannine Letters written? Clearly this is related to the date of John's Gospel, so this must be discussed briefly here too.

The Gospel was probably only finished (by adding Jn 21, though this may have existed in an earlier form) and published after the death of John the Elder, and so in its *final* form it is later than the Letters.[147] However, a strong

---

[145] See in general Bauer 1971, p86-7; Robinson 1988, p98; Lohse 1991, p365; see also Aune 1997, p 1; Dahl 2000, p457. Note that in Ant 20.256, Josephus, speaking of the Procuratorship of Gessius Florus (64-66 CE), writes: "The ill-fated Jews [of the province of Judaea], unable to endure the devastation by brigands that went on were one and all forced to abandon their own country and flee, for they thought that it would be better to settle among gentiles, no matter where." See also Josephus, JW 7.410-19. It seems likely that some of these refugees went to Asia Minor, and Ephesus in particular. Note also that Polycrates (See Eusebius, HE 3.31.3; 5.24.2) gives evidence that Philip the evangelist, who had left Jerusalem after the persecution of Stephen and gone to Caesarea (Acts 8:40, where he was still living sometime later, see Acts 21:8-10) emigrated at some point to Hierapolis with his daughters. John the elder may well have similarly emigrated to Western Asia Minor at this time. Günther (1995, p121, 211) accepts that the Presbyter John came to Ephesus around 70 CE, but because he thinks there was no Pauline community in the city and the original community founded by Apollos had developed to a position he calls "Hyperpaulinismus" (p85), he sees the arrival of John as involving the founding of Ephesian Christianity a second time. But this is very unlikely.

[146] The likelihood that John and others with him travelled from elsewhere to Ephesus, and so had some sense of group cohesion prior to arriving in Ephesus, reinforces the probability that this community remained as a distinct group there.

[147] See Hengel 1989, p105-8. On Jn 21 as a later addition to the Gospel, see Schnelle 1998, p490-1.

case can be made that the Letters were written after at least the vast majority of the Fourth Gospel had been composed. We will argue below that the Christology of the secessionists can best be understood as a development from the Christology of the Fourth Gospel, which suggests 1 Jn is later than the Gospel. Secondly, at a number of points (eg 1 Jn 1:1-4) the letters seem to clearly presuppose the Gospel and to be influenced by it.[148]

What then is the date of the Gospel? The very earliest papyrus fragment of any part of the NT is P^{52}, which contains Jn 18:31-33, 37, 38. It is dated by papyrologists (on the basis of writing, ink and lay-out) to around 130 CE.[149] This suggests that John cannot have been written later than the end of the first or the very beginning of the second century.[150] But overall, a date between 80-90 CE seems the most likely; we have insufficient evidence to be more precise than this.[151] Given that the secessionists have probably developed their views in dialogue with the Fourth Gospel (or perhaps an earlier form of it) and that they are a crucial feature in 1 Jn, then this suggests we should date the letters around 90-100 CE.[152]

What about the date of 2 and 3 Jn? 2 Jn deals with the same problem as 1 Jn: those who have "gone out" and deny Jesus has come in the flesh. This argues that it was written about the same time as 1 Jn. Similarly 3 Jn deals with some similar issues to 2 Jn – travelling teachers. Further, the linguistic connections noted above between 2 and 3 Jn suggest they were written at the same time, or very close in time to one another. This suggests all three letters were written in close proximity. Thus, although the order of letters is debated

---

[148] For further discussion see Brown 1979a, p97; 1982, p32-5, 90-100; Edwards 1996, p53-5; Rensberger 1997, p20; cf. Schnelle 1998, p456-9. See also Lieu 1986, p74, who notes that the love command in John's Gospel is a "new" command (Jn 13:34) but in 1 Jn 2:7-8 it is said to be "no new commandment" but rather an old one that the readers have had from the beginning, although it is *also* new because it belongs to the new age (1 Jn 2:8; see also 2 Jn 5). This argues that 1 Jn was written after the Gospel. Note that 1 Jn may have been written before the final redaction of the Gospel that incorporated, for example, Jn 21; see Brown 1997, p390.

[149] Stanton 2002, p120.

[150] Papyrus Egerton 2 depends partly on Jn; it suggests that Jn was circulating in Egypt well before the middle of the second century CE; see Stanton 2002, p120.

[151] Stanton 2002, p120 suggests 80-100 CE; Brown 1979a, p23 favours 90 CE.

[152] This is supported by the fact that the docetists whom Ignatius opposes around 110 CE have more developed views than the secessionists, though this observation is weakened by the fact that ideas may develop at a different rate in different places. Brown (1982, p101) dates the Gospel (without the redactor's additions) to around 90 CE and 1 Jn to around 100 CE. He dates 3 Jn to 100-110 CE. Smalley (1984, pxxxii) opts for 90-100. Strecker (1996, pxli-xliii) argues for 2 and 3 Jn around 100 or later, and 1 Jn (along with the Fourth Gospel) "in the first half of the second century". Edwards (1996, p56) favours "a date towards the end of the first century".

(is 3 Jn earlier than the others, for example?),[153] we will treat them as a group, since it seems likely that they were written at roughly the same time.

5. The situation of the community at the time 1 Jn was written, and the opponents

We now turn to discuss the situation of the addressees at the time 1 Jn was written, and will also discuss events that have occurred recently among the addressees, as far as these can be discerned from the letter. While 2 and 3 Jn relate primarily to travelling teachers, here we will discuss 2 Jn 7, which also relates to the secessionists. We will discuss 2 and 3 Jn in more detail in subsequent chapters as what is said there relates to the themes we discuss.

5.1 What has happened before 1 John was written?

It seems clear from 1 John that there had been some recent troubles within the group that the author addresses. The key passage here is 1 John 2:18-19: "Children, it is the last hour! As you have heard that antichrist is coming, so now *many antichrists have come.* From this we know that it is the last hour. *They went out from us,* but they did not belong to us; for if *they* had belonged to us, *they* would have remained with us. But by going out *they* made it plain that none of *them* belongs to us."

It seems then that a group has "gone out" from the group addressed, whom we will call the Johannine community.[154] The author claims that these secessionists, as Brown calls them, never really belonged to the community. However, it seems likely that before their departure, they regarded themselves as part of the community, and were probably so regarded by others. It was their actual departure that led to the verdict by the author of 1 Jn that "none of them belongs to us". But it is clear that the secessionists were Christians, who had been part of the Johannine community, and not for example, Jews who denied the Messiahship of Jesus, as 2:22 might suggest.

This naturally leads to the question of why the secessionists left? What were the issues over which the split occurred? In 2:18-19 the secessionists are called "antichrists"; 2:22 further defines the antichrist: "Who is the liar but the one who denies that Jesus is the Christ? This is the antichrist, the one who denies the Father and the Son." But what does it mean to deny "that Jesus is

---

[153] See Thomas 1995, p68-75, with reference to the many suggestions with regard to order, along with his own view; see also Olsson 1987, p34.

[154] Of course the secessionists may have argued that the author's group left them, or that they were unjustly excluded.

the Christ"? It could mean they deny that Jesus is the Messiah. However, I Jn 4:1-3 is more explicit:

"Beloved, do not believe every spirit, but test the spirits to see whether they are from God; for *many false prophets have gone out into the world.* By this you know the Spirit of God: every spirit that confesses *that Jesus Christ has come in the flesh* is from God, and *every spirit that does not confess Jesus is not from God.* And *this is the spirit of the antichrist, of which you have heard that it is coming; and now it is already in the world.*"

Here again we have a reference to the antichrist, this time, "the spirit of the antichrist",[155] which is said to be a spirit that "does not confess Jesus"; such a spirit is not from God. This ties in to the similar statement in 2:22.[156] The spirit of the antichrist is here related to false prophets; it seems that the two designations of "antichrists" and "false prophets" are different terms for the same people, terms which arise from different perspectives, the one being eschatological (antichrist) and the other pneumatic (prophets and distinguishing spirits).[157] It seems that specific people are in mind, since the author speaks of "false prophets" as well as the "antichrist". Since they are given these designations, which are the reverse of honourable titles which could be given to key figures, it seems likely that those who have left included Church leaders whose Christological teaching the author of 1 Jn sees as erroneous.[158] We note also that the origin of the group the author opposes is the Christian community which is addressed; the false prophets have "gone out" from the group (1 Jn 4:1; 2 Jn 7).

The author also says that a spirit that is from God is one that "confesses that Jesus Christ has come in the flesh" (4:2). It seems likely then that, when the author says that the spirit of the antichrist "does not confess Jesus" (4:3), this means that the spirit does not confess that Jesus has come in the flesh. That this inference is probable is implied by the similar language found in 2 John 7:

"Many *deceivers* have gone out into the world, *those who do not confess that Jesus Christ has come in the flesh*; any such person is *the deceiver and the antichrist!*"

It seems reasonable to connect 1 Jn 2:18-20 and 4:1-6 with 2 Jn 7. We note the related language of someone being a liar (1 Jn 2:22), a false prophet (1 Jn 4:1) or a deceiver (2 Jn 7) and of denying (1 Jn 2:22) and not confessing (1 Jn 4:3; 2 Jn 7) something concerning Jesus. Most scholars therefore regard it as

---

[155] On the term "antichrist" see Strecker 1996, p236-41.

[156] Returning to a theme treated earlier is typical of the style of our author; see Schnackenburg 1992, p17-18.

[157] See Schnackenburg 1992, p17.

[158] See Edwards 1996, p59.

reasonable to connect these verses from 1 and 2 Jn and to suggest that the secessionists (of 1 John 2:18-22) deny that Jesus Christ has come in the flesh (as is made explicit in 1 Jn 4:1-6 and 2 Jn 7).[159] The strength and reality of the conflict between the author and his community on the one hand and the "secessionists" on the other is seen in the way the secessionists are described as "antichrists", "liars" and "false prophets" in 2:18-23; 4:1-6. It seems undeniable that the opponents are not simply a literary creation, but rather that this is a real conflict in the experience of the author and his readers.[160]

We also note that it is clear that the secessionists are no longer among the addressees. This is clear from 1 Jn 4:4-6 where we have the alternation from "you are from God" to "they are from the world"; in context, "they" refers to the secessionists, who are here called the false prophets. Clearly the secessionists are a separate group, which is not addressed by the author.[161]

But what more can we say about the secessionists than this? I will now turn to the influential work of Raymond Brown on 1 John, and present his view of the group he calls the secessionists and will then question some aspects of this way of reading the letter.

5.2 The view of Raymond Brown on the secessionists

Brown in his commentary on 1 John gives a chart which he entitles "Epistolary Statements Pertinent to the Adversaries' Views".[162] This supports his analysis that the secessionists disagree with the author of 1 Jn in four fundamental areas.

Firstly, in Brown's view the secessionists and the author disagree over Christology. Here he draws on texts we have just discussed. As we noted, the secessionists are accused of neglecting the "flesh" or humanity of Jesus (1 Jn 4:2; 2 Jn 7). Brown suggests the secessionists "so stress the divine principle in Jesus that the earthly career of the divine principle is neglected."[163] Thus, while they regarded the human existence of Jesus as real, they did not think it was salvifically significant. Brown argues that the secessionists read Jn 3:16-17 to mean that the entrance of Jesus into the world was what gave eternal life

---

[159] Note the author of 1 Jn does not state their teaching and then refute it with arguments; rather he discredits his opponents by the use of pejorative language (false prophets, antichrist).

[160] See Painter 1993, p439; cf. Neufeld 1994, p96-112.

[161] Other statements which assert something, often very positive, about the readers show that the secessionists are not among the addressees; see 1 Jn 2:7,13-14, 20-1, 24, 27, 29; 3:5, 11, 15; 4:3-4; 5:13.

[162] Brown 1982, p762-3. See further Brown 1982, p47-68, who also reviews previous discussions of the secessionists.

[163] Brown 1979a, p112.

to those who believe. The subsequent deeds, including the death of Jesus, were thus unimportant.[164]

Secondly, Brown argues that moral behaviour was also at the heart of the disagreement between the secessionists and the author of 1 John. To the secessionists, the only sin was refusing to believe in Jesus. The secessionists interpreted passages such as Jn 3:18 and 5:24 to mean that the believer is already judged and already has eternal life.[165] Through believing, they claimed they had an intimacy with God to the point of being sinless or perfect.[166] Hence, the secessionists gave no salvific importance to ethical behaviour or to obeying commandments; for them there was no sin provided one believed (I John 1:8,10).[167] Thus, "although they claim communion with God, they do not see any importance in keeping commandments and pretend to be free from the guilt of sin (1:6,8; 2:4)."[168]

Thirdly, Brown argues that the secessionists and the author of 1 John disagree about eschatology with there being no place in the secessionists' theology for future eschatology. While the author of 1 John holds to a realized eschatology, he adds the ethical requirement of, for example, walking in the light (1:7) and keeping God's word (2:5) to the claims of realized eschatology. He also emphasizes future eschatology in passages like 1 Jn 2:28; 3:2-3, 18-19; 4:17, where future eschatology is used as a corrective of the secessionists' ethics.[169]

Finally, primarily on the basis of 1 Jn 4:1-3 Brown thinks the secessionists claimed to speak under the guidance of the Spirit.[170] He sees this as an explanation for the author of 1 John's failure to mention the Spirit with any frequency.

On this reading of 1 John, the overall reason the author wrote was to refute the secessionists,[171] and "to reinforce the readers"[172] against the secessionists, who are still trying to win more adherents. Similarly, a number of other commentators have regarded the conflict with the secessionists as *the key* to the interpretation of the Letter. Thus, for example, Schnackenburg writes that

---

[164] See further in Brown 1979a, p114f. He also notes verses like Jn 17:3, 8.

[165] Brown, 1984, p111.

[166] Brown 1979a, p123.

[167] Brown 1979a, p128-30; 1984, p111. This flowed from their christology. "If they did not attribute salvific importance to the earthly career of Jesus, ... why should the earthly life of the Christian be pertinent to salvation?" (Brown 1979a, p129).

[168] Brown 1979a, p94. For Brown's view that the secessionists ignored the command to "love the brother or sister" (2:9-11; 3:11-18; 4:20), see Brown 1979a, p131-5; see also Schnackenburg 1992, p23-4.

[169] See Brown 1979a, p135-8.

[170] Brown 1979a, p97, 138-44.

[171] Brown 1984, p113.

[172] Brown 1979a, p94.

"The polemic against these antagonists ... in fact pervades the entire document."[173]

However, this analysis depends on reading most of the antithetical statements in 1 John as aimed at the secessionists. Brown admits this when he writes: "Our only knowledge of them [the secessionists] is derived from the assumption that they held the opinions against which the author of I John argues, and such a mirror-image approach has many perils."[174] It is this approach to 1 John, which has been the dominant one in recent scholarship, that we will now question.[175]

5.3 Reading the rhetoric of 1 John

The author of 1 John repeatedly uses a number of formulae. These can be analysed into four categories.:

a) *"ἐὰν εἴπωμεν"*: *"If we say"*, which occurs three times. For example 1:6 *"If we say* (ἐὰν εἴπωμεν) *that we have fellowship with him while we are walking in darkness, we lie and do not do what is true"*.[176]

b) *"ὁ λέγων"* or *"ἐάν τις εἴπῃ"*: *"The one who says"* or *"If anyone says"*, which occurs four times. For example 2:4 *"The one who says* (ὁ λέγων) 'I have come to know him,' *but does not obey his commandments, is a liar, and in such a person the truth does not exist;"*[177] or 4:20 *"If anyone says* (ἐάν τις εἴπῃ) 'I love God' *and hates his brother, he is a liar"*.[178]

---

[173] Schnackenburg 1992, p3; see also for example Bonnard, 1983, p14; Painter 1993, p439 (who suggests (1993, p441) that the author may have been concerned with those amongst his adherents who were tempted to follow his opponents). For a very helpful survey of past scholarship with regard to general approaches to 1 Jn and the opponents see Neufeld 1994, p6-29.

[174] Brown 1979a, p103-4. He goes on: "For [p104] instance, it is uncertain that every idea that the author opposes in the Epistle is accepted by the secessionists. ... Nevertheless, it is a working hypothesis to separate the statements against which the author directly polemicizes and to see whether, taken together, they present a consistent body of thought. It is my contention that they do."

[175] That the primary purpose of the Johannine Letters is polemical has been denied by Lieu 1981, p210-28; 1991, p8-16; Neufeld 1994, p30 and passim; Edwards 1996, p57-68; Griffith 1998, 253-76.

[176] See also 1:8, 10.

[177] See also 2:5-6, 9-10.

[178] Brown (1979a, p104) notes: "Presumably the disputes that caused the secession led the adversaries to shape lapidary statements expressive of their thought. The author has gathered these statements almost as slogans and used them in his rebuttal."

c) "ὁ μισῶν ..." or "ὁ ἀρνούμενος ...": "The one who ... (article + participle - with negative meaning), which is used negatively in twelve verses. For example, 2:10-11: "The one who loves his brother lives in the light ... But *the one who hates his brother* (ὁ δὲ μισῶν τὸν ἀδελφὸν αὐτοῦ) is in the darkness, and does not know the way to go, because the darkness has brought on blindness." Or 2:22 "Who is the liar but *the one who denies* that Jesus is the Christ (ὁ ἀρνούμενος ὅτι Ἰησοῦς οὐκ ἔστιν ὁ Χριστός)? This is the antichrist, the one who denies the Father and the Son."[179]

d) "πᾶς ὁ ...": "Everyone who ...", which is used negatively seven times. For example 2:23 *Everyone who denies the Son* does not have the Father (πᾶς ὁ ἀρνούμενος τὸν υἱὸν οὐδὲ τὸν πατέρα ἔχει). The one who confesses the Son has the Father also." Or 3:4: "*Everyone who commits sin* is guilty of lawlessness; sin is lawlessness (πᾶς ὁ ποιῶν τὴν ἁμαρτίαν καὶ τὴν ἀνομίαν ποιεῖ, καὶ ἡ ἁμαρτία ἐστὶν ἡ ἀνομία)."[180]

These introductory formula often (but not always) introduce constructions exhibiting antithetical parallelism or pure antithesis. Antithetical parallelism occurs when the same thought is expressed, first positively and then negatively in a phrase which does not add significantly to the development of the thought (eg 1:5-10; 2:4, 7, 10-11; 4:7-8). This gives emphasis to the statement. For example, note the antithetical parallelism in 5:12: "*The one who has* the Son has life; *the one who does not* have the Son of God does not have life (ὁ ἔχων τὸν υἱὸν ἔχει τὴν ζωήν· ὁ μὴ ἔχων τὸν υἱὸν τοῦ θεοῦ τὴν ζωὴν οὐκ ἔχει)."[181] A pure antithesis occurs when we have the use of opposite pairs of terms rather than the reversal of the original phrase. For example, in 1 Jn 3:7-8 we read: "The one who does righteousness is righteous, just as he is righteous. The one who does sin is from the devil."[182] This is a device which is based on the author's theological dualism.[183]

There are fifteen examples of antithetical parallelism or pure antithesis in 1 Jn, and each example begins with one of the above four formulae of introduction.[184] It is these verses which are at the heart of Brown's

---

[179] See also 3:8, 10, 14; 4:6, 7-8, 16-18, 20; 5:10, 12; 3 Jn 11.

[180] See also 3:6, 10, 15; 4:2-3 (where the reference is to "every spirit"); 2 Jn 9. Similar expressions are also used positively in 2:29; 3:3, 9; 4:7; 5:1 (twice), 4, 18; cf also 2 Jn 1; 1 Jn 4:2-3.

[181] See also for example, 4:7-8; see further Jones 1970, p440-1. The antithetical couplets in 1 Jn have been the basis of source theories by Bultmann and others; see Brown 1982, p38-43.

[182] See also for example, 3:7-10; 4:4-6; 3 Jn 11.

[183] On this see Edwards 1996, p12-13. Note, for example, the absolute distinction between truth and falsehood and between light and darkness; see 1 Jn 1:5.

[184] See Jones 1970, p440-1; see also Wendland 1998, p50-5.

reconstruction of the secessionists, although I should note that he subsequently draws into his reconstruction a number of other verses as well. But primarily, his case depends on each of these phrases ("If we say ..."; "The one who ..." and so on) and their associated antithetical parallelism or pure antithesis referring to the secessionists.

But how do we read the verses in each of my four categories? This becomes a question of whether the views of the secessionists can be read off each passage? Thus, when the author says, "If we say *x*, we are wrong; if we say *a* we are right" or "Everyone who does *y* is mistaken, everyone who does *b* is right" does this mean that someone is actually saying *x* and doing *y*? Brown explicitly notes the difficulty of this process of mirror reading, with reference for example to 1 Jn 2:15-17, when he writes: "But it is very difficult to be sure that this passage is directed against the opponents, since it may be simply a general pastoral warning to his own followers."[185]

Most scholars would agree that in the three passages discussed at the beginning of this section (1 Jn 2:18-19; 4:1-3 and 2 Jn 7) the author does have the secessionists in view, and therefore that a Christological issue is at stake between the author of 1 Jn and the secessionists. But to go beyond this single issue to construct a more rounded position for the secessionists, we must assume that someone - the secessionists - is saying x and doing y in my four categories above. Hence the claims or actions which are denied are assumed to be the slogans, or to depict the behaviour, of the secessionists, which the author answers.[186]

However, it could be that this manner of expression is simply part of the forthright rhetorical style of the author, in which case we would be wrong to argue that the formula and associated antitheses and antithetical parallelism can be used to reconstruct the views of the secessionists. So how do we read these formulae? In particular, do they indicate the views of the secessionists? In my view, we are wrong to take these formulae as indicative of the views of the secessionists for the following reasons.

Firstly, note the wording in 1 Jn 1:8-9: "If we say (ἐὰν εἴπωμεν) that we have no sin, we deceive ourselves and the truth is not in us. If we confess our sins, he who is faithful and just will forgive us our sins and cleanse us from all unrighteousness." In this regard, Edwards notes: "Those who see this as polemic fail to take the 'we' seriously. Rather than attacking a specific group of 'opponents' who claim to be sinless, the author is warning *his own*

---

[185] Brown 1979a, p128; see also 1982, p48. However, Brown (1982, p762) includes 2:15-17 in his chart of "Epistolary Statements Pertinent to the Adversaries Views".

[186] Hence Neufeld (1994, p22) notes "the commitment that commentators have to the assumption that the antithetical statements represent the boasts of the enemies."

community that they must not make this claim."[187] Hence, to interpret the
conditional clauses of the type "If we say ..." as polemical "fails to allow
sufficiently for the author's vigorous and ... idiosyncratic 'upfront' style".[188]
Here then the author uses the "If we say ..." slogan and an antithesis to speak
to his own community.[189] Hence the "slogans" which the author uses (eg in
1:6, 8, 10) are not necessarily quotes from the secessionists,[190] but part of the
author's rhetorical style.

Another important example of "we" comes in 2:3-4: "Now by this *we* may
be sure that we know him, if we obey his commandments. The one who says
(ὁ λεγῶν), 'I have come to know him', but does not obey his
commandments, is a liar, and in such a person the truth does not exist." Here
we have a switch from "we" in 2:3 to the more impersonal "the one who says"
in 2:4. However, the impersonal form in 2:4 does not mean that the
community are not involved in this debate, as the continuity between "we"
and "the one who" in 2:3-4 shows. These verses strongly suggest it is the
same group, the community of addressees, who are in mind in 2:4, as they are
in 2:3. As Lieu notes, "The pattern of religious experience and behaviour
being explored here [in 2:4] are again those characteristic of the
community."[191] This suggests the impersonal forms "the one who ...",
"everyone who ..." and so on, are not to be read as concerning the
secessionists, but are simply another, more impersonal way of speaking about
the community.

Secondly, Griffiths has shown that the expressions "If we say ...", "The
one who says ..." and "If anyone says ..." are found in non-Christian Greek
literature, such as the Greek commentaries on Aristotle and in Philo, in non-
polemical contexts. In this non-Christian literature, these formula are used "in
the service of advancing [the author's] arguments within a shared
worldview",[192] and as a way of debating and transmitting traditions which are
important for the communities concerned. It is significant then that in the

---

[187] Edwards 1996, p58; emphasis added. See also Lieu 1991, p50; Neufeld 1994, p82-95;
Strecker 1996, p28-9; 69-76.

[188] Edwards 1996, p58. Edwards (1996, p45) helpfully notes about the author's style:
"The memorable, rhythmic, antithetical style and frequent repetitions suggest the inclusion of
material designed for oral delivery and perhaps memorization." See also Perkins 1979, pxxi-
xxii. On the rhetoric of 1 Jn see Wendland 1998, p43-64.

[189] Lieu (1991, p64) notes that 1:8-10 can be understood as addressed to the community:
"Denial of guilt or of sinfulness, or the refusal to acknowledge misbehaviour as 'sin', may
indeed have been a temptation for the community - hence the antithetical style of 1:8-10, 'If
we say ...'; this would be hardly surprising in view of the tendencies to assurance and to
realised eschatology which we have emphasised."

[190] Brown 1979a, p107 argues this.

[191] Lieu 1991, p51.

[192] Griffith 1998, p260.

closest parallels to 1 Jn, these formulae are used in a non-polemical way and in order to pass on traditions. This suggests that the formulae in 1 Jn need not be interpreted polemically.

Thirdly, what about the antitheses in general, of which Brown and others make so much? Do they refer to the secessionists? At times, the author can use antitheses, and the formula which he uses with the antitheses, when there is no obvious hint of a debate with opposing views. In these cases, the antitheses seem to arise out of the prior non-antithetical material. In this regard, it is helpful to look at 2:3-5 again: "Now by this we may be sure that we know him, if we obey his commandments. The one who says, 'I have come to know him', but *does not obey his commandments*, is a liar, ... but whoever *keeps his word*, in that one truly the love of God is perfected." As Lieu points out, the antithesis in verses 4-5 explains what is meant by 2:3, where it is said that the test of the knowledge of God is keeping his commandments.[193] No opponents need be inferred from 2:4-5; rather what we have here is instruction of the community, using antitheses, about knowing and obeying God.

Similarly, in 2:8-11 we read: "Yet I am writing you a new commandment that is true in him and in you, because the darkness is passing away and the true light is already shining. The one who says (ὁ λέγων), 'I am in the light', while hating a brother or sister, is still in the darkness. The one who loves (ὁ ἀγαπῶν) a brother lives in the light, and in such a person there is no cause for stumbling. But the one who hates (ὁ δὲ μισῶν) his brother is in the darkness, walks in the darkness, and does not know the way to go, because the darkness has brought on blindness." Here we note the use of an antithesis along with the regular occurrence of one of our formulae. Are both the antithesis and the formula used with regard to the secessionists? It seems more likely that the antithesis in 2:9-11 arises out of the affirmation in 2:8 that the light is already shining. Verses 9-11 can best be seen as describing what is appropriate and inappropriate behaviour, and thus as giving instruction for the community of readers. With regard to the negative portrayal of a "brother" in 2:11, Edwards notes that specific individuals may be in mind "but more probably this is a general warning, aimed at inculcating consistency between what people claim and how they live."[194] Further, as Neufeld notes, the antithetical statements (often regarded as "slogans" of the opponents) are "rhetorical devices by which he [the author] engages the audience to consider carefully what he has to say with the hope of persuading them to accept his views."[195]

---

[193] See Lieu 1991, p6; see also Edwards 1996, p73.

[194] Edwards 1996, p74.

[195] Neufeld 1994, p89; see also p88. Lieu (1991, p16) also notes "[t]he antithetical, debating style is all part of the thought and theological pattern of 1 John."

Lieu also suggests there is no hint of a debate with opposing views in the antithesis in 5:12: "The one who has the Son has life; the one who has not the Son of God has not life".[196] Rather than being directed against the secessionists who are seen as no longer possessing the Son of God,[197] this can be seen as a statement of the author's faith, expressed characteristically using antithetical parallelism.[198]

Thus, we see that the author adopts the antithetical form and the associated formulae, such as "The one who says ....", as a regular and preferred feature of his style.[199] We need not see the antithetical form, or the associated formulae, as referring to the opponents.[200]

Fourthly, it is noteworthy that the secessionists are first explicitly mentioned in 2:18-19,[201] and in these verses they seem to be introduced as a new factor. It would be strange then if the secessionists were actually in view in 1:6, 8, 10; 2:4, 6, 9. This point also argues against the whole letter being seen as polemical.

We can suggest then that the four formulae given above and their associated antitheses, are a natural part of the author's style. Thus, the author has a preference for emphasizing a theological view either by stating the positive and denying the negative of a position, or by the use of opposite pairs of terms. Further, using antitheses is in keeping with the author's fundamental dualism. Hence one cannot insist *on the basis of these expressions alone*, that the secessionists are actually saying x or doing y in the formulae. Accordingly, we cannot use what we suggest are rhetorical devices as evidence to reconstruct the views of the secessionists. Rather, some other evidence is needed that opponents are in view in the passages beyond 1 Jn 2:18-19; 4:1-3 (and 5:6-8 as we will argue) and 2 Jn 7, and this evidence is not forthcoming. By contrast, it is likely that they are in view in these four

---

[196] See Lieu 1991, p5.

[197] This is how Brown 1982, p602 reads this verse.

[198] Further examples could be given here. For example, Lieu (1991, p5-6) suggests that "in 3:4-10 the antitheses seem to be his own assessment of the case, not the contrasting views of two groups." See further in Lieu 1981, p222-3, on 4:7-8; see also 5:12.

[199] The use of the antithesis is a feature of the style of the Fourth Gospel. Antithetical parallelism is found for example in John 3:18a-b, 20-1, 36a-b; 5:22-3, 43-7; 6:53-4; 10:4-5; 12:44-9; 14:23-4; 15:6-7, 19a-b. Pure antithesis is found in John 3:3-5, 11-13, 19-21, 31-2; 5:24-9 8:41-7; 9:29; 10:25-6; 15:18-25; 16:20-2; 17:14-15; 18:36,7; see Schnackenburg 1992, p7. Similarly, the phrase, "πᾶς ὁ ...": "Everyone who ..." is regularly found in the Fourth Gospel, where it is often part of an antithesis; see Jn 3:7-8, 15, 16, 20; 4:13; 6:40, 45; 8:34; 11:26; 12:46; 16:2, 18:37; 19:12; cf also 5:28; 18:20. Thus, the antithesis and the phrase "πᾶς ὁ ..." may be used in the Johannine Letters because they have become characteristic rhetorical features of Johannine style.

[200] We note that Brown sees the examples we have dealt with (2:4-5, 2:11 and 5:12) as against the secessionists in each case; see Brown 1982, p253, 291, 602.

[201] See Neufeld 1994, p30.

passages because of the statement that "they went out from us", and references to antichrists and false prophets.

This does not mean that the secessionists were only a minor issue for the author. The refusal to greet someone who brings a different teaching (2 Jn 10-11) shows how serious this matter was for the author. Our point is that, beyond Christological issues that the author clearly attributes to the secessionists, we cannot be certain about the beliefs of the secessionists.

5.4 What was the purpose of 1 John, if it is not fundamentally polemic against the secessionists?

Before we consider what we can say about the secessionists, this discussion raises one other issue which we need to address briefly. The view that the secessionists are being opposed in the antitheses and other formulae leads naturally to the view that 1 John was primarily written against the secessionists, and thus to refute them, or to prevent them from making any further impact on the Johannine community.[202] Hence 1 Jn is fundamentally seen as a polemical letter, engaging in polemic with outsiders and with their views, with this polemic controlling the thought of the letter. However, since we see the secessionists as only mentioned in a few places, on our view this is very unlikely.

We should note at this point that we agree with Brown, and virtually all scholars, in seeing the secessionists as *one* issue that the author addresses. We will develop the point in the next section that the main, or perhaps the only, cause of disagreement between the secessionists and the author was christology. As we will note there, in this area the author of 1 John does answer the secessionists' view that the human existence of Jesus was not salvifically significant (see 1 Jn 1:7; 2:2; 3:16; 4:10; 5:6). Although in these passages the author is not involved in direct polemic against the secessionists, he is concerned to answer some of their teaching and its consequences. However, this is the only area in which we can be confident about the views of the secessionists. Why then did the author write the letter?

Although we cannot argue the point in detail here, it seems most likely that 1 John was written to offer assurance to its readers and to reinforce them in their faith. This is certainly related to the secessionists. 1 Jn 2:19 convincingly shows that they have left the community and we can suggest that those who remained are now less certain about their faith, and less convinced about their salvation. The author writes then, not to refute the secessionists (in such a way that their theology can be read off every antithesis) but to convince the readers of the truth of the community's beliefs and practices. The document is thus to

---

[202] See Painter 1986, p48-71; see also Schnackenburg 1992, p17-24; Bultmann 1973, p35; Brown 1982, p90.

shore up the ideology of the group. If you like, the departure of the secessionists left a considerable "hole" in the identity of the group and the author now seeks reinforce that identity with the letter of 1 John.

Some evidence for this can be noted. The emphasis at the beginning, middle and end of the letter is on the proclamation of eternal life, and the author underlines at these points that readers can know that they have eternal life. Thus, the letter begins with a resounding affirmation of the Johannine tradition: the testimony that eternal life was revealed to the community, and that what has been heard, seen and touched concerning the word of life forms the foundation of the community and its faith (1:1-3). Note the tenor of reassurance and confidence here, created by the frequent use of verbs of perception in the first person plural. The body of the letter closes in 5:11 with the same theme, and the Epilogue begins similarly in 5:13: "I write these things to you who believe in the name of the Son of God, so that you may *know* that you have eternal life."[203] 1 Jn 5:20, the penultimate verse in the Epilogue, is also a confession of where eternal life may be found. There is an inclusio then, with the theme of assurance concerning eternal life bracketing the whole letter. The other key verses which relate to eternal life are 2:24-5, which come directly after the first passage which relates to the secessionists. So we can suggest that the departure of the secessionists has shaken the community. How can they know that they have eternal life? By remaining in the Johannine tradition which they heard from the beginning, and so in the Son and in the Father, and thus receiving eternal life. Hence, the concept of "eternal life" constitutes the basic framework of the letter.[204]

Other factors reinforce this view. We note the prevalence of $o\tilde{\iota}\delta\alpha$ and $\gamma\iota\nu\acute{\omega}\sigma\kappa\omega$,[205] the call back to "what was from the beginning" (1:1; 2:7; 2:24; 3:11; 2 Jn 5, 6), which reassures the readers that what they have believed all along has been true, the many "tests" mentioned in the letter which seem to be designed to enable the readers to ascertain whether they "walk in the light" (1:7), or "know God" (2:3), or have passed from death to life (3:14),[206] assurances concerning what may be called their current spiritual state,[207] and that opposition and persecution does not indicate that the community is on the wrong track.[208]

---

[203] Note the subtle, but highly significant contrast between 1 Jn 5:13 and Jn 20:31. The issue in 1 Jn is no longer advocating belief in Jesus so that they might have life (as it was in Jn 20:31), but rather assurance, knowing that they do have eternal life.

[204] See Lieu 1991, p22-3; see also Olsson 1987, p41.

[205] The verbs $o\tilde{\iota}\delta\alpha$ or $\gamma\iota\nu\acute{\omega}\sigma\kappa\omega$ appear 36 times in 1 Jn.

[206] Jones (1970, p440) suggests there are 27 such tests in 1 John.

[207] This is clearest in 2:12-14; see also 2:20-1, 27; 3:1; 4:4, 14, 16-17; 5:1, 13-14, 18-20.

[208] See 2:15-17; 3:1, 13; 4:5. Data which could have been disconfirming of confidence is thus turned around into confirmatory data, which reinforces assurance.

From the view that one of the primary reasons that the author wrote was to reinforce the readers in their belief, to assure and convince them that they can know they have eternal life, we can, I think, gain a perspective from which to grasp the theological thought of the letter as a whole.[209] Further, much of the material that is often seen as answering the secessionists (and so used to build up a picture of the secessionists' theology) is actually better seen as material designed to assure the community itself about their salvation. It tells us nothing about the secessionists' ideology, but a lot about the author's purposes. That our basically non-polemical reading of the letter can provide a satisfactory explanation for why the author wrote to the readers, supports our overall reading that the secessionists are only to be seen in a few verses.

5.5 What can we say about the secessionists?

We have argued that we cannot use the formulae and antitheses discussed in section 5.3 above to determine what the secessionists believed and did. This means that the only area in which we can gain some idea of the secessionists' views is in the area of Christology. We have also noted that the texts we can legitimately draw on to reconstruct the secessionists' position are 1 Jn 2:18-23; 4:1-6 and 2 Jn 7-9. We will also see that there are good reasons to include 1 Jn 5:6-8 too.

Some have argued that the secessionists were Jews who denied that Jesus was the Messiah, the Son of God. This would be in view in 2:22: "Who is the liar but the one who denies that Jesus is the Christ?" This might suggest that the secessionists were Jews who rejected Jesus as the Messiah. However, this is very unlikely. Firstly, 2:19 shows that the secessionists had once been within the community, which shows that they were not non-Christian Jews. Secondly, if the secessionists were Jews who rejected Jesus as the Messiah, we would expect the author to deal with the Scriptures at some length, but in fact there are no OT quotations in 1 and 2 John.

It seems clear then that the secessionists are Christians with a different Christology. The key verses here are 1 Jn 4:3 and 2 Jn 7. It seems most likely that the secessionists did not deny the reality of Jesus' flesh; the contrast we will note shortly with the docetists discussed by Ignatius, suggests that the secessionists were different from Ignatius' docetists, who did deny the reality of Jesus' flesh and of his earthly life. Rather, it seems more likely that the Johannine secessionists denied that Jesus' life in the flesh (including his death) mattered theologically. As Brown notes, we can suggest "the secessionists admitted the reality of Jesus' humanity, but refused to acknowledge that his being in the flesh was essential to the picture of Jesus *as*

---

[209] Of course, the author focuses on other things besides assurance.

the Christ, the Son of God.”[210] This is why the author writes that they “do not confess that Jesus Christ has come in the flesh” (1 Jn 4:3; 2 Jn 7); in the view of the author of 1 and 2 Jn the secessionists so stress the divinity of Jesus that their position is tantamount to not confessing, or denying that Jesus has come in the flesh. The best explanation is then that they so stressed the significance of Jesus’ pre-existence and of his divinity that they neglected the humanity of Jesus. Further, we can suggest that the secessionists saw Jesus’ flesh and his life in general, as salvifically insignificant. This can be seen to be compatible with a lack of emphasis on Jesus’ humanity and also explains why the author of 1 Jn stresses the significance of Jesus’ death for salvation, for there is much more emphasis in the letter than in the Gospel of John on the redemptive death of Jesus (see 1 Jn 1:7; 2:2; 3:16; 4:10; 5:6).[211]

The secessionists can thus be thought of as having “an exaggeratedly high christology”.[212] This also explains the emphasis in 2 Jn 9 that the secessionists are “progressives” who have gone too far and not remained rooted in the original teaching.

But how does this view explain 2:22 which suggests that the secessionists are denying that “Jesus is the Christ”. Brown suggests that “the adversaries had trouble not with the predicate but with the subject in such confessions: *Jesus* is the Christ, the Son of God. The author would have been talking about the subject as a Jesus-come-in-the-flesh [2 Jn 7; 1 Jn 4:1-3] and thus insisting on the importance of the human career, including the death, of the Word become flesh.”[213] This means that Jesus’ earthly career, including his death, was given no great importance in their theology. For the author of 1 Jn, to refuse to confess that *Jesus* is the Christ, is actually to “deny the Son” (2:23),[214] and to do this is to deny both the Father and the Son (2:22).

In their denial of the significance of the “flesh of Jesus” the secessionists are close to later docetists. Docetists considered that the humanity and suffering of Jesus was apparent, rather than real, but the secessionists of 1 John do not fit this group exactly, as we know it from later sources.[215] Note

---

[210] Brown 1982, p76 (emphasis original).

[211] See further Brown 1979a, p120-3.

[212] Brown 1982, p55; see also Neufeld 1994, p34; Günther 1995, p116; cf. Lalleman 1998, p247-53 who thinks the opponents denied the human aspect of Christ entirely, but if this was the case, we would expect the author to respond differently.

[213] Brown 1982, p54. He refers also to 1 Jn 5:5-6. By contrast, Strecker (1996, p74) thinks the secessionists “distinguished between the earthly Jesus and the heavenly Christ”. But then we would expect a clearer affirmation of the reality of incarnation from the author of 1 Jn.

[214] We can suggest that for the author of 1 Jn, although the secessionists probably believed (along with the author) that the Son was preexistent, to deny that the fleshly life of the Son was significant is tantamount to “denying the Son”.

[215] Brown 1979a, p105. On docetism see Strecker 1996, p71-6; Klauck 2000, p475-8, with bibliography.

the contrast between the relativising of the significance of Jesus' flesh suggested by 1 John 4:2 and the Trimorphic Protenoia (13.50:12-15) written around 200 in which the heavenly Word says "I put on Jesus. I extracted him from the accursed wood and I made him stand at rest in the dwelling places of his parent."[216] The closest parallels to the secessionists' Christology are rather found in the opponents of Ignatius of Antioch, whose writing is to be dated around 105-110 CE.[217] However, the docetists whom Ignatius combatted probably argued that the humanity of Jesus was only apparent and not real, which again goes beyond the secessionists. Note the following passages:

Smyrnaeans 1.1 "I give glory to Jesus Christ .... for I have observed that you are established in immoveable faith .... being fully persuaded as touching our Lord, that he is in truth of the family of David according to the flesh, God's son by the will and power of God, truly born of a Virgin, baptised by John ... 1.2 truly nailed to a tree in the flesh for our sakes under Pontius Pilate and Herod the Tetrarch ... 2.1 For he suffered all these things for us that we might attain salvation, and he truly suffered even as he also truly raised himself, not as some unbelievers say, that his Passion was merely in semblance - but it is they who are merely in semblance, and even according to their opinions it shall happen to them, and they shall be without bodies and phantasmal .... 4.2 For if it is merely in semblance that these things were done by our Lord I am also a prisoner in semblance. 5.2 For what does anyone profit me if he praise me but blaspheme my Lord, and do not confess that he was clothed in flesh?"[218]

There is no evidence that the secessionists of 1 and 2 Jn had adopted such radical docetism. The author of 1 Jn argues for the salvific importance of Jesus' flesh and death, rather than for the reality of Jesus' humanity. Further, if the author of 1 Jn was seeking to refute docetism of the form found in Ignatius, he seems to be doing so very obscurely. In that case, we would have expected explicit references to Jesus' birth, death and resurrection, such as we do find in Ignatius.[219]

It seems then that we should speak of the docetic-type views of the secessionists, rather than seeing them as reflecting developed docetism. But it is interesting that there are geographical and chronological links here. We have argued that the author of the Johannine Letters is in Ephesus, and the secessionists are in this same area. The docetists mentioned by Ignatius are

---

[216] Reference from Brown 1979a, p112; Text from Layton 1987, p100. See also the Acts of John 88-93.

[217] Brown (1979a, p113) thinks the greatest obstacle to identifying the secessionists with later docetists is that the author of 1 Jn should have had no difficulty in refuting late docetists from John's Gospel, since there is no suggestion in that Gospel that Jesus' body only seemed to be real, although we will note that the Gospel can be read in such a way as to relativize the significance of Jesus' humanity.

[218] See also IgnTr 9-11.

[219] See Edwards 1996, p62. Strecker (1996, p134-5) sees the secessionists as docetists with very similar views to those in Ignatius and so thinks 1 Jn 4:2 indicates that the secessionists deny Jesus' fleshly existence. But this is unlikely.

also present in Asia Minor - in Smyrna and Tralles. Ignatius is to be dated around 105-110, and 1 Jn perhaps 90-100. It is possible then that the secessionists later had some connection to the docetists combatted by Ignatius.[220]

We can also note that in the history of scholarship there have been many attempts to identify the secessionists with known groups. Proposals have included that they were charismatics, Jews, Cerinthians, the Docetists combatted by Ignatius or Gnostics.[221] Some scholars have argued that there was more than one group of opponents.[222] We must conclude that these attempts are misguided. We simply do not know enough about the secessionists to identify them with a known group.[223] They are closest to the docetists combatted by Ignatius, but are not to be identified with this group.

This means we simply do not know enough about the secessionists to relate them to any other group which we discuss in this book. We have no evidence that they are related to the opponents of the Pastor or to the Nicolaitans whom we will discuss in the next chapter, although we know nothing about the Christology of either group. The Jewish dimension of the teaching of the Pastor's opponents makes it unlikely that they had an exaggeratedly high Christology. Further, judging from 1 Jn 2:19-20, the secessionists seem to be an internal Johannine development. We can be fairly clear then that they are not to be identified with any other group we discuss here.

5.6 So what has happened in the community addressed, prior to 1 John being written?

Firstly, prior to 1 Jn being written, a group within the community have left - the secessionists. We cannot construct their thought in full. All we can note is that they had a different Christology from the author of 1 John, a Christology that saw Jesus' flesh as salvifically insignificant. The secessionists were a significant group and 1 Jn 4:5 – "the world listens to them" - suggests that they subsequently had some success in evangelism.[224]

Secondly, the departure of the secessionists (and perhaps their success in evangelism) has had a profoundly destabilising influence on the remaining members of the Johannine community addressed by 1 John. As a response to this, the author of 1 John writes to the community to answer the Christology

---

[220] See Brown 1982, p57-9 further on this.

[221] See the reviews of past scholarship in Brown 1982, p55-68; Neufeld 1994, p6-36; Edwards 1996, p60-3.

[222] See Smalley 1984, pxxiii-xxviii.

[223] We must recall that the recipients of 1 John probably knew a good deal about the secessionists, and so did not need to be reminded about their nature in writing.

[224] See Schnackenburg 1992, p24.

of the secessionists, but primarily to assure the remaining community of the reality of their salvation. Further, the elder also wrote 2 Jn to warn another community (or perhaps other communities) where the secessionists' missionaries have not yet arrived, of the threat of these secessionists (2 Jn 7-11).

5.7 Can we understand how the secessionists developed their theology?

Can we go one step further and suggest how the secessionists developed their theology? Following Brown, we can suggest that both the secessionists and the community of the author of 1 John have been reading the Gospel of John. This seems reasonable, since 2:19-20 shows that the secessionists had been part of the author's group. However, the author's community and the secessionists interpreted the Gospel differently, and we can suggest that both justified their current theology from the Gospel. Thus the secessionists' thought could have arisen as a particular way of interpreting the Johannine tradition as it is found in the Gospel of John.[225]

As we have noted, 1 Jn 4:2 and 2 Jn 7 suggest that the secessionists denied that Jesus' life in the flesh (including his death) mattered theologically, a position which the Johannine author could describe as not acknowledging the coming of Jesus "in the flesh". We can see how the secessionists' view could be developed from the Fourth Gospel. As Brown shows, Jn 1:14 can be interpreted in such a way "that the real purpose of Jesus' earthly life was simply to reveal God's glory in human terms (Jn 7:18; 8:50; 11:40; 14:9; 17:5, 24),"[226] a revelation achieved simply by the Word becoming flesh (1:14b). Further, the secessionists could argue that the sending of Jesus, the preexistent Son, was what brought salvation (Jn 3:17) and through this it was possible to have eternal life (Jn 17:3). These passages show that what we have suggested was the secessionists' view – that nothing Jesus actually did in his life in the flesh was of salvific significance – could have been developed from the Gospel.

If the salvific value of Jesus' life "in the flesh" was what was the difference between the author and the secessionists, then the secessionists' attitude to Jesus' death will be significant. 1 Jn 5:6 is helpful in this regard: "This is the one who came by water and blood, Jesus Christ, not with the water only, but with the water and the blood." Since this is connected to Jesus Christ and his "coming", which is the subject of 1 Jn 4:2-3 and 2 Jn 7, and since the author's strong insistence that Jesus did not come by water alone but

---

[225] See Brown 1982, p69-79. It is possible that they have been working with traditions that later became the Gospel. See also Houlden 1973, p17-20, although he also allows for external influences.

[226] Brown 1982, p75.

by water and blood seems to be aimed at someone who denied this, it seems legitimate to connect the verse to the secessionists.[227] It suggests that for the secessionists Jesus came "in water" whereas John insists Jesus came "in water and in blood". "In water" is best seen as a reference to Jesus' baptism, and suggests that the secessionist thought the incarnation of the preexistent Son took place in connection with Jesus' baptism; Brown suggests that it is possible to read the Fourth Gospel as meaning that this is how Jesus' baptism is to be understood.[228] By contrast, the statement in 1 Jn 5:6 that Jesus came "in water and in blood" is best seen as a reference to Jesus' crucifixion, and the water and blood that flowed from Jesus' side in Jn 19:34. The author thus insists on the significance of Jesus' death, and is probably doing so against the secessionists. Further, their lack of interest in the salvific significance of Jesus' death can also be seen as an interpretation of the Fourth Gospel, particularly its emphasis on glory with respect to Jesus' death.[229]

That the secessionists developed their views as an interpretation of the Fourth Gospel also enables us to understand the way the author discusses the Christology of the secessionists. He shares the same fundamental basis for his views – John's Gospel – and so his attack on the secessionists Christology is limited in scope. We can thus adequately account for the secessionists Christology as a development from the Fourth Gospel.[230]

6. Cerinthus

We need to discuss Cerinthus here briefly, since he has often been connected with Ephesus, specifically as one of the Johannine secessionists. As we noted above, in Adv Haer 3.3.4 (=HE 4.14.3-8) Irenaeus writes: "There are also those who heard from him [Polycarp] that John, the disciple of the Lord, going to bathe at Ephesus, and perceiving Cerinthus within, rushed out of the

---

[227] Edwards (1996, p60) and Strecker (1996, p69-70) also see 1 Jn 5:6-8 as polemical. See also Neufeld 1994, p27-9.

[228] See Brown 1982, p77-8. He notes for example that before the statement that the light was coming into the world in 1:9, John discusses the role of John the Baptist in 1:6-8 and that after Jn 1:14 in which the Word becomes flesh we have the statement in which John the Baptist testifies to the incarnate Word by proclaiming his preexistence (1:15).

[229] Brown (1982, p78-9) shows that there are features of the Fourth Gospel that could have led the secessionists to down play the significance of the crucifixion as a salvific event and to regard it simply as a revelation of glory. John's account of the passion and death of Jesus emphasises revelation and victory rather than suffering; see 10:17-181 12:32-3; 16:32; 18:6; 19:11, 30. On Jesus' death and glory see also Smith 1995, p115-122. See the different interpretation in Strecker 1996, p182-5 who thinks this verse refers to the docetic secessionists' rejection of the eucharist.

[230] Note Pervo's (1992, p62 n91) comment: "Most reconstructions of the opponents of the writer of *1 John* now regard them as 'johannine' in inspiration."

bath-house without bathing, exclaiming, 'Let us fly, lest even the bath-house fall down, because Cerinthus, the enemy of the truth, is within.'"

We have already noted that we do not know enough about the secessionists to associate them with Cerinthus. However, it also seems clear that we do not have much reliable information about Cerinthus himself, although we have no reason to doubt his connection with Ephesus.[231] Brown discusses the evidence from patristic sources and shows that Cerinthus is generally presented either as a gnostic or a Jewish Christian, with the gnostic presentation being the earliest attested, and Brown and Hill suggest, the most reliable.[232] We do not have any clear evidence which dates Cerinthus' activity, and Brown suggests he was active in the first quarter of the second century.[233] Further, the only likely contact between Cerinthus' views and those of the secessionists is found in 1 Jn 5:6, since according to Irenaeus (Adv Haer 1.26.1), Cerinthus thought that "Christ descended upon him [Jesus] in the form of a dove from the Supreme Rule".[234] However, if 1 Jn had Cerinthus in view in 1 Jn 5:6, we would have expected him to write of the coming of Christ on Jesus, not of the coming of Jesus Christ.[235] Thus, it seems very unlikely that there was any connection between Cerinthus and the secessionists.[236] However, Brown suggests that Cerinthus was active after 1 Jn was written and that at some point the secessionists joined Cerinthus, taking John's Gospel with them. This would be one factor in explaining the popularity of John's Gospel with Gnostics,[237] and Cerinthus' thought would in part be a development of the secessionists' views. This is possible, but it can be no more than a suggestion. Further, although it is likely that Cerinthus gained some sort of a following in Ephesus, we do not know whether there was a "Cerinthus group" in the city.[238]

---

[231] See Hill 2000, p137.

[232] Brown 1982, p770; see also Hill 2000, p135-72, who also argues for the authenticity of Cerinthus' chiliasm. See also Brown 1982, p65-8, 766-71; Bardy 1921, p344-73; Hultgren and Haggmark 1996, p34-6; Klauck 2000, p450-1

[233] Brown 1982, p65-6; Klauck (2000, p450) dates his activity to 100-120 CE.

[234] Hill (2000, p149-59) defends the reliability of Irenaeus' account.

[235] See Brown 1982, p67. He also notes "Moreover, since Cerinthus held that Christ descended upon Jesus after the baptism, would the author not have been making a partial concession to Cerinthus when he said that there was a coming of Jesus Christ in water (at baptism)?"

[236] See Neufeld 1994, p16-17.

[237] He suggests (1982, p105) that Irenaeus' report that John opposed Cerinthus "may be a historicizing simplification of the fact that opponents of 1 John became Cerinthians."

[238] Hultgren (1994, p99) notes that Cerinthus does not seem to have been the founder of a school or community.

7. Overall Conclusions

We have argued that all four Johannine documents can be seen as the work of one author, John the Elder; at the very least they are all part of the one tradition, and belong in the one location. Although we do not think we can speak of a "Johannine community" on the basis of the Fourth Gospel, clearly 1-3 Jn are addressed to a specific group of "Johannine" Christians. Given the connection between John's Gospel and Ephesus, the additional evidence that locates 1 Jn in Ephesus, and the connections between 1-3 Jn, we can proceed with confidence to use the Letters as evidence for Christians in the city.

We have also argued that we should not read 1 Jn primarily as a polemical letter and so we can say far less about the secessionists than many recent scholars. However, we have argued that the secessionists have docetic tendencies, although we cannot identify them with any known group.

But did the secessionists continue to exist in Ephesus? We can suggest that they did. They have leaders (who are spoken of as "many antichrists" (1 Jn 2:18) and as false prophets (1 Jn 4:1)), at least one distinctive theological position (and we can certainly suggest that they had further theological views), they seem to have had some success in mission (1 Jn 4:5), and to have been sending out some missionaries to other outlying Johannine groups (2 Jn 7-11). These are all signs of the formation of a group. Further, the author of 1 Jn does not try to convince the secessionists to change their minds; as far as he is concerned, they have gone "into the world" and he does not seek to refute their theology in detail. It seems likely then that the secessionists continued to exist as a separate group in Ephesus, and perhaps also elsewhere. This also explains both 1 Jn 2:26 and 3:7, where the author warns against "those who would deceive you" (2:26). These two verses suggest that the secessionists continued to exist as a group and imply some continuing interaction between them and the Johannine community addressed by the author of 1 Jn.[239]

We have therefore gained evidence for two groups in Ephesus – the Johannine community which is centred in Ephesus, but has house churches in outlying areas, and the secessionists. We will draw further on 1-3 Jn in Part Three of this work.

---

[239] See Lieu 1991, p13; see also Bauer 1971, p92; Brown 1982, p104-6.

Chapter 7

Revelation 2:1-7: The Proclamation to the Church in Ephesus and the Nicolaitans

1. Introductory questions

1.1 Authorship

The author of Revelation identifies himself simply as "John" (1:1, 4, 9; 22:8). That he adds no further details suggests he was well known to the readers of the book. There is no internal evidence which suggests that the author was, or wanted to present himself as, the author of John's Gospel or the letters of John, and it is very unlikely that the Gospel of John and Revelation were written by the same person.[1] We cannot identify "John" the author of Revelation with any other known figure.

However, it is likely that the author was a Palestinian Jew. The apocalypse as a genre was commonly found within Palestinian Judaism, while we have no known examples from the eastern or western Diaspora. The author has a distinctive style of Semitizing Greek, which suggests his first language was Aramaic or perhaps Hebrew.[2] We also know that many Jews fled from Palestine after the first Jewish revolt of 66-73 CE., and many thousands were sold into slavery.[3] Thus it seems likely that the author was a refugee to Asia Minor from Palestine after the revolt.

---

[1] For discussions see Yarbro Collins 1984, p28-9; 31-2; Aune 1997, pl-liii. That the author of Revelation speaks of the twelve apostles as figures of the past in 21:14 means it is very unlikely that he was the son of Zebedee. Further, we have argued that the Fourth Gospel was written by John the Elder, and a number of factors argue against common authorship of Rev and John's Gospel. These include that different words are used to refer to the same thing (eg. "lamb" and Jerusalem); differences in theological outlook and eschatological perspectives; differences in syntax, style and vocabulary.

[2] For further points see Charles 1920, 1, pxliii-xliv; Aune 1997, pl. The author also has detailed knowledge of the Hebrew OT; see Aune 1998, pcxxi.

[3] Josephus, Ant 20:256; JW 7:410-19. Aune (1997, pcxxi) compares Trypho's departure from Palestine to Asia Minor because of the Bar Kosiba revolt; see Justin, Dial. 1.3.

1.2 Dating

Irenaeus, who was born in Asia Minor and knew Polycarp, bishop of Smryna (d. c. 155 CE), said that John saw the apocalyptic vision "towards the end of Domitian's reign".[4] Since Domitian ruled from 81 to 96 CE, this would be around 95-6. This external evidence is supported by a number of other factors which argue that this is the most likely date. Firstly, the use of the symbolic name "Babylon" for Rome (14:8; 16:19; 17:5; 18:2, 10, 21) points decisively to a date after 70 CE. Secondly, the legend of Nero *redivius* is reflected in 13:3; 17:11; Nero died in 68, and the legend is attested in 69, but since Rev presupposes widespread knowledge of the legend, a somewhat later date seems to be required. Thirdly, the earliest attestation of the phrase "οἱ δώδεκα ἀπόστολοι" used in Rev 21:14, is 80-95 CE, which suggests a date for Revelation after 80 CE.[5] Finally, factors which some scholars have thought favoured the earlier dating at the end of Nero's reign (c. 68 CE) can be interpreted plausibly against the background of Domitian's reign.[6] The evidence then suggests that the traditional date towards the end of Domitian's reign (c. 95-96 CE) is the most likely one. A date in the early 90's is favoured by most scholars today.[7]

---

[4] Irenaeus, *Adv. Haer.* 5.30.3, written around 180 CE. It is not clear whether Irenaeus thought the text containing the vision was written at the same time, or a little later, but with no positive evidence for a later date, his remark supports a date of 95-96; see Yarbro Collins 1984, p76.

[5] See Aune 1997, plxiv.

[6] For example, references to the temple and Jerusalem in Rev 11:1-2, 8, which seem to presuppose that the temple is still standing, do not require that the book was written before 70. Further, John's reuse of earlier materials in the book accounts for the features which have led some scholars to argue for a date in the late 60s.

[7] Yarbro Collins 1984, p54-83; Beasley-Murray 1974, p37-8 favours a date of around 95; Thompson 1990, p13-15 for between 92-96; Court 1994, p96-103 leaves the issue open. For a review of the date see Friesen 2001, p136-51. As we will note below, there is no reliable evidence supporting the theory that Domitian persecuted Christians; that he was thought to have persecuted Christians has been one factor in dating Rev to his reign. However, Revelation does not portray a universal persecution but rather shows John's expectation of persecution. The past incidents of persecution in Rev are part of the sporadic opposition encountered by Christians in the first century. See also Biguzzi 1998, p276-90, for support of a Domitianic date and a connection with the temple of the Sebastoi. The other options are the reign of Trajan (98-117 CE) or the reign of Nero (54-68 CE; see previous footnote). Hengel 1989, p81 suggests a Trajanic date for the completion of a work begun under Nero. Farrer (1964, p32-7) favours an early Trajanic date around 100 CE. These are all dates for the completion of Rev. Aune (1997, pcxviii-cxxxiv) gives a detailed proposal of stages of composition, which helps to explain the existence of features in Rev which have led some scholars to date Rev to the late 60s. Aune (1997, pcxxxii) dates the completion of Revelation to "the last decade of the first century A.D., perhaps even after the turn of the century during the reign of Trajan (A.D. 98-117)."

1.3 Did John know the Christian community in Ephesus to which he writes?

Given the differences between the proclamations, and their details about people and the circumstances of each community, there seems little doubt that John knew the situation of each of the communities he addresses well.[8] It also seems very likely that John was personally known to each of the communities, and may have had an itinerant prophetic ministry in these centres.[9] We noted above that in 1:4 John simply gives his name and adds no further introduction; that he writes in his own name, in contrast to most other writers of apocalypses,[10] suggests that the author must already have been well known to the members of the seven churches as a reliable and authoritative person.[11] We should regard him as a reliable source of information for the situation at Ephesus. It is also possible that John lived in Ephesus before he was exiled to Patmos, but we have no definite evidence for this.[12]

1.4 The unity of Rev 2-3 with the rest of the book

R.H. Charles suggested that the letters were written earlier than the rest of Revelation and were originally seven real letters sent independently to the churches addressed. Later the letters were collected by the author, the endings and parts of the beginnings of the letters were added, and they were used at the beginning of the book.[13] This would mean that 2:1-7 would not provide

---

[8] Ramsay (1904a) and Hemer (1986) sought to show that John used features of the history, economics and topography of the individual cities to which he wrote. However, see the critical remarks, particularly about Hemer's work, in Thompson 1990, p202-4 and Friesen 1995b, p291-306. But John clearly knows the communities to which he writes well.

[9] See Aune 1981, p26-7; 1997, p131; Yarbro Collins 1984, p46; Schnackenburg 1991, p56.

[10] Other apocalyptic writers generally wrote in the name of a great figure of the past, such as Moses, Enoch, Ezra or Baruch.

[11] See Kirby 1988, p199. Further, Aune (1990, p203-4) notes: "The implicit function of these proclamations [Rev 2-3], ... is to demonstrate that the risen Christ, speaking through the prophet John in the Spirit, knows precisely the situation of each and every one of the seven communities." We will note below that John was probably an itinerant prophet who regularly travelled a particular circuit, which would explain why he knew all seven churches.

[12] See Aune 1981, p27-8; Yarbro Collins 1984, p46, 53, n47, 103. Patmos, which is off the coast of Miletus, was closer to Ephesus than to any of the other seven churches, which suggests that John was exiled from Ephesus. Eusebius reports the tradition that when Nerva succeeded Domitian, John "took up his residence at Ephesus"; see HE 3.18.1; 20.7-9; 23.1. However, it is uncertain if this tradition is reliable.

[13] See Charles 1920, 1, p37-47. He thought the letters expected the congregations to survive until Christ's advent (2.25; 3:3) but that 3:10 presupposed a universal martyrdom, as did Rev 4-22. Rev 3:10 was thus added later, when the author's views had changed. However, we note that 4-22 does not expect all Christians to die, so the supposed contradiction disappears. Further, Charles thought Rev 4-22 pointed to a worldwide persecution in connection with the imperial cult, an issue which was absent from the letter.

evidence for the Ephesian Christians in 95 CE, but rather at some earlier period.

However, the letters are intimately connected with the rest of the book. In particular, the way Jesus Christ is spoken of at the beginning of each of the seven letters repeats features of the vision of the one like a Son of Man in 1:12-20 and the images used in the promises to the one who conquers at the end of each of the letters are all repeated in Rev 19:5-22:21.[14] Further, a number of key images, symbols and motifs used later in the visions are introduced in the seven letters.[15] Finally, a very regular pattern is followed in each letter and there are strong connections between them.[16] These factors suggests that the letters were composed together for their present context and at the same time as the rest of the book.[17]

2. The proclamation to Ephesus (Rev 2:1-7)

Here we will discuss what the letter to "the church in Ephesus" tells us about the Christians in the city to whom John writes.

2.1 Introduction

The risen Christ communicates a prophetic proclamation to each of the seven churches through John. These communications have often been characterised as letters (as we have been calling them up to now), but this is somewhat inaccurate since they do not follow the pattern of ancient letters. It is better to regard them as proclamations by the risen Christ.[18] A number of points need to be made before we examine the proclamation to Ephesus.

However, the concentration on the imperial cult in Rev 4-22 is probably part of the author's strategy and the imperial cult was probably not being systematically forced on Christians in Asia at this time; see Yarbro Collins, 1984, p74.

[14] See Enroth 1990, p600 n15; see also Court 1994, p108; Schüssler Fiorenza 1991, p34 and for example the correspondence between 2:7 and 22:2, 14; 2:11 and 21:8; 22:14.

[15] See Thompson 1990, p180. He notes terms such as blasphemy, deception, fornication and Satan. Thus "Later usages loop back recursively to the messages given to the seven churches." (p180) See also Feuillet 1963, p30.

[16] For connections note for example: 2:5 and 2:9 (first works); 3:8 and 3:20 (a door); 2:9 and 3:17 (being rich and poor).

[17] Thompson 1990, p41-52 discusses the narrative and metaphoric unity of Revelation; some of the features he points to connect Rev 2-3 with the rest of the book. See also Thompson 1990, p179-81; Yarbro Collins 1984, p73-5; Court 1979, p21-4; Beasley-Murray 1974, p70-1; Schüssler Fiorenza 1991, p45-7. Aune (1997, pcxxxii) suggests that 2:1-3:22 was added at the final stage of composition of the book; on this view the proclamations would provide evidence for Ephesian Christians at the time of composition.

[18] This term is favoured by Aune 1990, p182-204; see also Schüssler Fiorenza 1991, p46. Aune notes that the seven proclamations exhibit few features derived from the

2.1.1 Why seven churches, and why these seven?

John addresses seven churches, but the fact that he chooses seven, the number which for him is symbolic of completeness or wholeness, suggests that John is writing with other churches in Asia, and probably the whole church, in mind.[19] While each proclamation is in a sense addressed to each of the seven churches and so has a wider relevance, as the plural ἐκκλησίαις in 2:7 and parallels show (and note also 2:23), the distinctiveness of each proclamation shows that each is primarily addressed to a particular, named church, which is in a unique situation and is facing particular problems.

But why has John chosen these seven congregations? We cannot ultimately say why, since he does not tell us. But two reasons suggest themselves. Firstly, perhaps these were the most important Christian communities in the province of Asia at this time.[20] Secondly, perhaps these seven churches, which were all within one hundred miles of Ephesus, constituted a circuit travelled regularly by itinerant Christian teachers and prophets, including John, who was probably an itinerant prophet who clearly knew these seven churches well.[21]

Certainly it is likely that John wrote to Ephesus because it was the capital of the province of Asia and hence the Christian community there was of particular significance. Secondly, it was the closest major community to the

---

Hellenistic epistolary tradition and are clearly distinct in form from a Hellenistic letter. Ramsay 1904a, p38-40 was influential in establishing the tradition of calling them "letters".

[19] See Feuillet 1963, p41-2; Court 1994, p35; Friesen 2001, p136; Rev 2:23 supports this view. Schüssler Fiorenza 1991, p53 notes that the number seven, which John uses a great deal, "symbolically indicates their [the proclamations] universal character"; see also Beagley 1987, p30; Enroth 1990, p603. Note however that this does not *necessarily* mean that John is writing to *all* the Christians in each place, such as Ephesus; we will discuss this issue below.

[20] There were other Christian communities in the province of Asia by this time, certainly at Troas (Acts 20:5-12), Colossae (Col 1:2) and Hierapolis (Col 4:13) and almost certainly at Magnesia and Tralles since the churches there were well established when Ignatius wrote to them ten-fifteen years later.

[21] Court (1994, p34-5) suggests these seven churches "were probably centres of the Johannine mission field - perhaps the only churches acknowledging John." But this is an argument from silence. Ramsay (1904a, p185-96) suggested these seven churches were located on a circuit which could be followed by the person who carried the proclamations, a suggestion which would also explain the order of the seven proclamations. However, as Aune notes (1997, p131) "Ramsay's hypothesis of a circular post road has no firm basis in archaeological fact but is rather an inference based on the location of cities." See also Friesen 1995b, p300. But a number of roads radiated out from Ephesus and so the six cities may all have been accessible on these roads. Bauer (1971, p78) thought that John "selected the most prominent communities from those in his area which met the prerequisite of seeming to afford him the possibility of exerting a real influence"; even then he had to include churches "which only to a very limited degree belonged to the sphere of his influence" so as to be able to write to *seven* churches. Thus, those which are not included were, in Bauer's view, "heretical". But clearly this is an argument from silence; see further Robinson 1988, p145-61.

island of Patmos, and so the most logical place for the carrier of the proclamations to begin his or her travels. That the proclamation to Ephesus is the first proclamation is probably due to both of these factors.

2.1.2 The structure of the proclamations

Each of the proclamations follows a regular pattern, which Aune has analysed into the following structural features, while noting that there is considerable variety in content and some variety in order. Here we also give in brackets the sections in Rev 2:1-7 which correspond to this structure.

(1) the *adscriptio,* which states the destination of the proclamation (2:1a);
(2) the command to write, expressed by the aorist imperative γράψον (2:1b);
(3) the τάδε λέγει formula, a prophetic messenger formula and also a proclamation formula characteristic of edicts issued by Roman magistrates and emperors,[22] which provides justification for the use of the first person in the rest of the proclamation (2:1c);
(4) the Christological predications, which show that the speaker is the exalted Christ of the vision in 1:12-20 (2:1c);
(5) the *narratio,* or narrative, which provides a brief outline of the situation of each congregation (2:2-3 and resumed in v6);
(6) the *dispositio* or arrangement, which is the central section of each of the proclamations; the narratio serves as the basis for the assertions made in this section (2:4-5);
(7) the proclamation formula ("Let anyone who has an ear listen to what the Spirit is saying to the churches"), which is an injunction to the audience to pay attention to the message (2:7a);
(8) the promise-to-the-Victor formula (2:7b).[23]

2.2 What does the proclamation to Ephesus tell us about the addressees in Ephesus?

Here we will not give a word by word exegesis, but will rather highlight the features of the proclamation to Ephesus which are relevant to our overall discussion.

---

[22] See Aune 1990, p187-9. τάδε λέγει is perhaps best translated as 'thus says', since it was obsolete in Koine Greek, and thus was an intentional archaism at the time.
[23] See Aune 1990, p183-94; 1997, p119-124; for other suggestions see Thompson 1991, p38; Schüssler Fiorenza 1991, p46, Grové 2000, p193-210.

2.2.1 The ἄγγελος of the adscriptio *(v1a)*

The proclamation is addressed by the risen Christ to the ἄγγελος of the community in Ephesus; a similar pattern is found in each of the proclamations (see also 1:20).

Who is the ἄγγελος? It has been suggested that the angels are to be identified with bishops or elders of these communities.[24] However, this is unlikely, given that there is no precedent for such leaders being addressed as "ἄγγελος", and that Rev does not mention bishops elsewhere.[25] Further, since John consistently uses ἄγγελος elsewhere of supernatural beings, it is likely that the term has this meaning in 2:1-3:22.[26] Most scholars see these angels as heavenly beings who are, in a sense, the patron angels of the congregations, or representatives of the churches *in* the heavenly world. This idea is seen as based on the Jewish apocalyptic idea that each nation had its angelic representative, who presided over its fortunes. John has adapted this familiar notion to a new situation.[27] Thus they are best seen as the spiritual counterparts or personifications of the communities as a whole. This also explains why most of what is said in the seven proclamations applies to the whole community and not just to leaders. In any case, the verse does not give evidence for community leaders of some sort.

Since the proclamation to Ephesus is addressed to "the angel" it contains second person singular pronouns and verb forms.[28]

2.2.2 The narratio *(v2-3)*

The *narratio*, or narrative, which is introduced by an οἶδα clause, describes the situation of the community in the past and the present. It serves as a basis

---

[24] See the comprehensive survey of views, including this one, in Aune 1997, p108-112. For example, Barrett (1985, p45) asks "Were the *angeloi* members of the churches to whom was committed the task of sending messages to other churches, and correspondingly of receiving messages from other churches?" Compare Clement in Hermas, Vis II.4.3, whose job it was to receive and transmit messengers. However Barrett (1985, p45) notes: "it is against it that elsewhere in Revelation angels, *angeloi*, are undoubtedly supernatural beings." Alternatively, the term could mean "messenger" and so refer to the person John sent as his representative to each of the seven churches with a copy of his apocalypse. But again John's normal usage of ἄγγελος goes against this.

[25] See Schüssler Fiorenza 1985, p145; Enroth, 1990 p603-4.

[26] See Aune 1997, p131. See for example 1:1; 5:2, 11; 7:1,2, 11; 8:2-13.

[27] See Caird 1966, p24; Satake 1966, p150-55; Yarbro Collins 1984, p40-1; Aune 1997, p131-2. Schüssler Fiorenza (1985, p145-6; 1991, p52-3) suggests that the seven angels to whom the proclamations are addressed are the visionary counterparts of the prophets of each community; on this see Yarbro Collins 1984, p40-3. Feuillet 1963, p41 gives a summary of all the options.

[28] In some of the other proclamations the address occasionally shifts to second and third person plural forms, eg 2:10, 13. John can also address a particular group within a community; see 2:10, 14-15, 20-22, 24; see also Satake 1966, p152-3.

for the *dispositio* or response which follows, and gives the actual situation of
the Ephesian community from the perspective of the risen Christ.

2.2.2.1 Commendation about testing the "false apostles"

The risen Jesus begins by commending the hearers in Ephesus: "I know your
works, namely, your toil and endurance (οἶδα τὰ ἔργα σου καὶ τὸν κόπον
καὶ τὴν ὑπομονήν σου; v2)."[29] Such expressions occur regularly in the seven
proclamations;[30] their referent in each case is closely related to the wider
situation of the church addressed. Accordingly, we need firstly to examine the
rest of v2 where it is said that the addressees cannot tolerate "evil people",
which is clearly a reference to those "who call themselves apostles but are
not" whom the readers have tested and found to be false (v2:2c). Thus, some
outsiders have come to the community claiming to be "apostles", which has
the basic meaning of "envoy" or "emissary". As a significant centre on
important trade routes, it is understandable that itinerant "apostles" visited
Ephesus.[31] Can we say anything about them?

John uses the term "ἀπόστολος" in two other places. In 18:20 "saints,
apostles and prophets" are said to witness the destruction of "Babylon". Here
"apostles" seems to be a special group of "messengers", which Aune suggests
includes the Twelve, but could also include other "apostles".[32] In 21:14 John
speaks of "the twelve names of the twelve apostles of the Lamb", which is
clearly a reference to "the Twelve" who followed Jesus, and so excludes, for
example, Paul.

What is the meaning of the term in 2:2? It is unlikely that John means the
term "apostle" to have the restricted sense of "the Twelve apostles" in 2:2,
since it is hard to believe that in the nineties anyone went about claiming to be
one of the Twelve.[33] However, there are many examples in the NT of the use
of the term "ἀπόστολος" to refer to a broader group of messengers, envoys,
or itinerant missionaries. This included people like James, Barnabas, Paul,
Silas, Andronicus and Junia.[34] It is likely that those "who call themselves

---

[29] Here the καί is epexegetical, and κόπος and ὑπομονή are two aspects of the "ἔργα" of
the Ephesian Christians; see Aune 1997, p143.

[30] ἔργον also occurs in 2:19, 22, 23, 26; 3:1,2, 8,15; it is used positively in 14:23;
15:3; negatively in 9:20; 16:11; 18:6. People are judged by their works; see 20:12, 13;
22:12. κόπος is found only here and in 14:13, where it is used positively. ὑπομονή is used
in 1:9; 2:19; 3:10, 13:10; 14:12. In 13:10 and 14:12 it is called for in the face of severe
difficulties faced by the saints. βαστάζω is found only here and in 17:7 where it has a
different sense. κοπιάω is used only here.

[31] See Mounce 1977, p87.

[32] See Aune 1997, p144.

[33] See Caird 1966, p30.

[34] See Acts 14:14; 1 Cor 15:7; 2 Cor 8:23; Gal 1:19; Phil 2:25; 1 Thess 2:6; Rom 16:7;
see also 1 Cor 12:28; 15:7; 2 Cor 12:11f; see also Caird 1966, p30; Prigent 2001, p158. For

apostles" were claiming to belong to this wider group and that they were itinerant, since apostles of this type in the early church generally travelled from place to place; further John's language suggests they arrived at some point in Ephesus and were then tested.[35] Clearly then itinerant Christian teachers, who called themselves "apostles" and can be seen as part of the wider phenomenon of travelling Christian apostles, prophets and teachers, have attempted to gain a hearing in the Ephesian church but have been rejected there.

John clearly thinks these self-styled apostles had no right to call themselves "apostles", but we do not know why he thinks they are "wicked people."[36] We do not know if they claimed the support of particular Christian leaders, or what sort of message they preached.[37] Further, we do not know if other streams of the early Church of this period would also have considered them to be false apostles. Or was the heart of the issue here one on which John (and the Ephesian Christians who seem to agree with him, at least about these "apostles" and the Nicolaitans), was out of step with many others Christians of his time?[38]

We also do not know what sort of test the Ephesians used to determine that these apostles were false. Was it a doctrinal one (cf. 1 Jn 2:22) or one that concerned "the signs of a true apostle" (cf. 2 Cor 12:12), or did it concern an ethical matter, or something else?[39] Thus we cannot say whether these apostles were teaching a different gospel, or rather a different praxis, or something else again.[40] If these apostles tried to impose themselves on the Ephesians by claiming the authority of apostles, then the Ephesian Christians showed some strength of character in opposing them. Further, it is clear that these Ephesian Christians have had firsthand experience of conflict with other

---

a discussion of the term see Aune 1997, p144-6 and the literature referred to there. For travelling teachers of various sorts see also 3 Jn 5-8; Hermas, Mand 11.12; Did 11-13.

[35] See Yarbro Collins 1984, p43, 136-7; Aune 1997, p144; Müller 1984, p101-2.

[36] Aune (1997, p145) notes that "Since Ephesus may have been the center of his [John's] activity, he may actually have had personal experience in the testing and rejection of these 'apostles'."

[37] The case of those who came to Corinth and claimed to be apostles (2 Cor 11:13) and produced impressive credentials (2 Cor 11:22f) may be comparable.

[38] Aune (1997, p155) notes that Christianity was "a diverse movement, and beliefs and practices thought perfectly appropriate in one region might be regarded as deviant in another." It is anachronistic to speak of the Ephesians' "hatred of heresy" on the basis of this verse, as Caird 1966, p31 does.

[39] Schüssler Fiorenza (1985, p115) notes that the criteria for testing these itinerant apostles is not given; cf. Didache 11-13. Prigent (2001, p158) suggests the test is related to 2:2 and so "consisted of the observation of a refusal on the part of these individuals to risk their comfort, their liberty or their lives for the confession of their faith."

[40] Thus Beasley-Murray (1974, p74) is too certain when he says that they are "evil" not so much because of their unorthodox doctrinal opinions but because of the "moral evil which resulted from their doctrine".

Christians who claimed some form of authority, but whom the Ephesians chose to reject.

Some scholars have connected these apostles with the Nicolaitans of Rev 2:6, and thus claimed that the Nicolaitans had itinerant apostles.[41] However, this is unlikely. Firstly, John makes no connection between the apostles and the Nicolaitans, apart from praising the church in Ephesus for rejecting both groups, which is clearly an insecure basis on which to identify them.[42] Secondly, John writes that the apostles have been "tested" and "found" to be false using Aorists (ἐπείρασας, εὗρες), indicating that the events of testing and discerning belonged in the past, while he speaks of the Nicolaitans in the present tense (μισεῖς, μισῶ), showing they are an on-going threat.[43] Thirdly, John begins v6 with the adversative ἀλλά, showing that this verse begins a new train of thought, again suggesting the apostles and Nicolaitans are different groups.[44] Fourthly, when John mentions the Nicolaitans in Pergamum, nothing is said of apostles, and when he speaks of what is almost certainly the same group in Thyatira he speaks of their prophet (2:20), not their apostles. Thus it is very unlikely that the "apostles" of 2:2 are Nicolaitans.

It has also been suggest that these "apostles" were supporters of Paul, or even Paul himself.[45] However, there is no positive evidence to support this proposal. Unfortunately, then, we know no details about these apostles who had been active in Ephesus.

We noted above that the risen Jesus commends the Ephesians for their works, their toil and patient endurance and not growing weary (v2-3) and that the meaning of such terms is related to the situation in the church.[46] It seems

---

[41] Bousset 1906, p237; Lohmeyer 1970 p22; Kraft 1974, p56; Müller 1984, p102; Schüssler Fiorenza 1985, p115; Enroth 1990, p604; Thompson 1990, p123 see them as Nicolaitans.

[42] See Yarbro Collins 1984, p43. The basis for identifying the Nicolaitans, Balaam and Jezebel (see below) is that the teaching ascribed to them is the same, which is clearly a more secure basis for an identification.

[43] See Aune 1997, p143.

[44] See Aune 1997, p147.

[45] Aune (1997, p144) notes that the Tübingen school proposed this. Hort (1908, p21) notes that "This is one of the passages supposed to shew antipathy to St Paul. No doubt that (e.g. in Gal.) he has occasion to plead his apostleship against Judaizers, 1 Cor. ix.2; 2 Cor. xi.5=xii.11; xii.12; and two or three passages in *Hom. Clem.* at a much later time shew a very bitter feeling against him and his claims. But St Paul himself had occasion to say in like manner of others that they were pseudapostles (sic), no apostles of Christ (2 Cor. xi.13f.), doubtless Judaizers. The words here may just as well apply to Judaizers, or indeed to any who put forward false claims to apostleship."

[46] The meaning of ἔργον is particularly related to its context. In 2:19, 26 it is positive, but in 2:22, 23, it relates to the works of Jezebel. In 3:1,2 it is negative and probably relates to the "soiling of garments" (3:4). In 3:8 it is positive; in 3:15 negative. Often "I know your works" simply indicates that the risen Christ knows about the church; the rest of the proclamation indicates what he knows, and whether it leads to commendation or judgement.

likely that these expressions are closely related to the presence of these false apostles and that the toil, patient endurance and not growing weary for which they are commended is that which is involved in resisting the false apostles.[47]

2.2.2.2 Endurance and Suffering (v3)

In v3 the risen Christ says that he knows that the Ephesians are enduring patiently, bearing up "for the sake of my name" and not growing weary (v3). But what are they enduring? The phrase "because of my name (διὰ τὸ ὄνομά μου)" means "because of me", since "name" refers to the exalted Christ.[48] References to being hated or suffering "because of my name" are found in Mt 10:22; Mk 13:13; Hermas Vis 3.2.1; Sim 9.28.3; Pol, Phil 8:2; the phrase can thus be used in the context of suffering and martyrdom. So this phrase in 2:3, along with mention of "having endurance (ὑπομονὴν ἔχεις)" suggests that the thought here is of suffering and persecution.[49] Since John explicitly speaks of difficulties caused by Jews elsewhere in the proclamations (2:9 and 3:9), we can suggest that the suffering spoken of here was caused by pagans. However, we cannot say any more than this.

2.2.3 The dispositio (v4-5)

2.2.3.1 An Accusation (v4)

The *dispositio* ("arrangement"), which is marked by the use of imperatives and future indicatives,[50] is the central section of each of the proclamations and gives the risen Christ's verdict on the situation of the Christian community. As we have noted, the *narratio* gives the basis for the assertions made in this section.

In v4 the risen Christ makes an accusation against the Ephesians: "you have abandoned the love you had at first". Is this love for God,[51] love for one another within the community,[52] or love for those not in the community (by no means impossible given the emphasis on mission in Revelation)?[53]

---

[47] See Beasley-Murray 1974, p74.

[48] Aune 1997, p146.

[49] See Yarbro Collins 1984, p113.

[50] Aune 1990, p192. The *dispositiones* are not marked by a stereotypical phrase used in all the proclamations.

[51] See Prigent 2001, p159.

[52] This is the view of Müller 1984, p103.

[53] See Beale 1999, p230. He relates this to 2:1: as lampstands "their primary role in relation to their Lord should be that of a light of witness to the outside world." Falwell sees the reference to their first love to be a love for non-Christians which had lead to first works of evangelism. John is thus indicating "a lack of missionary fervor" and was calling them to return to this; see Falwell 1948, p193; see also p191. He sees evangelism as a particular

Beasley-Murray connects the reference to love with the comment in v5 that they are to "do the works you did at first". This seems reasonable, since both the love and the works were done "at first". This suggests to him that it is a love for other people that the community has abandoned, and that the loss of early love for others was accompanied by the cessation of early works of love.[54] Rev 2:5 ("do the works you did at first") would be a call to do loving works and thus to right the accusation made in v4 ("you have abandoned the love you had at first"). Beasley-Murray then connects this loss of love with their testing of the false apostles: "If the price paid by the Ephesians for the preservation of true Christianity was the loss of love, the price was too high, for Christianity without love is a perverted faith."[55] Their zeal for truth had led them to lose love.

While this is possible, it is clear that John is very general at this point, a point which is underlined by the different possibilities of love for God, love for the community and love for others which commentators support. Perhaps we are best to see the reference at this point as general. But the important point that Beasley-Murray recognises is the link between v4 and v5 with regard to love and works "at first". It seems likely then that John wants to indicate at this stage is that something is amiss with regard to love, and that it is linked in some way with "works" (v5). We will make a more specific suggestion below about the nature of this love, after noting what John says about works.

2.2.3.2 A Remedy: Remember, Repent, Do (v5)

The community is called to remember what they were once like, to repent, and to "do the works you did at first" (v5a). The use of the verb "μνημονεύειν", also found in 3:3, suggests that the author has a significant knowledge of the history of the community.[56]

As noted above, the connection between v4 and v5 suggests the latter verse involves works that are linked in some way to love. We can develop this

---

characteristic of the Christians in Ephesus (and in so doing is too dependent on Acts), but it is not clear that this verse must refer to love for outsiders. ἀγάπη is only found here and in 2:19, where the term is also undefined. In Rev 1:5 and 3:9 ἀγαπάω refers to Christ's love for the believer; φιλέω is used in this way in 3:19. In 12:11 ἀγαπάω is used of the martyrs who "loved not their lives even unto death"; in 20:9 we read of the "beloved city". Thus, the wider usage of ἀγάπη and related terms does not help us here.

[54] Beasley-Murray 1974, p75. Hort 1908, p22 suggests the love is "the characteristic ἀγάπη of Christian brotherhood, which poured itself forth in the first fervour of their faith." He compares 1 Thess 1:3; 3:6; 2 Thess 1:3; Phil 1:9; Col 1:4. Trevett (1992, p80) sees losing their first love as "a decline in ardour'.

[55] Beasley-Murray 1974, p75. See also Caird 1966, p31 – "their hatred of heresy had bred an inquisitorial spirit which left no room for love."

[56] See Aune 1997, p147.

interpretation of the call to "do the works you did at first" (v5a) a little further. We will note in section 3 below that the "works" (ἔργα) of the Nicolaitans spoken of in v6 concern eating food offered to idols and idolatry. The Ephesians "hate" these "works". This context suggests the "works" which the Ephesians did at first (v5a) concern actions which showed they were in agreement with John about the necessity for Christians to avoid all contact with idolatry, works which were the exact opposite of the "works" of the Nicolaitans.[57] These works which John calls the Ephesians to do again as they had at first would then involve avoiding idolatry, not attending pagan festivals, devoted worship of God alone and so on. Such "works" would also show their love for God and so this interpretation provides firmer ground for determining the meaning of the "love you had at first" of v4: it refers to love for God, which leads them to a total abandonment of all idolatry. At the time of writing, however, although they hate the idolatry of the Nicolaitans, some at least of the Ephesians are no longer acting as they did at first, and as John wants them to, with respect to involvement in idolatry and society.[58] They are called to return to these "first works" and thus to this "first love".

Aune thus sees this verse as indicating that there is a group of Christians in Ephesus who are not in the Nicolaitan camp, but who, as far as John is concerned, are not in agreement with him either and have departed from "the works done at first" (2:5), and so need to repent.[59] Aune also sees this group in some of the other churches mentioned in Rev 2-3, notably in Sardis (their works are imperfect in God's sight (3:2)) and in Laodicea (they are neither cold nor hot (3:15f)). When all of the seven churches are considered, Aune regards this centrist group as being the majority.[60]

The call to "do the works you did at first" (v5a) would thus be a call to be part of a Christian community that had no interactions with pagan idolatry, that avoided all contact with trade guilds, festivals and so on. In short, the call would be to works that identified the Ephesians as members of a tight-knit Christian community and to reinforce the boundaries with the world, which for John had become too lax, although as we will see, they were not as open as the boundaries of the Nicolaitan group. This interpretation has the merit of seeing "works" in 2:5 and 2:6 as having the same general referent, and of

---

[57] This is to develop an interpretation suggested by Aune 1981, p28-9.

[58] See also Thompson 1998, p65 who notes: "'The works you did at first' (when first becoming Christians) contrast with 'the works of the Nicolaitans,' as 'love' contrasts with 'hate' … The Likeness of a Human exhorts those at Ephesus to express that exclusivism that they had at first."

[59] Aune 1981, p29. In Aune 1997, p155 he notes that 2:5 may "point to the fact that second-generation Christians had developed a comfortable accommodation with the pagan world. John himself appears to be a separatist and intolerant of any other stance."

[60] Aune 1981, p29.

detecting an underlying consistency within 2:4-6 with regard to both actions "at first" and "works".[61]

If they do not repent, Christ will come "and remove your lampstand from its place" (v5b).[62] This is an allusion back to the opening of the proclamation (2:1): the threat here is that the one who walks among the seven lampstands will remove the Ephesians' lampstand from its place.[63] As Aune notes "This is nothing less than a threat to obliterate the Ephesian congregation as an empirical Christian community."[64]

It has also been suggested that the reference to Christ removing the lampstand of the church from its place is an allusion to the history of Ephesus as one of movement. The site of the city had been changed around 550 and again c. 281 BCE because navigation of the harbour was threatened by the silting up of the Cayster river. The risen Christ was alluding to this well-known feature of the city.[65] But this may be seeing too much in what is an image of judgement.

2.2.4 Resumed narratio (v6)

Rev 2:6 is a further part of the *narratio* since it has verbs in the present tense, a characteristic of the *narratio*, whereas the *dispositio* is marked by the use of imperatives and future indicatives, which are not found in v6.[66] Hence v6 is a further description of the situation of the community. We see then that the author here breaks the pattern found in most of the other proclamations in that the *narratio* follows the *dispositio*, as well as preceding it, as occurs also in 3:4.[67] We can also note that in 2:4 we have the phrase ἀλλὰ ἔχω κατὰ σοῦ

---

[61] Note however that ἔργα is used in a different sense in 2:2, where John commends them for "works", which are related to on-going endurance, whereas in v5 John complains of the current lack of the particular "works" he is referring to in that verse; see Kraft 1974, p56.

[62] The prediction that Christ will "come" could be to the second coming of Christ, as it is in 2:25 and 3:11. However, here the coming of Christ is conditional on their reaction to his words: if they do not repent, then he will come. Christ's coming envisaged here is thus a coming to the Christian community in Ephesus in judgement. See Caird 1966, p32; Court 1994, p35. The coming of Christ mentioned in the proclamations to Pergamum (2:16) and Sardis (3:3) is to be understood similarly.

[63] In the proclamation to Pergamum the threat to the church (2:16) also alludes to the opening of the communication (2:12); see Farrer 1964, p74.

[64] Aune 1997, p147.

[65] See Ramsay 1904a, p210-36, 243-6; Hemer 1986, p52-4; Court (1994, p35) comments: "Theological threats and promises thus can be seen to satirize the local environment of the church."

[66] See Aune 1990, p191-2.

[67] The fifth proclamation exhibits a similar disruption of the normal pattern with 3:1b being *narratio*, 3:2-3 *dispositio* and 3:4 part *narratio*, part *dispositio*; see Aune 1990, p190, 192. The *narratio* is generally introduced by the οἶδα clause, and so the finite verbs in the *narratio* "are limited to past and present tenses in the indicative"; see Aune 1990, p190. In

ὅτι ... and in 2:6 ἀλλὰ τοῦτο ἔχεις, ὅτι ... . Aune comments: "There can be little doubt that the author has intentionally used these positive and negative versions of this saying as an *inclusio* to frame the *dispositio*."[68]

In v6 the risen Christ commends the Ephesians for hating the works of the Nicolaitans, "which I also hate". We will consider the question of the identity of the Nicolaitans and their works in the next section.

2.2.5 The promise of victory (v7b)

Each of the proclamations closes with a promise which varies in form and structure. In the proclamation to Ephesus the promise is that to the one who conquers "I will grant to eat of the tree of life, which is in the paradise of God."[69]

The promise to the conqueror is a clear reference to Gen 2-3. There are perhaps additional allusions in this promise. As well as there being an allusion to the fruit from the tree of life which was not to be eaten by Adam and Eve in the "paradise of God" (Gen 3:22-4), perhaps there is also an allusion to the similarly attractive offer of food "offered to idols" being made by the Nicolaitans.[70] Such idol food for John means death. Yet there is rich compensation for those who refuse the forbidden food offered by the Nicolaitans, for those who refuse this food will receive much more treasured fruit from the true tree of life in the paradise of God, which is here clearly a symbol of the enjoyment of eternal life.[71]

3. The Nicolaitans

In Rev 2:6, addressed to the church in Ephesus, we read: "Yet this is to your credit: you hate the works of the Nicolaitans, which I also hate (ἀλλὰ τοῦτο

2:6 we have present indicative verbs, but not an οἶδα clause; in the *narratio* in 3:4 we also do not have an οἶδα clause.

[68] Aune 1990, p191.

[69] Caird argues that the conqueror "is the victim of persecution, whose martyr's death is his victory, just as the Cross was the victory of Christ." (See Caird 1966, p33; he bases this on 2:26; 3:21; 7:14; 12:11; 15:2.) But John does not imply that all Christians would undergo martyrdom, or that only martyrs enter Paradise, since the proclamations include general promises to all Christians (see 2:10b; 3:4; 3:10 (the whole church will be kept safe); 3:20), and all whose names are written in the book of life enter the heavenly city. Those who conquer are thus all Christians.

[70] See Farrer 1964, p71. For discussions of the phrase "tree of life" see Aune 1997, p151-4; Wong 1998, p211-26.

[71] The promise to eat from the tree of life is repeated at the end of Rev in 22:2, 14, as are all the promises in the proclamations. It has also been suggested that there is an allusion to the tree-shrine of Artemis and of its sacred enclosure which offered asylum; see Hemer 1986, p41-50, Court 1994, p35; Worth 1999b, p64-8.

ἔχεις, ὅτι μισεῖς τὰ ἔργα τῶν Νικολαϊτῶν ἃ κἀγὼ μισῶ)." What did the Nicolaitans stand for? Why have the Ephesian Christians addressed by John rejected them and what does this rejection say about these Ephesian Christians and their theology and life in the city? These are the questions we will explore here.

3.1 Were there any Nicolaitans in Ephesus?

But firstly we need to discuss the relationship between John's addressees in Ephesus and the Nicolaitans. The Ephesians are said to hate the works of the Nicolaitans, with "ἔργα" here referring to behaviour and lifestyle. That the Ephesians hate these works clearly means that they have rejected the Nicolaitans.[72]

But it is important to note that the Nicolaitans are clearly within the communities addressed at Pergamum and Thyatira. This is clearest in 2:16 – "If not, I will come to you soon [ie. the community] and war against them [ie. the Nicolaitans]." Thus, the Nicolaitans are Christians within these communities who thought it was acceptable (as we will argue) to eat food offered to idols, and to be in contexts that John regarded as idolatrous. We will note below that the Nicolaitans are a sub-group which is present at the time of writing *within* the churches in Pergamum and Thyatira (2:14-16, 20-5). It is possible that the Nicolaitans were also a sub-group within the church addressed in Ephesus, but the language of "hating the Nicolaitans" makes it more likely that the Ephesian Christian community addressed by John had rejected the Nicolaitans as a group.

Yet clearly there had been some contact between the Ephesian Christians addressed and the Nicolaitans. This can be explained in three possible ways. Firstly, that a group of itinerant Nicolaitans[73] had tried to be received by the Ephesian Christians but had been unsuccessful. Secondly, the Ephesian Christians had refused to have anything to do with the Nicolaitans who were established in Ephesus as a separate group with its own identity. Or thirdly, there had been a Nicolaitan sub-group within the group of Ephesian Christians addressed by John (as there currently was at Pergamum and Thyatira), but this sub-group had been rejected by those whom John now addresses, and have formed their own group.[74]

---

[72] See Malina and Pilch 2000, p52.

[73] We will see below that the Nicolaitans have prophets; this and the fact that the Nicolaitans existed in two churches and have been rejected in a third, suggests they were itinerant, although they also "settled down" in some places.

[74] We will discuss who John is addressing in Ephesus in section 4 below.

In any case, it seems very likely that a group of Nicolaitans existed in Ephesus at the time John writes, but were not among John's addressees.[75] The present tenses in 2:6 seem most decisive here – ἔχεις, μισεῖς, μισῶ; they suggest that those addressed by John hate a group which is in existence in the city at the time of writing, but which was not included among John's addressees and so was independent of them.[76] Further, as Aune notes, these present tenses used in v 6 to describe the Nicolaitans indicate that they are "a continuing threat."[77] It seems very likely then that there was a group of Nicolaitan Christians in Ephesus who had been rejected by the Ephesian Christians John addresses, but that they continued to exist and were a continuing presence and challenge to these Ephesian Christians.[78]

We can suggest that the Nicolaitans consisted of at least one house church, perhaps more. Such a group could have been founded by itinerant Nicolaitan leaders, and is now established outside rather than within the "ἐκκλησία" John addresses – whether it had originally been a part of those whom John addresses or not, we do not know. But for our purposes, two points emerge. Firstly, that a group of Nicolaitans currently existed in Ephesus. Secondly, the Christians John addresses "hate" these Nicolaitans, and so reject the Nicolaitans' teaching, while considering them to be an on-going threat. With these points in mind, we will discuss what we can know of the Nicolaitans.

3.2 Patristic testimony

Before proceeding further, we need to note that a group called the Nicolaitans are mentioned by a number of patristic sources. For example, Irenaeus (Haer 1.26.3; cf 3.11.1) basically repeats the biblical material, although he adds that the Nicolaitans were followers of Nicolaus, the proselyte of Antioch

---

[75] Thus, if our first option above is correct, then the itinerant Nicolaitans established a group of their own in Ephesus, and it was this group which was now "hated".

[76] Koester 1971, p155; 1995, p132; Fox 1994, p486, 496; Boxall 1998, p202 see a group of Nicolaitans in Ephesus. With respect to Pergamum and Thyatira, Thompson (1990, p122) notes that John is in conflict with local church members, not outsiders. He adds: "One could perhaps argue that they belong to different house churches in those cities, but there is no indication of that." With respect to Ephesus he notes (p122) that "the Ephesian Christians 'hate the works of the Nicolaitans' and thus do not allow them to be part of the church at Ephesus. There the Nicolaitans seem to be outsiders seeking to establish themselves in the Ephesian church." He does not consider the possibility of Nicolaitan house churches in Ephesus and does not consider the suggestion raised in the text. Farrer 1964, p74 envisages a group of Nicolaitans in Ephesus – "Nicolaitanism has taken root at Pergamum, as at Ephesus ..." Brown (1982, p104 n243) also sees the Nicolaitans as "a distinct group (to be hated) in the church at Ephesus".

[77] Aune 1997, p143; he notes by contrast that the verbs relating to the "apostles" of 2:2 are aorists, showing that the testing spoken of there was a past event.

[78] Aune (1997, p147) suggests "The Nicolaitans appear to be a minority group of Christians trying to gain a hearing and a more extensive following in the Ephesian church."

mentioned in Acts 6:5. Further, Clement of Alexandria (Str 2.20; 3.4) claims that Nicolaus was an ascetic, and that the Nicolaitans known to him had misunderstood a story about Nicolaus in which he was recorded to have said that one "ought to despise the flesh" (Strom 3.4.25).[79] However, the information given by these authors seems to have been derived from Revelation itself, from the name "Nicolaus" found in Acts 6:5, and from knowledge of the group which called itself the "Nicolaitans" in the time of these patristic authors. There is no indication that they had reliable historical information concerning the group about which John writes in Rev. Nor is there any strong evidence for a solid link between the Nicolaitans of Revelation and the later group of the same name mentioned by these patristic authors.[80] Given this situation, it seems clear that nothing can be confidently concluded about the Nicolaitans of Revelation from this later evidence.[81] Thus, the teaching of the Nicolaitans of Rev 2 can only be inferred from the book of Revelation itself.

3.3 The Nicolaitans – at Ephesus, Pergamum and Thyatira

Rev 2:6 tells us nothing about who the Nicolaitans were, but Rev 2:14-16 to the church in Pergamum is more helpful:

"But I have a few things against you: you have some there who hold to the teaching of Balaam, who taught Balak to put a stumbling block before the people of Israel, so that they would eat food sacrificed to idols and practice fornication (φαγεῖν εἰδωλόθυτα καὶ πορνεῦσαι). So you also have some who hold the teaching of the Nicolaitans as well (οὕτως ἔχεις καὶ σὺ κρατοῦντας τὴν διδαχὴν [τῶν] Νικολαϊτῶν ὁμοίως).[82] Repent then."

---

[79] See also Hippolytus (Haer 7.36.3); The Apostolic Constitutions 6:8; Tertullian (Adv. Marc. 1.29; De praescr. haeret. 33; De Pudic. 19); Eusebius (HE 3.29).

[80] von Harnack (1923, p413-22) maintained that the Nicolaitans of Revelation and the second century sect of the Nicolaitans were the same continuously existing gnostic sect. But his grounds for doing so were highly tenuous.

[81] See Caird 1966, p31; Farrer 1964, p71; Yarbro Collins 1984, p43; Watson 1992, p1107. Note also that we have no evidence for an historical connection between the Nicolaitans of Rev and the Nicolaus of Acts 6:5. The connection with Nicolaus made in patristic sources probably arose from the concern of Gnostic groups like the Nicolaitans to trace their origins back to biblical figures; see Fox 1994, p493-4.

[82] Aune (1997, p188) notes that the οὕτως, "so, thus, in this way", "coordinates the phrase that it introduces with the statement that immediately precedes in v 15, by way of interpretation or explanation. Thus, 'the teaching of Balaam' is the same as 'the teaching of the Nicolaitans'. ... The καὶ σύ, 'you too,' refers to the presence of this influence in Ephesus previously mentioned in 2:6; the concluding ὁμοίως, 'as well, likewise, similarly,' also compares the situation in Pergamon with that in Ephesus." Thus it is clear that the teaching of the Nicolaitans is described in v14.

Thus, some members of the church at Pergamum hold the teaching of the Nicolaitans which is here equated with the teaching of the Balaam. The teaching of Balaam is said to have two dimensions: eating food sacrificed to idols and practicing fornication (πορνεῦσαι; Rev 2:14). These two sins are further listed as the teaching of the prophet Jezebel at Thyatira in Rev 2:20:

"But I have this against you: you tolerate that woman Jezebel, who calls herself a prophetess and is teaching and beguiling my servants to practice fornication and to eat food sacrificed to idols (πορνεῦσαι καὶ φαγεῖν εἰδωλόθυτα)."

We seem therefore to have an equation: the teaching of the Nicolaitans is further defined as the teaching of Balaam (2:14-15), and the prophet Jezebel is also said to hold this same teaching (2:20). It is generally agreed then that Jezebel and her associates were Nicolaitans and that the group called the Nicolaitans was discussed by John in the proclamations to three cities - Ephesus, Pergamum and Thyatira.[83]

What more can we say about their teaching? John describes the teaching of the Nicolaitans as concerning "eating food sacrificed to idols and practicing fornication (φαγεῖν εἰδωλόθυτα καὶ πορνεῦσαι)". We will discuss these points in reverse order, since πορνεῦσαι casts light on what John means by "eating food sacrificed to idols".

3.4 "Practicing fornication"

There are three possible interpretations of πορνεῦσαι – "practicing fornication". Firstly, it could be taken literally, and would thus refer to sexual immorality. Secondly, it could be a metaphor for idolatry. Thirdly, it could be meant both literally and metaphorically and thus imply both fornication and idolatry. Which of these three options seems preferable?[84]

It is important to note that πορνεύω and its cognates are nearly always used metaphorically in Revelation; when πορν– cognates are used with a

---

[83] This equation is generally agreed; see Schüssler Fiorenza 1985, p116; 1991, p55-6; Aune, 1981, p27-8; 1997, p148; Yarbro Collins 1984, p43; Beasley-Murray 1974, p86; Räisänen 1995, p1606. Mackay (1973, p111-15) is unconvincing in attempting to distinguish rigidly between the Nicolaitans, the teaching of Balaam, and Jezebel and her followers. Beasley-Murray (1974, p96) suggests there is a reference to Nicolaitans in the comment that people had "soiled their garments" in Sardis (3:4). This is possible, but if the Nicolaitans were present in Sardis, it seems more likely that John would have made this explicit.

[84] Commentators are divided between the three options. Those who argue that it means sexual immorality include Beasley-Murray 1974, p86-7; Watson 1992, p1106-7. Those who argue that it means idolatry include Caird 1966, p39; Yarbro Collins 1984, p46, 107 n5; Thompson 1990, p122; Malina and Pilch 2000, p58. Those who argue that it means both idolatry and sexual immorality include Schüssler Fiorenza 1985, p116; Lohmeyer 1970, p31; Farrer 1964, p71, 74.

literal sense, it is as part of vice lists, where a literal use is understandable.[85] This strongly suggests a metaphorical sense in Rev 2:14, 20-22.[86] This is in keeping with one of its senses in Jewish usage, where the term came to have a standard metaphorical sense of idolatry, and thus of apostasy.[87]

Further, while either meaning is possible in 2:14, it is much more likely that the metaphorical meaning is in view in 2:20 (and hence in 2:14 also). In Rev 2:21-22 we read: "I gave her [Jezebel] time to repent, but she refuses to repent of her fornication (ἐκ τῆς πορνείας αὐτῆς). Beware, I am throwing her on a bed, and those who commit adultery with her (τοὺς μοιχεύοντας μετ᾽ αὐτῆς) I am throwing into great distress, unless they repent of her doings (ἐκ τῶν ἔργων αὐτῆς)." While "those who commit adultery with her" could be taken literally,[88] it is more likely to refer to Jezebel leading others into idolatry.[89] Further, the phrase "unless they repent of *her* doings" strongly suggests "fornication" is metaphorical, because, as Aune asks, on a literal reading, "why should those who commit fornication with 'Jezebel' repent of *her* behavior?"[90]

Thus, with strong OT precedent, John is using πορνεῦσαι – practicing fornication – as a metaphor for committing idolatry.[91]

3.5 Eating food offered to idols

When an animal was sacrificed in a Greek temple, only a small part was actually burned; generally some of the animal was consumed in the Temple by priests and worshippers and the rest was sold in the market or, on festival days, distributed to the public. Aune notes that "to eat meat sacrificed to idols (φαγεῖν εἰδωλόθυτα)" can refer to four possible situations. Firstly,

---

[85] For πορνεύω see 2:14, 20; 17:2; 18:3, 9; for πορνεία see 2:21; 9:21; 14:8; 17:2, 4; 18:3; 19:2; πόρνη (harlot) is used figuratively of a power that is hostile to God and God's people in Rev 17:1, 5, 15-16; 19:2. The exceptional literal use in vice lists are in 9:21; 21:8; 22:15 (πορνεία in 9:21; πόρνος (one who practices sexual immorality) in 21:8 and 22:15).

[86] See Aune 1997, p204; Caird 1966, p39; Yarbro Collins 1984, p107 n5.

[87] The image of the harlot was applied by the prophets to the people of God; see Hos 4:12-18; Isa 1:21; Jer 3:3-10; Ezek 16:15-58; 23:1-49; it was also applied to Israel's enemies; see Nah 3:4; Isa 23:15-18; see also Yarbro Collins 1984, p107 n5; 121; Schüssler Fiorenza 1991, p131.

[88] In which case it could mean a) other followers (plural) of Jezebel were having sexual relations with Jezebel or b) other followers of Jezebel were joining her in having sexual relations with say, cultic prostitutes.

[89] Boxall (1998, p207) notes "to take the language literally in this case would mean to postulate a situation in Thyatira far worse than anything Paul found in Corinth (multiple adultery or fornication), despite the fact that John can praise the Thyatirans for their 'love, faith, service, and patient endurance' (2.19)." See also Farrer 1966, p77.

[90] See Aune 1997, p205.

[91] See, for example, Thompson 1990, p122, 227 n33; Räisänen 1995, p1616-17; Aune 1997, p148; Boxall 1998, p207-8; Malina and Pilch 2000, p58.

participating in a sacral meal in a temple; secondly, eating sacrificial meat distributed during a public religious festival; thirdly, buying meat which had been offered to an idol at the market place and eating it, or eating such meat at a friend's house; fourthly, participating in a sacral meal held by members of a club or association.[92] Which of these are involved here?

John could be saying that the Nicolaitans purchased meat in the market place which had been offered to idols and in doing so, in John's view, are involved in idolatry, which he also describes as "practicing fornication". However, three points argue against this somewhat "minimalist" interpretation of the Nicolaitans' activity. Firstly, this means the *one* activity is described by two different terms; that is, that eating (in one's private home) meat offered to idols (φαγεῖν εἰδωλόθυτα) is also described as πορνεῦσαι. This is possible, but it seems at least as likely that the two expressions, co-ordinated with καί, indicate two different (though linked) activities. Secondly, while in 2:14 John speaks of φαγεῖν εἰδωλόθυτα καὶ πορνεῦσαι, in 2:20 he reverses the order and speaks of πορνεῦσαι καὶ φαγεῖν εἰδωλόθυτα. This suggests that although the two activities are linked by their very nature, they are in some way independent and so the order can be reversed.[93] This suggests there is more to "idolatry" than simply eating meat offered to idols at home. Thirdly, as we will note below, there is a huge amount of polemic against "idolatry" in Revelation, and although it is possible that all that Christians are doing is eating idol meat, it seems much more likely that the Nicolaitans, who as we will see are associated with the "harlotries of Babylon", are actually involved in worshipping idols in some way.

Thus we suggest that the Nicolaitans were eating food offered to idols, but were *also* involved in some additional activities or facets of pagan worship that could be described as "πορνεῦσαι".[94] There are a range of possibilities here, which relate to the different contexts outlined by Aune in which meat offered to idols was consumed, as well as to other cultic activities. They may have been involved in associations or trade guilds, which we know were very

---

[92] Aune 1997, p186; see also p192-4; see also Theissen 1982, p127-8; Thompson 1990, p122-4.

[93] This reversal of order in 2:20 compared with 2:14 argues against the καί in 2:14 being epexegetical.

[94] Note that the Apostolic Decree instructs Gentiles to abstain from the pollution of idols and from sexual immorality, along with what is strangled and from blood; see Acts 15:20, 28-9; 21:25. Farrer (1964, p77; see also Charles 1920, 1, p74) also notes the similarity between Rev 2:24 and Acts 15:28 with its mention of a burden (βάρος). He suggests that the wording and occasion are so similar that it is difficult not to suppose a direct reference by John to the Decree. This is possible, but we have noted that John probably understands πορνεύω metaphorically, and he does not refer to the other two elements of the Decree, which make any direct allusion to the Decree by John improbable. See also Yarbro Collins 1987, p87; Aune 1997, p187, 208.

significant in some cities.[95] They may have participated in cultic meals in pagan temples, or perhaps taken part in pagan cultic worship. Or perhaps in addition to eating idol meat in some situations, they took part in pagan festivals for various deities and rulers in the city.[96] All we can say is that at least something like this is probably indicated by the fact that John speaks of the Nicolaitans as being involved in "idolatry" *in addition to* their consumption of meat which had been offered to idols.[97]

3.6 Further preliminary observations

We can make four further observations at this point. Firstly, John presents the Nicolaitans as a serious threat to the churches. The church at Ephesus is commended for hating the Nicolaitans (Rev 2:6). To the church in Pergamum the risen Lord says that if they do not repent, he will come and war against them with the sword of his mouth (Rev 2:16).[98] Those in the church at Thyatira who do not follow the teaching of Jezebel are encouraged to hold fast until the risen Lord comes, and are reassured that they will not have to carry any other burden (Rev 2:24-5). Further, Jezebel herself will become sick, and if they do not repent, those who commit adultery with her will be thrown into great distress and those who are described as "her children" will die (Rev 2:22-3).[99] The Nicolaitans are thus seen as a very serious threat.

Secondly, the evidence suggests that Balaam, Jezebel and perhaps other leaders of the Nicolaitans were itinerant. The fact that several communities were affected by the same teaching points in this direction. Further, Jezebel is not portrayed as settled in Thyatira, but rather the Thyatirans are admonished for "allowing" or "permitting" (ἀφεῖς) the activities of "that woman Jezebel, who calls herself a prophet" (2:20). Perhaps the community has allowed her to stay in the home of a community member and to prophesy and teach the community (2:20), which again suggests she is an itinerant leader. Thus it is likely that the Nicolaitans were not a purely local phenomenon, but rather

---

[95] See Harland 2000, p118-120.

[96] See Klauck 2000, p330; Friesen 2001, p157.

[97] Thus for example Beasley-Murray (1974, p86) thinks the Nicolaitans, as well as eating idol meat, also participated in pagan religious festivals where meat offered to an idol was served. Aune (1997, p186) suggests "Though it is not completely clear precisely what is involved, it would appear that actual participation in sacrificing and eating victims in Greek temples is less likely than participating in the ritual banquets associated with public holy days and festivals or buying sacrificial meat from the market and eating it at home." But he does not consider the arguments given in the text.

[98] Farrer (1964, p74) points out that this punishment with the sword alludes to the Balaam story, since the angel confronted Balaam with a drawn sword (Num 22:22-35) and Balaam was finally killed with the sword (Num 31:8).

[99] It is somewhat surprising that Jezebel is not threatened with death, since false prophets are to be executed; see Dt 13:5-11; 4Q375; 11QTemple 54.10-15; Aune 1997, p205.

were a movement that was spread by itinerant leaders, and may have been influential elsewhere as well.[100]

Thirdly, according to John the Nicolaitans presented a "teaching" (διδαχή - Rev 2:15; see also 2:14, 20, 24). This indicates that they were concerned with more than moral practice, but also advocated certain theological positions.[101] We should also note that they seem to be an organised group. They have leaders: Balaam and Jezebel, who was also a prophet. Jezebel has "children" (Rev 2:23), which suggests disciples or followers who were devoted to her teaching.[102] They therefore probably existed within the communities at Pergamum and Thyatira as a well organised sub-group within the wider fellowship, but could have also existed as a separate entity in their own right in other places since they seem to be an organised, structured movement.

Fourthly, it is interesting to note that Jezebel was clearly a leader among the Nicolaitans. She is a prophet, and is also said to be a teacher (2:20). John writes about her at length, which is testimony to her influence and significance in the group.[103] We will discuss the significance of her role as a woman leader in Chapter 11.

3.7 The names "Balaam", "Jezebel" and "the Nicolaitans"

It is very unlikely that "Balaam" and "Jezebel" were the real names of a teacher in Pergamum and a prophet in Thyatira respectively. Apart from the fact that it is unlikely that a Jew or a Christian would adopt these names from the OT, we should note that John regularly uses the OT as a source for his symbolic names, alludes to it a great deal, and is involved in a good deal of interpretation and application of the OT.[104] Thus, "Balaam" and "Jezebel" are symbolic names that John, or perhaps someone before him, has given to the people concerned, names which reflect John's understanding of the

---

[100] See Yarbro Collins 1984, p137.

[101] We can thus already rule out the view that they were preaching only a "practical error" (see Beckwith 1919, p459).

[102] See Caird 1966, p44; Yarbro Collins 1984, p40. Aune (1997, p203) suggests that Jezebel was a patroness or hostess of one of the house churches at Thyatira. While this is likely, we should note that she is clearly a teacher, as well as a patron. She is to be compared to other significant early Christian women like Junia (Rom 16:7), Phoebe (Rom 16:1-2), Prisca (see chapter 2), the four daughters of Philip who were prophets (Acts 21:8-9), the women who were Montanist prophets and Ammia, a Christian prophet active in Philadelphia (Eusebius, HE 5.17.3-4).

[103] Schüssler Fiorenza (1991, p133) notes that "such influential leadership of women in the Asian churches is quite in keeping with the general religious and political position as well as sociocultural influence women had in Asia Minor."

[104] See Schüssler Fiorenza, 1985, p118. On John's use of the OT see Beale 1988 p318-36; Thompson 1990, p50-1; Schmidt 1991, p592-603; Court 1994, p88-9.

Nicolaitans and their two leaders, rather than their own self-understanding.[105] Why, then, does John use these particular names and what do they tell us about the people concerned? And is the name "Nicolaitans" itself a symbolic name?

3.7.1 "Balaam"

In Rev 2:14 Balaam is said to have "taught Balak to put a stumbling block before the people of Israel, so that they would eat food sacrificed to idols and practice fornication." The reference is to passages in Num 22-25 and 31. After Balak had tried to persuade Balaam to curse Israel (Num 22-24), we read in Num 24:14 that Balaam said to Balak: "So now, I am going to my people; let me advise you what this people will do to your people in days to come." Then Num 25:1-2 goes on: "While Israel was staying at Shittim, the people began to have sexual relations [ἐκπορνεῦσαι in the LXX] with the women of Moab. These invited the people to the sacrifices of their gods, and the people ate and bowed down to their gods." No connection is made with Balaam in this passage from Num 25:1-2, but in Num 31:16 we read: "These women here, on Balaam's advice, made the Israelites act treacherously against the Lord in the affair of Peor, so that the plague came among the congregation of the Lord." By reading these verses together, we see that Balaam was associated with leading Israel to commit immorality, to worship foreign gods and to eat food offered to these gods. It is likely then that John has called the teacher of the Nicolaitans at Pergamum "Balaam" because in John's eyes this teacher was committing the same offences as the Balaam of Numbers: putting a stumbling block before the people, and encouraging them to eat food sacrificed to idols and to "practice immorality".[106]

But in addition, we note that Balaam's supposed responsibility for the events at Baal-peor meant that he came to be seen as the father of religious syncretism, and in both early Jewish and early Christian literature he is regarded as a paradigmatic false prophet.[107] By identifying the unnamed teacher at Pergamum with this infamous character, John was depicting him in an exceedingly negative way, and was loading on to him all the odious baggage that was associated by the first century CE with the name "Balaam". In

---

[105] Similarly, he calls Rome "Babylon" (14:8; 16:19; 17:5; 18:2, 10, 21).

[106] That Balaam led the people into actual sexual immorality (ie the word is not used as a metaphor in Num 25:1-2) is the strongest reason for thinking of πορνεῦσαι in Rev 2 as meaning sexual immorality. But as we have seen, John's consistent use of the term to mean idolatry, and the context in Rev 2:22 suggest it is used metaphorically in this passage.

[107] See Philo, Vit Mos 1.53-55; 263-304; Josephus, Ant 4.126-30; Ps.-Philo Bib. Ant 18:13; see also Jude 11; 2 Pet 2:15-16. Balaam's acceptance of Balak's bribe also meant he was seen as an example of the mercenary spirit, but that is not in view here; see Caird 1966, p39. However, he was seen positively in some texts; see Boxall 1998, p211-12.

reality, he may have been a well-intentioned, honourable teacher, but John was denouncing him and his teaching, and was seeking to convince his readers that he was as mischievous as Balaam of old was thought to have been.

3.7.2 "Jezebel"

In the OT, Jezebel features prominently. She was the wife of king Ahab and is said to have killed prophets of Yahweh (1 Kgs 18:4, 13) and opposed Elijah (1 Kgs 19:1-2), arranged for Naboth's death (1 Kgs 21:5-26) and promoted worship of Baal (1 Kgs 18:19). In 2 Kgs 9:22 Jehu speaks of "the many whoredoms (αἱ πορνεῖαι ... τὰ πολλά) and sorceries" of Jezebel; the reference is probably to the cult of Baal which she championed in Israel, and thus "committed adultery" against Yahweh.[108] Jehu also calls her a cursed woman (2 Kgs 9:34) and after her death Jehu says: "This is the word of the Lord, which he spoke by his servant Elijah the Tishbite, 'In the territory of Jezreel the dogs shall eat the flesh of Jezebel; the corpse of Jezebel shall be like dung on the field in the territory of Jezreel, so that no one can say, This is Jezebel.'" (2 Kgs 9:36-7; see also 1 Kgs 21:23; 2 Kgs 9:7, 10)

Again then, John seems to have chosen the name "Jezebel" because of what he regards as the parallels between the biblical Jezebel and the prophet in Thyatira. Just as the biblical Jezebel led the people to worship foreign gods (1 Kgs 18:19; 16:31-2), so too did the prophet of Thyatira. Perhaps the parallel was also chosen because Jezebel killed the prophets of Yahweh and opposed Elijah, just as the prophet at Thyatira was opposing John.[109]

But John may have wished to suggest something more through making the association. Jezebel is cursed in the OT, and dies as one who is cursed and her posterity was extirpated by Jehu (2 Kgs 9:8-9; 10:1-17). John seems to be implying that "Jezebel" of Thyatira is deserving of a similar fate if she does not repent,[110] and indeed the proclamation contains the judgement that "I will strike her children dead" (Rev 2:23), because they have been committing "adultery" with her.

Yarbro Collins' comment with respect to "Balaam" and "Jezebel" is helpful here:

---

[108] Aune (1997, p203) notes that there is nothing in the accounts of Jezebel to support these charges if taken literally, which suggests they are to be taken metaphorically; see also Farrer 1964, p77; Beasley-Murray 1974, p90.

[109] Schüssler Fiorenza (1991, p134) suggests John may also have likened the prophetess of Thyatira to Queen Jezebel because of the high status and wealth of the Queen. This would then be part of John's critique of wealth. This is possible, but cannot be more than a suggestion.

[110] Note that in v21 it is said that she has already been called to repent, but has refused. No further call to repentance is issued, but rather she will be thrown on a "bed" (κλίνη). The implication is perhaps that she will become sick and will not recover, because she is under judgement.

The hearers were being invited to see analogies between classic situations in Israel's past and their own situations. They were being called upon to think typologically. ... The nameless man who had a following in Pergamum is no longer a fellow Christian who holds opinions and teaches practices that must be evaluated on their merits. Suddenly he is Balaam who led Israel into idolatry and harlotry; these deeds angered the Lord and provoked him to send a plague upon Israel (Num 25:1-9; 31:16). The implication for the hearers is plain: if they listen to this man's teaching they will be punished by God. The same dynamic is present in giving the name "Jezebel" to the prophet who had a following in Thyatira.[111]

Thus calling the Nicolaitan teachers "Balaam" and "Jezebel" is a further dimension in John's denunciation of these leaders and their teaching.

3.7.3 "The Nicolaitans"

If "Balaam" and "Jezebel" were both names John gave to the people concerned, then this raises the question of whether the name "Nicolaitan" was also a name John, or others before him, gave to the group, rather than the self-designation of the group concerned.

In Rev 2:14-15 John equates the teaching of Balaam with the teaching of the Nicolaitans. Thus it has been suggested that the Greek name "Nicolaitan" is an etymological word play on the Hebrew name "Balaam". We note that Balaam = בלע עם = he has consumed the people, while Νικόλαος = νικᾷ λαόν = he has conquered the people. Thus the names are roughly etymological equivalents.[112] Therefore, John, or someone before him, could have chosen the cryptic name "Nicolaitan" because of its etymological similarity to the name Balaam, so as to associate the group with the negative traditions about Balaam. However, it is not clear that readers of Rev would have understood this etymological derivation.[113]

Bauckham has another suggestion, which better explains the name. He notes that the name "Nicolaitan" shows they are followers of Nicolaus, meaning "conquer the people", which is an allusion to Revelation's key word νικάω, to conquer. He goes on: "Their teaching made it possible for Christians to be successful in pagan society, but this was the beast's success, a real conquest of the saints, winning them to his side, rather than the only apparent conquest he achieved by putting them to death. Hence the name Nicolaus is aptly explained by that of Balaam (2:14), the Old Testament false

---

[111] Yarbro Collins 1984, p147.

[112] See Charles 1920, p52-3; Schüssler Fiorenza 1985, p127 n13. Farrer (1964, p74) assumes a somewhat different translation: "St John produces a second play on the name: this 'victor of the people' [Nicolaus] is a Balaam (='master of the people')." A similar word play with the name Balaam is found in t.b. Sanh. 105a. There are other word plays using Balaam in the first century; see Philo Cher 32. There are comparable uses of Hebrew in Rev 9:11; 13:18 and 16:16.

[113] See Schüssler Fiorenza, 1985, p127 n13

prophet who destroyed many of the Israelites by his plan to lure them into idolatry and fornication (Num. 25). Bauckham notes: "With reference to this event, Jewish exegesis explained the name Balaam as meaning 'destroy the people' (b. Sanh. 105a)."[114]

Thus, the use (or creation) of probably all three names by John is part of his response to the Nicolaitans. By using these names he sought to denounce the group, and to warn the communities he addresses of the severe repercussions which will follow from continued contact with the Nicolaitans.

3.8 Understanding the Nicolaitans' position

In Revelation we hear only John's polemic against the Nicolaitans. Can we understand the position the Nicolaitans adopted? Although the conflict between John and the Nicolaitans appears at first to be a practical one over eating meat offered to idols, and idolatry, these factors point towards a deeper difference in attitude towards cultural and religious accommodation.[115] Christians, particularly gentile Christians, clearly grappled with the question of which pagan customs they could be involved in for the sake of economic survival or simple sociability.[116] Pagan religions pervaded virtually all spheres of city life. Economic life was often connected with pagan religion, particularly the trade guilds for artisans, whose meetings involved sacrifices to a god. Cultural and social life was inextricably interwoven with religious practices; participating in cultic meals formed a bond between oneself and others; intentionally avoiding such occasions created barriers. Banqueting with a non-Christian friend, going to the theatre, attending a city festival, being part of a voluntary association which existed for the mutual benefit of its members - all these aspects of city life were connected with pagan religiosity.

What was the Christian to do? Take the trade guilds for example. There were real economic, professional and social advantages to be had from being part of the guild. But the guild had a religious dimension, which involved pagan sacrifice, and meat sacrificed to idols was served at meetings of trade guilds and business associations as well as at private receptions. It seems unlikely that a Christian could be part of a guild, but could also absent themselves from every pagan sacrifice. As a Christian linen-worker, for example, one could refuse to join the guild, and suffer economically as a result

---

[114] Bauckham 1993d, p124. Compare Farrer 1964, p76; Aune 1997, p149 who think it is much more likely that "Nicolaus" is an actual rather than a symbolic name.

[115] See also Lohmeyer 1970, p31; Caird 1966, p38-41, 44.

[116] This is shown by how often the issue is mentioned not only in the NT (1 Cor 8:1, 4, 7, 10; 10:19; Acts 15:20, 29; 21:25) but also in early Christian writings (Did 6.3; Aristides, Apol 15.5; Justin, Dial 35; Tertullian, Apol 9; Clement Alex, Strom 4.16; Paed. 2.1; Origen, Contra Cels 8.28-30); see also Yarbro Collins 1984, p88.

of this isolation, or join the guild and reap the advantages, but also participate in the religious dimension of the organisation.

Further, what was the Christian's attitude to meat offered to idols? If most of the meat available in the market had been "offered to idols" and one was served meat at the home of a non-Christian friend, what did you do? If one was invited to eat with non-Christian friends at an eating establishment connected to a temple, what did you do in this situation? Clearly the apparently simple issue of eating meat in a variety of contexts raised huge questions for a Christian about how they should relate to the wider city and to its social and professional institutions.

And what about the imperial cult? We have noted in Chapter 1 that worship of the emperor was a very significant and prominent feature of city life in Ephesus towards the end of the first century CE. Christians living in the city of Ephesus, and elsewhere in Asia Minor where the cult was also prominent, would have been confronted with this very obvious feature of civic life. Although we have no evidence that Christians were compelled to be involved in the cult at this period, did the Christian have to avoid any involvement, and thus risk whatever consequences this might bring, perhaps including persecution which we know occurred slightly later (recall Pliny's letter)? Or could a Christian be involved in the imperial cult with a good conscience?[117] These were real issues facing Christians in Asia.

We have seen that, according to John, the Nicolaitans taught that it was acceptable for Christians to eat food which had been offered to idols and to be involved in some undefined way in pagan worship, perhaps including the imperial cult. How could the Nicolaitans have argued for such views? Although we do not know what traditions from Jesus or Paul were available to the Nicolaitans in the 90s, they could have used some of the following arguments:[118]

1) They could have pointed out that Jesus had argued that it was possible to be loyal to both God and to Caesar (Mk 12:13-17), which could be taken as precedent for involvement in the imperial cult.
2) In the controversy over meat offered to idols at Corinth one side had argued that since pagan gods did not exist, it was irrelevant that meat had been offered to an idol in pagan worship. Others had said that to eat such meat was to be involved in idolatry. But had not Paul shown sympathy with the strong, and urged them that the only obstacle to eating such meat was the conscience of the weak (1 Cor 8-10; cf Rom 14:13-23)?

---

[117] See Beasley-Murray 1974, p86-7.
[118] See Caird 1966, p40-1; Schüssler Fiorenza 1991, p56-7, 86, 133; see also Beasley-Murray 1974, p86-7, 91.

3) In writing to the Corinthians Paul had in fact said that "An idol has no real existence" and that "there is no God but one" (1 Cor 8:4). Did this not mean that there was no need for the Christian to refuse to pay honour to the emperor or to refuse to participate in pagan worship?

4) Even when Paul spoke of the need for the Corinthians to keep themselves pure, he had said that this did not mean leaving the world altogether (1 Cor 5:10). When pagan cults were such a pervasive part of city life, did this not mean that Paul was tacitly supporting the Nicolaitans' stand of not trying to avoid all contact with paganism?

5) Had not Paul taught that the authorities of the state were ordained by God and therefore that the Christian should be subject to them (Rom 13:1-7)?[119] Surely one should therefore make a gesture of political loyalty to Rome and take part in the imperial cult as part of one's civic duty.

While such arguments may one-sidedly interpret a passage, one could understand that some could read a passage in this particular way. The Nicolaitans could thus conclude that they could eat food previously sacrificed to "idols", or that the patron gods of the guilds were of no account and so they could participate in the pagan religious ceremonies of the trade guild,[120] or that the imperial cult was a meaningless and harmless ritual, in which one could be involved with a clear conscience, even if other Christians regarded such actions as idolatry. Such views, given on the authority of the Spirit by a prophet like Jezebel, would have been very welcome to Christians.[121] We should also note that participation in the cults of the cities or the imperial cult consisted mainly in participation in cultic acts and ceremonies, rather than adherence to certain credal statements, so it could be argued that one could honour the emperor, or sacrifice to an idol, without having to agree to any doctrinal formula, which might have been more difficult. Thus the Nicolaitans could argue theologically for their support of integration into pagan society and that they could enter fully into the social, commercial and political life of their city without fear of contamination.

An additional reason that the Nicolaitans adopted their position on idolatry may have been the desire to get on better with others in their city, and to avoid persecution.[122] We have clear evidence from the second century that

---

[119] Note the similar point made in 1 Peter 2:13f, 17 and 1 Tim 2:1-2, which were also addressed to Christians in Asia Minor.

[120] The trade guilds were prominent in Thyatira; see Hemer 1986, p107-9, 127-8. It is tempting to speculate that the Nicolaitans were successful there (see Rev 2:20-23) because their teaching enabled Christians to take part in the guilds and thus improve their economic situation (see Yarbro Collins 1984, p132; Ramsay 1904a, p350), although we have no firm evidence to support this theory.

[121] See Beasley-Murray 1974, p91. There is also a connection between prophecy and eating meat offered to idols in Philo, Spec Leg 1.315-17.

[122] For a discussion of antipathy towards Christians by local Gentiles, one reason for which was that they ignored the city's gods see Thompson 1990, p129-32.

many people hated Christians for a variety of reasons. The most fundamental charge was of "hatred of the human race", a charge which seems to have grown out of Christian exclusiveness, and their refusal to respect other gods and to take part in Gentile social and political life.[123] These concerns and attitudes were probably already fairly widespread at the end of the first century.[124] The participation in civic life which the Nicolaitans advocated, and the concomitant involvement in pagan worship, could therefore have been a response adopted in order to counter this antipathy towards Christians. By involvement in pagan worship, action which they could support with various arguments as we have seen, they could convince pagans that they were good neighbours.

The Nicolaitans thus seem to have been able to participate in activities which were necessary for social intercourse in the Greco-Roman city. Through involvement in pagan worship, the Nicolaitans were able to take part actively in the social, economic and political life of their cities. And they could perhaps point to the great benefits they reaped from this policy - harmonious relations with non-Christians, a break down of antipathy, and perhaps even advantages for evangelism. We can understand then why the Nicolaitans gained a hearing and were popular in Thyatira and Pergamum; we have also suggested that they existed as a separate group in Ephesus at the time John wrote. They presented an answer to a felt need.

3.9 The deep things of Satan

In Rev 2:24 we read: "But to the rest of you in Thyatira, who do not hold this teaching, who have not learned what some call 'the deep things of Satan,' (οἵτινες οὐκ ἔγνωσαν τὰ βαθέα τοῦ σατανᾶ ὡς λέγουσιν) to you I say, I do not lay on you any other burden." Given that 2:20-23 concerns Jezebel and her followers, the reference in v24 ("this teaching"), is to Jezebel's teaching. Thus it seems clear that according to John, Jezebel and her followers have "learned what some call 'the deep things of Satan'." There are two ways of interpreting this phrase.

Firstly, Jezebel herself could be claiming to know and teach "the deep things of Satan". If Jezebel and her group described "the deep things" as being "of Satan", then it could be a claim to know the mysteries and secrets of Satan.[125] Secondly, John (or some other opponent in the first instance) could

---

[123] Note that Tacitus said Nero chose the Christians as a scapegoat because there was already antipathy towards them. Christians were also accused of such crimes as arson, incest and cannibalism, charges which were also made against other associations such as the worshippers of Dionysius. See Yarbro Collins 1984, p87.

[124] See Yarbro Collins 1984, p87.

[125] Schüssler Fiorenza, 1985, p116-17, 124; Yarbro Collins 1987, p82 and Taeger 1998, p196 favour this interpretation of the phrase.

have labelled Jezebel's teaching as "the deep things of Satan". In this case, she may have claimed to know "the deep things of God", or simply "the deep things".[126] However, John believed that these things were actually of Satan, and thus involved knowledge, not of the divine, but of demonic realities. Hence John would have described them as "the deep things of Satan" in order to denigrate Jezebel's teaching and to express his opposition to it. By labeling the teaching as "of Satan" John would also be associating the teaching with the negative portrayal of Satan in the rest of Rev, including Satan's judgement in Rev 20:7-10. Another example of such labeling of opponents by John is found in Rev 2:9, 3:9. The Jews would have claimed to be the synagogue of God, but John believed that in reality they were the "synagogue of Satan".[127]

Is there any connection between this claim to know the deep things of God or of Satan, and the teaching concerning eating food offered to idols and idolatry? On either interpretation this is likely. If Jezebel herself claimed to know "the deep things of Satan" then this could mean that she and her followers claimed to possess knowledge which prevented them from being overcome by Satan. Hence they could associate with evil as well as good, and show their superiority over so-called sin. Thus they could be involved in what others saw as idolatry and could be significantly involved in city life, since they were immune from any effects of participation in what others saw as the things of Satan, because they knew his mysteries and so were confident of their protection from Satan.[128] Alternatively, if Jezebel claimed to know "the deep things of God", then the possession of such special knowledge could have led to the belief that they were assured of salvation. Hence they were free to participate in idolatrous worship, while also believing in the Christian God, because of their certain salvation. In any case, it seems likely that Jezebel was basing her actions and teaching on a claim to knowledge.[129]

3.10 John's Response to the Nicolaitans[130]

However, for John the beliefs and actions of the Nicolaitans were totally unacceptable, for the risen Christ declares that he hates the works of the Nicolaitans and approves of the Ephesians' hatred of those works (Rev 2:6).

---

[126] Some later Gnostics claimed to know "the deep things of God"; see Irenaeus *Adv haer* 2.28.9; Hippolytus *Haer* 5.6; further in Aune 1997, p207-8. Compare also 1 Cor 2:10.

[127] See Räisänen 1995, p1619-21 (who favours the second interpretation given above). Note also Polycarp, Phil 7:1-2, of false teachers: "and whosoever perverts the oracles of the Lord for his own lusts, and says that there is neither resurrection nor judgement - this man is the first-born of Satan. Wherefore, leaving the foolishness of the crowd, and their false teaching, let us turn back to the word."

[128] See Caird 1966, p44; see also Farrer 1964, p77.

[129] See Taeger 1998, p196.

[130] We of course do not know how the Nicolaitans would have viewed John.

Similarly, statements of future judgement against the Nicolaitans are given in 2:16 and 2:20-23. Since, according to Rev 2:6 some of the Ephesian Christians shared John's attitude to the Nicolaitans, we will discuss John's attitude here.

As we have seen, John describes one element of the Nicolaitans' teaching as πορνεῦσαι – "practicing fornication". It is important to note that πορνεύω and its cognates are used of Babylon/Rome, who is called the Great Whore (17:1) and who holds in her hand "a golden cup full of abominations and the impurities of her fornication" (17:4).[131] Thus, the Nicolaitans are associated with the one whose judgement is described extensively in Rev.[132] Through the use of πορνεύω for both the Nicolaitans and Babylon, John adds another dimension to his condemnation of the Nicolaitans. We have also noted that John uses the pejorative names "Balaam" and "Jezebel" as a form of polemic against the Nicolaitans and also in an endeavour to warn the communities he addresses of the severe repercussions of following the Nicolaitans.

For John there seems to have been no exceptions to the rule that meat sacrificed to idols must be avoided. Since avoiding such meat would have been awkward and perhaps even insulting in many pagan social contexts, John's solution to the problems posed by pagan worship for the Christian seems to have been to have as little as possible to do with pagan social and cultural life. For only in this way could one avoid contact with idolatry. To John, the openness to the surrounding Greco-Roman culture that the Nicolaitans advocated, and which John sees as symbolized by eating meat which had been sacrificed to idols and involvement in other forms of idolatry, was totally unacceptable, as he makes clear.[133] Christians could not join any of the widespread unofficial societies for mutual benefit, nor be part of trade guilds. If possible, they must have no contact with any form of idolatry. Hence John is calling for exclusivism with regard to Greco-Roman culture, especially its polytheism. Christians should withdraw from Greco-Roman professional and civic life and form exclusive groups. No accommodation to polytheistic culture was permissible.[134] That John was calling for social, political and

---

[131] See Rev 14:8; 17:2, 4; 18:3, 9; 19:2.

[132] See for example Rev 14:8; 16:10-11, 17-21; 17:1-18:24. Thompson (1990, p180) comments that from John's perspective, "The prophetess Jezebel at Thyatira is understood properly when she becomes a homologue to Babylon the Whore." Thompson (1990, p80) also notes that "The prophetess Jezebel ...deceives those at Thyatira [2:20] - an activity [ie deception] practiced only by Satan, the beast of the earth, and Babylon the Whore."

[133] Yarbro Collins 1984, p88.

[134] See Yarbro Collins 1984, p137; Thompson 1990, p123-5. It has been noted that the communities which receive approval and encouragement from Christ seem to be economically poor and powerless in society (Smyrna, 2:9; Philadephia, 3:8), while those which are censured are rich and complacent (Laodicea, 3:17). Further, the wealthy Laodiceans (3:17) have nothing to fear from the authorities, whereas the poor in Smyrna (2:9) are threatened with persecution (2:10). Yarbro Collins (1984, p133) notes: "The underlying

economic withdrawal from the life of the Greco-Roman city is confirmed by 18:4-5, in the context of a description of the fall of Babylon: "Then I heard another voice from heaven saying, 'Come out of her, my people, so that you do not take part in her sins, and so that you do not share in her plagues; for her sins are heaped high as heaven, and God has remembered her iniquities'". This does not seem to be a call to avoid corruption by retreating to the desert like the Essenes, but rather a call to social exclusivism.[135]

The polemic in the rest of Rev against idolatry, and the imperial cult in particular, can also be seen in part as a continuation of John's reaction to and polemic against the Nicolaitans.[136] The whole of Revelation, and not just Rev 2-3, is directed against this teaching, as well as addressing other issues. We cannot deal here with all John says about pagan worship but we can note the following elements in his polemic.

Firstly, one element of this polemic is the announcement of judgement on those who are involved in the imperial cult (14:9-11),[137] or who are idolaters (21:8; 22:15). In 16:2 it is said that the first angel poured the first of the seven bowls of God's wrath on those who bore the mark of the beast and worshiped its image.[138] One reason for the announcement of judgement on Babylon/Rome in Rev 17-18[139] is her idolatry. This is clear, for example, in 17:4 which speaks of a golden cup "full of abominations ($\gamma\acute{\epsilon}\mu o\nu$ $\beta\delta\epsilon\lambda\upsilon\gamma\mu\acute{\alpha}\tau\omega\nu$)" since $\beta\delta\acute{\epsilon}\lambda\upsilon\gamma\mu\alpha$ is traditional language used to express the horror of idolatry.[140] One reason for Rome's judgement then is the idolatry which she spreads throughout the world.[141] The call to "Come out of her" (18:4) is a call to separate from her idolatry, as well her injustice and murder.[142]

---

reason seems to be that it was possible to get and to maintain wealth only by accommodating to the polytheistic culture." See also Thompson 1990, p124-5; Schüssler Fiorenza 1991, p57. This observation supports the view that John opposed the Nicolaitans because they accommodated to society, whereas he argued that Christians should form exclusive groups. We will discuss this issue in further detail in Chapter 9.

[135] See Yarbro Collins 1984, p127; she also sees a call to economic separatism in 13:17 and 14:9-11; see Yarbro Collins 1984, p125-7.

[136] See Schüssler Fiorenza, 1985, p117.

[137] There is general agreement that John is referring to the imperial cult when he speaks of worshipping the beast and its image (eg. in 14:9).

[138] Further, it seems likely that all of the seven bowls of God's wrath (16:1-21) are directed against the community of those who worship the beast; see Schüssler Fiorenza 1991, p93.

[139] This judgement is announced earlier in 14:8 and in the seventh bowl (16:19).

[140] See Mk 13:14; Mt 24:15; Dan 9:27; 11:31; 12:11; see also Caird 1966, p214.

[141] Other reasons for her judgement include her misuse of political power (this is her fornication in 17:1-6; on it see Schüssler Fiorenza 1991, p96), her abuse of wealth (18:3, 11-19) and her persecution of Christians; see 17:6; 18:24.

[142] See Schüssler Fiorenza 1991, p100.

We see then that there is a repeated announcement of judgement on idolatry. This functions as a warning not to worship idols and not to participate in the imperial cult. John seeks to show those who follow the Nicolaitans what will be the result of their teaching: they will be judged as the followers of the beast are. It is a call to Christians to steadfast resistance and loyal endurance, as is made explicit in 16:15. It is those who conquer the beast and its image who will sing the song of Moses and the Lamb (15:2-3).

Secondly, John stresses that behind the cult of the emperor stands Satan. Perhaps this is in contrast to the Nicolaitan's claim that an idol had no real existence. Thus John pictures the second beast, who probably represents the imperial cult functionaries (13:11-18), seeking to lead the whole world to worship the image of the first beast (13:12) who represents the imperial power. But John has already made it clear that the image of the first beast is not an empty idol, but that behind the first beast stands Satan, the dragon, for in 13:2 we read that the dragon had given to the first beast "his power and his throne and great authority".[143] This beast is then the viceroy of Satan's powers; John is saying that when people worship the image of the beast they are, in effect, worshipping Satan.[144] So this too is part of John's polemic against the Nicolaitans and idolatry.[145]

Thirdly, that Christians must not be involved in any way in the imperial cult is stressed by mention of the mark on the foreheads and right hands of the beast's followers (13:16-17; 14:9, 11; 16:2; 19:20; 20:4). This functions as a counterimage to the sealing of the 144,000 (7:1-8) or the writing of God's name on their foreheads (14:1). The contrast makes it clear that the worshippers of the beast are the rivals of the Lamb's followers.[146] Thus John emphasises that Christians cannot "go along with" the imperial cult since worshipping the beast or remaining loyal to God and the Lamb are strict alternatives.

Fourthly, 19:10 can be seen as part of this polemic against idolatry. When John fell down at the feet of the angel, the angel replies: "You must not do that! ... Worship God." Only God and the Lamb may receive worship, and to prostrate oneself before an angel or the image of the emperor, would be to give to them worship that was due only to God. Again, the underlying point is to stand fast and avoid idolatry.[147] To emphasize the point, 22:8-9 reports an encounter between John and an angel which is almost identical to 19:10.

---

[143] See also 13:4; cf. 12:9; 16:13, 20:2; the beast is allowed to make war on believers in 13:7.

[144] On these passages see Schüssler Fiorenza 1991, p83-7.

[145] Judgement on the second beast is announced in 19:20; for the Judgement of Satan see 20:1-3, 7-11.

[146] See Schüssler Fiorenza 1991, p86.

[147] Schüssler Fiorenza 1991, p102-3; see also Thompson 1990, p69-70.

Fifthly, Rev 20:4-6 shows that those who had refused to worship the beast, that is to participate in the imperial cult, and had been killed as a result, will receive justice and will be priests of God and of Christ. This serves to strengthen the readers' resolve in their resistance to the imperial cult and their loyalty to God and the Lamb.

Thus throughout Rev John is calling his readers, including the followers of the Nicolaitans,[148] to repent of idolatry. Further, he is seeking to motivate his readers to worship God and the Lamb, and not to participate in any form of idolatry, particularly the imperial cult. He calls for resistance and endeavours to encourage and exhort his readers to avoid the worship of idols, and not to be like those in 9:20-21 who did not repent of their idolatry.[149]

3.11 The relation to the wider city - three views

We can thus see that three positions on the issues of participation in pagan worship and involvement in the wider city are clear in the Rev 2-3.[150] Firstly, John's views about eating meat sacrificed to idols and his denunciation of "practising fornication" make it plain that he was calling upon Christians to avoid membership in guilds or other Gentile associations and to avoid anything in society that was connected to idolatry. He represented strict nonconformist behaviour with respect to the question of accommodation to paganism, and opposed participation by Christians in the civic life of Asia Minor.[151] Judging by the proclamations, he had a following in the church in Ephesus (2:6); and a smaller following in Pergamum (2:15) and Thyatira (2:24f).

Secondly, Jezebel and the Nicolaitans represent the "accommodationist" approach of involvement with paganism.[152] They advocated a policy whereby their followers could live peacefully within pagan society. They have their strongest influence in Pergamum and Thyatira, where the adherents of Balaam's teaching and the followers of Jezebel are an integral part of these Christian communities. We have argued that a group of Nicolaitans existed in Ephesus at the time John writes, but were not among the addressees. Rather, the group of Nicolaitan Christians in Ephesus had been rejected by the

---

[148] This is at least the case in Pergamum and Thyatira, where the Nicolaitans were within the groups addressed; see section 4. below for a discussion of the situation in Ephesus.

[149] See Schüssler Fiorenza 1991, p109.

[150] Aune 1981, p28-9.

[151] See Yarbro Collins 1984, p124. Aune (1981, p28) attributes John's attitude to "his apocalyptic tradition of nonconformity and opposition to the influence of the dominant alien culture".

[152] Yarbro Collins 1984, p88 speaks of assimilation; Aune 1981, p29 of cultural and religious accommodation.

Ephesian Christians John addresses, but the Nicolaitans were an on-going threat and continuing challenge to these Ephesian Christians.

Thirdly, there is the group of Christians who take a "centrist" position, and they are clearly in view in Ephesus. They are not in the Nicolaitan camp, but, as far as John is concerned they have departed from the works done at first (2:5), and so he calls them to repent. Aune suggests that a battle is going on for the members of this centrist party between the two movements, led by John on the one hand and Jezebel on the other, both of whom claim to be prophets.[153] We will discuss this group further in Section 4 below.

3.12 Rival Prophets?

According to John, Jezebel "calls herself a prophet" (2:20), but the way John expresses this shows that he does not agree with the claim made by Jezebel. However, she was apparently recognized by many as a prophet, since she is said to be "teaching and beguiling my servants" (2:20) and to have "children" (2:23). Further, the name "Balaam" which John gave to the teacher in Thyatira suggests that this man may have had or claimed a prophetic role, since the Balaam of the OT was known as a (false) prophet in early Jewish and early Christian literature. The connection with the Balaam of the OT could have been made by John partly because of this link with prophecy.[154] These points suggest then that members of the Nicolaitans were prophets.[155] Further, as we have noted, Jezebel, Balaam and any other Nicolaitan prophets may have legitimated their activity of eating food offered to idols and condoning idolatry by pointing to prophecies and thus claimed prophetic inspiration for their teaching.

John does not explicitly claim to be a prophet in Rev, but he clearly sees himself as a prophet. This is suggested by the fact that he describes the book he is writing as "prophecy" (1:3) and a "prophetic book" (22.7, 10, 18, 19). Further, in 22:9 an angel says to John: "I am a fellow servant with you and your comrades the prophets". This certainly implies that John was a prophet.[156] Further, it seems likely that John was an itinerant prophet who

---

[153] Aune, 1981, p29.

[154] Aune 1981, p28.

[155] This does not mean that all the leaders of the Nicolaitans were prophets.

[156] See Aune 1981, p18-19, 27; 1989, p109; see also Fekkes 1994, p37-58. See below on 22:9. It is important to note that he does not introduce himself as a prophet or a teacher, but rather as a brother and partner (1:9). John derives his authority to address the churches, not from holding an institutional position, such as "prophet", but from his prophetic inspiration, which is emphasised in 1:9-11; see Schüssler Fiorenza 1991, p50. See further in Chapter 10.

regularly travelled a particular circuit, since he knows the seven churches well, but does not seem to associate closely with any one of them.[157]

A more difficult question is whether John is one of a number of prophets in the churches of Asia Minor. A key verse here is Rev 22.16: "It is I, Jesus, who sent my angel ὑμῖν with this testimony for (ἐπί) the churches." In particular, to whom does ὑμεῖς refer here? It can be taken to refer either to the members of the seven churches addressed by John or to a group of Christian prophets who mediated John's message to the churches. Aune has argued that the second interpretation is correct for the following reasons. Firstly, ὑμεῖς and "the churches" cannot both refer to Christians in general because the presence of ἐπί in the phrase ἐπὶ ταῖς ἐκκλησίαις makes it almost certain that it refers to a different group from that referred to by ὑμεῖς. Since αἱ ἐκκλησίαι almost certainly refers to the seven churches in Asia, ὑμεῖς must refer to a different group.[158] Secondly, ὑμεῖς could refer to the seven churches, and αἱ ἐκκλησίαι to the wider, universal church. However, in Rev αἱ ἐκκλησίαι clearly refers primarily to the seven churches, which means this is its most likely referent in 22:16.[159] Thirdly, if ὑμεῖς in 22:16 cannot refer to the seven Christian communities, it must refer to a different group. Aune suggests ὑμεῖς could refer to potential martyrs, lectors, envoys (who delivered Rev to each of the seven churches) or to a group of prophets associated with John. Aune favours the latter option. Rev 22:9 is an important verse to support this reading of 22:16. With reference to an angel, Rev 22:9 reads "I am a fellow servant with you and your comrades the prophets, and with those who keep the words of this book." This seems to indicate that John was one of several Christian prophets.

Yarbro Collins has argued that the reference to prophets in 22:9 is to the classical prophets of Israel.[160] However, as Aune points out, the phrase "your comrades the prophets" is co-ordinated in 22:9 with "those who keep the words of this book". This is a group contemporaneous with John, so it is likely that the first phrase ("your comrades the prophets") also concerns

---

[157] See Yarbro Collins 1984, p136-7; Thompson 1990, p12; other features of Rev, especially John's condemnation of the wealth of Rome (Rev 18) are explained by this suggestion. On itinerant prophets see Didache 11-13; Yarbro Collins 1984, p134-6.

[158] Aune 1989, p104-5; cf Yarbro Collins 1984, p39.

[159] In 1.4,11,20 (x2) the seven churches are in view. In 2.7,11,17,29; 3.6,12,22 we have the formula "what the Spirit says to the churches". This refers primarily to the seven churches; that it may have a wider reference too does not invalidate our point that the most natural reading of αἱ ἐκκλησίαι in 22:16 is that it refers to the seven churches. In 2:23 αἱ ἐκκλησίαι most naturally refers to the seven churches. See Aune 1989, p107. He notes "There is no evidence to suggest that αἱ ἐκκλησίαι as a collective term refers to any group other than the seven specific Christian communities to whom the book as a whole is addressed."

[160] Yarbro Collins 1984, p44-6. Yarbro Collins (1984, p40-3) argues against John leading a prophetic school or circle with members in each of the churches. She is refuted by Aune 1989.

John's contemporaries, that is, a group of prophets associated with himself.[161] This in turn suggests that ὑμεῖς in 22:16 also refers to a group of Christian prophets known by John.

On this reading of 22:16, the community prophets (ὑμεῖς) have received the testimony of the Book of Revelation for the churches. Thus, they probably deliver, read and perhaps also interpret John's written revelation to the seven churches.[162] On this view prophets were active in each of the seven churches;[163] it is also likely that such prophets were actually members of at least some of the seven churches. In any case, we can suggest that John is a member of a prophetic circle or guild in the churches of Asia.[164] We have no specific evidence that any of John's prophetic colleagues were active in the Ephesian Christian community, but this is likely.[165]

This discussion suggests that two opposing prophet circles or schools were active in the churches of Asia, one school associated with John, another with Jezebel, Balaam and the Nicolaitans. The conflict between John and the Nicolaitans then is probably a battle between rival schools of prophets and their followers, as well as a conflict over theology and praxis.[166] We also note what is said in Rev 2:21: "And I have given her time to repent (καὶ ἔδωκα αὐτῇ χρόνον ἵνα μετανοήσῃ), but she refuses to repent of her fornication." This implies that at some point in the past the risen Christ had denounced Jezebel's activity and called on her to repent, probably through John or one of his prophetic associates, but that Jezebel had refused to repent.[167] This suggests that there has been a previous relationship between John and Jezebel and probably a history of conflict between these two "schools".

We should recall of course that John is a "travelling outsider" in the same way as the Nicolaitans are (and the false "apostles" of 2:2 as well). "Jezebel", "Balaam" and their followers can thus be seen as John's chief opponents or

---

[161] See Aune 1989, p109. This interpretation of 22:9 is reinforced by Rev 19:10 which is parallel to 22:9. In 19:10 "your brothers who hold the testimony of Jesus" are shown to be prophets by the phrase "For the testimony of Jesus is the spirit of prophecy". This makes it more likely that the "prophets" of 22:9 are Christian prophets of John's time.

[162] See Aune 1989, p111.

[163] See Court 1994, p35-6.

[164] See Aune 1981, p18-19, 29; 1989, p104f; Hill 1971-72, p406-11; Prigent 2001, p79-84; cf. Yarbro Collins 1984, p45. 1 Cor 14:29-33 suggests that a group of prophets functioned in a special way in the Corinthian church.

[165] The other references to prophets (apart from the reference to the two prophets in 11:10; cf 11:3) are 10:7; 11:18; 16:6; 18:20, 24; 22:6. Rev 10:17 is probably a reference to classical Israelite prophets; in Rev 11:18; 16:6; 18:20, 24; 22:6 the reference could be to Christian as well as Jewish prophets. For the view that many of the classical prophets had been martyred see Mt 5:12; 23:29-39; Lk 11:47-51; Acts 7:51-3. This explains the references to the blood of the prophets.

[166] See Aune 1981, p28; Schüssler Fiorenza, 1985, p117; cf. Yarbro Collins 1984, p43-4, 157, who thinks we can only speak of rival prophets, not rival prophetic schools.

[167] See Charles 1920, 1, p71; Lohmeyer 1970, p28; Aune 1981, p27; 1997, p204.

competitors in the churches; their teaching seems to have been the alternative to John's own teaching in at least three of the seven churches. That John is in a conflict situation with others who also claim to be recipients of divine revelation, in part explains the emphasis on authentication in the book, particularly in Rev 1 and 22. At a number of points the narrative underlines John's authority and legitimates his prophecy, perhaps because the author knows that the voice of his prophecy has been and will be contested by other Christians.[168]

3.13 Locating the Nicolaitans within Early Christianity

We will now consider if the Nicolaitans, whom we have argued existed in Ephesus, were similar to any other groups we know about in Early Christianity?

3.13.1 Were the Nicolaitans Paulinists?

Some scholars have regarded the Nicolaitans as Paulinists, since, like Paul, they ignored the Apostolic Decree of Acts 15. Thus, Renan thought "Nicolaus" was a nickname for Paul.[169] However, while Paul was more open to Christians eating food offered to idols, he does not advocate the same stance as that advocated by the Nicolaitans. But we will consider below the view that the Nicolaitans are related to "the strong" at Corinth, and so that there may be some Pauline connection.

3.13.2 Were the Nicolaitans Gnostics?

Were the Nicolaitans Gnostics (or gnostics)? Certainly they bear some affinity with later Gnostics, particularly in the claim to know "the deep things", since later Gnostics, according to the church fathers, claimed to know "the depths of God",[170] and made the more general claim to secret knowledge. We know that later Gnostics were accused of eating food offered to idols and

---

[168] See 1:1-2 (a chain of communication) 1:4-7 (divine initiative in the revelatory process) 1:9-20 (John's call narrative, which is his direct commissioning); see also Thompson 1990, p177-9; Aune 1981, p19; Court 1994, p18. In Rev 22 the authority of the prophecy is emphasised (22:6, 18-19) and Christ witnesses to and guarantees the content of the prophecy (22:16, 18). We will discuss this further in Chapter 10.

[169] Renan 1869, p303-4, 367-70. See also Simon 1978, p74-5, who thinks the Nicolaitans are second generation Paulinists, and also notes the relation of John's polemic to the Apostolic Decree. Note also, Genouillac (1907, p210) notes that John thought the position of the Nicolaitans with regard to meat offered to idols and "fornication" was scandalous, and writes: "Il est possible qu'il ait voulu encourager les judéo-chrétiens d'Éphèse contre les partisans excessifs ou imprudents du libéralisme paulinien".

[170] See Schlier TDNT 1, p517-18; see also Räisänen 1995, p1622.

of being involved in idolatry.[171] However, the name "Nicolaitans" does not occur in any surviving Gnostic texts,[172] and it is unlikely that what became full-blown Gnosticism existed in the 90's.[173] We also do not know enough about the Nicolaitans to call them Gnostic.[174] Further, Aune notes with regard to the Nicolaitans that rather than being a gnostic group: "their use of prophecy to legitimate accommodationism suggests that they also stood within some kind of definite prophetic or oracular tradition."[175]

3.13.3 A Judaising group?

Koester describes the Nicolaitans as a "hostile Judaizing group".[176] This is based firstly on the view that the references to Balaam and Jezebel (Rev 2:14, 20) indicate the self-understanding of the Nicolaitans and show that they were involved in "daring interpretations of Scripture" and secondly, on the identification of the Nicolaitans with those who claim to be true Jews in Rev 2:9; 3:9.

With regard to the first point, it is more likely, as we have noted, that the references to Balaam and Jezebel were contributed by John, since he uses the OT as a source for his symbolic names, alludes to the OT a great deal, and is himself involved in a good deal of "daring interpretation" and application of the OT.[177] Thus, the references to the OT probably indicate John's understanding of the Nicolaitans, rather than their own self-understanding.

With regard to Koester's second point, this would mean that the "Jews" referred to by John were actually Jewish Christians. However, when we look at the references to Jews in Rev 2:9 and 3:9 this seems unlikely. In both cases,

---

[171] According to some church fathers, the libertine direction of Gnosticism was expressed in the eating of food sacrificed to idols; eg Justin (Dial 35.6) claims that Valentinians, Basilidians and Saturnilians eat sacrificial meat and attend pagan festivals; see also Irenaeus, Adv Haer 1.6.3; 1.24.5; 1.28.2; see Schüssler Fiorenza 1985, p117; Theissen 1982, p132-6. Further, if πορνεύω is to be understood as actual immorality, this would create another link, since many Gnostics were accused of being libertine. Note however, that no surviving Gnostic text mentions eating meat which had been sacrificed to idols, so this makes it unlikely that the Nicolaitans were Gnostic; see Aune 1997, p149, 193; Heiligenthal 1991, p135-6.

[172] See Aune 1997, p148-9.

[173] See Prigent 2001, p153.

[174] A number of scholars have applied the label Gnostic to the Nicolaitans: see Beasley-Murray 1974, p86; Smith 1957, p190-1; Harnack 1923, p413-22. Irenaeus (Haer. 3.11.1; see also 1.26.3) thought that the Nicolaitan's doctrine was similar to that taught by the later gnostic Cerinthus.

[175] Aune 1981, p29.

[176] Koester 1971, p148. He thinks that Ignatius may be combating one group in IgnMag 8-11; IgnPhd 6, 8; IgnTr 10; IgnSm 2. But Ignatius is almost certainly combating two groups and we have insufficient information to identify either with the Nicolaitans.

[177] See Schüssler Fiorenza, 1985, p118.

the Jewish communities probably claim to be the synagogue of God, but because they oppose the Christians, John calls them "the synagogue of Satan". It is clear from Rev 2:9 that, in John's view, the Jews actively slandered the Christians in Smyrna, and this was probably also the case in Philadelphia (hence the Jews there will acknowledge that the Christians were right, and they were wrong).

If the Nicolaitans were to be identified with these "Jews" of Rev 2:9 and 3:9, as Koester claims, then we would expect something similar to be said of the churches which had had contact with the Nicolaitans. However, John does not criticise the churches of Ephesus, Pergamum and Thyatira for giving in to persecution from the Nicolaitans (as Koester's theory would require) but rather criticises them for being invaded by the Nicolaitans. The Jews endanger the churches from outside as a persecuting group, but the Nicolaitans, according to John, endanger the church from within by means of their teaching. The "Jews" in 2:9 and 3:9 are in fact better understood as the Jewish communities of these cities.[178] We conclude, therefore, that the "Jews" and the Nicolaitans are not to be identified, since John keeps them distinct, but are rather to be seen as two distinct groups.[179] There is thus no evidence which suggests that the Nicolaitans were Judaisers.

3.13.4 The Nicolaitans and "the strong" in Corinth

Schüssler Fiorenza[180] has noted that there are striking parallels between the Nicolaitans and the problems posed for Paul by the "strong" mentioned in 1 Cor.[181] In 1 Cor 8:1-9:23 and 10:23-11:1 Paul discusses knowledge and freedom with respect to eating food sacrificed to idols. In 1 Cor 10:14-22 he raises the related question of participation in pagan cults. He argues that Christian freedom needs to take into account the effect of one's actions on other Christians. Paul does not reject the claim to "knowledge", but wants such knowledge to be limited by love. But his whole discussion suggests the strong at Corinth both ate food offered to idols and attended pagan cultic festivals. It is very likely that the "strong" at Corinth believed that their Christian freedom meant they could eat meat offered to idols and participate in pagan festivals with impunity.[182]

---

[178] We have some other evidence that Jews in Asia Minor opposed Christians; see Trebilco 1991, p20-32; eg. Martyrdom of Polycarp 12.2; 13.2; Eusebius HE, 4.15.26, 29.

[179] See Schüssler Fiorenza, 1985, p118-19.

[180] Schüssler Fiorenza 1985, p119-20; see also Prigent 2001, p153-4.

[181] Schüssler Fiorenza; see also Räisänen 1995, p1627-31. Note that we should not speak of "Gnosis" at Corinth (see Räisänen 1995, p1627-8) just as we have argued that this is inappropriate with regard to the Nicolaitans.

[182] See further Räisänen 1995, p1628-31. In 1 Cor 6:12-20 Paul also discusses the problem of immorality (πορνεία), again in such a way as to suggest that the enthusiasts at

We see then that there were significant similarities between the Nicolaitans and the strong in Corinth.[183] Given the likelihood that the strong at Corinth were a group which had misunderstood Pauline teaching, or had drawn from what Paul says conclusions that he did not wish to draw, this makes it likely that the Nicolaitans were similarly a group whose origins lay in a misunderstanding or development of Pauline teaching.[184]

3.14 Are the Nicolaitans related to the opponents of the Pastor?

We have noted that the closest parallel to opponents of the Pastor and the Nicolaitans are both "the strong" in Corinth. This raises the possibility that the Pastor's opponents and the Nicolaitans may be the same group; the similarity of both groups to "the strong" in Corinth would be explained by them actually being one and the same group over time.

Corinth considered that "All things are lawful for me" (1 Cor 6:12) and so that the Christian could act immorally with impunity. However, we have argued that πορνεῦσαι in Rev 2:14, 21 does not refer to literal sexual immorality. Boxall (1998, p198-218) has also argued that the Nicolaitans are best seen as in the Pauline tradition, and shows how this view is compatible with much that John writes in Rev.

[183] Schüssler Fiorenza (1985, p120-6) goes on to discuss the similarities between Paul and Rev with respect to the answers given to the similar problems posed by the strong at Corinth and the Nicolaitans. The comparable way in which Paul and Rev answer these groups (that is, by both stressing "eschatological reservation" (although in their different ways) and that redemption must be lived out in everyday life) is a further indication that the Nicolaitans and the opponents of Paul in 1 Cor were similar. Schüssler Fiorenza (1985, p119-20) notes another possible point of contact between the two groups. In 1 Cor 2:10a Paul refers to "the depths of God (τὰ βάθη τοῦ θεοῦ)" which can only be searched by the Spirit of God (cf. Rom 11:33). Schüssler Fiorenza implies that the strong in Corinth claimed to know these "depths of God", and hence that Paul was saying this was impossible, and that this is comparable to Rev 2:24. She notes other less plausible parallels on Schüssler Fiorenza 1985, p119-20. It has been thought that the Nicolaitans and the strong at Corinth had a similar social position and were from the wealthier stratum of early Christian churches; see Thompson 1990, p123-4; Theissen 1982, p127-32. However, Meggitt (1998, p107-113) has shown that eating meat was not an issue that related exclusively to the wealthier members of society, but that the poor also ate meat. We have no grounds for talking about the socio-economic level of the Nicolaitans therefore. Meggitt also challenges the reading of 1 Cor that sees the strong there as wealthy. Further, the Nicolaitans could well have attracted the "ordinary" members of the Christian community since they could have advocated that one could participate in the civic and private festivities associated with Hellenistic religion, something that all Christians, regardless of social level, may have been attracted to; see Aune 1997, p193. Finally, it is noteworthy that John does not accuse the Nicolaitans of being wealthy (cf Rev 3:17-18); nor are the two communities in which the Nicolaitans are most influential – Thyatira and Pergamum – accused of being wealthy. So the link between wealth and the Nicolaitans is unsubstantiated.

[184] Farrer (1964, p77) notes: "This antinomianism [of the Nicolaitans] may be a misrepresentation of the Pauline doctrine of liberty, as was the case with the antinomians of 2 Peter, who are also likened to Balaam (2:15; 3:15-16; cf Jude 11)." See also Swete 1906, p36-7; Vanni 1980, p32; Fox 1994, p495-6; Taeger 1998, p196.

A speculative scenario would be that the group which began as opponents of the Pastor in 65-80 split off from the Pauline community, became established as a separate group in Ephesus, adopted the name or was nicknamed "Nicolaitans", and spread its influence to Pergamum and Thyatira. We know that women were attracted to the teaching of the opponents of the Pastor and were themselves teachers among those opponents; the impact of women teachers could then be seen to continue with the impact of Jezebel in Thyatira, although we note that women were clearly prominent in a number of movements in the early Church. This hypothesis would have the advantage of "not multiplying entities beyond what is necessary", since we would then be dealing with one group, not two.

However, the main point against this (admittedly speculative) proposal is our lack of information. All we know about the Nicolaitans concerns food offered to idols and idolatry. We have no indication that either of these were matters on which the opponents of the Pastor had an opinion. But what we do know counts against equating the two groups. In fact, the opponents of the Pastor advocated abstention from some food (1 Tim 4:1-5), probably because of their view that the Jewish law continued to have some relevance (1 Tim 1:7-11).[185] This seems to be very different from advocating eating idol meat.[186] Further, since the Jewish law continued to be relevant for the Pastor's opponents in some way, it seems unlikely that they would also have advocated eating idol meat and involvement in idolatry. Thus, that the Pastor's opponents became the group that John calls the Nicolaitans, while possible, seems unlikely.

4. Who are John's addressees in Revelation?

We are now able to address the issue of who are John's addressees? We have two basic options here.

Firstly, that John is writing to only some of the Christians in each of the cities, or that in some cities where there are different groups of Christians, such as may be the case at Ephesus, he is only writing to one group and is not

---

[185] Although we noted a negative view of the material world may also be a factor.

[186] Although the Corinthian strong held together eating idol meat and over-realized eschatology (since the latter opened the way to libertine behaviour), the opponents of the Pastor do not seem to be particularly libertine, since the catalogues of vices in the Pastorals seem to be dependent on the polemical schema the Pastor has adopted, rather than descriptions of actual behaviour by the opponents. If we did have evidence for libertine behaviour by the Pastor's opponents then this would add to the hypothetical case given above, since libertine attitudes could allow eating idol meat and involvement in idolatry.

writing to others.[187] In this regard, Koester thinks that one of the Christian groups present in Ephesus was "a Jewish-Christian conventicle which was led by the prophet John, and which produced the book of apocalyptic revelations which has been preserved under his name."[188] Similarly, Thompson notes that one of the questions about John which is still debated is "Did he head a conventicle splinter group of Christians in each of these [seven] cities?"[189]

Secondly, that John addresses his book to all Christians in each city, but is aware that he will gain a positive hearing from only some of the Christians or some of the Christian groups to which he writes. He is aware that the Christians who will not receive his book positively belong to various "traditions", but he intentionally writes to them in any case, wanting to convince them about his view of the world and so on. On this view, his work is not itself evidence for a "John of Revelation community", since he is writing to all Christians. Clearly, there are some Christians who agree with John and so he had "supporters". But these are people who agree with John ideologically, rather than those who owe allegiance to John in some way as the founder of their group, or as the leader of a clearly defined community. Hence these people do not "belong" to John as it were.

We need to note that we have argued that a separate group of Nicolaitans existed in Ephesus, while in Pergamum and Thyatira, the Nicolaitans were within the group addressed. It seems likely that John is not writing to the Nicolaitans in Ephesus. To him, they are beyond repentance (as Jezebel seems to be since she is not called on the repent).[190]

---

[187] In some small cities, he may be writing to all Christians, since the group he knows may be the only group in the city.

[188] Koester 1971, p155.

[189] Thompson 1990, p12-13; he argues for a diverse Christian audience on p191-7, and suggests (p196) "John operates within the existing churches of the Asian cities." By contrast, Court (1994, p108) suggests the seven proclamations were perhaps addressed to "house churches set up by John in these cities". Satake (1966, p193) also speaks of "Die Gemeinden der Apokalypse" as a separate community from other Christian communities. Prigent (2001, p81) writes: "it is possible that small Johannine communities [ie relating to John of Revelation] existed alongside other Christian Churches in the larger Asian cities without entering into any true relationship with them." Of course, we have suggested that John was part of a group of prophets, but clearly his audience in Rev was not this group. Klassen (1999, p404) also writes with regard to Rev: "The Johannine community rejected all forms of violence. Instead they urged their people to endure suffering and to follow the Lamb in steadfastness and faithfulness." Here Klassen shows that he sees what John writes in Rev as a mirror in which to see a "Johannine community" which is addressed in Rev. See also Bornkamm in TDNT VI, p669-70; Trevett 1989a, p123; Smalley 1994, esp p15-20, 57-69. By contrast Hartman (1996, p123) notes: "The apocalypses are commonly assumed to have been produced by conventicles and to reflect their attitudes. I am afraid this reflects a form-critical axiom which, to my mind, should not be accepted so easily, viz. that a type of literature presupposes a certain type of community as its *Sitz im Leben.*"

[190] This suggests John has a different attitude to the Nicolaitans and Jezebel than he does to those who are Nicolaitans in Pergamum and the Nicolaitans in Thyatira called on to repent

How do we decide between these two options? The opening line of each proclamation, normally translated "To the angel of the church in Ephesus", could be translated simply: "To the angel of the assembly in Ephesus", a translation which need not imply that all Christians in Ephesus were being addressed. This would be in line with one meaning of ἐκκλησία which is "a specific Christian group, assembly, gathering",[191] as in 1 Cor 11:18; 3 Jn 6, 9. Rev 2:1 would then be to an assembly of Christians who are in Ephesus, a group known to John and who recognise John as "one of their own" without necessarily implying anything about the presence or absence of other Christians in the city. Note that the Bauer-Danker lexicon sees Rev 2:1 as an example of ἐκκλησία meaning "congregation or church as the totality of Christians living and meeting in a particular locality or larger geographical area, but not necessarily limited to one meeting place".[192] However, John's usage of ἐκκλησία in Rev is limited to Rev 1:4, 11, 20; 2-3 and 22:16 and he never makes it clear in which sense he uses the term. We must therefore consider wider factors.

In order to decide between these two options then, we need to consider first of all the relationship between John and the communities he addresses. As we have noted, it is clear that John is aware of the situation of each of the seven churches and it is most likely that he was personally known to these communities.[193] It is equally clear that he was deeply unhappy with many aspects of the life of the seven churches. This is seen firstly in the tone of the seven proclamations. While a proclamation often begins with some form of commendation,[194] John often goes on to state: "But I have this against you … (Rev 2:4, 14, 20; 3:3 ("Remember then …)),[195] or to write some form of accusation against the community (3:1, 15). This is followed up by a call to change and then a threat that, "If not, I will come to you …" in an act of judgement.[196] Clearly then, there is much happening in the life of the seven churches with which John does not agree.

Further evidence of John's attitude to his readers is found in Rev 4-22 when what John says is occasionally addressed directly to his readers in the

---

in 2:22. John's different attitude with regard to whether repentance was possible may be related to his assessment of whether they would respond; Jezebel has clearly not responded to a previous call to repent (2:21), and perhaps John had previously called on the Ephesian Nicolaitans to repent without success.

[191] BDAG, p305, 3.b.α.

[192] BDAG p304, 3.b.β.

[193] See Aune 1981, p26-7. He suggests that John was an itinerant prophet who "traveled a restricted circuit to a limited number of Christian congregations." (p27)

[194] In the proclamation to Sardis the commendation comes towards the end in 3:4; there is no commendation in the proclamation to Laodicea, 3:14-22.

[195] John is entirely positive in the proclamations to Smyrna and Philadelphia.

[196] Rev 2:5, 16; 3:3, 16; in the proclamation to Thyatira the judgement solely concerns the followers of Jezebel (Rev 2:18-29).

seven churches. Thus for example in Rev 18:4 we read: "Then I heard another voice from heaven saying, 'Come out of her, my people, lest you take part in her sins, lest you share in her plagues....'" In the context, this is clearly addressed directly to the readers in the seven churches. We note also the exhortations addressed to the readers in 13:9; 14:12 and 16:15.

Another dimension of John's attitude to the seven churches is discussed by Aune, who analyses how John presents his own role vis-à-vis the communities he addresses. John calls himself simply "John" (1:1, 4, 9; 22:8), presents himself as God's "servant" (1:1) and describes himself to his readers as "your brother" (1:9), thus building rapport with them. But, as we have noted above, although John does not designate himself as a "prophet", he implies that he fulfils this role in calling the book a "prophecy" (προφητεία) in 1:3; 22:7, 10, 18, 19. John comes closest to calling himself a prophet in 22:9 where an angel says to John "I am a fellow servant with you and your brothers the prophets ...". That John is part of a circle of prophets is confirmed by 22:16: "I Jesus have sent my angel to you (ὑμῖν) with this testimony for the churches";[197] we have argued above that ὑμεῖς refers to a group of prophets to which John belongs, who transmitted John's revelation to the churches.[198] We see then that John is making an indirect claim to the role of prophet.

In this regard, Aune notes: "John's chief opponent in the churches is 'Jezebel,' who calls herself a prophetess (2:20). This direct claim to prophetic authority by 'Jezebel' is countered by John's greater claim to mediate divine revelation from Jesus Christ to the seven churches."[199] Accordingly, the two call narratives in 1:9-20 and 10:8-11:2 legitimate John as the receiver of revelation and show that he wanted his readers to accept his book as a revelation from Jesus Christ. Further, John regularly refers to what he hears or sees in visions and auditions from various heavenly sources. In addition, John's message is declared to be reliable by God (21:5; 22:6). We can suggest that this emphasis on mediating divine authority is to counter opponents and to convince readers of the veracity of what he says.[200]

Thus, although building rapport with his readers is important, we also see that to some extent John stands over against them as did the prophets of Israel, although he does so not on his own authority, but as the bearer of divine revelation. He has known opposition in the past (cf 2:14f, 20-23) and

---

[197] See Aune 1981, p19.

[198] See Aune 1998, p1225-6.

[199] Aune 1981, p19.

[200] We will discuss this in more detail in Chapter 10. Schüssler Fiorenza (1991, p138) argues that John's repeated stress on "heavenly ratification and divine sanction evidence a great anxiety about the authority and influence of his work. They characterize John's discourse as belonging to that of a cognitive minority within the Christian community of Asia."

he does not now anticipate an easy hearing. Hence as Aune comments: "it is presumably for the purpose of overcoming a reluctance to accept and act on his message that he so carefully focuses on the divine authority of that message."[201]

But there is one other important feature that we can discern of the relationship between John and his readers. We note that, although it is clear that John is very familiar with his readers, the only specific indication of a previous relationship comes in 2:21, where we read that John gave Jezebel "time to repent", which we have noted suggests an earlier oracle directed by John, or his associates to Jezebel.[202] As we have noted, it is likely that both John and Jezebel are heads of prophetic groups and that the two groups are rivals.

Aune suggests that we read the seven proclamations through the lens of this conflict. Many of the communities then appear, from John's perspective, to be made up of two or three "tendencies".[203] Behind the issue of eating meat offered to idols and "practising immorality" is the wider issue of the attitude towards cultural and religious accommodation. John represents a "non-accommodationist stance" while Jezebel and the Nicolaitans represent the opposite attitude.

Where do the communities stand? Judging by the tone of the proclamations, John has allies in Ephesus, Smyrna and Philadelphia, some in Thyatira (2:24f) and a few in Pergamum, Sardis (3:4) and Laodicea. The Nicolaitans have their strongest influence in Pergamum and Thyatira but have been "generally unsuccessful"[204] among the addressees in Ephesus, where we have suggested the Nicolaitans existed as a separate group.

But Aune goes on: "The majority of Christians, however, seem to belong to a centrist tendency or party,[205] which has not yet moved into the camp of the Nicolaitans, but which (from John's perspective) has departed from the works done at first (2:5), or whose works are imperfect in God's sight (3:2), or who are neither cold nor hot (3:15f.). If this centrist party dominated most of the churches of Asia Minor, these congregations would clearly have provided a battleground for the divinely-legitimated movements led by John on the one hand and "Jezebel" and the Nicolaitans on the other."[206] So this centrist party, which espouses neither cultural accommodation nor strict

---

[201] Aune 1981, p22.

[202] See Aune 1981, p27.

[203] Aune 1981, p28.

[204] Aune 1981, p28.

[205] We will go on to argue that among John's addressees are people belonging to a Pauline community and others who belong to a Johannine community, so that among the addressees there is more than simply a "tendency" but rather defined groups.

[206] Aune 1981, p28-9.

nonconformist behaviour, is probably in the majority (or at the least, a significant presence) in most of the churches.

What this means is that John has a battle on his hands as he tries to convince his readers.[207] This situation also makes sense of the fact that John cannot presume he will receive a hearing, but rather presents his message so carefully as having divine authority. It also means that we cannot equate John's attitudes on a whole range of matters with the attitudes to these matters to be found among his readers! In fact, John's attitudes are likely to be quite different from the attitudes of some of his readers.

What light does this shed on who John's addressees are? It raises the likelihood that John is not writing to "his group in Ephesus" or "in Thyatira" and so on. He rather seems to be embattled in a deeply conflictual situation – not only with a rival "school" of Nicolaitans, but also with the majority (or at least a very significant number) of Christians among his readers. Given this situation, it is certainly possible that John is in a deeply conflictual situation with "his own community", but, given what we have said up to now in this section about John's expectation of opposition and about different attitudes to society, it seem much more likely that he is writing to all the Christians in the seven cities.

Further, there are a range of positive reasons why it is likely that John is writing to all the Christians in the city of Ephesus and in the other six cities (while noting as he writes that most of his readers will not entirely agree with him).

Firstly, John's universal language strongly suggests he is thinking of all Christians as he writes.[208] It is certainly inherently unlikely that one who thinks in such "cosmic" terms as John does, and writes of Christians from "every tribe, language, people and nation", [209] (as well as thinking of the church as the "true Israel"[210]) would then simply write to one-third (say) of the Christians in Ephesus, while ignoring all the others. Of course, he may not be writing to those who consider themselves Christians but whom John thinks are "irredeemable", but the centrist group we have identified in Rev 2-3 clearly does not come into this category.

Secondly, we have argued that John knows the local geography and the local communities in the seven cities well and may have lived in more than one

---

[207] Aune 1981, p29 thus concludes: "The Apocalypse constitutes a final, culminating statement of the values, norms and behaviors advocated by John in which the author seeks acceptance by his readers of the divine revelation he mediates."

[208] Note the varied lists which includes "every tribe, language, people and nation" in 5:9; 7:9; 10:11; 11:9; 13:7; 14:6; 17:15; and the positive references (for example) to people from every nation standing before the Lamb or to the nations; see 5:9; 7:9; 21:24, 26; 22:2.

[209] See Bauckham 1993d, p86-7, 137-40; Court 1994, p106 and note Rev 7:9-14; 11:13; 14.6.

[210] See for example, Rev 2:9; 3:9; 21:12

of the seven cities.[211] If, for example, he had been in Ephesus for some years, or if he had visited the city on a number of occasions, it seems most likely that he would have know the different Christian groups in the city. Indeed our analysis suggests just this – he knows both his friends and his "Christian enemies" in each of the cities. It is inherently unlikely then that an itinerant prophet like John who has "been around" for some time, would *not* know all the Christian groups in Ephesus, even if he knew some better than others.[212] And given the universal scope of Revelation and John's concern that *all* Christians avoid accommodation with Greco-Roman society, it seems likely that if he knows of Christians in these cities, then he would want to address them, provided of course they are not, in his view, "beyond the pale" in the way the Nicolaitans are.[213]

Thirdly, we need to note that although Rev shares features of the letter genre, it is not simply a letter. Rather, it also bears characteristics of a prophecy and, primarily, of an apocalypse.[214] If it were solely a letter, then we could argue that it was written to a small group within a city. However, it is not solely a letter, and so its genre does not require us to postulate "John's community" to which it is written.

Fourthly, we have already argued that John knows that many Christians in the communities to which he writes do not agree with him. He is not only writing to like-minded Christians and while there could be a huge crisis in "John's community", given the other points we have made above (such as his universalism), it seems more likely that he is writing to all Christians in each of the cities. In addition, that John anticipates much opposition but still writes his book, suggests that even if some groups disagreed with him, he would still want to address them.

Finally, the issue of the relationship between John's addressees and the readers of the Pastorals and the Johannine letters will be the focus of chapters 8-13. We will note there that there are no clear grounds on which we can say that John is writing to a particular group of Ephesian Christians and that there is no evidence which would contradict our hypothesis that John is writing to

---

[211] We might ask if John would have known all the Christians in seven cities, three of which were very large (Ephesus, Smyrna, Pergamum)? But it is clear that much of what John knows about some of the groups is reasonably general, and quite compatible with the knowledge a prophet would acquire while travelling around a number of groups. It is certainly not impossible that John would know at least something about all the Christian groups.

[212] Note also our argument in Chapter 13 section 2.1.1 where we argue that because of the level of communication and travel between Christian groups, it is unlikely that Christians in one group in a city would be unaware of the existence of another Christian group in the same city.

[213] Although they are currently tolerated by Christians in Pergamum and Thyatira, but of course John wishes to change this situation.

[214] On the genre of Revelation see Thompson 1990, p18-24; Aune 1997, plxx-xc.

all Christians in Ephesus, or at least all those who for him were "within the pale".

We conclude then that John is writing to all the Christians who, in his view, are not "beyond the pale" in each of the cities. But he anticipates that many will disagree with him. As Aune has shown, he thinks that the majority of Christians in Ephesus have "departed from the works done at first" (2:5) and that John had a battle on his hands as he tried to convince his readers.

This makes it likely that John is writing to a variety of Christian groups. We can suggest that he is writing to Pauline Christians, who were addressed in the Pastorals (and will be addressed by Ignatius), and that he also has some "Johannine Christians" in view (who may have been or will be addressed by 1-3 John, depending on how we date the letters). Perhaps he also thinks of those who were the opponents of the Pastor or the Johannine secessionists. (We have suggested he is not writing to the Nicolaitans in Ephesus.) Thus, the indications that John disagrees with the majority of his readers testifies to a diversity of Christian groups in Ephesus. This is a hypothesis that we will test in our discussions in Chapters 8-13.

5. What does Revelation tell us about the Christians in Ephesus addressed by John: Were they facing a crisis?

We would be wrong to think that the seven churches are addressed only in Rev 2-3, for clearly the whole of Rev is written to the seven churches (1:11). Can we then say something about the seven churches, and in particular the Christian community in Ephesus, from what is said in the book as a whole?

Rev as a whole tells us a good deal about John's theology, and about other issues such as his use of the OT. However, it is difficult to determine the theology and situation of the Christian community in Ephesus addressed by John from the book. We have already noted that John anticipates that many of his readers do not share his views, at least on some matters. Further, at times John is probably expressing views he shared with many in the seven communities, but it is difficult to determine when this is the case. We must also recall that John is a creative theologian, who is not simply reflecting the beliefs of other communities around him. Hence it would be precarious to read simplicter, say the Christology of the Ephesian Christians from Revelation.[215]

---

[215] Thompson (1990, p72) notes that Rev was meant to be read in worship (see 1:3; 22:18) and thus that "the book itself becomes liturgical material for the churches of western Asia Minor." Were the hymns in the book then actually sung in the worship of the Ephesian community? This seems possible, but we do not know. Or were the hymns in Rev in some way a reflection of the worshipping life of the Christians in Ephesus, or some of the other seven churches, and so familiar to them? Given that John knew these churches well, this seems a possibility, but we cannot say anything with certainty with respect to Ephesus.

However, there are some issues on which we can draw some conclusions about the Christian community in Ephesus addressed by John from what he wrote and these will be dealt with in Chapter 8-13. Here we will discuss the issue of whether John's readers in Ephesus were facing a crisis.

5.1 Were John's readers in Ephesus facing a crisis?

Here we are interested in the question of whether John's readers in Ephesus were facing a crisis.

5.1.1 Did Domitian persecute Christians?

Firstly, we need to note that it seems clear that no far-reaching persecution occurred under Domitian. The standard portrait of Domitian that has come down to us from writers such as Pliny the Younger, Tacitus, Suetonius and Dio Cassius presents Domitian as a megalomaniac and a tyrant, whose cruelty, unbridled passions, insecurity and madness were legendary and whose reign was a period of confusion, disorder and chaos.[216] However, Thompson has argued that the epigraphical, numismatic and prosopographical evidence shows that these standard literary sources distort virtually every aspect of Domitian's public and state activities as Emperor. In particular, there is no evidence that Domitian demanded greater divine honours than his predecessors,[217] and there is no evidence for widespread oppression and persecution of Asian Christians by Domitian.[218] Further, when we look at Rev itself, there are only two possible examples of actual persecution in the

---

[216] Thompson 1990, p96-101 gives a summary of the standard portrait. Eusebius, writing in the fourth century, said that "many were the victims of Domitian's appalling cruelty" and notes that even non-Christian historians recorded the persecution and martyrdom of Christians (HE 3.17-20). Thompson (1990, p136) suggests he drew on Dio Cassius as a source concerning persecution by Domitian. For the views of other Christians about Domitian's reign see Thompson 1990, p136-7; Tertullian, Apol. 5.

[217] Thompson 1990, p106-7; cf. Caird 1966, p23; Schüssler Fiorenza 1991, p54. Hence, while Christians in Asia probably found the imperial cult objectionable, it was just as objectionable under Claudius as under Domitian.

[218] See Thompson 1990, p101-9, 171-2; see also Aune 1997, plxiv-lxix; Prigent 2001, p71-4. The authors concerned were writing under Trajan, whom they contrasted with Domitian. Thompson (1990, p115) concludes that for these writers "a retrospective presentation of Domitian and his reign serves as a foil in the present praise of Trajan. Their relationship is constructed to form contrasting pairs in which each member reciprocally shapes the other. Domitian has to be the opposite of Trajan - the more evil Domitian, the better the Optimus. Domitian's evil tyranny displays the life of liberty under Trajan, just as Trajan's humanness requires Domitian's exaggerated divinity." See further Thompson 1990, p109-115. It is also clear that in most respects, Trajan continued the policies and administration of Domitian. Domitian was, however, more rigorous than his predecessors in administering the Jewish tax, but there is no evidence for a Domitianic persecution of Jews or converts to Judaism; see Thompson 1990, p133-7.

past by the state. John himself is "on the island called Patmos because of the
word of God and the testimony of Jesus" (1:9b),[219] which probably means he
was in exile on Patmos as a punishment for his witness to Jesus.[220] Antipas
almost certainly had been killed because he was a Christian (2:13 – "my
witness, my faithful one, who was killed among you"). Thus, it seems very
unlikely that the background to Revelation was the significant persecution of
Asian, including Ephesians, Christians.

5.1.2 Other elements of conflict in the social situation of Ephesian Christians addressed by John

However, we can see from Rev itself, and we can suggest from other evidence,
that there were other difficulties and conflicts encountered by the readers.

Firstly, we have already discussed the conflict between John and the
Nicolaitans. This was one dimension of perceived crisis from John's
perspective, and was also one dimension of the crisis for some of his readers.
Further, we have noted that the Ephesian Christians have tested and rejected
"apostles"; clearly this was an element of conflict for this community.

Secondly, it is clear that the Christian communities in Smyrna and
Philadelphia seem to have been in conflict with their local Jewish communities
(Rev 2:9; 3:9). The most likely interpretation of these verses is that they
concern people who are non-Christian Jews, but whom John considers have
now forfeited the right to call themselves Jews because they reject Christ and
attack his followers. Because they actively oppose and slander Christians
(βλασφημία; 2:9),[221] John regards them as aligning themselves with Satan, the
Great Accuser (Rev 12:10). Hence for John they are a synagogue not of God
but of Satan.[222] In John's eyes, it is the members of the church who are the
true Jews.[223]

---

[219] 1:9a probably refers simply to the fact that for John the Christian life means
participation in Jesus' affliction, victory and steadfastness, rather than to specific persecution.
This is suggested by the fact that John says he shares these things with his readers; see
Thompson 1990, p172.

[220] See Farrer 1964, p64; Beagley 1987, p31; Schüssler Fiorenza 1991, p50. Thompson
1990, p173 disputes this meaning. He notes that no Roman source designates Patmos as an
island for banishment, and he could have been on Patmos because he wanted to preach there.
While it is possible that John went to Patmos in order to preach the Gospel there, or to
receive prophetic inspiration, it seems more likely that he was exiled there.

[221] βλασφημία is strong language, elsewhere used of the activity of the beast and the
Whore; see 13:1, 5, 6, 17:3; Lambrecht 2001a, p329-39 argues that here it refers to slander
against Christians, rather than blasphemy against God and Christ.

[222] See Caird 1966, p35; Schüssler Fiorenza 1985, p116; Beagley 1987, p32. For a
review of past discussion on the identity of "the Jews" see Beagley 1987, p31-4. We have
noted above that Koester (1971, p148) thinks the "synagogue of Satan" is a reference to the
Nicolaitans who are Jewish Christians, but this is unlikely. Further, note the parallel between
2:9 and 3:9 and the false apostles of Rev 2:2: these people were almost certainly apostles in

What is the significance of the fact that John does not mention Jews in the proclamation to Ephesus? Here we have two options. Firstly, that because John is silent about conflict between Christians and Jews in Ephesus, such conflict was not an issue for the addressees (as it was for Christians in Smryna and Philadelphia). However, we note that this is an argument from John's silence. Secondly, that John's letters, to some extent at least, have an exemplary character.[224] This would mean that what is said to one church has a representative or paradigmatic function for the other six churches in Asia (and elsewhere in the province, and further afield too). Thus, what is said of one church, in this case about conflict with the Jews, may well apply to others, though probably to a lesser degree. This is hinted at by John at the end of each proclamation when he writes "Let anyone who has an ear listen to what the Spirit is saying to the *churches*" (eg Rev 2:7).

This second option seems more likely. Certainly, just because nothing is said on a topic to one particular church, does not mean that that church was totally innocent or uninvolved in that regard. Clearly what is said to one church applies to that church, but what is said to a particular church has at least some relevance to another, as the refrain in 2:7 and so on suggests. In particular, we cannot say that there was no conflict between Christians in Ephesus and the Jewish community in the city at the time of Revelation *solely* on the basis of John's silence. We do not have positive evidence for that conflict, but it seems likely, and the fact that it occurred in Smryna and Philadelphia reinforces this likelihood.

Thirdly, we have some evidence for antipathy towards Christians from Gentile neighbours in Asia. It is clear from Pliny's correspondence with

---

their own eyes, but John denies them that title. The case is the same with the Jews of Rev 2:9 and 3:9; see Kraabel 1968, p183 n2. Thompson 1990, p138 thinks John is also condemning Jewish accommodation to Greek city life in Rev 2:9; 3:9, but this is by no means clear in these verses. Further, in his discussion of Jews in Asia (1990, p133-45) he does not take seriously the fact that most of our evidence for Jewish accommodation comes from after the time of Revelation.

[223] See Thompson 1990, p90; see also Lambrecht 2001b, p341-56. It has been suggested that some Jewish Christians had been expelled from the synagogue, and so could no longer claim the protection granted by Roman law to Judaism, in which case their situation with respect to Rome could be vulnerable. That Jews in Smyrna were acting as informers to the Roman authorities about the Christians, could be suggested by 2:10. However, while this interpretation is possible, it is not demanded by the text. It may rather reflect a conflict situation in which Jews at Smyrna 'slandered' or spoke against Christians in the sense of being generally opposed to them, just as Christians, including John, spoke against Jews. See further Yarbro Collins 1984, p85; Sweet 1979, p85; Schüssler Fiorenza 1991, p55; Farrer 1964, p72. Perhaps the Jews in Philadephia had also expelled the Christians from the synagogue, which would explain the reference in 3:7 to the keys of David, and to the risen Christ as the one "who opens and no one shall shut, who shuts and no one opens", but this may be reading too much into the text. See Yarbro Collins 1984, p86; Beale 1988, p330-1; Thompson 1990, p174; cf. Lambrecht 2001a, 329-39.

[224] See Hirschberg 1999, p117-18.

Trajan in 111 CE that opposition to Christians came primarily from local people, since Pliny says that people were brought to him with charges (*deferebantur*), and that "these accusations spread (as is usually the case) from the mere fact of the matter being investigated and several forms of the mischief came to light. A placard was put up, without any signature, accusing a large number of persons by name."[225] His letter shows that Christians aroused a deep suspicion and uneasiness among their Gentile neighbours, and that they could be regarded as endangering the fabric of society. Further, because many Christians would not participate in any form of pagan worship, they were in a vulnerable position, and open to the charges of atheism and hatred of humanity. Whether or not Christians were asked to worship the emperor (which seems unlikely), some Christians may have been only too aware that they could not participate in many aspects of city life. This may have led to somewhat precarious relations between Christians and Roman officials.[226] Thus, although overt conflict between Christians and their non-Christian neighbours was rare,[227] it would not be surprising if Christians on some occasions felt vulnerable in their pagan cities, to say the least. The situation would be even more difficult if the Christians had been repudiated by the local Jewish community and so could not claim shelter there.

We can also note that many scholars argue that John wrote in order to awaken his readers to dimensions of crisis that John perceived in their situation, dimensions that many of his readers currently did not perceive in this way. The crisis may become visible only through the knowledge revealed in an apocalypse. This means that we need not see the readers' situation in Ephesus (or elsewhere) as currently being one of overwhelming crisis. Nor need the readers perceive Rome, for example, to be the hugely threatening beast that John depicts. Many readers undoubtedly perceived Roman rule quite positively. But we have noted that there were some dimensions of conflict in the current situation of the Ephesian readers.[228]

What can we say then about the situation of the Christians in Ephesus addressed by John? Firstly, we cannot be sure that they understood their situation as one of crisis. Certainly this was how John perceived their situation, but many Ephesian Christian readers probably did not share John's

---

[225] See Pliny, *Ep.* 10.96.4-5; Thompson 1990, p130-2; Schüssler Fiorenza 1991, p127.

[226] See Yarbro Collins 1984, p84-99.

[227] See Thompson 1990, p132; Wilken 1984, p132.

[228] See Thompson 1990, p25-8, 194-6 cf. Schüssler Fiorenza 1985, p6. Thus, in Rev John anticipates major trials in the near future, caused by the outside world and makes it clear that he expects tribulation and oppression from political and economic institutions of his world. But in these visions he is anticipating conflict, conflict which in his view stems from the fundamental opposition between the church and urban society and the Roman Empire; see Thompson 1990, p174, 189; Schüssler Fiorenza 1991, p54. It is not evidence for all these dimensions of crisis in the present experience of his hearers.

view before hearing Rev. Secondly, it seems clear that they had not suffered in an empire-wide persecution instigated by Domitian. Thirdly, we have already discussed the conflict they experienced with other Christians, namely the "apostles" (2:2) and the Nicolaitans (2:6). Fourthly, we do not have positive evidence for conflict between Ephesian Christian readers of Rev and the Jewish community in Ephesus, but such conflict seems likely. Fifthly, given that the readers in Ephesus have knowledge of the Nicolaitans, and so probably of the significance of the issue of relations between Christians and pagan worship in general, we can suggest that they were aware of their vulnerability as people who did not participate in local cults. Finally, we have no knowledge of other experiences of trauma for Ephesian Christians such as local persecution.

6. Overall Conclusions

Firstly, Revelation was almost certainly written towards the end of Domitian's reign. Its author John clearly knew the seven churches addressed well, and so can be regarded as a reliable witness concerning the Christian community he writes to in Ephesus.

Secondly, the risen Christ addresses the Christian community in Ephesus in the first of the seven proclamations (2:1-7). The Ephesians are commended for testing and rejecting people whom John considers to be false apostles. We know nothing about the teaching of these apostles, or by what criteria the Ephesians tested them and considered them to be false, but it seems likely that they were itinerant, and claimed to belong to the wider group of apostles which included people like Barnabas, Paul, Andronicus and Junia.

Thirdly, we gain some idea of a group of Christians in Asia, who had a form of organisation and were called "the Nicolaitans" by John. They advocated that Christians could participate in pagan cults, and thus could be involved in society and need not form an exclusive group. They presented an answer to a felt need, and may have marshaled a number of arguments based on Christian tradition to support their position. One of their leaders, who was a prophet and teacher, was a woman whom John calls "Jezebel". The Nicolaitans are not to be thought of as "gnostic"; rather their closest affinity seems to be with the "strong" at Corinth. The Nicolaitans had gained a significant hearing in Thyatira and Pergamum where they were a part of the Christian community John addressed. We have argued that a group of Nicolaitans were established in Ephesus, as a separate group rather than within the group addressed by John.

To John the Nicolaitans were idolatrous, and the risen Lord "hated" them, and the Ephesian addressees are said to hate them too (Rev 2:6). This suggests that many of the Christians John addressed in Ephesus did not accept the "accommodationist" position of the Nicolaitans. However, while the Ephesian addressees were not in the Nicolaitan camp, as far as John was concerned they had departed from the works done at first (2:5). We have suggested that this means that although they do not agree with the Nicolaitans, nor do they see the issue of the relationship to society in the same clear-cut terms as John does.[229] John was writing to convince them of his position and to call them to repent. This suggests that perhaps the majority of the Ephesian Christians did not agree with John that Christians should form an exclusive group which was withdrawn from society rather than be involved in the life of the Greco-Roman city. Thus the call to "do the works you did at first" (v5a) is probably a call to do the works commensurate with belonging to a tight-knit, exclusive Christian community which had no interactions with pagan idolatry.

We have also noted that it is unlikely that the Nicolaitans and the opponents of the author of the Pastoral epistles are the same group.

Fourthly, we can know something of the situation of the Christians in Ephesus addressed by John. John perceived that their situation was one of crisis, but we cannot be sure that the Ephesian readers understood their situation in this way. They almost certainly had not suffered in an empire-wide persecution instigated by Domitian, nor is there evidence that they had experienced conflict from the Jewish community in Ephesus. However, some at least of the Ephesians would have been aware of conflict between themselves and other Christians, namely the "apostles" (2:2) and the Nicolaitans (2:6). They were probably aware of their vulnerability as a group which did not participate in local cults. Beyond this we have no knowledge of other experiences of trauma for Ephesian Christians.

Finally, this raises the issue of to whom John is writing. We have suggested that John is writing to all the Christians in each of the cities, but that he anticipates that many will disagree with him. With regard to Ephesus, this makes it likely that John is writing to a variety of Christian groups. We can suggest that he is writing to Pauline Christians, who were addressed (or will be addressed, depending on dating) in the Pastorals (and will be addressed by Ignatius), and that he also has some "Johannine Christians" in view. Perhaps he also thinks of those who were the opponents of the Pastor or the Johannine secessionists. But we have suggested he is not writing to the Nicolaitans in Ephesus, since he regards this group as "beyond the pale".

---

[229] Note Thompson's (1990, p195) comment, with which I am in general agreement: "It is true that John, like Ignatius, tries to polarize the churches in Asia ... ; that is, John draws sharp boundaries within the churches by claiming that there is only one proper attitude to take towards the world. Those who accept the necessity (and pleasure) of living quietly with their neighbours are in the wrong; good Christians assimilate the Roman world as demonic. In fact, one could argue that John's major challenge comes not from outside the church but from Christians who are open to living in the world."

However, he clearly wants to oppose the influence of the Nicolaitans and so we can suggest that he aims much of his polemic against their views. Thus, the indications that John disagrees with many of his readers is in keeping with my suggestion that there is a diversity of Christian groups in Ephesus.

In Part Three, we will test this hypothesis – that in Ephesus the Pastorals and the Johannine Letters are to distinct groups (recall that we date the Pastorals around 80-100 and the Johannine Letters 90-100 so they may well be contemporaneous),[230] while John in Revelation is writing to a variety of Christians in the city. In addition, we will seek to describe various facets of the life of the Christians, as this is accessible to us.

I need to note that there is another possible view with regard to the relationship of the original Pauline community, and the readers of the Pastorals, the Johannine Letters and Revelation. It is possible that these documents may reflect what was happening in only one Christian "community" in Ephesus. This could be called the "merger" or "take over" theory. If all the Ephesian connections which we have discussed are allowed, then on this "take over" view, the original Pauline community would be addressed by the Pastoral Epistles, it would then be "taken over" by John the Evangelist when (as we have suggested) he arrived in the city, addressed by John the Seer in Revelation, it would split in two according to the Johannine Letters and finally be addressed by Ignatius. On this reading all the Christians in Ephesus at any one time and over time would see themselves as part of one community, and there would then be continuity between the addressees of all the literature connected with Ephesus.

A number of scholars have held this "takeover" theory in various forms,[231] of whom Lohse is a good example. In order to explain the fact that there is no explicit trace of Pauline theology in the book of Rev, he writes:

"A historical reflection might help to explain this lack of specific Pauline influence in the book of Revelation. The Jewish war and the capture and destruction of Jerusalem in 70 CE made quite a number of Palestinian Christians leave their country and come to Asia Minor. Their arrival changed the character of the congregations in that region. It is to be supposed that the prophetic traditions that stand behind the author of the book of Revelation are of Palestinian origin and became influential when the time of the Pauline mission had passed.

---

[230] Recall our discussion of what we mean by the term "group" in the Introduction and our discussion of house churches and the way they fostered diversity in Chapter 2.

[231] A number of scholars think that the one group is addressed by at least most of the documents written to Ephesus; see for example Falwell 1948, p191; Bruce 1988, p393; Mussies 1990, p188-193. Moule (1981, p204) clearly holds the "take over" theory when he writes of "the seething diversity of Ephesus where the Pauline churches were to be quickly invaded by antinomianism, Judaizing Christianity, and influences of a Johannine type (see Acts xx. 29f., ? Ephesians, Rev. ii. 1ff., and the Gospel and Epistles of John)." Günther (1995, p5) notes that something like this view (although he does not describe it as a "take over theory") goes back to Schwegler in 1846. See Strelan (1996, p301-2) for further discussion of others who have held this view.

In these traditions the name and theology of Paul were nearly unknown. They were entirely related to the inheritance of the twelve apostles."[232]

Clearly Lohse means this to apply to Ephesus, as to elsewhere in Western Asia Minor. What he says implies that the group that had been founded by Paul came under the influence of John the Seer, so that Paul became "nearly unknown".

Similarly, Prigent, in outlining the background to Rev 2:1-7 speaks of "the Church of Ephesus" in relation to Paul, and then of the arrival of "the apostle John", of 1 Timothy, and of "the Church in Ephesus" in relation to Ignatius; clearly for him all these people and documents relate to the one "Church".[233]

In Part Three we will be arguing against this view, by seeking to show that there were in fact different Christian groups in Ephesus. We will also, as we proceed, be constructing a profile of the nature of these groups, by outlining the different character of the groups with regard to a range of identity-defining issues. Hence in Part Three I will argue, not only that the Pastoral Epistles and the Johannine Letters are to different communities, but I will also seek to give a description of facets of the life of these different communities.

Finally, a further note of introduction to Part Three. Some readers will undoubtedly disagree with my view that 1-3 Jn should be located in Ephesus, and others may well disagree with locating the Pastorals there too. For these readers, I hope that Part Three of this study remains a way of shedding light on the second-third generation period of early Christianity when these documents were produced. For even if some would wish to locate these documents elsewhere, they clearly provide evidence for the early Christian movement and can be read alongside one another, and also in conversation with Rev. Thus my hope is that even if my geographical arguments are rejected, Part Three remains interesting as a dialogue between three sets of documents in second-third generation Christianity, a dialogue which reveals the commonalties and differences that characterised this period.

---

[232] Lohse 1991, p365. We will note in our Overall Conclusions that here he is in large measure reflecting Bauer's view. There are a number of possible variants of what I have called the "merger" or "take over" theory. Lohse's version, as seen above, is clearly a "take over" of Pauline Christianity by John. A variant could be that some Pauline influence was retained – and so it was more nearly a "merger", with the resultant community reflecting both Pauline and Johannine strands. The important point for us is that this view advocates that all the Christians in Ephesus would identify themselves as being part of only one Christian community at any one time.

[233] Prigent 2001, p156.

Part 3

The relationships between the readers of the Pastorals, the Johannine Letters and Revelation

Chapter 8

The wider culture and the readers of the Pastorals, the Johannine Letters and Revelation: Acculturation, Assimilation and Accommodation

1. Introduction

The early Christians in Ephesus lived geographically as part of the city of Ephesus. However, groups of any sort can have a variety of relations to the wider culture of the city in which they live. At one extreme, a group could have as little as possible to do with the wider culture, perhaps by retaining a different language within the group, and insulating themselves from the ideals and traditions of the wider culture as much as they could. At the other extreme, a group could participate fully in the wider culture, to the extent that the group's language, values and practices are identical with those of the wider culture, and all that distinguishes them is that they gather together as a group.[1]

In order to understand this variety of possible interactions between a group and its wider culture, and to discuss the situation of the Christians in Ephesus, we need to outline some conceptual tools. The category of "Hellenization" has often been used in the past in this regard, but it suffers from a lack of specificity as an analytical tool. Further, because it involves a whole range of different aspects – political, social, linguistic, educational and religious - a group could be significantly "Hellenised" in some areas but not others.[2] We need some other way to discuss social and cultural interaction.

In response to this difficulty, Barclay has used the concepts of acculturation, assimilation and accommodation in order to analyse the ways in

---

[1] For a discussion of how we understand the term "group", see the Introduction.
[2] See the discussion in Barclay 1996, p88-91 with regard to Hellenization and Diaspora Judaism. See also Stevenson 2001, p216-18, whose analysis would be aided by the use of Barclay's categories.

which a group might react to its wider environment.[3] We will briefly discuss these three terms and will then use them in this analysis.

Acculturation refers to "the linguistic, educational and ideological aspects of a given cultural matrix".[4] This is confined to the non-material aspects of the wider culture, and so relates to language, values and intellectual traditions, including cultural ideals, and the idea of what constituted virtue.[5]

Assimilation refers to social integration ("becoming 'similar' to one's neighbour"[6]) and concerns social contacts, interactions, and practices, and involves the political, social, material and religious aspects of Hellenization. Assimilation points to the degree to which a group is integrated into, or holds aloof from, their social contexts. Did they participate in the activities of the dominant culture and if so in what ways? This involves not just frequency of contact, but also the quality of those contacts, since a small number of close relationships with family or close friends may be of much greater significance than many secondary relationships.[7]

Accommodation concerns the use a group made of the "cultural tools", such as language, concepts and frameworks of thought, which it acquired from the wider environment. This involves the way acculturation is used and "the sort of cultural engagement to which .. [a group] devoted their acculturation".[8] Does the group seek to merge with the wider culture through its use of cultural tools? Does it aim at cultural convergence? This would involve the integrative use of acculturation to build bridges with the wider culture. With respect to Judaism, Barclay notes that such cultural convergence may include "the imitation of Hellenistic culture, its internalization and its

---

[3] See Barclay 1996, p92-102, but also his use of these concepts throughout the book. For positive discussions of Barclay's terminology see Zetterholm 2001, p86-99 (who responds to Rutgers 1998, p34-8) and Sanders 2000, p143-4, who writes (p144) that Barclay provides "by far the best model of Jewish life in the Roman Diaspora that we have, and he has developed it on the basis of the evidence." For further discussion of these concepts, although they are not always used in exactly the same way as Barclay uses them, see Siegel 1955; Hutnik 1991, p25-59, 153-69; Stier and Greén 1992, p41-50; Snyder 1999, p2-5.

[4] Barclay 1996, p92.

[5] Barclay (1996, p95) constructs a scale for acculturation. The points from the "high" level of acculturation downwards are: scholarly expertise; familiarity with Greek literature, rhetoric, philosophy and theology; acquaintance with common moral values; no facility in Greek.

[6] Barclay 1996, p92.

[7] See Barclay 1996, p93. With regard to Diaspora Jews, Barclay (1996, p93) creates an assimilation scale which goes from high to low assimilation. The points from the "high" level of assimilation downwards are: abandonment of key Jewish social distinctives; gymnasium education; attendance at Greek athletics/theatre; commercial employment with non-Jews; social life confined to the Jewish community.

[8] Barclay 1996, p97-8.

employment in reinterpreting the Jewish tradition";[9] clearly similar things can be said with regard to early Christianity.

Alternatively, a group could use cultural tools to underline the difference between itself and the wider culture, and so for the purpose of furthering polemic, antagonism and even polarization between the group and the wider culture. In this case, the group would be building, not bridges, but defensive walls against the majority culture, and this could involve the use of cultural tools in polemic against the wider culture. This is the oppositional use of acculturation, and can be seen as cultural antagonism. Of course there are many positions on a scale between these two extremes,[10] with this scale measuring "how, not how much" a group uses its acculturation.[11]

I will seek to use these categories to analyse the relationship between the readers of the Pastoral Epistles and their wider environment in the city of Ephesus and I will then do the same for the readers of the Johannine Letters. I will then compare the results obtained. Does this analysis suggest that the readers of these two sets of documents are different groups, as I have proposed? I will also use these categories for a discussion of John the Seer's work in Revelation, and will compare the results obtained with those for the Pastorals and the Johannine Letters. Are these results suggestive with regard to my hypothesis that John is addressing all the Christians in Ephesus? Further, this analysis will contribute to the overall description of the early Christians in Ephesus.

While we run the risk of oversimplifying complex phenomena and missing the subtlety of a situation, I hope that the use of the categories of acculturation, assimilation and accommodation is an advance over concepts of "Hellenization". We also need to note how limited our evidence here is, since we are seeking to analyse comparatively short texts. Nonetheless, I believe the comparisons between the documents are revealing.

We also need to note here that we do not see "culture", and hence categories such as "acculturation" and "assimilation", as a static phenomenon, but rather as a constantly developing and evolving phenomenon. Thus, when we speak of the interaction between Christian groups and their wider culture, we should not think of either the Christian group, or the culture with which they are engaging, as static entities. Rather, we perhaps should think of the interaction between two moving objects.

---

[9] Barclay 1996, p96-7.

[10] See Barclay 1996, p96-8. The centre point of the scale for accommodation which involves neither integrative nor oppositional trends is described by Barclay as "reinterpretation of Judaism preserving some uniqueness". He calls the integrative end of the scale "Submersion of Jewish cultural uniqueness" and the oppositional end "Antagonism to Graeco-Roman culture".

[11] Barclay 1996, p97.

2. The Pastoral Epistles

2.1 Acculturation and the readers

It has often been noted that in the Pastorals there is a much higher level of vocabulary and allusions which can be paralleled in other Hellenistic texts than is found in most of the rest of the NT. In this regard, A.D. Nock comments with respect to vocabulary that "as we pass from the Pauline Epistles to the Pastorals ... there is an approximation to the phraseology of the world around, a lessening of the feeling of isolation, and an increase in intelligibility to the ordinary contemporary man, had he happened upon these books."[12]

It also seems clear that the author presupposes that the language and concepts that he uses are familiar to his readers. For example, the Pastor does not explain the epiphany Christology that we will shortly discuss; rather he assumes that his readers are familiar with it and with the conceptual background that it presupposes. Similarly, concepts like εὐσέβεια and σώφρων, which we will discuss, are not explained but are simply utilised. It seems clear then that the author presupposes that his readers are familiar with this language. It is therefore good evidence for the significant level of acculturation of the readers.

Many examples of the considerable exposure in the Pastorals to the language and thought forms of the Greco-Roman world could be given, but the following are sufficient to demonstrate this feature of the Pastorals. We should note here that as well as exhibiting the language and thought forms of the Greco-Roman world, the Pastorals are clearly indebted to the language and literature of Hellenistic Judaism.[13] It is quite possible then that, although we have sought to choose examples where the language has not been much used within Hellenistic Judaism (as far as we know), some of the examples which we will discuss of the use of language which was at home in the wider Greco-Roman context may have been mediated through Hellenistic Judaism, rather than coming more directly from the Greco-Roman world. But ultimately it is the presence of a concentration of such language, often not found in the rest of the NT and very much at home in the wider culture, which is of concern to us here.

---

[12] Nock 1972, p342-3. He notes by contrast (p347) that "in the vulgar Greek of the Levant there was nothing corresponding to the Semitic flavor of the early Christian writers. ... Paul ... is writing the Greek of a man who has the Septuagint in his blood." See also Turner 1976, p102-5; Young 1994, p20.

[13] See Marshall 1999, p78; see also Dibelius-Conzelmann 1972, p30-1.

2.1.1 Epiphany Christology – translation of the Gospel into a new idiom

In the area of Christology, the author uses the term ἐπιφάνεια in 1 Tim 6:14; 2 Tim 1:10; 4:1,8; Tit 2:13 and the associated verb ἐπιφαίνω in Tit 2:11; 3:4. It is clear that these two terms are vital components of his christology.[14] ἐπιφάνεια is used of the first "appearance" of Jesus in 2 Tim 1:10, and in Tit 2:11 ("For the grace of God has appeared for the salvation of all people") and 3:4 ("but when the goodness and loving kindness of God our Saviour appeared") the verb refers to a result of the first "appearance" of Jesus.[15] ἐπιφάνεια is used in 1 Tim 6:14; 2 Tim 4:1; 4:8; Tit 2:13 to refer to the second "appearance" of Christ, which is elsewhere called his "παρουσία". Hence, for the Pastor God's saving activity in Jesus is bracketed by two epiphanies with a period in between which stretches from the first epiphany to the second. Using ἐπιφάνεια and ἐπιφαίνω, the Pastor speaks of Christ as a divine figure who is the manifestation in this world of the unseen and transcendent God (eg 1 Tim 6:14-16).[16]

What can we say about the use of these two terms? Firstly, ἐπιφάνεια occurs elsewhere in the NT with this sense only in 2 Thess 2:8, and the verb ἐπιφαίνω has a different sense in its other two occurrence in Lk 1:79 and Acts 27:20. Secondly, while the verb is found in the LXX and the noun in 2 and 3 Macc, and similar ideas are found in Jewish apocalyptic,[17] the concept of "epiphany" cannot be said to be important in Jewish literature.

By contrast, in Greco-Roman religion, ἐπιφάνεια is often used of the self-manifestation of a divine being in this world, with appropriate signs of majesty and power. It can refer to the appearance of a god, for example,

---

[14] Marshall (1988, p169) sees the concept of epiphany as "the controlling factor in the christology of the Pastorals." See also Lau 1996; Stettler 1998, p139-49; Marshall 1999, p287-96.

[15] Marshall (1988, p171) notes in connection with these two verses that it is "the whole saving event inaugurated by the coming of Jesus and continuing in the witness of the church to individuals that is meant." 2 Tim 1:9-10 shows that God's grace and kindness are understood in personal terms as referring to Christ. 1 Tim 1:15; 3:16 show that "epiphany means the appearance of the previously hidden divine figure who already existed rather than that some characteristic of God, namely his grace, is manifested in Jesus." (Marshall 1988, p172).

[16] Marshall (1988, p170) notes "Christ is seen as reflecting God and is understood in relation to God who thus occupies the central position." Marshall argues (1988, p171-5) that the Pastor's epiphany christology can be seen as equivalent to an incarnation christology. Therefore, although we cannot discuss the matter further here, we should not think that in the translation process the Pastor has radically altered the understanding of Christ which he received in the tradition. Further, Marshall (1988, p174) notes on the basis of Tit 2:13; 2 Tim 1:9f; 1 Tim 3:16 that "what we have is not an epiphany of a quality of God but of one who is identified in some way with God."

[17] See Marshall 1988, p169.

during processions or to help people in time of need, or as the motivation for the foundation of a cult.[18] It can also be used to refer to the emperor.

Both ἐπιφάνεια and ἐπιφαίνω are also found in Ephesian inscriptions. In 48 BCE the cities of Asia set up an inscription at Ephesus in which they honoured Julius Caesar as "the manifest god descending from Ares and Aphrodite (τὸν ἀπὸ ῎Αρεως καὶ ᾿Αφροδε[ί]της θεὸν ἐπιφανῆ)".[19] The Salutaris inscription of 104 CE speaks of Salutaris' decision "to adorn and reverence the religious and public realms of your greatest and most notable city, for the honour and reverence of the most manifest goddess Artemis (εἴ]ς τε τειμὴν καὶ εὐσέβ[ειαν τῆ]ς ἐπιφανεσ[τάτης θεᾶς] ᾿Αρτέμιδος)".[20] A very similar expression is also used earlier in the same inscription.[21] An edict of 162-4 CE speaks of temples being founded and altars dedicated to her among both Greeks and barbarians "because of the visible manifestations effected by her (διὰ τὰς ὑπ᾿ αὐτῆς γεινομένας ἐναργεῖς ἐπιφανείας)".[22] ἐπιφανής was also used of Aphrodite,[23] and one inscription to Hygeia reads ἐπιφανεῖ θεᾷ ῾Υγεία.[24]

An architectural detail of the temple of Artemis is also significant here. A number of coins represent the temple with one to three openings in the pediment.[25] It has been suggested that these openings were ritual doors or windows for Artemis' epiphany and that her followers would assemble in the court below waiting for her epiphany or for a symbol of her divinity in the window. Evidence for this comes from some Ephesian coins which depict a female figure in the central doorway of the pediment; it has been suggested that the female figure is either Artemis or her priestess as her surrogate.[26] It seems likely then that these doorways were places where it was believed the epiphany of Artemis occurred. As Stevenson notes: "Their appearance on the coinage of Ephesus represents a symbolic expression of the deeply-held belief that the goddess is accessible and comes to the aid of her people."[27]

---

[18] See Picard 1922, p362-4; Dibelius-Conzelmann 1972, p104; New Docs 4, p80-1; Lau 1996, p182-9; Stevenson 2001, p52-4.

[19] SIG 760.

[20] See IvEph 27, lines 384-5; translation from Rogers 1991, p173; see also New Docs 4, p80-81; Oster 1990a, p1724.

[21] IvEph 27, lines 344-5.

[22] IvEph 24B, lines 13-14; see also New Docs 4, p75-6; Engelmann 1994, p299.

[23] IvEph 251.

[24] IvEph 1212; see also IvEph 987, 988, 3825. The term can also be used of people and places with the meaning of "distinguished"; see for example IvEph 2055, 3080.

[25] See Trell 1945, plates 1-3. Coins depicting the temple of Artemis Leukophryene at Magnesia on the Maeander show similar openings and other temples may also have had them; see Trell 1945, p12-14; see also Bingöl 1999, p233-40.

[26] See Price and Trell 1977, p129-30; Trell 1988, p96; Oster 1982b, p217; Stevenson 2001, p53-4.

[27] Stevenson 2001, p54.

Descriptions of epiphanies are not restricted to the use of the two terms we have been discussing (or Latin equivalents). Two examples here will suffice. Strabo, (*Geog.* 4.1.4.) writing around 20 C.E. describes the establishment of an Artemis cult at Massilia. As part of this he writes of an event that occurred in Ephesus: "Now the goddess, in a dream (κατ᾽ ὄναρ), it is said, had stood beside Aristarcha, one of the women held in very high honour, and commanded her to sail away [from Ephesus] with the Phocaeans ..."[28] Pliny also records an epiphany which occurred during the building of the Temple of Artemis in Ephesus; this occurred in the fourth century BCE, but the story had clearly been treasured. Chersiphron, the architect of the temple, had been unable to set the lintel over the door of the temple correctly. Pliny writes: "The architect was in anguish as he debated whether suicide should be his final decision. The story goes that in the course of his reflections he became weary, and that while he slept at night he saw before him the goddess for whom the temple was being built; she was urging him to live because, as she said, she herself had laid the stone. And on the next day this was seen to be the case."[29] This again shows that Artemis was believed to be god who "appeared" to her worshippers.

It is significant then that the Pastor uses ἐπιφάνεια and ἐπιφαίνω. Given the prominence of the terms in Hellenistic religions, and their comparative unimportance in Jewish literature, a strong case can be made that here the concept of epiphany, and the associated epiphany scheme, has been adopted from the sphere of Hellenistic religions and used by the author as a vehicle for the expression of his Christology.[30] Accordingly, it is an example of the adoption of a concept and associated vocabulary from the wider milieu, and so of acculturation, one that is not found in other NT documents.

2.1.2 Language for God

There are a number of examples in the Pastorals where the language used for God is probably influenced by Hellenistic concepts. In 1 Tim 6:14-16 we read

---

[28] Strabo, Geog. 4.1.4. The Phocaeans, who founded Massilia, had been commanded to take from Artemis of Ephesus someone to conduct them on their voyage to found Massilia. They then travelled to Ephesus to ask how they could obtain from the goddess what had been commanded of them.

[29] See Pliny, NH 36.97.

[30] See Marshall 1988, p168-9; Barrett 1963, p116. Marshall (1993, p18) notes that the concept of epiphany "is one which would have been particularly effective in the Hellenistic world. It is used to speak to new readers and it develops the concept that Jesus has appeared as god manifest and will reappear." Barrett (1963, p96) notes of 2 Tim 1:9-10: "most of the language of vv 9f belongs to contemporary Hellenistic religious vocabulary, which knew of the formal and majestic appearance of divine kings who bore the title Saviour and of religions which offered illumination and immortal life."

that Timothy is to keep the commandments "until the manifestation of our Lord Jesus Christ, which he [God] will bring about at the right time - he who is the blessed and only Sovereign, the King of kings and Lord of lords. It is he alone who has immortality and dwells in unapproachable light, whom no one has ever seen or can see." Although much here is paralleled in the OT and in Hellenistic Judaism, the ideas are also found in Hellenistic thought.[31] In particular, the idea that God is unapproachable and unseen and thus hidden, but has been made manifest in Jesus, is part of the epiphany schema in Hellenistic religions.[32]

We note also the phrase "ὁ μόνος ἔχων ἀθανασίαν - it is he alone who has immortality" (1 Tim 6:16). As Marshall notes "This is a Hellenistic way of saying that God alone has and can confer life. … it rejects claims made for other divine beings and heroes. It is not a description of God that is found in Hellenistic Judaism and has therefore been taken over from the language used of gods and emperors."[33] Thus, the description of God in 6:15-16 is closely related to Hellenistic ideas.

Another example is given in 1 Tim 1:11 and 6:15 where God is called μακάριος, "blessed". These are the only occurrences of the term in the NT with respect to God. But μακάριος is also used in non-biblical Greek for the condition of the gods,[34] and its usage here probably reflects the influence of Greek speaking Judaism or of Hellenistic religious language.[35]

In Tit 3:4 (and so admittedly relating to Crete) the term φιλανθρωπία "love for humanity" is used of God.[36] In the Greco-Roman world, φιλανθρωπία was regarded as a virtue to be found in the gods, but also one to be looked for in rulers in relation to their subjects. Luck suggests that here "the phraseology is influenced by the worship of manifested gods as seen especially in emperor worship",[37] and Marshall thinks the imperial cult background is convincing.[38]

---

[31] See Barrett 1963, p88; Roloff 1988, p354-7. Marshall (1988, p169) notes that in 1 Tim 6:14 "the Hellenistic sense is present, as appears from the accompanying mention of God in his transcendence as the One who will reveal Christ, and we note that the same concept of God which is part of this scheme already appears in 1 Tim 1,17."

[32] See Dibelius-Conzelmann 1972, p104.

[33] Marshall 1999, p667; see also Roloff 1988, p356; Hanson 1982, p112-13.

[34] See the references in BDAG p610-11. It is only used in the inscriptions in Ephesus in IvEph 46, line 8 and 1353, line 9, both of which are Christian.

[35] See Marshall 1999, p383.

[36] In is only found elsewhere in the NT in Acts 28:2, where it is used of the people of Malta who welcome Paul.

[37] TDNT IX, p111; see also Barrett 1963, p141.

[38] Marshall 1999, p313; see also Dibelius-Conzelmann 1972, p144-5.

Φιλάνθρωπος ("loving humankind, humane") is found in inscriptions in Ephesus,[39] and in one inscription Artemis is described as "τ]ὴν σεμνοτάτην καὶ φιλανθρωπο[τάτην"[40] – "the most revered and loving towards humankind".

It seems very likely then that some of the language used for God in these letters has been influenced by the wider Hellenistic environment.

2.1.3 God and Jesus as "Saviour"

The Pastor uses σωτήρ of both God and Christ. God is called σωτήρ at the beginning of both 1 Tim (1:1) and Tit (1:3), perhaps in order to establish God's character as "Saviour" as the basis for what follows.[41] The term is also used of God in 1 Tim 2:3; 4:10; Tit 2:10; 3:4 and is arguably the most important term for God in the letters.[42] However, σωτήρ is also used of Jesus in 2 Tim 1:10; Tit 1:4; 2:13;[43] 3:6, emphasizing that salvation is achieved through his life and death.[44]

What can we say about the use of the term? Firstly, in the rest of the Pauline corpus, σωτήρ is used of Jesus only in Phil 3:20 and Eph 5:23. However, it is found in Lk 1:47; 2:11; Jn 4:42; Acts 5:31; 13:23; 1 Jn 4:14 and Jude 25.[45] Further, Paul's letters show that σώζω and σωτηρία were used from an early period,[46] and so, as Marshall puts it, it "can only have been a matter of time until the noun «Saviour» came into use to designate the one who saves."[47] Secondly, σωτήρ is found in the OT and in Jewish literature,[48] and σώζω and σωτηρία are also found in this literature. This

---

[39] See IvEph 8 lines 18, 41; 17 line 58; 18, a15; 1352 line 13; 3214, line18; 3801, I line 12. φιλανθρωπία is suggested in IvEph 27 line 79 and found in IvEph 4135 (Christian).

[40] See IvEph 3211.

[41] See Marshall 1988, p168.

[42] See Taylor 1993, p68; Young 1994, p50-5. The verb σώζω is also used in 1 Tim 1:15; 2:4, 15; 4:16; 2 Tim 1:9; 4:18; Tit 3:5.

[43] Regardless of the translation adopted in Tit 2:13 (on which see below), σωτήρ applies to Jesus here.

[44] On the term "Saviour" see in particular Donelson 1986, p135-41. Note that there is a link here with epiphany language. As Donelson (1986, p136) notes the idea of salvation by the intervention of the god "occurs in the emperor cult and elsewhere, frequently in conjunction with the term ἐπιφάνεια, so that a deity 'appears' and by that epiphany effects salvation, and thus is termed savior." For an example see SIG 760, cited above in our discussion of epiphany language, which also calls Julius Caesar "σωτήρ".

[45] Marshall (1988, p168) notes "It would be wrong to assume that all these texts are necessarily late."

[46] See for example 1 Thess 2:16; 5:8-9; Rom 1:16; 5:9-10; 8:24; 10:1.

[47] Marshall 1988, p168.

[48] See Dt 32:15; Ps 24:5; 27:1; Is 12:2; 17:10 with reference to God's deliverance from Egypt. The term emphasizes that God is the originator and initiator of salvation.

explains its use in passages like Lk 1:47 and 2:11; further, its use in Acts 13:23 seems to be an echo of Jud 3:9, 15.

However, σωτήρ is also widely used in the Hellenistic world. It could be used of people who were regarded as deliverers, of guides such as Epicurus, the philosophers, as well as of deified rulers (such as Augustus, when he brought peace) and gods such as Zeus, or Athena who guarded the Acropolis, or Asclepius, the god of healing and helper of the distressed.[49] Σωτήρ is also used in Ephesian inscriptions. Van Tilborg notes that it is used in honour of Zeus Soter and of Roman commanders.[50] We note the following. Firstly, Julius Caesar is called "τοῦ ἀνθρωπίνου βίου σωτῆρα" (IvEph 251). Secondly, Gallus son of Publius is called "saviour and benefactor" in the name of "the people from Italy who trade in Ephesus" (IvEph 800). Thirdly, in IvEph 3435 the people of Metropolis honour Sextus Appuleius as σωτήρ; he was proconsul in 23-22 BCE. Fourthly, in IvEph 713 the proconsul in 123-4 CE is honoured as "benefactor and saviour". Fifthly, Hadrian is called σωτήρ a number of times.[51] Sixthly, IvEph 1243 simply reads: "Διὸς Σωτῆρος". Seventhly, in IvEph 3271 it is not clear if Zeus or Hadrian is called σωτήρ. Finally, we also note that σώτειρα was used of Artemis in Ephesus.[52]

Given the occurrence of σωτήρ and its cognates in the OT and Jewish literature, its use in the Pastorals is not necessarily a sign of acculturation. However, as Wilson notes, "Saviour, in the Pastorals, whether used of God or Jesus, recalls Hellenistic rather than OT language as the associations in 2 Tim 1.10 (*photisantos de zoen kai aphtharsian*) and Tit 3.4 (*chrestotes, philanthropia*) indicate."[53] Thus, although there is Jewish precedent for the use of the term, the contexts in which "Saviour" is used and that we have already discerned examples of acculturation in what is said of both Jesus and God in the Pastorals, suggests that here too, Hellenistic language has had an

---

[49] On σωτήρ in the Hellenistic world see Nock 1972, p720-35; Dibelius-Conzelmann 1972, p100-3; Marshall 1999, p131.

[50] See van Tilborg 1996, p47-50. Van Tilborg 1996, p47-8 notes that σωτήρ is found in inscriptions from the time of Julius Caesar and the reign of Augustus, but that there is a gap then until the time of Hadrian, with no emperors in the first century receiving the title. It is hard to see this as significant however.

[51] σωτήρ πάσης τῆς οἰκουμένης καὶ εὐεργέτης (IvEph 271F); σωτήρ καὶ εὐεργέτης (IvEph 1501 and 3271); σωτήρ καὶ κτίστης (IvEph 272, 274, 3410; SEG 1983, no 943; 1989, no 1212).

[52] IvEph 1255 is a dedication to Artemis Soteira and Agathos Demon; 1265 is "to Artemis Soteira from the family of the Sebastos". See also Oster 1990, p1724; Strelan 1996, p52. In the novel of Achilles Tatius entitled *Leuciplle and Clitophon* we read of Artemis: αὐτὴ μόνη τοὺς ἐπ᾽ αὐτὴν καταφεύγοντας ἔξεστι σώζειν "She alone has had the power, until now, of affording an asylum to those who fly to her for help (8.8, 9; LCL translation). See also IvEph. 26.4, 18

[53] Wilson 1979, p81.

impact. Further, the marked prominence of σωτήρ in the Pastorals, where it has probably become *the* key term for God, is not really explained by the Jewish background. Why is the term relatively rare in most of the NT, but found here in the Pastorals? And why should the author of the Pastorals use it so often, when it was comparatively rare in the Jewish background? An explanation from his context seems to be required: we can suggest that the much more pronounced usage of σωτήρ in the Pastorals compared with other books of the NT is another indication of acculturation.[54]

In the three cases we have discussed so far, the Pastor does not explain his language but simply uses it. This suggests that it was known to the readers and so suggests that we are seeing the acculturation of both the author and the readers.

2.1.4 Eusebeia[55]

The term εὐσέβεια and its cognates, are used thirteen times in the Pastorals: εὐσέβεια in 1 Tim 2:2; 3:16; 4:7-8; 6:3, 5, 6, 11; 2 Tim 3:5; Tit 1:1; εὐσεβέω in 1 Tim 5:4; εὐσεβῶς in 2 Tim 3:12; Tit 2:12. These terms are not found in the undisputed Paulines, but are used, though fairly rarely, elsewhere in the NT (in Acts and 2 Pet) and in the LXX.[56]

Εὐσέβεια was a popular term in the Hellenistic world, where it expressed the attitude of reverence or respect that a person should demonstrate towards the gods, to other people including rulers, and to the orders of society which were sanctioned by the gods. But in general usage εὐσέβεια came to mean the actual worship paid to the gods in cultic activities rather than a reverent attitude, although outward actions were seen as the expression of inner attitudes.[57] Further, in the Greco-Roman world, εὐσέβεια came to be seen as both a duty and a highly important virtue, which was often referred to in inscriptions.

We also find εὐσέβεια in inscriptions in Ephesus. For example, as part of the Salutaris inscription, the proconsul of Asia in 103/4 CE, C. Aquillius Proculus, writes: "May I congratulate him that his piety toward the goddess [Artemis] and the Augusti (τή[ν τ]ε πρὸς τὴν θεὸν εὐσέβειαν [καὶ τὴν

---

[54] See Marshall 1988, p168; Taylor 1993, p67. Dibelius-Conzelmann (1972, p101) note with regard to the use of σωτήρ in the Pastorals: "it is necessary to assume that non-Jewish influences have been predominant." Hanson (1982, p39) comments "there can be little doubt that this latter title has been deliberately borrowed from the imperial cult." In general see Quinn 1990, p304-15.

[55] On the term see Foerster in TDNT VII, p168-96; Quinn 1990, p282-91; Taylor 1993, p68; Wilson1979, p33-4, 50-1; Marshall 1999, p135-44.

[56] εὐσέβεια is found in Acts 3:12; 2 Pet 1:3, 6; 3:11; εὐσεβέω in Acts 17:23; εὐσεβής in Acts 10:2; 2 Pet 2:9. On the LXX usage see below.

[57] See Marshall 1999, p136-9; Quinn 1990, p287; Friesen 1995, p39.

πρὸς τοὺς Σ]εβαστού[ς), and his goodwill toward the city in the theatre now become clear to all."[58] On five other occasions εὐσέβεια or εὐσεβής are used with reference to Salutaris or others.[59] Note also an inscription of 162-4 CE in which Gaius Popillius Carus Pedo, the proconsul writes: "since I also have regard for the reverence of the goddess (εἰς τε τὴν εὐσέβειαν τῆς θεοῦ) and for the honour of the most illustrious city of the Ephesians".[60] On numerous other occasions the two terms are used of individuals to describe their character.[61]

In Hellenistic Judaism εὐσέβεια was used to translate traditional Jewish concepts into contemporary Greek.[62] In these texts εὐσέβεια "appears to gather together into one comprehensive idea the knowledge of God and the appropriate response."[63] Although in Greek thought it was seen as a virtue with a strong connection to cultic acts, εὐσέβεια seems to have been a sufficiently broad concept for Hellenistic Judaism to use it to refer to knowledge of and loyalty to God, as well as to conduct which flowed from the "fear of the Lord"; thus the term could express the Jewish concept of the spiritual life of piety. It comes closest to the idea of "religion", a term which is lacking in both Hebrew and Greek. We should note however that εὐσέβεια and εὐσεβής are only found comparatively rarely in Jewish writings, and are predominantly found in Sirach, and 3 and 4 Macc.[64]

The Pastor uses εὐσέβεια to express his understanding of the Christian life and of ethics. For him, it encapsulates both reverent knowledge of God and the appropriate conduct which flows from that knowledge. For the Pastor, the term is rooted in the Christ-event (1 Tim 3:16; 2 Tim 3:12) and is closely

---

[58] IvEph 27, line 367.

[59] For εὐσέβεια see IvEph 27, lines 118 (reconstructed) 367, 384; for εὐσεβής see IvEph 27, lines 84, 418, 429.

[60] See IvEph 24a, line 11; translation from New Docs 4, p74-8, which gives a full discussion of the inscription.

[61] For εὐσέβεια see IvEph 21 II, line 5; 26 line 13, 233 line 12; 236 line 7; 237 line13; 666a line 17; 683a, line 4; 702 line 14; 853 line 10; 886; 1024 line 8; 1380; 1480 line 16; 1538 line 7; 3041 line 5; 3419 line 2. For εὐσεβής see IvEph 11a3; 17, line 69; 21 I line 17; 203; 217; 296/9; 302-4a; 300; 314/5; 666a.b; 680; 690; 824; 892; 941, 942; 957; 989a; 1001-6; 1008-10; 1012-24; 1028-30; 1032-8; 1040-4; 1047-51/3; 1065-7/8; 1084; 1352; 1565; 1578b; 1579; 1588; 1590a; 1598; 1859; 2090; 2426; 3059; 3118; 3263; 3408; 3418a; 4336. See also Rogers 1999, p244. For other examples from elsewhere see New Docs 2, p55-6; New Docs 7, p233-41.

[62] See in particular Quinn 1990, p282-91; Marshall 1999, p139-41.

[63] Marshall 1999, p141.

[64] εὐσέβεια is found 4 times in the canonical books (Prov 1:7; 13:11; Isa 11:2; 33:6) 5 times in the Apocrypha (1 Esdr 1:23; Wis 10:12; Sir 49:3; 2 Macc 3:1), 3 times in 3 Macc, 47 times in 4 Macc. For εὐσεβής the figures are canonical books 10 times; other books, 2 Macc 1:19; 12:45; Sir 15 times, 4 Macc 11 times. εὐσεβέω and εὐσεβῶς occur 6 times and once respectively in the LXX.

related to the knowledge of God or of the Gospel (1 Tim 6:3, 5, 11; Tit 1:1). Thus while the Pastor's opponents display superficial "godliness" (2 Tim 3:5), true εὐσέβεια arises from commitment to and true understanding of God.[65] But the term is also used by the Pastor as a comprehensive term to describe the Christian life. Thus εὐσέβεια is seen as something in which a person must train themselves, or something they should pursue (1 Tim 4:7-8; 6:11; Tit 2:12). It can also be seen in specific ways, such as honouring parents (1 Tim 5:4). Thus, while the term is drawn from the environment, the author does "Christianise" it to quite some extent. It is linked to Christ and the Gospel (1 Tim 3:16), and expresses both faith in God and the observable conduct that should flow from that.[66]

Although the usage of εὐσέβεια in Hellenistic Judaism could, of itself, have led the Pastor to adopt the term, given that it is only found in a small selection of Jewish works, it seems more likely that its wide currency in the Greco-Roman world has led the Pastor to use it.[67] As Hellenistic Jews had adopted the term, so too does the Pastor.

We note too that the Pastor never explains how he understands εὐσέβεια, but presupposes that his readers are familiar with it. This suggests that his readers knew the term and thus we are not simply seeing the Pastor's acculturation to the Greco-Roman world here, but also the acculturation of his readers.

2.1.5 Virtues

The Pastor regularly discusses virtues that Christians should demonstrate. These virtues are generally the civic virtues which were widely acknowledged and highly prized in the Greco-Roman world, although at times they are leavened by more specifically Christian virtues, as seen in 2 Tim 1:7 where love stands alongside self-discipline.

One key concept for the Pastor is self-control or moderation. This ideal is most commonly expressed by the σώφρων word group, which is used 10 times.[68] In 1 Tim 3:2 we read that "a bishop must be above reproach, married only once, temperate, sensible (σώφρωνα), respectable ..." In Tit 2:11-12 the Pastor states that the grace of God has appeared "training us to renounce impiety and worldly passions, and in the present age to live lives that are self-controlled (σωφρόνως), upright, and godly." As Marshall notes, the term has become "a fundamental characteristic of the Christian life ... [which]

---

[65] See Marshall 1999, p143.

[66] See further Barrett 1963, p50; Wilson 1979, p51; Marshall 1990b, p86.

[67] See Quinn 1990, p288.

[68] It is only used 16 times in total in the NT, so as Marshall notes (1999, p182), the word group "is thus both characteristic and distinctive of the PE."

communicates in readily understandable terms the idea of 'a suitable restraint in every respect', a self-control which leads to behaviour appropriate to the situation."[69]

The word-group is rare in the LXX, where it is found only as one of a list of cardinal virtues.[70] However, it is very common in Hellenistic Greek where it represented the virtue of restraint of desire. It is found regularly in Ephesian inscriptions as one of the virtues of particular people. Thus, for example, in IvEph 614c, line 23-4 a woman is described as "βιώσαντα σωφρόνως καὶ κοσμίως".[71]

Although it is possible that the usage of the term in Hellenistic Judaism has influenced the Pastor to use the σώφρων word group so extensively, it seems more likely that here he "has probably been influenced by the language of popular Hellenistic philosophy."[72]

We also note that σώφρων, δίκαιος and εὐσεβής, which are each significant in the Pastorals, comprise three of the four standard Greek virtues (only ἀνδρεῖος courage, is lacking).[73] Key facets of the Christian life for the Pastor are thus expressed in the language used at the time to describe the virtuous life and we see a "rapprochement between the Hellenistic moral ideal ... and Christian living".[74]

A number of other terms are also used in the Pastorals to express the ideas of self-discipline and moderation. Note ἐγκρατής "disciplined" (Tit 1:8), νηφάλιος "sober" (Tit 2:2; 1 Tim 3:2, 11), νήφω "to be sober" (2 Tim 4:5), ἀνανήφω "to become sober" (2 Tim 2:26)[75]; σεμνότης "seriousness, respectfulness" (1 Tim 2:2; 3:4; Tit 2:7); σεμνός "worthy of respect, serious" (1 Tim 3:8, 11; Tit 2:2).

Although again there are some examples of the use of this language in the LXX and other Jewish writings, these terms were all very much at home in the Hellenistic world as noteworthy virtues. Marshall comments on the σώφρων word group and these terms: "The piling up of terms which are not found earlier in the NT and which are more at home in Greek culture indicates

---

[69] Marshall 1999, p184; see also Johnson 1996, p50. All the occurrences of the word group are 1 Tim 2:9, 15; 3:2; 2 Tim 1:7; Tit 1:8; 2:2, 4, 5, 6, 12. On the term see Marshall 1999, p182-4.

[70] See 4 Macc 1:3, 6, 18, 30-1; 2:2, 16, 18; 3:17; 5:23; 15:10; Wis 8:7

[71] κόσμιος is found in 1 Tim 2:9; 3:2. Note also σώφρων in IvEph 614b, line 18 where a woman is described as "σώφρονα καὶ κόσμιον ζήσασαν βίον"; 1606, line 10; 2488, line 1; 2579, line 2. σωφροσύνη in IvEph 683a, line 10; σωφρονίζω in IvEph 215, line 6; σωφρονισμός in IvEph 1340B, line 4; σωφροσύνη in IvEph 6A, line 14.

[72] Marshall 1999, p184.

[73] See Kidd 1990, p17-18.

[74] Kidd 1990, p203; see also Barrett 1963, p135.

[75] These terms related to sobriety are probably meant both literally (cf. 1 Tim 3:3, 8; Tit 1:7; 2:3) and figuratively.

a significant change in vocabulary in the PE. Clearly they are using the language of Hellenism, but equally clearly they are doing so to make points that were made in Judaism and in the early church in other ways."[76] Again then we see a translation process at work, whereby more acculturated language is used to express key theological ideas.[77] Further, this language is used extensively by the author without explanation. Although some of it is in response to the opponents, it is unlikely that this is the case with all of it. We can again suggest that it reflects the acculturation of the readers therefore.

2.1.6 Lists of qualities required of leaders

In 1 Tim 3:1-13 and Tit 1:5-9 the Pastor gives lists of the personal qualities required of leaders. In 1 Tim 3:2 and Tit 1:6-7 the idea of being "above reproach (ἀνεπίλημπτος)" (1 Tim 3:2) or "blameless (ἀνέγκλητος)" (Tit 1:6-7) express a guiding principle which is then spelled out concretely in the remainder of the lists.[78] The same general principle is reiterated in 1 Tim 3:7 at the end of the list with regard to the episkopos when it is said that "he must be well thought of by outsiders (δεῖ δὲ καὶ μαρτυρίαν καλὴν ἔχειν ἀπὸ τῶν ἔξωθεν)". Clearly, the Pastor is concerned that no moral failure by the leaders would tarnish the church's reputation.

Although character outlines for leaders are found in both Greco-Roman and Jewish sources (eg the list in 1QS 4), the models that give most insight into the lists in the Pastorals are from the former. In these sources we find the idea of being both above reproach and well thought of by others, as well as the concern to avoid moral failure in leaders. Dibelius and Conzelmann quote a passage from Onosander in which he writes about choosing a general in this way:

"I believe, then, that we must choose a general, not because of noble birth as priests are chosen, nor because of wealth as the superintendents of the gymnasia, but because he is temperate, self-restrained, vigilant, frugal, hardened to labour, alert, free from avarice, neither

---

[76] Marshall 1999, p189.

[77] It might be thought that the concept of αὐτάρκεια in 1 Tim 6:6, which was popular among the Stoics and Epicureans (although the word is also found in Hellenistic Judaism), has been adopted from Hellenistic thought (see eg. Diog Laert 6.11). While this is possible, in 1 Tim 6:6 the word is not used with the meaning of "self-sufficiency", which it has in Stoicism, but rather refers to the virtue of "contentment". Since it is associated with εὐσέβεια in 1 Tim 6:6, the implication is that godliness provides all that is necessary, and so αὐτάρκεια here does not involve "self-sufficiency"; see Marshall 1999, p644-5. On the term see also Hengel 1974, p54-7. But perhaps the use of the word at all reflects its popularity in non-Christian circles.

[78] ἀνέγκλητος is also used of deacons in 1 Tim 3:10.

too young nor too old, indeed a father of children if possible, a ready speaker, and a man with a good reputation."[79]

Marshall notes that of the eleven qualities called for here, seven (or their close equivalents) are also represented in the Pastorals.[80] Onosander then goes on to discuss why each of these characteristics are important in a general. He concludes in the following way:

"The general should be a man of good reputation ... It is absolutely essential, then, that a general be such a man, of such excellent traits of character as I have enumerated, and besides this, that he have a good reputation."[81]

Another text in Lucian is also of interest. It concerns the qualities of a dancer, but most of the traits looked for are very general ("unexceptionable, impeccable, not wanting in any way, blent of the highest qualities, keen in his ideas, profound in his culture ..."[82]) rather than relating specifically to dancing. Thus many of the qualities in these lists in Onosander and Lucian are relatively unspecific and do not relate directly to a particular function; rather the lists could be applied to a whole range of professions or offices, since they describe a generally virtuous person. This is exactly the situation in the Pastorals.[83]

However there are some features of the qualifications for office-holders in the Pastorals which are not found in standard lists, most notably the emphasis on being a skilled teacher (1 Tim 3:2). The Pastor's emphasis on marriage is also noteworthy (1 Tim 3:2, 12; 5:9; Tit 1:6) although Onosander does note "I should prefer our general to be a father". The Pastor has to some extent adapted the lists for his own purposes, probably with his opponents in mind, since they promoted celibacy and their activity meant leaders needed to be able teachers. But it seems most likely that in these lists the Pastor has generally adopted the normal standards of society with regard to the qualities sought for in leaders.[84] Again, then, this is an example of acculturation.

But is the Pastor here trying to change the characteristics of leaders because of the activity of the opponents, and so in using a standard schema of leadership qualities is he more acculturated in this area than his readers? We have noted that he is responding to the opponents with regard to marriage and

---

[79] Onosander, *De imperatoris officio* 1.1, quoted in Dibelius-Conzelmann 1972, p158; see also p50-1; Taylor 1993, p84.

[80] Marshall 1999, p183.

[81] Onosander, *De imperatoris officio* 1.17, quoted in Dibelius-Conzelmann 1972, p160.

[82] Lucian, Salt. 81, quoted in Dibelius-Conzelmann 1972, p160.

[83] See Stiefel 1995, p443; Dibelius-Conzelmann 1972, p50-1.

[84] Taylor (1993, p84) notes "The personal qualifications are not created in a vacuum but are essentially adopted from society."

the leader being an apt teacher, and his emphasis on some virtues (and so his use of acculturation with regard to leadership qualities) is probably in contrast to the "profane chatter and contradictions" (1 Tim 6:20) and "stupid and senseless controversies" (2 Tim 2:23) of the opponents. So it may be that in this area we are seeing primarily the acculturation of the Pastor, rather than that of both the author and the readers, which we have argued for in other cases.

2.1.7 Women and the ideal household

It seems clear that the Pastor adopts the attitude of society with regard to the role of women in the household and in society. As we will see in Chapter 11, although his attitude towards women in this regard may primarily be a response to his opponents and the much more positive role they advocated for women (rather than simply motivated by the desire to be acculturated to society), it remains clear that in this area the Pastor adopts the societal role assigned to women by society of wife and mother and thus reflects the values of the society around him.[85] For clearly the contemporary society followed hierarchical and patriarchal norms. Another dimension of this is that the author seems to be seeking to conform the social structure of the community to that of the normal Greco-Roman household, that is, the household managed prudently by the male householder, who has authority over his wife, children and slaves. We note also that instructions are only given to the subordinate members of the community (eg. 1 Tim 5:14; 6:1-2) in contrast to the Haustafeln in Col 3:18-4:1 and Eph 5:22-6:9 where, for example, wives and husbands and slaves and masters are addressed.

Similarly, the Pastor's attitude towards slaves conforms to the ideal household structure of the wider society. Slaves are told to "regard their masters as worthy of all honour" (1 Tim 6:1) and "to be submissive to their masters and to give satisfaction in every respect; they are not to talk back" (Tit 2:9). In calling for the submission of slaves to masters, the Pastor is adopting the standard social structure of the society in which the church lived.

However, in this regard we are most likely seeing the attitude of the author, not of all the readers. We will note in Chapter 11 that a number of women are currently teachers in the community and we will also note the activity of the widow's order. Similarly, 1 Tim 6:1-2 strongly suggests that some slaves are not currently regarding their masters as worthy of all honour. Probably at least to some extent because of the opponents, some of the readers have a much

---

[85] Thus, for example, with regard to Tit 2:5, Barrett (1963, p135) notes "The language used is paralleled in many honorific inscriptions, i.e. the author considers the civic virtues acknowledged in the Hellenistic world worthy of Christian imitation." See also 1 Tim 2:15; 1 Tim 5:10, 14; Maloney 1994, p366-7; Dewey 1998, p446; MacDonald 1999b, p246.

more egalitarian attitude towards relationships within the household than the Pastor has. We cannot say then that the readers are acculturated in this area in the way that the Pastor is.[86]

2.1.8 Conclusions

It seems likely then that in a number of cases the author has adopted terms, forms of thought, concepts and attitudes from the Hellenistic world.[87] Does this evidence really indicate a significant degree of acculturation? For example, one could imagine an introverted group that was very marginal within the wider society, which still spoke the language of that wider society. However, we have not only discussed significant linguistic evidence, but we have also seen that the author shares attitudes, standards and patterns of behaviour with the wider society (eg regarding qualities sought for in leaders and what it meant to be virtuous). The sum total of this evidence about language, concepts, attitudes and behaviour, strongly suggests that the author was acculturated to a significant degree.

But are we seeing here only the relative acculturation of the author? Are the readers *also* acculturated with respect to language, concepts and attitudes? We note that in most cases the Pastor does not introduce any of the language or concepts as "new".[88] The two probable exceptions that we have noted here are that the Pastor is clearly trying to alter attitudes among his readers towards women and thus to bring about a more hierarchical structure in the church, and he also seems to be trying to alter the required qualities sought in leaders, and so in these two areas his readers are probably not as acculturated as he is. In these areas other factors, particularly what is said about the opponents, mean the author is reflecting primarily his own position in what he says. But generally, the Pastor assumes that the language he uses will communicate with his readers and that they will be able to understand it. Otherwise he will simply fail to communicate with them. We can suggest, therefore, that they too know this language and are at home with it. Hence, the language of the

---

[86] Verner (1983, p182) fails to distinguish between the Pastor and the readers when he writes that the "prevailing domestic ideal in the church of the Pastorals reflected the dominant social values of the larger society, namely prosperity and propriety." There is another similar case. We have already noted that in much of what he says about his opponents, the Pastor is dependent on the standard polemic of philosophers against sophists; see Karris 1972, p549-64. That the Pastor has taken over this standard schema shows that he is familiar with such polemic, at least in some form, and so participates in this feature of wider culture. However, in this case we cannot say that the readers are necessarily familiar with the schema.

[87] Other examples could be given. Note that the Pastor regards holding office in the church as socially prestigious in the same way that citizens of Greek cities and members of associations regarded office holding; see 1 Tim 3:1, 13; Verner 1983, p160.

[88] See MacDonald 1988, p211.

community, and of the Pastor himself, reflects the fact that the community is acculturated to the wider society to a significant extent.

2.2 Assimilation – participation in wider cultural life?

Did the readers of the Pastorals participate in noteworthy aspects of Greco-Roman city life? To what degree were they integrated into their social context or did they remain aloof from it? Here we are concerned with their social contacts and interactions with the wider culture and the extent to which they participated in the activities of that dominant culture.

2.2.1 Silence in most areas

The Pastor says nothing about the issue of idolatry (cf. 1 Tim 1:17), and there is no evidence in the letters that the readers attended festivals, or participated in any other way in idolatry.[89] But how would the Pastor or his readers have reacted when faced with pagan worship? Would they have argued that it was meaningless and therefore that observing such worship was harmless? We do not know.

It is worth noting that in the Pastorals, the predominant threat comes, not from "the world" but from "false" Christians (eg. 1 Tim 4:1-5; 6:3-6; 2 Tim 3:1-9). But in 2 Timothy the readers are instructed to expect persecution (2 Tim 1:8; 2:3, 9; 3:11-13; 4:5), which suggests that they are not so integrated socially as to avoid persecution.[90] But the Pastor does not give us his view with regard to why or the ground on which, readers will be persecuted.

In most areas then there is silence with regard to the level of assimilation of the readers. But there is one area in which we gain some information, and we now turn to that.

2.2.2 The Pastor's concern about what outsiders think and the desire not to cause offense

The Pastor is very conscious of the outside world and what the wider society thinks of the community. In particular, he is concerned that the community and its teaching should not be discredited in the eyes of outsiders but rather that they should have a respectable reputation and should avoid giving offense to outsiders. It seems likely that the readers share his views, since he regularly

---

[89] Note that the Pastor speaks of the oneness of God; see 1 Tim 1:17: "the only God"; 1 Tim 6:15: "the blessed and only Sovereign"; see also 1 Tim 3:15; 4:10: "the living God". But none of this seems to be polemical.

[90] For a discussion of what 2 Tim says with regard to Paul's suffering and martyrdom see Wilson 1979, p110-14; see also MacDonald 1988, p205.

mentions not giving offense, but never argues at length that this should be a key motivation for action, but simply assumes that it is.[91]

With regard to assimilation, this concern for the opinion of outsiders at least shows that social life was not confined to the Christian community; rather the community has some interactions with the wider community, to the extent that what that wider community thinks, and in particular that the wider community views the Christian group positively, is regarded as important. This is all evidence for some assimilation therefore.

With regard to concern for the opinion of outsiders, note 1 Tim 3:7, with regard to an overseer: "Moreover, he must be well thought of by outsiders, so that he may not fall into disgrace and the snare of the devil." Here we see the concern for what outsiders think, in this case, of leaders of the community. Note also 1 Tim 6:1: "Let all who are under the yolk of slavery regard their masters as worthy of all honour, so that the name of God and the teaching may not be blasphemed." Here the reason given for slaves to be respectful towards their masters, is that otherwise, both God and Christian teaching will be "blasphemed"[92] by outsiders and thus the church's reputation will be damaged. As Verner notes: "slaves, especially those with pagan masters, risked damaging the public image of the church, if they expressed their Christian freedom by attempting to loosen or break the yoke of slavery."[93] Rather, by obeying and showing "complete and perfect fidelity" they could "be an ornament to the doctrine of God our Saviour" (Tit 2:9-10) .[94] Accordingly, the Pastor instructs readers to behave in an appropriate way for the sake of the church's reputation and to avoid unnecessary slander being directed at the church. [95]

In Chapter 11 we will discuss in more detail what is said of widows in 1 Tim 5, but we note some relevant points here. The lifestyle of many widows in the Christian group, particularly the fact that they have been going from house to house teaching (v13), seems to have led to a negative reaction from

---

[91] See for example 1 Tim 6:1-2.

[92] Barrett (1963, p135) recalls the accusations made against Christians in Tacitus, *Annals* 15.44; Pliny, *Letters* 10.96.

[93] Verner 1983, p144.

[94] Verner (1983, p145) notes: "Of course, insubordination among slaves would damage the church's image primarily, if not exclusively, among the slave-owning class."

[95] See for example Barrett 1963, p135; Wilson 1979, p47; MacDonald 1988, p167-70. Note that in 1 Tim 3:7 διάβολος could well mean "slanderer"; see MacDonald 1988, p167. See also Tit 2:3-5, 7-8. Recall that Roman society saw Christianity as an atheistic superstition that corrupted households and thereby could be a threat to the entire society. Since the household was the basic building block of society anything that threatened that building block was therefore suspect; see MacDonald 1988, p189. Note that Paul is also concerned with the reputation of the community with outsiders (see for example 1 Cor 14:15-16, 23) but that this seems to have become a much more crucial theme in the Pastorals.

the wider society; such very visible behaviour which did not conform to the submissive domesticity preferred by society, would have been considered as offensive by many outside the Christian group. In response the Pastor writes in 1 Tim 5:14: "So I would have younger widows marry, bear children, and manage their households, so as to give the enemy no occasion to revile us." Here "the enemy" is probably the non-Christian, rather than Satan (cf 3:7).[96] Clearly the Pastor advocates a lifestyle for the widows which would not lead to offense among outsiders, whereas currently this seems to be what is happening.[97] 1 Tim 5:7 is also revealing: "Give these commands as well, so that they [the widows] may be above reproach." The outsider is thus seen as a real or potential objector to indiscreet behaviour.

We have noted above that standard qualities required for leaders in the wider society have been adopted by the Pastor (and that this is one feature of acculturation). One reason for this is to combat the opponents. But it *also* seems likely that concern for outside opinion is a key factor in adopting these standard qualities for those who will fulfil the offices of presbyter-overseer (1 Tim 3:1-7; Tit 1:5-9) and deacon (1 Tim 3:8-13) and that this concern about outsiders is shared by the Pastor and his readers alike.[98] We have noted the key requirement that leaders be "above reproach", "well thought of by outsiders", and "blameless" (1 Tim 3:2, 7; Tit 1:6-7). In fact, the list of qualifications for a presbyter-overseer is framed by an expression of concern about what outsiders think of the potential leader (1 Tim 3:2, 7) and the list of qualities themselves is designed precisely so that the leaders chosen will "be well thought of by outsiders", since the qualities are so close to other such lists, as we have seen.[99] The motivation for this is most likely so that no offense will be caused by leaders, who would be seen as acceptable leaders by the wider society.

Bassler sums up this attitude in the following way: "The advice to bishops (1 Tim 3:7), young widows (1 Tim 5:14), young wives (Titus 2:5), young men (Titus 2:8), and slaves (1 Tim 6:1; Tit 2:10) betrays ... an anxiety about the effect of the behavior of these groups of Christians on the reputation of the church. ... We find a concern for the obedient submissiveness of slaves toward their masters (Titus 2:9-10), of children toward their fathers (1 Tim 3:4), and of women toward their husbands (Titus 2:5) and their ministers (1 Tim 2:11). Women are admonished to be 'sensible, chaste, domestic, kind, and submissive to their husbands' (Titus 2:5), 'to adorn themselves modestly

---

[96] See MacDonald 1988, p167-8; Towner 1994, p122.

[97] See Bassler 1984, p36.

[98] For a discussion of leadership and the titles given to leaders see Chapter 10.

[99] Towner (1994, p30) notes: "The office codes and the instructions concerning the selection of elders aim at establishing 'blamelessness' of reputation and, as far as possible, a proven track record."

and sensibly ... and to learn in silence with all submissiveness' (1 Tim 2:9-11). The explicit motivation for this advice, ... is the concern for the opinion of outsiders."[100] Because it seems to matter a great deal that the behaviour adopted by the members of the community should be acceptable in the eyes of outsiders, the Pastor advocates society-sanctioned behaviour that will lead to acceptability.

Strongly connected to this desire not to cause offence is the desire to make a positive impression on others. Tit 3:1-2 sums up the required attitude: "Remind them to be subject to rulers and authorities, to be obedient, to be ready for every good work, to speak evil of no one, to avoid quarrelling, to be gentle and to show every courtesy to everyone." Clearly, the author has attitudes towards outsiders in view here, and desires that a positive impression will be made on outsiders. Passages like 1 Tim 6:14 and Tit 2:14 and 3:8,14 can be seen to be part of the same theme of making a positive impression on others.

Also part of the same attitude is the desire for peaceful coexistence in the world, expressed in 1 Tim 2:1-2 where we read that "I urge that supplications, prayers, intercessions and thanksgivings be made for everyone, for kings and all who are in high positions, so that we may lead a quiet and peaceable life in all godliness and dignity." This can be seen to be part of the same mindset that calls for no offense to be given to outsiders and for Christians "to show every courtesy to everyone" (Tit 3:2).

Thus, Bassler writes that the Pastorals "are permeated with a strong concern for the opinion of contemporary society."[101] Again we note that the Pastor can take it for granted that the opinion of outsiders provides a sufficient motivation among his readers for the adoption of a certain course of action. That the opinion of outsiders matters so much, not just to the Pastor but also to the community, suggests that the community is significantly in contact with outsiders and open to the opinions of the wider society. Social life was not confined to the Christian community and we can suggest that members were sufficiently involved in the wider society to be concerned about what outsiders think. We suggest then that this shows a degree of social integration and hence of assimilation on the part of the Pastor and the community.

We can note that the evidence we have discussed here suggests that the community is currently causing some offence to those in the wider society, at

---

[100] Bassler 1984, p31-2.

[101] Bassler 1984, p31; see also Streete 1999, p309. As Taylor (1993, p76) puts it: "In the Pastorals one has a constant sense that the 'world' is looking over the shoulder of the author." Bassler (1984, p31 n31) notes that Paul was concerned about the opinion of outsiders (1 Thess 4:11-12; 1 Cor 14:23-25), "but his concern was characteristically addressed to the whole church, not to subunits of it."

least in part because of the opponents' views.[102] For example, that the behaviour of some widows has caused offense in the wider society is suggested by 1 Tim 5:13-14 with its reference to widows marrying "so as to give the adversary no occasion to revile us". Currently, widows "gadding about from house to house" was probably leading precisely to this. We will suggest in Chapter 11 that the opponents had advocated a much more counter-cultural role for women, and this had led to a negative reaction from the wider society (eg 1 Tim 5:7, 14). The Pastor counters this by not only saying that the opponents were wrong, but also by instructing women to adopt society-sanctioned roles and thus seeks to curtail actions on their part that were offensive. So the problem was the involvement of some women in the opponents' teaching, but part of the Pastor's solution was the adoption of a place for women in keeping with the wider society's evaluation. Similarly, 1 Tim 6:1-2 suggests some of the behaviour of slaves may have caused offence in the wider community.

2.2.3 Conclusions

We have suggested that the Pastor and the community demonstrate a degree of social integration and hence of assimilation. Currently the community was causing some offence in the wider society.

2.3 Accommodation: Using acculturation in an integrative way

We have seen that the Pastor is somewhat acculturated and have suggested that his readers are too. But how did the Pastor use his acculturation? This is the question of accommodation. We will argue here that the Pastor and his readers used cultural tools in an integrative way in order to build bridges of communication and will discuss further evidence for cultural convergence. But in section 2.4 we will discuss evidence that suggests there is also an oppositional dimension with regard to accommodation in the Pastorals.

2.3.1 Translating the tradition into a more acculturated form

We have noted the acculturation of the Pastor and (to perhaps a slightly lesser extent) his readers. Why does the Pastor use language with such strong resonance in the Greco-Roman world in his letters? Perhaps this was his only vocabulary, but I would suggest there are two more compelling reasons for the use of this language.

---

[102] This may explain the references to persecution in 2 Tim; see 1:8; 2:3, 9-10; 3:11-12; 4:5; see also Dewey 1998, p446.

The language of epiphany provides a good example here. We have noted that this is language that is well known within the wider society and its use can be seen as a translation of Christology into the language and thought forms of the Hellenistic world. Why did the Pastor use this particular language to express beliefs about Christ? We can suggest two complementary motives. Firstly, that the author uses this sort of Hellenised terminology suggests that the readers found the sort of language used in the letters intelligible; hence the author used it because he believed it would speak to his readers.[103] As we have shown, the Pastor is expressing many elements of what he regards as "the faith" in a more acculturated, Hellenised form, and we suggest that readers who seem themselves to be somewhat immersed in the wider culture would find this a helpful way of elaborating the Gospel. The author thus seeks to enable the gospel to be more of a part of the readers' conceptual worldview, rather than being an "alien" philosophy. However, we note that this translation process has probably happened in the past for the readers – there is no sense that the author must elaborate on this language; it seems to be commonplace for the readers. They already know it and are at home with it and so it is a good vehicle for communication.[104] This is why we have suggested that the readers themselves are acculturated to some extent.

But a second and probably additional reason is likely, since the two explanations are not mutually exclusive. This language is probably used so that the Gospel will be more comprehensible to outsiders, and so we can suggest there was a concern for communication with outsiders and the use of this language has a motivation in mission. This suggestion is supported by the evidence which suggests that mission was important to the Pastor and his readers, as we will note below. This, combined with the fact that the Gospel they are seeking to make known is translated into at least some Hellenistic terms and so is in a more acculturated idiom, suggests the author and community were using acculturation in an integrational way, to build bridges with the wider society.

This can be said, not only for the use of epiphany language, but also for concepts like "Saviour", other language for God, eusebeia[105] and the list of virtues. These can all be seen as ways of interpreting Christ, the Christian life

---

[103] See Marshall 1988, p169.

[104] This does not mean that the readers were all Gentile Christians, but if they included Jews, then they were Hellenised Jews to whom this sort of language was understandable.

[105] Thus Marshall (1999, p144) suggests with regard to εὐσέβεια: "the word-group may have been chosen because it provided a contact point with pagan society (Greek or Roman). Ironically, it may well have been the currency of the language in Graeco-Roman thought that delayed and then limited its use in the early church's vocabulary."

and other elements of the tradition within the wider linguistic culture, both to Christian readers who are part of that culture and to outsiders.[106]

We can suggest then that one use of acculturation for the author, and the community to which he speaks, was to build bridges with the wider society. These "linguistic bridges" were of assistance to outsiders and were of use in mission. We will seek to argue for the importance of mission in more detail shortly, but will firstly discuss other matters relating to accommodation.

2.3.2 A further indication of the integrative use of acculturation

We have already noted the Pastor's concern about what outsiders think and the desire not to cause offense, and argued that this is relevant with regard to assimilation. It seems likely that in the present time, the community is in fact causing some offense and is receiving unfavourable notice because of some facets of the behaviour of its members.

We can outline how we see the overall situation as follows, and will then argue for two features of this outline that we have not yet discussed:

a) as discussed in 2.2.2 above, the Pastor shows a concern for the opinion of outsiders and does not wish to give offense, which shows a concern for some assimilation;
b) again as we showed in 2.2.2 above, currently, the community is giving some offense to outsiders;
c) this has led to the desire for greater acculturation precisely so that that acculturation can be used in an integrative way (ie. accommodation) and the offense to outsiders can be reduced;
d) this, along with acculturated language (which we have already discussed under 2.1 above), leads to
e) the goal that mission might be effective;
f) mission itself is also facilitated by the translation of elements of the Gospel into more acculturated language, as we have shown in 2.3.1 above.

We will address c) briefly, and will then turn to point e).

We suggest then that, in order to curtail offense the Pastor advocates acculturation, so that acculturation can be used for integrative accommodation. We have noted the Pastor's concern about what outsiders think and the desire not to cause offense in section 2.2.2 above. It is clear that

---

[106] Barrett (1963, p33) comments that the Pastorals attempt to "restate the convictions of the first, apostolic generation, in a new era and a new environment." Marshall (1999, p89) notes that the Pastor was "able to present the Christian message in the language and categories of the Hellenistic world." See also Spicq 1969a, p295, 676-84; Taylor 1993, p65.

in order for the community to be "above reproach", the Pastor adopts some attitudes and behaviour that will lead to the approval of society, so that the group will "fit" better in society and "the name of God and the teaching may not be blasphemed" (1 Tim 6:1). Hence, as we have noted in our discussion of acculturation, the Pastor adopts or echoes attitudes and standards of respectable behaviour in the wider society in a number of areas. This includes broad areas concerning "piety" and virtues, attitudes to women, household values, the behaviour of slaves, and the personal qualities sought for in church leaders. Further, the desire not to cause offence is often cited as the direct motivation for some aspects of behaviour, behaviour which can be seen as acculturated. We can suggest then that current offense (caused at least in part by the influence of the opponents' teaching), has led to the desire for *further* acculturation on the part of the author, by adopting attitudes and the standards of respectable behaviour in the wider society and being part of the society's language and attitudes to a greater extent. It seems likely that this is a strategy to ensure that outsiders view the group positively.

All of this means that at least some of these elements of acculturation have been adopted precisely so that they can be used in an integrative way to bring about some cultural convergence, so that the community is not overly marginalised in society (as a "scandalous" group could well be), but rather is more a part of mainstream city life. This integrative use of acculturation is accommodation. At least one of the intended uses of some of the cultural tools we discussed above under acculturation is for integration then.

But we have also suggested that the community is concerned for mission, and that one goal of integration (and hence of the acculturated attitudes and behaviour which leads to integration) is mission. We will now turn to this.

2.3.3 A goal of integrative accommodation is mission

Towner has argued that the main motivation for behaviour that was "respectable" in the eyes of the world, and so was not offensive, was mission.[107] The deeper motive for the Pastor's teaching concerning respectable behaviour was that many might come to hear the message, and thus ultimately come to a "knowledge of the truth" through the community's message. Hence, the Pastor was anxious to avoid behaviour that would put people off and to encourage behaviour that would make it easier for people to join the group. The Pastor seems to have argued that if the group was seen to

---

[107] See Towner 1989, p169-99. Note also Streete (1999, p313): "the great concern of the Pastoral Epistles is the prescription of right conduct for the purpose of inducing, rather than coercing, the rest of the world to adopt its *bios*, its way of life".

be completely disruptive within society, then their message would become disreputable and they would have little prospect of wide scale mission.[108]

The teaching given to slaves is helpful here. Note 1 Tim 6:1: "Let all who are under the yoke of slavery regard their masters as worthy of all honour, so that the name of God and the teaching may not be blasphemed." This suggests that some Christian slaves were failing to honour their non-Christian masters; v2 similarly suggests that some slaves were being disrespectful to Christian masters. But in response, the Pastor calls for submission and conformity to the social structure of the day. The reason for the call for conformity is given in 1 Tim 6:1: "so that the name of God and the teaching may not be blasphemed." Clearly the concern is that because of the rebelliousness of Christian slaves, non-Christian slave owners would "mock the God and the doctrine that produced such behaviour".[109] And if they were to mock and blaspheme, they would not be attracted to the Christian community. Towner also shows that in the parenesis to various other groups "mission provides the impulse for the concern for outsiders."[110]

In support of this view, Towner argues that salvation is a key theme in the Pastoral Epistles and calls it "the centrepoint of the message".[111] Note for example 1 Tim 1:15: "The saying is sure and worthy of full acceptance, that Christ Jesus came into the world to save sinners", and 1 Tim 4:10: "For to this end we toil and struggle, because we have our hope set on the living God, who is the Saviour of all people, namely of those who believe."[112] Note also that in 2 Tim, Paul is portrayed as a model to be imitated, and a clear focus of Paul's activity is presented as mission.[113]

---

[108] Note the parallel with 1 Cor 10:33 where Paul speaks of limiting his own behaviour, that others may be saved.

[109] Towner 1989, p177; see also MacDonald 1988, p168.

[110] Towner 1989, p197, where the quotation refers to Tit 3:1-2, but it also sums up his view on other groups. With regard to the mission motivation of instructions to widows and to other groups see Towner 1989, p187-90 and p197-8 respectively.

[111] See Towner 1989, p75-119; the quotation is the title of chapter 5, see p75. Donelson (1986, p140) argues that the concept of salvation "determines directly the content and direction of the ethical and ecclesiastical life-style promulgated in the letters." See also MacDonald 1988, p174-5; Young 1994, p50-9. A further indication of the significance of mission comes in 2 Tim 4:2. There we read "proclaim the message; be persistent in season and out of season (εὐκαίρως ἀκαίρως)". Malherbe (1984,p235-43) argues that this command to speak "out of season" goes against the advice of philosophical moralists, who advocated that one should only speak at an opportune time. Why then does the Pastor defy convention by advocating speaking "out of season"? MacDonald (1988, p170-6) suggests that although rebuking the opponents is in view, 2 Tim 4:2 also reflects the significance of the community's mission, and 2 Tim 4:5 certainly supports this.

[112] See also 1 Tim 2:4-7; 3:16; 4:10; 2 Tim 1:9-10; 2:8-13; 3:15; Tit 2:11-14; 3:4-7.

[113] See MacDonald 1988, p174-5; see 2 Tim 1:8, 11-13; 2:8-9

Given the key role that salvation plays in the letters, it seems likely that the concern for what outsiders think and the adoption of a respectable lifestyle is so that outsiders might not be put off, but rather ultimately might be saved. Scandalous behaviour by the standards of the time would lead to the church being criticised and ignored. Rather people were to participate in the social structures of the day because the church's mission continued to be vital. The motivation for not causing offence was mission, and acculturation to (some of) the standards and values of society is being put to use for this goal. As Towner notes: "The lifestyle of respectability was mission-oriented, designed to maintain a working relationship with the world by living in ways that it approved."[114] In the Pastor's opinion, the readers are to live in such a way as to commend the gospel which the church proclaims.

Thus we can suggest that causing no offense and the associated acculturation were mission-oriented. We have already noted that in the Pastorals the Gospel is translated into at least some Hellenistic terms and so is presented in a more acculturated idiom. All of this suggests that acculturation was used for bridge building, that is for a form of convergence. Thus the form of accommodation that we see in this document has a strong dimension of what we can call convergence, albeit convergence with an aim, that is mission.

But were the readers likewise using acculturation in an integrative way? We have noted the readers' familiarity with much acculturated language, and we have suggested that one reason for the use of this acculturated language, both by the Pastor and the readers, was so that their faith could be explained to outsiders, which we have suggested is a form of convergence. Secondly, we can suggest that just as the author adopted some elements of acculturation so that they can be used in an integrative way to bring about some cultural convergence, so too the community had this same motivation in their adoption of elements of acculturation. Further, the emphasis on salvation and mission

---

[114] Towner 1989, p243. Towner (1994, p30) notes with regard to the author [Paul for Towner]: "For him to encourage the churches to live a life that would measure up even to pagans' critical estimate was sound evangelistic technique. The mission motive behind the life he called for is obvious." Tit 2:1-10 (and so to Crete) is also interesting in this regard. Here we have teaching which calls older men and women, younger men and women, and slaves to adopt a lifestyle which is respectable and socially acceptable. But in v5, 8 and 10 it is said that they should adopt such behaviour that "the word of God may not be discredited" (v5) or something similar. Clearly the outsider is in view. Yet why are they concerned with what the outsider thinks? The basic motivation for behaviour which will not offend the outsider again seems to be mission. The book of Titus begins by speaking of God and Jesus Christ as Saviour (1:3-4). Further, Tit 2:10 speaks of a slave's behaviour being "an ornament to the doctrine of God our Saviour", and then immediately adds "For the grace of God has appeared, bringing salvation to all" (Tit 2:11). (See also Tit 3:3-8.) The Pastor thus wants to avoid any behaviour which will discredit the Gospel and so hinder mission. Mission provides the impulse for the concern for outsiders therefore.

often comes in traditional sayings, including "faithful" sayings which are introduced by the formula, "the saying is sure",[115] and so it seems likely that these sayings were well known to the readers, and were probably key credal elements which express their faith; we may suggest that they are a part of their contemporary Christian praxis. With respect to accommodation then, these points suggest that the readers used acculturation in an integrative way.

2.4 Evidence that the Pastor and his readers are also using acculturation in an antagonistic way

However, the Pastor does not simply become acculturated and adopt or reflect Greco-Roman culture indiscriminately. For example, he is insistent about monotheism (see 1 Tim 2:5; 6:15-16) , and about the centrality of Jesus Christ and the Gospel message. But there are also some key areas in which he maintains a polemical or counter-cultural edge against some facets of the wider culture. Thus he does not use acculturation in an exclusively integrative way, but also sustains antagonistic and oppositional accommodation in some key areas. The evidence thus suggests that the author is not unconsciously acculturated, but rather is discriminating in what he adopts from his environment, and at times polemicizes against society. We will examine two areas here.

2.4.1 Christ as "our Great God and Saviour"

In Tit 2:13 the Pastor writes that "we wait for the blessed hope and the manifestation of the glory of our great God and Saviour, Jesus Christ." Although the meaning of this verse is disputed, it is most likely that here the Pastor asserts that Jesus Christ is "our great God and Saviour".[116] The phrase "God and Saviour" was current in religious writings of the period, usually denoting a single deity.[117] For example, the phrase is applied to Julius Caesar, and to Zeus.[118] However, the Pastor here affirms that not the emperor, nor Zeus, but Jesus was "God and Saviour", and not only this, but "*our great God*

---

[115] See 1 Tim 1:15; 3:1; 4:9; 2 Tim 2:11; Tit 3:8; see Knight 1992, p99-102. Note that the saying in 3:1 does not concern salvation. Other sayings, which are probably from tradition and are about salvation include 1 Tim 2:5-7; 3:16; Tit 2:11-14.

[116] See Spicq 1969a, p640-1; Marshall 1988, p174; 1999, p274-82. The understanding of the verse given above is supported by the fact that this recognises the presence of the stereotyped formula "God and Saviour", that this gives the best explanation of the absence of the article before σωτῆρος and that elsewhere in the New Testament "epiphany" is applied to the appearing of the Son, not of God.

[117] See Towner 1994, p247.

[118] See Spicq 1969a, p251-2, 640. Θεός and Σωτήρ are both found in IvEph 251, but they are used some distance apart and Θεός refers to Aphrodite and Σωτήρ to Julius Caesar.

and Saviour".[119] Hellenistic language is probably being used polemically against Hellenistic religion here.[120] The author is thus using acculturation polemically against one facet of his context.

2.4.2 Wealth

Another area in which the author adopts a polemical edge towards society and thus uses his acculturation in a counter-cultural way is with regard to wealth in 1 Tim 6:17-19. These verses show that the Pastor clearly knows a good deal about the position of the wealthy in contemporary culture and reflects some contemporary values with regard to wealth which the wealthy would have found congenial. These include that one should not set one's hope on wealth, since it provides a precarious foundation (v17c; cf. Menander, *Dyskolos* 285), that wealth should be used for the benefit of others and that the wealthy person should be liberal and generous (v18c).[121] In v17-19 then, the wealthy are being asked to play the same role in the Christian community as they would be expected to play in other social or political groupings. Thus wealthy Christians are to express their faith in a way that is familiar to the readers.

However, there are other features of the Pastor's instructions with regard to wealth which go against contemporary expectations and so exhibit a polemical edge against the culture. Firstly, the Pastor charges the rich "not to be haughty" (v17b). This "stands against a social world that lends social power to wealth by conferring on its possessors a presumption of moral superiority. Whatever else our author will concede to them, he will not have wealthy Christians thinking of themselves, to cite Dio Chrysostom again, as οἱ βελτίους 'the better people' (*Oration* 48.9)."[122]

---

[119] See Harris 1992, p179.

[120] See Spicq 1969a, p245-54; Marshall 1988, p157, 160. Hanson (1982, p187) notes that here we are: "driven to conclude that the author was trying to counter the imperial cult. ... the author was consciously attempting to present Christ as the true saviour of the human race over against the false saviour Caesar."

[121] Aristotle held that wealth's power consisted in it being used to benefit others (*Rhetoric* 1361a28). Kidd (1990, p198-9) notes: "the instructions to wealthy Christians in these epistles do presuppose cultural norms about how the well-off should use their resources and about the sort of relationships that should exist between benefactors and their clientele. Principal motifs we have found to reside in Aristotle (the relationship between wealth, beneficence, and honor) Menander (the wisdom of securing the future through friendships), Dio Chrysostom (the moral worth of the wealthy), and the inscriptions (the quest for lasting glory through beneficence)." See further Kidd 1990, p126-30.

[122] Kidd 1990, p131.

Secondly, in the Greco-Roman city, the wealthy were expected to lavish money and time on their cities and thus to become benefactors.[123] Those who were not wealthy responded by giving public honour to benefactors, whose reward consisted largely of the honour and glory of being known as a benefactor. Patrons of clubs or associations also expected deference and perhaps the bestowal of a title such as "εὐεργέτης" on them in an inscription because of their benefactions. We note the reciprocity of this – the benefactor gave, and in turn received glory from those who received from his or her benefactions. As Kidd notes: "εὐεργεσία deserves τιμή, financial burdens should be adequately compensated by honor. ... [T]he best way to secure one's posterity is not through the accumulation of wealth, but through the bestowal of benefactions on others in order to create reciprocal bonds of service, or friendship."[124]

It is also clear that the practice of bestowing honour on benefactors was alive and well in Ephesus. Thus the term εὐεργέτης – benefactor - is regularly found in inscriptions,[125] as is εὐεργεσία – public service, and the verb "εὐεργέτεω" – to do good service or to be proclaimed as a benefactor.[126] For example, in the mid-first century CE the Procurator Tiberius Claudius Balbillus was honoured by the council and people of Ephesus "[διὰ τὴ]ν ἀδιάλειπτον [αὐτοῦ εἰς τε τὴν] θεὸν εὐσέβειαν [καὶ εἰς τὴν πόλ]ιν εὐεργεσίαν."[127] Around 25/26 CE one Alexandros set up an honorary inscription for M. Aurelius Cotta Maximus Messalinus, proconsul of Asia, as his personal friend and benefactor.[128] In the Salutaris inscription, the

---

[123] Kearsley in New Docs 7, p238, in discussing a late first century BCE or early first century CE inscription from Kyme in Asia Minor which records the benefactions of one Kleanax, notes "a wealthy individual's manner of making a mark in office was manifest in three or four common ways: supplying the necessities for sacrifices; financing banquets for large numbers of people; providing spectacles as civic entertainments and taking on the general funding of the festivals in the city's calendar."

[124] Kidd 1990, p115, 117. On the role of the ideal benefactor and reciprocity see Nock 1972, p724-35; Danker 1982, esp p170-2, 317-92; Stevenson 1992, p421-36; Joubert 2000, p37-58; New Docs 7, p233-41. For a discussion of the normal responses to benefactors, see Danker 1982, p436-86. Kearsley (in New Docs 7, p236) writes: "The hundreds of honorific inscriptions from the cities in Asia Minor show that benefactors were a dominating feature of Graeco-Roman society." Further Danker (1982, p436) notes: "Ingratitude is the cardinal social and political sin in the Graeco-Roman world, and failure to memorialize benefactions conferred by generous people is its flipside."

[125] See for example, IvEph 22, line 70; 277; 286a, 297-8, 509, 614, 616, 619, 620, 621; see further IvEph vol 8.1, p31.

[126] For εὐεργεσία see IvEph 212.10, 258, 1442.10. 1493.14. 3041, 3431, 3466. For εὐεργέτεω see IvEph 695.4, 1087.6, 1419.2, 1440.12, 1442.9. 1449 .9, 1455.11, 1458.7, 3048.15, 3110.8, 3251.11.

[127] IvEph 3041.

[128] See IvEph 3022 on which see Rogers 1999, p244.

proconsul Aquillius Proculus is twice described as "the benefactor (ὁ εὐεργέτης)"[129]

By contrast, what the author says in 1 Tim 6:17-19 makes it clear that there is to be no earthly glory for Christian benefactors. They are not to expect any conferred honours or reciprocity from those who benefited from their gifts. Rather, as Countryman notes, the rich are "denied the honors, powers and rewards which Greco-Roman culture led them to expect in return for their beneficence."[130] Any reward for the rich (or anyone else for that matter) is not immediate but belongs to another age and is from God (1 Tim 6:17-19). This is decidedly oppositional to the contemporary culture.[131]

Thirdly, honour *is* to be given to three groups of people in the community: real widows (1 Tim 5:3); elders who preach and teach (1 Tim 5:17) and (presumably non-Christian) masters of Christian slaves (1 Tim 6:1), who could defame the teaching. It is noteworthy that it is these groups, rather than the rich, who are to be honoured.[132]

Kidd sums up the overall approach of the Pastor in this way:

"against the backdrop of the normal function benefactions had in cementing reciprocal relationships between wealthy people and their dependents, the ideal held before wealthy Christians in the Pastorals is far less culturally integrative than mere vocabulary and reticence to demand a heroic divestment of possessions suggest. In fact, because wealthy *Bürger* are challenged to assume a familiar *noblesse oblige* yet are simultaneously discouraged from expecting a culturally recognizable return on their generosity, there is as much to horrify as to attract them. In a word, cultural notions of the role of benefactors are shared in part and repudiated in part – the content of the ideal is transformed even as its language is appropriated. ... [I]n these letters language of the ideal *Bürger* is used in such an anti-*bürgerlich* way ...By cutting the philotimic heart out of a culturally assumed social bond without absolving the wealthy of their responsibility for liberality and generosity, the Pastorals accept precisely the sort of tension between loyalty to cultural demands and loyalty to Christ which one expects from the Pauline mind."[133]

Thus, the Pastor is aware of the position of the rich in society and acculturated in this area to some extent, but his thought also has a counter-cultural dimension to it and so exhibits oppositional accommodation. To quote Kidd

---

[129] IvEph 27, lines 76 and 327.

[130] Countryman 1980, p210.

[131] Kidd notes (1990, p157): "the whole web of human reciprocity is dismantled if it is indeed in the next age rather than in this one and from God himself rather than from earthly friends that the wealthy can expect a return on their beneficences."

[132] Kidd (1990, p140) notes that each of these groups represent "contributions of critical concern to him [the Pastor]: domesticity, ideational integrity, reputation in the community."

[133] Kidd 1990, p200.

again, "The Pastorals repudiate the presuppositions even as they appropriate the language of the cultural ideal of the wealthy *Bürger*."[134]

But were the readers likewise using acculturation in an oppositional way? We will argue in Chapter 9 that wealth is currently being given away by some of the wealthy in the community. This suggests that they are acting as benefactors, but whether they were being honoured or not is unclear. It is hard to say what the readers' current attitude was with regard to polemic against other "gods and saviours". We can be less certain then that the readers were involved in this polemic against society.

2.5 "Christliche Bürgerlichkeit"?[135]

We need to comment briefly on a much debated topic with regard to the Pastorals which relates to our current discussion. A number of scholars have suggested that the Pastor's goal is simply to settle down in the world, particularly because of the delay of the parousia and in order to reduce persecution.[136] Thus the Pastor was seen as adapting the Christian life to Greco-Roman society, by the adoption of a moral code and lifestyle which was in harmony with the surrounding culture. The evidence for this is seen in a number of the factors that we have discussed under the topic of acculturation. While we cannot discuss this view at length here, we can simply note three points which suggest this line of interpretation is flawed.

Firstly, the Pastor maintains a forward looking eschatology, which has a significant place in his overall theology.[137] It is unlikely then that the delay of the parousia has been a significant factor in the development of his ethics. Secondly, we have shown that, although the Pastor and his readers are significantly acculturated, and have used their acculturation for integrative purposes in some areas, they also maintain opposition to the wider culture in

---

[134] Kidd, 1990, p158. The Pastorals are also counter-cultural in the exhortations concerning suffering in 2 Tim 1.8-12, 16; 2:3, 9; 3:11-12; 4.6-8; see also Wilson 1979, p42. However, although in arguing that Christians should be willing to suffer he is broadly demonstrating difference from the wider culture, and showing that there are limits to integration, there is no sense in which the author is using cultural tools in these exhortations. Further the Pastorals are somewhat counter-cultural in maintaining a strict sexual ethic for male leaders, who are to be "the husband of one wife" (1 Tim 3:2, 12; Tit 1:6), which probably refers to fidelity in marriage; see Johnson 2001, p213-14.

[135] The phrase is from the German original of the commentary by Dibelius and Conzelmann. In the translation (1972, p40) it is given as "the ideal of good Christian citizenship".

[136] This view has been forcefully expressed by Dibelius and Conzelmann 1972, p8-10, 39-41. It has been very influential; see for example Kee 1980, p119; Koester 2000, p305. For full discussions of this topic see Schwarz 1983; Towner 1989; Kidd 1990.

[137] See Towner 1989, p61-74; Kidd 1990, p181-94; Young 1994, p70-2. Note for example 1 Tim 6:14; Tit 2:13.

some areas. It is inadequate to say that the Pastor's goal is simply to settle down in the world then. Thirdly, we have noted that in a number of areas the author shares language with the wider society or endorses positions which conformed to social convention (and so to some extent does represent christliche Bürgerlichkeit), but that the main motivation for this is to commend the faith to outsiders and so for the furtherance of mission, or as a specific response to the opponents.

2.6 Conclusions

We have suggested that the Pastor, and to a slightly lesser extent his readers, show significant facets of acculturation to the wider society. This acculturation involves some key theological concepts and key attitudes and facets of behaviour. We have noted that there was probably a desire for some social integration and hence for some assimilation on the part of the Pastor and the community. Currently the community was causing some offence in the wider society.

Finally with regard to accommodation, we have suggested that the Pastor and the community were using acculturation to build bridges with the wider society and that a key goal of this integrative accommodation was mission. However, there was also a less prominent but nonetheless significant oppositional dimension to accommodation (although we can be less certain about the readers in this regard), and accordingly we should not see accommodation as indiscriminate.

3. The Johannine Letters

3.1 Acculturation and the readers

3.1.1 1 John - a Jewish book

We turn now to assess the acculturation of the Johannine Letters. Dodd claimed that the language of the Johannine Letters is more Hellenised in its mode of thought than that of the Gospel of Jn.[138] However, this assessment was dependent on the view that some concepts, such as the ideas of the divine "seed" (3:9) and of the "anointing" (2:20,27), were derived from Gnostic sources,[139] an assessment which is unlikely.[140] Further, as Brown notes "Key

---

[138] Dodd 1946, plii-liii; see also Wilder 1957, p213.

[139] See further Dodd 1946, pxx; Dodd thought the meaning of such terms was different in 1 Jn from that in Gnostic sources. As another example, Dodd (1946, pliii) also thought that 3:2 rested "upon presuppositions characteristic of 'Hellenistic mysticism'", and that the

concepts of I John like 'truth' are not modeled on Platonic lines but on apocalypticism and Jewish intertestamental thought, and a close affinity has been detected between ideas in I John and those found in the Dead Sea Scrolls."[141]

Although we must be aware of seeing a hard and fast distinction between things "Jewish" and things "Hellenistic", it is important to note that despite the fact that 1 Jn has no quotations from the OT, it can be seen as thoroughly at home within a Jewish setting and Jewish parallels give much insight into its language.[142] Further, Turner suggests that "there is evidence that the Greek is Jewish, without however being exclusively Aramaic or Hebrew."[143] For example, the phrase "to do the Truth" (1:6) is a Hebraism. There is certainly nothing comparable to the translation of dimensions of the gospel into Hellenistic language which is found in the Pastorals. But we will note below that 2 and 3 Jn exhibit examples of Hellenistic epistolary conventions.

3.1.2 Evidence of "in-group" language

However, the most significant feature of the Johannine Letters from our perspective is the presence of what can be called "in-group" language. Thus for example, note the use of the following language: light-darkness dualism (1 Jn 1:5-7; 2:8-11); "born of God" or "of him" (1 Jn 2:29, 3:9; 4:7; 5:1, 4, 18); being "of God" (eg. ἐκ τοῦ θεοῦ; 4:1)", or "of the Father" (1 Jn 2:16; 3:10; 4:1-4, 6-7; 5:19; 3 Jn 11); truth (1 Jn 1:6, 8; 2:4, 21; 3:18, 19; 4:6; 5:6; 2 Jn 1-4; 3 Jn 1, 3-4, 8, 12); old/ new commandment (1 Jn 2:7-8); "from the beginning"(1 Jn 1:1; 2:7, 13-14, 24; 3:8, 11; 2 Jn 5-6); antichrists (1 Jn 2:18,

---

statement "God is love" "appears to have been moulded upon lines traceable directly to ideas of Hellenistic thinkers about the divine nature."

[140] See Turner 1976, p132-3.

[141] Brown 1982, p28; see also Schnackenburg 1992, p26-30. On 1 Jn and the Dead Sea Scrolls see Boismard 1972, p156-65; Brown 1965, p138-73; but note the cautions of Bauckham 1997, p267-79, who argues that the similarities between Johannine literature and Qumran texts (p271) "is much more plausibly attributed to common dependence on the Hebrew Bible and general Jewish tradition than to any closer relationship between John and Qumran." The same would apply to 2-3 Jn.

[142] See Lieu 1991, p20; Schnackenburg 1992, p8; Stamps 1997, p625. Further, the reference to the story of Cain shapes 1 Jn 3:12-18 and the OT covenant theme has been influential in the book; see Brown 1982, p28; see also Boismard 1949, p365-91; Malatesta 1978. For possible reasons for the lack of references to the OT see Schnackenburg 1992, p27.

[143] Turner 1976, p135; he gives examples on p135-7, including asyndeton, parataxis and the use of periphrastic tenses; see also Héring 1956, p113-21; Schnackenburg 1992, p9. Note by contrast Turner's comment on the Pastorals (1976, p102, 104): "the vocabulary of the Pastorals is nearer to Hellenistic literary writers, such as Epictetus, and especially to the Hellenistic-Jewish wisdom books. ... The style of the Pastorals is not completely free from Semitisms but, compared with the rest of the NT, that element is fairly slight."

22; 4:3; 2 Jn 7); anointing (1 Jn 2:20, 27); abide (1 Jn 2:6, 10, 14, 17, 19, 24, 27-8; 3:6, 9, 14-15, 17, 24; 4:12-13, 15-16; 2 Jn 2, 9); to overcome (1 Jn 2:13-14; 4:4; 5:4-5). This language is often not unique to the Johannine Letters, but it does give the indication of being "in-group" language that has been shaped by the experiences of a group and is understood within that group, but which outsiders would not necessarily understand immediately.[144]

It may well be then that the fact that the author uses "in-group" language to a significant degree could mask the extent to which the author and the addressees can also use language which was a part of the wider world's discourse.[145] Thus we should not conclude that the author and the readers were not acculturated to some extent. But that the author (and we can suggest the readers, since this sort of language must be understandable to them) uses this sort of language is revealing and suggests that this (rather than any more acculturated language) was his preferred mode of discourse.

We conclude that the language of 1 Jn shows few signs of acculturation to the Greco-Roman world, although that the author writes in an "in-group" language may mask the extent to which the group could actually participate in the wider discourse of the society in which they lived. But that the author chooses to use in-group language and that overall his language shows little sign of acculturation is significant.

3.1.3 The letter form of 2 and 3 John

2 and 3 Jn provide some interesting additional evidence here. Both letters closely follow the form of the Hellenistic private letter. Firstly, the form of the address and the close of the letter follow the standard pattern of the Hellenistic private letter, although this is often the case in the NT. Secondly, in 2 Jn 4 and 3 Jn 3 we have the expression "ἐχάρην λίαν"; the expression of joy upon receiving a letter was common in replies during the Hellenistic-Roman period.[146] Thirdly, ἐρωτᾶν used in 2 Jn 5 is one of the four common verbs of petition found in Hellenistic letters. Fourthly, in 3 Jn 2 we have the conventional health wish, including the verb ὑγιαίνειν. This health wish, which appears in papyri in the early second century CE and shows great variety in detail, is not found elsewhere in the NT or in the Apostolic Fathers and thus is a feature that 3 Jn alone shares with the Hellenistic private letter. As Funk notes "The conventional health wish in III John 2 marks this letter as

---

[144] Of course, here 1-3 Jn are very similar to Jn's Gospel which has much "in-group" language; see Meeks 1972, p44-72; Lieu 1986, p186-8.

[145] Much of this in-group language is dualistic (eg. light-darkness, truth-error) and so has similarities with language from Qumran; see Boismard 1972, p156-65.

[146] See Funk 1967, p425; cf. Phil 4:10; Polycarp to Philippians 1.1.

the most secularized in the NT."[147] Fifthly, in 3 Jn 6 we find the idiom καλῶς ποιήσεις which Funk notes "is also very commonly used in the papyri in polite forms of petition, and is to be translated there as 'please' or 'I beg you'."[148] Thus Funk concludes: "It may then be said that the letter bodies of both II and III John are opened with forms and structures entirely characteristic of the common letter tradition. ... There are thus certain formal and structural respects in which II and III John follow the common letter tradition, more closely, perhaps, than other letters in the NT, including those of Paul."[149] We should also note however, that "in-group" language is also not lacking in 2 and 3 John.[150]

We have noted that there are few signs of acculturation in 1 Jn. But the acculturated letter form of 2 and 3 Jn suggests that the author (recall that we think John the Elder wrote all three letters),[151] and probably the readers in the wider Johannine group (which we have noted included some readers in nearby geographical locations), had more interaction with the wider cultural world than 1 Jn suggests. Perhaps then it is the contents, genre or audience of 1 Jn that has led the author, in writing that "letter", to show few signs of acculturation. But it is significant that, although 2 and 3 Jn show considerable signs of acculturation, we do not see the same phenomenon of translating very significant theological ideas into more acculturated forms that we encountered in the Pastorals. We will return to this point below in discussing accommodation.

3.2 Assimilation – participation in wider cultural life?

3.2.1 "Keep yourselves from idols" 1 Jn 5:21

There are two areas that merit discussion with regard to assimilation. Firstly, the very last sentence in 1 Jn (5:21) reads: "Little children, keep yourselves from idols (Τεκνία, φυλάξατε ἑαυτὰ ἀπὸ τῶν εἰδώλων)." If this was a

---

[147] Funk 1967, p430.

[148] Funk 1967, p427; he gives examples on p427-8. Funk (1967, p428) also notes that the phrase καλῶς ποιήσεις "occurs so frequently in common letters, especially as a polite way of introducing requests, and so often in the sequence indicated, i.e., background / καλῶς ποιήσεις / request, as to merit the characterization 'epistolese'." This sequence is also found in 3 Jn.

[149] Funk 1967, p428; see also Deissmann 1927, p241-2; Turner 1976, p132, 134; Lieu 1986, p37-51.

[150] Note for example being "of God" (3 Jn 11); truth (2 Jn 1-4; 3 Jn 1, 3-4, 8, 12); "from the beginning"(2 Jn 5-6); antichrists (2 Jn 7); abide (2 Jn 2, 9).

[151] Even if the author of 2 and 3 Jn is a different person from 1 Jn, the two authors would clearly be related (probably as members of a school) and so the evidence of 2 and 3 Jn can shed light back on 1 Jn.

reference to real idols (as opposed to a metaphorical reference) then it could suggest either that at least some of the readers were currently involved in such idolatry or that the author thought they might be tempted to revert to paganism. Either possibility – real or potential worship of idols - could suggest a significant degree of assimilation on the part of the addressees.

However, it is very unlikely that we should see a reference to the worship of idols here. Firstly, nothing in the letter as a whole prepares us for a reference in its conclusion to a temptation to worship idols, or actual involvement in idol worship, on the part of the readers.[152] Secondly, references to "idols" with a metaphorical meaning are found in Qumran; for example, an apostate is spoken of as one who walks "among the idols of his heart" (1QS 2:11) and CD 20:8-10 speaks of those who "set up idols in their hearts ... they shall have no share in the House of the Law". It is quite reasonable then to see the reference to "idols" in 1 Jn as metaphorical. Thirdly, such a metaphorical meaning fits with the context of 1 Jn 5:14-21 much better than a literal meaning. The metaphorical "idol" would then be a reference to a different understanding of God, and thus to a false God, and would probably be a reference to the secessionists who by their teaching have propounded what to John was an idol.[153] Thus, 1 Jn 5:21 gives no evidence of assimilation on the part of the readers.

3.2.2 The community and "the world"

A second area is more fruitful with regard to the level of assimilation of the addressees and this concerns what John writes about "the world".

It is clear in the Letters that there is a sharp delineation between the community and "the world" with the latter regularly being seen in oppositional terms. Firstly, in 1 Jn 2:16 "all that is in the world" is said to have its origin not in God but "from the world". Secondly, the world is said to "not recognise us" (ὁ κόσμος οὐ γινώσκει ἡμᾶς), just as it does not recognise God (1 Jn 3:1). But thirdly, worse than this, the world "hates" the community (1 Jn 3:13). Here "the world" clearly refers to people who are not "of God". Fourthly, in 1 Jn 5:19 we read: "We know that we are God's children, and that the whole world lies under the power of the evil one." Thus "the world" is seen as under the control of the power that opposes God. Further the world, like the darkness, is passing away (1 Jn 2:8, 17). Given the strong sense of opposition between the community and "the world", and

---

[152] See Lieu 1991, p57.

[153] See Brown 1982, p627-9 (who also gives a discussion of the many suggestions about the meaning of this verse made by commentators); Loader 1992, p79-80. Schnackenburg (1992, p263-4) argues for a connection between idols and sin and so takes the verse to mean "keep yourselves from sin".

between God and the evil one, we can understand why "the world" is seen as hostile to the community,[154] and also why 1 Jn 2:15-17 commands that "the world" is to be avoided.

Fifthly, and connected with this, it is revealing that in 1 Jn 4:4-6 being "of the world" is contrasted with being "of God" rather than with being "not of the world": "ὑμεῖς ἐκ τοῦ θεοῦ ἐστε ... αὐτοὶ ἐκ τοῦ κόσμου εἰσίν ... ἡμεῖς ἐκ τοῦ θεοῦ ἐσμεν ..." This clearly demonstrates that John sees "the world" as diametrically opposed to God;[155] similarly, believers who are "of God", and the world, are in direct opposition here.[156]

Sixthly, in 1 Jn 2:15-17 there is a strong concern against members of the community loving the world: "Do not love the world or the things in the world. The love of the Father is not in those who love the world; for all that is in the world - the desire of the flesh, the desire of the eyes, the pride in riches - comes not from the Father but from the world." Here the focus is on the attractions of the material world, and of society apart from God. These are to be shunned, although we note that 1 Jn 3:17 shows that worldly goods are still to be used for the good of the community.

Finally, although in 1 Jn 5:19 "the world" is seen as under the control of the evil one, the Christian community knows that it has overcome the evil one and conquered the world because of Christ (see 1 Jn 2:13; 4:4; 5:4-5,20).[157] This too is part of the opposition between the world and God/the community.[158]

Against this background we can also understand what is said of the secessionists. They are said to have "gone out into the world" (2 Jn 7; see also 1 Jn 4:1, 3); since they are no longer part of the community, they have become part of the opposition and so are said to be in "the world". This is made explicit in 1 Jn 4:5-6, which clearly refers to the secessionists: "They are from the world (αὐτοὶ ἐκ τοῦ κόσμου εἰσίν); therefore what they say is from the world (διὰ τοῦτο ἐκ τοῦ κόσμου λαλοῦσιν), and the world listens

---

[154] Schnackenburg (1992, p29) notes: "One has the feeling of being in the middle of a conflict between the powers of good and evil, a conflict involving not only human beings but also superhuman spirits."

[155] Note the opposition between God and the devil in 1 Jn 3:8-10. By contrast in 4:4-6 the world replaces "the devil", who is spoken of as the opposition to God in 3:8-10; see Lieu 1991, p83.

[156] Connected to this is the strong sense of election and hence of "us" and "them" seen, for example, in 1 Jn 5:19. Note also the strong sense of being "of God" and possessing knowledge (2.20f, 27).

[157] Note 1 Jn 5:4-5 in particular.

[158] Lieu (1986, p184) notes that this negative attitude to the world is to be distinguished from the gnostic rejection of the world. On "the world" and the Johannine Letters see also Cassem 1972-73, p81-91; Smith 1974-75, p223-4; Schnackenburg 1992, p125-8; Neufeld 1994, p136; Wheeler 1995, p113.

to them. We are from God." The secessionists are seen as having some
success in the world, for the world listens to them. As Lieu notes, "the success
of the 'antichrists' there is an indication of their true character (4.1,5). They
belong to the world and no appeal is made to them nor even any prayer for
them."[159] All of this language underlines the strong sense of opposition
between the community and the world, with the latter term including the
secessionists.

However, positive statements about "the world", such as those found in the
Gospel of Jn,[160] are still found in 1 Jn. In 1 Jn 4:9 we read: "God's love was
revealed among us in this way: God sent his only Son into the world so that
we might live through him". Although the purpose of the "sending" of the
Son is that "*we* might live", the verse still suggests that God loves the
world.[161] Further in 4:14 it is said that "the Father has sent his Son as the
Saviour of the world" and in 2:2 it is said that Jesus "is (ἐστιν) the atoning
sacrifice for our sins, and not for ours only but also for the sins of the whole
world." We note the present tense here – Jesus deals in the present with the
sins of the whole world.

Overall then the world is seen in strongly oppositional terms, although
some positive statements are made about the world. But there is little to
suggest that the community was involved in mission.[162]

All of these factors suggest that the community to which the letters are
addressed had a strong sense of separateness from the world.[163] 1 Jn 5:19
sums up both the community's sense of election (and hence that "we" possess
the truth), and their separateness from the world: "We know that we are God's
children, and that the whole world lies under the power of the evil one." The
community seems to see themselves as a bastion preserving those who know
the truth. Certainly, we get the strong sense that the community is not

[159] Lieu 1986, p146.

[160] See for example Jn 1:9; 3:16, 19; 4:26; 6:14; 8:12; 9:39; 11:27; 12:46; 16:28; 17:2.

[161] See Brown 1982, p518: "the difference between 'the world' of 4:9b and the 'we' of 9c
reflects salvation history. God had a real love for the world; but some preferred darkness and
rejected God's love, and so only the Christian 'we' received life."

[162] See Lieu (1991, p85) who suggests that the community lacked "any real concern for
the world: missionary language is used of the appearance of the false prophets who 'have
gone out into the world' (4:1) – there is little to suggest that the community would seek to
join them." See also Lieu 1986, p182-6; Hahn 1965, p152-63; see further the conclusions of
Cassem (1972-73, p89) which show the predominance of the negative evaluation of the world
in 1 Jn.

[163] We avoid the term "sectarian" because of its problematic nature, on which see Edwards
1996, p108-111; cf. Lieu 1986, p147-8.

interacting with "the world", but rather sees "the world" as its enemy, an enemy who is to be shunned and who hates the community.[164]

Another sign of the "separateness" of the community is that relations with non-Christians are never addressed in 1 Jn.[165] Rather the letter is concerned with the community, with mutual love between members and with the secessionists and the problems they have caused.[166] While this reflects the situation of the community and its recent history of schism, it does show that the interests and concerns of the author, and we may suggest the community too, have turned inwards and are preoccupied with internal matters.

We can also note the strong sense of "community" in the letters, which confirms the impression of an inward-focussed group. Much is said about "loving one another", with the reference being to love for those within the community of addressees (eg. 1 Jn 2:10; 4:7-12). Terms such as "brother and sister", "beloved" and "κοινωνία" (1 Jn 1:3, 6-7) express the sense of a tightly-knit group.[167] It seems clear then that there are very close and significant relationships within the group; perhaps members had few significant relationships outside the group.

Another significant factor here is hostility towards those with whom the group disagrees theologically, of whom pejorative language is used. We have already noted that in 1 Jn 2:19 and 4:5 the secessionists, who are other Christians, are condemned as not being part of the group, but rather as being "of the world". In 2 Jn 9-11 we have the command not to receive or even greet someone who does not "abide in the teaching of Christ" as the author understands it. These are further indications of a very clear demarcation of group boundaries and testifies to the strong sense of community in the group.

This evidence clearly indicates that the group had strong internal boundaries (both against "the world" and at least some "other Christians"), held aloof from its social context and did not participate to any significant extent in the activities of the dominant culture. This is therefore evidence of a low level of assimilation.

We also note that the author of 1 Jn can regularly speak of himself as a member of the community.[168] There is no sense in which he seems to be trying to convince the readers to share his attitude to the world. We can

---

[164] Lieu (1991, p84) notes with regard to "the world": "Whether we are to think of active hostility or passive unconcern, of official action or popular reaction, of Jew or of Greek, or both, for the author it is undifferentiated 'world'."

[165] By itself this would be an argument from silence, but in connection with the language we have discussed, it becomes significant.

[166] Lieu (1991, p57) notes that 1 Jn is "focussed only on intra-communal relations." See also Edwards 1996, p112.

[167] See Edwards 1996, p110.

[168] See for example 1 Jn 4:4-6 and 5:19. See further in Chapter 10.

therefore suggest that the readers similarly saw themselves as "separate" and also had a low level of assimilation.

3.3 Accommodation?

We turn now to the question of how the author of 1-3 Jn uses cultural tools? Firstly, we have argued that the extent of acculturation of the author and readers is certainly not high, although 2-3 Jn suggest that the language of 1 Jn may not reveal the true level of acculturation of the author and readers of 1-3 Jn.

We have also noted that the letters show a focus on relations within the community and that even in 2-3 Jn with their more acculturated form, we do not see the same phenomenon of translating very significant theological ideas into more acculturated forms that we encountered in the Pastorals. When discussing the Pastorals we suggested that one goal of this translation process was mission and so the author and readers were using acculturation in an integrational way, to build bridges with the wider society. It is precisely this sort of integrational use of acculturation that we do not find in 2 and 3 Jn, although of course we are dealing with short documents. But the features of acculturation that we do find in 2-3 Jn – forms of the health wish and particular epistolary idioms and so on – although significant in themselves, do not suggest that the author is trying to build bridges with the wider society. Perhaps the instances we see of acculturation are used primarily because this is language the author and readers know and appreciate, rather than it being used in an integrational way with respect to society. Thus there is no evidence for an integrational use of acculturation, in order to further mission or for some other purpose. This is in keeping with the sense of opposition between the community and the world which we have discerned in 1 Jn in particular. But nor is there any obvious case for the antagonistic use of acculturation either,[169] although this may be partly because there is only limited evidence for acculturation in the first place.

3.4 Conclusion

There are few signs of acculturation in 1 Jn, although 2 and 3 Jn suggest that the author and his readers in the wider Johannine group had more interaction with the wider cultural world than 1 Jn suggests. We have argued that the evidence suggests the group addressed in 1-3 Jn had a low level of assimilation since they had strong internal boundaries and did not participate to any significant extent in the activities of the dominant culture.

---

[169] For example, the rhetoric against "the world" does not exhibit any clear instances of acculturated language.

We have also suggested with regard to accommodation, that the author of 1-3 Jn is not seeking to use the cultural tools he has obtained in an integrational way, although we must recall that we are dealing with short documents here. But it is significant that, although 2 and 3 Jn show significant signs of acculturation, we do not see the same phenomenon of translating very important theological ideas into more acculturated forms that we encountered in the Pastorals.

The evidence discussed here with regard to acculturation, assimilation and accommodation is thus in strong contrast to the Pastorals and suggests that the two sets of documents are to different communities.

4. Revelation

We turn now to discuss acculturation, assimilation and accommodation of John the Seer in Rev and his readers. What can we discern in this area, and does the evidence support our hypothesis that Rev was written to a range of Christians in Ephesus, including the readers of the Pastoral Epistles and the Johannine Letters?

4.1 Acculturation and the readers.

John is of course steeped in the OT and makes many allusions to a whole range of OT texts. He assumes that, at least to some extent, his readers are also familiar with the OT.[170] He is also indebted to past and contemporary Jewish religious and apocalyptic traditions and to early Christian tradition and practice. But John also incorporates into his work a variety of other traditional symbols and myths derived from a wide range of non-Jewish sources.

The debate between Betz and Yarbro Collins is instructive in this regard. Betz suggested that Jewish and Christian apocalyptic texts have been particularly shaped by the Hellenistic environment and so the perspectives provided by that environment were crucial for interpretation.[171] In reply, Yarbro Collins argued that "any treatment of the background of Revelation which limits itself either to Jewish or to Hellenistic tradition will be one-sided and misleading. The actual situation was characterized by a complex interaction of inherited tradition and environment. ... [T]he history-of-

---

[170] See for example Provan 1996, p81-100. On the OT in Rev see Beale 1988 p318-36; Thompson 1990, p50-1; Schmidt 1991, p592-603; Paulien 2001, p5-22; Beale 2001, p23-34; Moyise 2001, p35-40. Kirby (1988, p202) notes with respect to the OT images John uses that "In some cases these images may be not so much direct citations as part of a general religious currency that John could employ with his readers."

[171] Betz 1969, p134-56.

religions background of Revelation is best understood in terms of a fusion of diverse traditions."[172] To support this view, she showed that Rev 16:4-7 combines a traditional Jewish cosmology with the four elements, which is a Hellenistic cosmological motif. "This procedure reflects a certain internationalism, a more or less deliberate fusion of diverse traditions. Such an approach to the pluralistic culture of the early Roman empire is characteristic of Revelation as a whole."[173] One further example of this is Rev 22:16 where Jesus is called "the bright morning star". The image was prominent in Judaism, where it was used of an eschatological saviour figure because of Num 24:17. But in Greco-Roman religions stars were deified, and the morning star was usually identified with Ishtar or Venus. As Yarbro Collins notes: "The fact that Jesus is identified with the *morning star*, which had a rather negative connotation in Jewish tradition because of Isa 14:3-20, supports the hypothesis that non-Jewish tradition played a role in the selection of this epithet."[174]

Thus it is clear that John was familiar with both the Jewish and the Greco-Roman thought worlds (which should of course be seen as inter-related in any case), and as Yarbro Collins suggests, the question of "influences" with regard to John's work "must be seen in the context of a complex process of cultural interaction".[175] We also need to note that some of these Hellenistic elements would have been mediated to John via Judaism, which of course had already had centuries of engagement and interaction with Hellenism to various degrees and in various ways.[176] But, as we will seek to show, it also seems likely that John interacted directly with Greco-Roman thought, as well as with Greco-Roman thought mediated via Judaism.

We turn now to give some examples of areas in which it seems clear that John has been directly influenced by Greco-Roman thought or concepts, areas which are thus examples of acculturation. Here we can only discuss a sample of this evidence, but it will hopefully be sufficient to show that John is more acculturated and participates more in the wider culture's mythic and symbolic world than one might think at first. We will also seek to show that he presupposes that his readers are also acculturated to some extent.

---

[172] Yarbro Collins 1977, p367-8.

[173] Yarbro Collins 1977, p379.

[174] Yarbro Collins 1977, p380. Her emphasis.

[175] Yarbro Collins 1977, p380. See also Aune 1983a, p22-3; Hartman 1996, p113-133; cf. Prigent 2001, p50-68.

[176] See Aune 1987, p481. This is particularly noticeable with Jewish apocalypticism, since apocalyptic was close to an international phenomenon.

4.1.1 The imperial cult (Rev 4-5)

Aune has shown that John's depiction of the ceremonies in the heavenly throne room in Rev 4-5 and elsewhere has been significantly influenced by popular images of the ideas, ceremonies and activities associated with the Roman imperial court.[177] For example, in Rev 4:4, 10 it is said that the twenty-four elders wear golden crowns on their heads, which they then cast before the throne, and are clothed in white. As Aune notes, the presentation of gold crowns to a king was a well-known ceremony to the Romans and white was the sacred colour. He suggests: "The heavenly scene of the twenty-four elders throwing down their crowns before the throne has no parallel in Israelite-Jewish literature and becomes comprehensible only in light of the ceremonial traditions of Hellenistic and Roman ruler worship."[178]

4.1.2 The combat myths (Rev 12)

Yarbro Collins has shown that John makes significant use of the "combat myth". This is an ancient myth of combat involving a struggle between two divine beings for universal kingship, for example between Apollo and Python in Greece, or Horus and Seth in Egypt.[179] John uses the myth in Rev 12 in particular in order to depict the struggle between the woman who gives birth to a son and the red dragon. Although the combat myth is found in the OT, Yarbro Collins has shown that some key motifs in Revelation cannot be explained as being derived from the OT or from Semitic mythology alone. Rather, these motifs can only be explained as elements taken from a variety of traditions, with strong affinities being able to be discerned with the combat myth found in Syro-Phoenician, Egyptian and Greco-Roman traditions. It seems then that John was adopting an international perspective by composing the narrative using traditions from a variety of cultural contexts.[180] However, the closest parallel for the dragon's attack on the woman in Revelation 12 is the myth of the dragon Python's attack on Leto at the time of the birth of her

---

[177] See Aune 1983a, p5-26; see also Barnett 1989a, p113-116; Charles 1993, p85-97; Borgen 1996, p146. For a discussion of titles used in the imperial cult and Revelation, see Cuss 1974, p53-74.

[178] Aune 1983a, p13. Aune (1983a, p6-7) shows that residents of Asia Minor could have been aware of a combination of real and ideal images of the ceremonial of the Roman imperial court. See also Borgen (1996, p145-59) who compares Philo's portrait of Moses as a divine king with what is said about Jesus in Rev 4-5. He suggests (1996, p157) that in some areas what Philo says about Moses and what John says about Jesus "has its background in ideas associated with the political milieu surrounding emperors and kings".

[179] On the myth see Yarbro Collins 1976, p57-100. There were a number of versions of the combat myth in circulation in the first century CE and they had a common pattern.

[180] Yarbro Collins 1976, p2, 187.

son Apollo, particularly as it is found in Hyginus.[181] The striking similarities between the two stories indicate that Rev 12 "at least in part, is an adaptation of the myth of the birth of Apollo."[182] It seems then that John was familiar with this Leto-Apollo myth, which was well-known in Western Asia Minor in the first centuries BCE and CE,[183] and has adapted it for his purposes.

4.1.3 Greco-Roman magic

Aune has shown that there are a number of parallels in Rev with the techniques, formulas and motifs of magic of the period.[184] Magic was an international phenomenon and a key concern of magic was magical revelation. Aune suggests that the image of the risen Jesus as key-bearer in Rev 1:18b has been influenced by the depiction of Hekate, who was very popular in Asia Minor, was the primary figure associated in myth with the possession of the keys to the gates of Hades and was often regarded as the patron deity of magic and sorcery.[185] Further, the phrase "I am the Alpha and the Omega" (Rev 1:8; 21:6; 22:13) has close associations with magical revelation, where A and Ω feature prominently, and the phrase "Surely I am coming quickly" (Rev 2:16; 3:11; 22:7, 12, 20) has parallels in magical divination, where the deity is often asked "to come".[186] Accordingly, these motifs in Rev have significant parallels with the language and motifs of magical revelation in the Greco-Roman world. Aune notes that these passages in Rev are all unique in early Christian writings, "a fact which suggests (but does not prove) that John has not derived them intact from Christian tradition, but has consciously adapted them from Graeco-Roman tradition."[187] It seems very likely then that John, and probably his audience (as we will note below), were aware of this aspect of popular culture.[188]

---

[181] Yarbro Collins 1976, p188; see also Garrett 1998, p471.

[182] Yarbro Collins 1976, p67. This does not mean however that John has taken over the story unaltered. Unlike most of the other female figures in these combat myths, the woman of Rev 12 does not fight the dragon, is not the ally of the hero and is not involved in his recovery or victory. Yarbro Collins (1976, p71-5) also argues that the description of the woman in Rev 12:1 as "Queen of Heaven" is probably influenced by the iconography of Isis. Thus in Rev 12 we probably have a fusion of Leto and Isis traditions.

[183] Yarbro Collins 1976, p70-1; see also Garrett 1998, p472. On Apollo in Ephesus see Oster 1990, p1668-9.

[184] Aune 1987, p481-501.

[185] Aune 1987, p484-9. On Hecate in Ephesus see Oster 1990, p1696 and for example IvEph 567; 1223.

[186] Aune 1987, p489-93; see also Garrett 1989, p94.

[187] Aune 1987, p494.

[188] In Rev 13 and 17 John makes use of the legend about Nero's return which was very common in the period after Nero's death. However, Bauckham has shown that John uses Jewish forms of the tradition of Nero's return (see SibOr 5:28-34, 93-110, 137-54, 214-227.

4.1.4 Conclusions

We conclude that John uses imagery from the Greco-Roman world to communicate aspects of his visions, using mythical and symbolic language which had a wide currency in his contemporary world. Thus, while John is embedded in the OT and in contemporary Jewish tradition, he is also a participant in the wider culture and its language.[189] John also regularly assumes that at least some of this contemporary culture will be familiar to his readers.[190] The addressees must be able to understand some of these "cultural codes" for there to be communication between John and his readers.[191] Further, as we will see, John is often polemicizing against, for example, the imperial cult, in his use of the language derived from that cult and if his readers knew absolutely nothing about the cult and its language, one of John's key points in some passages would be lost to his readers. It is much more likely that they have some knowledge about these facets of wider culture and are able to appreciate John's polemic. Otherwise we would expect John to spell out the point of his polemic more in, for example, Rev 4-5. It seems likely then that John's hearers, including the Ephesian Christian addressees, had some familiarity with the wider culture of their day.[192]

361-380, and a different Jewish tradition also found in the Christian Ascension of Isaiah 4:2-14). Thus, although it seems very likely that John knew of the traditions about Nero independently of Jewish sources, we cannot show this, and so cannot include this as an example here. But we can note that John portrays Nero the beast's claim to divinity as a parody of Christ's death and resurrection. Thus, as we will argue below with regard to his use of acculturation, John is again polemicising against the wider culture. See Bauckham 1993c, p384-452; see also Aune 1998a, p737-40.

[189] Paulien (1988, p47-8) notes: "Much of his use of earlier [pagan and apocalyptic] literature should probably be attributed to previous reading and the natural exposure he would have had to ideas that were 'in the air' in Asia Minor. The imagery that originated in these sources was buried deep in John's mind and was called up and transformed in the course of his visionary experience." Stevenson (2001, p217) also notes that Rev is "a document that is immersed in the Hellenistic environment of Asia Minor."

[190] Note that although John's readers probably included some Jewish Christians, they certainly also would have included Gentile Christians, as is shown by the emphasis on "the nations" among the people of God in Rev 5:9; 14:6; 15:4; 21:4, 26; 22:2 cf 15:4; see also Paulien 1988, p48; Stevenson 2001, p216.

[191] Paulien (1988, p33) notes: "the author did not give free rein to his fantasies, but grounded his language firmly in the cultural milieu with which his readers were familiar. Such a procedure would be quite natural for a prophet who sought to communicate a word from God in a specific time and place."

[192] Thus Schüssler Fiorenza (1991, p30-1) comments that a variety of traditions, including Greco-Roman, and Asian mythological traditions "were readily available and unconsciously present to the original recipients of the book. ... By working with associations and with allusions to divergent mythic and religious-political traditions, Revelation seeks to appeal to the imagination of people steeped in Jewish as well as Greco-Roman culture and religion."

4.2 Assimilation – participation in wider cultural life?

As we have seen in Chapter 7, John the Seer is wholeheartedly against any significant form of social integration by Christians and is seeking to convince his readers also to take this approach and participate as little as possible in the social intercourse of the wider culture. Although the key focus of John's concern is idolatry and "worshipping the beast", we will argue in Chapter 9 that the call to "Come out of her my people" (Rev 18:4) also relates to significant participation in economic life; in John's view Christians should not participate in the web of relations that were intrinsic to the economic life of the Roman empire. Thus, although John is acculturated to some extent, he opposes any significant degree of assimilation. Of course, it is unclear how possible this was, and John does not spell out how Christians were actually to live and undertake the practicalities of life (food? money?) since his concern in Rev is not to answer such questions. But his principles are clear.

By contrast, we have shown in Chapter 7 that the Nicolaitans ate food offered to idols and were also involved in some additional activities or facets of pagan worship that could be described as "πορνεῦσαι", such as involvement in associations or trade guilds, participation in pagan festivals in the city, in cultic meals in pagan temples, or perhaps in pagan cultic worship. This suggests that they were integrated socially into the life of the city in some significant ways and participated in some facets of wider cultural life.

With regard to the Christians in Ephesus to whom John writes, we have suggested that currently some of them are more involved in the majority culture than John would like. This is suggested by the call to "repent and do the works you did at first" (Rev 2:5), as well as by the fact that overall in the seven churches John seems to anticipate that the majority of Christians are neither his opponents, nor his supporters; rather he thinks of the majority as somewhat unconcerned about the issues which divide him from the Nicolaitans, and so he calls this majority to "Come out of her my people" (18:4).

4.3 Accommodation: using cultural tools in an antagonistic way to further polemic

As we have noted briefly above, in Revelation John uses the cultural tools he has acquired from the wider environment in a vigorous polemic against that environment. We will now seek to show this for each of the three topics we have discussed in the section on acculturation.

4.3.1 The imperial cult (Rev 4-5)

There is a polemical edge to John's use of the ideas associated with the Roman imperial court. John is convinced that Jesus ranks above the Roman emperors, even if emperors like Gaius claimed divine authority. Thus, Aune argues that John parodies the ceremonial of the imperial court and cult in order to show that the claims of Caesar and of Christ were antithetical, and that the claims of Christ were legitimate, while those of the emperor were not.[193] The parody can be seen, for example, when the twenty-four elders throw down their crowns before the throne in Rev 4:10, a direct parody of a ceremony performed before the emperor. John's use of language from the Roman imperial court thus shows that "the sovereignty of God and the Lamb have been elevated so far above all pretensions and claims of earthly rulers that the latter, upon comparison, become only pale, even diabolical imitations of the transcendent majesty of the King of kings and Lord of lords."[194] Here then John uses his acculturation – in this case his knowledge of the Roman imperial court - in an antagonistic way.[195]

4.3.2 The combat myths (Rev 12)

We have noted that in Rev 12 John has incorporated the Leto-Apollo myth. Caird suggested that the myths reflected in Revelation 12 were deliberately adopted and rewritten by John to contradict their contemporary political application. The emperor is not the one who kills the dragon and embodies the triumph of order over chaos; rather Christ turns out to have the legitimate claim to this role and the emperor is seen to be "one of the dragon's minions".[196]

In developing this idea, Yarbro Collins notes that Augustus' rule was regarded as a golden age and that myths about Apollo were used as political propaganda in support of the empire during his rule.[197] Further Nero later identified himself with Apollo, and Apollo myths and the Apollo cult were used during Nero's reign as imperial propaganda. Against this background, it

---

[193] See Aune 1983a, p5-26; 1987, p481; see also Charles 1993, p93-7; Borgen 1996, p158-9.

[194] Aune 1983a, p22.

[195] Aune (1997, p126-9) notes that the seven proclamations in 2:1-3:22 are closest to the genre of royal or imperial edicts. He notes (1997, p129): "The author's [ie John's] use of the royal/imperial edict form is part of his strategy to polarize God/Jesus and the Roman emperor, who is but a pale and diabolical imitation of God. In his role as the eternal sovereign and king of kings, Jesus is presented as issuing solemn and authoritative edicts befitting his status." Thus, in 2:1-3:22 John is again using cultural tools and thus his acculturation in a polemical way, in this case, against the emperor.

[196] Caird 1966, p148.

[197] See Yarbro Collins 1976, p188.

is significant that Rev 12 is to some extent at least, an adaptation of the myth of Apollo's birth. Yarbro Collins firstly discusses John's reinterpretation of the Jewish source which used the Apollo myth, and then goes on to suggest with regard to Rev 12: "By incorporating and reinterpreting the Jewish source which used the Apollo myth to depict the birth of the messiah, the author of Revelation formulated a further element in the antithesis of Christ and Nero. The claims of the Apollonian Nero are rejected by the depiction of Christ as the true bringer of order and light."[198] Thus we see that John incorporates Greco-Roman and other myths and traditions in order to polemicise against Greco-Roman culture and pagan worship. Since the Leto-Apollo myth was well-known in Western Asia Minor, we can suggest that John expected at least some of his readers to recognise the polemic against Greco-Roman culture in which he was engaged here.

4.3.3 Greco-Roman magic

It seems likely that John has incorporated Hellenistic magical traditions in Rev in order to engage in an extensive anti-magical polemic. In Rev 1:18b John depicts Jesus, the key-bearer, as the one who has taken over the role assigned in Greco-Roman magic to Hekate.[199] It is Christ who is the A and Ω (Rev 1:8; 21:6; 22:13), showing that he cannot be controlled by magical incantations. We have noted that in magical divination the deity is asked "to come"; in using the phrase "Surely I am coming quickly" (Rev 2:16; 3:11; 22:7, 12, 20), "John turns the table on contemporary magical practice and places the promise to come on the lips of the risen Jesus, adding the adverb 'quickly' to make the parody obvious."[200] Further, Aune notes that the way the language and motifs have been used by John suggests that "the validity of the religious and magical assumptions behind them are implicitly denied. In other words, the author has devised an extensive and creative anti-magical polemic the purpose of which is to nullify the revelatory claims of the pagan competitors of Christian prophets."[201]

4.4 Conclusions

We see then that John incorporates elements of Greco-Roman culture and traditions in order to polemicise against Greco-Roman culture (both practices

---

[198] Yarbro Collins 1976, p190.

[199] Aune 1987, p485.

[200] Aune 1987, p493.

[201] Aune 1987, p494. This is part of John's depiction of magic, also seen in Rev 9:21, 21:8, 22:15, as well as in the depiction of the magic practiced by the beast (13:13-15; 19:20).

and ideas) and pagan worship.[202] His use of acculturation is thus oppositional and he uses elements of culture in order to polemicise against dimensions of his environment.

But what of the readers with regard to accommodation? Are they involved in an antagonistic or oppositional relationship with their environment? Are they using acculturation against the wider society for oppositional purposes? It is difficult to say, but given the repeated calls to "repent" in the seven proclamations, which often seem to suggest the readers (in John's view) have compromised with the wider world (eg Rev 2:5; 3:2-4, 15-17) and that John anticipates he has a battle on his hands in order to convince his readers, it seems unlikely that they were as diametrically opposed to the wider society as John was.

But to whom is John writing? Does this evidence suggest he is writing to a particular community, or to all the Christians in Ephesus (or as many as possible)? There is certainly nothing in what we have discussed in this section that requires the conclusion that John is writing to his own community.[203] Further, that he is significantly acculturated, and presupposes that his readers are too, argues strongly against the view of Bornkamm and Satake, which we will discuss in greater detail in Chapter 10, that John is writing to groups of Jewish Christians who migrated from Palestine shortly after the fall of Jerusalem and who maintained a distinct identity as groups in Asia Minor.[204]

We have argued that one element in John's intended audience is the Nicolaitans and those who are under their influence and much of what John writes with regard to assimilation and accommodation can be understood as directed against them. But we have also argued in Chapter 7 that there is a significant number of readers (including many in Ephesus) who are not part of the Nicolaitans, but also do not agree with John. What we have discerned in this Chapter about John and his understanding of his readers fits well with the view that some of this centrist group which John has in mind as he writes are readers of the Pastorals in particular. John can assume that his readers are acculturated to some extent, and we have argued that the readers of the Pastorals were precisely this. Further, we have argued that the readers of the Pastorals were assimilated to the extent that what the wider community thought of the group, and in particular that the wider community viewed the Christian group positively, was regarded as important. Even though we cannot

---

[202] Aune 1987, p481 notes that John "used pagan imagery and practices as part of a broad apologetic assault on Graeco-Roman culture itself." See also Paulien 1988, p46, 48; Barnett 1989a, p111-20; Schüssler Fiorenza 1985, p195-6.

[203] We could build up a profile of readers and their acculturation and perhaps assimilation and accommodation from what John writes, but then one could do this for any document. The more important matter is whether the evidence requires one to build up such a profile.

[204] See Bornkamm in TDNT 6, p669f; Satake 1966, p155-95; see also Schweizer 1961, p135-6; Bauer 1971, p84.

say that the readers of the Pastorals were involved in idolatry in any way, we could understand that John the Seer would want to argue against this somewhat assimilationist stance of the community of the Pastorals therefore. And John's antagonistic use of acculturation is also understandable with regard to the readers of the Pastorals - he could well think that their use of acculturation to build bridges with society for the purpose of mission was dangerous.

The situation is more complex with regard to the readers of the Johannine Letters. We have argued that they were not significantly acculturated, so perhaps they would miss some of the allusions John the Seer makes to the myths and culture of the wider world, although the evidence of 2-3 Jn suggests they could have been more acculturated than 1 Jn suggests. Similarly, they seem to not be assimilated, and so John's polemic against social integration would not be particularly aimed at them.

We suggest then that while this evidence does not require our hypothesis that Rev was written to all the Christians in Ephesus, it is compatible with it.

5. Overall Conclusions

We have argued that the author and readers of the Pastoral Epistles are acculturated to a significant degree and that since they are concerned that the wider community views the Christian group positively, this is an indication of some assimilation. The cultural tools they had acquired were predominantly used to build bridges with the wider culture but there was also a less prominent although nonetheless significant note of polemic. Thus with regard to accommodation, their use of acculturation was predominantly, though not exclusively, integrative.

The author of the Johannine Letters is only acculturated to a limited degree, although 2 and 3 Jn suggest that the author and his readers in the wider Johannine group were more acculturated and had more interaction with the wider cultural world than 1 Jn suggests. The group addressed in 1-3 Jn had a low level of assimilation with strong internal boundaries and did not participate to any significant extent in the activities of the dominant culture. With regard to accommodation, the author of 1-3 Jn is not seeking to use the cultural tools he has obtained in an integrational way, nor do we see evidence of the translation of theological ideas into more acculturated forms.

These strong contrasts suggest that the Pastorals and the Johannine Letters are to distinct and different groups in Ephesus. Since these matters of acculturation, assimilation and accommodation are very significant features of group identity, in this chapter we have also begun to give a description of facets of the life of these two groups.

The author of Revelation was acculturated to a moderate degree and he presupposes that (at least some of) his readers are too. The author is wholeheartedly against any form of social integration and is seeking to convince his readers to take this approach. Currently, some of them are more involved in the majority culture than he would like. By contrast with John, the Nicolaitans are significantly involved in social integration. Further, in Revelation John uses his cultural tools from the wider environment in a vigorous polemic against that environment. His use of acculturation is thus oppositional.

Although this evidence from Revelation does not require that John is writing to all the Christians in the city, it is certainly compatible with that hypothesis. In particular, the readers of the Pastorals with their significant degree of acculturation, some assimilation and an integrative approach with regard to accommodation, can be seen as one group to whom John is directing his work, although there is no reason why we should not see the readers of 1-3 John as also addressed in Revelation.

Chapter 9

Material Possessions and the readers of the Pastorals, the Johannine Letters and Revelation

My focus in this chapter will be on the material possessions of the readers addressed in the Pastoral Epistles, the Johannine Letters and Revelation. I will not be discussing the wider and more complex issue of social status, because in my view, we do not have enough evidence to discuss the details of the social status of the readers of these documents.[1] My focus will be on attempting to discern what the author says about the material possessions, or lack thereof, of the addressees of these documents and then to ask the question about how material possessions were being used by the addressees.[2] Again we will be testing our hypothesis that the Pastorals and the Johannine Letters were to different communities, but that in Revelation John is addressing all the Christians in Ephesus.

1. Material Possessions and the Pastoral Epistles

I will argue in this section that there was considerable diversity with regard to material possessions in the community addressed in the Pastorals and that the community had a significant community fund.

The Pastorals show a considerable amount of interest in the wealth of individuals and of the community. Kidd notes the extent to which learning "how to behave in the household of God" (1 Timothy 3:15) "involves managing the church's financial resources and learning how to minister to the

---

[1] Note Kidd's remark (1990, p50) that the Pastorals are "light on the sort of data – e.g., level and source of income – that would allow the placing of anyone in a particular stratum", such as upper class or lower class. This is even more the case with the addressees of the Johannine Letters and Revelation.

[2] We have noted in Chapter 1 that the city of Ephesus flourished in the first and second century. Clearly it contained both wealthy and poorer people. For the housing of some of the rich see Hueber 1997, p53-64.

congregations wealthier members."[3] This suggests material possessions and wealth in general was a real issue in the community.[4]

1.1 Wealthy members of the community

Some members of the community addressed by the Pastor seem to be relatively well off. Note the following evidence:

1.1.1 Instructions to the "rich"

Firstly, in 1 Tim 6:17-19 the author writes "To the rich in this age (Τοῖς πλουσίοις ἐν τῷ νῦν αἰῶνι)".[5] What does the author mean by πλούσιος? The word means "having an abundance of earthly possessions that exceeds normal experience, rich, wealthy".[6] In the NT the term is used, for example, for Joseph of Arimathea in Mt 27:57, where BDAG suggests that what is meant is "one who does not need to work for a living".[7] But clearly πλούσιος is a relative term which does not by itself specify how wealthy a person is. Similarly, in 1 Tim 6:17 the wealthy are also told not to set their hopes on "uncertain riches" (πλούτου ἀδηλότητι), with πλοῦτος being defined by BDAG as an "abundance of many earthly goods, wealth".[8] Clearly this again is unspecific. It is enough for us here that there were members of the community who could be regarded as πλούσιος.[9]

The author tells Timothy to "charge them not to be haughty (παράγγελλε μὴ ὑψηλοφρονεῖν)"; haughtiness was regarded as something to which the wealthy were particularly prone.[10] These rich Christians are rather "to do

---

[3] Kidd 1990, p92-3.

[4] Note that I am not endeavouring to compare the Pastorals with the undisputed Paulines on this matter and so will only occasionally make comparisons with these letters.

[5] Kidd 1990, p93-100 argues that 1 Tim 6:9-10 and v17-19 address the one group – the rich. However, from what is actually said in these two passages, it seems much more likely that there are two different groups; see Brox 1969, p219; Verner 1983, p174.

[6] BDAG, p831; for πλούσιος and πλοῦτος see also TDNT VI, p318-332; EDNT III, p114-17; on the terms "rich" and "poor" see also Malina 1987, p354-67; Hollenbach 1987, p50-63.

[7] BDAG, p831. See also, for example, Lk 12:16 ("The land of a rich man brought forth plentifully .."); 14:12 (rich neighbours); 16:1 (the rich man and the dishonest steward); 16:19 (the rich man and Lazarus); 18:23 (the rich ruler, who is described as "πλούσιος σφόδρα", very rich); 19:2 (Zacchaeus); Mk 12:41 ("Many rich people put in large sums" to the Temple treasury); James 2:6; 5:1.

[8] See BDAG, p832, with reference to Mt 13:22; Mk 4:19; Lk 8:14; Js 5:2; Rev 18:17.

[9] Countryman (1980, p24) notes "To be rich, in terms of classical society, meant to live on one's investments and by the labor of others."

[10] Hermas, in Sim 8.9.1 writes of those who "became rich and in honour among the heathen; then they put on great haughtiness (ὑψηλόφρονες) and became high-minded, and

good, to be rich in good deeds, generous and ready to share (ἀγαθοεργεῖν, πλουτεῖν ἐν ἔργοις καλοῖς, εὐμεταδότους εἶναι, κοινωνικούς)".[11] We will discuss later who are to be the recipients of the wealthy people's gifts. Here we simply need to note that they are in the church, and are not told to give all their money away. Rather, they are to use what they have as benefactors for others; but it seems likely that they will remain rich. They are clearly important in the community.[12]

1.1.2 Wealthy Women's adornment

In 1 Tim 2:9 women are told that in the context of worship they should not adorn themselves "with braided hair or gold or pearls or costly attire" (μὴ ἐν πλέγμασιν καὶ χρυσίῳ ἢ μαργαρίταις ἢ ἱματισμῷ πολυτελεῖ; 1 Tim 2:9).[13] We gain little specific information, but it is clear that these women are wealthy. We note, for example, that Pliny regularly writes of pearls as "the epitome of extravagant luxury";[14] further, with regard to "costly (πολυτελής) attire" πολυτελής means "being of great value or worth, ordinarily of relatively high degree on a monetary scale, (very) expensive, costly".[15] The same word is used of the alabaster flask of ointment of pure nard used to anoint Jesus' head in Mk 14:3; it is said in Mk 14:5 that the ointment could have been sold for more than three hundred denarii, with the denarii being a worker's average daily wage.[16]

Clearly, the Pastor thinks it was possible for women to come to worship dressed in this way, and it seems likely that some women among the addressees had in fact been doing so. As Verner notes: "Only well-to-do women could have been the object of this exhortation since only they could

---

abandoned the truth, and did not cleave to the righteous." On haughtiness and the wealthy see Philo Mos 1:31; 1 Clem 59:3; Herm. Mand. 8:3.

[11] See similar instruction in Rom 12:8; Hermas, Mand 2.6; Sim 9.30.5; 1 Clem 38.2.

[12] Countryman (1980, p153) suggests that the rich are an important theme for the Pastor, since "he returned to them at the end of that letter [1 Timothy] with a final exhortation, in emphatic position just before his final salutation". He notes on p176 n11: "Surely, even a pseudepigraphical author would say something of significance to himself as his last word."

[13] πλέγμα is a wave or plait of hair, which indicates an elaborate hair style. We note that the Pastor instructs the women to adorn themselves "modestly and sensibly in seemly apparel". This may be in contrast to the opponents' arrogance (2 Tim 3:2) and divisiveness (Tit 1:11 ; 3:9-11). See further in Chapter 11. Concern for modesty in dress was a standard virtue for Greco-Roman women and the contrast between outward and inward adornment of women was a topos of Hellenistic literature; see Xenophon, Econ. 7.43; Plutarch, Praec.conj. 26; see Spicq 1969a, p377-8.

[14] Bauckham 1993, p354; see Pliny N.H. 9.105, 112-114, 117-122, 37.14-17.

[15] BDAG, p850; it is also used metaphorically of inward adornment in 1 Pet 3:4; see also Jos CAp 2.191.

[16] See BDAG, p223.

have afforded such ostentation."[17] Thus, some members of the community were able to afford very expensive luxury items of clothing and so were clearly rich.

1.1.3 Women who can assist widows

Some members of the community were wealthier women who could be expected to assist widows in need of financial help. Thus in 1 Tim 5:16 the Pastor writes: "If any believing woman has widows (εἴ τις πιστὴ ἔχει χήρας), let her assist them; let the church not be burdened, so that it may assist those who are real widows."[18] That such women can assist widows (plural), to the extent that because of the financial support of such a "believing woman" the church will not need to support the widows concerned, suggests that these "believing women" have significant wealth at their disposable. Thus Kidd writes of them as "service patronesses".[19]

1.2 Evidence which has been thought to indicate wealth, but in my view does not

I turn now to evidence which has been thought to indicate the wealth of certain groups, but where I think the evidence is insufficient to make this claim.

1.2.1 Christian Slave owners

1 Tim 6:2 clearly implies that the community included Christian slave owners: "Those who have believing masters must not be disrespectful to them on the ground that they are ἀδελφοί." It has been thought that owning a slave indicated a significant degree of wealth.[20] Thus, Kidd thinks that these slave owners are people of some means who "will be numbered among the 'rich in

---

[17] Verner 1983, p168; Kidd (1990, p106) notes that these are "prosperous and socially powerful women"; see also Spicq 1969a, p376-7, 424-5; Countryman 1980, p153; Verner 1983, p180; Padgett 1987, p19-31; Kidd 1990, p85-6, 102. Note the descriptions of wealthy women in Juvenal Sat. 6.492 (note the social implications of this since this is a satire on wealthy upper class women); Petronius Sat. 67. On wealthy women in Ephesus see Rogers 1992, p215-223; van Bremen 1996, p193-296; Friesen 1999, p107-113.

[18] The meaning of εἴ τις πιστή here is debated; see Dibelius and Conzelmann 1972, p76; Marshall 1999, p606-7. See further Chapter 11.

[19] Kidd 1990, p105. Verner (1983, p139) notes "the author urges them [the believing woman] to take full responsibility for the support of widows in their care so that the church will not have to shoulder this burden. He thus regards them as women of means who have the power to take actions that can affect the financial health of the church."

[20] The work of Theissen 1982, p83-7 has been very influential here.

this world' (1 Timothy 6:17)."[21] Further, Verner thinks that the actual houses
in which most lower class households lived could not accommodate both the
family and slaves.[22] In addition, in Verner's opinion slaves were expensive to
buy and look after and so "it thus appears unlikely that more than twenty-five
percent of households included slaves ... [T]he household which possessed
even one slave stood higher on the socio-economic pyramid than most of its
neighbors."[23]

However, Meggitt has shown that we should not think that slave owners
were necessarily wealthy. He notes that "a slave could be obtained in the first-
century Graeco-Roman world without incurring substantial expenditure,"[24] by
for example bringing up an exposed baby or buying an infant. Accordingly
slave ownership was quite possible for the non-elite; artisans, soldiers,
peasants and even other slaves owned slaves. Meggitt concludes that "the
inclusion of a slave in a person's household can therefore indicate little about
the householder's socio-economic status."[25]

1.2.2 Leaders who were heads of households

Again, some of what the Pastor says about the qualities required for
leadership has been thought to presupposes that at least some of the leaders
were reasonably wealthy, but again this is to go beyond the actual evidence.

In 1 Tim 3:12 among the requirements for deacons we read: "Let deacons
be the husband of one wife and let them manage their children and their
households well (τέκνων καλῶς προϊστάμενοι καὶ τῶν ἰδίων οἴκων)". As
Kidd notes, unless καὶ τῶν ἰδίων οἴκων is superfluous, this indicates that
the Pastor is assuming that slaves as well as wives and children are part of the
deacon's household.[26] Since it is thought that only the well-to-do owned
household slaves,[27] it is suggested that the fact that deacons owned slaves
shows that they are relatively wealthy and of relatively high social standing.[28]
However, as we noted in the previous section, that a householder owns a slave
indicates little about the householder's socio-economic status.

We can also note that the fact that leaders are assumed to be
"householders" and so to have "houses" (see 1 Tim 3:4-5 with regard to

---

[21] Kidd 1990, p140; see also p83, 86; Verner 1983, p56-61. Verner (1983, p141) notes
that this exhortation to Christian slave-owners is unparalleled in other Haustafeln.

[22] See Verner 1983, p57-60.

[23] Verner 1983, p61.

[24] Meggitt 1998, p129.

[25] Meggitt 1998, p131.

[26] Kidd 1990, p83; see also Verner 1983, p133; Theissen 1982, p83-7.

[27] Verner 1983, p134.

[28] Verner 1983, p133.

overseers) also does not mean that they are wealthy.[29] Meggitt notes that although οἶκος and οἰκία could be used of households that included slaves, households could vary in size a great deal. He notes: "The 'household' of a poor person, for example, could be as small as two family members and the majority were no doubt equally modest in size."[30] And even if the "household" did include slaves, we have noted this does not necessarily mean that the householder was wealthy.

There is another reason that it seems unlikely that office holders were necessarily wealthy. In 1 Tim 5:17 we read that elders who govern well are considered worthy of "double honour" (διπλῆ τιμή), namely those who labour in preaching and teaching. That some sort of financial or material payment is in view here is indicated by the two scriptural quotes which follow, including the statement that "The labourer deserves his wages". Clearly, then, it is presupposed that some elders will receive some form of payment from the community.[31]

However, we need to recall that the rich would not have wanted to have received some form of tangible material reward, but rather would have seen

---

[29] Compare Theissen 1982, p87 who thinks that "Reference to someone's house is hardly a sure criterion for that person's high social status; but it is a probable one, particularly if other criteria point in the same direction."

[30] Meggitt 1998, p129.

[31] Dibelius and Conzelmann (1972, p78) note: "A financial compensation is certainly intended here ... The next verse makes the connection with material reimbursement unmistakably clear." See also Brox 1969, p199; Schwarz 1983, p38; Marshall 1999, p612-5 (who reviews all the options); Johnson 2001, p277-8. τιμή with the meaning of price, money or salary is witnessed to in the NT, papyri and inscriptions; see Mt 27:6,9; Acts 5:2-3; 1 Cor 6:20; 7:23; SEG 22.485; Spicq 1969a, p542. Schöllgen (1989, p232-9) notes that there is no evidence that τιμή mean a regular salary or stipend, since the term is attested only for one-off payments, not a regular salary. Nor should we think of sufficient material assistance so that the officeholder did not have to work to earn a living. Since the support of widows is proving burdensome, it is unlikely that the community could also support elders (plural) to the extent that they did not have to work. Schöllgen (1989, p235-9) agrees that 5:18 indicates that some form of material payment is meant but thinks it refers to the elders receiving a double portion at the community's Agape meal; he cites support for such a practice from Tertullian and Greco-Roman collegia. This is possible, but as Marshall notes (1999, p615), something more than an honorific portion of food seems to be implied by v18. It seems best then to conclude that some form of material and/or financial payment, is involved, though we cannot be more specific than this. That leaders are not to be "lovers of money" or "greedy for gain" (1 Tim 3:3; 8; Tit 1:7) and that some people expected to make money out of teaching εὐσέβεια (1 Tim 6:3-5, esp 5) also suggests leaders received financial rewards. The "double honour" is thus probably a reference to respect (received by all elders, including those who do not preach and teach), and some material payment; see Mounce 2000, p309. 2 Tim 2:6 may also suggest financial reward for leaders; see Blomberg 1999, p210. That some form of gift was made to leaders in the early Church is also clear in 1 Cor 9:7-14; 2 Cor 11:8-11; Gal 6:6; Didache 13. For a discussion of μάλιστα here see Chapter 10.

their leadership roles as benefactions.[32] That some elders receive a material reward suggests then that they are not wealthy.[33] Clearly then the author does not presuppose that all leaders are wealthy and we have seen that the fact that some leaders own slaves and have households do not give grounds for this assumption either. This does not mean that leaders were not wealthy, but we have no unequivocal evidence which confirms this and it is certainly not a requirement of office. The leaders are not destitute – they do have households – but we cannot say that they are wealthy either.[34]

While hard data is unfortunately not available to us, we conclude that a significant group of the addressees were wealthy, although I think this group is smaller than both Verner and Kidd imply. Further, it is not the case that the leadership of the group necessarily comes from among the wealthy.[35]

---

[32] See Kidd 1990, p107. He writes: "The images of a muzzled ox and of a laborer and his wages would not be attractive to a wealthy person, who would see wage labor as little more than slavery." He refers to Aristotle *Rhetoric* 1367a32; Cicero, *De officiis* 1.150-151.

[33] Kidd (1990, p106) notes that this mention of pay "must somehow affect the characterization of the leadership as coming exclusively from the upper echelons of municipal society." But we wish to go further than he does in denying that the leaders are necessarily wealthy. See also Malherbe 1983, p99

[34] See also Davies 1996a, p76-9. The discussion in Kidd 1990, p106-8 about how to reconcile the mention of payment in 1 Tim 5:17 with his view that leaders are wealthy is accordingly unnecessary. Kidd (1990, p84) also suggests that the way "aspiring to the office of bishop" is seen as "desiring a noble task" in 1 Tim 3:1 suggests office holders were wealthy, since the Pastor adopts language used in the Greco-Roman city of wealthier citizens who "aspired" to the "noble task" of municipal office; see also Verner 1983, p151. However, 1 Tim 5:17 seems to provide stronger evidence about the socio-economic situation of leaders, and clearly the less-well-off can aspire to office as a noble task (for example, in associations) just as the wealthy can, and perhaps in imitation of the attitudes of the wealthy. There is no necessary inference here that the leaders spoken of in 1 Tim 3:1 were wealthy then. 1 Tim 3:13 (gaining a "good standing") also need not be read as indicating deacons were wealthy. We also note that one of the qualifications looked for in an overseer was that they were hospitable (φιλόξενος; 1 Tim 3:2; Tit 1:8). This might suggest that the person had to have some financial means, but we should beware of thinking that only the rich can be hospitable and clearly poorer people can also demonstrate hospitality; see Meggitt 1998, p132-3. It is therefore not an indicator of wealth. Further, it has been argued that those who were able to host house churches in their own homes often became leaders (see for example Filson 1939, p111-12) but Malherbe 1983, p99 notes that "the Pastorals do not provide evidence that the bishops derived authority from providing hospitality to the church."

[35] Therefore I think Kidd (1990, p86) is going beyond the evidence when he suggests that "there are more than casual links between three prominent groups in this community: the leadership (1 Timothy 3:1-13; Titus 1:5-9), Christian slave owners (1 Timothy 6:2), and the rich in this world (1 Timothy 6:17-19)."

1.3 The less well off in the community: the real widows

It is also clear that at least one group in the community are among the destitute, or that they would be destitute without the assistance offered them by the community.

What the Pastor writes about widows is complex, but it is clear that the community includes women whom the Pastor calls "real widows" (τὰς ὄντως χήρας - 1 Tim 5:3, 5, 16).[36] These are women who are "all alone" (v5), and who do not have children, grandchildren (v4) or other family members (v8) who might support them. Clearly, they are in need of assistance from the church (v16). We can suggest that the death of the woman's husband has left her with insufficient financial resources to be self-supporting. Without the help of the church, they would be in dire straits. Kidd notes that "this is the only place [in the Pastorals] where truly destitute people surface in the epistles."[37]

1.4 Those who are neither wealthy nor destitute

1.4.1 Supporting family members

In 1 Tim 5:4 the Pastor instructs children and grandchildren of widows to support these women, since this is their "religious duty" (εὐσέβεια) and in this way they make some return to their parents. In 1 Tim 5:8 the author writes: "And whoever does not provide for relatives, namely for family members, has denied the faith and is worse than an unbeliever."[38] What is in view is a family supporting a widow who is part of that family.

We note the very strong terms in which the Pastor puts this injunction - failure to support a widow in one's family means one has disowned the faith and is worse than an unbeliever. This suggests that some families have been unwilling to support their own (now destitute) widows.[39] Why was this? Perhaps at least one reason was that some families were of very modest economic means and perhaps had suffered economic strain in the attempt to care for widowed relatives and had finally given up providing economic support in the hope that the (reasonably wealthy?) church would support the

---

[36] For further discussion of this passage, see Chapter 11.

[37] Kidd 1990, p103; see also Countryman 1980, p107.

[38] For this translation of καὶ μάλιστα see Marshall 1999, p590. This also means we do not have to envisage a significant difference between ἴδιοι and οἰκεῖοι. For a different interpretation see Campbell 1995, p157-60 (who thinks "οἰκεῖοι" refers to fellow Christians, but the use of "οἰκεῖοι" without qualification makes this unlikely); Mounce 2000, p285-6.

[39] See Kidd 1990, p105. The Pastor is quite clear that the "household of God" should not take over what he regarded as the role of household/family.

widows.[40] Perhaps one result was that the church was "burdened" (1 Tim 5:16). It certainly suggests that some families, while not being destitute, had very modest means and that subsistence was a struggle.

1.4.2 The slaves

Some of the addressees were slaves (1 Tim 6:1-2; Tit 2:9-10, where they are told not to pilfer). Thus, although the Pastor only addresses these groups briefly, they are clearly present in the community as well. It is impossible to generalise about the economic position of slaves, since we know of some very wealthy slaves.[41] But clearly these were the exception and we can suggest that most of the slaves addressed here were neither wealthy, nor destitute.

1.4.3 Those who want to be rich and the polemic against the love of money

In response to what he says is the view of the opponents that "godliness is a means of gain" (1 Tim 6:5), the Pastor replies that there is "great gain in godliness with contentment" (αὐτάρκεια).[42] This leads to teaching on the correct attitude to wealth, which is that those who desire to be rich fall into temptation and that the love of money is "a root of all kinds of evil" (1 Tim 6:7-10).

The level of argumentation against the love of money in 1 Tim 6:6-10 is noteworthy.[43] Clearly, the author considered that the love of wealth was a real problem among his addressees because, as he saw it, great problems stemmed from it. Although one factor here is that, as we noted in Chapter 5, the Pastor's opponents seem to have regard "godliness as a means of gain" (1 Tim 6:5; Tit 1:11), 1 Tim 6:9-10 certainly suggests that there was a significant group among the readers who could be characterised as "those who desire to be rich" and for whom, in the Pastor's view, the "love of money" was a problem. This is clearly a different group from "the wealthy" of 1 Tim 6:17-19. Verner speaks of them as "entrepreneurs, ... perhaps both free and slave, who were attempting to advance into the circle of wealthy."[44]

---

[40] See Verner 1983, p146.

[41] See González 1990, pxiv.

[42] On αὐτάρκεια see Brenk 1990, p39-51.

[43] We also note a polemic against the inappropriate use of wealth in 1 Tim 5:6 and 2 Tim 3:2. Note also the assertion of the "better way" than the "love of money" in 1 Tim 6:17-19. However, as Barrett (1963, p85, italics original) notes: "The author, it seems, is careful not to condemn those who are rich ([1 Tim 6] v. 9) or riches (v. 10). It is the desire to become rich, and the *love* of money, that lead not only to *temptations* and thus to *ruin and perdition*, but also to much unhappiness." See also Verner 1983, p174; Marshall 1990b, p90; 1993, p17.

[44] Verner 1983, p181. It is possible that some of the Pastor's opponents belong in this group. In 1 Tim 6:5, and so just before the passage which speaks of those who want to be

1.5 The Wealth of individuals and of the community, and how it was used

1.5.1 Individual possessions

We note firstly that there were clearly wealthy people who use wealth for themselves. According to the Pastor in 1 Tim 2:8, some women were using their wealth for what the Pastor regards as ostentation. Clearly also the wealthy addressed in 1 Tim 6:17-19 would retain a good deal of their wealth for their own needs – they are told to be generous, not to give the majority of their money away.[45]

1.5.2 Individual wealth used for other Christians

It is clear that some wealthy individuals used their wealth for other Christians. In 2 Tim 1:16-18 the Pastor writes of Onesiphorus: "May the Lord grant mercy to the household of Onesiphorus, because he often refreshed me (ὅτι πολλάκις με ἀνέψυξεν) and was not ashamed of my chain; when he arrived in Rome, he eagerly searched for me and found me – may the Lord grant that he will find mercy from the Lord on that day! And you know very well how much service he rendered in Ephesus (καὶ ὅσα ἐν Ἐφέσῳ διηκόνησεν)". The verb διακονέω, used of the help given by Onesiphorus, indicates service generally, and so probably indicates service of various kinds, with ὅσα indicating the number and variety of services offered by Onesiphorus.[46] He is being commended for the proper use of his material wealth - in service to others. He may well function as an exemplary benefactor from whom the readers are to learn the correct use of wealth.[47] A similar use of material possessions is in view in Titus 3:13: "Make every effort to send Zenas the lawyer and Apollos on their way, and see that they lack nothing." The readers are being asked to supply the necessities of life for other Christians in these

---

rich, the Pastor writes that the opponents imagine "that godliness is a means of gain". Further, Tit 1:11 notes that the opponents "must be silenced, since they are upsetting whole families by teaching for sordid gain what it is not right to teach". Note also what is said about people being "lovers of money ... lovers of pleasure" in 2 Tim 3:2-4, where the opponents are in view (see 2 Tim 3:5-9).

[45] Note that the attitude expressed in 1 Tim 4:4: ("for everything created by God is good, and nothing is to be rejected, provided it is received with thanksgiving") could also be seen as an encouragement that being wealthy was acceptable.

[46] See Knight 1992, p387. He suggests the "refreshment" offered in Rome may have been with food (Knight 1992, p384) and by his personal presence, but it clearly could have been broader than this.

[47] Knight (1992, p384) writes with regard to 1:16 "Paul wants Onesiphorus's family, which probably enabled Onesiphorus to provide for Paul's needs, to receive the same in return, i.e., 'mercy,' in the sense of having their own needs met."

cases.[48] In the pseudepigraphical situation in which we envisage the letters, these statements function as paradigms, demonstrating exemplary behaviour that the readers should emulate.

But we note that the author is concerned that some families in the community seem to be failing to support their widows and we have suggested some reasons as to why this might have been the case. The Pastor exhorts them in very strong terms that they must support their own widows if they are able to (see 1 Tim 5:8).

1.5.3 The community's common fund used for the community

As well as wealthy individuals using their wealth for others, it is clear that the community as a whole possessed some sort of common fund and used this fund internally for the community. Although the common fund is not spoken of in so many words, it is clear that it existed and that the community as a community had some financial responsibilities. We have evidence for this in two different areas, although undoubtedly the fund was used in other ways too.

Firstly, the community's common fund was used to support the "real widows" who were genuinely destitute. As we have noted, 1 Tim 5:3-16 gives regulations concerning widows, including those who are to be regarded as "true widows". It appears that a list was kept of these "true widows" (1 Tim 5:9), and that they were entitled to financial support by the community, as 1 Tim 5:16 shows.[49]

However, in 1 Tim 5:3-16 the Pastor is, along with other things, trying to limit the number of widows who were dependent on the church. Thus, for example, a widow with children or grandchildren is to be looked after by those family members (1 Tim 5:4, 8), believing women who "have widows" should support them (1 Tim 5:16) and a widow who is enrolled and receives support must be sixty years old (1 Tim 5:9). This suggests that there was pressure on the resources of the community, as does the mention of the need to avoid the church being burdened (βαρέω; 1 Tim 5:16). The community then seems to have had some resources, but these were clearly limited.[50]

Secondly, as we have noted, according to 1 Tim 5:17, some presbyters who "labour in preaching and teaching" received some form of payment from the community, presumably from the community fund. We also note that the lists of qualities for leaders include references to attitudes to money. Thus in 1 Tim 3:3 we read that an overseer must not be a "lover of money (ἀφιλάργυρος)" and in 1 Tim 3:8 and Tit 1:7 we read that a diakonos and a presbyter-overseer

---

[48] See Knight 1992, p358.
[49] See Dibelius and Conzelmann 1972, p71.
[50] See Barrett 1963, p77.

respectively must not be "greedy for gain (αἰσχροκερδής)". This shows the great problems the Pastor saw as stemming from the love of money, and the opponents' attitudes to money is probably an additional issue here too.[51] But that these qualities were sought for in leaders also suggests that a leader might be able to gain monetary advantage from holding office if they were a "lover of money". This implies again that the community did have some wealth.

Thus we see that the community needed to have a collective fund to support widows, who otherwise would be totally destitute, but also because the church wanted to be able to pay elders who preached and taught. Undoubtedly the fund was used in other areas too.

We do not know how the common fund was collected or distributed. Presumably contributions were voluntary.[52] But clearly the existence of the fund, which seems to have been limited (since the author exhorts families to support their own widows), but must have been of some significant size (since the community did support some widows and some elders from it), shows the importance of the richer people in the community, since presumably the poorer members would not have been able to contribute large amounts of money.

If the church was unable to support its own (otherwise destitute) widows, or was unable to pay needy leaders, then this would clearly be a blow to its sense of community, cohesion and morale. The concern about families supporting widows in 1 Tim 5 is thus a concern for the well-being of the whole community. But we also see that the rich were important with regard to the financial life of the church. In addition, we can suggest that community resources were an important enrichment of their common life which would have fostered the sense of group identity and reinforced the boundaries of the group.

1.5.4 Wealth used beyond the community

Did individuals only use their wealth within the community, and did they only give to the community's common fund? Could it be that in 1 Tim 6:18 when the rich are told "to do good, to be rich in good works, generous and ready to share" the Pastor has in mind being generous *beyond* the community, as well as within it?

We turn to the question then of who benefits from "the good works" of the rich? In some passages it is clear that "good works" are to be done within the Christian community. Thus in 1 Tim 5:16 where a believing woman who "has widows" is called on to assist them, it is clear that these widows are

---

[51] See 1 Tim 6:3-5.

[52] The arrangements Paul made for various churches to contribute to the collection may provide a parallel here; see for example 1 Cor 16:1-4. We also do not know who controlled the common fund.

Christians, since if they are not cared for by the believing woman, they become the responsibility of the church (1 Tim 5:16). This suggests the widows are themselves Christians, and that here it is a case of doing good within the Christian circle. Do we have any evidence which suggests that the rich should be generous beyond the community?

Firstly, we note the very general way the Pastor writes in 1 Tim 6:18: the rich "are to do good, to be rich in good works, generous and ready to share". There is no indication here that the author is thinking *only* of doing good to Christians. In a group which is so open to outsiders and what outsiders think (eg 1 Tim 3:7; 5:7, 14; 6:1; Tit 2:5, 9-10), and so is far from "sectarian", the most natural meaning of such language is quite general – doing good to lots of people, not just "the in-group". Thus it is noteworthy that no limitation, along the lines of the recipients of "good works" being "the saints" or something similar, is made in 1 Tim 6.[53]

Secondly, we note in what general terms the Pastor speaks of "good works" in these letters. For example, in 2 Tim 2:21 we read that people who cleanse themselves will be "ready for every good work" (εἰς πᾶν ἔργον ἀγαθὸν ἡτοιμασμένον); in 2 Tim 3:17 we read of being "equipped for every good work" and Tit 2:14 speaks of "a people of his own who are zealous for good deeds".[54] It seems unlikely that "good works", which clearly could involve helping people in material ways and so involve financial outlay, are to be limited only to "Christians". The author gives no indication of such a limitation which suggests that in these passages "good works" should be thought of in the most general possible way, and so as including outsiders.[55]

Thirdly, in fact there are indications that "good works" are to be done to and for outsiders, and hence that material possessions are being used for their benefit. Tit 3:1-5 is important in this regard.[56] Verse 1 speaks of being subject

---

[53] Hanson (1982, p114) suggests this verse is reminiscent of Rom 12:13-16. In Rom 12:13 we read "contribute (κοινωνοῦντες) to the needs of the saints", which is to be compared with the call to be "generous" (κοινωνικούς) in 1 Tim 6:18. Further in Rom 12:16 we read "do not be haughty (μὴ τὰ ὑψηλὰ φρονοῦντες)" whereas in 1 Tim 6:17 the rich are commanded "not to be haughty (μὴ ὑψηλοφρονεῖν)". Thus Hanson suggests "it is quite possible that the author had the Romans passage in mind", which seems plausible. But, if this is the case, it is particularly noteworthy that the Pastor does not limit the generosity to "the saints" in 1 Tim 6:18, as Romans 12:13 does. Even if the Pastor is not recalling Rom 12:13-16 here, as we state in the text it is significant that no limitation to "the saints" or something similar is made in 1 Tim 6.

[54] See also the emphasis on "good works" in 1 Tim 2:10; 3:1; 5:10, 25; Tit1:16; 2:7; 3:1, 8, 14; see also Marshall 1999, p227-9.

[55] See also the discussion of 1 Tim 5:10 below; note also 2 Tim 2:24 "And the Lord's servant must not be quarrelsome but kindly to everyone …"

[56] Even though Tit is addressed to Crete, there seems to be no difference between 1 and 2 Tim and Tit with regard to "good works" and so it can be used to illuminate the situation with regard to the rich and good works in Ephesus.

and obedient to rulers and authorities. The author then speaks of being "ready for every good work" and goes on to instruct readers "to speak evil of no one … to show every courtesy to all people (πᾶσαν ἐνδεικνυμένους πραΰτητα πρὸς πάντας ἀνθρώπους)". That non-Christians are particularly in view when the Pastor speaks of "πάντας ἀνθρώπους" is shown by the fact that the author goes on to speak of the readers' pre-Christian lives. Why should they "show every courtesy to all people"? Because "we ourselves were *once* foolish, disobedient, led astray …" (v3) and so should understand the pre-Christian life, and hence behave in appropriate ways in society (v1-2), since that was the life the readers once lived. Clearly then the passage concerns Christians' relationships with rulers and with the wider society in general.[57]

In this context what does the author mean in v1 by "being ready for every good work"? The reference is clearly very general. Since it is preceded by instruction to be obedient to rulers, and followed by instructions about attitudes to non-Christians ("to speak evil of no one"),[58] showing "all" gentleness to "all people", (clearly including non-Christians), it must include "good work" "in society" and thus to people in general, as well as "good work" for other Christians. As Kelly comments, the author means that "Christians should be to the fore, as far as possible, in showing public spirit in their district."[59] The Pastor returns to emphasize this at the end of the passage in v8, where he states: "I desire that you insist on these things, so that those who have come to believe in God may be careful to devote themselves to good works; these things are excellent and profitable to everyone (τοῖς ἀνθρώποις)", where "τοῖς ἀνθρώποις" clearly includes non-Christians.[60] Again then we can suggest that the phrase "good works" includes works for non-Christians.

Fourthly, just before giving the final greetings in the letter, the author returns to this theme in Titus 3:14 where we read: "And let our people learn to

---

[57] See Brox 1969, p304; Knight 1992, p334.

[58] Knight notes (1992, p333) "the indefiniteness and breadth of the word μηδένα 'no one'."

[59] Kelly 1963, p249; see also Brox 1969, p303. Knight 1992, p333 notes with that the phrase "to be ready for every good deed" "could be a request for readiness to perform good deeds in society in general or could refer to a readiness to do so in relation to government in particular. The general form of the statement would incline one to regard it as relating to society in general, but its position immediately after the demand to obey authorities suggests that it goes with this demand and explains what such obedience entails." He goes on to note that "doing good" is not restricted to that which relates directly to government, but seems to involves "doing good" in the larger context.

[60] Knight (1992, p352) notes that "profitable to everyone" refers "especially to the benefit that 'good deeds' have for 'people,' i.e., non-Christians, ἀνθρώποις here picking up the previous use of the word in v. 2, where non-Christians are primarily in view".

devote themselves to good works in order to meet urgent needs,[61] so that they may not be unproductive". In this context, such general exhortation clearly picks up the theme of Titus 3:1-8 – that is, of doing "good works"; as in 3:1-8, it seems likely that in 3:14 "good works" includes actions beyond the Christian sphere. Thus in Tit 3:14 we can suggest this involves "good works" when unbelievers are in "urgent need", as well as assisting needy Christians, including travelling Christian missionaries.[62] Thus Hanson comments that in 3:14: "the author may be urging the Christians to take part in relief work in the community at large."[63] But perhaps nothing quite so large-scale is envisaged. The verse could simply mean that Christians are to assist non-Christian neighbours when they are in need. Certainly, given the link with Tit 3:1-2, which has such a strong "society-facing" dimension to it, it seems unlikely that we should limit the "urgent need" to which the readers are to respond to the needs of Christians.

This suggests that when the author calls for "good works" in Tit 3:14 he includes in this phrase, "good deeds" done to and for outsiders, which clearly may have financial implications. Again then, this suggest that the general call in 1 Tim 6:18 for the wealthy to be rich in good deeds has in view using their material possessions both within and beyond the community of faith.

Finally, at times, there is a contextual connection between "good deeds" and the opinion of outsiders, which suggests that the "good deeds" may be done to or for outsiders. For example, in Tit 2:7-8 we read: "Show yourself in all respects a model of *good works*, and in your teaching show integrity, gravity, and sound speech that cannot be censured; then *any opponent* (ὁ ἐξ ἐναντίας) will be put to shame, having nothing evil to say of us."[64] It is unclear who the Pastor has in mind in writing of "ὁ ἐξ ἐναντίας". But given that the Pastor is concerned about the opinion of outsiders in Tit 2:5 and 10 and that the word of God may not be discredited (Tit 2:5), but rather that the behaviour of Christians might enhance their teaching (Tit 2:10), it seems likely that outsiders are included among "opponents" here, even if the Pastor has the teachers who oppose him in mind as well.[65] Clearly here, being a

---

[61] χρεία in the plural refers to things like food and clothes, which are needed for daily life. Εἰς τὰς ἀναγκαίας χρείας, literally "for the necessary need", could mean that "Christians ought to be urged to work, so as to be able to supply their own daily needs"; see Hanson 1982, p197. But he notes the translation given above is more likely; see also Marshall 1999, p345-6.

[62] In the immediate context, the "good deed" in view is assisting Zenas and Apollos (v13). But, given the link with verses 1 and 8, which are clearly echoed here, it seems most likely that the general exhortation of v14 also covers doing "good deeds" to non-Christians.

[63] Hanson 1982, p197; see also Spicq 1969a, p693f.

[64] Note also the concern for opinion of outsiders in Tit 2:5, 10.

[65] See Mounce 2000, p414, who argues that both outsiders and the author's Christian opponents are meant.

"model of good works" is regarded as important (as is teaching) so that outsiders (and Christian opponents) will see the group positively. But how will "showing himself a model of good deeds" mean that outside opponents will have nothing evil to say of the group? It could simply mean that the deeds are done to other Christians ("see how they love each other"), but it would be clearest if some of the good deeds which the Pastor advocates are done to outsiders. The hoped-for result of such actions would be that outsiders would see the group positively.[66]

All of this suggests that at least some of the actions via which the wealthy are "to be rich in good deeds" (1 Tim 6:18) are to be done by the rich for outsiders.[67] Further, some of the passages we have discussed about "good works" have financial implications in themselves. Thus, when in Tit 3:14 the readers are urged "to meet urgent needs", this clearly would involve money in some cases, and we have suggested the verse means both insiders and outsiders are to be assisted. Tit 3:1 has similar implications. So it seems likely that some of the "good deeds" that the general members of the community are exhorted to do, which at times may well have financial implications, are for outsiders too.[68]

But are the rich among the readers already using their money for the benefit of outsiders? Two points suggest this. Firstly, 1 Tim 6:17-19 comes after 1 Tim 6:6-16 which concerns the danger of wanting to be rich and the love of money, and then goes on to positive teaching (v11-16). It seems clear from this section that the danger of wanting to be rich is seen by the author as a real problem among the opponents whom he accuses of thinking that godliness can be a source of wealth (v9-10). By contrast, the instruction to the wealthy in v17-19 is comparatively brief, with only v18 giving actual concrete directions. From this Roloff concludes that this is already familiar

---

[66] Although Knight (1992, p313) does not consider the issue of whether any of the good works are done to outsiders, his comment is in keeping with the view put forward here. He notes re 2:8b "The ἵνα clause reminds Titus that his life must be lived purposefully, so that what he does is not only intrinsically good and in accord with the 'sound teaching' (v. 1), but also *so that it has effect for good*, with reference to the gospel, *on those who observe him, especially those seeking an occasion to fault Christianity*. Titus's conduct should not give any grounds for Christians to be accused of evil." (emphasis added). Clearly this applies most fully if the good works are done to "outsiders".

[67] This is also in accord with the emphasis in the Pastorals on the salvation of all, on which see Towner 1989, p75-119.

[68] Contrast Countryman (1980, p154, his italics) who thinks that in 1 Tim 6:17-19 the author "concentrates on telling the rich Christians what their *proper* role is—to support the church generously." But he does not give reasons for his view that their generosity is to be limited to giving within the community.

teaching which here is being summarised.[69] Given that there are a number of wealthy people among the readers, if this was entirely new teaching which instructed them to make a significant change from current behaviour, then we would expect more detail. Further, the teaching given has similarities to Luke 12:16-21; 16:1-14 and so we can suggest it was known to the readers from tradition.[70] These points suggest (though they do no more than this) that this passage serves as a reminder to the rich, and to some extent they were already doing what the Pastor here instructs.

Secondly, we note what is said about the widows in 1 Tim 5:10. There we read that a widow who is enrolled must "be well attested for her good works, as one who has brought up children, shown hospitality, washed the saints' feet, helped the afflicted, and devoted herself to doing good in every way (εἰ παντὶ ἔργῳ ἀγαθῷ ἐπηκολούθησεν)." "Washed the saints' feet" involves doing literally that, but probably also indicates willingness to serve "the saints" (ie. other Christians) in humble ways. This suggests that by the phrase "helped the afflicted" the author could well include the non-Christian afflicted. Certainly, the final very general statement – "and devoted herself to doing good in every way", coming as it does after several references to "good works" to Christians ("shown hospitality, washed the saints' feet"), is best seen as a reference to good works which are not limited in any way, and so include helping "outsiders".

The important matter for us at this point is that the author is describing the widow's past life. The Pastor envisages that a widow's "good works" have included activities beyond the group, and it seems that some use of financial resources could at times have been involved, since hospitality and "helping the afflicted" could at times include money. Hanson implies this, when he says with regard to the phrase "well attested for her good deeds": "presumably these good deeds will have been performed in the days of her prosperity while her husband was still alive."[71]

Clearly then, the author assumes that widows who are to be enrolled have used their financial resources, however meagre they may have been, for outsiders. This suggests that this sort of outward-looking generosity may have been customary in the community. Although we cannot argue more strongly than this, it does suggest that the rich had in the past used some of their

---

[69] Roloff (1988, p366) notes: "im Grunde bleibt es bei einem stichwortartigen Gerüst von Paränese, dessen Hauptfunktion sein dürfte, an ausgeführte, den Gemeinden bereits bekannte paränetische Tradition zu erinnern, die hier bloß in Abbreviatur erscheinen."

[70] See Roloff 1988, p366-7; Marshall 1999, p669.

[71] Hanson 1982, p98. But note that we should not think of such widows as necessarily wealthy in the past; they may simply have provided what they could with what little they had. Marshall (1999, p597) also notes "The reference is very broad, to whatever kind of good works the widow could find to do."

material possessions for outsiders and that others in the community (including some women who were now widowed) did too.

What this means is that wealth is not simply being used within the community, but also outside the community as well.[72] We have noted in the previous section that the community had a common fund and that its use would have fostered the sense of group identity and reinforced the boundaries of the group. But we see now that material possessions are not being used only to reinforce the boundary definition of the group – we give our money to ourselves, but not to outsiders. Rather material possessions were probably being used for the benefit of outsiders too. This would have the opposite effect of opening the community to outsiders and so of countering internal boundaries. Material possessions are being used in both ways then.[73]

1.5.5 Wealth and the selection of leaders

We have noted that we cannot say that leaders were necessarily wealthy. However, it is interesting that being "greedy for gain" or having a "love of money" was *not* acceptable for leaders.[74] So the desire for wealth, avariciousness, was used to discount potential leaders. Thus wealth – in this case the *lack* of desire for it - is being used as a criterion for selection of leaders. Whether the potential leaders are wealthy or not, they must not see leadership as a route to monetary gain. So wealth has a connection with leadership, but not the connection that is often suggested.[75]

1.6 Conclusions

It is clear that there was significant stratification with regard to wealth among the addressees of the Pastorals.[76] Thus, as we have seen there are some rich

---

[72] This is not to suggest that all that Christians do for outsiders will be well received. We recall the emphasis on suffering in 2 Tim (eg 2 Tim 1:8; 2:3, 9-10), which clearly suggests some relations with outsiders were problematic.

[73] In view of what we have said it seems likely that in 1 Tim 5:4 ("If a widow has children or grandchildren, they should first learn their religious duty to their own family and make some repayment to their parents ...") the Pastor would also be thinking of Christian children supporting their non-Christian mothers if the latter were widows. In this way too, members of the community would be supporting non-Christians, but since they would be family members this is clearly a different sort of case from 1 Tim 6:18.

[74] See 1 Tim 3:8; Tit 1:7; 1 Tim 3:3.

[75] See for example Verner 1983, p159, who thinks "The assumption in the Pastorals is that the official leaders came from among the well-to-do householders of the church". See also Maier 1991, p38, 45-7. In the background here with regard to not being greedy for gain becoming a criteria for leadership are the Pastor's opponents, who are accused precisely of this matter (see 1 Tim 6:3-5). The leaders of the community must not show this characteristic, which in the opinion of the Pastor has led his opponents into such dire straits.

[76] See also Marshall 1990b, p89; Taylor 1993, p72-3; Kidd 1990, p112.

Christians, a few potentially destitute people, and some who are in between. We can also note that, although there is stratification in the community with regard to wealth, the rich are not said to be the leaders, nor is wealth a criteria for leadership – in fact the lack of desire for wealth is a criterion for leadership. Nor are the wealthy, who are addressed in 1 Tim 6:17-19, told to seek positions of leadership. The rich are not equated with leaders and the poor with those who are led.

Further we note that the community had a communal fund, which was used for the support of widows and of elders. This would have had the effect of increasing the solidarity of the group, since via its money the community could make a real difference for some of its members. If it had been unable to support widows in particular (a situation which the author was concerned about) then this would have been an embarrassment for the group and would have undermined its self-confidence. Wealth functioned positively in the group therefore to enhance the sense of belonging and of group identity and reinforced the boundaries of the group.

But we have also argued that when the Pastor instructed the wealthy to do "good works", this would have included financial help for people *outside* the group. We have argued that to some extent this was already happening within the group. This would have had the effect of opening the group to the interests and needs of those outside itself. So while the communal fund enhanced the group's solidarity, wealth was not only used simply to reinforce group boundaries. In some ways wealth reinforced the boundaries of the group, in other ways its use countered internal boundaries by opening the group up to the needs of outsiders. We see wealth being used in various ways therefore.

2. Material possessions and the Johannine Letters

2.1 Material possessions in 1 John

2.1.1 1 Jn 3:16-18: The brother and sister in need and group boundary reinforcement

In 1 Jn 3:16-18 we have the exhortation to love given in this way:

"We know love by this, that he laid down his life for us – and we ought to lay down our lives for one another. How does God's love abide in anyone who has the world's goods (τὸν βίον τοῦ κόσμου)[77] and sees a brother or sister in need (θεωρῇ τὸν ἀδελφὸν αὐτοῦ χρείαν

---

[77] Schnackenburg (1992, p122) notes βίος here means "income, property or wealth"; Brown (1982, p449) defines it as "livelihood, material life".

ἔχοντα) and yet refuses help? Little children, let us love, not in word or speech, but in truth and action."

In 1 Jn 3:11-15 John has discussed love of the community and the negative example of Cain, who murdered his brother; in 3:16 he turns to the positive example of Christ who laid down his life for "us". This leads to the exhortation that Christians should "lay down their lives for their brothers and sisters" (1 Jn 3:16c). Having received life in an act of love, this life must be expressed in love for one another.[78] For the author, this is part of "doing the truth" (see 1 Jn 1:6; cf. 2 Jn 4; 3 Jn 3, 4; Jn 3:21). To show the reality of love by loving "ὁ ἀδελφός" is to be confident and assured before God (1 Jn 3:18-23).[79]

In 1 Jn 3:16-17 John relates "laying down one's life" to sharing one's material possessions. This could be an "*a maiore ad minus* argument: If one is obliged to give up one's life for one's brother, one is obliged to the lesser gift of the means of livelihood."[80] However, Brown thinks this may not be in the author's mind: "If he equates the secessionists with the Antichrist and hatred with murder, he may *equate* giving one's livelihood with laying down one's life."[81] So John may have historicized apocalyptic ideals here. But in any case, he clearly sees the crucial need for the readers to have compassion on "brothers and sisters" in need.[82] This is not a new moral demand, but is based on the author's Jewish heritage.[83] But John expresses this demand in his own way in 3:17c when he criticises the person who "closes his heart against" the brother or sister in need.[84]

---

[78] See 1 Jn 3:23; 4:7, 11, 20; cf Jn 3:16; 15:12-13; 17:26; see also Hengel 1974, p69. That the readers are said in 3:17a to have received love suggests that "ἡ ἀγάπη τοῦ θεοῦ" in 3:17 is a subjective genitive, and refers to God's love; see Brown 1982, p475; cf. Sandnes 1994, p114-15; see also 1 Jn 4:7.

[79] See Wheeler 1995, p113.

[80] Brown 1982, p474.

[81] Brown 1982, p474. His emphasis.

[82] Brown 1982, p450 notes: "The author is envisioning a situation where a person not only does not help his brother in need, but actually shuts off a feeling of compassion that the needy would instinctively arouse." Such a person is blocking God's love, "which would lead him to treat his brother as Christ treated us, so divine love does not function in such a person." For the appeal to love of brothers and sisters as a motive for almsgiving, see also 1 Thess 4:9-10; Rom 12:10-13; 2 Clem 4:1-3; Hengel 1974, p68.

[83] See Dt 15:7; CD 14:14-16; Mk 10:21; Lk 10:25-37; James 2:15-16; IgnSm 6:2.

[84] Brown (1982, p475) thinks the secessionists are behind this issue. He writes of this criticism against someone who sees a brother or sister in need and does nothing: "This insistence [against someone who has no compassion] makes sense if the secession has created a problem of need so urgent that the author may well think it reflects the last hour. The passage raises the *possibility* that the members of the Johannine Community with 'enough of this world's livelihood' (3:17a) had joined the secession, leaving the author's adherents in dire need." But we have questioned the approach which sees the secessionists behind such

In this passage John presupposes that there are (at least) two types of people in the community – those who "have need" and those who have enough of this world's possessions to be of real assistance to those who are in need, although this does not mean those who are able to assist the needy were necessarily wealthy.[85]

But the crucial thing here is that the recipient of assistance is said to be "the brother". Who is ὁ ἀδελφός? We will seek to show that in these Letters the term refers to a member of the group addressed, the Johannine community, rather than to Christians in general, or to outsiders.[86] We note for example 1 Jn 3:10-11:

"The children of God and the children of the devil are revealed in this way:
all who do not do what is right are not from God, nor *the one who does not love his brother or sister* (ὁ μὴ ἀγαπῶν τὸν ἀδελφὸν αὐτοῦ).
For this is the message you have heard from the beginning, *that we should love one another* (ἵνα ἀγαπῶμεν ἀλλήλους)."

Here, "to love his brother or sister" and "to love one another" are clearly in parallel, showing that "ἀδελφός" and "ἀλλήλους" – ie. the community members, are equivalent.[87] Thus we can agree with Brown when he calls "ἀδελφός", "a term of inner-Johannine affection",[88] which refers to fellow

---

phrases. Particularly significant is the point that 1 Jn 3:17 speaks of a person "seeing a brother or sister in need". The author makes it clear that neither the community addressed in 1 Jn nor the secessionists saw the other group as a "brother" any longer, since the secessionists had "gone out from us" and by this fact had shown that they were never a part of us (1 Jn 2:19). Hence, it is unlikely that the author has the secessionists and their material possessions (and their implied unwillingness to share these with the author's community) in mind in 3:17. It is much more likely that 3:17 is paraenesis to the community, dealing with some practicalities of real love within the community.

[85] See Blomberg 1999, p234-5. The phrase χρείαν ἔχοντα is used in Mk 2:25; Acts 2:45; 4:35; Eph 4:28, but clearly does not provide any details about the extent of the need. In 1 Jn 2:17 the phrase contrasts with "anyone who has the world's goods". Rensberger (1999, p134) notes: "The gospel [of John] does not, for instance, speak of renouncing one's possessions in order to sustain one's brothers and sisters, although something like this is found in 1 John 3:16-17." However, Countryman (1999, p391 n4) leans towards the view that the passage speaks of a sharing of abundance rather than "a radical divestment of worldly goods".

[86] See Brown 1982, p450; Meeks 1993, p61; Gundry 2002, p105-6. ἀδελφός is used 16 times in 1 Jn; see 1 Jn 2:9, 10, 11; 3:10, 13, 14, 15, 16, 17; 4:20 (x2), 21; 5:16; 3 Jn 3, 5, 10. In all these cases it seems most likely that it refers to community members. The term is used twice in 1 Jn 3:12 to refer to Cain murdering his brother Abel.

[87] See Brown 1982, p441. For the command to "love one another" (ἀλλήλους) see 1 Jn 3:23; 4:7, 11, 12, and for "loving the brother" see for example 1 Jn 4:20-21.

[88] See Brown 1982, p270 and on the term see p269-73. Lieu (1981, p227) notes "love is restricted within the community thus preserving the strong, exclusive community-sense." See also Strecker 1996, p107. For a similar, but slightly different attitude see from Qumran 1QS 1:3-4, 9-10; CD 2:15; 6:20-21; 1 QH 14:9-11.

Johannine community members, either male or female.[89] So ἀδελφός is not used for non-Christians, nor, we may suggest, for other Christians who belong to different groups.[90] It is particularly not to be used of the secessionists, since they "have gone out from us" but in any case they "were not of us" (1 Jn 2:19). Rather it is used for "those who belong" to our group.

We thus see that by restricting who one is to help to "ὁ ἀδελφός", giving is "in-house". For the author, failure to do this was significant, for it was not loving the brother or sister whom they have seen; failure to do this raised the question of how such a person can love God whom they have not seen (1 Jn 4:20). Thus material resources ("the world's goods") are to be used for "the brother or sister in my group". In this way, the boundary of the group is reinforced and maintained.

But what did the readers currently do? Were they loving one another? And were they doing so "in truth and action" by sharing possessions with brothers and sisters in need?

Here we need to consider the form of Johannine rhetoric. Does the command to "love one another" mean that the readers were not currently doing so at all? This seems unlikely. That at least to some extent they are currently "loving one another" is suggested by 1 Jn 3:13-14: "Do not be astonished, brothers and sisters, that the world hates you. We know that we have passed from death to life because we love one another. Whoever does not love abides in death." In contrast to the hatred the community experiences from outsiders, from "the world", the love they have for one another is real and assures them that they have life in the present. That loving one another is one of the "Tests of Life" that the readers are encouraged to use to gain assurance about salvation in the present suggests that they are currently "loving one another" in some significant ways.[91] However, John's call to

---

[89] We note then that the primary concern is love for the insider. It is because ἀδελφός has this meaning of insider that the author regards hating "one's brother" as a contradiction to the light (1 Jn 2:9b, 11a); see Brown 1982, p273. The usage in 3 Jn 5 is also particularly interesting: "Beloved, you do faithfully whatever you do for the *brothers and sisters*, even though they are strangers to you; they have testified to your love before the church. You will do well to send them on in a manner worthy of God." These "brothers" are unknown to the readers. They are only "brothers" because of the faith they share and because they belong to the same movement. Clearly, even if the "brother" did not belong to one's own immediate group, ἀδελφός could be used because they belong to the same wider group. Rather they were a "brother", not because of personal knowledge, but because of mutual belonging to this wider group.' Ἀδελφός then, is here a designation of members of the wider Johannine community, rather than just immediate and local group members.

[90] See Chapter 12 for further discussion relating to this.

[91] We find a similar "test", which also suggests the readers are currently loving one another in 1 Jn 4:7b-8: "Everyone who loves is born of God and knows God. Whoever does not love does not know God, for God is love." Note also 1 Jn 4:19: "We love, because he first loved us." See also 1 Jn 5:2.

"love one another" in a number of passages (eg. 1 Jn 4:7-12; 16-21) suggests that, in his view, this is certainly an area where the community could improve.[92]

What is said in 2 Jn 4-5 reinforces this conclusion. There we read: "I was overjoyed to find some of your children walking in the truth, just as we have been commanded by the Father. But now, dear lady, I ask you, not as though I were writing you a new commandment, but one we have had from the beginning, let us love one another." Here the elder begins by saying some of the readers are "walking in the truth". This means much more than that they are believing the right things. It also involves "walking", that is living out the faith as the Johannine community understands this.[93] Given that the commandment they have had from the beginning is that they "love one another" (2 Jn 5; see also 1 Jn 2:7-11), we can suggest that "walking in the truth" involves love for the brothers and sisters to at least some extent. But the elder goes on to encourage them to love one another more. Clearly, in the author's opinion they are currently faithful, and loving, but they could always do more in this area. This is what he means by saying in 2 Jn 5 that this is not a new commandment. They know it, and obey it – but they can always improve.

So we can suggest that the readers are currently "loving one another". But are they "loving one another" by sharing material possessions with those "brothers and sisters" who are in need? It could be again that some of the community are doing this, but that John sees this as an area in which they could improve, or it could be that they have not seen "loving one another" as involving the practical dimension of sharing "the world's goods".

3 Jn 5-6 is helpful here. There we read: "Beloved you do faithfully whatever you do for the brothers and sisters (τοὺς ἀδελφούς), even though they are strangers to you; they have testified to your love (οἱ ἐμαρτύρησάν σου τῇ ἀγάπῃ) before the church." We will discuss this passage in more detail below. But here we can note that the "brothers and sisters" are Johannine Christians from the elder's group or house church who have visited Gaius' house church. Although they are "strangers to you" and thus personally unknown to Gaius' house church, they have clearly supported them

---

[92] Brown (1982, p762-3) sees secessionists in view here; for example in 1 Jn 4:20 the secessionists are saying "I love God", but do not love the author's community. However, in Chapter 6 we have argued that we should not see the secessionists as in view in such statements. Further 1 Jn 3:18-19 is explicitly addressed to the community: "Little children let *us* love … And by this *we* will know …" But perhaps the departure of the secessionists has led to the community loving one another less because of suspicion, or simply because of the trauma of schism.

[93] See Brown 1982, p661-2.

in material ways with hospitality. Significantly, the elder describes this as showing love.[94]

We can tentatively suggest then that within the wider Johannine community that we see in 1 –3 Jn, it had become customary to "love one another" in practical ways. This is the case in 3 Jn 5-6. We can suggest then that 1 Jn 3:17-18 should not be read as meaning that currently no one was sharing the world's goods with needy community members. Rather, although this was already being done to some extent, John calls for greater attention to this area. Certainly there is no evidence that they are sharing material possessions beyond the community. The problem is not over-generosity with outsiders, but that generosity towards insiders could be improved.

2.1.2 1 Jn 2:15: Detachment from possessions

Before we leave 1 Jn, we need to discuss 1 Jn 2:15-17: "Do not love the world or the things in the world. The love of the Father is not in those who love the world; for all that is in the world – the desire of the flesh, the desire of the eyes, the pride in riches – comes not from the Father but from the world. And the world and its desire are passing away, but those who do the will of God live for ever."

Here the antithesis between the Father and "the world" is fundamental to the passage with the author drawing a sharp distinction between the Father and those who love the Father and are of the Father and "the world", with the latter clearly including wealth or riches. Brown reads this passage in accordance with Johannine dualism between what is above and what is below and as a description of "a world into which the light of God's son has not yet penetrated".[95] Thus, "the flesh" would refer to "human nature incapable of attaining to God unless it is re-created by His Spirit",[96] "the desires of the eyes" means seeing only the visible and missing what is invisible and pertains to the light of God, and "life" would be biological life, which is distinct from eternal life. Hence "'the pride of life' is contentment with material life and not reaching out for God's own life."[97] So the verse is a description of life outside the life of the community of faith, a life characterised by "an absence of the otherworldly".[98] However, as Lieu notes, this reading "pays insufficient attention to the use of 'desire' and 'pride', while 'flesh' is not opposed to

---

[94] Note also that in 3 Jn 4 the readers are also said to be "walking in the truth".

[95] Brown 1982, p312.

[96] Brown 1982, p326.

[97] Brown 1982, p326.

[98] Brown 1982, p326.

spirit in this Epistle – it otherwise occurs only at 4:2 – and in its remaining use 'life' means wealth (3:17)."[99]

A different interpretation notes that "desire" is used in a negative sense in the OT (Num 11:4; Ps 106:14) and in the NT is used of the pre-Christian way of life (Gal 5:16; Eph 2:3). So "desire of the flesh" probably refers to sinful tendencies, a sense found in Paul (Gal 5:19) and one which is close to Jn 8:15. The "desire of the eyes" perhaps refers to greed or lust and "pride in riches" "is best taken to refer to arrogance and rash confidence concerning worldly goods".[100] The passage is somewhat unspecific because the author wishes to stress that the world is full of evil desires, rather than to give a list specifying them in detail. But it is clear that "flesh", "eyes" and "riches" are not wrong in themselves. Rather, "they become evil and objectionable only when they excite evil impulses in human beings."[101] The passage then calls for the readers not to "love" these things and so not to desire sinful tendencies and sensory pleasures, and not to have confidence in worldly goods. The basis for this is that "all that is in the world .... is not of the Father (οὐκ ἔστιν ἐκ τοῦ πατρός)..." (2:16). Hence the members of the community are exhorted not to love the material world, but rather to exhibit a real inner detachment from material possessions as well as to shun the values of the world.[102] It is this sort of detachment that would lead those who have "the world's goods (τὸν βίον τοῦ κόσμου)" (3:17) to be able to give to "a brother or sister in need". But we cannot say that the readers are currently attached to possessions.

We conclude then that in 1 John the author calls for material resources to be used for "the brother or sister in my group". Currently the readers are probably doing this to some extent, but, as with all dimensions of "loving one another", they are called to do so more. But most significantly, material resources are being used within the group and so the boundary of the group is reinforced and maintained through their use.

2.2 Material possessions in 2-3 John: Hospitality and group boundary definition

In this section I will seek to show that in 2 and 3 John we see the use of hospitality as a tool in boundary establishment and in disputes about group boundaries. Thus material resources, required in hospitality, are being used by the author and by some of the readers in the service of group definition.

---

[99] Lieu 1991, p54.

[100] Houlden 1973, p74.

[101] Schnackenburg 1992, p121. Countryman (1980, p70) writes that v15-17 is "a warning directed not against material things as such, but rather against one's attachment to these things. ... Thus it is not the object of lust, but the lust itself that is sinful."

[102] See Schnackenburg 1992, p126; Lieu 1991, p57.

Hospitality was very significant within early Christianity. Travelling teachers were dependent on the hospitality of other Christians, since there was a real lack of adequate accommodation for travellers. Indeed, 3 Jn 5-7 indicates that the hospitality offered to travelling teachers by Gaius was essential for their very survival. A range of texts show that hospitality was a regular feature of early Christian life and was particularly significant for travelling teachers and prophets.[103] Hospitality was also a form of fellowship and acceptance. Here we recall the significance of table fellowship in the Jewish world of the NT and in the NT itself. By eating with someone, and also by sharing your home with them, you were creating a bond of fellowship and acceptance.[104]

2.2.1 2 John 10-11: Do not offer hospitality

Both 2 and 3 John are concerned with travelling teachers and their acceptance or rejection.[105] In 2 John 10-11 we read:

"Do not receive into the house or welcome anyone who comes to you and does not bring this teaching; for to welcome is to participate in the evil deeds of such a person."

The elder envisages people who come with a different "teaching of Christ (τῇ διδαχῇ τοῦ Χριστοῦ)" (2 John 9). As we have noted in Chapter 6, 2 John does not suggest that there has been an outbreak of "false teaching" among those addressed. Rather the elder writes to a house church which is some distance from him, with instructions about how to deal with anticipated visitors who are suspected of "going beyond" the teaching of Christ (v9) of which the elder approves. Evidently, the author thinks the opponents' teaching is an innovation. These opponents are not "walking in the truth" (v4) but rather, as deceivers, are leading people astray (v7). The elder warns that such opponents who propagate this different Christology should not be received, or even welcomed. By contrast, the elder calls on the readers to hold on to what they have heard "from the beginning" (2 Jn 5-6), which 2 Jn 7 shows concerns the teaching about Jesus Christ "coming in flesh."[106]

In 2 Jn 10-11, the elder uses two key phrases with regard to the person who brings a different doctrine. Firstly, "Do not receive him into the house (μὴ

---

[103] See Rom12:13; Phlm 22; 1 Tim 3:2; 5:10, Tit 1:8; Heb 13:2; 1 Pet 4:9; Didache 11-13; 1 Clem 1:2; 10:7; 11:1; 12:1.3; 35:5; Hermas Sim 9.27.2; Mand. 8.10.

[104] On Hospitality see Malherbe 1983, p65-70, 92-112; Koenig 1985; Sandnes 1994, p147-8; Osiek and Balch 1997, p206-14.

[105] Note that testing travelling teachers in connection with Ephesus is also spoken of in Rev 2.2 where they are called "apostles". But it is very unlikely that there is any connection between the two passages.

[106] Rensberger 1997, p154-5.

λαμβάνετε αὐτὸν εἰς οἰκίαν)". This is probably a reference both to private hospitality and to being received into the house where a house church met.[107] Thus, they are not to receive any material support for the present or the future, nor are they to be granted a hearing. Secondly, "(do not) give him any greeting (χαίρειν αὐτῷ μὴ λέγετε); for to welcome is to participate in the evil deeds of such a person." Envisaged here is the normal greeting to any stranger. Clearly for the author, any form of co-operation with the those who go beyond "the teaching of Christ" has dire consequences. Even to greet or welcome such a person is to participate in their evil, which seems to threaten one's reward (v8). As Lieu notes, for the elder, "Heretical teaching is so insidious and lethal a danger that total avoidance is the only solution, as it was also for Ignatius".[108]

The situation then is that the elder is telling the readers "not to offer the hospitality and base of operations usually afforded such travelers, if they do not bring the appropriate Christology."[109] Clearly, material possessions, used in hospitality, are not to be used for those who "do not bring this teaching". Rather, 2 Jn suggests that material possessions are only to be used for the benefit of those whose held an approved theology.[110] The use or non-use of material possessions has been caught up in the issue of defining the group: there are some people – those "beyond the pale" for the group - on whom one will not spend one's resources. Material possessions have become a way of constructing boundaries.

2.2.2 3 John: The actions of Gaius and Demetrius

We turn now to 3 John. Firstly, we note that the Elder praises Gaius for his hospitality in 3 Jn 5-8:

"Beloved you do faithfully whatever you do for the brothers and sisters (εἰς τοὺς ἀδελφούς), even though they are strangers to you; they have testified to your love before the church. You will do well to send them on in a manner worthy of God; for they began their journey for the sake of the name, accepting no support from non-believers. Therefore we ought to support such people, so that we may become co-workers with the truth."

Although v5 is somewhat indefinite with regard to exactly how Gaius has shown love, the addition of "even though they are strangers to you", the request to "send them on" and noting that "they began their journey for the sake of the name" (v7) indicate that what Gaius has done for the brothers and

---

[107] Lieu 1986, p97 notes "the two are not mutually exclusive".

[108] Lieu 1986, p97; see IgnSm 4.1; 7.2.

[109] Rensberger 1997, p26.

[110] 2 Jn does not make it entirely clear exactly who would make the assessment of which theology was "approved".

sisters is to provide hospitality. Even though the travelling brothers and sisters were unknown to Gaius, he showed them love (v6) by welcoming them and providing essential hospitality because they were fellow Christians. The elder also hopes that Gaius will continue to provide hospitality on a subsequent visit, and so Gaius is now requested to "send them [the brothers and sisters] on in a manner worthy of God" (v6b).[111] Support of these and other brothers and sisters will mean that Gaius and those like him will become "co-workers with the truth" (v8).[112]

Again, then hospitality is a key matter. Gaius has provided hospitality for travelling missionaries and is being urged to provide hospitality again. It is not stated, but in view of what follows in 3 Jn 9-10, it is clear that from both the elders' and Gaius' perspective, these travellers preached "the doctrine of Christ" (2 Jn 9). Again then, hospitality has a part in group identity, in this case as part of the definition and clarification of group boundaries. Those who are within the group, even if they are personally unknown, are offered hospitality; we have seen from 2 Jn 10-11 that those who are excluded from the group are denied such hospitality.

We note that Gaius clearly had the material resources to show hospitality to the brothers and sisters and to do so again (3 Jn 5-8). Although he may not have been wealthy, he is not destitute either. The phrase in v6 "You will do well to send them on their journey as befits God's service (οὓς καλῶς ποιήσεις προπέμψας ἀξίως τοῦ θεοῦ)" is interesting in this regard. To "send them on" means to give them concrete assistance, including hospitality.[113] This reinforces that Gaius has some financial means at his disposal.

Hospitality features again in 3 John 9-10, but this time the elder clearly disapproves of what has happened. We learn that the otherwise unknown Diotrephes has done exactly what the elder in 2 John recommends (see 2 Jn 10-11), but in doing so has acted against the "brothers and sisters" of whom the elder approves. In 3 John 9-10 we read:

"I have written something to the church; but Diotrephes, who likes to put himself first, does not receive us.[114] So if I come, I will call attention to what he is doing in spreading false

---

[111] We will comment on this further below.

[112] This is the reverse of 2 Jn 10-11, where the refusal of hospitality means one is refusing to participate in spreading a different teaching about Christ; see Rensberger 1997, p161.

[113] See Acts 15:3; Rom 15:24; 1 Cor 16:6, 11; 2 Cor 1:16; Tit 3:13; *Poly.* Phil 1.1; and for example Smalley 1984, p350.

[114] Mitchell (1998, p299-320) argues convincingly that there is no lexicographical support for translating ἐπιδέχεσθαι in 3 Jn 9 as "to recognise one's authority", as for example, both RSV and NRSV do, and that it should be translated as "receive". She also notes that the verb was commonly used to refer to diplomatic acceptance or rejection, but that it does not inform us of the motivation for such actions (p318). 3 Jn 9-10 can best be understood within this

charges against us. And not content with those charges, he does not himself receive the brothers and sisters (τοὺς ἀδελφούς), and even prevents those who want to do so and expels them from the church."

What has been happening here focuses on "the brothers and sisters" of 3 Jn 3, 5, 10. There has clearly been a breakdown in the relationship between the elder and Diotrephes and as a result of this the elder seeks Gaius' help. Gaius is probably not a member of Diotrephes' house church, since the elder tells Gaius what has been happening in that house church. Nor does the elder ask Gaius to speak with Diotrephes about the conflict, which suggests that Gaius does not have any influence over Diotrephes or his house church. However, clearly Gaius is on good terms with the elder, and seems to be one of his children (v4). Having provided hospitality for the elder's messenger once (v5-6), we now see that the request in v6 for further hospitality for the "brothers and sisters" is because they have been rebuffed by Diotrephes. The purpose of 3 John then may well be to encourage Gaius to provide this hospitality, perhaps especially to Demetrius (v12), who seems to be contrasted with Diotrephes as a model whom Gaius should imitate.[115]

It is also clear from 3 Jn 9-10 that the elder had previously sent "brothers and sisters" to communicate to Diotrephes' community, but that Diotrephes had refused to accept the letter or the letter-carriers. In not receiving the "brothers and sisters" Diotrephes is denying them both entry into the community and hospitality. In ignoring the letter and those whom the elder supports, Diotrephes had turned his back on the elder and all he stood for.[116] Further, Diotrephes had not only refused to welcome the brothers and sisters (v10); he had added to this insult by spreading malicious talk about the elder. He had also prevented other members of the community from offering the messengers hospitality, by putting those who want to welcome the travellers out of the church (whether in actual fact, or only as a threat). Clearly, this refusal of hospitality also meant refusal to support the mission in which the brothers and sisters were involved.

---

framework of diplomatic relations in the Greco-Roman world, as we seek to do below. See also Osiek and Balch 1997, p284 n72.

[115] See Rensberger 1997, p159.

[116] Mitchell (1998, p319) notes: "In rejecting the letter and envoys of the elder and denying them a hospitable reception into his house-church, Diotrephes was rejecting the elder himself and breaking off relations with him. ... in not receiving the brothers whom he sent, Diotrephes did not receive the elder whom they represented." This is clearly how the Elder has interpreted Diotrephes actions. Note also that in 3 Jn 10 we read that Diotrephes refuses to welcome the brothers and sisters because he is "not content with those charges" against the elder. Lieu (1986, p113) notes "the implication may be that it was their link with the Elder which told so heavily against 'the brethren'."

In all of this, the parallel with 2 Jn 10-11 is strikingly clear. There the elder advises that hospitality or a greeting is to be denied one who does not have the right doctrine, while here in 3 Jn travelling missionaries are denied hospitality or entry to the house church, and even those who wish to help them and thus, in Diotrephes' view, share their errors, are to be excluded from the house church. As Rensberger comments, this amounted to "using the tactics of 2 John 10-11 against the elder, though it is not certain who originated these tactics, since the chronological relationship between 2 and 3 John is unclear."[117] Further, although nothing is said about beliefs, this parallel "may suggest that Diotrephes suspected them [the travelling teachers] of false belief or rejected their status and rights as Christian missionaries for reasons not stated."[118]

Although in this case the Elder disapproves of what has happened, we again see that hospitality – or the denial of hospitality in this case – has been used as a mechanism of boundary definition. Diotrephes has used material possessions, in the form of denying hospitality essential for missionary work, as a way of defining who he finds unacceptable. By contrast, the elder urges Gaius to continue to provide hospitality, as he has done in the past, for "the brothers and sisters" who are part of the elder's group. In doing so, Gaius will show himself to be a "fellow worker in the truth" (v8) and thus an honoured part of the same group.

Thus we see that material possessions are connected with some form of doctrinal test and are being used in the service of group definition by both sides in this dispute. Hospitality is being used to define whom a group accepts, and whom they reject, and so plays a crucial part in group boundary definition.[119]

It is interesting to observe that this is similar to but distinct from the way that we saw material possessions being used in 1 Jn. For there we saw material possessions being used only *within* the group for the "brothers or sisters in need" (1 Jn 3:17) and thus in the service of group boundary reinforcement and maintenance. Here, again they are being used in connection with group identity, but this time in the service of the actual boundary definition of the group.

---

[117] Rensberger 1997, p162.

[118] Lieu 1986, p114; she suggests that this may have constituted the much resented "slander". See Lieu 1986, p113 for other possibilities. Mitchell (1998, p297-320) has shown that the issue is not that Diotrephes rejects the authority of the elder. The elder's response to all of this is surprisingly mild. He does not defend himself, or the "brothers and sisters". He speaks simply of a possible visit, where he will "call attention" to what Diotrephes is doing, which suggests giving his side of the story rather than a public rebuke. It seems that the Elder can only rely on his personal influence and prestige against the influence and prestige of Diotrephes; see Lieu 1986, p114-15; Dodd 1946, p165.

[119] See Countryman 1980, p160-1.

2.3 Conclusions

We conclude then that we cannot say much about the stratification of the community addressed in the Johannine Letters, apart from the fact that some were in need and others were able to supply that need; some could also provide hospitality. In these cases we do not need to speak of people being wealthy, nor actually destitute. But we do see material possessions being used in group boundary definition (2 and 3 Jn) and reinforcement (1 Jn). This contrasts significantly with what we suggested was the use of material possessions among the readers of the Pastoral Epistles.

3. Material Possessions and the Christians in Ephesus according to Revelation

3.1 John's relationship to the Seven Churches

My interest here is in the Christians in Ephesus addressed by John of Revelation and their material possessions or lack thereof. But firstly we need to recall the discussion in Chapter 7 about the relationship between John and the communities he addresses. We argued there that John was deeply unhappy with many aspects of the life of the seven churches. Not only does he face major opponents, such as the Nicolaitans, but we also suggested that the majority of members of the seven churches agree neither with John nor the Nicolaitans. Factors such as the tone of the seven proclamations, with their frequent calls to repentance, and exhortations such as those found in 16:15 and 18:4, suggest that John has a battle on his hands as he tried to convince his readers about many matters.

It follows from this that we cannot equate John's attitudes on a whole range of matters, including material possessions, with the attitudes to these matters to be found among his readers. Rather, John's attitudes to material possessions could well be quite different from the attitudes of some of his readers. We will need to bear this in mind in the following discussion where we will seek to discern what can be said about the material possessions of John's readers and about John's attitude to wealth. Finally I will address the issue of his Ephesian readers' attitudes on this matter, and how they used material possessions.

3.2 Material possessions and the readers in the seven Churches (according to John)

3.2.1 Rev 2:9 to Smyrna

In Rev 2:9 we read: "I know your affliction and your poverty, even though you are rich (οἶδά σου τὴν θλῖψιν καὶ τὴν πτωχείαν, ἀλλὰ πλούσιος εἶ)." Clearly this involves paradox – the addressees in Smyrna cannot literally be both poor and rich, and so either πτωχεία or πλούσιος is being used metaphorically. In context, it seems most likely that they are economically poor,[120] but John says that they are metaphorically rich, with the reference to riches being to eschatological riches.[121] Aune comments: "The fact that no mention is made of the economic poverty of the other six Christian communities suggests that the situation of this congregation is unusual."[122]

Several possible reasons for their economic poverty can be given. Firstly, Hemer suggests that one reason may be that since converts were often made "among the poorer classes they could represent the lowest classes of society (1 Cor. 1.26; James 2.5)".[123] We note that Meggitt has recently suggested that Christians did indeed come from the lowest classes. But this does not explain why it is *only* the Christians in Smyrna who are said to be poor. Perhaps on this view, their poverty could relate to the foundation of the community, in that from the beginning only the poor were converted.[124] Secondly, it could be

---

[120] Aune (1997, p175) suggests that the community "apparently had few if any wealthy members". For this interpretation see also Aune 1997, p161; Royalty 1998, p87; Beale 1999, p239. The term πτωχοί, "poor", is used literally in 13:16 (in opposition to "rich") and figuratively in 3:17.

[121] See Aune 1997, p161; see also Lk 6:20=Mt 5:3; Mt 6:19-21=Lk 12:33-4; Lk 12:21; 2 Cor 6:10; Jas 2:5. He notes that the Stoics used Greek and Latin terms for wealth figuratively; see Seneca Ep. 62.3. See also Philo Praem 104; Som 1.179; Plant 69. Royalty (1998, p160) asks why Christ sees the Smyrneans as rich? "The clue to the Smyrnan's (sic) wealth is Christ himself; he wears gold and appears among golden lampstands that signify the seven Churches of Asia. The Smyrnans acknowledge a wealthy Lord ... And they are rich in deeds, in suffering and endurance." Note also that they are clearly suffering, something on which John places considerable significance. Royalty (1998, p162) comments: "It is because of their suffering, not their poverty, that the Smyrnans rank high in Christ's characterization of the seven Churches and are therefore called rich."

[122] Aune 1997, p161.

[123] Hemer 1986, p68.

[124] However, Aune (1997, p161) suggests Hemer's view is problematic since "it is now recognised that early Christianity was not a movement restricted to the lower classes; it encompassed the social spectrum .., though no generalization can reveal the social and economic status of the Christians in Smyrna". But Aune is here relying on the "consensus" view that Meggitt has so strongly challenged; see Meggitt 1998. Even if Meggitt is wrong, and there was more of a spread of social classes among Christian communities in general, there is no reason why this particular community could not come from the lowest classes.

that many of the material possessions of the community had been confiscated or stolen during persecution.[125] This is possible, but perhaps John would have made the point clear. Finally, Aune notes that "[u]ncompromising Christians found it difficult to make a living in a pagan environment",[126] a view which is thought by many to be the reason for the poverty of the Smyrnaeans.[127]

We also note that Christ commends this church. Kraybill comments: "The socio-economic status of any Christian church John mentions seems inversely related to the book's level of approval toward it."[128] We will see that the only group that is said to be rich is roundly condemned by Christ.

3.2.2 Rev 3:17-18 to Laodicea

In Rev 3:17-18 we read:

For you say, "I am rich (πλούσιός εἰμι), I have prospered, and I need nothing." You do not realize that you are wretched, pitiable, poor (πτωχός), blind, and naked. Therefore I counsel you to buy from me gold refined by fire so that you may be rich (ἵνα πλουτήσῃς); and white robes to clothe you and to keep the shame of your nakedness from being seen; and salve to anoint your eyes so that you may see.

Again it seems clear that the community cannot be literally rich and poor simultaneously, but rather that one term is literal and the other metaphorical. It seems most likely that the community is in fact literally wealthy, but that the risen Christ berates them for being materially rich but spiritually poor, blind and naked,[129] and advises them to become spiritually rich.[130] Thus, the

---

[125] See Hemer 1986, p68 who notes the mention of slander of Jews in 2:9b and writes: "It has often been observed that the poverty of the Christians may have been at least partly due to the despoliation of their property by mobs, whether Jewish or pagan." But we would expect to hear more of this in Revelation and elsewhere. Aune (1997, p161) thinks this suggestion is improbable. Beale (1999, p239) thinks the church at Smyrna "is suffering economic hardship because of Jewish slander."

[126] Aune 1997, p161; see also Caird 1966, p35.

[127] Aune 1997, p161. Hemer (1986, p68) also suggests that "devoted Christians on occasion reduced themselves to penury by the liberality of their own giving (2 Cor 2:8)". But Aune (1997, p161) again notes that this seems improbable.

[128] Kraybill 1996, p25.

[129] See Aune 1997, p259. Philo has a similar metaphorical use of the term "poor" in Quod Omn. Prob. 9: "You call those poor who are surrounded with silver and gold and a huge amount of landed possessions."

[130] They are to do this by buying gold "that you might be rich". As Aune (1997, p259) notes, there is paradox involved here too, for how can the "poor" purchase expensive gold. Obviously, "poverty, purchasing , and gold are used as metaphors."

Christian community in Laodicea is saying "I am rich", and in fact they are wealthy.[131]

It is worth noting the significance of local factors here. Laodicea was situated on prominent trade routes at the crossroads between the route from Ephesus to the East and from Pergamum and Sardis to the south coast. It was also a centre of trade and manufacturing and was known for its export of expensive garments made of black wool.[132] It became prosperous during the last part of the first century BCE, and although it suffered from earthquakes during the time of Tiberius and Nero, Laodicea became a major city by the second century CE. The wealth of a significant number of its inhabitants is indicated by the fact that, although it was destroyed by an earthquake in 60 CE, it refused imperial financial assistance for a considerable rebuilding programme.[133] It was also a banking centre and the capital of the Cibyratic conventus, which meant it was the juridical centre for 25 communities.[134] It is understandable then that some Christians in the city were wealthy; further as Hemer notes: "The church was evidently influenced by the material self-sufficiency which characterized the city".[135]

It seems clear then that the community at Laodicea was wealthy, at least in John's eyes. Beale argues that they had become wealthy because they had been willing to cooperate with the worship of the trade guilds and the economic institutions of their culture. This sort of spiritual compromise for economic gain meant that their witness was ineffective, which is why Christ is introduced as the "faithful and true witness" at the beginning of the letter to Laodicea in 3:14. Whereas the Christians of Smyrna have refused to conform to the pressures of idolatry, the Laodiceans are the mirror opposite.[136] This

---

[131] On the material wealth of the Laodiceans, see Countryman 1980, p135; Yarbro Collins 1980, p202; Wheeler 1995, p113; Kraybill 1996, p25. Aune 1997, p258 cities parallels to the statement "I am rich", from Hos 12:9; 1 Enoch 97:8-9 and Arrian, *Epict Diss* 3.7.29. Beale (1999, p304) suggests "they might have believed that their healthy spiritual welfare was indicated by their economic prosperity. For a precedent they could have appealed to the OT, in which Israel's material welfare in the land was a barometer of their covenant faithfulness to Yahweh. That some kind of boast about material welfare is in mind is likely from the observation that wherever πλούσιος ("rich") and πλουτέω ("I am rich") are used negatively in Revelation, the reference is to unbelievers who have prospered materially because of their willing intercourse with the ungodly world system (6:15; 13:16; 18:3, 15, 19)."

[132] See Strabo 12.8.16.

[133] See Tacitus, Annals 14.27.

[134] See Hemer 1986, p180-2, 191-201; Aune 1997, p249.

[135] Hemer 1986, p191. Note that Smyrna was also a wealthy city, although the Christians there were poor; John does not see an automatic correlation between the city and the Christian community therefore. But John does seem to suggest that the Laodicean Christians mirrored the self-sufficiency of the city.

[136] Beale 1999, p304-5. Yarbro Collins (1984, p133) also notes with regard to John's condemnation of wealth here: "The underlying reason seems to be that it was possible to get

seems the most likely explanation of both the source of wealth of the Laodiceans, and the fact that John is strongly opposed to them being wealthy.[137]

3.3 Indications about the material possessions of the addressees from Rev 4-22

3.3.1 Revelation 18: Judgement on Rome

The indications of the wealth or poverty of the addressees are not limited to the seven letters. In particular we note Rev 18, where judgement is pronounced on "Babylon the great" (18:2), that is, Rome. Take Rev 18:16-17 for example: "Alas, alas, the great city, clothed in fine linen, in purple and scarlet, adorned with gold, with jewels, and with pearls! For in one hour all this wealth has been laid waste!" Included in the chapter is a portrayal of kings, merchants and shippers who brought goods to Rome weeping over the demise of the great city (Rev 18:9-11, 15-19), and a cargo list of luxury items that merchants brought to Rome (18:11-13).[138] But it is strange that in Rev 18, a climactic point of judgement in the book, John gives the perspective of merchants and sailors (Rev 18:15-19), people who depended for their livelihood on their involvement with Rome's economic system. Bauckham notes:

Why then does John give us the perspective of Rome's collaborators in evil: the ruling classes, the mercantile magnates, the shipping industry? Part of the reason may be that, although the perspective was certainly not John's, it could rather easily be that of some of his readers. If it is not likely that many were among the ruling classes, it is not unlikely that John's readers would include merchants and others whose business or livelihood was closely involved with the Roman political and economic system. For such readers John has set a kind of hermeneutical trap. Any reader who finds himself sharing the perspective of Rome's mourners – viewing the prospect of the fall of Rome with dismay – should thereby discover, with a shock, where he stands, and the peril in which he stands. And for such readers, it is of the utmost significance that, prior to the picture of the mourners, comes the command: Come out of her my people, lest you take part in her sins, lest you share in her plagues (18:4).[139]

Kraybill similarly thinks that some Christians were involved in trade and that Rev 18 is a call for Christians to sever all economic and political ties with

and to maintain wealth only by accommodating to the polytheistic culture." See also Thompson 1990, p124-5; Schüssler Fiorenza 1991, p57; deSilva 1992, p291.

[137] It has been suggested that the Nicolaitans included wealthy Christians, but we have shown in Chapter 7 that there is no compelling evidence for this.

[138] On the lists see in particular Bauckham 1993c, p338-83. On Rev 18 see also Yarbro Collins 1980, p185-204.

[139] Bauckham 1993c, p376; see also Kraybill 1996, p15; cf Yarbro Collins 1980, p195

Rome. He argues that John intended his warning in Rev 18:4 "as practical pastoral instruction: if Christians had (or were tempted to have) dealings with Rome through maritime trade or other commercial ties, they should withdraw immediately or they would share both in Rome's guilt and her punishment".[140] Rev 18 "probably addresses not only a distant imperial society ('them'), but also fellow Christians within John's faith community ('us')."[141]

This view explains the chapter as a whole; for it is not simply a dirge on Rome, or a description of Rome's downfall,[142] since verses 4-8 are clearly addressed to readers. Further, the detailed attention given to the perspective of merchants and sailors in Rev 18:15-19 is startling. Both features are comprehensible if some of the readers were actually involved in forms of trade with Rome, or at the least were involved in the web of trade, even local trade, which had at its centre the centre of the Empire. So John is calling some of his readers to give up their involvement in trade, and hence their presumably profitable incomes. This is reinforced by what John has already said to the church at Laodicea.

3.3.2 Revelation 11:18 – the small and great

There is another indication of the position of the readers with regard to material possessions. In Rev 11:18 we read:

"The nations raged, but your wrath has come,
and the time for judging the dead,
for rewarding your servants, the prophets and saints,
and those who fear your name, both small and great,
and for destroying those who destroy the earth."

Lines 3-4 here refer to Christians in general as "your servants" and "those who fear your name". John suggests here that "those who fear your name", that is, all Christians, are made up of "both small and great (τοὺς μικροὺς καὶ τοὺς μεγάλους)". As Aune notes "the phrase 'small and great' is an

---

[140] Kraybill 1996, p16; see also Bauckham 1993c, p377: "The command is for readers to *dissociate* themselves from Rome's evil" (his emphasis). Provan (1996, p81-100) thinks it is economics as an aspect of idolatry which is condemned in Rev 18 rather than Rome's economic exploitation. But Rev 18:15-19 suggests some sort of hermeneutical trap for Christians involved in commerce (as well as in its consequent idolatry); that Christians were involved in this way is reinforced by the call of Rev 18:4.

[141] Kraybill 1996, p23.

[142] Yarbro Collins (1980, p203) helpfully summarises the reasons for Rome's judgment in Revelation: "(1) the idolatrous and blasphemous worship offered and encouraged by Rome, especially the emperor cult; (2) the violence perpetrated by Rome, especially against Jews and Christians; (3) Rome's blasphemous self-glorification; and (4) Roman wealth."

idiom occurring frequently in the Apocalypse and the OT and means a group comprised of those from various social stations".[143] This is another hint that, in John's view, among his addressees there are people of differing social status, of which we may suggest that wealth was one component. This confirms what we have already seen: that both wealthy and poorer people are among the readers.

3.4 John's attitude to material possessions

Since we wish to draw some conclusions from John's overall attitude to material possessions in the next section, we need to make some brief comments on the matter here. We have already discerned a good deal about John's attitude to wealth from his commendation of the poor Christians in Smyrna, his condemnation of the rich Laodiceans, and his judgement on the wealth of Rome in Rev 18. Clearly John announces God's judgement on the wealthy, and on Rome.

Rev 13:16-17 shows that a key reason for John's condemnation is that he sees an unavoidable connection between economic activity and idolatry. In Rev 13:16-17 we read: "Also it [the second beast] causes all, both small and great, both rich and poor, both free and slave, to be marked on the right hand or the forehead, so that no one can buy or sell unless he has the mark, that is, the name of the beast or the number of its name." Thus, in John's prophecy, without the "mark of the beast" one is unable to conduct trade. It seems clear that the mark is a sign of allegiance of some sort.[144] It is the counter-image of the "seal" on the foreheads of believers in 7:3-8 or the divine name, written on the foreheads of true believers of 14:1; 22:4; 3:12.

Thus, in John's view, in order to be involved in trade or general economic relations, one must offer allegiance to the beast. John believes there is an unavoidable connection between "the mark of the beast", that is allegiance to the emperor and his cult, and commerce.[145] This is John's clearest statement that for him, trade and economic relations are inextricably connected with idolatry. This seems to be the strongest reason why he calls on Christians to avoid commerce, and why he condemns wealthy Christians. Rather than receiving "the mark of the beast", Christians should have the divine name on their forehead, but without the mark of the beast, they cannot buy and sell, and so should not be wealthy, or significantly involved in trade. Faithful Christians should not be involved in the prosperity of Roman society. If they

---

[143] Aune 1981, p19. See Rev 13:16; 19:5, 18; 20:12; in the OT see Gen 19:11; Dt 1:17; 25:13f; 1 Sam 5:9; 20:2; 30:2, 19; 1 Kgs 22:31.

[144] Beale 1999, p715. For discussions of the "mark of the beast" see Judge 1991, p160; Kraybill 1996, p135-41.

[145] See Countryman 1980, p83.

are, they are involved in "idolatrous allegiances"[146] to economic institutions. Any Christians in this situation must "Come out of her, my people, lest you take part in her sins ..." (Rev 18:4).[147] But we should also note that there is a strong link between wealth and injustice for John. His condemnation of Rome is driven at least in part by his view that Roman wealth is gained through injustice.[148]

But is John against wealth per se? Does he want Christians to live some form of ascetic life involving the renunciation of (most) material possessions? If one could be significantly wealthy and integrated into city life, without involvement in idolatry, would John be willing for Christians to be wealthy – but of course, for John the question is purely theoretical. Or is the key point renunciation of idolatry and of the idolizing of wealth?[149] Is he envisaging some form of self-sufficiency within the Christian community?[150] Or for John is it simply that "the truly faithful are expected to be poor".[151] We cannot say. But clearly to be as rich as the Christians of Laodicea, or to be as involved in trade as the (Christian) merchants of Rev 18 were, is unacceptable to John. So for John the call is to "Come out of her, my people..." (Rev 18:4), and so for Christians to be as uninvolved in city life as possible.[152]

---

[146] Kraybill 1996, p22; see also Blomberg 1999, p236.

[147] Note that although they are not necessarily wealthy, John attacks the Nicolaitans for the same underlying reason – in his view they are involved in idolatry.

[148] See Kraybill 1996, p200-5.

[149] Bauckham (1993d, p123), suggests that the Laodicean Christians' repentance of "the idolizing of material prosperity ... will be equivalent to coming out of Babylon, as God's people are urged to do" (with reference to 18:4). Aune (1998b, p991) thinks the summons to flight "refers to the necessity of Christians disentangling themselves and distancing themselves morally, and perhaps even socially, from the corrupt and seductive influences of Roman rule in Asia" and compares it with 2 Cor 6:17 which he thinks is a call "to abstain from the idolatrous practices of pagan society."

[150] See Blomberg 1999, p237; see also Klauck 1992, p179.

[151] Yarbro Collins 1980, p202. Note that John in Revelation can use the symbols of material riches to convey the power of God's reign, for example in Rev 21:2, 18-21; see Wheeler 1995, p114; Royalty 1998. But clearly this symbolic use of riches to depict the new Jerusalem (for example), does not enable us to determine John's actual attitude to wealth in the present.

[152] Of course John does see a positive place for wealth of a kind. For example, the one like a Son of Man is clearly pictured as wealthy (1:13), the Lamb receives wealth (5:12) and the new Jerusalem is pictured as a place of great wealth (21:10-21; see also 21:24, 26). We cannot discuss this in detail here, but clearly a certain sort of wealth, under particular circumstances, can function positively for John.

3.5 Material possessions and the Christians in Ephesus?

We have noted that John describes the Christians in Smyrna as poor and the Christians in Laodicea as rich. He gives economic information about none of the other 5 churches, including Ephesus. Yet we have also seen that John stresses at some significant points in Rev 4-22 that Christians should not be wealthy, should not have the mark of the beast, and should not be involved in the idolatrous alliances which in his view were integral to being part of the commercial networks of the empire.

What does the absence of socio-economic information about Ephesus signify? Does it mean that the community was neither poor nor rich? That the community (along with the other 4 communities where the issue is not raised) agreed with John on this issue? Does it mean that what is said in Rev 4-22 on the dangers of idolatrous wealth is not addressed to the Ephesians (or the other 4 churches), or is addressed to them only as a prophylactic? Are we to take it that none of the Ephesian Christians are being called to "Come out of her, my people?" But is it likely that the emphasis John puts on economic matters throughout the book is *only* for the benefit of Christians in Laodicea, the only church in which John highlights the presence of rich Christians?

It seems much more likely that, from John's perspective, although the problem of idolatrous wealth is a particular issue in Laodicea, it is *also* an issue in the other five churches. We can suggest that in John's view this is a problem for *all* Christians who must live in the Empire.[153] Note for example that in Rev 13:16-17 John writes that the second beast causes "*all*, both small and great, both rich and poor, both free and slave, to be marked on the right hand or the forehead, so that no one can buy or sell who does not have the mark ..." This is a contentious issue for all Christians, as John sees it. He thinks that all Christians must refuse to compromise on the issue of idolatrous wealth, but clearly the connection between economics and idolatry as John saw it, was a particular problem for the wealthy. We can suggest that at least some Christians in Asia Minor beyond Laodicea (including Ephesus) were involved to some extent in commerce, and possessed at least some wealth. We can suggest that at least some of these Christians did not see the connection between money and idolatry as John did, but rather would argue that a Christian can be involved in trade and not be idolatrous. They are addressed in passages like Rev 18.

But clearly we cannot say anything for certain with regard to the particular economic situation of the addressees in Ephesus, beyond the suggestion that some of them may have been wealthy in John's eyes. As we have noted in

---

[153] Kraybill (1996, p17) notes: "John warned Christians to sever or to avoid economic and political ties with Rome because institutions and structures of the Roman Empire were saturated with unholy allegiances to an Emperor who claimed to be divine (or was treated as such)."

Chapter 7, we can say that, from the way John writes in Rev 2-3, he seems to have a battle on his hands, and the Ephesians, like other Christians, are called by John to repent – and in their case to "remember then from what you have fallen, repent and do the works you did at first." (Rev 2:5) This tells us that, in John's opinion, the Ephesian Christians needed to read the whole book – and we may suggest needed to adopt his attitude to idolatrous wealth as much as any of his other readers. It also suggests that he knew they did not agree with him on many issues, and we may suggest that that included this issue of wealth as it did other issues too. But we cannot be more specific than this.

3.6 How is wealth being used in the seven Churches then?

John would like the lack of material possessions to be a boundary marker or a sign of identity for Christians. Those within the community should not have the mark of the beast, which John thinks will be necessary for involvement in commerce, on their right hand or forehead. Hence they should avoid economic contacts with the empire, so as to avoid the idolatry that for John was inescapably connected with economics. If John had his way, then Christians in each of the seven cities would "Come out of her" and would have as few dealings as possible with the economic life of their cities.

Clearly in Smyrna this was less of an issue for the poor Christians. We may suggest that for John it was a particularly acute issue for the rich Christians of Laodicea. But what about the Christians in the other five churches, including Ephesus?

We can suggest that the majority of John's readers in the seven churches did not share his views on economic matters. Wealth was probably not an issue for them in the way that it was for John. The lack of material possessions was probably not functioning as a distinctive identity marker in the seven churches, and John would like it to. This would explain the fervent condemnation of wealth in the book, and in particular the call in Rev 18:4-5. Perhaps the addressees in Ephesus, like those elsewhere, did not see wealth as a boundary marker, and were happy to be involved in commerce, whether they were rich or poor.

4. Overall Conclusions

Firstly, we need to acknowledge that we have very limited information on this matter with regard to Christians in Ephesus from Revelation. We can suggest that John does not see his addressees in Ephesus as either "rich" or "poor", but more than this we cannot say (although we have made a couple of suggestions).

We have proposed in Chapter 7 that in Revelation John is writing to all the Christians in Ephesus, but is aware that many will disagree with him on a range of matters. On this view, John is writing to the recipients of the Pastorals and the Johannine Letters as well as to others. The alternative hypothesis is that John is writing to a separate group from those addressed in the Pastorals and the Johannine Letters – a "John of Revelation community". Given how little he says about material possessions and Ephesus, we have no information which strongly supports or contradicts either hypothesis. However, given that there are rich and poor among the addressees of the Pastorals, and some stratification on this issue among the readers of the Johannine Letters, if they were all being addressed by Rev 2:1-7 we can understand why John called them neither "rich" nor "poor"; this would be in keeping with the view we favoured in Chapter 7 (that John is addressing all Christians in Ephesus), but more than this we cannot say.

Secondly, we note that the addressees of the Pastorals and the Johannine Letters show stratification with regard to material possessions. Although this is clearest in the Pastorals, where we also have much more detail, the Johannine Letters also show there are "haves" and "have nots" in the community addressed.

Thirdly, there are significant differences between the addressees of the Pastorals and the Johannine Letters with regard to the ways in which material possessions were used. In the Pastoral Epistles wealth was used within the community for widows and to pay elders, and hence to reinforce the sense of belonging and solidarity and thus of group boundaries. However, I have argued that the rich were being called on to do "good works" with their money *outside* the group, and that to some extent at least, the rich were currently doing this. This would have tended to deconstruct group boundaries. Thus, in some ways wealth reinforced the identity of the group, in other ways its use countered internal boundaries by opening the group up to the needs of outsiders.

By contrast, in the Johannine Letters we have suggested that currently material possessions were being used in the definition and reinforcement of group boundaries. Material possessions were being used in hospitality to define whom a group accepts, and whom they reject, and so played a crucial part in group boundary definition. Further, "the world's goods" were being shared with needy community members to some extent (John calls for greater attention to this area) and so reinforced group boundaries. These differences with regard to material possessions testify to the differences between these two communities in late first century Ephesus.

But fourthly, we can also note that in Revelation John's attitude was different from that displayed by either of these two communities. In Revelation, John is seeking to make material possessions themselves a boundary marker – Christians should not have wealth, since for him it was inextricably connected with idolatry. If his readers did include the addressees of the Pastoral Epistles and the Johannine Letters, the view we favoured in Chapter 7, then we can suggest that neither group saw material possessions themselves as a boundary defining issue. John's is thus yet another, and quite different "voice" on this matter in Ephesus, where (via his text) he was seeking a hearing among the Christians.

Finally, we can ask why there were significant differences between the addressees of the Pastoral Epistles and the Johannine Letters on the matter of the use of material possessions? Here we can draw some correlations with what we discussed in the previous chapter. There we suggested that the addressees of the Pastoral Epistles were significantly acculturated and were seeking to use that acculturation to construct bridges with the wider world, and thus were an outward-facing community involved in integrative accommodation, particularly with a focus on mission. We can suggest that the use of material possessions beyond the group fits in with this. They were interacting positively with the wider world; their use of material possessions beyond the group is of a piece with this.

By contrast, we suggested in the previous chapter that the addresses of the Johannine Letters may have been acculturated to some extent – 2 and 3 Jn suggested this – but that their use of "in-group language" made this difficult to determine. When it came to assimilation, we argued that their attitude to "the world" suggests that as a group they were somewhat turned in on themselves and maintained a separateness from others. We can note that their use of material possessions is of a piece with this attitude, since they seemed to only use possessions for themselves. In fact, we can suggest that material possessions were enlisted to aid in the process of "turning in on themselves", since the evidence suggests they only used them within the community.

Thus through our delineation of assimilation and accommodation in the respective communities in the previous chapter, we can understand *why* material possessions were used in each group in the ways we have suggested. The different uses of material possessions are comprehensible within the wider framework we established in Chapter 8. But we have also added one more dimension to the case we argued in the previous chapter with regard to the integrative bridge building of the addressees of the Pastorals and the very limited assimilation of the addressees of the Johannine Letters. Further, we have added another dimension to our description of facets of the life of these two groups.

Chapter 10

Leadership and Authority and the readers of the Pastoral Epistles, the Johannine Letters and Revelation

One dimension of group identity concerns the way a group is organised and led. For a group to persist, it needs to have some form of leadership and some way of managing conflict.[1] This involves leadership structures and an answer to questions such as "what sort of persons are in a position to issue effective imperatives?"[2] In this chapter we will address this issue and will seek to discern what we can say about leadership and group structure with regard to the Pastorals, the Johannine Letters and Revelation. In particular, does the evidence support our hypothesis that the Pastorals and the Johannine Letters are written to two different groups. Clearly, if the respective authors presuppose that the leadership structure of the communities they address are quite different, then we can suggest that the communities are different. Further, we will also see if the evidence supports our hypothesis that in Revelation John the Seer is writing to all the Christians in Ephesus?

We will not be discussing the understanding of the church demonstrated by each book, since this is clearly part of the author's theology, which may or may not be shared by the readers. Rather we are interested in what the author says or presumes about current leadership structures among the readers. This gives us a better indication as to whether each author is writing to the same or different readers. Through this discussion we also hope to further our descriptive task of gaining insight into the nature of particular communities in Ephesus.

In addition to discussing leadership structures, we will also discuss the locus of authority among the addresses. As well as talking about leaders and offices[3], we want to discern (as far as this is possible) what the author and the addressees see as "bedrock" when it comes to authority. In particular, where

---

[1] See Meeks 1983, p111-39.

[2] See Meeks 1983, p131.

[3] Holmberg (1978, p110-11), drawing on Brockhaus' work, gives the formal characteristics of "office" as "1. the element of permanency, 2. the element of recognition by the church (an indication of permanency and recognition is the established title of office), 3. the position apart ("Sonderstellung") of individuals in regard to the church (position of authority or dignity), 4. the regular commission (imposition of hands), 5. the legal element, the legal securing of the function in question." See also Giles 1989, p12.

is authority seen to reside? This question is intricately connected with leadership structures and by going beyond a discussion of leadership into this question of the locus of authority, we can shed further light on the group concerned but we are also able to understand why a particular leadership structure is favoured in a particular document.

1. Leadership and authority in the Pastorals[4]

Here we will address the question of what the Pastor says about leaders in the community in Ephesus addressed in 1 and 2 Tim? We will also draw on Tit where it sheds light on the situation in the other two epistles.

1.1 The role of Timothy and Titus

How do we understand what is said to Timothy and Titus in these letters? We note that Timothy and Titus are not given any title and it is very unlikely that they are to be thought of as fulfilling the role of "overseer/bishop" or something similar, since nothing suggests that they bore the designation of "overseer" and no indication is given that Timothy and Titus are to be seen as residential (rather than itinerant) leaders.[5] However, as those with leadership responsibility (albeit, the sort undertaken by itinerants), we can suggest that at times Timothy and Titus also function as paradigms for local settled leaders with regard to their character traits, behaviour and general responsibilities (such as opposing some forms of teaching). We turn now to what we can say about these leaders of local communities.

---

[4] We should not see the Pastorals as "on the way" to *the* three-fold church order of the second century, as found in Ignatius (overseer/bishop, presiding over elders and deacons), because in fact there was considerable variety with regard to the development of office in the Apostolic Fathers. In these writings we see the following nomenclature: 1 Clement: overseers and deacons, with a plurality of overseers and their equivalence with elders/"seniors" (see 1 Clem 42:4-5; 44:1 with 44:4-5; 47:6; 57:1; cf. also Clement, *Quis Dives* 42); Ignatius: overseer, elders, deacons (IgnMag 6.2; IgnTr 2.2-4; 3.1; IgnPhd, inscr., IgnSm 12.2; IgnPol 6.1); Polycarp: elders and deacons (Polycarp 5.3); Hermas: apostles, overseers, teachers and deacons (Vis 3.5.1). See Marshall 1999, p177.

[5] Meier (1973, p345) notes: "It would be strange indeed to want Timothy and Titus to represent the later monarchical *episkopos,* and yet to apply that title only to a number of officials below Timothy and Titus, while never applying the title to the 'apostolic delegates'." See also Verner 1983, p148-9, 157; Marshall 1999, p180, 519-20; cf. von Campenhausen 1969, p107-8.

1.2 Πρεσβύτερος and ἐπίσκοπος and the relationship between the two terms

The Pastor discusses qualifications required of an ἐπίσκοπος in 1 Tim 3:1-7, without mention of πρεσβύτεροι. In 1 Tim 5:17 he speaks of πρεσβύτεροι, without discussing ἐπίσκοπος. In Titus 1:5 he speaks of appointing elders (πρεσβύτεροι) in every town but then goes on in Tit 1:7: "For an overseer must be blameless (δεῖ γὰρ τὸν ἐπίσκοπον ἀνέγκλητον εἶναι), as God's steward, ...", apparently equating presbuteros and episkopos, but using πρεσβύτερος in the plural and ἐπίσκοπος in the singular. How do we explain this usage? We need firstly to outline a little about the two crucial terms, presbuteros and episkopos.

1.2.1 Πρεσβύτερος

In the Greco-Roman world, "πρεσβύτεροι" generally means "older men", with both respect for older people and older folk fulfilling the role of leaders being noteworthy features of society. However, "πρεσβύτεροι" does not generally designate an appointed official of some kind. Within Judaism, authority was often exercised by a community of older men.[6] In this context, "elders" were "senior men in a community, the leaders of the influential families, and their position is one that is recognised by custom and wont, and not by any kind of official appointment to a definable office."[7] Hence the term "does not so much denote an office as connote prestige".[8] Further, elders within the synagogue do not seem to have had a key role with regard to worship and organisation, although they did have some broader administrative roles.[9] It seems unlikely then that there was a group of appointed "officeholders" called "elders" in the synagogue which provided the model for Christian presbyters.[10] Rather Jewish "elders" were senior men who exercised leadership by virtue of their age, rather than because they had been appointed to a particular "office". Thus the term basically connotes seniority.

---

[6] On the term "elder" see Harvey 1974, p318-32; Campbell 1994a, p20-66; Young 1994b, p145. Campbell (1994a, p66) notes that not all elders were necessarily old. "Their authority did not rest on age alone, but on the prestige of the families whose heads they were." Apart from the Pastorals, Johannine Letters and Revelation, the term is found in Jas 5:14; 1 Pet 5:1, 5; 1 Clem 44.5; 47.6; 54.2; 57.1; 2 Clem 17.3, 5; IgnMag. 2; 3.1; 6.1 et al; IgnPol inscr; 5.3.

[7] Marshall 1999, p172.

[8] Campbell 1994a, p65. See also Harvey 1974, p318-32, especially p326.

[9] Marshall 1999, p173.

[10] See Harvey 1974, p318-32; Marshall 1999, p173.

1.2.2 Ἐπίσκοπος

Ἐπίσκοπος means "guardian" or "overseer" and can be used in the Greco-Roman world to describe supervisors or leaders in different contexts.[11] In the LXX it was used of those who had civil, military or religious oversight (see Num 4:16; 31:14; 2 Kgs 11:15, 18). It seems that early Christians may have adopted the term from two possible sources. Firstly, directly from the model of the supervisor in the Greco-Roman world, as a result of the church's interaction with Hellenistic culture, although the use of the term in the LXX may have facilitated this adoption. Or secondly, the use of title in the early Church may be linked to the use of the title mebaqqer in some Jewish circles, as shown by the Dead Sea Scrolls,[12] since the roles of the mebaqqer and the ἐπίσκοπος in early Christianity are similar.

We now need to determine how these terms were used in 1 and 2 Tim and thus in Ephesus. However, the best place to begin, as I hope will become clear in due course, is a discussion of the situation in Crete as shown by Titus.

1.2.3 Crete

In Chapter 5 we have noted that there are some distinctions between 1 and 2 Tim addressed to Ephesus on the one hand, and Tit addressed to Crete on the other. We will seek to show here that this distinction is also found with regard to leadership, and that it seems likely the terms presbuteros and episkopos are not used in exactly the same way in 1 Tim (Ephesus) as they are in Tit (Crete).

Meier notes the following differences between the two situations.[13] Firstly, in Titus a much less developed church structure seems to be described. This is understandable given that the Pauline community in Ephesus was clearly established during Paul's ministry whereas we do not know when the community was actually founded in Crete and so the presentation of it as of recent origin in Titus is reasonable. Secondly, there is a group of deacons and an order of widows in Ephesus (1 Tim 3:8-13; 5:3-16), with no mention being made of either group in Crete. Thirdly, in 1 Tim 3:6 it is said that a new convert must not become an episkopos; that there is no echo of this in Tit suggests that the community on Crete was of too recent a foundation for such a requirement to be implemented. Accordingly, as Meier notes, we need to avoid "automatically reading what we know about the Ephesian church into

---

[11] See BDAG, p379-80. It is only found in Ephesus in later Christian inscriptions; see IvEph 3705, 3842, 4270.

[12] See CD 9.18, 19, 22; 13.6, 7, 16; 14.8, 11, 13, 20; 15.8, 11, 14; 1QS 6.12, 20; see Spicq 1969, p448-9; Thiering 1981, p59-74. Note however, that the term episkopos is not found within Christian sources relating to Palestine.

[13] Meier 1973, p337-8; see also Giles 1989, p85-9.

the Cretan communities".[14] Further, these difference can all be explained by the suggestion that the Ephesian community addressed in 1 and 2 Tim had been in existence for much longer than the Cretan community addressed in Tit. This also means that there could be differences in the way the two terms for leaders are used.

We begin then with a discussion of Tit 1:5-7, since this text clarifies the situation in Crete with regard to the relationship of episkopos and presbuteros.[15] In Tit 1:5 Titus is told to "appoint elders in each town (καταστήσῃς κατὰ πόλιν πρεσβυτέρους)". We note that πρεσβύτερος is used in the plural, and thus each town is to have a group of presbyters. But v6a switches from plural to singular: the Pastor writes of "someone who is blameless (εἴ τίς ἐστιν ἀνέγκλητος) ...". Clearly the plural "πρεσβύτεροι" in v5 are to be identified with the τίς of v6a; this change from plural to singular occurs quite frequently in the Pastorals and so is not particularly surprising here.[16]

In v6 the Pastor calls for the presbyter to be "blameless" (ἀνέγκλητος) and gives a short list of the qualities which are called for in a presbyter relating to his wife and children. Why are the qualities relating to family called for in v6? In v7, which begins with γάρ, the Pastor goes on to speak of the "episkopos" in the singular as the manager of God's household (θεοῦ οἰκονόμου). Because he is over God's household, he must be blameless in the way he has managed his *own* household. We thus see a strong connection between v5-6 and v7. To emphasise this, it is also said that the "episkopos" must be above reproach - ἀνέγκλητος – using the same word used of the "presbyter" in v6. This connection is also expressed by γάρ at the beginning of v7.[17] Given these links, it seems clear that the presbyters of v5-6 are equated with the episkopos of v7; one office is being spoken of, not two. Meier represents this as follows:[18]

---

[14] Meier 1973, p337.

[15] Recall that in Chapter 5, section 5.6 we have argued that there is a distinction between the opponents' teaching presupposed in 1 and 2 Tim, and so relating to Ephesus, and Tit, which we think relates to Crete. Therefore we begin here by seeing what the situation is in Crete (Tit) with regard to leadership, and seeking to discern if it is different from Ephesus (1 and 2 Tim); that such a distinction is indeed discernible, as we will see, reinforces our earlier findings and justifies our approach here.

[16] For example, in 1 Tim 2:9-15 we have plural, singular, plural; in 1 Tim 5:1 the change from singular to plural; in 1 Tim 5:3-16 there is the oscillation between singular and plural; and in 1 Tim 5:19-20 singular (πρεσβυτέρου) changes to plural (τοὺς ἁμαρτάνοντας) in 5:20. Meier (1973, p332) thus writes of "the frequent alternation between singular and plural with no ostensible reason".

[17] Meier (1973, p338) notes the rough syntax here: "vs. 6 is either tacked on loosely to vs. 5 or simply left hanging without any apodosis".

[18] Meier 1973, p338; cf. Giles 1989, p88-9.

$$(\gamma \acute{\alpha} \rho)$$

$$\pi \rho \epsilon \sigma \beta \upsilon \tau \acute{\epsilon} \rho \upsilon \varsigma - \tau \acute{\iota} \varsigma - \dot{\alpha} \nu \acute{\epsilon} \gamma \kappa \lambda \eta \tau \upsilon \varsigma \rightarrow \rightarrow \tau \dot{\upsilon} \nu \dot{\epsilon} \pi \acute{\iota} \sigma \kappa \upsilon \pi \upsilon \nu - \dot{\alpha} \nu \acute{\epsilon} \gamma \kappa \lambda \eta \tau \upsilon \varsigma.$$

v5   v6   v7

The switch from plural to singular is unproblematic here then and does not indicate that there was "one overseer". As Meier notes the switch "takes place in vs. 6, with *tis*, so that there is nothing at all surprising about the singular *ton episkopon* in vs. 7"[19] Further, as we have noted above, switches from plural to singular are not uncommon in the Pastorals and here an additional reason for the singular may be that the Pastor is quoting a list of requirements from tradition, and that this list spoke of "τὸν ἐπίσκοπον". These sorts of lists were well known in the Greco-Roman world. Thus the singular in Tit 1:7 should be seen as generic.

We conclude then that in Crete there was a group of leaders who could be known as presbuteroi or episkopoi, the former term indicating their status and the latter their function.[20]

1.2.4 But what was the situation at Ephesus?

We note first of all that in 1 Tim 3:1-7 the Pastor speaks of the task of the overseer (ἐπισκοπή) and gives the qualities required in an episkopos.[21] Here again the Pastor speaks in the singular. This is because he speaks of the "task of an overseer", which naturally involves a singular reference. Further, as in Tit 1:7 he is probably using a tradition which referred generically to an overseer using the singular τὸν ἐπίσκοπον, which means that "the number holding this office in the church cannot be determined from the instructions."[22] The Pastor then goes on to speak of the qualities looked for in a deacon (1 Tim 3:8-13). No mention is made of "presbuteroi" in this chapter.

In 1 Tim 5:1 πρεσβύτερος is clearly used of an older man, a point to which we will return. Then in 1 Tim 5:17-25, presbuteroi are spoken of, and an office is clearly in view.

---

[19] Meier 1973, p338.

[20] See also for example Wilson 1979, p54-5.

[21] We need not see ἐπισκοπή as referring to a status or an "office" (we see presbuteros as more of a status designation), but rather as designating a task here; see Marshall 1999, p476. BDAG, p379 think the meaning of ἐπισκοπή here is "engagement in oversight, supervision".

[22] Marshall 1999, p477; see also Wilson 1979, p55. Meier (1973, p328 n13) notes that its use in the singular may well be dependent on a set list of qualities. It is often commented on that episkopos is only ever used in the Pastorals in the singular, and this is used as an argument against seeing a group of episkopoi here. However, we note that the word episkopos is in fact only used twice in the Pastorals (1 Tim 3:2 and Tit 1:7) and so this point loses its force.

What then is the relation of episkopos and presbuteros in 1 Timothy? And what can we say about the role and function of leaders? We have already noted that in Titus, relating to Crete, the two terms are equated. Is this the case here too? If so, then the Pastor simply uses the alternative titles, episkopos first in 1 Tim 3, then presbuteros in 1 Tim 5. However, we have already noted that there are some differences between the situation on Crete and that in Ephesus with regard to community structure, probably relating to the Ephesian community having been established for much longer (which was probably historically the case). So it could be that there are differences with regard to these two terms too.

1 Tim 5:17 is most helpful here: "Let the elders who rule well be considered worthy of double honour (οἱ καλῶς προεστῶτες πρεσβύτεροι διπλῆς τιμῆς ἀξιούσθωσαν), namely (μάλιστα) those who labour (οἱ κοπιῶντες) in preaching and teaching." The word προΐστημι – "rule" is crucial here. According to BDAG, it means "to exercise a position of leadership, rule, direct, be at the head (of)";[23] it has a similar sense in 1 Thess 5:12. Clearly, in 1 Tim 5:17, it is being used in the technical sense of some form of leadership.[24] The verb κοπιάω is also significant. In 1 Tim 4:10 it refers to the hard labour of missionary work and it is often used in the undisputed Paulines as a term for the demanding activity of ministry or leadership.[25] The use of both προΐστημι and κοπιάω here confirms that πρεσβύτεροι, after having been used in the non-technical sense in 1 Tim 5:1, is being used here in 5:17 in the technical sense with reference to leadership.

The meaning of μάλιστα in 1 Tim 5:17 is important with regard to the overall sense of the verse. It can mean either "namely" (in which case it gives further definition of what is meant), or "especially", with the former meaning being most likely here. The meaning "especially" leaves it ambiguous as to whether those who do not labour in teaching receive the "double honour" or not,[26] and so this sense does not give a clear unambiguous reading. By contrast, μάλιστα with the meaning of "namely" is used elsewhere by the Pastor.[27] Further, this meaning identifies those who "rule well" with those who "labour in preaching and teaching" and as Marshall notes, "With the

---

[23] BDAG, p870. It is used in this sense in Amos 6:10; 1 Macc 5:19; 1 Tim 3:4, 12; Hermas Vis 2.4.3; Josephus Ant 8.300; Vita 93, 168. It has the sense of caring for those under one's direction in Rom 12:8; 1 Thess 5:12; see Marshall 1999, p331 n97.

[24] Meier (1973, p326) translates προΐστημι as "those presbyters who preside .." and notes the verb has "the technical, ministerial sense" here. 1 Tim 3:4, 5, 12; Tit 3:8, 14 show that the non-technical sense of the verb is known to the Pastor.

[25] See 1 Thess 5:12; 1 Cor 15:10; Gal 4:11; Rom 16:12; Phil 2:16; Col 1:29.

[26] See Marshall 1999, p612.

[27] See Skeat 1979, p173-7; Campbell 1995, p157-60; see 1 Tim 4:10; 2 Tim 4:13; Tit 1:10-11.

author's stress on the importance of teaching, he is likely to have regarded the outstanding elders as those who performed this duty."[28]

This means that the Pastor envisages two different groups of presbyters: those who do not rule, and those who rule and also labour in preaching and teaching, with this latter group being the subject of 1 Tim 5:17 where they are said to receive "double honour".[29] This suggests there was some differentiation in who was called a "presbuteros" in Ephesus. We can suggest the following.

Firstly, we have noted that "presbyters" originally meant "senior members" and that this meaning is found in the Pastorals in 1 Tim 5:1. We also note that "seniors" were the natural leaders in most groups of the period, including early Christian groups.[30] "Presbyters who do not rule" would then be senior men who have, over time, come to have less and less of the leadership role which the group as a whole would have naturally assumed should fall to them. That this group of non-ruling "seniors" existed is shown by the fact that lists of qualities are given for leadership roles in the Pastorals and that potential leaders are tested (see later); it is not automatic then that older men, "seniors", would lead. Given these lists, and "testing" before appointment, it is likely that there were some "seniors" who did not possess the required qualities and so did not lead. This is the group who "do not rule", which I will call group one.

Secondly, there was the group of presbyters who rule and also "labour in preaching and teaching"; they are group two.[31] They are to receive "double honour" and that this should happen is then argued for by the Pastor in 1 Tim 5:18, using two quotations.[32]

---

[28] Marshall 1999, p612; see also Roloff 1988, p307.

[29] See Marshall 1999, p173. Meier (1973, p326-7) envisages the following three-fold division: "presbyters who (simply) preside, presbyters who preside with great diligence or notable success, and those in this second group who exercise their leadership especially by preaching and teaching." However, this is dependent on μάλιστα meaning "especially" and we have noted above why μάλιστα is more likely to mean "namely". Marshall (1999, p612) also notes that such a three-fold division is "complex and hard to envisage in practice." Meier (1973, p326) also thinks "'presiding' is the very definition of what a presbyter is", and so all presbyters must be involved in some form of ruling. By contrast, following the work of Campbell (1994, for example, p65-6) and others, I would see the "very definition" of "presbuteros" as being "senior member" and so it need not require a person to preside. After all, this non-technical sense of the term is found in 1 Tim 5:1. Hence one group is presbyters (= seniors) who do not preside, rather than presbyters who (simply) preside. On my reading of the text, it remains possible that there is a third group in mind in 1 Tim 5:17 – those who rule, but do so poorly. But this seems overly subtle.

[30] See for example Campbell 1994a, p241-2.

[31] Because "labouring in preaching and teaching" is so important they are described as ruling καλῶς.

[32] See the discussion in Chapter 9 about "double honour".

If there were these two groups, did the title of "ἐπίσκοπος (overseer)", which designates a function, apply to either or both groups? In other words, were all "presbyters" "overseers", as seems to have been the case in Crete according to Titus? It seems that group one did not "oversee", since they did not "rule" and so it is unlikely that they were regarded as "overseers". So at the very least we see that some "presbyters", used in the sense of "seniors", did not "oversee", so there is some differentiation between these two terms.[33] But it is likely that group two, the "presbyters who ruled well and taught", were also called by their functional name of "overseers" and so the same group is referred to in 1 Tim 3. This is most likely for the following reasons.

Firstly, we note that in 1 Tim 3:2 it is said that an overseer must be "an apt teacher" (διδακτικός). This suggests that the "presbyters" of 1 Tim 5:17 who teach and preach (οἱ κοπιῶντες ἐν λόγῳ καὶ διδασκαλίᾳ) are the same as the "overseers" of 1 Tim 3, who are clearly involved in teaching.[34]

Secondly, that the "overseer" of 1 Tim 3 is involved in "ruling", and so that we are right to see a connection between the "overseer" of 1 Tim 3 and the ruling presbyters of 1 Tim 5:17, is implied by 1 Tim 3:4-5. For there we read: "He must manage (προϊστάμενον) his own household well, keeping his children submissive and respectful in every way - for if someone does not know how to manage (προστῆναι) his own household, how can he take care of (ἐπιμελήσεται) God's church?" Although the overseer is said to "take care of God's church" rather than to "manage" it, clearly there is a close similarity between the two activities, because it is only if he can show that he can "manage" his household well that he will be able to go on to undertake the clearly related role of "caring for" God's church. We also note that the same verb προΐστημι, is used of the presbyter "ruling well" in 1 Tim 5:17 and the overseer "managing his house" (related to "caring for God's church") in 1 Tim 3:4-5.[35] This suggests we are right to equate the "ruling presbyters" of 1 Tim 5:17 and the "overseers" of 1 Tim 3.

Thirdly, the overseers are not to be recent converts (1 Tim 3:6), which again suggests they need to know the faith because they will "labour in teaching and preaching" (1 Tim 5:17).

Finally, if we do not equate the "ruling, teaching presbyters" and the "overseers", then on the one hand we have overseers who "care for God's

---

[33] It is often argued that presbyter and episkopos are synonymous in the Pastorals; see for example Gibaut 2000, p17.

[34] Note also that in Tit 1:9 it is said of the presbyter-overseers on Crete: "He must have a firm grasp of the word that is trustworthy in accordance with the teaching, so that he may be able both to preach with sound doctrine and to refute those who contradict it." But we have noted that there are differences in the way presbuteros and episkopos are used in Ephesus and Crete and so this cannot be used as evidence for the meaning of the terms in Ephesus.

[35] But note the verb is also used in 1 Tim 3:12 with regard to deacons "managing their children".

church" (which is related to "managing" (προΐστημι)) and are apt teachers (1 Tim 3) and on the other hand a separate group of presbyters who "rule (προΐστημι)" and teach and preach (1 Tim 5:17). It seems much better to equate the two groups.[36] Further, if we do not equate ruling presbyters with overseers but rather differentiate between the two groups, then the Pastor has *not* given a list of qualities for presbyters in Ephesus, which seems strange given that the opponents, who are most certainly leaders and teachers,[37] are causing such difficulties. The only difference then between the situation in Ephesus and in Crete is that it is implied that in Ephesus there are some "presbyters" who are simply "older men" and are not fulfilling the function of overseers. Further, as we will see, in Ephesus some "presbyters" are probably also deacons.

We need to ask why the Pastor called these leaders "presbyters" in 1 Tim 5:17 and not "overseers", the term he used in 1 Tim 3? We note that in the Pastorals "episkopos" has *only* the technical sense of a function fulfilled by one in a leadership position and that the author also uses the abstract term ἐπισκοπή in 1 Tim 3:1, whereas presbuteros has a dual sense. Perhaps this is the reason the author uses the more technical and therefore less ambiguous "episkopos" in 1 Tim 3. But we can understand him reverting to the perhaps more established term of "elder",[38] in 1 Tim 5:17-19;[39] yet we also see that in this passage he needs to make it clear he is talking, not about "elders" in general, but about "elders who rule". On the supposition that "elder" was the more established, but also the more ambiguous term, we can thus understand the usage in 1 Tim.

We conclude then that the "presbyters" who according to 1 Tim 5:17-19 are to rule well and teach are the same group as the "overseers" in 1 Tim 3, where the functional name is used. We should not think then that there are three groups of leaders in Ephesus – overseers, presbyters and deacons. Rather, there are two groups of leaders – presbyter-overseers, and deacons. Further, we have suggested that at Ephesus "πρεσβύτερος" was used in two senses. Firstly, it was used without any additional term, of "elders", with the meaning of "senior men"; people designated *only* by this term did not exercise active leadership, and so were simply "presbyters/ seniors" (1 Tim 5:1) and not "presbyter-overseers". Secondly it was used of "elders" who fulfilled an office which involved ruling and teaching and who were *also* designated by

---

[36] We have noted above that τὸν ἐπίσκοπον in 1 Tim 3:2 is a generic singular.

[37] See Chapter 5.

[38] It may be more established since leadership would be exercised in early Christian groups from the beginning by older people. Further, that the term πρεσβυτέριον "council of elders" (1 Tim 4:14) is also known in Ephesus suggests that presbuteros was an established and regularly used term among the addressees.

[39] Perhaps the fact that he had spoken of "elders" in the sense of "older men" in 1 Tim 5:1 also led him to use presbuteros in 1 Tim 5:17.

their function as "overseers". We have also suggested that the technical sense of "presbyter" (="presbyter as office") and "episkopos" were equated.[40] But we need to note that while all "overseers" were elders, not all elders were overseers.[41]

We can also note that 1 Tim 4:14 speaks of a body of presbyters. There we read: "Do not neglect the gift that is in you, which was given to you through prophecy with the laying on of hands by the council of elders (τοῦ πρεσβυτερίου)."[42] This could either be a group of all "older men"[43] regardless of whether they were active in leadership, or it could be a group of "presbyter-overseers", that is, those older men active in leadership.[44]

1.2.5 What did the presbyter-overseers do?

In writing the Pastorals, the Pastor is not establishing any office, nor is his primary concern with what leaders did, and so the details of their functions and duties are not described directly. Rather he is regulating an existing office to ensure that the right sort of people become leaders and so he is preoccupied with aspects of character, probably because some of his opponents had been leaders and he wished to avoid further leaders abandoning what he regarded as "the faith". Thus, roughly the same qualities are listed for presbyter-overseers as for deacons. The concentration on qualities makes it difficult to determine what these leaders did. We should also note that the addressees presumably knew what presbyter-overseers did, and the need was to regulate who would take up this office, not to give a job description.

However, we have already gained some indications in this area. The presbyter-overseers are to "rule well" (προΐστημι; 1 Tim 5:17) and this is also said to involve "caring for (ἐπιμελήσεται)" God's church (1 Tim 3:5). In addition, "ruling well" is said to particularly involve labouring in preaching and teaching (1 Tim 5:17; 3:2). We can suggest that this involved general oversight of the teaching given in the community, as well as being involved in

---

[40] In any case, in Ephesus the episkopos and the presbuteros are not to be identified completely, as they seem to have been on Crete. Rather the episkopoi are a specialised group within the presbyters in Ephesus.

[41] For a critique of the view of Campbell (1994, p176-205) that the Pastorals reflect the development of monepiscopacy (in the sense of a "town-church leader" (p205)) and the differentiation of the roles of overseer and presbyter see Marshall 1999, p179-80, who notes that the terminological distinction Campbell suggests does not become clear until Ignatius' time, that his view involves a very difficult interpretation of Tit 1:5, and that it makes the place of Timothy and Titus problematic.

[42] The alternative reading πρεσβύτερου, found in the original of Sinaiticus "is obviously a later attempt at creating an easier reading" (Meier 1973, p339 n38).

[43] This is the sense of the term in Josephus, CAp 2.206.

[44] For a discussion of 1 Tim 4:14 see Meier 1973, p339-42; Marshall 1999, p564-9.

teaching oneself.[45] Against the background of 1 Tim 5:17 and 1 Tim 3:2, it also seems likely that 2 Tim 2:2 applies to leaders: the faithful people to whom Timothy is to entrust the Gospel are presbyter-overseers, who will teach the Gospel to other leaders, and so on. This verse need not apply exclusively to leaders, and so may well have others in mind too, but given the leaders' role in teaching and that leaders are to be faithful,[46] we may suggest it applied primarily to them.[47] Further, the discussion of discipline and the testing of presbyters in 1 Tim 5:19-25 suggests that, because the presbyter-overseers were significant leaders with real responsibilities, and so had considerable potential for good or ill, great care must be taken in both these matters. But it does not assist us further in clarifying their role.[48] Finally, we have noted that in 1 Tim 4:14 the group of presbyters laid their hands on Timothy and laying on of hands is also mentioned in 1 Tim 5:22 and 2 Tim 1:6.[49] This suggest that one of the duties of presbyter-overseers was the laying on of hands in connection with a person taking up a position of leadership, although we have suggested that elders who were simply "older men" may have also been involved in the laying on of hands.[50]

Thus, although the leadership role of the presbyter-overseers is spoken of in fairly general terms, we can say that the role entailed considerable responsibility with regard to general oversight of the community (the meaning of "episkopos" after all) and particular responsibility for teaching sound doctrine.[51]

---

[45] Note that it is not said that only leaders can teach. Further, as we will discuss in more detail below, that in 1 Tim 3:2 a prospective overseer is required to be "an apt teacher", and so to have taught before he became a recognised leader, suggests that some of those who were not appointed leaders were involved in teaching in the community.

[46] See 1 Tim 3:11, where it is said that women deacons must be "faithful in all things".

[47] See Marshall 1999, p175.

[48] For a discussion of the duties of the overseer, see Young 1994, p99-104; Marshall 1999, p175-6. That some of the qualities looked for in leaders relate to them not misusing money (1 Tim 3:3, 8; Tit 1:7) does not indicate that their primary responsibility was for the community's finances, but rather is to be seen against the background of the community's common fund and the common charge in antiquity that leaders sought to gain money from those they taught; see 1 Thess 2:5-9. It is not to be doubted that they may have had some financial responsibility, but this was not their major role.

[49] On the differences between these passages see Marshall 1999, p567-9.

[50] See Wilson 1979, p54.

[51] 1 Tim 5:19-20 speaks about disciplining a sinning elder. It is not clear who undertakes this task, and it may be that the elders together had responsibility in this area.

1.3 Deacons

In 1 Tim 3:8, 12 the term διάκονος clearly refers to a specific function that is fulfilled alongside that of the presbyter-overseers.[52] It seems likely that deacons were appointed from among the "seniors", since they too are said to be householders and heads of families.[53] We note the following points in relation to deacons.

1.3.1 What did the deacons do?

As was the case with the presbyter-overseers, the Pastor is not establishing a new office, but rather regulating an existing office. Further, the emphasis in the discussion in 1 Tim 3:8-13 is again on the qualities looked for in deacons, rather than the role they fulfilled, so it is difficult to be sure about their duties and functions. But again we can deduce some points.

Firstly, since one of the prerequisites of office is "let them manage (προϊστάμενοι) their children and their household well", using the same verb used in 1 Tim 3:4-5 and 5:17 of the presbyter-overseers, it is likely that they had some "managing" or "ruling" responsibilities in the community. We should not think that presbyter-overseers did all the "ruling" therefore. But the particular "managing" responsibilities of deacons remain unknown. Secondly, the title "διάκονος" itself indicates some form of action as an agent or an assistant of someone else,[54] but since the word group "is used in the NT of practically every sort of ministry",[55] the word in itself does not assist us here.[56] Because of this breadth of usage, we certainly cannot say on the basis of the word "διάκονος" itself that the deacon's tasks were restricted to practical needs.

---

[52] In 1 Tim 3:10, 13 the verb διακονέω has the meaning of "to serve as a διάκονος".

[53] See Campbell 1994, p200.

[54] See BDAG, p230-1. For a discussion of the meaning of the term see Collins 1990, p73-252. It is found in inscriptions in Ephesus. In IvEph 3414-8 it occurs in a non-Christian context, probably with the meaning of an attendant or official in a temple or religious guild. Other inscriptions which contain the term are almost certainly Christian; see IvEph 495; 543; 1363; 3286; 3305; 4144; 4206-8; 4214; 4281; 4304; 4320.

[55] Marshall 1999, p487.

[56] Marshall (1999, p487) notes: "the claim that the omission of any reference to teaching or authority in the list of the deacons' qualifications (cf. 3.2; 5.17; Tit 1.7) implies that they were restricted to tasks pertaining to practical needs ... lacks any foundation." Collins shows that it is wrong to see διακονία, διακονεῖν and διάκονος as referring primarily to humble service of other people. He suggests (1990, p194) that "the root idea expressed by the words is that of the go-between ... in commonly signifying that an action is done for someone, the words do not speak of benefit either to the person authorising the action or to the recipient of the action but of an action done in the name of another."

Thirdly, it may be that we should see deacons as having some role with regard to doctrine, since in 1 Tim 3:9 it is said that "they must hold fast to the mystery of the faith with a clear conscience".[57] However, since they are not said to be teachers, it may simply be that, for the Pastor, every person with responsibility in the community needs to hold to "sound teaching", since they have influence both within and beyond the community by virtue of their leadership office.

So, with regard to function, it seems that the deacons had a role with regard to "managing/ruling" and acted as some form of assistant. Perhaps they had some role with regard to doctrine, but more than this we cannot say.[58]

1.3.2 How do deacons relate to presbyter-overseers?

The Pastor does not explicitly relate deacons in status to presbyter-overseers and so deacons are not explicitly said to be under the authority of presbyter-overseers. There is only one indication in this regard. In 1 Tim 3 the episkopos is discussed first, which perhaps indicates this was a more important function and so that the presbyter-overseers had precedence over the deacons or that the deacon's role was a less responsible position than that of the presbyter-overseers.[59] Collins thinks we can be more specific than this; he notes that deacons are discussed after the overseers and suggests: "even if this indicates little more than that the two offices are in some way coordinated, it would at least suggest that the deacon is the assistant of the other."[60]

---

[57] Note the equivalent in Tit 1:9. Marshall (1999, p487-8) thinks that 1 Tim 3:9 implies that the deacon has "some responsibility within the gospel ministry".

[58] Note that Acts 6:1-6 is often seen as relevant here, but the term διάκονος is not found there. We will make some further observations with regard to function in Chapter 11, when we discuss women deacons.

[59] The same order is found in Phil 1:1, so the order in both passages is probably significant; see also Collins 1990, p236; Gibaut 2000, p17-18. Marshall (1999, p488) writes that "the comparative brevity of the description [of deacons] may well suggest a subordinate appointment", but 1 Tim 3:8-13 is not really much shorter than 1 Tim 3:1-7. Note too that in 1 Tim 3:13 the author writes: "for those who serve well as deacons gain a good standing for themselves and great boldness in the faith that is in Christ Jesus". Gibaut (2000, p17-18) notes that later generations took this as a reference to the promotion of a deacon to the office of bishop, but that it is very unlikely that this is what the verse means. Rather Gibaut (2000, p18) suggests the author "probably intended to say that deacons who are competent and fervent will win the respect and gratitude of the church."

[60] Collins 1990, p237; see also Giles 1989, p60. Given the meaning of the term, deacons could be assistants of the overseers or of God/Jesus Christ. In this regard, Beyer (TDNT 2, p91) cites the analogy of the servant of the synagogue accompanying the head of the synagogue, but this hardly seems relevant. Campbell (1994, p199-200) thinks deacons were the assistant of the overseers and suggests that they were those leaders of house churches who

There are two other significant points with regard to the deacons in relation to the presbyter-overseers, but neither relate to status. Firstly, nothing is said in 1 Tim 5:17-19 about deacons receiving payment. This may, but need not, indicate that deacons were of secondary importance; it could simply indicate that the tasks of the deacon were not so time consuming that they needed to receive compensatory payment. Secondly, nothing is said of deacons in Crete, which suggests that they were not as vital as presbyter-overseers to the life of a new community, or perhaps came at a later stage of development when more differentiation of functions occurred as a community grew in size.

1.3.3 Women deacons

We will note in Chapter 11 that 1 Tim 3:11 shows that there were almost certainly women deacons in the community addressed in Ephesus. We will argue there that some women were currently teachers and leaders in the community and that some women were also deacons is a further indication that women were fulfilling leadership functions within the community.

1.3.4 Prophets

It seems likely that prophets also had a role in the community. In 1 Tim 1:18 it is said that Paul is entrusting the charge to Timothy "according to the earlier prophecies made concerning you". This suggests that Spirit-inspired prophecies pointed to Timothy as having this role of leadership. Similarly what is envisaged in 1 Tim 4:14 is that the prior Spirit-inspired prophecy pointed to Timothy, and thus indicated on whom the council of elders should lay their hands. The result was that Timothy was given a special gift, probably a gift for ministry. Alternatively, the prophecy could confirm prior giftedness by the Spirit and the laying on of hands would involve recognition by the community.[61]

It is unlikely that these verses only relate to the past; rather Timothy here probably functions as a paradigm for contemporary leaders. Hence, both 1 Tim 1:18 and 4:14 imply that the Pastor envisages prophets having a role in indicating who should lead the contemporary community.[62] As Hanson notes: "There is no trace in the Pastorals of any tension between prophets and

---

assisted the overseer (whom Campbell sees as the person set over a group of house churches) by continuing to lead their own house churches. But this is to go beyond our very limited evidence at this point.

[61] See Fee 1994, p773-6. 1 Tim 3:1 also indicates that people could, on occasions, volunteer as candidates for office, while 1 Tim 1:18 and 4:14 suggest they were then confirmed (or not) through the activity of a prophet; see Maloney 1994, p368.

[62] See Brox 1969, p180; Hanson 1982, p38, 94.

ordained ministers. Indeed there is no reason why a church officer should not himself be a prophet. Thus we have no justification for speaking of 'an order of prophets'. At the time when the Pastorals were written, prophecy was a charisma not an office."[63] But we note that it seems likely that prophets exercised some form of leadership in the community, even if only to indicate who should be ordained to formal leadership positions.[64]

1.4 A degree of institutionalisation with regard to leadership in the Pastoral Epistles

Having outlined the general structure of leadership in the community addressed by the Pastorals, we now turn to a general feature of the situation.[65] It is clear that the Pastorals exhibit a degree of institutionalisation with regard to leadership structures. For in the Pastorals we see a situation in which apostles are no longer present to exercise supervision and where time and perhaps the growth of the church has led to the need for greater structure than seems to have been the case in the undisputed Paulines. However, as Marshall notes, the Pastorals "stand at the beginning of this process, and what we see is the beginning of a co-ordination of the organisation and ministry of the congregations."[66]

Here then we will discuss "institutionalisation". MacDonald helpfully defines "institutionalisation" in the following way: "the transformation of the early church from its loosely-organized, charismatic beginnings to its more tightly-structured nature in the second century. ... As time passes and groups grow, greater organization is required. Communal forms become increasingly 'solid'. As the body of tradition expands, the possibilities for innovation decrease. With the existence of a fairly solidified symbolic universe, creativity is no longer necessary, nor perhaps even possible, in the same way."[67] Accordingly, in this section we will note that there are a number of

---

[63] Hanson 1982, p38.

[64] Note also the mention of the "evangelist" in 2 Tim 4:5.

[65] We have discussed the issue of the economic position of leaders in Chapter 9. Note also that the patriarchal structure of the household has become more evident in the life of the church in the Pastorals, including its leadership. This springs in part from understanding the church as the "household of God". We will discuss this further in Chapter 11.

[66] Marshall 1999, p171; see also Meier 1973, p345.

[67] MacDonald 1988, p235. Note that we are not suggesting there was no "leadership structure" in the earliest period, nor that we should see this development as occurring everywhere at the same pace, or in the same direction. MacDonald (1988, p11) quotes the definition of institutionalisation given by Berger and Luckmann: "Institutionalization occurs whenever there is a reciprocal typification of habitualized actions by types of actors. Put differently, any such typification is an institution." MacDonald gives a thorough discussion of institutionalisation in 1988, p10-18. With regard to the Pastorals Marshall (1999, p170) notes:

signs of a significant degree of institutionalisation with regard to leadership structures in the Pastorals.

We are not suggesting that there were no signs of institutionalisation in the undisputed Paulines. Clearly there were local church leaders who had recognised positions of authority in some of Paul's communities (eg 1 Thess 5:12; 1 Cor 16:15-16; Phil 1:1), although the tasks of ministry was not confined to these leaders (see 1 Cor 12:28-30 and Rom 12:6-11). We should not draw a rigid distinction between an earlier charismatic ministry and a later institutional form of leadership.[68] But our point is that there is *greater* institutionalisation in the Pastorals.

1.4.1 Signs of a degree of institutionalisation

Firstly, it is clear that in the community addressed in 1 and 2 Tim there are established and formal leadership positions; we have argued that these are presbyter-overseers and deacons. Rather than someone fulfilling particular functions (and perhaps then being given a "title"), the community has leaders with particular designations, who, by virtue of being a "presbyter-overseer" or "deacon" fulfil those functions. Further someone can "aspire to the task (or position) of overseer" (ἐπισκοπή; 1 Tim 3:1), and thus the position of being a presbyter-overseer is one which a person might seek. In Tit 1:5 (which relates to Crete) we learn that Titus is to look for suitable people and "appoint elders"; Titus is to look for people to fill what the Pastor understands as a position. Although we do not wish to overplay the difference, rather than someone arising naturally to fulfil a function, there are thus designated positions of leadership to which one can aspire, or be appointed. Further, it seems very likely that the community as a whole looks to the people who hold the positions of presbyter-overseers or deacons for leadership. Accordingly, we see the emergence of designated and formalised positions of leadership.

Secondly, the Pastor gives a lists of qualifications for those who would hold these offices (1 Tim 3:1-13; Tit 1:5-9). That those who become office holders need first to satisfy a list of what we may call character attributes testifies to a degree of formality.

Thirdly, the Pastor speaks of testing potential office-holders prior to them taking up office. Thus, in 1 Tim 3:10 he writes with regard to deacons: "And let them first be tested (καὶ οὗτοι δὲ δοκιμαζέσθωσαν πρῶτον); then, if they prove themselves blameless, let them serve as deacons (εἶτα διακονείτωσαν ἀνέγκλητοι ὄντες)." Some form of investigation of the person's attributes, using the list of required character traits in 1 Tim 3:8-12,

---

"The PE represent a stage in the history of the church when the contours of organisation are becoming more pronounced."

[68] See Marshall 1999, p176; Campbell 1994a, p248-54.

is envisaged.[69] Similarly, in 1 Tim 5:22, 24-5, having spoken of the disciplining of presbyter-overseers (1 Tim 5:20-1),[70] the Pastor goes on to discuss the careful investigation of potential presbyter-overseers prior to the laying on of hands in ordination.[71] The Pastor is suggesting that if presbyter-overseers are carefully chosen then discipline should not be an issue; that is, "prevention is better than a cure".[72] Hence in verse 22 the Pastor writes with respect to presbyter-overseers: "Do not be hasty in the laying on of hands, do not participate in the sins of others ...". Clearly this presupposes time for an investigation of the potential presbyter-overseer's life. In v24-5 the Pastor goes on to advise that this is complex because sin can be evident or hidden. "Timothy is to avoid ordination of the wrong candidates by carrying out careful investigation. It is to be careful precisely because, while some sins are so public that they cry out like denouncers running to the tribunal, other failings show up belatedly, only after prolonged inquiry."[73] Thus, for both the presbyter-overseer and the deacon we see that a procedure for testing prior to selection for office has developed.

Fourthly, 1 Tim 4:14 and 2 Tim 1:6, which both clearly refer to ordination through the laying on of hands, show that ordination has developed as a ritual for the commencement of ministry.[74]

Fifthly, we have argued in Chapter 9 that the reference to those presbyters who rule well in teaching and preaching receiving "double honour (διπλῆ τιμή)" (1 Tim 5:17) almost certainly refers to some sort of financial or material payment. This is particularly indicated by the two scriptural quotations which follow, including the statement that "The labourer deserves his wages". Thus, we see that leaders are receiving payment, which is another indication of institutionalisation.

---

[69] See MacDonald 1988, p213.

[70] Meier (1973, p330-2) argues that in 1 Tim 5:20 the reference to the discipline of those persisting in sin is much more likely to refer to presbyters rather than to all sinners. He notes that 5:1-6:2 concerns different groups and that it would be strange if in 5:20 the Pastor suddenly discussed sinners in general, rather than continuing to discuss particular groups of people.

[71] 1 Tim 5:22 is much more likely to refer to ordination and preparation for it than to the reconciliation of penitents; see Meier 1973, p333-4; Marshall 1999, p620-2.

[72] Meier 1973, p334.

[73] Meier 1973, p335. That 1 Tim 5:22, 24-5 refers to testing of presbyters is argued by Meier 1973, p333-5. Verse 23 is probably best seen as a digression occasioned by the remark at the end of v22: "Keep yourself pure". The remark about purity might be thought to mean that Timothy should adopt ascetic practices of avoidance of certain food (and drink), which were followed by the opponents (1 Tim 4:1-5); v23 then clarifies that the Pastor does not mean this.

[74] That in 1 Tim 4:14 the reference to the presbuterion laying on hands involved ordination, see Young 1994b, p144.

Sixthly, although the Spirit remains active in the community,[75] we see a particular connection made between the Spirit and leadership. In 2 Timothy 1:6-7 we read: "For this reason I remind you to rekindle the gift of God that is within you through the laying on of my hands; for God did not give us a Spirit of cowardice but of power and of love and of self-discipline (δυνάμεως καὶ ἀγάπης καὶ σωφρονισμοῦ)." Thus Timothy has been given "τὸ χάρισμα τοῦ θεοῦ" through the laying on of hands. The image of rekindling and so of fire, often used with regard to the Spirit, the use of χάρισμα and πνεῦμα in close proximity,[76] and the use of δίδωμι, which is often used of God giving the Spirit,[77] argue that the "gift of God" is here envisaged as given by the Spirit. Thus the Pastor envisages the Spirit giving gifts to leaders and we can suggest that the same thought is present in 1 Tim 4:14, where the link between "gift" and "Spirit" is confirmed by the mention of prophecy. So we note that the Spirit is connected with both leadership office and the institution of the church, since the gift of the Spirit for leadership comes through the laying on of hands by the council of elders (1 Tim 4:14) or by an individual in authority (Paul in 2 Tim 1:6; Timothy in 1 Tim 5:22). Thus there is a movement towards the institutionalisation of the Spirit's gift, since it is those who are in office who are said to receive "charisma" for ministry.[78] This may not be the only sense in which the Pastor would have used the word "charisma", and so we cannot conclude that in his view no one else receives a gift from the Spirit, but it does reflect one of his emphases. Clearly then there are links between the institution of the Church and the Spirit and leadership; this can also be seen as a sign of greater institutionalisation with regard to leadership.

These points are all indications of institutionalisation with regard to the leadership structure of the church. Since the Pastor does not argue for most of these matters, but, for example, assumes that leadership is in the hands of those who hold positions as presbyter-overseers and deacons and that these people have been ordained, we can note that the Pastor is reflecting the situation among the addressees with regard to the developing institutionalisation of leadership structures.

---

[75] Note Marshall's warning (1999, p176): "Suggestions that the Holy Spirit is no longer active except in those appointed to office represent an argument from silence; those who adopt them have to find ways of explaining away the reference to prophets in 1 Tim 4:14."

[76] Cf. 1 Cor 12:5,7.

[77] See Luke 11:13; Acts 5:32; 8:18; 15:8; Rom. 5:5; 1 Cor. 1:22; 5:5; Eph. 1:17; 1 Thess. 4:8; cf also 1 Tim. 4:14.

[78] See in particular Käsemann 1964, p86-9; Dunn 1975, p347-50.

1.4.2 Yet the institutionalisation of the leadership and structure of the church has only really begun

However, there are important indications that the community is on the way to, rather than having arrived at, institutionalisation with regard to leadership and structure.[79]

Firstly, an important matter here is that πρεσβύτερος is used both as a title for a leadership position and with reference to an "older man". In 1 Tim 5:1-2, the contrast with "younger men" (νεώτεροι) and the parallelism with the feminine form πρεσβυτέρα in v2 indicate that πρεσβύτερος in v1 refers to older men in general. By contrast, as we have noted, in 1 Tim 5:17 the discussion of "πρεσβύτεροι who have presided well" must refer to some kind of official "elder". Clearly then the term is still somewhat flexible; it had not become so much of a technical term for a leadership position that it could not be used, without any special explanation, in the more established sense with regard to age.[80]

Similarly, the διάκονος/ διακονία/ διακονέω word group is used in various ways in the Pastorals. Although in 1 Tim 3:8, 12 διάκονος is used of people who hold a specific office alongside the presbyter-overseers, in 1 Tim 4:6 διάκονος is used in a very general way to refer to Timothy as a servant or assistant of Jesus Christ.[81] The verb διακονέω is also used in the specialised sense of "to serve as a διάκονος" in 1 Tim 3:10, 13, but it has a more general sense of "to render assistance" in 2 Tim 1:18. Further, διακονία is used in the general sense of "assistance" or "ministry" in 1 Tim 1:12; 2 Tim 4:5, 11.[82] Again then, we see that terms which can be used for a leadership position can also be used with a different sense. This is a sign that institutionalisation is in progress (evidenced by the development of technical terms themselves for leaders) but has not proceeded so far as to result in a single meaning for key terms.

Secondly, and related to this is the point that, if we are correct in our earlier discussion of the titles "presbuteros" and "episkopos", we have two terms for the one position. It is significant that there is no one title for presbyter-overseers. Rather, we see them being referred to at first in 1 Tim 3 by their function of "overseer" and then later in 1 Tim 5 by the term

---

[79] See Marshall 1999, p171.

[80] See Meier 1973, p324-5; Harvey 1974, p326-8. Marshall (1999, p174) notes it "is in course of transition from a general to a more technical meaning". Cf. 1 Peter 5:1-4.

[81] He is also called a δοῦλος Κυρίου in 2 Tim 2:24 and Paul is called a δοῦλος θεοῦ in Tit 1:1.

[82] See Collins (1990, p237), who suggests that with the possible exception of 2 Tim 1:18 "these uses refer to activity in the direct interest of the gospel by those with a commission of a missionary or local nature." Note that Ignatius can also use διακονία of the "ministry" of the bishop; see eg IgnPhd 1:1

"presbyter", which is emerging as a status designation for leaders (though this term can still be used in its more general sense of "old man"). This variety indicates that institutionalisation has only really begun.

Thirdly, it is not said that deacons should obey presbyter-overseers, and as we have noted there is no clear attempt to relate presbyter-overseers and deacons to each other in an hierarchical order.[83] This lack of clear hierarchy with regard to the two offices, particularly in view of the later developments seen for example in Ignatius, indicates again that institutionalisation of leadership positions is only beginning.

Fourthly, we note that leadership is "plural" in the Pastorals. We have argued that the singular use of "episkopos" is generic, and we note that both presbuteros and diakonos are either used in the plural, or on the one occasion when presbuteros is used in the singular it is clear from the context that a plurality of leaders is still in view.[84] We suggest therefore that among the addressees, leadership was seen as undertaken by a group, rather than by a single individual.[85] Again, particularly in view of later developments with the emergence of the monepiscopacy, and in the light of plural leadership in the undisputed Pauline letters, this suggests that institutionalisation is only beginning.

Fifthly, although leaders (presbyter-overseers) were involved in teaching (1 Tim 5:17), and probably had oversight of what was taught (as 2 Tim 2:2 suggests), they are not the only people who can teach the community. This is clearest in the fact that one of the qualities required of a prospective episkopos in 1 Tim 3:2 is that he is an apt teacher. This makes best sense if the person has already actually been involved in teaching in the community before they were appointed as an episkopos, rather than being an assessment based on no

---

[83] We have noted that the deacons may be the assistants of the presbyter-overseers, but that it is not said that the deacons must obey the presbyter-overseers, and no clear instruction with regard to hierarchy is given, is significant.

[84] In 1 Tim 5:17 we have the plural ("Let the elders ...) and then in 5:19 "Never accept any accusation against an elder (κατὰ πρεσβυτέρου ...) ..." Clearly the singular "elder" in 5:19 is one of the group of 5:17. Presbuteros is plural in Tit 1:5. Diakonos is plural in 1 Tim 3:8 and 12; it is used in the singular of Timothy in 1 Tim 4:6. Διακονέω is used in the plural of serving as deacons in 1 Tim 3:10, 13 and in the non-technical sense in the singular in 2 Tim 1:18; διακονία is used of Paul (1 Tim 1:12), Timothy (2 Tim 4:5) and Mark (2 Tim 4:11), all in the singular.

[85] This does not mean that there was always, for example, two "leaders" in a house church. But even if there was only one leader in such a situation, we can suggest that such a person was not seen as *the* locus of authority in and of themselves, but rather community members understood that leadership was a shared task. Thus, even if one person led a house church, we can suggest that the members of that house church would also recognise the authority of leaders of other house churches which made up the whole community.

evidence.[86] That all the teaching is not centralised in the leaders again indicates that institutionalisation has not proceeded very far.

We conclude therefore that, although institutionalisation of the leadership and structure of the church has begun, it has only begun and there remains a good deal of elasticity and some informality in this area.

1.5 The locus of authority in the Pastorals

In this section, and in corresponding sections relating to the Johannine Letters and Revelation, we will discuss what we can discern about what the author and readers regard as the locus of authority. What does the author and the addressees see as "bedrock" when it comes to authority?[87]

There were different forms of authority in the early Church. Clearly one was that of apostleship, with apostles like Paul tracing their sense of authority back to a commission by the risen Lord (1 Cor 9:1). There is also the authority of the prophet who claims inspiration from the Spirit and the more general phenomenon of authority based in charismatic gifts. Other forms of authority are that of office or appointment, spiritual maturity, seniority or age, or where authority is seen to reside in the community as a whole, rather than in any particular individuals.

We also need to note that we should not see a fundamental opposition between "charismatic" and "institutional" ordering of the life of the early Church. As Giles notes, "While it is true that the more charismatic forms of leadership such as seen at Corinth did give way to more ordered institutional leadership with the passing of time, the data suggest that the charismatic and the institutional existed side by side from the beginning ... There never were two diametrically opposed patterns but differing degrees of emphasis and a tendency for the process of institutionalization to become more pronounced."[88]

Related to this, more than one loci of authority can function simultaneously in any one community. It then becomes significant to see the relationship between them. What can we say about the Pastorals in this regard?

---

[86] See Marshall 1999, p176. Note also that the Pastor never says that teaching is only to be done by those holding an official position, although this is an argument from silence.

[87] On authority in the early Church see Meeks 1983, p136-9; Holmberg 1978, especially p196-208; Chilton and Neusner 1999 (who use the three categories of institutional, charismatic and scriptural authority). Weber (1978, p215-16) argued that there are three "pure types of authority": rational, traditional, and charismatic. These were seen as abstractions or ideal types, and a particular example can show traits of more than one ideal type; see further Giles 1989, p175-7. However, Weber's terminology does not quite fit the situation we find in our texts. For discussion of the relationship of power and authority, see Holmberg 1978, p124-35; Hack Polaski 1999, p35-51.

[88] Giles 1997, p220.

Clearly, foundational for the community in the Pastorals is what has occurred in the Christ-event that has led to salvation. This is summed up in a number of statements that can be regarded as creeds or elements of tradition; a good example is 1 Tim 3:16.[89] These statements encapsulate the faith of the community which is centred in the Christ-event, which is itself an expression of the "goodness and loving kindness of God our Saviour" (Tit 3:4) and is made real in the believer's life through the Holy Spirit (Tit 3:5-6).[90]

But beyond this it is clear that the Pastorals look back to Paul as the key guide to the Gospel. Paul is the key authority figure of the past who was "appointed a herald and an apostle and a teacher" of this Gospel (2 Tim 1:11; see also 1 Tim 1:12-13; 2:7).[91] This suggests that he is highly respected in the community and is regarded as the fountain-head of what we will see is "the tradition". Accordingly, Paul, who is designated as an "apostle of Christ Jesus" (1 Tim 1:1; 2 Tim 1:1; Tit 1:1), is spoken of as the one to whom the Gospel has been entrusted (1 Tim 1:11; Tit 1:3).[92] That Paul is spoken of as an example,[93] is connected with this – he is the paradigm for the addressees as the "herald, apostle and teacher". The authority of Paul among the addressees is also suggested by the direct "charges" within the letters: for example in 1 Tim 5:21 we read: "In the presence of God and of Christ Jesus and of the elect angels I charge you to keep these rules…"[94] In all of this, Paul is important, not only in his own right, but also because he is the one who has been entrusted with the Gospel. Since the Gospel and Jesus Christ are the final loci of authority, Paul derives key significance as the true guide to and teacher of this Gospel, and thus has himself become a locus of authority for the community from the past.

A key phrase to describe the content of what is believed is "sound" or "healthy teaching". This is what Paul has been entrusted with and what the Pastor now says he is passing on. We suggest that it is this "sound teaching" that has become the crucial "operational" locus of authority in the community. Given that Paul is no longer present, this "sound teaching" or tradition which

---

[89] See also 1 Tim 1:15; 2:3-6; 6:13-16; 2 Tim 1:9-10; 2:11-13; Tit 3:4-7. On traditions in the Pastorals see Ellis 1999, p406-18 (who is somewhat overconfident about our ability to discern traditions); on salvation see Towner 1989, p75-119; Young 1994, p50-68; on the faithful sayings see Knight 1968.

[90] Thus, ultimate assurance is said by the Pastor to be in God (see 2 Tim 1:12).

[91] Young (1994, p121) notes: "Paul is the guarantor, and the real authority behind these texts." See also Collins 1988, p124-9; Beker 1991, p36-9. Note that Paul is described as "διδάσκαλος" twice in the Pastorals (1 Tim 2:7; 2 Tim 1:11), but the term is not used of Paul in the undisputed Paulines.

[92] This need not be seen in an exclusive sense, as if Paul is necessarily regarded as the only true preserver of "the Gospel".

[93] Note 1 Tim 1:16; see also 2 Tim 3:10: "Now you have observed my teaching …"

[94] See also Tit 3:8.

is said to derive from Paul, has become the actual present and operational guide for the community with regard to the content of the true Gospel of Jesus Christ and how one should live. Thus teaching must be in accordance with "sound doctrine", and people are exhorted that they might live in such a way as to show that they adhere to "sound teaching".[95]

This emphasis on "sound teaching" is clear in 1 Tim 1:9-11 where it is said that the law "is laid down not for the innocent but for the lawless and disobedient, ... and whatever else is contrary to the sound teaching that conforms to the glorious gospel of the blessed God". Here "sound teaching" is equated with "the glorious gospel". Note also 1 Tim 4:6: "If you put these instructions before the brothers and sisters, you will be a good servant of Christ Jesus, nourished on the words of the faith and of the sound teaching that you have followed", and the instruction in Tit 2:1 to "teach what is consistent with sound teaching".[96]

Much of the stress on "sound doctrine" arises because the Pastor's opponents have abandoned such teaching and now contradict it (eg 1 Tim 1:19-20). This leads to injunctions to have nothing to do with godless and silly myths, or with the Pastor's opponents (1 Tim 4:7; 2 Tim 2:23; 4:3-4). It is because the opponents have abandoned this tradition for myths and speculations and in so doing are following Satan that they are condemned (eg 1 Tim 1:19-20; 5:15). As we have noted in Chapter 5, it seems likely that the opponents also saw Paul as an authority figure and would have seen themselves as in the Pauline tradition. As Young notes: "The fundamental issue between these letters and those they oppose [ie the opponents] concerns the proper interpretation of the life and teaching of Paul."[97] In a situation where both sides wanted to claim Paul's mantle, the Pastor responds by strongly criticising the opponents, giving traditions which he thinks contain "sound teaching", emphasising the importance of this latter concept and giving detailed instructions (which he clearly also regards as "sound teaching") about matters such as leadership, exemplary behaviour and ethics.

Paul is clearly thought of as the one who preached this "sound doctrine" and, as we have noted, is thus the source or fountainhead of the tradition. This is clear in 1 Tim 1:11, where "sound teaching" (v10) is said to conform "to the glorious gospel of the blessed God, which *he entrusted to me*." Note also 2

---

[95] On "sound teaching" see Malherbe 1980, p121-36; Young 1994, p74-96; Young sets the concept of sound teaching in a helpful social context.

[96] See also 1 Tim 4:6; 6:3; 2 Tim 4:3; Tit 1:9; 2:1, 7-8; note also the emphasis on teaching in 1 Tim 4:12-13, 16; 5:17; 6:1; 2 Tim 3:10-16; Tit 2:10. Further, in 1 Tim 6:1 slaves are told to regard their masters as worthy of all honour "so that the name of God and the teaching may not be blasphemed". Here we see that "the teaching" is a shorthand expression for what the community believes, that is, the gospel. This shows again how central the idea of "teaching" is for the community.

[97] Young 1994, p88.

Tim 1:13: "Hold to the standard of sound teaching that you *have heard from me* .." and 2 Tim 2:8: "Remember Jesus Christ, raised from the dead, a descendent of David – that is *my gospel*."[98]

But the author also stresses that "sound teaching" or tradition must be passed on faithfully to others. This is understandable given that the opponents are claiming another version of the "Pauline tradition". Thus in the letters, Paul is presented as passing on the tradition to "Timothy" (or "Titus"),[99] who is to pass it on to other teachers, who in turn will teach others. Thus a chain of tradition is envisaged – from Paul to Timothy and Titus, to other teachers, with still others beyond them. This is expressed in 2 Tim 2:2: "what you have heard from me through many witnesses entrust to faithful people who will be able to teach others as well." As part of this, Timothy (and others entrusted with the Gospel) must "guard what has been entrusted to you", that is the gospel (1 Tim 6:20). We see here then an emphasis on the authority of the tradition, and linked with this is the authority of carefully selected and recognised teachers.

In conjunction with this, we note that an overseer must be "an apt teacher" (1 Tim 3:2),[100] and in Tit 1:9 we read "He [a presbyter-overseer] must have a firm grasp of the word that is trustworthy in accordance with the teaching, so that he may be able both to preach with sound doctrine and to refute those who contradict it." Further, it seems most likely that Timothy and Titus both function as paradigms for leaders in the community,[101] and thus what is said to them applies to leaders among the addressees. We note that in 2 Tim 2:24 we read: "And the Lord's servant must not be quarrelsome but kindly to everyone, an apt teacher, patient, correcting opponents with gentleness." Similarly in 2 Tim 3:14 we read: "But as for you, continue in what you have learned and firmly believed, knowing from whom you have learned it ...". Thus, leaders have a responsibility as teachers and are to "guard the good

---

[98] See also 1 Tim 1:3; 2 Tim 2:2; Tit 1:3.

[99] See the idea of Paul handing on the "deposit (παραθήκη)" in 1 Tim 6:20; 2 Tim 1:12, 14. The "deposit" is the tradition of what is believed, that is, the gospel. As Marshall (1999, p518) notes, the community, faced with the challenge of the opponents, emphasised the need to teach the truth and oppose error: "But this raises the questions of where the truth is to be found and how it is to be preserved. It is not surprising, then, that the church is called back to the deposit handed down by Paul."

[100] We note however, the lack of any other explicit mention of expertise with regard to the content of faith as a quality called for in leaders; the only other point at which this is mentioned is that the overseer is not to be a recent convert (1 Tim 3:6), but the motivation given is that he might not become conceited. This is because of the huge stress in the letters on respectable behaviour.

[101] Although we do not think that Timothy and Titus are meant to be representatives of monepiscopacy, it is clear that what is said directly to them (eg in 1 Tim 4:15-16) also has wider application for others among the addressees with leadership responsibilities. On the paradigmatic function of such examples see Fiore 1986, p191-236.

treasure" and to "pass on the tradition".[102] But we should also note the concern about the character of the leaders (eg 1 Tim 3:1-13). Those who are leaders should set an example of correct ethical behaviour (which includes living in the proper hierarchical relationships), because of the strong connection in these letters between "teaching" and "conduct" (see, for example, 2 Tim 3:10-14) – teaching is "sound teaching" precisely because it leads to a "sound life". Thus it was crucial for leaders themselves to be living out the obligations and duties which were such an important part of "sound teaching" for the Pastor.

We conclude then that authority in the community lies primarily in the tradition of "sound teaching", itself connected to Paul, but that this tradition is to be passed on from authoritative teacher to authoritative teacher.[103] It is this "sound doctrine" which the Pastor's opponents have jettisoned, which is the reason why they are so roundly condemned.

Other factors do have a role with respect to being loci of authority, although these other factors are not emphasised to the same extent as the Pauline tradition and the authorised teachers of the tradition. We note here briefly the role of the Spirit, Scripture, and the church.

The Spirit has guided the community in its interpretation of the present and so functions as an authority; thus in 1 Tim 4:1 we read: "Now the Spirit expressly says that in later times some will renounce the faith". Further in 2 Tim 1:14 we read: "Guard the good treasure entrusted to you, with the help of the Holy Spirit living in us." We may suggest the Pastor believes that leaders will be enabled by the Spirit in the crucial task of guarding the deposit of Pauline tradition, which is a key locus of authority. The Spirit also has a role in enabling leaders, since the Spirit is said to give a gift through the laying on of hands (1 Tim 4:13-16; 2 Tim 1:6). 1 Tim 4:13-16 shows that the gift relates to teaching and perhaps ministry more generally;[104] this shows that the Spirit enables and empowers those who function as authoritative teachers of the tradition. But we also note from 1 Tim 4:1 that there are "deceitful spirits". This means that the Spirit's role with regard to authority is not

---

[102] See Marshall 1999, p521.

[103] Note Wilson (1979, p62): "In the Pastorals the importance and authority of church offices are ultimately secondary to the 'sound teaching', the apostolic tradition. It is this which provides the rationale for the existence of offices, for it is to the preservation and dissemination of sound teaching that church leaders are committed." See also Marshall 1988, p165.

[104] Given that in 2 Tim 1:8 the author goes on to write about "testifying to our Lord", the gift in v6-7 is probably again teaching and preaching; see also v13. In 1 Tim. 5:22 the context is leadership and the concern lest a leader be compromised by a wrong choice of successor. Fee (1988b, p673) suggests that the gift "refers first to the Spirit (2 Tim. 1:6-7) but is also broadened to refer to the gift for ministry that came by the Spirit (1 Tim. 4:14)."

straightforward; there are also false spirits, and so discernment must be exercised in this area.[105]

The authority of Scripture is also emphasised at times and clearly the Scriptures are seen as valuable for every aspect of the church's teaching.[106] But we may suggest that a crucial question is who can interpret Scripture in what the Pastor regards as the correct way? Clearly, in the Pastor's opinion the opponents misread the law (1 Tim 1:7-11) and their "myths and genealogies" are probably based on the OT. So, we may suggest, "authorised teachers" are important in that they can interpret Scripture correctly (see 2 Tim 3:14-17);[107] so although Scripture is a key authority, it needs to be read in the right way, by those who teach in accordance with "sound teaching".[108]

The church is also said to be the "pillar and bulwark of the truth" (1 Tim 3:15). As Marshall notes, "the church is closely associated with the gospel and is the guardian of the true message which leads to salvation."[109] But crucial to the life of the church is the tradition and the authoritative leaders who teach the sound deposit, so we probably should not see the church in itself as an independent authority here.

In all of what he says about the tradition and authoritative teachers, is the Pastor reflecting only his own views, or is he reflecting the situation of the community? It seems very likely that the community reveres Paul and regards him as the key exponent of the Gospel; the Pastor seems to be able to take this for granted. Further, the Pastor is not creating the positions of leadership that he discusses – there are already leaders in the community and he is simply discussing who should become leaders. Clearly leaders also currently have a teaching role, since some leaders have become "false teachers" (1 Tim 1:3). All of this suggests that currently the community addressed does see the locus of authority as in the tradition of which Paul was the fountainhead, and that that tradition is carried on by authoritative leaders. The challenging situation faced by the Pastor is rather created by the fact that a group has come into existence which claimed a different understanding of the tradition.

---

[105] On the Spirit in the Pastorals see in particular Quinn 1979, p345-68; Haykin 1985, p291-305; Donelson 1986, p143-5; Young 1994, p68-70.

[106] See 1 Tim 4:4-5; 4:13; 2 Tim 3:15-17. On 1 Tim 4:4-5 in this regard see Trebilco 2000, p204-220.

[107] Just as the Pastorals seek to show how correctly to "read" Paul's teaching and example, against the opponents' use of traditions about Paul.

[108] Thus the "teaching" mentioned in 1 Tim 4:13 is clearly from Scripture, and for the Pastor would be "sound teaching"; this is also in view in 1 Tim 4:16.

[109] Marshall 1999, p521.

1.6 Conclusion

We have already noted that the leadership roles of presbyter-overseers and deacons have developed prior to the Pastor writing the Pastorals. We have discussed various aspects of these positions. We have also concluded that although institutionalisation of the leadership and structure of the community of the addressees has begun, it has only begun and there remains a good deal of elasticity and some informality in this area.

We have also argued that in the Pastorals the locus of authority with regard to the gospel is seen to be Paul, but that in the current post-Pauline situation, authority resides in the tradition of "sound teaching" and in the "authoritative teachers" who have been carefully selected, taught and commissioned and who pass on this tradition. Given this emphasis on teaching and on carefully selected and authoritative teachers as the locus of authority, we can understand why the particular leadership structure (presbyter-overseers and deacons) we see in the Pastorals was favoured. The author sees a strong and respected leadership structure as the crucial way of maintaining the integrity of the community. Such stress is laid on leadership because much is at stake here – they are a crucial part of the locus of authority.

The development of leadership structures among the readers that we have discerned may have been in part a consequence of time and that leaders were now predominantly local rather than both local and itinerant as they had been in Paul's day. But we can also suggest that one reason for both the development of a more structured leadership and for seeing the locus of authority in authoritative teachers has been the influence of the Pastor's opponents. Although it does not seem that formalised leadership positions are particularly new among the addressees, no doubt a good deal of the emphasis the Pastor puts on leaders and their authority is because of the rise of the opponents, which has suggested to the Pastor that more formality was required in some features of leadership (perhaps with regard to testing prior to appointment and discipline) and that the leaders needed to be more and more the locus of authority, provided of course they had "a firm grasp of the word that is trustworthy in accordance with the teaching" (Tit 1:9). Thus we can see why there was an increasing stress on leadership and the authority of teachers.

2. Leadership and authority in the Johannine Letters

Although we will argue that 1-3 Jn are related with regard to the matters of leadership and authority, we will distinguish here between 1 Jn on the one hand and 2-3 Jn on the other. We will accordingly treat them in order.

2.1 Leadership in the community addressed in 1 John

The author of 1 John, traditionally called "John", does not begin with the normal epistolary opening, and does not give his name, nor any designation such as "apostle" or "elder". No leadership position of any sort is mentioned in the letter.

What is said in fact undermines at least some potential "leadership offices". In 1 Jn 2 there are three reference to an "anointing". In 1 Jn 2:20-1 we read: "But you have been anointed (καὶ ὑμεῖς χρῖσμα ἔχετε) by the Holy One, and all of you have knowledge. I write to you, not because you do not know the truth, but because you know it, and you know that no lie comes from the truth." Further in 1 Jn 2:26-7 we read: "I write these things to you concerning those who would deceive you. As for you, the anointing that you received from him (καὶ ὑμεῖς τὸ χρῖσμα ὃ ἐλάβετε ἀπ᾽ αὐτοῦ) abides in you, and so you do not need anyone to teach you. But as his anointing teaches you (ἀλλ᾽ ὡς τὸ αὐτοῦ χρῖσμα διδάσκει ὑμᾶς) about all things, and is true and is not a lie, and just as it has taught you, abide in him."

What does "τὸ χρῖσμα", which generally means either "anointing" or "oil for anointing", refer to? Since the anointing "abides in you" (2:27), its meaning here seems to be metaphorical with the emphasis being on what is used or received.[110] This leads to two possible interpretations. Firstly, the anointing could be through the Holy Spirit, or secondly, the anointing could be through the word of God, the Gospel, or the teaching which is heard.[111] Whichever meaning is correct, the important point for us is that because all believers received "the anointing", which now abides in them, and because it teaches them about all things, they are said to have no need of a teacher and so it seems very likely that there is no office of "teacher" in the community. This is reinforced by the emphatic position of the personal pronoun ὑμεῖς at

---

[110] See Lieu 1991, p29.

[111] See Brown 1982, p345-7; Burge 1987, p174-5; Strecker 1996, p64-6, 76-7 (who favour the view that the anointing is by the Spirit); Lieu 1991, p28-30; Neufeld 1994, p107-8 (who favour the reference being to the word of God). 1 Jn 3:24 and 4:13 relate the Spirit to knowledge, which suggests the anointing is a reference to the Spirit. But the structure of 1 Jn 2:20-27 suggests the anointing is through the word/Gospel, since while v20, 27 speak of the anointing from the Holy One abiding in you, in v24 we read: "Let what you heard from the beginning abide in you". The parallel then suggests the anointing refers to the word of God. Further, this is in keeping with 1 Jn 4:1-5, as Lieu (1991, p30) notes: "Rather than the community's confidence being essentially 'charismatic', the spirit can pose problems (4:1f); it is the received teaching or tradition which is more likely to be at the heart of their confidence." Note that it has been suggested that the author here introduced a term which was used by his (gnostic (in the view of some)) opponents. Did they claim superior knowledge through some form of a rite? If this was the case then John replies that all believers know all that is necessary. But as Lieu (1991, p29, her emphasis) notes: "since the author can also speak of the 'anti*christ*', '*chris*ma' is probably a term which he himself has coined or which comes from the tradition of his own community."

the beginning of both v20 and v27. As Strecker comments with regard to v27 (and the point applies equally to v20), this position strengthens the address: "*you*, the members of the Christian community, who are addressed by this writing, and not the false teachers, who do not belong to us (v.19)–it is *you* who are in possession of the 'oil of anointing'".[112] This anointing leads the addressees to the knowledge of the truth, and hence the community knows what truth and lies are (v21), in contrast to the secessionists (v19, 22-3). Since all the members of the community have "the anointing" which teaches them everything, they have no need of a teacher.

But is this simply rhetoric? It seems not, since there is no evidence in 1 Jn for anyone holding the position of "teacher". Rather, as we will see shortly, statements about knowledge and about certainty are regularly in the plural and refer to the community as a whole. Further, the author generally does not distinguish himself from the community as a teacher who instructs them "from above" as it were, but rather regularly speaks of "us" and "we". Accordingly, he generally sees himself as part of the community.[113] Further, in what he says about knowledge and certainty, John affirms that the community is collectively the locus of knowledge and shows that he clearly believes what he says in 2:20-1 and 26-7 – that they have no need of a teacher.[114] We have already noted that no other leadership positions are mentioned either.

2.2 The locus of authority in 1 John

All of this raises the question of where authority is located in 1 Jn? What does the author and (as far as we can discern this) the community see as "bedrock" when it comes to authority? Of course in 1 Jn the locus of authority is first and foremost in God, the Christ event, and the Gospel message – "what we have seen with our eyes, what we have looked at and touched with our hands, concerning the word of life" (1 Jn 1:1). But how does the community translate this authority of God and the Gospel message in such a way that it governs its life, as it clearly wants it to? How is it practically embodied and applied for the community and its life?

---

[112] Strecker 1996, p76, emphasis original.

[113] We will discuss the significance of the fact the he addresses the community as "little children" below. It is a term used by a teacher of pupils, but at this point we simply note that he does not take the next step of calling himself "teacher" but rather says that they have no need of a teacher (2:27).

[114] Edwards (1996, p75) suggests "It may seem illogical for the author to say that his addressees need no teacher when he himself is teaching them, but probably he sees his own teaching as part of the 'anointing'." Alternatively he may have seen a "teacher" as someone "over" them, and since he was writing "alongside" the community, he did not see himself as a "teacher".

Firstly, in 1 Jn there is some sense of the authority of the author. The author regularly addresses his readers as τεκνία (little children),[115] or less frequently παιδία (children).[116] This is the language a wisdom teacher would use to pupils, or a spiritual father to spiritual children.[117] Clearly, this language suggests the author had a sense of implicit individual authority,[118] which is in keeping with our view that he is John the Elder. Such a sense of authority is not only found in this form of address. Lieu also notes with regard to the author that he can issue commands to his readers (2:28; 4:1), gives an authoritative interpretation of recent events (2:18f) and of Christian practice (5:16-17).[119] We will note below that this sense of authority is based in being a tradition bearer and witness. But Lieu goes on to note: "Yet alongside these notes of a spiritual authority exercised from above or outside stand others which place the author within the community, if not literally, then in spirit."[120] We will now look at the ways in which the author does this.

As we have noted, the author does not introduce himself, or give himself a title such as apostle or elder. With only one exception, his only use of the first person singular with reference to himself is with the verb γράφω, to write.[121] The only exception is in 5:16 where he writes: "I do not say that you should pray about that", thus using the first person singular only to express what he does not want to say! Even when he does issue commands and so exercises a form of authority, there is regularly an affirmation in the immediate context "to soften its impact".[122] Further, instructions or commands are often of the form: "And now, little children, abide in him, so that when he is revealed *we*

---

[115] See 1 Jn 2:1, 12, 28; 3:7, 18; 4:4; 5:21.

[116] See 1 Jn 2:14, 18. In 1 Jn 3:7 there is debate about the reading, which is either τεκνία or παιδία.

[117] See Sir 2:1; 3:1; Ps 34:11; Prov 4:1; 5:1; 7:24; 8:32; Tobit 4:3, 12, 13.

[118] See Brown 1982, p214; see also Schnackenburg 1992, p9; Strecker 1996, p56. The author can also call his readers ἀγαπητοί ("beloved"); see 1 Jn 2:7; 3:2, 21; 4:1, 7, 11; 3 Jn 1, 2, 5, 11. Lieu (1991, p24-5) notes the term is found in the exhortations of testament literature.

[119] Lieu 1991, p25.

[120] Lieu 1991, p25; see also Rensberger 1997, p19.

[121] See 1 Jn 2:1, 7-8, 12-14, 21, 26, 5:13. For example, 1 Jn 5:13: "I write these things to you who believe in the name of the Son of God, so that you may know that you have eternal life." But even here he then goes on "And this is the boldness *we* have in him, that if *we* ask …", that is, he quickly resumes the first person plural associating himself strongly with the readers. First person singular verbs are used in reporting what others might say, and so are not used of the author, in 1 Jn 2:4 (Whoever says, "I have come to know him" …) and 4:20.

[122] Lieu 1991, p27; see for example 2:15, following 2:12-14 and 2:28, following 2:27. Lieu (1991, p25) notes that he also gives "an authoritative interpretation of recent events (2:18f) and of Christian practice (5:16-17)."

may have confidence… " (2:28) and "Let *us* love one another" (1 Jn 4:7).[123] Further, by far the most common mode of communication in the letter is for the author to associate himself with his readers, and to place himself within the community, often using "we" and "us", even as he instructs them.[124] While it has sometimes been thought that this might not be a genuine "we", from both its frequency and the way it is used it seems clear that the author's intent is to include himself and his readers by using the first person plural.[125] Thus, in these ways the author does not stand above the community but rather places himself within it. We can suggest therefore that he does not see himself as the most significant locus of authority (although he does have authority of his own) but first and foremost as part of the group that includes the readers.

So where does authority lie? We will argue that the primary locus of authority is the community. This is seen in what the author writes about witness, about the anointing and about what was "from the beginning". What is important for us is that the *predominant* sense of the locus of authority that we gain from 1 Jn is of the collective authority of the community, with the individual authority of the author of 1 Jn that we have noted above being very much a subsidiary factor. We will now discuss this evidence for a collective locus of authority.

2.2.1 Witness

The author begins his letter in this way in 1 Jn 1:1-5: "*We* declare to you what was from the beginning, what *we* have heard, what *we* have seen with *our* eyes, what *we* have looked at and touched with *our* hands, concerning the word of life – this life was revealed, and *we* have seen it and *we* testify to it, and *we* declare to *you* the eternal life that was with the Father and was revealed to *us* - *we* declare to *you* what *we* have seen and *we* have heard so that *you* also may have fellowship with *us* … *We* are writing these things so that *our* joy may be complete. This is the message *we* have heard from him and *we* are proclaiming to *you* …"

---

[123] See also for example 3:18; 4:11; but note that the author does issue a very few direct commands to readers, eg the closing exhortation in 5:21: "Little children, keep yourselves from idols" and in 4:1 (but even here he goes on in 4:2: "By this *you* know …).

[124] Neufeld (1994, p72, 93 n30) notes that the first person plural used in verbs and pronouns occurs 53 times and appears in 51 of the 105 verses of 1 John. Of course the author can speak of his readers as "you" and for example, of what they know (2:7) or of what they have heard (3:11).

[125] See Brown 1982, p158-61, who notes that, apart from 1:1-4, the plural in 1 Jn is most often used of the author and his readers.

We get a clear sense here of "we"/"us" and "you".[126] There is a group of witnesses who have "seen" and "heard", and have become tradition-bearers who "testify"; they now pass on what has been seen and heard to "you", the readers. We thus get the impression of a group of authoritative bearers of witness and tradition.[127]

However, 1 Jn 4:14, 16 seems to undermine this: "And *we* have seen and do testify that the Father has sent his Son as the Saviour of the world. ... So *we* have known and believe the love that God has for *us*." The context shows that the "we" here is the whole community rather than any special group of eyewitnesses; the experience of witness of the whole community can thus be spoken of.[128] Further, as we have noted, throughout the letter it is this sense of the joint "we"/"us" of author *and* readers that predominates over the sense of a select "we"/"us" as opposed to "you" readers in 1 Jn 1:1-5.[129] It is as if, having briefly suggested in 1 Jn 1:1-5 that he *can* stand over against the community as a member of the select "we", in the rest of the letter, the author abandons this possible form of authoritative communication for a strategy which locates himself *within* the community, as part of the collective, communal "we".

So while there is a sense of the authority of the author (and he does actually teach and give commands in the letter), the much stronger idea is that of the authority of the whole community – that they together are the witnesses, that together they "know" and so forth. So the much stronger concept is of the community as the locus of authority, rather than this being the role of a select few, or of the author filling this role. We will suggest below how the author can see the community as fulfilling this role, a conception of the role of the community which we suggest the community itself shared.

---

[126] Although note the change to "we" language, which clearly includes both reader and author, in 1 Jn 1:6-10.

[127] This seems to be the language of eye-witness; but note that what is seen and touched is not Jesus but is rather "concerning the word of life". Thus we need not envisage that eyewitnesses are involved. Rather the issue is one of continuity of tradition-bearers. Thus later tradition-bearers, through historical links or unity of faith, can use the same language as the first eyewitnesses; see Lieu 1981, p213; Brown 1982, p160-1. For the various explanations offered for the first person plural in 1:1-4 see Brown 1982, p158-61; Neufeld 1994, p72 n37. Hills (1991, p373) sees this as an appeal to authoritative witness. See also Brown 1974-75, p236; Hutaff 1994, p413; cf. Neufeld 1994, p73-5, 93-4.

[128] See Lieu 1991, p24-5. Lieu (1991, p25) notes the whole community, "because of their experience of God's love and gifts, and indeed of mutual indwelling with God, can use the language of witness themselves."

[129] Note for example, the sustained "we" of 1 Jn 3:11-24. Hutaff (1994, p414) writes: "The authoritative 'we' used in 1:1-5 is replaced in 1:6-10 with a hortatory 'we,' used to instruct or reprimand; it really means 'you.'" But it is highly significant that in 1:6-10 (and from then on) the author so often actually speaks of "we".

2.2.2 Anointing

We return here briefly to the topic of anointing discussed above, and mentioned in 1 Jn 2:20-1 and 26-7. One might imagine that some communities that spoke of an "anointing" would argue that particular people were "anointed", and that the anointing was perhaps to inspire teachers or leaders, or ensure the veracity of witnesses. However, recall 1 Jn 2:27: "As for you, the anointing that you received from him abides in you, and so you do not need anyone to teach you. But as his anointing teaches you about all things, and is true and is not a lie, and just as it has taught you, abide in him." We note that on each occasion, "you" here is plural and refers to the community. So the most noticeable thing is that everybody, and *not* particular people, has the anointing and so the community does not need someone to fulfil the function of a "teacher", because the anointing teaches each one about all things (see also 1 Jn 2:20: "all of you have knowledge").

Further, I would suggest that what is said about the anointing can be connected with the author seeing himself as part of the community (rather than as over and above it, addressing it from the outside), and with the author seeing the whole community as the locus of authority. Since all community members possess the anointing which leads to knowledge, they function together as the locus of authority and hence the author wishes to see himself as part of the anointed whole. What is said about the anointing reinforces the community as the locus of authority and explains the author's way of writing.

2.2.3 "What was from the beginning"

John uses the phrase "what was from the beginning", or something similar, on several occasions. We have already quoted 1 Jn 1:1: "We declare to you what was from the beginning, what we have heard, what we have seen with our eyes …" 1 Jn 2:24 is also typical of what John writes in this regard: "Let what you heard from the beginning abide in you. If what you heard from the beginning abides in you, then you will abide in the Son and in the Father."[130]

Hills has argued that the meaning of ἀπ᾽ ἀρχῆς here is derived from OT prophetic texts such as Isa 43:13; Mic 5:2 and Hab 1:12, and that the meaning of the phrase to be derived from the prophetic tradition is "from of old".[131] Thus, "the message he declares is from of old and not some novelty that they [the readers] can afford to reject."[132] Further, Brown notes: "When the author speaks of 'the beginning,' he means the beginning of the revelation of Jesus to his followers during the ministry, but for his readers this means the beginning of their contact with the tradition that came with conversion/ initiation/

---

[130] See also 1 Jn 2:7, 13-14; 3:11; 2 Jn 5-6; see also 1 Jn 3:8
[131] See Hills 1989, p307.
[132] Neufeld 1994, p68.

baptism."[133] Thus the phrase "from the beginning" refers not to an absolute beginning, but to the beginning of the community's life and what it has "known" since then.[134] It refers then to the transmission of traditions about Jesus from the beginning of the community into the present.

But there is one important feature of these statements about that which is "from the beginning" which is significant for our current discussion. In each case, apart from in 1 Jn 1:1, the author notes what "*you* have had from the beginning" or "what *you* heard from the beginning", rather than what "*we*" (ie. a select few) or "*I*" have had from the beginning. Thus, the author implies that *the community as a whole* has known, for example, the commandment "from the beginning" (1 In 2:7), or has heard the message of loving one another "from the beginning" (1 Jn 3:11). The author affirms that the whole community together has known some key tradition or teaching "from the beginning". The whole community is thus the bearer of these vital aspects of tradition; it is not that only the author, or a particular group of readers, or a select group of leaders are tradition-bearers. Our author only expresses this idea in 1 Jn 1:1, and then does not pick it up again. Rather, the whole community is together the tradition-bearer.

How can this be? The author obviously has a very real sense of the continuity of the community, and the unity of contemporary community members with those who have gone before. Even if some are new to the community, then they are one with those who have actually, in reality, had the commandment (for example) "from the beginning", or those who knew those who did have the commandment "from the beginning". This language then expresses the vitality and power of tradition: because the community carries on the tradition so strongly, it can actually be said that all the community, even recent members, have heard the message "from the beginning".[135]

But the effect of this language is again to locate authority in the community, rather than in an individual (eg. the author) or a small group (eg. of leaders). This is entirely in keeping therefore with what is said about witness and about anointing.

Against the background of what we have said of witness, anointing and the vitality of communal tradition "from the beginning", we can understand how the author can attribute knowledge to the whole community and can speak so often and with such certainty of what "you (the community) know" or even

---

[133] Brown 1982, p434; he reviews all the options for the meaning of "ἀρχή" on p155-8. See also Neufeld 1994, p67-70.

[134] See Lieu 1986, p75; see also Ellis 1999, p185-6.

[135] Given this strong sense of the tradition of the community and the importance of the community as tradition-bearer, we can understand why the secession and thus the schism of the community was such a shattering experience for the author, and we may suspect, the community too.

more often of what "we know ...". For example, as part of the epilogue in 1 Jn 5:19-20 we read: "*We* know that *we* are God's children ... And *we* know that the Son of God has come and has given *us* understanding so that *we* may know him who is true; and *we* are in him who is true, in his Son Jesus Christ. He is the true God and eternal life."[136] The author can say that the community ("we") knows these things *because* they are in union with the witnesses of the word of life, because they all have the anointing and because they (sometimes through others in the community) have heard what was "from the beginning". These statements of conviction and certainty about the knowledge "we" share are understandable in the light of these other facets of what the author affirms about witness, anointing and the tradition.

Now this does not mean that everyone in the community is in fact equally certain about what they "know". In fact, we have argued in Chapter 6 that assurance was a problem among the readers and that the author writes to encourage the readers in this regard (eg. 5:13). But the author uses these concepts of witness, anointing and what was "from the beginning" in this re-assurance process and further, as Lieu notes "that assurance is always 'ours' or 'yours' and never 'mine'."[137]

None of this means that there were not some people who, on occasions, "took the lead" in the community, including our author. That the author wrote the letter to the community seems in itself to be an act of leadership. There could well have been a number of people who undertook some functions of leadership, and sociologically it seems that such people must have existed. But the important point is that the author of 1 Jn sees himself functioning within the group, and not over and above it, and we can suggest the same was true for others who functioned as leaders. Further, the community did not conceive of authority as primarily residing in these individuals but rather in the group as a whole, and theologically this was supported by the concepts of witness, anointing and carrying on the tradition of what was "from the beginning", which were all seen in corporate terms.

Thus we can agree with Lieu when she writes: "For 1 John authority lies within the life and experience of the believing community; finding the way forward is a shared enterprise, and examination of their present Christian life is done from within and not from outside."[138]

---

[136] See further statements about the knowledge of community in 2:3, 5, 18; 3:2, 14, 16, 19, 24; 4:6, 13, 16; 5:2, 15, 18-20. He speaks of what "you know", clearly with reference to the community in 2:13-14; 20-1, 29; 3:5, 15; 4:2; 5:13. He uses both οἶδα and γινώσκω. The alternation between "we know" (3:14) "you know" (3:15) and "we know" (3:16) shows that the 1ppl and 2ppl are used synonymously of the community.

[137] Lieu 1991, p26.

[138] Lieu 1991, p27. Lieu (1991, p25) also notes that since authority was not located "in appointed or inherited roles but in that awareness of witness, it must have been seen as an

We can also note again at this point that, although the author generally does not choose to stand over and above the community, in 1 Jn 1:1-5 he does express a sense of authority (though this is undermined to some extent in 1 Jn 4:14-16) and that there it is an authority based in witness. But he gives no sense of an authority which is exclusive to a small group or based in any sort of appointment or office.[139]

2.2.4 The ambiguity of the Spirit

Before we proceed, we need to note briefly what the author says about the Spirit. It might be thought that the Spirit was a source of authority and perhaps an additional factor that led to the locus of authority being the whole community, since the Spirit was given to all. 1 Jn 3:24 might suggest this: "And by this we know that he abides in us, by the Spirit that he has given us". 1 Jn 4:13 might be additional evidence here: "By this we know that we abide in him and he in us, because he has given us of his Spirit."[140]

However, 1 Jn 4:1-3 suggests that the Spirit is a problematic source of authority, since "spirits" must be tested to see whether they are from God, and some will be found to be false spirits.[141] Because of the experience of false spirits and false prophets, it seems less likely that the Spirit is currently the key locus of authority for the community.

2.3 Leadership in 2-3 Jn

The way the author begins in both 2 and 3 Jn by speaking of himself as "the elder", but without a personal name, is most striking. What can we say about the title or office and its use here?

In Chapter 6 we have argued from the evidence of Papias, Polycrates and Irenaeus that John the Elder, who was not one of the twelve, wrote the Gospel of John in Ephesus. We have also argued that John the Elder wrote 2-3 Jn (as well as 1 Jn). Thus, we suggest that the term "the elder" in 2-3 Jn has the same general meaning which we argued it has when applied to "John the Elder" by Papias; that is, it designates senior Christian teachers in the late first century CE who have received traditions from those who were Christians before them. The person who writes 2-3 Jn as "The elder" would then be a

---

authority not limited to certain individuals (although it may have been predicated particularly of them), but potentially available to every member of the community."

[139] See Lieu 1991, p91.

[140] Note also 1 Jn 5:6 "And the Spirit is the one that testifies, for the Spirit is the truth."

[141] See Burge 1987, p172-3.

tradition-bearer who could be called an "elder".[142] We will see that the evidence arising from 2-3 Jn suggests that this is indeed the meaning of the term "the elder".

In 2 and 3 Jn the author is writing to a community which is not his own (2 Jn 13; 3 Jn 15). That he begins 3 Jn simply with "The elder, to the beloved Gaius" shows that the designation "elder" must have been as well known as the author's own name. Further, the author gives instructions in the letters, and authority (particularly its use with respect to whom to include and whom to exclude) is a key matter in them both; this suggests the authority of the writer would need to be made clear at the beginning of each letter. Since the author establishes his authority in writing to another house church (although clearly one that is part of the wider Johannine movement) simply by calling himself "the elder", the title clearly has connotations of authority.[143]

As we have already noted in discussing the Pastorals, the title "elder" was widely used in the early Church. In at least some early churches, appointed officials in a local community could be called "presbyters", as we have argued was the case in the Pastorals (although there these leaders were also called "overseers"). But that the author of 2-3 Jn does not give his own name, or the name of a local church, means that he is probably not simply "one of the elders" responsible for such a local church.[144] He could be the leader among "the elders", and thus the person who has sole or primary responsibility for the community in which he is based (referred to as the "elect sister" in 2 Jn 13), who in these letters writes to members of other house churches which are under his overall authority.[145] However, 3 Jn shows that the problem for the elder is precisely that Diotrephes is in no sense structurally under the elder's authority. Further, Brown notes that Diotrephes is putting himself first in a local church (3 Jn 9) and the elder sees this as something to be resisted, so he is unlikely to himself be the prime leader in his own community.[146] Thus in 2-3 Jn the term does not seem to be used with the sense of "appointed officials".

It seems more likely then that, as we suggested at the beginning of this section, "the elder" designates one who is a tradition-bearer of some sort. We will seek to show in section 2.4 below that the way 2-3 Jn presents the locus of authority reinforces this. We will suggest that he is a tradition-bearer and as such, he has a sense of authority residing in his own possession of the tradition, and thus in his person. He uses the title "the elder" in order to

---

[142] Lieu (1986, p55-64) argues against the view that the "Elders" formed a clearly defined group in Asia Minor. Our view does not require that there was such a clearly defined group, but rather the existence of at least one person who could be called an "elder".

[143] See Lieu 1991, p9.

[144] See Lieu 1986, p53; 1991, p9.

[145] See Campbell 1994, p207-8 for this suggestion.

[146] See Brown 1982, p649.

reinforce his authority when writing to others who belong to his own tradition. As we have noted, the elder does not seem to belong to the sort of structure that we see in the Pastorals or Ignatius, where authority is strongly connected with appointment to an office. Rather in 2 and 3 John it seems likely that factors such as personality and contact with tradition were more significant than some sort of "office".

The events spoken of in 3 Jn add some details to this picture.[147] We learn that Diotrephes has refused to accept the elder's letter or some itinerant "brothers" and "likes to put himself first" (3 Jn 9-10). It has been suggested that Diotrephes represents the sort of structured local authority that we have not found in 1 Jn, and that in him we see an early form of monepiscopacy.[148] On this view Diotrephes is opposed to the elder's form of authority, since the elder would represent an authority which was not limited by appointment to a particular office or to a particular place, but was based in the individual, and their gifts, or in the fact that they were a tradition-bearer. In 3 Jn we would then be seeing a conflict between a form of institutional authority (found in Diotrephes) and "personal" authority (found in the elder).[149]

What do we make of this suggestion? The key here is perhaps that "personal" authority can be easily disregarded. Although the elder perceives himself as having authority in the way he writes 2 and 3 Jn and so as having authority beyond his own community, since (we suggest) it is personal authority, which resides in his person as a tradition-bearer, it is authority that must be acknowledged by the recipients. It is somewhat different then from authority conferred through an institution, by appointment to an office, which, if a person or group is also part of the institution, is harder to defy. In the situation revealed by 3 Jn, Diotrephes seems to have chosen to ignore this personal authority of the elder. Given Diotrephes' rejection of his personal authority, the elder shows that he is unable to appeal to his possession of any other form of authority in his dispute with Diotrephes, precisely because he has no such supra-local authority apart from his already-rejected personal authority. While he can write from his own group to another house church with explicit directives and thus with a sense of authority (and he presumes he has a right to concern himself with affairs in this other house church), it does

---

[147] See the thorough survey of all the approaches to these events by Brown 1982, p732-9. It seems highly unlikely that the issue between the elder and Diotrephes is a doctrinal one given that the elder (who can write the directive of 2 Jn 10) says nothing about doctrinal issues with regard to Diotrephes; see Rensberger 1997, p158-9.

[148] See for example Bornkamm TDNT 6, p671-2; von Campenhausen 1969, p121-3.

[149] Lieu (1991, p92) writes: "there is nothing in the title 'Elder' or in the letters to align their author with a particular 'non-institutional', and even less a charismatic, style of ministry." But while we agree about the "charismatic" style, there is clearly a dispute about authority going on, and it seems most likely that the author locates his own authority in being a tradition-bearer.

not seem that the elder has formal or official authority in that other community; if he did then he would surely respond to Diotrephes differently.[150] He clearly has authority in his own context, but with regard to Diotrephes' context he can do no more than threaten a visit (although this in itself may well have been effective). Thus the elder cannot "pull rank" over Diotrephes. In a situation in which Diotrephes does have some formal authority within his own sphere, to the extent that he can exclude "brothers" from "the church", the elder is powerless, since he lacks formal authority in Diotrephes' sphere. In fact, Diotrephes is able to act against the elder and his messengers with impunity it seems – precisely because he is the leader in this local context. All of this suggests that we have two different forms of authority at work and that the relationship between them has not been articulated. We cannot go so far as to see Diotrephes as an institutionalised "bishop", but he does seem to possess clear local authority.

So it seems we have two factors at work. Firstly, the issue of authority between a local leader and the elder, who would like his authority to be supra-local, but since it is personal and based in the tradition (see further below), it must be recognised by others. When his authority is not recognised, the elder has no other basis on which to assert authority over another context, since he has no official standing in that other context. But we should note that it is not as if the elder is totally powerless in this situation. In 3 Jn 10 he writes: "So if I come, I will call attention to what he [Diotrephes] is doing in spreading false charges against us." It is clearly implied that the elder will "call attention" to Diotrephes' behaviour before the church (cf. 3 Jn 6). This suggests that the elder will use his "personal authority" to confront Diotrephes. While there is an element of uncertainty about whether the elder will make the visit, perhaps because he is unsure how the community will react were he to confront Diotrephes before them,[151] that he proposes such a personal confrontation suggests again that he understands his own authority as residing in his person.[152]

But the second and equally important matter is that the whole overall institutional structure relating what were probably the house churches of the elder and of Diotrephes is not particularly clearly defined. The relationship between a local leader and a tradition-bearer who sees himself as having

---

[150] Thus as Brown (1982, p648) suggests, "One gets the impression of prestige but not of juridical authority." It is this that counts against Donfried's view (1977, p325-33) that the Elder was an "ecclesiastical officer" and the title indicated "office". Certainly, the Elder has authority, but since he cannot refer to any institutional roots for this authority and is powerless in the face of Diotrephes, his authority is not based in "office", but in some other factor.

[151] See Brown 1982, p719.

[152] Von Campenhausen (1969, p123) notes "He falls back on the living authority with which he is endowed by the 'truth'".

responsibilities of care beyond his own "home context",[153] has not been worked through. There is no overall structure of institutional authority; rather the overall framework in which both the elder and Diotrephes are operating seems to be embryonic and the situation reflects different claims of authority, power and influence.[154] There is no appeal to appointment or structural or institutional rank or position on the part of the elder. Rather the elder will simply use his personal authority to "call attention to" what Diotrephes is doing. This also reinforces the impression we have gained from the use of the title "the elder" in 2 and 3 Jn that we do not see here significant institutional development, but rather that the term points to John being a tradition-bearer.[155]

2.4 The locus of authority in 2 and 3 Jn

In 2 and 3 Jn we gain a stronger impression of the authority of the author than is clear in 1 Jn.[156] Brown[157] notes that in 2 Jn the elder judges when people are "following the truth" (2 Jn 4), re-issues the commandment they have had from the beginning (2 Jn 5), delineates the Christological error of those who "go beyond" "the teaching of Christ" (v7-9), gives a directive about not receiving false teachers (v9-10), assumes that those to whom he writes wish to hear more from him (v12), and passes on greetings from the Christians in the church where he lives (v13). In 3 Jn the elder praises Gaius, one of his "children" (v4), for hospitality shown to "the brothers" who seem to have come from the elder (v3, 5-8,12), requests that Gaius continues to show hospitality (v6-7), writes about Diotrephes, but seems to have no authority over him, and writes of Demetrius, who is coming to Gaius (v12). Further, that the elder sees himself as implicated in the hostile reception given to the itinerant "brothers" suggests he has some authority or jurisdiction over these brothers. This sense of authority leads the elder to be able to say in the greeting of 2 Jn 3 that "There *will be* with us grace, mercy and peace". This is particularly noteworthy since it expresses a greater degree of confidence than is found in the Pauline forms of this greeting, from which the greeting in 2 Jn

---

[153] Note "my children" in 3 Jn 4.

[154] See a similar suggestion in Lieu 1986, p156-8.

[155] Lieu 1986, p156 suggests with regard to 3 Jn that "we are in the sphere not of defined forms of institutional authority but of power and influence which have not been adequately theologically or institutionally interpreted."

[156] We have noted that in 1 Jn the author does have a sense of authority, but chooses not to use it; in 2 and 3 Jn the author (who we think is the same person as the author of 1 Jn) does choose to use his authority more. We will suggest below that the different audiences offer the best explanation for this different approach by the author.

[157] Brown 1982, p647-8.

3 has been developed.[158] It is clearly a statement given by one who regards himself as having the authority to mediate God's salvation, a confidence which is also seen in the addition of "in truth and love" at the end of the greeting.

Thus, the sense of the authority of the author is quite significant, although note that on some occasions, he puts himself "along side" the addressees.[159] But overall the stronger sense of personal authority in 2 and 3 Jn in comparison to 1 Jn is clear, and it is also in keeping with the author (who we think is the same person as the author of 1 Jn) calling himself "the elder" in 2-3 Jn, a title which, as we have seen, clearly has connotations of authority.

In what is his sense of authority based? We have noted above that the title "elder" is not an institutional title that reflects appointment or office. We have suggested that the elder has personal authority and it seems most likely that he speaks authoritatively about the tradition because of who he is.[160] Can we be more specific than this? His authority could be based in factors such as his role in tradition-bearing and witness, experience, or age. We will now seek to show that the indications of the significance of tradition and "the truth" in 2 and 3 Jn suggest that it is the author's role as tradition-bearer which is most significant.

The sense of tradition and truth is clear in a number of ways. In 2 Jn 5 we read of a commandment that "we have had from the beginning", a phrase which is repeated in 2 Jn 6. We have seen that in 1 Jn this phrase emphasizes the tradition of the community and the same sense is clear here. The sense of authoritative tradition is also present in the concept of the "teaching of Christ" in 2 Jn. We read in 2 Jn 9 that: "Everyone who does not abide in the teaching of Christ, but goes beyond it, does not have God; whoever abides in the teaching has both the Father and the Son." Further, in 2 Jn 10 the readers are told not to welcome anyone who "does not bring this teaching". Here then the idea of the importance of authoritative tradition is formulated in terms of the concept of the "teaching of Christ". It is noteworthy that in 2 Jn 9 we read of "the one who abides in *the teaching* (ὁ μένων ἐν τῇ διδαχῇ)". This is in contrast to 1 Jn where μένω is mainly used of "abiding" in God or Christ (but note 1 Jn 2:14); 2 Jn 9 is similar to the calls to faithfulness to tradition found for example in 1 Tim 2:15 and 2 Tim 3:14.[161]

---

[158] See Lieu 1986, p47-8; 69-70. See further in Chapter 13.

[159] See for example 2 Jn 5-6 "one *we* have had from the beginning, let *us* love one another. And this is love, that *we walk* ...; 3 Jn 8: "Therefore *we ought* ... so that *we may become co-workers with the truth*." See also 2 Jn 2.

[160] This is the case, rather than because he is "the elder". Indeed, he is "the elder" because of these personal factors.

[161] See Lieu 1991, p94. Lieu (p94) notes that διδαχή is not found in 1 Jn although loyalty to the tradition is found in the more dynamic language of "what you have heard" (2:24; 2:7). We will develop these points further in Chapter 13.

It is not said in (the very brief) 2 Jn who has prime responsibility for carrying on or preserving this teaching; the fact that the elder writes to the whole community suggests (but does not prove) that the whole community has at least some responsibility in this regard. Certainly the elder does not tell particular leaders to "Be on your guard" (v8) or to "not receive into the house …anyone who comes to you and does not bring this teaching" (v10), but seems to speak to the whole community. But we also note that the elder himself in writing 2 Jn gives a very strong sense that he has a clear responsibility for maintaining this tradition.

We also note that the concept of "truth (ἀλήθεια)" is used five times in 2 Jn 1-4 and six times in 3 Jn 1, 3 (twice), 4, 8, 12. While ἀλήθεια is found in 1 Jn, there it is regularly used of the contrast between truth and falsehood,[162] a contrast which is not found in 2 and 3 Jn.[163] In these latter two books, the link with "truth" and the tradition of the community is clear in several places. In 2 Jn 4 and 3 Jn 3 we have statements about "walking in the truth", which refer to living faithfully according to the tradition. The link with tradition is also found in 3 Jn 12 where we read that "the truth itself" has testified about Demetrius. It is also noteworthy that in 2 Jn 2 we read: "… because of the truth that abides *in us* (διὰ τὴν ἀλήθειαν τὴν μένουσαν ἐν ἡμῖν) and will be *with us* for ever." Just as they are to "abide in the teaching" (2 Jn 9-10), so also the "truth" abides "in us". Here then the author sees the community as closely connected with "the truth". This recalls the emphasis on the community and its knowledge in 1 Jn. It also suggests that we are right to see the community as having a role in preserving "the teaching", although again the elder, in the very act of writing, shows that he has a role here too.

One further point is significant. In discussing 1 Jn we noted that in 1 Jn 1:1-5 the author *does* speak of himself as part of an authoritative group of witnesses and tradition-bearers. While in the rest of the letter he speaks as part of the community, generally using "we" and "us", and thus sees the locus of authority as the community, he does show in 1:1-5 that he possesses his own form of authority, albeit as part of a group of witnesses. Since we suggest the same person wrote all three letters,[164] 1 Jn 1:1-5 sheds light on 2 and 3 Jn. We can suggest that in 2 and 3 Jn the author has decided to draw on this alternative form of authority, seen in 1 Jn 1:1-5 and based on being a tradition-bearer and witness. So in 2 and 3 Jn he is speaking on the basis of what we see in 1 Jn 1:1-5, an approach he generally declined to take in 1 Jn (except in his use of "children" as a term of address, and the occasional command). This explains the far greater sense of personal authority in 2 and 3

---

[162] See 1 Jn 1:6, 8; 2:4, 21; 3:18-19; 4:6; 5:6.

[163] Du Rand 1979, p128 notes that ἀλήθεια is the "dominant structural marker in 3 Jn"; see also Günther 1995, p118.

[164] See Chapter 6.

Jn.[165] However, in 1 Jn the author generally decided not to use his own *personal* authority as a tradition-bearer, and we can suggest this was primarily because he was writing to the local community in which he was resident, and where he (and they) saw authority as primarily communal, whereas 2-3 Jn are sent to outlying Johannine house churches.

But this also explains why, as we have already seen, the elder in 2 and 3 Jn cannot refer to an authority of office or institution – his authority is of a different nature from this and consists in being a tradition-bearer and witness, an authority that Diotrephes can choose to ignore, since he seems to represent a different sort of authority.

Thus we have noted that the elder has a clear sense of personal authority and we have suggested that his authority is based in the fact that he is a witness or a tradition-bearer for his own community; there is no evidence that it is an authority derived from an appointment to office, and much that suggests this is not the case.

But in that the elder writes to the whole community in 2 Jn and in what he writes about "the teaching" and "the truth" in relation to the community, we can suggest that, although the elder seems to have significant responsibility for the tradition, the community also has some responsibility for maintaining the tradition and so to some extent continues to be the locus of authority, as was the case in 1 Jn.

2.5 Conclusions

The following points emerge from this discussion. Firstly, we hear of no leaders in 1 Jn. This does not mean that there were not some people who, on occasions "took the lead", including our author. But the author of 1 Jn, and we can suggest others, primarily saw themselves as functioning within the group, and not over and above it.

Secondly, 1 Jn 1:1-5 shows that the author can speak as part of an authoritative group of witnesses and tradition-bearers. However, although he therefore has his own form of personal authority, in the rest of the letter he generally chooses to speak as part of the community, which he sees as the primary locus of authority. 1 Jn thus suggests that the community did not conceive of authority as residing in any individuals who functioned at times as leaders, but rather in the group as a whole. What the author says about witness, the anointing and tradition, which were all seen in corporate terms and were all related to the whole community, explains how the author could see the locus of authority as the community.

Thirdly, in 2 and 3 Jn "the elder" clearly has a sense of his own authority and has authority in some spheres (eg. with Gaius), but it is not an authority

---

[165] This also explains why he uses the title "the elder" at the beginning of both letters.

based in an institution or appointed office. Rather he is working within a different sort of framework, with his authority based in his own person, more specifically, we may suggest, in the fact that he is a tradition-bearer, as emerges in these two letters.

Fourthly, from the dispute between the elder and Diotrephes, we see that the overall organisational structure in which they both participate is embryonic. While Diotrephes may have considerable authority within his own house church, the elder clearly lacks institutional authority in Diotrephes' setting, and we can suggest that this is because the form of authority on which the elder relies (tradition-bearing, and thus something relating to him personally) is easily disregarded.

Fifthly, the locus of authority in 2 and 3 Jn seems to be in the "tradition", and although the elder seems to have significant responsibility for the tradition, the community also has some responsibility for its maintenance and so to some extent continues to be a locus of authority, as was the case in 1 Jn.

Finally, in all of these factors – leadership, locus of authority, but also institutional framework - we see a considerable contrast with the Pastoral Epistles. We will develop this in our conclusions to this chapter.

3. Leadership and Authority in Revelation, particularly among the addressees at Ephesus as this is reflected in Rev 2:1-7

We have suggested that in Revelation John the Seer is writing to all the Christians in Ephesus. Here we will discuss whether the evidence with regard to leadership structures and the locus of authority supports or contradicts this hypothesis.

3.1 Leadership in the Book of Revelation

What does Revelation tell us about the leadership structure of the Christians addressed in Ephesus? The proclamation of 2:1-7 makes no mention of any leaders among the addressees, and no reference is made to such officials as bishops, presbyters or deacons in the other six proclamations to the churches or in the rest of Revelation. Yet John does refer to "angels", "elders", "apostles" and "prophets".[166] Are any of these "leaders" of the churches? We will discuss them in turn.

---

[166] On the terms "servant" and "saint" which John uses for all Christians, see Chapter 12.

3.1.1 "ἄγγελος"

In Chapter 7, we have already discussed the reference to an "ἄγγελος" of the church. It is unlikely that the angels are to be identified with bishops or elders of these communities, since there is no precedent for such leaders being addressed as an "ἄγγελος" and John consistently uses the term of supernatural beings. The mention of an "ἄγγελος" does not give evidence for community leaders of some sort.

3.1.2 Elders

"Elders" (πρεσβύτεροι) are often mentioned in Rev,[167] and a number of suggestions have been made about their identity. It is unlikely that they are angels since angels are probably never called elders in the OT,[168] and are never said to be crowned. That there are twenty-four elders (4:4) has suggested that they represent the twelve sons of Israel and the twelve apostles of the Lamb (21:12-14) or that they may correspond to the 24 heads of priestly families in 1 Chron 24:4-18.[169] That they wear crowns (4:4, 10) shows that they are also represented as kingly figures. Despite debate about who they represent, one thing seems certain: these elders are heavenly beings, who have no relationship to any leadership structure of the church on earth and are never related to anyone in the seven churches. They give no evidence for the existence of presbyters in the Asian churches therefore.[170]

3.1.3 Apostles

John uses the term "ἀπόστολος" three times in Rev. In 2:2 the Ephesians are praised for testing and rejecting those who claim to be apostles, "but are not". As we have noted in Chapter 7, these seem to be contemporary, itinerant apostles comparable to Paul, Andronicus and Junia and others. They are not resident leaders of a church in Asia. Barrett notes the Ephesian addressees are commended for testing those who claimed to be apostles, but are not, and goes on: "the fact that it seems worthwhile to lay a false claim to be an apostle proves that there were also real ones, and proves at the same time that the apostles in question were not the Twelve Apostles of the Lamb, whom it

---

[167] See Rev 4:4, 10; 5:5, 6, 8, 11, 14; 7:11, 13; 11:16; 14:3; 19:4.

[168] Isa 24:23 may be an exception.

[169] When any number is given with regard to elders it is always 24; On the elders see Satake 1966, p137-50; Sweet 1979, p118; Thompson 1990, p58, 69-70; Court 1994, p113; Aune 1997, p288-92.

[170] See Satake 1966, p149-50; Bornkamm in TDNT 6, p669; Schweizer 1961, p135. Cf. Barrett 1985, p43-4.

would have been easy to identify and to distinguish from the shams."[171] So it seems likely that there were people who could legitimately call themselves "apostles" (since the term had a variety of meanings)[172] who circulated among the churches. But we note that they were itinerants, not resident leaders.

In Rev 18:20 we read "Rejoice over her [Babylon], O heaven, you saints and apostles and prophets! For God has given judgement for you against her." This is a very general reference, and seems to include all who could claim the title "apostle", which Aune suggests includes the Twelve, but could also include other "apostles".[173] It simply shows that the apostles form an identifiable group within the general framework of the "saints", but gives no evidence that "apostles" were local leaders in the churches.[174] Finally, in 21:14 it is said that "the wall of the [new] city has twelve foundations, and on them are the twelve names of the twelve apostles of the Lamb." Clearly, this is a reference to "the Twelve" who followed Jesus.[175] We conclude then that there is no positive evidence that "apostles" had a place within the leadership structure of the seven churches, although itinerants who could claim to be "apostles" were in the general area.

3.1.4 Prophets

In section 3.12 of Chapter 7 we suggested that John sees himself as a prophet since he speaks of his book as a "prophecy" (1:3) and a "prophetic book" (22.7, 10, 18, 19) and in 22:9 an angel says to John "I am a fellow servant with you and your comrades the prophets". We also suggested that John was one of a number of prophets in the churches of Asia Minor who formed an identifiable group (see 22:16). On this reading of 22:16, the community prophets (ὑμεῖς) have received the testimony of the Book of Revelation for the churches. Thus, they probably deliver, read and perhaps also interpret John's written revelation to the seven churches.[176] On this view prophets were active in each of the seven churches;[177] it is also likely that such prophets were actually members of at least some of the seven churches. Further, "Jezebel" was a prophet and "Balaam" may well have been a prophet too since the Balaam of the OT was known as a (false) prophet in early Jewish and Christian literature.

---

[171] Barrett 1985, p44.

[172] See Chapter 7.

[173] See Aune 1997, p144.

[174] Aune, 1981, p23.

[175] Yarbro Collins 1984, p27 notes that 21:14 reflects a situation when the time of the twelve apostles is past.

[176] See Aune 1989, p111.

[177] See Court 1994, p35-6; Giles 1997, p224.

This has led us to the suggestion that two opposing prophetic circles or schools were active in the churches of Asia, one school associated with John, another with Jezebel, Balaam and the Nicolaitans. The conflict between John and the Nicolaitans then can be seen as a battle between rival schools of prophets and their followers, as well as a conflict over theology and praxis.

Accordingly, we suggest that prophets were active in the seven churches; clearly John approves of some of these and strongly disagrees with others. It is likely that some of these prophets were itinerant, but it seems that the Nicolaitan prophets have settled down in one place and it is quite likely that some prophets of whom John approves had also settled down, and thus were active in and members of at least some of the seven churches.[178] So the pattern is a little different from that in Didache 11-13 where apostles and prophets are said to appear from time to time in local communities. We have no specific evidence that any of John's prophetic colleagues were active in the Ephesian Christian community, but this is likely.

This means that the only "earthly" Christian leaders that John mentions are prophets and perhaps apostles, of whom the latter and some of the former seem to be itinerant. No other form of local official is mentioned. *If* John accurately reflects the actual leadership structure of the seven churches (ie, that the only leaders are itinerant "apostles" and itinerant and resident "prophets") then this would diverge from other forms of Christianity known to us in Asia Minor.[179] Aune notes that various solutions to this divergence have been proposed, and we will now discuss this issue.

3.2 Does John reflect the actual leadership structure of the seven churches?

What was the leadership structure of the seven churches addressed in Revelation and does John reflect this structure? A number of answers to this question have been put forward.[180]

Firstly, it could be that the prophets mentioned in Rev are the only officials in these churches. Bornkamm and Satake suggest these groups would then probably be made up of Jewish Christians who migrated from Palestine shortly after the fall of Jerusalem.[181] Satake also suggests the form of church structure found in these churches originated in an apocalyptic tradition from

---

[178] See Aune 1989, p111; Court 1994, p35-6; cf. Barrett 1985, p44; see further in Chapter 7.

[179] See Aune 1981, p23-4. Aune suggests the Johannine Letters may be a possible exception here, but this seems unlikely.

[180] I am dependent on the excellent summary of this issue in Aune 1981, p24-6.

[181] See Bornkamm in TDNT 6, p669-70; Satake 1966, p155-95; see also Schweizer 1961, p135-6. In Chapter 6 we have suggested that some Christians did migrate to Ephesus at this time, and so are not in disagreement with this facet of Bornkamm and Satake's proposal.

Palestine in the period prior to James' control of the Jerusalem church.[182] Thus, when they migrated from Palestine, these Christians brought with them a community organisation which was similar to that of the very earliest Christian community, in which prophets alone were leaders.

However, there are a number of difficulties with this theory. Firstly, there is simply not enough positive evidence to support it, since it is largely built on conjecture.[183] Secondly, it assumes that prophets were "office bearers" in an institutional sense in these churches, but this is misguided. John claims only to be a mediator of revelation, and his authority lies solely in communicating the message with which he has been entrusted, and not in holding a local office.[184] Thirdly, the theory assumes that some Palestinian Jewish Christians continued the church structure of the earliest period, despite the changes brought about by the leadership of James, the brother of Jesus, in the Jerusalem church,[185] which seems very unlikely. Finally, this view makes the unlikely assumption that these immigrant communities were evenly scattered throughout western Asia Minor, and were not influenced by other forms of Christianity in these areas.[186]

A second view with regard to the leadership structure of the seven churches addressed in Revelation is that the structure presented by John, with prophets playing such a central role, is "an ideal portrait or literary fiction rooted in conceptions from an earlier period in Christian history".[187] However, that John uses his real name and not a pseudonym, and that the description of the situation of each of the seven churches in the seven proclamations does not seem to be a literary fiction but rather gives a strong impression of veracity,[188] argue strongly against this view.

Thirdly, John did not mention local church officials intentionally, since his role as a prophet transcended local community concerns and his message was directed to the whole church and not just to its leaders. On this view John tells us very little about local church structures, not because these were not present, but because he emphasised the supralocal character of saints, apostles and prophets. Aune argues for this view for the following reasons.[189] Firstly, as Aune notes, "early Christian literary convention did not necessitate the acknowledgment of the status, role, authority or even the existence of local officials."[190] Thus, for example, Paul's mention of local officials in Phil 1:1

---

[182] Satake 1966, p194.

[183] Yarbro Collins 1984, p37.

[184] See Aune 1981, p25; Yarbro Collins 1984, p37; cf. Court 1994, p35-6.

[185] See Yarbro Collins 1984, p36-7.

[186] See Aune 1981, p24.

[187] Aune 1981, p24. Aune rejects this possibility.

[188] See Aune, 1981, p24; Court 1979, p24-42; in general see Ramsay 1904; Hemer 1986.

[189] Aune 1981, p25-6; it is also favoured by Yarbro Collins 1984, p37; Smith 1957, p187.

[190] Aune 1981, p25.

appears "fortuitous".[191] Secondly, John does mention prophets and is a prophet himself, but we should not regard John, or other prophets as "office bearers". Rather John's only claim is to mediate divine revelation, and, as we will note below, he sees his authority as residing not in himself, or in an "office", but in God. Further, Aune notes that early Christian literature "suggests that prophets were never fully integrated into the organizational structure of the local churches, even though they occasionally played an important role in communal worship."[192] For example, in Pauline literature the supralocal role of apostles, prophets and teachers is emphasised (1 Cor 12:28-30; Eph 4:11) along with their foundational function (Eph 2:20; 3:5; cf. IgnPhd 9:1). Similarly, in Rev the foundational role of apostles is emphasised in Rev 21:14, while that of OT prophets is suggested in 10:7. The other references to prophets and apostles in Rev all emphasise their supralocal role.[193] Thus, in mentioning prophets, we should not think that John is interacting with local office bearers.

Thirdly, Aune suggests that John has chosen not to use the authority of local leaders (whatever leadership structure there may have been), as the communication vehicle for his message, but rather relies on the genre of the apocalypse, and its claim to be "the revelation of Jesus Christ".[194] Further, John uses the rhetorical device of placing himself on the same plane as his hearers (eg. in 1:9) and emphasises the close relationship between the saints (that is, all Christians) and the prophets in passages like 16:6, 18:24 in order to gain a hearing. By placing himself on the same plane as others he abandoned any appeal to personal or official authority. In keeping with this, he also does not single out leaders of the communities to which he writes, or call them and their authority to his aid, but rather uses the power of his words and of his chosen genre to communicate his message.

Finally, Aune notes that if John was an itinerant prophet, as seems likely,[195] then he would have relied on local officials when he visited a centre (cf. 2 and 3 John). One reason that John may refrain from criticising local officials, and thus does not even mention or name them, may be that he does not want to alienate people upon whom he might at some point be dependent.[196]

---

[191] Aune 1981, p25.

[192] Aune 1981, p25.

[193] Aune (1981, p25) writes that this "suggests that the ideological unity of the many scattered congregations of Christians found concrete expression in the view that God himself (through Jesus and/or the Spirit) was the central authority of the church and whose will and purposes were expedited by specially endowed persons."

[194] See Aune 1981, p26.

[195] See Chapter 7.

[196] See Aune 1981, p26. Yarbro Collins (1984, p137) also suggests that John did not mention any community leaders "because he was perhaps in competition with them [bishops,

We conclude then that the lack of reference in Rev to any church leadership structures should not be taken to mean that no such structure existed. It seems more likely that, for reasons of his own, John has chosen not to address any leaders in these churches, but rather has emphasised "the supralocal character of the saints, apostles and prophets."[197] This means that the actual structure of the community John addressed in Ephesus is veiled from us; John simply does not reveal the basic organisational structure of any of the seven groups of addressees. We have already noted, however, that prophets were almost certainly in existence in these communities and played a role in their life. We should not however see these prophets as "office bearers" in an institutional sense in these churches.[198] We have no specific evidence that any of John's prophetic colleagues were active in the Ephesian Christian community, but this is likely.

3.3 The locus of authority in Revelation

Where does authority lie in Revelation?[199] And can we say anything about the locus of authority as far as the readers of Revelation, particularly Rev 2:1-7, are concerned?

The overwhelming sense in Revelation is that authority is not located in John himself but rather is of divine origin. Clearly John does not speak or write on his own authority but as a bearer of God's prophetic word. This is emphasised in a number of ways.

Firstly, John begins the book in Rev 1:1-2 in the following way: "The revelation of Jesus Christ (᾽Αποκάλυψις ᾽Ιησοῦ Χριστοῦ), which God gave him to show his servants what must soon take place; he made it known by sending his angel to his servant John, who testified to the word of God and to the testimony of Jesus Christ, even to all that he saw." What does John mean by the phrase ᾽Αποκάλυψις ᾽Ιησοῦ Χριστοῦ at the beginning of the book? Since John goes on "which God gave him" ie. Jesus, the phrase is clearly a subjective genitive and should be translated as: "The revelation from Jesus

---

elders or deacons in any of the communities] in influencing the points of view of the other readers." Schüssler Fiorenza (1985, p142-4) suggests that the fact that John mentions prophets and not local leaders (such as those mentioned by Ignatius) "could be a sign that the author and the communities to whom he writes tend to disregard and ignore these officers as unimportant." (p143-4) Although this is possible, the evidence of the Pastorals suggests that such local leaders were important in Ephesus and it is more likely that John simply chooses not to engage such local leaders.

[197] Aune 1981, p26.

[198] Hill (1971-72, p410) notes that "while these prophets are in some way separable from the body of believers, the evidence is not such as to allow a distinction to be drawn in terms of precedence or position."

[199] For a recent study of this topic see Carey 1999.

Christ".[200] But in 1:1 John actually constructs a chain of revelation by which the content of the prophecy has come to John: God – Christ – angel – John. This makes it clear that the ultimate source of the revelation, and thus of the book, is God, while the agent of the revelation is Jesus Christ, who transmits it via an angel, to John, who transmits it to believers. This explains why in 1:2 John can describe himself as testifying to "the word of God and to the testimony of Jesus Christ";[201] what he writes has its origin in God, and is also the witness given by Jesus.[202] Clearly then, John indicates at the outset that what he writes is not ultimately his words but rather are of divine origin.

Secondly, John's chosen designation for his work is "the prophecy" (1:3) and in 22:7,10, 18-19 he describes it as a "prophetic book".[203] Given the strong link between prophecy and the Spirit, by using this language John underlines that what he writes are not his words, but words that are given to him by the activity of the Spirit. Four times John is said to receive visions "in the Spirit"; on two of these occasions he says that he was "in the Spirit" (1:10; 4:2) and on the other two that an angel "carried him away in the Spirit" (17:3; 21:10). Bauckham has convincingly argued that in each case the reference is to God's Spirit as "the agent of visionary experience", rather than to the human spirit.[204] By means of these references John is indicating that the Spirit has been the agent of his visionary experiences, and it was in these visions that he was given his prophetic revelations. They also make it clear that John believes his prophecy is divinely inspired, which complements the claim that the revelation came from God.[205]

Further, note 19:10: "the testimony of Jesus is the Spirit of prophecy". Bauckham notes, "this must mean that when the Spirit inspires prophecy, its content is the witness of Jesus."[206] Although this includes prophecy given by Christian prophets to the churches, it also clearly refers to John's own prophecy, the Book of Revelation (cf 1:3; 22:7, 18-19). So, as in 1:2, John

---

[200] See Charles 1920, 1, p6; Aune 1997, p6.

[201] The latter is again a subjective genitive: the witness born by Jesus; see Aune 1997, p19.

[202] The risen Jesus attests to the content of the book in 22:20: "The one who testifies to these things says, 'Surely I am coming soon.'" Note other guarantees of the reliability of the text: 19:9b; 21:5b; 22:6a.

[203] Note that in 1:1 John is not saying that his work belongs to the literary type called "apocalypse". Charles (1920, 1, p6) notes that "apocalypse" was not used as the title of any book before the time when Rev was written. Rather as Aune (1997, p12) notes, "On the basis of its occurrence in Rev 1:1. and particularly because the term became the title for John's composition, 'Apocalypse' came to be applied to a literary report of visions similar to those narrated in Revelation."

[204] Bauckham 1993d, p116.

[205] See Bauckham 1993d, p116-17; see also Bauckham 1993c, p150-59; Friesen 2001, p158.

[206] Bauckham 1993d, p119.

again sees Revelation as the witness of Jesus, but we note that he emphasises the Spirit's activity in this regard.

Thirdly, the seven proclamations are each introduced explicitly as the words of the risen Christ, who is described in a different way in each introduction (2:1, 8, 12, 18; 3:1, 7, 14). Thus when we read that "I know your works" in 2:2, this does not relate to John, but to the risen Christ. Yet we again see a connection with the Spirit, because in 2:7, and at the conclusion of each of the seven proclamations, we read: "Let anyone who has an ear listen to what the Spirit is saying to the churches."[207] The words are then also those of the Spirit. As Bauckham says, in this case "what the Spirit says is what the exalted Christ says".[208] Thus the risen Christ is to be seen as speaking to each of the churches through the Spirit.[209] Although John has written the words that are read, their ultimate source is not actually John.[210]

Fourthly, that these are not John's words, but have their origin in divine activity is emphasised by the command given to John to "write". Note the very general statement in 1:19: "Now write what you have seen, what is, and what is to take place after this." Note also 21:5, said by the one seated on the throne: "Also he said: 'Write this, for these words are trustworthy and true.'" These commands, along with 1:11, seem to have the entire book in view.[211] In this way John emphasises that the impetus to write is not his own; rather he writes the book in obedience to a direct divine command to do so. Further, as well as the commissioning of John in Rev 1:11-20, there is also an additional commissioning of John in 10:8-11. John is told to take a scroll and eat it, and as has been predicted it was sweet as honey in his mouth but made his stomach bitter. This is a "symbolic commission to prophecy",[212] based on

---

[207] The formula is also found in 2:11, 17, 29; 3:6, 13, 22 and see the variant form in 13:9.

[208] Bauckham 1993d, p117. Note that in 14:13b and 22:17a the Spirit's words are not the words of Christ.

[209] See further Aune 1997, p151. Schüssler Fiorenza (1985, p121) notes: "Just as Paul emphasized towards his opponents in Corinth that he also had the authority of an apostle and the spiritual experience of a pneumatic, so also the author of Rev. stresses that his authority is prophetic authority and his message an authentic pneumatic message, since the *pneuma* articulates the messages given to the communities."

[210] This is also emphasized in 1:20, where the interpretive key to what John writes is said to be given by the risen Christ (1:20), and in 17:7-18 where an angel gives John a long explanation; cf. 4:1 where a voice instructs John. We note also that the risen Christ directly addresses the readers, eg in 16:15. This direct address from Christ to the reader emphasises that the risen Christ is the ultimate source of the words which on the face of it are John's words. The overall effect of this language is to emphasize that this work is a prophecy and so its source is the risen Christ, not John. He is simply the one who "heard and saw these things" (22:8).

[211] See Aune 1998b, p1126.

[212] Aune 1998a, p574.

Ezek 2:8-3:3, a story which is integral to Ezekiel's prophetic call.[213] Then in 10:11 we read: "Then they said to me, 'You must prophecy again about many peoples and nations and languages and kings." This is a renewal of his commission to be a prophet and emphasises again that the origin of his work is not in John himself.

Fifthly, the words of a whole range of speakers are actually given in the book and it is noticeable that John himself "says" virtually nothing.[214] He records the words of others – heavenly actors such as God, the risen Christ, the elders, the four living creatures, angels, an eagle in heaven, unidentified heavenly voices, or "Christians" in heaven;[215] occasionally people on earth speak.[216] All of this emphasises that these are *not* (with very few insignificant exceptions) the words of John. The authority does not lie in him.

Sixthly, rather than distinguishing himself from his readers, as if he were *the* authority, John associates himself with them.[217] The effect of this, combined with what we have seen up to now, is to suggest that the authority of the book lies not in himself but in the risen Christ. We have noted Rev 1:1-2: "The revelation of Jesus Christ, which God gave him ... he made it known by sending his angel to his *servant* John, who testified to the word of God and to the testimony of Jesus Christ, even to all that he saw." Similarly, in 1:9 he writes "I John, your *brother, who share with you* in Jesus the persecution and the kingdom and the patient endurance ..." Here John associates himself with

---

[213] Aune 1998a, p575 notes with regard to Ezekiel: "There the act of eating the scroll is a metaphor symbolizing the prophetic word that enters into Ezekiel (see Ezek 3:1). The meaning is similar in Rev 10:10-11, for as soon as John has eaten the scroll he is commissioned to prophecy".

[214] Very occasionally, John is asked a question and responds briefly (eg. 7:13). What John says simply serves to move the plot along. Similarly, all the action is done by angels (eg 8:6-12), or the Lamb (8:1); very little is done by John (but see 10:10).

[215] Note the following range of speakers: God speaks in 21:5-8 and the risen Christ in 16:15; 22:7 (and perhaps 22:6, although this may be an angel), 22:12-13, 16, 20. "The Spirit and the Bride" speak in 22:17. The hymns are sung by heavenly elders (4:11; 7:13-17; 11:17-18), by heavenly elders and the four living creatures (5:9; 19:4), by the four living creatures (5:14; 6:1, 3, 5, 7). John hears the voices of angels (5:2, 11; 7:3, 12; 10:9, 11; 14:7-11, 15, 18; 16:5-6; 17:1-2, 7-18; 18:2-3, 21-4; 19:9-10, 17-18; 21:9; 22:9-11), or the heavenly elders (5:5), or "every creature in heaven and on earth and under the earth and in the sea" (5:13) or an eagle in heaven (8:13), or a "voice" of the horn of the altar (9:13-14; that this is the most likely meaning of the "voice" here; see Aune 1998a, p536), or an unidentified heavenly voice (10:4, 8, 11:1 –3, 12, 15; 12:10-12; 14:2, 13; 16:1, 7, 17; 18:4-8; 19:5; 21:3-4; on unidentified voices see Aune 1998a, p561-2). "Christians" in heaven speak, or sing: the slaughtered souls (6:10), a great multitude in heaven (7:10; 19:1-3, 6-8), those who had conquered the beast (15:3-4).

[216] Note the kings of the earth and the rich and the strong, and every one, slave and free (6:16-17); those who worship the beast (13:4); the kings of the earth (18:10); merchants (18:14, 16-17); sailors (18:18-20)

[217] See further Carey 1999, p118-28.

the readers; he seems anxious to avoid the impression that authority lies in his own person. We note further that although John makes it clear that he is writing a "prophecy" (eg. 1:3), he does not introduce himself as a prophet (although he clearly sees himself as one),[218] or a teacher, or as holding any "office". Rather, his chosen self-designation is a "servant" (1:1), a title given to all Christians,[219] and in 1:9 he emphasises that he is a brother and a partner with his hearers. John derives his authority to address the churches, not from holding an institutional position, but from the fact that he has heard (eg. 1:10) and seen (1:12) and hence has written the book (1:11). He clearly de-emphasises himself and locates the authority of what he writes in the one who gives him the experiences he has had - the risen Christ and the Spirit (1:10-20), and ultimately God (1:1). Further, he does not write a pseudonymous book in which he claims the authority of one of the great prophetic figures of the past, but rather writes in his own name.[220] All of this emphasises that he does not see authority as residing in himself.

Finally, we note that John uses the OT a great deal as a source, and this clearly functions as an authority for him and as a way to underline the authority of his work. However, as Friesen notes: "John expected the hearers to recognize him on both counts, as visionary and as a master of tradition. The ecstatic element is nevertheless primary, for even his handling of authoritative texts is affected by his visions. He does not so much quote scripture as build with them."[221] Again, we see the importance of what he receives from a divine source – his visions – rather than the importance of John himself.

But does John think that his readers, including those at Ephesus, will accept what he writes as a prophecy which is a "revelation from Jesus Christ"? Are they willing to accept the authority of "the book"? Clearly John is writing to Christians, and so it seems likely that in theory they would be willing to "hear" and grant authority to the words of the risen Christ and the Spirit. But would they see *this* "book" as the words of the risen Christ, as his revelation?

The very significant emphasis that we have discerned on the authority of the book, and on it being the words of the risen Christ and the Spirit, with its origin in God, written at the command of Christ and so on, strongly suggests that John saw the need to bolster the authority of the book by emphasising its source. While at least some of this presentation of divine authority is

---

[218] This is clearly implied in 22:9, where an angel says to John "I am a fellow servant with you and your comrades the prophets"; see Aune 1981, p18-19, 27; 1989, p109.

[219] See Chapter 12.

[220] See Schüssler Fiorenza 1988, p196.

[221] Friesen 2001, p158; see also Schüssler Fiorenza 1985, p135.

conditioned by fact that John is writing a prophecy,[222] and by what we can discern as features of the genre of "apocalypse", it is the way John underlines the divine authority of his message and then underlines it again which is noteworthy. This in itself suggests that some might reject the book as not "the revelation from Jesus Christ" (and so might see John as a false prophet) and John sought to counter this potential rejection.[223]

But note also what John writes in 1:3 and in 22:18. Rev 1:3 reads "Blessed are those who hear and who keep what is written in it" and in 22:18 we read: "I warn everyone who hears the words of the prophecy of this book; if anyone adds to them, God will add to that person the plagues described in this book; if anyone takes away from the words of the book of this prophecy, God will take away that person's share in the tree of life and in the holy city, which are described in this book."[224] These very strong claims to divine authority suggest that John is concerned that some readers will disregard what he writes, and that some will add or take away from his words. Clearly he anticipates opposition, not only to various aspects of what he writes from groups like the Nicolaitans and also the many readers of his book that he calls to "Repent" (as we have noted before) but he also anticipates opposition to or rejection of *the book itself.* Hence we have this inclusio in 1:3 and 22:18. This suggests that some will not regard it as authentically "the revelation from Jesus Christ".

We conclude then that some of John's readers may have rejected the authority of his book. Of course, some would have accepted it. But that John underlines to such a considerable extent the divine authority of the book strongly suggests that prophetic authority was not the exclusive form of authority recognized amongst the readers; it was almost certainly one authoritative source alongside others for at least some readers. This again suggests that John is not writing to a "prophetic conventicle" or something similar or that the book of Revelation testifies to a community which only recognised this form of authority. That John seems concerned that some readers will not recognise the authority of the book suggests that these readers valued some other form of authority – that of office or tradition for example. The rejection of one form of authority suggests the valuing of another form. We can note that the Nicolaitans valued the authority of other prophets; it may

---

[222] Aune (1981, p22) notes that early Christian prophets "characteristically claimed divine authority for their messages".

[223] The complex history of reception of Revelation into the canon does not help us here, since we are interested in the immediate reception of the book. But we can at least be sure it was not immediately rejected everywhere.

[224] With regard to 22:18, Aune (1998b, p1232) notes: "John may have had reason to believe that his revelation was in danger of being interpreted away or augmented by Christians within the various local communities who regarded themselves as prophetically gifted." He cites Jezebel and the Nicolaitans as one example here.

be that some of John's other readers valued other forms of authority. Against this background we can understand John's significant stress on authority. We will pursue this thought further below.

3.4 Conclusions

We conclude then that we are unable to say anything about the leadership structure of the addressees in the seven churches in Revelation, including Ephesus. We have evidence for a group of itinerant prophets and perhaps some apostles, but we have no evidence about the form of local leadership. This does not mean that such leadership did not exist; rather John has not chosen to articulate with that leadership in his writing. Thus, its form is veiled from us.

Secondly, we have noted that in the book of Revelation, authority lies with God, Jesus Christ and the Spirit. John does not claim authority in his own right, but rather emphasises in many ways the divine authority of his work. We have also suggested that his emphasis on this matter, along with other indications of disputes between John and other Christians in the seven churches, suggests that some of his addressees may have contested his claim to authority.

We also cannot say that there were communities in Asia Minor where the only form of authority that was recognised was prophetic authority. We have noted that Bornkamm and Satake have suggested this but that it is unlikely. The emphasis in Rev on the divine authority of prophecy should not be taken as a perfect mirror of an actual community therefore. Rather, it is understandable that a community would recognise prophetic authority as one form of authority alongside others. Perhaps at times it was a competing form of authority, or one that sat uneasily alongside other forms, but we cannot say that it was the exclusive form of authority in one community.[225] Just as John does not reveal the form of organisation among his readers, so he does not show what other forms of authority might have been recognized among those addressees.

All of this is compatible with our hypothesis that John is not writing to a "John of Revelation" community, but rather is writing to all Christians in Ephesus.

---

[225] One example here is that we may suggest it was quite possible that John could have written a letter to one of the churches in which he gave himself an explicit title and exhorts his readers or makes demands of them in his own name. But *in this document* John chooses to put all the emphasis on the risen Christ and his words, rather than rely on his own authority.

4. Overall conclusions

There are significant differences between both the authors and the addressees of the Pastoral Epistles and the Johannine Letters with regard to leadership structures and the locus of authority.

In the Pastorals we have the development of appointed leadership positions and what we have suggested is the beginnings of institutionalisation. The locus of authority is in the Pauline tradition, but this is mediated by recognised and authorised teachers. By contrast, the author can write 1 Jn without mentioning any leaders and indeed stresses that the community does not need a teacher. Further the locus of authority is the whole community. In 2 and 3 Jn "the elder" (who we think wrote 1 Jn too) asserts some form of authority, but we have argued that this is personal authority based in witness and being a tradition-bearer and not the authority of office or appointment. Further, the locus of authority in 2 and 3 Jn seems to be in the "tradition", and although the elder has clear responsibility for the tradition (and so to this extent is a locus of authority himself), the community also has some responsibility for its maintenance and so to some extent continues to be the locus of authority, as was the case in 1 Jn. There are significant differences here then, particularly between the Pastorals and 1 Jn. We also note that on this topic it seems clear that we are not seeing simply the views of the author, but the actual situation prevailing among the readers. Again, we can suggest that this indicates that these sets of documents are written to different communities.

We should also note some similarities between the two sets of documents, but we suggest these are somewhat superficial and actually indicate underlying differences. Note that in both the Pastorals and the Johannine Letters we have a sense of the tradition, of a "deposit", of "what was from the beginning". Both sets of documents show that they belong to the second (or third) generation and are looking back to the foundation of the faith. In both the Pastorals and the Johannine Letters we have "tradition-bearers" – authorised leaders in the Pastorals, and "the elder" in 2 and 3 Jn (and also in 1 Jn, but without giving himself a title). But the two groups of documents reveal something of a contrast in the way they conceive of this tradition being passed on and the way tradition functions as a locus of authority. For in the Pastorals, the tradition ("sound doctrine") is carried by carefully selected tradition-bearers – leaders. Further, these leaders gain their validation through having been taught as part of the chain of teaching (2 Tim 2:2) which goes back to Paul, through selection, the laying on of hands and through recognition as an "office-holder". Their authority is not in themselves so much as in their office and is based in appointment. Validation is the result of what we may call "an institution at work".

By contrast in 1 Jn the emphasis is on the community as a whole functioning as the tradition-bearer – the community as a whole is the witness, receives the anointing which enables them to "know", and the community as a whole has known or heard what was "from the beginning". The community itself functions as the "tradition-bearer". In 2 and 3 Jn we have argued that the community continues to have a role with regard to the tradition although we note that the elder becomes more of an authority figure, and the situation is closer to that in the Pastorals. But even here there is a contrast with the Pastorals. In 2 and 3 Jn, because of the connection with 1 Jn 1:1-5 (which is by the same author), we can suggest that it is because of witness that the elder is a tradition-bearer – because of what he has seen and heard – if not directly (which seems most likely) then from others before him. It is because of these things that he is "the elder". There is no suggestion of the elder being recognised in the community as the holder of an "office" or of a formal position, and many points count against this. Authority is not bestowed by appointment, nor is validation the work of people who are part of an institution; rather authority is based in personal tradition-bearing.

Although there are similarities then in that in both sets of documents we have tradition-bearers, and both value "tradition" or "the teaching", there are significant differences in the understanding of the tradition process. All of this strongly suggests that the two sets of documents are to two different communities (or groups of house churches in the case of the Johannine Letters). Again, we have added a further dimension to our description of facets of the life and identity of these two groups.

How does Revelation fit in here? We have noted that we cannot say anything about the leadership situation with regard to the readers of Rev 2:1-7 in Ephesus. Nor can we go from the fact that John sees the locus of authority with regard to his writing as being in God, Christ and the Spirit to deduce that there was a community in which "prophetic authority" was the only form of authority. Rather, the opposite is the case to at least some extent: John seems to be aware that some of his readers will not accept his words as "the revelation from Jesus Christ". It is because the work is a prophecy (and because John himself is a prophet) that John sees the locus of authority as divine, rather than that his work is a mirror in which we can see a community.

As we have noted, in Part Three of this work we are testing the hypothesis that the Pastorals and the Johannine Letters are to separate communities, and that John in Revelation is addressing both groups (and perhaps others). Given that we have been unable to discern any details about leadership structure in Rev, it is quite reasonable to suggest that John's addressees in Ephesus included the readers of the Pastorals and the Johannine Letters. In fact, if John was wanting to articulate with leaders in both the Pastorals and the Johannine Letters, how would he have done so? Given the very different leadership structures, at least between the Pastorals and 1 Jn, the path of wisdom was certainly not to articulate with them![226]

But we can also note that if our discussion of Rev had led to the conclusion that John understood that the leaders of the communities he addressed were, for example, people who had been appointed to an office and were called "diakonoi", and that there were no other leaders in these communities, then this would have counted against our view that John was writing to all Christians in Ephesus, and argued strongly in favour of John writing to a particular community with this sort of leadership structure. That our discussion has not led to evidence which would contradict our hypothesis is therefore significant.

What about the matter of the locus of authority? We could imagine that on receiving John's "Revelation", the readers of the Pastorals and the Johannine Letters might seek to discern whether the "revelation" was in keeping with "the faith" or "the teaching" (1 Tim 1:3), or might want to weigh the text to see if it was "of God" or in accordance with what they had heard "from the beginning" (see 1 Jn 1:1-5). Further, we could understand that they might not immediately accept John's book, because the locus of authority within which it operates is one that is different from that which is most fundamental in their own community.

However, we do note that both the readers of the Pastorals and of the Johannine Letters did acknowledge, and to some extent value, prophetic authority.[227] This is seen in the Pastorals in 1 Tim 4:1, where we hear that "the Spirit expressly says ...", which is a reference to some form of prophecy that has now been fulfilled in the community's present experience, and in the notes about prophecy in connection with leadership (1 Tim 1:18; 4:14).[228] Further the Johannine Letters clearly recognise the Spirit's activity.[229]

Yet in both the Pastorals and the Johannine Letters we have mention of false or deceitful spirits. 1 Tim 4:1 speaks of the opponents: "paying attention to deceitful spirits and teachings of demons"[230], and 1 Jn 4:1-3 speaks

---

[226] Note that we are not necessarily assuming that 1 Jn had already been written when John wrote Rev, but rather that if Rev was earlier, the trends 1 Jn reveals concerning leadership were already in evidence in the group that would later receive 1 Jn.

[227] There is no question that both sets of readers valued the revelation of Jesus Christ, and the authority of God. But we may suggest that in Rev the primarily question is whether this book as a prophecy, and hence inspired by the Spirit, gives this revelation reliably. So it turns back to the question of the readers' attitude to prophecy – which is after all the word John himself uses in Rev 1:3.

[228] Note also Tit 1:12.

[229] See 1 Jn 4:13;5:6-8; see further Coetzee 1979, p43-67; Lieu 1991, p45-9. We have suggested that the "anointing" in 1 Jn 2:20, 27 is probably not a reference to the Spirit. We will comment on 1 Jn 4:1-3 shortly.

[230] Note also "the snare of the devil" in 1 Tim 3:7; see also 2 Tim 2:26

explicitly about testing "spirits": "Beloved do not believe every spirit, but test the spirits to see whether they are from God; for many false prophets have gone out into the world. By this you know the Spirit of God: every spirit that confesses that Jesus Christ has come in the flesh is from God and every spirit that does not confess Jesus is not from God. And this is the spirit of the antichrist, of which you have head that it is coming; and now it is already in the world."[231] Although this originally applied to the secessionists, could it not easily be applied to John's work in the book of Revelation? Was the "spirit" that was claimed to be speaking here (eg. Rev 2:7, 11) from God? Was John a "false prophet"? John would presumably have passed the test given in 1 Jn 4 with regard to Christology,[232] but would this have itself been sufficient to convince readers of the Johannine Letters that John's Revelation was acceptable and trustworthy? Further, given the stress that we have discerned in different ways in the Pastorals and the Johannine Letters on "tradition", we can only guess how these different readers would have reacted to a book that claimed to be a (new) "revelation from Jesus Christ".

Thus, although we may suggest that prophecy or the activity of the Spirit is acknowledged or appreciated, it also has a decidedly ambiguous dimension to it for the readers of both sets of documents – there are deceitful spirits, or false prophets around. Thus although John's Revelation was not an utterly "foreign body" to them, and does key in to a recognised, if minor locus of authority, it is also one that is decidedly problematic for both sets of readers. Further, given that both communities allocate first place to a quite different locus of authority, the concern of John that we have discerned that his prophecy might not be accepted (and so his repeated underlining that its authority was from God, Christ and the Spirit) is seen to be well-founded.

Thus our discussions in this chapter are certainly compatible with our overall hypothesis, and we have also been able to discern further characteristics of the communities of readers of the Pastorals and the Johannine Letters.

---

[231] Note also the mention of the antichrist in 1 Jn 2:22; 2 Jn 7.

[232] Note the emphasis on the Lamb that was slain (eg Rev 5:12; 7:14; :12:11), although Rev hardly stresses the "flesh" of Jesus.

Chapter 11

The role of women among the readers of the Pastoral Epistles, the Johannine Letters and Revelation

In this chapter we are seeking to reconstruct the situation of Christian women in Ephesus as this is reflected in the Pastoral Epistles, the Johannine Letters and Revelation.[1] We are not attempting to outline all that the different authors say about women, but rather to discern the situation of women among the readers of these documents, as far as this is possible. As in previous Chapters we will also ask if what the authors say about the role of women is in keeping with, or contradicts our hypothesis that the readers of the Pastorals and the readers of the Johannine Letters are distinct communities, and that John in Revelation is writing to all the Christians in the city (apart from those he considers beyond the pale).

1. The Pastoral Epistles

Since the Pastor is reacting to the situation of the readers and attempting to prescribe new patterns of behaviour, we will see that through an analysis of his prescriptive rhetoric, we are able to discern a good deal about the current situation of women among the addressees.[2] As Maloney comments with regard to the Pastorals: "nowhere else do we find so much concentrated attention devoted to women's roles in early Christian communities: here, almost alone among Christian Testament writings, women actually take center stage from time to time."[3]

---

[1] The literature on women in the ancient Mediterranean world is extensive. See for example, van Bremen 1996; Hallett 1999, p13-34 (who discusses the ways in which women and their lives "were simultaneously likened to and differentiated from males and the existences of men" (p34)); LiDonnici 1999, p80-102. On women in Ephesus, see Rogers 1991, p215-23; Kirbihler 1994, p51-75; Strelan 1996, p118-25; van Tilborg 1996, p154-164; Friesen 1999a, p107-113; Solden 1999, p115-119.

[2] See Maloney 1994, p377.

[3] Maloney 1994, p361. MacDonald (1999b, p246) also notes: "One of the major priorities of the Pastoral Epistles is the management of women's behavior."

1.1 For the Pastor, leaders are Male

We note first of all that, although being male is not listed as a qualification for either presbyter-overseers or deacons, the author presupposes that leaders will be men (although we will argue that there are women deacons).[4] This is clearest in the list of qualities which the Pastor sets down as required of presbyter-overseers (1 Tim 3:1-7; Tit 1:5), particularly the requirements that they must be "the husband of one wife" (1 Tim 3:2, 12; Tit 1:6).[5] The emphasis on male leadership is probably connected to the concept of the church being the "household of God" and thus "(t)he ideal of the hierarchical Greco-Roman household is applied to the church".[6]

1.2 Women teachers in the community to which the author writes

As we have noted in Chapter 10, in 1 Timothy the Pastor is not writing to create new leadership offices, but is rather seeking to regulate matters relating to existing offices, particularly regarding what sort of people should be leaders. Despite the Pastor's view that leaders should be male, it seems clear, as we will show, that currently some women are teaching[7] in the Ephesian community addressed, but are teaching doctrine which the Pastor regards as false. Part of his aim is to curtail the activities of these women. Although teaching was not the exclusive preserve of leaders, since it was one of their key tasks (1 Tim 3:2; 5:17; Tit 1:9), it seems very likely that women were currently among the leaders of the community. We will now discuss the evidence for this.

We note first of all that in 2 Tim 3:6-7, after warning the readers about his opponents, the Pastor writes:

---

[4] Cardman 1999, p303 suggests that since 1 Tim 5:17 does not specify the gender of the "elders who rule well", there may have been female elders, "but the letter writer may have tried to obscure them in the text." She notes they would have been casualties of 1 Tim 2:11-13. Bailey 1998, p214-16 argues that πρεσβύτερος in 1 Tim 5:1 should be translated as male presbyters and πρεσβύτερας in 5:2 as female presbyters with the reference being to women elders ordained and engaged in ministry. However, this is unlikely since his analysis is based on seeing 4:6-5:22 as a chiasm, which seems questionable and we also note that women presbyters are clearly not in view in Tit 1:5-9, nor are women presbyter-overseers in view in 1 Tim 3:1-7.

[5] On the meaning of this phrase see Marshall 1999, p155-7; Johnson 2001, p213-14 (who both take it to refer to marital fidelity).

[6] Dewey 1998, p447.

[7] Schreiner (1995, p127) suggests that by "teaching" the Pastor understands "the public transmission of authoritative material (cf. 1 Tim. 4:13, 16; 6:2; 2 Tim. 4:2; Titus 2:7)."

"For among them [ie the opponents] are those who make their way into households and captivate silly women, overwhelmed by their sins and swayed by all kinds of desires, who are always being instructed and can never arrive at a knowledge of the truth."[8]

It is clear from this that the Pastor's opponents have gained a following among the women in the community.[9] But women are not only following the opponents; it seems likely that women are themselves, in the view of the Pastor, "false teachers". We will begin by discussing the activity of widows and will then turn to 1 Tim 2:8-15.

1.2.1 Widows and the teaching of the Pastor's opponents

After stating that younger widows should not be enrolled on the list of "real widows" because they eventually want to marry and so "violate their first pledge", the Pastor goes on in 1 Tim 5:13-15 to say:

"Besides that, they learn to be idle, gadding about from house to house (περιερχόμεναι τὰς οἰκίας); and they are not merely idle, but also gossips and busybodies, saying what they should not (λαλοῦσαι τὰ μὴ δέοντα). So I would have younger widows marry, bear children, and manage their households, so as to give the adversary no occasion to revile us. For some have already turned away to follow Satan."

We note firstly the reference to young widows having "turned away to follow Satan". Elsewhere, the Pastor associates his opponents with Satan, the devil or demons. In 2 Tim 2:26 it is said that the opponents (who are clearly in view) may "escape from the snare of the devil, having been held captive by him to do his will". In 1 Tim 4:1 the opponents are said to have renounced the faith "by paying attention to deceitful spirits and teachings of demons" and in 1 Tim 1:20 we read: "among them [the opponents] are Hymenaeus and Alexander, whom I have turned over to Satan, so that they may learn not to blaspheme."[10] Clearly then, in saying in 1 Tim 5:15 that some widows "have

---

[8] MacDonald (1999b, p246) notes that the Pastorals "reflect common stereotypes about the nature of the female character, such as the tendency for women to gossip (1 Tim 5:13) or their inclination for being easily duped (2 Tim 3:6)."

[9] Spicq (1969a, p777) thinks that this passage does not refer to Christian women, since they have not arrived at a knowledge of the truth. But clearly the Pastor has members of the community in view. Bassler (1988, p46) notes the success of the opponents in attracting women; see also MacDonald 1988, p176-80. Note also Tit 1:11 – opponents are "upsetting whole families by teaching for sordid gain what it is not right to teach". But this relates to Crete.

[10] This suggests they were already under Satan's influence. Note the use of διάβολος in 1 Tim 3:6, 7, 11; 2 Tim 3:3; Tit 2:3; in at least some of these references the word refers to "slanderers".

already turned away to follow Satan", the Pastor associates these widows with
his opponents.

But it is also clear that some of the younger widows are involved in
teaching. According to 1 Tim 5:13, they are "gadding about from house to
house (περιερχόμεναι τὰς οἰκίας)", which probably includes going from
house-church to house-church, and "saying what they should not (λαλοῦσαι
τὰ μὴ δέοντα)". Clearly these younger widows have a good deal of self-
autonomy, are moving about freely and are speaking openly.[11] But it is the
content of what they are saying that is most objectionable to the Pastor.[12]
While the Pastor does not explicitly say that they are "teaching", this seems
the most likely interpretation of 1 Tim 5:13, and we can understand why the
Pastor would not say in so many words that some widows were actually
currently functioning as teachers, since teaching the community is an activity
he wishes to associate solely with men.[13] We also note the parallel between
the widows "saying what they should not" and the opponents who
"blaspheme" (1 Tim 1:20), do not agree with "the sound words of our Lord
Jesus Christ" (1 Tim 6:3) and are involved in "profane chatter and
contradictions" (1 Tim 6:20).[14] This strongly suggests that some of these
widows are themselves part of the group of teachers which the Pastor regards
as his opponents, since they are both teaching doctrine of which the Pastor
disapproves and in that teaching are "straying after Satan".[15]

We note too that the opponents forbid marriage (1 Tim 4:3), and that the
widows are clearly (now) unmarried. Since it was unusual in Greco-Roman
culture for a young woman whose husband had died, or a young woman who
had never been married to remain unmarried,[16] (some of) these women seem
to have been choosing not to marry or remarry, in accordance with the
opponents' activity of "forbidding marriage" (1 Tim 4:3). If some of these
women were themselves teachers, then they are exemplifying their own
teaching. And as they teach from house to house, they are probably

---

[11] Streete (1999, p301) suggests "These young women perhaps occupy a rather high
position in the socially stratified Greco-Roman society, since they have enough leisure to go
from house to house".

[12] Bassler (1988, p52) notes that the condemnation of excessive speech, especially by
women, is found quite often (see Karris 1973, p553; Musonius Rufus, Or. 3; Juvenal, Sat. 6),
but here the emphasis is on the content of what the women say, not their manner of speaking.
Dewey (1998, p448) notes "From these widows' point of view, they are probably going about
teaching and proclaiming the faith, carrying out their Christian ministry (see 4:1-7 above)."

[13] See 1 Tim 3:2, 9; 5:17; Tit 1:9; see also 1 Tim 2:7; 4:11-16; 2 Tim 2:14-15, 24-5; Tit
2:1; the teaching activity of women spoken of in Tit 2:4-5 and implied in 2 Tim 1:5; 3:15 is
limited to teaching other women and children.

[14] See also 1 Tim 1:6; 3:1; 2 Tim 2:14-18, 23; 3:8, 13; 4:3-4; Tit 1:10-11; 3:9.

[15] See Dewey 1998, p450; Cardman 1999, p304. Schreiner 1995, p111-112 rejects this
view.

[16] We will note below that some of the "widows" may have been virgins.

advocating celibacy as part of their teaching, and so are seeking to increase the size of the widows' group and the number of adherents to this alternative teaching within the community.[17]

The Pastor's "solution" with regard to these teaching widows also points to the connection with the teaching of the Pastor's opponents. The Pastor instructs the widows that rather than abandoning marriage, and thus achieving a degree of autonomy (since they would not be under the direct authority of a husband), these young widows are to marry, have children and manage their households. That is, they are to take up the role the Pastor assigns to women,[18] and in so doing, he hopes, to put themselves beyond the influence of other (male) opponents.

All of these points indicate that some widows were themselves among the teachers opposing the Pastor, and thus were teachers in the community of the addressees. Of course the opponents are not only women (since men who are among the Pastor's opponents are named in 1 Tim 1:20 and 2 Tim 2:17-18), but it seems very likely that women are a part of the group of opponents.

Further, as we have noted in Chapter 10, teaching was a key component of the leader's role in the Pastorals (see 1 Tim 3:2; 5:17; Tit 1:9), and although people who were not "official" leaders probably were currently involved in teaching activity in the community, given the amount of time the Pastor devotes to this issue of women who are involved in teaching (in 1 Tim 2:11-15 and 5:3-16), it seems likely that women were among the *official* teachers and so that some women were currently leaders in the community.[19] Against this background, we can discuss 1 Tim 2:8-15.

1.2.2 "I permit no woman to teach ..." - 1 Tim 2:8-15

We do not need to go into all the issues which have been raised in conjunction with this passage, nor do we need to clarify all the aspects of what the Pastor writes in response to the situation of his readers. Our aim is to discern the situation of the women the Pastor addresses; what were their roles and activities?[20] Here we will discuss five aspects of v8-15.

---

[17] Bassler (1988, p53) notes that "It is interesting that the only place in the Pastoral Epistles that encourages women to speak limits the content of that speech to the distinctly anti-celibate topics of marital submissiveness and maternal love (Tit. 2:3-5)."

[18] MacDonald (1999b, p251) notes that in the Pastor's view, "believing women should emulate virtuous Roman matrons".

[19] That women were functioning as both teachers and leaders is argued for example by Maloney 1994, p370; Fee 1991, p55.

[20] For bibliography on this passage see Mounce 2000, p94-102. There is debate about whether v9 refers to women's adornment when they pray during worship, or whether it refers to women's adornment in worship in general, in which case the women might not be involved in praying during worship. For the debate see Bassler 1988, p47-8; Marshall 1999, p446-8.

a) In 1 Tim 2:11 the Pastor writes: "Let a woman learn in silence (γυνὴ ἐν
ἡσυχίᾳ μανθανέτω)".[21] 1 Tim 2:12 clarifies that they are to "learn in
silence" rather than teach. Taken with 2:12 then, the command in 2:11
suggests that women were not being silent, particularly given that the Pastor
reiterates the command to silence in v12.[22] Hence v11-12 together suggest
that some women were currently teaching. We now turn to 2:12 in more
detail.

b) In 1 Tim 2:12 the Pastor writes: "I permit no woman to teach or to have
authority over a man; she is to keep silent (διδάσκειν δὲ γυναικὶ οὐκ
ἐπιτρέπω οὐδὲ αὐθεντεῖν ἀνδρός, ἀλλ᾽ εἶναι ἐν ἡσυχίᾳ)." Firstly, some
have argued that γυνή here means "wife" rather than "woman", and thus
argue that the verse involves the subordination of a wife to her husband,
rather than women in general. This view is based on the fact that the singular
form of the word pair γυνή – ἀνήρ in v12 refers most naturally to wife and
husband (cf. the plurals in v8-10).[23] However, the lack of any possessive
pronouns or any other determinative clue that husbands and wives are
intended makes this view improbable.[24]

Rather, 1 Tim 2:12 seems to be a comprehensive prohibition of teaching by
women among the readers. Along with the evidence for widows teaching
"wrong doctrine" that we have examined, this shows that some women were
currently teaching in the community. As Dewey notes, "The fact that the
author spends so much time and effort [in 1 Tim 2:9-15] to enjoin silence on
Christian women suggests that the actual and accepted practice of women was
active and vocal and that the author was attempting to change this
behavior."[25] Given that some widows were advocating the opponents'
teaching (1 Tim 5:13-15), and that 1 Tim 2:12 shows women are currently
teaching, it seems most likely that the Pastor will primarily not allow these
women to teach because of the content of their teaching; that is, because some

---

Note that if v9 does not concern women during prayer, then the introduction of the topic of
women's adornment becomes an unrelated digression, which seems unlikely.

[21] Note that ἐν ἡσυχίᾳ here probably indicates "listening quietly with deference and
attentiveness to the one teaching"; see Marshall 1999, p453. See also Schreiner 1995, p123-4.
In the context of the whole passage, since "silence" is given as the natural antonym to
teaching, the injunction suggests that women need to learn, and so implies that they are
currently following the wrong teaching.

[22] See Dewey1998, p445-6

[23] For this view see for example Gritz 1991, p125, 131; Stratton 1996, p269.

[24] See Bassler 1988, p62, n13; Schreiner 1995, p115-17.

[25] Dewey 1998, p446. See also Schottroff, Schroer, Wacker, 1998, p232; Marshall 1999,
p520.

women are propagating the teaching the Pastor regards as "false".[26] The prohibition in 1 Tim 2:12 can thus be seen against the backdrop of the concern for sound teaching and sound teachers in the Pastorals.[27]

c) In 1 Tim 2:12 the Pastor writes : "I permit no woman to teach or *to have authority over a man*" (διδάσκειν δὲ γυναικὶ οὐκ ἐπιτρέπω οὐδὲ αὐθεντεῖν ἀνδρός)." Are teaching and the exercising of authority related here? It could be that the two infinitives (διδάσκειν and αὐθεντεῖν) envisage separate activities of (respectively) teaching and exercising the authority of general leadership, or that the exercise of authority takes place through teaching. Marshall notes that the relation of v11 to v12 suggests that "learning" and "teaching" are the main point of contrast. He goes on "αὐθεντεῖν as a reference to 'authority' (leadership) unrelated to teaching would exceed the scope of the discussion initiated at v.11. It is, therefore, more likely that the verb characterises the nature of the teaching rather than the role of the women in church leadership in general."[28] We suggest then that, from the Pastor's point of view, women were "having authority over a man" through teaching.

But what does αὐθεντεῖν mean here? Baldwin argues that the different meanings of αὐθεντέω are united by the idea of the possession or exercise of authority.[29] Further, Köstenberger has argued that "the conjunction οὐδέ coordinates activities of the same order, that is, activities that are either both viewed positively or negatively by the writer or speaker."[30] He suggests that there are only two possible ways of understanding 2:12: "(1) 'I do not permit a woman to teach [error] or to domineer over a man,' or (2) 'I do not permit a woman to teach or to exercise authority over a man.' In the first instance, both 'teaching error' and 'domineering a man' would be viewed negatively by the writer. In the latter case, both 'teaching' and 'exercising authority' would be

---

[26] Note that Towner (1989, p39, 216) and Schreiner (1995, p127) think that women were currently teaching, but not that the content of their teaching was wrong. But this gives insufficient weight to what is said about the widows and what is said about Eve in 2:13-14.

[27] See 1 Tim 1:3, 7; 2:7; 3:2; 4:11-16; 5:17; 6:1-3; 2 Tim 1:11; 2:2, 24; 3:10, 16; 4:2-3; Tit 1:9, 11; 2:1, 3, 7.

[28] Marshall 1999, p460. Schottroff, Schroer, Wacker (1998, p199) suggest women claimed to have the authority to teach men. Maloney (1994, p370) notes concerning 1 Tim 2: "We may see in the prohibition on women's 'exercising authority over men' an oblique reference to the prophet's role in the community, since in the early church it was the word of the Lord given through the prophets that was the true authority guiding the life of the churches." However, this is rather speculative.

[29] Baldwin 1995, p65-80. The different possibilities are: (1) to rule, to reign sovereignly; (2) to control, to dominate; (3) to act independently; (4) to be primarily responsible for or to instigate something; (5) (late) to commit a murder. He further divides up the possibilities with regard to senses 2 and 3. See also Baldwin 1995b, p269-305; he refers to previous studies.

[30] Köstenberger 1995, p85.

viewed positively in and of themselves, yet for reasons to be gleaned from the
context the writer does not permit these."[31]

But is αὐθεντεῖν – "to have authority" - used positively or negatively here?
Marshall notes that in the context, that Eve was deceived is cited as a parallel.
Hence "this strongly suggests the conclusion that behind the present
prohibition lies some particular false teaching by some women. Otherwise,
the reference to Eve's being deceived and sinning is pointless. The activity of
teaching here is thus judged negatively; it follows that the attitude expressed
in it towards the men [using αὐθεντεῖν] is also something of which the writer
disapproves."[32] This suggests that the issue is the manner in which women are
exercising the authority involved in teaching.[33] The most likely suggestion is
that we should see a connection here with the over-realised eschatology of the
opponents (2 Tim 2:18). Perhaps the belief that the resurrection had already
come "could encourage the women to assume roles apparently denied them by
the curse of Eve (... Gen 3:16), perhaps with the encouragement of false
teachers."[34]

Hence, 1 Tim 2:12 confirms that the issue is that the women are involved
in teaching, whose content the Pastor believed was wrong, and that the way
the teaching was being done by some women involved them having what the
Pastor thought was inappropriate authority.

d) The Pastor refers to Adam and Eve in v13-14: "For Adam was formed first,
then Eve; and Adam was not deceived, but the women was deceived
(ἐξαπατηθεῖσα) and became a transgressor." The key points for us are as
follows.

Firstly, the Pastor provides a justification for v11-12 by appealing to the
order of creation given in Genesis 2, noting that Adam was formed first.[35]
Bassler writes: "The sequence of creation, first Adam and secondly Eve, is
thus assumed to be a revelation of God's will for the relationship of the two
sexes. Thus women in roles of authority over men are viewed as flouting the

---

[31] Köstenberger 1995, p89.

[32] Marshall 1999, p458.

[33] See Marshall 1999, p459. Köstenberger (1995, p89-91) thinks διδάσκειν is used
positively, and so αὐθεντεῖν denotes an activity that is positive in and of itself. The
conclusion from this is that women are not advocating the opponents' teaching. However,
Marshall's observation given in the text, that Eve was deceived, and so the women in Ephesus
were too, argues against this view.

[34] Marshall 1999, p459. He goes on: "Within such a reconstruction αὐθεντέω is
understandable as a reference to the exuberant and excessive flaunting of freedom in the face
of men".

[35] For a discussion of intertestamental, rabbinic and Gnostic texts about Eve see Stratton
1996, p261-3.

divine will itself."[36] This verse reinforces the likelihood that women were claiming authority over men, and to refute this the Pastor asserts the primacy of Adam. Again we note that in context, the most likely way for women to "have authority over a man" is through their teaching activity.

Secondly the Pastor emphasises that Eve "was deceived and became a transgressor".[37] The point seems to be that in this Eve is analogous to the women in the community in Ephesus who are currently being "deceived" in that they are following the opponents.[38] In support of the connection in view here being that both Eve and the Ephesian women teachers are "deceived" we note that the Pastor describes the opponents as "deceiving others and being deceived" (πλανῶντες καὶ πλανώμενοι (2 Tim 3:13)), and as giving heed to "deceitful spirits" (1 Tim 4:1 (πνεύμασιν πλάνοις)).[39] It was because some women were currently being deceived that "it seemed unwise, in the Pastor's view, for women to occupy positions of authority or influence within the church."[40] The reference to Genesis 3 thus provides a scriptural warrant for the Pastor's instructions. Bassler concludes:

"Eve, the prototype of all women, was the one in the garden who was deceived, and her daughters, who seem to have inherited this proclivity, must therefore be excluded from positions in which this tendency could further endanger the church. The key points in this argument are thus (1) the prior identification of the heretics as deceivers, (2) the awareness that women in the church were far too frequently deceived by these heretics, and (3) the wording of Gen. 3:12-13, in which the primal woman, but not the primal man, admits to succumbing to deception."[41]

---

[36] Bassler 1988, p49.

[37] The statement that Adam was not deceived is probably a literal reading of Gen 3, since only the woman admits to being deceived there (Gen 3:13; LXX). By contrast, in Gen 3:12 Adam admits only to receiving and eating the fruit and says nothing about being deceived. Fee (1988a, p74) notes that it was Eve and not Adam who was deceived by the serpent. Marshall (1999, p463) notes "Here the point is simply either that Adam was not deceived by the serpent as Eve was, or that Adam was not [the first to be] deceived, but Eve was .." Others suggest that there is an allusion to the legend of Eve's seduction by the serpent here (2 Enoch 31:6; Protoevangelium Jacobi 13.1; b. Yebam 103b; b. 'Abod. Zar. 22b; b. Sabb. 146a), but this seems unlikely in the context and the parallels postdate the New Testament; see Towner 1989, p313-14 n78; Schreiner 1995, p143.

[38] See Bassler 1988, p50-1.

[39] See also the description of the opponents as "deceivers" (φρεναπάται) in Tit 1:10 and compare also 1 Tim 6:5.

[40] Bassler 1988, p50-1.

[41] Bassler 1988, p51. Bassler (1988, p52) also notes that in Gen 3:17 the punishment of Adam is based not only on his disobedience to God's command, but also on the fact that he listened to Eve. Bassler notes: "It is easy to see these words reflected in the Pastor's insistence not only on subordination, but also on *hesuchia*. The women must not be allowed to exercise this sort of verbal influence again."

The note about Eve's deception in 2:14 then again shows that some women are following the opponents. But how does this relate to the injunction that they should not teach (v12), as it clearly does since it is part of the explanation of v12? It suggests again that some of these women, whom the Pastor thinks have been deceived like Eve, should not teach (v12), precisely because they have themselves become "false teachers" (as 1 Tim 5:13 also suggests) and so must cease from this activity since they are not teaching "sound doctrine" but are rather themselves deceived.

e) Again we do not need to enter into all of the debates about v15.[42] Two points are relevant here. Firstly, although exactly what is meant by "she will be saved through childbearing" (1 Tim 2:15) is debated, the reference to childbearing clearly counters the opponents' emphasis on "forbidding marriage" (1 Tim 4:3). As a specific response to the opponents, the Pastor emphasises that rather than abandoning marriage, women are to bear children.[43]

Secondly, the Pastor emphasizes that "she will be saved through childbearing, provided they[44] continue in faith and love and holiness, with modesty". Again, this emphasises that they are not to be involved in the opponents' teaching, but are to continue to practice what the Pastor regards as the virtues of the Christian life.

We should note that the Pastor does not associate *all* women with the opponents (even if he wishes to silence all women). There are instructions to treat women with consideration (1 Tim 5:2-3) and Timothy's grandmother Lois and mother Eunice are warmly commended (2 Tim 1:5). We will suggest that some women were deacons (1 Tim 3:11) and the teaching skills of women "were not completely rejected but were redirected to a domestic arena where they countered rather than complemented heretical activities (Tit.

---

[42] For discussions of the many controversial issues associated with v15 see Bassler 1988, p53-6; Porter 1993, p87-102.

[43] See Fee 1988, p74-5; Gritz 1991, p143; Schreiner 1995, p150-1. Bassler (1988, p55-6, her emphasis) makes an interesting suggestion here: "It may be that because of the Pastor's concern to reject the celibate lifestyle advocated by his opponents, he sought here to *counter* the suggestion of Genesis that childbirth is a curse [Gen 3:16], an idea that would play into the hands of the heretics. Indeed, the heretics, who were skilled in manipulating Jewish myths, may have already exploited the potential of this idea. The Pastor then polemically transformed the Genesis curse into a Christian blessing, which may have operated on two levels. A woman will be saved *from the allure of the heretical message* by bearing children, and because she thus avoids making a shipwreck of her faith, she will also be saved in the absolute sense of the word, provided, of course, she continues in faith, love, and holiness."

[44] Note the shift from singular "she will be saved (sothesetai)" to the plural "if they continue …" The third person plural is best taken as a generic reference to women among the addressees. The singular may be explained by the reference to Eve in v13-14; see further Porter 1993, p98-9.

2:3-5)."[45] Thus all women are not associated with the opponents. It is not clear, however, whether there are some current women teachers who are not part of the group the Pastor regards as his opponents.

We conclude then that some women have followed the opponents and that some of these women have become teachers themselves in the community, and hence are leaders.[46]

1.2.3 Other matters regarding the Pastor's opponents and women

Three other matters need to be noted here. Firstly, in Chapter 8 we have already noted the importance the Pastor places on the opinion of outsiders. Here we note that the Pastor opposes the activity of women amongst the opponents not only because, from his point of view, they were teaching "unsound doctrine", but also because the opponents' teaching encouraged behaviour by women which was likely to attract the negative comment of outsiders. Thus in 1 Tim 5:13-14, we read that ceasing "gadding about from house to house" is linked with giving "the enemy no occasion to revile us". Here the "enemy" is clearly the outsider. As MacDonald notes "The desire of young women to remain unmarried and their active movements from house to house have apparently contributed to the community being viewed as suspicious."[47] We should recall that Greco-Roman society was "a society in which the modest behavior of women was vital to household honor and communal identity".[48] It seems clear therefore that the Pastor thinks the activities of widows is one of the reasons why the community has been and will be slandered by others. As well as countering the opponents' teaching, the Pastor's directives in 1 Tim 5 concerning widows are an attempt to curtail negative comments from outsiders and to reduce the mounting tension between the Christian community and society.

This desire to avoid negative comment is therefore connected to the author's attempt to control the behaviour of women so that the Christian community conforms to the ideal of the contemporary household. As Dewey notes, "The author is socially conservative, wanting ... conformity to an ideal

---

[45] Bassler 1988, p58. Dewey (1998, p452) comments on this verse: "older women are to teach young women their subordinate status in the household. The author wants to use women to teach other women to internalize their inferior status and their proper function as limited to the household."

[46] In the light of all of this we can suggest that some of those who "make their way into households and captivate silly women" (2 Tim 3:6-7), may themselves be women; see Streete 1999, p312-13; see also Maloney 1994, p373, 376.

[47] MacDonald 1999b, p248.

[48] MacDonald 1999b, p251.

of a hierarchical household that mirrors the public hierarchy established by the Roman imperial authorities."[49]

Secondly, a number of scholars have suggested a connection between the Pastorals and the second century *Acts of Paul and Thecla*. In this story, Paul preaches to Thecla, who abandons her household to follow Paul and adopt a celibate life and goes on to fulfil a prominent leadership role in her own right. Thecla's lack of regard for social respectability is met with hostility and violence from her family and others in the wider society. The *Acts* seem to be an alternative interpretation of the Pauline tradition to that found in the Pastorals or the Acts of the Apostles, and a tradition which continues the tradition of women's leadership, celibacy and greater social equality among Christians.[50] It has been suggested that when the Pastor argues against the teaching activity of women (1 Tim 2:9-15) against celibacy (1 Tim 4:3) and writes in 1 Tim 4:7 that his readers should "have nothing to do with profane myths and old wives' tales", the Pastor is countering the sorts of traditions about Paul which are later found in the *Acts of Paul and Thecla*, in which Paul is an advocate for women's leadership.[51] The Pastor presents counter-traditions, in which Paul advocates that women should adopt traditional gender roles.

It is also possible that there is a direct connection between the opponents (including the women among these teachers) and the traditions found in the *Acts*. Perhaps the opponents of the Pastor utilised Pauline traditions similar to those written later in the *Acts of Paul and Thecla*, as a justification for their teaching and lifestyle. In any case, the *Acts* certainly show that, in the generations after Paul's death, there were different perspectives on women within the Pauline tradition from those represented in the Pastorals.

---

[49] Dewey 1998, p445. It is clear in a number of passages in the Pastorals that the author wishes women to conform to traditional Greco-Roman roles (see 1 Tim 2:15; 1 Tim 5:10, 14; Tit 2:2-5; note also the importance that the Pastor puts on the family unit in 1 Tim 5:4-8). As Maloney (1994, p367) comments: "Instructions for the behavior of wives, not husbands (Titus 2:4-5; cf. 1 Tim 5:14) and for slaves, not masters (1 Tim 6:1-2; Titus 2:9-10) show that the particular 'hot spot,' in the author's view, was defiance of social convention on the part of traditionally low-status groups: married or marriageable women and slaves of both sexes." The Pastor's insistence on women confining their roles to the domestic sphere would also reduce the likelihood that women would be able to spread the opponents' teaching. But clearly the Pastor is also concerned that women conform to majority values so as to give no offence to outsiders (eg 1 Tim 5:14).

[50] See MacDonald 1999b, p238. She notes "It is useful to think in terms of several trajectories of the Pauline tradition emanating from the teaching and leadership of the apostle that would have had varying consequences for the lives of early Christian women."

[51] See Davies 1980, p70-94; Gordon 1997, p194-202; Dewey 1998, p445, 447-8; MacDonald 1999b, p249-51; Cardman 1999, p301-2; Streete 1999, p306; cf. Harding 2001, p38-44.

Thirdly, some scholars have sought to relate the opponents' teaching to Ephesian devotion to Artemis. Thus, Richard and Catherine Kroeger have argued that the opponents taught the priority of Eve over Adam and that Eve enlightened Adam with her teaching.[52] Similarly, Gritz argues that the restriction on women teaching was related to the influence of the cult of Artemis among the addressees in Ephesus.[53] However, both works go considerably beyond the evidence in their reconstructions of the opponents' teaching and its supposed connection with the context of Ephesian non-Christian religious life.[54]

1.2.4 Why were women attracted to the opponents' teaching?

It seems that the opponents' teaching was attractive to women. Why was this the case? The most likely suggestion is that it included "freedom from the oppressive patriarchal structure that characterized the Greco-Roman world and was increasingly characterizing the church."[55] Bassler goes on:

"Insofar as Gal. 3:28 was more than mere baptismal rhetoric, Christianity seems to have begun as a rather egalitarian movement, with equality affecting even the structure of Christian marriages. But Christianity did not long remain egalitarian. Social pressure both within and without the church soon forced a restructuring both of itself and of the families within it according to the hierarchical, patriarchal pattern of contemporary society. This is particularly evident in the Pastoral Epistles, and it is also evident from these epistles that some women sought to escape this pattern to some degree by embracing a celibate lifestyle. At first this was possible within the widows' office of the church, but increasingly it was the heretics, with their blanket renunciation of marriage, who offered the best avenue to freedom. Thus the success of the Pastor's opponents with the 'weak women' can be attributed in large measure to the real social benefits once promised by the church but now found primarily among the heretics."[56]

It seems most likely then that the opponents preserved at least some freedom for women because of what we have called their over-realized eschatology (2 Tim 2:18). This led to an emancipatory strand of their teaching, which in turn was attractive to women.[57]

---

[52] Kroeger and Kroeger 1992.

[53] Gritz 1991, especially p115-59; see also Bailey 1998, p219-226.

[54] For a discussion of these works see Schreiner 1995, p109-110 and the articles cited there. See also Strelan 1996, p154-5; Baugh 1999, p449-60.

[55] Bassler 1988, p46; for a discussion of the nature of the patriarchal society of the period see Sawyer 1996, p17-31.

[56] Bassler 1988, p46-7.

[57] Maloney (1994, p373) notes that "these women may well have shared the conviction of their sisters in Corinth that they were already enjoying the fruits of the resurrection (cf. 1 Cor 15:12ff)."

But there is another reason why women may have been attracted to the opponents' teaching. There is a clear link between leadership and wealth in the ancient world, and this is as true for women as it is for men, to the extent that the (few) women who were able to obtain influential positions were generally wealthy.[58] We have noted in Chapter 9 that some of the women among the addressees were wealthy (eg 1 Tim 2:9; 5:16); further it seems likely that some of the women who followed the opponents and themselves became teachers were wealthy.[59] Given the connection between wealth and leadership, these wealthier women (whether they were recent converts or not) would probably expect to have some influence within the Christian group.[60] It seems likely that the Pastor would not support this; however, that the opponents would have welcomed wealthier women, who would have become influential within their group, is suggested by the indications that some of the opponents were wealthy,[61] and that some wealthy women were themselves teachers amongst the opponents (1 Tim 2:9-15). We can suggest then that some wealthier women would naturally gravitate towards the opponents. This may then be an additional reason for the opponents' success amongst women.

1.3 Women Deacons?

In 1 Tim 3:11, in the middle of a discussion of deacons we read: "Women likewise must be serious, not slanderers, but temperate, faithful in all things (Γυναῖκας ὡσαύτως σεμνάς, μὴ διαβόλους, νηφαλίους, πιστὰς ἐν πᾶσιν)". There has been considerable debate about the identity of these "women". The reference could be to all the women in the community, to the wives of deacons or to women deacons. Which is the most likely?

In 1 Tim 3:8-13 we have qualifications for "deacons" and then for "women", and then for "deacons" again. The character traits required of these "women" are almost exactly the same as those required of "deacons" in 1 Tim

---

[58] See van Bremen 1995.

[59] Note the connection between wealth in 1 Tim 2:9 and women teaching what they should not in 2:11-15. It seems likely then that some of the women who are told to be silent are wealthy.

[60] We are not able to undertake a detailed comparison with Paul's letters here, but the level of wealth encountered among the addressees in the Pastorals seems higher than in Paul's letters (particularly when we take note of Meggitt's work on Paul (Meggitt 1998)). It seems likely that as women who were somewhat higher up the scale of wealth joined a group like that revealed in the Pastorals, they expected a higher level of involvement in leadership; see also Kidd 1990, p102-3.

[61] The accusation made by the Pastor that the opponents were greedy for gain (1 Tim 6:5; Tit 1:11) suggests that the opponents included wealthier Christians; see Chapter 5, section 5.7.

3:8-10,[62] but since similar qualities are looked for not only in episkopoi (1 Tim 3:1-7), but also in older women and older men (Tit 2:2), we can conclude nothing from this.

Stiefel notes that "the syntactical signals sent by the text itself [1 Tim 3:11] within its context are in fact ambiguous, orienting attention in different directions."[63] It is this ambiguity that has led to so many different interpretations of the verse, but which also needs to be explained. There are three important syntactical features of 3:8-13. Firstly, γυναῖκας is anarthrous and no indication is given of their specific relationship to the διάκονοι of 3:8-10. This may indicate that a whole class of women is meant, or secondly, it may show that wives are being spoken of, since a term of relationship "may be used without the article when spoken of in general".[64] A third possible reading of the anarthrous γυναῖκας "is based on the use of anarthrous γυνή to specify the female counterpart or equivalent of a male exercising a given occupation or status."[65] In this case, γυνή would be in apposition to a noun, which in 1 Tim 3:11 would be understood to be διάκονος. One reason for this use of language would be that feminine gender terms for "women deacons/deaconesses" are not attested until the fourth century.[66] However, we cannot decide between these three possibilities with regard to the anarthrous γυναῖκας without considering further factors.

The second syntactical feature is that 3:11 repeats the syntax of 3:8, and as in that verse, δεῖ εἶναι must be understood from 3:2. Further, the noun in both 3:8 and 3:11 is accompanied by the adverb ὡσαύτως. This structure shows that 3:11 begins another topic (just as 3:8 does), but one closely connected with 3:2-7 and 3:8-10.

The third syntactical feature is that in 3:12 the Pastor returns to the discussion of διάκονοι; thus the γυναῖκας are included within a discussion of "deacons". Stiefel also analyses the syntactical structure of 3:8-13, which consists of A (3:8-9), B (3:10), A' (3:11), B' (3:12), C (3:13). It is clear from this that 3:11 is an integral part of the passage, and can be seen as "an abbreviated mirror of 3.8-9".[67]

Given these three syntactical features of the passage, what is the most likely meaning of γυναῖκας? It is unlikely that the reference is to the women of the community as a whole, since the detailed structural integrity of 3:8-13 indicates that the γυναῖκας of 3:11 have a connection with the διάκονοι. Nor

---

[62] Bailey 1998, p211-12 notes that the only requirement given for deacons but absent in v11 is "not greedy for gain".

[63] Stiefel 1995, p445.

[64] Stiefel 1995, p446.

[65] Stiefel 1995, p446.

[66] See G. Stählin, 'χήρα' TDNT 9, 464 n231.

[67] Stiefel 1995, p450.

is there any reason why the author would speak about women in general at this point. It is also unlikely that the "women" are wives of the deacons,[68] since then we would expect some possessive, or a relative pronoun or adjective with γυναῖκας. Further, the [δεῖ] ... ὡσαύτως structure counts against this view since its presence in 3:11 suggests the beginning of the discussion of a third group related to episkopoi and diakonoi. We also note that nothing is said about requirements for the wives of episkopoi.[69]

The γυναῖκας could be a group who served the church in some capacity as "women deacons", a group which would be separate and distinct from the (male) διάκονοι.[70] In support of this view is the [δεῖ] ... ὡσαύτως structure of the passage, which would signal a third category of leaders; their inclusion within the topic of "deacons" would show their equivalent status to the male deacons. But this view does not really explain why they are mentioned within the discussion of (male) deacons (1 Tim 3:8-10, 12-13) if they are a separate and independent group of women deacons.

Another view would not see the γυναῖκας as a separate group, but rather as included within the group of διάκονοι; this view sees the γυναῖκας as women who minister along with men as deacons.[71] Stiefel notes "the inclusion of the women in the topic of διάκονοι and their syntactic integration into the passage speak strongly for their status as ministers as part of the group of διάκονοι. The suggestion that γυναῖκας may function in apposition with an understood διακόνους to specify female counterparts to the males gives an explanation for the anarthrous noun."[72]

But what about the [δεῖ] ... ὡσαύτως structure of the passage? Women are often categorised in 1 Timothy as a group (1 Tim 2:9-15; 5:3-16), so it would not be strange for the women deacons, who (we are suggesting) do not form an actual "separate group" but rather belong within the order of deacons, to be addressed separately.[73] But how is it that the Pastor, who is clearly opposed to women teachers/leaders, does not forbid women from being a full part of the order of deacons? Stiefel comments:

"the behaviours that attract notice to women in chapters 2 and 5 may not be so apparent among the women deacons. Neither they, nor the male deacons, are teaching in the congregation; that function is reserved for the ἐπίσκοπος. Nor are they functioning as a separate group of women, as the widows have been. The situation may thus indeed provoke unease [for the Pastor], yet not prohibition or redress. Thus the convoluted verse with its

---

[68] A view favoured, for example, by Hanson 1982, p80-1.

[69] See Stiefel 1995, p446, 452, 455.

[70] This view is favoured, for example, by Schweizer, Church Order, p86 n334.

[71] In support of this view see, for example, Roloff 1988, p164-6; Giles 1989, p61-2; Maloney 1994, p368; Stiefel 1995, p442, 455-6; Marshall 1999, p492-5

[72] Stiefel 1995, p454.

[73] See Stiefel 1995, p455-6.

multivalent signals images the ambivalent situation of the women described. It is probably their status within the diaconal order that shields the women deacons, a situation mirrored in their being wrapped about by the term and the syntactic structure of the διάκονοι."[74]

We conclude then that close attention to the syntax of 3:8-13 strongly suggests that women were involved in a diaconal ministry, and were part of the one group of "deacons" along with men. We note that one corollary of this interpretation is that deacons are not teachers (at least not formally), but this seems likely in any case, given that, as we have noted in Chapter 10, nothing is said about a teaching role for deacons.

In the Pastorals, deacons seem to have had a role with regard to managing or ruling and were involved in "service", although we note that they are not said to simply "serve" the community in a purely practical way. That they had significant responsibilities is shown by the Pastor's concern to regulate who should be a deacon. In Chapter 10, we suggested that the fact that the deacons are discussed after the episkopos in 1 Tim 3 may indicate that the presbyter-overseers had precedence over the deacons or that the deacon's role was a less responsible position than that of the presbyter-overseers. Further, it has been suggested that deacons may be assistants to the presbyter-overseers, although this is not certain. But clearly deacons hold positions of leadership in the community. We have argued that some women were currently teachers and leaders in the community and we now see that some women were also deacons; this is a further indication that women were fulfilling leadership functions within the community.

1.4 The widows' order (1 Tim 5:3-16)

We have discussed the group of widows in Chapter 9 and earlier in this chapter have argued that some widows have followed the Pastor's opponents and their teaching and some have themselves become teachers. Here we simply need to note further points that are relevant to this chapter.

Firstly, it is clear from 1 Tim 5:3-16 that the Pastor is not seeking to establish a new "order of widows". If this was the case, we would have expected him to describe the terms and conditions of the order more fully. Rather, he is seeking to regulate and limit an existing order,[75] which is a fairly developed organisation in which widows are "enrolled".[76] This is clear from 1 Tim 5:9: "Let a widow be enrolled (χήρα καταλεγέσθω) if she is not less

---

[74] Stiefel 1995, p456.

[75] See Bassler 1984, p34.

[76] Kraemer 1992, p182; Price 1997, p1-5; MacDonald 1999b, p246-9 see this passage as evidence for a formal group or order of widows; see also Davies 1980, p70-1. But the evidence is lacking to suggest that they were a "ministerial order".

than sixty years of age …"[77] Further, the qualities required for widows to be enrolled are very similar to those required for appointing people as episkopoi and diakonoi,[78] which suggests that the widows are part of an official group of some sort.

Secondly, in 1 Tim 5:16 we read: "If any believing woman has widows (εἴ τις πιστὴ ἔχει χήρας), let her assist them." It is likely that such a "believing woman" was herself a widow since she is spoken of as acting on her own without the involvement of a husband and is said to herself "have widows". MacDonald comments: "Because widows in Greco-Roman society were sometimes in charge of households and in control of considerable resources, there is good reason to believe that 1 Tim 5:16 refers to the situation of a widow of some means caring for poorer women in her own household."[79] Thus, as we have noted in Chapter 9, this verse suggests that some wealthy women were able to support a group of widows,[80] and that there were groups or "houses" of widows under the protection and patronage of wealthy widows.[81] Perhaps economic motives were to the fore here, since economically vulnerable widows would have been assisted in this way.[82] It is certainly further evidence of the significance of the group of widows.

Thirdly, it is clear that the Pastor is seeking to reduce the size of the official widows' group. We see this in the strict new requirements for enrolment introduced in 1 Tim 5:9-14, in the insistence that the children and grandchildren of a widow must support her (1 Tim 5:4-8), which seems to lead to a widow in this situation not being enrolled in the group, and that a "believing woman" who "has widows" must support them (v16), which again would result in such women not being enrolled. The result is that only "real widows" who are "all alone" (v5) would be enrolled in the order. The Pastor's goal seems to be to reduce the size of the order of widows "to a system of

---

[77] BDAG, p520 define καταλέγω as "to make a selection for membership in a group", but it is the context rather than simply the verb itself which suggests enrolment in a reasonably formal group is in view here.

[78] See Dewey 1998, p447.

[79] MacDonald 1999b, p247.

[80] MacDonald (1999b, p247) suggests: "It is probably best to think of the support of women extending beyond relatives when it came to caring for other women."

[81] Maloney 1994, p373; Dewey 1998, p448. MacDonald (1999b, p247) notes the reference to "the virgins called widows" in IgnSm 13.1 which "implies that celibate women of various ages sometimes lived together in a house, in contrast to the usual family arrangements." Tabitha (Acts 9:36-42) also seems to have acted as patron of a group of needy widows. The Pastor emphasizes that the "believing woman" should pay all the expenses herself, and not call on the church's finances (1 Tim 5:16), but prior to the time of writing, such groups of widows may have received some support from the church; the Pastor is changing this arrangement so that the church is not "burdened".

[82] See Schottroff, Schroer, Wacker, 1998, p186.

charity for older destitute women."[83] Previously it had probably been much more than this.

Why is the Pastor seeking to reduce the group? Finances may be one reason; the church's communal fund simply could not support too many widows. But it is likely that there is a more fundamental reason. Bassler has noted that widows had a significantly greater degree of autonomy than married woman.[84] She suggests that, as the community became more patriarchal, this encouraged women to join the widows' order. This would be a way of preserving some autonomy and freedom, both for women whose husbands had died, but probably also for women who had never married, since the word χήρα can refer to both these groups.[85] Hence, the group of widows blossomed.

But a further factor here was that the opponents' teaching advocated abstaining from marriage (1 Tim 4:3). This and the Pastor's prescription of marriage and childbearing for younger widows (1 Tim 5:14; cf. 1 Tim 2:15) suggest that at least some of the widows were women who eschewed married life in favour of celibacy and that the opponents' teaching may well have been the motivation for this. So, as we have already noted, the widows may have become key practitioners and advocates of the lifestyle promoted by the opposing teachers, some of whom, we have argued, were widows themselves (see 1 Tim 5:13-14).

So it is likely that these widows were particularly open to following the opponents' teaching and the widows' order was in effect becoming a "feeder" organisation for the opponents. In an attempt to counter the influence of the opponents, the Pastor sought to greatly reduce the number of women who could be enrolled in the widows' order. So, as well as saving the church money, curtailing the size of the widows' order and requiring some of the widows to return to a hierarchical household (of their sons, for example), would greatly curtail the freedom of these widows to be involved in teaching and other activities.[86] All of this also suggests that the widows' order was currently a significant group of women among the addressees and that it preserved an alternative vision to that of the Pastor with regard to the role of women in the community.

Fourthly, we have suggested above that some of the members of the widows' order may not have been previously married and so the term χήρα in 1 Tim 5 may refer both to widows as normally understood and to women who lived without any man.[87] Maloney notes "the reference to a 'first pledge' [1

---

[83] Dewey 1998, p448.

[84] Bassler 1984, p36

[85] We will investigate this likelihood below.

[86] See Dewey 1998, p448.

[87] Methuen (1997, p286-7) notes χήρα could mean "a woman who lives without a man".

Tim 5:12] is probably to a vow taken by those entering the widow's order; had the members all been married before, one could say that this would not have been their 'first' pledge, technically speaking, but a second vow".[88] Further, if many of the "young widows" had not been married before, then v9 and v14 become compatible. In v9 the Pastor insists that enrolled widows be married only once, whereas in v14 he instructs "young widows" to marry; if these "young widows" had already been married, this would disqualify them forever from joining the widows' order. However, if many of the "young widows" had in fact never been married, there is no tension between the two verses; v14 would then speak of their first marriage, thus not disqualifying them from later joining the order.[89] Finally, we know that shortly after the Pastorals, the group of "widows" included "virgins (παρθένοι)", who are clearly women who have never married.[90] These arguments are not conclusive, but certainly open the possibility that not all "widows" had been married before entering the order.[91] If this is correct, it suggests that the group was attractive to women who had never married as an alternative society, and as we have noted, the autonomy offered to members was probably a significant reason for its popularity.

Fifthly, what activities were currently undertaken by widows in the community, and what did the Pastor think they should do? The only suggestion about what enrolled widows did is given in 1 Tim 5:5 where it is implied that they are engaged in a ministry of prayer.[92] Apart from this, it seems that the Pastor has no clear expectations of what widows in the much-reduced widows' order should do. He outlines that they have already performed Christian service (v10) but does not say that they should continue to do so in their old age.[93] It seems that, apart from prayer, he has no expectations of them, which is perhaps a necessity since those who remained in the widow' order needed to be at least 60 years, which was considered an

---

[88] Maloney 1994, p372. On the meaning of the "pledge" see Barrett 1963, p76. MacDonald (1999b, p247) suggests it "probably refers to the breaking of a pledge to remain unmarried that was attached to the office [of widow]." We also note that in 1 Tim 5:11-12 the Pastor speaks about "widows" wanting "to marry" not "to remarry" so, as Maloney (1994, p372) notes, "it is at least possible that a first marriage is intended".

[89] See Maloney 1994, p372; Methuen 1997, p290-1. But Maloney (1994, p372) comments "But it remains probable that the author simply wanted to restrict the widows' order by disqualifying as many women as possible."

[90] IgnSm 13.1 speaks of "the virgins called widows".

[91] See Bassler 1984, p35; see also Methuen 1997, p290-1.

[92] In Polycarp, Phil 4.3 it is clear that the office of widow involved prayer for the community.

[93] See Barrett 1963, p74. MacDonald (1999b, p248) notes that the qualifications for enrolment include caring for children, showing hospitality and caring for the sick (1 Tim 5:10) and states "it seems reasonable to conclude that women would continue to provide such services once they were enrolled." But that this is not stated is significant.

advanced age in this period. We can suggest that currently the widows in the order undertook other activities.[94] We note that some widows went "from house to house" (1 Tim 5:13) and that for some this involved teaching. But we do not know if either activity was currently part of their "official duties" as enrolled widows and we do not know what other activities they were involved in.

1.5 Other women

It is interesting that the Pastor makes positive mention of some clearly significant women. In 2 Tim 1:5 Timothy's grandmother, Lois and his mother, Eunice, are commended for their faith.[95] In 2 Tim 4:19 Prisca and Aquila are said to give greetings; we have discussed Prisca in Chapters 2 and 3. We note that Prisca is mentioned first here, which may indicate her greater importance in the Christian community.[96] The otherwise unknown Claudia also gives greetings in 2 Tim 4:21.

Why does the Pastor mention these women, in a letter which is otherwise so opposed to women in significant positions of leadership? Perhaps the Pastor saw Lois and Eunice as models of women who teach children, which is a legitimate activity as far as the Pastor is concerned? But it seems likely that Prisca and Claudia featured significantly in the traditions which the addressees valued. We can confirm this in the case of Prisca, since Acts and 1 Corinthians show that she was active in Ephesus. It seems likely that the readers knew traditions about her, which is why the Pastor mentioned her. She was too significant to overlook; that she is mentioned before Aquila shows her significance.

This evidence suggests that the readers knew traditions about some significant women leaders. This is compatible with (though in itself does not require) our conclusion that there were currently some women leaders among

---

[94] Maloney (1994, p373, p379 n20) notes that "double honour" ($\delta\iota\pi\lambda o\tilde{\upsilon}\varsigma$ $\tau\iota\mu\dot{\eta}$) in 1 Tim 5:17 refers to payment of elders, and that the same word is used in 1 Tim 5:3 of widows. She concludes that widows "must have received a regular stipend from the church, regarded as proper compensation for their ministerial work (cf. 1 Tim 5:3 with 1 Tim 5:17)." See also Sawyer 1996, p109. However, while "double honour" seems to refer to both "honour" as in "give respect to" and "payment" it is not clear that $\tau\iota\mu\dot{\alpha}\omega$ with respect to widows ("single honour" as it were) also refers to payment.

[95] As Dewey (1998, p450) notes, "Whether or not the women's names are historically accurate, they do attest to the important role women played in the spread of Christianity." That Timothy's male forebears are not mentioned may imply that they were not Christians, a point perhaps supported by Acts 16:1 which says that Timothy's Jewish mother was a Christian, but makes no comment about his Greek father.

[96] See Dewey 1998, p450-1.

the addressees, for whom Prisca and Claudia were perhaps revered role models.

1.6 Conclusions

We can suggest that women had been active as teachers and leaders in the community addressed by the Pastorals, although from the Pastor's point of view some women were currently teaching what he regarded as "false doctrine". Some of these women teachers seem to have been active in going from "house to house", probably house church to house church.

Some of their behaviour can be seen as living out a more egalitarian vision of "the faith", but for the Pastor this behaviour involved a disruption of prescribed social and household norms which led to negative comment from outsiders. It is clear that the teaching activity and behaviour of women is one of the main concerns of the Pastor.

We have also noted that women were active as deacons and that there was an order of "widows", which may have included women who had never been married and which was currently a significant group among the addressees. This group preserved an alternative vision to that of the Pastor with regard to women's roles in the community.

2. The Johannine Letters

We turn now to seek to determine the situation of women among the addressees of the Johannine letters, although again this will first of all involve us in discussing what the author of the Johannine letters does, and does not say, about the situation of women.[97] This focuses on two passages. Firstly, are women mentioned in 1 Jn 2:12-14, and secondly, who is the "elect lady" of 2 Jn 1? This will lead us to ask why there is so little mention of women in these letters.

2.1 1 Jn 2:12-14

In 1 Jn 2:12-14 the author addresses the readers in this way:

"I am writing to you, little children (τεκνία), because your sins are forgiven on account of his name.

---

[97] Recall that in Chap 6, section 1 we have argued that, since the Gospel is an "open" text written to all Christians, we cannot conclude from the fact that women feature prominently in the narratives of the Fourth Gospel that women featured prominently in the community to which John the Elder belonged.

I am writing to you, πατέρες, because you know him who is from the beginning.
I am writing to you, νεανίσκοι, because you have conquered the evil one.
I write to you, children (παιδια), because you know the Father.
I write to you, πατέρες, because you know him who is from the beginning.
I write to you, νεανίσκοι, because you are strong, and the word of God abides in you, and you have overcome the evil one."

Following the condemnation of those who do not keep the commandments (2:4) and the threat against all who do not love their brother or sister (2:11), the author reassures his readers in 1 Jn 2:12-14 that they are forgiven, do know God and that they do have fellowship with God. The passage is divided in two; the first three clauses begin with γράφω and the last three with ἔγραψα.[98] But how many groups are addressed? And does the passage include or exclude women?

Firstly, it seems clear that the term τεκνία, "little children" includes the whole community addressed, since this term is used by the author elsewhere in 1 Jn to refer to all those to whom he writes (2:1, 28; 3:7, 18; 4:4; 5:21). Similarly παιδια "children" probably includes all the addressees, because this is the sense in which it is used in its only other occurrence in the letters, 1 Jn 2:18.[99] As Brown comments: "it is almost impossible that suddenly here, and here alone, *teknia* and *paidia* could refer only to one group constituting one-third of the audience."[100] This means that τεκνία and παιδια are alternative ways of addressing the whole group.[101]

But what does the author mean by πατέρες and νεανίσκοι?[102] These two terms, along with τεκνία and παιδια, could refer to all Christians.[103] Thus

---

[98] For discussions of the change from present to aorist see Brown 1982, p294-7; Watson 1989a, p104-5; Schnackenburg 1992, p118.

[99] Παιδια is also found in as a variant in 1 Jn 3:7. It could be that τεκνία and παιδια refer to new converts, with "fathers" being a reference to the mature and "neoteroi" to those making progress. However, then the order would be strange, since it would be neither from young to old, nor old to young, and so this, and the fact that the author uses both τεκνία and παιδια as terms of address elsewhere in the letter, counts against this view.

[100] Brown 1982, p298.

[101] This is in keeping with the use of the two terms in the Gospel of John, where they designate disciples.

[102] Some commentators suggest that 1 Jn 2:12-14, with its mention of "fathers", "young men" and "children", reflects the literary form of the *Haustafeln* or "household codes" directed to various members of Christian households found in Eph 5:22-6:9 and Col 3:18-4:1 and elsewhere. Thus Perkins (1979, p29) suggests "It seems that the various designations [fathers etc] derive from the literary form the author is using, while the content of the victory described could be applied to any member of the community." However, Brown (1982, p319) notes: "Yet, while not unrelated to that genre, the I John clauses are not primarily moral admonitions and the grouping is not clearly domestic." Further, given that both τεκνία and παιδια refer to the whole community, and not to literal children, it seems unlikely that the

Dodd suggests the threefold listing "is probably not much more than a rhetorical figure."[104] Like the stylistic alternation between γράφω and ἔγραψα, this too would then be a stylistic distinction. However, the order argues against all the terms (τεκνία, παιδία, πατέρες and νεανίσκοι) referring to one group, since it is neither ascending, nor descending with regard to age. Further, as Watson notes "neither πατέρες nor νεανίσκοι is used inclusively of an entire audience in the NT".[105]

It seems much more likely then that πατέρες and νεανίσκοι refer to two distinct subdivisions within the community. This makes best sense of the order of the terms of address. In each group of three, the whole community is addressed first as the author's children, and then two other groups are addressed, presumably in order of seniority. Further, the division of people into young (neaniskoi) and old (presbuteroi, presbutai) based on spiritual maturity, dignity and/or age is found in the OT, intertestamental literature and the NT.[106]

But if πατέρες and νεανίσκοι refer to distinct subgroups among the readers, we have three possible options with regard to the relationship between the subgroups and the whole group. We will also see that these options have different implications with regard to women within the community.

Firstly, the two groups of πατέρες and νεανίσκοι could together constitute *the whole community*, with no "remainder" as it were (since everyone can be regarded as either young or old), so they would refer to the whole community divided into two. If this was the case, then πατέρες and νεανίσκοι are being used generically and women are addressed in 1 Jn 2:12-14. I will call this *Option A*.

Secondly, the two groups of πατέρες and νεανίσκοι could be two prominent groups in the community, alongside other groups which are not mentioned. So the two groups of πατέρες and νεανίσκοι *along with other*

---

passage belongs to the literary form of the household code and so the meaning of the terms cannot be derived from their meaning in this literary form.

[103] See Brown 1982, p298 for those who have held this view.

[104] Dodd 1946, p38.

[105] Watson 1989a, p99.

[106] Gen 19:4; Ex 10:9; Josh 6:21; Isa 20:4; Ezek 9:6 LXX; 1QpHab 12:4-5; 1QS 6:13-24; CD 13:11-13; 1QSa 1:6-19; Acts 2:17; 1 Tim 5:1-2; Tit 2:1-8; 1 Pet 5:1-5; see also Brown 1982, p299-300. He argues (1982, p318) that "length of time as Christians underlies the distinction" between πατέρες and νεανίσκοι. Brown (1982, p300) notes that we might have expected the terms presbyteroi and neoteroi in 1 Jn. However he notes that Acts 5:6,10 shows that neaniskoi and neoteroi were interchangeable "and Johannine usage may have preferred to keep *presbyteroi* as a designation for members of the Johannine School who were disciples of the Beloved Disciple" (Brown 1982, p300). Further in passages like Judg 17:10; 18:19; 2 Kgs 2:12; 13:14 the term "father" is used as a reverential designation.

groups constitute the whole community of addressees. But within this there are two options with regard to women in the community. *Option B* involves the generic usage of the terms πατέρες and νεανίσκοι, so that whatever these terms mean (and we will see this would be difficult to determine), they include women.[107]

Option C would also see there as being other groups within the community apart from πατέρες and νεανίσκοι. With this option πατέρες and νεανίσκοι would be understood here as non-generic terms which referred solely to males. Accordingly, all the women in the community would be part of the "other groups", groups which are not mentioned in 1 Jn 2:12-14, and so would be excluded at this point. If this was the case, then it would suggest that the author conceived of his readers as being composed of male πατέρες and νεανίσκοι, with women not considered an important part of the audience.[108]

Which of these three options is most likely? We should note first of all that what is said of each of the three groups in 1 Jn 2:12-14 is fairly general and in each case represents important facets of the gospel from the author's perspective.[109] In terms of meaning, each phrase ("they know him who is from the beginning" etc) could arguably be applied to a specific group, or it could be applied to all Christians. Thus what is said about each group does not help us decide who πατέρες and νεανίσκοι refer too.[110]

With options A and B outlined above, the masculine plural nouns πατέρες and νεανίσκοι would be taken to be generic, and thus to include both genders.[111] In the NT, a masculine plural noun is often inclusive of both genders, so this reading is a possibility.[112] A number of scholars state or imply that πατέρες and νεανίσκοι include both men and women in our verses and

---

[107] Brown favours this view. He clearly thinks the terms are generic (Brown 1980, p300, p321 n15) but also argues: "If 'Fathers' and 'Young People' are two groups within the Community (even though logic requires that they must be fairly comprehensive, to the point of constituting a merism), they are not necessarily the only divisions." (Brown 1982, p319)

[108] Watson 1989a, p108 n17 notes that this could be implied, but opts for reading the masculine plurals as generic.

[109] See Brown 1982, p320-2.

[110] It is often noted that what is actually said about πατέρες and νεανίσκοι in v12-14 is consonant with them being older and younger Christians, for example. Thus, it would be appropriate to write of "fathers" that they "know him who is from the beginning" (v13, 14); they know the Father, because, as those who have been Christians for some time, they "are firmly anchored in fellowship with Christ" (see Schnackenburg 1992, p118). However, as we note in the text, each phrase could also be applied to all Johannine Christians.

[111] This is how Watson reads these masculine plurals; see Watson 1989a, p108 n17; see also Brown 1982, p300, p321 n15: ("While *neaniskoi* is masculine in form, probably it included young women as well.")

[112] See Turner 1963, p22: "Sometimes a pl. masc. noun covers masc. and fem. subjects: Lk 2:41 οἱ γονεῖς. Το 10:12 B τοὺς πενθερούς. So οἱ ἀδελφοί, οἱ παῖδες. Thus οἱ κύριοι (Lk 19:33 Ac 16:16. 19) may cover a man and woman owner."

so argue for either Option A or B.[113] But is it likely that these two nouns are generic here? If this was the case, even if we could not decide between Option A and B, it would exclude Option C, and would mean that women are addressed in 1 Jn 2:12-14.

2.1.1 For a generic usage and so for Option A or B

Firstly, we note that νεανίσκοι is only used in 1 Jn in these verses and the other occurrences of πατήρ in the Johannine letters are with reference to God. Hence this does not help us to decide if the usage in 2:12-14 is generic or not. But are there other arguments in favour of a generic usage of the two terms, and so for either Option A or B?

Does other Biblical usage help here? As we have noted, in some places in the LXX, the constituents of the *whole* people of Israel are described as old and young, using the terms πρεσβύτεροι or πρεσβυταί with νεανίσκοι (see Ex 10:9; Josh 6:21; Isa 20:4). In these cases, everyone is reckoned to be either "old" or "young", and the masculine plurals are clearly generic and include women. However, these two terms can also be used in Gen 19:4 and Ezek 9:6 to refer to men only.[114]

Similarly, the NT usage of πατέρες and νεανίσκοι and related terms does not support a generic usage in 1 Jn 2:12-14. πατήρ is normally used of males in the NT, although in Heb 11:23 we read that "By faith Moses was hidden by his parents (τῶν πατέρων αὐτοῦ) for three months after his birth", which is clearly a reference to both his mother and father. Further, a generic meaning of "ancestors (both male and female)" for πατήρ is possible (but not required) on some other occasions.[115] Apart from 1 Jn 2:13-14, νεανίσκος is always clearly used with reference to a male.[116] We also note that in Acts 2:17-18, quoting from Joel 3:1-5 in the LXX, we read: "I will pour out my Spirit upon all flesh and your sons and your daughters shall prophecy, and your young men (οἱ νεανίσκοι) shall see visions and your old men (οἱ πρεσβύτεροι) shall dream dreams. Even upon my slaves, both men and women, in those days I will pour out my Spirit." That women are mentioned separately (as "daughters" and "female servants") shows that the masculine

---

[113] Although note that they do not always clarify for which option they are arguing. For example, Schnackenburg (1992, p116) understands them to refer to "fathers and young people". He thus implies that women are included among the "young people"; he does not comment on whether he thinks women are included among the "fathers" or not, but this seems to be his implication when he writes that the author "tries to strengthen both young and old in the conflict over religion and morals."

[114] In Gen 19:4 this is indicated by the phrase "οἱ ἄνδρες τῆς πόλεως". See a similar usage in Ez 9:6.

[115] For example, perhaps in Lk 6:26; Jn 6:31;1 Cor 10:1; Heb 1:1; 8:9.

[116] See Mt 19:20, 22; Mk 14:51; Lk 7:14; Acts 5:10; 23:18, 22.

plurals νεανίσκοι and πρεσβύτεροι refer to males only and so are not generic here.[117]

What this shows is that we cannot assume that in using the terms πατέρες and νεανίσκοι John definitely meant "men and women" in both cases. The usage of these terms in the NT in fact makes it much more likely that in 1 Jn they are being used to refer to men only. So while πατέρες and νεανίσκοι can be generic masculine plurals, their usage in the NT is generally not generic, and this is clearly the most likely meaning here.[118]

So arguments for a generic usage and so for Options A and B are inconclusive at best.

2.1.2 Option A – the argument from a rhetorical standpoint

Are there other reasons for arguing for these being generic plurals? As well as arguing that πατέρες and νεανίσκοι are generic, Watson in effect argues for my Option A. He has analysed this passage from a rhetorical standpoint. He suggests that the two groups of three in 1 Jn 2:12-14 "can be explained as an example of the figure of thought called *distributio* … It derives its name from the fact that 'after mentioning a thing as a whole, the parts are afterwards enumerated'".[119] He suggests that the author "has begun the two sections with the inclusive grouping of children and then distributed it into the two constituent groups",[120] of πατέρες and νεανίσκοι, both of which he takes to be inclusive terms.[121] But although Watson gives two examples from the

---

[117] The use of other terms is similar. In 1 Peter 5:1-5 πρεσβύτεροι and νεώτεροι are used, but may only refer to men. In 1 Tim 5:1-2 we have "older man", "younger men", "older women" and "younger women", showing that πρεσβύτερος and νεώτερος refer to males alone and again are not generic plurals. Similarly, in Tit 2:1-6 we have instructions to "older men" (v2), "older women" (v3), reference to "younger women" (v4) and instructions to "younger men" (v6). This usage of related terms suggests that 1 Jn 2:13-14 *could* be a reference only to men.

[118] We note also by way of parallel that the author of John's Gospel is probably able to use masculine terms exclusively. In Jn 20:17 the risen Jesus says to Mary: "Do not hold me, for I have not yet ascended to the Father; but go to my ἀδελφούς and say to them, I am ascending to my Father and your Father, to my God and your God." (RSV) How are we to understand ἀδελφοί? Lieu (1996, p236 n2) suggests that here ἀδελφοί is used exclusively, because the reference seems to be to the twelve. As Lieu notes "John rarely speaks of 'the twelve' (6.67-71), but an experienced reader would have known that this was an exclusively male group; in turn, this suggests that 'brothers' (20.17) is exclusive."

[119] Watson 1989a, p99. The quotation is from Bullinger 1898, p435.

[120] Watson 1989a, p101 and p108 n17.

[121] Watson (1989a, p101) himself clearly thinks all the community is listed as "πατέρες" and "νεανίσκοι". He writes that the author "has used *distributio* in the form in which the inclusive group is listed first and is then distributed into constituents subgroups", (fathers and young men) and then supports this with the view that the masculine plurals are generic.

Rhetorica ad Herennium in which all the elements which make up a whole are enumerated in the *distributio*,[122] the examples of the *distributio* which he discerns in the Bible (Ex 10:9; Josh 6:21; Isa 20:4; Acts 2:16-21) do not consistently divide the whole group up into *all* the elements in the subcategories which are specified, but rather tend to divide the whole up several times in different ways in successive pairs.[123] But most importantly, the possibility (and it can be no more than this) that the passage might use the rhetorical figure of *distributio*,[124] and so divide the whole group up into two (generic) subcategories, cannot dictate the *actual* usage of πατέρες and νεανίσκοι in 1 Jn 2. Rather usage in 1 Jn is clearly crucial and we have noted so far a lack of any definitive indication that the two terms are generic.

2.1.3 *Against Option C and so for a generic usage (either Options A or B)*

Brown and Watson suggest that the masculine plural nouns πατέρες and νεανίσκοι must be taken as generic because of what they regard as the significant part played by women in John's Gospel and thus in the "Johannine community".[125] This is in effect to argue against my Option C and hence to argue for Options A or B. What do we make of this argument?

Even if we were to accept the reconstruction of the "Johannine community" and the reconstruction of the role of women in that community

---

[122] For example, the Senate, magistracy and voting populace, who together constitute all the elements of those who participate in government; see Watson 1989a, p100. But note that his other example from the *Rhetorica ad Herennium* is much less clear. It consists of the whole group, called the jury, with four subgroups then being mentioned: "(1) those who love the Senate; (2) those who favour the equestrian order; (3) those with parents; (4) those who are parents" (Watson 1989a, p100). Clearly, the first two categories are distinct, but the last two categories overlap with each other and the first two. Some people could be in three of the four categories.

[123] See Watson 1989a, p109 n18. He notes that in Ex 10:9 the "we" is inclusive and is specified in subcategories of young and old, sons and daughters, flocks and herds; in Jos 6:21 "all the city" is divided into subcategories of men-women, young-old, oxen-sheep-asses; in Isa 20:4 the inclusive category is Egyptians-Ethiopians and the subcategories are young-old, naked-barefoot; in Acts 2:17-21 'all flesh' is inclusive, and the subcategories are sons-daughters, young men-old men, menservants-maidservants.

[124] Edwards 1996, p38; see also Stamps 1997, p626.

[125] Brown (1980, p300) commenting on Houlden's view (see below) writes: "I disagree with his further surmise that since 1 John has no comparable feminine forms of address, the Johannine Community accorded women no prominence, unlike the Pauline churches where they played an important part! The grammatical argument is weak because frequently in NT Greek a plural masculine noun covers subjects of both genders (MGNTG 3, 22); and from an analysis of John I would conclude that women had a role of extraordinary importance in the Johannine tradition, outranking their role in the Pauline tradition." Watson 1989a, p108-9 n17 refers to Brown's discussion of the role of women in the "Johannine Community" in Brown 1979a, p183-98.

from the Gospel of John (which following Bauckham we do not), we cannot argue that women *must still* be prominent in the community to which 1 John was addressed just because they are thought to be prominent in John's Gospel. Clearly (on the hypothesis of a "Johannine community" to which John was written) time has elapsed between the Gospel and 1 John being written, most notably time to allow for the development of the secessionists, and then for their departure (1 Jn 2:19-23). Further, these events have meant considerable recent change for the readers of 1 John and there have also probably been new theological developments, at least by the author (for example, a greater stress on the atoning significance of Jesus' death).[126] This all raises the possibility that there could have been a significant change in the role and involvement of women in the community addressed by 1 John in the recent past and certainly since the Gospel was written.[127] It is also possible that the leading women in the community all joined the secessionists.[128]

This would mean that Option C, a corollary of which is that women were not regarded as an important part of the community, is quite possible. In any case, clearly we cannot argue, on the basis of the supposed prominence of women in John's Gospel and hence in the "Johannine community", that πατέρες and νεανίσκοι in 1 John 2:12-14 *must* be generic plurals which include women. Clearly, this attempt to argue against Option C is unconvincing.

2.1.4 For Option C

The invisibility of women elsewhere in the Johannine Letters argues in favour of Option C. But since these are short letters, and this is an argument from silence, it remains a weak argument.

---

[126] See Chapter 6, section 3.1, and see for example 1 Jn 1:7; 2:2.

[127] Note that one could argue that, because Revelation has some connection with John's Gospel, then women "should" have a valued and prominent role in the theology of the author of Revelation. Even if we cannot say that Jezebel (Rev 2:20) is condemned by John solely because she is a woman, we note that she is the only woman mentioned in Rev and that she is opposed by John. Clearly, just because a document is connected with Jn's Gospel in some way does not mean that it must share that Gospel's attitude to women. (This argument is weakened a little by the fact that the connection between Jn and 1 Jn is stronger than the connection between Jn and Rev.) Clearly, the argument that, because I Jn is connected to Jn, then women cannot be excluded from 1 Jn 2:12-14, is a weak argument.

[128] This possibility is raised by the fact that the secessionists are somewhat docetic, and that women were probably prominent in some early Gnostic communities, which had docetic elements. For a discussion of women in Gnostic communities see McGuire 1999, p257-99.

2.1.5 Who would πατέρες and νεανίσκοι refer to in Option C?

With Option C, πατέρες and νεανίσκοι refer to two male groups alongside other groups (including women) in the community. Who would the terms refer to? Clearly the cogency of possible explanation in this regard might help to evaluate this option.

There are various possibilities for the meaning of these two terms if they refer to two groups alongside others. Houlden, who argues for my Option C, suggests that πατέρες and νεανίσκοι refer to "the leading groups within the community".[129] He thinks that "In view of the signs of concern with the discipline and organization of the community shown in the Johannine Epistles, it is likely that the terms possess some degree of formality."[130] He suggests that the two terms designate church officials, and are the equivalents of the terms "presbyters" and "deacons" used elsewhere. Clearly, there would be other groups in the community: men who were not leaders, and all other women, with perhaps each of these group being subdivided in other ways. But Houlden's view of the meaning of πατέρες and νεανίσκοι seems unlikely. Given that leaders are not addressed anywhere else in 1 Jn, it seems unlikely that they are referred to here.[131] It is possible, however, that the usage is less formal than Houlden thinks, and that perhaps the two terms refer not to leaders, but to small (interest?) groups within the male sector of the community.[132]

But, given that no other explanation is cogent, it seems more likely that, if the two terms are non-generic and so the author is only addressing men, that he is addressing all the men as πατέρες and νεανίσκοι, with the groups being divided on the lines of spiritual maturity or age. Women would then be in "other groups".

2.1.6 Who would πατέρες and νεανίσκοι refer to in Option B?

With Option B, in which both πατέρες and νεανίσκοι include men and women but there are other groups too, so that the πατέρες and νεανίσκοι do not make up the whole of the community, there are various options for the meaning of these two terms. They could both be terms of leadership, but we have seen that this is quite unlikely, given that leaders are not addressed anywhere else. Perhaps they could be terms for the quite old and the rather young, with middle aged as the "other groups", but this seems forced. In fact,

---

[129] Houlden 1973, p70.

[130] Houlden 1973, p70-1.

[131] Schnackenburg (1992), p119 n191 thinks that Houlden's interpretation is "improbable". Brown (1982, p300) regards it as "a pure guess".

[132] BDAG, p667 notes that νεανίσκοι can be equated with νεός, a term used in the gymnasium.

under scrutiny, Option B seems unlikely – given that it is unlikely that he would single out leaders, then if the terms are generic, who is "left out" of the groups of πατέρες and νεανίσκοι?[133] This suggests that if one argues for a generic usage of the two terms (which we have seen is unlikely), then Option A seems more likely than Option B.

The lack of viable options for the meaning of πατέρες and νεανίσκοι with Option B, and that a generic meaning of the two terms is unlikely in any case (Options A and B) suggests that Option C is the most likely. In this case, πατέρες and νεανίσκοι would together include "all men", the older men as πατέρες and the younger men as νεανίσκοι, with all the women in "other groups".

2.1.7 Implications

We conclude then that we cannot say that women are included in the πατέρες and νεανίσκοι of 1 Jn 2:12-14. We can note that the author did not explicitly include women, as occurs, for example, in Acts 2:17-18, 1 Tim 5:1-2 and Tit 2:1-6. Although we cannot say that women are definitely excluded in 1 Jn 2:12-14, this seems the most likely explanation.

A number of scholars have supported my Option C, taking πατέρες and νεανίσκοι as non-generic. Thus, for example, Hutaff writes that the author "addresses 'fathers' and 'young men' (but no female counterparts)".[134] But if Option C is correct and πατέρες and νεανίσκοι refer only to men, then why does the author *not* include women? Osiek's comment with regard to an exclusively masculine address in Acts is also relevant here. She comments: "When the Paul of Acts addresses crowds as Ἄνδρες ἀδελφοί (men, brothers), he is not using what we would call gender-exclusive language as generic language that is meant to include women as well. On the contrary, women, though often present in public places in the biblical world, were socially invisible in public language that was addressed only to men as those with public power."[135]

---

[133] Thus Brown's uncertainty (1982, p300) about the meaning of "Father" is understandable. He thinks the two terms are generic, but is uncertain as to whom they refer: "It is impossible to determine the exact connotation that the title 'Father' had for the Johannine Community. Clearly it refers to more than heads of families (the meaning in the *Haustafel* or list of household offices in Eph 6:4)."

[134] Hutaff 1994, p411; see also Perkins 1979, px-xi; Strecker 1996, p56. Lieu (1991, p42) also seems to take the terms as exclusive when she writes: "The word of God abides in the young men (2:14)". Rensberger (1997, p71) notes it is possible that the author intended to include women but goes on: "it may also be that women in the community are already losing the prominence that is apparent in the Gospel of John".

[135] Osiek 1994, p60.

This seems to be what is happening here in 1 John – that the women are much less visible in this letter. Although women may well be included in terms like τεκνία, παιδία, ἀγαπητοί and ἀδελφός,[136] at this point in 1 Jn 2:12-14 they are excluded. We also note in this regard that 2 and 3 Jn refer exclusively to men – the elder, Gaius, Diotrephes, Demetrius, although the fact that these are short occasional letters needs to be kept in mind.[137] But Houlden's conclusion seems to follow: "Unlike the Pauline congregations, where women played an important part, this Johannine church accords them no prominence."[138]

But we need to note that we are seeing here the views of the author with regard to the probable lack of prominence accorded women. It is possible that the views of the addressees were quite different, and that women had a more significant place in the life of the community. But this emerges nowhere in the letters.

2.2 The "Elect Lady" of 2 Jn 1 and the "elect sister" of 2 Jn 13

2 Jn 1 is addressed "to an elect lady and her children (ἐκλεκτῇ κυρίᾳ καὶ τοῖς τέκνοις αὐτῆς)". There are a number of possible ways of reading this. Firstly, Klauck has suggested that κυρίᾳ here means "regular" or "general", in keeping with the meaning of κυρίᾳ as an adjective in Greco-Roman literature, where it has this meaning; the reference would then be to the "regular assembly" or "general meeting".[139] However, in arguing for this, Klauck draws exclusively on Greco-Roman texts which speak of the regular assembly of a city. Arguably, Jewish texts in which a collective is personified as a women,[140] provide the more proximate and therefore more likely background. Secondly, the letter could be addressed "to lady Eklecta", but this is unlikely since "ἐκλεκτός" is used in v13 as a modifier, not a name. Thirdly, it could be "to [the] elect Kyria". But if this was the meaning, we would expect the name to be given first, and we would also expect the article before ἐκλεκτός, as it is

---

[136] Note that there is no clear way of proving that these terms are inclusive, although it seems likely that they are in passages like 1 Jn 2:1 (Note for example that Phil 4:1-2 shows that Paul uses ἀδελφός inclusively.) For discussion of whether these terms are inclusive see for example Perkins 1979, px-xi; Hutaff 1994, p411. Hutaff (1994, p414) takes ἀδελφός in 2:9; 3:15; 4:20 to mean "one's fellow Christian" and so to include "sisters" and (on p411) suggests "beloved" is gender-inclusive.

[137] We will discuss the references to "the elect lady and her children" (2 Jn 1; cf v5) and "your elect sister" (2 Jn 13) below.

[138] Houlden 1973, p70.

[139] Klauck 1990, p135-8.

[140] For example virgin Israel (Jer 31:21); daughter Zion (Jer 4:31); or as a mother with children (Bar 4:32; 5:5; 4 Ezra 10:40-9).

in Rom 16:13.[141] Fourthly, the "elect lady" could be a term for a particular leader of a house church, a woman who would be similar to Chloe (1 Cor 1:11), Nympha (Col 4:15) or Prisca (Rom 16:3). The members of the house church would then be referred to as "her children".[142] However, in v13 we read: "The children of your elect sister send you their greetings." Here then, the image of a woman with children is used in a parallel way to v1. Hutaff notes: "If the 'lady' addressed [in v1] is an actual woman, then the 'sister' [v13] would likewise be a woman, by implication the letter's author. 'Elect sister' must not refer to the author, however, since he has already been identified by the masculine form of the term 'elder.' [v1]."[143]

The fifth option is more likely then: that "the terms 'elect lady' and 'elect sister' are communal metaphors for 'sister' churches, whose members, including the author, are seen as 'children,' probably following the Johannine convention of speaking of Christians as 'children of God.'"[144] In support of this view we also note that in the letter the author changes from "you" singular in v4-5 to "you" plural in v6-12 and back to singular in v13. This usage shows that he is addressing a whole community rather than a single person in charge of a community. Further, using the metaphor of an elect or chosen woman for a church is found in 1 Pet 5:13 of the church of Rome, and in the Shepherd of Hermas (Vis 2.4.1) the whole church is spoken of as a woman and is addressed as "lady" (Vis 3.1.3).[145]

We conclude then that 2 Jn is written to a church, which, as we have noted before, seems to be some distance from the author and his community.[146] The author uses feminine imagery for his own church ("your elect sister", v13) and for the community to which he writes ("elect lady", v1,5), with "Κυρία" and "ἀδελφή" thus being metaphors for the church. We also note that members of the community are referred to as "children" of the lady/sister church (v1, 4, 13). This continues the "family" imagery of 1 Jn, which uses the language of brother/sister and of "children of God".[147]

---

[141] See Hutaff 1994, p423; see also Schnackenburg 1992, p278. For the name given first in the epistolary openings see 1 Tim 1:2; 2 Tim 1:2; Titus 1:4, Philm 1-2, 3 Jn 1.

[142] See Schüssler Fiorenza 1994, p248.

[143] Hutaff 1994, p423.

[144] Hutaff 1994, p423.

[145] "Elect" or "chosen" is used as a self-designation of Christians in Rom 8:33; Col 3:12; 2 Tim 2:10; Tit 1:1; 1 Pet 1:1; Rev 17:13; Vis 1.3.4. Lieu (1996, p236) suggests that the personification of the church as an "elect lady" "may draw its imagery from the Song [of Songs]; for this woman too is 'elect' (Song 6.9)- and her love song was (to become) the song of Israel with her God." Note also the links between Song of Songs 5:6 and Jn 20:14; Song 5.5 and Jn 12:1-10; Song 5:3 and Jn 13:4-5. The echo of the Song of Songs in 2 Jn is also suggested by Hengel 1989, p170 n61; he has developed this argument in Hengel 2000b, p249-53.

[146] See Brown 1982, p651-5; Lieu 1986, p64-7; cf. Kraemer 1992, p176-7.

[147] O'Day 1998, p467.

How do we evaluate the significance of this use of feminine language for the church? O'Day comments on the use of kuria: "This language links 2 John with other New Testament writings that use feminine images for the church (e.g., Rev. 12:1-2; Eph 5:22-31). These images may show the value the early church placed on female experience, or they may indicate the beginning of patriarchal structures of governance in which the elder becomes 'lord' over lady church."[148] Certainly, 2 Jn gives no evidence with regard to the actual position of women among the addressees.

2.3 Conclusions

We note then the probable absence of any explicit mention of women in these letters.[149] Although seeing πατέρες and νεανίσκοι as referring exclusively to men is not certain, it is the most likely reading of 1 Jn 2:12-14. This is the author's perception, and it may not necessarily be the perception of the community. But, even as the view of the author, it is an interesting insight into one (male) "voice" in Ephesus. Further, it provides a considerable contrast to the Pastorals where, although the Pastor is seeking to severely curtail the activities of women, they are currently actively involved in leadership. It is very unlikely that this is the case in the community addressed in the Johannine Letters.

3. Women in Revelation

We recall here first of all our "hypothesis": that the Pastorals and the Johannine Letters are to different communities in Ephesus, but that John in Revelation is seeking to address a range of Christians in Ephesus, including the readers of the Pastorals and the Johannine Letters. We will seek to test this hypothesis by determining the situation of women among the readers of Revelation. Since we have found active women leaders in the Pastorals (whom the author seeks to restrict severely) and no women leaders in the Johannine Letters, it seems likely a variety of portrayals of the activity of women in Ephesus would be compatible with our hypothesis. If for example, John's Apocalypse showed that there were many active women leaders in Ephesus then this could still be compatible with our hypothesis, since we could suggest that the Pastor had not been successful in restricting women's

---

[148] O'Day 1998, p467.

[149] Hutaff 1994, p411 notes "the absence of any mention of women or issues related to women".

activity, or that women remained active among the Pastor's opponents.[150] If on the other hand, John's Apocalypse suggested that there were no active women leaders in Ephesus, then this could suggest that the Pastor had been reasonably successful in restricting women's activity, and that we are also correct to see women as uninvolved in leadership and marginalised within the Johannine community. However, if there are active women in leadership and John approves of this, it could suggest that he is writing to an entirely different community from the Pastorals or Johannine Letters, and to a community in which women continued to be active, well after the Pastorals were written. Thus, both John's attitude to women and the position of women among the addressees are important.

Accordingly, our purpose here is to discuss John's views with regard to women and to determine the situation of women among the addressees of Rev in Ephesus. Firstly, we will discuss Rev 2:1-7 to determine if this contributes anything to our topic. Secondly, we will note that actual historical women are invisible in Revelation, with two exceptions which we will discuss, Rev 2:20-24, and Rev 14:1-5. Thirdly, Revelation draws on feminine imagery in three passages, and these will be discussed briefly. Finally, we will try to determine if these other passages shed any light on the situation of women among the Ephesian readers addressed in Rev 2:1-7.

3.1 Women in Ephesus (Rev 2:1-7)

The letter to the congregation in Ephesus in Rev 2:1-7 contains no explicit reference to women. There are two possibilities however. Firstly, John notes that the readers have "tested those who claim to be apostles but are not, and have found them to be false" (2:2). Given that we know that Junia was an apostle (Rom 16:7) and that there may have been other apostles who were women, it is possible that some of those judged to be "false apostles" were women, but we have no evidence for this conjecture.

Secondly, the Ephesian addressees are said to "hate" the Nicolaitans (Rev 2:6), and we have shown in Chapter 7 that one of the two key Nicolaitan leaders was given the nickname "Jezebel" (Rev 2:20). Was the fact that one of their leaders was a woman a factor in the Ephesians "hating" the Nicolaitans? Again, we can simply pose the question, and will return to it in due course.

3.2 John's attitude towards women

It is important at this point to determine something about John's attitudes towards women since this will help us to determine if one factor in John's condemnation of Jezebel was that she was a woman. We are interested in the

---

[150] We would be assuming that Revelation was dated around 95 and that the Pastor wrote towards the beginning of our suggested range of dates for these letters of 80-100 CE.

possibility that there may have been comparable women in Ephesus. If John is opposed to women in ministry, then there may have been more active women leaders in the seven churches than he suggests. Accordingly, we will now briefly portray John's attitude to women and then see what we can conclude from this about actual women in Ephesus.

3.2.1 Jezebel the "false prophet"

In Rev 2:20 to the church in Thyatira we read: "But I have this against you: you tolerate that woman Jezebel, who calls herself a prophet and is teaching and beguiling my servants to practice fornication and to eat food sacrificed to idols." We have already discussed the Nicolaitans in detail. Here we need only focus on how the passage relates to our current investigation.

John's account is highly polemical against Jezebel; to him, she is a false prophet and an idolater.[151] But as Yarbro Collins comments, "A truly critical reading of this text must ask whether ... androcentric bias is playing a role."[152] We recall that the nickname "Jezebel" evokes the OT stories about a powerful woman who challenged the forces of Yahweh (1 Kgs 18:21-46). But unlike ancient Jezebel, who is the wife of a king, the Jezebel of Thyatira stands alone.[153] Jezebel calls herself a prophet (2:20) and she was probably recognized as a prophet by some Christians in the area (eg. her "children" (2:23)). We have also noted that John and Jezebel seem to be rival prophets, and the passage reflects a struggle between rival prophetic schools.[154] Jezebel is a teacher since she has "children" who are her disciples (v23), she is said to be "teaching and beguiling my servants ..." (v20)) and to be teaching "the deep things of Satan" (v24). She was also clearly an important and influential woman leader in the church of Thyatira. As Yarbro Collins notes, "If she had not been well received in at least Thyatira, John would not have been so concerned about her influence."[155] Jezebel also probably had an impact on communities beyond Thyatira, since in Rev 2:23, after speaking of judgement on Jezebel, John writes "And all the churches will know ...". That John

---

[151] Recall that her "immorality" (πορνεία Rev 2:21) is probably a reference to her worship of other gods; cf. Selvidge 1996, p278.

[152] Yarbro Collins 1987, p81.

[153] See Selvidge 1996, p277.

[154] See Yarbro Collins 1987, p81; Garrett 1998, p470. We know of other early Christian women with the gift of prophecy (see 1 Cor 11:2-16; and the 4 daughters of Philip mentioned in Acts 21:8-9). Yarbro Collins (1987, p84) suggests it is unlikely that Jezebel was the only woman to prophesy in the region in this period. Maloney (1994, p362) thinks Thyatira is a community "in which women play a central and authoritative role (see Rev 2:20)" and that John is "confronted with women in authority". But to speak about women in the plural is to go beyond the evidence.

[155] Yarbro Collins 1987, p83.

envisages her judgement having an impact beyond Thyatira, suggests her influence is likewise beyond Thyatira. In Rev 2:21 John suggests that there has been a history of conflict between himself and Jezebel when he writes "I gave her time to repent (καὶ ἔδωκα αὐτῇ χρόνον ἵνα μετανοήσῃ), but she refuses".[156]

John clearly condemns Jezebel, not only in what he says, but also by calling her "Jezebel" and thus identifying her with the woman who opposed Elijah and supported the prophets of Baal (1 Kgs 16:31; 19:1-3). He clearly condemns Jezebel because of her teaching, in the same way as he condemns the man "Balaam" because of his teaching.[157] But is the fact that she is a woman *also* a factor in John's opposition to Jezebel? Does John deny her the status of "prophet" simply because he disagrees with what she claims the Spirit was saying, or also because she is a woman? Would John deny the title προφήτης to any woman? Again we can ask if John is opposed to her because she is such a successful and influential *woman*?

We will return to these questions below, but we note here that John condemns Jezebel in much more strident terms than he condemns Balaam (compare 2:14-16 and 2:20-24; Jezebel is threatened with death), and it is certainly noticeable that the only actual woman who is spoken of by John is condemned.

3.2.2 Rev 14:1-5

The only other passage that speaks of actual Christian women is Rev 14:1-5. In Rev 14:4 it is said of the 144,000 spoken of in this passage that "It is these who have not defiled themselves with women, for they are virgins (οὗτοί εἰσιν οἱ μετὰ γυναικῶν οὐκ ἐμολύνθησαν, παρθένοι γάρ εἰσιν)." What does this passage indicate about John's view of women?

This is the fourth vision in the series of unnumbered visions beginning in 12:1. In 14:1 the 144,000 are said to have the Lamb's name and his Father's name written on their foreheads (14:1), in contrast to those who worship the beast and bear his mark (13:16). They are engaged in the pure worship of God (14:2-3). But who are they? The 144,000 mentioned here first appear in 7:1-8, where they are said to be made up of 12,000 people from each of the twelve

---

[156] See Aune 1981, p27. In Rev people sometimes do not repent; see Rev 16:8-9.

[157] See Rev 2:14-15. This comparison is not often made. Yarbro Collins (1987, p80-4) does not note that John condemns both Balaam and Jezebel and so does not ask if he condemns Jezebel because she is a woman, or because of what she teaches. However, Schüssler Fiorenza (1991, p133) notes concerning Jezebel: "John, however, does not argue against this woman prophet because she claimed prophetic office and leadership as a woman. Rather he calls her names because he does not agree with her teaching." But she does not discuss Balaam at this point (since he is not explicitly called a prophet) and so does not make any comparison with regard to the way John writes of Jezebel and Balaam.

tribes of Israel. However, the 144,000 probably do not refer to Jewish Christians, since in 2:9 and 3:9 John denies the title "Jews" to those who were probably Jews by birth,[158] and so clearly sees the church as able to claim the title "Jews". Hence the twelve times 12,000 probably represent those from every tribe, nation, tongue and people. Yet while the number 144,000 is probably not to be taken literally, it seems clear that it is a *different* group from all the faithful mentioned in 7:9-17, who are specifically said to be "a great multitude that no one could count" (7:9). The explicit contrast between the numbered group in 7:1-8 (and 14:1-5) and the numberless group in 7:9-17 suggests they are different groups, with the 144,000 being a specific group within the faithful.[159]

If the group portrayed in 14:1-5 do not represent all Christians, who are they? Yarbro Collins notes that they are said to "follow the Lamb wherever he goes" (14:4), and that "[a]ccording to chapter 5, the most distinctive characteristic of the Lamb is the fact that he was slain."[160] She suggests that the 144,000 are those who are called to suffer death because of their faith.[161] This would then be a presentation of "ideal discipleship",[162] which explains the contrast between the 144,000 and the innumerable multitude. Sacrificial terminology in 14:1-5 supports this interpretation that the 144,000 are the faithful who die for their faith.[163]

---

[158] Some have thought the allusion in 2:9 and 3:9 is to Judaising Christians, but this is unlikely; see Chapter 7.

[159] See Yarbro Collins 1987, p85. By contrast Pippin 1992, p70-1 thinks the 144,000 represent all the faithful and so females are excluded from the New Jerusalem. But it is very unlikely that the 144,000 represent all Christians. Dewey 1992, p87 argues that the 144,000 includes women: "I do not believe the Apocalypse excludes all women from its vision of heaven. The expression, '144,000 men who have not defiled themselves with women' is, in my opinion, simply the author's androcentric mindset in operation. Nowhere else in early Christianity do we find women excluded [from heaven]. I doubt they are excluded here." Schüssler Fiorenza (1991, p88) thinks "They are true followers of the Lamb because they refuse to participate in 'the lie' and deception of the beast."

[160] Yarbro Collins 1987, p84; see Rev 5:6.

[161] She notes (see Yarbro Collins 1987, p84-5) it is not clear whether some have already died, or whether the reference is solely to future events. See also Aune 1996, p274-6, who notes parallels like Lk 9:57-8; Jn 12:26; 13:36. However Aune (1996, p276-7, 283) thinks the 144,000 are all Christians, and "following the Lamb wherever he goes" is a reference to their willingness to suffer and die.

[162] Yarbro Collins 1987, p85.

[163] Yarbro Collins (1987, p81) notes that in v5 they are said to be unblemished (ἄμωμος), which is used of sacrificial animals and that the 144,000 are "first fruits" (ἀπαρχή), a sacrificial technical term which shows they are a sacrifice offered to God. "The statement that these were redeemed 'from humanity' (ἀπὸ τῶν ἀνθρώπων) suggests that this special group is the first fruits and the rest of humanity is the harvest." (p86) This is analogous to the first resurrection (20:4-6) of those beheaded because of their faith and the general resurrection (20:11-15). Thus, they are the first of a much larger number of faithful Christians. Garrett

The statement in 14:4 that the 144,000 "have not defiled themselves with women, for they are virgins" could be meant metaphorically. In the same way as "practicing immorality" is a reference to idolatry,[164] here those who have not worshipped other gods but rather been faithful to God could metaphorically be said to "have not defiled themselves with women."[165] The true followers of the Lamb would then be those who have not been involved in the spiritual fornication of the imperial cult. Schüssler Fiorenza argues that this must be the case, since a literal ascetic interpretation of 14:4 is unlikely because "such a misogynist stance is nowhere else found in Revelation."[166]

However, Yarbro Collins notes this argument is unconvincing: "In the messages and other visions, idolatry is symbolized by forbidden sexual acts: prostitution and adultery. Here any kind of heterosexual relation is portrayed as defiling. The distinctiveness of the language used here, along with its concreteness, suggests that the reference is to literal sexual relations."[167] Further, if the reference is metaphorical, it is not clear why the 144,000 are only men.[168]

The most likely meaning of 14:4 is that the 144,000 men are literally virgins. As Yarbro Collins notes, "the passage thus expresses a point of view in which the defiling potential of sexual relations with women [according to Leviticus 12, 15, 18] is to be avoided by avoiding such relations altogether. The question arises as to the occasion and rationale for this intensification of the quest for ritual purity and for the androcentric way in which the achievement of purity is expressed."[169]

(1998, p472) also sees them as an exclusive group who die rather than worship the beast. As "first fruits" they will participate in the first resurrection (20:4), with the "whole harvest" to follow at the second resurrection (20:13).

[164] For πορνεύω see 2:14, 20; 17:2; 18:3, 9; for πορνεία see 2:21; 9:21; 14:8; 17:2, 4; 18:3; 19:2; πόρνη (harlot) is used figuratively of a power that is hostile to God and God's people in Rev 17:1, 5, 15-16; 19:2. The exceptional literal use in vice lists are in 9:21; 21:8; 22:15 (πορνεία in 9:21; πόρνος (one who practices sexual immorality) in 21:8 and 22:15).

[165] This is argued by Schüssler Fiorenza 1985, p190; 1991, p88; see also Prigent 2001, p433-4.

[166] Schüssler Fiorenza 1991, p88; see also Klassen 1999, p394. Schüssler Fiorenza notes that celibacy is not stressed elsewhere in Revelation. She also notes that Philo (*De Cherub* 49-50) uses the masculine term virgins in a metaphorical sense for God's people, male and female. However, in Rev 14:4 the term clearly applies only to men. Klassen (1999, p394) also notes that for some early Christians marriage was honourable (eg Heb 13:4) and suggests "the reference in Rev. 14:4 could be to those who have been faithful to their spouses by refusing to commit adultery"; but this seems to go beyond the meaning of παρθένοι in the verse.

[167] Yarbro Collins 1987, p86.

[168] See Charles 1920, 2, p8-9 (who thinks most of the verse is an interpolation). Schüssler Fiorenza (1985, p190-1) suggests "The mention of 'women' could also allude to the prophetess in Thyatira called Jezebel, who in John's view 'seduces' Christians to idolatry and accommodation to pagan society." This is possible, but seems unlikely.

[169] Yarbro Collins 1987, p87.

Yarbro Collins notes that the intensification of purity may have been based on the adaptation in Revelation of the holy war tradition.[170] In this tradition, since Yahweh and the angels fought with Israel, those who fought in holy war alongside Yahweh had to temporarily refrain from sexual intercourse so as to be ritually pure (see Deut 23:9-14; Josh 3:5; 7:13; 1 Sam 21:5; 2 Sam 11:11). This tradition is known among the Maccabees and at Qumran, where the men seem to have kept themselves ritually pure in preparation for the eschatological battle.[171] The tradition is also used in Rev 19:11-21.[172] Thus "the expectation that the faithful were to have an active role in the eschatological battle (Rev 17:14) could be the occasion for the high value placed on sexual continence and for the androcentric point of view (warriors were normally men)."[173] But this tradition has been intensified here: "By describing the 144,000 as not merely *refraining* from sexual intercourse [as in the OT and Qumran] but as *virgins*, John implies that the men not only meet but exceed the standard of purity necessary for participation in holy war."[174]

Another factor in portraying the 144,000 as virgins may have been that the idea of the priesthood of all Christians is important in Revelation.[175] Hence the androcentric view of Rev 14:1-5 may reflect the fact that only men were priests in Israel, and that the priest had to be holy, and hence refrain from sexual intercourse with women, because of his relationship to Yahweh.[176] But again we note that the regulations for cultic purity call for temporary sexual abstinence rather than for virginity. Why does John call for the latter here?

Yarbro Collins has noted that Rev 14:1-5 has much in common with "The Book of Watchers" (1 Enoch 1-36, henceforth BW) and Olson has followed up this insight.[177] He suggests that the language of Rev 14:4a is best explained by John making a conscious allusion to the Book of Watchers at this point. 1 Enoch 15:2-7 shows that the angels were intended to remain perpetual virgins but that the angels who fell had sexual relations with women on earth and in this way "defiled themselves". Olson shows that John knows this story from BW,[178] and that Rev 14:4a is a conscious literary allusion to BW which

---

[170] Yarbro Collins 1987, p87; see also Garrett 1998, p472.

[171] See 1QM 7:3-7; see also Josephus War 2.120-1; Philo Apology, 11.14-17.

[172] See Yarbro Collins, Political Perspective 1977, p246-8.

[173] Yarbro Collins 1987, p88; see also Aune 1996, p271-4.

[174] Garrett 1998, p472, her emphasis.

[175] See Rev 1:6; 5:10; 20:6; Yarbro Collins 1987, p88.

[176] Yarbro Collins (1987, p88) notes the interesting parallel with Philo's On the Life of Moses 2.68-9 where it is said that Moses, in order to be a priest, must refrain from intercourse with women.

[177] Yarbro Collins 1987, p88-9; Olson 1997, 492-510.

[178] Olson 1997, p497-501.

"serves effectively as a trigger to call up an entire narrative".[179] John's point is then that "the redeemed 144,000 stand in radical opposition to the fallen angels of the BW".[180] In contrast to the angels, who have lost their priestly status (they were "defiled" (1 Enoch 15:2-7)) by taking wives, the 144,000 have *not* "defiled themselves with women". Olson suggests that John is showing that the church as a "kingdom of priests" replaces the fallen angelic priesthood of BW.[181]

Even if Olson is correct and there is a conscious allusion to BW here (which seems the best explanation for the call for celibacy rather than temporary sexual abstinence in 14:4), the import of John's very concrete language remains – it is clearly androcentric and implies that women are not among the 144,000 "special disciples".[182]

What do we conclude from this language about John's view of women? Yarbro Collins notes "the wording is one-sided. It assumes that the model Christians are male. .... [I]t is not just a matter of the generic masculine used to refer to both males and females. There is also a suggestion that males are more pure than females and that females are more defiling than males."[183]

3.2.3 John's symbolic language: Feminine imagery in Revelation

We move now to discuss John's use of feminine imagery. Again, this is a large topic in itself, but here our question is whether John's use of feminine imagery gives us any indication of his attitude to women in the seven communities, particularly Ephesus, and what part women might have played

---

[179] Olson 1997, p500. He comments (1997, p500): "the words are vivid, and they grab the reader's attention, but nothing can be found elsewhere in Revelation to which they point. Events of some kind are implied, and one naturally wants to ask, What defilement is meant? Which women? What opportunity for defilement have these male virgins passed over? ... In short, Rev 14:4 sends one off looking for a *story*. In the BW that story is found."

[180] Olson 1997, p500.

[181] That priestly imagery is used of both the 144,000 and the angels in BW confirms that the two groups are contrasted here. On the priestly imagery, see Olson 1997, p501. The 144,000 are also the anti-image of those who worship the beast and bear his mark on their foreheads (Rev 13:16-17).

[182] Olson (1997, p508-10) criticizes Yarbro Collins for reading data about John's audience from Rev 14:4 – that the text indicates that actual male celibates in the early church are meant. Even if this is to push the language too far, Rev 14:4 still indicates something of John's view on gender issues.

[183] Yarbro Collins 1987, p90. Yarbro Collins (1987, p91) goes on: this "reflect[s] something of the ordinary daily lives of women in the seven congregations addressed by the Apocalypse. Rev 14:1-5 makes these women worse than invisible. Not only are the ideal Christians portrayed in male terms, but women are depicted as dangerous: sexual contact with women is defiling. This passage suggests that women in these congregations be defined as inferior and subordinate to men." See also Pippin 1994, p113. But this is to assume that John here reflects the social reality of particular communities. We can only say with certainty that we see John's view here; the situation amongst the readers could be quite different.

in that community. John speaks of three archetypal women in the course of his visions – the woman clothed with the sun who gives birth to a son in Rev 12, the city of Babylon/Rome which is portrayed in Rev 17-18 as a whore, and the new Jerusalem pictured in Rev 21:2 "as a bride adorned for her husband" (see also 19:6-8; 22:17).

Some of John's feminine images are traditional.[184] As Garrett notes, some of the feminine images "presuppose a traditional symbolic use of the image of 'adultery' or 'fornication' to represent idolatry".[185] John utilises this scriptural pattern in portraying Jezebel and Rome as "whores" and when he depicts the heavenly Jerusalem as "a pure virgin", suggesting abstinence from any idolatry. But the overall impact of John's use of feminine images remains clear. Garrett notes in this regard:

"Studying the cultural background of this symbolism enables one to understand that John uses such language to represent certain basic concepts or realities: the worship of idols verses single-minded devotion to God; the people of Israel, 'mother' of the Messiah and the church; the pollution and sin of the Roman Empire versus the purity of the heavenly city of God. But even when one understands the 'point' of Revelation's various references to women, John's language remains disturbing and dangerous. He categorizes women into the wholly good (the woman clothed with the sun and the new Jerusalem) and the wholly bad ('Jezebel' and 'Babylon'). The wholly good are those whose sexuality is effectively controlled; the wholly bad are those whose sexuality escapes male management and manipulation. (The woman reader is thus divided: she wants to identify with the good but is reluctant to do so because the images deny female self-determination; she hesitates to identify with the bad but may endorse the defiance of the 'whores' against those who would control or destroy them.) John's feminine imagery is dangerous because (whether intentionally or not) it promotes an ethos in which women are not allowed to control their own bodies and their own destinies and in which violence against women is – at least in some cases – condoned."[186]

Pippin also writes: "all the females in the Apocalypse are victims; they are objects of desire and violence because they are all stereotyped, archetypal images of the female rather than the embodiment of power and control over their own lives in the real or fantastic worlds."[187]

---

[184] On feminine imagery in Rev see Pippin 1992a, p15-107; 1992b, p193-210; 1992c, p67-82; Robbins 1992, p211-17; Schaberg 1992, p219-226; Selvidge 1996, p274-85; Garrett 1998, p471-4; Kim 1999, p61-81. On the use of the two-women topos, see Rossing 1999.

[185] Garrett 1998, p470. For the feminization of a city in the OT prophetic tradition see Nah 3:4; Isa 23:15-18; Hos 2:1-13. Hosea uses fornication as metaphor; "to fornicate" became virtually synonymous with involvement in idolatry; see Hos 1:2; 2:1-13; 3:1; 4:12-14; Ex 34:16; Lev 17:7; 20:5; Deut 31:6; Judg 8:27; 2 Kgs 9:22; Isa 57:7-13; Jer 3:1-10; Ezek 16:15-58; 23:1-49.

[186] Garrett 1998, p474.

[187] Pippin 1992a, p72. Elsewhere she writes: "The roles of women in the male myth of the Apocalypse are virgin, whore, and mother-beloved and hated-but always under male control and domination." (Pippin 1992b, p200). Note also Schüssler Fiorenza 1985, p199: "Rev.

Thus a key point is that in each of these passages, women are portrayed as predominantly passive and as the object of actions by men. Clearly John's usage of imagery is problematic for contemporary women.[188] It also seems likely that the predominantly negative and exclusively passive roles that archetypal women play in these narratives suggest that John does not envisage women being active and innovative leaders in the churches to which he writes. But, although this seems likely, we need to be cautious. Recent study of the use of gendered imagery in Gnostic texts, suggests that we should be cautious in going from imagery in a text to social reality with regard to the social status of women in the real world of the readers.[189] The relationship between text and world is much more complex than this.

3.3 Conclusions and implications for women in Ephesus?

We return first of all to discuss John's condemnation of Jezebel. We note that Jezebel seems to be more influential and successful in Thyatira than Balaam is in Pergamum. Not only does John note Jezebel's "children", with no comparable remark being made about Balaam, but we note that in 2:14 "some" hold the teaching of Balaam, whereas in Thyatira the whole community is said to "tolerate the woman Jezebel" (2:20).[190] Further, Jezebel is a rival prophet to John and she was probably influential beyond Thyatira, while nothing is said about Balaam in either respect. Clearly then Jezebel is a more significant "opponent" in John's view than Balaam. Is this sufficient to explain John's more vehement condemnation of Jezebel?

We may suggest that the answer is probably not. What John says in 14:1-5 and his use of feminine symbolic language suggest that gender issues are a factor in the vigorous condemnation of Jezebel and that John would not be supportive of women in leadership. One reason that "Jezebel" is more vehemently condemned than "Balaam" then is probably because she is a woman. Balaam is bad because of his teaching. Jezebel is even worse – not only is her teaching wrong, but she is also a woman, who is claiming to be a

---

engages the imagination of the contemporary reader to perceive women in terms of good or evil, pure or impure, heavenly or destructive, helpless or powerful, bride or temptress, wife or whore." But note the comment of Jack (2002, p161): "in a text in which opposition and struggle are key, defining features, it is not surprising that stereotyping and even demonization are used as literary devices. In Revelation, it is not women alone who are subjected to such treatment. Many other images and symbols are offered as expressions of the forces of evil."

[188] It is also clear that John's images are part of his patriarchal world where they are "at home" and have a long history.

[189] See McGuire 1999, 258-9; see also Klauck 2000, p488-90.

[190] But note the reference in 2:24 to "the rest of you in Thyatira, who do not hold this teaching"; so clearly although all tolerate Jezebel, only some follow her.

prophet and exercising power. This may well be one of the reasons why John is more vehement in his critique of Jezebel in 2:20-4 than he is of Balaam in 2:14-16.[191]

But what might the condemnation of Jezebel, 14:1-5 and the use of feminine symbolism mean with regard to the situation of women among the addressees in Ephesus? It is impossible to be categorical. But if John did not comment on actual historical women, and only used feminine symbolic language, we could suggest that it was possible for John to use negative and passive images of women in his visions, but also accept some women in leadership in Ephesus (and elsewhere) without comment. However, given the negative implications of 14:1-5, that John has no positive things to say about *actual* women, and that he does not portray archetypal women in active roles, it seems very unlikely that he would accept women in leadership in Ephesus. We can very tentatively suggest then that his silence with regard to women in Ephesus means that there were no active women in leadership in Ephesus among John's addressees.

But we need to recall again that what we are reading in Revelation is John's view of women in the church. We are not seeing the actual situation of women in the community in Ephesus he addresses (or elsewhere apart from Thyatira, where Jezebel is clearly an active and influential leader). It could be that the actual situation of women in Ephesus was somewhat different, and perhaps included women who were active leaders teaching in accordance with John's views. And of course, since we have suggested that some of the members of the seven churches disagreed with John about relationships with the world, it is at the very least possible that his addressees could have totally disagreed with John about women in leadership.

Finally, we note that in Rev 2:6 it is said that the readers at Ephesus "hate" the Nicolaitans. Did Jezebel spend some time in Ephesus and was one of the reasons the Ephesian readers rejected the Nicolaitans that a woman was a key leader? We cannot say. Nor do we know if any of the rejected apostles in Ephesus were women.

4. Overall Conclusions

We note firstly that there are active women leaders in the community addressed in the Pastorals. Some of these leaders are clearly involved in teaching that the Pastor considers "false". His reaction to this, and to the potential for the activity of some women to draw negative comment from

---

[191] Compare Kraemer (1992, p176) who suggests that John "is only offended by the content of Jezebel's prophecy and teaching, and not the mere fact that she engages in either." Kraemer does not think John objects to women's leadership per se.

outsiders is to silence women teachers and to greatly restrict the widows' order. But we note that a number of women have been very active as leaders in this community and that there are probably women deacons, whose activities are not affected by the Pastor.

In the Johannine Letters we can suggest that the pendulum has swung from opposition to women to silence. As far as the author is concerned it seems that women can at times be invisible. There may be some significant women among the readers, but John does not address them. The women who must be part of the audience are almost lost from sight, although they are probably included in the corporate terms as "ἀγαπητοί" (1 Jn 2:7) and "ἀδελφοί" (1 Jn 3:13). The only people John does mention explicitly are men. We can suggest that women are not involved in leadership and the subject of women's ministry is "off the agenda". We can thus suggest again that the Pastorals and the Johannine Letters are to two quite different communities.[192]

In Revelation, Jezebel, the only woman who is active as a leader, teacher, and prophet is roundly condemned. Although a man is condemned for teaching the same doctrine, given what John says in 14:4-5 and his use of feminine imagery to portray passive women, it seems likely that one of the reasons for the vigour of John's opposition to Jezebel is that she was a woman who was also an active leader.

We do not know what the situation was among Ephesian readers of Revelation. Were some of the rejected apostles women, and were they rejected because they were women? Did the Ephesians addressed in Revelation "hate" the Nicolaitans because of the involvement of women like Jezebel? We cannot say. But certainly there is no positive evidence that women were active as leaders among the Ephesians addressed in Revelation.

If there were no active women leaders in Ephesus (which is highly speculative in itself), then is this compatible with our hypothesis that John is writing to all Christians in Ephesus? Two factors would have to be met for this to be the case. First, that Revelation was actually written a few years after the Pastorals, so there is time for the change to occur from active women teachers to the situation in Rev where there is no positive evidence that women were active as leaders among the Ephesians (although this itself is only a supposition since the evidence is very limited).

Second, and related to the first factor, for our hypothesis to be confirmed, all the women leaders from the Pastorals would need to have joined the

---

[192] It is possible that if we date the Pastorals at the earliest point in our possible dating range of 80-100 (ie. at 80), then the Johannine Letters, written 90-100, could be to the same community, with the Pastor's commands that women cease teaching and his restriction of the activities of widows having been completely effective. However, we have already noted considerable evidence which suggests that these two sets of documents are to different communities, and what we have discovered here is compatible with that.

Pastor's opponents (which John would then not have addressed) or to have ceased being leaders.[193]

If these two conditions are met, then the evidence from Rev would be compatible with our hypothesis that Rev is addressed to a range of Christians in Ephesus, including the readers addressed in the Pastorals and the Johannine Letters. But since the evidence about women in Ephesus from Revelation is so limited, it is really inadequate to either contradict or support our hypothesis.

---

[193] The first option is favoured by the indications of the activity of women in leadership in the Acts of Paul and Thecla.

Chapter 12

What shall we call each other? The issue of self-designation in the Pastoral Epistles, the Johannine Letters and Revelation

1. Introduction

Members of groups tend to develop "names" or "self-designations" that they use for one another. Within the group that became popularly known as "the Quakers", the terms "Children of the Light", "Friends in the Truth" or "Friends" became the preferred "self-designation" by members of the group themselves.[1] However, outsiders came to call the group "Quakers".[2]

What terms were used within earliest Christianity in this way to designate other members of the group? How did authors refer to members of the communities to whom they were writing, and how would these members have referred to each other? This is the issue we will address here.

We need to distinguish between three different sorts of terms. Firstly, there is "insider language" for self-designation; that is, the term or terms that would be used to designate other members of the group when speaking strictly within the group. Secondly, there is "out-facing language"; that is, the terms that would be used to designate members of the group when addressing outsiders, or to represent oneself to outsiders. Thirdly, there is "outsider-coined language";[3] that is language used *by* outsiders to designate a group.

---

[1] The earliest used term was "Children of the Light"; soon after "Friends" was used; see Braithwaite 1955, p44, 73, 131-2; *The Journal of George Fox* in Nickalls 1952, p26, 28. He notes (p131-2) "how carefully Friends had avoided describing themselves by terms with a denominational meaning. Their own names, of which the chief were 'Children of the Light' and 'Friends in the Truth,' or 'Friends,' belonged equally to all disciples with a living experience of Christ, and were not descriptive terms that would be naturally accepted or used by others." This was because they saw themselves as a movement for all and not as a sect.

[2] The name "Quakers" was a derisive nickname probably based on "the trembling of Friends under the powerful working of the Holy Ghost" (Braithwaite 1955, p57). Ingle (1994, p54) notes that a justice named Gervase Bennett applied the name "Quaker" to Fox and his followers and that Fox took umbrage to the label. He goes on "Fox preferred the name 'Children of the Light,' a phrase that he claimed Christ had bestowed on them and that they used for many years. He was creative in adopting other acceptable terms, such as 'People of God,' 'Royal Seed of God,' or 'Friends of the Truth,' the latter winning favor and becoming the basis of the modern name, 'Religious Society of Friends."

[3] I am grateful to John Barclay for suggesting this, and the previous term.

Such language is often derogatory and may begin as a nickname. Sometimes such names may be the same as either of our first two categories (particularly since a group may eventually adopt for itself a term coined by others), though they may also be different.[4]

Connected to this issue of self-designation are wider issues of group identity with which we are concerned here in Part Three. For terms of self-designation used by a group to represent itself, both to insiders and to outsiders, provide an important indicator of the nature of the group.[5] In particular, we are interested here in whether this language of self-designation sheds further light on whether the Pastoral Epistles and the Johannine Letters are written to different and distinct communities or not. Further, does this language help us with regard to whether Revelation is addressed to all Christians in Ephesus or to a particular community? Since investigating the language of self-designation is one way of looking at the significant issue of group identity, we hope that a discussion here will aid us in our overall enquiry.

Accordingly, we will ask what terms the authors of the Pastoral Epistles, the Johannine Letters and Revelation used as insider language and as out-facing language for self-designation? Further, can we discern from what the authors say anything about the terms for self-designation (as both insider language and out-facing language) that the *readers* of these books used? And can we discern anything about what names outsiders used for these readers – our third category above of "outsider-coined language"?

2. The name "Christian"

Does the name "Christian" provide an answer to our question? Would the readers of the Pastorals, the Johannine Letters and Revelation have known and used it? If so, in what way? We will argue here that the name "Christian"[6] seems to have been used in Antioch, for example, by outsiders for those within the "Christian" group, and so comes into our third category of "outsider-coined language". It may be that readers of the Pastorals, the Johannine Letters and Revelation would have been known by outsiders by this term. Further, while the term may have been used by these readers to

---

[4] The term "Quaker" is a classic example of our third category of "outsider-coined" language.

[5] Elliott (1993, p113) notes that one feature of the self-definition of a group is the "Use of collective terminology once applied to Israel or drawn from the sacred tradition". Similarly, Horrell (2001, p300) describes ἀδελφός as "a basic identity-designation of those who are members of the Christian communities".

[6] We will need to continue to use the term "Christian" for convenience.

designate themselves *to* outsiders and so could be an example of "out-facing language" (our second category), we have no explicit evidence for this. But we will argue that it is not the term that they would have used as "insider language" to designate other members of the group when speaking strictly within the group.

The name "Christian" occurs in the NT only in Acts 11:26, 26:28 and 1 Peter 4:16, although it is also found in Pliny the Younger (around 112 CE), Tacitus (in 115 CE) and Suetonius (before 130).[7] The crucial verse is Acts 11:25-6:

Then Barnabas went to Tarsus to look for Saul, and when he had found him, he brought him to Antioch. So it was that for an entire year they met with the church and taught a great many people, and it was in Antioch that the disciples were first called "Christians" (χρηματίσαι τε πρώτως ἐν Ἀντιοχεία τοὺς μαθητὰς Χριστιανούς).

According to Luke then, the name "Christian" originated in Syrian Antioch. But can we say *when* people at Antioch were first called "Christians"? It is possible that Luke is reflecting actual chronology at this point, and so the term's use in Antioch may date back to around 44 CE.[8] However, although Luke seems to imply this, as Mattingly comments: "we are not bound to press his [Luke's] allusion chronologically. He may simply have introduced it at the most suitable place in his narrative."[9]

But it is generally agreed that the name "Christian" was first coined by outsiders and, at least at first, comes firmly into our third category.[10] There are three reasons for arguing that the name "Christian" was an example of "outsider-coined language". Firstly, if it was used as "insider language" for purposes of self-designation within the group by "Christians" we would expect it to be found more often in the NT. Secondly, the infinitive "χρηματίσαι", used by Luke in Acts 11:26 is best translated as "were called" Christians, indicating that, as far as Luke was concerned, the name originated with outsiders.[11] Thirdly, the name Χριστιανοί is a Latin formation rather

---

[7] Pliny, *Epistles* 10.96; Tacitus, *Annals* 15.44; Suetonius, *Nero* 16.2 (for the date see Warmington 1977, p3-4); see also Lucian, *Alexander* 25, 38; *Peregrinus* 11, 12, 13, 16. Barrett (1994, p556) notes that it seems probable that the name was used in Pompeii in a graffito between 62 and 79 CE; see CIL 4.679.

[8] See Elliott 2000, p790. Agrippa is mentioned in Acts 12:1 and he reigned from 41-44 CE.

[9] Mattingly 1958, p26.

[10] See for example Barrett 1994, p556-7; Elliott 2000, p789-91.

[11] See Haenchen 1971, p367-8, note 3; see also Pilch 1997, p121. This is how the verb is used in Philo (Deus. 121; Leg ad Gaius 346) and Josephus (JW 2.488; Ant 8.157; 13.318; CAp 2.30).

than being of Greek or Aramaic origin; this, together with the two preceding points makes it unlikely that it was first created by "Christians".[12]

We can also suggest that the name "Christian" was coined as a derogatory name. In Acts 26:28 Agrippa uses it with a mocking sense, and in 1 Peter it is used in an outsider-facing situation with reference to persecution and again has a clearly pejorative meaning.[13] Elliot suggests "the label had a derogatory overtone from the outset, so that it meant, not simply 'partisans of Christ,' but something like 'Christ-lackeys,' shameful sycophants of Christ, a criminal put to ignominious death by the Romans years earlier".[14] Further, Roman sources indicate that the label "Christiani" had negative connotations.[15]

It seems likely that the name Christianoi was coined by Gentile non-Christians, because Jews would probably not call "Christians" Χριστιανοί since this would indicate acceptance of the belief that Jesus was the Messiah.[16] Further, as Barrett notes "It is a not unreasonable suggestion that it [the name "Christian"] reflects a situation in which Christians were becoming numerous and were clearly distinguishable from Jews."[17]

It is very unlikely then that the term "Christian" originated as "insider language" used for self-designation by the early Christians and it is certainly not the term that Christians *first* used of each other. It is possible that the term was picked up reasonably early by "Christians" as "out-facing language" for self-designation, and as time went on as "insider language", since it had the advantage of focussing on "Christos". Certainly in Ignatius we find Χριστιανοί being used as "insider language" to designate members of the groups to which he writes. Thus for example, in IgnEph 11.2 he expresses his hope that he will "be found in the lot of the Christians of Ephesus (ἐν κλήρῳ Ἐφεσίων εὑρεθῶ τῶν Χριστιανῶν) who also were ever of one mind with the Apostles in the power of Jesus Christ." Similarly in IgnMag 4.1 he writes: "It is right then, that we should be really Christians, and not merely have the

---

[12] See Mattingly 1958, p27-9; Barrett 1994, p556; Elliott 2000, p789-90. Analogies include *Caesariani, Pompeiani, Augustiani.*

[13] Pilch 1997, p121; Elliot 2000, p791-4.

[14] Elliot 2000, p790-1. Bickerman (1949, p109-24) argues that the name was created by disciples. However, his view that χρηματίζω means "to style oneself" is unlikely given the usage in Philo and Josephus; see Mattingly 1958, p28 n3. For other views of the origin of the term see Mattingly 1958, p26-37; Taylor 1994, p75-94. Lake and Cadbury 1933b, p385 think it is unclear whether it was coined as a derogatory name or not.

[15] See Pliny, *Epistles* 10.96-7; Tacitus, *Annals* 15.44; Suetonius, *Nero* 16.2; see also Elliot 2000, p791.

[16] The creation of a name by non-Christian Gentiles suggests that the "Christian" community had formed a sufficiently large and cohesive group for them to be recognized as a distinct entity, and also that they were a group which was sufficiently distinguished from the Jewish community for them to be given a different name.

[17] Barrett 1994, p556.

name."[18] This latter passage is interesting since it shows that his addressees are known by outsiders as "Christians" ("and not merely have the name"), but also that Ignatius used it as a self-designation in speaking to his readers ("we should be really Christians"). Thus, although Χριστιανοί originated as a nickname used by outsiders, by Ignatius' time it has become "insider language" for self-designation at least for Ignatius, but probably for some of his addressees too. We see then some "leakage" between our categories – outsider-coined language becomes insider language.[19]

But was the term "Christian" adopted as "insider language" for self-designation by the readers of the Pastorals, the Johannine Letters and Revelation? It is the lack of usage of the name "Christian" by Luke after Acts 11:26 *and* the lack of usage in the rest of the NT that is most decisive with regard to this question. If Luke used the term consistently from Acts 11 on we might feel confident that the term came to be widely used as insider language for self-designation - either in the time of which he is writing (the late 40s to the late 50s) or at the least, by the time when he was writing (perhaps 80-90).[20] But Luke only uses the term "Christian" once more - in Acts 26:28, which reads: "Agrippa said to Paul, 'Are you so quickly persuading me to become a Christian?'"[21] Elsewhere, as we have noted, it is only found in 1

---

[18] See also IgnMag 10.1: "let us learn to lead Christian lives"; IgnTr 6.1 "live only on Christian fare"; IgnRom 3:2: "that I may not only be called a Christian, but may also be found to be one."; IgnPol 7.3: "A Christian has no power over himself." It is also found in Did. 12.4: "so that no man shall live among you in idleness because he is a Christian." See also Diogn 6.1-10; Mart Pol 3.2; 10.1; 12.1-2.

[19] We see this sort of "leakage" in (the non-Christian) Lucian's Peregrinus 13, written around 165 (see Jones 1986, p117). He writes: "Furthermore, their first lawgiver persuaded them that they are all *brothers* of one another after they have transgressed once for all by denying the Greek gods ...". Similarly Tertullian (Apol. 39) writes: "And they [i.e. outsiders] are wroth with us, too, because we call each other *brethren*; for no other reason, as I think, than because among themselves names of consanguinity are assumed in mere pretence of affection." (I am grateful to John Barclay for both these references.) Here Tertullian shows that outsiders knew Christians called each other "brothers", and react to the term. Lucian, an outsider, shows this explicitly. In both examples then we see "leakage" from one category to another – a term used by Christians ("brother"), as we will see, comes to be used of them by outsiders. It is likely that other forms of transference from one category to another also occurred.

[20] Barrett (1999, p530) suggests Acts was written in "AD 90 or thereabouts".

[21] On the textual issues in 26:28 and its interpretation see Barrett 1998, p1169-71. Luke's statement in 11:26 ("and it was in Antioch that the disciples *were first* (πρώτως) *called* 'Christians'") implies that there were other occurrences known to Luke when the name "Christian" was used; see Lake and Cadbury 1933b, p386. But the fact that he avoids using it elsewhere in Acts, apart from in 26:28, may suggest he is deliberately avoiding it. This may in turn suggest that Luke was aware that it was used in a very limited way in this early period.

Peter 4:16.[22] It is noteworthy that in both Acts 26:28 and 1 Peter 4:16 the use of the name "Christian" again comes into the category of "outsider-coined language". Secondly, as Cadbury remarks "the absence of the word from the earliest Christian literature, including 1 Clement, and indeed from all the Apostolic Fathers except Ignatius, suggests that as a matter of fact it was not a name early accepted by the Christians themselves."[23] Thirdly, after Acts 11:26, Luke in fact uses a whole range of "insider language" for self-designation for "Christians", individually or corporately – "disciples",[24] "brothers and sisters",[25] "the friends",[26] "saints",[27] "believers",[28] "the saved",[29] "the church",[30] and "the assembly".[31] This variety of self-designations strongly suggests that Luke himself did not think "Christians" was the term used to designate other members of the group when speaking

---

[22] Mattingly (1958, p27 n2) suggests "The use of *Christianus* was clearly widespread and official when 1 Peter iv.14-16 was written", which he argues was during the reign of Trajan. But if it was widespread we would expect it to be used elsewhere in the NT.

[23] Lake and Cadbury 1933b, p386. Note that it is used in the Didache 12.4, and in the Epistle to Diognetus 6:1-10. As noted above, Tacitus uses the term (see Tac. Ann. xv.44). This usage leads Mattingly (1958, p28, 32) to think that by the time Luke wrote (sometime after 70, Mattingly is not precise), the name "Christian" was in use among the populace, but he suggests it was also used as an official, legal term. However, although this is possible, we need to recall that Tacitus wrote early in the second century. Hence, even though he was writing about events in 64 CE, we have no way of knowing if the term "Christian" was used in Rome in 64, although this seems likely (and is supported for example by Elliott 2000, p791). All we can say for sure is that Nero could identify a particular group as followers of Jesus at this point, but that they were called "Christians" in 64 is not proven. Even if they were called "Christians" in Rome at this time, that the term is not found outside Acts and 1 Peter in the NT, suggests the term was not widely used at this time elsewhere. It is not until Ignatius' writings around 110 CE that we get the impression that the name "Christian" is being more widely used.

[24] See Acts 11:29, 13:52; 14:20, 22, 28; 15:10; 16:1; 18:23, 27; 19:1, 9, 30; 20:1, 30; 21:4, 16, 16.

[25] See for example Acts 1:15; 11:1; 12:17; 21:17-18.

[26] Acts 27:3 is the sole occurrence.

[27] Acts 9:13, 32, 41; 26:10. Its use is comparatively rare; see Cadbury in Lake and Cadbury 1933b, p380.

[28] Cadbury (in Lake and Cadbury 1933b, p382) notes that a range of Greek expressions may be equivalent to the English term "believers", and that these are all found sporadically in early Christians literature. He goes on (p382) "None is unrepresented in Acts, but it is doubtful how far any of them are for the writer stereotyped into fixed terms." See the range of uses in Acts 2:44; 4:32; 15:5; 16:1, 15; 18:27; 19:18 21:,20, 25; 22:19. The absolute use of οἱ πιστοί occurs at 10:45.

[29] This is Barrett's translation (1994, p158) of τοὺς σῳζομένους in 2:47.

[30] See for example 12:1.

[31] See 4:32; 6:2, 5; 15:12, 30; 21:22. On names of Christians in Acts see Cadbury in Lake and Cadbury 1933b, p375-92. He also discusses Nazarenes, κοινωνία, αἵρεσις, "the whole flock" (Acts 20:28), εὐαγγέλιον, λόγος, πίστις and ὁδός.

strictly within the group. It is unlikely to have been insider language for the readers of our three sets of documents then.

We have noted that the name "Christian" originally comes into the category of "outsider-coined language". This, and the lack of usage in the rest of the New Testament that we have just noted, suggest that in the mid to late first century when our three sets of documents were written, the term "Christian" was predominantly a name used by outsiders. We have also noted that originally the term "Christian" was almost certainly a derogatory one – we can understand then why Christians did not quickly come to use it of themselves.[32] Thus, even though it is found in 1 Peter, which was written to Asia Minor, its use there in a derogatory sense suggests it may not in fact have been used as "insider language" by the readers of 1 Peter. Further, perhaps the term "Christian" was actually used *by outsiders* as a name for the readers of the Pastorals, the Johannine Letters or Revelation, which are similarly written to Asia Minor, but the authors of these documents give us no hint of the term's use by outsiders.[33] But that it was insider language used by the authors or readers of these three sets of documents seems very unlikely.

But we also need to note (as we will go on to show) that there are no other examples in our chosen documents of terms that we can easily recognise as being used to designate members of the group when addressing outsiders or of names used by outsiders for the group. This is probably a matter dictated by genre, since our documents are "insider" documents. Accordingly, for the remainder of this Chapter, we will focus on "insider language" - terms that would be used to designate other members of the group when speaking strictly within the group.

Before we leave Acts, one further point is worth considering. In Acts 11:26 Luke writes, "it was in Antioch that the *disciples* (τοὺς μαθητάς) were first called 'Christians' (Χριστιανούς)." Is Luke suggesting that, prior to the use of the name "Christians", the name "disciples" was used in some way? Was this "insider language" of self-designation that was being used in Ephesus, where we think readers of our three sets of documents are located? The term μαθητής is used extensively in the Gospels, including Luke, and is found 28 times in Acts. However, μαθητής does not occur outside of the Gospels and Acts. Luke uses it in connection with Christians in Ephesus (in Acts 19:1, 9, 30; 20:1, 30) but its lack of use by Paul means that its extensive use in the

---

[32] Elliott (2000, p791) suggests that the reason "Christian" was only slowly adopted as a self-designation by Christians and hence is absent from most of the NT, is that the term was coined by outsiders as "a term of opprobrium".

[33] Recall also that, as we noted above, the term "Christian" is used three times in the early second century by Greco-Roman authors, which suggests it was used by outsiders more than our documents suggest.

sections of Acts describing Paul's mission is due to Luke's penchant for the word, rather than to it probably being historical at these points. We have no evidence then that Paul's converts in Ephesus (and elsewhere), and other Christians in Ephesus too, would have described themselves as "μαθηταί".[34]

So we turn then to the Pastorals, the Johannine Letters and Revelation to see what these documents suggest about the sort of insider language that is used for self-designation. We will be considering what terms the respective authors used to designate other members of the group and will discuss whether these are terms the readers may have used of themselves for the purposes of self-identification. I will also seek to discuss why particular documents and the recipients of documents might use particular terms. We will also see if this investigation supports or contradicts our on-going probing of our hypotheses – that the Pastorals and the Johannine Letters are written to different groups, while Rev is written to both groups, along with other readers.

3. Insider terms designating members of the group in the Pastoral Epistles

In investigating the Pastorals with our question of insider language for self-designation in mind, we are immediately faced with the fact that each letter purports to be addressed to one individual. However, it is clear that these letters are intended to be read by a group, since, for example, the closing benediction in 1 Tim 6:21 is plural: "Grace be with you (ὑμῶν)".[35] The plural "we" is also used at various points (eg. 1 Tim 2:2; 4:10) indicating that the author has a Christian community in view and at times the author instructs "Timothy" about what to say to others (eg. 1 Tim 4:6; 6:1-10, 17-19). Clearly therefore we may ask what the letters say about insider terms for self-designation used by the author and the community.

---

[34] Luke also uses one of his favourite expressions, "the Way" with regard to Ephesus. For example in 19:23 he says that "no little disturbance broke out concerning the Way (περὶ τῆς ὁδοῦ)." He uses the phrase "the Way" three other times in connection with Ephesus: "the Way of the Lord" (18:25); "the Way of God" (18:26); "and spoke evil of the Way" (19:9). However, the expression "the Way" is not found elsewhere in the NT (see Barrett 1994, p448) and is clearly a Lucanism. It does not seem to reflect a name for "the Christian faith" in Ephesus in the 50s.

[35] See also 2 Tim 4:22; Tit 3:15.

3.1 "Brother and sister": ἀδελφός

As with the undisputed Pauline letters, here also we find the use of the term "ἀδελφός" as a way of referring to group members. The term is found four times in this way and ἀδελφή is used once. Note for example 1 Tim 4:6: "If you put these instructions before the brothers and sisters (ἀδελφοῖς), you will be a good servant of Christ Jesus."[36] 2 Tim 4:21, at the conclusion of 2 Timothy, is similar: "Eubulus sends greetings to you, as do Pudens and Linus and Claudia and all the brothers and sisters (καὶ οἱ ἀδελφοὶ πάντες)."[37]

While statistics can be misleading, it is worth noting that ἀδελφός is significantly more common in the undisputed Pauline letters than in the Pastorals.[38] While ἀδελφός or ἀδελφή is used as fictive kinship terms to refer to other "Christians" on average once per page of Nestle-Aland's 26th edition of the Greek New Testament, the usage in the Pastorals is 0.28 times per page.[39] Thus these two terms are used significantly less in the Pastorals than elsewhere in the Pauline corpus.

Can we explain why the title ἀδελφός is used in the Pastorals, but also why it is used less often than in the undisputed Paulines? In their use of the title ἀδελφός, the Pastorals are reflecting their links with the Pauline tradition, in which the label was very common.[40] But why is the title ἀδελφός noticeably less prominent in the Pastorals than it is in the

---

[36] That the reference here is to all members of the church and not just leaders is argued convincingly by Marshall 1999, p548-9.

[37] Note that this verse shows that οἱ ἀδελφοί is being used inclusively to refer to both men and women, since Claudia is clearly thought of as part of "οἱ ἀδελφοὶ πάντες". We are therefore justified in translating οἱ ἀδελφοί as "brothers and sisters". For a comparable example, see Phil 4:1-2.

[38] On the usage of ἀδελφός in Paul see Meeks 1983, p87; Sandnes 1994, p73-82; Aasgaard 1998, p129-312; Horrell 2001, p299-303. Note that in 1 Cor 6:6 ἀδελφός is the antonym of "unbelievers". See also for example Rom 14:10, 13, 15, 21; 1 Cor 8:11, 13; Philem 16. It is clear that Jews considered themselves as a fellowship of "brothers and sisters" or used ἀδελφοί with the broad sense of "compatriots" or "fellow Jews"; see Gen 13:8; Ex 2:11; Lev 25:35f; Dt 15:3, 7, 9, 11-12; 22:1-4; Jer 22:18; 2 Macc 15:14; Tobit 1.3, 5, 10, 16; 2:2, 3, 19 (on which see Skemp 1999, p92-103); Spec Leg. 2:79-80; Josephus, JW 2:122; 1QS 6:10, 22; CD 6:20; 7. von Soden (TDNT 1, p145) notes "There can be no doubt, however, that ἀδελφός is one of the religious titles of the people of Israel taken over by the Christian community."

[39] See Horrell 2001, p311 for the statistics. For example, the terms are used 5 times in the Pastorals, five times in Philemon, and 39 times in 1 Cor. The total in the undisputed Paulines is 112 times; it is the term Paul uses most often to refer to members of the communities to whom he writes. The figures exclude the use of the terms to describe a biological kinship relation.

[40] The Pastorals reflect broader traditions than simply the Pauline tradition (see Chapter 13), and as we note below, ἀδελφός was widely used in early Christianity, so it may be that this broad general usage of the term was also a factor in the use of ἀδελφός in the Pastorals.

undisputed Paulines? It could be that the reduction in usage is due to the fact that these letters are said to be written to individual church leaders, rather than to communities. However, this explanation is ruled out by the fact that the short letter of Philemon has more occurrences of ἀδελφός than the three Pastorals together. So the nature of the addressees does not explain the decline in usage.[41]

We suggest firstly, that the more hierarchical pattern of leadership and group structure in the Pastorals, reflected in the development of the office of presbyter-overseers and deacons, has led to the decline in the use of ἀδελφός, at least by the author.[42] But a second and related factor that is probably also at work here is the understanding of the church as a household. As has often been noted, the analogy between the church and the household is commonly found in the Pastorals.[43] But more than this, the church is regarded as the household of God, as we find in 1 Tim 3:14-15: "I am writing these instructions to you so that, if I am delayed you may know how one ought to behave in *the household of God, which is the church of the living God*, the pillar and bulwark of the truth."

Further, it seems that the author has applied or superimposed the contemporary household model to the church, so that, in the Pastor's view, the ethos and ordering of the church should reflect the values and ethos of the traditional household of the time.[44] Hence I suggest that the predominant view is *not* that members of the "household of God" are all regarded as "brothers and sisters", as we see in the undisputed Paulines.[45] Rather, as in the

---

[41] See Horrell 2001, p306.

[42] We are not suggesting that ἀδελφός does not contain some sense of hierarchy or superiority (cf. Horrell 2001, p297), since clearly there were older and younger ἀδελφοί and so there could be a sense of hierarchy in the use of the term. But, as we will note, the comprehensive use of the household model in the Pastorals, including the prominent place given to the male householder, reflects a greater level of hierarchy than is implicit in the use of the term ἀδελφός.

[43] This analogy underlies verses such as 1 Tim 3:4-5, 12; 5:14; 2 Tim 2:20-1. On the household character of the church in the Pastorals; see Brox 1969, p157-9; Verner 1983, p127-187; Sandnes 1994, p108; Horrell 2001, p307-9.

[44] See for example Bassler 1996a, p91, who notes "The author of this letter, though, applies conventional advice concerning relationships among household members to the church as the household of God." On the family in antiquity see Verner 1983, p27-81; Sandnes 1994, p47-64; Martin 1996, p40-60.

[45] We are not suggesting that the Pauline communities were egalitarian (a debate into which we cannot enter, on which see Horrell 2001, p303, 310), but rather that in the Pastorals we see a greater emphasis on hierarchical relationships than we see in the undisputed Paulines. Horrell (2001, p304) notes with regard to the undisputed Paulines that "the terms οἶκος and οἰκία are never used by Paul to describe the Christian community". Of course ἀδελφός language, and that of the "household" are closely related, but as Horrell (2001, p295-6) notes "they should not simply be treated together as varied forms of familial terminology. We need to ... take account of the ways in which the different terms may reflect

household, men are leaders and women are not, and there is a hierarchy even within the group of men - between those who are leaders and others who are not, between older men and younger men, older women and younger women.[46] This means that the place of the "father" has been reasserted, and so we get the emphasis on hierarchy within the "household of God".[47] This has led, I would suggest, to a lessening of the ethos of being "brothers and sisters" across the Christian community as a whole.[48]

Tit 2:2-6 represents this trend, but I think it is clearest in 1 Tim 5:1-2, a passage which uses the term ἀδελφός. In 1 Tim 5:1-2 we read: "Do not speak harshly to an older man, but speak to him as to a father (πατέρα), to younger men as brothers (ἀδελφούς), to older women as mothers (μητέρας), to younger women as sisters (ἀδελφάς) - with absolute purity."[49] Here we have the metaphorical use of ἀδελφός but we also have the metaphorical use of "father" and "mother". In particular, it is envisaged that a younger leader should speak in a very conciliatory way to one they should regard as a "father". Given the role and power of the "father" in the family of the period, this clearly suggests a different style of relationship from that of two "brothers" interacting with one another. Similarly, because of their seniority, older women are to be treated as "mothers". By contrast, it is only younger men (νεώτεροι) and younger women (νεώτεραι) who are to be treated as brothers and sisters respectively. Overall, relations are patterned according to seniority – probably of both age and faith. Thus, perceiving the church as the "household of God", seems to have led to the development of an internal hierarchy, in which the church reflects to quite some degree the hierarchical relationships found in a household, rather than just being "brothers and

---

different ideals with regard to the construction of social relationships in the Christian communities."

[46] We thus get the emergence of what may be called the "Christian hierarchical family"; see Young 1994, p89-90.

[47] Verner (1983, p79) notes: "in both [Greek and Roman] societies the household was conceived of as a patriarchal institution, whose male head (κύριος, *paterfamilias*) exercised sweeping, although not entirely unrestricted authority over the other members. These members fell into three main categories, namely, wife, children, and slaves." See also Horrell 2001, p297-9 who notes (p298) "when οἶκος is used to describe the human household it often denotes some kind of structured and stratified group."

[48] See also Horrell 2001, p306-11.

[49] Compare Tit 2:2-6, where different age groups are addressed, but ἀδελφός is not used. We will discuss below the only other use of ἀδελφός, which is in 1 Tim 6:2. The advice in 1 Tim 5:1-2 regarding attitudes to different age-groups contains conventional teaching found in popular moral philosophy; see Marshall 1999, p572-3; Dibelius-Conzelmann 1972, p72 for examples.

sisters".[50] By comparison, while Paul sees himself as the "father" of the Corinthians (1 Cor 4:16), or the Thessalonians (1 Thess 2:11) or of Timothy (Phil 2:22) or Onesimus (Phlm 10),[51] he never says that someone should be treated as a "father". It seems likely then that "ἀδελφός" is fading as an insider term for self-designation in the Pastorals for reasons which can be explained by other developments which are clear in the letters.

1 Tim 6:2 is also revealing in this regard. Here, it is acknowledged that both slaves and masters are "ἀδελφοί". But rather than arguing that being "ἀδελφοί" means that the Christian slave should be treated differently from non-Christian slaves by the Christian master, the Pastor warns slaves not to "be disrespectful (μὴ καταφρονείτωσαν)" to masters because they are ἀδελφοί, but rather to "serve them all the more, since those who benefit by their service are believers and beloved." This suggests that, in the Pastor's opinion, slaves should not seek the social consequences which could be claimed on the basis of ἀδελφοί language and implies that "ἀδελφοί" can be heard with connotations which the Pastor does not favour, that is, more egalitarian connotations that he thinks are inappropriate or unwise in his social context.[52] Rather the Pastor is anxious to avoid the suggestion that as "ἀδελφοί", Christian slaves should be treated differently by Christian masters. Here then we have the language of "brother-sister", but the social practice advocated is much more akin to that of the hierarchically structured household.[53]

What this also suggests is that the way in which ἀδελφός language was being used in the community may have been somewhat different from the way the Pastor used it. It seems likely that some slaves had been claiming that since they were ἀδελφοί of their masters, this should have real and practical social implications.[54] For the Pastor, advocating this is to be disrespectful (1 Tim 6:2), which clearly expresses the view of the slave owner "from above". This is probably not how the slaves would have put it; they probably wished "to act in a way subversive of the master-slave relationship, treating them

---

[50] Note also what is said to women (1 Tim 2:9-15; Tit 2:1-10) and to slaves (1 Tim 6:1-2); see also Bassler 1996a, p92. Sandnes (1994, p48) notes "The household is clearly a hierarchical model with given social roles".

[51] Compare also Phil 2:22.

[52] Note 1 Tim 6:1: slaves should regard their masters as worthy of all honour "so that the name of God and the teaching may not be blasphemed."

[53] Horrell (2001, p309) notes: "The socially subordinate are specifically warned against expecting their identity as ἀδελφοί to have an impact on conventional social relations." Compare Phlm 16.

[54] On the basis of this passage Towner (1989, p175) suggests "Christian slaves at Ephesus must have been pressing for emancipation." See also Verner 1983, p142-3; Kidd 1990, p140.

[masters] more like equal siblings, as ἀδελφοί."[55] We can conclude two things from this. Firstly, we again see that the Pastor is not a whole-hearted advocate of "ἀδελφός" language because of his more hierarchical views. Secondly, we can suggest that some in the community (slaves but perhaps others too) may have preferred the (more traditionally Pauline) self-designation of ἀδελφός and may have used it much more frequently than the Pastor did. In this regard then, the Pastor can be seen to be prescriptive rather than simply descriptive.

3.2 "The believers": οἱ πιστοί

A second "self-designation" used in the Pastorals is οἱ πιστοί, perhaps best translated as "the faithful ones". In 1 Tim 4:12 we read: "Let no one despise your youth, but set the faithful (τῶν πιστῶν)[56] an example in speech and conduct, in love, in faith, in purity." In 1 Tim 4:3 we read of food: "which God created to be received with thanksgiving by those who are faithful (τοῖς πιστοῖς) and know the truth." In Tit 1:6, among the qualifications for an elder, we read: "someone who is blameless ... whose children are believers [or "faithful [to God]"] (τέκνα ἔχων πιστά) ..." Note also 1 Tim 5:16: "If any believing woman [or woman who is faithful [to God]] (πιστή) has relatives ... ".[57]

Overall πιστός is used as a term designating a member of the group (with or without the article) seven times in the Pastorals.[58] It is much more prominent with the meaning of "the faithful one" or "the believer" in the Pastorals than it is in the undisputed Paulines, where it is found with this meaning only in 2 Cor 6:15 and Gal 3:9.[59]

---

[55] Horrell 2001, p307.

[56] Mounce (2000, p245) gives the translation "the faithful" here, which helpfully ties the usage into other occurrences of the πιστ- word group in the Pastorals.

[57] Note the variant here: πιστὸς ἢ πιστή, but the text as given above is clearly original; see Mounce 2000, p272-3. 2 Tim 2:2 also uses πιστός, although here a group within the wider group of "Christians" seems to be spoken of; the verse reads: "and what you have heard from me through many witnesses entrust to faithful people (πιστοῖς ἀνθρώποις) who will be able to teach others as well." The person is taught "the faith" and then must pass this on to others who will be "faithful" as is appropriate to holding "the faith". Note also 1 Tim 6:2 and compare Tit 2:10.

[58] πιστός is used as a label in 1 Tim 4:3, 10, 12; 5:16; 6:2; 2 Tim 2:2; Tit 1:6. Marshall (1999, p215) notes that "in some of these cases [of the use of πιστός] the usage is tantamount to categorising a person as 'Christian'." πιστός is used with the meaning of "faithful" in 1 Tim 1:12; 3:11. In Tit 1:9 one of the characteristics of a bishop is that "He must have a firm grasp of the word that is trustworthy (πιστοῦ λόγου) in accordance with the teaching". The "faithful" (πιστός) sayings are found in 1 Tim 1:15; 3:1; 4:9; 2 Tim 2:11; Tit 3:8.

[59] Eph 1:1 and Col 1:2 are related but different in usage of the term. A related usage is that of the verb πιστεύω which can be used to designate the group of believers; see Cadbury

Can we explain why the author uses οἱ πιστοί as a label? We note firstly the significance of the πιστ- word group in the Pastorals. πιστεύω occurs six times, πίστις 33 times, πιστός 17 times and πιστόω once, a total of 57 occurrences. Marshall notes that this is "a figure which is almost three times as high as one would have expected in comparison with the use of the word-group in the earlier epistles of Paul. This is a quite remarkable concentration of vocabulary, even when we make allowance for some specialized usages."[60] Clearly, the concepts of faith, to be faithful and to believe, are of central importance to the author and it is understandable that insider language of self-designation for "Christians" has emerged from this word group.

But secondly, we note the particular way in which πίστις is used in the Pastorals. Although πίστις can be used in the sense of "belief" (eg. 1 Tim 2:15; 2 Tim 3:15), in the Pastorals we find the expression "ἡ πίστις", "the faith", being used regularly as a term which summarises the content of what is believed. For example, in 1 Tim 1:19 we read that "certain persons have suffered shipwreck in the faith (περὶ τὴν πίστιν ἐναυάγησαν)". ἡ πίστις is used to refer to the content of what is believed a total of 15 times.[61] 2 Tim 2:2 is related to this, where we read that what is heard or believed, which is elsewhere in the Pastorals called "the faith", can be passed on from one person to another. Alternative expressions for "the content of what is believed" are "the deposit" (παραθήκη) which has been entrusted to a person,[62] or "the teaching (διδασκαλία)".[63]

---

in Lake and Cadbury 1933b, p382. For example in 1 Tim 1:16 we read: "to those who would come to believe in him (πιστεύειν ἐπ᾽ αὐτῷ) ..." Or note Tit 3:8: "I desire that you insist on these things, so that those who have come to believe in God (οἱ πεπιστευκότες θεῷ) may be careful to devote themselves to good works ..." See also 1 Tim 3:16; Tit 3:8. This usage is reasonably common in the undisputed Paulines; see for example, Rom 1:16; 3:22; 4:11, 24; 9:33; 10:4, 11; 1 Cor 1:21; 14:22. But the verb, which is used in this regard in a variety of linguistic ways, does not seem to have functioned as a "label" in the same way as οἱ πιστοί functions in the Pastorals. The opposite of the usage of πιστός discussed above is the use of the term ἄπιστος for an "unbeliever" who is outside the community. Note 1 Tim 5:8; Tit 1:15; this usage is also found in Paul; see for example 1 Cor 7:12-15. Further, note that one of God's key characteristics for our author is that God is faithful; see 2 Tim 2:11-13; this is also found in Paul; see for example 1 Cor 1:9; 10:13; 2 Cor 1:18.

[60] Marshall 1984, p211; see also Wilson 1979, p28-31; Towner 1989, 121-9; Marshall 1999, p213-17; Mounce 2000, pp. cxxx-cxxxii.

[61] See 1 Tim 1:19; 3:9; 4:1, 6; 5:8, 12; 6:10, 12, 21; 2 Tim 1:5; 2:18; 3:8; 4:7; Tit 1:13; 2:2. Marshall (1999, p214) notes that the anarthrous usage may also refer to the content of what is believed; see 1 Tim 2:7; 3:13; 2 Tim 1:13. Compare also the pronounced usage of the term "the truth"; see 1 Tim 2:4, 4:3; 6:5; 2 Tim 1:14; 2:15, 18, 25; 3:7-8; 4:4; Tit 1:1, 14. This usage of "the faith" is found in Paul; see Gal 1:23 (cf. 3:23, 25); 1 Cor 16:13; 2 Cor 13:5; Phil 1:27, but it does seem to be much more pronounced in the Pastorals.

[62] See 2 Tim 1:12-14; παραθήκη is used in 1 Tim 6:20; 2 Tim 1:12, 14. On the expression see Spicq 1931, p481-502.

Given the central place of "faith" or "belief" in the Pauline tradition, it seems likely that words from the πιστ - group would be used as a term for self-designation in this tradition at some point. But given this general possibility, we can suggest that in the particular case of the Pastorals, the use of οἱ πιστοί as a self-designation is related to the particular significance of the πιστ - word group for the Pastor, one facet of which is the use of ἡ πίστις as a technical term used to designate a body of doctrine or belief. Thus οἱ πιστοί ("the faithful ones") came to be used as an insider term for one who has faith and accepts "the faith" or lives by this body of doctrine. We see then that the group's distinguishing activity (having "faith") became a key "label" for the group. Clearly, for this group, "faith"/ "the faith" is central to the formation of their "Christian" identity, to the extent that their most prominent internal self-designation was derived from this term.

3.3 The use of other terms

Other terms are found as "insider" self-designations in the Pastorals, although they are not used very often. "The saints" is used as a label in 1 Tim 5:10, where it is said that a widow who is put on the list must have "washed the feet of the saints (ἁγίων)".[64] "The elect" (οἱ ἐκλεκτός) is also used as an insider name for "Christians" in 2 Tim 2:10: "Therefore I endure everything for the sake of the elect". This usage is also found in Tit 1:1: "Paul, a servant of God and an apostle of Jesus Christ, for the sake of the faith of God's elect ..."[65] The term ἐκκλησία is clearly in use as an insider term designating the group collectively, for example in 1 Tim 3:5: "for if someone does not know how to manage his own household, how can he take care of God's church."[66] The author can also speak of Christians as "a people" (λαός; Tit 2:14) and "the household of God", which we have already discussed, is used as a term for "Christians" collectively in 1 Tim 3:15.

---

[63] For example in Tit 2:10. Note also the expression "the sound words", which uses medical imagery to refer to the content of what is believed; see for example 1 Tim 6:3; 2 Tim 1:13; Tit 1:9; 2:1; Malherbe 1980, p19-35.

[64] Marshall (1999, p595-6) notes that ἅγιος is used here of Christians in general.

[65] The term is also used to refer to "the elect angels" in 1 Tim 5:21. There are also particular labels for individuals. As in the undisputed Paulines the term "τέκνον" "child" is used (1 Tim 1:2, 18; 2 Tim 1:2 (my beloved child – ἀγαπητῷ τέκνῳ); 2 Tim 2:1; Tit 1:4). Interestingly υἱός is not used at all. In 1 Tim 6:11 we read: "But as for you, man of God (ἄνθρωπε θεοῦ)..." and similarly in 2 Tim 3:17: "that the man/woman of God (ὁ τοῦ θεοῦ ἄνθρωπος) may be complete ..."

[66] The term is also found in 1 Tim 3:15; 5:16.

3.4 Conclusions

We conclude then that "brothers and sisters" and "the believers" are most commonly used for the purpose of "insider" self-designation in the Pastorals, with the latter being the most common, although other terms such as "the elect", "the household of God" are also used.

It is interesting to note that "ἀδελφός" can be seen to reflect "horizontal" identity and points to a certain form or kind of human community. By contrast "οἱ πιστοί" can be seen to reflect "vertical" identity, in the sense that it relates to God (we are "the believing ones" – by implication, believing in God), although in the Pastorals it also relates to a human religious activity of "believing". The two self-designations can thus be seen to be complementary, rather than in any sense "competitors".

In all of this, are we seeing simply the Pastor's understanding of what Christians should call themselves? Are these terms for self-designation simply the preferred terms of the Pastor and do they reflect only his perceptions? Or do we have grounds for suggesting that the Pastorals reflects the self-designations used by the addressees?

The Pastor clearly assumes, for example, that the audience will recognize themselves in the title "the faithful ones". This is most obvious in 1 Tim 4:3; 5:16; 6:2 and Tit 1:6. Thus, when we read in Titus 1:6 that it is important that an elder's children "are believers" or "are faithful [to God]", I think it is fairly clear that πιστός would have been a self-designation the readers would have owned. Otherwise there is a failure of communication. Further, the whole communication strategy of the Pastor is dependent on the readers identifying with these terms. That the author assumes that the audience will identity with "the faithful ones" or "the brothers and sisters" in the text, suggests these were self-designations of the audience. There is no sense that these terms need to be justified, or explained or spelt out; they are entirely self-evident. We can argue therefore that the labels are self-designations used by the readers.

We also need to note the significance of the letter genre of the Pastorals. As letters, they are part of an on-going conversation between author and readers, who share some form of relationship.[67] In writing a letter, we can suggest that an author would try to use terms that were recognised by the readers, terms with which they would be familiar and with which they would identify. We can assume this is the case, unless there are clear indications that the author is trying to introduce a new self-designation or is involved in polemic against the readers at a particular point. If this was the case, we would expect new or polemical terms to be justified, or to be glossed or argued for in some clear way. If new terms were introduced without such additional discussion, we can suggest there would be a failure of communication on the part of the author,

---

[67] This can be as true of pseudepigraphical letters, as it is of other letters.

with the point the author seeks to make being lost on the readers. We have good grounds then for suggesting that the readers of the letters would have used "brother and sister" and "the faithful ones" as self-designations.

But we should also note that there may well be a tendentious edge in regard to the use of ἀδελφός language in the Pastorals. We have noted that 1 Tim 6:2 suggests that slaves may have used ἀδελφός language differently from the Pastor. Although the Pastor uses ἀδελφός in 1 Tim 6:2 we can suggest that he also uses in that verse what he regards as preferable "self-designations" – πιστοί and (to a lesser degree since he only uses the term once more, of Timothy in 1 Tim 1:2) ἀγαπητοί; these are the terms he uses as he seeks to convince the slaves not to be "disrespectful". Certainly this verse suggests that the Pastor may not be entirely comfortable with "ἀδελφός" as a self-designation, or may be seeking to use it rarely. Further, we note that the group of widows of 1 Tim 5:3-16 may well have used different terms from ἀδελφός and ὁ πιστός as terms of self-designation. They may well have used terms that were more egalitarian or reflected a different view of gender relations. By contrast, we have suggested that the Pastor uses the more egalitarian ἀδελφός less often because of his overall views about the nature of the church. However, there is no indication that the use of πιστός has a tendentious edge to it, and given the significance of the πιστ- word group in the Pauline tradition, we can suggest that it was used by the readers.

4. Insider terms designating members of the group in the Johannine Letters

4.1 Terms probably used only by the author of the readers

The author of 1 Jn regularly addresses readers as τεκνία (little children),[68] or less frequently παιδία (children).[69] These two terms of endearment, which are *only* used as terms of address, may be more indicative of the relationship of the author to the readers, whom he considers his spiritual children, rather than an indication of a term that the readers would have used more generally of one another to designate other members of the group.[70] Thus, these two terms indicate how the author designates other members of the group; but they cannot be seen as "insider language" of anyone else in the community.

---

[68] See 1 Jn 2:1, 12, 28; 3:7, 18; 4:4; 5:21.

[69] See 1 Jn 2:14, 18. In 1 Jn 3:7 there is debate about the reading, which is either τεκνία or παιδία.

[70] See Schnackenburg 1992, p110. Brown (1982, p214) notes that this language need not mean that the author was an old man.

Another term which is used exclusively by the author of 1-3 Jn to address his readers is "beloved" (ἀγαπητόι), which is used ten times in the Letters.[71] 1 Jn 4:7, 9-11 is interesting in this regard:

Beloved (Ἀγαπητόι), let us love one another, because love is from God; everyone who loves is born of God and knows God. ... God's love was revealed among us in this way: God sent his only Son into the world so that we might live through him. In this is love, not that we loved God but that he loved us and sent his Son to be the atoning sacrifice for our sins. *Beloved* (Ἀγαπητόι), since God loved us so much, we also ought to love one another.

This passage explains why the author used the term "beloved". He sees his readers as "beloved" because God loves them, as has been shown by God sending his Son.[72] But is the term used as a self-designation by members of the group? Did they address one another as "Beloved", or identify themselves as "the Beloved"? We cannot really tell. Clearly for the author of 1 Jn, as a response to God's love, they "ought to love one another" (1 Jn 4:11, but also repeatedly emphasised in the letters)[73] and so *become* "beloved" of one another. Given this emphasis on God's love and on loving one another in the letters, we can suggest that the author thought "beloved" was a term of address that *should* be used within the group by one member to another. But whether it was actually used by members of the group as an insider self-designation or not is another matter. That the author *only* uses it as a plural address ("Beloved ...") suggests caution in this regard.[74]

---

[71] See 1 Jn 2:7; 3:2, 21; 4:1, 7, 11; 3 Jn 1, 2, 5, 11. It is not used in the Gospel of Jn or Rev. It is used as a term of address occasionally by Paul; see for example 1 Cor 10:14; 15:58; 2 Cor 7:1;12:19; Phil 2:12; 4:1; Col 1:7; 4:7, 9, 14; Phlm 1, 16. Brown (1982, p254) notes: "Another usage of agapetos in the Greek OT is as an adjective to describe God's beloved people (Jer 6:26; 31 [38]:20; Ps 60:7[5]; 108:7[6]; 127:2). This covenant designation is carried over to the NT epistles where Christians are 'God's beloved who are called saints' (Rom 1:7)."

[72] We can suggest then that this term of address arises directly from the author's theology. Brown (1982, p264) also suggests "granted the emphasis in 1 John on *agape*, 'love,' ... the author surely intends the title to have a theological connotation for a community whose model figure was 'the disciple whom Jesus loved.'"

[73] 1 Jn 3:11; 4:7, 11, 12; 2 Jn 5; see also 1 Jn 2:10; 3:10, 14, 18, 23; 4:19, 21; 5:2 which all emphasize loving the "brother or sister" or a similar idea.

[74] We do not read for example, "You should love a beloved ..." or "If you love a beloved ...".

4.2 "Brother and sister": ἀδελφός

There are two more likely candidates for terms the group would have used as "insider" self-designations. Firstly, ἀδελφός ("brother" or "sister")[75] is again a key term for another member of the community, being used 16 times in this way.[76] Note 1 Jn 2:9-11: "Whoever says 'I am in the light,' while hating a *brother or sister* (τὸν ἀδελφὸν αὐτοῦ μισῶν), is still in the darkness. Whoever loves a *brother or sister* (τὸν ἀδελφὸν αὐτοῦ) lives in the light ..." Also noteworthy is 1 Jn 3:13-18:

"Do not be astonished, *brothers and sisters* (ἀδελφοί), that the world hates you. We know that we have passed from death to life because we love one another. Whoever does not love abides in death. All who hate a *brother or sister* (τὸν ἀδελφὸν αὐτοῦ) are murderers, and you know that murderers do not have eternal life abiding in them. We know love by this, that he laid down his life for us —and we ought to lay down our lives for one another. How does God's love abide in anyone who has the world's goods and sees a *brother or sister* (τὸν ἀδελφὸν αὐτοῦ) in need and yet refuses help? Little children (τεκνία), let us love, not in word or speech, but in truth and action."

We see here an interesting switch from discussion of loving "ὁ ἀδελφός" in 3:13-17 to the author addressing readers as "little children" in 3:18. It seems that one member of the group can be designated as "brother or sister" of another, but the author addresses all the readers as "little children". This suggests that ἀδελφός is a term used by the members of the community of each other, while, as we have suggested, τεκνία is more restricted in its usage, being confined to the language the author uses to address the community, rather than a term individuals would use of each other.

But who is ὁ ἀδελφός here? It is clear from the Letters that the term refers to other Christians in the group addressed rather than to Christians in general, or to outsiders.[77] We note for example 1 Jn 3:10-11:

"The children of God and the children of the devil are revealed in this way:
all who do not do what is right are not from God, nor are *those who do not love their brother or sister* (ὁ μὴ ἀγαπῶν τὸν ἀδελφὸν αὐτοῦ).
For this is the message you have heard from the beginning, *that we should love one another.*"

---

[75] We cannot be certain that ἀδελφός is being used inclusively in the Johannine Letters, and it is beyond the scope of this Chapter to discuss this in detail. We will follow the usage of the NRSV in translations.

[76] All the occurrences are 1 Jn 2:9, 10, 11; 3:10, 13, 14, 15, 16, 17; 4:20 (x2), 21; 5:16; 3 Jn 3, 5, 10. The term is used twice in 1 Jn 3:12 to refer to Cain murdering his brother Abel.

[77] See Lieu 1981, p227; Brown 1982, p269-73; Strecker 1996, p107.

Here, "to love their brother or sister" and "to love one another" are clearly in parallel, showing that "ἀδελφός" and "one another" – i.e. the community members, are equivalent.[78] Thus we can agree with Brown when he calls "ἀδελφός", "a term of inner-Johannine affection",[79] which refers to fellow Johannine community members.[80]

So the term is not used for all Christians, but rather it is used as an insider self-designation for "those who belong" to "our group". It is particularly not to be used of the secessionists, since they "have gone out from us" but in any case they "were not of us" (1 Jn 2:19).

The usage in 3 Jn 5 is also particularly significant: "Beloved, you do faithfully whatever you do for the *brothers and sisters*, even though they are strangers to you (εἰς τοὺς ἀδελφοὺς καὶ τοῦτο ξένους); they have testified to your love before the church. You will do well to send them on in a manner worthy of God." These "brothers and sisters" are clearly unknown to the readers. They are only "brothers and sisters" because of the faith they share and because they were part of the same wider movement.[81] Clearly, ἀδελφός was a term used of a "fellow Christian" even if he or she did not belong to one's own immediate house church. Rather they were a "brother or sister", not because of personal knowledge, but because of mutual belonging to a wider group.[82] ἀδελφός then, is here a designation of a "Christian" who is part of a wider group, rather than just a term for a member of "my immediate house church". Clearly, ἀδελφός was an important "insider" self-designation in the community addressed in 1-3 Jn, which probably included a number of house churches.

Why do the Johannine Letters use the term ἀδελφός so often? We have already noted that the term is common in the Pauline tradition; in fact it is widely used throughout the NT, being found over 200 times for "coreligionists" and is used in every work except Titus and Jude.[83] Accordingly, its use in the Johannine Letters may simply be part of this wider phenomenon. However, there are factors which are more intrinsic to the Johannine writings at work here too. Firstly, the use of ἀδελφός probably

---

[78] See Brown 1982, p441. For the command to "love one another" (ἀλλήλους) see 1 Jn 3:23; 4:7, 11, 12, and for "loving the brother" see for example 1 Jn 4:20-21.

[79] See Brown 1982, p270 and on the term see p269-73. For a similar, but slightly different attitude see from Qumran 1QS 1:3-4, 9-10; CD 2:15; 6:20-21; 1 QH 14:9-11.

[80] We note then that the primary concern is love for the insider. It is because ἀδελφός has this meaning of "insider" that the author regards hating "one's brother" as a contradiction to the light (1 Jn 2:9b, 11a); see Brown 1982, p273.

[81] Note the "brothers" of 3 Jn 5 are contrasted with τῶν ἐθνικῶν (literally "the Gentiles") in 3 Jn 7.

[82] Recall here our definition of a "group" in the Introduction.

[83] See Brown 1982, p269.

reflects the love commands of John's Gospel (eg. 13:34, 15:12, 17),[84] where the command to love is expressed as loving "one another". Secondly, in the Gospel of John, ἀδελφός is generally used for physical relatives (eg. Jn 7:3) but in two instances -20:17 and 21:23, both after the resurrection - it is used for followers of Jesus. These two instances show the development of "ἀδελφός" language for "Christians". It is likely that this usage would influence readers of John's Gospel, and it is clear that we should include the readers of the Johannine Letters in this group.

Thirdly, in the Letters, "ἀδελφός" is used 5 times with ἀγαπάω, "to love," 5 times with μισέω, "to hate," and once in the expression "to lay down one's life for" (1 John 3:16). Thus, two-thirds of the significant uses of ἀδελφός in the Johannine Letters concern love or hate for one's "brother or sister",[85] with the injunctions not to hate a brother or sister serving to reinforce the importance of mutual love. We can suggest then that the use of ἀδελφός reflects the experiences of the group addressed. It seems likely that the experience of love of the brother or sister in the group addressed has reinforced and increased the use of the term "ἀδελφός". We can also note that this evidence suggests that "ἀδελφός" language points primarily to the sense of mutual belonging, rather than to a sense of equality.

4.3 "Children of God": τέκνα θεοῦ

A second candidate for a term that was used to designate other members of the group when speaking strictly within the group is τέκνα θεοῦ - "children of God". We have noted that the author uses τεκνία and παιδία to address readers directly. However, he uses the phrase τέκνα θεοῦ ("children of God") four times in 1 John in such a way as to suggest that it was a self-designation for Christians.[86]

In 1 John 3:1-2 we read: "See what love the Father has given us, that we should be called children of God (ἵνα τέκνα θεοῦ κληθῶμεν); and that is what are. The reason the world does not know us is that it did not know him. Beloved, we are children of God now (ἀγαπητοί, νῦν τέκνα θεοῦ ἐσμεν); what we will be has not yet been revealed." In 1 Jn 3:10 we read: "The children of God (τὰ τέκνα τοῦ θεοῦ) and the children of the devil are revealed

---

[84] It is very likely that the readers of 1 Jn are familiar with John's Gospel; see Brown 1982, p32-5.

[85] Brown 1982, p269. ἀδελφός is used with ἀγαπάω in 1 Jn 2:10; 3:10, 14; 4:20, 21; with μισέω in 1 Jn 2:9, 11; 3:13, 15; 4:20.

[86] 1 Jn 3:1, 2, 10; 5:2. On the background to the term see Culpepper 1980-81, p17-25. John uses the phrase "children of the devil" once (1 Jn 3:10). A similar distinction is found in Jn's Gospel which uses children of God or children of Abraham (1:12; 11:52; 8:39) with τέκνα but Jesus addresses his disciples as τεκνία or παιδία (13:33; 21:5). 2 and 3 Jn use only τέκνα, of members of the community. Jesus is of course υἱός.

in this way: all who do not do what is right are not from God, nor are those who do not love their brothers and sisters." Further in 1 Jn 5:2 we read: "By this we know that we love the children of God (τὰ τέκνα τοῦ θεοῦ), when we love God and obey his commandments." These three passages seem to indicate that "children of God" was a self-designation that was used by the group.[87] This is particularly likely, given that in 1 Jn 3:1, the author writes "See what love the Father has given us, that we should be called children of God".[88]

But why was "children of God" used as a self-designation? One reason may have been because of its use in John 1:12 and 11:52 (where τέκνα [τοῦ] θεοῦ is used).[89] But there is also a second reason that arises from the language of the Letters themselves. An emphasis found in the Letters which is related to being called "children of God" is the discussion of being "born of God".[90] This is found, for example, in 1 Jn 4:7, which reads: "Beloved, let us love one another, because love is from God; everyone who loves is born of God (ἐκ τοῦ θεοῦ γεγέννηται) and knows God." Note also 1 Jn 5:1: "Everyone who believes that Jesus is the Christ has been born of God (ἐκ τοῦ θεοῦ γεγέννηται)." Identical or similar expressions are found in 1 Jn 2:29; 3:9 (twice); 5:4 and 5:18 (once with reference to the "Christian" and once with reference to Jesus). It is clear then that members of the community regarded themselves as having been "born of God".

Although a specific self-designation does not seem to have been developed from this language or from the verb γεννάω, there does seem to have been a clear link between the concepts of being "born of God" and being a "child of God".[91] This is evident in the conjunction of both ideas in 1 Jn 3:9-10 and 5:1-2. Note the former verses: "Those who have been born of God (πᾶς ὁ γεγεννημένος ἐκ τοῦ θεοῦ) do not sin, because God's seed abides in them; they cannot sin, because they have been born of God (ὅτι ἐκ τοῦ θεοῦ γεγέννηται). The children of God (τὰ τέκνα τοῦ θεοῦ) and the children of

---

[87] Pancaro (1969-70, p127) notes it is used in the Letters of "all those who believe"; Culpepper (1980-81, p25) notes that "1 John provides some initial evidence that the Johannine community claimed the designation τέκνα θεοῦ for itself."

[88] Note that the Johannine Letters can use the opposite of this language and speak of the "children of the devil" (1 Jn 3:10) and of the one who commits sin as "of the devil" (1 Jn 3:8). For the author, it is not just being "children" that matters, but rather the question is "children of whom"?

[89] Although we should note that "children of God" is only used in these two passages in Jn's Gospel. See further Pancaro 1969-70, p126-9; Culpepper 1980-81, p26-31.

[90] On this expression see Lieu 1991, p33-8; Schnackenburg 1992, p162-9.

[91] Strecker (1996, p83) writes: "Although the notion and the concept of being 'born of God' is to be distinguished, both in terminology and in the history of tradition, from being 'children of God' (τέκνα θεοῦ) the latter spectrum of ideas can here be identified with the former (3:9-10; 5:1-2)." See also Brown 1982, p388-9; Lieu 1991, p34.

the devil are revealed in this way: all who do not do what is right are not from God, nor are those who do not love their brothers and sisters." These verses suggest that the notion of "being born of God" may have undergirded and supported the concept of being "children of God";[92] that is, the readers were children of God because they had been born of God. Thus, belief in being born of God may have facilitated the use of "children of God" as a self-designation. Certainly, the emphasis on "being born of God" in the letters reinforces the likelihood (evident from 1 Jn 3:1-2, 10 and 5:2), that "children of God" was used as a self-designation by the members of the community, since both ideas are clearly of great significance for the community.[93]

4.4 The use of other terms

τέκνα is also used in 2 Jn 1, 4, 13 as a designation of members of the local church, and in 3 Jn 4 we have the use of the term to speak of members of the community as the author's own children. For example in 2 Jn 1 we read: "The elder to the elect lady and her children (καὶ τοῖς τέκνοις αὐτῆς)". Given that "the elect lady" is almost certainly a symbolic designation for the church, her "children" are members of that church.[94] Perhaps this usage grew out of the use of "children of God" as a self-designation.

"The friends" is also a term designating other believers in 3 Jn 15: "Peace to you. The friends (οἱ φίλοι) send you their greetings. Greet the friends (τοὺς φίλους) there, each by name."[95] Although a reference to greeting friends by name is not unusual in contemporary letters, the usage found here has probably developed out the reference to "friends" in Jn 11:11 and especially 15:13-15.[96]

---

[92] While we cannot be sure which concept developed first, we note that the idea of being "children of God" is common in the OT and is found elsewhere in the NT, while the idea of being "begotten by God" is rare in the OT and limited to the Johannine literature in the NT; see Brown 1982, p384-5. This suggests that John developed the idea of being born of God to support the (much more common and already accepted) idea of being children of God. Thus, Brown (1982, p390) suggests "the Johannine writers developed the language of divine begetting to explain the origin of divine sonship/childhood."

[93] The use of the title "children of God" is in keeping with the general theocentricity of the letters; see Lieu 1981, p220-1. Note also that Christians are often said to be "of God" (ἐκ τοῦ θεοῦ; 3:10; 4:4, 6; 5:19) or "of the Father" (ἐκ τοῦ πατρός; 2:16).

[94] See Chapter 11, section 2.2. Brown (1982, p654) notes "The objection that a woman addressed in II John cannot herself represent a church and still have children who are members of that church does not respect the plasticity of symbols."

[95] Some manuscripts have altered this to ἀδελφοί, clearly on the basis of the use of this latter term in the letters.

[96] See Brown 1982, p726; cf. Rensberger 1997, p164. On "friendship" in John's Gospel see van der Watt 2000, p362-6. In general see Sandnes 1996, p95-111.

There are other terms which are used less often as self-designations. "Church" (ἐκκλησία) is used only in 3 Jn 6, 9, 10. In 2 Jn 1 we read: "The elder to the *elect* lady and her children ..." Perhaps "the elect" was another way the group could refer to itself.[97] We note that the author's opponents also receive a "label" – they are "anti-christs" (1 Jn 2:18, 22; 4:3; 2 Jn 7).

4.5 Conclusions

The two most prominent self-designations then are ἀδελφός and τέκνα θεοῦ. Again we can note that it is interesting that while "ἀδελφός" as a self-designation reflects what we might call "horizontal" identity and refers to a distinctive kind of community, by contrast, "τέκνα θεοῦ" reflects the idea that identity is related to a special "rebirth" actualized by God and relates to a particular religious experience, and so points to "vertical" identity. The two self-designations can again thus be seen to be complementary, rather than in any sense "competitors". But we also note that while "οἱ πιστοί" in the Pastorals related the "Christians" to God, and thus could be seen as vertical, it also clearly relates to a human activity. By contrast, "τέκνα θεοῦ" refers solely to a special relationship with God.

But again we need to ask, are these terms for self-designation simply the preferred terms of the author, reflecting only his perceptions? Or do we have grounds for suggesting that the Johannine Letters reflect the self-designations used by the addressees?

We have argued that τεκνία, παιδία and ἀγαπητοί indicate how the author designates other members of the group and cannot be seen as "insider language" of anyone else in the community. But with regard to ἀδελφός and τέκνα θεοῦ, it seems likely that these are self-designations that would be used by the readers. Again we can note that the whole communication strategy of the author is dependent on the readers identifying with these self-designations. For example, in 1 Jn when the author writes "See what love the Father has given *us*, that *we* should be *called* children of God" (1 Jn 3:1), if the readers do not agree that "they should be called children of God", or that "children of God" was an appropriate self-designation, then there is a considerable failure of communication on the part of the author. His whole point here turns on the reader agreeing that they can be called "children of God". This at least suggests that "children of God" was a self-designation the readers would have owned and that they would have seen themselves as caught up in the designation.

We note again the significance of the genre of the Johannine Letters. 2 and 3 Jn are genuine letters, and even though the genre of 1 John is debated, it seems

---

[97] On the terms children, fathers and young men in 1 Jn 2:13 see Chapter 11, section 2.1.

likely that its genre is closest to that of a letter.[98] Again we note that in writing a letter, we can suggest that an author would try to use terms with which readers would identify.[99] Otherwise there would be a failure of communication. We have good grounds then for suggesting that the readers of the letters would have used "brother and sister", and "children of God" as self-designations.

5. Insider terms designating members of the group in Revelation

5.1 "The saints": οἱ ἅγιοι

One of the most prominent terms designating "Christians" in the text of Revelation is "οἱ ἅγιοι", "the saints", which occurs thirteen times in all.[100] Thus for example in Rev 8:3-4 we read: "Another angel with a golden censer came and stood at the altar; he was given a great quantity of incense to offer with the prayers of all the saints (τῶν ἁγίων πάντων) on the golden altar that is before the throne. And the smoke of the incense, with the prayers of the saints (τῶν ἁγίων), rose before God from the hand of the angel."[101]

It could be argued that "the saints" here are a group of particularly pious "Christians". However, that John means to refer to all "Christians", including those who are alive on earth, with the designation "saints" is shown by Rev 13:10: "Here is a call for the endurance and faith of the saints (τῶν ἁγίων)". Rev 14:12 is very similar: "Here is a call for the endurance of the saints (τῶν ἁγίων), those who keep the commandments of God and hold fast to the faith of Jesus." In these two passages, the narrator addresses the audience directly; clearly in 14:12 he is calling *all* his readers to keep the commandments and to hold fast to the faith of Jesus; similarly he is calling all his audience to endure, and thus it is clear that he labels them all as "the saints".

Another helpful example is found in Rev 19:7-8. Here the marriage of the Lamb is spoken of; the text goes on " '... and his bride has made herself ready; to her it has been granted to be clothed with fine linen, bright and pure'—for the fine linen is the righteous deeds of the saints." Elsewhere in Rev it is clear

---

[98] On the genre of 1 Jn see Chapter 6.

[99] It is possible that an author could introduce new "self-designations" but we have noted above that we would expect this to be indicated by justification, explanation or elaboration of the self-designation by the author, none of which are found here.

[100] This term is found only once in Pastorals (1 Tim 5:10) and not at all in the Johannine Letters. In Rev it is found in 5:8; 8:3, 4; 11:18; 13:7, 10; 14:12; 16:6; 17:6; 18:20, 24; 19:8; 20:9; see also 22:11. It is used of Christ in 3:7; God in 4:8; 6:10; angels in 14:10; people in 20:6 and Jerusalem in 11:2; 21:2, 10; 22:19.

[101] The prayers of "the saints" are also mentioned in Rev 5:8.

that the bride is the church, and thus all Christians;[102] here it is clearly implied that the bride and "the saints" are synonymous. Again, then, "the saints" is a designation for all Christians.[103]

However, at times the author can speak of "the saints" alongside another group. We note the following passages. Firstly, Rev 16:6: "because they shed the blood of saints and prophets .." Secondly, Rev 17:6: "And I saw that the woman was drunk with the blood of the saints (τῶν ἁγίων) and the blood of the witnesses (τῶν μαρτύρων) to Jesus." Thirdly, Rev 18:20: "rejoice over her, O heaven, you saints and apostles and prophets! For God has given judgment for you against her." Finally, Rev 18:24: "And in you was found the blood of prophets and of saints, and of all who have been slaughtered on earth." All these passages seem to be linked, in that they describe the people of God and their suffering.[104]

In these passages, does the author speak of a small group of (particularly holy) "saints" and other small groups of "prophets" or "witnesses" or "apostles"? Given the passages discussed first of all in this section, in which we argued that "the saints" is a label for *all* "Christians", it seems more likely that in this second group of passages the author speaks of "the saints" as all Christians, but also speaks of a smaller group of leaders (that is, prophets, or witnesses, or apostles), who could be included within "the saints", but at this point in the narrative are distinguished from the mass of "saints".[105]

---

[102] See Rev 21:9, where the bride is clearly the New Jerusalem; see also Rev 22:17.

[103] McIlraith (1999, p526) notes that 19:8b helps us interpret who the wife (or Bride of 19:7) is and what the wedding garment is: "The wife [of 19:7] is identified with the 'saints,' all who respond positively to Christ and continue 'overcoming.' ... It implies that the wife is the entirety of all the redeemed." This clearly implies that "the saints" are also "all the redeemed". Other passages where all Christians are labelled as "the saints" are 13:7 and 20:9; there is a textual issue in 22:21, where some texts omit: "the saints".

[104] Note also that within this broader section of chapters 16-19 the Lamb's followers are described in 17:14 as "called and chosen and faithful" and are referred to as "my people" in 18:4 and "his servants" in 19:2, 5.

[105] This is the view of Aune; for example (1998, p886) he translates 16:6 as "because they poured out the blood of God's people and the prophets". See also Aune 1998, p937, 1007, 1010; Murphy (1998, p339) notes with regard to 16:6 that "The designation of the martyrs as 'saints and prophets' corresponds to how the seer speaks of the churches in general. The only office he mentions is that of prophet, and all Christians qualify as 'saints'." (Cf. Beale 1999, p616-17, 818 who thinks that "saints" and "prophets" are equated here and that, on the basis of 11:3-12 all Christians can be called "prophets"; see also Satake 1966, p49. However, although John affirms the prophetic witness of the church in 11:3-12, he seems to reserve the word "prophet" for particular people and nowhere uses it unambiguously of all Christians.) Perhaps the prophets, witnesses, or apostles are distinguished from the rest of "God's people" because these are the people who particularly suffer. This is supported by the theme of the rejection and death of the prophets; see Aune 1998, p886-7.

Can we discern why John's preferred title for "Christians" is "saints"? Aune suggests the term "is derived from Jewish tradition, where it can refer to both the people of God and angels".[106] But why has John chosen to use "saints" as a way of designating "Christians"? I think the designation "saints" resonated with a number of other features of John's theology.

Firstly, the most obvious reason is the influence of Dan 7 on John. The general influence of Dan 7, with its vision of the one like a Son of Man, on the author of Revelation has been clearly demonstrated.[107] A prominent dimension of Dan 7 is its use of the phrase "the saints of the Most High". Note Dan 7:18: "But the saints of the Most High (ἅγιοι ὑψίστου) shall receive the kingdom and posses the kingdom forever – forever and ever."[108] It is clear in Revelation that John has interpreted Jesus as the "one like a Son of Man" of Dan 7:13. Along with this has come the identification of "the saints of the Most High" with the people of God in Revelation.[109] This "fits" John's understanding of the present and future of the people of God, since in Dan 7 the small horn of the fourth beast makes war against "the saints" (7:21) and the saints are given into his power for three and a half "times" (7:25), but the saints are also said to receive judgment in their favour (7:22) and to gain the Kingdom (7:22, 27). Broadly speaking, this is the future John sees for God's people, and so we can understand why he calls them "saints".

A second and related point is that by using the title οἱ ἅγιοι John can underline the continuity between the "people of God" in the OT and the "new people of God" redeemed by the Lamb. Since this title is regularly associated with God's people in the OT, by using it of the "new people" John can strongly evoke this sense of continuity. Our first point and our next three points indicate why John wishes to underline *this* particular element of continuity.

A third reason why John uses the title "saints" is probably the prominence of cultic categories in Revelation. Thus, for example, the throne room vision of

---

[106] Aune 1997, p359. He refers to Ps 34:10 (MT), but goes on to note that "In early Jewish literature, 'holy ones' is often used of righteous Jews (1 Enoch 38:4, 5; 41:2; 43:4; 48:1; 50:1; 51:2; 58:3, 5; 62:8; 65:12; 99:16; 100:5; 1QM 6:6; 10:10; 12:1b; 16:10). Perhaps even more commonly, however, ἅγιοι or its equivalent is frequently used in early Jewish literature of angels".

[107] See Beale 1984a, p154-305; 1984b, p423.

[108] See also Dan 7:21-22, 25, 27.

[109] As Pattemore notes (2000, p230-1) "Whether the 'holy ones' in Daniel 7 are to be taken as human, as angelic or other heavenly beings, or as both, is a matter of ongoing discussion. But once again for our purposes here, the question is not how did the author of Daniel or his audience understand them, but how would John and his audience have done so. In Revelation ἅγιος used substantively always refers to the people of God."

Rev 4-5, shows how crucial cultic imagery is for John.[110] We may suggest that calling the people of God "saints" is another dimension of this use of cultic categories in Revelation.

Fourthly, and related to the second point, is probably the importance the author ascribes to God being "Holy". We note for example Rev 4:8: "Holy, holy, holy is the Lord God Almighty, who was and is and is to come!"[111] Pattemore describes their appeal to their sovereign as "holy" as "the grounds for their own identity as saints".[112]

Finally, we can suggest that Ex 19:6 has been influential in leading the author to describe "Christians" as "saints". Ex 19:6 has clearly been influential in Rev 1:6 and 5:10, for in these two texts John applies phrases drawn from Ex 19:6 to describe the new multi-ethnic people of God as a kingdom and priests.[113] But the LXX of Ex 19:6 also uses the phrase "a holy nation" (ἔθνος ἅγιον). Perhaps John has also been influenced to speak of the new people of God as "saints" by the description in Exodus of God's people as a "holy nation".

5.2 "Slave or servant": δοῦλος

A second label used in Revelation is δοῦλος, which is used fourteen times by John, three times literally,[114] and eleven times metaphorically. Probably on seven of these latter occasions John uses the title "slave" or "servant" (δοῦλος) for all Christians, though we will note that at times the exact referent is debatable.[115] Rev 19:5 reads: "Praise our God, all you his servants

---

[110] There are also strong cultic links for example in Rev 7:9-10 (palm branches) and note the occurrence of altars (6:9, 8:3, 5; 9:13; 11:1; 14:18; 16:7) and incense (8:3).

[111] See also Rev 6:10 - the only other passage.

[112] Pattemore 2000, p192. Note also that Rev 18:4 with its call to "Come out of her, my people" expresses the idea of "separateness" and thus of strong boundaries for God's people which is closely related to the concept of God's holiness.

[113] See Aune (1997, p47-8) for a discussion of the way John has understood the text of Ex 19:6 as referring to two distinct privileges - kingdom and priests - rather than the one privilege reflected in the MT and LXX.

[114] Rev 6:15; 13:16; 19:18.

[115] Aune (1997, p13) notes: "These metaphorical uses of δοῦλος refer to Moses (15:3), to John himself (1:1 [second time]), to prophets (10:7; 11:18), but most frequently to Christians generally (1:1 [2x]; 2:20; 7:3; 19:2, 5; 22:3, 6 ...), though at least two of the references in the last category may refer to Christian prophets (1:1 [first time]; 22:6; see Charles, 1:6), though the fact that the revelation is intended for those who hear it read aloud suggests that "servants" may rather mean *all* Christians." The term also refers to angels in 19:10 and 22:9. In the NT the term servant is used of Christians generally in 1 Cor 7:22; Gal 1:10; Eph 6:6; Col 4:12 and 1 Peter 2:16.

(πάντες οἱ δοῦλοι αὐτοῦ), all who fear him, small and great."[116] Note 22:3-4, which is part of the vision of the New Jerusalem: "Nothing accursed will be found there any more. But the throne of God and of the Lamb will be in it, and his servants (οἱ δοῦλοι αὐτοῦ) will worship him; they will see his face, and his name will be on their foreheads." In context, this passage clearly refers to all "Christians" who will worship God and the Lamb in the New Jerusalem.[117] Note also Rev 7:3: "Do not damage the earth or the sea or the trees, until we have marked the servants of our God (τοὺς δούλους τοῦ θεοῦ ἡμῶν) with a seal on their foreheads." It is most likely that this is a reference to all "Christians" still living on earth, for nothing in the context suggests to the reader that the reference should be limited in any way.[118] Rev 2:20 also seems to refer in a generic way to "Christians": "you tolerate that woman Jezebel, who calls herself a prophet and is teaching and beguiling my servants (δούλους) to practice fornication".

However, in other passages, "servant" seems to be a title given to a prophet. This is clearest in 10:7: "... as he announced to his servants the prophets (τοὺς ἑαυτοῦ δούλους τοὺς προφήτας)." Note also the related word in 22:9: "You must not do that! I am a fellow servant (σύνδουλός) with you and your brothers (ἀδελφῶν) the prophets, and with those who keep the words of this book."[119] What seems to have occurred is that "servant" has become an honorific title for those who particularly "serve" God as trusted representatives. In keeping with this, in 15:3 we read: "And they sing the song of Moses, the servant of God."[120] In some other passages it is somewhat

---

[116] There is a textual issue here, relating to whether or not καί should be in the text. The translation could be as given, or if the καί is included, it would read: "Praise our God, all you his servants, and all who fear him, small and great."

[117] Given this context, it seems likely that in 22:6 "servants" refers to all Christians ("for the Lord, the God of the spirits of the prophets, has sent his angel to show his servants what must soon take place").

[118] See Pattemore 2000, p245.

[119] Note also 19:10: "You must not do that! I am a fellow servant (σύνδουλός) with you and your brothers (ἀδελφῶν) who hold the testimony of Jesus. For the testimony of Jesus is the spirit of prophecy." Here "servant" seems to refer to a prophet. "Servant" in 11:18 may also refer to prophets. Aune (1997, p18) notes that the phrase "my/thy servants the prophets" is frequently found in the OT and occurs occasionally in the Pseudepigrapha and the Dead Sea Scrolls.

[120] Pattemore (2000, p196 n104) suggests: "The background of usage of δοῦλος in the LXX, particularly in passages describing the period of the kings and later, reflects both a broad sense in which all God's people are described as his δοῦλοι, as people who acknowledge his rule as king (e.g. 2 Chron. 6:3; Ezra 5:11; Neh. 1:6; Ps 33:23 (MT 34:22); Isa 42:19; Dan 3:26 Th.), and a narrower sense in which a prominent individual is described as δοῦλος κυρίου or δοῦλος θεοῦ (e.g. David, 2 Sam 3:18; Elijah, 1 Kgs 18:36; Moses, 2 Kgs 18:12). Where prophets are intended they are specifically mentioned as such (e.g. 2 Kgs 17:13; 21:10; Ezra 9:11; Amos 3:7; Zech 1:6). NT usage more strongly reflects the singular

problematic to ascertain the exact referent of δοῦλος.[121] But clearly John's predominant usage is that δοῦλος refers to "Christians" in general.

Why did John use the term "servants" of Christians? Like the people of God of the OT, the new people of God can be called God's "servants".[122] Thus, John is again making the continuity clearly between the people of Israel and the new multi-ethnic people of God. But why does John use this particular title of the many that applied to Israel, and not others?

Perhaps the prominence of the title "servant" should also be connected with the strong emphasis on worshipping God alone and not the beast. The slave - master relationship was an exclusive one and John may wish to emphasize that the Christian "servant" can only serve God and not the beast. As Pattemore notes the term "servants" identifies the audience as a whole "as

---

case (e.g. Rom. 1:1; Gal. 1:10; 2 Tim. 2:24) and, outside of Revelation, never refers to prophets."

[121] Note 1:1: "The revelation of Jesus Christ, which God gave him to show his servants (δούλοις) what must soon take place; he made it known by sending his angel to his servant (τῷ δούλῳ αὐτοῦ) John." Here it seems most likely that the first usage of δοῦλος refers to all "Christians", and the second gives the label of δοῦλος to John, who as a prophet is a particular type of servant. (See Pattemore 2000, p196 n104 who argues that the first occurrence refers to the whole of John's audience; see also Boring 1989 p66; Bauckham 1993, p85-86.) Note also 19:2 "for his [God's] judgements are true and just; he has judged the great whore who corrupted the earth with her fornication, and has avenged on her the blood of his servants." Here "servants" could be a label for all Christians. However, since John does not seem to anticipate that all Christians will die at the hands of Rome, it seems more likely that "his servants" is here an honorific title used, as the context suggests, of those who have been martyred. I suggest that the same usage is found in Rev 6:9-11. Rev 6:9 speaks of "the souls of those who had been slaughtered for the word of God and for the testimony they had given." In Rev 6:11 we read that these people "were each given a white robe and told to rest a little longer, until the number would be complete both of their fellow servants (οἱ σύνδουλοι αὐτῶν) and of their brothers and sisters who were soon to be killed as they themselves had been killed." In context σύνδουλος seems to refer to martyrs, but as Pattemore (2000, p196 n104) notes "the two subsequent [to 6:11] co-occurrences of σύνδουλοι and ἀδελφοί (19:10; 22:9) specifically imply that the angel shares a relationship with not only prophets, but also with all who hold the testimony of Jesus, or who obey the prophetic words of the book." But, in any case, that the term can be used particularly of martyrs does not mean that it cannot also be used of all Christians. Perhaps in these passages John wishes to connect the concepts of Christians as "servants" and their role as suffering witnesses. Finally, in 11:18 we read: "The nations raged, but your wrath has come, and the time for judging the dead, for rewarding your servants, the prophets and saints and those who fear your name, both small and great ..." Here, we can take "servants" with "prophets" ("your servants the prophets, and saints...") or with "the prophets and saints" ("your servants, namely, the prophets and the saints"); see Aune 1998, p645; cf. Beale 1999, p616-17.

[122] See for example 2 Chron. 6:3; Ezra 5:11; Neh. 1:6; Ps 33:23; Isa 42:19; 48:20; Dan 3:26 Th; Josephus, Ant. 11.90, 101; Philo, Mig. 45; cf. Mut 46. On the usage of δοῦλος in the NT see Combes 1998, p49-94.

those who owe allegiance to God as king".[123] We also note that the term "servant" is used in some passages that refer to the worship of God or refer to the sealing of the servants of God, the latter being an indication of ownership and security.[124] The term thus underlines the exclusivity of the relationship between God and God's people, which John wishes to emphasize. It also reflects the contest for ownership – God or the Beast – which we see in Revelation.

5.3 The use of other terms

We find a number of other terms used to designate "Christians" in Revelation. The term "ἀδελφός" is used five times in total. On two occasions it refers to "Christians" in general, as in 1:9 ("I John, your brother") and 12:10 ("for the accuser of our brothers (τῶν ἀδελφῶν ἡμῶν) has been thrown down"). On the other three occasions, "ἀδελφός" is used of a smaller group such as the martyrs, or the prophets.[125] The title "υἱός" is used once to refer to "Christians" in 21:7, and "children" (τὰ τέκνα αὐτῆς) is used of the followers of Jezebel in 2:23.[126] As an honorific, Antipas can be called "my witness, my faithful one (ὁ μάρτυς μου ὁ πιστός μου)" (2:13), but this does not seem to be a general label.[127]

We have a number of other collective designations used of "Christians". The name which occurs most often is "church" (ἐκκλησία) although this is only found once (in 22:16) outside of chapters 1-3.[128] Another corporate expression for "Christians" is found in 1:6: "and made us to be a kingdom, priests serving his God and Father ..."[129] Note also 5:9-10: "for you were slaughtered and by your blood you ransomed for God from every tribe and language and people and nation; you have made them to be a kingdom and priests serving our God, and they will reign on earth." (5:9-10). The designation "people" is used twice of "Christians", in Rev 18:4: "Come out of

---

[123] Pattemore 2000, p244.

[124] See 19:5; 22:3-4 (worship) and 7:3 (the sealing of "the servants of God"). That sealing indicates ownership and security is argued by Pattemore 2000, p244. The service to God which these servants perform is described in detail in 7:14-17, esp v15.

[125] For martyrs see 6:11 and prophets as "brothers" see 19:10; 22:9.

[126] See also 12:4-5 of the male child brought forth by the woman. Note the use of σπέρμα in 12:17.

[127] Compare the almost identical way Jesus is described in 1:5, 3:14; 19:11. See also 11:2: "And I will grant my two witnesses .." Compare also 17:14: "and those with him [the Lamb] are called and chosen and faithful."

[128] See 1:4, 11, 20; 2:1, 7, 8, 11, 12, 17, 18, 23, 29; 3:1, 6, 7, 13, 14, 22; 22:16.

[129] See also 1:9, which uses "kingdom". Note also 20:6 "they will be priests of God and of Christ".

her, my people (ὁ λαός μου) ...'' and 21:3: "See, the home of God is among mortals. He will dwell with them as their God; they will be his people."[130]

It is interesting to note that John has a name for a group which he opposes: the Nicolaitans (2:15).[131] Similarly, John objects to the use of the name "Jew" by people he clearly opposes in Smyrna and Philadephia. In both cases groups call themselves "Jews", but in John's view they should not use this self-designation but are rather "the synagogue of Satan" (2:9; 3:9). Clearly then "Jews" is a contested label, with John probably claiming that the Christian community is the true bearer of the title "Jew".

5.4 Conclusions

We have noted above that both the Pastorals and the Johannine Letters have a predominant horizontal and a predominant vertical self-designation – that is one that reflects the "community" dimension of the group, the other that reflects their relationship with God. It is interesting that the two terms in Rev – saints and servants – both relate to the vertical dimension. This perhaps reflects the concentration in Rev on the relationship of the readers to God, and polemic in the book against any idolatry.

But in all of this, are we seeing simply John's understanding of what Christians should call themselves? Or do we have grounds for suggesting that Revelation reflects the self-designations used by a particular community (the "John of Revelation community") or perhaps self-designations used by the various communities addressed in Asia Minor?

We have argued that the Pastorals and the Johannine Letters do reflect the terms for self-designation used by their readers. However, here we need to confront a fundamental difference between Revelation and our other documents. We have noted that the Pastorals and the Johannine Letters can best be seen as genuine letters and that the author of a letter would try to use terms with which readers would be familiar, unless there are clear indications to the contrary. But the situation is different with Revelation. Although it has features of the letter genre, it is also a prophecy and an apocalypse.[132] Further, the communication situation is somewhat different in Revelation from that which prevails in the Pastorals and the Johannine Letters. For in writing Revelation John is seeking to create and portray a different worldview

---

[130] Elsewhere it is used in the phrase "from every tribe and tongue and people and nation" (5:9; see also 7:9; 10:11; 11:9; 13:7; 14:6; 17:15.) A number of images are also used of "Christians" corporately. For example, note the "seven golden lampstands" of 1:12, which are clearly an image of the seven churches (1:20; see also 11:4). However, such imagery does not suggest any form of current self-designation.

[131] As we have seen in Chapter 7, the names "Balaam" and "Jezebel" are also nicknames developed by John, or someone else who opposed these two people and their followers.

[132] For a discussion of the genre of Revelation see Aune 1997, pp. lxx-xc.

from that which many of his readers currently hold. On the basis of this new worldview, John hopes his readers will be able to see their (real) world in a different light. He is thus attempting to shape a new imaginative world.[133] The fundamental problem for John is that his readers (or many of them) have adopted a worldview to which John is fundamentally opposed.

Hence because of the genre and the communication situation of Revelation, it is much harder to infer from the text what terms the readers themselves would have used as self-designations. Rather, the key terms of "saints" and "servants" may well have been chosen by John as part of the shaping of an alternative worldview for his readers. Thus, in John's view, readers *should* see themselves as "the holy ones" consecrated to God and "servants" dedicated to God alone, but currently some readers are involved in idolatry (2:14,20) and so are far from "holy". John also fears that some are so involved in the life of the Greco-Roman city that they need to "Come out of her, my people" (18:4) and so they are far from being "servants" dedicated exclusively to God. The readers may in due course come to see themselves in these titles (John certainly hopes so), but this may well involve a good deal of the "repentance" that John regularly calls for (see Rev 2:5; 16, 22; 3:3, 19). Certainly we cannot say that these self-designations are the readers' "self-designations of first choice". Rather, the readers may have quite different terms they would prefer and which they are currently using.

Thus, the "world-shaping" nature of Revelation means that we cannot read so easily from the text to "how it was among the readers" with regard to self-designations. Although John hopes that the readers will come to recognize themselves in the titles "saints",[134] and "servants" it is not at all clear that they will do so, or that they will all do so.

What does this mean with regard to our hypothesis that John is writing to all the Christians in Ephesus? John *could* be writing to his own group, which saw themselves as "saints" and "servants". Or John could be writing to a wide group of readers, and would not necessarily be reflecting their current self-designations, but would rather be seeking to shape their whole perception of

---

[133] This is most obvious in the repeated calls for repentance in Rev 2-3 (eg 2:5, 16; 22; 3:3, 19), but it is also clear that in Rev 4-22 John is seeking to transform the understanding of many of his readers (eg 14:12). See also Bauckham 1993, p17-22; for example p17: "Revelation provides a set of Christian counter-images which impress on its readers a different vision of the world: how it looks from the heaven to which John is caught up in chapter 4. The visual power of the book effects a kind of purging of the Christian imagination, refurbishing it with alternative visions of how the world is and will be." For the way in which John constructed an alternative view with regard to space and time, see Friesen 2001, p152-66.

[134] This is most obvious for example in Rev 5:8; 8:3-4; 13:10 (where the author addresses "the saints" directly), 14:12 (again a direct address to the saints) and 22:21, where we read "The grace of the Lord Jesus be with all the saints."

themselves and of the world, one element of which is the terms they are prepared to recognise as appropriate for themselves.

We have argued that the "world-view shaping" nature of Rev is such that we cannot go from John's preferred self-designations to that of the readers. The self-designations cannot be used as evidence for "John's own community" therefore. Again then, we have not found evidence here for a "John of Revelation community".

Further, we could well understand John using the titles "saints" and "servants" of the readers of the Pastorals and the Johannine Letters, in an attempt to "convert" their worldviews. Neither terms are prevalent in either document.[135] But by using them of these readers (and others) John would be seeking in an additional and complementary way to make his point about the "separateness" of the Christian community and the necessity of allegiance to God alone.

6. Overall Conclusions

The different labels or self-designations used by the respective authors in each document or groups of documents present an interesting window on to the theology of the documents themselves. We have also attempted to present a case for why particular labels were used, and to argue for the logical or theological connections between particular points an author makes and the terms of self-designation used. We have often been able to note a consistency between the use of a term and the wider structure of thought of an author.

With regard to terms for self-designation, it is noteworthy that our documents probably only give us "insider language", which we have suggested is language that would be used to designate other members of the group when speaking strictly within the group. It is clear, for example, that saying "I am a brother or sister" would have meant little to a "pagan" (to use another label!).[136] This probably reflects the genre of our documents – they are all written to Christian communities. Were any of the other self-designations that we have discussed used as "out-facing language", that is, terms that were used to designate members of the group when addressing outsiders, or which represented the group to the outside world? Perhaps "the believers" or "children of God" could have been used in this way eventually, but this is far

---

[135] "Saints" is used in 1 Tim 5:10, but not in the Johannine Letters. "Slave" is used literally in 1 Tim 6:1 and Tit 2:9, metaphorically of Timothy in 2 Tim 2:24 and Paul in Tit 1:1, but not in the Johannine Letters.

[136] Although we have noted above that Lucian was aware of the use of the term by Christians, but this was after the NT period.

from obvious.[137] In any case, in our documents they are used as "insider language".

We note that no one self-designation is predominant in our documents, although "brothers and sisters" comes closest to this. It is also interesting to note the plurality of terms of self-designation in each document, and across the documents. As befits a young movement, no one label or self-designation has been settled upon. We have also noted that in the Pastorals and the Johannine Letters we have one predominant "horizontal" self-designation, and one predominant "vertical" self-designation. Thus the two self-designations in each case can be seen as complementary.

In Part Three, we have been testing the hypothesis that the Pastorals and the Johannine Letters were written to different communities in Ephesus. The linguistic evidence discussed here would not, by itself, necessarily support our hypothesis that these documents are to different social communities. Clearly, different documents to the same community could use different linguistic self-designations.

But, in conjunction with all that we have discussed previously, with regard to matters like acculturation and assimilation, leadership, material possessions and so on, which are factors that more directly indicate different social communities in Ephesus, what we have discussed here with regard to self-designations reinforces the likelihood of our hypothesis. Note that we have argued that in the case of the Pastorals and the Johannine Letters we are not simply seeing the preferred terms for self-designation of the authors concerned. Rather, we have argued that the terms we have discussed would have been used for self-designation by the readers of these documents. The difference between these self-designations increases the likelihood that these documents were written to different communities in Ephesus and testifies to the differences between these communities. We can suggest that the addressees of the Pastorals and the Johannine Letters perceived their identity in somewhat different terms then. These different self-designations (particularly "the believers" and "children of God") reflect somewhat different self-images, and different ways of designating or recognizing the "specialness" or "difference" that the readers perceived to be at the heart of their movement as "Christians" – "difference" from non-Christians, but perhaps also from some other Christians. We can suggest that the readers of these documents would give different answers to the question, "What is distinctive about you?" The readers of the Pastorals might say "We are the believing ones" and might go on to talk about believing in Christ and in certain key points, which

---

[137] Barrett (1994, p556-7) notes of the early Christians that: "They might call themselves μαθηταί ... , or πιστεύοντες, or, in relation to one another, ἀδελφοί. These words were useless to outsiders unless it was made clear whose disciples they were, in whom they believed, in whose family they were brothers."

they may have wished to define credally. By contrast, the readers of the Johannine Letters may have answered the question by speaking of their relationship to God as "children of God". We see different views then about what is most significant to them.[138]

Note also, that although "brothers and sisters" is shared, "the believers" is not found in the Johannine Epistles,[139] and "children of God" is not found in the Pastorals.[140] But that "brother and sister" is shared may suggest that these communities may well not have been hostile to one another.[141] We will follow this suggestion up in Chapter 13.

What does this analysis of Rev say with regard to our hypothesis that Rev was not written to a "John of Ephesus" community, but rather to all the Christians in the city? We have argued that in Rev, John is hoping that his readers will come to see themselves in the text, and thus identify themselves as "saints" or "servants". Given the nature of Rev as a "world-shaping" document, we cannot say that the readers would currently be using these as terms for self-designation. We have not found evidence here for a John of Revelation community then. This analysis neither confirms nor denies our hypothesis therefore. But we could well understand John using the titles "saints" and "servants" of the readers of the Pastorals and the Johannine Letters, in an attempt to "convert" their worldviews.

---

[138] Note that we also see different ways of distinguishing the "other" and so of drawing boundaries. The Pastorals speak of "unbelievers" or apistoi (see 1 Tim 5:8; Tit 1:15). The Johannine Letters speak of the one who commits sin as "of the devil" (1 Jn 3:8) and of "children of the devil" (1 Jn 3:10), and of "antichrist" (1 Jn 2:18, 22; 4:3). These ways of distinguishing the "other" are clearly related to the way they distinguished themselves.

[139] In 1 Jn 1:9 we read "If we confess our sins, he who is faithful (πιστός) and just will forgive us our sins" and in 3 Jn 5 we read "Beloved, you do faithfully (πιστόν) whatever you do ..." The verb πιστεύω is used regularly in 1 Jn (note 5:1, 5, 10) reflecting its use in the Gospel of Jn, but it is never used in such a way as to suggest a self-designation.

[140] τέκνα θεοῦ is not found in the Pastorals, where τέκνον is used of literal children (eg 1 Tim 3:4), or as a metaphorical term for Timothy (eg 1 Tim 1:2). τεκνίον is not used.

[141] Although we note that we have argued that in the Johannine Letters "brother and sister" was only used of community members.

Chapter 13

The relationships between traditions and communities in Ephesus

1. Introduction

We have been suggesting that the Pastoral Epistles and the Johannine Letters were written to separate communities in Ephesus, while John did not address Revelation to a particular "John of Revelation" community, but rather wanted to address a range of Christians, including the readers of the Pastoral and the Johannine Letters. Here we will firstly discuss the relationships between the readers of the Pastorals and the Johannine letters and then will turn to the relationship between John in Revelation and the Pauline tradition.[1]

2. The relationship between the readers of the Pastorals and the Johannine letters

There are a number of possibilities with regard to the relationship between the readers of the Pastorals and the Johannine Letters. Firstly, they could be totally ignorant of each other's existence. Ephesus was after all a big city.[2] Secondly, they could be aware of each other's existence but hostile towards one another. In this case we would expect very little mutual interchange, little sharing of distinctive vocabulary, and perhaps some comment to be made explicitly about the other group in each group's documents. However, we note that there is no

---

[1] We have also discussed the evidence for other Christians groups in Ephesus – the Pastor's opponents (whom we have suggested formed a separate group), the secessionists from the Johannine community and probably the Nicolaitans. Unfortunately, because of our lack of information about these opponents, we are unable to make suggestions about the relationships between the Pastor's opponents, the Johannine secessionists, the Nicolaitans, and other groups.

[2] Schnackenburg (1991, p60) argues for the presence in Ephesus of both a Pauline and a Johannine community. He asks: "Wie ist es möglich, daß die «paulinische» Hauptgemeinde und die joh. Gemeinden keine Notiz voneinander nahmen?" He answers this in terms of small house churches in a large city; this situation suggests to him that groups could exist totally independently of each other. However, I will argue here that some contact is discernible between the two communities in the respective documents.

clear comment in each group's literature about the other group. For example, we find no clear polemic in the Johannine letters against a Pauline group.[3] Thirdly, and this is the view for which we will argue, they could be aware of each other's existence, and have what we will call "non-hostile" interactions. If this was the case, although we cannot say that relations were friendly and positive, I hope to be able to show that it is most likely that the two communities would not have been hermetically sealed off from one another, but would have had some "non-hostile" relations, although the distinctive identity of each community was also retained.[4] If the contact was sufficient then we might expect each group to adopt some of the distinctive vocabulary and ideology of the other group, since this was a period in which Christian communities in general were using and reusing a variety of traditions. One example of this is the non-hostile use of Mk by Mt and Luke when they wrote their Gospels.[5] In a similar way (if our overall hypothesis is correct), one group in Ephesus could be adopting (and perhaps adapting) the distinctive vocabulary, traditions and ideology of another group.

Accordingly in this section we will shortly be discussing possible examples of shared vocabulary and ideology between the Pastoral Epistles and the Johannine Letters. Our "working hypothesis" is that the addressees of the Pastoral Epistles and the Johannine Letters were not hostile towards one another and had at least some interactions. We will suggest below some reasons why this is likely. But we should note that sharing vocabulary does not automatically mean that the groups concerned had some positive social contact. Sharing of vocabulary between groups that were hostile towards one another is after all not impossible. But the *lack* of any shared vocabulary between the Pastoral Epistles and the Johannine Letters would certainly suggest that social contact between these Christian groups was non-existent or very limited.[6] So here we will argue for the likelihood of our hypothesis and then will attempt to discount a factor that would undermine it.

---

[3] See Schnackenburg 1991, p61.

[4] A fourth possibility is that they were not distinct communities, but perhaps sections of one wider community, or that each document was addressed to the same community. But our studies in Chapters 8-12 have attempted to show that the documents were to distinct communities, which formed distinct social entities. Of course the communities could be in different locations and show no influence on each other, or they could be in different locations and show some mutual influence through the transmission of traditions by travelling Christians. But we have attempted to show in Chapters 5 and 6 that it is most likely that the readers of both 1 and 2 Tim and 1-3 Jn are in or around Ephesus.

[5] The point of non-hostile use of one Synoptic Gospel by another Evangelist holds even if one adopts a different view of Synoptic relations.

[6] Of course shared vocabulary could also come from tradition – perhaps even tradition received in some other location.

We also need to note that it seems likely that there were a lot of traditions "in the air" in this period. To show that one group has adopted vocabulary from another requires us to show that the vocabulary was originally the exclusive preserve of the first group and that the second group could not have developed it independently. Further, we are dealing with very short texts. We should not expect to be able to show a large body of shared vocabulary therefore and perhaps even meagre results will be significant.

We should also note at this point that chronological factors are reasonably straightforward. We have suggested that the Pastorals were written between 80-100 and the Johannine Letters between 90-100, although the dating for the Johannine Letters in particular lacks a firm foundation and could be earlier. The group that became the community addressed in the Pastorals has probably been in Ephesus since the foundation of Paul's mission in the early 50s, and as we have noted a number of scholars have suggested that the Johannine group arrived in Ephesus during or shortly after the Jewish war of 66-70.[7] It seems likely then that by the time the Pastorals and the Johannine Letters were written, the respective groups of addressees could have been in contact with the other group for a significant number of years. We are justified then in asking if contact occurred between the two groups and if it left any discernible impact in the respective documents.

2.1 Examining the hypothesis that the addressees of the Pastoral Epistles and the Johannine Letters had at least some non-hostile interactions

In order to show that this, our "working hypothesis", is likely, we need to begin by discussing two factors. Firstly, that it is likely that the addressees of the Pastoral Epistles and the Johannine Letters knew of each other's existence. Secondly, that it is not likely that they would have been hostile towards one another but rather would have had at least some non-hostile interactions.

2.1.1 Why it is unlikely the author and readers of the Pastorals and the author and readers of the Johannine Letters would be totally ignorant of each other's existence

As we have noted in Chapter 6, in *The Gospels for all Christians*, Bauckham and Thompson have shown how very extensive were the contacts between early Christian groups. We note our knowledge of the extensive travels of a number of early Christian leaders, which led to different groups being aware

---

[7] We will note in Chapter 14 that Ignatius clearly thinks (at least some of) his readers revere Paul, which suggests that the Pauline group addressed in the Pastorals continued to exist after that document was written and so during the period the Johannine letters were written (if that was after the Pastorals).

of events and developments elsewhere, the frequent exchange of letters (and hence messengers) between different Christian centres, and the way in which different ideas spread from one place to another, one dimension of which is the evidence for rivalry and conflict in early Christianity.[8] Thus Bauckham suggests we should not think of early Christianity as "a scattering of relatively isolated, introverted communities, but a network of communities in constant, close communication with each other."[9]

Given this level of contact between early Christian groups it seems very unlikely that two contemporaneous communities in Ephesus would be totally unaware that there was another reasonably sizeable Christian group in the city.[10]

---

[8] See Bauckham 1998b, p30-44; Thompson 1998, p49-70 and Chapter 6 here.

[9] Bauckham 1998a, p2.

[10] Data about the number of Christians in Ephesus and elsewhere in this period is very sparse. Pliny (*Ep.* 10.96), writing in 112 CE, shows that by this time Christians were numerous in the province of Pontus and Bythinia, and that this had led to the comparative neglect of pagan cults. Given the early date at which the Gospel was first preached in Asia, we may expect that it also gained a hold there, and we have seen some indications of a sizeable community at the end of Paul's mission. Further, Verner (1982, p181) notes the indications of the size and diversity of the community addressed in the Pastorals: "There were three [we would argue for two] classifications of major offices in the church. One group at least among the officers received financial compensation for their work. There was also an office of widows. Either directly or indirectly through its individual members the church was supporting what was, one gains the impression, a large group of widows. Thus the financial resources of this Christian community must have been considerable. Although the leadership tended to be drawn from among older adults, both young men and young women were probably present in the church in significant numbers. At any rate there were enough young widows among the membership that the leadership was becoming uneasy about their presence and their activities, if the author's attitude may be taken as characteristic. Finally the size of the membership is suggested by the possibility that it may have been large enough that it met for worship in several different groups in the same city." Note Verner (1983, p167) takes 1 Tim 2:8 as evidence that the author thinks of the addressees in Ephesus as worshipping in a number of different locations in smaller groups. Hence he speaks (1983, p181) of "this rather large and diverse Christian community". Data for the size of the Johannine community addressed in 1-3 Jn is lacking, but it clearly consisted of some house churches, some of which were in outlying areas. Ignatius speaks of his addressees in Ephesus as πολυπλήθεια - great in quantity or number (see IgnEph 1.3; cf. 2 Macc 8:16). Robinson (1988, p120) has suggested that in Ephesus by 100 CE there could have been dozens or even scores of house churches of around 30 people each. This is only a guess, but it may well be realistic. Muddiman (2001, p45) suggests at the end of the first century there may have been around 500 Christians in Ephesus, in a dozen or so house churches. Günther (1995, p26-7) estimates there were 2000 Christians in Ephesus at the end of the second century and notes how sparse our data is for the earlier period. See also Countryman (1980, p169) who suggests that at the end of the first century the church at Rome was around 1,000 members. Aune (1997, p164) estimates that at the end of the first century there were fifty thousand Christians in total; cf. Aune 1997, p131 where he gives Reicke's estimate of eighty thousand for Asia, which is also accepted by Elliot 2000, p89. See Mitchell 1993, 2, p36-7, 62-3 for references to discussions of the number of

But if the two groups were aware of each other's existence, given the documents we have, can we suggest what relationships between them might have been like?

2.2.2 Why it is likely that relations between the readers of the Pastorals and the readers of the Johannine Letters would not be hostile

We have noted in Chapters 5 and 6 that both the Pastorals and the Johannine Letters were written with "opponents" in view, and accordingly in the Pastorals the author sought to draw boundary lines around the group and in the case of 1 Jn, we noted that a group had already left the community addressed and showed what the basis for their departure had been. We thus see lines of exclusion emerging in both cases. For the Pastor, the crucial matters concerned eschatology, asceticism, the Law and behaviour. We have suggested that the Pastor's opponents had an over-realised eschatology and so thought the resurrection had already arrived, that they practised asceticism, maintained the validity of part of the Jewish Law and that their behaviour led to adverse comment from outsiders. For 1 John, the crucial matter was the christology of the secessionists, and we have suggested that they so emphasised the divinity of Christ that they marginalised his humanity.

It is noteworthy that neither group would have regarded the other in the same way as they saw their "opponents". Neither group would have failed the particular "litmus tests" that the other group had used with regard to their "opponents" and which their respective opponents had failed, leading to their exclusion (or departure in the case of the secessionists). Or to use a different metaphor, the two communities are drawing the "faultlines" in different places. In fact, the views or behaviour for which they excluded their opponents were quite different from the views or behaviour displayed by the other group.

Each group would also rate well on some of the key factors behind these exclusionary principles. For example, it seems unlikely that the Johannine community followed the Law in the way the Pastor takes exception to, and we have no evidence that they were ascetic. Further, the readers of the Pastorals certainly seemed to "love one another" (for example, some widows) with their material possessions and their Christology gave some place to the humanity of Christ (eg. 1 Tim 2:5; 3:16; 6:13).[11]

Christians in later periods. The discussion of numbers in Stark 1996, p3-27 is too general to be of assistance here. For further discussion see Meggitt 1998, p121 n227; Hopkins 1998, p185-226.

[11] The eschatology of 1 Jn, which has a future dimension (eg 1 Jn 2:28; 3:2-3; 4:17-18), is also different from the eschatology of the Pastor's opponents; on eschatology in 1 Jn see Brown 1982, p27-8, 99-100; Lieu 1991, p87-90.

Now clearly there are very significant differences between these two group; we have noted very different attitudes to the wider world, different group structures and concepts of authority, different self-designations and so on. It is these differences which have led us to suggest that they are different groups and that the "merger" thesis is invalid, and so that the Johannine Letters are not addressed to the readers of the Pastorals.

But it is significant that, while the two groups would have clearly had significant arguments about matters on which they were quite different (such as the relationship with the world,[12] and group structure and authority), neither group would have immediately excluded the other on the basis of their established "litmus tests". We can suggest too that they might have found that they had significant underlying similarities and commonalities. We cannot be certain of these because of the uncertainty as to whether, for example, the Christology espoused by the respective authors was actually shared by their communities, but it seems likely that they might have discovered that they shared a good deal in common. We certainly cannot say that they would have refused contact with each other at first sight because the other group contravened some clear principle. We can suggest then that social and theological relationships between the readers of the Pastorals and of the Johannine Letters would not have been hostile.

2.3 The evidence of vocabulary

We turn now to seek to discount a negative argument. As noted above, the *lack* of any shared vocabulary between the Pastoral Epistles and the Johannine Letters would suggest that social contact between these Christian groups was non-existent or very limited. Here we will seek to show that there was some influence from one community to the other with regard to vocabulary, and so we are seeking to discount a factor that would undermine our hypothesis. Further, although linguistic contact does not prove that there was social contact, given the two factors we have just raised which argue that each group was aware of the existence of the other and that there were "non-hostile" relations between them, we can raise the possibility that there was some (positive) social contact. We will firstly discuss influences on the Pastorals and then will turn to the Johannine Letters.

---

[12] But note that 3 Jn 5-8 speaks of mission in a way of which the Pastor might have approved.

2.3.1 Influences on the Pastoral Epistles

The Pastorals are influenced by and utilise a range of Christian traditions.[13] It is clear that the Pastor utilises Pauline tradition extensively, although on occasions this has been modified or translated into different language.[14] Further, traditions found in the Synoptics are also very important for the Pastor. For example, 1 Tim 1:15 echoes Lk 19:10 and 1 Tim 2:6 is based on Mk 10:45, which is also echoed in Tit 2:14. In these cases, the Pastor uses traditional Christological material which is found in the Synoptic gospels.[15] Further, we note the evidence for linguistic and other connections between Luke-Acts and the Pastorals; although I am not convinced that Luke wrote the Pastorals, this evidence shows the considerable similarities between the two works. At the very least, it shows that some traditions which are found in Luke-Acts were also known to the Pastor.[16]

But in this section our particular interest is in the relationship between the Pastorals and the Johannine Letters. We are not presupposing that John's Gospel and the Johannine Letters have necessarily been written by the time the Pastorals were written, although this may well have been the case. Rather, we are interested in whether there were oral (or perhaps some written) traditions

---

[13] General Christian tradition, including perhaps creeds or preaching formulas, is found in 1 Tim 1:15-16; 2:3-6; 3:16; 2 Tim 1:9-10; 2:8-13; Tit 2:11-14; 3:5-7. In Chapter 8 we have noted briefly that the Pastorals are also influenced by Jewish thought and have shown that they use language and concepts which are thoroughly at home in the Greco-Roman world.

[14] Note for example 2 Tim 2:11; cf. Rom 6:8. Marshall (1993, p12-24) argues that the Pastorals are a faithful and creative application of Pauline theology to a new and specific situation. Note also Marshall's comment (1988, p167) on the relationship between the Pastorals and Paul with regard to Christology: "The Pastor is not making use of the Pauline epistles in his christology, although he does use traditions which were also used by Paul and he can be said himself to stand close to Paul in his general outlook."

[15] See Marshall 1988, p164-7; see also Stettler 1998, p322-5. Note also that 1 Tim 5:18 uses a Q tradition in its Lucan form; see Lk 10:7; cf. Mt 10:10; 1 Tim 6:19 echoes Jesus' teaching in Mt 6:19-21; Mk 10:21 and parallels. We note that these three synoptic passages are not echoed by Paul. But note that, rather than being woodenly repeated, traditions are often reshaped creatively by the Pastor in the light of the current situation. Marshall (1993, p18) writes: "It is notable that the traditional material is generally not betrayed as such by a distinctive vocabulary and syntax which would indicate that the writer was quoting material which he himself had not composed. On the contrary, it is significant that time and again the traditional material is couched in the typical vocabulary and style of the Pastoral Epistles and that it applies very directly to the situation which is being addressed." An example is 1 Tim 2:4-6, which is clearly based on tradition (Mk 10:45) but elaborated and expanded so it bears specifically on the theme of salvation for all, which is appropriate to the context. The same tradition is developed in Tit 2:14 to suit the context of godly living expressed in good works. This approach to tradition by the Pastor also makes our task of discerning Johannine traditions in the Pastorals more complex.

[16] See Wilson 1979; see also Price 1997, pxx-xxix.

that influenced the Pastor and are (perhaps) later found in the Johannine Gospel and Letters.

2.3.2 The influence of the Fourth Gospel and the Johannine Letters on the Pastorals

Here we need to recall our position with regard to John's Gospel. We have argued that the Gospel was written in Ephesus, but, following Bauckham et al, that we cannot use it to determine the history of the community to which the Gospel was addressed, since we think that the Gospel was not written for a specific community. We are not disputing that the author of John's Gospel was part of a particular community; we simply do not think we can read from the Gospel to the life of that community, since the author had the needs and interests of all (or most) Christians in mind when he wrote (and may have been influenced by the experiences of several early Christian communities). However, we have argued that the author of the Fourth Gospel also wrote 1-3 Jn. This means that the language of John's Gospel can be used here, since the Gospel gives further evidence of the "linguistic world" of the author of 1-3 Jn.[17] Hence we will use both John's Gospel and the Johannine Letters when it comes to attempting to determine any relationship between the Johannine literature and the Pastorals.[18]

Hanna Stettler has recently proposed that the influence of the Johannine literature on the Pastorals can be observed at the linguistic and thematic level on a number of occasions.[19] I regard the following examples as convincing.

2.3.2.1 The good confession before Pilate (1 Tim 6:13-14)

In 1 Tim 6:13-14 we read: "In the presence of God, who gives life to all things, and of Christ Jesus, who in his testimony (τοῦ μαρτυρήσαντος) before[20] Pontius Pilate made the good confession (τὴν καλὴν ὁμολογίαν), I charge you to keep the commandment ..." Stettler notes that in 1 Tim 6:13 the author diverges from the Synoptic tradition and that it is likely that the Pastor is here influenced by Jn 18:36-7.[21] In Jn 18:36-7, after Jesus has given an

---

[17] Even if one holds that different authors wrote the Gospel and 1-3 Jn, then clearly their linguistic worlds are closely connected.

[18] We are not then using the Gospel as evidence for a "Johannine community". Rather we are using the Gospel (and 1-3 Jn) as evidence when looking for linguistic connections between its author and traditions found in the Pastorals.

[19] See Stettler 1998, p325-8.

[20] Marshall 1999, p663 argues that ἐπί must mean "in the presence of" not "in the time of" because the court context is so strong here; see also Turner 1927, p270-3.

[21] Stettler 1998, p327.

initial reply to Pilate's question "Are you the King of the Jews", and then Pilate has commented and asked Jesus "What have you done", we read:

"Jesus answered, 'My kingdom is not from this world. If my kingdom were from this world, my followers would be fighting to keep me from being handed over to the Jews. But as it is, my kingdom is not from here.' Pilate asked him, 'So you are a king?' Jesus answered, 'You say that I am a king. For this I was born, and for this I came into the world, to testify to the truth (ἵνα μαρτυρήσω τῇ αληθείᾳ). Everyone who belongs to the truth listens to my voice.'"

Although the linguistic connection is purely with the verb μαρτυρέω, it is straight forward to see how what Jesus says in Jn 18:36-7 can be regarded as "the good confession" in 1 Tim 6:13. Further, contrast Jn 18:36-7 with the Synoptic accounts. Mk 15:2-5 reads:

"Pilate asked him, 'Are you the King of the Jews?' He answered him, 'You say so.' Then the chief priests accused him of many things. Pilate asked him again, 'Have you no answer? See how many charges they bring against you.' But Jesus made no further reply, so that Pilate was amazed."

No additional conversation takes place between Jesus and Pilate in Mark. Further, the accounts in Mt 27:11-14 and Lk 23:1-5 are in agreement with Mark with respect to Jesus saying only one thing to Pilate, along the lines of "You have said so". It certainly seems unlikely that one could deduce from the accounts in the Synoptics, or from the traditions that were later written in the Synoptics, that Jesus could be said to have "made the good confession" before Pilate. It is *only* in John's version of the interrogation before Pilate that Jesus can be said to have done this.[22] Further in 1 Tim 6:12, the "good confession" of Jesus is put in parallel by the Pastor with the "good confession" of Timothy.[23] When speaking of the latter, it seems most likely that the Pastor has more in mind than Jesus' "You have said so" in the Synoptics, and so it must be Jn 18:36-7 that he has in mind.[24] Here then is a clear example of the

---

[22] Note also the very strong emphasis in John's Gospel on witness in conjunction with Jesus, on which see for example Jn 5:31-9; 8:13-18; see also Harvey 1976. 1 Tim 6:12 may also reflect this wider Johannine theme.

[23] Marshall (1999, p663) writes: "The phrase draws a parallel between Jesus appearing before a hostile ruler and Timothy (and Paul) bearing witness before hostile people inside and outside the church." Note also the use of ὁμολογέω in 1 Tim 6:12 and the related noun ὁμολογία twice in 1 Tim 6:12-13. The verb is used in Jn 1:20; 9:22; 12:42; 1 Jn 1:9; 4:2, 3, 15; 2 Jn 7, but in Paul only in Rom 10:9-10. The noun is only found in Paul in 2 Cor 9:13.

[24] Marshall (1999, p662-3) notes "The sense is presumably that Jesus made 'the good confession' in that he held fast to his self-testimony as Messiah and Son of man despite the risk entailed ..; to be sure, if we are to think of a testimony 'before Pontius Pilate', then it is the acknowledgment by Jesus that he was 'the king of the Jews' (Mk 15:2 ..). ... Another possibility is that the witness of Jesus to the truth (Jn 18.33-37) is in mind. ... In any case, it is the faithfulness of Jesus which is stressed rather than the precise content of what he said." But

influence of a Johannine tradition on 1 Tim.[25] Some dependence of the Pastor on the tradition found in John's Gospel seems most likely then.[26]

2.3.2.2 μένειν ἐν (1 Tim 2:15; 2 Tim 3:14)

Stettler notes the use of μένειν ἐν in the sense of "festhalten an" (to hold on to) in 1 Tim 2:15 and 2 Tim 3:14 and suggests a connection with Johannine usage.[27] In 1 Tim 2:15 we read "Yet she will be saved through childbearing, provided they continue in faith and love and holiness (ἐὰν μείνωσιν ἐν τίστει καὶ ἀγάπῃ καὶ ἀγιασμῷ) with modesty." In 2 Tim 3:14 we read "But as for you, continue in what you have learned (σὺ δὲ μένε ἐν οἷς ἔμαθες) and firmly believed, knowing from whom you learned it, .."[28] The expression μένειν ἐν does not occur in Paul, and according to BDAG, μένω is only found with the sense "of someone who does not leave a certain realm or sphere: remain, continue, abide",[29] in our two passages from the Pastorals and in Jn and 1-3 Jn.[30]

We can be more specific about Johannine usage. As Brown notes, μένειν ἐν is very common in the Johannine literature, being used 19 times explicitly or implicitly in the Gospel, 22 times in 1 Jn and twice in 2 Jn.[31] The phrase μένειν ἐν is often used of the believer's relationship with Jesus or with God.[32] However, there are noteworthy Johannine parallels to our two passages from the Pastorals. In 1 Tim 2:15 we have the idea of abiding in faith, love and holiness. This is paralleled by Jn 15:9,10 ("abide in my love ... just as I have

---

as we have noted, in Mk (and Mt and Lk) Jesus does not really "hold fast to his self-testimony" since he simply says "You have said so" – which, while not denying what Pilate said, is hard to sum up as a "good confession". The Pastor can really only have Jn in mind.

[25] It could be that John and the Pastor are independently drawing on a common tradition here. But it is noteworthy that it is a common tradition that no one else in the NT has had access to, which suggests that its source is a collection of traditions about Jesus, that is, Johannine tradition.

[26] Stettler 1998, p327.

[27] Stettler 1998, p326.

[28] The verb is used in two other places in the Pastorals with a different sense. In 2 Tim 2:13 we read: "he remains faithful (ἐκεῖνος πιστὸς μένει)" (for μένω with an adjective see 1 Cor 7:11; Acts 27:41; Jn 12:24). In 2 Tim 4:20 we read: "Erastus remained in Corinth (ἔμεινεν ἐν Κορίνθω)".

[29] See BDAG, p631, 1aβ.

[30] On abiding in 1 Jn see Lieu 1991, p41-5; on this concept in the LXX see Malatesta 1978, p58-64.

[31] Brown 1982, p259-60. He divides the occurrences up into the categories of "indwelling pertinent to God", "indwelling of other realities in the Christian" and "miscellaneous theological uses".

[32] See for example Jn 6:56; 15:4-7; 1 Jn 2:6, 24 (relationship with Jesus); 1 Jn 2:24 (relationship with God).

kept my Father's commandments and abide in his love") and 1 Jn 4:16 ("those who abide in love abide in God").[33]

In 2 Tim 3:14 we have the concept of abiding in "what you have learned", that is, in teaching or tradition. This is paralleled by Jn 8:31 ("If you abide in my word ...") and by 2 Jn 9a, 9b ("Everyone who does not abide in the teaching of Christ (μὴ μένων ἐν τῇ διδαχῇ τοῦ Χριστοῦ), but goes beyond it, does not have God; whoever abides in the teaching (ὁ μένων ἐν τῇ διδαχῇ) has both the Father and the Son").[34] We also find the related but somewhat different concept of "the word" or "truth" abiding in a person on a number of occasions in the Johannine Literature.[35] Lieu notes that "abiding in teaching", as we find it in 2 Jn 9, is "a very different concept",[36] from abiding in a person. What we see in 2 Jn 9 concerns "the steadfast maintenance of unity with the teaching or tradition received",[37] rather than "going beyond" it into a different theological position. This is precisely the idea in 2 Tim 3:14. Certainly the links between 2 Jn 9 and 2 Tim 3:14 are strong. We can fully concur with Marshall then when he comments that the use of μένω in 2 Tim 3:14 "is characteristic of Johannine expression".[38]

In these cases we could be seeing the independent development of language to emphasise tradition, a concept which is clearly important in both sets of documents. But that in two passages the Pastorals make this emphasis by using language which is new in the Pauline tradition, and which is identical to an established Johannine usage which is not found elsewhere in the NT, does strongly suggest that the Pastorals have here been influenced by distinctive Johannine vocabulary.

---

[33] Note also 1 Jn 3:17 ("How does God's love abide in anyone ..."): cf. 1 Jn 3:14 (one without love abides in death); 1 Jn 2:10 (abides in light).

[34] Note that 1 Jn 2:27 ends with "μένετε ἐν αὐτῷ", which could be translated "abide in it" (rather than "abide in him"), which would refer to abiding in the anointing (cf. Brown 1982, p361); we have noted in Chapter 10 that the anointing could be through the word of God, or the teaching which is heard. This would then be another example of the use of μένω which is comparable to 2 Tim 3:14.

[35] See Jn 15:7b ("If you abide in me, and my words abide in you ..."); Jn 5:38 ("you do not have his word abiding in you ..."); 1 Jn 2:14 ("the word of God abides in you"); 2:24 ("Let what you heard from the beginning abide in you"); 2 Jn 2 ("because of the truth that abides in us ..."). See also 1 Jn 2:27 ("the anointing that you received from him abides in you ..."); 3:9 ("God's seed abides in them ..").

[36] Lieu 1986, p93.

[37] Lieu 1986, p94. Lieu (1986, p94 n114) notes that Conzelmann (see 1954, p201) "labels 1 John a 'Johannine Pastoral' because of its interest in tradition, but 2 John has a better claim to the title".

[38] Marshall 1999, p787.

2.3.2.3 Cases of possible influence of the Johannine literature on the Pastorals

There are a two other instances where it is probable or possible that there has been influence from the Johannine literature on the Pastorals. We will deal with these more briefly.

Firstly, in 1 Tim 1:15 we read: "Christ Jesus came into the world (ἦλθεν εἰς τὸν κόσμον) to save sinners". We note the parallels with John here (see Jn 1:9; 3:19; 6:14; 9:39; 11:27; 12:46; 16:28). It is noteworthy that one parallel is Jn 18:37, which we have already argued has influenced 1 Tim 6:13. Jn 18:37 reads: "For this I was born, and for this I came into the world (ἐλήλυθα εἰς τὸν κόσμον), to testify to the truth."[39] Thus, as Knight notes with regard to ἦλθεν εἰς τὸν κόσμον, "the expression (especially in application to Jesus) is not distinctly Pauline but is particularly Johannine".[40]

Although there are Synoptic parallels such as Lk 19:10 ("For the Son of Man came to seek out and to save the lost")[41] the concept of Jesus "coming into the world" is only found in the Johannine writings. It is possible that the Pastor (or the tradition he has utilised, since this is a "faithful saying") has developed the expression "coming into the world" from the Synoptic sayings, independent of Johannine influence.[42] This is possible because of the connection in Lk 19:10 and Mk 2:17 between Jesus coming and his activity of saving or calling sinners, which is said to be the purpose of Jesus' "coming into the world" in 1 Tim 1:15. But given that none of the Synoptic passages speak of Jesus "coming into the world", which is found only in John, where it occurs regularly, and that we have already noted two instances where a strong case can be made for Johannine influence on the Pastorals, it seems that Johannine influence is very likely here, even if there has also been influence from the Synoptic tradition.[43]

Secondly, Barrett notes that in 2 Tim 1:14 the Spirit is said to assist in guarding the Gospel. He writes: "It is noteworthy that when he [the Pastor] does mention the Holy Spirit it is as an agent who preserves tradition"[44] and compares this with John 16:14f. We note also the activity of the Paraclete in Jn

---

[39] Linguistically, Jn 9:39 is closer: "εἰς τὸν κόσμον τοῦτον ἦλθεν".

[40] Knight 1992, p101. εἰς τὸν κόσμον εἰσῆλθεν is found in Rom 5:12, but with reference to sin. Mounce (2000, p57) notes: ἦλθεν εἰς τὸν κόσμον "is language reminiscent of the Fourth Gospel ... as it joins the incarnation and redemption." Marshall (1999, p398) writes: "The resemblance to Johannine phraseology should be noted, but most commentators give it little weight." One commentator in the latter category is Roloff 1988, p90-1.

[41] See also Mt 9:13; Mk 2:17; Lk 5:32.

[42] This seems to be Knight's (1992, p102) view when he writes: "Paul quotes this brief objective statement based on Jesus' self-testimony". See also, for example, Brox 1969, p111, who sees Lk 19:10 as the source of 1 Tim 1:15.

[43] Stettler suggests (1998, p326) with regard to 1 Tim 1:15: "kann man kaum umhin, auch hier johanneischen Einfluß anzunehmen ...".

[44] Barrett 1963, p98.

14:26 of teaching believers "everything", and that the Paraclete will "remind you of all that I have said to you". The Spirit is not said in the Pauline epistles to have a role in guarding the tradition. This parallel is noteworthy, and may be an independent development in the Pastorals, or may show the influence of Johannine thinking about the Spirit on the Pastor.[45]

---

[45] There are also a number of more dubious examples:

1) In 1 Tim 5:10, one of the requirements for a woman who is to be enrolled in the widows' order is that she must have "washed the feet of the saints (εἰ ἁγίων πόδας ἔνιψεν)". "Saints" here is a reference to Christians in general (see Marshall 1999, p595, against the interpretation of Wagener 1994, p188f). The action is probably to be associated with hospitality, since the reference occurs between notes which concern caring actions for the needy. As Marshall (1999, p597) notes "it is not an activity especially ascribed to widows, since the verse deals with their life before being enrolled as widows (and therefore possibly while their husbands were still alive)." It is not said to be a mutual action, so a cultic or symbolic act is probably not in view here. This reference to foot-washing could clearly be a reference to John 13 and Barrett (1963, p76) suggests "The allusion here makes it very probable that the author either had read John 13:14, or had heard some oral tradition to the same effect." Foot washing may have been practised in the Johannine community, but there is no certain evidence for it elsewhere before the time of Augustine and Ambrose (see Fee 1988a, p125). However, washing of feet is widely attested as a menial act and a symbol of humble service (Marshall 1999, p596 n73 lists Gen 18:4; 19:2; 43:24; 1 Sam 25:41; Josephus Ant 6.308; Herodotus 6.19; Plutarch, Pomp. 73.7; Jn 13:5f, 8-10, 12, 14; cf Lk 7.44). Note also that ἅγιοι as a word to describe Christians is particularly associated with Paul (eg Rom 8:27; 12:13; 1 Cor 6:1; Phil 1:1) and Rev (eg. Rev 5:8; 8:3; 11:2) and is not used in John's Gospel or Letters with this sense.

2) In 1 Tim 6:13-14 we read: "I charge you to keep the commandment (τηρῆσαί σε τὴν ἐντολήν) without spot or blame ..." Stettler (1998, p325) notes that the request to τηρεῖν the ἐντολήν "sounds Johannine". She notes ἐντολή in the singular is found in a number of Johannine passages (Jn 10:18; 12:49f; 13:34; 15:12; 1 Jn 2:7-8; 3:23; 4:21; 2 Jn 4:5-6) and comparable expressions, which also use τηρεῖν and ἐντολή are found in Jn 14:15; 15:10; 1 Jn 2:3-4; 3:22, 24; 5:3; Rev 12:17; 14:12. Apart from the Johannine writings, this combination of τηρεῖν and ἐντολή is only found in Mt 19:17, and it is not found again in the Pastorals, although she notes that 1 Cor 7:19 is comparable. This is a possible example of Johannine influence, but given that 1 Cor 7:19 (τήρησις ἐντολῶν Θεοῦ) is similar, and that the expression is found elsewhere in Mt 19:17 (τήρησον τὰς ἐντολάς) and that both τηρεῖν and ἐντολή are very common in the NT, we cannot be certain that the Pastor is dependent on Johannine tradition here.

3) In Tit 3:5 we read: "he saved us ... through the water of rebirth and renewal (διὰ λουτροῦ παλιγγεννεσίας καὶ ἀνακαινώσεως) by the Holy Spirit". παλιγγεννεσία is only found here and in Mt 19:28 where it has the sense of the renewal of the world in the Messianic age. Stettler (1998, p328) suggests that in Tit 3:5 παλιγγεννεσία probably picks up language from Jn 3:3-8; 1 Jn 2:29; 3:9; 4:7; 5:1, 4, 18 with regard to being born from above, of God, of the Spirit and so on. However, its usage in Tit 3:5 can be adequately accounted for on the basis of early Christian language associated with baptism and conversion and/or by its frequency in philosophical writings and common language of the day; see Marshall 1999, p319-20; Mounce 2000, p449. Thus note the careful statements of Dunn 1970, p169 and Barrett 1985, p87-8 about possible links between Jn and the Pastorals here.

2.3.2.4 Conclusion

Thus we have two examples which can be best explained as the influence of Johannine tradition on the Pastorals. In addition, we have two other cases where influence is possible. This certainly does not mean that there *must* have been social contact between the author and community of the Pastorals and the author and/or the community of the Johannine Letters. After all, we have noted that Synoptic tradition is utilised in the Pastorals, and I am not suggesting that there was somehow social contact between the author of the Pastorals and the authors of Mt, Mk and Lk! So that the influence of Johannine literature can be detected in the Pastorals does not necessarily mean actual contact with "Johannine tradition bearers". Further, we do not know what early Christian traditions were "in the air" in Ephesus at this time, or where such traditions came from. Traditions found in the Pastorals could after all have come in a number of ways, even through the travels of one person. But that we have discerned this influence means we have removed a possible argument against our theory of non-hostile social relations. We will now look at influence in the other direction – from the Pastorals and the Pauline tradition on the Johannine Letters and will then draw conclusions from the instances of influence that we have detected.

---

4) Stettler (1998, p326) suggests there may be a distant parallel between ἔργον πονηρόν in 2 Tim 4:18 and the Johannine usage of the expression in Jn 3:19 ("and people loved darkness rather than light because their deeds were evil (πονηρὰ τὰ ἔργα)"); 1 Jn 3:12b; 2 Jn 11; cf 3 Jn 10. The phrase only occurs in these passages in the NT, apart from one passage (Col 1:21) where the sense is different (cf also Hermas Vis 3.7.6; 3.8.4; Vis 1.22.4b). It is possible then that there is some Johannine influence here, but as Marshall (1999, p825) notes: "The language may possibly echo that of the Lord's Prayer".

Stettler also suggests other examples which we think are unlikely. For example, in 2 Tim 1:10 we read of Jesus: "who abolished death and brought life and immortality to light (φωτίσαντος δὲ ζωὴν καὶ ἀφθαρσίαν) through the gospel". Stettler (1998, p325) suggests that the imagery of light used in connection with "life" is otherwise found above all in the Johannine writings, such as Jn 1:9 and so suggests this is another linguistic connection between the Pastorals and the Johannine literature. However, as Marshall (1999, p708) notes "ζωή" is "a thematic word for salvation in the PE" where it is regularly used (see 1 Tim 1:16; 4:8; 6:12, 19; 2 Tim 1:1, 10; Tit 1:2; 3:7), which means its occurrence here may simply be because it is a favourite of the Pastor. Further, the verb φωτίζω is also found elsewhere (for example in Eph 1:18; 3:9; cf 1 Cor 4:5) so we cannot say that 2 Tim 1:10 is directly influenced by Jn, although it is possible. Further, φωτίζω is only found in Johannine Literature in Jn 1:9.

2.4 Influences on the Johannine Letters

2.4.1 Links between the Johannine letters and John's Gospel and other New Testament traditions

As we have noted in Chapter 6, the Johannine Letters share with John's Gospel a significant range of vocabulary and expressions and exhibit a common fund of theological ideas, although there are some differences between the Gospel and Letters.[46] It is clear then that the most significant "influence" on the Johannine Letters is John's Gospel, or the traditions which came to be written in that Gospel. Further, although we will note some interesting features of the language of 2 and 3 Jn in particular below, there are many links between 2 and 3 Jn on the one hand and the Gospel and 1 John on the other, so there is no doubt that 2 and 3 Jn are clearly "Johannine".[47]

We also need to note that while there are parallels between 1 Jn and the rest of NT,[48] they are at the general level of theological ideas, rather than clear

---

[46] See for example Brown 1982, p20-8; Schnackenburg 1992, p34-9; Edwards 1996, p50-3.

[47] Note the following examples of links between 2 Jn and the Johannine tradition. Firstly, the echo of Jn 10:18 in 2 Jn 4; see Lieu 1986, p72, who thinks "the echo may be a conscious appeal to the authoritative language of the Gospel". Secondly, 2 Jn 4-6 with discussion of "the command" is clearly Johannine, even if there has been development from the Gospel in what is said. Thirdly, in 2 Jn 12 we read that the elder wishes to visit the addressees "that our joy may be fulfilled". This reflects Jn 15:11; 16:24; 17:13 and 1 Jn 1:4; see further in Lieu 1986, p99. Fourthly, "to have God" in 2 Jn 9 is a clear echo of 1 Jn 2:22-23; see also 5:12. Note the following examples of 3 John's strong links with the Johannine tradition. Firstly, with regard to the expression, "whom I love in truth" in 3 Jn 1, Lieu (1986, p102) writes that the phrase "probably here also expresses not sincere affection so much as a relationship determined by membership of the Johannine circle for which 'truth' was a characterising term." Secondly, note that in 3 Jn 3-6 we have "truth" and "love" used in parallel; Lieu (1986, p104) notes: "The parallel linking of 'truth' and 'love' recalls the way they are brought together at the close of the greetings of 2 John; they are the cardinal and characteristic virtues of Johannine Christianity. ... It is important that, despite the high proportion of non-Johannine vocabulary we shall find in 3 John, Gaius's integrity is being measured by Johannine standards." Thirdly, 3 Jn 11-12 with its antithetical style is reminiscent of 1 Jn 3:6-10. Lieu (1986, p116) notes: "In both [passages] the antithesis explores the relationship between behaviour ('doing') and being 'of God' or seeing 'him'; since being 'of God' is a typically Johannine idiom with no precise parallel in other New Testament writings the link between the two passages appears particularly strong." However, she also notes some significant points of difference between the two passages.

[48] Piper (1947, p437-51) has argued that there are many parallels to 1 Jn's credal statements, theological axioms and moral commandments in the rest of the NT, but that these parallels "differ in their verbal expression in a such a way as to make literary dependence highly improbable" (p440). Note for example the similarity between 1 Jn 3:16 and Mk 10:45 (= Mt 20:28) and Rom 5:8; 1 Jn 4:2-3 and 1 Cor 12:3. But in none of these cases is influence from another text on 1 Jn clear. See further Dodd 1937, p142-8; 1946, pxxviii-xlii; Rensberger 1997, p21. The view that 1 Jn seems closer to "primitive preaching" (Smith 1991, p12) than

instances of the influence of particular passages or traditions on 1 Jn. Thus for example, in 1 Jn 4:9 we read: "God sent his only Son into the world" (and see also 4:10, 14). This has parallels in Gal 4:4; Rom 8:3; Mk 9:37, but rather than this being an example of the influence of these texts, it is much more likely that 1 Jn here shows its affinity with John's Gospel, where the expression is very common (eg. Jn 3:17; 5:36, 38; 6:57; 17:18). Further although 1 Jn reflects some sayings of Jesus, we cannot conclude that the author of 1 Jn knows any of the Synoptic gospels or actual oral sayings in their Synoptic forms.[49]

Brown, following Boismard, has also shown the similarities between 1 Jn 2:28-3:11; 1 Pet 1:3-5, 13-15, 18-23 and 2:9; and Tit 2:11-14; 3:4-7. Similarities consist in concepts such as the revelation or appearance of Christ, being begotten anew or regeneration by God, the love of God, hope, that the Christian is to be pure, and taking away sins. Although it is possible that 1 Jn drew from 1 Peter, Brown notes that the similarities consist of ideas rather than wording.[50] Brown suggests: "the similarities between the two works are neither accidental nor the result of direct copying but are best explained if these works (and Titus as well) represent exhortations drawn from a common body of ideas. The most plausible locus for such a body of ideas would be the process of entrance into the Christian community. ... [that is] conversion/ initiation/ baptism. While the Johannine theological proclamation had its peculiarities, it shared many features with other Christian baptismal proclamations, whence the parallels just discussed."[51] Thus these similarities can be explained by both documents incorporating similar oral traditions or drawing from "a common body of ideas" (perhaps relating to baptism), rather than the direct influence of one text or tradition on another.

---

the Gospel of John (eg. with regard to the atonement and eschatology) has been based at least in part on the recognition of the presence of these credal statements and elements from general Christian tradition in 1 Jn.

[49] Dodd (1946, pxxxviii-xlii) has shown that there are resemblances between Synoptic passages and 1 Jn (note Mk 12:29-31 and 1 Jn 4:21; Mt 7:21 and 1 Jn 2:17; Mt 24:11 and 1 Jn 4:1; Mt 7:7-8, Mk 11:24 and 1 Jn 3:22). But it seems likely, as Dodd suggests (1946, pxli) that 1 Jn is drawing on "a body of traditional Sayings of Jesus similar to that which we have in the Synoptic Gospels" rather than on a particular written gospel, or a singular tradition that was later written down in a particular gospel. An interesting example here is σκάνδαλον in 1 Jn 2:10: "Whoever loves a brother or sister lives in the light, and in such a person there is no cause for stumbling (σκάνδαλον ἐν αὐτῷ οὐκ ἔστιν)." σκάνδαλον is only found here in the Johannine literature, and it is found in Mt 13:41; 16:23; 18:7 for example; in this regard Dodd (1946, pxli) thinks its appearance in 1 Jn is a "reminiscence" of Synoptic tradition. However, the term is found in Lev 19:14, and the verb is found in Jn 6:61 and 16:1; see Brown 1982, p274. The influence of either Lev or Jn seems more likely than Mt, or Matthean traditions therefore.

[50] Brown 1982, p432. See Boismard 1956, p200-4 on 1 Jn.

[51] Brown 1982, p432-4.

Thus we can see some openness in 1 Jn to other Christian traditions and ideas which has resulted in some commonalities and parallels with a range of NT documents. However, this can be explained by general oral traditions of Jesus' sayings and similar sources, rather than by the influence of particular NT documents on 1 Jn.

2.4.2 The influence of the Pastorals and the Pauline tradition on the Johannine Letters

In this section we will seek to show that, rather than simply the parallels between documents we noted in the previous section, there has also been some influence from Pauline texts on the Johannine Letters. We note firstly, that we cannot detect any clear examples of the direct influence of Pauline texts on 1 Jn.[52] However, I will seek to show that there are some clear examples of Pauline vocabulary in 2 and 3 John.

2.4.2.1 The greetings in 2 John

The greeting in 2 Jn 3 reads "Grace, mercy, and peace will be with us from God the Father and from Jesus Christ the Son of the Father, in truth and love (ἔσται μεθ᾽ ἡμῶν χάρις ἔλεος εἰρήνη παρὰ Θεοῦ πατρὸς καὶ παρὰ Ἰησοῦ Χριστου τοῦ υἱοῦ τοῦ πατρὸς ἐν ἀληθείᾳ καὶ ἀγάπῃ)." The majority of Greek letters of the period begin with "A to B greetings (χαίρειν)."[53] Paul probably developed the use of "grace (χάρις)" in the letter opening of Christian letters, although there are some similar pre-Christian examples.[54] But Paul's way of beginning the letter with the "grace" formula seems to have influenced other New Testament letters which contain greetings, since apart from 3 Jn and James, they contain very similar formulae.[55] Thus the opening of 2 John follows the precedent of most other NT letters.

The standard Pauline greeting is χάρις ὑμῖν καὶ εἰρήνη ἀπό Θεοῦ πατρὸς ἡμῶν καὶ κυρίου Ἰησοῦ Χριστοῦ.[56] Influence from a form of the Pauline formula in 2 Jn 3 seems clear. "Grace" is rare in the Johannine

---

[52] One possible example relating to 1 Jn 5:4 and the use of πίστις in the Pauline corpus will be discussed below.

[53] The standard salutation of "χαίρειν" is found in Jas 1:1; Acts 15:23; 23:26.

[54] See Lieu 1986, p45. As we will note in more detail below, the "grace and peace" formula has parallels (although they are not verbally identical) in 2 Apoc Bar 78.2 and LXX Esth 9.30; see Aune 1997, p29.

[55] See Lieu 1986, p46. Note for example 1 Pet 1:1; 2 Pet 1:1; Rev 1:4.

[56] It is found in Rom 1:7; 1 Cor 1:3; 2 Cor 1:2; Gal 1:3; Eph 1:2; Phil 1:2; 2 Thess 1:2 (note variant); Phlm 3 (Col 1:2 lacks "and Jesus Christ our Lord"; 1 Thess 1:1 has simply χάρις ὑμῖν καὶ εἰρήνη).

literature, and the phrase "Θεοῦ πατρὸς" in 2 Jn 3 is not Johannine.[57] Thus, as Lieu notes with regard to 2 Jn 3: "Dependence on the Pauline-type greeting is obvious".[58]

However, we can be more specific than this. "Mercy" is added to the standard Pauline formula in the greeting in 1 Tim 1:2 and 2 Tim 1:2, which are identical and both read: χάρις ἔλεος εἰρήνη ἀπὸ Θεοῦ πατρὸς καὶ Χριστοῦ Ἰησοῦ τοῦ κυρίου ἡμῶν.[59] Only the greetings in 2 Jn 3, 1 Tim 1:2 and 2 Tim 1:2 add "ἔλεος", which occurs only in 2 Jn 3 in the Johannine literature (ἐλεέω is not used at all), to the "grace and peace" greeting and thus read χάρις ἔλεος εἰρήνη.[60] Further 2 Jn 3, 1 Tim 1:2 and 2 Tim 1:2 all omit *both* ὑμῖν and καὶ after χάρις and replace the two words with ἔλεος *and* describe God simply as "Father" (as does Tit 1:3) rather than as "our Father" which is found a number of times in Paul.[61] We have noted that the resultant "Θεοῦ πατρὸς" in 2 Jn 3 is not Johannine. This number of clear connections between the three passages suggests that while 2 Jn 3 shows the influence of the Pauline tradition, the contact has been between 2 Jn and 1 and 2 Tim in particular, rather than between 2 Jn and the general Pauline tradition.[62]

However, as Lieu notes, the author of 2 John has made (what we suggest is) the greeting of the Pastorals his own by adding the Johannine "in truth and love", the replacement of ἀπό found in the Pauline greetings with παρά which is common in John (and is repeated here before υἱός), the omission of κύριος with reference to Jesus and its replacement by the unique phrase "Son

---

[57] χάρις is only found in Jn 1:14-17 (three times), in 2 Jn 3 and as a variant reading in 3 Jn 4. While God as Father is found in Jn, the phrase Θεὸς πατήρ is not used at all.

[58] Lieu 1986, p47. Funk (1967, p430) also notes with regard to the greeting formula in 2 and 3 Jn: "Since the Pauline structure, so far as is now known, is a unique development in the history of the letter, it is possible that the author has been influenced by Paul or the Christian letter tradition stemming from him." But we can be more specific than this, as we will show in the text.

[59] Note that Tit 1:4 is almost identical but lacks ἔλεος. For discussion of the addition of ἔλεος in 1 and 2 Tim see Marshall 1999, p357-8; Mounce 2000, p8-12. It is common in the LXX and occurs in the Pauline benediction in Gal 6:6 and in Jewish usage in 2 Apoc Bar 78:2. Wis 3:9 and 4:15 use χάρις καὶ ἔλεος. Note that ἔλεος is stressed in 2 Tim 1:16, 18 (and Tit 3:5, but then why was it omitted in the greeting there?) and ἐλεέω is used in 1 Tim 1:13, 16, so the reason for the addition may be the theology of 1 and 2 Tim. ἔλεος is also found in Jude 2.

[60] Note that Jude 2 reads: ἔλεος ὑμῖν καὶ εἰρήνη καὶ ἀγάπη πληθυνθείη which seems to be independent of either 2 Jn or 1 and 2 Tim. The series χάρις ἔλεος εἰρήνη is not found in the LXX; χάρις καὶ ἔλεος occurs in Wis 3:9; 4:15.

[61] See also Lieu 1986, p47 n43. Note "our Father" is not Johannine. For "our Father" in Paul see for example, Rom 1:7; 1 Cor 1:3; 2 Cor 1:2; Gal 1:4; Phil 1:2.

[62] Lieu (1986, p47) notes the linguistic evidence and goes on "more particularly, the addition of 'mercy' (also not Johannine) and the description of God as 'the Father' rather than 'our Father' parallel the development of the formula in the Pastoral Epistles." But dependence on the Pastorals seems more likely.

of the Father",[63] and in the confident statement that grace, mercy and peace "will be with us". This last phrase is to be contrasted with the Pauline greetings (also found in the Pastorals) which contain an expression of hope rather than the certainty of 2 Jn 3. This certainty in 2 Jn 3 is in keeping with 2 Jn 2 ("because of the truth that abides in us and will be with us for ever") and with the author's desire to give assurance to his readers.[64]

So we may suggest that we see a modified form of a Pauline formula in 1 and 2 Tim and that we see significant features of that modified form of 1 and 2 Tim in 2 Jn, although with alterations by which the elder has made it his own.[65] The evidence seems strong enough to suggest dependence of some form on 1 and 2 Tim (or on the traditions written there) by 2 Jn; it seems very unlikely that the significant and verbally identical modifications of the standard Pauline formula we find in 1 and 2 Tim on the one hand and 2 Jn on the other have come about independently.

How would such dependence of 2 Jn on 1 and 2 Tim have come about? Here we are clearly in the realm of speculation. But 2 Jn could have consciously copied 1 and 2 Tim – indeed literary dependence seems possible. Or it could be that this form of greeting was also used in worship among the addressees of the Pastorals, where it had become standardised, and that the author of 2 Jn (or someone known to him) heard it and adopted it.[66]

2.4.2.2 Mission language in 3 Jn and the Pauline tradition

There is further evidence of the influence of Pauline texts on 3 Jn. In 3 Jn 6-8 we read: "You will do well to send them [the brothers and sisters] on in a manner worthy of God (οὓς καλῶς ποιήσεις προπέμψας ἀξίως τοῦ Θεοῦ); for they have set out for the sake of the name, accepting no support from non-believers. Therefore we ought to support such people, so that we

---

[63] See Lieu 1986, p47, 79. "Truth" and "love" are found together in 2 Jn 1 and 3 Jn 1, and are of course both very common in Johannine literature. παρά is used 33 times in Jn, not at all in 1 Jn. Lieu also notes (1986, p70 n60): "The omission of the Pauline 'Lord' (κύριος) before Jesus Christ and the stress on him as Son of the Father is characteristic of Johannine thought".

[64] See Brown 1982, p659, 681-2. Note his comment (p682): "An author faithful to the Johannine tradition might well be uncomfortable with the usual Christian epistolary wish that the addressee receive grace, mercy, and peace; for Johannine Christians should already possess these gifts." Other features of the opening, such as "all who know the truth" and "because of the truth that abides in us" are also distinctively Johannine; see Lieu 1986, p68-70.

[65] Thus Hutaff (1994, p424) notes with regard to 2 Jn 3: "This verse is a Johannine version of the greeting in 1 Tim 1:2 and 2 Tim 1:2".

[66] It could be that the elder is consciously trying to appeal to the readers of the Pastorals with this phrase, but we would need further evidence of the language of the Pastorals in 2 Jn to support this, and such evidence is lacking.

may become co-workers with the truth (ἵνα συνεργοὶ γινώμεθα τῇ ἀληθείᾳ)."

The verb προπέμπω can mean to conduct or escort someone to a destination, a sense it has in Acts 20:28 and 21:5. However, it also "acquired a technical meaning in missionary contexts of patronage or financial sponsorship for the journey, a meaning it does not have in its non-biblical background."[67] Given that the elder goes on to speak of "supporting" these people in 3 Jn 8, this is clearly the intended meaning here. Apart from in 3 Jn 8, προπέμπω is found with this meaning in Acts 15:3; Rom 15:24; 1 Cor 16:6, 11; 2 Cor 1:16; Tit 3:13; Polycarp, Phil 1.1.[68] It is noteworthy then that it is predominantly used with this sense in Pauline writings.

Further, συνεργός - co-worker, or fellow-worker - is used in 3 Jn 8: if we support these travelling missionaries, we will "become co-workers with the truth". Apart from its occurrence here, the term is exclusively found in Pauline writings.[69] Co-workers were a very important part of Paul's missionary team, and in Chapter 2 we noted the number of co-workers present in the original Pauline mission in Ephesus, although the actual term συνεργός is not used in regard to that mission. But it is noteworthy that συνεργός is a Pauline term.

Also of interest here is the use of ἀξίως "worthy" in 3 Jn 6. This is only found elsewhere in the NT in Paul.[70] Further, note the significant parallels in 1 Thess 2:11-12 and Col 1:10. In 1 Thess 2:11-12 we read "As you know, we dealt with each of you like a father with his children, urging and encouraging you and pleading that you should lead a life worthy of God (ἀξίως τοῦ Θεοῦ)." Brown notes that this is "an impressive parallel since in III John 4 the Presbyter has rejoiced that his 'children are walking in the truth' and now he is urging such a child to help others on the journey 'in a way worthy of God'."[71] The parallel with Col 1:10 is also noteworthy.[72]

Further, the whole thrust of 3 Jn on missionary work, and the support of travelling missionaries and missionary activity, is somewhat unexpected in

---

[67] Lieu 1986, p106; see also Hutaff 1994, p409.

[68] BDAG also note that it has this sense in 1 Macc 12:4; 1 Esdr 4:47; Ep Arist 172.

[69] See Rom 16:3, 9, 21; 1 Cor 3:9; 2 Cor 1:24; 8:23; Phil 2:25; 4:3; Col 4:11; 1 Thess 3:2; Philm 1, 24. It is not found in the Apostolic Fathers. Note that in Paul συνεργός is used with the genitive and not the dative of person or thing as it is here in 3 John and some classical authors; see Lieu 1986, p107 n141, p109 n150. See also de la Potterie 1959, p286, who sees the construction as Jewish; cf. Clem Hom XVII.9; See also Hall 1973-74, p119-20.

[70] See Rom 16:2; Eph 4:1; Phil 1:27; Col 1:10; 1 Thess 2:12. The related ἄξιος is more frequent (Mt, Lk, Acts, Paul, Heb, Rev) but is only found in Johannine literature in Jn 1:27.

[71] Brown 1982, p711.

[72] With regard to the parallels in Paul's writings, Lieu (1986, p107) thinks that "the frequency of the phrase 'worthily of God' (ἀξίως τοῦ θεοῦ) in non-biblical Greek makes this of less significance." See also Deissmann 1909, p248. However, the parallels in 1 Thess 2:11-12 and Col 1:10 are very noteworthy, particularly given the other connections with Pauline writings.

one of the Johannine Letters. Although there is a good deal of interest in mission in Jn's Gospel,[73] given the attitude to "the world" (see Chapter 8) and the apparent complete lack of interest in mission in 1 Jn, the topic of missionary work is a surprising one in 3 Jn.[74] Perhaps in 3 Jn it is purely a reaction to 2 Jn, which seems to suggest that the secessionists have sent out "missionaries" in support of their message, about whom the elder warns in his letter.[75] But even if this is the case, this new topic is discussed in 3 Jn using some significant Pauline language. Thus Lieu comments with regard to 3 Jn 3-8: "We have in this section a catena of words and phrases otherwise foreign to the Johannine corpus, often having more in common with the Pauline writings".[76]

We conclude that this language certainly suggests some influence from the Pauline sphere. And, as with 2 Jn 3, it is a cumulative case - προπέμπω, συνεργός, and perhaps to a lesser extent ἀξίως are to be associated with Paul. Furthermore, these words are used in the service of a discussion about missionaries, a topic we would not have expected given the attitude of 1 Jn to "the world".

Since we have already discerned contact between 2 Jn 3 and the Pastorals, it is not unreasonable to suggest that there is also contact here between 3 Jn and the Pauline tradition. Was this contact with the more general Pauline tradition mediated by the community addressed by the Pastorals, since they had a concern for mission?[77] This may well be the case. But there is other noteworthy language in 1 and 3 Jn in this regard.

2.4.2.3 Tentative evidence for the influence of non-Johannine traditions in 1 Jn and 3 Jn

The following are examples in which there may have been influence on 3 Jn from beyond the Johannine sphere.[78] Firstly, in 3 Jn 11 we read: "Beloved, do

---

[73] See Okure 1988.

[74] See Lieu 1986, p106-7. One interesting example in this regard is ἐξέρχεσθαι used in 3 Jn 7 of the travelling missionaries: "for they have set out for the sake of the name (ὑπὲρ γὰρ τοῦ ὀνόματος ἐξῆλθον) ..." Lieu (1986, p107) notes that "In 1 and 2 John 'to go out' (ἐξέρχεσθαι) is used only of the antichrists and the use of this 'mission' terminology of them may reflect the ambivalence of those letters towards missionary work." (The verb is found in 1 Jn 2:19; 4:1; 2 Jn 7 and extensively in the NT.) Yet in 3 Jn 7, the verb is clearly used by the elder of missionary work.

[75] But note also that 1 Jn 4:5 suggests that the secessionists have had some success in "the world", for "the world listens to them".

[76] Lieu 1986, p109; see also Rensberger 1997, p160.

[77] See Chapter 8.

[78] Earlier in section 2.4.1 we discussed parallels between 1 Jn and the rest of the NT at the general level of ideas, rather than instances of the influence of particular texts on 1 Jn (which is very difficult to detect). Here we are discussing influence from particular *texts* on 3 Jn.

not imitate (μὴ μιμοῦ) what is evil but imitate what is good." Neither the verb μιμέομαι nor the related μιμητής (imitator) are found elsewhere in the Johannine literature. However, μιμέομαι is found in 2 Thess 3:7, 9 and Heb 13:7 while μιμητής is found in 1 Cor 4:16; 11:1; Eph 5:1; 1 Thess 1:6; 2:14; Heb 6:12. We see then that here we have a non-Johannine word that is found in Pauline literature, but also in Hebrews.[79]

Secondly, in 3 Jn 6 we read that the brothers and sisters "have testified to your love before the church (ενώπιον ἐκκλησίας)". The word "ἐκκλησία" is found three times in 3 Jn: of the elder's community (v6) and twice of the "ἐκκλησία" dominated by Diotrephes (v9-10). However, ἐκκλησία does not occur at all in John's Gospel or in 1 and 2 Jn; it is used in Mt (3), Acts (23), Pauline writings (59, including Eph, excluding the Pastorals), Pastorals (3), Hebrews (2), James (1) and Revelation (20). Hence it is a word which 3 Jn shares with much of the rest of the NT, but which is not found elsewhere in the Johannine literature. While its absence in Jn's Gospel is understandable in the light of its absence from Mk and Lk,[80] that it is absent in the Gospel and in 1-2 Jn but present in 3 Jn can be seen as part of the wider phenomenon of new and different language usage in 3 Jn.

Thirdly, in 3 Jn 11 we read "Beloved, do no imitate what is evil but imitate what is good (Ἀγαπητέ, μὴ μιμοῦ τὸ κακὸν ἀλλὰ τὸ ἀγαθόν). Whoever does good is from God; whoever does evil has not seen God (ὁ ἀγαθοποιῶν ἐκ τοῦ Θεοῦ ἐστιν· ὁ κακοποιῶν οὐχ ἑώρακεν τὸν Θεόν)." This language of "doing good" and "doing evil" is again non-Johannine. "Good" (ἀγαθός) occurs here in 3 Jn 11, in Jn's Gp only in Jn 1:46; 5:29; 7:12 and is not found in 1 and 2 Jn. "Evil" (κακός) occurs here in 3 Jn 11 in the Gp only in Jn 18:23, 30 and again not in 1 and 2 Jn. The compound verbs used here in 3 Jn 11 are not found in the rest of the Johannine corpus, which speak rather of "doing the truth", "walking in the light", "loving one another" and in 1 Jn 3:6-10, "doing righteousness".[81] Lieu notes with regard to ἀγαθοποιέω: "Reflecting its use in the Septuagint meaning 'to show favour to' or 'to benefit', it is used in Mark and Luke, but it is only in 1 Peter and the Apostolic Fathers that it comes to gain the more explicit sense of 'doing what is morally right' and to be seen as a necessary qualification for Christians."[82] This is the sense it has in 3 Jn 11, with "to do evil" being used for the opposite of "to do good". Lieu notes "It would seem that although 3 John can use Johannine terminology and

---

[79] See Lieu 1986, p117.

[80] See Brown (1982, p709-10) who does not consider that its use in 3 Jn is part of a wider phenomenon of the use of different language in 3 Jn.

[81] See Lieu 1986, p116-17.

[82] Lieu 1986, p117. See Mk 3:4; Lk 6:9, 33, 35; in LXX Num 10:32; Jud 17:13; Zeph 1:12. "To do right" is the meaning in 1 Pet 2:15, 20; 3:6, 17; (cf. 4:19); 2 Clem 10:2; Hermas Vis III.4.5; 9.5; Sim IX.18.1; Ep. Diognetus 5:16.

values, these are being combined with language from the developing ethical terminology of non-Johannine Christianity".[83]

Fourthly, within the Johannine literature, the predominant usage of the πιστ- word group is with πιστεύω, which is used 98 times in the Gospel of Jn and nine times in 1 Jn. By contrast, πίστις is *only* found in the Johannine corpus in 1 Jn 5:4: "And this is the victory that conquers the world, our faith (ἡ πίστις ἡμῶν)." Thus, Hutaff calls πίστις here "a notably un-Johannine noun".[84] Further, contrast 1 Jn 5:4 with Jn 16:33, where Jesus says: "In the world you face persecution. But take courage; I have conquered the world!'". Here it is Jesus who conquers the world; in 1 Jn 5:4 this is said of "our faith".

Further, note the use of πιστός in 3 Jn 5, where we read, "Beloved, you do faithfully (πιστὸν ποιεῖς) whatever you do for the friends, even though they are strangers to you". Apart from this passage, πιστός is used in the Johannine literature only in Jn 20:27 and 1 Jn 1:9. Although this small usage in other Johannine works may have led to the use of πιστός in 3 Jn 5, Lieu notes with regard to this verse: "The phrase itself is unusual with no obvious parallels, but most probably it reflects the common use of 'πιστός' as an attribute or epithet of Christians, believing and faithful. Here the neuter adjective is being used adverbially and means to act as a believer should – a non-Johannine equivalent for 'walking in truth'."[85] Further, we note that the most "common use of 'πιστός' as an attribute or epithet of Christians" is in the Pastorals; see 1 Tim 1:12; 3:11; 4:3, 10; 5:16; 6:2; 2 Tim 2:2, 13; Tit 1:6, 9. However, πιστός is used as an epithet for "faithful" Christians in passages like Acts 10:45; 16:1 1 Pet 5:12; Rev 2:13; 17:14; cf. Heb 3:2.[86] And we recall the significance of πίστις and πιστός in Paul and especially in the Pastorals.[87] We can only wonder if the reason for the use of these two terms in 1 Jn and 3 Jn, when they are either very rare or not used elsewhere in the Johannine Letters, is because of the significant use of these terms in the Pastorals? Or is it because they were becoming more common in general Christian language? But of course their use in 1 and 3 Jn could be explained as "natural developments" from the stress on πιστεύω in Jn's Gospel and 1 Jn.

Now perhaps each of these four cases are debatable: are we seeing here simply a development of new language by a creative author (drawing perhaps on Christian tradition known to him, or on the LXX), or are we seeing the influence of wider Christian traditions?[88] But our case is cumulative (and we

---

[83] Lieu 1986, p117.

[84] Hutaff 1994, p421. πίστις is common in the Synoptics, Acts, Paul, Heb, James, 1 and 2 Peter, Jude, Rev.

[85] Lieu 1986, p105-6.

[86] Passages like Mt 25:21, 23; Lk 12:42 are less explicit in this regard.

[87] See Chapter 12.

[88] There are some examples in 2 and 3 Jn where there *may* be influence from beyond the Johannine sphere, but where we cannot be confident that this is the case. Some examples will

must not forget that we are dealing with very short letters and so cannot expect vast amounts of evidence). It seems unlikely that the greetings in 2 Jn, the missionary language in 3 Jn and these less certain examples in 1 and 3 Jn can *all* be seen as "indigenous" developments by a creative author. It seems more likely that the greetings in 2 Jn and the missionary language in 3 Jn reflect influence from Pauline texts, and thus show the author was open to wider influences. Having gained this perspective on the documents, we can suggest that the four probable examples of non-Johannine influence in 1 and 3 Jn do show the influence of wider Christian traditions.

We also recall that in Chapter 8 we discussed the greater openness in 3 Jn to "the world", reflected for example in the conventional "health wish" in 3 Jn 2, the expression of joy in 3 Jn 3 ("ἐχάρην λίαν") and the idiom καλῶς ποιήσεις in 3 Jn 6. We suggest that in 3 Jn the elder is more open to the outside world *and* to wider Christian language.[89]

2.4.2.4 Conclusions

This evidence – both of Christian influence and influence from the wider world – suggests that to some extent "the shutters have opened" in 3 Jn and we have some fresh linguistic air being breathed. What is the significance of this? We have noted that 2 and 3 Jn are clearly "Johannine", and show that some key Johannine concepts remain alive and well; but what we see here is the marriage of the old (Johannine) concepts with some new-to-the-community ideas – Pauline and others. It seems that in 3 Jn there is an adoption not just of the language of Paul, but more generally of other Christians too, as well as language from the wider world. This evidence thus suggests an openness to the wider Christian sphere, and to the wider world, and a willingness to adopt ideas and language from those wider spheres. One feature of these wider

---

suffice. Firstly, in 2 Jn 1 the elder addresses his recipients as "the elect lady and her children" and in 2 Jn 13 we have "the children of your elect sister send you their greetings". ἐκλεκτός is only found in Jn 1:34 in the Gp of Jesus in a variant reading, although the verb ἐκλεγομαι "to choose" is used in Jn 6:70; 13:18; 15:16, 19 emphasising Jesus' choice of the disciples. Thus ἐκλεκτός in 2 Jn 1 could have developed out of the usage of the Gp. However, ἐκλεκτός is used 24 times in the NT, often for Christians (eg 2 Tim 2:10; Tit 1:1; 1 Peter 1:1; 2:4, 9) and the use in 2 Jn 1 and 13 could reflect this developing trend with regard to the word in the NT, and thus usage in the wider Christian sphere. Secondly, "walking in truth", which is peculiar to 2 Jn 4 and 3 Jn 3-4 in the Johannine literature, is similar to the figurative use of "walking" for a manner of life found in Paul (eg Rom 6:4; 2 Cor 4:2). This contrasts with Jn and 1 Jn which speak of "doing the truth" or "being of the truth" and use the image of walking for "walking in the light"; see further Lieu 1986, p71. Thirdly, the language in 2 Jn 8-9 is rare in the Johannine writings, particularly "working" (ἐργάζεσθαι), "reward" (μισθός) and "losing" (ἀπολλύναι), but we cannot say that there must be influence from beyond the Johannine literature; see Lieu 1986, p88; Rensberger 1997, p154.

[89] See also Lieu 1986, p123.

spheres is the Pauline sphere, and we can suggest that this influence has come from the most available source – the Ephesian community of the Pastorals.[90]

This evidence contributes to our argument here by removing a potential objection to it. Recall that the *lack* of any shared vocabulary between the Pastoral Epistles and the Johannine Letters would place a question mark against our view that there were non-hostile social relations between the readers of the Pastorals and the Johannine Letters. We have rather discovered probable linguistic influence in both directions: the likely influence of the Johannine tradition on the Pastorals and the likely influence of the Pastorals and the Pauline tradition on 2 and 3 Jn. This linguistic evidence removes a potential question mark against our view, although as we have noted the presence of such shared vocabulary does not of itself prove such non-hostile social contact.

It may be helpful to outline our overall argument here. It seems very likely that the community of the Pastorals and of the Johannine Letters are in the same city of Ephesus. We have suggested from other evidence that these are two distinct communities, rather than that the different documents are addressed to the same community over time. Is it likely that these two communities had any social contact? Evidence of linguistic contact is not the basis for our claim of non-hostile social contact – that suggestion comes from other factors such as proximity in time and place, the likelihood of mutual knowledge, and that neither community would have failed the "litmus tests" of the other community and so they had no clear reason to see each other negatively. Rather, as we have noted above, the linguistic evidence is marshalled here in an attempt to remove a counter argument to our hypothesis of non-hostile relations between the two groups. Thus, I am not suggesting social contact on the basis of linguistic contact alone.

Further, we have observed positive evidence in 2 and 3 Jn of an openness to other Christian (including Pauline) language and to the wider world in 3 Jn. This suggests that such an author would be open to non-hostile relations with another local Christian community, and to this extent provides positive evidence for our hypothesis. This language also shows that the community of readers of 2 and 3 Jn were not hermetically sealed against all other Christians.

We can suggest the differences with regard to openness to influence from the wider Christian sphere that we have observed between 1 Jn and 2-3 Jn,

---

[90] Is it possible that Gaius or Diotrephes are in the Pauline tradition, and so the elder picks up their language in 3 Jn? This is unlikely. Gaius seems to be one of the elder's "children" (v4) and the elder uses much Johannine language of him (eg "whom I love in the truth" (v1); see Lieu 1986, p102) so it is not likely that he is in the Pauline tradition. If Diotrephes was in that tradition, why would the elder use Pauline language here since he is not writing to Diotrephes, but only about him? Further, the elder uses Pauline language of his own activity of mission, not with regard to what Diotrephes has done. So this is an unlikely explanation.

which we think were written by the same author, are attributable to the different audience of these letters and to their different genres. As we have noted before, 1 Jn seems to be written to the grouping of house churches to which the author belongs, whereas 2 and 3 Jn are to house churches at a distance. Further, probably because of the different reasons the respective letters were written, their genres are somewhat different. Although 1 Jn is clearly to a specific group (see 1 Jn 2:19), it has tract-like qualities, whereas 2 and 3 Jn are clearly straight-forward letters. Perhaps in 1 Jn, because of both of these points, the author has used "in-house" language more[91] (although we have discussed an openness in 1 Jn to some other Christian traditions, but not at the linguistic level), since he is writing a "tract" to his own group; in 2-3 Jn he reflects the fact that he and his wider audience (which is still part of the Johannine movement) are aware of wider and more varied Christian language. These different audiences and the distinctions in genre thus help to explain the differences with regard to language that we have observed.

3. Influences on Revelation

We have argued that in Rev John is addressing quite a broad group of readers including the readers of the Pastorals and the Johannine Letters, but is anticipating a hostile reaction from some. In this situation, what might we expect with regard to vocabulary? Would we expect him to adopt some of the linguistic world of at least some of his readers?

John is of course influenced himself by Johannine language to some extent, as we will show below. We should also note that Vos has argued that John shows knowledge of a number of sayings of Jesus that are now found in the Synoptic Gospels.[92] Clearly, then John does know and use a variety of Christian traditions. But is he influenced by Pauline language? We will shortly consider this question.

---

[91] Recall our discussion of this in Chapter 8.

[92] See Vos 1965. Note for example, Rev 3:5c in relation to Mt 10:32 and Lk 12:8 (Vos 1965, p85-94); Rev 13:10 in relation to Mt 26:52b (Vos 1965, p104-109). See also Aune 1990, p194; Bauckham 1993c, p92-117; Ellis 1999, p226-8. Ellis notes (1999, p227-8): "That John knew a number of preformed Synoptic traditions is not improbable but, if so, he used them much in the same way that he used the books of the 'Old Testament' (II Cor 3:14). That is, he adapted them to his own theme and setting so that it is difficult if not impossible to say whether they were written or oral, derived from formulated traditions or from his memory of Jesus' teachings".

3.1 Revelation and the Gospel of John

The relationship of Revelation to John's Gospel has been a subject of on-going debate.[93] Firstly, we note that there are considerable differences between them. As Prigent notes, the differences between the Gospel and Rev at a linguistic level "are such that they cannot be explained by the linguistic evolution of one single person, even when spread out over a considerable duration".[94] It seems almost certain then that they were written by different authors.

Yet there are what Prigent calls "obvious signs of kinship" in the phraseology between the books.[95] Note for example the parallelism between Jn 7:37 and Rev 22:17, and the similar expressions "do the truth" in Jn 3:21 and "do a lie" in Rev 22:15. But there are also key parallels with regard to themes and expressions. Note the shared use of "Ἐγώ εἰμι" (Rev 1:8, 17; 2:23; 21:6; 22:13, 16 cf Jn 6:35; 8:12 etc) and the designation of Christ as logos (Rev 19:13; Jn 1:1, 14; 1 Jn 1:10; 2:14). Prigent also notes that additional parallels "which concern elements that are far from being marginal, have bearing on key metaphors such as the bride (Jn 3:29; several times in Rev), the mother (Jn 16:21; Rev 12:2), light (several times in the Gospel; Rev 21:23), the door (Jn 10 *passim*; Rev 3:8), the shepherd (Jn 10; Rev 7:17), the use of the root σκην- (Jn 1:14; Rev 21:3), the spirit as a witness to Jesus (Jn 15:26; Rev 19:10)".[96] He thus suggests the Gospel and Rev "present the marks of a common family".[97] Although the relationship is more distant than the relationship of Jn's Gospel to 1-3 Jn, clearly there is an affinity between Rev on the one hand and the Gospel of Jn and 1-3 Jn on the other.

3.2 Pauline Influence on Revelation?

Are there any clear connections between Paul and Pauline traditions and Revelation? Of course Paul was active in Ephesus, and we have argued that at the conclusion of his ministry the Pauline community was well established in the city. We have also noted that his mission had an impact elsewhere in Western Asia Minor (Colossae, Hierapolis, Laodicea) forty or so years before John wrote Revelation. Further, we have argued that the Pastorals are in the Pauline tradition and to Ephesus, and so that the Pauline tradition continued to

---

[93] See Prigent 2001, p36-50; Prigent is drawing on the excellent discussion of Frey in Hengel 1993, p326-429. See also Aune 1997, pliv-lvi; Schnelle 1998, p436-7; cf. Schüssler Fiorenza 1985, p85-113.

[94] Prigent 2001, p40. He notes for example that different words are chosen for the same entity; eg ἀρνός/ ἀρνίον; Ἱεροσόλυμα/ Ἱερουσαλήμ; ἴδε in preference to ἰδού.

[95] Prigent 2001, p40-1.

[96] Prigent 2001, p42; see also Böcher 1980, p295-301; Schnackenburg 1991, p57-8.

[97] Prigent 2001, p41. He also argues that the eschatology of Jn and Rev are not as dissimilar as is often thought; see Prigent 2001, p46-50. See also for example Olsson 1987, p33-4.

have an impact on the area. We will note in Chapter 14 that the Ephesian community to which Ignatius wrote is familiar with Paul's ministry. But can we discern any influence from Paul or Pauline traditions in Rev, written to Western Asia Minor, including Ephesus? If John was consciously addressing readers in the Pauline tradition, and trying to convince them to adopt his theological positions, as our hypothesis suggests, then would it not be reasonable to suggest that John might have mentioned Paul or adopted some Pauline language? We will investigate this here.

There are no explicit reference to Paul in Revelation. Perhaps this is not surprising, since outside of his own writings and Acts, Paul is only mentioned in 2 Pet 3:15-16.[98] But there have been a number of suggestions with regard to possible examples of the influence of Paul's writings in Rev to which we now turn.

3.2.1 Possible examples of Pauline influence on Revelation[99]

Firstly, in Rev 1:4-5a we read: "John to the seven churches that are in Asia: Grace to you and peace from him who is (χάρις ὑμῖν καὶ εἰρήνη ἀπό ὁ ὤν) and who was and who is to come, and from the seven spirits who are before his throne, and from Jesus Christ ..." As was the case with 2 Jn 3, here we have an example of the Christian modification of the standard Greek letter greeting of χαίρειν. Has John been influenced by Paul and the Pauline letter tradition in this greeting?[100]

In Rev 1:4-5a the description of the source of grace and peace has clearly been shaped by John; it is quite distinctive with its mention of three divine sources of "grace and peace".[101] However, Aune suggests the grace and peace formula in Rev 1 "is typical of Pauline and some Deutero-Pauline letters".[102] The exact wording of Rev 1:4 "χάρις ὑμῖν καὶ εἰρήνη ἀπο ...", is found in Rom 1:7b; 1 Cor 1:3; 2 Cor 1:2; Gal 1:3; Eph 1:2; Phil 1:2; Col 1:2b; 2 Thess 1:2; Philem 3. 1 Thess 1:1 reads simply "χάρις ὑμῖν καὶ εἰρήνη", while Tit 1:4b reads "χάρις καὶ εἰρήνη ἀπό ...". We have already noted that 1 Tim 1:2b, 2 Tim 1:2b and 2 Jn 3 read "χάρις ἔλεος εἰρήνη ἀπό ...". 1 Pet 1:2 and 2 Pet 1:2 read "χάρις ὑμῖν καὶ εἰρήνη πληθυνθείη" while Jude 2 reads

---

[98] He is mentioned by Ignatius in IgnEph 12:2 and Polycarp in Phil 3.2; 9.1; 11.2-3.

[99] Note the full list of "Passages [in Rev] in some cases directly dependent on and in others parallel with earlier books of the NT" given in Charles 1920, 1, plxxxiii-lxxxvi (see also Mitton 1955, p36-7). But in most cases it is unlikely that there was direct dependence by John on an earlier work, as we will show below.

[100] We might suggest that Jn used the letter form itself because Paul wrote letters and hence because of Pauline influence. But it is more likely that John wanted to write to seven churches and that the letter form was the obvious way to do so.

[101] See Taeger 1998, p189.

[102] Aune 1997, p27.

"ἔλεος ὑμῖν καὶ εἰρήνη καὶ ἀγάπη πληθυνθείη." Thus, the greeting in Rev is certainly closest to Paul's letters and that found in Eph and is somewhat different from 1 and 2 Tim. But we also note that "χάρις ὑμῖν καὶ εἰρήνη" is found in 1 and 2 Peter.

How do we explain the greeting in Rev? There are three possibilities. Firstly, that John is directly dependent on the Pauline letter greeting. Secondly, that he has created the letter greeting himself. Thirdly, that he has adopted what has become the customary greeting when Christians wrote letters; on this view, this custom of a specific Christian modification of the standard letter form would go back to Paul, but was widely adopted by different Christian groups with the result that the "Christian form" of the letter became common. In writing as he does John would then be dependent on letter writing (or liturgical) practices among Christians in the 80s and 90s rather than being dependent on Paul or Pauline tradition directly. Can we decide between these three options?

Given the similarity to Paul, it is unlikely that John has created the greeting himself. But that a very similar greeting is found in both 1 and 2 Pet means this feature cannot be used to show an exclusive connection between Rev and Paul or Pauline tradition.[103] It is just as likely that 1 and 2 Pet and Rev reflect standard practice among Christians, which may indeed go back to Paul as the originator of the now-customary formula, but that John is here dependent on contemporary practice rather than Paul himself. To complicate matters further, Aune suggests that although the "grace and peace" formula may have been created by Paul, "this appears doubtful since the formula already appears in the superscription of Paul's first letter (1 Thess 1:1), and it has parallels (if not verbally identical parallels) in 2 Apoc Bar 78.2 and LXX Esth 9.30."[104] So it is also possible that John may be dependent on a wider custom than that found in the earliest Christian letters.

Thus we cannot say that John has definitely been influenced by Paul. It is just as likely, and perhaps more so, that John reflects Christian practice here, with that practice being originally shaped by Paul.[105]

A second possible instance of the influence of Paul's writings in Rev is found in Rev 22:20-1. There we read: "The one who testifies to these things says, 'Surely I am coming soon.' Amen. Come, Lord Jesus! The grace of the

---

[103] Of course 1 and 2 Pet may themselves be influenced by Pauline tradition, but even if this was the case, the use of the formula still extends beyond Paul's own letters (whether they are all by him or some are written in his name).

[104] Aune 1997, p29.

[105] Thus, Lohse (1991, p361) for example, is quite careful in his wording in this regard. He notes with regard to Rev 1:4: "the possibility of a connection with the common Christian practice as shaped by Paul the apostle cannot be overlooked." See also Schüssler Fiorenza 1985, p121.

Lord Jesus be with all (Ἡ χάρις τοῦ κυρίου Ἰησοῦ μετὰ πάντων)."[106] Lohse suggests that in this final passage of the book "the author follows the pattern as developed by Paul"[107] and suggests a comparison with 1 Cor 16:22-23 ("Let anyone be accursed who has no love for the Lord. Our Lord come! The grace of the Lord Jesus be with you.").

However, is John here dependent directly on Paul, or are both Paul and John dependent on early Christian tradition and perhaps liturgy? Paul may have inherited the benediction formula from tradition, and John may have adopted it from this same source. Thus, as Aune notes, although John may have adopted Paul's benediction-formula, "it is also possible to conclude that John is using a variant of the traditional epistolary benediction that had been popularized in Asia Minor (and elsewhere) by Paul."[108] If this is the case, then we need see no direct dependence of John on Paul.

Further, note that the standard Pauline benediction is "The grace of our (or the) Lord Jesus *Christ* (Ἡ χάρις τοῦ κυρίου ἡμῶν Ἰησου Χριστοῦ)..."[109] whereas John writes "The grace of the Lord Jesus (Ἡ χάρις τοῦ κυρίου Ἰησοῦ)." It is noteworthy that in Rev 22:21 John writes "Lord Jesus", a phrase he uses elsewhere only in 22:20, which is part of a traditional formula.[110] In 22:21 John does *not* say "Lord Jesus Christ", which is found in all the Pauline benedictions except 1 Cor 16:23. That "Lord Jesus" is not a phrase regularly used by John suggests he is using tradition here in 22:21; but that Paul's normal expression is "The grace of our/the Lord Jesus *Christ* .." suggests John is not directly quoting Paul.[111] Further, outside the Pauline corpus, "grace" in the letter closing is found in Heb 13:25 which reads: "Grace be with all of you." Although this wording is further removed from Rev 22:21 than the examples in Paul, it does show that a grace-benediction-formula was used in other early Christian letters, further weakening an argument which would see John as directly dependent on Paul here.

Thus we cannot say that in Rev 22:21 John is definitely dependent on Paul or Pauline tradition. This is possible, but it is no more than that.[112]

---

[106] Note the variant readings here with regard to πάντων; on which see Metzger 1971, p766-7, who argues for the text as given above.

[107] Lohse 1991, p363.

[108] Aune 1998, p1240-1.

[109] "The" in 1 Cor 16:23; 2 Cor 13:14; Phil 4:23; "our" in Rom 16:20; Gal 6:18; 1 Thess 5:28; 2 Thess 3:18; Philm 25 (though note the variants in Rom 16:20).

[110] See Aune 1998b, p1234-6, 1241.

[111] John has clearly made the grace-formula his own, since he says that the recipients of grace are "all the saints", a term which is otherwise not found in the benedictions of NT letters and which we have shown in Chapter 12 was one of John's favourite designations for "Christians" (he uses it 13 times in Rev), although it is also used by Paul.

[112] Note the view of Taeger (1998, p189): "Die briefliche Rahmung der Apk (1,4.5a; 22,21) zeigt zweifellos eine auffällige Nähe zur paulinischen und deuteropaulinischen

Thirdly, Aune thinks another instance of "possible Pauline influence" is the use of the phrase ἐν κυρίῳ "in the Lord" in 14:13. This phrase is "found almost exclusively in the Pauline corpus with the exception of this passage and Ignatius Pol. 8.3." But Aune goes on to note that in 14:13 it is not clear whether κύριος refers to God or Christ.[113] Clearly, if it refers to God, it is not a reflection of Pauline vocabulary.

We conclude that Pauline influence on Rev is not proven in any of these cases.[114]

3.2.2 Dubious examples of Pauline influence on Rev

There are a number of other places in Rev where Pauline influence is possible but unlikely. Firstly, Taeger notes that the designation of Christ as "ὁ πρωτότοκος τῶν νεκρῶν" in Rev 1:5 could be related to Col 1:18 where we read "πρωτότοκος ἐκ τῶν νεκρῶν".[115] However, Taeger suggests this title for Christ has been influenced by Ps 88:28 in the LXX and notes that the title "faithful witness" in Rev 1:5 is also an allusion to Ps 88:38. Thus in calling Christ "ὁ πρωτότοκος τῶν νεκρῶν", John has probably himself adapted the verse in Psalm 88 by adding τῶν νεκρῶν (cf. Rev 1:18) and so it is unlikely that we should see Pauline influence here.[116] Secondly, although the doxology to Christ in Rev 1:5b-6 has Pauline parallels (eg. Gal 2:20; Eph 5:25), it has probably been brought together by John and influence from Paul here is unproven.[117] Thirdly, a direct connection between Rev 20:6 ("the first resurrection") and 1 Cor 15:20f and Col 1:18 is also very unlikely. Fourthly, although only Paul/Pauline tradition (2 Cor 11:2; Eph 5:31f) and John the Seer (Rev 19:7-9; 21:2, 9; 22:17) portray the Christian community explicitly as the "bride", the representation of the community as a woman or bride is already present in the OT (eg. Isa 61:10; cf 4 Esd 7:26). A similar motif is also found in Jn 3:29 and we also note John's depiction of the opponent of the bride,

---

Breifkonvention." Taeger does not speak of dependence on Paul by Rev however. See also Schüssler Fiorenza 1985, p121.

[113] Aune 1997, pcxxvii. Beale (1999, p767) simply notes: "a similar spheric or incorporative dative occurs in 1 Cor 15:22 and 1 Thess 4:16".

[114] See for example Aune (1997, pcxxvi –cxxvii) who notes: "There are few if any reflections of Pauline influence within Revelation as many scholars have recognized". Note that Schüssler Fiorenza (1985, p122) argues for some underlying similarity between John and Paul, rather than for direct dependence of John on Paul.

[115] Compare also 1 Cor 15:20; Rom 8:29; Acts 26:23.

[116] Taeger 1998, p190.

[117] See Taeger 1998, p192-3. Alternatively, it is possible that in Rev 1:5-6 John is recalling a baptismal liturgy known to him; see Vanni 1980, p33. This would also mean that recourse to Pauline influence to explain these similarities is unnecessary. Note that there is "a general structural relationship" between Rev 1:5d-6 and Tit 2:14; see Aune 1997, p45-6, but direct influence of Tit on Rev seems unlikely.

Babylon, as a woman in Rev 17. Again, then, Pauline influence is not required to explain John's language in this regard.[118] Fifthly, the use of "Amen" in Rev 3:14, 22:20 is probably derived from contemporary liturgy and from Isa 65:16, rather than being dependent on 2 Cor 1:20.[119] Sixthly, Mounce has suggested that in Rev 3:14 (ἡ ἀρχὴ τῆς κτίσεως) John is dependent on Col 1:18 (ὅς ἐστιν ἀρχή).[120] However, Vanni notes: "Ces similitudes peuvent être cependant expliquées plus généralement et de manière plus convaincante par un substrat (liturgique) commun."[121]

Finally, an interesting cameo here is provided by Rev 17:14, where we read of the Lamb that "he is Lord of lords and King of kings, and those with him are called and chosen and faithful." At first sight in English translation this appears similar to 1 Tim 6:15: "he who is the blessed and only Sovereign, the King of kings and Lord of lords." However, the Greek in each case reads as follows: Rev 17:14: "ὅτι κύριος κυρίων ἐστὶν καὶ βασιλεὺς βασιλέων ..." (Rev 19:16 is very similar); 1 Tim 6:15: "ὁ βασιλεὺς τῶν βασιλευόντων καὶ κύριος τῶν κυριευόντων ..." In addition, parallels to Rev 17:14 are found in Dt 10:17; Ps 135:3; 2 Macc 13:4; 3 Macc 5:35. Hence the apparent parallel between Rev and 1 Tim 6:15 is better explained as the independent use of the LXX by each author.

3.2.3 Counter evidence

Here we can note two pieces of counter-evidence to the suggestion that John shows some influence from Paul and Pauline writings in Rev. Firstly, some words found in Paul are used in quite different ways in Rev. Aune notes: "The absence of Pauline influence throughout the body of Revelation is reinforced by the two unusual uses of the active verb εὐαγγελίζειν, 'to announce good news' (10:7; 14:6), and the unusual use of the noun εὐαγγέλιον, 'good news, gospel,' in the phrase εὐαγγελίζειν εὐαγγέλιον, 'announce good news' (14:6), where there is not only no trace of Pauline influence but also no trace of the conventional use of this verb and noun in other early Christian literature."[122]

Secondly, Lohse raises a key objection to the view that would see Pauline influence in Rev. Lohse writes: "John the prophet speaks of the twelve apostles in 18:20 and 21:14 without even mentioning that Paul too had been called to be an apostle. John points to the Twelve as to a circle that was

---

[118] See Taeger 1998, p193-4.

[119] See Taeger 1998, p194-5; Fekkes 1994, p137-40.

[120] Mounce 1977, p124-5. He thinks (p124) "it all but certain that the writer of Revelation knew the Colossian epistle".

[121] Vanni 1980, p32.

[122] Aune 1997, p cxxvii. See also Aune 1998, p570, 825-6.

closed.[123] The names of the twelve apostles are written on the twelve foundations of the heavenly city of God, but the name of Paul the apostle is not mentioned. Was he forgotten? Or why is there not anywhere in the book of Revelation an allusion that would point either to the person or to the theology of Paul?"[124] We will shortly seek to explain this observation, which certainly counts against Pauline influence.

We can therefore agree with Lohse when he writes that "no explicit traces of Pauline theology are found in the book of Revelation. ... Although there are some similarities in the interpretation of the common creed between the Pauline letters and the book of Revelation, John the prophet writes his message without taking notice of the work of Paul the apostle."[125] Similarly, Taeger concludes his extensive discussion of this matter with the following summary: "Vor allem lassen sich solche Berührungspunkte – mit Ausnahme vielleicht der brieflichen Rahmung – nicht im Sinne einer bewußten Stellungsnahme des Apk-Autors zu Paulus bzw. zum paulinischen Erbe interpretieren."[126]

3.3 Why is Paul ignored in Revelation?

Earlier in the article from which we have quoted above, Lohse wrote of "the failure to mention a single syllable of Pauline thought" and went on: "This fact is all the more astonishing in view of the fact that at the end of the first century CE there were some influential persons in Ephesus who were informed about Pauline theology and doctrine. We read in the Pastoral letters a clear testimony that Paul's work and theology were not entirely forgotten in this period. They were still being spoken of and discussed in order to find answers to new problems. Reading the book of Revelation, on the other hand, gives the impression that its author had never heard about Paul the apostle and his theology."[127]

Is this evidence that Rev is written to a "John of Revelation community", one that had no contact with Pauline tradition, which is why John includes no reference to Paul? In fact on this view, John himself would have had nothing to do with Pauline tradition. Or is this evidence that Rev was written to a group that *had* been "Pauline" many years before, but which had now completely forgotten him?[128]

---

[123] See further Taeger 1998, p188 and references cited there.

[124] Lohse 1991, p360.

[125] Lohse 1991, p365, 366.

[126] Taeger 1998, p195; see also Vanni 1980, p32; Ellis 1999, p229-30 who suggests similarities can be explained by John using traditions which were also known to others, rather than by John's direct use of Pauline letters.

[127] Lohse 1991, p360; cf. Berger 1995, p595-602.

[128] We will discuss this in more detail below.

All of this leads to the question of why Paul is ignored in Revelation? There are a number of possible explanations for the silence about Paul in Rev. Firstly, as we have noted, the evidence we have discussed is compatible with the view that John in Rev is writing to "his own community" – and hence does not write of Paul at all. Perhaps then John and his readers are simply embedded in a different theological tradition from Paul?

Or secondly, perhaps John simply does not know Paul well – has he come from Palestine recently, and not moved before in circles in which Paul was active? But we have suggested in Chapter 7 that John knows the communities to which he writes very well, and so even if John did not know Paul well before he arrived in the area, that he does not write of Paul would suggest that the communities he got to know had perhaps once known Paul, but now his influence lies completely in the past and he has been completely forgotten in Western Asia Minor?[129] Hence John did not know Paul before he arrived and did not get to know him from the communities with which he interacted and to whom he wrote. This could lead back to the first explanation – that John was writing to only some Christians in these cities, and these communities were now "John of Revelation communities". Or it could mean that although these were not his "own" communities as it were, whatever stance they were theologically, they were not "Pauline".

But there is a third and completely different explanation. We have suggested that John is addressing the readers of the Pastoral Epistles, along with other Christians (including the readers of the Johannine Letters). If this was the case, then we might expect some linguistic contact with the Pauline community. But this is not forthcoming. Is John hostile towards Paul? Or does this lack of reference to Paul undermine our hypothesis? Or perhaps John's readers do know Pauline tradition, and John (despite perhaps not knowing about Paul when he arrived?) has now got to know Pauline tradition from them but has chosen not to speak of Paul or Pauline tradition.

It is this last scenario – that some of John's readers know the Pauline tradition, but John has chosen not to speak of that tradition – which we will now develop. Taeger thinks that it is very unlikely that John the Seer, who was clearly connected with the communities to which he wrote in Asia Minor, completely lacked knowledge of the person and theology of Paul.[130] We note in this regard the continuing influence of Paul in Ephesus in particular, shown

---

[129] See Bauer 1971, p83-4 for this view. We will discuss Bauer's view further in the Conclusions to this book.

[130] Taeger 1998, p195; see also Schüssler Fiorenza 1985, p122; Boxall 1998, p201. Muddiman (2001, p37) thinks there was a Pauline group in Ephesus at the end of the first century, and a "Johannine circle" which included the addressees of the Johannine epistles and Rev and writes of these two groups: "It is impossible that the two groups would not have known of each other's existence."

by the Pastorals and later by Ignatius. It seems unlikely that Paul has been completely forgotten in Western Asia Minor.[131] Taeger thinks rather that John made no use of the knowledge of Paul that he did have. Why would this be?

We have noted in Chapter 7 that John has opposition in the seven churches and we have suggested that the Nicolaitans may have been influenced by Paul, or may have radicalised Paul's teaching. We have also argued that the views of the Nicolaitans are closest to those found among the group at Corinth with whom Paul argued at length in 1 Corinthians.[132] This suggests that the Nicolaitans might be an off-shot of Pauline Christianity, or might have found their inspiration there (even if they have misinterpreted Paul's own views). Thus the development of the Nicolaitans to which John objects, may well have its origins in a Christianity that was originally shaped by Paul. We have also noted that John can be seen to be combating the Nicolaitans throughout Rev, and not just in three places in the seven proclamations. In Rev then, John could well be tackling trends or developments in post-Pauline Christianity.[133] As Taeger comments "Vor dem Hinterground dieser Kontroverse mag es verständlich erscheinen, daß sich der Apk-Autor nicht auf Paulus und paulinischer Tradition bezieht."[134] As he faces in the Nicolaitans a version of Christianity which perhaps still regarded Paul as its chief inspiration, John must be reserved with regard to Paul and Pauline tradition. It seems reasonable to suggest that John has avoided any reference to Paul precisely because he is influential among John's opponents. It may be that John objects, not so much to Paul, as to the way Paul is currently being used by John's opponents and that this has led to John's silence about Paul. If he used Pauline tradition, or referred to Paul, he would be playing into the hands of his opponents, who themselves looked back to Paul.

But there is further evidence which suggests that John chose not to make use of the knowledge of Paul that he had. Here we will argue that Paul and the Pauline tradition were not an ally in the battle John was involved in with

---

[131] Note also the Apocryphal Acts of Paul and Thecla from Asia Minor in the second century, which suggest Paul was not forgotten; see further Bremmer 1996.

[132] See Chapter 7, section 3.13.4. See also Taeger 1998, p196; Vanni 1980, p32. Taeger (1998, p197) also notes that in addition to the opposition group of the Nicolaitans, John strongly opposes other communities. For example in Laodicea the community thinks it is rich, but is deceived (3:17). Taeger suggests this "illusionäres Vollendungsbewußtein" may be similar to the enthusiastic tendency which Paul criticises in 1 Cor 4:8 (see also Schüssler Fiorenza 1985, p119). Thus it may be that there is Pauline influence to which John objects not only with respect to the Nicolaitans, but also in some communities where the Nicolaitans are not mentioned. Thus, some features of community life to which John objects (and not just the Nicolaitans) may be traceable back to Pauline influence. But this is uncertain.

[133] Taeger 1998, p198.

[134] Traeger 1998, p198.

regard to attitudes to outsiders and to Rome in particular, and so John did not mention Paul or enlist his name in his support.

Taeger notes that the relationship with the world which John envisages, and which is summarized in Rev 18:4 ("Come out of her, my people, so that you do not take part in her sins"), contradicts the understanding that Paul had of the relationship between the world and Christian communities.[135] Thus, for example, in 1 Cor 10:32-3 we read: "Give no offense to Jews or to Greeks, or to the church of God, just as I try to please everyone in everything I do, not seeking my own advantage, but that of many, so that they may be saved." Note also 1 Thess 4:10-12: "But we urge you ... to aspire to live quietly, to mind your own affairs ... so that you may behave properly toward outsiders and be dependent on no one."

Although these verses are not all that Paul would want to say on the matter,[136] it is clear that the opinions of outsiders are important to Paul. Paul's attitude to the world is quite nuanced (see eg. Rom 12:2), and cannot be discussed in detail here, but it is clear that John does not express sentiments like those found in these two passages by Paul. By contrast, Taeger suggests that the irreconcilable gulf that John sees between those "who have been redeemed from the earth" (Rev 14:3) and the "inhabitants of the earth" (Rev 13:8, 12, 14) should, in John's view, continue (see Rev 22:11) and should also be perpetuated as a result of his book.[137] Further, Taeger suggests that John's attitudes to "outsiders" is clearly different from the expression of Paulinism found in his own time in the Pastorals, which, as we have seen in Chapter 8, present quite a different relationship with the wider world from that argued for in Rev.

We also note that in Rev the fundamental attitude to Rome, expressed in Rev 17:1f, is of judgement, for according to Rev 17:6 Rome is "drunk with the blood of the saints and the blood of the witnesses to Jesus". The woman of Rev 17, who represents Rome, is carried by the beast (17:7) and it has already been revealed to John that the beast has been given its power by the dragon, who is Satan (13:2; 12:9). Thus John has a very definite view about the Roman Empire, and this view is fundamental to his work. This is strongly contrasted with the attitude to the state expressed in the Pastorals. In Tit 3:1 we read: "Remind them to be subject to rulers and authorities, to be obedient, to be ready for every good work", and in 1 Tim 2:1-2 we read "First of all, I urge that supplications, prayer, intercessions, and thanksgiving be made for

---

[135] See Taeger 1998, p200-2.

[136] Note the different emphasis in 2 Cor 6:14-7:1, which is clearly aimed at the Corinthian situation; see for example, Thrall 1994, p475.

[137] See Taeger 1998, p201. But note that John clearly believes in mission on a world scale (note John regularly speaks of believers from "the nations"; see Rev 5:9; 7:9; 14:6; 15:4; 21:24, 26), but he does not spell out how this is to come about.

everyone, for kings and all who are in high positions, so that we may lead a quiet and peaceable life in all godliness ..." While it is not suggested in the Pastorals that the state is ordered by God, nor does the Pastor see the state as doing God's will, we see here what Roloff calls a "postiv-vertrauensvolle Haltung".[138] Although the Pastor might have had more to say on the subject of relations with the state, there is clearly a contrast with Revelation here.[139]

What all this means is that Paul and the Pauline tradition is hardly an ally in the battle John is involved in with regard to attitudes to outsiders and to Rome in particular. Accordingly, we can suggest that the silence about Paul and Paulinism in Rev is probably because Paul is seen as their inspiration by the opponents of Jn and because Paul, and the Pauline tradition as seen in the Pastorals, did not support the position Jn took. Hence John did not see Paul as an ally, and in fact to allude to him would be to look for support to the person that the Nicolaitans also looked to – which would not further John's case but would rather play into the hands of his opponents. They could well reply to John, "But this Paul of whom you speak, and of whom you obviously approve, actually supports our position with regard to food offered to idols and the Roman empire". Accordingly Taeger entitles his article on this topic "Begründetes Schweigen" – well-founded silence.

Given that we can explain this silence, we should not conclude that John does not know of Paul, or that there were no Christians in the seven churches who regarded themselves as followers of Paul. The lack of reference to Paul or allusion to Pauline tradition in Rev then does not require the conclusions that John is writing to a community that does not know Paul, or that his addressees are a sectarian community. Since the lack of reference can be adequately accounted for, it does not undermine our hypothesis that John is writing to readers of the Pastorals, who are Christians who would see themselves as in the Pauline tradition (along with others). Because John's main Christian opposition *also* see themselves as Paul's spiritual children (at least to some extent), we may suggest that John has decided not to refer to Paul. Clearly such a suggestion cannot be proved, but it is does account for the known evidence. Thus John could well be writing to those who were readers of the Pastorals, along with Johannine Christians and others.

---

[138] Roloff 1988, p115.

[139] See Taeger 1998, p202-3. He also compares Rev to Rom 13:1-7 and 1 Pet 2:13-17. He suggests (p203) that it cannot be excluded: "daß Johannes auf Bestrebungen im zeitgenössischen Paulinismus reagiert und sich entschieden von ihnen absetzt." See also Boxall 1998, p215-17, who notes (p217) with regard to 1 Tim 2:1-2: "This is a far cry from Revelation's denunciation of the Roman Empire as Babylon the Great, seated on the beast!"

4. Overall Conclusions

We have suggested that the readers of the Pastorals and the readers of the Johannine Letters would have been aware of each other's existence and would not have refused contact with one another (since they did not fail the other's litmus tests). The (admittedly limited, though they are small documents) evidence for linguistic contact removes a possible counterargument against our thesis of "non-hostile relations" between these two communities, since if there had been no linguistic contact this would suggest the communities had nothing to do with one another. We can suggest then that there was some contact between the two communities and that we should not envisage communities that were water-tight and hermetically sealed off against each other and unexposed to other influences. We cannot argue that there were positive relations between the two groups, but we have suggested that at the least the evidence is compatible with relations between the two groups not being hostile.[140]

We have also suggested that the silence of John in Rev about Paul does not undermine our hypothesis that John is writing to the readers of the Pastorals and the Johannine letters. This silence could be taken to mean that John is writing to his own community which did not know anything about Paul, but given the probable presence of the community of the Pastorals in Ephesus, it seems unlikely that John would be totally ignorant of Paul. Further, we can give an explanation for this silence that is compatible with our hypothesis – that John's opponents looked to Paul as their inspiration and saw themselves at least to some extent as Paul's spiritual children and so to mention Paul would be to play into their hands; in addition the position of Paul and the author of the Pastorals on attitudes to outsiders and Rome was quite different from John's and so did not offer him any assistance in his battle with his opponents, or his attempt to convince his other readers that they should "Come out of her, my people".[141] We have also noted in previous chapters that there is no positive evidence which suggests that John was writing to "his own community".

We can note here the far-reaching conclusions that Lohse develops from the silence towards Paul in Rev. Although we have quoted the passage below at the end of Chapter 7, it is also highly relevant here. In attempting to explain

---

[140] Note also that none of the cases of sharing of vocabulary that we have discussed suggest that one group has appropriated the language of the other in order to polemicise against that other group.

[141] This suggests that some contemporary followers of the Pauline tradition (ie. those who had (probably) earlier been recipients of the Pastorals) could be part of the centrist party which we have suggested is implied by Rev 2:4-5, and that John is trying to convince this group (and others) in Ephesus to adopt his own position.

the fact that there is no explicit trace of Pauline theology in book of Rev, Lohse writes: "A historical reflection might help to explain this lack of specific Pauline influence in the book of Revelation. The Jewish war and the capture and destruction of Jerusalem in 70 CE made quite a number of Palestinian Christians leave their country and come to Asia Minor. Their arrival changed the character of the congregations in that region. It is to be supposed that the prophetic traditions that stand behind the author of the book of Revelation are of Palestinian origin and became influential when the time of the Pauline mission had passed. In these traditions the name and theology of Paul were nearly unknown."[142]

On this view, by 95 CE, all Christians in Asia Minor would have forgotten Paul. Not only does Ignatius, and later Polycarp, contradict this,[143] but this thesis would also require that the Christians who belonged to the community of the Pastorals (80-100 CE) had by 95 completely forgotten Paul. But we have also noted that there is a much more likely explanation for this silence: that John knows of Paul and his theology, but chooses not to refer to him.

We can put forward our hypothesis with some confidence then and suggest that there were non-hostile relations between the readers of the Pastorals and the Johannine Letters and that in Rev John is writing to both communities, as well as to others.

---

[142] Lohse 1991, p365.

[143] As noted above Paul is mentioned by Ignatius in IgnEph 12:2 and Polycarp in Phil 3.2; 9.1; 11.2-3.

Part 4

Ignatius' letter to Ephesus

Chapter 14

Who are the addressees of Ignatius' letter to Ephesus?

Early in the second century, Ignatius, bishop of Antioch, travelled in Asia Minor on his way to martyrdom in Rome. Before reaching Rome, he wrote seven letters to Christians in Asia Minor, one of which was to Ephesus. In this chapter we will discuss some introductory issues and will discuss what Ignatius says about leaders in Ephesus. We will then ask to whom was Ignatius writing in Ephesus? Was he writing to all the Christians in the city, or to a particular Christian community, and if so, which community? Answering this question will also tell us a good deal about the Christians in Ephesus at the time. In the following Chapter, we will discuss additional facets of the life of the Christians in Ephesus.

1. Introductory matters

We need to turn first of all to some introductory matters.

1.1 Ignatius' journey

In the early second century Ignatius, the bishop of Antioch was arrested in Antioch in Syria and taken to Rome where he expected to suffer martyrdom. He probably travelled by ship from Antioch to a port on the southern coast of Asia Minor, although he could have gone by land. Ignatius then passed through Philadephia, where he met Christians from that community (IgnPhd 7.1).[1] He then travelled to Smyrna where there was a delay and where his stay was long enough for him to get to know a number of different individuals and family groups (IgnSm 13; IgnPol 8.2-3). In Smyrna he was supported by Polycarp, the bishop of Smyrna, and the local Christians. While in Smyrna he was visited by Christians from Ephesus, Magnesia and Tralles, whom he had

---

[1] It is most likely that IgnPhd 7 refers to a debate Ignatius had in Philadephia with some Christians there, although some scholars think the debate occurred in Antioch.

contacted to inform them of his journey.[2] He then wrote letters to each of these communities in return (IgnEph 21.1; IgnMag 15.1; IgnTr 12.1) and also wrote to the church in Rome to tell them of his impending arrival and to urge them not to attempt to prevent his martyrdom.[3]

He then went on to Troas, and from there he wrote to the churches of Philadelphia and Smyrna and also to Polycarp. His time in Troas was brief, and abruptly terminated when he sailed suddenly from Troas (IgnPol 8.1).[4] While there he learned that "peace" had returned to the church in Antioch.[5] We know that he was then taken to Philippi (Polycarp, Phil 9.1), since some Christians of that city wrote to Polycarp and seem to have mentioned that he had passed through the city.[6] We do not know for certain that he was martyred in Rome, although we have no reason to doubt this.[7]

1.2 Dating

Eusebius in his *Chronicon,* written early in the fourth century, dates both Ignatius' martyrdom and Pliny's letter to Trajan in the tenth year of Trajan's reign, which was 107 CE. However, we see from Eusebius' Ecclesiastical History (HE 3.33, 36) that his chronological information on these two matters was not at all precise.[8] It seems likely that Eusebius knew of the persecution

---

[2] Ephesus, Magnesia and Tralles did not lie on Ignatius' direct route, as he notes in IgnRom 9.3. Hence Schoedel (1985, p12) notes "en route across Asia Minor someone had gone on to Ephesus, Magnesia and Tralles to alert the Christians of those communities to Ignatius' arrival in Smyrna." See also Corwin 1960, p16. Further, messengers who had previously been sent to Rome to prepare for Ignatius' arrival there are probably referred to in IgnRom 10.2 (see Schoedel 1985, p191), which increases the likelihood that messengers had also been sent to Ephesus, Magnesia, and Tralles to encourage the Christians in those places to send representatives to see Ignatius. Note also that while IgnEph 1.2 does not say that Ignatius sent a messenger to the Ephesians, this is certainly implied. We do not know if Ignatius contacted other Christian communities who did not send representatives to visit him. IgnMag 15 suggests he did not have the opportunity to write to all the churches who sent representatives to visit him in Smyrna. Schoedel (1985, p132) notes: "He probably gave special attention to those whose representation seemed most to demand it."

[3] The Greek text followed here is from Lake 1912; English quotations will generally follow the translation given by Schoedel 1985, with the occasional modifications.

[4] Ignatius had hoped to write to "all the churches", but was unable to since he was suddenly moved from Troas to Neapolis; see IgnPol 8.1.

[5] On the situation at Antioch see section 1.5 below.

[6] Polycarp, Phil 3:1; 9:1; 13:1-2.

[7] Polycarp, in writing to the Philippians presumed that Ignatius had died a martyr's death but was not certain (9:2; 13:2). Similarly, Eusebius (HE 3.36.3) noted only that "The story goes that he was sent from Syria to Rome to be eaten by beasts."

[8] He introduces his note on Pliny's letter by saying "the persecution which at that time was extended against us ..." (HE 3.33.1); the previous time reference is simply to "the reign of the Emperor Trajan" (HE 3.32.6). Similarly in introducing his story of Ignatius (HE

under Trajan spoken of by Pliny and hypothesized that Ignatius had been
arrested during this same persecution. It was thus Eusebius who placed the
two events in the same year. With no other evidence for this, we cannot rely
on Eusebius' dating of the Ignatius' death to 107. However, there seems no
compelling reason to reject Eusebius' placement of the arrest during Trajan's
reign, and so the majority of scholars have dated the letters between 98 and
117 CE.[9] But can we be more precise than this?

The letters themselves offer very little evidence which would help us to
establish their date.[10] That Ignatius was arrested suggests that some action
was being taken against Christians, although it may have been on a very
limited scale,[11] and his letters to Asian communities do not suggest that they
were being persecuted, nor that any accusations were being made against
Christians.[12] Further, Ignatius calls for Christians to meet more frequently
(IgnPol 4.2; IgnEph 13.1) which suggests Christianity was not regarded as an
illegal *collegium* at this time.[13] We should contrast this implied situation with
Pliny's remark to Trajan: "Even this practice [partaking of food], however,
they had abandoned after the publication of my edict, by which according to
your orders, I had forbidden political associations."[14] This shows that in
Pontus and Bithynia in Pliny's time some Christians had stopped meeting for
communal meals because of pressure from the Romans. Since it is likely that
Pliny wrote Ep 10.96 in 110 CE,[15] Trevett notes: "if such an edict had not

---

3.36.1), Eusebius writes "At this time ..." In HE 3.22.1 he speaks of Ignatius as the second
bishop of Antioch. See further in Munier 1981, p126-31. Eusebius is, however, the earliest
writer to date Ignatius' death.

[9] Trevett (1992, p8) notes that the scholars who have suggested different dates for the
letters have argued that they are forgeries to varying degrees.

[10] Apart from the date of August 24, with no year given, in IgnRom 10.3.

[11] He says in IgnEph 3.1 that "I have been bound in the name" (cf. IgnPhd 10.2), which
suggests he was a captive because he was a Christian. However, we will note below that the
restoration of "peace" at Antioch probably does not refer to the cessation of persecution but
rather to the cessation of internal hostility in the Christian community, so we should not see
his arrest as part of an on-going persecution. For the suggestion that Ignatius gave himself up
to the authorities see Trevett 1992, p61-6.

[12] Trevett 1992, p6-7 notes that there are no references to apostasy, only one call to pray
for outsiders (IgnEph 10.1) and only one warning against giving occasion to gentiles (IgnTr
8.2). Ignatius also notes that Ephesus was "a passage for those slain for God" (IgnEph 12.2)
and Christianity was greatest when the world hated it (IgnRom 3.3). These passages suggest
tension between Christian communities and their environments, but do not suggest there was
officially sanctioned persecution. Ignatius makes no reference to the hostility of the
authorities or of the populace and does not discuss the attitude of "the world" at length.

[13] Note also his frequent mention of meetings in IgnEph 5; IgnMag 4, 6, 7; IgnTr 2-3,
7, 13,2; IgnPhd inscr., 3-4; IgnPol 4.1. None of these passages suggest holding meetings
was a problem.

[14] Pliny the Younger, Ep. 10.96.

[15] See Sherwin-White 1966, p80-1, 691.

been applied in the eastern provinces before the time of which Pliny wrote, then possibly (given Ignatius's seeming lack of fear of action against such gatherings) a pre-111 CE date for the letters is indicated."[16] Thus a date before 111, and perhaps between 105-110 seems to be the most plausible, although the lack of information in the letters means we cannot rule out a date either a little earlier or a little later than this.[17]

1.3 The authenticity of his writings

Lightfoot[18] argued that the so-called middle recension of Ignatius' letters is authentic. Although this view has gained the support of most scholars, it has recently been challenged by Hübner. He argues that the letters are pseudepigraphic compositions written to give a new basis for the episcopate and to argue against the Gnosticism of the later second century. He thinks that parts of Ignatius' letters are dependent on Noetus of Smyrna, although Noetus was dead by the time one of his followers wrote the Ignatian letters. This leads to a proposed date for the letters of 170-180 CE.[19]

However, Hübner's points have been answered by a number of others.[20] His view that some of the language of the Ignatian letters fits better into the late second century and is to be seen as influenced by Noetus (for example,

---

[16] Trevett 1992, p6. See the discussion of the rest of the evidence in Trevett 1980, p46-58; 1992, p3-8. There was a major earthquake in Antioch in 115 CE (see Harrison 1936, p227), and since no mention is made of this in the letters it could be argued that Ignatius was writing before 115. However, there is no necessary reason why Ignatius should have mentioned an earthquake, so the point is not decisive.

[17] Trevett 1992, p9 suggests a date of c. 107 CE is the most plausible, but this seems to be putting too much weight on the evidence of Eusebius and the Antiochene and Roman Ignatian *Acts of Martyrdom* (which she acknowledges "inspire no confidence" (p4)). In Trevett 1980, p58 she suggests 107-109 CE. Lightfoot (1889b, Vol 2, p435-72) and Schoedel (1985, p5) argue for 100-118 CE; Corwin 1960, p3 dates the letters between 108 and 117 CE. Brown and Meier 1983, p163 date the letters ca. 110; Grant 1964, p48 and Genouillac 1907, p x, date the letters in the reign of Trajan. Hengel 1989, p14 and p152 n84 opts for a date not later than 113 because Trajan left Rome in that year in preparation for his Parthian campaigns, never to return. However, 113 need not be a *terminus ante quem* since the authorities in Antioch would not know that Trajan was not going to return to Rome and in any event an appeal case (if that is what it was) would be delegated to the *praefectus urbi*; see Trevett 1989b, p36. Davies 1976, p178-80 argues for 113 but on speculative grounds.

[18] Lightfoot 1889b, Vol 1, p328-430. The seven letters were extensively interpolated, probably in the fourth century, and at some point five other letters were added to the seven.

[19] Hübner 1997, p44-72.

[20] See Lindemann 1997, p185-94; Edwards 1998, p214-226; Schöllgen 1998, p16-25; Vogt 1999, p50-63. On earlier challenges to authenticity see Schoedel 1985, p5-7; Trevett 1992, p9-15.

IgnEph 7.2 and IgnPol 3.2) has been shown to be unconvincing.[21] Further, it has been shown that some other features of Ignatius' letters are much more likely to be dated early in the second century, rather than late in that century as proposed by Hübner. For example, what Ignatius says about silence in IgnMag 8.2 is best seen, not as anti-Gnostic polemic, but rather as something that belongs credibly in the early second century.[22] Finally, on Hübner's view, prior to the production of the letters, Ignatius would only be known through a very brief mention in Polycarp's letter (Polycarp, Phil 9.1); it seems highly unlikely that a pseudepigrapher would choose such an unknown figure as the supposed author of the letters, since he would not have the prior authority required for a pseudepigraphic writing to be convincing. This argues strongly against Hübner's view.[23] Thus, we can continue to regard the middle recension of Ignatius' letters as authentic and to be dated around 105-110.

1.4 Ignatius' source of information about the Christians in Ephesus to whom he wrote.

As we have noted, Ignatius visited Christians in Philadelphia and stayed for a short period in Smyrna, which meant that he was able to meet groups and individuals in these two cities. However, Ignatius did not visit Ephesus and so his knowledge of the Christians there was secondhand.[24] While it is possible that Christians in Philadelphia or Smyrna (especially Polycarp) passed on to Ignatius information about the Christians in Ephesus, his main source of information was Onesimus the "bishop of Ephesus", and four other Christian leaders from Ephesus, who visited Ignatius while he was in Smyrna (IgnEph

---

[21] See Edwards 1998, p219-26. Edwards (1998, p217) notes that the contents of Ignatius' letters "are not such as a prudent forger of that epoch [near the end of the second century] would contrive." Note also that Vogt (1999, p54-6) argues that Ign.Eph 7.2 is better explained against the background of NT passages like Rom 1:3-4 and Jn 1:1-14; 11:25; 14:6 rather than by postulating the influence of Noetus. On Hübner's argument that the Ignatian letters are dependent on Noetus, see Vogt 1999, p50-63.

[22] See Edwards 1998, p222-4; Vogt 1999, p50-3; cf. Hübner 1997, p51-2. Note also that Ignatius' conferring of the title "θεός" on Jesus has parallels in the NT, which Hübner (1997, p61) does not take sufficiently into account; see Lindemann 1997, p190.

[23] See Lindemann 1997, p190-2. Hübner thinks Polycarp's Phil 13 is not authentic. Another question against Hübner's view is why the pseudepigrapher did not write of the apostolic origin of the office of bishop, if one key reason he wrote was to legitimate the office; see Lindemann 1997, p192.

[24] Rius-Camps 1980, p67f, 113f, 136-8 argues that Ignatius passed through Ephesus, but this is based on his view that the original letter to the Ephesians contained most of our IgnEph, IgnSm and some of IgnPol, including the greetings in IgnSm 13.1-2 and IgnPol 8.2-3. However, Rius-Camps' view is highly unlikely as a number of scholars have shown.

1.3-2.1).[25] It seems likely that all Ignatius' information did not come from Onesimus, since one of the topics Ignatius raises in writing to the Ephesians was the "silence" of Onesimus in Ephesus, which was clearly regarded as a problem by some of the Ephesians (IgnEph 6.1; 15.1-3). It is possible Onesimus told Ignatius about his "silence", but it is perhaps more likely that one of the other leaders was an additional source for Ignatius at this point.

It is likely then that in what he says about the Ephesian Christians, Ignatius is reflecting, with an unknown degree of accuracy, the views of the leaders of the Ephesian Christians with which he has had contact. We must also keep in mind the possibility that these leaders passed on an overly optimistic picture of the Christians in the city, or an unnecessarily negative view.[26]

Further, given that Ignatius is an advocate of hierarchical church structures and that, as we will see, some Christians in Ephesus probably disagreed with his views on church structure, it is perhaps significant that Ignatius' informants about Ephesus were already on his side of the argument. It is unlikely that they would give a sympathetic account of those who were "non-hierarchically" inclined in Ephesus, even if they could have done so. Thus, it is important to note that in all he says Ignatius is dependent for his information on people who were already sympathetic to his own views.

It is also important to note here that when Ignatius writes about a problem to a particular Christian community, it seems most likely that he does so because the matter is relevant to that community. There is no reason to doubt that Ignatius was aware of the differing situations of the churches in Asia. He is clearly addressing local problems and writing letters that are tailored to individual needs rather than simply offering a uniform message to each of the churches. Thus, as we shall see, when he addresses the issue of staying away from the eucharist in Ephesus, it is clear that this was a problem in Ephesus, even if it was also a problem elsewhere. Thus, although what Ignatius wrote to churches in Asia was partly conditioned by his experiences in Antioch, and

---

[25] In IgnEph 1.1 Ignatius writes: 'Having received (Ἀποδεξάμενος) in God your much loved name'. Schoedel (1985, p40-1) comments on ἀποδεξάμενος: "that is, he has received a report - no doubt from the bishop". Lake in LCL translates the participle as "I became acquainted". Note also IgnEph 6.2: "Now indeed Onesimus himself praises highly your godly orderliness." See also IgnEph 9:1. Ignatius is explicit in IgnTr 1.1 that he received information about the church at Tralles from their bishop Polybius; see also IgnMag 1.1; 2.1.

[26] His knowledge of other churches is either derived from having visited them (IgnPhd and IgnSm) or from those who visited him (IgnMag, IgnTr). He is less well informed about the Roman church. He often says that he knows something about a community; see IgnMag 12.1; 14.1; IgnSm 4.1; IgnPol 7.3. He knew most about the Christians in Smyrna, and named a number of individuals in the church there; see IgnSm 13.1; IgnPol 8.2.

Christian practices there,[27] and in his theology he reflects primarily contemporary thinking in Syria rather than Asia, when he wrote to Asian Christians Ignatius made use of information and insights which he had gained locally. Thus, he is also a witness to the church situation in Asia.[28]

1.5 The Situation at Antioch

Ignatius asks for prayer for the church in Syria in IgnEph 21:2; IgnMag 14; IgnTr 13:1; IgnRom 9:1. Then, after he has gone to Troas and Philo, a deacon from Cilicia, and Rheus Agathopous, from Syria had arrived (IgnPhd 11:1), Ignatius speaks of "peace" in Antioch and calls on the churches to send representatives to Antioch to rejoice with the church "because they are at peace".[29]

The nature of the "peace" in Antioch has been much debated. It seems most likely that Ignatius had failed to preserve unity and concord in Antioch where there had been very significant opposition to him, particularly to his concept of church order and the role of the bishop. It seems likely that there had been a challenge to Ignatius' authority in the church in Antioch; for Ignatius, such evidence of disunity seems to have called into question the value of his whole ministry. This explains why he does not write directly of his experiences in Antioch and why he does not write (as far as we know) to the community there. Further, his warnings in his letters about troublesome elements and divisions, combined with his language of self-depreciation all point in this direction. Thus "peace" in Antioch probably involved the cessation of internal division and dissension and the recovery of peace and harmony in the Christian community, rather than the cessation of persecution.[30] This provides an important background which will enable us to understand some of the statements Ignatius makes.

1.6 Reading Ignatius' rhetoric

1.6.1 The rhetorical device of ascribing fulfillment of a command in advance

Before we proceed further, we need to discuss two features of Ignatius' rhetoric: firstly, that he often makes a recommendation, but says that it is already achieved, and secondly, that he often praises a community lavishly,

---

[27] See Barnard 1966, p20-30; Trevett 1989a, p128; 1989b, p38.

[28] See Trevett 1992, p43, 52, 76; cf. Corwin 1960, p52-87.

[29] See IgnPhd 10.1-11.1; IgnSm 11.2-3; IgnPol 7.1-2; 8.2; see also Pol. Phil 13.1.

[30] See Trevett 1989b, p37-43; 1992, p56-66, who considers the other options; see also Schoedel 1985, p10-11, 13, 212-13, 250-1; Corwin 1960, p25-8. Cf. Grant 1964, p52-3; 1966, p107-8; Mellink 1999, p127-65.

but later shows that the situation is not actually as positive as it sounds at first. Here we will propose a perspective with regard to how to read these rhetorical devices.

In a number of places in the letters Ignatius makes a recommendation, but says that it is in principle already achieved. For example, in IgnEph 4:1 he writes: "Consequently it is right for you to run together with the purpose of the bishop, which you indeed do." However, we will suggest later that this is a rhetorical device, whereby he says that a community is already doing something when in fact they are not, or are not all doing so. Schoedel points to two parallels to this practice. Firstly, Demosthenes defined one function of an orator as "to see things getting a foothold, to foresee what is coming, and to forewarn others."[31] Schoedel notes: "Rhetoricians continued to play this role in Hellenistic cities, and it seems likely that Ignatius' self-understanding is partly shaped by such models."[32] Thus, when he states that his readers are already doing something, he is actually "foreseeing what is coming", or what he hopes is coming, just as Demosthenes had advised, rather than necessarily describing things exactly as they currently are.

Secondly, phrases like "which indeed you do (ὅπερ καὶ ποιεῖτε)", which Ignatius uses in IgnEph 4.1, are found in both private and official Hellenistic letters which were written to make a firm but polite request. Note the following example from P. Freib. 39: "So then I request you earnestly and exhort you to take good care of my horse, as indeed you always do (ὡς καὶ πάντοτε ποιεῖς), and I thank you profusely and will again thank you ..."[33] It seems likely then that in the following examples in which Ignatius makes a recommendation, but says that it is in principle already achieved, he is a following a well established convention of his day.[34]

The question is then, whether the Ephesians had actually been doing what Ignatius ascribes to them, or whether he is rather using the rhetorical device of ascribing fulfillment-in-advance in order to soften what is actually a command that they should start acting in a certain way. Here we will give two examples where Ignatius is clearly ascribing "fulfillment-in-advance", which suggests this is also the case on some occasions in his letter to the Ephesians, which we will discuss below.

Firstly, in IgnSm 4.1, in introducing his discussion of docetism, he writes: "Now I urge these things on you, beloved, knowing that you are of the same mind (εἰδὼς ὅτι καὶ ὑμεῖς οὕτως ἔχετε); but I am guarding you in advance from beasts in human form, whom not only ought you not receive,

---

[31] Demosthenes, Coron. 246; see Schoedel 1985, p129.

[32] Schoedel 1985, p129.

[33] Cited by Schoedel, 1985, p51.

[34] Schoedel (1985, p7) comments that Ignatius shows "the habit of driving home requests by ascribing the fulfillment of them to Ignatius' addressees in advance".

but if possible not even meet." Thus, Ignatius begins by saying that his addressees agree with him and that he is simply guarding them in advance of any trouble. He is not trying to change their minds, since they already see things his way.

However, in IgnSm 5.3 of those who do not confess that Jesus Christ is "the bearer of flesh", he writes: "Their names, which are faithless, it did not seem right to me to record; indeed, I would rather not even remember them until they repent in regard to the passion, which is our resurrection." This suggests that Ignatius is contending against people known to the Smyrnaeans, who know of whom he is speaking.[35] Further, in IgnSm 6.1 Ignatius speaks of one who has τόπος, which probably refers to a position of leadership in the Christian community, who has used his position to promote docetism. What Ignatius says assumes that the person was a member of the church, and the reference to τόπος suggests he was an elder.[36] He was probably a leader of those who were "remaining aloof from eucharist and prayers", who are mentioned in IgnSm 7.1. All of this suggests that in IgnSm 4.1-8.2 Ignatius is not guarding the Smyrnaeans in advance against docetism, but rather contending against a real and present threat. His comment in IgnSm 4.1 that he knows that they are of the same mind and that he is "guarding you in advance" cannot be taken at face value then, but must be seen as rhetorical. Thus Schoedel says "this kind of statement cannot be taken too literally".[37] Rather Ignatius is following the convention of saying that a recommendation he makes is in principle already achieved.

Secondly, in IgnTr 2.2 he write: "It is necessary then (as is your practice (ὥσπερ ποιεῖτε)) to do nothing without the bishop; but be subject also to the presbytery as to the apostles of Jesus Christ." Further, in IgnTr 3.1-2 he writes: "Similarly let everyone respect the deacons as Jesus Christ, as also the bishop who is a type of the Father, and the presbyters as the council of God and as the band of the apostles. Nothing can be called a church without these, concerning which I am persuaded that you are so disposed (περὶ ὧν πέπεισμαι ὑμᾶς οὕτως ἔχειν)." He suggests then that the Trallians are agreed with his understanding of church order.

However, in IgnTr 7.2 he writes: "He who is within the altar is pure - that is, the person who does anything apart from the bishop, presbytery and deacon, is not pure in conscience." This certainly hints at the presence in

---

[35] This is also suggested by IgnSm 7.2 where they are told to remain aloof from docetists and "to speak about them neither privately nor publicly." Clearly Ignatius presupposes that the people concerned are known to the Smyrnaeans.

[36] See Schoedel 1985, p235-6. It is unlikely that he was a gnostic anti-bishop as Bauer (1971, p32) suggested.

[37] Schoedel 1985, p231. He does note however, that overall the language suggests a significant sense of security against the opponents. Compare Trevett 1992, p102-3 who sees IgnSm 4.1 as prophylactic.

Tralles of Christians who acted apart from their leaders.[38] In IgnTr 12.2 Ignatius called for loyalty from the presbyters in particular, which suggests that some of the presbyters were not supporting the bishop. Further, in IgnTr 12.3 he writes: "I pray you to listen to me in love that I may not be a witness against you by having written". This shows that there are significant divisions and tensions within the church at Tralles.[39] These points suggest that when Ignatius says it is their current practice to do nothing without the bishop in IgnTr 3.1-2, he is using the rhetorical device of ascribing fulfillment-in-advance in order to soften a recommendation.[40] In fact, some of them are acting apart from the bishop.[41]

Thus at times Ignatius writes that his addressees are already doing what he recommends, or already agree with him.[42] But in some of these cases it is very likely that in fact they were *not* currently doing what he said, and so he was using the rhetorical device of ascribing fulfillment-in-advance in order to soften what was a command that they should act in a certain way. Currently, for example, his addressees were actually following the teaching of people Ignatius regarded as opponents, or were not already doing what he said.

When we turn to Ignatius' letter to the Ephesians, we find two passages where Ignatius may be using the fulfillment-in-advance rhetorical device in order to soften a command. These are in IgnEph 4.1 and 8.1. We will recall our findings in this section when we discuss these two passages in due course.

1.6.2 Ignatius underplays the extent to which the situation is not to his liking

In a number of places in the letters Ignatius makes a very positive statement about a church and is lavish in his praise, but during the course of the letter it becomes clear that all is not quite as he made it sound at first. This means he tends to minimize the success of teachers who do not adopt his own

---

[38] See Trevett 1992, p89.

[39] See Schoedel 1985, p160.

[40] See Schoedel 1985, p51.

[41] Trevett (1992, p90) sees IgnTr 7.2 as "a warning to Christians against forming conventicles for worship separate from the officers (also IgnEph 5.2 and IgnSm 8), prophylactic rather than for certain a description of what was actually happening in Tralles." But this takes insufficient account of the strength of Ignatius' language here.

[42] Ignatius probably uses the idea of fulfillment in advance on other occasions. 1) Compare IgnMag 11 with the concerns about Judaisers expressed in IgnMag 8-10, which suggest that in 11 Ignatius is addressing a real problem in the community; see Schoedel 1985, p129. 2) Compare IgnTr 8:1 with IgnTr 7:2; 9-11. This comparison suggests that Ignatius' words in IgnTr 8:1 are meant to be read as a recommendation which he is tactfully saying they already follow in principle, in which case his words are not to be taken literally; see Schoedel 1985, p231. 3) Schoedel sees IgnPol 4.1 as another example of the softening of a command; see Schoedel 1985, p269.

theological position or who are not in harmony with the local bishop. We note the following examples.

Firstly, we have already seen that in IgnSm 4.1, although Ignatius writes that the Smyrnaeans "are of the same mind" with respect to Christ's death and resurrection, and that he is simply "guarding you in advance" with respect to docetism, it becomes clear from IgnSm 4.2-8.2 that Ignatius is contending against a real and present threat in Smyrna. Thus in IgnSm 4.1 he significantly underplays the impact of docetism in the Christian community in Smyrna.

Secondly, in IgnMag 11 Ignatius comments with respect to Judaizing that he writes "not because I know that some of you are so disposed, but as one less than you I wish to forewarn you not to get caught on the hooks of vain opinion." However, what Ignatius writes in IgnMag 8-10 suggests that he is actually addressing a real problem within the community. Again he seems to be minimising the success of those who disagreed with him theologically.[43]

Thirdly, at the beginning of the letter to Tralles Ignatius writes about the stability and endurance of the Trallians. They are "at peace in flesh and spirit" (inscr) and they have "a mind blameless and unwavering in endurance, not on loan but according to nature" (1:1). Ignatius also says that he saw "your whole congregation" in Polybius the bishop. Yet in IgnTr 3:3-5:2 it seems that some who have claimed to have esoteric knowledge have had a considerable impact on the Trallians.[44] The community is not as stable as he suggests at first. Further, after having said that "the person who does anything apart from the bishop, presbytery and deacon, is not pure in conscience" (IgnTr 7.2), Ignatius goes on in IgnTr 8.1 to say "Not because I know of any such things among you". However, in view of IgnTr 2.2 and 12.3 it seems likely that some of the Trallians were in fact acting apart from the bishop. Further, in IgnTr 12.2 Ignatius called for loyalty from the presbyters in particular, which suggests that some of the presbyters were not supporting the bishop. They are not as united as Ignatius implies in IgnTr insc-1.1.

Finally, in IgnPhd 3:1 Ignatius corrects what would have been a misleading impression from IgnPhd 2:1-3:1: there was no real division in Philadelphia, only a "filtering out" of alien elements. However, since Ignatius met in one group those who opposed him along with those who agreed with him (IgnPhd 7:1-3), and since some in the community opposed Philo and Rheus Agathopous after Ignatius had visited the community (IgnPhd 11:1) it seems likely that there had not in fact been a "filtering out". It also seems that the Philadelphians were not as concerned about the situation as Ignatius was. Here then his tendency to underplay the extent to which the situation is not to his liking exhibits itself not in underplaying the influence of the opposition but rather in his overplaying the extent of separation. He would in fact like

---

[43] See Schoedel 1985, p129
[44] See Schoedel 1985, p143

them to be more divided at Philadelphia than they are, so that those who opposed him did not "contaminate" the group, just as he would like the opponents to be less successful in Smyrna.

It seems then that we would be wrong to always take Ignatius at face value, for he tends to underplay the extent to which the situation is not to his liking. When he is lavish in his praise, or insists that his readers are not actually suffering from "false teaching" (IgnSm 4.1; IgnMag 11; IgnTr 8.1) and that he is simply writing to give them warning in advance (IgnTr 8.1; IgnSm 4.1), we must investigate further to see if we should take him at face value. Often the letter as a whole shows that he is actually praising them lavishly before telling them that things are not as he would like them to be. As Schoedel comments, "Ignatius seems anxious to avoid leaving the impression that the opposition has had any success at all. Evidently even to concede danger is dangerous."[45] We must keep this tendency in mind as we read the letters.

In his letter to the Ephesians, Ignatius insists that his readers are not suffering from "false teaching" in 6.2 and 8.1. When we examine these passages we will need to ask if Ignatius is again being too lavish with his praise, and is minimizing the success of opponents, or if his praise is genuine.

2. The leadership of the Christians in Ephesus

2.1 The bishop, elders, and deacons

Ignatius regards the leaders of the churches as the focus of unity. Faced in the Asian churches with theological views which he opposed, one feature of Ignatius' strategy against these other views was to argue for a tight organisational structure for the church and obedience by the people to their leaders in order that there might be unity.

The letter to Ephesus gives us the names of some of the leaders, and a little about the organisational structure of Christians in Ephesus.[46] There is a bishop, Onesimus (IgnEph 1.3),[47] a presbytery (πρεσβυτέριον; IgnEph 2.2;

---

[45] Schoedel 1985, p58.

[46] On the names of these leaders see Schoedel 1985, p44-6. Some of the names are Latin, others Greek; Schoedel (1985, p46) describes them as "a mixed bag".

[47] Knox (1960, p85-92) suggested that Onesimus was the slave of Paul's letter to Philemon, partly because of IgnEph 1.1: "Having received in God your much-loved name". Knox thought the mention of a "much-loved name" was a reference to Onesimus, but this is very unlikely particularly since Onesimus was a relatively common name, especially though not exclusively for slaves; see Grant 1966, p31; Schoedel 1985, p44; Martens 1992, p73-86. The papyri mention many people who were farmers and merchants with this name; see Schoedel 1985, p44 n24; Livy 44.16. For suggestions about the meaning of the "name" in

4.1; 20.2),[48] and at least one deacon named Burrhus,[49] who travelled to Smryna to visit Ignatius.[50] Crocus,[51] who also travelled to Smryna was probably also a deacon, since he served Ignatius in the same way as Burrhus did.[52] Other members of the Ephesian community who travelled to Smryna were Euplous and Fronto (IgnEph 2.1). Ignatius says that he "saw all" of the Ephesian Christians through these five men (IgnEph 2.1).[53] This suggests they were all leaders, including Euplous and Fronto, since Ignatius regularly "sees" congregations in their leaders.[54] Thus five leaders had travelled to Smryna to met Ignatius (IgnEph 2.1; see also 21.1).

Ignatius' letters show that the three-fold ministry of bishop, elders and deacons existed in the communities known to him in Asia.[55] In IgnTr 3.1 he writes: "Similarly let everyone respect the deacons as Jesus Christ, as also the bishop who is a type of the Father, and the presbyters as the council of God and as the band of the apostles. Nothing can be called a church without these." He did not create this structure,[56] but found it already in place in the churches to which he wrote. However, we will note below that this structure was not universally accepted in Asia at the time.

What he says gives us some indication of the way the different ministries related to one another and to the people of the community. In some passages Ignatius speaks solely in terms of the authority of the bishop. Thus in IgnEph

---

IgnEph 1.1 see Schoedel 1964, p308-16; 1985, p40-1. It probably refers to the firmness and affection of the Ephesians, and so is a further dimension of Ignatius' portrayal of the Ephesians as a prominent Christian community.

[48] Ignatius does not name any individual presbyters in Ephesus, perhaps simply because none of those who visited him were presbyters. For presbyters elsewhere see IgnMag 2; 13.1; IgnTr 2.2; 7.2; 13.2; IgnPhd 4; 7.1; IgnSm 8.1; 12.2; cf. 1 Tim 4:14.

[49] Ignatius calls Burrhus a deacon, and also calls him a fellow slave (2.1; σύνδουλος), a term Ignatius uses only of deacons (see IgnMag 2; IgnPhd 4; IgnSm 12.2).

[50] For deacons elsewhere see IgnMag 2; 6.1; 13.1; IgnTr 2.3; 3.1; 7.2; IgnPhd insc; 4; 7.1; 10.1f; 11.1; IgnSm 8.1; 10.1; 12.2; IgnPol 6.1.

[51] As he writes, Ignatius wants Burrhus and Crocus to continue to stay with him. We learn from IgnPhd 11.2 and IgnSm 12.1 that Burrhus went on with Ignatius at least as far as Troas and acted as his scribe or as carrier for his letters; see Schoedel 1985, p45. This was financially supported by the Ephesians and the Smyrnaeans. Crocus is also mentioned in IgnRom 10.1; it is likely that he was the carrier of Ignatius' letter to the Romans.

[52] Schoedel 1985, p46.

[53] This broadens the statement in 1.3 which refers to receiving the whole congregation through the bishop.

[54] See IgnMag 2; 6.1; IgnTr 1.1; see also Schoedel 1985, p46.

[55] We will discuss exactly what Ignatius understood by the term episkopos below.

[56] Schoedel (1985, p142) comments on IgnTr 3.1 "He must have found them [bishop, presbyters and deacons] in place wherever he went to make this statement in the matter-of-fact way that he does. It is only his exaltation of the role of the bishop that sometimes strikes us as going beyond what was commonly accepted." Note also IgnPhd 10.2. We can also note that he never mentions a bishop in writing to the Romans.

5.3-6.1 he writes: "Let us be eager, then, not to resist the bishop that we may be obedient to God ... Clearly, then, one must regard the bishop as the Lord himself."[57] In other passages Ignatius speaks of being subject "to the bishop and the presbytery". Thus in IgnEph 2.2 he writes: "It is right, then, in every way to glorify Jesus Christ who glorified you, so that being joined in one obedience, subject to the bishop and the presbytery, you may be holy in every respect."[58]

To be able to appreciate the relationship between the three offices and the community we must turn to Ignatius' other letters. His basic position is shown by these passages from his letter to the Magnesians:
(3.1) "And you are not to take advantage of the youth of your bishop, but to show him all respect in accordance with the power of God the Father, just as I know that also your holy presbyters have not presumed on his apparent youthfulness but, as men wise in God, yield to him ..."
(2.1) "Since, then, I was thought worthy to see ... my fellow slave the deacon Zotion, from whom may I benefit, because he is subject to the bishop as to the grace of God and to the presbytery as to the law of Jesus Christ. ..."
(6.1) ".. I exhort you, be eager to do all things in godly concord, with the bishop set over you in the place of God, and the presbyters in the place of the council of the apostles, and the deacons, most sweet to me, entrusted with the service of Jesus Christ, ... (6.2) ... be united to the bishop and those set over you .."

The hierarchy of office is clear here. The bishop is at the top and the presbyters yield to him (IgnMag 3.1); the deacons are subject to the bishop and the presbyters (IgnMag 2.1);[59] the people are to be subject to the bishop (IgnMag 3.1-4.1; 6.2), but also to the presbyters (IgnMag 6.1, 7.1) and deacons (IgnMag 6.1), who are likewise set over the people,[60] and elsewhere Ignatius can include the deacons among those whom a congregation should obey.[61]

---

[57] See also IgnMag 3.1; 4; IgnTr 2.1; IgnPol 6.1.

[58] See also IgnEph 20.2; IgnMag 2.1; 7.1; IgnTr 2.2; 13.2; Schoedel 1985, p22; Richardson 1937, p439.

[59] Thus for Ignatius deacons are lower in rank than the bishop or the presbyters. It is primarily a serving ministry; see IgnMag 6.1; IgnTr 2.3; see also Schoedel 1985, p141; Genouillac 1907, p169-71.

[60] In IgnMag 13.2 he can also say: "Be subject to the bishop and to each other".

[61] See IgnMag 6.1-2; IgnTr 3.1, 7.2; IgnPhd inscr, 7.1; IgnPol 6.1; see also IgnMag 13.1; IgnPhd 4.1. But note that in IgnSm 8.1 he tells the community to follow the bishop and the presbytery, but to respect the deacons. Ignatius regularly compares the bishop with God or Christ (IgnMag 3.1; 6.1; 13.2; IgnTr 2.1; 3.1; IgnSm 8.1), the presbyters with the NT apostles (IgnPhd 5.1; IgnMag 6.1; IgnTr 2.2; 3.1; IgnSm 8.1; cf 12.1), and the deacons with Jesus Christ (see IgnTr 2.3; 3.1; IgnMag 6.1; cf. IgnSm 8.1); see Genouillac 1907, p132-6.

Thus it is important to note that, while these passages show that the head position belongs to the bishop, the leadership of the community is provided by the three offices of bishop, presbyters and deacons. The bishop, presbyters and deacons taken together are the seat of unity in the church. For Ignatius leadership was collegial to the extent that the bishop was not the only leader the people were to be subject to, nor was he the sole authority in the community. This is clear from the passages quoted above which show that the people are to be subject to the bishop and the presbytery, or to the bishop, presbytery and deacons. Thus in IgnEph 2.2 Ignatius can take it for granted that the congregation should obey the presbytery along with the bishop, and as we have noted, elsewhere Ignatius can include the deacons among those whom a congregation should obey. But another important dimension here is shown by IgnEph 2.1-4.2. As we will note below, in this section Ignatius requests that the Ephesian deacon Burrhus accompany him. While the bishop and presbyters have agreed to this, it seems clear that the congregation needed to agree too, since there were financial repercussions involved. This shows that the bishop cannot really act alone in a matter like this, but must act with the support of the community.

The bishop then is far from an autocratic ruler and to at least some extent needs to work with the elders in particular in a collaborative way.[62] We conclude that with Ignatius we have not gone as far along the road towards a "ruling bishop" (monarchical episcopacy) as is often thought.[63]

---

[62] Only in IgnMag 3.1 does Ignatius say that presbyters should be submissive to the bishop, (although in IgnTr 12.3 it is said that they should refresh the bishop) but this seems to be implied in the distinction between the two orders. But the basic emphasis is collegial. The close connection between the bishop and the presbyters is expressed in the imagery of IgnEph 4.1.

[63] See Schoedel 1985, p23, 46; Richardson 1937, p440; Corwin 1960, p82; Trevett 1992, p202-3. Note the distinction between a ruling bishop ("monarchical episcopacy") in a strictly hierarchical relationship to presbyters, deacons and the congregation and "monepiscopacy" – one bishop who may be little more than a chair of a group of presbyters; see Trevett 1992, p202-3. As we will see, even monepiscopacy is not firmly established in some Asian churches. There is another indication that with Ignatius we have not gone far along the road towards monarchical episcopacy. In IgnPol 7.2, Ignatius instructs Polycarp to call together a "godly council" to elect a delegate to send to Antioch. In IgnPhd 10.1 and IgnSm 11.2 he also spoke of the *church* appointing someone to go to Antioch. That a delegate is not simply selected by the bishop is an indication of the collegial nature of ministry. Schoedel (1985, p23) also comments: "The situation in the Pastoral Epistles is not entirely clear, but it appears that the churches known to Ignatius have moved at most but a step beyond them." Compare Rius-Camps (1980, p32) who reads the letters as implying that the bishops of Ephesus, Magnesia and Tralles are monarchical bishops in the main cities. This is to misread the evidence. See also Genouillac 1907, p137-45, 157-8. It is difficult to determine the function of the presbyters in Ignatius. They function primarily as a group (IgnTr 3.1) and the bishop may have authorised some of their number to conduct the

In writing to the Ephesians Ignatius emphasizes that the presbyters were loyal to the bishop (IgnEph 4.1; see also 5.1). IgnTr 12.2 and IgnSm 6.1 suggest that in these churches there were some uncooperative or even rebellious presbyters. One could understand how difficult such a situation would be for a bishop and why presbyterial loyalty was an important matter for Ignatius.[64] It is noteworthy then that in Ephesus the presbyters were "attuned to the bishop like strings to a cithara" (IgnEph 4.1).

2.2 What is meant by the title "ἐπίσκοπος" when it is used by Ignatius of Onesimus?

At this point we need to clarify what Ignatius means by the title "ἐπίσκοπος", since it is a term which can be used with different senses. Ignatius describes Onesimus as "your bishop" (IgnEph 1.3; 2.1; 5.1) and "the bishop" (IgnEph 4.1, 5.3, 6.1). Onesimus is never called "the bishop of Ephesus". However, Polycarp is called "bishop of the church of the Smyrnaeans" in IgnPol inscr, although none of the other bishops are described as bishop of their city.[65] Further, Ignatius seems to have thought of himself as the one bishop of Antioch,[66] although as we have noted, some in Antioch disagreed with him on church structure.

It is also clear that Ignatius thinks of a bishop as in principle a single "overseer" over a particular area and does not envisage there being two bishops over one geographical area. This is implied by a number of statements. In IgnSm 8 he writes: "You must all follow the bishop as Jesus

---

eucharist (IgnSm 8.1), and perhaps baptism and the agape (IgnSm 8.2). See Genouillac 1907, p166-9.

[64] See Trevett 1992, p81.

[65] Damas is called "your godworthy bishop" in IgnMag 2; Polybius "your bishop" in IgnTr 1.1. The bishop of Philadelphia is not named in IgnPhd 1.1 where we read " Ὁν ἐπίσκοπος ἔγνων ... – "Of which bishop I know ...". Polycarp is called "bishop" in IgnSm 8, 12.

[66] See especially IgnRom 9.1: "Remember in your prayer the church in Syria which has God instead of me for its shepherd"; see also IgnEph 21.2; IgnMag 14; IgnTr 13.1. Notice that in IgnPhd 10.1 he writes that "the church at Antioch in Syria is at peace", which again suggests that he is speaking of all the Christians in Antioch; see also IgnSm 11.1; IgnPol 7.1; Corwin 1960, p44-5. Ignatius calls himself "the bishop of Syria" in IgnRom 2.2 (cf. IgnRom 9.1). This does not mean that he necessarily has responsibility over a wider area, as Grant (1966, p88) thinks (cf. Serapion of Antioch who directs the affairs of the nearby seacoast town of Rhossus at the end of the second century; see Eus HE 6.12.3-6). It is more likely that he speaks of the church of Syria prior to hearing news of the peace at Antioch because only after he heard that news "can he bring himself to utter a name previously linked with such painful memories" (Schoedel 1985, p100). Hence, in IgnPhd 10.1; IgnSm 11.1 and IgnPol 7.1 he speaks of "the church at Antioch in Syria". See also Lightfoot 1889b, Vol 1, p390; Richardson 1937, p438; Trevett 1992, p197-8.

Christ (followed) the Father, and (follow) the presbytery as the apostles; respect the deacons as the commandment of God. Let no one do anything apart from the bishop that has to do with the church. Let that be regarded as a valid eucharist which is held under the bishop or to whomever he entrusts it. Wherever the bishop appears, there let the congregation be; just as wherever Jesus Christ is, there is the whole church.[67] It is not permissible apart from the bishop either to baptize or to celebrate the love-feast; but whatever he approves is also pleasing to God, that everything you do may be sure and valid." Ignatius here shows that he assumes that there was only one person who claimed the office of bishop in Smyrna. In IgnPhd 4.1 he writes: "Be eager, then, to celebrate one eucharist; for one is the flesh of our Lord Jesus Christ, and one the cup for union through his blood; one the altar, *just as one the bishop* along with the presbytery and deacons, my fellow slaves." Given passages like these, it is difficult to imagine that Ignatius thought there could be two "bishops" in any one city. Note in IgnPhd insc and 1.1 we read "Ignatius ... to the church of God the Father ... which is in Philadelphia in Asia, ... which church I greet in the blood of Jesus Christ, which is eternal and abiding joy, especially if they are one with the bishop and with the presbyters and deacons with him .... Of which bishop I know that he obtained a ministry for the community." This again suggests the bishop is over all the Christians in the city of Philadelphia.

Further, in IgnEph 3.2 Ignatius writes: "Indeed Jesus Christ, our inseparable life, is the Father's purpose; as also the bishops, appointed in every quarter, are in the purpose of Jesus Christ." This should not be taken to mean that monepiscopacy was established everywhere,[68] but it does strongly suggest that bishops like Onesimus and Ignatius wanted to claim that they were the sole bishops of Ephesus or Antioch respectively.

Thus it seems likely that, in Ignatius' view, Onesimus was the only one in Ephesus who could be thought of as the episkopos of all Christians in Ephesus. Others may have used the title in a different sense, as episkopos over a house church, but for Ignatius only Onesimus had the right to be seen as episkopos over "the church most worthily blessed which is in Ephesus in Asia" (IgnEph inscr). Only he is "your bishop" (IgnEph 1:3).

Now this was how Ignatius thought the situation should have been. However, we will note below that some people "resisted the bishop" and did

---

[67] Here in IgnSm 8.2 Ignatius refers to the "whole or catholic (καθολική)" church. In the context a reference to universality is required by the comparison between the "catholic church" and the local congregation. Schoedel (1985, p244) notes: "the 'catholic' church here is not the universal church opposed to heresy, but the whole church resistant by its very nature to division." Thus organic unity and opposition to division is implied by the word, rather than geographical extension.

[68] See Schoedel 1985, p49 who notes "Ignatius tends to shape the world about him in his own image."

not acknowledge his authority. For Ignatius this was wrong, but it seems to have been the situation. Of course, it is not certain that Onesimus saw himself as necessarily bishop over all the Christians; he may have been willing to accept that some groups would not acknowledge him. But it does not seem likely that there were other rival claimants to the office of "bishop of Ephesus".

2.3 Teachers, Apostles and Prophets?

The only teacher Ignatius speaks of is Jesus (IgnEph 15.1; IgnMag 9.1); he says nothing about a current office of teacher (cf. Did 1-6), although clearly contemporary leaders had teaching roles. When he speaks of apostles he is referring to a group which belongs to the past, and includes people like Peter and Paul (IgnRom 4.3; see also IgnEph 11.2; IgnMag 7.1; 13.2; IgnTr 7.1; IgnPhd 9.1). Present day itinerant apostles are not in view therefore (cf. Did 11-13).[69] For Ignatius the apostles have been replaced by the presbyters (IgnMag 6.1; IgnTr 2.2; 3.1; IgnPhd 5.1; IgnSm 8.1).[70]

The only prophets Ignatius explicitly mentions are the OT prophets (IgnMag 8.1; 9.2; IgnPhd 5.2; 9.1-2; IgnSm 5.1; 7.2 cf. Did 10.7; 11.7-12). However, it seems clear that Ignatius was himself a prophet (see IgnPhd 7.1-2), and we will comment later about the interest of some of Ignatius' addressees in charismata.

3. To whom is Ignatius of Antioch writing in his letter to Ephesus?

Ignatius begins his letter to Ephesus in this way: "Ignatius, also called Theophorus, to her who has been blessed with greatness by the fullness of God the Father, to her who has been foreordained before the ages, to be forever destined for enduring (and) unchanging glory ... to the church most worthily blessed which is in Ephesus in Asia (τῇ ἐκκλησίᾳ τῇ ἀξιομακαρίστῳ, τῇ οὔσῃ ἐν Ἐφέσῳ τῆς Ἀσίας), abundant greetings ..." (IgnEph, inscr). But who is he actually writing to in Ephesus? There are basically two options. Firstly, he could be writing to all Christians in

---

[69] Ignatius himself does not give commands as if he were an apostle; see IgnTr 3.3; IgnRom 4.3; cf IgnEph 3.1.

[70] However he can also apply the language of the Gospels about apostles "being sent" to the bishop (IgnEph 6.1) which suggests that the bishop is to some extent also analogous to the apostle.

Ephesus.[71] Secondly, he could be writing to one group of Christians in the city. We have argued in Parts Two and Three that there were a number of distinct Christian groups in Ephesus over time and probably at any one time. At the time of Ignatius there could well have existed in Ephesus the descendants of the group addressed by the Pastor who valued Paul, the descendants of the opponents of the Pastor (who probably formed a separate group), the Johannine community addressed in the Johannine letters, and the group which has split from it,[72] perhaps descendants of the Nicolaitans, and perhaps others as well.[73] Although all these groups may not have continued to exist at the time Ignatius wrote, it is most likely that at least some of them did. If Ignatius was just writing to one group (or to several groups, but not to all the Christians in the city), then this could be identified as the same group that the Pastor wrote to, or that 1 John was addressed to, or so forth.[74] Which of these two options is most likely?

Since Ignatius mentions Paul explicitly (see IgnEph 12.2), it might be thought that he was writing to Pauline Christians.[75] However, there are a number of indications in the letter that Ignatius wants to address all the Christians in Ephesus, which suggests that the first view is correct. Firstly, as we have noted, in IgnEph inscr he writes "to the church most worthily blessed which is in Ephesus in Asia (τῇ ἐκκλησίᾳ τῇ ἀξιομακαρίστῳ, τῇ οὔσῃ ἐν Ἐφέσῳ τῆς Ἀσίας)". Given Ignatius' stress on the importance of

---

[71] This is generally assumed by those who write about the letter. For example, Stander (1989, p209) writes that the letter is "to the believers at Eph". Grant (1964, p48) writes "The letters to churches are addressed to entire communities - like most of the Pauline epistles." Clearly he thinks Ignatius was writing to all the Christians in a city.

[72] It is hard to date both when that split occurred, and when Ignatius wrote his letter. But it seems most likely that the split occurred some years before Ignatius wrote.

[73] See Trevett (1992, p80) who suggests with regard to Ignatius' time: "There were, then, competing claims to Christian community in Ephesus." Koester (1971, p155) sees the following rival groups active simultaneously: "the original Pauline church, supported by the circle of Qumran-influenced Paulinist who wrote Ephesians, but also represented by the author of Luke-Acts ..., a Jewish-Christian 'school' engaging in a daring interpretation of the Old Testament (an early gnostic like Cerinthus would fit this description rather well); a heretical sect, called the Nicolaitans ...; and finally, a Jewish-Christian conventicle which was led by the prophet John". See a slightly different list in Koester 1995, p133 (which we quote in Chapter 16, our Overall Conclusions, note 1). This has of course also been the subject of Part Three and we will comment on it further in Chapter 16.

[74] Trevett (1992, p80) speaks of "the particular Ephesian group which our bishop was addressing".

[75] This is the view of Koester 1995, p133: "The congregation that Paul founded and that held on to the tradition of its founder is mentioned in the letter of Ignatius of Antioch to the Ephesians, but this congregation does not seem to have been the only – and perhaps not even the dominating – group of Christians in Ephesos." However, he does not argue for this position. He thinks there were five different groups in Ephesus at the end of the first century CE.

unity in the church, this inscription suggests he sees himself as writing to all the Christians in Ephesus, or at least all those in Ephesus whom he regarded as Christians.[76] It is difficult to see that he could address just one group among many in this way. Secondly, in IgnEph 11.2 he writes of his hope: "that I may be found a participant in the lot of the Christians of Ephesus (ἵνα ἐν κλήρῳ Ἐφεσίων εὑρεθῶ τῶν Χριστιανῶν) who always agreed with the very apostles in the power of Jesus Christ." That he can speak simply of "the Christians in Ephesus" strongly suggests that he has all the Christians in the city in mind. Thirdly, in IgnEph 12.2 he writes: "You are a passage for those slain for God; (you are) fellow initiates of Paul ... who in every letter remembers you in Christ Jesus." Although this could be taken as indicating that Ignatius is addressing a Pauline group, it is also compatible with seeing the addressees as all Ephesian Christians, who, in Ignatius' view can all trace their spiritual lineage back to Paul. Finally, in IgnEph 5.2 he writes: "for if the prayer of one or two has such power, how much more that of the bishop and the whole church (καὶ πάσης τῆς ἐκκλησίας)." This is not definitive, since he could simply be referring to a gathering of a number of house churches under one leader, but that he writes of "πάσης τῆς ἐκκλησίας" does suggest that Ignatius is thinking of all the Christians in the city.

Thus, we propose as a working hypothesis that Ignatius is writing to all the Christians, and thus all the Christian groups, in the city. We will now seek to show that this hypothesis is supported by the letter to the Ephesians and adequately explains what Ignatius writes. We will also seek to determine for which of the possible groups in Ephesus Ignatius provides us with evidence.

3.1 Non-attendance at the assembly and "Resisting the Bishop"

In IgnEph 5.1-6.1 Ignatius writes of Christians who "resist the bishop". Here we will discuss this situation, and will argue that, while some Christians in Ephesus are probably not opposing the developments in church structure which are in process, others are not in agreement with these developments and so "resist the bishop". Those who oppose these developments may well have included some who favoured a greater emphasis on the forms of authority which John the Seer made use of in Revelation and others who were from the Johannine community and so favoured a much more collegial church structure.

---

[76] There could have been others who regarded themselves as Christians, but whom Ignatius regarded as "atheists"; see IgnTr 10.1.

3.1.1 The Problem

In IgnEph 5.1 Ignatius writes of how blessed the Ephesians were to have such a spiritual bishop as Onesimus, and then goes on in 5.2-3:

> Let no one deceive himself: if anyone is not within the altar, he lacks the bread of God; for if the prayer of one or two has such power, how much more that of the bishop and the whole church (καὶ πάσης τῆς ἐκκλησίας)! 3) He, then, who does not come to the assembly (ἐπὶ τὸ αὐτό), by that very fact displays arrogance and has judged himself. For it is written, 'God resists the arrogant.' Let us be eager, then, not to resist the bishop that we may be obedient to God.

That Ignatius regards what he says as a very serious matter is shown by his introductory words: "Let no one deceive himself" (IgnEph 5.2).[77] However, he does not seem to be thinking of external opponents here (see IgnEph 7, 9, 16-17), since his language is much harsher when they are in view.[78] If it is not a matter of different beliefs, what is the passage about?

When Ignatius says "if anyone is not within the altar (θυσιαστήριον)", it is most unlikely that he has a physical altar in mind,[79] since elsewhere he uses θυσιαστήριον symbolically to refer to the church (IgnMag 7.2; IgnTr 7.2). This seems to be the meaning here also, since Ignatius goes on to emphasize the importance of corporate prayer. The passage thus suggests that a small number of people are meeting together, but apart from the bishop and the rest of the church. This is implied by the phrase "for if the prayer of one or two has such power, how much more that of the bishop and the whole church (καὶ πάσης τῆς ἐκκλησίας)!" (IgnEph 5.2). Thus some people are praying together, and Ignatius acknowledges that their prayer is powerful. They are not, however, coming to the assembly (IgnEph 5.3), which is the gathering under the bishop,[80] since these people are said to "resist the bishop". Nor are they "within the altar", that is, they are not a part of the community over which the bishop presides, and so lack, in Ignatius' opinion, the true bread of God (IgnEph 5.2). Thus, Ignatius exhorts them to join with the bishop and the whole church, for then their prayer will be even more powerful.[81] This is in

---

[77] Similar formulae are found elsewhere: IgnEph 16.1; IgnMag 8.1; IgnPhd 3.3; IgnSm 6.1; and in the NT in 1 Cor 6:9; 15:33; Gal 6:7; Jas 1:16.

[78] Schoedel 1985, p54.

[79] Some early Christian writers deny that there were such altars in the church; see Minucius Felix Oct. 32.1; Origen Cels 8.17. τράπεζα (table) was used in connection with the eucharist; see Schoedel, p55. Johanny 1978, p55 sees it as a physical altar; Kieffer 2000, p294 interprets it symbolically.

[80] We will show below that for Ignatius the only valid assembly is under the bishop.

[81] There is also more than one group at prayer in Magnesia; see IgnMag 7.1; 14. Note also IgnTr 12.2, which may suggest that some are praying separately at Tralles too, particularly in view of the indications in IgnTr 2.2; 7.2; 12.2-3 that there was a significant rift in the church there.

keeping with Ignatius' emphasis elsewhere on the power of corporate prayer.[82]

We see then that some Christians in Ephesus had a measure of independence from the bishop.[83] Ignatius regards such independence as arrogance (IgnEph 5.3) and answers it with a quotation from Prov 3:34 to the effect that God resists the arrogant. Hence the offenders should obey the bishop by coming together in unity in order that they may be obedient to God rather than arrogant. But the arrogance of these people seems to be simply that they believe they can worship apart from the bishop. To Ignatius this was arrogance, but of course those who worshipped apart from the bishop would not have seen themselves in this light, but may well have regarded the bishop as presumptuous.

In two other passages in the letter Ignatius repeats this theme of the necessity for all the Ephesian Christians to meet together, which shows how significant this problem of some not attending the assembly was for Ignatius. Firstly, in IgnEph 13.1-2 we read: "Be eager, then, to meet more often for thanksgiving (εὐχαριστίαν) and glory to God; for when you come together often, the powers of Satan are broken, and his destructiveness is shattered by the concord of your faith. Nothing is better than peace, by which all warfare of heavenly and earthly beings is destroyed."[84] Clearly, for Ignatius their lack of unity in worship, and, in view of 5.2-3, we may suggest their lack of concord about the importance of worshipping with the bishop, hindered the effectiveness of their spiritual lives. He urges them to meet more frequently since meetings would promote unity (see also IgnPol 4.2). Further, in saying that "nothing is better than peace", he may be indicating that currently there is considerable disagreement between Christians, and that this is a key reason that they are not worshipping together.

Secondly, in IgnEph 20.2 as part of the closing of the letter, Ignatius writes: "All of you,[85] severally and in common, continue to come together

---

[82] He sees corporate prayer as an expression of the unity of the community; see IgnMag 7.1; IgnTr 12.2; IgnSm 7.1. It will lead to conversion of the pagan (IgnEph 10.1-2) and of opponents (IgnSm 4.1) and the destruction of Satan's powers (IgnEph 13). He also asks for corporate prayer for the success of his martyrdom and peace in Antioch; see Schoedel 1985, p55.

[83] Schoedel (1985, p54) speaks of some Ephesians who "exercised a measure of independent judgment." See also Bauer 1971, p68.

[84] Schoedel (1985, p74) notes that both εὐχαριστία and "glory" are primarily terms for prayer to God at the celebration of the eucharist; see also IgnPhd 4; IgnSm 7.1; 8.1; IgnEph 5.2.

[85] Following Zahn's suggested emendation of the text from ὅτι to τι; see Schoedel 1985, p95-6; cf. Grant 1966, p52 who translates 20.2: "especially if the Lord reveals to me that individually you are all joining ... in one faith and in Jesus Christ." Trevett (1992, p82) follows Grant.

(συνέρχεσθε) in grace, as individuals, in one faith and in Jesus Christ ... that you may obey the bishop and the presbytery with undistracted mind, breaking one bread, which is the medicine of immortality". Again Ignatius emphasizes the need to come together in unity in obedience to the bishop and the presbytery. In this context, and in this context alone, should they "break one bread" together. Other eucharists are unacceptable; it is only this one bread broken by the bishop which is the medicine of immortality.[86]

We see then that the fact that some were "resisting the bishop" and not meeting together with him and the rest of the church was, in Ignatius' eyes, a significant problem in the Ephesian Christian community.[87] We will seek to explain this situation in more depth.

3.1.2 Their own gatherings

We have noted that IgnEph 5.2 suggests that some Ephesian Christians were meeting together, but apart from the bishop and the rest of the church. It is likely that these Christians were actually meeting together separately in one or more house churches. Although Ignatius does not say directly that the Christians he addressed met in house churches, this was clearly the case.[88] Given that we know of the importance of house churches in this period, and that there seems to have been a reasonable number of addressees in Ephesus,

---

[86] See Snyder 1963, p10.

[87] A significant part of the difficulty Ignatius had in Antioch probably concerned his view of the church and his advocacy of monepiscopacy; see Trevett 1992, p48. Thus, it is possible that he was particularly aware of this issue and sensitive to it. However, in view of the amount he says on the topic, and that adequate explanation can be given for the situation in the Asian churches he presupposes, it seems very likely that in speaking of people "resisting the bishop" he was also reflecting the actual state of affairs in Asian churches; see Trevett 1992, p81.

[88] We will note below that this is suggested by IgnEph 5.2. Further, in IgnEph 20.2 we read: "All of you, severally and in common (οἱ κατ᾽ ἄνδρα κοινῇ πάντες), continue to come together in grace". That Ignatius speaks of coming together "severally and in common" suggests that on some occasions they met as house churches ("severally") and on other occasions they met in larger groups ("in common"), which were perhaps the meeting of a several house churches. (Note also that the "bishop and the whole church" in IgnEph 5.2 may refer to the gathering together in one place of a number of house churches, or they may be the different house groups united around the bishop. IgnMag 7.2 ("All of you, hurry together as to one temple of God, as to one altar, to one Jesus Christ") may also suggest that a number of house churches came together on some occasions.) But these references, and all that we know of early Christianity in this period, make it likely that the Christians Ignatius was writing to met in house churches. Thus Corwin (1960, p85) comments: "Private houses probably still serve as the normal meeting places for the congregation (IgnEph 5.2, 20) of which he speaks directly more than once." Schoedel (1985, p240) comments: "there can be little doubt that separate meetings in different houses were usual in the early period." See also Schoedel 1985, p243.

since a number of leaders are mentioned, we must suppose that the addressees met in a number of house churches, and the bishop went from one to another on different occasions, or exercised authority and granted approval in some similar way, probably through authorizing others as his agents.[89] So those who are not meeting with the bishop, are probably meeting together in one or more house churches, but apart from the bishop or without his approval.[90] This is suggested by IgnEph 5.2 where the contrast between "the whole church" with the bishop and the powerful prayer of one or two apart from the rest of the church suggests that these one or two were meeting separately in a house church. That Ignatius often underplays the extent to which a situation is not to his liking suggests that there were significantly more than "one or two" involved. Thus the Ephesian Christians were not united, but rather different groups seem to have existed, groups which were not all under the bishop Onesimus.

Before we go on to discuss the reasons why some were "resisting the bishop" in Ephesus, we will note parallel examples in other cities addressed by Ignatius. That, in Ignatius' opinion, this phenomenon occurred in other places, means that we are right to see "resisting the bishop" as a problem in Ephesus.

3.1.3 Meeting "apart from the bishop" elsewhere in Asia

It is not only in the letter to the Ephesians that Ignatius refers to Christians resisting the bishop or meeting apart from him. Here we will note three examples.

Firstly, in IgnMag 4.1 we read: "It is right, then, not only to be called Christians but also to be Christians; just as some certainly use the title 'bishop' but do everything apart from him. Such people do not seem to me to act in good conscience because they do not meet validly in accordance with the commandment." The passage suggests that some people used the title bishop, but "do everything apart from him" and thus were in actual fact

---

[89] In IgnSm 7.1 we read "Let no one do anything apart from the bishop that has to do with the church. Let that be regarded as a valid eucharist which is held under the bishop or to whomever he entrusts it." This last clause suggests that the bishop was not at all the eucharists, which may well have been physically impossible, in Ephesus at least, but that all eucharists were held with his approval and so "under the bishop", either personally or through the supervision of his agents.

[90] Note Ignatius addresses his letter "to the church ... which is in Ephesus" (IgnEph inscr). But this does not suggest there were no house churches, since Paul can similarly address the Corinthians as "To the church of God which is at Corinth" (1 Cor 1:2; see also 2 Cor 1:1) and we know of the existence of house churches in Corinth. The ἐκκλησία is then the group of Christians in the city, the sum total of house churches, in both Paul and Ignatius.

ignoring the bishop, probably in matters of worship, but perhaps in other matters as well. This explains Ignatius' long digression in IgnMag 3.1-5.2 on episcopal authority. Further, in IgnMag 7.1-2 Ignatius writes: "As, then, the Lord did nothing without the Father - being united (with him) - neither by himself nor through the apostles, so you too do nothing without the bishop and presbyters, nor try to have anything appear right by yourselves (ἰδίᾳ ὑμῖν); but (let there be) one prayer in common, one petition, one mind, one hope in love, in blameless joy. ... All of you, hurry together as to one temple of God, as to one altar, to one Jesus Christ, who proceeded from the one Father and was with the one and returned (to him)." Schoedel notes in this regard: "the division that Ignatius fears is one that has to do with groups - not individuals - that go their own way. The expression ἰδίᾳ ('individually') when used with plurals (ὑμῖν 'yourselves') refers to the private meeting of groups."[91] Thus Ignatius refers here to Christians meeting apart from the bishop in Magnesia, meetings which he opposed.[92] In this context, that he speaks of the need for there to be "one prayer in common" suggests that a group was worshipping apart from the bishop.

Secondly, in IgnPhd 4, after having warned about fleeing divisions and the teaching of opponents, and not following a schismatic (IgnPhd 2.1-3.3) Ignatius writes: "Be eager, then, to celebrate one eucharist; for one is the flesh of our Lord Jesus Christ, and one the cup for union through his blood; one the altar, just as one the bishop along with the presbytery and deacons." This suggests that there were rival eucharists in Philadephia,[93] and the likelihood of this is confirmed by IgnPhd 7.2-8.1: "Do nothing without the bishop, keep your flesh as the temple of God. Love union, flee division (τοὺς μερισμοὺς φεύγετε). ... I then did my part as a man set on union. Where there is division and anger, God does not dwell. All, then, who repent the Lord forgives, if they turn in repentance to the unity of God and the council of the bishop."[94]

---

[91] Schoedel 1985, p116.

[92] Compare the situation at Philadelphia on which Schoedel (1985, p196) comments: "the bishop of Philadelphia is not in full control of the situation (cf. IgnPhd. 6-8) and apparently cannot deal to Ignatius' satisfaction with those who 'talk vanity'."

[93] Corwin (1960, p58) notes (her emphasis): "the emphasis on the *one* eucharist clearly suggests the existence of competing forms." See also Snyder 1963, p10.

[94] Trevett (1989c, p315) comments with respect to the situation at Philadelphia that "there was the possibility of meetings organised apart from the bishop and his circle, something Ignatius deplored (1; 3.2-3; 7.1; 8.1)." Note also IgnPhd inscr "which (church) I greet in the blood of Jesus Christ, which is eternal and abiding joy, especially if they are at one with the bishop and with the presbyters and deacons with him". The stress on unity with the ministry here is because Ignatius thought there was a grave threat to authority in IgnPhd from dissident members of the community. However, Bauer (1971, p70) was wrong to translate this as "'Polycarp and those presbyters who are with him' - that is, who are on his side", thus suggesting that some presbyters and deacons resisted the bishop, since the Greek means simply "those presbyters with him".

The term μερισμός ("division") occurs five times in IgnPhd and only once elsewhere (IgnSm 7.2).[95] From the letter it seems clear that the "divisions" involved "false teaching" to some extent, in this case people Ignatius regarded as Judaizers (IgnPhd 6-9). However, Schoedel shows that there was no serious theological disagreement between Ignatius and these opponents (such as disagreement about the person of Christ or the place of the law).[96] Rather their expertise in scriptural interpretation probably posed a threat to leaders. In addition, it is clear that a key issue with regard to "division" focussed on church governance. These opponents were the people who tried to deceive Ignatius (IgnPhd 7.1) and against whom he said: "Do nothing without the bishop" (IgnPhd 7.2), a proclamation the Spirit made through him. Thus IgnPhd 7.2-8.1 together with IgnPhd 4 suggest that there was a group within the community who acted apart from the bishop.[97]

Thirdly, in IgnSm 7.1-8.2, after having spoken of docetists who hold "erroneous opinions" Ignatius writes: "They remain aloof from eucharist and prayers because they do not confess that the eucharist is the flesh of our saviour Jesus Christ ... You must all follow the bishop as Jesus Christ (followed) the Father, and (follow) the presbytery as the apostles; respect the deacons as the commandment of God. Let no one do anything apart from the bishop that has to do with the church. Let that be regarded as a valid eucharist which is held under the bishop or to whomever he entrusts it. Wherever the bishop appears, there let the congregation be; just as wherever Jesus Christ is, there is the whole church. It is not permissible apart from the bishop either to baptize or to celebrate the love-feast; but whatever he approves is also pleasing to God, that everything you do may be sure and valid."

Further, in IgnSm 9.1 we read: "It is good to acknowledge God and the bishop: he who honors the bishop is honored by God; he who does anything without the bishop's knowledge serves the devil." Again this suggests Ignatius has in mind those who resist the authority of the one bishop. That the docetists remained aloof from the eucharist (IgnSm 7.1), that Ignatius writes of no one doing anything apart from the bishop and of valid eucharists being those held under the bishop or his appointees, strongly suggests that the docetists held their own eucharist without reference to the bishop.[98] This suggests that there were docetic house churches, probably led by an elder (see IgnSm 6.1), which would explain what is said about separate meetings. It

---

[95] See Schoedel 1985, p197.

[96] See Schoedel 1985, p205.

[97] See Trevett 1992, p92-9.

[98] See Corwin 1960, p56, 208; Grant 1966, p120; Schoedel 1985, p240-4; Trevett 1992, p102. In IgnTr 11.1 Ignatius calls the docetic teachers extraneous "side-growths" or "suckers" (παραφυάδες), which shows that he views them as illegitimate offshoots of the Christian community; see Schoedel 1985, p156. But the image also suggests that the docetists are meeting in separate groups.

seems likely that they also avoided eucharists in other settings because of the eucharistic theology involved.[99]

That people seem to have been meeting "apart from the bishop" in Magnesia, Philadephia and Smyrna reinforces the likelihood that this was what was occurring in Ephesus and thus corroborates our view that some Ephesian Christians were meeting apart from the bishop.[100]

3.2 The motives for independence from the bishop

Why did some Ephesian Christians "resist the bishop"? Why would they pray and worship apart from him and not come to the bishop's assembly or an assembly authorised by him? We will now seek to address these questions, and they will lead us to an answer to the question of who Ignatius'addressees were.

3.2.1 Those who "resist the bishop" still "live according to the truth"

In some places theological differences led some Christians to worship apart from the bishop. We have noted that those who did not follow the bishop in Smyrna were docetists and that in Philadelphia they were Judaizers. Further, the disunity Ignatius opposed in Magnesia (see especially IgnMag 4 and 7) may have been related to the Judaizers there (IgnMag 6-10), although this was probably not the only source of disunity.[101] In each case, one of Ignatius' strategies for combating these opponents was that there should be only one eucharist under the bishop.[102]

However, it seems unlikely that doctrinal differences were a factor in people resisting the bishop in Ephesus. After discussing the problem of those who "resist the bishop" in 5.1-6.1 Ignatius then writes in 6.2: "Now indeed Onesimus himself praises highly your godly orderliness (ὑμῶν τὴν ἐν θεῷ εὐταξίαν) - that you all live according to the truth (ὅτι πάντες κατὰ ἀλήθειαν ζῆτε), and that no heresy dwells among you (καὶ ὅτι ἐν ὑμῖν

---

[99] It is also likely that instructions for Christians to meet frequently are connected with the problem of people meeting apart from the bishop. In IgnPol 4.2 we read: "Let meetings be held more often; seek out all individually." Cf. IgnEph 13.1; Didache 16.2; 2 Clem 17:3; see also Grant 1966, p44. We will discuss the situation in Philadelphia and Smyrna, and the position of the bishop in each case, in more detail below.

[100] IgnTr 7.2 and 12.3 suggest that there may have been a similar situation in Tralles, in which case in IgnTr 2.2 Ignatius would be using the rhetorical device of ascribing fulfillment in advance in order to soften a recommendation.

[101] See Trevett 1992, p85-7.

[102] Ignatius never considers the possibility that a bishop may be a Docetist or Judaizer, which perhaps in itself points to the numerical strength of those who followed Ignatius' line theologically; cf. Bauer 1971, p61-76.

οὐδεμία αἵρεσις κατοικεῖ);[103] but you do not even listen to anyone except him who speaks truly concerning Jesus Christ." Further, he emphasizes that they have not listened to the opponents (IgnEph 9.1), so it is unlikely that some are "resisting the bishop" because they were docetists.

Here Ignatius makes it clear that, in his view, the Christian community he addressed did not tolerate false doctrine. Although we will suggest in Chapter 15 that it was not quite as straightforward as this, it does seem clear that the Ephesians were not following other teaching in the way that had occurred in Smyrna and Philadelphia. Thus, the problem of "resisting the bishop" was not a doctrinal one and Ignatius has no theological argument with those who do not come to the bishop's assembly, nor does he give any indication that he regards these independent Ephesians as deficient in belief. But he strongly disagreed with the disunity that they created and, given Ignatius' overall insistence that unity with the bishop was the way to avoid "false teaching", he may regard such independence as potentially dangerous since in his opinion those who are not united with the bishop will be vulnerable to what he regards as heresy. This is also suggested by the fact that in IgnEph 7.1f he turns his attention to precisely this problem of opponents who threaten the Christian community but who clearly had made little progress. If the reason for people "resisting the bishop" was not a doctrinal disagreement, then what was it? We will suggest there were two reasons.

3.2.2 The silence of Onesimus

At least one reason why some Ephesian Christians "resisted the bishop" is suggested by IgnEph 6.1, where Ignatius addresses the matter of the "silence" of the bishop Onesimus. He writes: "And the more anyone sees a bishop keep silence, the more he should fear him. For everyone whom the householder sends into his stewardship, him must we receive as the one who

---

[103] Schoedel (1985, p58 n3) thinks αἵρεσις "points back to the absence of strife ('faction') just discussed (cf. 4.1) and forward to the inability of false teachers ('heresy') to make inroads in Ephesus." However, in referring back to IgnEph 4.1 Schoedel overlooks the fact that in IgnEph 5.1-6.1 Ignatius had addressed precisely the issue of some not coming to the assembly and resisting the bishop - i.e. factionalism. Thus it is difficult to think that καὶ ὅτι ἐν ὑμῖν οὐδεμία αἵρεσις κατοικεῖ means here "that no faction dwells among you", since this seems to be contradicted by IgnEph 5.1-6.1. It seems much more appropriate here then to translate αἵρεσις as "heresy". The likelihood of this translation is reinforced by the previous phrase in IgnEph 6.2 – "that you all live according to the truth" and by the reference immediately afterwards, not to a lack of division (eg. "but you are all subject to the bishop"), but to a doctrinal matter - only listening to someone speaking truly concerning Jesus Christ. This meaning for αἵρεσις is also more suitable in the context of IgnTr 6.1, as Schoedel himself recognises (1985, p12 n65). Note that Trevett (1992, p80) translates αἵρεσις as "heresy" and takes it to refer in IgnEph 6.2 and IgnTr 6.1 specifically to docetic teaching.

sent him. Clearly, then, one must regard the bishop as the Lord himself." The fact that immediately after speaking in 5.2-3 of those who do not come to the assembly Ignatius goes on to speak of the silence of the bishop, strongly suggests that the two matters are linked, and that part of the reason for people staying away and maintaining their own groups is the bishop's silence.[104] This is one reason why they "resist the bishop".

The argument of IgnEph 6.1 deserves closer attention, since it is compressed. The argument seems to be:[105]

1) The bishop keeps silent.

2) The bishop is to be respected all the more when he shows himself willing to remain silent.

3) For in doing so the bishop points to the authority of the one who sent him.

4) To show silence is therefore the mark of Christ's servant.

5) Therefore he should be feared all the more.

Here then Ignatius argues that the bishop's silence is a virtue, and not a reason to disregard him. He makes a virtue out of what others seem to have seen as a weakness.[106] Ignatius returns to the subject of the silence of the bishop in IgnEph 15:1-2 where he writes: "It is better to be silent and to be (καὶ εἶναι)[107] than while speaking not to be. To teach is good if the one who

---

[104] See Trevett 1992, p82. It seems that in Philadelphia the silence of the bishop was also a problem which led some to stay away from the bishop's gatherings (IgnPhd 1.1). Similarly in Magnesia it may have been the youthfulness of the bishop Damas (see IgnMag 3.1) which led some people to feign obedience to the bishop, but to stay away from the bishop's circle; see Trevett 1992, p85.

[105] See Schoedel 1985, p56. Others have filled in the unexpressed part of this argument quite differently. Chadwick (1950, p169-72) discusses the references to the silence of bishops in IgnEph 6.1; 15; IgnPhd 1.1. He suggests that the argument was that since God is silence (IgnEph 19.1; IgnMag 8.2) and the bishop is the earthly representative of God (eg IgnMag 6.1; IgnTr 3; IgnRom 9.1), therefore Ignatius attributed to the bishop characteristics which he also predicates of God. Chadwick (1950, p171-2) writes: "Silence being therefore a primary characteristic of God Himself, Ignatius is led by his theory that the bishop is the earthly counterpart of the divine archetype to his notion that the silence of the bishop is a matter of the profoundest significance. God is silence, therefore when men see their bishop silent, the more reverence should they feel towards him, for it is then that he is most like God." See also Barnard 1966, p26-7; Corwin 1960, p123. However, in IgnEph 5.3-6.1 Ignatius does not refer to God's silence, but rather to the idea of the householder sending someone into his stewardship; see also Schoedel 1985, p57. The silence of God was a very important theme in Gnosticism, but an examination of this is beyond the scope of our inquiry here; see further Schoedel 1985, p120-2; Paulsen 1978, p110-18. Note that the reference to "in the stillness of God" in IgnEph 19.1 may be derived from Wis 18:14-15; see Cabaniss 1956, p97-102.

[106] Grant (1966, p37) comments: "Ignatius' argument is really rather ad hoc, since he himself possesses spiritual knowledge (Trall 5:2) and can speak with God's voice, that is, the Spirit can speak through him (Philad. 7:1-2)."

[107] Schoedel, p77 regards the meaning of "to be" as "to be what one professes (a Christian)".

speaks acts. One, then, is the teacher who 'spoke and it was so,' and also what he has effected in silence is worthy of the Father. He who truly possesses the word of Jesus is able also to hear his silence, that he may be perfect, that he may act through what he says, and may be known through that in which he is silent."

It seems very likely that again it is the silence of the bishop which is in view, and that he is the one who is silent, and who hears Christ's "silence" (cf. IgnEph 6.1). The very fact that Ignatius returns to this subject suggests it was a matter of some embarrassment and reinforces the suggestion that it is one of the reasons for some not meeting with the bishop. Further, Ignatius seems to have the bishop in mind when he writes in IgnEph 15.1: "To teach is good if the one who speaks acts". The implication may be that talk without action characterizes the opponents,[108] while the bishop does not speak without backing up what he says with deeds. Ignatius implies that Christ is the one true teacher, whose silent deeds speak volumes, as compared to these opponents, who are only words.[109]

Ignatius also says that Christ's silent deeds are regarded as worthy of the Father, for Christ is clearly "the teacher who 'spoke and it was so'" (IgnEph 15.1). This means Ignatius is able to attribute great significance to the silence of the bishop. Further, when he says in IgnEph 15.2 that: "He who truly possesses the word of Jesus is able also to hear his silence" then this is another argument in support of Onesimus' silence. Only one who is silent him or herself can hear another's silence; if the person speaks, the other person's silence is lost. It is Onesimus then, the silent one, who truly possesses the word of Jesus. He is the one who "may be perfect, ... and may be known through that in which he is silent" (IgnEph 15.2). Again then, Ignatius is supporting Onesimus in his silence. However, it seems that, at least to some extent, Ignatius is making a virtue out of necessity, and that the silence of Onesimus was indeed a problem for some of the Ephesian Christians, since Ignatius goes to such lengths to see it positively.[110]

---

[108] See Schoedel 1985, p77. We will discuss the opponents, who are in view in IgnEph 16-19, in Chapter 15.

[109] Schoedel (1985, p77) comments: "Here again he [Ignatius] is probably trying to defend the bishop's failure to confront the opposition effectively. He is suggesting that evil of such dimension must be left to Christ and that the bishop's quiet demeanor is more in accord with the mind of Christ." Words are not devalued by Ignatius in this passage, but the silence of the bishop was the problem in view.

[110] Ignatius again seeks to make a virtue out of necessity in speaking of the silence of the bishop of Philadelphia in IgnPhd 1.1 where he attributes more power to silence than to words; see Schoedel 1985, p196. In IgnEph 15.3 Ignatius writes: "Nothing escapes the Lord's notice, but even our secrets are near him. Let us then do everything knowing that he dwells in us." Given that Ignatius has just spoken about silence, almost certainly with the

What does Ignatius mean by saying that Onesimus was silent, and why was his silence a factor which led to some staying away from the assembly over which Onesimus presided, as Ignatius clearly implies (IgnEph 5.3-6.1)? A number of suggestions have been made. Perhaps Onesimus had a retiring nature,[111] or was ineloquent.[112] Perhaps he lacked spiritual gifts and was not able to pray and prophesy extemporaneously and so was forced to remain silent (cf. Did 10.7), in which case his silence meant he was unable to give the "word of the Lord" expected of those "sent" in his name (IgnEph 6, 15; Mt 10:16-20; Didache 4.1; 11.1-6; 12.1-5).[113] Finally, the discussion of Onesimus' silence along with the mention of Christ as the one physician (IgnEph 7.2) and the only teacher (IgnEph 15.1), with these roles not being attributed to any human in addition to Christ, suggests that Onesimus lacked the ability to be able to refute the opponents in debate.[114] If this was the case, his silence would have included the avoidance of what he regarded as dangerous debate with opponents.

In any case, it seems that the bishop's silence was one reason why some Ephesian Christians "resisted the bishop" and did not come to the bishop's assembly. Schoedel suggests: "We may conjecture that those who stayed away from worship found little in their inarticulate bishop to interest them."[115]

3.2.3 Evidence from Ephesus for a time of transition in church structure

We have already noted that some in Ephesus were "resisting the bishop" (IgnEph 5.2-6.1) and that one reason for this was Onesimus' silence.

---

bishop's silence in view, it seems likely that here he warns that even the silent thoughts of those inclined to resist the bishop are known to God, who hears even silent opposition.

[111] See Lightfoot 1889b, Vol 2, p46

[112] See Corwin 1960, p123.

[113] See Grant 1966, p37; Meinhold 1979, p19-25; Trevett 1989c, p320. In Meinhold's view, Ignatius defends the bishop by interpreting his silence in semi-Gnostic fashion. Trevett (1989c, p320) adds: "As in Jn 13:52 [sic, read 13:20] and elsewhere Ignatius used *pempo*. Indeed this was probably precisely the kind of 'word' which Asian Christians had received from the Seer and the prophets referred to in the Apocalypse. And the later Montanists would appeal to that tradition."

[114] See Schoedel 1985, p56.

[115] Schoedel, p56. In IgnEph 1.3 Ignatius writes that Onesimus is "indescribable in love, yet your bishop in the flesh". Schoedel (1985, p44) comments: "It is likely that Ignatius wants to say that there is much more to the man than meets the eye." This seems to be a further indication that Onesimus is not appreciated by some in Ephesus. All of this raises the question of why Onesimus became bishop of Ephesus? Perhaps Onesimus had other qualities (in IgnEph 1.3 Ignatius praises Onesmius' love), or perhaps he was the best person available. Or were the Ephesians used to great eloquence in their leaders and so had extremely high expectations of Onesimus. We simply do not know.

However, it seems likely that there was another factor behind the resistance of some towards the bishop. The evidence suggests that this was a time of transition in Ephesus with regard to church structure, and that one reason that some were "resisting the bishop" was that they were resisting these changes.

In IgnEph 6.1 Ignatius refers to someone being sent in this way: "For everyone whom the householder sends into his stewardship, him must we receive as the one who sent him. Clearly, then, one must regard the bishop as the Lord himself." Here, using material from Christian tradition, Ignatius is saying that the bishop has been "sent" by God the householder, and "must be received" by the Ephesians, since, according to tradition, the one sent by God must be received as God himself.[116] This, and the comment that "one must regard the bishop as the Lord himself" suggest that some Christians in Ephesus disagreed that the bishop had indeed been sent to them by God, and so did not receive him. Even if Onesimus was silent, Ignatius argues, he should be received, and his authority respected because he was sent by God. However, the passage suggests that one reason some Ephesians resisted the bishop was because they did not see him as one with God-given authority.[117]

This suggests that some Ephesian Christians were resisting a change in church structure, which involved the bishop claiming to have authority over all the Christians in Ephesus. We have noted that the church structure which Ignatius presupposes was a long way from the actual rule of the one bishop over all Christians in one city, since the bishop needs to work with the elders in particular in a collaborative way and the views of the people are significant.[118] But even monepiscopacy would have been a significant development for Christians used to leadership being provided by a group of presbyters, with no one person being regarded as the leader of the leaders. Thus, some Ephesian Christians seem to have argued that the one bishop had not been "sent" to them by God, and need not be received. Thus they need

---

[116] Schoedel (1985, p56 n 15) points out that there are two elements from tradition here. Firstly, Mt 21:33-41 where the householder sends servants into the vineyard. Secondly in Mt 10:40 and Gal 4:14 we read of receiving Christ's representatives as Christ himself, and in Jn 13:20 of accepting the one whom he sends. Schoedel (1985, p56 n15) argues that since the term οἰκοδεσπότης occurs only here in Ignatius, and οἰκονομία only in a different sense in IgnEph 18.2; 20.1, it is likely that Ignatius is here reliant on a source. Perhaps the source was Onesimus, who had used the argument himself in Ephesus? Note also that Didache 11.2, 4; 12.1 say that those sent in the Lord's name were to be received accordingly; cf. John 13:20; 20:21. Trevett (1992, p48) notes "It is interesting that Ignatius, too, made the same point, but that he did so with special reference to willingness to receive *bishops* (Eph 6)."

[117] Trevett (1989c, p319) notes Ignatius' language in IgnEph 5.2-6.1 (cf. Jn 13:20) suggests the refusal to receive "as the Lord" those who were "sent" to them. She writes: "Bishops, in particular (and especially silent ones?) should be so received, Ignatius argued."

[118] Trevett (1992, p113 n74) notes: "Developing monepiscopacy rather than episcopacy of the full-blown monarchical kind is reflected in these letters."

not come to the bishop's assembly, but rather could continue to meet separately.

This points to a time of transition in church structure in Ephesus, a transition that was resisted by some Christians. Some were resisting the bishop because they did not agree with this change in church structure. This would also explain the great attention Ignatius gives to explaining away Onesimus' silence. This is understandable if some groups of Christians in Ephesus did not want to grant to Onesimus the right to be episkopos over them. Ignatius wanted to show Onesimus, in his eyes the bishop over all Ephesian Christians, in the best possible light and to explain away his shortcomings in order to convince everyone that they should acknowledge Onesimus.

We will now examine other evidence which strongly suggests that some were "resisting the bishop" in Ephesus because they were resisting a change in church structure.

3.2.4 Resistance to the development of monepiscopacy

We have suggested that a further reason why some acted apart from the bishop was probably that some Christians were resisting the development of monepiscopacy and thus were opposed to the office of one bishop in a city.

We have already discussed leadership in Chapter 10 in detail. Here we need only note some points briefly. In Paul's letter to the Philippians 1:1 we read of "bishops" in the plural, and although the reference to "elders" in Acts 20:28 is probably anachronistic, we need not doubt that at the conclusion of Paul's ministry around 55 CE, there was a group of leaders in the Pauline community in Ephesus. At the time of the Pastorals, there were presbyter-overseers and deacons among the addressees in Ephesus. We have also noted the quite different form of leadership which is evident in the Johannine Letters.

It seems likely that, before Ignatius' travels in Asia Minor, the title "episkopos" was used in Asia to distinguish one leader in a Christian community. This is clearly the sense the term has in Ignatius' letters, and it is a sense that he presupposes, when, for example, he calls Polycarp "bishop of the church of the Smyrnaeans" (IgnPol, insc). But, as we will note below, the evidence of Ignatius' letters suggests that Polycarp was not the acknowledged head of all the Christians in Smyrna, and it is interesting that in his letter to Philippi Polycarp does not call himself "bishop of Smyrna".[119]

---

[119] In the inscription he writes: "Polycarp and the Elders with him to the Church of God sojourning in Philippi"; see also 6.1; in 9.1 and 13.1-2 he refers to Ignatius, but does not call him a bishop. The title of the book names Polycarp as "Saint Polycarp, Bishop of Smyrna and Holy Martyr" but it was undoubtedly added later.

However, we suggest that the time of Ignatius seems to be a time of a particular transition with regard to church structure and in his letters we are witnessing a struggle for monepiscopacy. Thus, those who "resist the bishop" may well have been actually resisting change, and probably wanted to hold on to a different church order. Perhaps they met apart from the bishop because they did not recognise his authority over them. Or perhaps this was how they had always met, and they were now resisting the attempts of a bishop to, as they saw it, "interfere" in their Christian group.

We will now examine further evidence which suggests that the time of Ignatius was a time of transition with regard to monepiscopacy. The evidence also suggests that the transition to monepiscopacy was not easily achieved in Asia,[120] and that in Ignatius' time, the churches in Asia to which he wrote were at varying points in this transition process to monepiscopacy.[121] We have a number of reasons for suggesting that in Ignatius we are seeing a time of transition to a different structure as regards leadership and that there was resistance to this.

3.2.4.1 Weighty justification of the office

We note first of all the weighty justification that Ignatius gives for the authority of the bishop in the following passages.

1) IgnEph 3.2: Bishops have been appointed "in every quarter" and "are in the purpose of Jesus Christ".

2) IgnMag 3.1-2: "yield to him [their youthful bishop] - not indeed to him but to the Father of Jesus Christ, the bishop of all. Thus to the honour of him who took pleasure in us it is right to obey without hypocrisy; for the point is not that a man deceives this bishop who is visible, but that he tries to cheat him who is unseen; in such a matter the reckoning is not with flesh but with God who knows our secrets." This is very powerful legitimation. God is the "episkopos of all", and the person who lies to the bishop does not just deceive the human and visible bishop, but despises the invisible bishop, God.

---

[120] Of course at the time Ignatius wrote it was not clear that monepiscopacy would "win" as it were.

[121] Trevett (1989b, p43-8) suggests that the transition to the Ignatian model of the Church was not easily achieved in Antioch, judging by Mt, which probably originated in this region, and the advice of Didache 15. Another indication that the office of bishop was in a state of transition is shown by the fact that the youthfulness of the bishop at Magnesia was considered a problem; see IgnMag 3.1-2. The impression we gain is that youthful bishops were exceptional. Schoedel (1985, p109) notes: "The fact that they were to be found at all indicates that the episcopacy was beginning to be placed on a different footing from that of the presbyterate: the criterion of age had (at least in principle) lost its significance. The office is in an important state of transition."

3) IgnMag 4.1: "It is right, then, not only to be called Christians but also to be Christians; just as some certainly use the title 'bishop' but do everything apart from him. Such people do not seem to me to act in good conscience because they do not meet validly in accordance with the commandment." As Schoedel notes, "obedience to the bishop is of such decisive importance to Ignatius that he goes on virtually to define being Christian in terms of it."[122] The passage also suggests that Ignatius was more concerned about people meeting apart from the bishop than many of his contemporaries, since he shows that for some using the title "bishop" did not mean doing everything with him, as it did for Ignatius.

4) In IgnMag 6.1 we read that the bishop is "set over you in the place of God".

5) IgnMag 13.2: "Be subject to the bishop and to each other as Jesus Christ (was subject) to the Father ..., and the apostles to Christ ... that there may be a union both fleshly and spiritual."

6) IgnTr 2.1: "For when you are subject to the bishop as to Jesus Christ, it is clear to me that you are living not in human fashion but in the fashion of Jesus Christ who died for us."

7) In IgnTr 3.1 we read that the bishop is a "type ($\tau \acute{u}\pi o \varsigma$) of the Father"; Ignatius goes on: "Nothing can be called a church" without the bishop, presbyters and deacons. A group which failed to acknowledge the bishop then was no "church."

8) IgnPhd 3.2: "For all who are of God and Jesus Christ, these are with the bishop". This shows how closely Ignatius identified being in the church with being with the bishop. This is very weighty justification for being with the bishop, for clearly the implication is that if one is not with the bishop, then one is not of God and Jesus Christ.

9) IgnSm 8.1-2: "You must all follow the bishop as Jesus Christ (followed) the Father, and (follow) the presbytery as the apostles".

10) IgnSm 9.1: "It is good to acknowledge God and the bishop: he who honours the bishop is honoured by God; he who does anything without the bishop's knowledge serves the devil." It is clear from this that for Ignatius it is not acceptable to act apart from the bishop; in fact to act in any way without the sanction of the bishop is to serve the devil.

11) IgnPol 6.1 "Heed the bishop, that God may also heed you. I am an expiation of those subject to the bishop, presbyters and deacons."[123]

That Ignatius gives such weighty justification throughout his letters for the authority of the bishop suggests that this was a contentious point, and that others disagreed with him about the bishop's authority. Indeed this is clear in

---

[122] Schoedel 1985, p109.

[123] See also IgnTr 13.2; IgnPhd inscr; IgnPhd 1.1.

the indications we have already noted that some were resisting the bishop. Further, the sheer number of times that Ignatius reinforces the authority of the bishop suggests that Ignatius was aware that his advocacy of monepiscopacy was controversial among at least some of his readers and that his was a time of transition with regard to monepiscopacy.

3.2.4.2 The scope of the bishop's control

Ignatius envisages the bishop having very broad and widespread control over the life of the community. Thus Ignatius often explicitly says that Christians must "do nothing without the bishop",[124] and also that anyone who acts apart from the bishop, "is not pure in conscience".[125] This means that a valid eucharist is that which is held under the bishop's control, or the person to whom the bishop entrusts the eucharist,[126] and that one cannot baptise or celebrate the love-feast apart from the bishop.[127] Community prayer was to be one prayer around the bishop,[128] at one altar.[129] Further, Ignatius makes it clear that it is the bishop who calls the council of the church (IgnPol 7.2), that only the bishop is to know if anyone remains celibate (IgnPol 5.2),[130] and that those who marry must do so with the approval of the bishop (IgnPol 5.2). Schoedel comments on this last measure: "This development put into the hands of the bishop a potent instrument of social control – 'group endogamy' - and no doubt contributed significantly to the tightly knit texture of the Christian community."[131]

That the scope of the bishop's control as envisaged by Ignatius was broader than that we see elsewhere at this time, and that he gave such weighty justification for the office and against "resisting the bishop" as we have seen, suggest that Ignatius was trying to consolidate and extend the authority of the bishop over the life of the church.

---

[124] See IgnMag 7.1; IgnTr 2.2; IgnPhd 7.2; IgnSm 8.1 ("Let no one do anything apart from the bishop that has to do with the church. .."); IgnSm 8.2; IgnPol 4.1 ("Let nothing take place without your approval".)

[125] IgnTr 7.2: "He who is within the altar is pure - that is, the person who does anything apart from the bishop, presbytery and deacon, is not pure in conscience."

[126] See IgnSm 8.1; IgnEph 5.2; 20.2; IgnPhd 4.1; see Gibbard 1966, p215.

[127] IgnSm 8.2: "It is not permissible apart from the bishop either to baptize or to celebrate the love-feast; but whatever he approves is also pleasing to God, that everything you do may be sure and valid."

[128] IgnEph 5.2; IgnMag 7.1.

[129] IgnMag 7.2; IgnTr 7.2; IgnPhd 4. On the emphasis that Ignatius gives to unity under the bishop see Anderson 1996, p119-23.

[130] Trevett (1992, p54) notes "The episcopal control over such things may have been new, however, and possibly resented by some".

[131] Schoedel 1985, p273.

We will now look at two other situations with regard to the bishop about which Ignatius writes, before returning to discuss the situation in Ephesus in the light of what we have discovered. Here we will develop further some of the points we made in section 3.1.3 which concerned the evidence for meeting "apart from the bishop" elsewhere in Asia. These examples will show that elsewhere in Asia there was on-going disagreement about the role of the bishop and that Ignatius saw the authority of the bishop in more elevated terms than many of his readers. This suggests that his was a time of transition with regard to church structure, and many did not agree with his views on the matter. This in turn confirms that this was the situation in Ephesus.

3.2.4.3 The situation in Philadelphia

The letter to Philadelphia is most revealing in this regard. In IgnPhd 6.3 he issues a strong warning to a group he met with in Philadephia, which shows that the meeting had not been pleasant. As he writes, Ignatius fears that those concerned may continue to disregard their bishop, and thus that what Ignatius had said will "witness against them". He reports that he had felt moved by the Spirit to say "Attend to the bishop and the presbytery and the deacons" (IgnPhd 7.1) and "Do nothing without the bishop" (IgnPhd 7.2). As we have noted above, this shows that the contentious issue focussed on church order, and in particular, the place of the bishop.

Yet IgnPhd 7.1-3 shows that those who disagreed with Ignatius' understanding of church order were part of the Christian community, since they were present when he met with some members of the community. In addition, it seems that Ignatius' opponents in Philadelphia were not radically at variance with other members of the community since Ignatius himself says that these opponents tried to deceive him and seem to have almost succeeded (IgnPhd 7.1).[132] Thus they were not hugely different from others in the group, which again also suggests that these opponents were part of the Christian community. This and what Ignatius was moved by the Spirit to say (IgnPhd 7.1-2) shows that no serious theological disagreement was involved but rather the issue was predominantly church order, particularly separatism from the bishop. The only other clear issue that was involved was that the opponents were experts in scriptural interpretation (see IgnPhd 8.2; 9.1); Schoedel suggests this skill may have posed a threat to their leaders and would explain why there was division without any signs of a clear theological dispute.[133]

But it does seem likely that these opponents were in some sense distinct from other members of the community. We have already noted that passages in IgnPhd suggest that some Christians in Philadelphia were "resisting the

---

[132] See Schoedel 1985, p205.
[133] Schoedel 1985, p205; cf. Malina 1978, p78-9.

bishop" and doing things apart from the bishop.[134] But they seem to have been doing so as a sub-group *within* the Christian community, since they met with Ignatius, along with all the other Christians. But it is this sort of sub-group that Ignatius disliked, and is arguing against in IgnPhd 7.1-3.

This suggests that this group who opposed Ignatius in Philadelphia, and in fact the bishop himself, may have seen the authority of the bishop in less absolute terms than did Ignatius.[135] In fact many in the community may have seen things differently from Ignatius. In IgnPhd 3.1 he speaks of a "filtering out" of evil elements. But it is unlikely that this had actually occurred, since his opponents were clearly present when he met with the community (IgnPhd 7.1-3) and later when Philo and Rheus Agathopous passed through Philadelphia on their way to see Ignatius they were dishonoured by some members of the community (IgnPhd 11.1). Clearly then, at this point after Ignatius' visit, those who disagreed with Ignatius' views on church order were still present within the community. This suggests that it was Ignatius, and not the Philadelphians themselves, who regarded Ignatius' opponents as "filtered out" or excluded from the community (IgnPhd 3.1-2).[136] Since it is against these people that Ignatius spoke the words recorded in IgnPhd 7.1 "Do nothing without the bishop ... love union, flee division", the issue focussed on church order and the role of the bishop in particular, and it was about this matter that there was an on-going disagreement.

It seems likely then that Ignatius saw the authority of the bishop in more elevated terms than many in Philadelphia. Again, we can suggest that his was a time of transition with regard to church structure, and many did not agree with his views on the matter.

3.2.4.4 The situation in Smyrna

The authority of the one bishop was also not firmly established in Smyrna. We have noted the indications that the docetists remained aloof from the eucharist (IgnSm 7.1-9.1) in Smyrna and in fact probably held their own eucharists. Even though the group of docetists had their own distinct identity and their own eucharists, it also seems likely that the docetists regarded themselves as part of the wider Christian community, rather than as a group quite apart from the other Christians in the city.[137] That this is the case is

---

[134] See IgnPhd 2.1-3.3 with its suggestion of rival eucharists; see section 3.1.3.

[135] See Schoedel 1985, p205

[136] See Schoedel 1985, p214.

[137] IgnSm 5.3 also suggests that Ignatius is opposing individuals known to the Smyrnaeans, which suggests they had links with the rest of the Christians in the city. IgnSm 6.2 only suggests that the docetist did not have concern for all the needy Christians. In view of IgnSm 5.2, which suggests that the docetists had been friendly to Ignatius, IgnSm 6.2 need not imply that the docetists formed a completely separate group. It rather seems to be

suggested by IgnSm 6.1: "Let no one be deceived: even heavenly powers and the glory of angels and the rulers, both visible and invisible, if they do not believe in the blood of Christ, are also subject to judgement. He who can receive this, let him receive it. Let (high) place (τόπος) inflate no one; for faith and love are everything, to which nothing is preferable." Here Ignatius suggests that the real problem is caused by someone who has τόπος, which here refers to a position of leadership and thus to someone with ecclesiastical prestige within the community, perhaps as one who held the office of elder.[138] It seems likely that the person concerned used his or her position within the community to further docetism. He or she may also have been behind the separate meetings in Smyrna (IgnSm 7.1, 9.1).

In this regard we can also note that in IgnSm 8.1 Ignatius writes: "Let that be regarded as a valid eucharist which is held under the bishop or to whomever he entrusts it." In the context of the letter to Smyrna with its mention of rival eucharists (IgnSm 7.1, 8.2), this additional phrase ("or to whomever he entrusts it") suggests that the rival eucharists had been held by the docetists under the leadership of the person mentioned in IgnSm 6.1. Hence, Ignatius wishes to make it clear that only the bishop can approve the person holding such eucharists. This is understandable if the person of IgnSm 6.1 was an elder, since elders probably presided over church events held in house churches.[139] The whole situation is comprehensible in terms of house churches, with one or several house churches in Smyrna being docetic in character, presided over by elders of this theological persuasion. It seems that Ignatius assumes that the elder concerned in IgnSm 6.1 was a member of the wider Christian community of the city, and hence should have come under the bishop, but that the person concerned actually maintained his independence from the bishop.

All of this suggests that Polycarp, bishop of Smyrna, was not in complete control of the situation, probably because the office of bishop did not mean as much in Smyrna as Ignatius thought it should have meant. [140] Certainly, it seems that the presbyters retained a considerable degree of freedom from the bishop, certainly more than Ignatius thought suitable.

Ignatius who polarizes the situation. Schoedel (1985, p241-2) notes that the eucharist often served as the occasion when the needs of the poor, especially widows and orphans, were attended to. Avoiding the common meal would involve neglecting works of love for the whole community.

[138] See Schoedel 1985, p235-6, 243; Trevett 1992, p104. Bauer (1971, p69) thought the unnamed opponent was "something like a gnostic anti-bishop in Smyrna", but this is unlikely, since if it was the case we would have expected Ignatius to have taken the offensive more strongly. Further, in IgnSm 8.1 he assumes there is only one bishop in Smyrna.

[139] See Schoedel 1985, p243.

[140] We can also note that in writing to the Philippians, Polycarp did not mention the office of bishop.

We see then that one factor behind a group of docetists meeting apart from the bishop in Smyrna was probably the fact that the structure of one bishop, who had direction over all that was happening in the Christian community, was not firmly in place. Rather, an elder, who seems to have been a docetist, and his followers, had the freedom to meet independently from the rest of the community, and apart from the bishop. Indeed one of the reasons that Ignatius argued for the authority of the one bishop was precisely to avoid elders and other leaders fostering what he regarded as "false teaching".[141] But the indications that the authority of the one bishop was not firmly established again points to this as a time of transition and suggests some were "resisting the bishop" because they did not agree with what to them was a new structure.

Ignatius' letter to Polycarp is also interesting in this regard. The letter suggests that Polycarp's position as bishop of Smyrna was not well established nor was it universally respected.[142] Thus Ignatius tells Polycarp to "Justify your office (Ἐκδίκει σου τὸν τόπον)[143] with all diligence, both fleshly and spiritual; be concerned about union (τῆς ἑνώσεως φρόντιζε), than which nothing is better." (IgnPol 1.2) This certainly suggests that Ignatius anticipated that some would dispute Polycarp's office of bishop and so he needed to "justify" it; further, the unity for which Polycarp is to be concerned is unity with the bishop.[144] Since Ignatius had stayed in Smyrna

---

[141] Hence Ignatius ends IgnSm 7.2 by saying "Flee divisions as the beginning of evils". Clearly, unity remains one of his dominant concerns. However, in IgnSm 9.2 Ignatius shows his satisfaction with the majority of his addressees in Smyrna; see Schoedel 1984, p245.

[142] Note Trevett's (1992, p103) comment : "I do not think we should assume that Ignatius and Polycarp (or Ignatius and all the other bishops he had met) shared precisely the same vision of episcopacy." See also Bauer 1971, p68-76.

[143] Schoedel (1985, p260) regards Ἐκδίκει as a legal metaphor which concerns "the advocacy of the cause of episcopal authority." Trevett (1992, p133) translates Ἐκδίκει as "vindicate" and notes: "The term used was peculiar to Ignatius among the Apostolic Fathers, but such *ekdikesis* was proclaimed with prophetic authority in early Christianity, offering 'parenetic warning or prophetic threat' and using 'casuistic legal expression' (*ei tis, ean tis* or similar) followed by a statement of the hearer's punishment." Trevett (1992, p102) also notes with respect to this passage that Ignatius "wished Polycarp would be more dynamic and insistent in (creation and ?) defence of" his office.

[144] In IgnPol 2:1 Ignatius speaks of difficulty from "troublemakers"; these may include people to whom Polycarp has to "justify his office" (IgnPol 1.2), that is advocate the cause of episcopal authority with those who object to the office of one bishop. See also IgnPol 6.1 where Ignatius calls on the Smyrnaeans to "heed the bishop", which, when combined with the other passages we have discussed, suggests Polycarp's position as bishop of Smyrna was not well established.

(IgnSm 13; IgnPol 8.2-3), it is likely that he had good grounds for these concerns. The letter to Polycarp then gives us some further insight into the task a bishop faced with a divided community, not all of whom were convinced about monepiscopacy.[145]

All of this reinforces the likelihood that the order that Ignatius advocated was neither so well established nor so well supported as he would have liked and points to a time of development and transition in church structure.[146]

3.2.4.5 Conclusions

This evidence builds into a strong cumulative case that this was a time of transition with regard to church structure in the congregations to which Ignatius wrote in Asia. He knew that many of his addressees were acting apart from the bishop, but also that they did not think this was wrong and so did not agree with Ignatius about the city-wide authority of the bishop. This suggests that some of his addressees were currently convinced about the rightness of a different, more collegial model of church order. This in turn suggests that monepiscopacy was not well established in Asia, and in fact that one of the reasons that Ignatius was writing was to attempt to establish it more securely.[147]

---

[145] This means that when Ignatius writes to Polycarp that "Let nothing take place without your approval" (IgnPol 4.1), we are right to think that currently some things did happen without his approval and that Ignatius wanted Polycarp to try and wrest control from individuals and groups in the Christian community and to hold such control himself.

[146] The Didache shows a preference for prophets, teachers and apostles (Did 11.1-12.5), but 15:1-2 suggests that when prophets and teachers were in short supply, then bishops (in the plural), and deacons were to be appointed. But in Didache 15.1-2 we read: "Appoint therefore for yourselves bishops and deacons ... Therefore *do not despise them*, for they are your honourable men together with the prophets and teachers." This suggests that some were non-cooperative or hostile towards this change which involved accepting the new authority of resident bishops and deacons; see Trevett 1992, p47-8. This is a comparative example of the difficulties caused in a time of change with regard to church structure.

Further comparative data is valuable, but not decisive, since the situation in Asia could well have been quite different from that elsewhere. But the following evidence is noteworthy. Firstly, Clement in his letter to Corinth mentions only a plurality of bishops at Corinth (See 1 Clem 42:4-5). Secondly, Ignatius does not mention a bishop in connection with Rome, and when Clement (writing from Rome) mentions a plurality of bishops at Corinth he does so without censure, which suggests monepiscopacy was not yet the norm in Rome (see Ehrhardt 1945, p114). Thirdly, when Polycarp wrote to Philippi he did not mention a bishop in the city, but rather spoke of presbyters and deacons; see Phil 5.3. It is also noticeable that Polycarp does not call himself a bishop in the letter. It seems likely then that Asia Minor and Syria had developed monepiscopacy more quickly than other areas. This would make it more likely that Asia itself was in a period of transition towards monepiscopacy.

[147] Compare Strand (1991, p144) who writes on the basis of Ignatius' letters that by ca. 115 CE monepiscopacy "was already firmly entrenched in the Roman province of Asia". See also Strand 1966, p72-5; 1992, p60.

We have seen that this was also the situation in Ephesus. Some were resisting the bishop and seem to have disagreed that he was "sent" by God. It seems very likely that they were resisting a change in church structure. But who were these Christians in Ephesus who were resisting such a change?

3.2.5 Support for a different form of church order

We can also suggest that some Christians in Ephesus may have wanted to resist the change to monepiscopacy because they valued their current, or currently threatened, system of church order.

The readers of the Pastorals may have been willing to accept the authority of the one bishop quite readily. As we have seen in Chapter 10, at the time the Pastorals were written the community of the addressees had begun the process of greater institutionalisation, and presbyter-overseers and deacons were recognised offices. We noted that leadership was plural, so the emergence of one episkopos as the key leader would involve some change, but change, we may suggest, which was only an extension of developments which they had experienced already in the emergence of more established leadership.

But one aspect of the opposition to the growth of the power of the one bishop in Ephesus may have been from those who belonged to the Johannine community, and another dimension of this opposition may have been from those who valued the prophetic model of leadership demonstrated by John the Seer. We will now discuss these two possibilities. This will lead us to the confirm our hypothesis that Ignatius is writing to all the Christians in Ephesus.

3.2.5.1 The Johannine communities addressed in 1-3 Jn

We have argued that 1-3 Jn were addressed to readers in and around Ephesus. We have shown in Chapter 10 that, although they valued tradition-bearers like the elder, they seem not to have had leaders who were appointed to particular offices, and the locus of authority was generally in the wider group. We can suggest that they would have resisted the developments towards a much more institutionalized church structure, including the development of monepiscopacy with the bishop claiming to having authority over all the Christians in Ephesus. They would have valued a much freer model of collegiality and monepiscopacy would have been a very significant development for them. We have argued that some of those who resisted the bishop continued to meet separately in house churches, as IgnEph 5.2-3 indicates.

We have noted the use of sending language in IgnEph 6.1. It is noticeable that this picks up Johannine language, particularly in Jn 13:20, but also more widely of the Father sending the Son.[148] It is possible then that Ignatius is aware that a group of Johannine believers were "resisting the bishop", primarily because they valued a freer church structure. Ignatius was arguing that they should come under the bishop, as a way of guarding against the growth of what he regarded as false teaching.

We can also note that two matters we have dealt with - not thinking the bishop had been "sent" by the Lord and wanting to retain a more collegial form of church structure - may be linked and may both apply to Johannine Christians. We could well understand if Johannine Christians argued for both of these points.[149] This makes our suggestion that Johannine Christians were at least a significant group among those who resisted the bishop more plausible. Ignatius was encouraging these Johannine Christians to come under the authority of the bishop.[150]

3.2.5.2 Those who valued the prophetic model of leadership demonstrated by John the Seer.

There is an additional likely background for those who "resist the bishop". Trevett[151] has noted that John wrote Revelation for Christians in Asia, including communities in Ephesus, Philadelphia and Smyrna. We can suggest that at least some of these Christians were convinced by what John wrote, although we have argued that John expected a considerable group in Ephesus and elsewhere to disagree with him. But it seems likely that at least some of his readers were also convinced about and valued prophetic activity and associated charismata.

How would those who reacted positively to Rev, and their spiritual children in Ephesus, Philadelphia and Smyrna, have received Ignatius views about church structure? It would not be surprising if in Ignatius' time some of the Christians of Asia continued to value prophecy, the on-going transmission of the risen Lord's words, and the leadership given by prophets.[152] Such Christians could well have been at least ambivalent in their attitude to emerging episcopal leaders, particularly if the relation of office to charismatic authority was in doubt or unclear. These believers may have been concerned

---

[148] See Schoedel 1985, p56 n15; see also Mt 10:40; Gal 4:4.

[149] Note they accepted "sending", but not of "bishops".

[150] We will discuss the question of why Ignatius does not mention John below.

[151] See Trevett 1989c, p316-21, 330; see also 1989a, p128. Eno 1976, p43-8 discusses conflict in the church from the second century onwards, conflict which focuses on the question of who are the bearers of authority. One particular example is conflict between church officials and prophetic movements, which is seen in Montanism and elsewhere. The possible example of this in Ignatius would then be part of a wider phenomenon.

[152] See Aune 1983b, p291-316 on prophecy in early Christianity in the period from 90-150 CE.

about the erosion of a form of leadership which they valued and may have felt free to act apart from the bishop and without his authority. Thus Christians who appreciated John's Revelation may lie behind some of the opposition to Ignatius and his fellow episcopal officials.

This view is supported by evidence in the letters that Ignatius was aware of the need to take account of the emphases of the kinds of Christians who found conducive the claim to prophetic inspiration which is fundamental to Revelation.[153] The following passages suggest that Ignatius was aware that some of his readers valued charismata and in particular prophecy, and that some of the rival claims of others to authority derived not from ecclesiastical position but rather from the claim to possess the Spirit. These passages also suggest that Ignatius was trying to reassure these Christians concerning the new structure of monepiscopacy, of which he was such an ardent advocate.

Firstly, on a number of occasions Ignatius defended his own status as a "charismatic".[154] Thus in IgnEph 5.1 he writes: "For if I in a short time had such fellowship with your bishop, as was not human but spiritual (οὐκ ἀνθρωπίνην οὖσαν, ἀλλὰ πνευματικήν), how much more do I count you blessed who are mingled together with him". Ignatius is here claiming that not only he himself, but also Onesimus were "spiritual", *pneumatikos*.[155] In IgnEph 20.2 he says that he will write a second document "particularly if the Lord reveals anything to me (μάλιστα ἐὰν ὁ κύριός μοι ἀποκαλύψῃ)". This suggests that he is the recipient of revelations from God.[156] Further, in IgnPhd 7 he claims that the activity of the Spirit in him prevented him from being deceived, for "the Spirit which is from God, is not deceived." He also says that he had spoken two prophetic utterances through the Spirit - "with a loud voice - the voice of God" - when he was in Philadelphia. Clearly his claim to inspiration by the Spirit was contested at the time, but Ignatius emphasises that "It was the Spirit who made proclamation" (IgnPhd 7.2). This language suggests that Ignatius was taking into account the emphases of the kinds of Christians who appreciated charismata and who would have agreed with John's claim in Revelation to be speaking a revelation or a prophecy, or to be

---

[153] See Trevett 1989a, p128.

[154] See Trevett 1989c, p319; Genouillac 1907, p151-3.

[155] Note also Ignatius' comparison of the flesh and the spirit, and of fleshly and spiritual things elsewhere; see IgnEph 7.2; 8.2; IgnSm 3.3; 13.1; IgnMag 1.2; 13.1; IgnTr insc; 13.3; IgnRom insc; see also Genouillac 1907, p119-20. However, such language is not necessarily connected with an emphasis on gifts and things charismatic, although as we have noted IgnEph 5.1 does seem to be relevant to this theme.

[156] Note also IgnTr 4.1-5.2: "Surely I am not unable to write to you of heavenly things? No, but I fear inflicting harm on you who are infants. Even in my case, not because I am in bonds and am able to know heavenly things, both the angelic locations and the archontic formations, things both visible and invisible ..." Clearly, Ignatius implies he knows complex heavenly things.

in the possession of gifts.[157] This and his defensiveness in IgnPhd 7.1-2 suggest that charismata were valued by some of his addressees, and that Ignatius was wanting to show them that he too possessed these gifts.[158]

Secondly, that he is aware that some of his readers valued charismata is also shown by the salutation to the church in Smyrna, where he writes of the church there that it "has been shown mercy in every gift ($\dot{\varepsilon}\nu$ $\pi\alpha\nu\tau\grave{\iota}$ $\chi\alpha\rho\acute{\iota}\sigma\mu\alpha\tau\iota$), which has been filled with faith and love, which is not lacking in any gift ($\dot{\alpha}\nu\upsilon\sigma\tau\epsilon\rho\acute{\eta}\tau\omega$ $o\ddot{\upsilon}\sigma\eta$ $\pi\alpha\nu\tau\grave{o}\varsigma$ $\chi\alpha\rho\acute{\iota}\sigma\mu\alpha\tau\sigma\varsigma$) ..." (IgnSm inscr).[159]

Thirdly, we have noted that while he was in Philadephia Ignatius defended his advocacy of hierarchy by uttering a prophecy (IgnPhd 7.1-2).[160] There were some present who were not convinced that it was a genuine prophecy, and claimed that Ignatius had had prior information about the situation in Philadelphia. Ignatius' insistence that it was the Spirit who spoke through him,[161] shows that the Christians in Philadelphia accepted and valued prophecy, but did not think that the Spirit had actually spoken through Ignatius. The proclamation made by the Spirit through Ignatius advocated obedience to the bishop, loving unity and fleeing division, which suggests that those who did not think the Spirit was speaking through Ignatius opposed his view of church structure and in particular his emphasis on the authority of the bishop (IgnPhd 7.1-8.1).[162] The passage therefore suggests that it was those

---

[157] Note also the emphasis on the Spirit's activity in leading into all truth in John's Gospel; see Jn 14:26; 15:26; 16:13-15. One should not think that Rev is alone in its emphasis on the Spirit and prophecy.

[158] Of course charismata play a very significant part in Paul, and we have noted that they still have a role in the Pastorals. It is possible then that this language also appeals to those in the Pauline tradition.

[159] See also IgnPol 2.2. $\chi\acute{\alpha}\rho\iota\sigma\mu\alpha$ is also mentioned in IgnEph 17.2. We may wonder if the mention of the silence of the bishop (IgnEph 6; IgnPhd 1) may also be interpreted in this context. If some Christians valued the manifestations of the Spirit, then a silent and lacklustre bishop would be particularly unattractive; see Trevett 1992, p50.

[160] Ignatius does not explicitly call it a prophecy, but it is clearly implied; see Trevett 1989c, p317-18.

[161] IgnPhd 7.1-2: "For although some desired to deceive me at the fleshly level, yet the Spirit, which is from God, is not deceived; ... I cried out while among you, I spoke with a loud voice - the voice of God: 'Attend to the bishop and the presbytery and the deacons.' Those who suspected me of saying this because I had advance information about the division of some - he is my witness in whom I am bound that I did not learn it from any human being. It was the Spirit who made proclamation, saying these words: 'Do nothing without the bishop, keep your flesh as the temple of God. Love union, flee divisions. ...'"

[162] IgnPhd 11 (see also IgnSm 10) shows that Ignatius' viewpoint was disliked in Philadephia and that he and two of his supporters had been treated in a disrespectful way. Ignatius does not give the exact reasons for this, but it seems to have been connected with IgnPhd 7.1-2, and to concern the issue of church structure, and perhaps a hierarchical as opposed to a more charismatic structure.

who emphasised charismatic authority in Philadelphia who resisted Ignatius' advocacy of the position of the bishop.[163]

In this context the IgnPhd insc is significant. Ignatius writes to the church in Philadelphia of the bishop, the presbyters and deacons "who have been appointed in the purpose of Jesus Christ, whom according to his own will he established in strength by his Holy Spirit (οὓς κατὰ τὸ ἴδιον θέλημα ἐστήριξεν ἐν βεβαιωσύνῃ τῷ ἁγίῳ αὐτοῦ πνεύματι)." He is thus saying that Jesus Christ and the Holy Spirit have established the three-fold church order and that the ministry of bishop, presbyters and deacons is now operative through the Holy Spirit. This can be seen as an answer to the Philadelphians' unwillingness to see the Spirit as active in church officials, which was a significant part of their opposition to Ignatius, as IgnPhd 7.1-2 shows.

Fourthly, Trevett notes that in IgnEph 15.2 Ignatius writes "He who truly possesses the word of Jesus is able also to hear his silence, that he may be perfect, that he may act through what he says, and may be known through that in which he is silent." Trevett comments on this passage: "Ignatius was responding negatively to those who claimed to have 'the word of Jesus' for a true possession ..., for in his view they had failed to 'hear' Jesus' silence. A ministry of teaching (in this case a suspect one, and something also associated with Christian prophets) was involved and in IgnEph 15, as elsewhere in the letters, Ignatius was contrasting mere 'words' and deeds. I wonder whether we should look to the Apocalypse to explain at least part of the background to this enigmatic passage."[164] For Trevett then, this passage seems to imply opposition by Ignatius to the claims of prophets and teachers.

Trevett goes on to point out that, given the emphasis in Rev on the *logos tou theou,* the declaration that John has "heard" something, and the formulas "τάδε λέγει" and "The one who has an ear, let them hear what the Spirit says to the churches (Ὁ ἔχων οὖς ἀκουσάτω τί τὸ πνεῦμα λέγει ταῖς ἐκκλησίαις)",[165] "the word", as John understood it, may well have been an important concept for some of the readers of Revelation in Asia.[166] This

---

[163] We can also note the way in which Ignatius speaks of the bishop of Philadelphia in IgnPhd 1.1: "Of which bishop I know that he obtained a ministry for the community, not of himself, nor yet through any human beings, nor yet for vainglory, but in the love of God the Father and the Lord Jesus Christ." Schoedel (1985, p196) writes that the bishop's authority "is viewed as essentially charismatic". He compares this passage with Gal 1:1.

[164] Trevett 1989a, p129. Trevett (1989a, p119-31) notes that there are many differences and few points of contact between Rev and Ignatius' letters. There are particularly interesting points of contact between Rev 12 and Ignatius' Eph 19 (p126-8).

[165] "I hear" occurs 27 times; τάδε λέγει in Rev 2:1, 8, 12, 18; 3:1, 7, 14 and "The one who has an ear, let them hear what the Spirit says to the churches" in Rev 2:7, 11, 17, 29; 3:6, 13, 22.

[166] Trevett 1989a, p129.

suggests that some of the Christians in Asia who were unsympathetic to Ignatius' views on church structure (whether in person or by report), may have been recipients of Rev who were attuned to what it represented.[167] These supporters of John the Seer's views may have had a reverence for the traditional roles of prophets and teachers, and concepts like "the word of Jesus". This is then additional evidence which suggests that those in conflict with Ignatius' emphasis on officialdom could well have valued prophetic authority.[168]

We can suggest then that those who valued the ministry of prophets, or charismatic gifts more generally, formed one dimension of the opposition in Asia to the form of church order advocated by Ignatius. These people did not necessarily disagree with Ignatius theologically,[169] but rather they seem to have been ambivalent in their attitude to the office of bishop and may have felt free to "resist the bishop" and to act apart from him and without his authority. As office and order were changing these Christians may well have sought to retain their traditional freedoms for it seems clear that the order Ignatius advocated would limit the freedom that had previously been accorded to charismatics in some earlier forms of order.

As we have seen above, the language of "resisting the bishop" is also found in Ignatius' letter to the Ephesians and in IgnEph 5.1 Ignatius claims that he and the bishop Onesimus were "spiritual" and in IgnEph 20.2 he notes that he is the recipient of revelations from God and uses the verb ἀποκαλύπτω. This suggests that, as elsewhere, some of those who "resisted the bishop" in Ephesus may well have valued prophecy and spiritual gifts and the sort of authority on which John relied in Rev. We have argued that John in Rev is not writing to a specific "John of Revelation community" but rather to all Christians in Ephesus and elsewhere. We suggested in Chapter 7 that some readers in Ephesus did agree with John, though many others did not. We are suggesting that some of those who agreed with John, and who accepted prophetic authority and their spiritual children, are among those in Ephesus who are "resisting the bishop".

---

[167] Trevett 1989a, p130. Trevett (1989a, p130) suggests that there are other points in IgnPhd and IgnMag which make her proposal more likely. Note in particular Ignatius' concern about Judaizers and their "myths", and their concern for the prophets, which could reflect that he is again opposing those who valued Rev. She notes that there is no clear evidence that Ignatius knew Rev.

[168] Trevett (1989a, p131) also notes there may have been tension between Ignatius' supporters and supporters of John the Seer concerning the appropriation of the insights and promises of Judaism, but this seems to have been more of an issue in Philadelphia than in Ephesus.

[169] Although we have noted above that one group of those who acted apart from the bishop were docetists, but clearly not all were.

We should note here that prophecy and charismatic gifts are of course part of the Pauline heritage. Both prophecy and a gift for ministry are mentioned in the Pastorals. Is it likely that readers of the Pastorals might also be among those who resist the bishop in favour of prophetic and charismatic concepts? This is possible, but in the Pastorals, prophecy and χάρισμα (in the singular on both occasions it is used) are both mentioned in connection with office and leadership.[170] It seems less likely then that the sort of opposition we seem to see in Ignatius' writings between prophecy and charismata on the one hand and leadership office on the other, would occur amongst readers of the Pastorals, where these two facets have already been brought into partnership.

3.2.5.3 Conclusion

We suggest then that those who were resisting the bishop in Ephesus included some from the Johannine community (who may have been meeting in separate house churches (IgnEph 5.2-3)), and some of those who had received Revelation and valued the prophetic authority which is fundamental to that book. We have also suggested that some of those who did not "resist the bishop" may have been the spiritual children of those who read the Pastoral Epistles.

We have argued in Chapter 7 that Revelation was sent to all Christians in Ephesus, so those who valued prophetic authority may have been *part* of the Johannine community, or some may have been in the Pastorals' community, or in another group. This means that we can suggest that Ignatius is writing to all the Christians in Ephesus, including the Johannine community and the community which received the Pastorals; his intended audience would include readers in both the Johannine community and the Pastorals (and perhaps others too) who received and agreed with Revelation.

It may be that Ignatius is also writing to other Christian groups in the city – perhaps the opponents of the Pastor if they still existed and were a separate group, or the Johannine secessionists, or the Nicolaitans (again if they were still a separate group). However, Ignatius gives no clear signs of the existence of these other groups and he may well have regarded some of these groups as "beyond the pale" and so not included in "the church which is in Ephesus".[171]

---

[170] For prophecy see 1 Tim 1:18; 4:14; for χάρισμα see 1 Tim 4:14; 2 Tim 1:6.

[171] We may also wonder if Onesimus and the other Ephesians who met Ignatius would have told him about them if they regarded them as not part of the wider Christian communities of the city.

3.2.6 Answering issues that could undermine our hypothesis

There are two issues we need to discuss which could undermine our hypothesis that Ignatius is addressing all the Christians in Ephesus, and that some of those who are "resisting the bishop" may have included those who belonged to the community addressed in 1-3 Jn and others who appreciated prophecy and charismata. We will now address these two issues.

3.2.6.1 If Ignatius is writing to all the Christians in Ephesus, why does he not mention John?

While Ignatius mentions Paul in IgnEph 12.2, he makes no mention in his letter to the Ephesians or elsewhere of "John" or "the elder", whom we have argued probably wrote Jn's Gospel and 2-3 Jn. If Ignatius was writing to all Christians in the city, including the community which received the Johannine letters, would we not expect him to mention "John"?[172]

However, we may suggest that there are four possible reasons why Ignatius does not mention John.[173] Firstly, we have argued that "John" is John the elder, not John the apostle, son of Zebedee. This would mean that "John" was not automatically seen by his contemporaries or those who lived shortly after him as a figure of absolutely crucial significance. Rather, he was not an apostle, and not one of the key figures of Christian tradition, but at the time when Ignatius wrote he was a personality from the more recent past. Even if he was a significant figure for some readers in Ephesus, he was not of such importance that he simply had to be mentioned (as Paul clearly was).[174] Thus, if "John" was in fact John the elder, we can understand why Ignatius does not mention him.

Secondly, even if "John" was John the son of Zebedee, we can suggest a reason why he was not mentioned. Ignatius' appeal to Paul in IgnEph 12.2 is significant in this regard. There Ignatius writes: "(you are) fellow initiates of Paul, (a man) sanctified, approved, worthy of blessing, in whose steps may it be mine to be found when I reach God, who in every letter remembers you in

---

[172] I am assuming that John and the Johannine community were located in Ephesus; see Chapter 6.

[173] Nothing in the letters indicates that Ignatius knew John personally; see Camelot 1958, p57. Trevett (1992, p21) notes "Ignatius shows some affinity with the thought and language of the Fourth Gospel but ... common terminology was sometimes used differently. In recent decades there have been fewer claims for literary dependence on Ignatius's part ..." Thus the affinity Ignatius does show with the Fourth Gospel is to be explained by factors such as a common background rather than literary dependence. See also Schoedel 1985, p9 and n52, 185 n29; Paulsen 1978, p36-7; Schnackenburg 1991, p56; cf. Corwin 1960, p69-71.

[174] He would perhaps be comparable then to John the Seer, who is not mentioned by Ignatius either; see further Hengel 1989, p14-15.

Christ Jesus." Ignatius thus sees Paul as a unifying figure from the past for all the Christians in Ephesus. Given that the Ephesians were currently divided and that Ignatius wants them to unite, it seem likely that he sees Paul as a figure with whom all of them can identify. He may be suggesting that they look beyond their present divisions to their "glorious past" when they "always agreed with the very apostles" (IgnEph 11.2). Their apostle, in particular, was Paul. As the one who established Christianity in the city, he can provide a unifying focus for them.[175] By contrast, John's activity in Ephesus came later (even if he too was one of "the apostles" with whom they agreed (IgnEph 11.2)). Thus, even though (we have suggested) at the time Ignatius wrote, one group in Ephesus looked back to Paul (the spiritual children of the addressees of the Pastorals), and another looked back to "John" (the spiritual children of the addressees of 1-3 Jn), it was Paul who was the stronger focus for unity because he established the Christian group in the city.[176] Perhaps another factor was that we have suggested the Pauline group agreed with Ignatius about church structure, while the Johannine group did not.

Thirdly, we have suggested that some "Johannine Christians" were among those who "resisted the bishop". If this is correct, we can understand why Ignatius does not mention John: he would not want to draw direct attention to a person or factor which promoted "resisting the bishop" and thus contemporary disunity among the Ephesian Christians.

Fourthly, we should note that the only "worthies" of the past mentioned by Ignatius are Paul (IgnEph 12.2; IgnRom 4.3) and Peter (IgnRom 4.3). Ignatius seems to model himself on Paul,[177] and the reference to Paul in IgnEph 12.2 is clearly in the context of Ignatius' forthcoming martyrdom. Further, Ignatius only mentions Peter in connection with his martyrdom in Rome (IgnRom 4.3). With regard to IgnRom 4.3, Schoedel notes "the selection here of Peter and Paul no doubt reflects Ignatius' awareness of a tradition about their joint presence and their martyrdom in Rome which significantly bolstered the prestige of that city's Christian community."[178] Further, Culpepper suggests that "Ignatius did not mention John because John had not been martyred."[179] Thus, that Ignatius only mentions Peter and Paul, and then

---

[175] Ignatius admired Paul as an apostle (see IgnEph 11.2-12.2; IgnRom 4.3) and compares and contrasts himself to Paul (IgnEph 12,2; IgnTr 5.1; cf 1 Cor 9:27; Rom 9:2). But this does not preclude him being aware of the special relationship between Ephesus and Paul.

[176] And if John was "the elder", Paul was much better known.

[177] See Rom 9.2 cf. 1 Cor 15:8-9.

[178] Schoedel 1985, p176.

[179] Culpepper 1994, p109. He also suggests the absence of reference to John may be explained "on the assumption .. that John the apostle had not worked in Ephesus".

clearly with reference to their martyrdom, means we should not give too much significance to Ignatius' silence about "John". Such silence does not necessarily mean that he does not know of a "John" who wrote the Fourth Gospel.[180]

Thus, we can suggest reasons why Ignatius does not allude to John. Further, we note that Ignatius makes no mention of the Book of Revelation, which was definitely written on Patmos, near Ephesus, by (a different) "John", who was thus definitely active in Western Asia Minor. As Culpepper concludes from this: "Therefore, Ignatius's silence [about "John" of the Fourth Gospel] can hardly be turned into testimony that Ephesus was not the home of the Johannine tradition."[181] This silence on his part does not require the conclusion that there was no Johannine community in Ephesus when Ignatius wrote. Nor does it undermine our hypothesis that Ignatius wrote to all the Christians in Ephesus, including the Johannine community.

3.2.6.2 The unity of the church

The unity of the church is a major theme in Ignatius' letters.[182] As we have noted, in his view a united church, with the people being obedient to their leaders, was crucial if the church was to meet the challenge of "false teaching". He expresses this clearly in IgnPhd 8.1 when he writes "I, then, did my part as a man set on union."[183] Ignatius writes at length about unity with the bishop, or with the bishop, presbyters and deacons, and, as we have seen, often goes on to speak of those who worship apart from the bishop. Ignatius "conceives of unity in terms of the complete subordination of individual interests to the group and the suppression or elimination of dissent."[184] Often it is difficult to determine if Ignatius is giving general exhortation on this, one of his major emphases, or if he is referring to a specific problem of disunity in the community he is addressing.

---

[180] Hengel (1989, p15) also notes the difference in attitude to church structures between the Fourth Gospel and Ignatius. Thus "Possibly Ignatius does not mention the 'Elder John' because he had been an antihierarchical, charismatic teacher, without any interest whatsoever in ecclesiastical offices like bishops, presbyters and deacons."

[181] Culpepper 1994, p109.

[182] See Richardson 1935, p33-9; 1937, p428-43; Camelot 1958, p20-55; Corwin 1960, p247-71; Grant 1964, p138; Paulsen 1978, p132-44; Schoedel 1985, p12, 21-2; Lindemann, 1990, p39.

[183] In all the letters we find exhortations to unity. Thus in writing to Polycarp Ignatius says (IgnPol 1.2): "Be concerned about union, than which nothing is better." See also for example IgnMag 1.2; 6.2-7.2; IgnPhd 3.2; 4, 7.2-8.2; IgnSm 7.2. Note also that unity is symbolized by the image of the one altar; see IgnEph 5.2; IgnMag 7.2; IgnTr 7.2; IgnPhd 4

[184] Schoedel 1985, p259.

He says a good deal about this theme in his letter to the Ephesians. Here we will discuss whether what Ignatius says about unity with regard to Ephesian Christians undermines or reinforces our hypothesis that he was actually addressing several distinct Christian groups?

In IgnEph 2.2 Ignatius writes: "It is right, then, in every way to glorify Jesus Christ who glorified you, so that being joined in one obedience, subject to the bishop and the presbytery, you may be holy in every respect." This passage must be related to Ignatius' request in IgnEph 2.1 that the Ephesian deacon Burrhus accompany him. It seems that the bishop and presbyters were happy about this, but that the congregation needed to agree, since there were financial repercussions involved. Hence the exhortation to be "joined in one obedience, subject to the bishop and the presbytery" does not necessarily mean that they are currently disunited. Rather Ignatius is saying that they should agree with the Ephesian leaders on this matter concerning Burrhus.

In IgnEph 3.2 Ignatius exhorts the Ephesians that they "might run together with God's purpose." He goes on to say that all the bishops in the world are in agreement with the purpose of God and thus "it is right for you to run together with the purpose of the bishop, which indeed you do (ὅπερ καὶ ποιεῖτε)." (IgnEph 4.1)

We have noted in section 1.6.1 above that Ignatius often softens a recommendation by saying that his addressees already comply with it. Is this the case here? Does the statement "it is right for you to run together with the purpose of the bishop, *which indeed you do*" mean that all the Ephesians do currently "run together with the bishop", or could it mean that some do not and Ignatius is softening what is actually a command by ascribing its fulfillment in advance? In IgnEph 4.1 Ignatius goes on to emphasize that currently it is primarily the presbytery who "run together" with the bishop, for he says "for your worthily reputed presbytery, worthy of God, is attuned to the bishop like strings to a cithara." The lack of mention of the wider Christian community here is significant. This suggests that in IgnEph 4.1 he is making a recommendation that the community should in fact be united with the bishop and presbytery. That this is a likely interpretation is confirmed by IgnEph 4.2 where he exhorts the congregation to unity by saying: "Now do each of you join (γίνεσθε) in this choir,[185] .... It is profitable, then, for you to be in blameless unity that you may always participate also in God."[186] Hence,

---

[185] Following Lake's translation for this phrase. Schoedel translates it as "And may each of you remain (γίνεσθε) joined in chorus." The present imperative γίνεσθε may emphasize the continuation of a presumed current state of affairs; see Schoedel 1985, p51. However, its use here is probably part of Ignatius' strategy of softening a request by stating that it is already fulfilled. Hence, Lake's translation, given above is preferable.

[186] On the imagery of the united chorus and its use elsewhere see Schoedel 1985, p52-3. The purpose of congregational unity is that they "may always participate also in God".

IgnEph 4.1 is likely to be another example of Ignatius making a recommendation, in this case that they be united with the bishop, but softening it by saying that they already comply with the recommendation in advance. What he says remains nonetheless a firm but polite request. Given his use of this fulfillment-in-advance rhetorical device, IgnEph 4.1 cannot be used to say that the other passages in the letter, which we have already discussed and which suggest that some members of the community do not in fact "run together with the bishop", do *not* mean that there is some disunity and division in the community.

What is behind this section in IgnEph 4.1-2? To some extent Ignatius still seems to have in mind his request that Burrhus should stay with him (IgnEph 2.1-2).[187] On this matter the bishop and presbytery are agreed (IgnEph 2.2) and Ignatius is again calling the community to agree with them too (IgnEph 4.1-2). However, in IgnEph 5.1-6.1 he will address the problem of those who "do not come to the assembly" and thus "resist the bishop". Probably then in IgnEph 4.1-2 he is both looking backwards and reinforcing his call for the community to be subject to the bishop and presbytery over the matter of Burrhus (2.1-2) *and* introducing what he will say in IgnEph 5.1-6.1 about the need for some to cease "resisting the bishop".

There are three further passages that concerns the Ephesians' unity. In IgnEph 11.2 Ignatius writes of his hope "that I may be found a participant in the lot of the Ephesian Christians who always agreed with the very apostles in the power of Jesus Christ." We will discuss this passage in detail in Chapter 15 with regard to the significance of the Christian community in Ephesus. Here we note that as far as Ignatius is concerned, the Ephesians have always preserved the ideal of apostolic unity and "still participate in the ideal of unity and order that their glorious past represents."[188] However, we may wonder if Ignatius knew a great deal about the past decades of the life of Ephesian Christians. Further, although in IgnEph 11.2 he writes of the Ephesians' unity, as we will note in Chapter 15, one reason for his lavish praise of the community was that his community in Antioch was divided. Further, given that he has clearly spoken of divisions and those who "do not come to the assembly" in IgnEph 5.1-6.1, he seems here in 11.2 to be using the other rhetorical device we discussed in section 1.6: that he underplays the extent to which the situation is not to his liking. Given what he says about "resisting the bishop" in IgnEph 5.2-6.1, it could well be that in IgnEph 11.2-12.2 he is partly trying to recall them to unity around the bishop by reminding them of what he envisages was their past glory.

We have now gained a perspective from which we can evaluate the remaining two passages which mention unity, which are both at the beginning

---

187 See Schoedel 1985, p49 with reference to IgnEph 3.2.
188 Schoedel 1985, p72.

of the letter. In the salutation to the letter Ignatius describes the Ephesians as "united (ἡνωμένη)" (IgnEph, inscr),[189] and in IgnEph 1.3 he says that he "received in God's name your whole congregation in Onesimus" the bishop.[190] In both passages Ignatius simply claims that the addressees were united. However, given the divisions we have discussed, it seems likely that these are examples of Ignatius' use of fulsome praise for the communities to which he writes, and thus of his rhetorical device of underplaying the extent to which the situation is not to his liking. Certainly to discount what he says later about "resisting the bishop" in IgnEph 5.2-6.1 on the basis of these two brief notes of "unity" would be to overlook the fact that Ignatius is clearly "building up" the community at this early point in the letter by using one of his characteristic rhetorical devices.

Thus, what Ignatius says about unity does not undermine our hypothesis that he is in fact writing to several distinct and different Christian groups, and that some of his readers were currently "resisting the bishop".

4. Overall Conclusions

We thus suggest that Ignatius is writing to all the Christians, and thus all the Christian groups, in Ephesus.[191] However, he is currently aware that some Christians in the city are "resisting the bishop" and are not coming to the bishop's assembly, or assemblies of which the bishop approves. Rather, they are continuing to meet separately in house churches which are independent of Onesimus. The issue does not seem to be a theological one, since Ignatius does not criticize a group within the community for its theology, but rather emphasises the need for one eucharist. This suggests that important doctrinal issues were not at stake but simply that different groups were not united under one bishop. We have noted that Ignatius goes into detail about the silence of Onesimus. This suggests that some Ephesian Christians found little in Onesimus that attracted them to worship under his direction. This seems to have been a factor in "resisting the bishop".

---

[189] Ignatius remarks on the unity of the community only in the inscription to IgnEph and IgnRom.

[190] There are similar expressions in IgnMag 2 and IgnTr 1.1. It is noticeable that he does not say this about the unnamed bishop of Philadelphia (see IgnPhd 1). It is clear that Ignatius thought the community in Philadelphia was deeply divided; see Trevett 1992, p94-99, who notes (p97): "Disunity and the need for co-operation with the bishop and his fellow officers are constant themes of this letter."

[191] This was also our suggestion with regard to Revelation. Of course there are considerable differences between the writings of Ignatius and Revelation; see Trevett 1989a, p119-23. These differences are to be explained by the differences in the respective authors, not by their works being addressed to different audiences.

But further, we have suggested that this period was one of transition in church leadership and structure in Ephesus, and some Christians were opposed to changes that were occurring and so were "resisting the bishop". We have argued that some Ephesian Christians seem to have disagreed that Onesimus had been "sent" to them by God and so did not think that he had to be received and regarded "as the Lord himself" (IgnEph 6.1). We have suggested that some of those who did not think the bishop had been "sent" by God may have been Johannine Christians who received to 1-3 Jn, who were currently "resisting the bishop" and maintaining a separate group identity. Ignatius was encouraging them to come under the authority of the bishop. We have also argued that some of those who "resisted the bishop" in Ephesus may have done so because they valued prophetic authority; these may be people who accepted and endorsed John the Seer's Apocalypse. We have suggested that the spiritual children of the addressees of the Pastorals probably would not have "resisted the bishop".

All of this suggests that Ignatius is writing to a variety of distinct groups in Ephesus – a Pauline group, a Johannine group, readers amongst both groups perhaps who valued prophetic authority as demonstrated by John the Seer, and perhaps other Christians too. Currently, Onesimus, the bishop of Ephesus, was not actually "overseer" over all these Christians,[192] but some were "resisting" his authority, because for them it represented an unwanted innovation. Ignatius is arguing in the letter that they should all be united under one episkopos, and that the eucharist in particular should only be conducted by the bishop, or by people he authorised.

However, we must ask a further question. Would Ignatius' letter be read by all the Christians in Ephesus? Clearly this is what Ignatius hopes. But the letter was probably carried back to Ephesus by Onesimus and his fellow leaders.[193] It would be read first of all by those with whom they were in direct contact. Would it be read by those who "resist the bishop", and do not go to the assembly? Were there other Christians in Ephesus entirely beyond Onesimus' sphere of influence? Presumably Onesimus would endeavour to make sure that it was read widely. But would the letter and its contents be

---

[192] Of course, Onesimus may have been very happy with this situation and it may be that all the "push" for the developments we are suggesting came from Ignatius.

[193] The bearer of the letter to the Ephesians was probably the Ephesian representatives themselves. This is suggested by the fact that Ignatius speaks of writing a letter "through (διά)" someone in IgnRom, IgnPhd and IgnSm (eg through the Ephesians, in IgnRom (10.1); see also IgnPhd (11.2) and IgnSm (12.1)), but not in IgnEph, IgnMag and IgnTr. Since Ignatius probably had an amanuensis for all of his letters, the reference to a person "through" whom he wrote is probably to the person who carried the letter. This means that when no one is mentioned, the letter would have been carried by that community's representatives; see Schoedel 1985, p191 n18.

accepted by all the Christians in Ephesus? Would they all acknowledge Ignatius' right to address them? We do not know.

But we may suggest that Ignatius writes with what he believes is a message for all the Christians in Ephesus. This is the concomitant of his belief that there should be one bishop over all the Christians in the city and is also indicated by the passages discussed in this Chapter. However, the letter itself shows that all the Christians in Ephesus do not accept that Onesimus should be the one bishop in Ephesus. Ignatius writes to all the Christians in the city, hoping that many will actually listen, and accept his message. Ignatius hopes that the letter will be a crucial weapon in the hands of Onesimus and others to advance the cause of monepiscopacy in Ephesus.

Chapter 15

Ignatius and additional facets of the life of the Christians in Ephesus

In the previous chapter we have discussed some introductory issues in relation to Ignatius' letters, the leadership of Christians in Ephesus, and then have argued that Ignatius is writing to all the Christians in the city, but that currently they are divided into some distinct groups, with some Christians acknowledging Onesimus the bishop and other "resisting" the bishop and meeting separately. In this Chapter we will discuss what we can discern about other facets of the life of the Christians in Ephesus from what Ignatius writes.

Ignatius says a good deal about "the church in Ephesus", by which *he* means "all Christians in the city". To some extent, this is Ignatius' own construct and we have argued in the previous Chapter that although some Christians in the city acknowledged Onesimus as their bishop, others did not. Currently Christians identified primarily with one of several different and distinct groups. We need to bear this in mind here.

1. The significance of "the church" of Ephesus

In his greetings to "the church" at Ephesus Ignatius writes: "to her who has been blessed with greatness (τῇ εὐλογημένῃ ἐν μεγέθει) ... to her who has been foreordained before the ages, to be forever destined for enduring (and) unchanging glory, united and elect in (the) true suffering ... to the church most worthily blessed (τῇ ἐκκλησίᾳ τῇ ἀξιομακαρίστῳ) which is in Ephesus in Asia."[1]

Ignatius here speaks of the significance of "the church" in Ephesus in his eyes.[2] A comparison with the greetings to the other churches to which

---

[1] In IgnRom 10.1 Ignatius says the Ephesians are "most worthy of blessing", probably because they had sent Crocus, who probably carried the letter to Rome, to assist Ignatius. In IgnEph 4.1 he also writes of "your worthily reputed presbytery, worthy of God". We will generally avoid the term "church" because it suggests a unified and single organisation, whereas we have shown in Chapter 14 that we do not think this is the case in Ephesus.

[2] As Schoedel points out (1985, p37), some of this language reflects the opening of Paul's letter to the Ephesians. Schoedel writes: "It is tempting to think that ... Ignatius felt it appropriate to address the Ephesians with language from an apostolic writing regarded as

Ignatius writes suggests that he regarded the Christians in Ephesus as more important than the other churches in Asia.[3] Only the salutation to the Romans is more elaborate than that to the Ephesians, testifying to Ignatius' high regard for the Christian community in Rome.[4] Further, it is only the Christian communities of Rome (IgnRom 1.2-3.2, 5.3-6.3) and Ephesus (IgnEph 11.2-12.2) which Ignatius sees as playing a role in lending significance and meaning to his journey to his death.[5] This again shows the pre-eminence of these two communities in Ignatius' eyes.[6]

In IgnEph 8.1 Ignatius emphasises further the importance of the Ephesian Christians: "I am your lowly offering and I dedicate myself to you, church of the Ephesians, famous to the ages." He goes on in IgnEph 8.2 to give what is perhaps his strongest affirmation of the Ephesians: "Fleshly people cannot do spiritual things, nor yet spiritual people fleshly things; ... But what you do

---

directed to them." However, Ignatius uses the ideas in different ways; for example in Eph 1:19 μέγεθος refers to God's power at work in believers; here it refers to the Christians in Ephesus. So Ignatius is emphasizing the significance of the church, not simply repeating earlier themes. See also Grant 1966, p30.

[3] In other circumstances Ignatius may have wished to visit the Christians in Ephesus, but his route was decided by the soldiers escorting him, and may have been determined by their need to pick up other prisoners on the way, since by the time they reached Philippi there were probably at least two other prisoners with Ignatius; see Polycarp, Phil 9.1. It might be thought that the fact that the letter to the Ephesian comes first in our collection of Ignatius' letters reflects the significance of the Christians in Ephesus. However, the modern order of Ignatius' letters is not derived from the manuscript tradition, in which the order of the letters varies widely, but rather from Eusebius (H.E. 3.36), who worked out an order on internal grounds. He rightly saw that IgnEph, IgnMag, IgnTr and IgnRom were written from Smyrna and IgnPhd, IgnSm and IgnPol from Troas. It is understandable to put IgnRom at the end of the first group; it is likely that Eusebius ordered IgnEph, IgnMag and IgnTr on the basis of their length, which in the Bihlmeyer text is 186, 111 and 102 lines respectively. The order is artificial and IgnMag 15 and IgnTr 13 suggest IgnMag and IgnTr were written before Eph; see Schoedel 1985, p132.

[4] Trevett (1992, p62) notes that the Roman church is addressed "in a way which was qualitatively and quantitatively more fulsome than the other churches." See also Quasten 1950, p68-70; Schoedel 1985, p165-7.

[5] See Schoedel 1985, p166.

[6] In IgnEph 1.1 Ignatius writes "Having received in God your much loved name, which you possess by a just nature according to faith and love in Christ Jesus ..." Schoedel suggests their "much loved name" refers to "the firmness and godly affection of the Ephesians, especially as shown on Ignatius' behalf". (Schoedel 1985, p41, who notes that the parallels in IgnTr 1.2 and IgnPol 1.1 suggest this, and discusses the less likely possibility that there is a hidden reference to the name Ephesus here, or to the name of Christ or Christian.) Lightfoot (1889a, Vol 2, p28) suggests the name is equivalent to the "'personality,' 'character,' 'worth'" of the Ephesians themselves. In the context the point is that the Ephesians have shown their Christian character by sending their bishop to greet Ignatius. Ignatius often emphasises the godly character of those he is writing to (for example in IgnTr 1.1), so this is not unusual here.

even according to the flesh, that is spiritual; for you do all things in Jesus Christ." This is a striking statement, for Ignatius had begun by speaking of the contrast between flesh and spirit in a Pauline way.[7] Yet at the end of IgnEph 8.2 he affirms that even what they do "according to the flesh" is spiritual. Ignatius thus thinks of the Ephesians as essentially spiritual, doing "all things in Jesus Christ".

In IgnEph 9.2 Ignatius is similarly very positive about the Ephesians: "So you are all companions on the way, God-bearers, and temple-bearers, Christ-bearers, bearers of holy things, in every way adorned with the commandments of Jesus Christ - you in whom I am very glad, that I was counted worthy through what I write to converse with you and rejoice together, that in your new way of life you love nothing except God alone."

In 11.2-12.2 Ignatius gives further reasons for the Ephesians' greatness: "Let nothing have any attraction for you without him, in whom I carry about my bonds as spiritual pearls, in which may it be mine to rise by your prayer, of which may I always have a share, that I may be found a participant in the lot of the Ephesian Christians who always agreed with the very apostles in the power of Jesus Christ. (12.1) I know who I am and to whom I write: I am condemned, you have been shown mercy; I am in danger, you have been strengthened. (12.2) You are a passage for those slain for God; (you are) fellow initiates of Paul, (a man) sanctified, approved, worthy of blessing, in whose steps may it be mine to be found when I reach God, who in every letter remembers you in Christ Jesus."

This passage gives us considerable insight into Ignatius' view of the Ephesians. Here he highlights the Ephesians' unity by saying that they have always been in agreement "with the very apostles" (11.2).[8] As we have noted in Chapter 14, it seems likely that, when Ignatius left Antioch, and for some time prior to that point, the Christian community in Antioch was divided, particularly about the issue of the office of bishop. This is then one of the reasons why the Ephesians are superior to Ignatius: his church in Antioch was divided,[9] while in Ignatius' view (which we have seen is overly optimistic)

---

[7] See Rom 8:5; 1 Cor 2:14-15; Gal 5:16-25 Schoedel (1985, p64) suggests "An almost conscious correction of the Pauline antithesis lies before us." See also Grant 1966, p40.

[8] By "the apostles" he may mean Paul and the twelve, or perhaps the wider group of the established leaders of the earliest church. He certainly means a group wider than the twelve, since he includes Paul among the apostles in IgnRom 4.3; see Schoedel 1985, p73; Corwin 1960, p196.

[9] See Trevett 1992, p59-66. That he is "in danger" (IgnEph 12.1) refers in the first instance to the possibility that his martyrdom may not succeed (IgnRom 6.2; 7.2), but probably also to his loss of control of the church in Antioch and the emergence of a group opposed to him; see Schoedel 1985, p10, 13. Such a challenge to his authority and such evidence of disunity seems, for Ignatius, to have called into question the value of his whole ministry. He thus now looks to the united Christians of Ephesus who are still in agreement

the Ephesians were united "with the very apostles". He continues this theme of their unity in 12.1 in saying that "you have been shown mercy ... you have been strengthened." Schoedel comments: "The superiority of the Ephesians consists in their preservation of apostolic unity. The disunity that seems to have threatened Ignatius' own ministry ... is probably what brings him to view the Ephesians so favourably in this connection."[10] Hence, his high evaluation of the Ephesians is to some extent the reverse side of his own powerful sense of unworthiness, which is itself connected with his failure as bishop of Antioch to create and preserve unity in his own community.[11] Thus his high evaluation of the Ephesians is, to some extent at least, connected to his own situation, and would not necessarily be shared by others.

In IgnEph 12.2 Ignatius also says that the Ephesians are a passage or highway (πάροδος) for martyrs, which probably refers to Acts 20:38 where the Ephesian elders formally farewelled Paul, aware that they would never see him again.[12] They are also fellow initiates (συμμύσται) with Paul, which again probably simply refers to the strong links Paul has with Ephesus.[13] Clearly the link between Paul and Ephesus was alive (perhaps through both oral traditions and in written texts) at this time and the greatness of the Ephesians in Ignatius' eyes was in part due to the strength of this link. Finally, Ignatius says that in every letter Paul remembered the Ephesians. Since Paul only mentions the Ephesians in 1 Cor 15:32; 16:8; Eph 1:1; 1 Tim 1:3; 2 Tim 1:18; 4:12, and it is unlikely that Ignatius knew each of these letters in any case,[14] it seems that here he generalises on the basis of a few instances.[15]

---

with the apostles and to other communities to confirm the value of his mission by supporting him in his martyrdom.

[10] Schoedel 1985, p73.

[11] On his sense of unworthiness and its connection to what had happened in Antioch see Schoedel 1985, p13-14, 213; Corwin 1960, p25-8; Trevett 1992, p61-6; IgnEph 2.2; 21.2; IgnMag 12.1; 14.1; IgnTr 4.2; 13.1; IgnRom 9.2. Note that Ignatius' self-depreciation was most marked in the letters written from Smyrna. His tone is different in the letters written from Troas after he had heard news of the peace in Antioch and his confidence increased; see for example IgnSm 11.1. Corwin (1960, p28) comments: "An occurrence disastrous enough to have produced such a sense of failure is more likely to have been a struggle within the church than persecution visited upon it from outside. For the former, as bishop, he would rightly have had a special sense of responsibility, and the failure to heal the breach might well have brought about the kind of self-torment he reveals. Nothing less serious can account for his self-reproach. Behind this mood of self-abnegation, then, we can probably see evidence for some serious trouble in the Antioch church, and it is natural to surmise that it was a schism."

[12] See Schoedel 1985, p73.

[13] Schoedel 1985, p73.

[14] It is debated as to how many of Paul's letters Ignatius actually knew. Schoedel (1985, p9-10) thinks certain usage can be established only for 1 Cor, although he may have known Ephesians (see Schoedel 1985, p37) and from the current passage it is clear he knew Paul was the author of more than one letter. He may know of a collection of Paul's letters. Lindemann

However, Ignatius' point is clear; he is not seeking "to give precise information on the frequency of the word *Ephesus* in the Pauline corpus. Ignatius is simply trying to link the Apostle Paul and the Christians of Ephesus as intimately as possible."[16]

Thus, Ignatius speaks very warmly of the Ephesian Christians, and emphasises their greatness, their worthiness and spiritual nature, their unity, and that they were strongly and intimately linked with Paul. Clearly for Ignatius they are a very significant community.

But is Ignatius overly zealous in speaking of the greatness of the Ephesians? Would other Christians necessarily have agreed with him? We have noted in Chapter 14, section 1.6 that Ignatius is often lavish in his praise, but that we should be cautious about taking him at face value since the whole of a letter often reveals that the situation is more complex than he suggests at first. Further, we have already noted in Chapter 14 that the Ephesians were not as united as Ignatius suggests. To some extent his praise of their unity (see 11.2-12.1) is meant as an encouragement to them to in fact be united. All is not quite as Ignatius suggests then. In addition, we can give two further reasons why some other Christians would probably not have been so lavish in their praise as Ignatius.

Firstly, we have noted that Ignatius' positive view of the Ephesians is the reverse side of his own sense of unworthiness and failure at Antioch. He sees them as so great, partly because he sees himself as such a failure.

Secondly, it seems clear that it was the Ephesians and the Smyrnaeans who experienced the most affinity with Ignatius, perhaps because they agreed with him on many things. This is shown by the high level of assistance given to Ignatius by the Ephesians and the Smyrnaeans. Note in particular the support offered by Crocus and Burrhus.[17] Further, it seems that the Ephesians spent longer in Smyrna with Ignatius than the Trallians or Magnesians, since greetings from Ephesus are sent to the latter two churches (IgnTr 13.1; Mag

---

(1990, p36) thinks Ignatius knew 1 Cor and probably Ephesians. Trevett (1992, p19-20) notes that "in every letter may indicate a knowledge of Eph and 1 Cor. Ignatius also said that Paul had instructed the Roman church (IgnRom 4.3) which may, but need not, refer to Paul's Romans". Paulsen (1978, p32-4) and Corwin 1960, p66-7) think the case is strong only for 1 Cor. By contrast, Grant (1964, p57) thinks Ignatius knew Rom, 1 Cor, 2 Cor, Gal, Eph, Phil, Col, 1 Thess and possibly 1 and 2 Tim.

[15] Schoedel 1985, p73. Schoedel (1985 p73 n7) also suggests that Ignatius may be thinking of Paul's use of the verb μνημονεύω. Thus Ignatius could consider that the Ephesians were included in every apostolic reminiscence; see for example Eph 1:16. In this way he could think that Paul never ceased remembering the Ephesians.

[16] Lindemann 1990, p36.

[17] Burrhus was financed by the Ephesians and the Smyrnaeans; see IgnEph 2.1-2; IgnRom 10.1; IgnPhd 11.2; IgnSm 12.1; Crocus was probably financed solely by the Ephesians; see section 3.2 below. Ignatius speaks in particularly glowing terms of these two men.

15), but not from Tralles or Magnesia to Ephesus, which suggests that by the time Ignatius wrote the letter to the Ephesians the one Trallian representative and the two from Magnesia had left for home. Thus, the Ephesian representatives stayed longer than did the others. This seems to indicate the enthusiastic support the Ephesians offered to Ignatius.[18]

No doubt, the Ephesians' affinity with Ignatius and the high level of support they offered him made Ignatius more positive towards the Ephesians. This suggests that Ignatius may well have been more glowing in praise of the Ephesians than many of his contemporaries.

Conclusions

Ignatius suggests four points which are of interest for us here. Firstly, that the Ephesian addressees were the most important, or at the least one of the most important Christian communities in Asia, is shown by the salutation of the letter. It is likely that this had a basis in reality, since Ignatius does not speak so lavishly of other Asian congregations.

Secondly, his emphasis on the strength and intimacy of their links with Paul suggests that the memory of Paul was alive among at least some of the Christians to whom he wrote.[19]

Thirdly, the way in which Ignatius speaks of the Ephesians' worthiness and spiritual nature and his general tone of praise suggest that many of them agreed with him theologically. This would rule out any thought that the majority of them were docetic, for example.

Fourthly, although we have noted that others would probably not have been as lavish as Ignatius was in his praise of the Ephesians, Ignatius' tone towards the Ephesians suggests that at this time the Ephesian community he addressed was respected by a number of other Christians.

2. "Opponents"

In IgnEph 6.2-9.2 and again in IgnEph 16-19 Ignatius addresses the problem of opponents who threaten his Ephesian addressees. In this section we will discuss the nature of these opponents and the impact they had in Ephesus.

---

[18] See Schoedel 1985, p132, 161. Schoedel (1985, p249) notes that in IgnSm 11.1 and IgnEph 21.2 Ignatius balances a statement about his worthiness and his unworthiness, whereas in IgnRom 9.2, IgnTr 13.1; IgnMag 14 he speaks only of his unworthiness. He suggests the more balanced statement in IgnSm and IgnEph reflects the fact that Ignatius had his most active supporters in the Ephesians and Smyrnaeans.

[19] We do not know if he is here reflecting something of the general reputation the Ephesian Christians had among Syrian Christians or if what he says about Paul was based on what he heard from the Ephesians who visited him.

2.1 Did Ignatius oppose one group or two in his letters?

In a number of passages in the letters Ignatius addresses the subject of teachers whom he regarded as false. There is an on-going debate as to whether Ignatius faced one group in which docetic and Judaizing ideas were mixed or whether he opposed two separate groups: Judaizers in Magnesia and Philadelphia, and docetists in Tralles and Smyrna and of whom he warned in Ephesus. However, overall the evidence suggests that he faced at least two different groups, the docetists and the Judaizers. Those who argue that he faced a composite teaching base this view primarily on the links between Judaizing and docetism found in Mag 9.1 and 11 but it seems likely that these links were formed by Ignatius himself, rather than being a reflection of a composite teaching there.[20] It is Ignatius then, who sees Judaizing as implying the denial of the birth, death and resurrection of Jesus Christ (see Mag 9.1, 11), which suggests that overall he is actually facing two distinct groups. Further, as Schoedel remarks, "If he [Ignatius] had been able to make a direct charge against the Judaizers of holding a docetic doctrine of Christ, he would surely have done so."[21] It is this lack of clear anti-docetic polemic in IgnMag and IgnPhd, the two letters which deal with Judaizing, which argues decisively that Ignatius is facing two groups.

We will now examine the passages in IgnEph in which Ignatius discusses these opponents.[22]

2.2 Opponents who regard themselves as Christians, are in Ephesus

In IgnEph 7-9 Ignatius addressed the issue of theological opponents. He writes (IgnEph 7.1): "For some are accustomed with evil deceit to carry about the name, at the same time doing things unworthy of God, whom you must avoid as wild beasts; for they are rabid dogs, biting without warning, whom you must guard against since they are almost incurable." Since Ignatius says they "carry about the name", it seems clear that he is referring to itinerant

---

[20] See Schoedel 1985, p118, 154.

[21] See Schoedel 1985, p200 n1. Those who have argued that he is facing two groups include Richardson 1935, p51-4; 79-85; Grant 1964, p54-55; 1966, p22; Rius-Camps 1980, p40-51; Schoedel 1985, p12, 118, 234; Sumney 1993, p345-65; Brown 2000, p176-197. Those who have argued that he is facing one group include Lightfoot 1889b, Vol 1, p373-7; Genouillac 1907, p240-57; Molland 1954, p1-6; Barnard 1966, p22-6.

[22] We can note that there are considerable differences between the letters concerning what Ignatius says on the issue of opponents. This shows that specific teaching is a problem in particular churches, and that Ignatius is not simply writing about opponents in general who may or may not be a problem in the particular church addressed. We have noted that Ignatius had good sources of information for each of the churches.

teachers.[23] This is confirmed by IgnEph 9.1, where he writes, "I know that some have passed by (παροδεύσαντάς) on their way from there (ἐκεῖθεν) [ie. Ephesus] with evil teaching", which is a further reference to the itinerancy of these teachers. However, this does not mean that none of these teachers are resident in Ephesus, and we will turn to this possibility shortly.

We also note that in IgnEph 7.1 he says these itinerant teachers carry about "the name", which is a reference to the name of Christ (cf. IgnEph 3.1) or "Christian" (cf. Mag 4.1). Thus, these teachers claimed to be Christians.

2.3 The opponents were docetists[24]

Firstly, we must ask if Ignatius knew the nature of the teaching which he regarded as false. In IgnEph 9.1 Ignatius gives an indication that he was reliably informed about it. As we have noted, he begins IgnEph 9.1 by saying: "I know (ἔγνων) that some have passed by on their way from there (ἐκεῖθεν) with evil teaching ..." ἔγνων here introduces a disclosure formula which is commonly found in letters.[25] What Ignatius wants to indicate by using it is that some teachers who had been in Ephesus have come to Smyrna "from there" (ἐκεῖθεν), that is, from Ephesus, and so Ignatius knows about them because he is now in Smyrna himself.[26] Hence Ignatius was probably reliably informed of some details about the teachers from Ephesus.

---

[23] See Trevett 1992, p80. Schoedel (1985, p59) notes that Ignatius uses περιφέρω in IgnEph 11.2; IgnMag 1.2; IgnTr 12.2 to refer to travel. Cf. Bauer (1971, p89), who insisted that the opponents ("sectarians" as he called them), were within the community.

[24] Since Ignatius seems to have been more or less prepared with arguments against the docetists (and the Judaizers), it is likely that he had already known such groups in Antioch; see Schoedel 1985, p11 n62. However, Corwin (1960, p52-87) takes this one step further and sees three groups in the church in Antioch: the Judaisers, the Docetists, and a central group to which Ignatius belongs. While this is possible, it is by no means certain, and it is methodologically unjustifiable to read statements written for example to Smyrna, as a straight-forward description of what had happened in Antioch (eg Corwin 1960, p53-4 re IgnSm 7.1). However, our interest here is in the situation in Asia, and it seems quite clear that both groups are in view there in different churches.

[25] See White 1972, p11-15.

[26] See Grant 1966, p40; Schoedel 1985, p65. Genouillac (1907, p213 n2 who suggests it refers to Antioch) does not agree with this interpretation of ἐκεῖθεν but Schoedel argues that ἐκεῖθεν in IgnEph 9.1 means "from where you are". There are a number of links between what is said of the opponents in IgnEph and IgnSm (see IgnSm 4.1; IgnEph 7.1; 9.1; 10.1), which suggests that the opponents of IgnSm 4.1 may have had some sort of connection with those mentioned in IgnEph 9.1, some of whom had travelled from Ephesus to Smyrna. However, the opponents in Smyrna may have been local people (see IgnSm 5.3; 6.1; 7.1; 8.1), and it is important that we do not read the situation in Smyrna into that in Ephesus, which seems to have been distinctively different. Overall it seems likely that some docetists had gone from Ephesus to Smyrna, but that there were already docetists within the Smyrnaean community at the time.

In IgnEph 6.2 Ignatius says that "no heresy (αἵρεσις) dwells among you."
In using the word αἵρεσις Ignatius seems to be referring specifically to
docetic teaching. This is made clear by the fact that he goes on to speak about
docetic teachers in IgnEph 7-9, as we will see, and says there that the
Ephesians have not listened to the docetists (IgnEph 9.1), which tallies with
his remark in 6.2 that no "heresy" dwells among you. Further, in IgnTr 6.1 he
also speaks of αἵρεσις and it is clear from IgnTr 9-11 that he is again
referring to docetism in particular.[27]
   We gain some further indications of the teaching of the opponents as the
letter to Ephesus progresses. In IgnEph 7, after introducing the subject of the
opponents (IgnEph 7.1) he goes on to emphasize the historical side of Christ's
being, as compared with the exalted Christ (IgnEph 7.2). This suggests that
these issues were at the heart of his contention with the opponents and thus
that they were docetists.[28]
   Further, in IgnEph 17-19 Ignatius goes on to answer the opponents'
teaching as he understands it, and thus gives us further indications of the
nature of the teaching. In IgnEph 17.2 he asks two rhetorical questions: "Why
do we not all become wise, receiving the knowledge of God which is Jesus
Christ? Why do we foolishly perish, being ignorant of the gift which the Lord
has truly sent (ὃ πέπομφεν ἀληθῶς ὁ κύριος;)?" These questions hint at the
content of the opponents' teaching in Ephesus. In both questions Ignatius
emphasizes that Jesus Christ is the source of true knowledge of God. Further,
he emphasises that Jesus Christ was truly (ἀληθῶς) sent, which suggests he
was opposing docetism, since he uses ἀληθῶς to deny docetism elsewhere.[29]
That this is the most likely interpretation is shown by IgnEph 18.1-19.3 where
he emphasizes the reality and centrality of Christ's birth and passion, which is
significant since these were matters that were probably denied by the docetists
of Ignatius' day.[30] It seems likely then that the opponents who had been
threatening the (or some) Ephesian Christians were docetists. In addition, it is
clear from other passages in Ignatius' letters, that docetists were a threat to the
churches in Smyrna (IgnSm 2-7) and Tralles (IgnTr 9-11), which makes it
likely that the Christians in Ephesus were facing a similar threat.[31]

---

[27] Trevett (1992, p80) and Rius-Camps (1980, p50-1) take αἵρεσις to refer specifically to
docetic teaching in IgnEph 6.2 and IgnTr 6.1. In speaking of the Judaizers he uses the terms
μερίζω (IgnMag 6.2), μερισμός (IgnPhd 2.1; 3.1; 7.2; 8.1) and σχίζω (IgnPhd 3.3).

[28] See Schoedel 1985, p61.

[29] See IgnTr 9.1-2; IgnSm 1.1-2.1.

[30] Schoedel 1985, p84. Schoedel (1985, p87-94) shows that in 19.1-3 in particular,
Ignatius is making a vigorous anti-docetic statement. Schoedel refutes the view that Ignatius
is here reflecting the Gnostic myth of redemption.

[31] On the docetists see Quasten 1950, p65-6; Gibbard 1966, p218; Schoedel 1985, p152-8,
220-46.

2.4 Did the opponents gain a following among Ignatius' addressees in Ephesus?

In IgnEph 6.2 we read: "Now indeed (μὲν οὖν) Onesimus himself praises highly your godly orderliness - that you all live according to the truth and that no heresy dwells among you; but (ἀλλά) you do not even listen to anyone except him who speaks truly concerning Jesus Christ."

Here Ignatius states that the Christian community he addressed tolerated no false doctrine. Ignatius begins the section with μὲν οὖν; the next main clause begins with ἀλλά. This grammatical structure shows that Ignatius intended to conclude one line of argument and to go on to make a contrasting point.[32] Schoedel suggests this structure indicates that Ignatius intended to say something like "Now indeed there is no faction among you, but there are dangers (which increase when you do not listen to your bishop)."[33] However, the actual contrasting point does not come until IgnEph 7.1, where it becomes clear that Ignatius' attention has shifted to the problem of teachers who endanger the Christian community from without. Instead of making this contrast in IgnEph 6.2 he reiterated his point that they all live according to the truth by saying that "you do not even listen to anyone except him who speaks truly concerning Jesus Christ." His intended contrast (as shown by his grammatical structure) has become a repetition of the previous point, in order to avoid the impression that the opponents he will speak of had made any headway at all.

Thus, Ignatius is very anxious to avoid the impression that the opponents he will speak of had made any impact.[34] But is this the whole story? We have noted in Chapter 14 that one of the features of Ignatius' rhetoric is that he can underplay the extent to which the situation is not to his liking. Is that the case here?

In Chapter 6 we discussed the Johannine secessionists for whom we have evidence in 1-2 Jn (probably to be dated around 90-100 CE), and there we suggested that they were tending towards docetism. Is *this* group still in existence in Ephesus when Ignatius writes? Have they now developed their thinking, so that it has become the docetism that Ignatius has in mind in what he writes? With these questions in view, we will now turn to the evidence which suggests that although there were no docetists within the group that

---

[32] See Schoedel 1985, p58.

[33] Schoedel 1985, p58.

[34] Note also that in IgnEph 9.1 Ignatius emphasises the inability of the opponents to gain a hearing in Ephesus when he writes: "I know that some have passed by on their way from there with evil teaching, whom you did not allow to sow among you, stopping your ears that you might not receive what was sown by them, since you are stones of the Father's temple." Ignatius here emphasises that the Ephesians have not even listened to these teachers. But we will suggest below that the situation is more complex than this.

Ignatius addresses, there was actually a docetic group in the city, which existed as a group beyond and outside Ignatius' addressees.[35] This group clearly poses something of a threat to his readers.

2.5 Were any docetists actually resident in Ephesus?

In IgnEph 9.1 we read: "I know that some have passed by on their way from there with evil teaching".[36] We have noted that these teachers have come from Ephesus to Smyrna. But have all of them come to Smyrna? It is certainly possible that some, but not all, have gone to Smyrna, and a group have remained in Ephesus. Ignatius would then be warning his Ephesian readers about the teachers who had remained in Ephesus.

We note the warnings that Ignatius writes to the Ephesians:

7.1-2 "For some are accustomed with evil deceit to carry about the name, at the same time doing things unworthy of God, *whom you must avoid as wild beasts*; for they are rabid dogs, biting without warning, *whom you must guard against* since they are almost incurable. There is one physician, both fleshly and spiritual ..."
8.1 "*So let no one deceive you*, as indeed you are not deceived ..."
16.1-2 "*Be not deceived*, my brothers: corrupters of homes 'will not inherit the Kingdom of God'; if then they died who did these things in the realm of the flesh, how much more if someone by evil teaching corrupts faith in God for which Jesus Christ was crucified? Such a filthy being will go into the unquenchable fire, *likewise also the person who listens to him*."
17.1-2 "*Do not be anointed with the ill odour of the teaching* of the ruler of the age lest he lead you captive from the life set before you. ... Why do we foolishly perish, being ignorant of the gift which the Lord has truly sent?" (emphasis added in each case)

We note the command to avoid these teachers and guard against them, not to be deceived and also that even one who *listens* to them will go into the "unquenchable fire". It is hard to explain the repetition and strength of this language to Ephesian readers, if all the docetists have actually left Ephesus. Why speak of those "whom you *must guard against* since they are almost incurable" (7.1) if they are not currently in Ephesus? Why warn the readers not to be deceived, and particularly not to listen (with such a dire warning that the fate of those who listen is the same as that of the docetists themselves), if *all* the docetists had departed Ephesus for elsewhere? We also note that in IgnEph 7.2 and 16-19 Ignatius gives a comparatively substantial refutation of

---

[35] When in IgnTr 11.1 Ignatius writes "Flee, then, the evil side-growths which bear death-dealing fruit" he seems to be calling for his addressees to have nothing to do with docetists resident in Tralles. IgnSm 5.1-6.1 also suggest this with regard to Smyrna.
[36] Similarly, as we have noted, in IgnEph 7.1 he speaks of those who "carry about the name".

docetism, which indicates his concern to "guard" his readers against opponents. This makes perfect sense if a docetic group was in existence in the city.

It seems very likely then that a separate group of docetists still lives in Ephesus, and as we have noted, the Johannine secessionists come readily to mind. Although we cannot be certain that they are in view, this seems very probable, particularly given that we have dated the Johannine letters around 90-100 and Ignatius' letters between 105-110.

But if there are such docetists in Ephesus, are they among Ignatius' addressees? This seems unlikely, since Ignatius seems to be warning the readers about outsiders, and since we have already seen that Ignatius suggests his readers have not been "deceived" by the docetists (see IgnEph 6.2 and 9.1).[37] We have also argued in the preceding Chapter that Ignatius is writing to a variety of distinct groups in Ephesus – a Pauline group, a Johannine group, and perhaps other Christians too; currently, Onesimus is not actually "overseer" over all these Christians. But since we have argued that Onesimus wishes to be "bishop" over the Johannine group that was earlier addressed by 1 Jn, it seems unlikely that he would *also* wish to be "bishop" over a group that had clearly split from the 1 Jn group some years before, and indeed had been condemned by that group as theologically aberrant. So it seems unlikely that Ignatius is writing to the docetists, whom we have suggested have evolved from the Johannine secessionists; having split from the Johannine Christians, they are "beyond the pale" for this group, and also for Onesimus and Ignatius. But, we may suggest that what Ignatius says about the *current* threat of docetists as he writes shows that the Johannine secessionists are still in town, have developed their teaching further in the docetic direction, and that Ignatius is concerned that they might continue to gain a hearing. Only this sort of "in-town situation" explains the strength of Ignatius' concern that his readers do not even listen to the opponents. We can also note that the secessionists in 1 Jn have gone into "the world" and "the world listens to them" (1 Jn 4:5), which suggests they are involved in mission. That they are still sending out itinerant missionaries (in this case to Smyrna) is in keeping with this.[38] But such itinerancy does not mean that they have *all* left Ephesus.

---

[37] Although we will note below that the situation is probably not quite as straight-forward as this.

[38] Schoedel (1985, p59) seems to assume that the docetists are *all* itinerants. But this seems to be based only on the idea that they "carry about the name" (IgnEph 7.1) and that they have come to Smyrna from Ephesus (IgnEph 9.1). Although the language used suggests some travel, it does not necessarily need to mean that the teachers concerned were always itinerant, nor that they did not have a "base". Indeed, IgnEph 9.1 (Ἔγνων δὲ παροδεύσαντάς τινας ἐκεῖθεν) is perhaps best translated as "I know that some have passed through [ie Smyrna] from there [ie Ephesus]"; this could certainly mean that the people

We conclude then that the strength of Ignatius' warning in IgnEph 7.1-2; 8.1; 16:1-2 and 17.1-2 strongly suggests that the Johannine docetic-tending secessionists are still in Ephesus, that they have developed further towards docetism and that Ignatius does not address them directly, but that he wishes to warn his readers about them. Ignatius is clearly concerned that the docetists in Ephesus pose a threat to his readers.

We have also noted in Chapter 14, section 1.6.2, that Ignatius tends to underplay the extent to which a situation is not to his liking. Thus, although he can say that they "all live according to the truth" and "no heresy dwells among you" (IgnEph 6.2), all is not quite as he made it sound and the docetists in Ephesus pose a real threat to his addressees. This explains the severity of 16.1-2 and other passages discussed above. We can suggest then that the impact of the opponents had been somewhat greater than Ignatius was prepared to admit.

We have now gained a perspective which helps us to understand IgnEph 8.1 better. After having spoken of docetic teachers (see IgnEph 7.1-2), Ignatius writes in IgnEph 8.1: "So let no one deceive you, as indeed you are not deceived, being entirely of God (Μὴ οὖν τις ὑμᾶς ἐξαπατάτω, ὥσπερ οὐδὲ ἐξαπατᾶσθε, ὅλοι ὄντες θεοῦ); for when no strife has become fixed among you that can torment you, then you live in a godly way." Here, Ignatius gives a command (that they stand firm against docetism and are not deceived by docetic teachers), but says that it is already being fulfilled.

In Chapter 14, section 1.6.1 we discussed the rhetorical use of fulfilment-in-advance language. The question that discussion raises about IgnEph 16.1 is whether or not the Ephesians are actually already literally fulfilling the command, and thus are not deceived by any opponents, specifically by the docetists whom we have suggested are resident in Ephesus? Ignatius would then simply be commending them for standing fast against the docetists, and encouraging them to continue to do so. However, it is also possible that the ascription of the fulfilment of a command in-advance here is a rhetorical device, in which case some at least among them are not currently obeying his injunction. In this case, Ignatius would be seeking to soften the command to them by the use of this rhetorical device and thus by saying that "you are not deceived". Can we say what the actual situation is? We must look at the whole letter to enable us to decide if we should take Ignatius literally, or if he is using a rhetorical device here.

The important point to note is that the strength of Ignatius' polemic against the docetists in the passages discussed above (7.1-2, 16.1-2; 17.1-2) suggests that, if the addressees were not deceived, then they were very close to being deceived. We will note below that the docetists were probably not answered

---

spoken of were resident in Ephesus. Given the strength of the language we have reviewed about the threat to Ephesian Christians, we would suggest that their base was indeed Ephesus.

by theological argument; further, the very evidence which suggested to us that the docetists were resident in Ephesus also suggests that they had had a considerably impact on the addressees. So, although we cannot say that the addressees were actually deceived (since there is no crystal clear evidence of this), when Ignatius adds in 8.1 "as indeed you are not deceived", we can suggest that this is another use of the fulfilment-in-advance rhetorical device. Ignatius *hopes* they will not be deceived; currently they must be commanded to avoid the docetists as if they were wild beasts (7.1) and that those who listen to them are as bad as the docetists themselves (16.1-2). Clearly Ignatius sees the readers as in a vulnerable position.

2.6 Christ (and not Onesimus) is the only physician

As we have noted, in IgnEph 7.1 Ignatius says the opponents "are rabid dogs, biting without warning,[39] whom you must guard against since they are almost incurable."[40] Docetists are thus dangerous to their hearers, but, since they are "almost incurable" it is also very unlikely that they will be convinced if Ignatius' addressees converse with them. In Ignatius' opinion, the best tactic in dealing with the opponents is accordingly neither to listen to them, nor to converse with them.[41]

In IgnEph 7.2 Ignatius goes on to say: "There is one physician ... Jesus Christ our Lord." In this context, this emphasis on Christ as the only healer, and thus the only one who can cure the "almost incurable", suggests that Ignatius has in mind the attempts of the Ephesians (and perhaps others elsewhere) to reply to the opponents' teaching. Ignatius' implied advice is that

---

[39] According to Schoedel (1985, p59) "a dog biting without warning" was a proverb that referred to "fawning behaviour masking an intent to do harm". This suggests they were quite attractive teachers, although such language could simply be a standard way of speaking of opponents since in IgnPhd 2.2 he speaks of wolves and in IgnSm 4.1 of beasts in human form.

[40] Ignatius has a similar attitude to docetists elsewhere. In IgnSm 4.1, in speaking of docetists he writes that rather than meeting them "only pray for them if somehow they may repent, which is difficult." In IgnSm 5.2 he says of docetists: "Anyone who does not say this denies him [Jesus Christ] completely and is the bearer of a corpse." In IgnSm 7.1 we read: "They, then, who speak against the gift of God die in their disputing." In IgnSm 5.3 he regards docetists as faithless and in IgnTr 10.1 writes "But if as some who are atheists - that is unbelievers - say, that he suffered in appearance ...", again clearly with reference to docetists; see also IgnSm 2; cf. IgnEph 18.1. Trevett (1989b, p43) comments: "The harshest language in these letters is reserved for the error of docetism." In fact, Ignatius holds out much higher hopes for the repentance of non-Christians; see IgnEph 10.1. We can also note that when the problem concerns those who resist the bishop and create division, Ignatius can speak of repentance with a different tone; see IgnPhd 3.2; 8.1; IgnSm 9.1.

[41] See IgnTr 11.1; IgnSm 4.1; 5.3; 7.2.

such a cure should be left to Christ's healing power since some things are too difficult and dangerous for human beings.[42]

Schoedel also suggests that Ignatius may again have Onesimus' silence in view in IgnEph 7.2, and may be pointing out that Onesimus' silence before his opponents is the wisest strategy.[43] This suggests that although the Ephesians did not adopt the opponents' views (IgnEph 6.2; 9.1), they also did not have an answer to their teaching. Specifically, it seems likely that Onesimus was silent before them; his failure to answer the docetists in debate (cf. IgnEph 6.1; 15.1-2) has probably not helped matters. This seems to have meant that the Ephesian addressees were rather vulnerable to the opponents. Perhaps it also explains why in IgnEph 7.2 and 16-19 Ignatius gives a substantial discussion which contains a number of elements which refute docetism,[44] and why in IgnEph 20.1 he also promises a second book in which he would write "further explanation of the (divine) plan which I was getting into regarding the new human being, Jesus Christ, having to do with faith in him and love of him, with his suffering and resurrection." Clearly a document on these themes from Ignatius would be anti-docetic.

Given that we have suggested that the docetists continued to exist in Ephesus as a separate group, and that they were unanswered, we can understand the concern that Ignatius expressed in the passages discussed in section 2.5 above. The problem in Ephesus is unanswered teaching and interest by the listeners; given this situation, Ignatius *hopes* they will not be deceived. The issue as Ignatius sees it is thus the real threat the docetists posed to his addressees in Ephesus and their overall vulnerability to docetic teaching.

2.7 No Judaisers in Ephesus

It seems clear that the Judaizers had been a problem in Philadelphia (IgnPhd 6, 8-9) and Magnesia (IgnMag 8-11). They were Christians (since they "professed Jesus Christ"; IgnMag 10.3; see also IgnPhd 6.1), some of whom were Gentiles (IgnPhd 6.1). They seem to have been committed to Jewish praxis to varying degrees (see IgnMag 9.1; 10.3), although they may have been more interested in the idea of Judaism rather than actual Jewish practices. At Philadelphia, they gave a very high place to the "archives",

---

[42] See Schoedel 1985, p60. Ignatius is here picking up an older theme; for example, Philo had complained that people try medical solutions before looking to God; see Sacr. 70.

[43] Schoedel 1985, p60.

[44] It is more substantial than in IgnTr 9-11. His treatment is also extensive in IgnSm 4-8, where docetism was clearly a real problem and hence required a substantial refutation. It is interesting then that, despite his own advice not to engage in discussion with the docetists, Ignatius gives the Ephesians some weapons with which to do just that. This again makes it likely that there are some resident docetists in Ephesus.

which included the Old Testament (IgnPhd 8.2).[45] Ignatius and the Judaizers differed in their interpretation of the prophets (see IgnMag 8.2; IgnPhd 5.2; 9.2) and the Judaizers also seem to have given special attention to the biblical priesthood (IgnPhd 9.1). It is also significant to note that the Judaisers were still a part of the Philadelphian congregation after Ignatius had left (see IgnPhd 11.1). It seems likely then that it was Ignatius, rather than the Philadelphians, who regarded the Judaizers as excluded from the community (cf. IgnPhd 3.1-2).[46] Ignatius thought the Judaizers could repent and be forgiven.[47]

However, there is nothing to suggest that the Judaizers were a threat in Ephesus. We do not know why, according to Ignatius, the Christian Judaizers had had an impact in Philadelphia and Magnesia and not in Ephesus, Tralles or Smyrna. Perhaps the Judaizing movement was started by travelling teachers, who had not yet arrived in these latter three cities. Perhaps the presence of Christian Judaizers in Philadelphia and Magnesia was due to local factors, such as the particular impact of the local Jewish community. Or perhaps the presence of Christian Judaizers was due entirely to developments and theological interests within the congregations concerned.

2.8 Conclusions

It is notable then that while various other teachings had made inroads into neighbouring churches, Ignatius regards his Ephesian Christian addressees as free from teaching with which he disagreed. However, we have suggested that there was a docetic group of Christians in Ephesus which had developed from the Johannine secessionists but that this group was not among Ignatius' addressees. Some of his addressees had probably listened to these docetists, and had been unable to answer them and Ignatius clearly regards the docetists as a current threat to his readers. But it does seem that at the time Ignatius wrote his readers had not capitulated to docetism, nor were they influenced by Judaizers.

---

[45] See also IgnPhd 5.1-2, 9.1; Schoedel 1978, p97-106; 1985, p207-9; Paulsen 1978, p56-9; Trevett 1989c, p323-5; 1992, p26.

[46] See Schoedel 1985, p214.

[47] See IgnPhd 8.1. On the Judaizers see Trevett 1992, p169-94, Schoedel 1985, p118-27; 200-11; Grant 1966, p103-4. Corwin's view (1960, p58-64) that the Judaizers are Christians who had been Essene Jews is unsubstantiated.

3. Other matters relating to the life of the Christians in Ephesus

We will now deal with a range of other issues on which Ignatius comments in
his letter to the Ephesians. Where Ignatius provides sufficient information,
these will include some of the themes that we dealt with in Part Three, which
we have not covered elsewhere.[48]

3.1 Outsiders

Ignatius suggests that Christians in Ephesus experienced hostility from their
pagan neighbours. Thus in IgnEph 10.2 where he is speaking of non-
Christians, we read: "Before their anger (ὀργάς) be gentle ... before their
slanderings (βλασφημίας) (offer) prayers, ... before their fierceness (ἄγριον)
be mild." This could be general advice, perhaps reflecting Ignatius' own
experience in Antioch. But it does suggest the Ephesian Christians
experienced a degree of rejection from their society. Further, in IgnEph 12.2
he writes that the Ephesians are "a passage for those slain for God (πάροδός
ἐστε τῶν εἰς θεὸν ἀναιρουμένων)". This suggests that Asian Christians, and
in particular Christians in Ephesus, were well aware of the realities of witness
to death.[49]

However, despite these indications of some hostility and awareness of
martyrdom, there is a relative lack of reference in Ignatius' letters to external
pressures on the Asian churches to which he writes. Ignatius gives no
indication that the churches were currently experiencing, or that they had
recently experienced, a concerted persecution campaign. Only Jesus and the

---

[48] We have already discussed the leadership structure amongst the readers and have
attempted to discuss the relationship between traditions and communities in that we have tried
to show that Ignatius is writing to all the Christians in Ephesus, including the Johannine
community and the community which received the Pastorals and that his intended audience
would include readers in both the Johannine community and the Pastorals (and perhaps others
too) who received Revelation. With regard to self-designation, we see only Ignatius'
preferred terms, not those of Ephesian readers. The terms he uses in writing to the Ephesians
are the following. In IgnEph 10.1 he writes: "Suffer them therefore to become your disciples
(μαθητευθῆναι)"; he uses "Christian" in IgnEph 11.2, "members of his Son" in IgnEph 4.2,
"brothers" in IgnEph 16.1, and regularly uses the term "Church" (IgnEph 5.2; 8.1; 17.1). His
use of the phrase "the Name" is also interesting. In IgnEph 1.2 he writes: "that I had been sent
a prisoner from Syria for the sake of our common name and hope"; IgnEph 3.1 "I am a
prisoner for the Name"; IgnEph 7.1: "For there are some who make a practice of carrying
about the Name with wicked guile".

[49] See Trevett 1989a, p120; 1989c, p329. Schoedel (1985, 73) thinks the reference to
Ephesus being a highway for martyrs in IgnEph 12.2 may simply be to Acts 20:38, where the
Ephesian elders formally sent Paul off, aware that they would never see him again. However,
this seems to do less than justice to the plural τῶν ... ἀναιρουμένων.

prophets are described as "persecuted" (IgnMag 8.2; IgnTr 9.1),[50] and Ignatius offers no guidance on relations with the authorities,[51] nor on behaviour under persecution. He also seems to presuppose that Christians were entirely free to hold meetings since he exhorted them to meet together more frequently (IgnEph 13.1; IgnPol 4.2) with no hint that such meetings might cause opposition or that Christians constituted an illicit *collegium*. His concern as we have seen, is rather with unity, church order with regard to the establishment of episcopal authority and the danger of what he regarded as unacceptable teaching. This suggests that at the time Ignatius wrote the Christian communities in Asia, including the Ephesians, were not currently suffering persecution from outsiders.

The response Ignatius advocates to hostility from outsiders in the letter to the Ephesians is also interesting. In IgnEph 10.1-3, the passage in which he suggests that Asian Christians have experienced hostility, he writes: "But pray on behalf of other people unceasingly, for there is hope of repentance in them that they may attain God. Let them learn at least from your deeds to become disciples. ... Let us be found their brothers in gentleness; let us be eager to be imitators of the Lord - who was wronged more?" Here Ignatius encourages the Ephesians to have a very open attitude to outsiders. However, this is an expression of Ignatius' attitude and we do not know if the Ephesians shared his views on the matter. But it is worth noting that if the Ephesians followed his advice then their attitude to outsiders would have been much more in keeping with that expressed in the Pastorals than with the attitudes found in Rev. Although Ignatius writes on this subject elsewhere (see IgnTr 8.2) it is worth noting that this is his most extensive discussion of the attitude to outsiders in any of his letters. One can only wonder why.[52]

3.2 The financial situation of the Christian addressees at Ephesus

In IgnEph 2.1 Ignatius requests that the deacon Burrhus stay with Ignatius in Smyrna: "Now concerning my fellow slave Burrhus, your godly deacon blessed in all things: I pray that he stay here to the glory of you and your bishop." The Ephesians seem to have agreed to this request, since it is clear from IgnPhd 11.2 and IgnSm 12.1 that Burrhus went on with Ignatius at least

---

[50] See Trevett 1989b, p35, 38-9.

[51] Ignatius was probably dictating his letters in the presence of Roman soldiers, perhaps with other prisoners and various members of the visiting delegations and the churches in Smyrna or Troas also present; see Corwin 1960, p20. This suggests that he would be tactful about relations with the authorities, but would not preclude some comment on the topic.

[52] Schoedel (1985, p14, 17) notes Ignatius' relative openness to his environment and shows that this is reflected in the extent to which elements of popular culture may be found in his thought.

as far as Troas and served as his scribe or carried his letters.[53] However, in IgnPhd 11.2 Ignatius says that he writes to the Philadelphians "through Burrhus who was sent with me by the Ephesians and Smyrnaeans as a token of honour." Thus, it turned out that Burrhus did stay, but not just because of the Ephesians (IgnEph 2.1), but also because of the Smyrnaeans. It seems likely that expense was an issue and that the Ephesians agreed to Burrhus staying on with Ignatius only after the Smyrnaeans cooperated by contributing financially.[54] The expenses involved would be in travel, and perhaps also in assisting Burrhus' family in Ephesus during his absence.

It might be tempting to think that the Ephesian Christians were not very well off therefore, since the expenses of one person seem to have been an issue for them. However, Crocus from Ephesus seems also to have accompanied Ignatius. In IgnEph 2.1 he writes: "And Crocus too, worthy of God and you, whom I received as an exemplar of your love, refreshed me in every way." Since Ignatius does not ask for Crocus to accompany him, but simply praises him for his concern for Ignatius, and since Crocus clearly did accompany Ignatius,[55] it seems likely that this had already been agreed to by the Ephesian congregation.[56] This is also shown to be the case by the letter to the Romans (written at the same time as the letter to the Ephesians), in which Ignatius says: "I write you these things from Smyrna through the Ephesians, most worthy of blessing; and there is also with me, along with many others, Crocus, a name dear to me." (IgnRom 10:1)[57] Crocus was probably the one who carried the letter to Rome, and made sure that it got there before Ignatius did.[58]

---

[53] ὅθεν καὶ γράφω ὑμῖν διὰ Βούρρου in IgnPhd 11.2 is ambiguous, as is the identical expression in IgnSm 12.1. Ignatius asks for Burrhus' continued service in IgnEph 2.1, but it is not clear whether this is so that he may be a scribe or may carry his letters. In IgnRom 10.1 we read: "I write you these things from Smyrna through the Ephesians (δι' Ἐφεσίων)," which, in view of the plural, probably means that the Ephesian representatives carried the letter, presumably to Ephesus, and sent it on from there; see Schoedel 1985, p191. The special mention of Crocus in IgnRom 10.1 suggests he carried the letter on to Rome. This suggests that Phld 11.2 and IgnSm 12.1 are to be taken to say that Burrhus was the carrier of these letters. If expense was a question, as we argue here, then he may have turned back from Troas and delivered the letters to the Philadelphians and the Smyrnaeans as he returned to Ephesus. See also Grant 1966, p106; Schoedel 1985, p214-5; Trevett 1992, p100.

[54] See Schoedel 1985, p12, 45.

[55] Ignatius uses the same language of Burrhus in IgnSm 12.1 (Burrhus "refreshed me in every way. Would that all imitated him, since he is an exemplar of service to God") which he here uses of Crocus, which suggests that Crocus attended Ignatius.

[56] Schoedel (1985, p45) suggests agreement about this was reached when Ignatius' representatives first contacted the Ephesian Christians.

[57] Here "through (διά) the Ephesians" seems to indicate that the Ephesian representatives carried the letter; see Schoedel 1985, p191 and n18.

[58] See Schoedel 1985, p191.

If it had been decided earlier that Crocus should accompany Ignatius and be of service to him, then we can understand why there would have been discussion about further expense involving Burrhus. But certainly, that the Ephesian Christians required the assistance of the Christians of Smyrna in order to release a second person to travel with Ignatius does suggest that the community in Ephesus was not financially strong,[59] or at least that the resources of those who were fully behind Onesimus and the other leaders who travelled to see Ignatius (and who did not "resist the bishop") were not substantial.

In Chapter 9 we discussed the material possessions of the readers of the Pastorals and the Johannine Letters (as well as with regard to readers of Revelation). While we could say little about the financial resources of the readers of the Johannine Letters, it is noteworthy that some of the addressees of the Pastorals were wealthy. However, we would be wrong to conclude much from the contrast between the wealth of some readers of the Pastorals and the apparent lack of wealth of Ignatius' Ephesians since there is too much that we do not know. It could simply be that the Ephesians spoken of by Ignatius were fully committed financially (for example, in supporting leaders, the poor, or widows) or it could be that the few wealthy people of an earlier period had now fallen on difficult times.

3.3 Women in Asian Churches

Ignatius had had more opportunity to get to know Christians in Smyrna, so it is not surprising that his letter to this church and the letter to Polycarp contain personal greetings. Included in these are two sets of greetings to women. Firstly, in IgnSm 13.2 we read: "I greet the house of Tavia, whom I boast is established in faith and love both fleshly and spiritual. I greet Alce, a name dear to me." Secondly, in IgnPol 8.2-3 we read: "I greet all individually,

---

[59] The evident caution with which Ignatius treats the subject of Burrhus accompanying him in IgnEph 2.1-2 is probably due not only to the financial implications of the matter, but also to the fact that he does not want to further strain the relations between the Ephesian community and their leaders. It seems that Onesimus and the other leaders with him wanted to support Ignatius but felt that caution was necessary in view of the threat to unity in Ephesus, of which Ignatius writes in IgnEph 5.1-6.1; see Schoedel 1985, p45. In this context, Ignatius' statement that the Ephesians should be "subject to the bishop and the presbytery" (IgnEph 2.2) thus means that they should agree with their leaders that Burrhus accompany Ignatius. It is also worth noting that Ignatius mentions slaves who were members of the community in Smyrna and who wanted to be set free with money from the common fund; see IgnPol 4.3. There was also a concern that the widows might be neglected; see IgnPol 4.1. Clearly then the community included slaves and some widows who were not well off. This however, does not tell us anything about the situation in Ephesus.

including the wife of Epitropus[60] with the whole household of her and her children ... I greet Alce, a name dear to me."

The wife of Epitropus seems to be a widow since she is pictured as in charge of the whole household. Similarly, Tavia may be a widow, although it could be that her husband was not a Christian. An "Alce" is mentioned in the MartPol 17.2: "Nicetes the father of Herod [the police official responsible for the arrest of Polycarp], brother of Alce". If she is the same Alce mentioned here, which seems likely since it is a rare name,[61] then she came from a family of some standing since Herod was an eirenarch, an office that was filled by people of some standing in this period.[62]

Ignatius' greetings to these three women are friendly and sincere. Further, it seems likely that Alce was a woman of some social standing.[63] Ignatius does not mention any women in writing to Ephesus, so we do not know if women of social standing were also members of the Ephesian community.

After noting the greetings to the women in Smyrna, Trevett comments: "It is not impossible ... that women in such Asian Christian communities functioned as deacons (cf. the slave women *ministrae* tortured by Pliny the Younger) or even presbyters."[64] However, Ignatius made no reference to any women leaders, so we do not know if he approved or disapproved of the public religious activity and leadership of women. He may have taken the public activity of women for granted, or he may have thought it aberrant and not wanted to draw attention to it. Yet the impression we gain from his letters is that all the officials in the churches addressed were men. Certainly it was men who were commissioned to visit Ignatius.[65]

Ignatius mentions what was probably an order of widows in IgnSm 13.1 and IgnPol 4.1.[66] We do not know if such a group also existed in Ephesus, or

---

[60] The name Epitropus is unusual. Since the "wife of Epitropus" is head of a household (IgnPol 8.2), as is Tavia (IgnSm 13.2), it is possible that τὴν τοῦ Ἐπιτρόπου should be translated "wife of the procurator" in which case she could be the Tavia of IgnSm 13.2, and there would only be two women greeted; see Schoedel 1985, p280 n14.

[61] See for example Fraser and Matthew 1987, p28 (where it occurs once); 1997, p28 (where it occurs twice); BDAG p44.

[62] See Schoedel 1985, p253; Trebilco 1991, p64. Alce was "a name dear to me" (IgnSm 13.2; IgnPol 8.3); cf. Crocus in IgnRom 10.1; IgnEph 2.1. She had probably visited Ignatius, but we do not know why she was "a name dear" to Ignatius. Compare also Polycarp, Phil 14, on the sister of Crescens.

[63] See Trevett 1992, p53.

[64] Trevett 1992, p53; see also MacDonald 1999, p238 who suggests that these women may have been influential.

[65] Trevett (1992, p111 n49) comments: "It may well be that Ignatius's understanding of the Church was such that it precluded the autonomous activity of women, but the evidence of the letters themselves does not make this evident." See also Trevett 1992, p94.

[66] On the order and the unusual expression "virgins called widows" see Schoedel 1985, p252, 269. Probably the phrase indicates that virgins who had no other means of support were

if it was unique to Smyrna. As we have noted, Ignatius was better acquainted with the situation at Smyrna, so his silence about widows at Ephesus means little.

We cannot draw any firm correlation between what Ignatius says with regard to women and what we concluded about women in the Ephesian communities in Chapter 11. If there was an order of widows in Ephesus similar to the order in IgnSm 13.1 then this would be an obvious link with the Pastorals, but Ignatius only mentions the order in connection with Smyrna. The lack of women in leadership in Ignatius' letter to the Ephesians (and probably elsewhere) may suggest that the Pastor succeeded in curtailing the leadership activity of women, or that we were right to suggest that women were not involved in leadership in the community addressed by the Johannine Letters. However, since we only have Ignatius' silence on this matter we are unable to do anything other than note the possible continuation in Ignatius of the trend that is evident in the Pastorals and perhaps continued in the Johannine Letters of the exclusion of women from leadership office.

3.4 The size of the communities addressed by Ignatius

Unfortunately, Ignatius does not tell us how many Christians there were in the communities to which he wrote.[67] It may be that he himself did not know this information. But some passages relating to the community in Smyrna provide some tantalizing hints.

In IgnPol 1.3 Ignatius advises Polycarp to "speak to people individually (τοῖς κατ' ἄνδρα ... κάλει)" and in IgnPol 4.2 he writes "Let meetings be held more often; seek out all by name (ἐξ ὀνόματος πάντας ζήτει)."[68] The fact that Ignatius needs to give such an exhortation suggests that the community was of a size such that the bishop might not know everyone individually. Since Ignatius stayed in Smyrna and so got to know some people there, he gives greetings to these people in IgnSm 12.2-13.2 and IgnPol 8.2-3. The number of people greeted indicates a reasonably sizeable community.[69]

---

able to join the order of widows. Schüssler Fiorenza (1983, p314) suggests Ignatius is strengthening the control and supervision of the bishop over their activities; cf. Trevett 1992, p53.

[67] Trevett (1992, p84) says of those to whom Ignatius wrote: "we do not know where, in what manner or in what numbers these Christians gathered."

[68] Ignatius uses the expression ἐξ ὀνόματος elsewhere to mean "individually" (see IgnEph 20.2), which could be the meaning here. But in this context the translation given seems to be called for. Camelot (1958, p 175) translates the phrase as "invite tous les frères par leur nom." Compare Schoedel 1985, p269-70. The expression occurs again in IgnPol 8.2, where it also seems to mean "individually".

[69] In IgnPol 8.2 we read "Ἀσπάζομαι πάντας ἐξ ὀνόματος" and in IgnSm 13.2 "I greet ... πάντας κατ' ὄνομα." (see also IgnSm 12.2) These phrases could again indicate that

Hence Trevett notes: "The advice he [Ignatius] gave to Polycarp about knowing all by name (*Pol.* 4.3), rather than as one of a category of 'young men', 'widows', perhaps 'slaves' and the like (*Smyrn.* 13.1; cf *Pol.* 4.1; 4.3; 5.1; *1 Timothy* 5:1ff), spoke of Christian communities with quite large numbers of believers, sufficient, at least, for a bishop possibly to lose track of individuals."[70] It is of course likely that the number of Christians differed in each of the five Asian cities, so the evidence from Smyrna simply indicates that one of the Christian communities was of some size.

With regard to Ephesus, we have noted that five leaders from Ephesus travelled to Smryna to met Ignatius (IgnEph 2.1; see also 21.1); this suggests the community in Ephesus they represented was of some size, although again it gives no hard data.[71] But it suggests we should not think of a small community.[72] The one other indication we have with regard to Ephesus is that in IgnEph 1.3 Ignatius uses πολυπληθεία: "Now since I received in God's name your whole congregation (πολυπλήθειαν) in Onesimus ..." BDAG defines πολυπληθεία as a "large crowd", and translates IgnEph 1.3 as "I have received your whole (large) congregation".[73] Genouillac takes this as an indication of "une église considérable par le nombre de ses chrétiens",[74] and Trevett notes "There would seem to have been a considerable number of Christians in the churches to which Ignatius wrote".[75] In the absence of hard data, this and the comparable indications from Smyrna, at least suggest that the number of Christians in Ephesus at the time was not small, but rather could be described as πολυπληθεία - a large crowd.

---

the community was quite sizeable, but need not be interpreted this way since similar greetings could be given to a small group.

[70] Trevett 1992, p52. The term Ignatius used for the local congregation was often πλῆθος; see IgnSm 8.2; IgnMag 6.1; IgnTr 1.1; 8.2. It is also used in other writings of the period as a technical term "for the whole body of their members, fellowship, community, congregation" (BDAG p825, 2.b.d). For Ignatius the term refers not only to the full number of members, but also to their organic unity; see Schoedel 1985, p244 n22. But does the term also suggest the communities were of at least some size?

[71] Four representatives travelled from Magnesia to see Ignatius (IgnMag 2), and one from Tralles (IgnTr 1.1-2). It might be thought that this gives some indication of the relative size of the Christian communities concerned. However, Trevett (1992, p87) points out that "the number of Christians coming [to see Ignatius in Smyrna] is in inverse proportion to the distance to be travelled." (See also Lightfoot 1889b, Vol 1, p365.) Trevett also refers to Circero, *Ad Att.* 5.14, who had travelled between Magnesia and Tralles at the same time of year (August; see IgnRom 10.3) and said that the roads were burning and dusty. It is understandable then that the Ephesians sent a larger group.

[72] Barnard (1966, p20) speaks of "these small Christian communities" addressed by Ignatius and Corwin (1960, p13) of "The little churches in Antioch and the other cities ...."

[73] BDAG, p846.

[74] Genouillac 1907, p211.

[75] Trevett 1980, p54-5.

3.5 Contact between Christian communities

Ignatius' letters reveal a significant amount of contact between the different communities of his day. Note the following:[76]

a) A messenger had been sent on ahead from Syria to Rome to tell the Romans of Ignatius' situation (IgnRom 10.2).[77]

b) Ignatius himself travelled from Antioch to Smyrna via Philadelphia.

c) Messengers travelled ahead of Ignatius to tell the communities at Ephesus, Magnesia and Tralles of Ignatius' journey, and representatives from these communities were sent to Smyrna to greet him there.

d) Ignatius wrote letters to Ephesus, Magnesia, Tralles and Rome.

e) Ignatius travelled from Smyrna to Troas.

f) While in Troas, Ignatius was met by Philo from Cilicia and Rheus Agathopous from Syria (who had followed him through Philadelphia (IgnPhd 11.1) and Smyrna (IgnSm 10.1)) who told him that "peace" had been restored in Antioch (IgnPhd 10.1; IgnSm 11.1-3; IgnPol 7.1).

g) Ignatius wrote from Troas to Philadelphia, Smyrna and to Polycarp. He asked these churches to send letters and/or personal messengers to Antioch to congratulate the church on the restoration of "peace" (IgnPhd 10.1-2; IgnSm 11.2-3; IgnPol 7.2). In writing to the Philadelphians Ignatius also said that "the neighbouring churches [ie those nearer Antioch][78] have sent bishops, and others presbyters and deacons" to Antioch (IgnPhd 10.2). In addition we can note that Ignatius wrote to Polycarp as follows: "Thus since I was unable to write to all the churches because I am sailing any moment from Troas to Neapolis, as the (divine) will requires, you [singular] will write to the churches on this side (ταῖς ἔμπροσθεν ἐκκλησίαις) as one who has the purpose of God, that they may also do the same thing, those who can by sending messengers, others (by sending) letters through those whom you [singular] send" (IgnPol 8.1). Thus, Polycarp is to finish the task of writing to "all the churches" to ask them to send representatives to Antioch, a task Ignatius could not undertake since he was suddenly moved on from Troas. By ταῖς ἔμπροσθεν ἐκκλησίαις Ignatius probably means the Christian communities of Ephesus, Magnesia and Tralles, which were churches between Smyrna (where Polycarp was) and Antioch.[79]

---

[76] See also Schoedel 1985, p12; Bauckham 1998, p40-2.

[77] See Schoedel 1985, p191.

[78] See Corwin 1960, p18; see also Camelot 1958, p49-50. Ignatius asks the Philadelphians to send a deacon to Antioch, and says this to show that he is not being unreasonable. If churches nearby in Syria have sent bishops or at least presbyters and deacons, then it is not unreasonable for the Philadelphians to send a deacon.

[79] See Schoedel 1985, p279-80.

h) We learn from Polycarp's letter to Philippi (Polycarp, Phil 13.1) that Ignatius also asked the church at Philippi to contact the church at Antioch following the peace there. We learn from Polycarp that the Philippians sent a letter of congratulations as far as Smyrna, and it was carried on from there to Antioch.

i) In four of the letters Ignatius passes on greetings from one church in Asia to another. Thus, for example, in IgnMag 15 he writes: "The Ephesians greet you from Smyrna .... And the rest of the churches also greet you in honour of Jesus Christ."[80] It is interesting that no such greetings are found in IgnRom, which suggests that Ignatius only passes on greetings when the addressees are known by those who greet them. This suggests that the members of the churches in Asia knew each other well and were in the habit of communicating with one another.[81]

This is very interesting information. Clearly much of this travel and letter writing was associated with Ignatius' unique situation, and the sending of representatives of Asian churches to Antioch was part of an elaborate plan by Ignatius to cement the "peace" in Antioch.[82] However, we do not gain the impression that it was altogether unusual for one church to send a representative to another, or for Christians from one centre to travel to another to greet a fellow Christian. We may then be catching a glimpse of connections, contacts and travels that were not extraordinary.

We can also note Ignatius' requests for prayer for the church in Antioch prior to his hearing of the peace there (see IgnEph 21.2; IgnTr 13.1; IgnRom 9.1). Further, after the peace, he reports that the prayers of the churches have been answered (see IgnPhd 10.1; IgnSm 11.1; IgnPol 7.1). We do not know how unusual such prayer for other communities was, but this evidence suggests again that the churches in different places were intimately connected with one another.

We can suggest then that churches, at least those in the larger cities, were in regular contact with one another and had a sense of fellowship with each other. They probably would have known of changes and developments in the different communities.[83] The evidence also suggests that Christians in

---

[80] See also IgnTr 13.1; IgnPhd 11.2; IgnSm 12.1. The "rest of the churches" in IgnMag 15 are probably others, such as the Trallians, who sent representatives to Smyrna. There may have been others who visited Ignatius to whom he did not write letters, who are also included in the greetings.

[81] See Genouillac 1907, p71.

[82] See Schoedel 1985, p213-14.

[83] See also Corwin 1960, p190. It is interesting that Christians from one city (say Antioch) could actually find Christians in another (say Ephesus). This in itself suggests there were good Christian networks in place.

Ephesus would not have been insular and isolated, but rather would have heard of new ideas and new church practices from elsewhere.[84]

This reinforces some points we have made earlier. We have drawn on this evidence in suggesting that John would not have written his Gospel solely for his own community, but would have had a much wider group of Christians in mind. Further, we have suggested that this sort of contact between groups (and other evidence for contact in an earlier period) would mean that it is unlikely that the Pauline community of the Pastorals would not have known of the existence of Johannine community of 1-3 Jn in Ephesus. We can also suggest here that this evidence for extensive contact suggests that Onesimus and other Christian leaders would be aware of at least most of the Christian groups in Ephesus. Given that we can see that Christians across Asia Minor and in Antioch are closely in contact with each other, it is improbable that Christians in Asia were totally out of touch with other Christians in their own cities; even if they did not wish to maintain strong contact with some groups for theological reasons, we can suggest that they would still know of each other's existence.

3.6 Does Ignatius show any knowledge of the city of Ephesus?

Does Ignatius give any hints in his letter to the Ephesians that he knows anything about the city? We note the following possibilities.

Firstly, during Ignatius' lifetime there was a surge of building activity in the cities of Asia.[85] When he speaks of stone "carried up to the heights by the crane of Jesus Christ (which is the cross), using the Holy Spirit as a rope" (IgnEph 9.1) the image he is using would have been a familiar sight to his Ephesian readers. However, it is not an image that is unique to Ephesus.

Secondly, in IgnEph 9.2 he writes about religious processions and describes the Christians as "God-bearers (θεοφόροι) and temple-bearers (ναοφόροι)". The reference seems to be to small religious objects such as statues of gods and goddesses and miniature temples which were carried in the processions in honour of deities, including Ephesian Artemis, and would have been a familiar Ephesian sight.[86] Pagan authors also used this idea of the "bearer of sacred vessels" symbolically.[87] However, while the passage does suggest a picture of pagan Ephesus, it relates equally to pagan religiosity in

---

[84] There is other evidence for this contact between Christians at this time; see Bauckham 1998b, p39-43. Note for example also the travelling prophets of the Didache; see Didache 11-13.

[85] See further in Chapter 1; see also Magie 1950, p582f; Trevett 1992, p78.

[86] See Acts 19:24; Genouillac 1907, p32-3, 211-12; Kieffer 2000, p290-1. Note the number of statuettes of deities carried in the procession established by Salutaris in 104 CE; see Rogers 1992, p80-126.

[87] Plutarch *De Iside* 3, p352b; Grant 1966, p41.

general. Ignatius need not have ceremonies in Ephesus in particular in mind in IgnEph 9.2 therefore.[88]

Thirdly, Ephesus was a centre for study of philosophy and rhetoric.[89] Perhaps it was for this reason that Ignatius wrote of wisdom and mysteries in IgnEph 17-19.[90] Fourthly, Ignatius wrote most extensively of Mary's virginity and giving birth in his letter to Ephesus (see especially IgnEph 19.1; also IgnEph 7.2; 18.1; cf. IgnTr 9.1; IgnSm 1.1). Was he aware of the fact that Artemis was thought of as a virgin goddess?[91] Finally, in IgnEph 19.3 one effect of the revelation of Christ is said to be: "Thence was destroyed all magic". This is the only mention of magic in Ignatius' letters and may show that he is aware of the strong connection between Ephesus and magic.[92] However, magic is mentioned by other apostolic fathers in general contexts,[93] and so Ignatius may not be making any specific link with Ephesus here.

All of these possible points of contact are elusive and need not imply any great knowledge of Ephesus by Ignatius. However, they may indicate his knowledge of the city and his sensitivity to the situations of its Christians.[94]

---

[88] Cf. Trevett 1989a, p121. Note Ignatius' use of imagery from pagan sacrifice in IgnRom 2.2. Again this is not related to Rome in particular, but is clearly imagery that residents of a Greco-Roman city would understand.

[89] Trevett 1992, p78.

[90] See Trevett 1992, p78.

[91] Note that one inscription from Rome calls Artemis of Ephesus παρθένος; see IG 14, 964; see also Achilles Tatius 6.21.2. Trevett (1992, p78) notes that "To the city of the virgin goddess he [Ignatius] wrote of the mystery of Mary's virginity and parturition". See also Genouillac 1907, p211-12.

[92] On the connection between Ephesus and magic see Trebilco 1994, p314-15; Kraabel 1968, p54-9. Schoedel (1985, p93) points out that the theme is at home in the apocalyptic tradition, but does not mention a possible Ephesian connection here. Kraabel (1968, p55) notes that the Ephesia grammata "typified to the popular mind a particularly Ephesian magic" and notes (1968, p55 n2) that perhaps Ignatius associated Ephesus and magic. He goes on: "his only use of the word *mageia* occurs in his letter to the Ephesian congregation, 19:3; .... But Ignatius may be thinking only of the story behind this text from Acts [19:11-20]." However, we have no clear evidence that Ignatius knew Acts, and we can only wonder if he would have known of this story independently of Acts?

[93] For example, magic is mentioned in Didache 2:2, 5:1 and in Barnabas 20:1.

[94] Trevett (1989c, p337 n83) notes the parallels between Rev 2:1-7 and IgnEph. In both letters the Christians are commended for their orthodoxy (Rev 2:2; IgnEph 6.2-7.1; 9.1; 10.3) and ναός occurs in IgnEph 15.3; cf. Rev 21:3 and 1 Cor 3:16 also. Trevett (1989a, p126-8) discusses parallels between IgnEph 19 and Rev 12 but notes (p127) that "so many of the 'points of contact' seem at best commonplace, are elusive or tenuous." She does not think Ignatius shows evidence of literary dependence on Rev, although she suggests he may have discussed some of its teaching.

4. Overall Conclusions

We have here gained some additional insight into the life of the Christians in Ephesus. Ignatius indicates that in his view the Christians in Ephesus were very significant and he shows that the memory of Paul was alive among at least some of the Christians to whom he wrote in the city. Many of the Ephesians seem to have agreed with him theologically, and Ignatius' tone in writing to them suggests that at this time the Ephesian community he addressed was respected by a number of other Christians.

We have argued that there was a group of docetic Christians in Ephesus and have suggested that this group had developed from the Johannine secessionists of 1-2 Jn. However, this group was not included among Ignatius' addressees, whom Ignatius thinks are free from teaching to which he objects. But some of his readers had probably listened to the docetists, who had been unanswered. Ignatius currently regarded the docetists as a very real threat to his somewhat vulnerable readers.

The addressees in Ephesus do not seem to be facing any external threat and Ignatius encourages a very open attitude to outsiders; the addressees also seem to have been of modest financial means. We have noted that all the officials Ignatius mentions were men, but that we cannot say anything else about the place of women among the addressees in Ephesus. In the absence of hard data, we have suggested that the number of Christians in Ephesus in Ignatius' time was not small, but rather could appropriately be described as πολυπληθεία - a large crowd. However, we cannot be more specific than this. Ignatius provides evidence for extensive contact between Christian communities and his letter to Ephesus may reflect some knowledge on his part of the city of Ephesus itself, but this is not certain.

Chapter 16

Conclusions

We have sought to give conclusions at various points throughout this book. It remains here to summarise some of our findings, and to suggest the relevance of what we have discussed to some wider debates.

We have discussed the beginnings of the life of the early Christians in Ephesus, both before the Pauline mission and during that mission. We have suggested that at the conclusion of the Pauline mission, the Pauline community was well established and that there were some indications of diversity within this group. Further, although by around 55 CE most of the Christians in Ephesus were "Pauline", we have noted that all the Christians in Ephesus at this time did not owe their allegiance to Paul. In Parts Two and Three we have sought to show that in the period from around 80-100 CE there were a number of different groups in Ephesus who regarded themselves as Christians – the Pauline group addressed by the Pastorals, the Johannine group spoken of in 1-3 Jn, the opponents of the Pastor who perhaps formed a separate group, the Johannine secessionists, and the Nicolaitans. It is clear that there were considerable differences between some of these groups, although we need to recall that there are many details about them for which we have no information.

We have also sought to argue that the Pauline group and the Johannine group were distinct and separate communities, although they maintained non-hostile contact.[1] Thus, we have argued against the "merger" or "takeover" theory which has been advocated by some scholars, which would suggest that the Pauline and Johannine groups merged, or that the Pauline group was taken over by Johannine influence and that there was only one Christian community

---

[1] This view is similar to that of Schnackenburg 1991b, p41-64, who also argues for the co-existence of the Pauline and Johannine communities in Ephesus. Koester (1971, p154-5; 1995, p133) similarly argues for the simultaneous existence of a number of Christian groups, but he thinks the groups are quite different, and does not locate the community of 1-3 Jn in Ephesus. In 1995, p133 he writes: "At the end of the first century, a variety of groups and sects existed in Ephesos: disciples of John the Baptist, a circle of Christians that claimed allegiance to Apollos, a church that derived its origin from Paul. To these groups one should add a prophetic conventicle, to which the prophet John sent his book from Patmos, and a sect called the Nikolaites." His views (especially 1971, p174-5) have been very influential; see for example Aune (1997, p140) who reports Koester's view (including that John is writing to "a Jewish-Christian group led by John of Patmos") without comment.

in Ephesus at any one time. We have also described a number of features of the distinctive identity of the Pauline and Johannine groups.

Further, we have argued that John the Seer in Revelation, and Ignatius in his letter to Ephesus were both seeking to address all Christians in the city. Thus in my view, there was no "John of Revelation community" in Ephesus. We have tried to counter views that might undermine these suggestions.

With regard to our view that John is writing to all the Christians in Ephesus (or at least to all those he thought were "within the pale"), although the evidence we have discussed in Part Three was compatible with this hypothesis, on no occasion have we been able to argue that the evidence *requires* it. But we have noted in our discussion of leadership, if John had described a particular situation among the readers (eg. that they were led only by people appointed to the office of "diakonos") then this could have counted against our view that John was writing to all Christians in Ephesus, and would have argued strongly in favour of the view that John was writing to a particular community with this sort of leadership structure. That our discussion has not led to evidence which would contradict our hypothesis is therefore significant. The same could be said with regard to wealth and the situation of women – in neither case did the evidence contradict our hypothesis that John was writing to all Christians in Ephesus, nor did it support an alternative hypothesis. In both cases, evidence could have been forthcoming that would do both. We can have some confidence therefore in putting forward the view that John was writing to all the Christians in the city.

We have also sought to delineate the nature of the various groups that we have discussed. This has involved an exposition of the nature of the Pastor's opponents, the Johannine secessionists, and the Nicolaitans. But we have also sought to discuss some key features of the life of the community to which the Pastor wrote, and to which the author of 1-3 Jn wrote. As we have noted, we have described these two latter groups in terms of their attitude to the wider world, their material possessions and the use to which they were put, the leadership structure and understanding of the locus of authority, the position of women, and their use of self-designations. In each case, we have been able to describe somewhat different attitudes and behaviours on the part of the community of the Pastorals on the one hand, and the Johannine community on the other. These discussions have constituted a description of some facets of the life of these two different groups. This evidence also testifies to the diversity of early Christianity in Ephesus.

Views about early Christians in Ephesus played a significant part in the highly influential work of Walter Bauer, and here we want to make some comments on how our conclusions compare with his. Bauer writes: "Even *Ephesus* cannot be considered as a center of orthodoxy, but is rather a particularly instructive example of how the life of an ancient Christian community, even one of apostolic origin, could erode when caught in the turbulent crosscurrents of orthodoxy and heresy."[2] How does he arrive at this view?

Firstly, Bauer notes that Paul established the community in Ephesus, and notes Paul's warning in Acts 20:30 to the Ephesian elders that "from their own midst there will arise men speaking perverse things to draw away the Christians for themselves",[3] which Bauer takes as a description of the situation at the time Luke wrote. He also thinks Ignatius' reference to Paul in IgnEph 12:2 could be a result of Ignatius reading 1 Cor rather than indicating Paul's continuing influence in Ephesus.[4] But more significant for Bauer's case is his view of Rev. He writes:

"we find as we turn to the Apocalypse that in this book the recollection of the Pauline establishment of the church of Ephesus appears to have been completely lost, or perhaps even deliberately suppressed. ... And as far as Paul is concerned, in the Apocalypse only the names of the twelve apostles are found on the foundations of the new Jerusalem (21.14); there is no room for Paul. And at the very least, it will be but a short time before the Apostle to the Gentiles will have been totally displaced in the consciousness of the church of Ephesus in favor of one of the twelve apostles, John. In Ephesus, Paul had turned out to be too weak to drive the enemies of the church from the battlefield."[5]

This view is open to criticism at a number of points. Firstly, we have argued in Chapter 13 that we can offer adequate explanations for John's silence about Paul in Rev and so this silence does not mean that Paul has been completely forgotten in Ephesus. Secondly, Bauer dates the Pastorals after the time of Marcion,[6] but such a late date is exceedingly unlikely, and we have argued for 80-100 as the most reasonable date. This means that we can affirm a trajectory of Pauline influence in Ephesus from Paul, through the Pastorals and on to Ignatius, since in the light of the Pastorals, it seems likely that Ignatius' comment about Paul in IgnEph 12.2 shows that Paul was still remembered in the Ephesian Pauline community in Ignatius' day, rather than simply being based on 1 Cor as Bauer suggests.[7]

---

[2] Bauer 1971, p82.

[3] Bauer 1971, p82-3.

[4] Bauer 1971, p83.

[5] Bauer 1971, p83-4. Satake (1966, p192) and Lohse (1991, p365) for example, also think that Paul's influence has declined in Asia Minor at end of the first century CE.

[6] See Bauer 1971, p84, 222-8.

[7] Bauer takes 2 Tim 1:15 as evidence of the opposition of Cerinthus to Paul and that "in the second century, the Apostle had lost the contest in Ephesus" (Bauer 1971, p84-5; see also Günther 1995, p81-5). However, this depends on dating the Pastorals after the time of Marcion and it is much more likely that 2 Tim 1:15 is a reminiscence of some events at the end of Paul's life. Further, in 1:15 ἀποστρέφειν probably means "deserted" rather than

Thirdly, Bauer is an exponent of what we have called the "takeover theory" – that at any point in time there was only one "community" of Christians in Ephesus.[8] Thus, in the quote given above, Bauer suggests that "John" (the author of the Fourth Gospel) will "displace" Paul in the consciousness of the church of Ephesus. As we have noted, given the trajectory from Paul to the Pastorals to Ignatius, that Paul was forgotten seems most unlikely. But we have argued that the Johannine Letters, which Bauer locates in Syria,[9] belong in Ephesus and in Part Three we have argued in opposition to the takeover theory that the Pauline and Johannine communities in Ephesus remained distinct.

Finally, Bauer sees those who, according to Ignatius, "resist the bishop" in Ephesus and elsewhere as "heretics" or "false believers".[10] By contrast, we have argued that in Ephesus it is more likely that they are other Christians who are resisting a change in church order, and so that we need not see the differences between those who are "with the bishop" and those who resist him as reflecting theological matters. Further, we have suggested that those who "resist the bishop" in Ephesus include Johannine Christians, and people who found the prophetic locus of authority of John of Rev conducive, while those who are willing to cooperate with the bishop include those addressed earlier by the Pastorals. This means that we cannot use what Ignatius says in this regard as evidence that in Ephesus at this time there was a very significant

---

"apostatised" (from the Gospel), particularly since the Pastor writes ἀπεστράφησάν με: ie, the verb applies to something that happened to Paul and nothing requires "gospel" to be the object of the verb. Thus the verse does not suggest all of Asia "apostatised from the Gospel"; see Mounce 2000, p493-4, who suggests the prime motive for the "desertion" may have been to avoid suffering. It is certainly not evidence for widespread apostasy from Christianity in Asia. Note also Dibelius-Conzelmann (1972, p106): "The phrase 'all have turned away from me' ... cannot be understood to imply apostasy from the gospel, because of the comparatively mild terminology and because of the word 'all' (πάντες). The phrase probably refers to an event like that described in 2 Tim 4:10f."

[8] This is also explicit in the following quote (Bauer 1971, p85): "in Ephesus a community of apostolic origin has, through its struggles with external enemies and above all through internal discord and controversies ... [ie as shown in Rev 2:1-7], suffered such setbacks and transformations that for many, even the name of its founder became lost. Orthodox Christianity underwent reorganization and now found an apostolic patron in that member of the twelve who shared his name with the apocalyptist and who established close connection with Jesus more securely than had Paul, which was considered to be the highest trump in the struggle with heresy."

[9] Bauer (1971, p92) thinks that the Gospel of John and 1 Jn were written in Syria, and so does not draw on 1-3 Jn with regard to Ephesus. However, he suggests (1971, p233) "in the second century the 'church' sought also to appropriate Ephesus by means of John as one of the twelve apostles."

[10] See Bauer 1971, p67-70. Bauer (1971, p69) sees the bishop in Ephesus (as in Magnesia, Tralles and Philadelphia) as the leader of "ecclesiastically oriented people" who "may have gathered larger or smaller majorities of the local Christians around them."

group of Christians whom Ignatius regards as "heretics". However, we have suggested that, in Ignatius' time, there was a group of docetic Christians in Ephesus and have suggested that this group had developed from the Johannine secessionists of 1-2 Jn. We have also noted that this group was probably not included among Ignatius' addressees.

Thus, our overall assessment of the early Christians in Ephesus is quite different from that propounded by Bauer.

But we have shown (in a way that Bauer did not) the diversity of early Christians in Ephesus, and the presence of a number of different groups. We have discussed above the range of features where quite different attitudes and patterns of behaviour are discernible among Christian groups in Ephesus. We also note that in texts related to Ephesus authors are regularly arguing against another group that they regard as "opponents". Thus in Ephesus, as elsewhere, from at least the time of the Pastorals there was a drawing of lines by some Christians in order to exclude others who regarded themselves as Christians. This is a clear tendency of our documents – the Pastorals, the Johannine Letters, Rev and Ignatius. Thus, one continuing element in the life of Christians in Ephesus was conflict between Christians, and the presence of differing strands of Christian faith.[11] A focus on admissible and inadmissible belief – and clarifying what was meant in both cases – is clearly a feature of Ephesian Christian communities. But we would not want to claim that this is a distinctive feature of Ephesus – clearly it was going on elsewhere too. But such drawing of internal boundaries within the Christian movement is certainly a feature of the Christian groups of Ephesus.

However, we should not think solely in terms of the opposition of one group to another. We have suggested, at least in the case of the readers of the Pastorals and the readers of 1-3 Jn, that they would have been aware of each other's existence, would not have refused contact with one another since they did not fail the other's litmus tests, and would have had "non-hostile relations". Further, the evidence for linguistic contact between the two groups removes a possible argument against our thesis of non-hostile relations between these two communities, since if there had been no linguistic contact this would suggest the communities had nothing to do with one another.

We cannot call this "unity" – they clearly retained the distinct identity of their separate groups. We can perhaps speak of commonality – that, while preserving their distinctive identity, we can suggest that they would have been willing to acknowledge the validity of each other's claim to be part of the

---

[11] Recall also the prophecy in Acts 20:29-30: "I know that after I have gone, fierce wolves will come in among you, not sparing the flock. Some even from your own group will come distorting the truth in order to entice the disciples to follow them." We have argued that Luke thought this was fulfilled in his own day.

wider movement that we call early Christianity. Further, we should certainly not envisage these groups as hermetically sealed against each other.

Bibliography

The Abbreviations used can be found in Alexander, P.H. et al., 1999. *The* SBL *Handbook of Style for Ancient Near Eastern, Biblical, and Early Christian Studies.* Peabody, Massachusetts: Hendrickson Publishers.

Aasgaard, R. 1998. '*My beloved brothers and sisters!' A study of the meaning and function of Christian siblingship in Paul, in its Greco-Roman and Jewish context.* D.Th. Thesis, University of Oslo.

Akurgal, E. 1990. *Ancient Civilizations and Ruins of Turkey.* Istanbul: Net Turistik Yayinlar.

Alexander, L.C.A. 1993. "Chronology of Paul." In *Dictionary of Paul and His Letters*, ed. G. F. Hawthorne, Martin, R.P., Reid, D.G.:115-23. Downers Grove: IVP.

_____. 1998. "Ancient Book Production and the Circulation of the Gospels." In *The Gospels for All Christians. Rethinking the Gospel Audiences*, ed. R. Bauckham:71-111. Grand Rapids, Michigan: Eerdmans.

Allo, P. E. B. 1956a. *Saint Paul Première Épitre aux Corinthiens.* EBib. Paris: Librairie Lecoffre.

_____. 1956b. *Saint Paul Seconde Épitre aux Corinthiens.* EBib. Paris: Librairie Lecoffre.

Alzinger, W. 1970. "Ephesos B." In *Paulys Realencyclopädie der Classischen Altertumswissenschaft*, ed. K. Ziegler, Supplementband XII:1588-1704. Stuttgart: Alfred Druckenmüller Verlag.

_____. 1974. *Augusteische Architektur in Ephesos.* Sonderschriften Band 16. Wien: Österreichischen Archäologischen Institut.

Ameling, W. 1988. "Drei Studien zu den Gerichtsbezirken der Provinz Asia in republikanischer Zeit." *Epigraphica Anatolica* 12: 9-24.

_____. 1996. "Die jüdischen Gemeinden im antiken Kleinasien." In *Jüdische Gemeinden und Organisationsformen von der Antike bis zur Gegenwart*, ed. R. Jütte, Kustermann, A.P.:29-55. Vienna: Böhlau.

Anderson, P.N. 1996. *The Christology of the Fourth Gospel.* WUNT 2.78. Tübingen: J.C.B. Mohr (Paul Siebeck).

Antonopoulou, T. 1999. "A Quantitative Survey of the Christian-Byzantine Inscriptions of Ephesus and Thessalonica." In *100 Jahre Österreichische Forschungen in Ephesos. Akten des Symposions Wien 1995*, ed. H. Friesinger, Krinzinger, F.:169-78. Wien: Verlag der Österreichischen Akademie der Wissenschaften.

Arnold, C. E. 1989. *Ephesians: Power and Magic. The Concept of Power in Ephesians in the Light of its Historical Setting.* SNTSMS 63. Cambridge: Cambridge University Press.

Arnold, I. R. 1972. "Festivals of Ephesus." *AJA* 76: 17-22.

Ashton, J. 2000. *The Religion of Paul the Apostle.* New Haven: Yale University Press.

Attridge, H. W. 1989. *The Epistle to the Hebrews.* Hermeneia. Philadelphia: Fortress Press.

Aune, D. E. 1981. "The Social Matrix of the Apocalypse of John." *BR* 26: 16-32.

_____. 1983a. "The Influence of Roman Imperial Court Ceremonial on the Apocalypse of John." *BR* 28: 5-26.

_____. 1983b. *Prophecy in Early Christianity and the Ancient Mediterranean World.* Grand Rapids: Eerdmans.

_____. 1987. "The Apocalypse of John and Graeco-Roman Revelatory Magic." *NTS* 33: 481-501.

_____. 1989. "The Prophetic Circle of John of Patmos and the Exegesis of Revelation 22.16." *JSNT* 37: 103-116.

_____. 1990. "The Form and Function of the Proclamations to the Seven Churches (Revelation 2-3)." *NTS* 36: 182-204.

_____. 1996. "Following the Lamb: Discipleship in the Apocalypse." In *Patterns of Discipleship in the New Testament*, ed. R. N. Longenecker:269-84. Grand Rapids, Michigan: Eerdmans.

_____. 1997. *Revelation 1-5.* WBC. Dallas, Texas: Word Books.

_____. 1998a. *Revelation 6-16.* WBC. Nashville: Thomas Nelson.

_____. 1998b. *Revelation 17-22.* WBC. Nashville: Thomas Nelson.

Aurenhammer, M. 1995. "Sculptures of Gods and Heroes from Ephesos." In *Ephesos: Metropolis of Asia. An Interdisciplinary Approach to its Archaeology, Religion, and Culture*, ed. H. Koester:251-80. Valley Forge, Pennsylvania: Trinity Press International.

Babcock, W.S., ed. 1990. *Paul and the Legacies of Paul.* Dallas: Southern Methodist University Press.

Bailey, K.E. 1998. "Women in the New Testament: A Middle Eastern Cultural View." *Evangelical Review of Theology* 22: 208-226.

Baldwin, H.S. 1995a. "A Difficult Word: αὐθεντέω ιν 1 Timothy 2:12." In *Women in the Church. A Fresh Analysis of 1 Timothy 2:9-15*, ed. A. J. Köstenberger, Schreiner, T.R., Baldwin, H.S.:65-80. Grand Rapids, Michigan: Baker Books.

_____. 1995b. "Appendix 2: αὐθεντέω in Ancient Greek Literature." In *Women in the Church. A Fresh Analysis of 1 Timothy 2:9-15*, ed. A. J. Köstenberger, Schreiner, T.R., Baldwin, H.S.:269-305. Grand Rapids, Michigan: Baker Books.

Ballhorn, G. 2001. "Die Miletrede - ein Literaturbericht." In *Das Ende des Paulus. Historische, theologische und literaturgeschichtliche Aspekte*, ed. F.W. Horn:37-47. Berlin: Walter de Gruyter.

Bammer, A. 1972. *Die Architektur des jüngeren Artemision von Ephesos.* Wiesbaden: Franz Steiner.

_____. 1982. "Forschungen im Artemision von Ephesus von 1976 bis 1981." *AnSt* 32: 61-87.

_____. 1984. *Das Heiligtum der Artemis von Ephesos.* Graz: Akademische Druck - u. Verlagsanstalt.

_____. 1988. *Ephesos, Stadt an Fluß und Meer.* Graz: Akademische.

Bammer, A., R. Fleischer, and D. Knibbe. 1974. *Führer durch das Archäologische Museum in Selçuk-Ephesos.* Wien: Österreichisches Archäologisches Institut.

Banks, R. 1980. *Paul's Idea of Community: The Early House Churches in their Historical Setting.* Exeter: Paternoster Press.

_____. 1985. *Going to Church in the First Century.* Paramatta, NSW: Hexagon Press.

Banks, R. and J. 1989. *The Church Comes Home. A New Base for Community and Mission.* Sutherland, Australia: Albatross Books.

Barclay, J.M.G. 1996. *Jews in the Mediterranean Diaspora from Alexander to Trajan (323 BCE - 117 CE).* Edinburgh: T & T Clark.

_____. 1998. "Review of R. Strelan, *Paul, Artemis and the Jews in Ephesus.*" *JTS* ns 49: 260-3.

Bardy, G. 1921. "Cérinthe." *RB* 30: 344-73.

Barnard, L. W. 1966. "The Background of St. Ignatius of Antioch." In *Studies in the Apostolic Fathers and their Background*, ed. L. W. Barnard:19 30. Oxford: Basil Blackwell.

Barnett, A.E. 1941. *Paul Becomes a Literary Influence*. Chicago, Illinois: University of Chicago Press.

Barnett, P.W. 1989a. "Polemical Parallelism: Some Further Reflections on the Apocalypse." *JSNT* 35: 111-20.

_____. 1989b. "Wives and Women's Ministry (1 Tim 2:11-15)." *EvQ* 61: 225-38.

Barrett, C. K. 1963. *The Pastoral Epistles in the New English Bible, with introduction and commentary*. New Clarendon Bible. Oxford: Clarendon Press.

_____. 1968. *A Commentary on The First Epistle to the Corinthians*. BNTC. London: A & C Black.

_____. 1973. *A Commentary on The Second Epistle to the Corinthians*. BNTC. London: A & C Black.

_____. 1976. "Jews and Judaizers in the Epistles of Ignatius." In *Jews, Greeks and Christians, Religious Cultures in Late Antiquity. Essays in Honor of William David Davies*, ed. R. Hamerton-Kelly, Scroggs, R.:220-44. Leiden: Brill.

_____. 1976-77. "Acts and the Pauline Corpus." *ExpTim* 78: 2-5.

_____. 1977. "Paul's Address to the Ephesian Elders." In *God's Christ and His People. Studies in Honour of Nils Alstrup Dahl*, ed. J. Jervell, Meeks, W. A.:107-21. Oslo, Bergen, Tromsö: Universitetsforlaget.

_____. 1978. *The Gospel According to St John. An Introduction with Commentary and Notes on the Greek Text*. London: SPCK.

_____. 1984. "Apollos and the Twelve Disciples of Ephesus." In *The New Testament Age: Essays in Honor of Bo Reicke*, ed. W.C. Weinrich:29-39. Macon: Mercer University Press.

_____. 1985. *Church, Ministry and Sacraments in the New Testament*. Exeter: Paternoster Press.

_____. 1994, 1998. *A Critical and Exegetical Commentary on The Acts of the Apostles; Two Volumes*. ICC. Edinburgh: T & T Clark.

_____. 1999. "The Historicity of Acts." *JTS* ns 50: 515-34.

Barth, M., Blanke, H. 2000. *The Letter to Philemon. A New Translation with Notes and Commentary*. Eerdmans Critical Commentary. Grand Rapids, Michigan: Eerdmans.

Barton, S. C. 1992. "The Communal Dimension of Earliest Christianity: A Critical Survey of the Field." *JTS* ns 43: 399-427.

_____. 1998. "Can We Identify the Gospel Audiences?" In *The Gospels for All Christians. Rethinking the Gospel Audiences*, ed. R. Bauckham:173-94. Grand Rapids, Michigan: Eerdmans.

Bassler, J. M. 1984. "The Widows' Tale: A Fresh Look at 1 Tim 5:3-16." *JBL* 103: 23-41.

_____. 1988. "Adam, Eve, and the Pastor. The Use of Genesis 2-3 in the Pastoral Epistles." In *Genesis 1-3 in the History of Exegesis. Intrigue in the Garden*, ed. G.A. Robbins:43-65. Lewiston, Queenston: The Edwin Mellen Press.

_____. 1996a. *1 Timothy, 2 Timothy, Titus*. ANTC. Nashville: Abingdon Press.

_____. 1996b. "A Plethora of Epiphanies: Christology in the Pastoral Letters." *PSB* 17: 310-25.

Batey, R. 1963. "The Destination of Ephesians." *JBL* 82: 101.

Bauckham, R. 1988. "Pseudo-Apostolic Letters." *JBL* 107: 469-94.

_____. 1992. "Mary of Clopas (John 19:25)." In *Women in the Biblical Tradition*, ed. G.J. Brooke:231-55. Lewiston: Edwin Mellen Press.

_____. 1993a. "Papias and Polycrates on the Origin of the Fourth Gospel." *JTS* ns 44: 24-69.

_____. 1993b. "The Beloved Disciple as Ideal Author." *JSNT* 49: 21-44.

_____. 1993c. *The Climax of Prophecy. Studies on the Book of Revelation*. Edinburgh: T & T Clark.

_____. 1993d. *The Theology of the Book of Revelation*. Cambridge: Cambridge University Press.

_____. 1997. "Qumran and the Fourth Gospel: Is There a Connection?" In *The Scrolls and the Scriptures. Qumran Fifty Years After*, ed. S. E. Porter, Evans, C.A.:267-79. Sheffield: Sheffield Academic Press.

_____. 1998a. "Introduction." In *The Gospels for All Christians. Rethinking the Gospel Audiences*, ed. R. Bauckham:1-7. Grand Rapids, Michigan: Eerdmans.

_____. 1998b. "For Whom Were Gospels Written?" In *The Gospels for All Christians. Rethinking the Gospel Audiences*, ed. R. Bauckham:9-48. Grand Rapids, Michigan: Eerdmans.

_____. 1998c. "Response to Philip Esler." *SJT* 51: 249-53.

Bauer, W. 1971. *Orthodoxy and Heresy in Earliest Christianity*. Philadelphia: Fortress.

Baugh, S. M. 1990. "Phraseology and the reliability of Acts." *NTS* 36: 290-94.

_____. 1992. ""Savior of All People": 1 Tim 4:10 in Context." *WTJ* 54: 331-40.

_____. 1994. "The Apostle Among the Amazons." *WTJ* 56: 153-71.

_____. 1995. "A Foreign World: Ephesus in the First Century." In *Women in the Church. A Fresh Analysis of 1 Timothy 2:9-15*, ed. A. J. Köstenberger, Schreiner, T.R., Baldwin, H.S.:13-52. Grand Rapids, Michigan: Baker Books.

_____. 1999. "Cult Prostitution in New Testament Ephesus: A Reappraisal." *JETS* 42: 443-60.

Beagley, A. J. 1987. *The 'Sitz im Leben' of the Apocalypse with Particular Reference to the Role of the Church's Enemies*. BZNW 50. New York: Walter de Gruyter.

Beale, G. K. 1984a. *The Use of Daniel in Jewish Apocalyptic Literature and in the Revelation of St. John*. Lanham, MD: University Press of America.

_____. 1984b. "The Influence of Daniel upon the Structure and Theology of John's Apocalypse." *JETS* 27: 413-23.

_____. 1988. "Revelation." In *It is Written: Scripture Citing Scripture. Essays in Honour of Barnabas Lindars*, ed. D.A. Carson, Williamson, H. G. M.:318-36. Cambridge: Cambridge University Press.

_____. 1999. *The Book of Revelation. A Commentary on the Greek Text*. NIGTC. Grand Rapids, Michigan; Carlisle: Eerdmans; Paternoster Press.

_____. 2001. "A Response to Jon Paulien on the Use of the Old Testament in Revelation." *AUSS* 39: 23-34.

Bean, G. 1984. *Aegean Turkey: An Archaeological Guide*. London: Ernest Benn.

Beasley-Murray, G. R. 1974. *The Book of Revelation*. NCB. London: Marshall Morgan & Scott.

_____. 1987. *John*. WBC. Waco: Word Books.

Becker, J. 1993. *Paul Apostle to the Gentiles*. Kentucky: Westminster/ John Knox Press.

Beckwith, I.T. 1919. *The Apocalypse of John*. London: Macmillan.

Behr, C.A., translator. 1981. *P. Aelius Aristides, The Complete Works*. Leiden: E.J. Brill.

Beker, J.C. 1991. *Heirs of Paul. Paul's Legacy in the New Testament and the Church Today*. Minneapolis: Fortress Press.

Benoit, P. 1961. "Les origines de l'episcopat dans le Nouveau Testament." In *Exégèse et Théologie 2*, ed. P. Benoit:232-46. Paris: Les Éditions du Cerf.

Bérard, J. 1935. "Recherches sur les itinéraires de Saint Paul en Asie Mineure." *RAr, 6th Series* 5: 57-90.

Berger, K. 1995. *Theologiegeschichte des Urchristentums. Theologie des Neuen Testaments.* Tübingen, Basel: Francke Verlag.

Best, E. 1987. "Recipients and Title of the Letter to the Ephesians: Why and When the Designation 'Ephesians'?" In *ANRW*, II.25.4:3246-3279. Berlin: Walter de Gruyter.

_____. 1997. *Essays on Ephesians.* Edinburgh: T & T Clark.

_____. 1998. *A Critical and Exegetical Commentary on Ephesians.* ICC. Edinburgh: T & T Clark.

Betz, H. D. 1969. "On the Problem of the Religio-Historical Understanding of Apocalypticism." *JTC* 6: 134-56.

_____, ed. 1992. *The Greek Magical Papyri in Translation.* Chicago: University of Chicago Press.

Beyschlag, K. 1971. "Zur Simon-Magus-Frage." *ZTK* 68: 395-426.

Bickerman, E. 1949. "The Name of Christians." *HTR* 42: 109-24.

Bieder, W. 1956. "Zur Deutung des kirchlichen Schweigens bei Ignatius von Antiochia." *TZ* 12: 28-43.

Biguzzi, G. 1998. "Ephesus, its Artemision, its Temple to the Flavian Emperors, and Idolatry in Revelation." *NovT* 40: 276-90.

Binder, D.D. 1999. *Into the Temple Courts. The Place of the Synagogues in the Second Temple Period.* SBLDS 169. Atlanta, GA: Scholars Press.

Bingöl, O. 1999. "Epiphanie an den Artemistempeln von Ephesos und Magnesia am Mäander." In *100 Jahre Österreichische Forschungen in Ephesos. Akten des Symposions Wien 1995*, ed. H. Friesinger, Krinzinger, F.:233-40. Wien: Verlag der Österreichischen Akademie der Wissenschaften.

Bird, A. E. 1997. "The Authorship of the Pastoral Epistles - Quantifying Literary Style." *RTR* 56: 118-37.

Blackburn, B.L. 1993. "The Identity of the 'Women' in 1 Tim. 3:11." In *Essays on Women in Earliest Christianity. Volume One*, ed. C.D. Osburn:303-19. Joplin, Missouri: College Press.

Blanchetiere, François. 1981. *Le Christianisme Asiate aux II ème et III ème siecles.* L'Universite de Strasbourg.

Blasi, A.J. 1995. "Office Charisma in Early Christian Ephesus." *Sociology of Religion* 56: 245-55.

Blevins, J. L. 1990. "Acts 13-19: The Tale of Three Cities." *RevExp* 87: 439-450.

Blomberg, C.L. 1999. *Neither Poverty nor Riches. A Biblical Theology of Material Possessions.* New Studies in Biblical Theology 7. Downers Grove, Illinois; Leicester: IVP; Apollos.

Blue, B. 1994. "Acts and the House Church." In *The Book of Acts in its Greco-Roman Setting*, ed. D.W.J. Gill, Gempf, C.:119-222. Grand Rapids, Michigan.

Böcher, O. 1980. "Der Verhältnis der Apokalypse des Johannes zum Evangelium des Johannes." In *L'Apocalypse johannique et l'Apocalyptique dans le Nouveau Testament*, ed. J. Lambrecht:289-301. Gembloux; Leuven: Duculot; Leuven University Press.

Bogart, J. L. 1977. *Orthodox and Heretical Perfectionism in the Johannine Community as Evident in the First Epistle of John.* SBLDS 33. Missoula, Montana: Scholars Press.

Boismard, M.-É. 1949. "La connaissance de Dieu dans L'Alliance Nouvelle, d'après la première lettre de saint Jean." *RB* 56: 365-91.
_____. 1956. "Une liturgie baptismale dans la Prima Petri." *RB* 63: 182-208.
_____. 1972. "The First Epistle of John and the Writings of Qumran." In *John and Qumran*, ed. J. H. Charlesworth:156-65. London: Geoffrey Chapman.
_____. 2000. "Rm 16.17-20: Vocabulaire et Style." *Bib* 107: 548-57.
Bonnard, P. 1983. *Les épîtres johanniques*. CNT 13c. Genève: Labor et Fides.
Borgen, P. 1995. "'Yes,' 'No,' 'How Far?': The Participation of Jews and Christians in Pagan Cults." In *Paul in his Hellenistic Context*, ed. T. Engberg-Pedersen:30-59. Minneapolis: Fortress Press.
_____. 1996. "Moses, Jesus, and the Roman Emperor: Observations in Philo's Writings and the Revelation of John." *NovT* 38: 145-59.
Boring, M.E. 1989. *Revelation*. IBC. Louisville: John Knox Press.
Bornkamm, G. 1971. *Paul*. New York: Harper & Row.
Botermann, H. 1991. "Paulus und das Urchristentum in der antiken Welt." *TRu* 56: 296-305.
Botha, J.E. 1996. "A review of current research on group formation in early Christianity." *HvTSt* 52: 252-69.
Bousset, W. 1906. *Die Offenbarung Johannis*. KEK. Göttingen: Vandenhoeck und Ruprecht.
Bovon, F. 1987. *Luke The Theologian. Thiry-three years of research (1950-1983)*. Translated by K. McKinney. Allison Park: Pickwick.
Bowe, B.E. 1999. "Dancing into the Divine: The Hymn of the Dance in the *Acts of John*." *JECS* 7: 83-104.
Bowen, C. R. 1920. "Are Paul's Prison Letters from Ephesus?" *AJT* 24: 112-35, 277-87.
_____. 1923. "I Fought with Beasts at Ephesus." *JBL* 42: 59-68.
Bowers, P. 1987. "Fulfilling the Gospel: The Scope of the Pauline Mission." *JETS* 30: 185-98.
Bowman, A. L. 1992. "Women in Ministry: An Exegetical Study of 1 Timothy 2:11-15." *Biblotheca Sacra* 149: 193-213.
Boxall, I. 1998. "'For Paul' or 'For Cephas'? The Book of Revelation and Early Asian Christianity." In *Understanding, Studying and Reading. New Testament Essays in Honour of John Ashton*, ed. C. Rowland, Fletcher-Louis, C.H.T.:198-218. Sheffield: Sheffield Academic Press.
Boyer, J. L. 1985. "Are the Seven Letters of Revelation 2-3 Prophetic?" *Grace Theological Journal* 6: 267-73.
Braithwaite, W.C. 1955. *The Beginnings of Quakerism*. Cambridge: Cambridge University Press.
Branick, V. 1989. *The House Church in the Writings of Paul*. Zacchaeus Studies: New Testament. Wilmington, Delaware: Michael Glazier.
Braun, F. 1988. *Terms of Address. Problems of patterns and usage in various language and cultures*. Contributions to the Sociology of Language 50. Berlin, New York, Amsterdam: Mouton de Gruyter.
Bremmer, J.N. 1995a. "Pauper or Patroness. The Widow in the Early Christian Church." In *Between Poverty and the Pyre. Moments in the history of Widowhood*, ed. J. Bremmer, van den Bosch, L.:31-57. London and New York: Routledge.
_____. 1995b. "Women in the Apocryphal Acts of John." In *The Apocryphal Acts of John*, ed. J.N. Bremmer:37-56. Kampen: Kok Pharos.
_____, ed. 1996. *The Apocryphal Acts of Paul*. Kampen: Kok Pharos.
Brenk, F. E. 1990. "Old Wineskins Recycled: *Autarkeia* in I Timothy 6.5-10." *Filología Neotestamentaria* 3: 39-51.
_____. 1998. "Artemis of Ephesos: An Avant Garde Goddess." *Kernos* 11: 157-71.

Brent, A. 1992. *Cultural Episcopacy and Ecumenism. Representative Ministry in Church History from the Age of Ignatius of Antioch to the Reformation With Special Reference to Contemporary Ecumenism.* Studies in Christian Mission 6. Leiden: Brill.

Briggs, R. C. 1970. "Contemporary Study of the Johannine Epistles." *RevExp* 67: 411-22.

Brooke, A. E. 1912. *A Critical and Exegetical Commentary on the Johannine Epistles.* ICC. Edinburgh: T & T Clark.

Brooten, B.J. 1982. *Women Leaders in the Ancient Synagogue. Inscriptional Evidence and Background Issues.* BJS 36. Chico, California: Scholars Press.

Broughton, T.R.S. 1938. "Roman Asia Minor." In *An Economic Survey of Ancient Rome,* ed. T. Frank, 4:499-916. Baltimore: John Hopkins Press.

Brown, C.T. 2000. *The Gospel and Ignatius of Antioch.* Studies in Biblical Literature 12. New York: Peter Lang.

Brown, L.A. 1992. "Asceticism and Ideology: The Language of Power in the Pastoral Epistles." *Semeia* 57: 77-94.

Brown, R. E. 1965. "The Qumran Scrolls and the Johannine Gospel and Epistles." In *New Testament Essays,* ed. R. E. Brown:138-73. Garden City, New York: The Bruce Publishing Co.

_____. 1966. *The Gospel According to John. Introduction, Translation, and Notes.* AB. Garden City, New York: Doubleday.

_____. 1977. "Johannine Ecclesiology - The Community's Origins." *Int* 31: 379-393.

_____. 1978. "'Other Sheep Not of This Fold': The Johannine Perspective on Christian Diversity in the Late First Century." *JBL* 97: 5-22.

_____. 1979a. *The Community of the Beloved Disciple.* New York: Paulist.

_____. 1979b. "The Relationship to the Fourth Gospel Shared by the Author of 1 John and by his Opponents." In *Text and Interpretation,* ed. E. Best, Wilson, R. McL.:57-68. Cambridge: Cambridge University Press.

_____. 1982. *The Epistles of John. Translated with Introduction, Notes and Commentary.* AB. Garden City, New York: Doubleday.

_____. 1984. *The Churches the Apostles Left Behind.* London: Geoffrey Chapman.

_____. 1988. *The Gospel and Epistles of John*: Collegeville: Liturgical Press.

_____. 1990. "Further Reflections on the Origins of the Church in Rome." In *The Conversation Continues. Studies in Paul and John in Honor of J. Louis Martyn,* ed. R.T. Fortna, Gaventa, B. R.:98-115. Nashville: Abingdon Press.

_____. 1997. *An Introduction to the New Testament.* ABRL. New York: Doubleday.

Brown, R. E. and J. P. Meier. 1983. *Antioch and Rome. New Testament Cradles of Catholic Christianity.* New York: Paulist Press.

Brown, S. 1977. "'Water-Baptism' and 'Spirit-Baptism' in Luke-Acts." *ATR* 59: 135-51.

Brownlee, W. H. 1972. "Whence the Gospel According to John?" In *John and Qumran,* ed. J. H. Charlesworth:166-94. London: Geoffrey Chapman.

Brox, N. 1965. "Nikolaos und Nikolaiten." *VC* 19: 23-30.

_____. 1989. *Die Pastoralbriefe.* RNT 7. Regensburg: Friedrich Pustet.

Bruce, F. F. 1942. *The Speeches in the Acts of the Apostles.* London: The Tyndale Press.

_____. 1967. "St Paul in Rome: 4. The Epistle to the Ephesians." *BJRL* 49: 303 22.

_____. 1971. *1 and 2 Corinthians.* NCB. London: Marshall Morgan and Scott.

_____. 1976. "Is the Paul of Acts the Real Paul?" *BJRL* 58: 282-305.

_____. 1977-78. "St John at Ephesus." *BJRL* 60: 339-61.

_____. 1982. "The Acts of Apostles Today." *BJRL* 65: 36-56.

_____. 1984. "Jews and Christians in the Lycus Valley." *BSac* 141: 3-15.

_____. 1984. *The Epistle to the Colossians, to Philemon, and to the Ephesians*. NICNT. Michigan: Eerdmans.

_____. 1985. "The Acts of the Apostles: Historical Record or Theological Reconstruction?" In *ANRW*, II.25.3:2569-2603. Berlin: Walter de Gruyter.

_____. 1988. *The Book of the Acts*. NICNT. Grand Rapids, Michigan: Eerdmans.

_____. 1989. *Philippians*. NIBC. Peabody, Massachusetts: Hendrickson.

_____. 1990. *Paul, Apostle of the Heart Set Free*. Grand Rapids: Eerdmans.

Bruns, J.E. 1967. "A Note on John 16:33 and 1 John 2:13-14." *JBL* 86: 451-3.

Brunt, P. A. 1979. "Marcus Aurelius and the Christians." In *Studies in Latin Literature and Roman History 1*, ed. C. Deroux:483-520. Bruxelles: Latomus Revue d'Études Latines.

Bryskog, S. 1996. "Co-Senders, Co-Authors and Paul's Use of the First Person Plural." *ZNW* 87: 230-50.

Budesheim, T. L. 1976. "Paul's Abschiedsrede in the Acts of the Apostles." *HTR* 69: 9-30.

Bullinger, E. W. 1898. *Figures of Speech Used in the Bible: Explained and Illustrated*. London; New York: Eyre & Spottiswoode; E. & J.B. Young & Co.

Bultmann, R. 1973. *The Johannine Epistles*. Hermeneia. Philadephia: Fortress Press.

_____. 1985. *The Second Letter to the Corinthians*. Minneapolis: Augsburg Publishing House.

Burchard, C. 1975. "Paulus in der Apostelgeschichte." *TLZ* 12: 881-95.

Burge, G.M. 1987. *The Anointed Community: The Holy Spirit in the Johannine Tradition*. Grand Rapids, Michigan: Eerdmans.

Burkert, W. 1999. "Die Artemis der Epheser: Wirkungsmacht und Gestalt einer Großen Göttin." In *100 Jahre Österreichische Forschungen in Ephesos. Akten des Symposions Wien 1995*, ed. H. Friesinger, Krinzinger, F.:59-70. Wien: Verlag der Österreichischen Akademie der Wissenschaften.

Burney, C. F. 1922. *The Aramaic Origin of the Fourth Gospel*. Oxford: Clarendon Press.

Burridge, R.A. 1992. *What Are the Gospels? A Comparison with Graeco-Roman Biography*. SNTSMS 70. Cambridge: Cambridge University Press.

_____. 1998. "About People, by People, for People: Gospel Genre and Audiences." In *The Gospels for All Christians. Rethinking the Gospel Audiences*, ed. R. Bauckham:113-145. Grand Rapids, Michigan: Eerdmans.

Burton, G.P. 1975. "Proconsuls, Assizes and the Administration of Justice under the Empire." *JRS* 65: 92-106.

Cabaniss, A. 1956. "Wisdom 18:14f.: An Early Christmas Text." *VC* 10: 97-102.

Cadbury, H. J. 1920. *The Style and Literary Method of Luke*. HTS 6. Cambridge: Harvard University Press.

Cadoux, C. J. 1925. *The Early Church and the World. A History of the Christian Attitude to Pagan Society and the State Down to the Time of Constantinus*. Edinburgh: T & T Clark.

Caird, G. B. 1966. *A Commentary on The Revelation of St. John the Divine*. BNTC. London: A & C Black.

_____. 1980. *The Language and Imagery of the Bible*. London: Duckworth.

Camelot, P. Th. 1958. *Ignace d'Antioche, Polycarpe de Smyrne, Lettres. Martyre de Polycarpe*. 3rd ed., Sources Chrétiennes 10. Paris: Éditions du Cerf.

Campbell, R. A. 1994. *The Elders: Seniority within Earliest Christianity*. Studies of the NT and its World. Edinburgh: T & T Clark.

_____. 1995. "ΚΑΙ ΜΑΛΙΣΤΑ ΟΙΚΕΙΩΝ - A New Look at 1 Timothy 5.8." *NTS* 41: 157-60.

Campbell, T. H. 1955. "Paul's 'Missionary Journeys' as Reflected in His Letters." *JBL* 74: 80-7.

Cardman, F. 1999. "Women, Ministry, and Church Order in Early Christianity." In *Women and Christian Origins*, ed. R.S. Kraemer, D'Angelo, M.R.:300-329. New York and Oxford: Oxford University Press.

Carey, G. 1999. *Elusive Apocalypse. Reading Authority in the Revelation to John*. Studies in American Biblical Hermeneutics 15. Macon, Georgia: Mercer University Press.

Carrez, M. 1979. "Le "Nous" en 2 Corinthiens." *NTS* 26: 474-86.

_____. 1985. "Note sur les événements d'Éphèse et l'appel de Paul à sa citoyenneté romaine." In *À Cause de l'Evangile. Études sur les Synoptiques et les Actes offertes au P. Jacques Dupont, O.S.B. à l'occasion de son 70e anniversaire*:769-77. Paris: Cerf.

_____. 1986. *La Deuxième Épitre de Saint Paul aux Corinthiens*. CNT, deuxième série. Genève: Labor et Fides.

_____. 1996. "La parcours christologique des discours de Paul dans le livre des Actes coïncide-t-il avec celui de l'Apôtre dans ses épîtres authentiques?" In *L'Évangile Exploré. Mélanges offerts à Simon Légasse à l'occasion de ses soixante-dix ans*, ed. A. Marchadour:357-74. Paris: Les Éditions du Cerf.

Carrington, P. 1957. *The Early Christian Church*. Cambridge: Cambridge University Press.

Carruth, S. 1996. "Praise for the Churches: The Rhetorical Function of the Opening Sections of the Letters of Ignatius of Antioch." In *Reimagining Christian Origins. A Colloquium Honoring Burton L. Mack*, ed. E.A. Castelli, Taussig, H.:295-310. Valley Forge, PA: Trinity Press International.

Carson, D. A., Moo, D. J., Morris, L. 1992. *An Introduction to the New Testament*. Grand Rapids, Michigan: Zondervan.

Carter, T.L. 1997. "'Big Men' in Corinth." *JSNT* 66: 45-71.

Cassem, N. H. 1972-73. "A Grammatical and Contextual Inventory of the Use of κόσμος in the Johannine Corpus with some Implications for a Johannine Cosmic Theology." *NTS* 19: 81-91.

Chadwick, H. 1950. "The Silence of Bishops in Ignatius." *HTR* 43: 169-72.

Chapman, J. 1911. *John the Presbyter and the Fourth Gospel*. Oxford: Clarendon Press.

Chapot, V. 1904. *La province romaine proconsulaire d'Asie*. Bibliothèque de l'École des Hautes Études 150. Paris: Librairie Émile Bouillon.

Charles, J.D. 1993. "Imperial Pretensions and the Throne-Vision of the Lamb: Observations on the Function of Revelation 5." *CTR* 7: 85-97.

Charles, R.H. 1920. *A Critical and Exegetical Commentary on The Revelation of St. John, 2 Vols*. ICC. Edinburgh: T & T Clark.

Charlesworth, J. H., Culpepper, R. A. 1973. "The Odes of Solomon and the Gospel of John." *CBQ* 35: 298-322.

Charlesworth, J. H. 1995. *The Beloved Disciple. Whose Witness Validates the Gospel of John?* Valley Forge, Pennsylvania: Trinity Press International.

Chilton, B., Neusner, J. 1999. *Types of Authority in Formative Christianity and Judaism*. London and New York: Routledge.

Clavier, H. 1953. "La sante de l'Apôtre Paul." In *Studia Paulina in Honorem Johannis de Zwaan*:66-82. Haarlem: De Erven F. Bohn N.V.

Clemen, C. 1905. "The sojourn of the Apostle John at Ephesus." *AJT* 9: 643-76.

Coetzee, J. C. 1979. "The Holy Spirit in 1 John." *Neot* 13: 43-67.

Coffin, C. P. 1924. "The Meaning of 1 Cor. 15:32." *JBL* 43: 172-6.

Cohen, S. J. D. 1982. "Masada: Literary Tradition, Archaeological Remains, and the Credibility of Josephus." *JJS* 33: 385-405.

_____. 1996. "Ioudaios: 'Judaean' and 'Jew' in Susanna, First Maccabees, and Second Maccabees." In *Geschichte - Tradition - Reflexion. Festschrift für Martin Hengel zum 70. Geburtstag*, ed. P. Schäfer, Band 1: Judentum:211-220. Tübingen: J.C.B. Mohr (Paul Siebeck).

Cole, D. P. 1988. "Corinth and Ephesis. Why Did Paul Spend Half his Journeys in these cities?" *BRev* 4, no. 6: 20-30.

Collins, J.N. 1990. *Diakonia. Re-interpreting the Ancient Sources*. New York, Oxford: Oxford University Press.

Collins, R.F. 1988. *Letters That Paul Did Not Write: The Epistle to the Hebrews and the Pauline Pseudepigrapha*. GNS 28. Wilmington, Delaware: Michael Glazier.

_____. 1999. *First Corinthians*. SP. Collegeville, Minnesota: Liturgical Press.

_____. 2002. *1 & 2 Timothy and Titus*. New Testament Library. Louisville: Westminster John Knox Press.

Combes, I.A.H. 1998. *The Metaphor of Slavery in the Writings of the Early Church from the New Testament to the Beginning of the Fifth Century*. JSNTSS 156. Sheffield: Sheffield Academic Press.

Conybeare, W. J. 1872. *The Life and Epistles of St. Paul*. London: Longmans.

Conzelmann, H. 1954. "'Was von Anfang war'." In *Neutestamentliche Studien für Rudolf Bultmann zu seinem Siebzigsten Geburtsteg, 20, August 1954*, ed. W. Eltester: 194-201: Munich: Chr. Kaiser Verlag.

_____. 1965. "Paulus und die Weisheit." *NTS* 12: 231-44.

_____. 1975. *1 Corinthians*. Hermeneia. Philadelphia: Fortress Press.

_____. 1987. *Acts of the Apostles*. Hermeneia. Philadelphia: Fortress Press.

Cook, D. 1984. "The Pastoral Fragments Reconsidered." *JTS* ns 35: 120-31.

Cook, J. I. 1981. *Edgar Johnson Goodspeed Articulate Scholar*. SBL Biblical Scholarship in North America 4. California: Scholars Press.

Corwin, V. 1960. *St. Ignatius and Christianity in Antioch*. Yale Publications in Religion 1. New Haven: Yale University Press.

Countryman, L.W. 1980. *The Rich Christian in the Church of the Early Empire: Contradictions and Accommodations*. Texts and Studies in Relgion 7. New York and Toronto: Edwin Mellen Press.

_____. 1999. "Asceticism in the Johannine Letters?" In *Asceticism and the New Testament*, ed. L.E. Vaage, Wimbush, V.L.:383-91. New York, London: Routledge.

Court, J. M. 1979. *Myth and History in the Book of Revelation*. London: SPCK.

_____. 1994. *Revelation*. NTG. Sheffield: JSOT Press.

Cranford, L. 1980. "Encountering Heresy: Insight from the Pastoral Epistles." *SwJT* 22: 23-40.

Crocker, P. T. 1987. "Ephesus: its silversmiths, its tradesmen, and its riots." *BurH* 23: 76-8.

Crutchfield, L. V. 1988. "The Apostle John and Asia Minor as a Source of Premillenianism in the Early Church Fathers." *JETS* 31: 411-27.

Cullmann, O. 1976. *The Johannine Circle*. London: SCM Press.

_____. 1988. *Unity through Diversity*: Fortress Press.

Culpepper, R. A. 1975. *The Johannine School*. SBLDS 26. Missoula: Montana: Scholars Press.

_____. 1980-81. "The Pivot of John's Prologue." *NTS* 27: 1-31.

_____. 1983. *Anatomy of the Fourth Gospel: A Study in Literary Design*. Philadelphia: Fortress.

_____. 1985. *1 John, 2 John, 3 John*. Knox Preaching Guides. Atlanta: John Knox Press.

_____. 1994. *John, the Son of Zebedee*. Columbia: University of South Carolina Press.

Cunningham, R. B. 1992. "Wide Open Doors and Many Adversaries (1 Corinthians 16:9; Acts 19)." *RevExp* 89: 89-98.

Cuss, D. 1974. *Imperial Cult and Honorary Terms in the New Testament*. Paradosis 23. Fribourg: Fribourg University Press.

D'Angelo, M.R. 1990. "Women in Luke-Acts: A Redactional View." *JBL* 109: 441-61.

Dahl, N. A. 2000. *Studies in Ephesians. Introductory Questions, Text- & Edition-Critical Issues, Interpretation of Texts and Themes*. WUNT 131. Tübingen: Mohr Siebeck.

Dalmeyda, G. 1926. *Xénophon d'Éphèse, Les Éphésiaques. Texte Établi et Traduit*. Paris: Société d'Édition "Les Belles Lettres".

Danker, F. W. 1982. *Benefactor: Epigraphic Study of a Greco-Roman and New Testament Semantic Field*. St Louis, Missouri: Clayton Publishing House.

_____. 1989. *2 Corinthians*. ACNT. Minnesota: Augsburg Publishing House.

Dassmann, E. 1990. "Archeological Traces of Early Christian Veneration of Paul." In *Paul and the Legacies of Paul*, ed. W.S. Babcock:281-306. Dallas: Southern Methodist University Press.

Davies, M. 1996a. *The Pastoral Epistles*. NTG. Sheffield: Sheffield Academic Press.

_____. 1996b. *The Pastoral Epistles*. Epworth NT Commentaries. London: Epworth.

Davies, S. L. 1976. "The Predicament of Ignatius of Antioch." *VC* 30: 175-80.

_____. 1980. *The Revolt of the Widows. The Social World of the Apocryphal Acts*. Carbondale and Edwardsville: Southern Illinois University Press.

Davies, W.D. 1953. "'Knowledge' in the Dead Sea Scrolls and Matthew 11:25-30." *HTR* 46: 113-39.

de la Potterie, I. 1959. "L'arriere-fond du theme johannique de verite." In *Studia Evangelica I,*, ed. K. Aland, et al:277-94. Berlin: Akademie Verlag.

_____. 1969. "La connaissance de Dieu dans le dualisme eschatologique d'après 1Jn II, 12-14." In *Au Service de la Parole de Dieu. Mélanges offerts à Monseigneur A.-M. Charue*:77-99. Gembloux: J. Duculot.

_____. 1978. "La notion de 'commencement' dans les écrits johanniques." In *Die Kirche des Anfangs für H. Schürmann*, ed. R. Schnackenburg, Ernst, J., Wanke, J.:379-403. Freiburg: Herder.

Deissmann, A. 1909. *Bible Studies*. Edinburgh: T&T Clark.

_____. 1927. *Light from the Ancient East. The New Testament Illustrated by Recently Discovered Texts of the Graeco-Roman Wolrd*. London: Hodder and Stoughton.

Delebecque, É. 1982. "La mésaventure des fils de Scévas selon ses deux versions (Actes 19, 13-20)." *RSPT* 66: 225-32.

_____. 1983. "La révolte des orfèvres à Éphèse et ses deux versions (Acts des Apôtres, xix, 24-40)." *RThom* 83: 419-29.

DeSilva, D. A. 1991. "The 'Image of the Beast' and the Christians in Asia Minor: Escalation of Sectarian Tension in Revelation 13." *TJ* 12: 185-208.

_____. 1992a. "The Revelation to John: A Case Study in Apocalyptic Propaganda and the Maintenance of Sectarian Identity." *Sociological Analysis* 53: 375-95.

_____. 1992b. "The Social Setting of the Revelation to John: Conflicts Within, Fears Without." *WTJ* 54: 273-302.

Dewey, J. 1992. "Response: Fantasy and the New Testament." *Semeia* 60: 83-9.

_____. 1998. "1 Timothy, 2 Timothy, Titus." In *Women's Bible Commentary*, ed. C.A. Newsom, Ringe, S.H.:444-52. Louisville, Kentucky: Westminster John Knox Press.

Dibelius, M. 1956. *Studies in the Acts of the Apostles*. London: SCM Press.

Dibelius, M., Conzelmann. H. 1972. *The Pastoral Epistles*. Hermeneia. Philadelphia: Fortress Press.

Dickey, S. 1928. "Some Economic and Social Conditions of Asia Minor Affecting the Expansion of Christianity." In *Studies in Early Christianity Presented to Frank Chamberlin Porter and Benjamin Wisner Bacon*, ed. S.J. Case:393-416. New York and London: The Century Co.

Dodd, C. H. 1934. "The Mind of Paul: Change and Development." *BJRL* 18: 69-110.

_____. 1937. "The First Epistle of John and the Fourth Gospel." *BJRL* 21: 129-56.

_____. 1946. *The Johannine Epistles*. MNTC. London: Hodder and Stoughton.

Donahue, P. J. 1978. "Jewish Christianity in the Letters of Ignatius of Antioch." *VC* 32: 81-93.

Donelson, L.W. 1986. *Pseudepigraphy and Ethical Argument in the Pastoral Epistles*. HUT 22. Tübingen: J.C.B. Mohr (Paul Siebeck).

Donfried, K. P. 1977. "Ecclesiastical Authority in 2-3 John." In *L'Évangile de Jean. Sources, rédaction, théologie*, ed. M. de Jonge:325-33. Gembloux; Leuven: J. Duculot; Leuven University Press.

_____. 1992. "Chronology, New Testament." In *Anchor Bible Dictionary*, ed. D.N Freedman, 1:1011-1022. New York: Doubleday.

Du Rand, J. A. 1979. "The Structure of 3 John." *Neot* 13: 121-31.

_____. 1991. *Johannine Perspectives. Introduction to the Johannine writings, Part 1.* Doornfontein: Orion.

Du Toit, A.B. 1986. "Hyperbolical Contrasts: A Neglected Aspect of Paul's Style." In *A South African Perspective on the New Testament. Essays by South African New Testament Scholars presented to Bruce Manning Metzger during his Visit to South Africa in 1985*, ed. J.H. Petzer, Hartin, P.J.:178-86. Leiden: E.J. Brill.

Dubois, J. D. 1976. "L'hérésie dans les lettres aux Eglises (Ap. 2-3)." *FoiVie* 75: 3-11.

Duncan, G. S. 1929. *St Paul's Ephesian Ministry*. London: Hodder & Stoughton.

_____. 1931. "A New Setting for St. Paul's Epistle to the Philippians." *ExpTim* 43: 7-11.

_____. 1934. "The Epistles of the Imprisonment in Recent Discussion." *ExpTim* 46: 293-8.

_____. 1955. "Were Paul's Imprisonment Epistles Written from Ephesus?" *ExpTim* 67: 163-66.

_____. 1956. "Paul's Ministry in Asia - The Last Phase." *NTS* 3: 211-18.

_____. 1958. "Chronological Table to Illustrate Paul's Ministry in Asia." *NTS* 5: 43-45.

Duncan-Jones, R. 1974. *The Economy of the Roman Empire. Quantitative Studies*. Cambridge: Cambridge University Press.

Dunn, J. D. G. 1970. *Baptism in the Holy Spirit*. London: SCM Press.

_____. 1975. *Jesus and the Spirit*. London: SCM Press.

_____. 1977. *Unity and Diversity in the New Testament*. London: SCM Press.

_____. 1987. *The Living Word*. London: SCM Press.

_____. 1988. *Romans 1-8, Romans 9-16, 2 Vols*. WBC. Dallas, Texas: Word.

_____. 1989. *Christology in the Making*. London: SCM Press.

_____. 1996. *The Epistles to the Colossians and to Philemon. A Commentary on the Greek Text*. NIGTC. Grand Rapids, Michigan; Carlisle: Eerdmans; Paternoster Press.

_____. 2000. "Jesus in Oral Memory: The Initial Stages of the Jesus Tradition." In *SBLSP 2000*: 287-326. Atlanta: SBL.

Dupont, J. 1962. *Le discours de Milet, testament pastoral de saint Paul (Actes 20: 18-36)* LD 32 Paris: Les Éditions du Cerf.

_____. 1984. "La construction du discours de Milet." In *Nouvelles Études sur les Actes des Apôtres*, ed. J. Dupont:424-45. Paris: Les Éditions du Cerf.

Dupuy, B. 1982. "Aux origines de l'époscopat. Le corpus des Lettres d'Ignace d'Antioche et le ministère d'unité." *Istina* 27: 269-77.

Easton, B.S. 1948. *The Pastoral Epistles*. London: SCM Press.

Edwards, M. J. 1989. "Martyrdom and the First Epistle of John." *NovT* 31: 164-171.

_____. 1998. "Ignatius and the Second Century: An Answer to R. Hübner." *ZAC* 2: 214-226.

Edwards, R. B. 1996. *The Johannine Epistles*. NTG. Sheffield: Sheffield Academic Press.

Ehrhardt, A. 1945. "The Beginnings of Mon-Episcopacy." *CQR* 140: 113-26.

_____. 1969. *The Acts of the Apostles*. Manchester: Manchester University Press.

Elliger, W. 1992. *Ephesos: Geschichte einer antiken Weldstadt*. Urban-Taschenbücher 375. Stuttgart, Berlin, Köln: W. Kohlhammer.

Elliott, J. H. 1981. *A Home for the Homeless. A Sociological Exegesis of 1 Peter, Its Situation and Strategy*. Philadelphia: Fortress Press.

_____. 1993. *What is Social-Scientific Criticism?* Guides to Biblical Scholarship; New Testament Series. Minneapolis: Fortress Press.

_____. 1998. "Phases in the Social Formation of Early Christianity: From Faction to Sect - A Social Science Perspective." In *Recruitment, Conquest and Conflict. Strategies in Judaism, Early Christianity, and the Greco-Roman World*, ed. P. Borgen, Robbins, V.K., Gowler, D.B.:273-313. Atlanta, Georgia: Scholars Press.

_____. 2000. *1 Peter. A New Translation with Introduction and Commentary*. AB. New York: Doubleday.

Elliott, J. K. 1993. *The Apocryphal New Testament. A Collection of Apocryphal Christian Literature in an English Translation*. Oxford: Clarendon Press.

Ellis, E. E. 1970. "Paul and His Co-Workers." *NTS* 17: 437-52.

_____. 1987. "Traditions in the Pastoral Epistles." In *Early Jewish and Christian Exegesis. Studies in Memory of William Hugh Brownlee*, ed. C.A. Evans, Stinespring, W. F.:237-53. Atlanta, Georgia: Scholars Press.

_____. 1992a. "The Pastorals and Paul." *ExpTim* 104: 45-7.

_____. 1992b. "Pseudonymity and Canonicity of New Testament Documents." In *Worship, Theology, Ministry in the Early Church. Essays on Honor of Ralph P. Martin*, ed. M.J. Wilkins, Paige, T.:212-24. JSNTSS 87. Sheffield: JSOT Press.

_____. 1999. *The Making of the New Testament Documents*. Biblical Interpretation Series 39. Leiden: Brill.

Engelmann, H. 1993a. "Celsusbibliothek und Auditorium in Ephesos (IK 17, 3009)." *JÖAI* 62: 105-111.

_____. 1993b. "Zum Kaiserkult in Ephesos." *ZPE* 97: 279-89.

_____. 1994. "Ephesos und die Johannesakten." *ZPE* 103: 297-302.

_____. 2000. "Neue Inschriften aus Ephesos XIII." *JÖAI* 69: 77-93.

Engelmann, H., Knibbe, D. 1989. "Der Zollgesetz der Provinz Asia. Eine neue Inschriften aus Ephesos." *Epigraphica Anatolia* 14: 1-209.

Eno, R. B. 1976. "Authority and Conflict in the Early Church." *EgT* 7: 41-60.

Enroth, A. M. 1990. "The Hearing Formula in the Book of Revelation." *NTS* 36: 598-608.

Erdemgil, S. 1992. *Ephesus*. Istanbul: Net Turistik Yayinlar.

Esler, P.F. 1998. "Community and Gospel in Early Christianity: A Response to Richard Bauckham's *Gospels for all Christians*." *SJT* 51: 235-48.

Evans, M. 1983. *Women in the Bible*. Exeter: Paternoster.

Exum, C., Talbert C. 1967. "The Structure of Paul's Speech to the Ephesian Elders (Acts 20, 18-35)." *CBQ* 29: 233-6.

Eybers, I. H. 1970. "Some examples of hyperbole in Biblical Hebrew." *Semitics* 1: 38 49.

Falwell, R.H. 1948. *The Place of Ephesus in the Propagation of Christianity in New Testament Times.* D.Th. Thesis, Southern Baptist Theological Seminary.

Farrer, A. 1964. *The Revelation of St. John the Divine.* Oxford: Clarendon Press.

Fascher, E. 1980. *Der erste Brief des Paulus an die Korinther. Erster Teil: Einführung und Auslegung der Kapitel 1-7.* THKNT. Berlin: Evangelische Verlagsanstalt.

Fearghail, F.Ó. 2002. "The Jews in the Hellenistic cities of Acts." In *Jews in the Hellenistic and Roman Cities,* ed. J.R. Bartlett:39-54. London, New York: Routledge.

Fee, G. D. 1985. "Reflections on Church Order in the Pastoral Epistles, with Further Reflection on the Hermeneutics of Ad Hoc Documents." *JETS* 28: 141-51.

_____. 1987. *The First Epistle to the Corinthians.* NICNT. Michigan: Eerdmans.

_____. 1988a. *1 and 2 Timothy, Titus.* NIBC. Peabody, Massachusetts: Hendrickson.

_____. 1988b. "Pauline Literature." In *Dictionary of Pentecostal and Charismatic Movements,* ed. S.M. Burgess:665-83. Grand Rapids: Zondervan.

_____. 1990. "Women in Ministry: The Meaning of 1 Timothy 2:8-15 in Light of the Purpose of 1 Timothy." *Journal of the Christian Brethren Research Fellowship* 122: 11-18.

_____. 1991. *Gospel and Spirit. Issues in New Testament Hermeneutics.* Peabody: Hendickson.

_____. 1994. *God's Empowering Presence. The Holy Spirit in the Letters of Paul.* Peabody: Hendrickson.

_____. 1995. *Paul's Letter to the Philippians.* NICNT Grand Rapids, Michigan: Eerdmans.

Fekkes, J. 1994. *Isaiah and Prophetic Traditions in the Book of Revelation. Visionary Antecedents and their Development.* JSNTSS 93. Sheffield: JSOT Press.

Ferguson, E. 1973. "'When You Come Together': Epi To Auto in Early Christian Literature." *ResQ* 16: 202-8.

_____. 1991. "Τόπος in 1 Timothy 2:8." *ResQ* 33: 65-73.

Feuillet, A. 1963. *L'Apocalypse. État de la question.* Studia Neotestamentica Subsidia 3. Paris: Desclée de Brouwer.

Fieger, M. 1998. *Im Schatten der Artemis. Glaube und Ungehorsam in Ephesus.* Bern: Peter Lang.

Filson, F. V. 1939. "The Significance of the Early House Churches." *JBL* 58: 109-12.

_____. 1945. "Ephesus and the New Testament." *BA* 8: 73-80.

Finegan, J. 1956. "The Original Form of the Pauline Collection." *HTR* 49: 85-103.

_____. 1981. *The Archaeology of the New Testament. The Mediterranean World of the Early Christian Apostles.* Boulder. Colordo: Westview Press.

Fiore, B. 1986. *The Function of Personal Example in the Socratic and Pastoral Epistles.* AnBib 105. Rome: Biblical Institute Press.

Fitzgerald, J. T. 1988. *Cracks in an Earthen Vessel: An Examination of the Catalogues of Hardships in the Corinthian Correspondence.* SBLDS 99. Georgia: Scholars Press.

Fitzmyer, J. A. 1971. *Essays on the Semitic Background of the New Testament.* London: Geoffrey Chapman.

_____. 1989. *Paul and His Theology. A Brief Sketch.* 2nd ed.; Englewood Cliffs: Prentice Hall.

_____. 1993. *Romans. A New Translation with Introduction and Commentary.* AB. New York: Doubleday.

_____. 1998. *The Acts of the Apostles. A New Translation with Introduction and Commentary.* AB. New York: Doubleday.

_____. 2000. *The Letter to Philemon. A New Translation with Introduction and Commentary*. AB. New York: Doubleday.

Fitzpatrick-McKinley, A. 2002. "Synagogue Communities in the Graeco-Roman Cities." In *Jews in the Hellenistic and Roman Cities*, ed. J.R. Bartlett:55-87. London, New York: Routledge.

Fleischer, R. 1973. *Artemis von Ephesus und verwandte Kultstatuen aus Anatolien und Syrien*. EPRO 35. Leiden: E.J. Brill.

_____. 1999. "Neues zum Kultbild der Artemis von Ephesos." In *100 Jahre Österreichische Forschungen in Ephesos. Akten des Symposions Wien 1995*, ed. H. Friesinger, Krinzinger, F.:605-9. Wien: Verlag der Österreichischen Akademie der Wissenschaften.

Forbes, C. A. 1936. "Books for the Burning." *TAPA* 67: 114-25.

Ford, J. M. 1970-71. "A Note on Proto-Monatanism in the Pastoral Epistles." *NTS* 17: 338-46.

_____. 1975. *Revelation*. AB. Garden City: Doubleday.

Foss, C. 1979. *Ephesus after Antiquity: A Late Antique, Byzantine and Turkish City*. Cambridge: Cambridge University Press.

Fox, K.A. 1994. "The Nicolaitans, Nicolaus and the early Church." *SR* 23: 485-96.

Fraser, P.M., Matthews, E. 1987. *A Lexicon of Greek Personal Names. Volume 1 The Aegean Islands, Cyprus, Cyrenaica*. Oxford: Clarendon Press.

_____. 1997. *A Lexicon of Greek Personal Names, Vol IIIA The Peloponnese, Western Greece, Sicily and Magna Graecia*. Oxford: Clarendon Press.

Frend, W. H. C. 1984. *The Rise of Christianity*. London: Darton Longman and Todd.

Friedrich, N.P. 2002. "Adapt or Resist? A Socio-Political Reading of Revelation 2.18-29." *JSNT* 25.2: 185-211.

Friesen, S. J. 1993a. *Twice Neokoros. Ephesus, Asia and the Cult of the Flavian Imperial Family*. Religions in the Graeco-Roman World 116. Leiden: E.J. Brill.

_____. 1993b. "Ephesus: Key to a Vision in Revelation." *BAR* 19, no. 3: 24-37.

_____. 1995a. "The Cult of the Roman Emperors in Ephesos: Temple Wardens, City Titles, and the Interpretation of the Revelation of John." In *Ephesos: Metropolis of Asia. An Interdisciplinary Approach to its Archaeology, Religion, and Culture*, ed. H. Koester:229-50. Valley Forge, Pennsylvania: Trinity Press International.

_____. 1995b. "Revelation, Realia, and Religion: Archaeology in the Interpretation of the Apocalypse." *HTR* 88: 291-314.

_____. 1999a. "Ephesian Women and Men in Public Office during the Roman Imperial Period." In *100 Jahre Österreichische Forschungen in Ephesos. Akten des Symposions Wien 1995*, ed. H. Friesinger, Krinzinger, F.:107-113. Wien: Verlag der Österreichischen Akademie der Wissenschaften.

_____. 1999b. "Highpriests of Asia and Asiarchs: Farewell to the Identification Theory." In *Steine und Weg: Festschrift für Dieter Knibbe zum 65. Geburtstag*, ed. P. Scherrer, Taeuber, H., Thür, H.:303-7. Wien: Österreichisches Archäologisches Institut.

_____. 1999c. "Asiarchs." *ZPE* 126: 275-90.

_____. 2001. *Imperial Cults and the Apocalypse of John. Reading Revelation in the Ruins*. New York, Oxford: Oxford University Press.

Fung, R. Y. K. 1984. "Function or Office: a Survey of the New Testament Evidence." *Evangelical Review of Theology* 8: 16-39.

Funk, R.W. 1967. "The Form and Structure of II and III John." *JBL* 86: 424-30.

Furnish, V. P. 1979. *The Moral Teaching of Paul*. Nashville: Abingdon Press.

_____. 1984. *II Corinthians*. AB. New York: Doubleday & Co.

Gamble, H. 1977. *The Textual History of the Letter to the Romans: A Study in Textual and Literary Criticism*. SD. Grand Rapids, Michigan: Eerdmans.

Gardner, P. 1915. *The Ephesian Gospel*. London: Williams and Norgate.

Garrett, S. R. 1989. *The Demise of the Devil. Magic and the Demonic in Luke's Writings*. Minneapolis: Fortress Press.

_____. 1998. "Revelation." In *Women's Bible Commentary*, ed. C.A. Newsom, Ringe, S.H.:469-74. Louisville, Kentucky: Westminster John Knox Press.

Garrison, R. 1993. *Redemptive Almsgiving in Early Christianity*. JSNTSS 77. Sheffield: JSOT Press.

Gasque, W. W. 1975. *A History of the Criticism of the Acts of the Apostles*. BGBE 17. Tübingen: J.C.B. Mohr (Paul Siebeck).

_____. 1989. "The Historical Valus of Acts." *TynBul* 40: 136-57.

Geer, T.C. 1993. "Admonitions to Women in 1 Tim. 2:8-15." In *Essays on Women in Earliest Christianity. Volume One*, ed. C.D. Osburn:281-302. Joplin, Missouri: College Press.

Gempf, C.H. 1988. *Historical and Literary Appropriateness in the Mission Speeches of Paul in Acts*. PhD Thesis, University of Aberdeen.

Genouillac, H. de. 1907. *L'Église Chrétienne au temps de Saint Ignace d'Antioche*. Paris: Beauchesne.

Georgi, D. 1986. *The Opponents of Paul in Second Corinthians*. Studies of the NT and its World. Edinburgh: T & T Clark.

Gibaut, J.St.H. 2000. *The Cursus Honorum. A Study of the Origins and Evolution of Sequential Ordination*. Patristic Studies 3. New York: Peter Lang.

Gibbard, S. M. 1966. "The Eucharist in the Ignatian Epistles." In *Studia Patristica Vol VIII*, ed. F.L. Cross, part II:214-8. Berlin: Akademie-Verlag.

Gielen, M. 1986. "Zur Intrepretation der paulinischen Formel ἡ κατ᾽ οἶκον ἐκκλησία." *ZNW* 77: 109-25.

Giles, K.N. 1989. *Patterns of Ministry Among the First Christians*. North Blackburn, Victoria: Collins Dove.

_____. 1995. *What on Earth is the Church? A Biblical and Theological Inquiry*. London: SPCK.

_____. 1997. "Church Order, Government." In *Dictionary of the Later New Testament and Its Developments*, ed. P.H. Davids, Martin, R.P.:219-26. Downers Grove, Illinois: IVP.

Glare, P.G.W, ed. 1976. *Oxford Latin Dictionary*. Oxford: Clarendon Press.

González, J. L. 1990. *Faith and Wealth. A History of Early Christian Ideas on the Origin, Significance, and Use of Money*. San Francisco: Harper & Row.

Goodenough, E.R. 1953. *Jewish Symbols in the Greco-Roman Period, Volumes 2-3*. New York: Pantheon Books.

Goodspeed, E. J. 1933. *The Meaning of Ephesians*. Chicago: University of Chicago Press.

_____. 1937. *New Chapters in New Testament Study*. New York: Macmillan.

_____. 1951a. "Ephesians and the First Edition of Paul." *JBL* 70: 285-91.

_____. 1951b. "Phoebe's Letter of Introduction." *HTR* 44: 55-7.

Goranson, S. 1997. "Essene Polemic in the Apocalypse of John." In *Legal Texts and Legal Issues. Proceedings of the Second Meeting of the International Organization for Qumran Studies Cambridge 1995 Published in Honour of Joseph M. Baumgarten*, ed. M Bernstein, García Martínez, F. Kampen, J.:453-60. Leiden: Brill.

Gordon, J.D. 1997. *Sister or Wife? 1 Corinthians 7 and Cultural Anthropology*. JSNTSS 149. Sheffield: Sheffield Academic Press.

Goulder, M. 1996. "The Pastor's Wolves. Jewish Christian Visionaries behind the Pastoral Epistles." *NovT* 38: 242-56.

Graf, F. 1997. *Magic in the Ancient World*. Cambridge, Massachusetts: Harvard University Press.

Grant, F. C. 1950. *An Introduction to New Testament Thought*. New York: Abingdon Press.

Grant, R. M. 1946. *Second-Century Christianity. A Collection of Fragments*. London: SPCK.

_____. 1964. *The Apostolic Fathers. A New Translation and Commentary. Volume 1. An Introduction*. New York: Thomas Nelson & Sons.

_____. 1966. *The Apostolic Fathers. A New Translation and Commentary. Volume 4. Ignatius of Antioch*. N.J.: Thomas Nelson & Sons.

Grayston, K. 1984. *The Johannine Epistles*. NCB. Grand Rapids, Michigan: Eerdmans.

Griffith, T. 1998. "A Non-Polemical Reading of 1 John: Sin, Christology and the Limits of Johannine Christianity." *TynBul* 49: 253-76.

Griggs, C. W. 1990. *Early Egyptian Christianity from its origin to 451 C.E.* Coptic Studies 2. Leiden: Brill.

Gritz, S. H. 1991. *Paul, Women Teachers, and the Mother Goddess at Ephesus: A Study of 1 Timothy 2:9-15 in Light of The Religious and Cultural Milieu of The First Century*. Lanham: University Press of America.

Grosheide, F. W. 1953. *Commentary on the First Epistle to the Corinthians*. NICNT|. Michigan: Eerdmans.

Grové, A.H. 2000. "Revelation 2 and 3 - Uniformly Structured or Not?" *Scriptura* 73: 193-210.

Gruen, E.S. 2002. *Diaspora. Jews amidst Greeks and Romans*. Cambridge, Massachusetts: Harvard University Press.

Grundmann, W. 1964. "Paulus in Ephesus." *Helikon* 4: 46-82.

Gryson, R. 1976. *The Ministry of Women in the Early Church*. Collegeville, Minnesota: The Liturgical Press.

Gundry, R. H. 1970. "The Form, Meaning and Background of the Hymn Quoted in 1 Timothy 3,16." In *Apostolic History and the Gospel*, ed. W.W. Gasque, Martin, R.P.:203-22. Exeter: Paternoster Press.

_____. 2002. *Jesus the Word According to John the Sectarian*. Grand Rapids, Michigan: Eerdmans.

Gunther, J. J. 1972. *Paul: Messenger and Exile: A Study in the Chronology of His Life and Letters*. Valley Forge: Judson.

_____. 1973. *St Paul's Opponents and Their Background. A Study of Apocalyptic and Jewish Sectarian Teachings*. NovTSup 35. Leiden: E.J. Brill.

_____. 1979. "The Alexandrian Gospel and Letters of John." *CBQ* 41: 581-603.

_____. 1980. "Early Identifications of Authorship in the Johannine Writings." *JEH* 31: 407-27.

Günther, M. 1995. *Die Frühgeschichte des Christentums in Ephesus*. Arbeiten zur Religion und Geschichte des Urchristentums 1. Frankfurt am Main: Peter Lang.

_____. 1999. "Die paulinische Mission in Ephesos." In *100 Jahre Österreichische Forschungen in Ephesos. Akten des Symposions Wien 1995*, ed. H. Friesinger, Krinzinger, F.:289-95. Wien: Verlag der Österreichischen Akademie der Wissenschaften.

Habicht, C. 1975. "New Evidence on the Province of Asia." *JRS* 65: 64-91.

Hack Polaski, S. 1999. *Paul and the Discourse of Power*. Gender, Culture, Theory 8; The Biblical Seminar 62. Sheffield: Sheffield Academic Press.

Hadas, M. 1953. *Three Greek Romances*. Indianapolis: Bobbs-Merrill.

Haenchen, E. 1971. *The Acts of the Apostles. A Commentary*. Oxford: Basil Blackwell.

Hägerland, T. 2003. "John's Gospel: A Two-Level Drama?" *JSNT* 25.3: 309-322.

Hahn, F. 1971. "Die Sendschreiben der Johannesapokalypse. Ein Beitrag zur Bestimmung prophetischer Redeformen." In *Tradition und Glaube. Das frühe Christentum in seiner Umwelt. Festgabe für Karl Georg Kuhn zum 65. Geburtstag*, eds. G. Jeremias, Kuhn, H.W., Stegemann, H.:357-94. Göttingen: Vandenhoeck & Ruprecht.

Hall, D.R. 1973-74. "Fellow-Workers with the Gospel." *ExpTim* 85: 119-20.

Hallett, J.P. 1999. "Women's Lives in the Ancient Mediterranean." In *Women and Christian Origins*, ed. R.S. Kraemer, D'Angelo, M.R.:13-34. New York, Oxford: Oxford University Press.

Halleux, A. de. 1982. "'L'Église Catholique' dans la lettre Ignacienne aux Smyrniotes." *ETL* 58: 5-24.

Hann, R. R. 1987. "Judaism and Jewish Christianity in Antioch: Charisma and Conflict in the First Century." *JRH* 14: 341-60.

Hanson, A. T. 1968. *Studies in the Pastoral Epistles*. London: SPCK.

_____. 1981. "The Domestication of Paul: A Study in the Development of Early Christian Theology." *BJRL* 63: 402-18.

_____. 1982. *The Pastoral Epistles*. NCB. Grand Rapids, Michigan: Eerdmans.

Harding, M. 2001. *What Are They Saying About the Pastoral Epistles?* New York: Paulist Press.

Harland, P.A. 1996. "Honours and worship: Emperors, imperial cults and associations at Ephesus (first to third centuries C.E.)." *SR* 25: 319-334.

_____. 2000. "Honouring the Emperor or Assailing the Beast: Participation in Civic Life Among Associations (Jewish, Christian and Other) in Asia Minor and the Apocalypse of John." *JSNT* 77: 99-121.

Harrington, D. J. 1973. "The 'Early Catholic' Writings of the New Testament: The Church Adjusting to World-History." In *The Word in the World. Essays in Honor of Frederick L. Moriarty S.J.*, ed. R.J. Clifford, MacRae, G.W.:97-113. Cambridge, Massachusetts: Weston College Press.

_____. 1982. *Light of All Nations. Essays on the Church in New Testament Research*. Wilmington, Delaware: Michael Glazier.

_____. 1996. *Wisdom Texts from Qumran*. London and New York: Routledge.

_____. 1997. "Ten Reasons Why the Qumran Wisdom Texts are Important." *DSD* 4: 245-54.

Harris, M. J. 1970. *The Interpretation of 2 Corinthians 5:1-10, and its Place in Pauline Eschatology*. PhD Thesis, University of Manchester.

_____. 1971. "2 Corinthians 5:1-10: Watershed in Paul's Eschatology?" *TynBul* 22: 32-57.

_____. 1992. *Jesus as God. The New Testament Use of Theos in Reference to Jesus*. Grand Rapids, Michigan: Baker.

Harrison, P. N. 1921. *The Problem of the Pastoral Epistles*. Oxford: Oxford University Press.

_____. 1936. *Polycarp's Two Epistles to the Philippians*. Cambridge: Cambridge University Press.

_____. 1955. "Important Hypotheses Reconsidered: The Authorship of the Pastoral Epistles." *ExpTim* 67: 77-81.

_____. 1955-56a. "The Authorship of the Pastoral Epistles." *ExpTim* 67: 77-81.

_____. 1955-56b. "The Pastoral Epistles and Duncan's Ephesian Theory." *NTS* 2: 250-61.

Harrisville, R. A. 1987. *1 Corinthians*. ACNT. Minnesota: Augsburg.

Hartman, L. 1996. "Hellenistic Elements in Apocalyptic Texts." In *The New Testament in Its Hellenistic Context. Proceedings of a Nordic Conference of New Testament Scholars, held in Skálholt*, ed. G.A. Jónsson:113-133. Reykjavík: Gudfraedistofnun Háskóla Islands.

Hartman, L, Olsson, B. 1997. *"Into the Name of the Lord Jesus". Baptism in the Early Church*. Studies of the New Testament and its World. Edinburgh: T & T Clark.

Hartog, P. 2002. *Polycarp and the New Testament. The Occasion, Rhetoric, Theme, and Unity of the Epistle to the Philippians and its Allusions to New Testament Literature*. WUNT 2.134. Tübingen: Mohr Siebeck.

Harvey, A.E. 1974. "Elders." *JTS* ns 25: 318-32.

_____. 1976. *Jesus on Trial. A Study in the Fourth Gospel*. London: SPCK.

Hasler, V. 1977. "Epiphanie und Christologie in den Pastoralbriefen." *TZ* 33: 193-209.

Hawthorne, G. F. 1983. *Philippians*. WBC. Texas: Word.

Haykin, M.A.G. 1985. "The Fading Vision? The Spirit and Freedom in the Pastoral Epistles." *EvQ* 57: 291-305.

Hays, R.B. 1997. *First Corinthians*. IBC. Louisville, Kentucky: John Knox Press.

Head, B.V. 1880. *On the Chronological Sequence of the Coins of Ephesus*. Chicago: Obol International.

_____. 1892. *Catalogue of the Greek Coins of Ionia Catalogue of the Greek Coins in the British Museum: Ephesus*. London: British Museum.

Heberdey, R. 1904. "Vorläufiger Bericht über die Grabungen in Ephesus 1902/3." *JÖAI* 7: 38-55.

Heberdey, R., Niemann, G., Wilberg, W. 1912. *Das Theatre in Ephesos*. FiE 2. Wien: Alfred Holder.

Heckel, U. 1993. *Kraft in Schwachheit. Untersuchungen zu 2. Kor 10-13*. WUNT 2. Reihe 56. Tübingen: J.C.B. Mohr (Paul Siebeck).

Heiligenthal, von R. 1991. "Wer Waren die 'Nikolaiten'? Ein Beitrag zur Theologiegeschichte des frühen Christentums." *ZNW* 82: 133-7.

Helton, S.N. 1993. "Titus 2:5 - Must Women Stay at Home?" In *Essays on Women in Earliest Christianity. Volume One*, ed. C.D. Osburn:367-76. Joplin, Missouri: College Press.

Hemer, C. J. 1972. "A Note on 2 Corinthians 1:9." *TynBul* 23: 103-7.

_____. 1973. "Audeitorion." *TynBul* 24: 128.

_____. 1975. "Unto the Angels of the Churches. 1. Introduction and Ephesus." *BurH* 11: 4-27.

_____. 1977. "Luke the Historian." *BJRL* 60: 28-51.

_____. 1986. *The Letters to the Seven Churches of Asia in Their Local Setting*. JSNTSS 11. Sheffield: JSOT Press.

_____. 1989a. *The Book of Acts in the Setting of Hellenistic History*. Edited by C.H. Gempf. Tübingen: J.C.B. Mohr (Paul Siebeck).

_____. 1989b. "The Speeches of Acts I: The Ephesian Elders at Miletus." *TynBul* 40: 77-85.

Hempel, C., Lange, A., Lichtenberger, H. eds. 2002. *The Wisdom Texts from Qumran and the Development of Sapiential Thought*. BETL 159. Leuven: Leuven University Press; Uitgeverij Peeters.

Hengel, M. 1974. *Property and Riches in the Early Church. Aspects of a Social History of Early Christianity*. London: SCM Press.

_____. 1979. *Acts and the History of Earliest Christianity*. London: SCM Press.

_____. 1989. *The Johannine Question*. London: SCM Press.

_____. 1991. *The Pre-Christian Paul.* London; Philadelphia: SCM Press; TPI.

_____. 1993. *Die johanneische Frage. Ein Lösungsversuch mit einem Beitrag zur Apokalypse von J. Frey.* WUNT 67. Tübingen: J.C.B. Mohr (Paul Siebeck).

_____. 2000a. "Ἰουδαία in the Geographical List of Acts 2:9-11 and Syria as "Greater Judea"." *BBR* 10: 161-80.

_____. 2000b. "Die »auserwählte Herrin«. Die »Braut«, die »Mutter« und die »Gottesstadt«." In *La Cité de Dieu, Die Stadt Gottes,* ed. M. Hengel, Mittmann, S., Schwemer, A.M.:245-85. Tübingen: Mohr Siebeck.

Henneck, Schneemelcher. 1964. *New Testament Apocrypha.* Philadelphia: Westminster Press.

Héring, J. 1956. "Y a-t-il des aramaïsmes dans la première épître johannique?" *RHPR* 36: 113-21.

_____. 1962. *The First Epistle of Saint Paul to the Corinthians.* London: Epworth Press.

_____. 1967. *The Second Epistle of Saint Paul to the Corinthians.* London: Epworth Press.

Hicks, E. L. 1890a. *The Collection of Ancient Greek Inscriptions in the British Museum. Part III, Priene, Iasos and Ephesus.* Oxford: Clarendon Press.

_____. 1890b. "Demetrius the Silversmith. An Ephesian Study." *The Expositor, Fourth Series* 1: 401-22.

_____. 1890c. "Ephesus, A Postscript." *The Expositor, Fourth Series* 2: 144-9.

Hill, C.E. 2000. "Cerinthus, Gnostic or Chiliast? A New Solution to an Old Problem." *JECS* 8: 135-72.

Hill, D. 1971-72. "Prophecy and Prophets in The Revelation of St John." *NTS* 18: 401-18.

_____. 1979. *New Testament Prophecy.* London: Marshall, Morgan and Scott.

Hills, J.V. 1989. "'Little children, keep yourselves from idols'. 1 John 5,21 Reconsidered." *CBQ* 51: 285-310.

_____. 1991. "A Genre for 1 John." In *The Future of Early Christianity. Essays in Honor of Helmut Koester,* ed. B. A. Pearson, in collaboration with A.T. Kraabel, G.W.E. Nickelsburg, N.R. Petersen:367-77. Minneapolis: Fortress Press.

Hirschberg, P. 1999. *Das eschatologische Israel. Untersuchungen zum Gottesvolkverständnis der Johannesoffenbarung.* WMANT 84. Neukirchen-Vluyn: Neukirchener Verlag.

Hitchcock, F. R. M. 1925. "Who are 'The People of Chloe' in 1 Cor. i 11." *JTS* 25: 163-7.

Hock, R. F. 1980. *The Social Context of Paul's Ministry: Tentmaking and Apostleship.* Philadelphia: Fortress Press.

Hoffman, T. A. 1978. "I John and the Qumran Scrolls." *BTB* 8: 117-25.

Hogarth, D.G. et al. 1908. *Excavations at Ephesus. The Archaic Artemision.* London: British Museum.

Hollenbach, P. 1987. "Defining Rich and Poor Using Social Sciences." In *SBLSP 1987,* ed. K.H. Richards:50-63. Atlanta, Georgia: Scholars Press.

Holman, C. L. 1996. "Titus 3.5-6: A Window on Worldwide Pentecost." *Journal of Pentecostal Theology* 8: 53-62.

Holmberg, B. 1978. *Paul and Power. The Structure of Authority in the Primitive Church as Reflected in the Pauline Epistles.* ConBibNT 11. Lund: CWK Gleerup.

_____. 1998. "Jewish *Versus* Christian Identity in the Early Church?" *RB* 105: 397-425.

Hopkins, K. 1998. "Christian Number and Its Implications." *JECS* 6: 185-226.

Horbury, W., Noy, D. 1992. *Jewish Inscriptions of Graeco-Roman Egypt.* Cambridge: Cambridge University Press.

Horrell, D.G. 2001. "From ἀδελφοί to οἶκος θεοῦ: Social Transformation in Pauline Christianity." *JBL* 120: 293-311.

Horsley, G. H. R. 1992a. "The Inscriptions of Ephesos and the New Testament." *NovT*34: 105-168.

————. 1992b. "The Mysteries of Artemis Ephesia in Pisidia: A New Inscribed Relief." *AnSt* 42: 119-50.

Hort, F. J. A. 1908. *The Apocalypse of St John I-III. The Greek Text with Introduction, Commentary and Additional Notes.* London: Macmillan and Co.

Horvath, T. 1973-74. "3 Jn 11b: An Early Ecumenical Creed?" *ExpTim* 85: 339-40.

Houlden, J. L. 1973. *A Commentary on the Johannine Epistles.* BNTC Series. London: A & C Black.

Hübner, R.M. 1997. "Thesen zur Echtheit und Datierung der sieben Briefe des Ignatius von Antiochen." *ZAC* 1: 44-72.

Hueber, F. 1997a. *Ephesos: gebaute Geschichte.* Zaberns Bildbände zur Archäologie. Mainz am Rhein: von Zabern.

————. 1997b. "Zur städtebaulichen Entwicklung des hellenistisch-römischen Ephesos." *MDAI, Istanbul Abteilung* 47: 251-69.

Huffman, N. A. 1978. "Atypical Features in the Parables of Jesus." *JBL* 97: 207-20.

Hugenberger, G. P. 1992. "Women in Church Office: Hermeneutics or Exegesis? A Survey of Approaches to 1 Tim 2:8-15." *JETS* 35: 341-60.

Hughes, J.H. 1972. "John the Baptist: The Forerunner of God Himself." *NovT*14: 191-218.

Hultgren, A. J. 1994. *The Rise of Normative Christianity.* Minneapolis: Fortress Press.

Hultgren, A. J., Haggmark, S.A., ed. 1996. *The Earliest Christian Heretics. Readings from Their Opponents.* Minneapolis: Fortress Press.

Hultgren, A. J. Aus R. 1984. *1-11 Timothy, Titus, II Thessalonians.* ACNT. Minneapolis: Augsburg.

Hunkin, J. W. 1927. "1 Corinthians 15:32." *ExpTim* 39: 281-2.

Hurd, J. C. 1965. *The Origin of 1 Corinthians.* London: SPCK.

Hutaff, M.D. 1994. "The Johannine Epistles." In *Searching the Scriptures. Volume Two: A Feminist Commentary,* ed. E. Schüssler Fiorenza:406-27. New York: Crossroad.

Hutnik, N. 1991. *Ethnic Minority Identity. A Social Psychological Perspective.* Oxford: Clarendon Press.

Ingle, H.L. 1994. *First Among Friends. George Fox and the Creation of Quakerism.* New York; Oxford: Oxford University Press.

Jack, A. 2002. "Out of the Wilderness: Feminist Perspectives on the Book of Revelation." In *Studies in the Book of Revelation,* ed. S. Moyise:149-162. Edinburgh & New York: T & T Clark.

Jay, E. G. 1981. "From Presbyter-Bishops to Bishops and Presbyters. Christian Ministry in the Second Century: A Survey." *SecCent* 1: 125-62.

Jeffers, J. S. 1991. *Conflict at Rome: Social Order and Hierarchy in Early Christianity.* Minneapolis: Fortress.

Jefford, C. N. 1989. "Presbyters in the Community of the Didache." In *Studia Patristica Vol XXI,* ed. E.A. Livingstone:122-8. Leuven: Peeters Press.

Jewett, R. 1979. *Dating Paul's Life.* London: SCM Press.

————. 1988. "Paul, Phoebe and the Spanish Mission." In *The Social World of Formative Christianity and Judaism. Essays in Tribute to Howard Clark Kee,* ed. J. Neusner, Frerichs, E.S., Borgen, P., Horsley, R.:142-61. Philadelphia: Fortress Press.

Jobst, W. 1977. *Römischen Mosaiken aus Ephesos I. Die Hanghäuser des Embolos.* FiE 8.2. Wien: Österreichischen Akademie der Wissenschaften.

Johanny, R. 1978. "Ignatius of Antioch." In *The Eucharist of the Early Christians,* ed. W. Rordorf et al: 48-70. New York: Pueblo Publishing Company.

Johnson, L. T. 1978-79. "II Timothy and the Polemic Against False Teachers: A Re-examination." *JRelS* 6-7: 1-26.
_____. 1986. *The Writings of the New Testament: An Interpretation*. Philadelphia: Fortress Press.
_____. 1987. *1 Timothy, 2 Timothy, Titus*. Knox Preaching Guides. Atlanta: John Knox Press.
_____. 1992. *The Acts of the Apostles*. SP. Collegeville, Minnesota: The Liturgical Press.
_____. 1996. *Letters to Paul's Delegates: 1 Timothy, 2 Timothy, Titus*. The NT in Context. Valley Forge: Trinity Press International.
_____. 2001. *The First and Second Letters to Timothy. A New Translation with Introduction and Commentary*. AB. New York: Doubleday.
Johnson, S. E. 1972. "Unsolved Questions about Early Christianity in Anatolia." In *Studies in New Testament and Early Christian Literature*, ed. D. E. Aune: 181-93. NovTSup 33, Leiden: Brill.
_____. 1975. "Asia Minor and Early Christianity." In *Judaism, Christianity and Other Graeco-Roman Cults: Studies for Mortin Smith at Sixty*, ed. J. Neusner, 2:77-145. SJLA 12, Leiden: Brill.
_____. 1979. "The Apostle Paul and the Riot in Ephesus." *LTQ* 14: 79-88.
_____. 1987a. *Paul the Apostle and His Cities*. Wilmington: Michael Glazier.
_____. 1987b. "Parallels Between the Letters of Ignatius and the Johannine Epistles." In *Perspectives on Language and Text. Essays and Poems in Honor of Francis I. Andersen's Sixtieth Birthday July 28, 1985*, ed. E.W. Conrad, Newing, E.G.:327-38. Winona Lake, Indiana: Eisenbrauns.
Jones, A.H.M. 1971. *The Cities of the Eastern Roman Provinces*. Oxford: Clarendon Press.
Jones, C.P. 1978. *The Roman World of Dio Chrysostom*. Cambridge, Massachuesetts: Harvard University Press.
_____. 1986. *Culture and Society in Lucian*. Cambridge, Massachusetts: Harvard University Press.
Jones, P. R. 1970. "A Structural Analysis of 1 John." *RevExp* 67: 433-44.
Jones, S. 1998. "Identities in Practice: Towards an Archaeological Perspective on Jewish Identity in Antiquity." In *Jewish Local Patriotism and Self-Identification in the Graeco-Roman Period*, ed. S. Jones, Pearce, S.:29-49. Sheffield: Sheffield Academic Press.
Joubert, S. 2000. *Paul as Benefactor. Reciprocity, Strategy and Theological Reflection in Paul's Collection*. WUNT 2.124. Tübingen: Mohr Siebeck.
Joüon, P. 1938. "1 Jean 2,16: he alazoneia tou biou. 'La présomption des richesses'." *RSR* 28: 479-81.
Judge, E. A. 1961. "The Early Christians as a Scholastic Community: Part II." *JRH* 1: 125-137.
_____. 1969. *The Social Patterns of Christian Groups in the First Century*. London: Tyndale Press.
_____. 1980. "The Social Identity of the First Christians: A Question of Method in Religious History." *JRH* 11: 201-17.
_____. 1991. "The Mark of the Beast, Revelation 13:16." *TynBul* 42: 158-60.
Juel, D. 1988. "Episkopé in the New Testament." *LQ* n.s. 2: 343-56.
Junod, E., Kaestli, J.-D. 1983. *Acta Iohannis*. Corpus Christianorum Series Apocryphorum 1-2. Brepols: Turnhout.
Kaiser, C. B. 1977. "The 'Rebaptism' of the Ephesian Twelve: Exegetical Study on Acts 19:1-7." *RTR* 31: 57-61.

Kalantzis, G. 1997. "Ephesus as a Roman, Christian, and Jewish Metropolis in the First and Second Centuries C.E." *Jian Dao* 8: 103-119.

Kalms, J.H. 2001. *Die Sturz des Gottesfeindes. Traditionsgeschichtliche Studien zu Apokalypse 12.* WMANT 93. Neukirchen-Vluyn: Neukirchener.

Kampen, J. 1986. "A Reconsideration of the Name 'Essene' in Greco-Jewish Literature in Light of Recent Perceptions of the Qumran Sect." *HUCA* 57: 61-81.

Kaplan, J., Bernays, A. 1997. *The Language of Names.* New York: Simon & Schuster.

Karrer, M. 1986. *Die Johannesoffenbarung als Brief. Studien zu ihrem literarischen, historischen und theologischen Ort.* FRLANT 140. Göttingen: Vandenhoeck & Ruprecht.

Karris, R. J. 1973. "The Background and Significance of the Polemic of the Pastoral Epistles." *JBL* 92: 549-64.

Karwiese, S. 1995a. "The Church of Mary and the Temple of Hadrian Olympius." In *Ephesos: Metropolis of Asia. An Interdisciplinary Approach to its Archaeology, Religion, and Culture*, ed. H. Koester:311-19. Valley Forge, Pennsylvania: Trinity Press International.

_____. 1995b. *Groß ist die Artemis von Ephesos. Die Geschichte einer der großen Städte der Antike.* Wien: Phoibos Verlag.

_____. 1999. "Gedanken zur Entstehung des römischen Ephesos." In *100 Jahre Österreichische Forschungen in Ephesos. Akten des Symposions Wien 1995*, ed. H. Friesinger, Krinzinger, F.:393-8. Wien: Verlag der Österreichischen Akademie der Wissenschaften.

Käsemann, E. 1964. *Essays on New Testament Themes.* London: SCM Press.

_____. 1980. *Commentary on Romans.* London: SCM Press.

Kearsley, R.A. 1994. "The Asiarchs." In *The Book of Acts in its Greco-Roman Setting*, ed. D.W.J. Gill, Gempf, C.:363-76. Grand Rapids, Michigan: Eerdmans.

_____. 1999. "Bilingual Inscriptions at Ephesos: The Statue Bases from the Harbour Gymnasium." In *100 Jahre Österreichische Forschungen in Ephesos. Akten des Symposions Wien 1995*, ed. H. Friesinger, Krinzinger, F.:147-55. Wien: Verlag der Österreichischen Akademie der Wissenschaften.

Keck, L.E. 1965. "The Poor among the Saints in the New Testament." *ZNW* 56: 100-129.

Keck, L. E., Martyn. J.L. 1966. *Studies in Luke-Acts.* Nashville: Abingdon Press.

Kee, H. C. 1980. *Christian Origins in Sociological Perspective.* London: SCM Press.

_____. 1986. *Medicine, Miracle and Magic in New Testament Times.* SNTSMS 55. Cambridge: Cambridge University Press.

Keil, J. 1905. "Ärzteinschriften aus Ephesos." *JÖAI* 8: 128-38.

_____. 1924. "Johannes von Ephesos und Polykarpos von Smyrna." In *Strena Bvliciana. Commentationes Gratvlatoriae Francisco Bulic*, ed. M. Abramic, Hoffiller, V.:367-72. Zagrebiae: Aspalathi.

_____. 1930. "XV. Vorläufiger Bericht über die Ausgrabungen in Ephesos." *JÖAI* 26, Beiblatt: 5-66.

_____. 1931. "Antike und Christentum in Ephesos." In *Von der Antike zum Christentum. Untersuchungen als Festgabe für Victor Schultze zum 80. Geburtstag*:95-102. Stettin: Verlag Fischer & Schmidt.

_____. 1939. "Kulte im Prytaneion von Ephesos." In *Anatolian Studies Presented to William Hepburn Buckler*, ed. W.M. Calder, Keil, J.:119-128. Manchester: Manchester University Press.

_____. 1940. "Ein rätselhaftes Amulett." *JÖAI (Beiblatt)* 32: 79-84.

_____. 1964. *Ephesos: Ein Führer durch die Ruinenstätte und ihre Geschichte.* Wien: Österreichisches Archäologisches Institut.

Kelly, J. N. D. 1963. *A Commentary on The Pastoral Epistles*. BNTC. London: A & C Black.

Ker, D.P. 2000. "Paul and Apollos - Colleagues of Rivals?" *JSNT* 77: 75-97.

Kidd, R. M. 1990. *Wealth and Beneficence in the Pastoral Epistles. A "Bourgeois" Form of Early Christianity?* SBLDS 122. Atlanta, Georgia: Scholars Press.

Kieffer, R. 2000. "La demeure divine dans le temple et sur l'autel chez Ignace d'Antioche." In *La Cité de Dieu, Die Stadt Gottes*, ed. M. Hengel, Mittmann, S., Schwemer, A.M.:287-301. Tübingen: Mohr Siebeck.

Kim, J.K. 1999. "'Uncovering Her Wickedness': An Inter(con)textual Reading of Revelation 17 from a Postcolonial Feminist Perspective." *JSNT* 73: 61-81.

Kirbihler, F. 1994. "Les femmes magistrats et liturges en Asie Mineure (IIe s. av. J.-C. - IIIe s. ap. J.-C.)." *Ktema* 19: 51-75.

Kirby, J. T. 1988. "The Rhetorical Situations of Revelation 1-3." *NTS* 34: 197-207.

Kistemaker, S. J. 1990. "The Speeches in Acts." *CTR* 5: 31-41.

Klassen, W. 1999. "The Ascetic Way: Reflections on Peace, Justice, and Vengeance in the Apocalypse of John." In *Asceticism and the New Testament*, ed. L.E. Vaage, Wimbush, V.L.:393-410. New York, London: Routledge.

Klauck, H. J. 1981. *Hausgemeinde und Hauskirche im frühen Christentum*. SBS 103. Stuttgart: Katholisches Bibelwerk.

————. 1984. *1. Korintherbrief*. Die Neue Echter Bible. Würzburg: Echter Verlag.

————. 1985. "Gemeinde ohne Amt? Erfahrungen mit der Kirche in den johanneischen Schriften." *BZ* 29: 193-220.

————. 1986. *2. Korintherbrief*. Die Neue Echter Bible. Würzburg: Echter Verlag.

————. 1988. "Internal opponents: the Treatment of the Secessionists in the First Epistle of John." In *Truth and Its Victims*, ed. W. Beuken, Freyne, S., Weiler, A.:55-65. Edinburgh: T & T Clark.

————. 1990. "Κυρία ἐκκλησία in Bauer's Wörterbuch und die Exegese des zweiten Johannesbriefes." *ZNW* 81: 135-8.

————. 1991. *Der Erste Johannesbrief*. EKKNT. Zürich; Neukirchen-Vluyn: Benziger Verlag; Neukirchener Verlag.

————. 1992. "Das Sendschreiben nach Pergamon und die Kaiserkult in der Johannesoffenbarung." *Bib* 73: 153-82.

————. 2000. *The Religious Context of Early Christianity. A Guide to Graeco-Roman Religions*. Studies of the New Testament and its World. Edinburgh: T & T Clark.

Klein, G. 1961. *Die Zwölf Apostel, Ursprung und Gehalt einer Idee*. FRLANT Neue Folge 59. Göttingen: Vandenhoeck & Ruprecht.

Klijn, A. F. J. and G. J. Reinink. 1973. *Patristic Evidence For Jewish Christian Sects*. E.J. Brill: Leiden.

Kloppenborg, J.S. 1996. "Egalitarianism in the Myth and Rhetoric of Pauline Churches." In *Reimagining Christian Origins. A Colloquium Honoring Burton L. Mack*, ed. E.A. Castelli, Taussig, H.:247-63. Valley Forge, PA: Trinity Press International.

Knibbe, D. 1978. "Ephesos - nicht nur die Stadt der Artemis. Die 'anderen' ephesischen Götter." In *Studien zur Religion und Kultur Kleinasiens. Festschrift für Friedrich Karl Dörner*, ed. S. Sahin, Schwertheim, E., Wagner, J.: 2, 489-503. Leiden: E.J. Brill.

————. 1981. *Der Staatsmarkt. Die Inschriften des Prytaneions*. FiE 9.1.1. Wien: Österreichischen Akademie der Wissenschaften.

_____. 1995. *"Via Sacra Ephesiaca*: New Aspects of the Cult of Artemis Ephesia." In *Ephesos: Metropolis of Asia. An Interdisciplinary Approach to its Archaeology, Religion, and Culture*, ed. H. Koester:141-55. Valley Forge, Pennsylvania: Trinity Press International.

Knibbe, D., Alzinger, W. 1980. "Ephesos vom Beginn der römischen Herrschaft in Kleinasien bis zum Ende der Principatszeit." In *ANRW*, II.7.2:748-830. Berlin: Walter de Gruyter.

Knibbe, D., Büyükkolanci, M. 1989. "Zur Bauinschrift der Basilica auf dem sog. Staatsmarkt von Ephesos." *JÖAI* 59: 43-5.

Knibbe, D., Engelmann, H., Iplikçioglu, B. 1989. "Neue Inscriften aus Ephesos XI." *JÖAI (Beiblatt)* 59: 161-238.

_____. 1993. "Neue Inschriften aus Ephesos XII." *JÖAI* 62: 113-50.

Knibbe, D., Iplikçioglu, B. 1984. "Neue Inschriften aus Ephesos IX." *JÖAI* 55: 107-49.

Knibbe, D., Meriç, R., Merkelbach, R. 1979. "Der Grundbesitz der ephesischen Artemis im Kaystrostal." *ZPE* 33: 139-47.

Knight, G. W. 1968. *The Faithful Sayings in the Pastoral Letters*. The Netherlands: J.H. Kok.

_____. 1992. *The Pastoral Epistles. A Commentary on the Greek Text*. NIGTC. Grand Rapids, Michigan: Eerdmans.

Knox, J. 1960. *Philemon Among the Letters of Paul*. London: Collins.

_____. 1987. *Chapters in a Life of Paul*. Macon, GA: Mercer University Press.

Knox, W. L. 1925. *St Paul and the Church of Jerusalem*. Cambridge: Cambridge University Press.

_____. 1939. *St Paul and the Church of the Gentiles*. Cambridge: Cambridge University Press.

Koenig, J. 1985. *New Testament Hospitality. Partnership with Strangers as Promise and Mission*. OBT. Philadelphia: Fortress Press.

Koester, H. 1965. "History and Cult in the Gospel of John and in Ignatius of Antioch." *JTC* 1: 111-23.

_____. 1971. "GNOMAI DIAPHORA: The Origin and Nature of Diversification in the History of Early Christianity." In *Trajectories Through Early Christianity*, ed. H. Koester, Robinson, J.M.:114-57. Philadelphia: Fortress.

_____. 1992. "The Story of the Johannine Tradition." *STRev* 36: 17-32.

_____. 1995a. *Introduction to the New Testament Volume One: History, Culture and Religion of the Hellenistic Age*. New York, Berlin: Walter de Gruyter.

_____. 1995b. "Ephesos in Early Christian Literature." In *Ephesos: Metropolis of Asia. An Interdisciplinary Approach to its Archaeology, Religion, and Culture*, ed. H. Koester:119-40. Valley Forge, Pennsylvania: Trinity Press International.

_____. 1999. "Ephesos und Paulus in der frühchristlichen Literatur." In *100 Jahre Österreichische Forschungen in Ephesos. Akten des Symposions Wien 1995*, ed. H. Friesinger, Krinzinger, F.:297-305. Wien: Verlag der Österreichischen Akademie der Wissenschaften.

_____. 2000. *Introduction to the New Testament Volume Two: History and Literature of Early Christianity*. New York; Berlin: Walter de Gruyter.

Kosmetatou, E. 1999. "The Mint of Ephesos under the Attalids of Pergamon (202-133 BC)." In *100 Jahre Österreichische Forschungen in Ephesos. Akten des Symposions Wien 1995*, ed. H. Friesinger, Krinzinger, F.:185-93. Wien: Verlag der Österreichischen Akademie der Wissenschaften.

Köstenberger, A. J. 1995. "A Complex Sentence Structure in 1 Timothy 2:12." In *Women in the Church. A Fresh Analysis of 1 Timothy 2:9-15*, ed. A. J. Köstenberger, Schreiner, T.R., Baldwin, H.S.:81-103. Grand Rapids, Michigan: Baker Books.

Kraabel, A.T. 1968. *Judaism in Western Asia Minor under the Roman Empire with a Preliminary Study of the Jewish Community at Sardis, Lydia.* D.Th. Thesis, Harvard University.

Kraemer, R.S. 1989. "On the meaning of the term 'Jew' in Graeco-Roman Inscriptions." *HTR* 82: 35-53.

————. 1992. *Her Share of the Blessings. Women's Religions among Pagans, Jews, and Christians in the Greco-Roman World.* New York, Oxford: Oxford University Press.

Kraft, H. 1955. "Die altkirchliche Prophetie und die Entstehung des Montanismus." *TZ* 11: 249-71.

————. 1974. *Die Offenbarung des Johannes.* HNT 16a. Tübingen: J.C.B. Mohr (Paul Siebeck).

Kraft, J.C., Kayan, I., Brückner, H., Rapp, G. 2000. "A Geologic Analysis of Ancient Landscapes and the Harbors of Ephesus and the Artemision in Anatolia." *JÖAI* 69: 175-233.

Kraybill, J.N. 1996. *Imperial Cult and Commerce in John's Apocalypse.* JSNTSS 132. Sheffield: Sheffield Academic Press.

Kreitzer, L. J. 1987. "A Numismatic Clue to Acts 19:23-41: The Ephesian Cistophori of Claudius and Agrippina." *JSNT* 30: 59-70.

————. 1998. "The Plutonium of Hierapolis and the Descent of Christ into the 'Lowermost Parts of the Earth' (Ephesians 4,9)." *Bib* 79: 381-93.

Kroeger, R. C., Kroeger, C.C. 1993. *I Suffer Not a Woman. Rethinking 1 Timothy 2:11-15 in Light of Ancient Evidence.* Grand Rapids: Baker.

Kroll, J.H. 2001. "The Greek Inscriptions of the Sardis Synagogue." *HTR* 94: 5-55.

Kümmel, W. G. 1975. *Introduction to the New Testament.* London: SCM Press.

Künzl, E. 1999. "Ärzte in Ephesos: Gräber und Instrumente." In *100 Jahre Österreichische Forschungen in Ephesos. Akten des Symposions Wien 1995*, ed. H. Friesinger, Krinzinger, F.:205-9. Wien: Verlag der Österreichischen Akademie der Wissenschaften.

Kurz, W. S. 1985. "Luke 22:14-38 and Greco-Roman and Biblical Farewell Addresses." *JBL* 104: 251-68.

Lähnemann, J. 1978. "Die Sieben Sendschreiben der Johannes-Apokalypse." In *Studien zur Religion und Kultur Kleinasiens Festschriften F.K. Dörner*, ed. E. Schwertheim, Wagner, J., Sahin, S.:516-39. Leiden: E.J. Brill.

Lake, K. 1912. *The Apostolic Fathers, with an English Translation.* LCL. London; New York: William Heinemann; Macmillan.

————. 1920. *Landmarks in the History of Early Christianity.* London: Macmillan and Co.

————. 1938. *An Introduction to the NT.* London: Christophers.

Lake, K. and H. J. Cadbury. 1933a. *The Beginnings of Christianity Part 1 The Acts of the Apostles. Vol IV English Translation and Commentary.* London: Macmillan and Co.

————. 1933b. *The Beginnings of Christianity Part 1 The Acts of the Apostles. Vol V Additional Notes to the Commentary.* London: Macmillan and Co.

Lalleman, P.J. 1995. "Polymorphy of Christ." In *The Apocryphal Acts of John*, ed. J.N. Bremmer:97-118. Kampen: Kok Pharos.

_____. 1998. *The Acts of John. A Two-Stage Initiation into Johannine Gnosticism.* Leuven: Peeters.

Lambrecht, J. 1979. "Paul's Farewell-Address at Miletus (Acts 20, 17-38)." In *Les Actes des Apôtres. Traditions rédactions, théologie,* ed. J. Kremer:307-337. Gembloux: J. Duculot.

_____. 2001a. "Jewish Slander: A Note on Rev 2,9-10." In *Collected Studies on Pauline Literature and on The Book of Revelation,* ed. J. Lambrecht:329-39. Rome: Pontificio Istituto Biblico.

_____. 2001b. "Synagogues of Satan (cf. Rev 2,9 and 3,9): Anti-Judaism in the Apocalypse." In *Collected Studies on Pauline Literature and on The Book of Revelation,* ed. J. Lambrecht:341-56. Rome: Pontificio Istituto Biblico.

Lampe, G. W. H. 1951. *The Seal of the Spirit. A Study in the Doctrine of Baptism and Confirmation in the New Testament and the Fathers.* London: Longmans, Green and Co.

_____. 1973. "'Grievous wolves' (Acts 20:29)." In *Christ and Spirit in the New Testament in Honour of Charles Francis Digby Moule,* ed. B. Lindars, Smalley, S.S.:253-68. Cambridge: Cambridge University Press.

Lampe, P. 1987. *Die stadtrömischen Christen in den ersten beiden Jahrhunderten. Untersuchungen zur Sozialgeschichte.* WUNT 2.18. Tübingen: J.C.B Mohr (Paul Siebeck).

_____. 1992. "Acta 19 im Spiegel der ephesischen Inschriften." *BZ* 36: 59-76.

Lane Fox, R. 1986. *Pagans and Christians.* Harmondsworth: Viking.

Lang, F. 1986. *Die Briefe an die Korinther.* NTD. Göttingen und Zürich: Vandenhoeck & Ruprecht.

Langmann, G. 1979. "Ephesos - du Leuchte Asiens Ein Rundblick." *Antike Welt* 10: 3-20.

Lanowski, J. 1965. "Weltwunder." In *Paulys Realencyclopädie der Classischen Altertumswissenschaft,* ed. K. Ziegler, Supplementband X:1020-30. Stuttgart: Alfred Druckenmüller Verlag.

Lau, A. Y. 1996. *Manifest in Flesh. The Epiphany Christology of the Pastoral Epistles.* WUNT 2.86. Tübingen: J.C.B. Mohr (Paul Siebeck).

Laurence, R., Berry, J. eds. 1998. *Cultural Identity in the Roman Empire.* London: Routledge.

Lausberg, H. 1998. *Handbook of Literary Rhetoric. A Foundation for Literary Study.* Translated by A. Jansen M.T. Bliss, D.E. Orton, edited by D.E. Orton, R.D. Anderson. Leiden: Brill.

Law, R. 1909. *The Tests of Life. A Study of the First Epistle of St John.* Edinburgh: T & T Clark.

Lawlor, H.J., Oulton, J.E.L. 1927. *Eusebius Bishop of Caesarea: The Ecclesiastical History and the Martyrs of Palestine.* London: SPCK.

Layton, B. 1987. *The Gnostic Scriptures: A New Translation.* London: SCM Press.

Le Roux, C.R. 1999. "Ephesus in the Acts of the Apostles: A Geographical and Theological Appraisal." In *100 Jahre Österreichische Forschungen in Ephesos. Akten des Symposions Wien 1995,* ed. H. Friesinger, Krinzinger, F.:307-313. Wien: Verlag der Österreichischen Akademie der Wissenschaften.

Leary, T. J. 1990. "The 'Aprons' of St Paul - Acts 19:12." *JTS* ns 41: 527-9.

_____. 1992. "'A Thorn in the Flesh' - 2 Corinthians 12:7." *JTS* ns 43: 520-2.

Leclercq, H. 1922. "Éphèse." In *DACL,* ed. F. Cabrol, Leclercq, H., 5.1:118-42. Paris: Librairie Letouzey et Ané.

Lemaire, A. 1971. *Les Ministères aux origines de l'Église. Naissance de la triple hiérarchie: évêques, presbytres, diacres.* LD 68. Paris: Les Editions du Cerf.

_____. 1972. "Pastoral Epistles: Redaction and Theology." *BTB* 2: 25-42.

Lemcio, E. 1986. "Ephesus and the New Testament Canon." *BJRL* 69: 210-34.

Leon, H.J. 1960. *The Jews of Ancient Rome*. Philadelphia: Jewish Publication Society of America.

Lessing, E., Oberleitner, W. 1978. *Ephesos Weltstadt der Antike*. Wien-Heidelberg: Überreuter.

Levick, B. M. 1967. *Roman Colonies in Southern Asia Minor*. Oxford: Clarendon Press.

Levinskaya, I. 1996. *The Book of Acts in its Diaspora Setting*. The Book of Acts in its First Century Setting. Grand Rapids, Michigan: Eerdmans.

LiDonnici, L. R. 1992. "The Images of Artemis Ephesia and Greco-Roman Worship: A Reconsideration." *HTR* 85: 389-415.

_____. 1999. "Women's Religions and Religious Lives in the Greco-Roman City." In *Women and Christian Origins*, ed. R.S. Kraemer, D'Angelo, M.R.:80-102. New York, Oxford: Oxford University Press.

Lieu, J. 1981. "Authority to Become Children of God." *NovT* 23: 210-28.

_____. 1986. *The Second and Third Epistles of John: History and Background*. Studies of the New Testament and its World. Edinburgh: T & T Clark.

_____. 1988. "Blindness in the Johannine Traditions." *NTS* 34: 83-95.

_____. 1991. *The Theology of the Johannine Epistles*. Cambridge: Cambridge University Press.

_____. 1993. "What was from the Beginning: Scripture and Tradition in the Johannine Epistles." *NTS* 39: 458-477.

_____. 1996. "Scripture and the Feminine in John." In *A Feminist Companion to the Hebrew Bible in the New Testament*, ed. A. Brenner:225-40. Sheffield: Sheffield Academic Press.

Lightfoot, J. B. 1889a. "Discoveries Illustrating the Acts of the Apostles." In *Essays on the Word Entitled Supernatural Religion*. London: Macmillan & Co.

_____. 1889b. *The Apostolic Fathers Pt II; S. Ignatius, S. Polycarp*. London: Macmillan and Co.

Lincoln, A. T. 1990. *Ephesians*. WBC. Dallas: Word Books.

Lindars, B. 1990. *John*. NTG. Sheffield: JSOT Press.

Lindemann, A. 1989. "Der Apostel Paulus im 2. Jahrhundert." In *The New Testament in Early Christianity. La réception des écrits néotestamentaires dans le christianisme primitif*, ed. J.M. Sevrin:39-67. Leuven: Leuven University Press; Uitgeverij Peeters.

_____. 1990. "Paul in the Writings of the Apostolic Fathers." In *Paul and the Legacies of Paul*, ed. W.S. Babcock:25-45. Dallas: Southern Methodist University Press.

_____. 1997. "Antwort auf die „Thesen zur Echtheit und Datierung der sieben Briefe des Ignatius von Antiochen"." *ZAC* 1: 185-94.

_____. 2000. *Der Erste Korintherbrief*. HNT 9/1. Tübingen: Mohr Siebeck.

Loader, William. 1992. *The Johannine Epistles*. London: Epworth.

Lohmeyer, E. 1970. *Die Offenbarung des Johannes*. HNT 16. Tübingen: J.C.B. Mohr (Paul Siebeck).

Lohse, E. 1971. *Colossians and Philemon*. Hermeneia. Philadelphia: Fortress Press.

_____. 1991. "The Revelation of John and Pauline Theology." In *The Future of Early Christianity. Essays in Honor of Helmut Koester*, ed. B. A. Pearson, in collaboration with A.T. Kraabel, G.W.E. Nickelsburg, N.R. Petersen:358-66. Minneapolis: Fortress Press.

Longenecker, R. N. 1981. "The Acts of the Apostles." In *The Expositor's Bible Commentary*, ed. F.E. Gaebelein, Grand Rapids: Zondervan.

_____. 1990. *Galatians*. WBC. Dallas, Texas: Word Books.

Lövestam, E. 1987. "Paul's Address at Miletus." *ST* 41: 1-10.

Lüdemann, G. 1984. *Paul, Apostle to the Gentiles: Studies in Chronology*. London: SCM Press.

_____. 1988. "Acts of the Apostles as a Historical Source." In *The Social World of Formative Christianity and Judaism. Essays in Tribute to Howard Clark Kee*, ed. J. Neusner, Borgen, P., Frerichs, E.S., Horsley, R.:109-125. Philadephia: Fortress Press.

_____. 1989. *Early Christianity according to the Traditions in Acts: A Commentary*. London: SCM Press.

Lüderitz, G. 1994. "What is the Politeuma?" In *Studies in Early Jewish Epigraphy*, ed. J.W. van Henten, van der Horst, P.W.:183-225. Leiden: Brill.

Lyonnet, S. 1981. "'La voie' dans les Actes des Apôtres." *RSR* 69: 149-64.

MacDonald, D. R. 1980. "A Conjectural Emendation of 1 Cor 15:31-32: Or the Case of the Misplaced Lion Fight." *HTR* 73: 265-76.

_____. 1983. *The Legend and the Apostle. The Battle for Paul in Story and Canon*. Philadephia: Westminster Press.

MacDonald, M. Y. 1988. *The Pauline Churches. A Socio-historical Study of Institutionalization in the Pauline and Deutero-Pauline Writings*. SNTSMS 60. Cambridge: Cambridge University Press.

_____. 1996. *Early Christian Women and Pagan Opinion. The Power of the Hysterical Woman*. Cambridge: Cambridge University Press.

_____. 1999a. "Reading Real Women Through the Undisputed Letters of Paul." In *Women and Christian Origins*, ed. R.S. Kraemer, D'Angelo, M.R.:199-220. New York and Oxford: Oxford University Press.

_____. 1999b. "Rereading Paul: Early Interpreters of Paul on Women and Gender." In *Women and Christian Origins*, ed. R.S. Kraemer, D'Angelo, M.R.:236-53. New York and Oxford: Oxford University Press.

_____. 2000. *Colossians and Ephesians*. SP. Collegeville, Minnesota: The Liturgical Press.

Mackay, W. M. 1973. "Another Look at the Nicolaitans." *EvQ* 45: 111-15.

MacMullen, R. 1981. *Paganism in the Roman Empire*. New Haven: Yale University Press.

Macro, A. D. 1983. "The Cities of Asia Minor under the Roman Imperium." In *ANRW*, II.7.2:658-97. Berlin: Walter de Gruyter.

Maddox, R. 1982. *The Purpose of Luke–Acts*. Studies of the New Testament and its World. Edinburgh: T & T Clark.

Magie, D. 1950. *Roman Rule in Asia Minor to the end of the third century after Christ*. Princeton: Princeton University Press.

Maier, H. O. 1991. *The Social Setting of the Ministry as Reflected in the Writings of Hermas, Clement and Ignatius*. Waterloo. Ontario: Wilfred Laurier University Press.

Maillot, A. 1990. *Marie, Ma Sœur. Étude sur la femme dans le Nouveau Testament*. Paris: Letouzey et Ané.

Malatesta, E. 1978. *Interiority and Covenant, A Study of* εἶναι ἐν *and* μένειν ἐν *in the First Letter of Saint John*. AnBib 69. Rome: Biblical Institute Press.

Malherbe, A. J. 1968. "The Beasts at Ephesus." *JBL* 87: 71-80.

_____. 1977. "The Inhospitality of Diotrephes." In *God's Christ and His People. Studies in Honour of Nils Alstrup Dahl*, ed. J. Jervell, Meeks, W.A.:222-32. Oslo, Bergen, Tromsö: Universitetsforlaget.

_____. 1980. "Medical Imagery in the Pastoral Epistles." In *Texts and Testaments:Critical Essays on the Bible and Early Church Fathers*, ed. W.E. March:19-35. San Antonio: Trinity University.

_____. 1983. *Social Aspects of Early Christianity*. Philadelphia: Fortress Press.

_____. 1984. "'In Season and out of Season': 2 Timothy 4:2." *JBL* 103: 235-43.

_____. 1995. "Paul's Self-Sufficiency (Philippians 4:11)." In *Texts and Contexts. Biblical Texts in Their Textual and Situational Contexts. Essays in Honor of Lars Hartman*, ed. T. Fornberg, Hellholm, D.:813-26. Oslo: Scandinavian University Press.

Malina, B. J. 1978. "The Social World Implied in the Letters of the Christian Bishop-Martyr (named Ignatius of Antioch)." In *SBLSP 1978*, ed. P.J Achtemeier, 2:71-119. Missoula, Montana: Scholars Press.

_____. 1986. "The Received View and What it Cannot Do: 3 John and Hospitality." *Semeia* 35: 171-94.

_____. 1987. "Wealth and Poverty in the New Testament and Its World." *Int* 41: 354-67.

Malina, B. J., Pilch, J.J. 2000. *Social-Science Commentary on the Book of Revelation*. Minneapolis: Fortress Press.

Maloney, L.M. 1994. "The Pastoral Epistles." In *Searching the Scriptures. Volume Two: A Feminist Companion*, ed. E. Schüssler Fiorenza:361-80. New York: Crossroad.

Manson, T. W. 1962. *Studies in the Gospels and Epistles,* ed., M. Black. Manchester: Manchester University Press.

Marcus, J. 2000. *Mark 1-8. A New Translation with Introduction and Commentary*. AB. New York: Doubleday.

Markschies, C. 1999. *Between Two Worlds. Structures of Early Christianity*. London: SCM Press.

Marshall, I. H. 1976. "Orthodoxy and heresy in earlier Christianity." *Them* 2: 5-14.

_____. 1978. *The Epistles of John*. NICNT. Grand Rapids, Michigan: Eerdmans.

_____. 1980. *Acts*. TNTC. Grand Rapids: Eerdmans.

_____. 1984. "Faith and Works in the Pastoral Epistles." *SNTSU* 9: 203-18.

_____. 1986. "Church and Ministry in 1 Timothy." In *Pulpit and People. Essays in honour of William Still on his 75th Birthday*, ed. N.M. de S. Cameron, Ferguson, S.B.:51-60. Edinburgh: Rutherford House Books.

_____. 1988. "The Christology of the Pastoral Epistles." *SNTSU* 13: 157-77.

_____. 1989. "Universal Grace and Atonement in the Pastoral Epistles." In *The Grace of God, The Will of Man. A Case for Arminianism*, ed. C.H. Pinnock:51-69. Grand Rapids, Michigan: Academie Books.

_____. 1990a. "Luke's View of Paul." *SwJT* 33: 41-51.

_____. 1990b. "The Christian Life in 1 Timothy." *RTR* 49: 81-90.

_____. 1992. *The Acts of the Apostles*. NTG. Sheffield: JSOT Press.

_____. 1993. "'Sometimes Only Orthodox' - Is there more to the Pastoral Epistles?" *Epworth Review* 20, no. 3: 11-24.

_____. 1994. "The Christology of Acts and the Pastoral Epistles." In *Crossing the Boundaries: Essays in Biblical Interpretation in Honour of Michael D. Goulder*, ed. S.E. Porter, Joyce, P., Orton, D.E.:167-82. Leiden: Brill.

_____. 1996. "Salvation, Grace and Works in the Later Writings in the Pauline Corpus." *NTS* 42: 339-358.

_____. 1996. "Prospects for the Pastoral Epistles." In *Doing Theology for the People of God. Studies in Honour of J.I. Packer*, ed. A.E. McGrath D.M Lewis:137-155. Leicester: Apollos.

Marshall, I. H., in collaboration with Towner, P.H. 1999. *A Critical and Exegetical Commentary on The Pastoral Epistles*. ICC. Edinburgh: T & T Clark.

Martens, J.W. 1992. "Ignatius and Onesimus: John Knox Reconsidered." *SecCent* 9: 73-86.

Martin, C.J. 1994. "The Acts of the Apostles." In *Searching the Scriptures. Volume Two: A Feminist Companion*, ed. E. Schüssler Fiorenza:763-99. New York: Crossroad.

Martin, D.B. 1996. "The Construction of the Ancient Family: Methodological Considerations." *JRS* 86: 40-60.

_____. 2001. "Review Essay: Justin J. Meggitt, *Paul, Poverty and Survival*." *JSNT* 84: 51-64.

Martin, R. P. 1976. *Philipians*. NCB. Grand Rapids: Eerdmans.

_____. 1978. *New Testament Foundations*. Grand Rapids, Michigan: Eerdmans.

_____. 1986. *2 Corinthians*. WBC. Texas: Word.

_____. 1991. *Ephesians, Colossians and Philemon*. Atlanta: John Knox Press.

Martyn, J.L. 1979. *History and Theology in the Fourth Gospel*. Nashville: Abingdon.

Massingberd, J. 1970. "A Note on Proto-Montanism in the Pastoral Epistles." *NTS* 17: 338-46.

Mastin, B. A. 1976. "Scaeva the Chief Priest." *JTS* ns 27: 405-12.

_____. 1978. "A Note on Acts 19,14." *Bib* 59: 97-9.

Mathewson, D. 1992. "Revelation in Recent Genre Criticism: Some Implications for Interpretation." *TJ* 13: 193-213.

Mattill, A. J. 1978. "The Value of Acts as a Source for the Study of Paul." In *Perspectives on Luke-Acts*, ed. C. H. Talbert. Danville: Association of Baptist Professors of Religion.

Mattingly, H.B. 1958. "The Origin of The Name Christiani." *JTS* ns 9: 26-37.

McArthur, A. A. 1961. "The Office of Bishop in the Ignatian Epistles and in the Didascalia Apostolorum compared." In *Studia Patristica Vol IV*, ed. F.L. Cross, part II:298-304. Berlin: Akademie-Verlag.

McCown, C. C. 1923. "The Ephesia Grammata in Popular Belief." *TAPA* 54: 128-40.

McEleney, N.J. 1974. "The Vice Lists of the Pastorals." *CBQ* 36: 203-19.

McGing, B. 2002. "Population and Proselytism: How many Jews were there in the ancient world?" In *Jews in the Hellenistic and Roman Cities*, ed. J.R. Bartlett:88-106. London, New York: Routledge.

McGuire, A. 1999. "Women, Gender, and Gnosis in Gnostic Texts and Traditions." In *Women and Christian Origins*, ed. R.S. Kraemer, D'Angelo, M.R.:257-99. New York and Oxford: Oxford University Press.

McIlraith, D.A. 1999. "'For the Fine Linen is the Righteous Deeds of the Saints': Works and Wife in Revelation 19:8." *CBQ* 61: 512-29.

McRay, J. 1991. *Archaeology and the New Testament*. Grand Rapids, Michigan: Baker.

Meade, D. G. 1986. *Pseudonymity and Canon: An Investigation into the Relationship of Authorship and Authority in Jewish and Early Christian Tradition*. WUNT 39. Tübingen: J.C.B. Mohr (Paul Siebeck).

Meeks, W. A. 1972. "The Man From Heaven in Johannine Sectarianism." *JBL* 91: 44-72.

_____. 1983. *The First Urban Christians*. New Haven: Yale University Press.

_____. 1993. *The Origins of Christian Morality: The First Two Centuries*. New Haven and London: Yale University Press.

Meggitt, J. J. 1994. "Meat Consumption and Social Conflict in Corinth." *JTS* ns 45: 137-41.

_____. 1998. *Paul, Poverty and Survival*. Studies of the New Testament and its World. Edinburgh: T & T Clark.

_____. 2001. "Response to Martin and Theissen." *JSNT* 84: 85-94.

Meier, J. P. 1973. "*Presbyteros* in the Pastoral Epistles." *CBQ* 35: 323-45.

Meijer, F., van Nijf, O. 1992. *Trade, Transport and Society in the Ancient World. A sourcebook*. London and New York: Routledge.

Meinardus, O. F. A. 1973. *St Paul in Ephesus and the Cities of Asia Minor*. Athens: Lycabettus Press.

_____. 1974. "The Christian Remains of the Seven Churches of the Apocalypse." *BA* 37: 69-82.

_____. 1979. *St. John of Patmos and the Seven Churches of the Apocalypse*. New Rochelle, New York: Caratzas Brothers.

Meinhold, P. 1979. *Studien zu Ignatius von Antiochien*. Veröffentlichungen des Instituts für Europäische Geschichte Mainz 97. Wiesbaden: Franz Steiner Verlag.

Merkel, H. 1991. *Die Pastoralbriefe*. NTD 9/1. Göttingen: Vandenhoeck & Ruprecht.

Merkelbach, R. 1992. "Aurelia Artemisia aus Ephesos, eine Geheilte Augenkranke." *Epigraphica Anatolia* 20: 55-6.

Methuen, C. 1997. "The 'Virgin Widow': A Problematic Social Role for the Early Church?" *HTR* 90: 285-98.

Metzger, B. M. 1944. "St. Paul and the Magicians." *PSB* 38: 27-30.

_____. 1945. "St. Paul and the Baptized Lion. Apocryphal vs. Canonical Books of the New Testament." *PSB* 39: 11-21.

_____. 1971. *A Textual Commentary on the Greek New Testament*. London: United Bible Societies.

Michaelis, W. 1928. "The Trial of St Paul at Ephesus." *JTS* 29: 368-75.

Michaels, J. R. 1988. *1 Peter*. WBC. Texas: Word.

_____. 1991. "Paul and John the Baptist: An Odd Couple." *TynBul* 42: 245-60.

Millar, F. with D. Berciu, R.N. Frye, G. Kossack, T.T. Rice. 1967. *The Roman Empire and its Neighbours*. London: Weidenfeld and Nicholson.

Miller, J. D. 1997. *The Pastoral Letters as Composite Documents*. SNTSMS 93. Cambridge: Cambridge University Press.

Miltner, F. 1958. *Ephesos. Stadt der Artemis und des Johannes*. Wien: Verlag Franz Deuticke.

Minear, P. S. 1968. *I Saw a New Earth. An Introduction to the Visions of the Apocalypse*. Washington: Corpus Books.

Mitchell, M.M. 1989. "Concerning ΠΕΡΙ ΔΕ in 1 Corinthians." *NovT* 31: 229-56.

Mitchell, S. 1993. *Anatolia. Land, Men and Gods in Asia Minor*. 2 Vols. Oxford: Clarendon Press.

_____. 1998-1999. "Archaeology in Asia Minor 1990-98." In *Archaeological Reports for 1998-1999*:125-91. London: Council of the Society for the Promotion of Hellenic Studies.

Mitton, C. L. 1951. *The Epistle to the Ephesians*. Oxford: Clarendon Press.

_____. 1955. *The Formation of the Pauline Corpus of Letters*. London: Epworth Press.

Moberly, R. B. 1992. "When was Revelation Conceived?" *Bib* 73: 376-93.

Moffatt, J. 1930. "Ignatius of Antioch - A Study in Personal Religion." *JR* 10: 169-86.

Molland, E. 1954. "The Heretics Combatted by Ignatius of Antioch." *JEH* 5: 1-6.

Montefiore, H. 1964. *A Commentary on the Epistle to the Hebrews*. BNTC. London: A & C Black.

Moo, D. J. 1980. "1 Timothy 2:11-15: Meaning and Significance." *TJ* 1: 62-83.

Moore, M.D. 1993. "The 'Widows' in 1 Tim. 5:3-16." In *Essays on Women in Earliest Christianity. Volume One*, ed. C.D. Osburn:321-66. Joplin, Missouri: College Press.

Moore, M.S. 1990. *The Balaam Traditions. Their Character and Development.* SBLDS 113. Atlanta, GA: Scholars Press.

Moritz, T. 1996. "Reasons for Ephesians." *Evangel* 14: 8-14.

Morton, H.V. 1936. *In the Steps of St Paul.* London: Rich & Cowan.

Moule, C. F. D. 1981. *The Birth of the New Testament.* London: A & C Black.

Mounce, R.H. 1977. *The Book of Revelation.* NICNT. Grand Rapids, Michigan: Eerdmans.

Mounce, W.D. 2000. *Pastoral Epistles.* WBC 46. Nashville: Thomas Nelson.

Moxnes, H. 1988. *The Economy of the Kingdom. Social Conflict and Economic Relations in Luke's Gospel.* OBT. Philadelphia: Fortress Press.

Moyise, S. 2001. "Authorial Intention and the Book of Revelation." *AUSS* 39: 35-40.

Muddiman, J. 2001. *A Commentary on The Epistle to the Ephesians.* BNTC. London and New York: Continuum.

Müller, U. B. 1976. *Zur frühchristlichen Theologiegeschichte: Judenchristentum und Paulinismus in Kleinasien an der Wende vom ersten zum zweiten Jahrhundert n. Chr.* Gütersloh: Gütersloher Verlagshaus Gerd Mohn.

_____. 1984. *Die Offenbarung des Johannes.* ÖTK 19. Gütersloh: Gütersloher Verlagshaus Gerd Mohn; Würzburg: Echter.

Munck, J. 1950. "Discours d'adieu dans le Nouveau Testament et dans la littérature biblique." In *Aux Sources de la tradition chrétienne. Mélanges offerts à M. Maurice Goguel à l'occasion de son soixante-dixième anniversaire,* ed. O. Cullmann, Menoud, P.:155-70. Neuchâtel, Paris: Delachaux & Niestlé.

Murphy, F.J. 1998. *Fallen is Babylon: The Revelation to John.* The NT in Context. Harrisburg, PA: Trinity Press International.

Murphy-O'Connor, J. 1983. *St Paul's Corinth. Texts and Archaeology.* GNS 6. Wilmington, Delaware: Michael Glazier.

_____. 1984. "Redactional Angels in 1 Tim 3,16." *RB* 91: 178-87.

_____. 1986. "Interpolations in 1 Corinthians." *CBQ* 48: 81-94.

_____. 1990. "John the Baptist and Jesus: History and Hypothesis." *NTS* 36: 359-74.

_____. 1991a. *The Theology of the Second Letter to the Corinthians.* New Testament Theology. Cambridge: Cambridge University Press.

_____. 1991b. "2 Timothy Contrasted with 1 Timothy and Titus." *RB* 98: 403-18.

_____. 1992. "Prisca and Aquila: Traveling Tentmakers and Church Builders." *BAR* 8, no. 6: 40-51, 62.

_____. 1996. *Paul: A Critical Life.* Oxford: Clarendon Press.

Muse, R. L. 1986. "Revelation 2-3: A Critical Analysis of Seven Prophetic Messages." *JETS* 29: 147-61.

Mussies, G. 1990. "Pagans, Jews and Christians at Ephesos." In *Studies on the Hellenistic Background of the New Testament,* ed. P.W. van der Horst, Mussies, G.:177-94. Utrecht: Faculteit der Godgeleerdheid Rijksuniversiteit Utrecht.

Myers, E. P. 1986. "Interpreting Figurative Language." In *Biblical Interpretation Principles and Practices. Studies in Honor of Jack Pearl Lewis,* ed. E. P. Myers T. D. Hadley eds F.F. Kearley:91-100. Grand Rapids, Michigan: Baker Book House.

Nauck, W. 1950. *Die Herkunft des Verfassers der Pastoralbriefe. Ein Beiträg zur Frage der Auslegung der Pastoralbriefe.* Inaugural Dissertation zur Erlangung des Doktorgrades, Georg August Universität.

_____. 1957. *Die Tradition und der Charakter des ersten Johannesbriefes. Zugleich ein Beitrag zur Taufe im Urchristentum und in der alten Kirche.* WUNT 3, Tübingen: J.C.B. Mohr (Paul Siebeck).

Neil, W. 1973. *The Acts of the Apostles.* NCB. London: Oliphants.

Nestle, E. 1901. "The Aprons and Handkerchiefs of St. Paul." *ExpTim* 13: 282.

Neufeld, D. 1994. *Reconceiving Texts as Speech Acts: An Analysis of 1 John*. Biblical Interpretation Series 7. Leiden: E.J. Brill.

Neumann, K. J. 1990. *The Authenticity of the Pauline Epistles in the Light of Stylostatistical Analysis*. SBLDS 120. Atlanta: Scholars Press.

Neusner, J. and E. S. Frerichs. 1985. *"To See Ourselves as Others See Us." Christians, Jews, "Others" in Late Antiquity*. Chico. California: Scholars Press.

Nickalls, J.L. 1952. *The Journal of George Fox*. Cambridge: Cambridge University Press.

Nickle, K. F. 1966. *The Collection. A Study in Paul's Strategy*. London: SCM Press.

Noack, B. 1959-60. "On 1 John II. 12-14." *NTS* 6: 236-41.

Nock, A. D. 1972. *Essays on Religion and the Ancient World*. Edited by Z. Stewart. Oxford: Clarendon Press.

Nodet, E., Taylor, J. 1998. *The Origins of Christianity: An Exploration*. Collegeville, Minnesota: Liturgical Press.

Norris, F. W. 1976. "Ignatius, Polycarp, and I Clement: Walter Bauer Reconsidered." *VC* 30: 23-44.

_____. 1982. "Asia Minor before Ignatius: Walter Bauer Reconsidered." In *Studia Evangelica VII*, ed. E.A. Livingstone:365-77. Berlin: Akademie-Verlag.

Noy, D. 1993. *Jewish Inscriptions of Western Europe. Volume 1: Italy (excluding the City of Rome), Spain and Gaul*. Cambridge: Cambridge University Press.

O'Brien, P. T. 1977. *Introductory Thanksgivings in the Letters of Paul*. NovTSup 49. Leiden: E J Brill.

_____. 1982. *Colossians, Philemon*. WBC. Texas: Word Books.

_____. 1991. *The Epistle to the Philippians. A Commentary on the Greek Text*. NIGTC. Michigan: Eerdmans.

O'Day, G.R. 1998. "1, 2, and 3 John." In *Women's Bible Commentary*, ed. C.A. Newsom, Ringe, S.H.:466-7. Louisville, Kentucky: Westminster John Knox Press.

Oates, W. E. 1959. "Conception of Ministry in the Pastoral Epistles." *RevExp* 56: 388-410.

Oberlinner, L. 1980. "Die »Epiphaneia« des Heilswillens Gottes in Christus Jesus. Zur Grundstruktur der Christologie der Pastoralbriefe." *ZNW* 71: 192-213.

Oden, T. C. 1989. *First and Second Timothy and Titus*. IBC. Louisville: John Knox Press.

Ogg, G. 1968. *The Chronology of the Life of Paul*. London: Epworth Press.

Okure, T. 1988. *The Johannine Approach to Mission. A Contextual Study of John 4:1-42*. WUNT 2.31. Tübingen: J.C.B. Mohr (Paul Siebeck).

Oliver, J.H. 1941. *The Sacred Gerusia*. Hesperia Supplement 6. Athens: American School of Classical Studies at Athens.

Olson, D.C. 1997. "'Those Who Have Not Defiled Themselves with Women': Revelation 14:4 and the Book of Enoch." *CBQ* 59: 492-510.

Olsson, B. 1987. "The History of the Johannine Movement." In *Aspects on the Johanine Literature*, ed. L Hartman, Olsson, B.:27-43. Uppsala: Almqvist & Wiksell.

Olszewski, M.-T. 1999. "L'Ephèse d'Artémidore: La société des patients d'Artémidore." In *100 Jahre Österreichische Forschungen in Ephesos. Akten des Symposions Wien 1995*, ed. H. Friesinger, Krinzinger, F.:275-82. Wien: Verlag der Österreichischen Akademie der Wissenschaften.

Önen, Ü. 1985. *Ephesus the way it was. The City viewed in reconstructions*. Ismir: Akademia Tanitma Merkezi.

Orr, W. F., Walther, J. A. 1976. *1 Corinthians*. AB. New York: Doubleday & Co.

Osborne, G. R. 1989. "Soteriology in the Gospel of John." In *The Grace of God*, ed. C.H. Pinnock:243-60. Grand Rapids, Michigan: Academie Books.

Osborne, R. E. 1966. "Paul and the Wild Beasts." *JBL* 85: 225-28.

Osiek, C. 1994. "Women in the Ancient Mediterranean World: State of the Question – New Testament." *BRev* 39: 57-61.

Osiek, C., Balch, D.L. 1997. *Families in the New Testament World. Households and House Churches.* Louisville, Kentucky: Westminster John Knox Press.

Oster, R. E. 1974. *A Historical Commentary on the Missionary Success Stories in Acts 19:11-40.* PhD Thesis, Princeton Theological Seminary.

_____ 1976. "The Ephesian Artemis as an Opponent of Early Christianity." *Jahrbuch für Antike und Christentum* 19: 24-44.

_____. 1982a. "Christianity and Emperor Veneration in Ephesus: Iconography of a Conflict." *ResQ* 25: 143-49.

_____. 1982b. "Numismatic Windows into the Social World of Early Christianity: A Methodological Inquiry." *JBL* 101: 195-223.

_____. 1984. "Acts 19:23-41 and an Ephesian Inscription." *HTR* 77: 233-37.

_____. 1987. *A Bibliography of Ancient Ephesus.* ATLA Bibliography Series 19. Metuchen: American Theological Library Association and The Scarecrow Press.

_____. 1990a. "Ephesus as a religious Center under the Principate, I. Paganism before Constantine." *ANRW*, II.18.3: 1661-1728. Berlin: Walter de Gruyter.

_____. 1990b. "Ephesus, Ephesians." In *Encyclopedia of Early Christianity*, ed. E. Ferguson:300-303. New York, London: Garland Publishing.

_____. 1992a. "Ephesus." In *Anchor Bible Dictionary*, ed. D.N. Freedman, 2:542-9. New York: Doubleday.

_____. 1992b. "Christianity in Asia Minor." In *Anchor Bible Dictionary*, ed. D.N. Freedman, 1:938-954. New York: Doubleday.

Outschar, U. 1999. "Zur Deutung des Hadrianstempels an der Kuretenstraße." In *100 Jahre Österreichische Forschungen in Ephesos. Akten des Symposions Wien 1995*, ed. H. Friesinger, Krinzinger, F.:443-8. Wien: Verlag der Österreichischen Akademie der Wissenschaften.

Padgett, A. 1987. "Wealthy Women at Ephesus: 1 Timothy 2:8-15 in Social Context." *Int* 41: 19-31.

Painter, J. 1979. *John: Witness and Theologian.* London: SPCK.

_____. 1986. "The 'Opponents' in 1 John." *NTS* 32: 48-71.

_____. 1993. *The Quest for the Messiah. The History, Literature and Theology of the Johannine Community.* Edinburgh: T & T Clark.

Pancaro, S. 1969-70. "'People of God' in St John's Gospel?" *NTS* 16: 114-129.

Pape, W., Benseler, G. E. 1911. *Worterbuch der griechischen Eigennamen.* Braunschweig: Friedr. Vieweg & Sohn.

Parratt, J. K. 1968. "The Rebaptism of the Ephesian Disciples." *ExpTim* 79: 182-3.

Parrish, D. 1999. "House (or Wohneinheit) 2 in Hanghaus 2 at Ephesos: A Few Issues of Interpretation." In *100 Jahre Österreichische Forschungen in Ephesos. Akten des Symposions Wien 1995*, ed. H. Friesinger, Krinzinger, F.:507-13. Wien: Verlag der Österreichischen Akademie der Wissenschaften.

Parvis, M. M. 1945. "Archaeology and St Paul's Journeys in Greek Lands. Part IV - Ephesus." *BA* 8: 62-73.

Pattemore, S.W. 2000. *The People of God in the Apocalypse: A Relevance-Theoretic Study.* PhD Thesis, University of Otago, New Zealand.

Patzia, A. G. 1980. "The Deutero-Pauline Hypothesis: An Attempt at Clarification." *EvQ* 52: 27-42.

Paulien, J. 1988. *Decoding Revelation's Trumpets. Literary Allusions and the Interpretation of Revelation 8:7-12.* Andrews University Seminary Doctoral Dissertation Series 11. Berrien Springs, Michigan: Andrews University Press.

_____. 2001. "Dreading the Whirlwind. Intertextuality and the Use of the Old Testament in Revelation." *AUSS* 39: 5-22.

Paulsen, H. 1978. *Studien zur Theologie des Ignatius von Antiochien.* Forschungen zur Kirchen- und Dogmengeschichte 29. Göttingen: Vandenhoeck & Ruprecht.

_____. 1985. *Die Briefe des Ignatius von Antiochia und der Brief des Polykarp von Smyrna.* HNT 18. Tübingen: J.C.B. Mohr (Paul Siebeck).

Payne, P. B. 1981. "Libertarian Women in Ephesus: A Response to D J Moo's Article '1 Tim 2:11-15: Meaning and Significance'." *TJ* 2: 169-97.

Pearson, B. A. 1987. "Early Christianity and Gnosticism: A Review Essay." *RelSRev* 13, no. 1: 1-8.

Pease, A. S. 1946. "Notes on Book-Burning." In *Munera Studiosa*, eds. S. E. Johnson, Shepherd, M.H.: 145-60. Cambridge MA: The Episcopal Theological School.

Pereira, F. 1983. *Ephesus. Climax of Universalism in Luke-Acts.* Jesuit Theological Forum Studies 1. Anand, India: Gujarat Sahitya Prakash.

Perkins, P. 1979. *The Johannine Epistles.* NT Message. Wilmington, DE: Michael Glazier.

Perkins, P. 1982. *Love Commands in the New Testament.* New York: Paulist Press.

_____. 1983. "Koinonia in 1 John 1.3-7: The Social Context of Division in the Johannine Letters." *CBQ* 45: 631-641.

_____. 1988. *Reading the New Testament.* New York: Paulist Press.

_____. 1992. "Apocalyptic Sectarianism and Love Commands: The Johannine Epistles and Revelation." In *The Love of Enemies and Nonretaliation in the New Testament,* ed. W.M. Swartley:287-96. Louisville, Kentucky: Westminster/John Knox Press.

Pervo, R. I. 1990. *Luke's Story of Paul.* Minneapolis: Fortress Press.

_____. 1992. "Joahnnine Trajectories in the *Acts of John.*" *Apocrypha* 3: 47-68.

Pesch, R. 1986. *Die Apostelgeschichte.* EKK, 2 Vols. Einsiedeln, Köln: Benziger Verlag; Neukirchen-Vluyn: Neukirchener Verlag.

Peterson, D. 1993. "The Motif of Fulfilment and the Purpose of Luke-Acts." In *The Book of Acts in Its Ancient Literary Settings*, ed. B. Winter, Clarke, A.D.:83-104. Grand Rapids, Michigan: Eerdmans.

Peterson, E. 1926. *ΕΙΣ ΘΕΟΣ. Epigraphische, formgeschichtliche und religionsgeschichtliche Untersuchungen.* FRLANT 24. Göttingen: Vandenhoeck & Ruprecht.

Pettersen, A. 1990. "Sending Heretics to Coventry? Ignatius of Antioch on Reverencing Silent Bishops." *VC* 44: 335-50.

Picard, Ch. 1922. *Éphèse et Claros. Recherches sur les Sanctuaires et les Cultes de L'Ionie du Nord.* Paris: de Boccard.

Pick, B. 1906. "Die Neokorien von Ephesos." In *Corolla Numismatica. Numismatic Essays in Honour of Barclay V. Head*:234-44. London: Oxford University Press.

Pietersen, L. 1997. "Despicable Deviants: Labelling Theory and the Polemic of the Pastorals." *Sociology of Religion* 58: 343-52.

Pilch, J.J. 1997. "Are there Jews and Christians in the Bible?" *HvTSt* 53: 119-125.

Pillinger, R., Kresten, O., Krinzinger, F. Russo, E., ed. 1999. *Efeso Paleocristiana e Bizantina - Frühchristliches und Byzantinisches Ephesos.* Österreichische Akademie der Wissenschaften Philosophisch-Historische Klasse Denkschriften, 282. Band. Archäologische Forschungen Band 3. Wien: Verlag der Österreichische Akademie der Wissenschaften.

Pincherle, A. 1928. "Paul à Éphèse." In *Congrès d'histoire du Christianisme: Jubilé Alfred Loisy*, ed. P.-. Couchoud:51-69. Paris: Les Éditions Rieder; Amsterdam: Van Holkema & Warendorf.

Piper, O.A. 1947. "I John and the Didache of the Primitive Church." *JBL* 66: 437-51.

Pippin, T. 1992a. *Death and Desire. The Rhetoric of Gender in the Apocalypse of John.* Literary Currents in Biblical Interpretation. Louisville, Kentucky: Westminster/John Knox Press.

_____. 1992b. "Eros and the End: Reading for Gender in the Apocalypse of John." *Semeia* 59: 193-210.

_____. 1992c. "The Heroine and the Whore: Fantasy and the Female in the Apocalypse of John." *Semeia* 60: 67-82.

_____. 1994. "The Revelation to John." In *Searching the Scriptures. Volume Two: A Feminist Commentary*, ed. E. Schüssler Fiorenza:109-30. New York: Crossroad.

_____. 1999. *Apocalyptic Bodies. The Biblical End of the World in Text and Image.* London and New York: Routledge.

Pleket, H.W. 1994. "The Roman state and the economy: the case of Ephesus." In *Entretiens d'Archéologie et d'Histoire, Économie Antique. Les échanges dans l'Antiquité: le rôle de l'État.*:115-26: Saint-Bertrand-de-Comminges.

Plummer, A. 1915. *A Critical and Exegetical Commentary on the Second Epistle of St Paul to the Corinthians.* ICC. Edinburgh: T & T Clark.

Pogoloff, S.M. 1992. *Logos and Sophia. The Rhetorical Situation of 1 Corinthians.* SBLDS 134. Atlanta, Georgia: Scholars Press.

Pokorny, P. 1992. *Der Brief des Paulus an die Epheser.* THKNT 10/II. Leipzig: Evangelische Verlagsanstalt.

Polhill, J.B. 1992. *Acts.* NAC. Nashville, Tennesse: Broadman Press.

Portefaix, L. 1999. "The Image of Artemis Ephesia - A Symbolic Configuration Related to her Mysteries?" In *100 Jahre Österreichische Forschungen in Ephesos. Akten des Symposions Wien 1995*, ed. H. Friesinger, Krinzinger, F.:611-17. Wien: Verlag der Österreichischen Akademie der Wissenschaften.

Porter, S. E. 1993. "What does it mean to be 'Saved by Childbirth' (1 Timothy 2.15)?" *JSNT* 49: 87-102.

_____. 1995. "Pauline Authorship and the Pastoral Epistles: Implications for Canon." *BBR* 5: 105-23.

_____. 1996. "Pauline Authorship and the Pastoral Epistles: A Response to R.W. Wall's Response." *BBR* 6: 133-8.

_____. 1999. *The Paul of Acts: Essays in Literary Criticism, Rhetoric and Theology.* WUNT 115. Tübingen: Mohr Siebeck.

Powell, D. 1975. "*Ordo Presbyterii.*" *JTS* ns 26: 290-328.

Prast, F. 1979. *Presbyter und Evangelium in nachapostolischer Zeit. Die Abschiedsrede des Paulus in Milet (Apg 20,17-38) im Rahmen der lukanischen Konzeption der Evangeliumsverkündigung.* Stuttgart: Verlag Katholisches Bibelwerk.

Preisendanz, K. 1931. *Papyri Graecae Magicae. Die Griechischen Zauberpapyri.* 2nd edn.; 2 vols.; reprint Stuttgart: Teubner 1974.

Price, M.J., Trell, B.L. 1977. *Coins and Their Cities. Architecture on the ancient coins of Greece, Rome, and Palestine.* London: V.C. Vecchi and Sons.

Price, R. M. 1989. "The Sitz-im-Leben of Third John - A New Reconstruction." *EvQ* 61: 109-19.

Price, R.M. 1997. *The Widow Traditions in Luke-Acts. A Feminist-Critical Scrutiny.* SBLDS 155. Atlanta, Georgia: Scholars Press.

Price, S.R.F. 1984. *Rituals and Power. The Roman imperial cult in Asia Minor.* Cambridge: Cambridge University Press.

Prigent, P. 1977. "L'Hérésie asiate et l'Église confessante de l'Apocalypse à Ignace." *VC* 31: 1-22.

_____. 2001. *Commentary on the Apocalypse of St John.* Tübingen: Mohr Siebeck.

Prior, M. 1989. *Paul the Letter-Writer and the Second Letter to Timothy.* JSNTSS 23. Sheffield: JSOT Press.

Provan, I. 1996. "Foul Spirits, Fornication and Finance: Revelation 18 from an Old Testament Perspective." *JSNT* 64: 81-100.

Pucci Ben Zeev, M. 1998. *Jewish Rights in the Roman World. The Greek and Roman Documents Quoted by Josephus Flavius.* TSAJ 74. Tübingen: Mohr Siebeck.

Quasten, J. 1950. *Patrology.* Brussels; Utrecht: Spectrum Publishers.

Quesnel, M. 1985. *Baptisés dans l'Esprit. Baptême et Esprit Saint dans les Actes des Apôtres.* LD 120. Paris: Les Éditions du Cerf.

Quinn, J. D. 1978a. "The Last Volume of Luke: The Relation of Luke-Acts to the Pastoral Epistles." In *Perspectives on Luke-Acts*, ed. C.H. Talbert. Edinburgh: T & T Clark.

_____. 1978b. "'Seven Times He Wore Chains' (1 Clem 5.6)." *JBL* 97: 574-6.

_____. 1979. "The Holy Spirit in the Pastoral Epistles." In *Sin, Salvation and the Spirit: Commemorating the Fiftieth Year of the Liturgical Press*, ed. D. Durken:345-68. Collegeville, Minnesota: The Liturgical Press.

_____. 1981. "Ordination in the Pastoral Epistles." *Communio* 8: 358-69.

_____. 1990. *The Letter to Titus.* AB. New York: Doubleday.

_____. 1992. "Timothy and Titus, Epistles to." In *Anchor Bible Dictionary*, ed. D.N. Freedman, 6:560-71. New York: Doubleday.

Quinn, J. D., Wacker, W.C. 2000. *The First and Second Letters to Timothy.* Eerdmans Critical Commentary. Grand Rapids, Michigan: Eerdmans.

Rackham, R.B. 1910. *The Acts of the Apostles.* WC. London: Methuen & Co.

Räisänen, H. 1995. "The Nicolaitans: Apoc. 2; Acta 6." In *ANRW*, II.26.2:1602-44. Berlin: Walter de Gruyter.

Rajak, T. 2001. *The Jewish Dialogue with Greece and Rome. Studies in Cultural and Social Interaction.* AGJU 48. Leiden: Brill.

_____. 2002. "Synagogue and community in the Graeco-Roman Diaspora." In *Jews in the Hellenistic and Roman Cities*, ed. J.R. Bartlett:22-38. London, New York: Routledge.

Ramsay, W. M. 1889. "Artemis-Leto and Apollo-Lairbenos." *JHS* 10: 216-30.

_____. 1890a. "St Paul at Ephesus." *The Expositor Series* 4, no. 2: 1-22.

_____. 1890b. *The Historical Geography of Asia Minor.* Royal Geographical Society Supplementary Papers 4. London: John Murray.

_____. 1900a. "Historical Commentary on the Epistles to the Corinthians." *The Expositor, Sixth Series* 1: 91-111.

_____. 1900b. "Some Recent Editions of the Acts of the Apostles." *The Expositor, Sixth Series* 2: 321-35.

_____. 1904a. *The Letters to the Seven Churches of Asia and their Place in the Plan of the Apocalypse.* London: Hodder & Stoughton.

_____. 1904b. *The Church in the Roman Empire before A.D. 170.* London: Hodder and Stoughton.

_____. 1905. *St Paul the Traveller and the Roman Citizen.* 8th ed.; London: Hodder and Stoughton.

Reed, J. T. 1992. "Cohesive Ties in 1 Timothy: In Defense of the Epistle's Unity." *Neot* 26: 131-47.

Renan, E. 1869. *Saint Paul.* Paris: Michel Levy.

Rensberger, D. 1988. *Johannine Faith and Liberating Community.* Philadelphia: Westminster.

_____. 1992. "Love for One Another and Love for Enemies in the Gospel of John." In *The Love of Enemies and Nonretaliation in the New Testament*, ed. W. M. Swartley ed:297-313. Louisville, Kentucky: Westminster/John Knox Press.

_____. 1997. *1 John, 2 John, 3 John*. ANTC. Nashville: Abingdon Press.

_____. 1999. "Asceticism and the Gospel of John." In *Asceticism and the New Testament*, ed. L.E. Vaage, Wimbush, V.L.:127-47. New York, London: Routledge.

Reynolds, J.M. 1999. "Ephesus in the Inscriptions of Aphrodisias and Aphrodisians." In *100 Jahre Österreichische Forschungen in Ephesos. Akten des Symposions Wien 1995*, ed. H. Friesinger, Krinzinger, F.:133-7. Wien: Verlag der Österreichischen Akademie der Wissenschaften.

Reynolds, J.M., Tannenbaum, R. 1987. *Jews and God-Fearers at Aphrodisias. Greek Inscriptions with Commentary*. PCPhS Supplementary Volume 12. Cambridge: Cambridge Philological Society.

Richardson, C. C. 1935. *The Christianity of Ignatius of Antioch*. New York: Columbia University Press.

_____. 1937. "The Church in Ignatius of Antioch." *JR* 17: 428-43.

_____. 1953. *Early Christian Fathers*. London: SCM Press.

Richardson, P. 1984. "The Thunderbolt in Q and the Wise Man in Corinth." In *From Jesus to Paul. Studies in Honour of Francis Wright Beare*, ed. P. Richarson, Hurd, J.C.:91-111. Waterloo, Ontario: Wilfred Laurier University Press.

Riesenfeld, H. 1961. "Reflections on the Style and the Theology of St. Ignatius of Antioch." In *Studia Patristica Vol IV*, ed. F.L. Cross, part II:312-22. Berlin: Akademie-Verlag.

Ringe, S.H. 1999. *Wisdom's Friends. Community and Christology in the Fourth Gospel*. Louisville, Kentucky: Westminster John Knox Press.

Rius-Camps, J. 1980. *The Four Authentic Letters of Ignatius, The Martyr*. OrChrAn 213. Rome: Pontificium Institutum Orientalium Studiorum.

Robbins, V.K. 1992. "A Male Reads a Feminist Reading: The Dialogical Nature of Pippin's Power." *Semeia* 59: 211-17.

Robert, L. 1960. *Hellenica. Recueil d'épigraphie de numismatique et d'antiquités grecques. Vol 11-12*. Paris: Libraire d'Amerique et d'Orient.

_____. 1982. "Dans une maison d'Éphèse, un serpent et un chiffre." *CRAI*,: 126-32.

Roberts, C.H. 1975. "Elders: A Note." *JTS* ns 26: 403-5.

Robertson, A., Plummer, A. 1914. *A Critical and Exegetical Commentary on the First Epistle of St Paul to the Corinthians*. ICC. Edinburgh: T & T Clark.

Robinson, B. W. 1910. "An Ephesian Imprisonment of Paul." *JBL* 29: 181-89.

Robinson, J. A. T. 1960-61. "The Destination and Purpose of the Johannine Epistles." *NTS* 7: 56-65.

_____. 1985. *The Priority of John*. London: SCM Press.

Robinson, J. M. 1971. "The Johannine Trajectory." In *Trajectories Through Early Christianity*, eds. J.M. Robinson, Koester, H.:231-68. Philadelphia: Fortress Press.

Robinson, T. A. 1988. *The Bauer Thesis Examined. The Geography of Heresy in the Early Christian Church*. Lewiston/Queenston: Edwin Mellen Press.

_____. 1990. "From the Apostolate to the Episcopate: Reflections on Development." In *Self-Definition and Self-Discovery in Early Christianity. A Study in Changing Horizons. Essays in appreciation of Ben F. Meyer from former students.*, eds. D.J. Hawkin, Robinson, T.:225-50. Lewiston. Queenston, Lampeter: Edwin Mellen Press.

Rogers, C. L. 1979. "The Dionysian Background of Ephesians 5:18." *BSac* 136: 249-57.

Rogers, G. M. 1986. "Demetrios of Ephesos: Silversmith and Neopoios?" *Belleten Türk Tarih Kurumu* 50: 877-83.

_____. 1991. *The Sacred Identity of Ephesos: Foundation Myths of a Roman City.* London and New York: Routledge.

_____. 1992. "The Constructions of Women at Ephesos." *ZPE* 90: 215-223.

_____. 1999. "The Mysteries of Artemis at Ephesos." In *100 Jahre Österreichische Forschungen in Ephesos. Akten des Symposions Wien 1995*, ed. H. Friesinger, Krinzinger, F.:241-50. Wien: Verlag der Österreichischen Akademie der Wissenschaften.

Roloff, J. 1981. *Die Apostelgeschichte.* NTD 5. Göttingen: Vandenhoeck & Ruprecht.

_____. 1988. *Der Erste Brief an Timotheus.* EKKNT XV. Zürich; Neukirchen-Vluyn: Benziger Verlag; Neukirchener Verlag.

_____. 1989. "Themen und Traditionen urchristlicher Amtsträgerparänese." In *Neues Testament und Ethik für Rudolf Schnackenburg*, ed. H. Merklein:507-26. Freiburg, Basel, Wien: Herder.

_____. 1997. "Review of W. Thiessen, *Christen in Ephesus*, und M. Günther, *Die Frühgeschichte des Christentums in Ephesus.*" *BZ* 41: 142-5.

Roozenbeek, H. 1993. "Another Archiatros from Ephesos?" *Epigraphica Anatolia* 21: 103-6.

Ross, J. M. 1992. "The Extra Words in Acts 18:21." *NovT* 34: 247-9.

Rossing, B.R. 1999. *The Choice Between Two Cities. Whore, Bride, and Empire in the Apocalypse.* HTS 48. Harrisburg, Pennsylvania: Trinity Press International.

Rowlingson, D. T. 1950. "Paul's Ephesian Imprisonment: An Evaluation of the Evidence." *ATR* 32: 1-7.

Royalty, R.M. 1998. *The Streets of Heaven. The Ideology of Wealth in the Apocalypse of John.* Macon, Georgia: Mercer University Press.

Rutgers, L.V. 1998. *The Hidden Heritage of Diaspora Judaism.* Leuven: Peeters.

Safrai, S. Stern, M. eds. 1974, 1976. *The Jewish People in the First Century. Historical Geography, Political History, Social, Cultural and Religious Life and Institutions.* CRINT. Assen: Van Gorcum.

Salom, A. P. 1955. "Some Aspects of the Grammatical Style of 1 John." *JBL* 74: 96-102.

Sanders, E.P. 1986. "Paul on the Law, His Opponents, and the Jewish People in Philippians 3 and 2 Corinthians 11." In *Anti-Judaism in Early Christianity. Volume 1: Paul and the Gospels*, ed. P. Richardson:75-90. Waterloo, Ontario: Wilfred Laurier University Press.

Sanders, J. N. 1943. *The Fourth Gospel in the Early Church.* Cambridge: Cambridge Univ. Press.

_____. 1962. "St John at Patmos." *NTS* 9: 75-85.

Sanders, J. T. 1992. "Christians and Jews in the Roman Empire: A Conversation with Rodney Stark." *Sociological Analysis* 53: 433-445.

_____. 2000. *Charisma, Converts, Competitors. Societal and Sociological Factors in the Success of Early Christianity.* London: SCM Press.

Sandnes, K.O. 1994. *A New Family. Conversion and Ecclesiology in the Early Church with Cross-Cultural Comparisons.* Studien zur Interkulturellen Geschichte des Christentums 91. Bern: Peter Lang.

_____. 1996. "'I have called you Friends'. An Aspect of the Christian Fellowship within the Context of the Antique Family." In *The New Testament in Its Hellenistic Context. Proceedings of a Nordic Conference of New Testament Scholars, held in Skálholt*, ed. G.A. Jónsson:95-111. Reykjavík: Gudfraedistofnun Háskóla Islands.

Satake, A. 1966. *Die Gemeindeordnung in der Johannesapokalypse.* WMANT 21. Neukirchen-Vluyn: Neukirchener Verlag.

Saulnier, C. 1981. "Lois romaines sur les juifs selon Flavius Josèphe." *RB* 87: 161-98.

Sawyer, D.F. 1996. *Women and Religion in the First Christian Centuries.* London, New York: Routledge.

Schaberg, J. 1992. "Response to Tina Pippin, 'Eros and the End'." *Semeia* 59: 219-226.

Scherrer, P. 1995a. "The City of Ephesos from the Roman Period to Late Antiquity." In *Ephesos: Metropolis of Asia. An Interdisciplinary Approach to its Archaeology, Religion, and Culture,* ed. H. Koester:1-25. Valley Forge, Pennsylvania: Trinity Press International.

_____. 1995b. *Ephesos: Der neue Führer. 100 Jahre österreichische Ausgrabungen 1895-1995.* Wien: Österreichisches Archäologisches Institut.

Schille, G. 1989. *Die Apostelgeschichte des Lukas.* THKNT 5. Berlin: Evangelische Verlagsanstalt.

Schlarb, E. 1990. *Die Gesunde Lehre. Häresie und Wahrheit im Spiegel der Pastoralbriefe.* Marburger Theologische Studien 28. Marburg: N.G. Elwert Verlag.

Schlatter, A. 1962. *Die Apostelgeschichte.* Erläuterungen zum Neuen Testament 4. Stuttgart: Calwer Verlag.

Schlier, H. 1929. *Religionsgeschichtliche Untersuchungen zu den Ignatiusbriefen.* BZNW 8. Gießen: Alfred Töpelmann.

Schmeling, G.L. 1980. *Xenophon of Ephesus.* Boston: Twayne.

Schmidt, D. D. 1991. "Semitisms and Septuagintalisms in the Book of Revelation." *NTS* 37: 592-603.

Schmithals, W. 1983. "The *Corpus Paulinum* and Gnosis." In *The New Testament and Gnosis: Essays in honour of Robert McL. Wilson,* ed. A.H.B. Logan, Wedderburn, A.J.M.:107-24. Edinburgh: T & T Clark.

Schnabel, E.J. 1999. "Die ersten Christen in Ephesus. Neuerscheinungen zur frühchristlichen Missionsgeschichte." *NovT* 41: 349-82.

Schnackenburg, R. 1965. *The Church in the New Testament.* New York: Herder and Herder.

_____. 1971. "Episkopos und Hirtenamt zu Apg 20,28." In *Schriften zum Neuen Testament. Exegese in Fortschritt und Wandel,* ed. R. Schnackenburg: 247-67. München: Kösel-Verlag.

_____. 1977. "Die johanneische Gemeinde und ihre Geisterfahrung." In *Die Kirche des Anfangs. Für Heinz Schürmann,* ed. R. Schnackenburg, Ernst, J., Wanke, J.:277-306. Freiburg, Basel, Wien: Herder.

_____. 1991a. *The Epistle to the Ephesians.* Edinburgh: T&T Clark.

_____. 1991b. "Ephesus: Entwicklung einer Gemeinde von Paulus zu Johannes." *BZ* 35: 41-64.

_____. 1992. *The Johannine Epistles. Introduction and Commentary.* New York: Crossroad.

Schneider, G. 1982. *Die Apostelgeschichte II. Teil.* HTKNT 5. Freiburg, Basel, Wien: Herder.

Schnelle, U. 1998. *The History and Theology of the New Testament Writings.* London: SCM.

Schoedel, W. R. 1964. "A Blameless Mind 'Not on Loan' but 'By Nature' (Ignatius, Trall. i.1)." *JTS* ns 15: 308-16.

_____. 1978. "Ignatius and the Archives." *HTR* 71: 97-106.

_____. 1985. *Ignatius of Antioch.* Hermeneia. Philadelphia: Fortress Press.

_____. 1992. "Ignatius, Epistles of." In *Anchor Bible Dictionary,* ed. D.N Freedman, 3:384-7. New York: Doubleday.

Scholer, D. M. 1986. "1 Timothy 2:9-15 and the Place of Women in the Church's Ministry." In *Women, Authority and the Bible*, ed. A. Mickelsen:193-224. Downers Grove: IVP.

Schöllgen, G. 1989. "Die διπλῆ τιμή von 1 Tim 5,17." *ZNW* 80: 232-9.

_____. 1998. "Die Ignatianen als pseudepigraphisches Briefcorpus. Anmerkeung zu den Thesen von Reinhard M. Hübner." *ZAC* 2: 16-25.

Schottroff, L., Schroer, S., Wacker, M.-T. 1998. *Feminist Interpretation. The Bible in Women's Perspective*. Minneapolis: Fortress Press.

Schowalter, D. 1999. "Honoring the Emperor: The Ephesians Respond to Trajan." In *100 Jahre Österreichische Forschungen in Ephesos. Akten des Symposions Wien 1995*, ed. H. Friesinger, Krinzinger, F.:121-6. Wien: Verlag der Österreichischen Akademie der Wissenschaften.

Schrage, W. 1991. *Der erste Brief an die Korinther 1. Teilband. 1 Kor 1,1-6,11*. EKK. Zurich und Braunschweig; Neukirchen-Vluyn: Benziger Verlag; Neukirchener Verlag.

_____. 2001. *Der Erste Brief an die Korinther (I Kor 15,1-16,24)*. EKK VII/4. Düsseldorf; Neukirchen-Vluyn: Benziger Verlag; Neukirchener Verlag.

Schreiner, T.R. 1995. "An Interpretation of 1 Timothy 2:9-15: A Dialogue with Scholarship." In *Women in the Church. A Fresh Analysis of 1 Timothy 2:9-15*, ed. A. J. Köstenberger, Schreiner, T.R., Baldwin, H.S.:105-54. Grand Rapids, Michigan: Baker Books.

Schultze, V. 1926. *Altchristliche Städte und Landschaften, II. Kleinasien*. Zweite Hälfte. Gütersloh: C. Bertelsmann.

Schürer, E. 1898. *Geschichte des Jüdischen Volkes im Zeitalter Jesu Christi, Volume 3*. Leipzig: J.C. Hinrichs.

Schürer, E., revised and edited by G. Vermes, F. Millar, M. Black, M. Goodman. 1986. *The History of the Jewish People in the Age of Jesus Christ (175 B.C. - A.D. 135)*. Edinburgh: T & T Clark.

Schurmann, H. 1968. "Das Testament des Paulus für die Kirche. Apg 20, 18-35." In *Traditionsgeschichtliche Untersuchungen zu den synoptischen Evangelien*, ed. H. Schürmann:310-40. Düsseldorf: Patmos-Verlag.

Schüssler Fiorenza, E. 1976. "Miracles, Mission, and Apologetics: An Introduction." In *Aspects of Religious Propaganda in Judaism and Early Christianity*, ed. E. Schüssler Fiorenza: 1-25. Notre Dame, Indiana: University of Notre Dame Press.

_____. 1985. *The Book of Revelation: Justice and Judgment*. Philadelphia: Fortress Press.

_____. 1987. "Rhetorical Situation and Historical Reconstruction in 1 Corinthians." *NTS* 33: 386-403.

_____. 1991. *Revelation Vision of a Just World*. Proclamation Commentaries. Minneapolis: Augsburg Fortress.

_____. 1995. *In Memory of Her. A Feminist Theological Reconstruction of Christian Origins*. London: SCM Press.

Schwabl, H. 1999. "Nachrichten über Ephesos im Traumbuch des Artemidor." In *100 Jahre Österreichische Forschungen in Ephesos. Akten des Symposions Wien 1995*, ed. H. Friesinger, Krinzinger, F.:283-7. Wien: Verlag der Österreichischen Akademie der Wissenschaften.

Schwarz, R. 1983. *Bürgerliches Christentum im Neuen Testament? Eine Studie zu Ethik, Amt und Recht in den Pastoralbriefen*. Klosterneuburg: Österreichisches Katholisches Bibelwerk.

Schweizer, E. 1955. "Die Bekehrung des Apollos." *EvT* 15: 247-54.

_____. 1961. *Church Order in the New Testament*. London: SCM Press.

_____. 1966. "Concerning the Speeches in Acts." In *Studies in Luke-Acts*, ed. L. E. Keck, Martin, J.L.:208-216. Nashville: Abingdon.

_____. 1982. *The Letter to the Colossians: A Commentary*. Minneapolis, Minnesota: Augsburg.

_____. 1987. "The Nature of Ministry in Reformed Understanding: New Testament Dimensions." *HBT* 9: 41-63.

Scobie, C. H. H. 1982. "Johannine Geography." *SR* 11: 77-84.

Scott, E. F. 1936. *The Pastoral Epistles*. London: Hodder & Stoughton.

Seesemann, L. 1893. "Die Nikolaiten. Ein Beitrag zur ältesten Häresiologie." *Theologische Studien und Kritiken* 66: 47-82.

Segovia, F. 1981. "Love and Hatred of Jesus and Johannine Sectarianism." *CBQ* 43: 259-272.

_____. 1982. *Love Relationships in the Johannine Tradition*. Chico: Scholars Press.

Seland, T. 1995. *Establishment Violence in Philo and Luke. A Study of Non-Conformity to the Torah and Jewish Vigilante Reactions*. Biblical Interpretation Series 15. Leiden: E.J. Brill.

Sellin, G. 1998. "Adresse und Intention des Epheserbriefes." In *Paulus, Apostel Jesu Christi. Festschrift für Günter Klein zum 70. Geburtstag*, ed. M Trowitzsch:171-86. Tübingen: Mohr Siebeck.

Seltman, C. 1958. *Riot in Ephesus: Writings on the Heritage of Greece*. London: Max Parrish.

Selvidge, M. J. 1992. "Powerful and Powerless Women in the Apocalypse." *Neot* 26: 157-67.

_____. 1996. "Reflections on Violence and Pornography: Misogyny in the Apocalypse and Ancient Hebrew Prophecy." In *A Feminist Companion to the Hebrew Bible in the New Testament*, ed. A. Brenner:274-85. Sheffield: Sheffield Academic Press.

Senft, C. 1979. *La Première Épitre de Saint Paul aux Corinthiens*. CNT, deuxième série. Neuchâtel: Delachaux & Niestlé.

Shelton, J.B. 1991. *Mighty in Word and Deed. The Role of the Holy Spirit in Luke-Acts*. Peabody, MA: Hendrickson.

Shepherd, W.H. 1994. *The Narrative Function of the Holy Spirit as a Character in Luke-Acts*. SBLDS 147. Atlanta, GA: Scholars Press.

Sherwin-White, A. N. 1963. *Roman Society and Roman Law in the New Testament*. Oxford: Clarendon Press.

_____. 1966. *Letters of Pliny: a historical and social commentary*. Oxford: Clarendon Press.

_____. 1984. *Roman Foreign Policy in the East 168 B.C. to A.D. 1*. London: Duckworth.

Siegel, B.J., ed. 1955. *Acculturation: Critical Abstracts, North America*. Stanford Anthropolgical Series 2. Stanford, California: Stanford University Press.

Sihler, E. G. 1926. "Some Notes on Ephesus." *Theological Monthly* 6: 161-5, 199-203.

Sim, D.C. 2001. "The Gospels for All Christians? A Response to Richard Bauckham." *JSNT* 84: 3-27.

Simon, M. 1978. "De l'observance rituelle à l'ascèse: recherches sur le Décret apostolique." *RHR* 193: 27-104.

_____. 1986. *Verus Israel. A study of the relations between Christians and Jews in the Roman Empire 135-425*. Oxford: Oxford University Press.

Simpson, E.K. 1954. *The Pastoral Epistles. The Greek Text with Introduction and Commentary*. London: Tyndale Press.

Skarsaune, O. 1994. "Heresy and the Pastoral Epistles." *Them* 20: 9-14.

Skeat, T.C. 1979. "'Especially the Parchments': A Note on 2 Tim 4.13." *JTS* ns 30: 173-7.

Skemp, V. 1999. "ΠΑΔΕΛΦΟΣ and the Theme of Kinship in Tobit." *ETL* 75: 92-103.

Slater, T.B. 1998. "On the Social Setting of the Revelation to John." *NTS* 44: 232-56.

Smalley, S. S. 1984. *1,2,3 John*. WBC. Waco, Texas: Word Books.

_____. 1988. "John's Revelation and John's Community." *BJRL* 69: 549-71.

_____. 1994. *Thunder and Love. John's Revelation and John's Community*. Milton Keynes: Word Publishing.

Smallwood, E. M. 1981. *The Jews under Roman Rule from Pompey to Diocletian*. Leiden: E.J. Brill.

Smith, B. T. D. 1914. "Apollos and the Twelve Disciples at Ephesus." *JTS* 16: 241-6.

Smith, D. M. 1974-75. "Johannine Christianity: Some Reflections on its Character and Delineation." *NTS* 21: 222-48.

_____. 1991. *First, Second, and Third John*. IBC. Louisville: John Knox Press.

_____. 1995. *The Theology of the Gospel of John*. Cambridge: CUP.

Smith, J.O. 1996. "The High Priests of the Temple of Artemis at Ephesus." In *Cybele, Attis and Related Cults. Essays in Memory of M.J. Vermaseren*, ed. E.N Lane:323-35. Leiden: E.J. Brill.

Snape, H. C. 1954. "The Fourth Gospel, Ephesus and Alexandria." *HTR* 47: 1-14.

Snyder, G. F. 1977. "The Tobspruch in the New Testament." *NTS* 23: 117-20.

_____. 1999. *Inculturation of the Jesus Tradition. The Impact of Jesus on Jewish and Roman Cultures*. Harrisburg, Pennsylvania: Trinity Press International.

Soards, M. L. 1994. *The Speeches in Acts. Their Content, Context, and Concerns*. Kentucky: Westminster/ John Knox Press.

Solden, U. 1999. "Frauen als Funktionsträgerinnen im kaiserzeitlichen Ephesos: Die weiblichen Prytaneis." In *100 Jahre Österreichische Forschungen in Ephesos. Akten des Symposions Wien 1995*, ed. H. Friesinger, Krinzinger, F.:115-119. Wien: Verlag der Österreichischen Akademie der Wissenschaften.

Songer, H. S. 1970. "The Life Situation of the Johannine Epistles." *RevExp* 67: 399-409.

Sparks, K.L. 1996. *Ethnicity and Identity in Ancient Israel. Prolegomena to the Study of Ethnic Sentiments and their Expression in the Hebrew Bible*. PhD Thesis, University of North Carolina at Chapel Hill.

Speigl, J. 1987. "Ignatius in Philadelphia. Ereignisse und Anliegen in den Ignatiusbriefen." *VC* 41: 360-76.

Spencer, A. B. D. 1974. "Eve at Ephesus." *JETS* 17: 215-22.

Spicq, C. 1931. "Saint Paul et la loi des dépôts." *RB* 40: 481-502.

_____. 1959a. "La justification du charitable (1 Jo. 3, 19-21)." *Bib* 40: 915-27.

_____. 1959b. "L'épitre aux Hébreux, Apollos, Jean-Baptiste, les Hellénistes et Qumran." *RevQ* 1: 365-90.

_____. 1969a. *Les Épîtres Pastorales*. EBib. Paris: J. Gabalda.

_____. 1969b. "La place ou le rôle des jeunes dans certaines communautés néotestamentaires." *RB* 76: 508-27.

_____. 1978. *Notes de Lexicographie Néo-Testamentaire*. OBO 22/1. Fribourg/Suisse: Editions Universitaires; Göttingen: Vandenhoeck und Ruprecht.

Stagg, F. 1970. "Orthodoxy and Orthopraxy in the Johannine Epistles." *RevExp* 67: 423-43.

Stahr, S. 1962. "Ephesos - ein Beitrag Österreichs zur Paulusforschung." *ThPQ* 110: 193-208.

Stamps, D.L. 1997. "The Johannine Writings." In *Handbook of Classical Rhetoric in the Hellenistic Period 330 B.C. - A.D. 400*, ed. S. E. Porter:609-32. Leiden: Brill.

Stander, H. F. 1989. "The Starhymn in the Epistle of Ignatius to the Ephesians (19:2-3)." *VC* 43: 209-14.

Stanley, C.D. 1991. "'Neither Jew nor Greek': Ethnic Conflict in Graeco-Roman Society." *JSNT* 64: 101-24.

Stanley, D. M. 1961. *Christ's Resurrection in Pauline Soteriology*. AnBib 13. Rome: Pontificio Instituto Biblico.

Stanton, G. N. 2002. *The Gospels and Jesus*. 2nd ed. Oxford Bible Series. Oxford: Oxford University Press.

Stark, R. 1991. "Christianizing the urban empire: an analysis based on 22 Greco Roman cities." *Sociological Analysis* 52: 77-88.

_____. 1996. *The Rise of Christianity: A Sociologist Reconsiders History*. Princeton: Princeton University Press.

Steinhauser, K. B. 1984. "Authority in the Primitive Church." *Patristic and Byzantine Review* 3: 89-100.

Steinmetz, F. J. 1968. "'... so daß wir keinen Ausweg mehr sahen' (2 Kor 1,8). Apostolische Mühsal bei Paulus - und heute." *Geist und Leben* 41: 321-6.

Stettler, H. 1998. *Die Christologie der Pastoralbriefe*. WUNT 2.105. Tübingen: Mohr Siebeck.

Stevenson, G. 2001. *Power and Place. Temple and Identity in the Book of Revelation*. BZNW 107. Berlin, New York: Walter de Gruyter.

Stevenson, T.R. 1992. "The Ideal Benefactor and the Father Analogy in Greek and Roman Thought." *CQ* 42: 421-36.

Stiefel, J. H. 1995. "Women Deacons in 1 Timothy: A Linguistic and Literary Look at 'Women Likewise ....' (1 Tim 3.11)." *NTS* 41: 442-57.

Stier, J., Greén, M. 1992. *Ethnic Minority Groups: A Comprehensive Framework*. Växjö, Sweden: Växjö University.

Stoops, R. F. 1989. "Riot and Assembly: The Social Context of Acts 19:23-41." *JBL* 108: 73-91.

Storm, Melvin R. 1993. "Diotrephes: A Study of Rivalry in the Apostolic Church." *ResQ* 35: 193-202.

Stowers, S.K. 1984. "Social Status, Public Speaking and Private Teaching: The Circumstances of Paul's Preaching Activity." *NovT* 26: 59-82.

_____. 1998. "A Cult from Philadelphia: Oikos Religion or Cultic Association?" In *The Early Church in its Context: Essays in Honor of Everett Ferguson*, ed. A. J. Malherbe, Norris, F.W., Thompson, J.W.:287-301. Leiden: Brill.

Strand, K. A. 1966. "The Rise of the Monarchical Episcopate." *AUSS* 4: 65-88.

_____. 1991. "Church Organization in First-Century Rome: A New Look at the Basic Data." *AUSS* 29: 139-60.

_____. 1992. "Governance in the First-Century Christian Church in Rome: Was it Collegial?" *AUSS* 30: 59-75.

Strange, W. A. 1987. "The Sons of Sceva and the Text of Acts 19:14." *JTS* ns 38: 97-106.

Stratton, B.J. 1996. "Eve Through Several Lenses: Truth in 1 Timothy 2.8-15." In *A Feminist Companion to the Hebrew Bible in the New Testament*, ed. A. Brenner:258-73. Sheffield: Sheffield Academic Press.

Strecker, G. 1996. *The Johannine Letters. A Commentary on 1, 2, and 3 John*. Hermeneia. Minneapolis: Fortress Press.

Streete, G.C. 1999. "*Askesis* and Resistance in the Pastoral Letters." In *Asceticism and the New Testament*, ed. L.E. Vaage, Wimbush, V.L.:299-316. New York, London.

Streeter, B.H. 1929. *The Primitive Church*. London: Macmillan and Co.

Strelan, R. 1996. *Paul, Artemis, and the Jews in Ephesus*. BZNW 80. Berlin, New York: Walter de Gruyter.

Strocka, V.M. 1977. *Die Wandermalerei der Hanghäuser in Ephesos*. FiE 8.1. Wien: Österreichischen Akademie der Wissenschaften.

Sumney, J.L. 1993. "Those Who 'Ignorantly Deny Him': The Opponents of Ignatius of Antioch." *JECS* 1: 345-65.

_____. 1999. *'Servants of Satan', 'False Brothers' and Other Opponents of Paul*. JSNTSS 188. Sheffield: Sheffield Academic Press.

Suys, V. 1998. "Déméter et le prytanée d'Éphèse." *Kernos* 11: 173-88.

Swete, H. B. 1906. *The Apocalypse of St John*. London: Macmillan.

Taeger, J.-W. 1998. "Begründetes Schweigen. Paulus und paulinische Tradition in der Johannesapokalypse." In *Paulus. Apostel Jesu Christi. Festschrift für Günter Klein*, ed. M. Trowitzsch:187-204. Tübingen: J.C.B. Mohr (Paul Siebeck).

Takács, S.A. 1999. "Isis and Sarapis in Ephesos." In *100 Jahre Österreichische Forschungen in Ephesos. Akten des Symposions Wien 1995*, ed. H. Friesinger, Krinzinger, F.:269-74. Wien: Verlag der Österreichischen Akademie der Wissenschaften.

Talbert, C. H. 1992. *Reading John: A Literary and Theological Commentary on the Fourth Gospel and the Johannine Epistles*: NY: Crossroads.

Taylor, J. 1994. "Why Were the Disciples First Called 'Christians' at Antioch? (Acts 11, 26)." *RB* 101: 75-94.

_____. 1996. *Les Actes des deux Apôtres VI. Commentaire Historique (Act. 18,23-28,31)*. EBib 30. Paris: Librairie Lecoffre.

_____. 1999. "The List of the Nations in Acts 2:9-11." *RB* 106: 408-20.

Taylor, J.E. 1997. *The Immerser. John the Baptist within Second Temple Judaism*. Studying the Historical Jesus. Grand Rapids, Michigan: Eerdmans.

Taylor, W. F. 1993. "1-2 Timothy, Titus." In *The Deutero-Pauline Letters. Ephesians, Colossians, 2 Thessalonians, 1-2 Timothy, Titus,*, ed. G. Krodel:59-93. Minneapolis: Fortress Press.

Taylor, W. F., Reumann. J. H. P. 1985. *Ephesians, Colossians*. ACNT. Minnesota: Augsburg.

Tcherikover, V. 1961. *Hellenistic Civilization and the Jews*. Philadelphia: Jewish Publication Society of America.

Tcherikover, V., Fuks, A., Stern, M. 1964. *Corpus Papyrorum Judaicarum Vol 111*. Cambridge, Massachusetts: Harvard University Press.

Thacker, A. 1991. "Note: Paul's Thorn in the Flesh." *Epworth Review* 18, no. 1: 67-9.

Theissen, G. 1982. *The Social Setting of Pauline Christianity. Essays on Corinth*. Philadelphia: Fortress Press.

_____. 2001. "The Social Structure of Pauline Communties: Some Critical Remarks on J.J. Meggitt, *Paul, Poverty and Survival*." *JSNT* 84: 65-84.

Thiering, B.E. 1981. "*Mebaqqer* and *Episkopos* in the Light of the Temple Scoll." *JBL* 100: 59-74.

Thiessen, W. 1995. *Christen in Ephesus. Die historische und theologische Situation in vorpaulinischer und paulinischer Zeit und zur Zeit der Apostelgeschichte und der Pastoralbriefe*. Texte und Arbeiten zum neutestamentlichen Zeitalter 12. Tübingen: Francke Verlag.

Thiselton, A.C. 2000. *The First Epistle to the Corinthians. A Commentary on the Greek Text*. NIGTC. Grand Rapids, Michigan: Eerdmans.

Thomas, C. 1995. "At Home in the City of Artemis: Religion in Ephesos in the Literary Imagination of the Roman Period." In *Ephesos: Metropolis of Asia. An Interdisciplinary Approach to its Archaeology, Religion, and Culture*, ed. H. Koester:81-117. Valley Forge, Pennsylvania: Trinity Press International.

Thomas, J.C. 1995. "The Order of the Composition of the Johannine Epistles." *NovT* 37: 68-75.

_____. 1996. "'An Angel from Satan': Paul's Thorn in the Flesh (2 Corinthians 12.7-10)." *Journal of Pentecostal Theology* 9: 39-52.

Thompson, L. L. 1990. *The Book of Revelation: Apocalypse and Empire*. Oxford: Oxford University Press.

_____. 1998. *Revelation*. ANTC. Nashville: Abingdon Press.

Thompson, M.B. 1998. "The Holy Internet: Communication Between Churches in the First Christian Generation." In *The Gospels for All Christians. Rethinking the Gospel Audiences*, ed. R. Bauckham:49-70. Grand Rapids, Michigan: Eerdmans.

Thrall, M.E. 1994. *A Critical and Exegetical Commentary on The Second Epistle to the Corinthians. Volume 1: Introduction and Commentary on II Corinthians I-VII*. ICC. Edinburgh: T & T Clark.

Thür, H. 1995. "The Processional Way in Ephesos as a Place of Cult and Burial." In *Ephesos: Metropolis of Asia. An Interdisciplinary Approach to its Archaeology, Religion, and Culture*, ed. H. Koester:157-99. Valley Forge, Pennsylvania: Trinity Press International.

Thurston, B. B. 1989. *The Widows: A Women's Ministry in the Early Church*. Minneapolis: Fortress Press.

Tierney, M. 1929. "Ephesus, Pagan and Christian." *Studies: An Irish Quarterly Review* 18: 449-63.

Tonneau, R.P.R. 1929. "Éphèse au temps de Saint Paul." *RB* 38: 5-34, 321-63.

Torjesen, K.J. 1993. "Reconstruction of Women's Early Christian History." In *Searching the Scriptures. Volume One: A Feminist Introduction*, ed. E. Schüssler Fiorenza:290-310. New York: Crossroad.

Towner, P. H. 1987. "Gnosis and Realised Eschatology in Ephesus (of the Pastoral Epistles) and the Corinthian Enthusiam." *JSNT* 31: 95-124.

_____. 1989. *The Goal of Our Instruction: The Structure of Theology and Ethics in the Pastorla Epistles*. JSNTSS 34. Sheffield: JSOT Press.

_____. 1994. *1-2 Timothy & Titus*. IVP NT Commentary Series. Downers Grove, Illinois: IVP.

_____. 1995. "Pauline Theology or Pauline Tradition in the Pastoral Epistles: The Question of Method." *TynBul* 46: 287-314.

_____. 1997. "Feminist Approaches to the New Testament, with 1 Timothy 2:8 15 as a Test Case." *Jian Dao* 7: 91-111.

Tragan, P. R. 1985. "Les «destinataires» du Discours de Milet. Une approche du cadre communautaire d'Ac 20, 18-35." In *À Cause de l'Evangile. Études sur les Synoptiques et les Actes offertes au P. Jacques Dupont, O.S.B. à l'occasion de son 70e anniversaire*:779-98. Paris: Cerf.

Trakatellis, D. 1991. "God Language in Ignatius of Antioch." In *The Future of Early Christianity. Essays in Honor of Helmut Koester*, ed. B. A. Pearson, in collaboration with A.T. Kraabel, G.W.E. Nickelsburg, N.R. Petersen:422-30. Minneapolis: Fortress Press.

Trebilco, P.R. 1991. *Jewish Communities in Asia Minor*. SNTSMS 69. Cambridge: Cambridge University Press.

_____. 1993. "Itineraries, travel plans, journeys, apostolic parousia." In *The Dictionary of Paul and His Letters*, ed. G. F. Hawthorne, Martin, R.P., Reid, D.G.:446-456. Downers Grove, Illinois: IVP.

_____. 1994. "Asia." In *The Book of Acts in its Greco-Roman Setting*, ed. D.W.J. Gill, Gempf, C.:291-362. Grand Rapids, Michigan: Eerdmans.

_____. 1997. "Diaspora Judaism." In *Dictionary of the Later New Testament and Its Developments*, ed. P.H. Davids, Martin, R.P.:287-300. Downers Grove, Illinois: IVP.

_____. 1999. "Jews, Christians and the Associations in Ephesos: A Comparative Study of Group Structures." In *100 Jahre Österreichische Forschungen in Ephesos. Akten des Symposions Wien 1995*, ed. H. Friesinger, Krinzinger, F.:325-34. Wien: Verlag der Österreichischen Akademie der Wissenschaften.

_____. 2000. "The Goodness and Holiness of the Earth and the Whole Creation (1 Tim. 4:1-5)." In *Readings from the Perspective of Earth. The Earth Bible, Volume 1*, ed. N. Habel:204-220. Sheffield: Sheffield Academic Press.

_____. 2001. "Timorati di Dio." In *Gli Ebrei nell'impero romano*, ed. A. Lewin:161-93. Florence: Editrice La Giuntina.

Trell, B.L. 1945. *The Temple of Artemis at Ephesos*. Numismatic Notes and Monographs 107. New York: The American Numismatic Society.

_____. 1988. "The Temple of Artemis at Ephesos." In *The Seven Wonders of the Ancient World*, ed. P.A. Clayton, Price, M.J.:78-99. London and New York: Routledge.

Trevett, C. 1980. *Ignatius and His Opponents in the Divided Church of Antioch in Relation to Some Aspects of the Early Syrian Christian Tradition: a study based on the text of the Middle Recension of the Ignatian Letters*. PhD Thesis, University of Sheffield.

_____. 1983. "Prophecy and Anti-Episcopal Activity: a Third Error Combatted by Ignatius?" *JEH* 34: 1-18.

_____. 1989a. "The Other Letters to the Churches of Asia: Apocalypse and Ignatius of Antioch." *JSNT* 37: 117-35.

_____. 1989b. "Ignatius 'To the Romans' and 1 Clement LIV-LVI." *VC* 43: 35-52.

_____. 1989c. "Apocalypse, Ignatius, Montanism: Seeking the Seeds." *VC* 43: 313-338.

_____. 1989d. "Ignatius and the Monstrous Regiment of Women." In *Studia Patristica Vol XXI*, ed. E.A. Livingstone:202-14. Leuven: Peeters Press.

_____. 1992. *A Study of Ignatius of Antioch in Syria and Asia*. Studies in the Bible and Early Christianity 29. Queenston, Lampeter: Edwin Mellen Press.

Trobisch, D. 1989. *Die Entstehung der Paulusbriefsammlung. Studien zu den Anfängen christlicher Publizistik*. NTOA 10. Freiburg, Schweiz; Göttingen: Universitätsverlag; Vandenhoeck & Ruprecht.

_____. 1994. *Paul's Letter Collection. Tracing the Origins*. Minneapolis: Fortress Press.

Trocmé, É. 1999. "La Jezabel de Thyatire (Apoc. 2/20-24)." *RHPR* 79: 51-5.

Trudinger, P. 1988. "The Ephesus Milieu." *DRev* 106: 286-96.

Turner, C.H. 1927. "1 Tim. vi 12, 13: ἐπὶ Ποντίου Πειλάτου." *JTS* 28: 270-3.

Turner, N. 1963. *A Grammar of New Testament Greek, by J.H. Moulton, Vol III, Syntax*. Edinburgh: T & T Clark.

_____. 1976. *A Grammar of New Testament Greek, by J.H. Moulton, Vol IV, Style*. Edinburgh: T & T Clark.

Usami, K. 1983. *Somatic Comprehension of Unity: The Church in Ephesus*: AnBib 101.

Uzel, I. 1999. "Les Instruments Medicaux et Chirurgicaux Conservés au Musée d'Ephèse." In *100 Jahre Österreichische Forschungen in Ephesos. Akten des Symposions Wien 1995*, ed. H. Friesinger, Krinzinger, F.:211-14. Wien: Verlag der Österreichischen Akademie der Wissenschaften.

van Bremen, R. 1996. *The Limits of Participation. Women and civic life in the Greek East in the Hellenistic and Roman periods*. Amsterdam: J.C. Gieben.

van der Horst, P. W. 1976. "Peter's Shadow, The Religio-Historical Background of Acts v.15." *NTS* 23: 204-12.

_____. 1981. *Aelius Aristides and the New Testament*. SCHNT 6. Leiden: E.J. Brill.

_____. 1991. *Ancient Jewish Epitaphs. An introductory survey of a millenium of Jewish funerary epigraphy (300 BCE - 700 CE)*. Kampen: Kok Pharos Publishing House.

van der Watt, J.G. 2000. *Family of the King. Dynamics of Metaphor in the Gospel according to John*. Biblical Interpretation Series 47. Leiden: Brill.

van Eck, E. 2000. "A Sitz for the Gospel of Mark? A critical reaction to Bauckham's theory on the universality of the Gospels." *HvTSt* 56: 973-1008.

van Tilborg, S. 1996. *Reading John in Ephesus*. NovTSup 83. Leiden: Brill.

van Unnik, W. C. 1960a. "The "Book of Acts" the Confirmation of the Gospel." *NovT* 4: 26-59.

_____. 1960b. "Die Rücksicht auf die Reaktion der Nicht-Christen als Motiv in der altchristlichen Paränese." In *Judentum, Urchristentum, Kirche. Festschrift für Joachim Jeremias*, ed. W. Eltester ed:221-34. Berlin: Alfred Töpelmann.

Vanni, U. 1980. "L'Apocalypse johannique. État de la question." In *L'Apocalypse johannique et l'Apocalyptique dans le Nouveau Testament*, ed. J. Lambrecht:21-46. Gembloux; Leuven: Duculot; Leuven University Press.

Vellanickal, M. 1977. *The Divine Sonship of Christians in the Johannine Writings*: AnBib72.

Verner, D. C. 1983. *The Household of God. The Social World of the Pastoral Epistles*. SBLDS 71. Chico, California: Scholars Press.

Vilela, A. 1973. "Le Presbytérium selon saint Ignace d'Antioche." *Bulletin de Littérature Ecclésiastique* 74: 161-86.

Vogt, H.J. 1978. "Ignatius von Antiochen über den Bischof und seine Gemeinde." *TQ* 158: 15-27.

_____. 1999. "Bemerkungen zur Echtheit der Ignatiusbriefe." *ZAC* 3: 50-63.

Vokes, F. E. 1982. "The Origin and Place of Presbyters in the New Testament Church." In *Studia Evangelica VII*, ed. E. A. Livingstone ed:541-5. Berlin: Akademie-Verlag.

von Campenhausen, H. 1969. *Ecclesiastical Authority and Spiritual Power in the Church of the First Three Centuries*. London: A & C Black.

von Harnack, A. 1908. *The Mission and Expansion of Christianity in the First Three Centuries*. London: Williams and Norgate.

_____. 1923. "The Sect of the Nicolaitans and Nicolaus, the Deacon in Jerusalem." *JR* 3: 413-22.

von Wahlde, U. C. 1990. *The Johannine Commandments: 1 John and the Struggle for the Johannine Tradition*. New York: Paulist.

_____. 2000. "'The Jews' in the Gospel of John. Fifteen Years of Research (1983-1998)." *ETL* 76: 30-55.

Vorster, W. S. 1975. "Heterodoxy in 1 John." *Neot* 9: 87-97.

Vos, L.A. 1965. *The Synoptic Traditions in the Apocalypse*. Kampen: J.H. Kok.

Vouga, F. 1988. "The Johannine School: A Gnostic Tradition in Primitive Christianity?" *Bib* 69: 371-85.

_____. 1990. *Die Johannesbriefe*. HNT 15/III. Tübingen: J.C.B. Mohr (Paul Siebeck).

Wainwright, J. J. 1993. "Eusebeia: Syncretism or Conservative Contextualization." *EvQ* 65: 211-24.

Wall, R. W. 1995. "Pauline Authorship and the Pastoral Epistles: A Response to S.E. Porter." *BBR* 5: 125-8.

Walters, J. 1995. "Egyptian Religions in Ephesos." In *Ephesos: Metropolis of Asia. An Interdisciplinary Approach to its Archaeology, Religion, and Culture*, ed. H. Koester:281-309. Valley Forge, Pennsylvania: Trinity Press International.

_____. 1999. "The Coincidence of the Expansion of Christianity and the Egyptian Cults in Imperial Ephesos." In *100 Jahre Österreichische Forschungen in Ephesos. Akten des Symposions Wien 1995*, ed. H. Friesinger, Krinzinger, F.:315-24. Wien: Verlag der Österreichischen Akademie der Wissenschaften.

Wankel, H. et al, ed. 1979-84. *Die Inschriften von Ephesos*. Inschriften griechischen Städte aus Kleinasien 11.1-17.4. Bonn: Rudolf Habelt.

Warden, P.D., Bagnall, R.S. 1988. "The Forty Thousand Citizens of Ephesus." *CP* 83: 220-3.

Warfield, B. B. 1885. "Some difficult passages in the First Chapter of 2 Corinthians." *JBL* 3: 27-39.

Warmington, B.H. 1977. *Suetonius: Nero. Text, with introduction and notes*. Bristol: Bristol Classical Press.

Watson, D.F. 1989a. "1 John 2.12-14 as *Distributio, Conduplicatio,* and *Expolitio*: A Rhetorical Understanding." *JSNT* 35: 97-110.

_____. 1989b. "A Rhetorical Analysis of 2 John according to Greco-Roman Convention." *NTS* 35: 104-30.

_____. 1989c. "A Rhetorical Analysis of 3 John: A Study in Epistolary Rhetoric." *CBQ* 51: 479-501.

_____. 1991. "Paul's Speech to the Ephesian Elders (Acts 20.17-38): Epideictic Rhetoric of Farewell." In *Persuasive Artistry. Studies in NT Rhetoric in Honor of George A. Kennedy*, ed. D.F. Watson:184-208. Sheffield: JSOT Press.

_____. 1992. "Nicolaitans." In *Anchor Bible Dictionary*, ed. D.N Freedman, 4:1106-7. New York: Doubleday.

_____. 1993. "Amplification Techniques in 1 John: The Interaction of Rhetorical Style and Invention." *JSNT* 51: 99-123.

Watson, D. F., Hauser, A.J. 1994. *Rhetorical Criticism of the Bible*. Leiden: E.J. Brill.

Watson, F. 1998. "Toward a Literal Reading of the Gospels." In *The Gospels for All Christians. Rethinking the Gospel Audiences*, ed. R. Bauckham:195-217. Grand Rapids, Michigan: Eerdmans.

Watson, N. 1992. *The First Epistle to the Corinthians*. Epworth Commentaries. London: Epworth Press.

_____. 1993. *The Second Epistle to the Corinthians*. Epworth Commentaries. London: Epworth Press.

Webb, R.L. 1991. *John the Baptizer and Prophet. A Socio-Historical Study*. JSNTSS 62. Sheffield: JSOT Press.

Weber, M. 1978. *Economy and Society: An Outline of Interpretive Sociology, 2 Vols*. Berkeley: University of California Press.

Weinreich, O. 1912. "'Θεοὶ ἐπήκοοι'." *MDAI, Athenische Abteilung* 37: 1-68.

Weiss, J. 1937. *The History of Primitive Christianity, 2 Vols*. London: MacMillan and Co.

Wendland, E.R. 1998. "'Dear Children' Verses the 'Antichrists': The Rhetoric of Reassurance in First John." *JOTT* 11: 40-84.

Wengst, K. 1976. *Häresie und Orthodoxie im Spiegel des ersten Johannesbriefes*. Gütersloh: Mohn.

_____. 1978. *Der erste, zweite und dritte Brief des Johannes*. ÖTK 16. Gütersloh; Würzburg:: Mohn; Echter Verlag.

_____. 1981. *Bedrangte Gemeinde und verherrlichte Christus: Der historische Ort des Johannesevangelium als Schussel zu seiner Interpretation*. Biblisch-theologische Studien 5; Neukirchen: Neukircener Verlag.

Wexler, P. 1981. "Terms for 'Synagogue' in Hebrew and Jewish Languages. Explorations in Historical Jewish Interlinguistics." *REJ* 140: 101-38.

Wheeler, S.E. 1995. *Wealth as Peril and Obligation. The New Testament on Possessions*. Grand Rapids: Eerdmans.

Whitacre, R. A. 1982. *Johannine Polemic: The Role of Tradition and Theology*. SBLDS 67. Chico, CA: Scholars Press.

White, J. L. 1972. *The Form and Function of the Body of the Greek Letter: A Study of the Letter-Body in the Non-Literary Papyri and in Paul the Apostle*. SBLDS 2. Missoula, Montana: Sbl.

White, L. M. 1988. "Shifting Sectarian Boundaries in Early Christianity." *BJRL* 70: 7-24.

_____. 1990. *The Social Origins of Christian Architecture. Volume 1: Building God's House in the Roman World: Architectural Adaptation among Pagans, Jews, and Christians*. HTS 42. Valley Forge, Pennsylvania: Trinity Press International.

_____. 1995. "Urban Development and Social Change in Imperial Ephesos." In *Ephesos: Metropolis of Asia. An Interdisciplinary Approach to its Archaeology, Religion, and Culture*, ed. H. Koester:27-79. Valley Forge, Pennsylvania: Trinity Press International.

Wiebe, B. 1994. "Two Texts on Women (1 Tim 2:11-15; Gal 3:26-9). A Test of Interpretation." *HBT* 16: 54-85.

Wilder, A.N. 1957. "The First, Second, and Third Epistles of John: Introduction and Exegesis." In *The Interpreter's Bible, Volume XII*, ed. G.A. Buttrick:209-313. New York: Abingdon Press.

Wiles, M. F. 1982. "Ignatius and the Church." In *Studia Patristica Vol XVII*, ed. E.A. Livingstone, Part Two:750-5. Oxford: Pergamon Press.

Williams, C.S.C. 1957. *A Commentary on the Acts of the Apostles*. BNTC. London: A & C Black.

Williams, D. J. 1990. *Acts*. NIBC. Peabody, Massachusetts: Hendrickson.

Williams, M.H. 1997. "The Meaning and Function of *Ioudaios* in Graeco-Roman Inscriptions." *ZPE* 116: 249-62.

Wilson, S. G. 1979. *Luke and the Pastoral Epistles*. London: SPCK.

Wimbush, A.L. 1996. ""... Not of This World ...": Early Christianities as Rhetorical and Social Formation." In *Reimagining Christian Origins. A Colloquium Honoring Burton L. Mack*, ed. E.A. Castelli, Taussig, H.:23-36. Valley Forge, PA: Trinity Press International.

Winter, B.W. 1988. "Providentia for the widows of 1 Timothy 5:3-16." *TynBul* 39: 83-99.

_____. 1994. "Acts and Roman Religion B: The Imperial Cult." In *The Book of Acts in its Greco-Roman Setting*, ed. D.W.J. Gill, Gempf, C.:93-103. Grand Rapids, Michigan: Eerdmans.

Wiplinger, G. 1999. "Neue Untersuchungen in Wohneinheit 1 und 2 des Hanghauses 2 in Ephesos." In *100 Jahre Österreichische Forschungen in Ephesos. Akten des Symposions Wien 1995*, ed. H. Friesinger, Krinzinger, F.:521-6. Wien: Verlag der Österreichischen Akademie der Wissenschaften.

Wiplinger, G., Wlach, G. 1996. *Ephesus. 100 Years of Austrian Research*. Vienna: Böhlau Verlag; Österreichisches Archäologisches Institut.

Wisse, F. 1971. "The Nag Hammadi Library and the Heresiologists." *VC* 25: 205-223.

Witherington, B. 1988. *Women in the Earliest Churches*. SNTSMS 59. Cambridge: Cambridge University Press.

————. 1995. *Conflict and Community in Corinth. A Socio-Rhetorical Commentary on 1 and 2 Corinthians*. Grand Rapids, Michigan; Carlisle: Eerdmans; Paternoster Press.

Wohlenberg, G. 1895. "Nikolaus von Antiochien und die Nikolaiten. Eine Studie." *NKZ* 6: 923-61.

Wolff, C. 1982. *Der erste Brief des Paulus an die Korinther. Zweiter Teil: Auslegung der Kapitel 8-16*. THKNT. Berlin: Evangelische Verlagsanstalt.

————. 1989. *Der zweite Brief des Paulus an die Korinther*. THKNT. Berlin: Evangelische Verlagsanstalt.

Wong, D.K.K. 1998. "The Tree of Life in Revelation 2:7." *BSac* 155: 211-26.

Wood, J. E. 1982. "Death at Work in Paul." *EvQ* 54: 151-5.

Wood, J.T. 1877. *Discoveries at Ephesus, including the sites and remains of the great Temple of Diana*. London: Longmans, Green & Co.

————. 1878. "On the Antiquities of Ephesus having relation to Christianity." *Transactions of the Society of Biblical Archaeology* 6: 327-33.

Woods, L. 1991. "Opposition to a Man and His Message: Paul's 'Thorn in the Flesh' (2 Cor 12:7)." *ABR* 39: 44-53.

Worth, R.H. 1999a. *The Seven Cities of the Apocalypse and Roman Culture*. New York/Mahwah, N.J.: Paulist Press.

————. 1999b. *The Seven Cities of the Apocalypse and Greco-Asian Culture*. New York/Mahwah, N.J.: Paulist Press.

Wright, A. 1897. "Apollos, a Study in Pre-Pauline Christianity." *ExpTim* 9: 8-12.

————. 1913. "Τάξει in Papias." *JTS* 14: 298-300.

Wright, B. G. 1984. "Cerinthus Apud Hippolytus: An Inquiry into the Traditions about Cerinthus' Provenance." *SecCent* 4: 103-115.

Yamauchi, E. 1980. *The Archaeology of New Testament Cities in Asia Minor*. London: Pickering & Inglis.

Yarbro Collins, A. 1976. *The Combat Myth in the Book of Revelation*. HTRHDR 9. Missoula, Montana: Scholars Press.

————. 1977. "The History-of-Religions Approach to Apocalypticism and the 'Angel of the Waters' (Rev 16:4-7)." *CBQ* 39: 367-81.

————. 1979. "Crisis and Community in John's Gospel." *TD* 27: 313-21.

————. 1980. "Revelation 18: Taunt-Song or Dirge?" In *L'Apocalypse johannique et l'Apocalyptique dans le Nouveau Testament*, ed. J. Lambrecht:185-204. Gembloux; Leuven: Duculot; Leuven University Press.

————. 1984. *Crisis and Catharsis: The Power of the Apocalypse*. Philadelphia: Westminster Press.

————. 1987. "Women's History and the Book of Revelation." In *SBLSP 1987*, ed. K.H. Richards: 80-91. Atlanta, Georgia: Scholars Press.

Yates, R. 1981. "Paul's Affliction in Asia: 2 Corinthians 1:8." *EvQ* 53: 241-5.

Young, F. 1994a. *The Theology of the Pastoral Letters*. Cambridge: Cambridge University Press.

————. 1994b. "On ΕΠΙΣΚΟΠΟΣ and ΠΡΕΣΒΥΤΕΡΟΣ." *JTS* ns 45: 142-8.

Zabehlicky, H. 1995. "Preliminary Views of the Ephesian Harbor." In *Ephesos: Metropolis of Asia. An Interdisciplinary Approach to its Archaeology, Religion, and Culture*, ed. H. Koester:201-15. Valley Forge, Pennsylvania: Trinity Press International.

Zahn, T. 1900. *Forschungen zur Geschichte des neutestamentlichen Kanons und der altkirchlichen Literatur*. Teil 6. Leipzig: A. Deichert'sche Verlagsbuchhandlung Nachf.

Zetterholm, M. 2001. *Synagogue and Separation. A Social-Scientific Approach to the Formation of Christianity in Antioch.* Lund: Teologiska institutionen, Lunds Universitet.

Zimmermann, G. A. 1874. *Ephesos im ersten christlichen Jahrhundert. Ein Beitrag zur neutestamentlichen Zeitgeschichte.* Leipzig: Druck von F.A. Brockhaus.

Zimmermann, H. 1962. "Christus und die Kirche in den Sendschreiben der Apokalypse." In *Unio Christianorum: Festschrift für Erzbischof Dr. Lorenz Jaeger zum 70. Geburtstag am 23. September 1962*, eds. H. Zimmermann, Schilling, O.: 176-97. Paderborn: Bonifacius - Druckerei.

Zumstein, J. 1990. "Visages de la communauté johannique." In *Origine et Postérité de l'Évangle de Jean*, ed. A. Marchadour:87-106. Paris: Les Éditions du Cerf.

Index of References

Old Testament

Jeremiah			12:11	325
4:23-6	137		*Hosea*	
Ezekiel			12:9	436
2:8-3:3	499		*Joel*	
9:6	532			
3:17-21	189		3:1-5 (LXX)	532
16:15-58	312			
23:1-49	312		*Amos*	
22:27	190			
27:18	175		6:10	452
33:2-9	189			
			Micah	
Daniel			5:2	479
7	579			
7:13	579		*Habakkuk*	
7:18	579			
7:21	579		1:12	479
7:22	579		2:17	60
7:25	579			
7:27	579		*Zephaniah*	
9:27	325			
11:31	325		3:3	190

New Testament

Matthew			21:26	131
			22:20	223
3:4	131		23:24	137
3:5	131		23:26	225
3:11	128		23:29-39	330
5:3	435		23:35	245
5:12	330		24:5	190
6:19-21	435		24:10-12	208
7:3-5	137		24:15	325
9:14	658		26:15	151
10:16-20	658		27:11-14	597
10:22	303		27:57	405
10:40	670		27:6	409
11:2	658		27:9	409
11:9	131			
13:22	405		*Mark*	
14:12	658			
17:10-13	131		1:5	131
18:23-5	137		1:6	131
20:1-6	137		2:17	600

Dead Sea Scrolls, Josephus, Philo and Rabbinic texts

Christian writings

Other Ancient Literature

Major Sources of Inscriptions

Index of Authors

Index of Subjects and Places